1992

Gale's Auto
SOURCEBOOK

**A Guide to Information on
1987-92 Cars and Light Trucks**

ISSN 1056-4330

1992

Gale's Auto

SOURCEBOOK

A Guide to Information on 1987-92 Cars and Light Trucks

Karen Hill, Editor

Joseph M. Palmisano, Associate Editor

Second Edition

Gale Research Inc. · DETROIT · LONDON

Editor: Karen Hill
Associate Editor: Joseph M. Palmisano
Assistant Editors: Ned Burels, Joyce Jakubiak
Contributing Editors: Annette Novallo, Annette Piccirelli
Senior Editor: Linda S. Hubbard

Research Manager: Victoria Cariappa
Research Supervisor: Maureen Richards
Editorial Associate: Mary Beth McElmeel
Editorial Assistants: Andrea Ghorai, Daniel Jankowski, Julie Karmazin,
Robert Lazich, Tamara C. Nott, Julie Synkonis
Aided by: Cynthia Grayson

Production Manager: Mary Beth Trimper
Production Assistant: Mary Winterhalter

Permissions and Production Manager: Jeanne Gough
Picture Permissions Supervisor: Margaret Chamberlain

Art Director: Arthur Chartow
Graphic Designer: Bernadette M. Gornie
Keyliner: C.J. Jonik

Data Entry Supervisor: Benita Spight
Data Entry Associates: Civie Ann Green, Pauline Sieli

Supervisor of Systems and Programming: Theresa A. Rocklin
Programmers: Wilmont C. Belfry, Thomas E. Potts

While every effort has been made to ensure the reliability of the information presented in this publication, Gale Research Inc. does not guarantee the accuracy of the data contained herein. Gale accepts no payment for listing; and inclusion in the publication of any organization, agency, institution, publication, service, or individual does not imply endorsement by the editors or publisher. Errors brought to the attention of the publisher and verified to the satisfaction of the publisher will be corrected in future editions.

Appreciation is extended to the automobile manufacturers and promotional agencies who readily supplied us with the photos and product information that appear in this edition.

ISBN 0-8013-8326-8
ISSN 1056-4330

The paper used in this publication meets the minimum requirements of American National Standard for Information Sciences—Permanence Paper for Printed Library Materials, ANSI Z39.48-1984. ∞™

Published simultaneously in the United Kingdom by
Gale Research International Limited
(An affiliated company of Gale Research Inc.)

CONTENTS

Highlights vii

Introduction ix

User's Guide xi

Master List of Cars and Light Trucks xvii

Part One: Car and Light Truck Profiles. 1
   (models listed alphabetically; consult the Master List of Profiled Cars and Trucks
   for specific page numbers)

Part Two: General Information Sources 441
   (includes publications, databases, videos, and associations)

Part Three: Manufacturer Profiles 529
   (includes contact information)

Part Four: Rankings Appendix. 549

Index to Information Sources 557

HIGHLIGHTS

Value-conscious car buyers and others seeking information on motor vehicles can turn to *Gale's Auto Sourcebook* as the one-stop resource for researching the car market.

The Complete Guide to Cars and Light Trucks

Gale's Auto Sourcebook provides all the facts, figures, and opinions you need on more than 320 models of cars and light trucks manufactured since 1987 for purchase in the U.S. Each model profile presents vital data and information sources on the vehicle's features, reliability, maintenance, and operation, organized into 11 easy-to-use categories:

- Model Descriptions
- Major Features
- Price History *(new feature)*
- Dimensions
- Engines
- Evaluations, Tests, and Rankings
- Recalls
- Safety and Repairs
- Repair Manuals
- Other Information Sources
- Associations

A Master List of Profiled Cars and Light Trucks identifies alternate, popular, and special model names, and links them to the models profiled in the *Sourcebook*.

Overview of Expert Evaluations

Gale's Auto Sourcebook provides a quick overview of how the experts rate each model by presenting excerpts from published evaluations and rankings from more than 35 reviewing sources. A special Appendix of selected lists, such as "Ten Best Imports," is also included.

New in This Edition

In addition to adding the pricing history of every make and model, the second edition of *Gale's Auto Sourcebook* provides:

- All the newest 1992 vehicle descriptions, including specifications
- More photos than ever—over 20% more
- All the latest recall and repair notices, including some problems that were spotted on new 1992 models
- Completely revised and updated manufacturer contact numbers
- Enhanced resource sections that now list 160 associations and more than 1,500 publications and other information sources
- More rankings and statistics to review—50% more in the Appendix alone

Arrangement and Index

Gale's Auto Sourcebook is arranged into four parts:

- Car and Light Truck Profiles
- General Information Sources
- Manufacturer Profiles
- Rankings Appendix

Consult the User's Guide for complete information on these descriptive sections. A single, alphabetic Index to Information Sources located at the end of the book speeds access to the resources listed throughout the book.

INTRODUCTION

Gale's Auto Sourcebook is the most comprehensive guide to cars and light trucks manufactured from 1987 through 1992 and sold in the U.S. Car and truck owners, buyers, enthusiasts, and others interested in automobiles will find a complete picture of the wide selection of vehicles available for purchase, as well as an overview of the automotive marketplace.

Gale's Auto Sourcebook can be used by information seekers at all levels—the first-time car buyer, the most dedicated auto buff, the industry professional, or the librarian or researcher—to:

• Look at a particular car model in detail—or quickly compare the features and reliability of several models—through the comprehensive profiles presented on over 320 cars and light trucks.

• Obtain a comprehensive and convenient overview of how the experts rate each of the car and truck models listed, through the brief excerpts from articles appearing in over 35 major automotive reviewing sources.

• Identify and access essential sources of automotive information—many of which are readily available in libraries—through the extensive citations to auto-related newspapers, magazines, and other publications and materials.

• Learn how to get in touch with the auto companies and their executives, and who to contact to register complaints or obtain marketing, consumer, or other information, by consulting the Manufacturers Profiles.

• Compare the performance of high-interest vehicles, through the lists provided in the Rankings Appendix.

Comprehensive Coverage and Convenient Arrangement

Information in *Gale's Auto Sourcebook* is conveniently arranged into four parts, which are followed by a master Index to Information Sources.

1. **CAR AND LIGHT TRUCK PROFILES** present facts and figures about each car and light truck listed. Each profile includes information on:

   • body styles and dimensions
   • major features
   • price history
   • engine specifications
   • excerpts from published reviews and rankings
   • government recall data
   • articles on safety and repairs
   • model-specific publications, such as repair manuals
   • model-specific associations

2. **GENERAL INFORMATION SOURCES** catalogs information sources that pertain to all types of automobiles and the automotive marketplace, organized by: associations; automotive industry directories; buyers guides; and general publications and materials on some 40 specific subjects. These include:

   • accessories
   • automotive engineering
   • automotive law
   • automotive safety
   • body repair
   • drivetrains
   • engines/transmissions

   • fuel systems
   • ignition systems
   • parts
   • restraint systems
   • security systems
   • sport utility vehicles
   • undercar repair/maintenance

3. MANUFACTURER PROFILES list contact and descriptive information for the companies that manufacture the models included. Entries include such data on market share, recent sales histories, and other business activities; customer service offices, consumer hotlines, and toll-free numbers are also provided when available.

4. RANKINGS APPENDIX provides a representative overview of the models and manufacturers judged to be the best (and worst) performers and sellers from 1987 through 1992 by major automotive reviewers.

INDEX TO INFORMATION SOURCES lists all of the publications, audio-visual materials, associations, and manufacturers cited in the Car and Light Truck Profiles, General Information Sources, and Manufacturers Profiles sections in one convenient location—speeding the search for a specific topic or title.

Please consult the User's Guide that follows this Introduction for more information on the *Sourcebook's* arrangement, content, and indexing.

Compilation

Data on the cars and trucks profiled in *Gale's Auto Sourcebook* was selected from a wide range of authoritative sources, including publications issued by the Environmental Protection Agency, the National Highway Traffic Safety Administration, and the vehicles' manufacturers. Excerpted evaluations, rankings, and citations to safety and repair information were compiled from a variety of well-known automotive publications and other major reviewing sources. Entries on associations and publications were drawn from reliable secondary sources and from selected information from other Gale databases.

Comments and Suggestions

Questions, comments, and suggestions for improving *Gale's Auto Sourcebook* are welcome. Please contact:

Editor
Gale's Auto Sourcebook
Gale Research Inc.
835 Penobscot Bldg.
Detroit, MI 48226-4094
Telephone: (313)961-2242
Toll-free: 800-347-GALE
Fax: (313)961-6815

USER'S GUIDE

Gale's Auto Sourcebook (GAS) is divided into four parts:

Part One: Car and Light Truck Profiles
Part Two: General Information Sources
Part Three: Manufacturer Profiles
Part Four: Rankings Appendix

Access to entries is facilitated by the Master List of Cars and Light Trucks, and an Index to Information Sources. Each of these sections is described in detail below.

Master List of Cars and Light Trucks

The Master List of Cars and Light Trucks provides, in a single alphabetic sequence, the names used to identify the more than 320 models profiled in Part One. Also included are alternate, synonymous, and related model names; these citations include "See" references to the appropriate model profiles (for example, users seeking information on the Mazda Protege will be referenced to the Mazda 323/Protege profile). The Master List also serves as an expanded table of contents, referencing the beginning page numbers for each model profile.

Part One: Car and Light Truck Profiles

This section features descriptions, specifications, evaluations, safety and repair data, and sources of additional information on more than 300 specific vehicle models. Vehicles are profiled separately if they have been given separate nameplates by the manufacturer (for example, the Ford Taurus and the Mercury Sable, well-known "corporate twins," are profiled separately). Vehicles are profiled together if the manufacturer considers them to be part of the same series (for example, the Audi 100 and the Audi 100 Quattro are covered in a single profile).

Consult the Master List of Cars and Light Trucks (which immediately follows this User's Guide) for a complete list of the models profiled and each profile's beginning page number.

Content of Car and Light Truck Profiles

Each profile contains up to 11 categories of information as described below:

▶ **Model Description.** Provides general introductory notes, including general descriptive information, awards and inclusion in significant ranked lists, and production sites and model years available.

▶ **Major Features.** Describes the entire model line, from coupe to wagon, and the standard equipment featured in each of these model versions. Included are items such as engine type, transmission, suspension, steering, brakes, and accessories. Coverage of standard equipment serves to illustrate the comparative features found on various versions of the model, and is not intended to be comprehensive.

▶ **Price History.** Provides new base model prices, if available, for production years listed. Prices are intended for general reference and comparisons, not as a precise indication of the cost of the vehicle.

▶ **Dimensions.** Presents, in chart form, data on the model's body dimensions. The dimensions included were chosen to indicate the overall size of the vehicle, its interior roominess, and factors affecting general operating costs. Data is listed by body style; dimensions are in inches unless otherwise noted. Included are:

- Years Available
- Vehicle Wheelbase
- Length
- Height
- Average Weight (lbs.)
- Fuel capacity (U.S. gal.)
- Front Headroom
- Front Legroom

Note: Slight variations in body design within a model year or between years may not be noted; major design variations are listed separately, following their specific years of availability. "Average Weight" refers to curb weight for cars and Gross Vehicle Weight Rating (GVWR) for light trucks.

▶ **Engines.** Presents common engine specifications in chart form, listed by engine type. Each engine description may include:

- Displacement (in liters)
- Horsepower @ RPM
- Torque (ft/lbs) @ RPM
- EPA Estimated Gas Mileage (City/Hwy)
- Type of Fuel Delivery
- Years Available

NOTE: EPA gas mileage estimates are for comparison purposes only. Estimates are for the latest year in which the engine was available and are for engines installed in standard-equipped models. Individual mileage may vary. Options, such as automatic transmission, age and condition of vehicle, and driving habits may affect actual mileage for any particular vehicle.

▶ **Evaluations, Tests, and Rankings.** Offers brief excerpts from articles that evaluate or rank the model's performance, from over 35 automotive reviewing sources, providing a quick and convenient overview of the reviewer's assessments. Entries for each evaluation include:

- Model year of tested/evaluated vehicle
- Evaluation excerpt
- Source (citation showing where the complete evaluation may be found, including article name, publication name, date, and page numbers)

Entries are arranged chronologically, with most recent first.

NOTE: Descriptive entries, including contact information, on the automotive-oriented publications cited in these entries are provided in Part Two: General Information Sources. Consult the Index to Information Sources at the back of this volume to locate entries on these publications.

Evaluations appearing in buyers guides and other annual automobile compilations—such as the Consumer Reports annual auto issue and Motor Trend's annual buyers guides—are not excerpted here, since these publications are well-known and readily available (exceptions are sometimes made for rarely reviewed or unique models). Descriptive entries on these publications are provided in Part Two: General Information Sources.

▶ **Recalls.** Provides excerpts from National Highway Traffic Safety Administration (NHTSA) vehicle recall campaigns. Each entry may include:

- Model year(s) of the recalled vehicle
- Number of vehicles recalled
- Vehicle description
- Defect description
- Corrective action
- NHTSA campaign number

Entries are arranged chronologically by model years, with most recent first. If no recalls are on record, this is also noted.

▶ **Safety and Repairs.** Cites articles from automotive and repair publications that contain model-specific repair tips and announcements of government safety investigations and manufacturer service bulletins. Each entry includes:

- Model year
- Source (citation showing where the complete article may be found, including article title, publication title, dates, and page numbers)
- Brief note describing the topic of the article (if the article title is not descriptive)

Entries are arranged chronologically by model year, with most recent first.

NOTE: Descriptive entries, including contact information, on all automotive-oriented publications cited in these entries are provided in Part Two: General Information Sources. Consult the Index to Information Sources at the back of this volume to locate entries on these specific publications.

▶ **Repair Manuals.** Contains entries on manuals, books, and other materials that provide model-specific repair instructions, advice, and tips. Entries may include:

- Title and publisher or distributor name, address, and phone number
- Editor or author's name
- Publication date or frequency
- Description of contents
- Additional phone numbers
- Price

Entries are arranged alphabetically by title. A book entry number, which is used to refer to that entry in the Index to Information Sources, precedes each entry.

▶ **Other Information Sources.** Provides entries on books, directories, magazines, newspapers, newsletters, databases, videos, and other model-specific information sources.
Entries may include:

- Title and publisher or distributor name, address, and phone number
- Editor or author's name
- Publication date or frequency
- Description of contacts
- Additional phone numbers
- Price

Entries are arranged alphabetically by title. Bracketed notes following the title indicate geographic coverage. A book entry number, which is used to refer to that entry in the Index to Information Sources, precedes each entry.

▶ **Associations.** Lists and describes organizations interested in preserving, restoring, or enjoying the described model. Entries may include:

- Organization name, address, and phone number
- Contact name and title
- Founding Date
- Membership
- Description of activities and services

Entries are arranged alphabetically by organization name. Bracketed notes following the organization name indicate geographic coverage. A book entry number, which is used to refer to that entry in the Index to Information Sources, precedes each entry.

Part Two: General Information Sources

This section covers general automotive associations, publications, and materials on topics of general interest to automobile owners or enthusiasts. A book entry number, which is used to refer to each entry in the Index to Information Sources, precedes entries in this section.

Content of General Information Sources

Entries in this section are organized into the following four categories:

▶ **Associations.** Consists of organizations, groups, and clubs affiliated with or related to either the automotive industry or automobile ownership. Entries are arranged alphabetically by organization name. Bracketed notes following the organization name indicate geographic coverage.

Entries for associations include: name, address, and phone number; contact name and title; founding date; membership; activities and services; and additional phone numbers.

▶ **Automotive Industry Directories.** Includes directories that list industry professionals, companies, associations, and other organizations. Bracketed notes following the title indicate geographic coverage. Entries are arranged alphabetically within the following eight categories:

- Auto auctions
- Automotive body shops
- Automotive consultants
- Automotive dealers
- Automotive associations
- Automotive parts retailers
- Automotive products manufacturers
- Automotive salvage dealers
- Automotive service and maintenance firms

▶ **Buyers Guides and Classifieds.** Includes books, periodicals, and newspapers that are solely devoted to listings of interest to buyers.

Entries are arranged alphabetically by publication title.

▶ **General Publications and Materials.** Includes books, manuals, directories, newspapers, magazines, newsletters, and videos. Entries are arranged alphabetically into the following 49 subject categories:

- Accessories
- Automotive aftermarket parts
- Automotive design
- Automotive engineering
- Automotive history
- Automotive industry
- Automotive law
- Automotive reconditioning
- Automotive road service
- Automotive safety
- Body repair
- Brakes
- Bumpers
- Crankshafts
- Diagnostics
- Diesel engines
- Drivetrains
- Electrical systems
- Electronic systems
- Emission systems
- Engines/transmissions
- Four-wheel drive
- Fuel systems
- Fuels
- General automotive
- General repair/maintenance
- Headlamps
- Heating/cooling systems
- Ignition systems
- Import cars
- Instrument panels
- Lubricants
- Parts
- Radiators
- Restraint systems
- Security systems
- Shock absorbers
- Sound systems
- Sport utility vehicles
- Sports and exotic cars
- Station wagons
- Steering systems
- Suspension systems
- Tires
- Trucks and vans
- Turbocharging
- Undercar repair/maintenance
- Wheels
- Windows

Entries for publications and materials may include: publication title or product name; name, address and phone number of its publisher, distributor, or producer; editor or author's name; publication date or frequency; descriptive information; and additional phone numbers.

Part Three: Manufacturer Profiles

This section provides descriptive and contact information for the manufacturers of each vehicle profiled in Part One. Entries on international manufacturers include contact information for their U.S. headquarters or offices. Entries in this section are arranged alphabetically by manufacturer name. A book entry number, used to refer to the entries in the Index to Information Sources, precedes each entry in this section.

Content of Manufacturer Profiles

- **Headquarters Information.** Provides manufacturer name, main address, and phone and fax numbers.

- **Description.** Contains a brief description that can include historical and organizational information, engineering and other innovations, awards and inclusion in significant ranked lists, and production statistics.

- **Additional Numbers.** Provides alternate national contact numbers, such as telex and toll-free numbers.

- **Corporate Contacts.** Provides names, titles, and office phone numbers of various executives and managers in departments such as administration, finance, marketing, sales, public relations, and human resources. National consumer hotline numbers are also listed here.

- **Off-Site Operations.** Contains the names, addresses, and phone numbers of production sites, manufacturing divisions, regional offices, and other corporate facilities. The executives and managers of these operations may also be listed.

- **Customer Services Offices.** Contains the names, addresses, and phone numbers of customer service regional offices, customer service zone offices, and customer service centers.

Part Four: Rankings Appendix

The Rankings Appendix presents representative published lists of vehicles that are considered to be the best and worst performers and sellers by major automotive reviewers. Also included are evaluative rankings of automobile manufacturers. The lists are arranged alphabetically by title within the following six categories:

- **1987 Model Year**
- **1988 Model Year**
- **1989 Model Year**
- **1990 Model Year**
- **1991 Model Year**
- **1992 Model Year**
- **General Auto Rankings**

These lists can be used to obtain a quick overview of how high-interest models have fared over the years. They are also usually cited in the Model Description section of the individual model profiles.

Index to Information Sources

Gale's Auto Sourcebook includes a comprehensive Index to Information Sources that lists all associations, manufacturers, publications, and audio-visual materials (cross-referenced by main keyword) cited in Part One: Car and Light Truck Profiles, Part Two: General Information Sources, and Part Three: Manufacturers Profiles. Entries are arranged alphabetically and are referenced by their entry numbers, not page numbers.

Master List of Cars and Light Trucks

This list outlines the approximately 320 automobiles described in Part One of *Gale's Auto Sourcebook (GAS)*. The beginning page number of each profile is provided for the convenience of the user and the list provides reference to the model or series name.

Acclaim, Plymouth *See* Plymouth Acclaim 328
Accord, Honda *See* Honda Accord 206
Achieva, Oldsmobile *See* Oldsmobile Achieva 310
Acura Integra 1
Acura Legend 2
Acura NSX 3
Acura Vigor 4
Aerostar, Ford *See* Ford Aerostar 166
Alfa Romeo 164 5
Alfa Romeo 6V America *See* Alfa Romeo Milano 7
Alfa Romeo Milano 7
Alfa Romeo Spider 9
Allante, Cadillac *See* Cadillac Allante 70
Alliance, Renault *See* Renault Alliance 388
AMC Eagle 12
Amigo, Isuzu *See* Isuzu Amigo 218
Aries, Dodge *See* Dodge Aries 127
Aston Martin Lagonda 13
Aston Martin Saloon 13
Aston Martin V-8 Coupe 14
Aston Martin Vantage 14
Aston Martin Virage Coupe 15
Aston Martin Volante 15
Astro, Chevrolet *See* Chevrolet Astro 82
Audi 80 16
Audi 90 17
Audi 100 18
Audi 200 19
Audi 4000 20
Audi 5000 21
Audi Coupe 22
Audi S4 23
Audi V8 Quattro 24
Avanti 25
Axxess, Nissan *See* Nissan Axxess 302

Bentley Continental 25
Bentley Eight 26
Bentley Mulsanne S 27
Bentley Turbo R 28
Beretta, Chevrolet *See* Chevrolet Beretta 83
Bertone X1/9 29
Blazer, Chevrolet *See* Chevrolet Blazer 85
BMW 3-Series 29
BMW 318i *See* BMW 3-Series 29
BMW 318is *See* BMW 3-Series 29
BMW 325 *See* BMW 3-Series 29
BMW 325i *See* BMW 3-Series 29
BMW 325i Convertible *See* BMW 3-Series 29
BMW 325is *See* BMW 3-Series 29
BMW 325iX *See* BMW 3-Series 29
BMW 5-Series 31
BMW 525i *See* BMW 5-Series 31
BMW 535i *See* BMW 5-Series 31
BMW 6-Series 33
BMW 635SCi *See* BMW 6-Series 33
BMW 7-Series 34
BMW 735i *See* BMW 7-Series 34

BMW 735iL *See* BMW 7-Series 34
BMW 750iL *See* BMW 7-Series 34
BMW 8-Series 36
BMW 850i *See* BMW 8-Series 36
BMW M3 *See* BMW 3-Series 29
BMW M5 *See* BMW 5-Series 31
BMW M6 *See* BMW 6-Series 33
Bonneville, Pontiac *See* Pontiac Bonneville 346
Brat, Subaru *See* Subaru Brat 399
Bravada, Oldsmobile *See* Oldsmobile Bravada 311
Bronco, Ford *See* Ford Bronco 169
Bronco II, Ford *See* Ford Bronco II 170
Brougham, Cadillac *See* Cadillac Brougham 72
Buick Century 37
Buick Electra 40
Buick LeSabre 43
Buick Park Avenue 47
Buick Reatta 49
Buick Regal Custom 52
Buick Riviera 56
Buick Roadmaster 59
Buick Skyhawk 62
Buick Skylark 65
Buick Somerset 68

Cabriolet, Volkswagen *See* Volkswagen Cabriolet 422
Cadillac Allante 70
Cadillac Brougham 72
Cadillac Cimarron 74
Cadillac De Ville 75
Cadillac Eldorado 77
Cadillac Fleetwood 79
Cadillac Seville 80
Camaro, Chevrolet *See* Chevrolet Camaro 86
Camry, Toyota *See* Toyota Camry 409
Capri, Mercury *See* Mercury Capri 277
Caprice, Chevrolet *See* Chevrolet Caprice 89
Caravan, Dodge *See* Dodge Caravan 128
Caravelle, Plymouth *See* Plymouth Caravelle 329
Cavalier, Chevrolet *See* Chevrolet Cavalier 91
Celebrity, Chevrolet *See* Chevrolet Celebrity 93
Celica, Toyota *See* Toyota Celica 411
Century, Buick *See* Buick Century 37
Charade, Daihatsu *See* Daihatsu Charade 125
Charger, Dodge *See* Dodge Charger 130
Cherokee, Jeep *See* Jeep Cherokee 228
Chevette, Chevrolet *See* Chevrolet Chevette 94
Chevrolet Astro 82
Chevrolet Beretta 83
Chevrolet Blazer 85
Chevrolet Camaro 68
Chevrolet Caprice 89
Chevrolet Cavalier 91
Chevrolet Celebrity 93
Chevrolet Chevette 94
Chevrolet Corsica 95
Chevrolet Corvette 96
Chevrolet Lumina 100

Chevrolet Lumina APV 102
Chevrolet Monte Carlo 103
Chevrolet Nova 104
Chevrolet S10 Pickup 105
Chevrolet Spectrum 106
Chevrolet Sportvan 107
Chevrolet Sprint 108
Chevrolet Suburban 109
Chrysler Conquest 111
Chrysler Fifth Avenue 113
Chrysler Imperial 114
Chrysler LeBaron Coupe/Convertible 115
Chrysler LeBaron Sedan 117
Chrysler New Yorker 120
Chrysler New Yorker Fifth Avenue See
    Chrysler New Yorker 120
Chrysler TC by Maserati 122
Chrysler Town & Country 123
Cimarron, Cadillac See Cadillac Cimarron 74
Civic, Honda See Honda Civic 208
Club Wagon, Ford See Ford Club Wagon 172
Colt, Dodge See Dodge Colt 131
Colt, Plymouth See Plymouth Colt 330
Comanche, Jeep See Jeep Comanche 231
Conquest, Chrysler See Chrysler Conquest 111
Continental, Bentley See Bentley Continental 25
Continental, Lincoln See Lincoln Continental 243
Cordia, Mitsubishi See Mitsubishi Cordia 289
Corniche Series, Rolls-Royce See Rolls-Royce
    Corniche Series 391
Corolla, Toyota See Toyota Corolla 412
Corrado, Volkswagen See Volkswagen Corrado 423
Corsica, Chevrolet See Chevrolet Corsica 95
Corvette, Chevrolet See Chevrolet Corvette 96
Cougar, Mercury See Mercury Cougar 278
Countach, Lamborghini See Lamborghini Countach . . . 237
Cressida, Toyota See Toyota Cressida 414
CRX, Honda See Honda CRX 210
Custom Cruiser, Oldsmobile See Oldsmobile
    Custom Cruiser 312
Cutlass Calais, Oldsmobile See Oldsmobile
    Cutlass Calais 313
Cutlass Ciera, Oldsmobile See Oldsmobile
    Cutlass Ciera 315
Cutlass Supreme, Oldsmobile See Oldsmobile
    Cutlass Supreme 316

Daihatsu Charade 125
Daihatsu Rocky 126
Dakota, Dodge See Dodge Dakota 133
Daytona, Dodge See Dodge Daytona 134
De Ville, Cadillac See Cadillac De Ville 75
Diablo, Lamborghini See Lamborghini Diablo 238
Diamante, Mitsubishi See Mitsubishi Diamante 290
Diplomat, Dodge See Dodge Diplomat 136
Dodge 600 126
Dodge Aries 127
Dodge Caravan 128
Dodge Charger 130
Dodge Colt 131
Dodge Colt Vista Wagon See Dodge Colt 131
Dodge Dakota 133
Dodge Daytona 134
Dodge Diplomat 136
Dodge Dynasty 137
Dodge Grand Caravan See Dodge Caravan 128
Dodge Lancer 138
Dodge Mini Ram Van See Dodge Caravan 128

Dodge Monaco 139
Dodge Omni 141
Dodge Power Ram 50 See Dodge Ram 50 143
Dodge Raider 142
Dodge Ram 50 143
Dodge Ram Van/Wagon 144
Dodge Ramcharger 145
Dodge Shadow 146
Dodge Shelby CSX See Dodge Shadow 146
Dodge Spirit 148
Dodge Stealth 150
Dodge Viper 151
Dynasty, Dodge See Dodge Dynasty 137

Eagle, AMC See AMC Eagle 12
Eagle Medallion 152
Eagle Premier 153
Eagle Summit 154
Eagle Talon 156
Eclipse, Mitsubishi See Mitsubishi Eclipse 291
Elan, Lotus See Lotus Elan 249
Elantra, Hyundai See Hyundai Elantra 212
Eldorado, Cadillac See Cadillac Eldorado 77
Electra, Buick See Buick Electra 40
Escort, Ford See Ford Escort 173
Esprit, Lotus See Lotus Esprit 250
Excel, Hyundai See Hyundai Excel 213
Explorer, Ford See Ford Explorer 176
Expo, Mitsubishi See Mitsubishi Expo LRV 292
Expo LRV, Mitsubishi See Mitsubishi Expo LRV 292

Ferrari 328 157
Ferrari 348 159
Ferrari F40 161
Ferrari Mondial 163
Ferrari Testarossa 164
Festiva, Ford See Ford Festiva 177
Fiero, Pontiac See Pontiac Fiero 350
Fifth Avenue, Chrysler See Chrysler Fifth Avenue 113
Firebird, Pontiac See Pontiac Firebird 353
Firenza, Oldsmobile See Oldsmobile Firenza 320
Fleetwood, Cadillac See Cadillac Fleetwood 79
Ford Aerostar 166
Ford Bronco 169
Ford Bronco II 170
Ford Club Wagon 172
Ford Country Squire Wagon See Ford LTD
    Crown Victoria 178
Ford Escort 173
Ford Explorer 176
Ford Festiva 177
Ford LTD Crown Victoria 178
Ford Mustang 180
Ford Probe 184
Ford Ranger 186
Ford Taurus 188
Ford Tempo 191
Ford Thunderbird 193
4-Runner, Toyota See Toyota 4-Runner 408
Fox, Volkswagen See Volkswagen Fox 425

Galant, Mitsubishi See Mitsubishi Galant 293
Geo Metro 196
Geo Prizm 197
Geo Spectrum 197
Geo Storm 198
Geo Tracker 199
GMC Jimmy 200

GMC Rally 201
GMC Safari 202
GMC Sonoma 203
GMC Suburban 205
GMC Syclone *See* GMC Sonoma 203
GMC Typhoon *See* GMC Jimmy 200
Golf, Volkswagen *See* Volkswagen Golf 426
Gran Fury, Plymouth *See* Plymouth Gran Fury 331
Grand Am, Pontiac *See* Pontiac Grand Am 357
Grand Marquis, Mercury *See* Mercury Grand Marquis . 280
Grand Prix, Pontiac *See* Pontiac Grand Prix 360
Grand Wagoneer, Jeep *See* Jeep Grand Wagoneer . . . 232

Honda Accord 206
Honda Civic 208
Honda CRX 210
Honda Prelude 211
Horizon, Plymouth *See* Plymouth Horizon 332
Hyundai Elantra 212
Hyundai Excel 213
Hyundai Scoupe 214
Hyundai Sonata 215

I-Mark, Isuzu *See* Isuzu I-Mark 219
Imperial, Chrysler *See* Chrysler Imperial 114
Impulse, Isuzu *See* Isuzu Impulse 220
Infiniti G20 216
Infiniti M30 217
Infiniti Q45 217
Integra, Acura *See* Acura Integra 1
Isuzu Amigo 218
Isuzu I-Mark 219
Isuzu Impulse 220
Isuzu Pickup 221
Isuzu P'up *See* Isuzu Pickup 221
Isuzu Rodeo 221
Isuzu Stylus 222
Isuzu Trooper 223

Jaguar XJ-6 224
Jaguar XJ-S 226
Jeep Cherokee 228
Jeep Comanche 231
Jeep Grand Wagoneer 232
Jeep Wagoneer 233
Jeep Wrangler 235
Jetta, Volkswagen *See* Volkswagen Jetta 429
Jimmy, GMC *See* GMC Jimmy 200
Justy, Subaru *See* Subaru Justy 400

Karif, Maserati *See* Maserati Karif 254
237

LaForza 13
Lagonda, Aston Martin *See* Aston Martin Lagonda 13
Lamborghini Countach 237
Lamborghini Diablo 238
Lamborghini LM002 239
Lancer, Dodge *See* Dodge Lancer 138
Laser, Plymouth *See* Plymouth Laser 333
LeBaron Coupe/Convertible, Chrysler *See*
    Chrysler LeBaron Coupe/Convertible 115
LeBaron Sedan, Chrysler *See* Chrysler LeBaron Sedan . 117
Legacy, Subaru *See* Subaru Legacy 401
Legend, Acura *See* Acura Legend 2
Lemans, Pontiac *See* Pontiac Lemans 364
LeSabre, Buick *See* Buick LeSabre 43
Lexus ES 250 240

Lexus ES 300 241
Lexus LS 400 241
Lexus SC 300/400 242
Lincoln Continental 243
Lincoln Mark VII 245
Lincoln Town Car 247
Lotus Elan 249
Lotus Esprit 250
Loyale, Subaru *See* Subaru Loyale 403
LTD Crown Victoria, Ford *See* Ford LTD Crown
    Victoria 178
Lumina, Chevrolet *See* Chevrolet Lumina 100
Lumina APV, Chevrolet *See* Chevrolet Lumina APV . . . 102
Lynx, Mercury *See* Mercury Lynx 281

Mark VII, Lincoln *See* Lincoln Mark VII 245
Maserati 222 251
Maserati 228 252
Maserati 425 253
Maserati 430 253
Maserati Karif 254
Maserati Shamal 255
Maserati Spyder 256
Maxima, Nissan *See* Nissan Maxima 303
Mazda 323/Protege 257
Mazda 626 258
Mazda 929 259
Mazda B2000 Series 260
Mazda B2200 *See* Mazda B2000 Series 260
Mazda B2600i *See* Mazda B2000 Series 260
Mazda MPV 261
Mazda MX-3 262
Mazda MX-5 Miata 263
Mazda MX-6 264
Mazda Navajo 265
Mazda Protege *See* Mazda 323/Protege 257
Mazda RX-7 266
Medallion, Eagle *See* Eagle Medallion 152
Mercedes-Benz 190 267
Mercedes-Benz 190D 2.5 *See* Mercedes-Benz 190 . . . 267
Mercedes-Benz 190D 2.5 Turbo *See*
    Mercedes-Benz 190 267
Mercedes-Benz 190E 2.3 *See* Mercedes-Benz 190 267
Mercedes-Benz 190E 2.5-16 Evolution II *See*
    Mercedes-Benz 190 267
Mercedes-Benz 190E 2.6 *See* Mercedes-Benz 190 267
Mercedes-Benz 260E 268
Mercedes-Benz 300 269
Mercedes-Benz 300CE *See* Mercedes-Benz 300 269
Mercedes-Benz 300D 2.5 *See* Mercedes-Benz 300 269
Mercedes-Benz 300E 2.6 *See* Mercedes-Benz 300 269
Mercedes-Benz 300E/4MATIC *See*
    Mercedes-Benz 300 269
Mercedes-Benz 300SE *See* Mercedes-Benz 300 269
Mercedes-Benz 300SEL *See* Mercedes-Benz 300 269
Mercedes-Benz 300SL *See* Mercedes-Benz 300 269
Mercedes-Benz 300TE/4MATIC *See*
    Mercedes-Benz 300 269
Mercedes-Benz 350SD *See* Mercedes-Benz 300 269
Mercedes-Benz 350SDL *See* Mercedes-Benz 300 269
Mercedes-Benz 400 271
Mercedes-Benz 400E *See* Mercedes-Benz 400 271
Mercedes-Benz 400SE *See* Mercedes-Benz 400 271
Mercedes-Benz 420SEL *See* Mercedes-Benz 400 271
Mercedes-Benz 500 273
Mercedes-Benz 500E *See* Mercedes-Benz 500 273
Mercedes-Benz 500SEC *See* Mercedes-Benz 500 273
Mercedes-Benz 500SEL *See* Mercedes-Benz 500 273

Mercedes-Benz 500SL See Mercedes-Benz 500 273
Mercedes-Benz 560 275
Mercedes-Benz 560SEC See Mercedes-Benz 560 275
Mercedes-Benz 560SEL See Mercedes-Benz 560 275
Mercedes-Benz 560SL See Mercedes-Benz 560 275
Mercedes-Benz 600SEL 276
Mercury Capri 277
Mercury Colony Park See Mercury Grand Marquis ... 280
Mercury Cougar 278
Mercury Grand Marquis 280
Mercury Lynx 281
Mercury Sable 283
Mercury Topaz 284
Mercury Tracer 286
Merkur Scorpio 287
Merkur XR4TI 288
Metro, Geo See Geo Metro 196
Mighty Max, Mitsubishi See Mitsubishi Mighty Max ... 294
Milano, Alfa Romeo See Alfa Romeo Milano 7
Mirage, Mitsubishi See Mitsubishi Mirage 294
Mitsubishi 3000GT 289
Mitsubishi Cordia 289
Mitsubishi Diamante 290
Mitsubishi Eclipse 291
Mitsubishi Expo See Mitsubishi Expo LRV 292
Mitsubishi Expo LRV 292
Mitsubishi Galant 293
Mitsubishi Mighty Max 294
Mitsubishi Mirage 294
Mitsubishi Montero 295
Mitsubishi Precis 296
Mitsubishi Sigma 297
Mitsubishi Starion 297
Mitsubishi Tredia 297
Mitsubishi Van 298
Mitsubishi Wagon................................ 298
Monaco, Dodge See Dodge Monaco................. 139
Mondial, Ferrari See Ferrari Mondial 163
Monte Carlo, Chevrolet See Chevrolet Monte Carlo... 103
Montero, Mitsubishi See Mitsubishi Montero 295
MPV, Mazda See Mazda MPV 261
Mulsanne S, Bentley See Bentley Mulsanne S 27
Mustang, Ford See Ford Mustang 180

Navajo, Mazda See Mazda Navajo 265
New Yorker, Chrysler See Chrysler New Yorker 120
Nissan 200SX 299
Nissan 240SX 299
Nissan 300ZX 301
Nissan Axxess 302
Nissan Maxima 303
Nissan NX 1600/2000 304
Nissan NX Coupe See Nissan NX 1600/2000 304
Nissan Pathfinder 305
Nissan Pulsar See Nissan NX 1600/2000 304
Nissan Sentra 306
Nissan Stanza 307
Nissan Truck 308
Nissan Van 309
Nova, Chevrolet See Chevrolet Nova 104
NSX, Acura See Acura NSX 3
NX Coupe, Nissan See Nissan NX 1600/2000 304

Oldsmobile Achieva 310
Oldsmobile Bravada 311
Oldsmobile Custom Cruiser........................ 312
Oldsmobile Cutlass Calais 313
Oldsmobile Cutlass Ciera......................... 315

Oldsmobile Custom Cruiser See Oldsmobile
  Cutlass Ciera 312
Oldsmobile Cutlass Supreme...................... 316
Oldsmobile Eighty Eight Royale 319
Oldsmobile Firenza 320
Oldsmobile Ninety Eight 321
Oldsmobile Silhouette Van 323
Oldsmobile Toronado 324
Omni, Dodge See Dodge Omni 141

Park Avenue, Buick See Buick Park Avenue 47
Paseo, Toyota See Toyota Paseo 416
Passat, Volkswagen See Volkswagen Passat 431
Pathfinder, Nissan See Nissan Pathfinder 305
Peugeot 405 326
Peugeot 505 327
Plymouth Acclaim 328
Plymouth Caravelle 329
Plymouth Colt 330
Plymouth Colt Vista Wagon See Plymouth Colt....... 330
Plymouth Gran Fury 331
Plymouth Grand Voyager See Plymouth Voyager 338
Plymouth Horizon 332
Plymouth Laser 333
Plymouth Reliant 335
Plymouth Sundance 336
Plymouth Turismo 337
Plymouth Voyager 338
Pontiac 1000 340
Pontiac 6000 343
Pontiac Bonneville 346
Pontiac Fiero 350
Pontiac Firebird 353
Pontiac Formula Firehawk See Pontiac Firebird 353
Pontiac Grand Am 357
Pontiac Grand Prix 360
Pontiac LeMans 364
Pontiac Safari Wagon 367
Pontiac Sunbird 370
Pontiac Trans Am See Pontiac Firebird 353
Pontiac Trans Sport 373
Porsche 911 376
Porsche 924S 379
Porsche 928 381
Porsche 944 383
Porsche 968 385
Precis, Mitsubishi See Mitsubishi Precis 296
Prelude, Honda See Honda Prelude 211
Premier, Eagle See Eagle Premier 153
Previa, Toyota See Toyota Previa................... 417
Prizm, Geo See Geo Prizm 197
Probe, Ford See Ford Probe 184

Quantum, Volkswagen See Volkswagen Quantum 432

Raider, Dodge See Dodge Raider 142
Rally, GMC See GMC Rally 201
Ram 50, Dodge See Dodge Ram 50 143
Ram Van/Wagon, Dodge See Dodge Ram
  Van/Wagon 144
Ramcharger, Dodge See Dodge Ramcharger 145
Range Rover 386
Ranger, Ford See Ford Ranger 186
Reatta, Buick See Buick Reatta 49
Regal Custom, Buick See Buick Regal Custom 52
Reliant, Plymouth See Plymouth Reliant............. 335
Renault Alliance 388
Renault Medallion 389

Riviera, Buick *See* Buick Riviera 56
Roadmaster, Buick *See* Buick Roadmaster 59
Rocky, Daihatsu *See* Daihatsu Rocky 126
Rodeo, Isuzu *See* Isuzu Rodeo 221
Rolls-Royce Corniche Series 391
Rolls-Royce Silver Spirit Series 392
Rolls-Royce Silver Spur Series 393

S10 Pickup, Chevrolet *See* Chevrolet S10 Pickup 105
Saab 900 394
Saab 9000 395
Sable, Mercury *See* Mercury Sable 283
Safari, GMC *See* GMC Safari 202
Safari Wagon, Pontiac *See* Pontiac Safari Wagon 367
Saloon, Aston Martin *See* Aston Martin Saloon 13
Samurai, Suzuki *See* Suzuki Samurai 406
Saturn 397
Scirocco, Volkswagen *See* Volkswagen Scirocco 433
Scorpio, Merkur *See* Merkur Scorpio 287
Scoupe, Hyundai *See* Hyundai Scoupe 214
Sentra, Nissan *See* Nissan Sentra 306
Seville, Cadillac *See* Cadillac Seville 80
Shadow, Dodge *See* Dodge Shadow 146
Shamal, Maserati *See* Maserati Shamal 255
Sidekick, Suzuki *See* Suzuki Sidekick 407
Sigma, Mitsubishi *See* Mitsubishi Sigma 297
Silhouette Van, Oldsmobile *See* Oldsmobile
   Silhouette Van 323
Silver Spirit Series, Rolls-Royce *See* Rolls-Royce
   Silver Spirit Series 392
Silver Spur Series, Rolls-Royce *See* Rolls-Royce
   Silver Spur Series 393
Skyhawk, Buick *See* Buick Skyhawk 62
Skylark, Buick *See* Buick Skylark 65
Somerset, Buick *See* Buick Somerset 68
Sonoma, GMC *See* GMC Sonoma 203
Sonota, Hyundai *See* Hyundai Sonota 215
Spectrum, Chevrolet *See* Chevrolet Spectrum 106
Spectrum, Geo *See* Geo Spectrum 197
Spider, Alfa Romeo *See* Alfa Romeo Spider 9
Spirit, Dodge *See* Dodge Spirit 148
Sportvan, Chevrolet *See* Chevrolet Sportvan 107
Sprint, Chevrolet *See* Chevrolet Sprint 108
Spyder, Maserati *See* Maserati Spyder 256
Stanza, Nissan *See* Nissan Stanza 307
Starion, Mitsubishi *See* Mitsubishi Starion 297
Stealth, Dodge *See* Dodge Stealth 150
Sterling 825 398
Sterling 827 398
Storm, Geo *See* Geo Storm 198
Stylus, Isuzu *See* Isuzu Stylus 222
Subaru Brat 399
Subaru Coupe 399
Subaru Hatchback 400
Subaru Justy 400
Subaru Legacy 401
Subaru Loyale 403
Subaru Sedan 403
Subaru SVX 404
Subaru Wagon 405
Subaru XT 405
Suburban, Chevrolet *See* Chevrolet Suburban 109
Suburban, GMC *See* GMC Suburban 205
Summit, Dodge *See* Dodge Summit 154
Sunbird, Pontiac *See* Pontiac Sunbird 370
Sundance, Plymouth *See* Plymouth Sundance 336
Supra, Toyota *See* Toyota Supra 418
Suzuki Samurai 406

Suzuki Sidekick 407
Suzuki Swift 408
Swift, Suzuki *See* Suzuki Swift 408

Talon, Eagle *See* Eagle Talon 156
Taurus, Ford *See* Ford Taurus 188
TC by Maserati, Chrysler *See* Chrysler TC by Maserati . 122
Tempo, Ford *See* Ford Tempo 191
Tercel, Toyota *See* Toyota Tercel 419
Testarossa, Ferrari *See* Ferrari Testarossa 164
Thunderbird, Ford *See* Ford Thunderbird 193
Topaz, Mercury *See* Mercury Topaz 284
Toronado, Oldsmobile *See* Oldsmobile Toronado 324
Town Car, Lincoln *See* Lincoln Town Car 247
Town and Country, Chrysler *See* Chrysler
   Town and Country 123
Toyota 4-Runner 408
Toyota Camry 409
Toyota Celica 411
Toyota Corolla 412
Toyota Cressida 414
Toyota Land Cruiser Wagon 414
Toyota MR2 415
Toyota Paseo 416
Toyota Previa 417
Toyota Supra 418
Toyota Tercel 419
Toyota Truck 420
Toyota Van 421
Tracer, Mercury *See* Mercury Tracer 286
Tracker, Geo *See* Geo Tracker 199
Trans Sport, Pontiac *See* Pontiac Trans Sport 373
Tredia, Mitsubishi *See* Mitsubishi Tredia 297
Trooper, Isuzu *See* Isuzu Trooper 223
Turbo R, Bentley *See* Bentley Turbo R 28
Turismo, Plymouth *See* Plymouth Turismo 337

Vanagon, Volkswagen *See* Volkswagen Vanagon 434
Vantage, Aston Martin *See* Aston Martin Vantage 14
Vigor, Acura *See* Acura Vigor 4
Viper, Dodge *See* Dodge Viper 151
Virage Coupe, Aston Martin *See* Aston Martin
   Virage Coupe 15
Volante, Aston Martin *See* Aston Martin Volante 15
Volkswagen Cabriolet 422
Volkswagen Camper GL *See* Volkswagen Vanagon . . . 434
Volkswagen Corrado 423
Volkswagen Fox 425
Volkswagen Golf 426
Volkswagen GTI 428
Volkswagen Jetta 429
Volkswagen Passat 431
Volkswagen Quantum 432
Volkswagen Scirocco 433
Volkswagen Vanagon 434
Volvo 240 Series 436
Volvo 700 Series 437
Volvo 740 *See* Volvo 700 Series 437
Volvo 760 *See* Volvo 700 Series 437
Volvo 780 *See* Volvo 700 Series 437
Volvo 900 Series 438
Volvo 940 *See* Volvo 900 Series 438
Volvo 960 *See* Volvo 900 Series 438
Voyager, Plymouth *See* Plymouth Voyager 338

Wagoneer, Jeep *See* Jeep Wagoneer 233
Wrangler, Jeep *See* Jeep Wrangler 235

Yugo 440

1992

Gale's Auto
SOURCEBOOK

**A Guide to Information on
1987-92 Cars and Light Trucks**

Car and Light Truck Profiles

ACURA INTEGRA (1987-92)

Introduced as part of the Acura line, which is a division of American Honda Motor Co. Chosen as one of *Car and Driver's* Ten Best Cars of 1987 and 1988. Produced in Japan.

1991 Acura Integra GS

MAJOR FEATURES

● Acura Integra RS 1992 standard equipment includes: 5-speed manual transmission, rack and pinion steering, 4-wheel disc brakes, and tinted glass.

● Acura Integra LS adds as 1992 standard equipment: AM/FM stereo cassette, power windows, and cruise control.

● Acura Integra GS adds as 1992 standard equipment: anti-lock brakes, rear spoiler, alloy wheels, and power moonroof.

PRICE HISTORY

The following new car prices reflect the approximate retail cost of the base model: **1987** - $10,039; **1988** - $11,040; **1989** - $11,260; **1990** - $11,950; **1991** - $12,100; **1992** - $12,335.

DIMENSIONS

Body Style	Years Avail	Wheel Base (in)	Lgth (in)	Ht (in)	Avg Wt (lbs)	Fuel Cap (gal)	Front Hdrm (in)	Front Legrm (in)
2d lbk	87-89	96.5	168.7	53.8	2,326	13.2	38.0	41.3
2d lbk	90-90	100.4	172.9	52.2	2,549	13.2	38.5	43.6
2d lbk	91-92	100.4	172.9	50.0	2,560	13.2	38.5	41.8
4d sdn	87-89	99.2	171.5	52.9	2,390	13.2	38.0	41.3
4d sdn	90-90	102.4	176.5	52.8	2,604	13.2	38.7	43.5
4d sdn	91-92	102.4	176.5	50.6	2,606	13.2	38.7	41.6

ENGINES

Type	Displace-ment (L)	Fuel Dly	HP @rpm	Torque @rpm (ft/lbs)	MPG Cty/Hwy	Years Avail
I-4	1.6	FI	118@6500	103@5500	26/30	87-89
I-4	1.8	FI	130@6000	121@5000	24/28	90-91
I-4	1.8	FI	140@6300	126@5000	na	92-92

KEY: I=in-line engine; V=V engine; F=flat engine; FI=fuel injection; bbl=barrel carburetor; T=turbo; D=diesel; HP=horsepower; MPG=estimated average miles per gallon.

EVALUATIONS, TESTS, AND RANKINGS

1991: "Exceptional engine delivers exceptional performance. . .Exemplary trade-in values . . . hardware needs to communicate with the driver." **Source:** "Acura Integra: A Definite Edge In Performance," *Autoweek's Autofile 1991 Edition*, 1990, pp. 60-64.

1990: "Acura Integra, smooth and refined, never asking for more than the lightest fingertip touch at the controls . . . rod-operated gearshift is smooth almost beyond the point of having feedback." **Source:** "Three Translations of the Family Sedan," *Popular Science*, September 1990, pp. 79-83.

1989: "1986-88 Integras had the honor of showing no owner complaints of trouble in federal government files . . . a family sports sedan . . . leans more heavily toward the sports side than the family side . . . The ride was all sport, no cushiony, floating, feeling." **Source:** "Acura Integra Features Performance," *The Detroit News*, March 8, 1989, pp. F1-F2.

1989: "continues the same precision ride as the previous model . . . Gone are the . . . hidden headlamps, replaced by flush, wraparound lenses." **Source:** "Integra makes steady evolution," *The Detroit News*, October 11, 1989, pp. F1-F2.

1988: "is the best moderately priced sedan in the world . . . cockpit is one of the best in the industry . . . The ride is supple and nicely controlled over virtually any surface." **Source:** "Hunting for High Average," *Car and Driver*, August 1988, pp. 58-69.

1988: "J.D. Power and Associates . . . ranked Acura No. 1 in . . . the Customer Satisfaction Index . . . Each ranking is based on questionaires completed by buyers one year after they bought the car." **Source:** "Acura No. 1 in survey of 87 buyers," *The Detroit News*, August 2, 1988, p. D1.

1987: "We like everything about the Integras . . . their sporty good looks, their usefully roomy interiors, . . . the value they represent." **Source:** "Cars: Fun Work, But Somebody's Got To Do It," *Car and Driver*, January 1987, pp. 36-41.

1987: "[Integra LS] . . . The cushion of the front seat was far too narrow ... was so smooth that it felt part of the driver ... the ride was firm but not harsh." **Source:** "Sports coupes: nimble, quick ... and affordable," *Popular Science*, October 1986, pp. 26, 28, 30, 32, 34.

RECALLS

1987: (99,088 cars; includes Acura and Honda models): Sections 6A and 6B were omitted from owner's manual. **Corrective action:** Insert corrective pages. *(NHTSA Campaign No. 87V171000.)*

1987: (360,198 passenger vehicles; includes Honda Civic and Acura Integra; includes models made before 1987): Under high ambient temperatures front windshield wiper contact unit could loosen and become dislodged. This could result in windshield wiper failure and would affect driver visibility. **Corrective action:** Install contact unit holder that would prevent loosening. *(NHTSA Campaign No. 88V180000.)*

SAFETY AND REPAIRS

1992: "Honda to Fix Bad Oil Switch," *Automotive News*, January 27, 1992, p. 2.

OTHER INFORMATION SOURCES

1 ● **Acura Driving Club Magazine**
Acura Driving Club of America
W. 222 33rd Ave., Ste. 13
Spokane, WA 99203

Magazine for Acura owners. Quarterly. **Price:** $25.00.

ASSOCIATIONS

2 ● **Hondacar International**
P.O. Box 5242
Deptford, NJ 08096
John Blair, Pres.

Founded: 1976. **Membership:** 1,700. Persons interested in any model of the Honda or Acura automobile. Purpose is to inform owners of both the pleasures of and potential problems with their cars, and to suggest ways to avoid such problems. **Former Name(s):** Honda Civic Club.

ACURA LEGEND (1987-92)

Acura is a division of American Honda Motor Co. Legend Coupe was chosen as *Motor Trend's* Import Car of the Year for 1987, picked by *Road & Track* as Best High Performance Car ($22,500-$27,500) and as Best Sedan ($17,500-$22,500) for 1987, named to *Car and Driver's* 10 Best Cars list of 1988, and named to *Car and Driver's* Ten Best Cars list for 1990. Legend, restyled for 1991, incorporated a number of refinements for the 1992 model year. The two-door Legend Coupe is offered in L and LS models only.

1991 Acura Legend L

MAJOR FEATURES

● Acura Legend has as 1992 standard equipment: 5-speed manual transmission, 4-wheel independent suspension, 4-wheel disc brakes, power rack-and-pinion steering, driver's side airbag, rear window defroster, adjustable lumbar support and power height adjustment, air conditioning, AM/FM stereo/cassette, power antenna, power windows, power door locks, cruise control, and security system.

● Acura Legend L adds as 1992 standard equipment: anti-lock braking system, passenger's side air bag, 8-way power driver's seat with a memory function, steering wheel remote control for audio system, power sunroof, and overhead map lights.

● Acura Legend LS adds as 1992 standard equipment: automatic climate control, burled walnut trim, heated front seats, passenger's 4-way power seat, Acura/Bose music system, and illuminated entry system.

PRICE HISTORY

The following new car prices reflect the approximate retail cost of the base model: **1987** - $20,258; **1988** - $21,805; **1989** - $22,600; **1990** - $22,600; **1991** - $26,800; **1992** - $27,450.

DIMENSIONS

Body Style	Years Avail	Wheel Base (in)	Lgth (in)	Ht (in)	Avg Wt (lbs)	Fuel Cap (gal)	Front Hdrm (in)	Front Legrm (in)
2d cpe	87-90	106.5	188.0	53.9	3,139	18.0	37.2	42.9
2d cpe	91-92	111.4	192.5	53.5	3,424	18.0	37.3	42.9
4d sdn	87-90	108.7	190.6	54.7	3,170	18.0	38.4	43.4
4d sdn	91-92	114.6	194.9	55.1	3,402	18.0	39.3	42.7

ENGINES

Type	Displacement (L)	Fuel Dly	HP @rpm	Torque @rpm (ft/lbs)	MPG Cty/Hwy	Years Avail
V-6	2.5	FI	151@5800	154@4500	20/25	87-87
V-6	2.7	FI	160@5900	162@4500	19/24	87-90
V-6	3.2	FI	200@5500	210@4500	18/26	91-92

KEY: I=in-line engine; V=V engine; F=flat engine; FI=fuel injection; bbl=barrel carburetor; T=turbo; D=diesel; HP=horsepower; MPG=estimated average miles per gallon.

EVALUATIONS, TESTS, AND RANKINGS

1992: "the instrument by which the other sedans in this category have been setting their watches ... Still the dictionary definition of smooth, refined and reliable, the new Legend LS remains the benchmark." **Source:** "Real World 101, Six luxuriant sedans vie for a place in your life: Acura Legend LS, Audi 100 S, Mazda 929, Acura Vigor GS, Lexus ES 300, Mitsubishi Diamante LS," *Road & Track*, February 1992, pp. 59-67, 69.

1992: "quick and fast, quiet and comfortable. . .Inner- and outer-door panels are thicker. . .adding not only safety but resistance to minor dents." **Source:** "From Acura, A Legend to Live With," *New York Times,* February 2, 1992, Sec. 8, p. 11.

1991: "In the safety arena. . .Legends stand out sharply . . . anti-lock brakes and driver's-side airbags are standard . . . new Legends are longer, wider, lower, faster, smarter . . . quite impressive." **Source:** "Acura Legend Sedan and Coupe: Still worthy of the name," *Road & Track,* December 1990, pp. 62-63.

1991: "most impressive engine that's among the best in the world . . . Spacious rear seat comfortable enough for a full-grown adult. . .Bland interior." **Source:** "Acura Legend Coupe: Time, Rivals Catching Up," *Autoweek's Autofile 1991 Edition,* 1990, pp. 92-96.

1991: "the 1991 Acura Legend is wider, looks more dramatic, offers more legroom, and features a more luxuriant cabin . . . passenger volume is up . . . 9.4 cubic feet; trunk space is nearly unchanged." **Source:** "Acura Legend: Honda overhauls its groundbreaking concept," *Automobile Magazine,* December 1990, pp. 76-77, 80-81.

1991: "it delivers commendable control. . .has grown into a larger, softer car. . .pleasing to drive, and unquestionably well-engineered." **Source:** "Acura Legend: Honda's second-generation luxury car: growing up under pressure," *Car and Driver,* December 1990, pp. 115-119.

1991: "sedan bigger, roomier, heavier, more powerful and more expensive than the model it replaces.the '91 gets slightly better gas mileage . . . Most. . .models also will escape the new 10 percent luxury tax on new cars that sell for more than $30,000." **Source:** "Honda gives Legend roomier, heavier, more powerful makeover," *The Detroit News,* November 8, 1990, pp. E1-E2.

1991: "with a large dose of extra power, fuel economy has magically improved . . . offers reasonable leg room in back, and the trunk is cavernous . . . controls . . . are pretty much well arranged." **Source:** "Acura Creates a Couple of New Legends," *New York Times,* June 2, 1991.

1990: "Even after a few years on the market, the Legend remains as modern as tomorrow morning . . . Sit inside and the Legend at once springs to your service . . . From the outside, the Legend Coupe is low, sleek, and contemporary." **Source:** "Acura Legend Coupe vs. Infinity M30 Coupe: Slugging it Out—Softly," *Motor Trend,* September 1990, pp.98-100, 102-103.

1989: "The car sped us reliably everywhere . . . the arrangement of buttons and slots on the dash of the Acura Legend Coupe is confusing . . . Overall quality: Excellent." **Source:** "Acura: A Legend in Its Own Time," *Design News,* October 3, 1988, pp. 230-231.

1988: "never experienced a car that was more sure-footed in the rain. . .grip is tenacious, its handling predictable and its antilock braking system (ALB) awesome . . . driving environment is at once ergonomically sound and sensually pleasing." **Source:** "Sure-footed Acura dazzling when wet," *The Detroit News,* August 17, 1988, pp. F1-F2.

1988: "sublimely comfortable and fun to drive . . . extraordinary visibility from the driver's seat . . . less-than-dazzling looks." **Source:** "driving style: Sleek looks . . . all-star performance," *Vogue,* January 1988, p. 60.

1987: "The interior of the car is spacious and well appointed . . . ride is comfortable, but a little too soft for a car that's capable of driving as quickly and spiritedly as this one is . . . worth a serious look." **Source:** "Acura Legend: An old favorite goes upscale," *Home Mechanix,* November 1986, pp. 24-26.

RECALLS

1991: (14,230 four-door passenger cars): Transmission shift cable bracket can be damaged by the engine rocking forward on engine mounts in a minor collision. When the shift cable bracket is damaged, the shift lever position may not correctly indicate the transmission gear position, which could result in unanticipated movement of the car, causing an accident. **Corrective action:** Replace the transmission shift cable and attaching hardwre with redesigned assemblies. *(NHTSA Campaign No. 91V065000.)*

1988: (99,088 cars; includes Acura and Honda models): Sections 6A and 6B were omitted from owner's manual. **Corrective action:** Insert corrective pages. *(NHTSA Campaign No. 87V171000.)*

SAFETY AND REPAIRS

1992: "Honda to Fix Bad Oil Switch," *Automotive News,* January 27, 1992, p. 2.

OTHER INFORMATION SOURCES

3 ● **Acura Driving Club Magazine**
Acura Driving Club of America
W. 222 33rd Ave., Ste. 13
Spokane, WA 99203

Magazine for Acura owners. Quarterly. **Price:** $25.00.

ASSOCIATIONS

4 ● **Hondacar International**
P.O. Box 5242
Deptford, NJ 08096
John Blair, Pres.

Founded: 1976. **Membership:** 1,700. Persons interested in any model of the Honda or Acura automobile. Purpose is to inform owners of both the pleasures of and potential problems with their cars, and to suggest ways to avoid such problems. **Former Name(s):** Honda Civic Club.

ACURA NSX (1991-92)

Introduced as part of Acura line, which is a division of American Honda Motor Co. NSX is the two-seat, all-aluminum sport coupe of Acura; 3,000 units are built annually. Chosen by *Automobile Magazine* as the 1991 Automobile of the Year, 1991 Design of the Year, and 1992 All Star. Produced in Tochiga, Japan.

1991 Acura NSX

MAJOR FEATURES

● Acura NSX 1992 standard equipment includes: 5-speed

manual transmission, anti-lock brakes, alloy wheels, leather-trimmed power seats, automatic climate control, Acura/Bose music system, driver's side airbag, and security system.

PRICE HISTORY

The following new car prices reflect the approximate retail cost of the base model: **1991** - $61,000; **1992** - $63,000.

DIMENSIONS

Body Style	Years Avail	Wheel Base (in)	Lgth (in)	Ht (in)	Avg Wt (lbs)	Fuel Cap (gal)	Front Hdrm (in)	Front Legrm (in)
cpe	91-92	99.6	173.4	46.1	3,010	18.5	36.3	44.3

ENGINES

Type	Displacement (L)	Fuel Dly	HP @rpm	Torque @rpm (ft/lbs)	MPG Cty/Hwy	Years Avail
V-6	3.0	FI	252@6600	210@5300	18/24	91-91
V-6	3.0	FI	270@7100	210@5300	19/24	91-92

KEY: I=in-line engine; V=V engine; F=flat engine; FI=fuel injection; bbl=barrel carburetor; T=turbo; D=diesel; HP=horsepower; MPG=estimated average miles per gallon.

EVALUATIONS, TESTS, AND RANKINGS

1992: "This car takes F=ma to its highest streetgoing evolution . . . it rushes . . . it rips . . . it soars." **Source:** "Ten Best Cars to Move You," Car and Driver, January 1992, pp. 63-65, 67.

1992: "one of the finest cars on the planet." **Source:** "Acura NSX: A bullet-fast monument to success," Automobile Magazine, January 1992, p. 48.

1991: "Incredible performance, handling and stability . . . powerful engine ensured effortless cruising and eye-blink passing . . . On some pavement, the tires were dreadfully noisy, even for a sports car." **Source:** "NSX: 'Why not have it all,'" USA Today, August 3, 1990, p. B4.

1991: "scats to 60 mph in a mere 5.7 seconds." **Source:** "Acura NSX: One of the Ten Best Cars in the World, 1991," Road & Track, December 1990, p. 48.

1991: "all-around blend of speed. . .flawless handling and superb road manners is unique." **Source:** "Acura NSX," Popular Mechanics, December 1990, p. 26.

1991: "combines all the performance and mechanical intrigue you could wnat from a world-class exotic sports car, with the user-friendliness and innovation you've come to expect from Honda." **Source:** "Acura NSX," Motor Trend, December 1990, pp. 38-45.

1991: "With its lightweight aluminum body . . . the acceleration is phenomenal . . . high speed manners are impeccable." **Source:** "Acura NSX exotic but friendly," Detroit Free Press, December 6, 1990, p. E1.

1991: "the car's light weight and technology conspire to provide an economy rating of 19 m.p.g., city, and 24, highway, good enough to avoid America's gas-guzzler tax." **Source:** "Acura's NSX: All-Aluminum Exotica," The New York Times, November 11, 1990.

1991: "certain to become a milestone in sports car design . . . it's a model of stability in the 130-mph range, and remarkably quiet . . . superb sports car." **Source:** "Acura's NSX Challenges the Elite," Popular Mechanics, September 1990, pp. 106-107.

1991: "car will propel from zero to 60 mph in about 5.5 seconds . . . steering effort was a bit high at parking speeds, but not uncomfortable . . . cornered flatly and stayed nailed down at high speeds and on smooth or uneven surfaces." **Source:** "Glowing reports on Acura NSX right on track," Flint Journal, September 11, 1991, pp. D1-D2.

RECALLS

None to date.

OTHER INFORMATION SOURCES

5 • Acura Driving Club Magazine
Acura Driving Club of America
W. 222 33rd Ave., Ste. 13
Spokane, WA 99203

Magazine for Acura owners. Quarterly. **Price:** $25.00.

ASSOCIATIONS

6 • Hondacar International
P.O. Box 5242
Deptford, NJ 08096
John Blair, Pres.

Founded: 1976. **Membership:** 1,700. Persons interested in any model of the Honda or Acura automobile. Purpose is to inform owners of both the pleasures of and potential problems with their cars, and to suggest ways to avoid such problems. **Former Name(s):** Honda Civic Club.

ACURA VIGOR (1992)

Announced in the spring of 1991 as a 1992 model, the Vigor personal performance sports sedan is positioned between the Legend and Integra lines in both size and price. The Vigor, which is available in two trim models—LS and GS, utilized NASA's NASTRAN Computer-Aided Design in its structural design phase. This allowed engineers to design a structure with the highest rigidity, yet control the overall weight of the vehicle. The Vigor is assembled in Saitama, Japan.

1992 Acura Vigor LS

MAJOR FEATURES

● Vigor LS has as 1992 standard equipment: 2.5-liter 5-cylinder engine, 5-speed manual transmission, speed-sensitive rack-and-pinion steering, 4-wheel disc brakes with ABS, driver's side air bag, air conditioning, power windows; door locks, and mirrors; tilt steering, cruise control, and 8-speaker AM/FM cassette stereo system.

● Vigor GS adds as 1992 standard equipment: leather interior, power moonroof, and driver's 4-way power seat.

PRICE HISTORY

The following new car prices reflect the approximate retail cost of the base model: **1992 - $23,265.**

DIMENSIONS

Body Style	Years Avail	Wheel Base (in)	Lgth (in)	Ht (in)	Avg Wt (lbs)	Fuel Cap (gal)	Front Hdrm (in)	Front Legrm (in)
4d sdn	92-92	110.4	190.4	53.9	3,212	17.2	38.0	43.7

ENGINES

Type	Displacement (L)	Fuel Dly	HP @rpm	Torque @rpm (ft/lbs)	MPG Cty/Hwy	Years Avail
I-5	2.5	FI	175@6300	170@3900	20/25	92-92

KEY: I=in-line engine; V=V engine; F=flat engine; FI=fuel injection; bbl=barrel carburetor; T=turbo; D=diesel; HP=horsepower; MPG=estimated average miles per gallon.

EVALUATIONS, TESTS, AND RANKINGS

1992: "felt strangely unsatisfying ... lithe and nimble feel along with excellent road control ... Innovations abound." **Source:** "Vigor proves perfection can be perfectly boring," *Detroit News*, November 13, 1991, pp. 1E, 5E.

1992: "understeers a mite ... balanced, predictable, communicative and fun ... interior is the best of Japanese design efficiency at work." **Source:** "Real World 101," *Road & Track*, February 1992, pp. 59-67, 69.

RECALLS

None to date.

OTHER INFORMATION SOURCES

7 ● **Acura Driving Club Magazine**
Acura Driving Club of America
W. 222 33rd Ave., Ste. 13
Spokane, WA 99203

Magazine for Acura owners. Quarterly. **Price:** $25.00.

ASSOCIATIONS

8 ● **Hondacar International**
P.O. Box 5242
Deptford, NJ 08096
John Blair, Pres.

Founded: 1976. **Membership:** 1,700. Persons interested in any model of the Honda or Acura automobile. Purpose is to inform owners of both the pleasures of and potential problems with their cars, and to suggest ways to avoid such problems. **Former Name(s):** Honda Civic Club.

ALFA ROMEO 164 (1991-92)

High-performance sedan with Pininfarina styling introduced to U.S. market in 1991. Produced in Arese, Italy and distributed by Alpha Romeo Distributors of North America in Orlando, Florida.

1991 Alfa Romeo 164

MAJOR FEATURES

● Alfa Romeo 164L has as 1992 standard equipment: 5-speed manual overdrive transaxle, front-wheel drive, four-wheel power disc brakes, anti-lock brake system, power-assisted rack-and-pinion steering, independent front and rear suspension, driver's side airbag, air conditioning, electric rear window defroster, cruise control, and sound system.

● Alfa Romeo 164S, which provides higher performance and a more sporty feel, adds as 1992 standard equipment: electronic sport suspension, rear decklid spoiler, six-way powered adjustable sport bucket seats, and other exterior body stylings.

PRICE HISTORY

The following new car prices reflect the approximate retail cost of the base model: **1991 - $24,500; 1992 - $24,700.**

DIMENSIONS

Body Style	Years Avail	Wheel Base (in)	Lgth (in)	Ht (in)	Avg Wt (lbs)	Fuel Cap (gal)	Front Hdrm (in)	Front Legrm (in)
sdn	91-92	104.7	179.4	54.8	3,325	17.2	38.2	39.3

ENGINES

Type	Displacement (L)	Fuel Dly	HP @rpm	Torque @rpm (ft/lbs)	MPG Cty/Hwy	Years Avail
V-6	3.0	FI	183@5800	185@4400	18/27	91-92
V-6	3.0	FI	200@6000	189@4400	17/25	91-92

KEY: I=in-line engine; V=V engine; F=flat engine; FI=fuel injection; bbl=barrel carburetor; T=turbo; D=diesel; HP=horsepower; MPG=estimated average miles per gallon.

EVALUATIONS, TESTS, AND RANKINGS

1991: "The 164 has none of the quirkiness of recent Alfa Romeos ... combines high performance with ... comfort." **Source:** "Alfa Romeo 164: The last of its Type," *Car and Driver*, November 1990, p. 32.

1991: "chassis is incredibly rewarding to drive ... the gearbox, despite its recalcitrant engagement of reverse, is a joy ... subtle wedge shape, handsome from any angle." **Source:** "European Influence: Eight sporting sedans with price tags less than $30,000," *Road & Track*, August 1991, pp. 64-65, 66, 84.

1991: "[Alfa Romero 164L] steering's self-centering forces are curiously strong and artificial-feeling ... seats are decently comfortable ... Nice, but nowhere near the faster, sportier S-model." **Source:** "Foreigners in the Fast Lane," *Car and Driver*, July 1991, pp. 54-60, 62, 64, 66, 68-70.

RECALLS

1991: (4,500 vehicles): Headlight switch could malfunction causing sudden high beams failure. **Corrective action:** Replace headlights switch. (NHTSA Campaign No. 91V019000.)

REPAIR MANUALS

9 ● Alfa Romeo
Peter Allen Video Productions
38-C Otis St.
West Babylon, NY 11704   Ph:(516)643-4372

A video featuring information on how to tune-up, maintain, and perform minor repairs on the entitled vehicle. **Release date:** 1986. **Producer:** Peter Allen Productions. **Acquisition:** Purchase.

OTHER INFORMATION SOURCES

10 ● Alfa Club of Colorado—Newsletter
Alfa Club of Colorado
17227 E. Long Ave.
Aurora, CO 80016   Ph:(303)690-5287

Monthly.

11 ● Alfa Giornale
Alfa Romeo Owners Club, Detroit Chapter
282 Lake Village
Walled Lake, MI 48088   Ph:(313)624-3946

Monthly.

12 ● Alfa Owner
Alfa Romeo Owners Club
2468 Gum Tree Ln.
Fall Brock, CA 92028   Ph:(619)723-4875

Promotes the history and tradition of the Alfa Romeo automobile. Provides technical information and covers safe and skillful driving techniques. Reports on the Club's amateur driving events and socials. Monthly. **Editor(s):** Julie Nichols. **Price:** Available to members only.

13 ● Alfa Romeo Owners Club, Chicago Chapter— Membership Directory [Illinois]
Alfa Romeo Owners Club, Chicago Chapter
1804 Winthrop
Highland Park, IL 60035   Ph:(708)831-3561

Annual.

14 ● Alfa Romeo Owners Club—Membership Roster
Alfa Romeo Owners Club (AROC)
2468 Gum Tree Ln.
Fallbrook, CA 92028   Ph:(619)728-4875

Annual.

15 ● Alfa Romeo Owners Club, Northern California Chapter—Journal
Alfa Romeo Owners Club, Northern California Chapter
1116 18th St.   Ph:(916)483-4544
Sacramento, CA 95814-4111   Fax:(916)483-4088

Monthly.

16 ● Alfa Romeo Owners Club, Northern California Chapter—Newsletter
Alfa Romeo Owners Club, Northern California Chapter
1116 18th St.   Ph:(916)483-4544
Sacramento, CA 93814-4111   Fax:(916)483-4088

Quarterly.

17 ● Alfa Romeo Owners Club of Oklahoma—Newsletter
Alfa Romeo Owners Club of Oklahoma
4134 E. 37 Pl.
Tulsa, OK 74135   Ph:(918)743-4958

Monthly.

18 ● Alfa Romeo Owners Club of Texas—Newsletter
Alfa Romeo Owners Club of Texas
10100 S. Gessner., No. 714
Houston, TX 77071   Ph:(713)779-5129

Monthly.

19 ● Alfa Romeo Owners Club, Orange County Chapter— Newsletter [California]
Alfa Romeo Owners Club, Orange County Chapter
22692 Granite Way
Laguna Hills, CA 92653   Ph:(714)588-0500

Monthly.

20 ● Alfantics
Alfa Romeo Owners Club, Washington D.C. Chapter
7309 Delfield St.
Chevy Chase, MD 20815   Ph:(301)652-6287

Periodic.

21 ● Sotto Veloce
Alfa Romeo Owners Club, Chicago Chapter
1804 Winthrop
Highland Park, IL 60035   Ph:(708)831-3561

Newsletter. Monthly.

22 ● Tennessee Alfa—Newsletter
Tennessee Alfa
c/o Lee D. Thomas
2814 McNairy Ln.
Nashville, TN 37204   Ph:(615)269-3680

Periodic.

23 ● Voto Veloce
Alabama Alfa Romeo Owners Club
c/o Tad Bailey
4020 N. Cahaba Dr.
Birmingham, AL 35243   Ph:(205)836-8080

Newsletter. Periodic.

ASSOCIATIONS

24 ● Alabama Alfa Romeo Owners Club
c/o Tad Bailey
4020 N. Cahaba Dr.
Birmingham, AL 35243
Tad Bailey, Exec. Officer   Ph:(205)836-8080

Individuals interested in Alfa Romeo automobiles united for information exchange and fellowship. **Convention/Meeting:** Monthly.

25 ● Alfa Club of Colorado
17227 E. Long Ave.
Aurora, CO 80016
Richard Smith, Pres.   Ph:(303)690-5287

Founded: 1969. **Membership:** 90. Enthusiasts of the Alfa Romeo automobile organized to promote the marque. **Convention/Meeting:** Monthly.

26 ● Alfa Romeo Owners Club
2468 Gum Tree Ln.
Fallbrook, CA 92028
Glenna Garrett, Exec.Sec.   Ph:(619)728-4875

Founded: 1958. **Membership:** 5500. Owners and enthusiasts of Alfa Romeo automobiles. Promotes knowledge of the history and tradition of the Alfa Romeo marque; provides technical information for efficient and safe operation of Alfas. Chapters organize socials and amateur driving events and conduct technical seminars and driver's schools to teach safe and skillful driving on the highway and in competitions. Maintains library of technical manuals. **Convention/Meeting:** Annual.

27 ● Alfa Romeo Owners Club, Atlanta Chapter [Georgia]
6728 Cockridge Dr.
Atlanta, GA 30360
Chuck Lipper, Pres.   Ph:(404)399-6159

Founded: 1970. **Membership:** 120. Owners and enthusiasts of the Alfa Romeo automobile. Promotes safety and knowledge of the Alfa Romeo. **Convention/Meeting:** Monthly.

28 ● Alfa Romeo Owners Club, Northeastern Ohio Chapter
445 S. Green Rd.
South Euclid, OH 44121
Richard W. Gent, Pres.   Ph:(216)481-2334

Owners and enthusiasts of Alfa Romeo automobiles united to promote the history of the Italian car and provide technical information for its safe and efficient operation. Sponsors car shows, auto races, time trials, and other social events.

29 ● Alfa Romeo Owners Club, Northern California Chapter
1116 18th St.
Sacramento, CA 95814-4111
Mark Webber, Pres.   Ph:(916)483-4544

Membership: 5500. Owners of Alfa Romeo automobiles. To preserve, collect, and protect Alfa Romeos.

30 ● Alfa Romeo Owners Club of Oklahoma
4134 E. 37th Pl.
Tulsa, OK 74135
David Simmons, Exec. Officer

Owners and enthusiasts of Alfa Romeo automobiles.

31 ● Alfa Romeo Owners Club, Orange County Chapter [California]
22692 Granite Way
Laguna Hills, CA 92653
Carole Sandeman, Sec.   Ph:(714)588-0500

Founded: 1985. **Membership:** 100. Owners and enthusiasts of the Alfa Romeo automobile. Works to further technical knowledge and enjoyment of the automobile. Sponsors rallies, tours, concours, and other related events. **Convention/Meeting:** Monthly.

32 ● Alfa Romeo Owners Club, Washington D.C. Chapter
7309 Delfield St.
Chevy Chase, MD 20815
Steve Morrison, Pres.   Ph:(301)652-6287

Founded: 1959. **Membership:** 300. Alfa Romeo enthusiasts in northern Virginia, Maryland, southern Pennsylvania, and Washington, D.C. Provides social activities, competitive events, and technical sessions. Maintains print, video, and tool library. **Convention/Meeting:** Annual - always summer. Also holds monthly meeting - always first Monday of the month.

33 ● Deep South Alfa Romeo Club [Mississippi, Louisiana, and southwestern Tennessee]
P.O. Box 2162
Jackson, MS 39205
Alfonso Vasquez, Pres.   Ph:(601)636-3470

Founded: 1982. **Membership:** 30. Alfa Romeo enthusiasts in Mississippi, Louisiana, and southwestern Tennessee. Provides support, encouragement, and technical information to Alfa Romeo owners. Sponsors social activities and tours. **Convention/Meeting:** Annual; also holds monthly meeting.

ALFA ROMEO MILANO (1987-89)

High-performance sedan produced in Italy and offered in the U.S. through 1989.

MAJOR FEATURES

● Alfa Romeo Platinum had as 1989 standard equipment: 5-speed manual transmission, power steering, antilock brakes, air-conditioning, rear-window defroster, sunroof, leather interior, and stereo cassette system.

● Alfa Romeo Milano Verde added as 1989 standard equipment: 3.0 liter, V-6 engine, independent suspension, tilt steering, and heated driver's seat.

● Alfa Romeo Milano Gold added as 1989 standard equipment: 2.5 liter, V-6 engine and other exterior body stylings.

● Alfa Romeo 6V 3.0 America had as 1987 standard equipment: 3.0 V-6 engine, five-speed manual transmission, and front and rear anti-roll bars.

PRICE HISTORY

The following new car prices reflect the approximate retail cost of the base model: **1987** - $15,400; **1988** - $17,550; **1989** - $18,475.

DIMENSIONS

Body Style	Years Avail	Wheel Base (in)	Lgth (in)	Ht (in)	Avg Wt (lbs)	Fuel Cap (gal)	Front Hdrm (in)	Front Legrm (in)
4d sdn	87-89	98.8	170.5	53.1	2,907	17.6	38.2	37.2

ENGINES

Type	Displacement (L)	Fuel Dly	HP @rpm	Torque @rpm (ft/lbs)	MPG Cty/Hwy	Years Avail
V-6	2.5	FI	154@5500	152@3200	18/24	87-89
V-6	3.0	FI	183@5800	181@3000	18/25	87-89

KEY: I=in-line engine; V=V engine; F=flat engine; FI=fuel injection; bbl=barrel carburetor; T=turbo; D=diesel; HP=horsepower; MPG=estimated average miles per gallon.

EVALUATIONS, TESTS, AND RANKINGS

1989: "one of the most exotic cars that carries four doors . . . chassis is tuned for lots of suspension travel . . . ride quality is good, particularly on rough roads." **Source:** "Shankle Alfa Romeo Milano," *Motor Trend*, December 1988, pp. 78-79.

1988: "one fine handling sedan . . . This a car that truly looks like no other . . . backseat quite comfortable." **Source:** "Alfa Romeo Milano Verde: Love at second sight," *Motor Trend*, November 1987, pp. 94-95, 145.

1988: "Drive it at 55 mph, and you'll think it's a noisy, bouncy bore . . . not a great sports sedan, but is sure is fun." **Source:** "This Sportin' Life," *Popular Mechanics*, January 1987, pp. 60-64, 114.

1987: "our test car had over 8000 miles, hard ones, harder than you'll ever drive, and everything on it worked. There were no rattles. It started perfectly and ran hard." **Source:** "Alfa Romeo Milano: Speed in the afternoon," *Motor Trend*, February 1987, p. 86.

1987: "a quick . . . automobile . . . . the wheel is too far away, the pedals too close." **Source:** "Alfa Romeo Milano Verde: A special heritage is standard equipment," *Car and Driver*, September 1987, pp. 99-100.

1987: "joy to handle. . .test route included quite a number of rough roads with which the suspension dealt very competently. . .gear change was a good surprise." **Source:** "Letter from Europe: More Power to You [Alfa Romeo 6V 3.0 America]," *Road & Track*, June 1987, pp. 148, 152, 154, 156.

RECALLS

1987-88: (6,000 passenger cars): May be intermittent headlights stalk switch malfunction. This could result in sudden headlights failure without prior warning with potential for accident. **Corrective action:** Replace headlight switch, if necessary, and modify headlight switch wiring harness. *(NHTSA Campaign No. 88V070000.)*

REPAIR MANUALS

34 ● Alfa Romeo
Peter Allen Video Productions
38-C Otis St.
West Babylon, NY 11704   Ph:(516)643-4372

A video featuring information on how to tune-up, maintain, and perform minor repairs on the entitled vehicle. **Release date:** 1986. **Producer:** Peter Allen Productions. **Acquisition:** Purchase.

OTHER INFORMATION SOURCES

35 ● Alfa Club of Colorado—Newsletter
Alfa Club of Colorado
17227 E. Long Ave.
Aurora, CO 80016   Ph:(303)690-5287

Monthly.

36 ● Alfa Giornale
Alfa Romeo Owners Club, Detroit Chapter
282 Lake Village
Walled Lake, MI 48088   Ph:(313)624-3946

Monthly.

37 ● Alfa Owner
Alfa Romeo Owners Club
2468 Gum Tree Ln.
Fall Brock, CA 92028   Ph:(619)723-4875

Promotes the history and tradition of the Alfa Romeo automobile. Provides technical information and covers safe and skillful driving techniques. Reports on the Club's amateur driving events and socials. Monthly. **Editor(s):** Julie Nichols. **Price:** Available to members only.

38 ● Alfa Romeo Owners Club, Chicago Chapter—Membership Directory [Illinois]
Alfa Romeo Owners Club, Chicago Chapter
1804 Winthrop
Highland Park, IL 60035   Ph:(708)831-3561

Annual.

39 ● Alfa Romeo Owners Club—Membership Roster
Alfa Romeo Owners Club (AROC)
2468 Gum Tree Ln.
Fallbrook, CA 92028   Ph:(619)728-4875

Annual.

40 ● Alfa Romeo Owners Club, Northern California Chapter—Journal
Alfa Romeo Owners Club, Northern California Chapter
1116 18th St.   Ph:(916)483-4544
Sacramento, CA 95814-4111   Fax:(916)483-4088

Monthly.

41 ● Alfa Romeo Owners Club, Northern California Chapter—Newsletter
Alfa Romeo Owners Club, Northern California Chapter
1116 18th St.   Ph:(916)483-4544
Sacramento, CA 93814-4111   Fax:(916)483-4088

Quarterly.

42 ● Alfa Romeo Owners Club of Oklahoma—Newsletter
Alfa Romeo Owners Club of Oklahoma
4134 E. 37 Pl.
Tulsa, OK 74135   Ph:(918)743-4958

Monthly.

43 ● Alfa Romeo Owners Club of Texas—Newsletter
Alfa Romeo Owners Club of Texas
10100 S. Gessner., No. 714
Houston, TX 77071   Ph:(713)779-5129

Monthly.

44 ● Alfa Romeo Owners Club, Orange County Chapter—Newsletter [California]
Alfa Romeo Owners Club, Orange County Chapter
22692 Granite Way
Laguna Hills, CA 92653   Ph:(714)588-0500

Monthly.

45 ● Alfantics
Alfa Romeo Owners Club, Washington D.C. Chapter
7309 Delfield St.
Chevy Chase, MD 20815   Ph:(301)652-6287

Periodic.

46 ● Sotto Veloce
Alfa Romeo Owners Club, Chicago Chapter
1804 Winthrop
Highland Park, IL 60035   Ph:(708)831-3561

Newsletter. Monthly.

47 ● Tennessee Alfa—Newsletter
Tennessee Alfa
c/o Lee D. Thomas
2814 McNairy Ln.
Nashville, TN 37204   Ph:(615)269-3680

Periodic.

48 ● Voto Veloce
Alabama Alfa Romeo Owners Club
c/o Tad Bailey
4020 N. Cahaba Dr.
Birmingham, AL 35243   Ph:(205)836-8080

Newsletter. Periodic.

ASSOCIATIONS

49 ● Alabama Alfa Romeo Owners Club
c/o Tad Bailey
4020 N. Cahaba Dr.
Birmingham, AL 35243
Tad Bailey, Exec. Officer   Ph:(205)836-8080

Individuals interested in Alfa Romeo automobiles united for information exchange and fellowship. **Convention/Meeting:** Monthly.

50 ● Alfa Club of Colorado
17227 E. Long Ave.
Aurora, CO 80016
Richard Smith, Pres.   Ph:(303)690-5287

Founded: 1969. **Membership:** 90. Enthusiasts of the Alfa Romeo automobile organized to promote the marque. **Convention/Meeting:** Monthly.

51 ● Alfa Romeo Owners Club
2468 Gum Tree Ln.
Fallbrook, CA 92028
Glenna Garrett, Exec.Sec.   Ph:(619)728-4875

Founded: 1958. **Membership:** 5500. Owners and enthusiasts of Alfa Romeo automobiles. Promotes knowledge of the history and tradition of the Alfa Romeo marque; provides technical information for efficient and safe operation of Alfas. Chapters organize socials and amateur driving events and conduct technical seminars and driver's schools to teach safe and skillful driving on the highway and in competitions. Maintains library of technical manuals. **Convention/Meeting:** Annual.

52 ● Alfa Romeo Owners Club, Atlanta Chapter [Georgia]
6728 Cockridge Dr.
Atlanta, GA 30360
Chuck Lipper, Pres.   Ph:(404)399-6159

Founded: 1970. **Membership:** 120. Owners and enthusiasts of the Alfa Romeo automobile. Promotes safety and knowledge of the Alfa Romeo. **Convention/Meeting:** Monthly.

53 ● Alfa Romeo Owners Club, Northeastern Ohio Chapter
445 S. Green Rd.
South Euclid, OH 44121
Richard W. Gent, Pres.   Ph:(216)481-2334

Owners and enthusiasts of Alfa Romeo automobiles united to

promote the history of the Italian car and provide technical information for its safe and efficient operation. Sponsors car shows, auto races, time trials, and other social events.

54 ● Alfa Romeo Owners Club, Northern California Chapter
1116 18th St.
Sacramento, CA 95814-4111
Mark Webber, Pres.   Ph:(916)483-4544

Membership: 5500. Owners of Alfa Romeo automobiles. To preserve, collect, and protect Alfa Romeos.

55 ● Alfa Romeo Owners Club of Oklahoma
4134 E. 37th Pl.
Tulsa, OK 74135
David Simmons, Exec. Officer

Owners and enthusiasts of Alfa Romeo automobiles.

56 ● Alfa Romeo Owners Club, Orange County Chapter [California]
22692 Granite Way
Laguna Hills, CA 92653
Carole Sandeman, Sec.   Ph:(714)588-0500

Founded: 1985. **Membership:** 100. Owners and enthusiasts of the Alfa Romeo automobile. Works to further technical knowledge and enjoyment of the automobile. Sponsors rallies, tours, concours, and other related events. **Convention/Meeting:** Monthly.

57 ● Alfa Romeo Owners Club, Washington D.C. Chapter
7309 Delfield St.
Chevy Chase, MD 20815
Steve Morrison, Pres.   Ph:(301)652-6287

Founded: 1959. **Membership:** 300. Alfa Romeo enthusiasts in northern Virginia, Maryland, southern Pennsylvania, and Washington, D.C. Provides social activities, competitive events, and technical sessions. Maintains print, video, and tool library. **Convention/Meeting:** Annual - always summer. Also holds monthly meeting - always first Monday of the month.

58 ● Deep South Alfa Romeo Club [Mississippi, Louisiana, and southwestern Tennessee]
P.O. Box 2162
Jackson, MS 39205
Alfonso Vasquez, Pres.   Ph:(601)636-3470

Founded: 1982. **Membership:** 30. Alfa Romeo enthusiasts in Mississippi, Louisiana, and southwestern Tennessee. Provides support, encouragement, and technical information to Alfa Romeo owners. Sponsors social activities and tours. **Convention/Meeting:** Annual; also holds monthly meeting.

ALFA ROMEO SPIDER (1987-92)

Spider was originally introduced as a 2-door convertible sports car. Spider Graduate and Spider Quadrifoglio were discontinued in 1990. The Alfa Romeo Spider Series was ranked as having the lowest fuel cost and the Alfa Romeo Spider Quadrifoglio had one of the highest repair cost among sport vehicles in 1990 according to *The Complete Car Cost Guide*. Produced in Torino, Italy and distributed by Alfa Romeo Distributors of North America in Orlando, Florida.

1991 Alfa Romeo Spider

MAJOR FEATURES

● Alfa Romeo Spider has as 1992 standard equipment: 5-speed manual overdrive transmission, independent front suspension, power steering, power four-wheel disc brakes, driver's side airbag, and power antenna.

● Alfa Romeo Spider Veloce adds as 1992 standard equipment: exterior body stylings, air conditioning, and additional interior accessories.

● Alfa Romeo Spider Graduate, which was the base model, had as 1990 standard equipment: air dam, four-wheel power disc brakes, rear fog lights, dual power remote control mirrors, and vinyl reclining bucket seats.

● Alfa Romeo Spider Quadrifoglio added as 1990 standard equipment: air conditioning, rear window defroster, power antenna, and power windows.

PRICE HISTORY

The following new car prices reflect the approximate retail cost of the base model: **1987** - $13,995; **1988** - $15,400; **1989** - $15,060; **1990** - $16,950; **1991** - $20,950; **1992** - $21,264.

DIMENSIONS

Body Style	Years Avail	Wheel Base (in)	Lgth (in)	Ht (in)	Avg Wt (lbs)	Fuel Cap (gal)	Front Hdrm (in)	Front Legrm (in)
2d conv	87-92	88.6	167.7	49.7	2,548	12.2	37.0	38.8

ENGINES

Type	Displacement (L)	Fuel Dly	HP @rpm	Torque @rpm (ft/lbs)	MPG Cty/Hwy	Years Avail
I-4	2.0	FI	115@5500	119@2750	22/30	87-91
I-4	2.0	FI	120@5800	117@2700	22/30	92-92

KEY: I=in-line engine; V=V engine; F=flat engine; FI=fuel injection; bbl=barrel carburetor; T=turbo; D=diesel; HP=horsepower; MPG=estimated average miles per gallon.

EVALUATIONS, TESTS, AND RANKINGS

1987: "a classic rendition of the ragtop, Italian style . . . Performance is good, but handling suffers." **Source:** "Topless Models: Let the good times roll—again," *Motor Trend*, May 1987, pp. 35-40.

RECALLS

1991: (500 vehicles): Casting flaw in steering box pitman or idle arm could result in sudden loss of control without warning with a potential for an accident. **Corrective action:** Replace components with casting flaw. *(NHTSA Campaign No. 91V007000.)*

REPAIR MANUALS

59 ● Alfa Romeo
Peter Allen Video Productions
38-C Otis St.
West Babylon, NY 11704   Ph:(516)643-4372

A video featuring information on how to tune-up, maintain, and perform minor repairs on the entitled vehicle. **Release date:** 1986. **Producer:** Peter Allen Productions. **Acquisition:** Purchase.

OTHER INFORMATION SOURCES

60 ● Alfa Club of Colorado—Newsletter
Alfa Club of Colorado
17227 E. Long Ave.
Aurora, CO 80016   Ph:(303)690-5287

Monthly.

61 ● Alfa Giornale
Alfa Romeo Owners Club, Detroit Chapter
282 Lake Village
Walled Lake, MI 48088   Ph:(313)624-3946

Monthly.

62 ● Alfa Owner
Alfa Romeo Owners Club
2468 Gum Tree Ln.
Fall Brock, CA 92028   Ph:(619)723-4875

Promotes the history and tradition of the Alfa Romeo automobile. Provides technical information and covers safe and skillful driving techniques. Reports on the Club's amateur driving events and socials. Monthly. **Editor(s):** Julie Nichols. **Price:** Available to members only.

63 ● Alfa Romeo Owners Club, Chicago Chapter—Membership Directory [Illinois]
Alfa Romeo Owners Club, Chicago Chapter
1804 Winthrop
Highland Park, IL 60035   Ph:(708)831-3561

Annual.

64 ● Alfa Romeo Owners Club—Membership Roster
Alfa Romeo Owners Club (AROC)
2468 Gum Tree Ln.
Fallbrook, CA 92028   Ph:(619)728-4875

Annual.

65 ● Alfa Romeo Owners Club, Northern California Chapter—Journal
Alfa Romeo Owners Club, Northern California Chapter
1116 18th St.   Ph:(916)483-4544
Sacramento, CA 95814-4111   Fax:(916)483-4088

Monthly.

66 ● Alfa Romeo Owners Club, Northern California Chapter—Newsletter
Alfa Romeo Owners Club, Northern California Chapter
1116 18th St.   Ph:(916)483-4544
Sacramento, CA 93814-4111   Fax:(916)483-4088

Quarterly.

67 ● Alfa Romeo Owners Club of Oklahoma—Newsletter
Alfa Romeo Owners Club of Oklahoma
4134 E. 37 Pl.
Tulsa, OK 74135   Ph:(918)743-4958

Monthly.

68 ● Alfa Romeo Owners Club of Texas—Newsletter
Alfa Romeo Owners Club of Texas
10100 S. Gessner., No. 714
Houston, TX 77071   Ph:(713)779-5129

Monthly.

69 ● Alfa Romeo Owners Club, Orange County Chapter—
    Newsletter [California]
Alfa Romeo Owners Club, Orange County Chapter
22692 Granite Way
Laguna Hills, CA 92653   Ph:(714)588-0500

Monthly.

70 ● Alfantics
Alfa Romeo Owners Club, Washington D.C. Chapter
7309 Delfield St.
Chevy Chase, MD 20815   Ph:(301)652-6287

Periodic.

71 ● Sotto Veloce
Alfa Romeo Owners Club, Chicago Chapter
1804 Winthrop
Highland Park, IL 60035   Ph:(708)831-3561

Newsletter. Monthly.

72 ● Tennessee Alfa—Newsletter
Tennessee Alfa
c/o Lee D. Thomas
2814 McNairy Ln.
Nashville, TN 37204   Ph:(615)269-3680

Periodic.

73 ● Voto Veloce
Alabama Alfa Romeo Owners Club
c/o Tad Bailey
4020 N. Cahaba Dr.
Birmingham, AL 35243   Ph:(205)836-8080

Newsletter. Periodic.

ASSOCIATIONS

74 ● Alabama Alfa Romeo Owners Club
c/o Tad Bailey
4020 N. Cahaba Dr.
Birmingham, AL 35243
Tad Bailey, Exec. Officer   Ph:(205)836-8080

Individuals interested in Alfa Romeo automobiles united for information exchange and fellowship. **Convention/Meeting:** Monthly.

75 ● Alfa Club of Colorado
17227 E. Long Ave.
Aurora, CO 80016
Richard Smith, Pres.   Ph:(303)690-5287

Founded: 1969. **Membership:** 90. Enthusiasts of the Alfa Romeo automobile organized to promote the marque. **Convention/Meeting:** Monthly.

76 ● Alfa Romeo Owners Club
2468 Gum Tree Ln.
Fallbrook, CA 92028
Glenna Garrett, Exec.Sec.   Ph:(619)728-4875

Founded: 1958. **Membership:** 5500. Owners and enthusiasts of Alfa Romeo automobiles. Promotes knowledge of the history and tradition of the Alfa Romeo marque; provides technical information for efficient and safe operation of Alfas. Chapters organize socials and amateur driving events and conduct technical seminars and driver's schools to teach safe and skillful driving on the highway and in competitions. Maintains library of technical manuals. **Convention/Meeting:** Annual.

77 ● Alfa Romeo Owners Club, Atlanta Chapter [Georgia]
6728 Cockridge Dr.
Atlanta, GA 30360
Chuck Lipper, Pres.   Ph:(404)399-6159

Founded: 1970. **Membership:** 120. Owners and enthusiasts of the Alfa Romeo automobile. Promotes safety and knowledge of the Alfa Romeo. **Convention/Meeting:** Monthly.

78 ● Alfa Romeo Owners Club, Northeastern Ohio Chapter
445 S. Green Rd.
South Euclid, OH 44121
Richard W. Gent, Pres.   Ph:(216)481-2334

Owners and enthusiasts of Alfa Romeo automobiles united to promote the history of the Italian car and provide technical information for its safe and efficient operation. Sponsors car shows, auto races, time trials, and other social events.

79 ● Alfa Romeo Owners Club, Northern California Chapter
1116 18th St.
Sacramento, CA 95814-4111
Mark Webber, Pres.   Ph:(916)483-4544

Membership: 5500. Owners of Alfa Romeo automobiles. To preserve, collect, and protect Alfa Romeos.

80 ● Alfa Romeo Owners Club of Oklahoma
4134 E. 37th Pl.
Tulsa, OK 74135
David Simmons, Exec. Officer

Owners and enthusiasts of Alfa Romeo automobiles.

81 ● Alfa Romeo Owners Club, Orange County Chapter
    [California]
22692 Granite Way
Laguna Hills, CA 92653
Carole Sandeman, Sec.   Ph:(714)588-0500

Founded: 1985. **Membership:** 100. Owners and enthusiasts of the Alfa Romeo automobile. Works to further technical knowledge and enjoyment of the automobile. Sponsors rallies, tours, concours, and other related events. **Convention/Meeting:** Monthly.

82 ● Alfa Romeo Owners Club, Washington D.C. Chapter
7309 Delfield St.
Chevy Chase, MD 20815
Steve Morrison, Pres.   Ph:(301)652-6287

Founded: 1959. **Membership:** 300. Alfa Romeo enthusiasts in northern Virginia, Maryland, southern Pennsylvania, and Washington, D.C. Provides social activities, competitive events, and technical sessions. Maintains print, video, and tool library. **Convention/Meeting:** Annual - always summer. Also holds monthly meeting - always first Monday of the month.

83 ● **Deep South Alfa Romeo Club [Mississippi, Louisiana, and southwestern Tennessee]**
P.O. Box 2162
Jackson, MS 39205
Alfonso Vasquez, Pres.   Ph:(601)636-3470

Founded: 1982. **Membership:** 30. Alfa Romeo enthusiasts in Mississippi, Louisiana, and southwestern Tennessee. Provides support, encouragement, and technical information to Alfa Romeo owners. Sponsors social activities and tours. **Convention/Meeting:** Annual; also holds monthly meeting.

AMC EAGLE (1987-88)

A product of the now-defunct American Motors Corporation, which briefly remained in the lineup after the 1987 takeover by Chrysler.

MAJOR FEATURES

● AMC Eagle (1987) and Eagle Wagon (1988) had as standard equipment: automatic transmission, air conditioning, tilt steering, roof rack, and rear window defogger.

PRICE HISTORY

The following new car prices reflect the approximate retail cost of the base model: **1987** - $11,485.

DIMENSIONS

Body Style	Years Avail	Wheel Base (in)	Lgth (in)	Ht (in)	Avg Wt (lbs)	Fuel Cap (gal)	Front Hdrm (in)	Front Legrm (in)
4d sdn	87-87	109.3	180.9	54.4	3,385	22.0	38.1	40.8
5d wgn	87-88	109.3	180.9	54.6	3,416	22.0	38.1	40.8

ENGINES

Type	Displacement (L)	Fuel Dly	HP @rpm	Torque @rpm (ft/lbs)	MPG Cty/Hwy	Years Avail
I-4	2.2	FI	103@5000	124@2500	25/33	88-88
I-6	4.2	2-bbl	112@3000	210@2000	17/21	87-87

KEY: I=in-line engine; V=V engine; F=flat engine; FI=fuel injection; bbl=barrel carburetor; T=turbo; D=diesel; HP=horsepower; MPG=estimated average miles per gallon.

EVALUATIONS, TESTS, AND RANKINGS

1987: "mediocre as a passenger car." **Source:** "AMC Eagle," *Consumer Guide: Complete Guide to Used Cars—1987 Edition*, 1987, p. 11-12.

RECALLS

None to date.

OTHER INFORMATION SOURCES

84 ● **AM-XTRA**
American Motorsport International
7963 Depew St.
Arvada, CO 80003   Ph:(303)428-8760

Newsletter. Bimonthly. **Price:** Available to members only.

85 ● **AMC Performance Car Club—Newsletter**
AMC Performance Car Club
2000 25th Ave.
Marion, IA 52302   Ph:(319)377-7510

Bimonthly.

86 ● **American Motoring Magazine**
American Motors Owners Association (AMO)
c/o Darryl A. Salisbury
517 New Hampshire
Portage, MI 49081   Ph:(616)342-9397

Bimonthly.

87 ● **American Motors Owners Association—Membership Roster**
American Motors Owners Association (AMO)
517 New Hampshire   Ph:(616)342-9397
Portage, MI 49081   Fax:(616)387-4806

About 1,000 owners of American Motors Corporation vehicles; international coverage. Irregular; latest edition March 1990. **Editor(s):** Valerie Fleming. **Price:** Available to members only.

88 ● **Americana: The American Motors Magazine**
American Motors Corp.
14250 Plymouth Rd.
Detroit, MI 48227

Bimonthly. **Editor(s):** Stephen Jacobs.

ASSOCIATIONS

89 ● **AMC Performance Car Club**
2000 25th Ave.
Marion, IA 52302
Ralph W. Toms, Sec.-Treas.   Ph:(319)377-7510

Founded: 1983. **Membership:** 10. To preserve, promote, and enjoy automobiles built by the American Motors Corporation. Sponsors car shows. **Convention/Meeting:** Monthly (April-October).

90 ● **American Motors Owners Association**
c/o Darryl A. Salisbury
517 New Hampshire
Portage, MI 49081
Darryl A. Salisbury, Pres.   Ph:(616)342-9397

Founded: 1974. **Membership:** 1,400. Owners and enthusiasts of AMC vehicles built from 1958 - 1988. To aid and encourage ownership, use, and enjoyment of AMC vehicles; to encourage preservation and restoration of these vehicles; and to increase communications and fellowship among owners. Maintains library; bestows awards. **Convention/Meeting:** Annual car show and swap meet - always July or August. 1992 Columbus, OH; 1993 Kenosha, WI.

91 ● **American Motorsport International**
7963 Depew St.
Arvada, CO 80003
Larry G. Mitchell, Director   Ph:(303)428-8760

Founded: 1986. **Membership:** 751. Collectors and admirers of AMC cars and Jeeps. Functions as a clearinghouse of information on all AMC products. Provides technical assistance to members involved in restoring or preserving AMC automobiles. Maintains library and archive of sales and engineering literature and artifacts pertaining to AMC products. Sponsors concours for AMC cars and Jeeps. Makes available novelty items and memorabilia. Bestows awards. **Convention/Meeting:** Annual.

92 ● **National American Motors Drivers and Racers Association**
PO Box 987
Twin Lakes, WI 53181-0987
Jock Jocewicz, Pres. Ph:(708)599-1255

Founded: 1978. **Membership:** 991. AMC automobile owners. Promotes use of AMC and Jeep vehicles in drag race competitions; sponsors car shows, swap meets, and races. Serves as information clearinghouse and parts exchange for members. Maintains library of owners' parts, shop manuals, and magazine articles on AMC vehicles. Bestows awards. **Former Name(s):** (1983) American Motors Drag Racing Association; (1985) National American Motors Drag Racing Association. **Convention/Meeting:** Annual (with exhibits) - usually summer.

ASTON MARTIN LAGONDA (1987-89)

Introduced as part of Aston Martin line. Produced at Newport Pugnell, England and sold in the U.S. through 1989.

MAJOR FEATURES

● Aston Martin Lagonda 1989 standard equipment included: Chrysler 3-speed Torqueflite transmission, front and rear vented power disc brakes, leather interior, walnut burl veneer, and front and rear independent suspension.

PRICE HISTORY

The following new car prices reflect the approximate retail cost of the base model: **1987** - $167,000; **1988** - $177,500; **1989** - $197,000.

DIMENSIONS

Body Style	Years Avail	Wheel Base (in)	Lgth (in)	Ht (in)	Avg Wt (lbs)	Fuel Cap (gal)	Front Hdrm (in)	Front Legrm (in)
4d sdn	87-87	115.0	207.9	51.2	4,400	33.3	37.8	42.2
4d sdn	88-89	115.0	208.0	52.0	4,622	27.5	37.8	42.2

ENGINES

Type	Displacement (L)	Fuel Dly	HP @rpm	Torque @rpm (ft/lbs)	MPG Cty/Hwy	Years Avail
V-8	5.3	FI	na	na	8/11	87-89

KEY: I=in-line engine; V=V engine; F=flat engine; FI=fuel injection; bbl=barrel carburetor; T=turbo; D=diesel; HP=horsepower; MPG=estimated average miles per gallon.

EVALUATIONS, TESTS, AND RANKINGS

1988: "flawless coachwork." **Source:** "Aston Martin Lagonda," *Car and Driver—Buyers Guide 1988*, 1988, p. 122.

1988: "engine hand-built and autographed by a single craftsman." **Source:** "Dream Cars," *Design News*, October 3, 1988, p. 145.

RECALLS

None to date.

REPAIR MANUALS

93 ● **Aston Martin and Lagonda**
Haynes Publications, Inc.
861 Lawrence Dr.
Newbury Park, CA 91320 Ph:(818)889-5400

Editor(s): Chris Harvey. **Price:** $34.95.

OTHER INFORMATION SOURCES

94 ● **Aston Martin Owners Club—Membership List**
Aston Martin Owners Club
1 A High St.
Sutton near Ely, Cambs. HP8 4BL, England Ph:2 404474-2

3,000 owners and enthusiasts of Aston Martin motorcars. Annual.

95 ● **Lagonda Club, U.S. Section—Bulletin**
Lagonda Club, U.S. Section (LC)
c/o Christopher M. Salyer
3237 Harvey Pkwy.
Oklahoma City, OK 73118-8652 Ph:(405)232-3100

Monthly.

96 ● **Lagonda Club, U.S. Section—Magazine**
Lagonda Club, U.S. Section (LC)
c/o Christopher M. Salyer
3237 Harvey Pkwy.
Oklahoma City, OK 73118-8652 Ph:(405)232-3100

Quarterly.

97 ● **Lagonda Club, U.S. Section—Newsletter**
Lagonda Club, U.S. Section (LC)
c/o Christopher M. Salyer
3237 Harvey Pkwy.
Oklahoma City, OK 73118-8652 Ph:(405)232-3100

Periodic.

ASSOCIATIONS

98 ● **Lagonda Club, U.S. Section**
c/o Christopher M. Salyer
3237 Harvey Pkwy.
Oklahoma City, OK 73118-8652 Ph:(405)232-3100
Christopher M. Salyer, Pres. Fax:(405)272-9381

Founded: 1950. **Membership:** 800. Individuals who own or are interested in Lagonda cars. Purpose is to promote and preserve these cars. Maintains spare parts program. **Convention/Meeting:** Annual - always Great Britain.

ASTON MARTIN SALOON (1987-89)

Produced at Newport Pagnell, England and sold in the U.S. through 1989.

MAJOR FEATURES

● Aston Martin Saloon had as 1989 standard equipment: 5-speed manual transmission, front and rear vented power disc brakes, and front and rear independent suspension.

PRICE HISTORY

The following new car prices reflect the approximate retail cost of the base model: **1987** - $125,000; **1989** - $145,000.

ASTON MARTIN V-8 COUPE

DIMENSIONS

Body Style	Years Avail	Wheel Base (in)	Lgth (in)	Ht (in)	Avg Wt (lbs)	Fuel Cap (gal)	Front Hdrm (in)	Front Legrm (in)
2d cpe	87-87	102.8	184.0	52.3	4,550	27.5	na	na
2d cpe	88-88	102.8	183.8	52.3	4,100	27.5	na	na
2d cpe	89-89	102.8	180.0	52.3	4,010	27.5	na	na

ENGINES

Type	Displace-ment (L)	Fuel Dly	HP @rpm	Torque @rpm (ft/lbs)	MPG Cty/Hwy	Years Avail
V-8	5.3	FI	300@5600	350@4500	9/na	87-88
V-8	5.3	FI	240@5500	288@5500	8/11	89-89

KEY: I=in-line engine; V=V engine; F=flat engine; FI=fuel injection; bbl=barrel carburetor; T=turbo; D=diesel; HP=horsepower; MPG=estimated average miles per gallon.

EVALUATIONS, TESTS, AND RANKINGS

1989: "the driver, in short, is well cared for." **Source:** "Aston Martin Saloon," *Road & Track—Buyer's Guide 1989,* 1988, p. 17.

RECALLS

None to date.

OTHER INFORMATION SOURCES

99 ● **Aston Martin Owners Club—Membership List**
Aston Martin Owners Club
1 A High St.
Sutton near Ely, Cambs. HP8 4BL, England Ph:2 404474-2

3,000 owners and enthusiasts of Aston Martin motorcars. Annual.

ASTON MARTIN V-8 COUPE (1987-88)

Produced at Newport Pagnell, England and sold in the U.S. through 1988.

MAJOR FEATURES

● Aston Martin V-8 Coupe had as 1988 standard equipment: 5-speed manual transmission, front and rear vented power disc brakes, and front and rear independent suspension.

PRICE HISTORY

The following new car prices reflect the approximate retail cost of the base model: **1987** - $112,000; **1988** - $127,000.

DIMENSIONS

Body Style	Years Avail	Wheel Base (in)	Lgth (in)	Ht (in)	Avg Wt (lbs)	Fuel Cap (gal)	Front Hdrm (in)	Front Legrm (in)
2d cpe	87-88	102.8	189.5	52.3	4,009	27.5	na	na

ENGINES

Type	Displace-ment (L)	Fuel Dly	HP @rpm	Torque @rpm (ft/lbs)	MPG Cty/Hwy	Years Avail
V-8	5.3	4x2 bbl	na	na	na	87-87
V-8	5.3	FI	na	na	na	88-88

KEY: I=in-line engine; V=V engine; F=flat engine; FI=fuel injection; bbl=barrel carburetor; T=turbo; D=diesel; HP=horsepower; MPG=estimated average miles per gallon.

EVALUATIONS, TESTS, AND RANKINGS

1988: "Old World craftsmanship." **Source:** "Aston Martin V-8," *Car and Driver—Buyers Guide 1988,* 1988, p. 52.

RECALLS

None to date.

OTHER INFORMATION SOURCES

100 ● **Aston Martin Owners Club—Membership List**
Aston Martin Owners Club
1 A High St.
Sutton near Ely, Cambs. HP8 4BL, England Ph:2 404474-2

3,000 owners and enthusiasts of Aston Martin motorcars. Annual.

ASTON MARTIN VANTAGE (1987-89)

Produced at Newport Pagnell, England and sold in the U.S. through 1989.

MAJOR FEATURES

● Aston Martin Vantage had as 1989 standard equipment: 5.3 liter, V-8 engine, 5-speed manual transmission, power-assisted rack-and-pinion steering, front and rear vented power disc brakes, and front and rear independent suspension.

PRICE HISTORY

The following new car prices reflect the approximate retail cost of the base model: **1987** - $127,000; **1988** - $143,000; **1989** - $197,000.

DIMENSIONS

Body Style	Years Avail	Wheel Base (in)	Lgth (in)	Ht (in)	Avg Wt (lbs)	Fuel Cap (gal)	Front Hdrm (in)	Front Legrm (in)
2d cpe	87-87	102.8	184.0	52.3	4,550	27.5	na	na
2d cpe	88-88	102.8	183.8	52.3	4,100	27.5	na	na
2d cpe	89-89	102.8	180.0	52.3	4,010	27.5	na	na

ENGINES

Type	Displace-ment (L)	Fuel Dly	HP @rpm	Torque @rpm (ft/lbs)	MPG Cty/Hwy	Years Avail
V-8	5.3	4x2 bbl	300@5600	350@4500	9/na	87-88
V-8	5.3	4x2 bbl	240@5500	288@5500	8/11	89-89

KEY: I=in-line engine; V=V engine; F=flat engine; FI=fuel injection; bbl=barrel carburetor; T=turbo; D=diesel; HP=horsepower; MPG=estimated average miles per gallon.

EVALUATIONS, TESTS, AND RANKINGS

1989: "a big bruiser, a powerful, stocky, intimidating, Sylvester Stallone of a car . . . occasional creaks and groans from the bodyshell . . . body roll is surprisingly well-contained." **Source:** "Aston Martin Vantage Volante: A luxury tourer in the grand style," *Motor Trend,* May 1989, pp. 168-170, 173-174.

1987: "these are very high performance cars." **Source:** "Aston Martin Vantage," *Road & Track—Buyer's Guide 1987,* 1986, p. 17.

RECALLS

None to date.

OTHER INFORMATION SOURCES

101 ● Aston Martin Owners Club—Membership List
Aston Martin Owners Club
1 A High St.
Sutton near Ely, Cambs. HP8 4BL, England Ph:2 404474-2

3,000 owners and enthusiasts of Aston Martin motorcars. Annual.

ASTON MARTIN VIRAGE COUPE (1990-92)

Hand-built at Newport Pagnell, Buckinghamshire, Great Britain.

1991 Aston Martin Virage Coupe

MAJOR FEATURES

● Aston Martin Virage has as 1992 standard equipment: all-aluminum body, 5-speed manual transmission, front and rear vented power disc brakes, and front and rear independent suspension.

PRICE HISTORY

The following new car prices reflect the approximate retail cost of the base model: **1990** - $170,000; **1991** - $227,250; **1992** - $227,250.

DIMENSIONS

Body Style	Years Avail	Wheel Base (in)	Lgth (in)	Ht (in)	Avg Wt (lbs)	Fuel Cap (gal)	Front Hdrm (in)	Front Legrm (in)
2d cpe	90-92	102.8	187.0	52.0	4,233	30.2	36.0	50.0

ENGINES

Type	Displacement (L)	Fuel Dly	HP @rpm	Torque @rpm (ft/lbs)	MPG Cty/Hwy	Years Avail
V-8	5.3	FI	330@6000	350@3700	12/17	90-92

KEY: I=in-line engine; V=V engine; F=flat engine; FI=fuel injection; bbl=barrel carburetor; T=turbo; D=diesel; HP=horsepower; MPG=estimated average miles per gallon.

EVALUATIONS, TESTS, AND RANKINGS

1991: "No thrills, perhaps, but plenty of satisfaction . . . power really comes on around 3000 rpm and builds smoothly, but rapidly, from there . . . You feel you have something substantial beneath you." **Source:** "Aston Martin Virage: An Allistair Cooke kind of car," *Road & Track,* April 1991, pp. 146, 148, 150.

1991: "An Aston fresh in shape, chassis, engine, and interior . . . Maybe it's expensive as hell, but it's also exclusive as hell . . . In some ways, Aston means great quality. In others, abysmal blacksmithing." **Source:** "Aston Martin Virage: This 2+2 equals a quarter-million," *Car and Driver,* May 1991, pp. 78-80, 84.

1990: "handbuilt . . . and costs as much as fourteen Mustangs." **Source:** "Aston Martin Virage," *Car and Driver—Buyers Guide 1990,* 1989, p. 64.

1990: "entirely new and is torsionally stiffer, lighter, and less complex . . . considerably more luggage area . . . much higher performance." **Source:** "Virage—Aston Martin of Tomorrow," *Motor Trend,* January 1989, p. 22.

RECALLS

None to date.

OTHER INFORMATION SOURCES

102 ● Aston Martin Owners Club—Membership List
Aston Martin Owners Club
1 A High St.
Sutton near Ely, Cambs. HP8 4BL, England Ph:2 404474-2

3,000 owners and enthusiasts of Aston Martin motorcars. Annual.

ASTON MARTIN VOLANTE (1987-89)

Hand-built at Newport Pagnell, Buckinghamshire, Great Britain.

MAJOR FEATURES

● Aston Martin Volante had as 1989 standard equipment: 5-speed manual transmission, front and rear vented power brakes, and front and rear independent suspension.

PRICE HISTORY

The following new car prices reflect the approximate retail cost of the base model: **1987** - $137,800; **1988** - $153,000; **1989** - $183,000.

DIMENSIONS

Body Style	Years Avail	Wheel Base (in)	Lgth (in)	Ht (in)	Avg Wt (lbs)	Fuel Cap (gal)	Front Hdrm (in)	Front Legrm (in)
2d conv	87-89	102.8	188.2	53.9	4,010	27.5	na	na

ENGINES

Type	Displacement (L)	Fuel Dly	HP @rpm	Torque @rpm (ft/lbs)	MPG Cty/Hwy	Years Avail
V-8	5.3	4x2 bbl	300@5600	350@4500	9/na	87-88
V-8	5.3	FI	240@5500	288@5500	8/11	89-89

KEY: I=in-line engine; V=V engine; F=flat engine; FI=fuel injection; bbl=barrel carburetor; T=turbo; D=diesel; HP=horsepower; MPG=estimated average miles per gallon.

EVALUATIONS, TESTS, AND RANKINGS

1988: "fuel economy [is] most remote of Aston Martin ambitions." **Source:** "Aston Martin Volante," *Car and Driver—Buyers Guide 1988,* 1988, p. 52.

RECALLS

None to date.

OTHER INFORMATION SOURCES

103 ● **Aston Martin Owners Club—Membership List**
Aston Martin Owners Club
1 A High St.
Sutton near Ely, Cambs. HP8 4BL, England Ph:2 404474-2

3,000 owners and enthusiasts of Aston Martin motorcars. Annual.

AUDI 80 (1988-92)

Audi 80 and 90 series replaced the 4000 series in 1988. The 4-wheel drive version is known as the Quattro. Included in *The Car Book* Best Bets among compacts in 1992. Among compact vehicles, the Audi 80 Quattro had the highest expected maintenance cost, according to *The Complete Car Guide* in 1990.

1991 Audi 80

MAJOR FEATURES

● Audi 80 has as 1992 standard equipment: 5-speed manual transmission, rack and pinion power steering, 4-wheel power disc brakes, driver's side airbag, power windows, air conditioning, rear window defogger, cruise control, power central locking system, and 6-speaker sound system.

● Audi 80 Quattro adds as 1992 standard equipment: anti-lock brakes and 4-wheel drive.

PRICE HISTORY

The following new car prices reflect the approximate retail cost of the base model: **1988** - $18,600; **1989** - $19,350; **1990** - $18,900; **1991** - $20,750; **1992** - $22,650.

DIMENSIONS

Body Style	Years Avail	Wheel Base (in)	Lgth (in)	Ht (in)	Avg Wt (lbs)	Fuel Cap (gal)	Front Hdrm (in)	Front Legrm (in)
4d sdn	88-92	100.2	176.3	54.8	2,906	15.9	37.8	42.2
4d sdn	88-92	99.9	176.3	54.8	3,087	18.5	37.8	42.2

ENGINES

Type	Displacement (L)	Fuel Dly	HP @rpm	Torque @rpm (ft/lbs)	MPG Cty/Hwy	Years Avail
I-4	2.0	FI	108@5300	121@3200	22/30	88-90
I-5	2.3	FI	130@5500	140@4500	20/26	88-92

KEY: I=in-line engine; V=V engine; F=flat engine; FI=fuel injection; bbl=barrel carburetor; T=turbo; D=diesel; HP=horsepower; MPG=estimated average miles per gallon.

EVALUATIONS, TESTS, AND RANKINGS

1991: "An excellent example of industrial design inside and out . . . Outstanding service program . . . Top-quality materials are used throughout." **Source:** "Audi 80/90: Perceptions Don't Match Reality," *Autoweek's Autofile 1991 Edition*, 1990, p. 135.

1990: "comfortable, sturdy, and fun to drive." **Source:** "Audi 80," *Car and Driver—Buyers Guide 1990*, 1989, p. 85.

1990: "not enough engine to justify their high prices . . . anti-lock brakes provide short, straight stops." **Source:** "Audi 80/90 Coupe Quatto," *Consumer Guide*, December 15, 1989, p. 10.

1989: "combines modern design with super-sleek, aerodynamically efficient bodywork . . . praises all around for the solid feel of the controls and the fine driving position . . . biggest problem is its price." **Source:** "Sensible Speed: A six-pack to go," *Car and Driver,* March 1989, pp. 46-50, 53-56.

1988: "Headroom . . . is barely adequate." **Source:** "Audi 80 Quattro: Flawless form, fearless function. At a price," *Car and Driver,* July 1988, p. 111-112.

1988: "wind noise at high speeds is extremely low." **Source:** "Audi 80/90: Onward and upward," *Car and Driver,* November 1987, p. 78.

RECALLS

1990: (6,600 cars with airbags; includes other Audi models): Steering lock bolts could break if driver applies excessive force to locked wheel. **Corrective action:** Replace complete steering lock assembly, including a modified lock bolt. *(NHTSA Campaign No. 90V070000.)*

1990: (600 vehicles; includes several Audi models): Improperly secured clip could cause safety belt hinge to separate from anchor in rear-end collision. **Corrective action:** Realign seat covering material where interference is present. *(NHTSA Campaign No. 90V069000.)*

REPAIR MANUALS

104 ● Audi 80, 90 Official Factory Repair Manual: 1988-91
Robert Bentley Publishing, Inc.
1000 Massachusetts Ave.
Cambridge, MA 02138   Ph:(617)547-4170

OTHER INFORMATION SOURCES

105 ● Audi Quattro: The Development and Competition History
Haynes Publications, Inc.
861 Lawrence Dr.
Newbury Park, CA 91320   Ph:(818)889-5400

Editor(s): Jeremy Walton. **Price:** $34.95.

106 ● European Car
Argus Publishers Corp.
12100 Wilshire Blvd., Ste. 250   Ph:(213)820-3601
Los Angeles, CA 90025   Fax:(213)207-9388

Magazine covering Volkswagen, Porsche, Mercedes-Benz, Audi, Ferrari, Jaguar, and BMW automobiles. Bimonthly.
Editor(s): Greg N. Brown. **Price:** $11.00 per year; $2.75 per issue.

ASSOCIATIONS

107 ● Audi International Motor Car Club
318 Harvard St., Ste. 10, Dept. 3
Brookline, MA 02146

Individuals interested in Audi automobiles. Promotes Audi cars and encourages communication among members. Provides discounts for accesories and parts.

AUDI 90 (1988-91, 1993)

Audi will not produce a 1992 version of the 90, but will offer the 1993 later in 1992. The Audi 90 was chosen by *The Complete Car Cost Guide* in 1990 as having a resale value after five years of 37%. The 90 series, in conjunction with the 80 series from Audi, replaced the 4000 series in 1988. Information on the 1993 version of the 90 sedan was unavailable at time of publication.

1991 Audi 90 Quattro

MAJOR FEATURES

● Audi 90 had as 1991 standard equipment: 4-speed automatic transmission with automatic shift lock, rack and pinion power steering, 4-wheel disc brakes with anti-lock braking system, driver's side airbag, climate control system, rear window defogger, power windows, power central locking system, power sunroof, and 6-speaker sound system.

● Audi 90 Quattro included as standard equipment: 4-wheel drive and 5-speed manual transmission.

● Audi 90 Quattro 20V had as 1990 standard equipment: 20-valve, 164-horsepower version of the five-cyclinder engine.

PRICE HISTORY

The following new car prices reflect the approximate retail cost of the base model: **1988** - $24,330; **1989** - $25,310; **1990** - $23,990; **1991** - $26,250.

DIMENSIONS

Body Style	Years Avail	Wheel Base (in)	Lgth (in)	Ht (in)	Avg Wt (lbs)	Fuel Cap (gal)	Front Hdrm (in)	Front Legrm (in)
4d sdn	88-91	100.2	176.3	54.8	2,999	15.9	37.8	42.2
4d sdn	88-91	99.9	176.3	54.8	3,197	18.5	37.8	42.2

ENGINES

Type	Displacement (L)	Fuel Dly	HP @rpm	Torque @rpm (ft/lbs)	MPG Cty/Hwy	Years Avail
I-5	2.3	FI	130@5500	140@4500	18/25	88-91
I-5	2.3	FI	164@6000	157@4500	17/24	90-91

KEY: I=in-line engine; V=V engine; F=flat engine; FI=fuel injection; bbl=barrel carburetor; T=turbo; D=diesel; HP=horsepower; MPG=estimated average miles per gallon.

EVALUATIONS, TESTS, AND RANKINGS

1991: "excellent example of industrial design inside and out . . . Outstanding service program . . . Top-quality materials are used throughout . . . Gearing . . . isn't too well suited for overall conditions . . . Oddly shaped trunk is impractical." **Source:** "Audi 80/90: Perceptions Don't Match Reality," *Autoweek's Autofile 1991 Edition*, 1990, pp. 135-139.

1991: "[Audi Quattro 90 has] . . . taut, direct feel; unmatched grip and foul-weather traction . . . [a] small, noisy cabin . . . The only clear sports sedan here, and a jewel anywhere." **Source:** "Foreigners in the Fast Lane: Seven pricey sedans undergo our acid test," *Car and Driver*, July 1991, pp. 54-60, 62, 64, 66, 68-70.

1989: "In the dry, the front-drive Audi 90 is stable almost to a fault . . . benefit of the Quattro layout is a smoother ride over road irregularities . . . With the rear-differential lock button punched. . .squirted to 20 mph in just 5.1 seconds." **Source:** "Snow Test: We compare the Audi 90 vs BMW 325is vs Audi 90 Quattro vs BMW 325iX," *Road & Track*, November 1988, pp. 88-89, 92-93, 96.

1989: "at speed, the Quattro 20V's ride is well controlled and creamy smooth . . . a snappy exhaust tone to remind you that this is a sedan built for high-speed cruising . . . Despite being tight, the 90 Quattro 20V is not cramped." **Source:** "Audi 90 Quattro 20V: Hans and Wolfgang will love it," *Car and Driver*, June 1989, pp. 150-152.

1988: "Audi 90 Quattro . . . this trip gave special opportunity to admire its low-rev gutsiness, useful for picking your way through sticky or slippery conditions . . . Our drivers praised the . . . light shift action, but criticized its notchy gates . . . the Quattro's ride can sometimes turn jiggly." **Source:** "Snow White And The Seven AWDs," *Road & Track*, May 1988, pp. 56-63, 67-70.

1988: "allows the driver to turn the ABS off . . . engineering also was evident in the sleek aerodynamic shape. . .Audi drag coefficient . . . was low . . . There were fasteners to keep the floor mats in place, and there were childproof rear door locks . . . the Audi 90 trunk . . . seemed small." **Source:** "New Audi 90 enters classical era," *The Detroit News*, June 1, 1988, pp. 1F-2F.

1988: "Quattro accelerates in almost a leisurely fashion; the engine revs must climb considerably before five-cylinder achieves full power. . .not a particularly quick automobile." **Source:** "High-priced Audi deserves a better engine," *Detroit Free Press*, July 25, 1988, p. 11C.

RECALLS

1990: (6,600 cars with airbags; includes other Audi models): Steering lock bolts could break if driver applies excessive force to locked wheel. **Corrective action:** Replace complete steering lock assembly, including a modified lock bolt. *(NHTSA Campaign No. 90V070000.)*

1990: (600 vehicles): Improperly secured clip could cause safety belt hinge to separate from anchor in rear-end collision. **Corrective action:** Realign seat covering material where interference is present. *(NHTSA Campaign No. 90V069000.)*

REPAIR MANUALS

108 ● **Audi 80, 90 Official Factory Repair Manual: 1988-91**
Robert Bentley Publishing, Inc.
1000 Massachusetts Ave.
Cambridge, MA 02138   Ph:(617)547-4170

OTHER INFORMATION SOURCES

109 ● **Audi Quattro: The Development and Competition History**
Haynes Publications, Inc.
861 Lawrence Dr.
Newbury Park, CA 91320   Ph:(818)889-5400

Editor(s): Jeremy Walton. **Price:** $34.95.

110 ● **European Car**
Argus Publishers Corp.
12100 Wilshire Blvd., Ste. 250   Ph:(213)820-3601
Los Angeles, CA 90025   Fax:(213)207-9388

Magazine covering Volkswagen, Porsche, Mercedes-Benz, Audi, Ferrari, Jaguar, and BMW automobiles. Bimonthly. **Editor(s):** Greg N. Brown. **Price:** $11.00 per year; $2.75 per issue.

ASSOCIATIONS

111 ● **Audi International Motor Car Club**
318 Harvard St., Ste. 10, Dept. 3
Brookline, MA 02146

Individuals interested in Audi automobiles. Promotes Audi cars and encourages communication among members. Provides discounts for accesories and parts.

AUDI 100 (1989-92)

Replaced the 5000 designation in 1989, with standard model called 100 and the turbo 200. Rated as one of the best performers among intermediate vehicles in a crash test performance by *The Car Book* in 1991.

1992 Audi 100

MAJOR FEATURES

● Audi 100 has as 1992 standard equipment: 5-speed automatic transmission with automatic shift lock, hydraulically-assisted power brakes and rack-and-pinion steering, 4-wheel disc brakes with anti-lock braking system, driver's side airbag, anti-theft vehicle alarm system, climate control system, rear window defogger, cruise control, power window, power central locking system, and 8-speaker sound system.

● Audi 100 Quattro adds as 1992 standard equipment: 5-speed manual transmission and 4-wheel drive.

● Audi 100 S adds as 1992 standard equipment: 8-way power front bucket seats with manual lumbar adjustments.

● Audi 100 CS adds as 1992 standard equipment: front fog lights, outside temperature gauge, and 6-function trip information computer.

● Audi 100 Wagon had as 1989 standard equipment: 3-speed automatic transmission, anti-lock braking system, automatic climate control, heavy-duty suspension, and rear window wiper/washer.

● Audi 100 E had as 1989 standard equipment: other exterior body stylings.

PRICE HISTORY

The following new car prices reflect the approximate retail cost of the base model: **1989** - $25,230; **1990** - $26,900; **1991** - $28,750; **1992** - $27,700.

DIMENSIONS

Body Style	Years Avail	Wheel Base (in)	Lgth (in)	Ht (in)	Avg Wt (lbs)	Fuel Cap (gal)	Front Hdrm (in)	Front Legrm (in)
4d sdn	89-91	105.2	192.2	55.9	3,153	21.1	37.9	41.1
4d sdn	92-92	105.8	192.6	56.3	3,385	21.1	38.4	42.2
5d wgn	89-89	105.2	192.2	55.9	3,042	21.1	37.9	41.1

ENGINES

Type	Displacement (L)	Fuel Dly	HP @rpm	Torque @rpm (ft/lbs)	MPG Cty/Hwy	Years Avail
I-5	2.3	FI	130@5600	140@4000	18/23	89-91
V-6	2.8	FI	172@5500	184@3000	19/26	92-92

KEY: I=in-line engine; V=V engine; F=flat engine; FI=fuel injection; bbl=barrel carburetor; T=turbo; D=diesel; HP=horsepower; MPG=estimated average miles per gallon.

EVALUATIONS, TESTS, AND RANKINGS

1992: "its widened track, fender flares and upright greenhouse give it a deceivingly smaller appearance . . . reacts calmly, never bobbing, but absorbing each dip." **Source:** "New for '92: More power and posh for Audi 100, Honda Civic, Volkswagen Golf and Mercedes 400E," *Road & Track*, December 1991, pp. 90, 92, 94.

1992: "noticeably nicer than its forebears . . . feels light on its feet . . . interior could not be more tasteful." **Source:** "Audi 100CS: A lean new thoroughbred prances out of Ingolstadt," *Car and Driver*, December 1991, pp. 109-110.

1992: "good performance from a new V-6 engine . . . ride is perfectly controlled, but not numb . . . ample rear seating and trunk space." **Source:** "Well-tooled Audi 100 can give the Japanese a scare," *The Detroit News*, December 4, 1991, pp. 1D, 3D.

1992: "looking into the realm of acceleration, you'll find the Audi in the cellar, not the tower . . . Audi 100 S will strike some potential buyers as being too firmly sprung . . . rear-seat passengers with long rides . . . will appreciate the charitable head and leg room." **Source:** "Real World 101: Six luxuriant sedans vie for a place in your life," *Road & Track*, February 1992, pp. 59-67, 69.

1989: "engine and gearbox are smooth and silent at highway speeds. . .seems in need of more power . . . ride is smooth and extremely well-insulated. Handling and braking is exemplary . . . driving position and pedal placement is excellent." **Source:** "Quattro boasts a confident ride," *The Detroit News*, July 19, 1989, pp. 1F-2F.

1989: "roomy cockpit curls into a gracefully broadened instrument nacelle . . . can now boast of appearing, at long last, near the top of J.D. Power's Customer Satisfaction Index." **Source:** "Audi 100/200," *Car and Driver*, September 1988, pp. 91-93.

RECALLS

1990: (6,600 cars with airbags; includes other Audi models): Steering lock bolts could break if driver applies excessive force to locked wheel. **Corrective action:** Replace complete steering lock assembly, including a modified lock bolt. *(NHTSA Campaign No. 90V070000.)*

1990: (600 vehicles; includes several Audi models): Improperly secured clip could cause safety belt hinge to separate from anchor in rear-end collision. **Corrective action:** Realign seat covering material where interference is present. *(NHTSA Campaign No. 90V069000.)*

1990: (5,900 passenger cars): The vehicle capacity weight was inadvertently omitted from placard located inside the gas filler door, as required by FMVSS 110. **Corrective action:** New labels containing the vehicle capacity weight will be affixed to the vehicles. *(NHTSA Campaign No. 91V156000.)*

1989-91: (20,800 passenger cars; includes the Audi 100, Audi 200, and Audi V-8): Instruction label in the trunk of vehicle is incorrect for the jack supplied with the vehicle. Incorrect use can result in the jack collapsing, with injury to individuals under or near vehicle during collapse. **Corrective action:** Supply insert to owner's manual noting correct usage, as well as a corrected instruction label for the trunk. *(NHTSA Campaign No. 91V050000.)*

REPAIR MANUALS

112 ● **Audi 100, 200 Official Factory Repair Manual: 1990, Including Quattro**
Robert Bentley Publishing, Inc.
1000 Massachusetts Ave.
Cambridge, MA 02138   Ph:(617)547-4170

Includes the Audi Quattro.

OTHER INFORMATION SOURCES

113 ● **Audi Quattro: The Development and Competition History**
Haynes Publications, Inc.
861 Lawrence Dr.
Newbury Park, CA 91320   Ph:(818)889-5400

Editor(s): Jeremy Walton. **Price:** $34.95.

114 ● **European Car**
Argus Publishers Corp.
12100 Wilshire Blvd., Ste. 250   Ph:(213)820-3601
Los Angeles, CA 90025   Fax:(213)207-9388

Magazine covering Volkswagen, Porsche, Mercedes-Benz, Audi, Ferrari, Jaguar, and BMW automobiles. Bimonthly. **Editor(s):** Greg N. Brown. **Price:** $11.00 per year; $2.75 per issue.

ASSOCIATIONS

115 ● **Audi International Motor Car Club**
318 Harvard St., Ste. 10, Dept. 3
Brookline, MA 02146

Individuals interested in Audi automobiles. Promotes Audi cars and encourages communication among members. Provides discounts for accesories and parts.

AUDI 200 (1989-91)

Replaced the Audi 5000; discontinued after the 1991 model. Competitive models included the Acura Legend and Nissan Maxima. Selected by *The Car Book* in 1991 as a good choice based on expected performance in six categories. Also named the best among intermediate vehicles in a crash test performance by the same publisher. Chosen by *The Complete Car Cost Guide* in 1990 as having the lowest resale value among luxury vehicles.

1991 Audi 200 Quattro Wagon

MAJOR FEATURES

● Audi 200 had as 1991 standard equipment: automatic transmission with automatic shift lock, hydraulically-assisted power brakes and steering, anti-lock braking system, driver's side airbag, anti-theft vehicle alarm system, cruise control, power windows, power central locking system, 2-way power sunroof, and Bose sound system.

● Audi 200 Quattro, which featured a larger body design, added as 1991 standard equipment: 4-wheel drive and 5-speed manual transmission.

● Audi 200 Quattro Wagon added as 1991 standard equipment: folding rear seat and rear window wiper/washer.

PRICE HISTORY

The following new car prices reflect the approximate retail cost of the base model: **1989** - $33,405; **1990** - $33,405; **1991** - $35,500.

DIMENSIONS

Body Style	Years Avail	Wheel Base (in)	Lgth (in)	Ht (in)	Avg Wt (lbs)	Fuel Cap (gal)	Front Hdrm (in)	Front Legrm (in)
4d sdn	89-91	105.6	192.7	55.9	3,263	21.1	37.9	41.1
4d sdn	89-91	106.1	193.4	56.1	3,627	21.1	37.9	41.1
5d wgn	89-91	106.1	193.4	56.1	3,726	21.1	37.9	41.1

ENGINES

Type	Displacement (L)	Fuel Dly	HP @rpm	Torque @rpm (ft/lbs)	MPG Cty/Hwy	Years Avail
I-5T	2.2	FI	162@5500	177@3000	18/22	89-91
I-5T	2.2	FI	217@5700	228@1950	18/24	91-91

KEY: I=in-line engine; V=V engine; F=flat engine; FI=fuel injection; bbl=barrel carburetor; T=turbo; D=diesel; HP=horsepower; MPG=estimated average miles per gallon.

EVALUATIONS, TESTS, AND RANKINGS

1991: "gobbling up Interstate miles rapidly and with ease. Potholes and railroad tracks are easily absorbed by the fully independent suspension." **Source:** "Audi 200 Quattro: A smooth car that deserves a fair shake," *Road & Track*, December 90, pp. 66, 68, 72-73.

1991: "prototype delivers nicely balanced, predictable, firm responses. . .chassis has changed much more in detail than in concept." **Source:** "Audi 200 Quattro: Fast like rocket, fine like sky," *Car and Driver*, November 1990, pp. 63-64.

1991: "demonstrated better grip . . . sleekly styled, tastefully decorated, and mechanically elegant . . . represents the superior value." **Source:** "4 Wheel Drive Wonderwagons," *Popular Science*, October 1990, pp. 88-90, 92.

1989: "Ride and handling . . . are first-rate, thanks to Audi's all-independent suspension, power rack-and-pinion steering . . . and four-wheel power disc brakes with anti-lock mechanism . . . four-wheel drive Quattro system provides an additional element of traction and safety." **Source:** "High-priced entry from Volkswagen stable," *Detroit Free Press*, October 10, 1988, p. 1F.

1989: "roomy cockpit curls into a gracefully broadened instrument nacelle . . . Audi can now boast of appearing. . .near the top of J.D. Power's Customer Satisfaction Index." **Source:** "Audi 100/200: Ingolstadt fights back," *Car and Driver*, September 1988, pp. 91-93.

1989: "what they lacked in power, they more than made up for with refined, well-balanced handling that has earned this comfortable sedan so much praise since its introduction in 1983. In the rain. . .simply phenomenal." **Source:** "Audi 200 Turbo: Comeback car or mirror trick," *Motor Trend*, November 1988, pp. 101-104.

RECALLS

1990: (6,600 cars with airbags; includes other Audi models): Steering lock bolts could break if driver applies excessive force to locked wheel. **Corrective action:** Replace complete steering lock assembly, including a modified lock bolt. *(NHTSA Campaign No. 90V070000.)*

1990: (600 vehicles; includes several Audi models): Improperly secured clip could cause safety belt hinge to separate from

anchor in rear-end collision. **Corrective action:** Realign seat covering material where interference is present. *(NHTSA Campaign No. 90V069000.)*

1990: (5,900 passenger cars): The vehicle capacity weight was inadvertantly omitted from placard located inside the gas filler door, as required by FMVSS 110. **Corrective action:** New labels containing the vehicle capacity weight will be affixed to the vehicles. *(NHTSA Campaign No. 91V156000.)*

1989-91: (20,800 passenger cars; includes the Audi 100, Audi 200, and Audi V-8 Quattro): Instruction label in the trunk of vehicle is incorrect for the jack supplied with the vehicle. Incorrect use can result in the jack collapsing, with injury to individuals under or near vehicle during collapse. **Corrective action:** Supply insert to owner's manual noting correct usage, as well as a corrected instruction label for the trunk. *(NHTSA Campaign No. 91V050000.)*

REPAIR MANUALS

116 ● **Audi 100, 200 Official Factory Repair Manual: 1990, Including Quattro**
Robert Bentley Publishing, Inc.
1000 Massachusetts Ave.
Cambridge, MA 02138   Ph:(617)547-4170

Includes the Audi Quattro.

OTHER INFORMATION SOURCES

117 ● **Audi Quattro: The Development and Competition History**
Haynes Publications, Inc.
861 Lawrence Dr.
Newbury Park, CA 91320   Ph:(818)889-5400
Editor(s): Jeremy Walton. **Price:** $34.95.

118 ● **European Car**
Argus Publishers Corp.
12100 Wilshire Blvd., Ste. 250   Ph:(213)820-3601
Los Angeles, CA 90025   Fax:(213)207-9388

Magazine covering Volkswagen, Porsche, Mercedes-Benz, Audi, Ferrari, Jaguar, and BMW automobiles. Bimonthly. **Editor(s):** Greg N. Brown. **Price:** $11.00 per year; $2.75 per issue.

ASSOCIATIONS

119 ● **Audi International Motor Car Club**
318 Harvard St., Ste. 10, Dept. 3
Brookline, MA 02146

Individuals interested in Audi automobiles. Promotes Audi cars and encourages communication among members. Provides discounts for accesories and parts.

AUDI 4000 (1987)

High performance sedan produced in Germany until 1987. It was replaced by the Audi 80 and 90 Series.

MAJOR FEATURES

● Audi 4000S had as 1987 standard equipment: 5-speed manual transmission, power-assisted front disc and rear drum brakes, air conditioning, cruise control, and power locks.

● Audi 4000CS Quattro added as 1987 standard equipment: 4-wheel drive.

PRICE HISTORY

The following new car prices reflect the approximate retail cost of the base model: **1987 - $15,875.**

DIMENSIONS

Body Style	Years Avail	Wheel Base (in)	Lgth (in)	Ht (in)	Avg Wt (lbs)	Fuel Cap (gal)	Front Hdrm (in)	Front Legrm (in)
4d sdn	87-87	99.8	176.6	54.3	2,337	15.8	38.1	40.9
4d sdn	87-87	99.4	176.6	54.3	2,824	18.5	38.1	40.9

ENGINES

Type	Displace-ment (L)	Fuel Dly	HP @rpm	Torque @rpm (ft/lbs)	MPG Cty/Hwy	Years Avail
I-4	1.8	FI	102@5500	111@3250	25/30	87-87
I-5	2.2	FI	115@5500	126@3000	18/22	87-87

KEY: I=in-line engine; V=V engine; F=flat engine; FI=fuel injection; bbl=barrel carburetor; T=turbo; D=diesel; HP=horsepower; MPG=estimated average miles per gallon.

EVALUATIONS, TESTS, AND RANKINGS

1987: "good combination of speed and gas mileage . . . almost eerie quietness, and wind noise remains remarkably low at highway speeds." **Source:** "1987 Audi 4000," *Car and Driver*, January 1987, p. 28.

1987: "Tremendous fun to drive . . . interior ergonomics brought raves from our testers." **Source:** "This Sportin' Life," *Popular Mechanics*, January 1987, pp. 60-64, 114.

RECALLS

None to date.

REPAIR MANUALS

120 ● **Audi 4000S, 4000CS and Coupe GT Official Factory Repair Manual: 1984-1987, Including Quattro and Quattro Turbo**
Robert Bentley Publishing, Inc.
1000 Massachusetts Ave.
Cambridge, MA 02138   Ph:(617)547-4170

Published 1989. **Price:** $94.95.

121 ● **Haynes Audi 4000 Owners Workshop Manual, No. 165: 1980-1987**
Haynes Publications, Inc.
861 Lawrence Dr.
Newbury Park, CA 91320   Ph:(818)889-5400

Editor(s): A. K. Legg. **Price:** $15.95.

OTHER INFORMATION SOURCES

122 ● **Audi Quattro: The Development and Competition History**
Haynes Publications, Inc.
861 Lawrence Dr.
Newbury Park, CA 91320   Ph:(818)889-5400

Editor(s): Jeremy Walton. **Price:** $34.95.

123 ● **European Car**
Argus Publishers Corp.
12100 Wilshire Blvd., Ste. 250   Ph:(213)820-3601
Los Angeles, CA 90025   Fax:(213)207-9388

Magazine covering Volkswagen, Porsche, Mercedes-Benz, Audi, Ferrari, Jaguar, and BMW automobiles. Bimonthly. **Editor(s):** Greg N. Brown. **Price:** $11.00 per year; $2.75 per issue.

ASSOCIATIONS

124 ● **Audi International Motor Car Club**
318 Harvard St., Ste. 10, Dept. 3
Brookline, MA 02146

Individuals interested in Audi automobiles. Promotes Audi cars and encourages communication among members. Provides discounts for accesories and parts.

AUDI 5000 (1987-88)

Produced in Germany. Chosen as one of the Ten Best Cars for 1987 by *Car and Driver*; and picked as one of the Top Ten Cars of the '80s by *Motor Trend*. For 1989, the 5000 designation was removed, with the standard model called 100 and 200 series.

MAJOR FEATURES

● Audi 5000S and 5000S Wagon had as 1988 standard equipment: 5-speed manual transmission, front disc and rear drum power-assisted brakes, rack-and-pinion power-assisted steering, digital climate control, power locks, and power windows.

● Audi 5000CS Turbo Quattro and 5000CS Turbo Quattro Wagon, which featured a larger body design, added as 1988 standard equipment: 4-wheel drive, anti-lock braking system, leather interior, sunroof, and 10-speaker sound system.

PRICE HISTORY

The following new car prices reflect the approximate retail cost of the base model: **1987 - $20,460; 1988 - $22,850.**

DIMENSIONS

Body Style	Years Avail	Wheel Base (in)	Lgth (in)	Ht (in)	Avg Wt (lbs)	Fuel Cap (gal)	Front Hdrm (in)	Front Legrm (in)
4d sdn	87-88	105.8	192.7	55.9	3,086	21.1	37.9	41.1
4d sdn	87-88	105.8	192.7	55.7	2,844	21.1	37.9	41.9
5d wgn	87-88	105.8	192.7	55.7	2,954	21.1	37.9	41.9

ENGINES

Type	Displace-ment (L)	Fuel Dly	HP @rpm	Torque @rpm (ft/lbs)	MPG Cty/Hwy	Years Avail
I-5	2.2	FI	158@5500	166@3000	17/25	87-87
I-5	2.2	FI	110@5500	122@2500	19/26	87-87
I-5	2.3	FI	130@5600	140@4000	20/25	88-88
I-5T	2.2	FI	162@5500	177@3000	18/26	87-88

KEY: I=in-line engine; V=V engine; F=flat engine; FI=fuel injection; bbl=barrel carburetor; T=turbo; D=diesel; HP=horsepower; MPG=estimated average miles per gallon.

EVALUATIONS, TESTS, AND RANKINGS

1988: "the most advanced production sedan in the world.

Brilliantly conceived and beautifully aerodynamic . . . The Audi 5000 set the standard for the modern, full-sized sedan, and was the ancestor of a host of followers." **Source:** "Top 10 cars of the '80s," *Motor Trend,* November 1989, pp. 100-103.

1987: "the silver-plated standard of modern sophisticated sedans. Its combination of clean, contemporary styling, functional interior design, and stirring performance has so far eluded imitation." **Source:** "Cars: Fun work, but somebody's got to do it," *Car and Driver,* January 1987, pp. 36-41.

1987: "on more slippery surfaces the Quattro would win . . . As surface traction improves, however, the advantages of the Quattro's four-wheel drive diminish . . . For drivers whose first priority is dry pavement performance—particularly handling—four-wheel drive does not amount to a great leap forward." **Source:** "Quattro Quandary," *Car and Driver,* February 1987, p. 81.

1987: "technical excellence, aesthetic appeal and scintillating performance . . . under the skin are the guts of a sports car." **Source:** "Audi Wagon: Excellence has its price," *Detroit Free Press,* November 24, 1986, p. 4C.

1987: "superb road manners." **Source:** "Audi 5000S Quattro: When the going gets tough, the tough get tiger paws," *Car and Driver,* October 1987, p. 123.

RECALLS

1987-88: (25,000 cars; includes models made before 1987): Repeated topping off of fuel tank during refueling, may allow vapors to escape from charcoal filter, which may ignite by exhaust system heat. **Corrective action:** Install redesigned filler neck, new vent valve, and hose for charcoal filter. *(NHTSA Campaign No. 87V157000.)*

1987-88: (35,000 cars with turbo; includes models made before 1987; includes other Audi models): Fuel injection seals may harden, allowing fuel into engine compartment. May result in fire. **Corrective action:** Replace with redesigned seals. *(NHTSA Campaign No. 89V006000.)*

1987: (16,000 cars; includes models made before 1987; includes other Audi models): Rear brake calipers may bind and overheat, affecting braking ability. **Corrective action:** Replace calipers. *(NHTSA Campaign No. 87V158000.)*

REPAIR MANUALS

125 ● **Audi 5000**
Peter Allen Video Productions
38-C Otis St.
West Babylon, NY 11704   Ph:(516)643-4372

How to tune-up, repair, and maintain the Audi. **Release date:** 1986. **Producer:** Peter Allen Productions. **Acquisition:** Purchase.

126 ● **Audi 5000S, 5000CS Official Factory Repair Manual: 1984-1988 Gasoline, Turbo and Turbo Diesel, Including Wagon and Quattro**
Robert Bentley Publishing, Inc.
1000 Massachusetts Ave.
Cambridge, MA 02138   Ph:(617)547-4170

Price: $94.95.

127 ● **Haynes Audi 5000, 1984-1988**
Haynes Publications, Inc.
861 Lawrence Dr.
Newbury Park, CA 91320   Ph:(818)889-5400

Published 1989. **Price:** $15.95.

OTHER INFORMATION SOURCES

128 ● **Audi Quattro: The Development and Competition History**
Haynes Publications, Inc.
861 Lawrence Dr.
Newbury Park, CA 91320   Ph:(818)889-5400

Editor(s): Jeremy Walton. **Price:** $34.95.

129 ● **European Car**
Argus Publishers Corp.
12100 Wilshire Blvd., Ste. 250   Ph:(213)820-3601
Los Angeles, CA 90025   Fax:(213)207-9388

Magazine covering Volkswagen, Porsche, Mercedes-Benz, Audi, Ferrari, Jaguar, and BMW automobiles. Bimonthly. **Editor(s):** Greg N. Brown. **Price:** $11.00 per year; $2.75 per issue.

ASSOCIATIONS

130 ● **Audi International Motor Car Club**
318 Harvard St., Ste. 10, Dept. 3
Brookline, MA 02146

Individuals interested in Audi automobiles. Promotes Audi cars and encourages communication among members. Provides discounts for accesories and parts.

AUDI COUPE (1987-91)

High performance 5-seater coupe based on the Audi 80 and 90 model series. Produced in Germany; discontinued after the 1991 model.

MAJOR FEATURES

● Audi Quattro Coupe had as 1991 standard equipment: 4-wheel drive, 5-speed manual transmission, hydraulically-assisted power brakes and steering, anti-lock braking system, driver's side airbag, anti-theft alarm system, climate control system, cruise control, power windows, sunroof, and power central locking system.

● Audi Coupe GT, discontinued in 1987, had as standard equipment: air conditioning, sunroof, cruise control, power locks, and AM/FM stereo cassette player.

PRICE HISTORY

The following new car prices reflect the approximate retail cost of the base model: **1990** - $29,750.

DIMENSIONS

Body Style	Years Avail	Wheel Base (in)	Lgth (in)	Ht (in)	Avg Wt (lbs)	Fuel Cap (gal)	Front Hdrm (in)	Front Legrm (in)
2d cpe	87-87	99.8	177.3	53.1	2,507	15.8	37.2	40.9
2d cpe	88-91	100.4	176.0	54.3	3,308	18.5	35.1	42.2

ENGINES

Type	Displace-ment (L)	Fuel Dly	HP @rpm	Torque @rpm (ft/lbs)	MPG Cty/Hwy	Years Avail
I-5	2.2	FI	110@5500	122@2500	19/25	87-87
I-5	2.3	FI	130@5500	140@4500	20/26	88-91
I-5	2.3	FI	164@6000	157@4500	17/24	90-91

KEY: I=in-line engine; V=V engine; F=flat engine; FI=fuel injection; bbl=barrel carburetor; T=turbo; D=diesel; HP=horsepower; MPG=estimated average miles per gallon.

EVALUATIONS, TESTS, AND RANKINGS

1989: "passenger compartment is isolated from both mechanical and wind noise . . . ergonomics are quite good . . . control is excellent and the ride compliant enough to soak up sizeable bumps." **Source:** "Audi Coupe Quattro: Taking the alternate performance route," *Motor Trend*, September 1989, pp. 61-64.

1989: "feels light, agile, stable and safe . . . understeers a bit and has more than a little body roll. But balance is quite good . . . the new Coupe can be tippy at its limits . . . not the sprint champ of sport coupes." **Source:** "Audi Coupe Quattro: Is sophisticated engineering sufficient," *Road & Track*, September 1989, pp. 62, 64-67.

1987: "The engine is mated to a superb, smooth-shifting five-speed manual transmission . . . side and rear vision is somewhat restricted." **Source:** "Revamped Audi Coupe GT is more racy," *Detroit Free Press*, September 14, 1987, p. 1D.

RECALLS

1990: (6,600 cars with airbags; includes other Audi models): Steering lock bolts could break if driver applies excessive force to locked wheel. **Corrective action:** Replace complete steering lock assembly, including a modified lock bolt. *(NHTSA Campaign No. 90V070000.)*

1990: (600 vehicles; includes several Audi models): Improperly secured clip could cause safety belt hinge to separate from anchor in rear-end collision. **Corrective action:** Realign seat covering material where interference is present. *(NHTSA Campaign No. 90V069000.)*

SAFETY AND REPAIRS

1987: "Growling Audi," *Road & Track*, May 1987, p. 214.
Note: Coupe GT with gear noise in 1st when decelerating.

REPAIR MANUALS

131 ● **Audi 4000S, 4000CS and Coupe GT Official Factory Repair Manual: 1984-1987, Including Quattro and Quattro Turbo**
Robert Bentley Publishing, Inc.
1000 Massachusetts Ave.
Cambridge, MA 02138　　　　Ph:(617)547-4170

Published 1989. **Price:** $94.95.

OTHER INFORMATION SOURCES

132 ● **Audi Quattro: The Development and Competition History**
Haynes Publications, Inc.
861 Lawrence Dr.
Newbury Park, CA 91320　　　Ph:(818)889-5400

Editor(s): Jeremy Walton. **Price:** $34.95.

133 ● **European Car**
Argus Publishers Corp.
12100 Wilshire Blvd., Ste. 250　　Ph:(213)820-3601
Los Angeles, CA 90025　　　　　Fax:(213)207-9388

Magazine covering Volkswagen, Porsche, Mercedes-Benz, Audi, Ferrari, Jaguar, and BMW automobiles. Bimonthly.
Editor(s): Greg N. Brown. **Price:** $11.00 per year; $2.75 per issue.

ASSOCIATIONS

134 ● **Audi International Motor Car Club**
318 Harvard St., Ste. 10, Dept. 3
Brookline, MA 02146

Individuals interested in Audi automobiles. Promotes Audi cars and encourages communication among members. Provides discounts for accesories and parts.

AUDI S4 (1992)

Successor to the 200 Quattro, the Audi S4 is the top performance version in the new 100 line. The front-engine, four-wheel-drive, 5-passenger, 4-door sedan competes against the BMW 535i and M5, Mercedes 300E, 300CE, and 500E, and the Infiniti Q45. Only 250 copies will be allocated to the U.S. in 1992, doubling to 500 in 1993.

MAJOR FEATURES

● Audi S4 has as 1992 standard equipment: turbocharged and intercooled 20-valve 5-cylinder engine, 5-speed manual transmission, independent front and rear suspension, power-assisted rack-and-pinion steering, vented disc brakes with anti-lock control, tilt/telescope steering wheel with hub-mounted air bag, climate control, and infrared remote locking.

PRICE HISTORY

The following new car prices reflect the approximate retail cost of the base model: **1992** - $45,570.

DIMENSIONS

Body Style	Years Avail	Wheel Base (in)	Lgth (in)	Ht (in)	Avg Wt (lbs)	Fuel Cap (gal)	Front Hdrm (in)	Front Legrm (in)
4d sdn	92-92	106.0	188.6	56.8	3,542	21.1	na	na

ENGINES

Type	Displace-ment (L)	Fuel Dly	HP @rpm	Torque @rpm (ft/lbs)	MPG Cty/Hwy	Years Avail
I-5	2.2	FI	230@5900	258@1950	18/23	92-92

KEY: I=in-line engine; V=V engine; F=flat engine; FI=fuel injection; bbl=barrel carburetor; T=turbo; D=diesel; HP=horsepower; MPG=estimated average miles per gallon.

EVALUATIONS, TESTS, AND RANKINGS

1992: "Terrific traction, seemingly endless grip, and impeccable stability . . . gearbox is occasionally stubborn, and the brakes feel spongy when hot . . . one of the most competent sports sedans on the market." **Source:** "Audi S4," *Automobile Magazine*, December 1991, p. 72.

1992: "Inside . . . all is civilized opulence . . . seems quiet, comfortable, roomy in front and back . . . as pleasant to drive in traffic as at speed." **Source:** "Audi S4," *Car and Driver,* March 1992, pp. 79-80.

RECALLS

None to date.

ASSOCIATIONS

135 ● **Audi International Motor Car Club**
318 Harvard St., Ste. 10, Dept. 3
Brookline, MA 02146

Individuals interested in Audi automobiles. Promotes Audi cars and encourages communication among members. Provides discounts for accesories and parts.

AUDI V8 QUATTRO (1990-92)

High performance sedan introduced to U.S. market in 1990. Produced in Germany.

MAJOR FEATURES

● Audi V8 Quattro 1992 standard equipment includes: 4-wheel drive, 4-speed automatic transmission, rack-and-pinion steering, anti-lock braking system, driver's side airbag, anti-theft alarm system, climate control system, cruise control, power windows, power central locking system, sunroof, cellular telephone, and Bose sound system.

PRICE HISTORY

The following new car prices reflect the approximate retail cost of the base model: **1990** - $47,450; **1991** - $51,500.

DIMENSIONS

Body Style	Years Avail	Wheel Base (in)	Lgth (in)	Ht (in)	Avg Wt (lbs)	Fuel Cap (gal)	Front Hdrm (in)	Front Legrm (in)
4d sdn	90-92	106.2	191.9	55.9	3,771	21.1	37.8	41.7

ENGINES

Type	Displacement (L)	Fuel Dly	HP @rpm	Torque @rpm (ft/lbs)	MPG Cty/Hwy	Years Avail
V-8	3.6	FI	240@5800	245@4000	14/20	90-91
V-8	4.2	FI	280@5800	289@4000	na	92-92

KEY: I=in-line engine; V=V engine; F=flat engine; FI=fuel injection; bbl=barrel carburetor; T=turbo; D=diesel; HP=horsepower; MPG=estimated average miles per gallon.

EVALUATIONS, TESTS, AND RANKINGS

1992: "the 4.2-liter version is notably quicker than the 3.6-liter model . . . automatic transmission harmonizes well with the Bavarian V-8 . . . appeals primarily to performance-oriented enthusiasts." **Source:** "Audi's U.S. Dilemma: Can a good car survive bad publicity," *Automobile Magazine,* December 1991, pp. 72-73, 76, 79.

1991: "Make no mistake, the Audi V-8 is one courageous automobile . . . Whether the venue is a treacherous mountain pass or a wide-open interstate . . . the Audi V8 is one of the most confidence-inspiring automobiles available at any price . . . exactly what you'd expect from the world's all-wheel-drive leader." **Source:** "Audi V-8 Five-Speed: The underdog scores a win," *Motor Trend,* May 1991, pp.96-98, 100.

1991: "Equipped with an automatic transmission, this car huffs

and puffs while running to 60 mph in a mediocre 9.3 seconds . . . stick-shift edition accelerates to 60 mph in 6.8 seconds . . . there isn't a better machine on the market." **Source:** "Audi V-8 Five-Speed: The Underdog Scores a Win," *Motor Trend,* May 1991, pp. 96-98, 100.

1990: "A gas guzzler tax of $1,050 . . . is added on to the base price . . . the person sitting in the rear middle seat would find the seat back a bit hard . . . On the other hand, the rear legroom was good." **Source:** "Audi flexes muscle with V-8 Quattro," *Detroit News,* March 7, 1990, p. 8C.

1990: "four-wheel drive system . . . worked like a charm . . . electronically controlled transmission . . . kept getting stuck in third gear; a second car was glitch-free . . . tied with Volvo for 12th place in the annual J. D. Power survey of customer satisfaction." **Source:** "Driving in the lap of luxury," *U.S. News & World Report,* January 8, 1990, pp. 59-62.

1990: "Audi built a compact, light-weight engine . . . drives like a rocket . . . has combined the fun of a manual . . . with the convenience of an automatic." **Source:** "Audi's New Flagship," *Design News,* October 2, 1989, pp. 146-147.

RECALLS

1990: (6,600 cars with airbags; includes other Audi models): Steering lock bolts could break if driver applies excessive force to locked wheel. **Corrective action:** Replace complete steering lock assembly, including a modified lock bolt. *(NHTSA Campaign No. 90V070000.)*

1990: (600 vehicles; includes several Audi models): Improperly secured clip could cause safety belt hinge to separate from anchor in rear-end collision. **Corrective action:** Realign seat covering material where interference is present. *(NHTSA Campaign No. 90V069000.)*

1989-91: (20,800 passenger cars; includes the Audi 100, Audi 200, and Audi V-8 Quattro): Instruction label in the trunk of vehicle is incorrect for the jack supplied with the vehicle. Incorrect use can result in the jack collapsing, with injury to individuals under or near vehicle during collapse. **Corrective action:** Supply insert to owner's manual noting correct usage, as well as a corrected instruction label for the trunk. *(NHTSA Campaign No. 91V050000.)*

OTHER INFORMATION SOURCES

136 ● **Audi Quattro: The Development and Competition History**
Haynes Publications, Inc.
861 Lawrence Dr.
Newbury Park, CA 91320   Ph:(818)889-5400
Editor(s): Jeremy Walton. **Price:** $34.95.

137 ● **European Car**
Argus Publishers Corp.
12100 Wilshire Blvd., Ste. 250   Ph:(213)820-3601
Los Angeles, CA 90025   Fax:(213)207-9388

Magazine covering Volkswagen, Porsche, Mercedes-Benz, Audi, Ferrari, Jaguar, and BMW automobiles. Bimonthly. **Editor(s):** Greg N. Brown. **Price:** $11.00 per year; $2.75 per issue.

ASSOCIATIONS

138 ● **Audi International Motor Car Club**
318 Harvard St., Ste. 10, Dept. 3
Brookline, MA 02146

Individuals interested in Audi automobiles. Promotes Audi cars and encourages communication among members. Provides discounts for accesories and parts.

AVANTI (1987-92)

Originally designed by Raymond Loewy for the Studebaker Corp. Except for the engine, chassis, and drive train, which are produced by General Motors Corp., the Avanti is built by hand in Youngstown, Ohio. Information on the 1992 models was unavailable at the time of publication.

MAJOR FEATURES

● Avanti Sport Coupe and Touring Sedan had as 1991 standard equipment: 4-speed automatic transmission, front disc and rear drum brakes, power windows, power door locks, air conditioning, AM/FM cassette stereo, and cruise control. Drivetrain by General Motors.

PRICE HISTORY

The following new car prices reflect the approximate retail cost of the base model: **1987** - $29,995; **1988** - $35,900; **1989** - $38,000.

DIMENSIONS

Body Style	Years Avail	Wheel Base (in)	Lgth (in)	Ht (in)	Avg Wt (lbs)	Fuel Cap (gal)	Front Hdrm (in)	Front Legrm (in)
2d cpe	87-91	109.0	193.0	55.0	3,550	na	34.0	45.0
4d sdn	87-91	109.0	200.0	55.0	4,504	na	34.0	45.0

ENGINES

Type	Displace- ment (L)	Fuel Dly	HP @rpm	Torque @rpm (ft/lbs)	MPG Cty/Hwy	Years Avail
V-8	5.0	FI	170@4400	250@2800	na	87-91

KEY: I=in-line engine; V=V engine; F=flat engine; FI=fuel injection; bbl=barrel carburetor; T=turbo; D=diesel; HP=horsepower; MPG=estimated average miles per gallon.

EVALUATIONS, TESTS, AND RANKINGS

1991: "a design so remarkable that it has survived more than a quarter century ... current Avanti has the power and the handling of a Caprice." **Source:** "The Impression of Speed, Even at Rest," *Gentlemen's Quarterly*, February 1991, pp. 50, 54.

1990: "imagine riding in a full-size '65 Galaxie convertible ... That's this car." **Source:** "Convertibles: Wind in your hair to lift your spirits," *Car and Driver—Buyers Guide 1990*, 1989, p. 136.

1987: "pleases simply because it's a classic." **Source:** "Avanti," *Road & Track—Buyer's Guide 1987*, 1986, p. 21.

RECALLS

None to date.

OTHER INFORMATION SOURCES

139 ● **Avanti**
Avanti Owners Association International (AOAI)
P.O. Box 322
Uxbridge, MA 01569   Ph:(508)278-3242

Magazine. Quarterly. **Price:** $18.00.

140 ● **Avanti Owners Association International— Membership Roster**
Avanti Owners Association International (AOAI)
P.O. Box 322
Uxbridge, MA 01569   Ph:(508)278-3242

Contains current information on the Avanti automobile, including articles on repair and new parts. Quarterly.

141 ● **Avanti Owners Association Newsletter**
Avanti Owners Assn. Intl.
P.O. Box 322
Uxbridge, MA 01569   Ph:(508)278-3242

Newsletter. Bimonthly.

ASSOCIATIONS

142 ● **Avanti Owners Association International**
1038 S. Stone Ave.
La Grange, IL 60525
Gene Rinck, President   Ph:(508)278-3242

Founded: 1965. **Membership:** 1,600. Owners of Avanti and Avanti II automobiles. Provides members with historical and technical data about the Avanti. Absorbed the Avanti Club of America in 1986.

BENTLEY CONTINENTAL (1988-92)

Part of Bentley line, the convertible is the corporate cousin to the Rolls-Royce Corniche. The Bentley Continental is produced in London, England. Along with other Rolls-Royce models, it made *The Car Book* 1989 top ten list of fuel economy losers. Information on the 1992 models was not available at time of publication.

MAJOR FEATURES

● Bentley Continental R has as 1992 standard equipment: turbo-charged engine. Fewer than 100 will be shipped to North America.

● Bentley Continental had as 1991 standard equipment: 3-speed automatic transmission, 4-wheel disc brakes with anti-lock brake system, power-assisted rack-and-pinion steering, climate control system, power door locks, power windows, driver's side airbag, cellular phone, stereo entertainment system including radio/cassette/compact disc player, and leather interior.

PRICE HISTORY

The following new car prices reflect the approximate retail cost of the base model: **1988** - $182,900; **1989** - $204,800; **1990** - $215,000; **1991** - $225,900; **1992** - $226,800.

DIMENSIONS

Body Style	Years Avail	Wheel Base (in)	Lgth (in)	Ht (in)	Avg Wt (lbs)	Fuel Cap (gal)	Front Hdrm (in)	Front Legrm (in)
2d conv	88-88	120.5	207.5	59.8	5,200	26.0	36.0	37.0
2d conv	89-89	120.5	207.5	59.8	5,340	28.5	36.0	39.0
2d conv	90-91	120.5	207.5	59.8	5,360	28.5	37.7	41.2

ENGINES

Type	Displace-ment (L)	Fuel Dly	HP @rpm	Torque @rpm (ft/lbs)	MPG Cty/Hwy	Years Avail
V-8	6.8	FI	na	na	10/13	88-91

KEY: I=in-line engine; V=V engine; F=flat engine; FI=fuel injection; bbl=barrel carburetor; T=turbo; D=diesel; HP=horsepower; MPG=estimated average miles per gallon.

EVALUATIONS, TESTS, AND RANKINGS

1990: ``superbly quiet-riding.'' **Source:** ``Bentley Continental,'' *Car and Driver—Buyers Guide 1990*, 1989, p. 139.

RECALLS

1988-89: (3,846 cars; includes models made before 1987; includes other Rolls-Royce Bentley models): Brake pedal micro switch may fail, resulting in failure of brake light. **Corrective action:** Install improved stop lamp switch and modify wiring. *(NHTSA Campaign No. 89V045000.)*

OTHER INFORMATION SOURCES

143 ● Autocar on Bentley Since 1919
Motorbooks International
729 Prospect Ave.
Osceola, WI 54020   Ph:(715)294-3345

Published 1988. **Editor(s):** Warren Alport. **Price:** $19.95.

144 ● Bentley Drivers Club—Members and Their Bentleys
Bentley Drivers Club
16 Chearsley Rd.
Long Crendon
Aylesbury, Bucks. HP18 9AW, England

2,800 owners of Bentley automobiles. Biennial. **Price:** Available to members only.

145 ● Illustrated Rolls-Royce and Bentley Buyer's Guide
Motorbooks International
729 Prospect Ave.
Osceola, WI 54020   Ph:(715)294-3345

Published 1987. **Editor(s):** Paul Woudenberg. **Price:** $15.95.

146 ● Rolls-Royce/Bentley Marketletter
Mary Ann Liebert, Inc.
1651 3rd Ave.
New York, NY 10128   Ph:(212)289-2300

Provides extensive listings of Rolls-Royce and Bentley cars for sale or trade. Monthly. **Price:** $53.00.

ASSOCIATIONS

147 ● Rolls-Royce Owners' Club
191 Hempt Rd.
Mechanicsburg, PA 17055
Timothy E. Younes, Exec.Dir.   Ph:(717)697-4671

Founded: 1951. **Membership:** 6,000. Persons interested in preserving and restoring automobiles produced by Rolls-Royce Ltd., Rolls-Royce Motors, Ltd., Rolls-Royce of America, and Bentley Motors (1931) Ltd. To exchange technical, historical, and general information. Reprints owners' manuals and technical materials.

BENTLEY EIGHT (1988-92)

Part of Bentley line manufactured in England, the Bentley Eight is the corporate twin of the Rolls-Royce Silver Spirit. Along with other Bentley models, listed by *The Car Book* in 1989 for poor fuel economy. Information on the 1992 model was not available at time of publication.

MAJOR FEATURES

● Bentley Eight 1991 standard equipment included: 3-speed automatic transmission, 4-wheel independent suspension with self-leveling system at the rear, 4-wheel disc brakes with anti-lock brake system, power-assisted rack-and-pinion steering, driver's side airbag, climate control system, security system, power front heated seats with four position memory, power windows, power door locks, AM/FM stereo cassette with 10-speaker sound system, and leather interior.

PRICE HISTORY

The following new car prices reflect the approximate retail cost of the base model: **1989** - $108,700; **1990** - $114,100; **1991** - $119,800; **1992** - $123,800.

DIMENSIONS

Body Style	Years Avail	Wheel Base (in)	Lgth (in)	Ht (in)	Avg Wt (lbs)	Fuel Cap (gal)	Front Hdrm (in)	Front Legrm (in)
4d sdn	88-88	120.5	207.8	58.5	4,900	28.5	36	41
4d sdn	89-90	120.5	207.8	58.5	5,180	28.5	37.5	39
4d sdn	91-91	120.5	207.4	58.5	5,120	na	na	na

ENGINES

Type	Displace-ment (L)	Fuel Dly	HP @rpm	Torque @rpm (ft/lbs)	MPG Cty/Hwy	Years Avail
V-8	6.8	FI	na	na	10/13	88-91

KEY: I=in-line engine; V=V engine; F=flat engine; FI=fuel injection; bbl=barrel carburetor; T=turbo; D=diesel; HP=horsepower; MPG=estimated average miles per gallon.

EVALUATIONS, TESTS, AND RANKINGS

1989: ``magnificent automobiles.'' **Source:** ``Rolls-Royce & Bentley,'' *Road & Track—Buyers Guide 1989*, 1988, p. 152.

RECALLS

1990: (364 cars; includes other Rolls-Royce and Bentley models): Amperage overload could cause fuse failure, causing loss of rear stop lamps. **Corrective action:** Install an additional fused circuit to handle the main stop lamps. *(NHTSA Campaign No. 90V039000.)*

1989-90: (1,785 cars; includes other Rolls-Royce and Bentley models): Contact between right front brake caliper hydraulic line and engine oil cooler line may damage brake line. **Corrective action:** Add a protective shield to prevent contact and replace any damaged hydraulic pipe. *(NHTSA Campaign No. 90V073000.)*

1988-89: (3,846 cars; includes models made before 1987; includes other Rolls-Royce Bentley models): Brake pedal micro switch may fail, resulting in failure of brake light. **Corrective action:** Install improved stop lamp switch and modify wiring. *(NHTSA Campaign No. 89V045000.)*

OTHER INFORMATION SOURCES

148 ● Autocar on Bentley Since 1919
Motorbooks International
729 Prospect Ave.
Osceola, WI 54020   Ph:(715)294-3345

Published 1988. **Editor(s):** Warren Alport. **Price:** $19.95.

149 ● Bentley Drivers Club—Members and Their Bentleys
Bentley Drivers Club
16 Chearsley Rd.
Long Crendon
Aylesbury, Bucks. HP18 9AW, England

2,800 owners of Bentley automobiles. Biennial. **Price:** Available to members only.

150 ● Illustrated Rolls-Royce and Bentley Buyer's Guide
Motorbooks International
729 Prospect Ave.
Osceola, WI 54020   Ph:(715)294-3345

Published 1987. **Editor(s):** Paul Woudenberg. **Price:** $15.95.

151 ● Rolls-Royce/Bentley Marketletter
Mary Ann Liebert, Inc.
1651 3rd Ave.
New York, NY 10128   Ph:(212)289-2300

Provides extensive listings of Rolls-Royce and Bentley cars for sale or trade. Monthly. **Price:** $53.00.

ASSOCIATIONS

152 ● Rolls-Royce Owners' Club
191 Hempt Rd.
Mechanicsburg, PA 17055
Timothy E. Younes, Exec.Dir.   Ph:(717)697-4671

Founded: 1951. **Membership:** 6,000. Persons interested in preserving and restoring automobiles produced by Rolls-Royce Ltd., Rolls-Royce Motors, Ltd., Rolls-Royce of America, and Bentley Motors (1931) Ltd. To exchange technical, historical, and general information. Reprints owners' manuals and technical materials.

BENTLEY MULSANNE S (1987-92)

Introduced as part of Bentley line. Manufactured in England, the Mulsanne S is the sport version of the Bentley Eight. Made EPA 1991 Bottom Ten list for gas mileage and *The Car Book* in 1989 for fuel economy losers. Information on the 1992 model was not available at time of publication.

1991 Bentley Mulsanne S

MAJOR FEATURES

● Bentley Mulsanne S had as 1991 standard equipment: 3-speed automatic transmission, 4-wheel disc brakes with anti-lock brake system, power-assisted rack-and-pinion steering, alarm system, driver's side airbag, power windows, power door locks, climate control system, AM/FM stereo cassette with 10-speaker sound system.

PRICE HISTORY

The following new car prices reflect the approximate retail cost of the base model: **1988** - $107,500; **1989** - $118,900; **1990** - $133,200; **1991** - $144,100.

DIMENSIONS

Body Style	Years Avail	Wheel Base (in)	Lgth (in)	Ht (in)	Avg Wt (lbs)	Fuel Cap (gal)	Front Hdrm (in)	Front Legrm (in)
4d sdn	87-88	120.5	209.2	58.5	4,900	28.5	36	41
4d sdn	89-90	120.5	207.8	58.1	5,180	28.5	37.5	39
4d sdn	91-91	120.5	207.4	58.5	5,120	na	na	na

ENGINES

Type	Displace-ment (L)	Fuel Dly	HP @rpm	Torque @rpm (ft/lbs)	MPG Cty/Hwy	Years Avail
V-8	6.8	FI	na	na	10/13	87-91

KEY: I=in-line engine; V=V engine; F=flat engine; FI=fuel injection; bbl=barrel carburetor; T=turbo; D=diesel; HP=horsepower; MPG=estimated average miles per gallon.

EVALUATIONS, TESTS, AND RANKINGS

1990: ``most finely finished ... Interior is ... enormous.'' **Source:** ``Bentley Eight/Mulsanne/Turbo R,'' *Car and Driver— Buyers Guide 1990*, 1989, p. 121.

RECALLS

1990: (364 cars; includes other Rolls-Royce and Bentley models): Amperage overload could cause fuse failure, causing loss of rear stop lamps. **Corrective action:** Install an additional fused circuit to handle the main stop lamps. *(NHTSA Campaign No. 90V039000.)*

1989-90: (1,785 vehicles; includes other Rolls-Royce and Bentley models): Contact between right front brake caliper hydraulic line and engine oil cooler line may damage brake line. **Corrective action:** Add protective shield to prevent contact and replace any damaged hydraulic pipe. *(NHTSA Campaign No. 90V073000.)*

1987-89: (3,846 cars; includes models made before 1987; includes other Rolls-Royce Bentley models): Brake pedal micro switch may fail, resulting in failure of brake light. **Corrective action:** Install improved stop lamp switch and modify wiring. *(NHTSA Campaign No. 89V045000.)*

OTHER INFORMATION SOURCES

153 ● Autocar on Bentley Since 1919
Motorbooks International
729 Prospect Ave.
Osceola, WI 54020   Ph:(715)294-3345

Published 1988. **Editor(s):** Warren Alport. **Price:** $19.95.

154 ● Bentley Drivers Club—Members and Their Bentleys
Bentley Drivers Club
16 Chearsley Rd.
Long Crendon
Aylesbury, Bucks. HP18 9AW, England

2,800 owners of Bentley automobiles. Biennial. **Price:** Available to members only.

155 ● Illustrated Rolls-Royce and Bentley Buyer's Guide
Motorbooks International
729 Prospect Ave.
Osceola, WI 54020   Ph:(715)294-3345

Published 1987. **Editor(s):** Paul Woudenberg. **Price:** $15.95.

156 ● Rolls-Royce/Bentley Marketletter
Mary Ann Liebert, Inc.
1651 3rd Ave.
New York, NY 10128   Ph:(212)289-2300

Provides extensive listings of Rolls-Royce and Bentley cars for sale or trade. Monthly. **Price:** $53.00.

ASSOCIATIONS

157 ● Rolls-Royce Owners' Club
191 Hempt Rd.
Mechanicsburg, PA 17055
Timothy E. Younes, Exec.Dir.   Ph:(717)697-4671

Founded: 1951. **Membership:** 6,000. Persons interested in preserving and restoring automobiles produced by Rolls-Royce Ltd., Rolls-Royce Motors, Ltd., Rolls-Royce of America, and Bentley Motors (1931) Ltd. To exchange technical, historical, and general information. Reprints owners' manuals and technical materials.

BENTLEY TURBO R (1989-1992)

Introduced as part of Bentley line as the turbocharged version of the Mulsanne, the Bentley Turbo R is manufactured in England. The 1989 edition of the Turbo R made the 1989 fuel economy loser list compiled by *The Car Book*, ranked fourth in EPA's Bottom Ten for 1991, and placed fourth in *Car and Driver* World's Best Sedan evaluation (see below). Information on the 1992 model was not available at time of publication.

1991 Bentley Turbo R

MAJOR FEATURES

● Bentley Turbo R had as 1991 standard equipment: 3-speed automatic transmission, 4-wheel independent suspension with self-leveling system at the rear, 4-wheel disc brakes with anti-lock brake system, driver's side airbag, security system, power windows, power door locks, climate control system, leather interior, and AM/FM stereo cassette with 10-speaker sound system.

PRICE HISTORY

The following new car prices reflect the approximate retail cost of the base model: **1989** - $149,500; **1990** - $167,400; **1991** - $181,900.

DIMENSIONS

Body Style	Years Avail	Wheel Base (in)	Lgth (in)	Ht (in)	Avg Wt (lbs)	Fuel Cap (gal)	Front Hdrm (in)	Front Legrm (in)
4d sdn	89-90	120.5	207.8	58.5	5,270	28.5	37.5	39
4d sdn	91-91	120.5	207.4	58.5	5,314	na	na	na

ENGINES

Type	Displace-ment (L)	Fuel Dly	HP @rpm	Torque @rpm (ft/lbs)	MPG Cty/Hwy	Years Avail
V-8T	6.8	FI	325@na	450@3200	10/13	89-91

KEY: I=in-line engine; V=V engine; F=flat engine; FI=fuel injection; bbl=barrel carburetor; T=turbo; D=diesel; HP=horsepower; MPG=estimated average miles per gallon.

EVALUATIONS, TESTS, AND RANKINGS

1990: "steering is well weighted and responsive to the task of trying to turn all that tonnage." **Source:** "Bentley Turbo R," *Road & Track*, March 1991, pp. 84-87.

1989: "unexpectedly quick for such a heavyweight . . . immediate throttle response . . . also had . . . wind noise." **Source:** "Finding the Best Sedan in the World: When price is no object, only excellence counts," *Car and Driver*, November 1990, p. 114.

1989: "The way the super-quiet Bentley Turbo R gripped the pavement. . .really amazed me." **Source:** "The People's Choice," *Regardie's*, July 1989, pp. 125-130.

RECALLS

1990: (364 cars; includes other Rolls-Royce and Bentley models): Amperage overload could cause fuse failure, causing loss of rear stop lamps. **Corrective action:** Install an additional fused circuit to handle the main stop lamps. *(NHTSA Campaign No. 90V039000.)*

1989-90: (1,785 cars; includes other Rolls-Royce Bentley models): Contact between right front brake caliper hydraulic line and engine oil cooler line may damage brake line. **Corrective action:** Add a protective shield to prevent contact and replace any damaged hydraulic pipe. *(NHTSA Campaign No. 90V073000.)*

1989: (187 Turbo R Sedans): May be insufficient clearance between vacuum hose clamp and throttle link, resulting in linkage binding against clamp and loss of acceleration. **Corrective action:** Reroute hose and shorten vacuum pipe. *(NHTSA Campaign No. 89V073000.)*

OTHER INFORMATION SOURCES

158 ● Autocar on Bentley Since 1919
Motorbooks International
729 Prospect Ave.
Osceola, WI 54020   Ph:(715)294-3345

Published 1988. **Editor(s):** Warren Alport. **Price:** $19.95.

159 ● Bentley Drivers Club—Members and Their Bentleys
Bentley Drivers Club
16 Chearsley Rd.
Long Crendon
Aylesbury, Bucks. HP18 9AW, England

2,800 owners of Bentley automobiles. Biennial. **Price:** Available to members only.

160 ● Illustrated Rolls-Royce and Bentley Buyer's Guide
Motorbooks International
729 Prospect Ave.
Osceola, WI 54020   Ph:(715)294-3345

Published 1987. **Editor(s):** Paul Woudenberg. **Price:** $15.95.

161 ● Rolls-Royce/Bentley Marketletter
Mary Ann Liebert, Inc.
1651 3rd Ave.
New York, NY 10128   Ph:(212)289-2300

Provides extensive listings of Rolls-Royce and Bentley cars for sale or trade. Monthly. **Price:** $53.00.

ASSOCIATIONS

162 ● Rolls-Royce Owners' Club
191 Hempt Rd.
Mechanicsburg, PA 17055
Timothy E. Younes, Exec.Dir.   Ph:(717)697-4671

Founded: 1951. **Membership:** 6,000. Persons interested in preserving and restoring automobiles produced by Rolls-Royce Ltd., Rolls-Royce Motors, Ltd., Rolls-Royce of America, and Bentley Motors (1931) Ltd. To exchange technical, historical, and general information. Reprints owners' manuals and technical materials.

BERTONE X1/9 (1987-89)

Originally produced by Fiat, then as part of the Bertone line; Bertone X1/9 ceased production after 1989. Produced in Bertone factories in Grugliasco, Italy and Caselle, Italy.

MAJOR FEATURES

● Bertone X1/9 1989 standard equipment: 5-speed manual transmission, rack-and-pinion steering, front and rear disc brakes, and 4-wheel independent suspension.

PRICE HISTORY

The following new car prices reflect the approximate retail cost of the base model: **1987** - $11,730; **1988** - $12,290; **1989** - $13,590.

DIMENSIONS

Body Style	Years Avail	Wheel Base (in)	Lgth (in)	Ht (in)	Avg Wt (lbs)	Fuel Cap (gal)	Front Hdrm (in)	Front Legrm (in)
2d trga	87-89	86.7	156.3	46.8	2,210	12.2	na	na

ENGINES

Type	Displacement (L)	Fuel Dly	HP @rpm	Torque @rpm (ft/lbs)	MPG Cty/Hwy	Years Avail
I-4	1.5	FI	75@5500	79@3000	23/28	87-89

KEY: I=in-line engine; V=V engine; F=flat engine; FI=fuel injection; bbl=barrel carburetor; T=turbo; D=diesel; HP=horsepower; MPG=estimated average miles per gallon.

EVALUATIONS, TESTS, AND RANKINGS

1989: "isn't the smoothest or quietest revver . . . it will pull to a 7000 rpm redline." **Source:** "Bertone X1/9: Still fun after all these years," *Road & Track,* July 1988, p. 80.

RECALLS

None to date.

OTHER INFORMATION SOURCES

163 ● X1/9 Newsletter
X1/9 Car Club
PO Box 901
Sun Valley, CA 91353-0901   Ph:(818)982-3420

Provides information on parts and technical assistance to owners of Bertone and Fiat X1/9 sports cars. Monthly. **Price:** Included in membership dues.

ASSOCIATIONS

164 ● X1/9 Car Club
P.O. Box 901
Sun Valley, CA 91353-0901   Ph:(818)982-3420
                                     Fax:(818)982-2634

Founded: 1984. Owners of Bertone and Fiat X 1/9 sports cars made from 1972-89. Provides information on parts and technical assistance. **Convention/Meeting:** Semiannual.

BMW 3-SERIES (1987-92)

Newly designed for the 1992 model year, the 3-series is the sporty line of BMW. 325is appears on *Car and Driver's* 1990 Ten Best Cars Nominee list. Dimensions listed below are for the 325i sedan.

1991 BMW 318is

MAJOR FEATURES

● BMW 318is, an entry-level 3-series coupe available in May 1992, has as 1992 standard equipment: 5-speed manual transmission, power-assisted rack-and-pinion steering, 4-wheel disc brakes, anti-lock braking system, power windows, AM/FM stereo cassette, and driver's side airbag.

● BMW 318i convertible has as 1992 standard equipment: 5-speed manual transmission, power assisted rack and pinion steering, 4-wheel disc brakes, anti-lock braking system, driver's side airbag, air conditioning, anti-theft system, and power windows and locks. The 318i sedan, previously sold in the U.S., will not be available for 1992 model year.

● The sportier BMW 325i sedan and convertible add as 1992 standard equipment: 5-speed manual or 4-speed automatic transmission, upgraded engine, power operated top (convertible), cruise control, cloth or leatherette upholstery.

● BMW 325is, a coupe available in April 1992, adds as 1992 standard equipment: electric two-way sunroof.

● BMW 325iX, not imported for the 1992 model year, added as 1991 standard equipment: 4-wheel drive, ski sack, 2-way sunroof, cloth or leatherette upholstery, and AM/FM stereo cassette.

● BMW M3, also not imported in 1992, had as 1991 standard equipment: same as 325i plus 2.3-liter DOHC 16-valve PFI 4-cylinder engine.

PRICE HISTORY

The following new car prices reflect the approximate retail cost of the base model: **1987** - $22,290; **1988** - $24,350; **1989** - $24,650; **1990** - $21,500; **1991** - $20,300; **1992** - $27,990.

DIMENSIONS

Body Style	Years Avail	Wheel Base (in)	Lgth (in)	Ht (in)	Avg Wt (lbs)	Fuel Cap (gal)	Front Hdrm (in)	Front Legrm (in)
4d sdn	87-87	101.2	175.6	54.3	2,765	14.5	37.7	39.6
4d sdn	88-88	101.2	172.2	54.3	2,765	16.4	37.7	39.6
4d sdn	89-91	101.2	170.3	54.3	2,844	16.4	37.7	39.6
4d sdn	92-92	106.3	174.5	54.8	3,021	17.2	na	na

ENGINES

Type	Displace-ment (L)	Fuel Dly	HP @rpm	Torque @rpm (ft/lbs)	MPG Cty/Hwy	Years Avail
I-4	2.3	FI	192@6750	170@4750	17/29	87-91
I-4	1.8	FI	134@6000	127@4600	20/26	91-92
I-6	2.7	FI	121@4250	170@3250	21/28	87-87
I-6	2.5	FI	168@5800	164@4300	17/24	87-92
I-6	2.5	FI	189@5900	181@4700	18/26	92-92

KEY: I=in-line engine; V=V engine; F=flat engine; FI=fuel injection; bbl=barrel carburetor; T=turbo; D=diesel; HP=horsepower; MPG=estimated average miles per gallon.

EVALUATIONS, TESTS, AND RANKINGS

1992: "performance of a wing-footed god, an engine that can sing Mozart, and German good looks . . . most handsome 3-series car ever." **Source:** "Ten Best Cars: And a glimpse into the future, too," *Car and Driver*, January 1992, pp. 35-43.

1992: "a car that shuns the garage and begs to take the long way home . . . overall ride quality is firm . . . shape is stocky, compact and powerful-looking." **Source:** "BMW 325i: A Bavarian cure for the sports-sedan blahs," *Road & Track*, October 1991, pp. 94-98.

1992: "It is fast. It is efficient. It is modern . . . tight and eager on the road . . . tendency to respond to the pavement with a little too much busyness." **Source:** "BMW 325i: An elegant application of intelligence," *Automobile Magazine*, January 1992, p. 49.

1992: "sleek shell . . . looks far sexier and more contemporary . . . road-holding ability and overall performance have been

markedly upgraded . . . ample, well-laid-out cockpit." **Source:** "325i Looks, Feels Like Larger Siblings," *Detroit Free Press*, September 5, 1991, p. 1E.

1991: "Responsive . . . steering and adroit handling . . . interior is fresh and refined . . . Ride quality is good." **Source:** "BMW 325i: A new generation carries on the flame," *Motor Trend*, March 1991, pp. 60-62.

1991: "bulges with the muscle . . . more engine noise and less fuel economy." **Source:** "BMW 325i: After nine years, there's a new kid on the block," *Car and Driver*, March 1991, pp. 61-63, 65.

1991: "looks miles better than . . . outgoing model . . . roomier and more aerodynamic . . . steering is . . . precise and responsive and lets you feel the road." **Source:** "First Drive: New 3-Series BMW," *Automobile Magazine*, March 1991, pp. 57-58, 60, 63.

1990: "as nimble as it is quick . . . rather cramped backseat . . . moderately priced route to the fast lane." **Source:** "A Classic Shifts Gears: BMW revs up the engine and downshifts the price," *House and Garden*, August 1990, p. 52.

1990: "the way it sounds, especially under hard acceleration, bespeaks successful development . . . little body roll to worry about . . . nimble in traffic." **Source:** "BMW 318is: Rewriting the Big Bang Theory," *Motor Trend*, September 1990, pp. 106-109, 111.

1989: "plenty of grip and stability . . . distinctly sporting flavor . . . long on sport and short on sedan." **Source:** "Sensible Speed: A six-pack to go," *Car and Driver*, March 1989, pp. 46-48, 50, 53-56.

1988: "BMW 325iX . . . starting was something the iX was reluctant to do in cold weather . . . did not perform better than significantly cheaper 4wds." **Source:** "Snow White and the Seven AWDs," *Road & Track*, May 1988, pp. 56-63, 67-70.

1987: "dramatically improved performance . . . reassuringly sure-footed . . . supple ride." **Source:** "325is: The spiritual return of the 2002tii," *Car and Driver*, August 1987, pp. 49-52.

RECALLS

1991: (13,500 passenger cars; includes the BMW 318is and BMW 318i): Incorrectly installed driver-side knee bolster prevented steering column from moving forward as designed to absorb impact energy. Chest deceleration exceeds maximum allowable limit, which results in increased risk of occupant injury in sudden stop or accident. **Corrective action:** Repair the knee bolster to allow clearance and avoid impedance of steering column movement during frontal impact. *(NHTSA Campaign No. 91V054000.)*

1988: (1,256 passenger vehicle; specifically BMW 325IX): Oil dipstick tube attaching bracket may have been bent during production or scheduled maintenance, reducing clearance between dipstick ring and throttle bellcrank lever. This reduced clearance may inhibit return of throttle to fully closed idle position, when accelerator pedal is released. **Corrective action:** Requires cutting off outboard end of throttle bellcrank lever to provide necessary clearance. *(NHTSA Campaign No. 88V031000.)*

REPAIR MANUALS

165 ● BMW 6 Cylinder
Peter Allen Video Productions
38-C Otis St.
West Babylon, NY 11704   Ph:(516)643-4372

How to tune-up, maintain, and pamper the entitled BMW

engines. **Release date:** 1986. **Producer:** Peter Allen Productions. **Acquisition:** Purchase.

OTHER INFORMATION SOURCES

166 ● BMW Automobile Club of America—Journal
BMW Automobile Club of America (BMW-ACA)
P.O. Box 3828
City of Industry, CA 91744-0828   Ph:(714)595-6699

(in English and German), quarterly.

167 ● BMW Magazine
Marque Publications
P.O. Box 2791
Fullerton, CA 92633   Ph:(714)771-7126

Offers feature articles on BMW automobiles, new products, aftermarket accessories, and travel and lifestyles involving BMW vehicles. Quarterly. **Editor(s):** Greg Pziuk, Publisher. **Price:** $12.50 per year; $3.95 per issue.

168 ● European Car
Argus Publishers Corp.
12100 Wilshire Blvd., Ste. 250   Ph:(213)820-3601
Los Angeles, CA 90025   Fax:(213)207-9388

Magazine covering Volkswagen, Porsche, Mercedes-Benz, Audi, Ferrari, Jaguar, and BMW automobiles. Bimonthly. **Editor(s):** Greg N. Brown. **Price:** $11.00 per year; $2.75 per issue.

169 ● Friends of BMW
BMW Car Club of America (BMWCCA)
345 Harvard St.
Cambridge, MA 02138   Ph:(617)492-2500

Directory. Annual. **Price:** Free to those included in listing; $3.00 per copy for other members.

170 ● Great Marques BMW
Book Sales, Inc.
110 Enterprise Ave.
Secaucus, NJ 070941995   Ph:(201)864-6341

Published 1989. **Price:** $10.98.

171 ● Roundel Magazine
BMW Car Club of America, Inc.
345 Harvard St.   Ph:(617)492-2500
Cambridge, MA 02138   Fax:(617)876-3424

Magazine for BMW enthusiasts; includes book reviews. Monthly. **Price:** $3.00.

172 ● Whispering Bomb
BMW Automobile Club of America, Los Angeles Region
P.O. Box 3828
City of Industry, CA 91744-0828   Ph:(714)595-6699

Contains information about the BMW (Bavarian Motor Works) automobile for owners and admirers. Covers news of new models, model changes, BMW racing results, factory developments, technical information, and Club activities. Monthly. **Editor(s):** James Tulk. **Price:** Available to members only.

ASSOCIATIONS

173 ● BMW Automobile Club of America
P.O. Box 3828
City of Industry, CA 91744-0828   Ph:(714)595-6699
Leif Anderberg, Pres.   Fax:(714)594-5178

Founded: 1970. **Membership:** 4280. Individuals who own a BMW (Bavarian Motor Works) automobile. Purposes are to further the BMW marque, to provide more enjoyment from the car, and to meet other owners of BMW automobiles. Sponsors two annual driving schools. Maintains library of factory manuals and related materials. Organizes competitions; bestows awards. Maintains charitable program. **Convention/Meeting:** Annual Oktoberfest - always September or October, Southern California; 1992 Lake Arrowhead.

174 ● BMW Car Club of America
345 Harvard St.
Cambridge, MA 02138   Ph:(617)492-2500
Mark L. Luckman, Exec.Dir.   Fax:(617)876-3424

Founded: 1969. **Membership:** 26,000. Owners of BMW (Bavarian Motor Works) automobiles and other interested persons. Promotes interest in BMW automobiles through technical, social, and competitive events; encourages the exchange of information among members. Club is independent of any commercial interests. **Convention/Meeting:** Annual Oktoberfest.

BMW 5-SERIES (1987-92)

The 5-series consists of three sedans: 525i, 535i, and M5. Positioned as BMW's mid-size vehicles, the 525i and 535i share the same body, but the 525i gets 189 horsepower from a twin-cam, 24-valve 2.5-liter while the 535i gets 208 from a single overhead-cam, 12-valve 3.4-liter. The M5, billed as an ultra-high performance vehicle, comes with enhanced 311-horsepower engine, and was chosen by *Road & Track* as One of the Ten Best Cars in the World, 1991; and Best Coupe/Sedan for more than $45,000.

1991 BMW 525i

MAJOR FEATURES

● BMW 525i has as 1992 standard equipment: 5-speed manual transmission, 4-wheel disc brakes, anti-lock braking system, recirculating ball steering, cruise control, power windows, adjustable steering wheel, air conditioning, 2-way power sunroof, improved central locking system, diversity antenna system, ventilation microfilter, and AM/FM stereo cassette.

● BMW 535i adds as 1992 standard equipment: 5-speed manual or 4-speed automatic transmission, remote-actuated alarm system, and automatic climate control.

● BMW M5 adds as 1992 standard equipment: upgraded

suspension and brakes, self-leveling rear suspension, and front sport seats.

PRICE HISTORY

The following new car prices reflect the approximate retail cost of the base model: **1987** - $28,330; **1988** - $31,950; **1989** - $37,000; **1990** - $33,200; **1991** - $34,900; **1992** - $35,600.

DIMENSIONS

Body Style	Years Avail	Wheel Base (in)	Lgth (in)	Ht (in)	Avg Wt (lbs)	Fuel Cap (gal)	Front Hdrm (in)	Front Legrm (in)
4d sdn	87-88	103.3	189.0	55.7	3,100	16.6	38.2	41.7
4d sdn	89-92	108.7	185.8	55.6	3,484	21.1	38.5	42.0

ENGINES

Type	Displacement (L)	Fuel Dly	HP @rpm	Torque @rpm (ft/lbs)	MPG Cty/Hwy	Years Avail
I-6	2.7	FI	121@4250	170@3250	20/24	87-87
I-6	3.5	FI	256@6500	243@4500	10/19	87-88
I-6	3.4	FI	182@5400	214@4000	15/23	87-88
I-6	2.7	FI	127@4800	170@3200	19/25	88-88
I-6	2.5	FI	168@5800	164@4300	18/25	89-90
I-6	3.4	FI	208@5700	225@4000	15/23	89-92
I-6	2.5	FI	189@5900	181@4700	17/25	91-92
I-6	3.5	FI	311@6900	265@4750	12/23	91-92

KEY: I=in-line engine; V=V engine; F=flat engine; FI=fuel injection; bbl=barrel carburetor; T=turbo; D=diesel; HP=horsepower; MPG=estimated average miles per gallon.

EVALUATIONS, TESTS, AND RANKINGS

1992: "leather seats are handsome and comfortable . . . angular execution of the body pleases the eye, as well as the spirit . . . isolation from road irregularities is good." **Source:** "BMW 325i vs. Acura Vigor GS: Sport sedans with split personalities," *Motor Trend,* November 1991, pp. 108-112.

1991: "Superbly balanced chassis coupled with strong engine . . . Outstanding noise insulation and ride quality." **Source:** "BMW 535i: Making it to the top," *Automobile Magazine,* January 1991, p. 154.

1991: "Beautifully luxurious . . . with the soul of a race car." **Source:** "BMW M5: One of the Ten Best Cars in the World, 1991," *Road & Track,* December 1991, p. 49.

1991: "the most expensive mid-level, mid-luxury car you can buy . . . the fastest four-door sedan in the world." **Source:** "BMW's M5: Performance—at a Price," *The New York Times,* October 28, 1990.

1990: "excels on winding, backcountry roads . . . brakes are superb . . . headlights . . . really light up the night." **Source:** "Driving in the lap of luxury," *U.S. News & World Report,* January 8, 1990, pp. 59-62.

1990: "nothing about the car's styling makes it instantly recognizable . . . Vision from the very comfortable driver's seat is excellent . . . backseat space for anyone more than 6 ft tall is inadequate." **Source:** "BMW 535i Does it All," *Design News,* October 2, 1989, pp. 134-135.

1989: "larger, roomier, and more powerful than the sedans they replace . . . aerodyamic performance has been improved." **Source:** "Faster Fives," *Popular Science,* January 1989, p. 52.

1989: "visibly sleeker shape helps decrease wind noise . . . one of the quietest passenger compartments on the road today . . . merits major kudos." **Source:** "BMW 535i: You pay for what

you get, but you get what you pay for," *Motor Trend,* April 1989, pp. 85-88.

RECALLS

1991: (5,644 BMW 525 vehicles): Insufficient axial clearance exists for throttle valve, shaft, and housing due to different thermal expansion rates of separate parts when vehicle reaches normal operating temperatures and ambient temperature is 40 degrees Fahrenheit or less. This could cause unexpected maintenance of speed and an accident. **Corrective action:** Inspect and repair by replacing throttle housing. *(NHTSA Campaign No. 91V029000.)*

1991: (480 M5 vehicles): Screws that attach wheel covers on original equipment wheels were not fully torqued and may gradually loosen and separate from wheels; could present a hazard to other vehicles and pedestrians in vicinity. **Corrective action:** Apply Loctite Z4Z (blue) to wheel cover to prevent screws from loosening. *(NHTSA Campaign No. 90V204000.)*

1989-90: (62,000 vehicles; includes BMW 525i, BMW 535i, BMW 735i, BMW 735iL, and BMW 750 models): Under certain conditions, front seat center, fold-down armrest may contact the safety belt buckle, causing damage to the release button and preventing the belt tongue from latching when buckling up; occupant would not be properly restrained and could be injured in sudden stop or accident. **Corrective action:** Replace front seat safety belt buckles with shorter version that will not contact the armrests. *(NHTSA Campaign No. 90V016000.)*

REPAIR MANUALS

175 ● BMW 6 Cylinder
Peter Allen Video Productions
38-C Otis St.
West Babylon, NY 11704   Ph:(516)643-4372

How to tune-up, maintain, and pamper the entitled BMW engines. **Release date:** 1986. **Producer:** Peter Allen Productions. **Acquisition:** Purchase.

OTHER INFORMATION SOURCES

176 ● BMW Automobile Club of America—Journal
BMW Automobile Club of America (BMW-ACA)
P.O. Box 3828
City of Industry, CA 91744-0828   Ph:(714)595-6699

(in English and German), quarterly.

177 ● BMW Magazine
Marque Publications
P.O. Box 2791
Fullerton, CA 92633   Ph:(714)771-7126

Offers feature articles on BMW automobiles, new products, aftermarket accessories, and travel and lifestyles involving BMW vehicles. Quarterly. **Editor(s):** Greg Pziuk, Publisher. **Price:** $12.50 per year; $3.95 per issue.

178 ● European Car
Argus Publishers Corp.
12100 Wilshire Blvd., Ste. 250   Ph:(213)820-3601
Los Angeles, CA 90025   Fax:(213)207-9388

Magazine covering Volkswagen, Porsche, Mercedes-Benz, Audi, Ferrari, Jaguar, and BMW automobiles. Bimonthly. **Editor(s):** Greg N. Brown. **Price:** $11.00 per year; $2.75 per issue.

179 ● Friends of BMW
BMW Car Club of America (BMWCCA)
345 Harvard St.
Cambridge, MA 02138   Ph:(617)492-2500

Directory. Annual. **Price:** Free to those included in listing;
$3.00 per copy for other members.

180 ● Great Marques BMW
Book Sales, Inc.
110 Enterprise Ave.
Secaucus, NJ 070941995   Ph:(201)864-6341

Published 1989. **Price:** $10.98.

181 ● Roundel Magazine
BMW Car Club of America, Inc.
345 Harvard St.   Ph:(617)492-2500
Cambridge, MA 02138   Fax:(617)876-3424

Magazine for BMW enthusiasts; includes book reviews.
Monthly. **Price:** $3.00.

182 ● Whispering Bomb
BMW Automobile Club of America, Los Angeles Region
P.O. Box 3828
City of Industry, CA 91744-0828   Ph:(714)595-6699

Contains information about the BMW (Bavarian Motor Works)
automobile for owners and admirers. Covers news of new
models, model changes, BMW racing results, factory
developments, technical information, and Club activities.
Monthly. **Editor(s):** James Tulk. **Price:** Available to members
only.

ASSOCIATIONS

183 ● BMW Automobile Club of America
P.O. Box 3828
City of Industry, CA 91744-0828   Ph:(714)595-6699
Leif Anderberg, Pres.   Fax:(714)594-5178

Founded: 1970. **Membership:** 4280. Individuals who own a
BMW (Bavarian Motor Works) automobile. Purposes are to
further the BMW marque, to provide more enjoyment from the
car, and to meet other owners of BMW automobiles. Sponsors
two annual driving schools. Maintains library of factory
manuals and related materials. Organizes competitions;
bestows awards. Maintains charitable program.
Convention/Meeting: Annual Oktoberfest - always September
or October, Southern California; 1992 Lake Arrowhead.

184 ● BMW Car Club of America
345 Harvard St.
Cambridge, MA 02138   Ph:(617)492-2500
Mark L. Luckman, Exec.Dir.   Fax:(617)876-3424

Founded: 1969. **Membership:** 26,000. Owners of BMW
(Bavarian Motor Works) automobiles and other interested
persons. Promotes interest in BMW automobiles through
technical, social, and competitive events; encourages the
exchange of information among members. Club is independent
of any commercial interests. **Convention/Meeting:** Annual
Oktoberfest.

BMW 6-SERIES (1987-89)

Introduced as part of BMW line, the series consisted of a
``luxury'' 635 and the M(otorsport)6. Phased out of production
in 1989.

MAJOR FEATURES

● BMW 635CSi and M6 had as 1989 standard equipment: 5-
speed manual or 4-speed automatic transmission, airbag,
AM/FM stereo cassette, power steering, power windows,
power locks, sunroof, cruise control, 4-wheel disc brakes, anti-
lock brake system, and air conditioning.

PRICE HISTORY

The following new car prices reflect the approximate retail cost
of the base model: **1987** - $46,965; **1988** - $46,000; **1989** -
$47,000.

DIMENSIONS

Body Style	Years Avail	Wheel Base (in)	Lgth (in)	Ht (in)	Avg Wt (lbs)	Fuel Cap (gal)	Front Hdrm (in)	Front Legrm (in)
2d cpe	87-87	103.3	193.8	53.7	3,490	16.6	37.7	41.7
2d cpe	87-89	103.3	189.6	53.3	3,570	16.6	37.7	41.7
2d cpe	88-89	103.3	189.6	53.7	3,530	16.6	37.7	41.7

ENGINES

Type	Displacement (L)	Fuel Dly	HP @rpm	Torque @rpm (ft/lbs)	MPG Cty/Hwy	Years Avail
I-6	3.4	FI	182@5400	214@4000	16/22	87-87
I-6	3.5	FI	256@6500	243@4500	10/19	88-89
I-6	3.4	FI	208@5700	225@4000	15/23	88-89

KEY: I=in-line engine; V=V engine; F=flat engine; FI=fuel injection;
bbl=barrel carburetor; T=turbo; D=diesel; HP=horsepower;
MPG=estimated average miles per gallon.

EVALUATIONS, TESTS, AND RANKINGS

1988: ``BMW M6 . . . feels precise . . . Not a hint of instability
on the banking.'' **Source:** ``Top-Speed 10: Indulging our go-fast
fetish again,'' *Motor Trend*, September 1988, pp. 36-37.

1987: ``the ride is reassuringly solid, the handling pin-sharp.''
Source: ``BMW M6: The joy of six,'' *Motor Trend*, September
1987, p. 56.

RECALLS

1988-89: (4,452 passenger cars equipped with air bags;
includes other BMW models): Threshold level of frontal impact
sensors too sensitive to severe vertical motion, resulting in
airbag deployment without actual crash. **Corrective action:**
Repair frontal impact sensors. *(NHTSA Campaign No.
89V179000.)*

REPAIR MANUALS

185 ● BMW 6 Cylinder
Peter Allen Video Productions
38-C Otis St.
West Babylon, NY 11704   Ph:(516)643-4372

How to tune-up, maintain, and pamper the entitled BMW
engines. **Release date:** 1986. **Producer:** Peter Allen
Productions. **Acquisition:** Purchase.

OTHER INFORMATION SOURCES

186 ● BMW Automobile Club of America—Journal
BMW Automobile Club of America (BMW-ACA)
P.O. Box 3828
City of Industry, CA 91744-0828   Ph:(714)595-6699

(in English and German), quarterly.

187 ● BMW Magazine
Marque Publications
P.O. Box 2791
Fullerton, CA 92633   Ph:(714)771-7126

Offers feature articles on BMW automobiles, new products, aftermarket accessories, and travel and lifestyles involving BMW vehicles. Quarterly. **Editor(s):** Greg Pziuk, Publisher. **Price:** $12.50 per year; $3.95 per issue.

188 ● European Car
Argus Publishers Corp.
12100 Wilshire Blvd., Ste. 250   Ph:(213)820-3601
Los Angeles, CA 90025   Fax:(213)207-9388

Magazine covering Volkswagen, Porsche, Mercedes-Benz, Audi, Ferrari, Jaguar, and BMW automobiles. Bimonthly. **Editor(s):** Greg N. Brown. **Price:** $11.00 per year; $2.75 per issue.

189 ● Friends of BMW
BMW Car Club of America (BMWCCA)
345 Harvard St.
Cambridge, MA 02138   Ph:(617)492-2500

Directory. Annual. **Price:** Free to those included in listing; $3.00 per copy for other members.

190 ● Great Marques BMW
Book Sales, Inc.
110 Enterprise Ave.
Secaucus, NJ 070941995   Ph:(201)864-6341

Published 1989. **Price:** $10.98.

191 ● Roundel Magazine
BMW Car Club of America, Inc.
345 Harvard St.   Ph:(617)492-2500
Cambridge, MA 02138   Fax:(617)876-3424

Magazine for BMW enthusiasts; includes book reviews. Monthly. **Price:** $3.00.

192 ● Whispering Bomb
BMW Automobile Club of America, Los Angeles Region
P.O. Box 3828
City of Industry, CA 91744-0828   Ph:(714)595-6699

Contains information about the BMW (Bavarian Motor Works) automobile for owners and admirers. Covers news of new models, model changes, BMW racing results, factory developments, technical information, and Club activities. Monthly. **Editor(s):** James Tulk. **Price:** Available to members only.

ASSOCIATIONS

193 ● BMW Automobile Club of America
P.O. Box 3828
City of Industry, CA 91744-0828   Ph:(714)595-6699
Leif Anderberg, Pres.   Fax:(714)594-5178

Founded: 1970. **Membership:** 4280. Individuals who own a BMW (Bavarian Motor Works) automobile. Purposes are to further the BMW marque, to provide more enjoyment from the car, and to meet other owners of BMW automobiles. Sponsors two annual driving schools. Maintains library of factory manuals and related materials. Organizes competitions; bestows awards. Maintains charitable program. **Convention/Meeting:** Annual Oktoberfest - always September or October, Southern California; 1992 Lake Arrowhead.

194 ● BMW Car Club of America
345 Harvard St.
Cambridge, MA 02138   Ph:(617)492-2500
Mark L. Luckman, Exec.Dir.   Fax:(617)876-3424

Founded: 1969. **Membership:** 26,000. Owners of BMW (Bavarian Motor Works) automobiles and other interested persons. Promotes interest in BMW automobiles through technical, social, and competitive events; encourages the exchange of information among members. Club is independent of any commercial interests. **Convention/Meeting:** Annual Oktoberfest.

BMW 7-SERIES (1987-92)

BMW's 7-series vehicles are the biggest of the BMW line. Picked by *Car and Driver* as Best Sedan in the World 1990. Named to *Car and Driver's* 1987 Ten Best Performers list as car with lowest interior sound level.

1992 BMW 735iL

MAJOR FEATURES

● BMW 735i has as 1992 standard equipment: 4-speed automatic transmission, power steering, 4-wheel disc brakes, driver's side airbag, automatic climate control system, leather upholstery, AM/FM stereo cassette, power windows, power locks, remote-actuated alarm system, diversity antenna system, and cruise control.

● BMW 735iL adds as 1992 standard equipment: self-leveling rear suspension.

● BMW 750iL, the flagship of the BMW line, will be introduced later in 1992 and will have as standard equipment: 735 standard equipment plus 5.0-liter PFI V-12, double-pane glass windows, cellular phone, and forged alloy wheels.

PRICE HISTORY

The following new car prices reflect the approximate retail cost of the base model: **1987** - $42,475; **1988** - $54,000; **1989** - $54,000; **1990** - $49,000; **1991** - $51,500; **1992** - $52,990.

DIMENSIONS

Body Style	Years Avail	Wheel Base (in)	Lgth (in)	Ht (in)	Avg Wt (lbs)	Fuel Cap (gal)	Front Hdrm (in)	Front Legrm (in)
4d sdn	87-92	111.5	193.3	55.6	3,795	21.5	38.3	na
4d sdn	88-92	116.0	197.8	55.1	4,165	24.0	38.3	na

ENGINES

Type	Displace-ment (L)	Fuel Dly	HP @rpm	Torque @rpm (ft/lbs)	MPG Cty/Hwy	Years Avail
I-6	3.4	FI	208@5700	225@4000	15/21	87-92
V-12	5.0	FI	296@5200	332@4100	12/18	88-92

KEY: I=in-line engine; V=V engine; F=flat engine; FI=fuel injection; bbl=barrel carburetor; T=turbo; D=diesel; HP=horsepower; MPG=estimated average miles per gallon.

EVALUATIONS, TESTS, AND RANKINGS

1990: "[750iLis] fast, it's responsive, it's comfortable. . .exudes smoothness in every mode." **Source:** "Finding the Best Sedan in the World," *Car and Driver,* November 1990, pp. 126-128.

1990: "handling is marked by clear signals to the driver, predictable response, and a suspension that's quite taut . . . steering . . . has a zone of insecurity on-center." **Source:** "Showdown: What happens when Lexus and Infiniti meet the world's best," *Car and Driver,* December 1989, pp. 41-43, 46-50, 52, 54-56.

1987: "Handling . . . was excellent . . . The car was easy to drive . . . The BMW 735i will find homes among those who seek a high quality, high performance sedan." **Source:** "BMW 735i," *Road & Track,* July 1987, p. 152.

RECALLS

1988-90: (62,000 vehicles; includes BMW 525i, BMW 535i, BMW 735i, BMW 735iL, and BMW 750 models): Under certain conditions, front seat center, fold-down armrest may contact the safety belt buckle, causing damage to the release button and preventing the belt tongue from latching when buckling up; occupant would not be properly restrained and could be injured in sudden stop or accident. **Corrective action:** Replace front seat safety belt buckles with shorter version that will not contact the armrests. *(NHTSA Campaign No. 90V016000.)*

1988-89: (4,729 passenger cars with 12 cylinder engines): Accelerator pedal may not have been properly attached to floor. Pedal may become stuck. **Corrective action:** Assure proper attachment of pedal. *(NHTSA Campaign No. 89V005000.)*

1988: (8,187 passenger vehicles; includes BMW 735 and 750): Driver and/or passenger seatbacks may not have been fully attached to seat base reclining arms (attaching brackets). There may be looseness of, or noise in, the seatback; also, during severe rear impact, seatback might not support occupant. **Corrective action:** Manually seat seatback on base. *(NHTSA Campaign No. 88V13500.)*

SAFETY AND REPAIRS

1988: "BMW 7-Series shaking," *Road & Track,* May 1989, pp. 194-197. **Note:** BMW 735i shakes in 50-55 mph range.

1988: "BMW 7-Series shakes," *Road & Track,* September 1989, p. 160. **Note:** BMW 735i shaking may be due to torque converter.

REPAIR MANUALS

195 ● BMW 6 Cylinder
Peter Allen Video Productions
38-C Otis St.
West Babylon, NY 11704   Ph:(516)643-4372

How to tune-up, maintain, and pamper the entitled BMW engines. **Release date:** 1986. **Producer:** Peter Allen Productions. **Acquisition:** Purchase.

OTHER INFORMATION SOURCES

196 ● BMW Automobile Club of America—Journal
BMW Automobile Club of America (BMW-ACA)
P.O. Box 3828
City of Industry, CA 91744-0828   Ph:(714)595-6699

(in English and German), quarterly.

197 ● BMW Magazine
Marque Publications
P.O. Box 2791
Fullerton, CA 92633   Ph:(714)771-7126

Offers feature articles on BMW automobiles, new products, aftermarket accessories, and travel and lifestyles involving BMW vehicles. Quarterly. **Editor(s):** Greg Pziuk, Publisher. **Price:** $12.50 per year; $3.95 per issue.

198 ● European Car
Argus Publishers Corp.
12100 Wilshire Blvd., Ste. 250   Ph:(213)820-3601
Los Angeles, CA 90025   Fax:(213)207-9388

Magazine covering Volkswagen, Porsche, Mercedes-Benz, Audi, Ferrari, Jaguar, and BMW automobiles. Bimonthly. **Editor(s):** Greg N. Brown. **Price:** $11.00 per year; $2.75 per issue.

199 ● Friends of BMW
BMW Car Club of America (BMWCCA)
345 Harvard St.
Cambridge, MA 02138   Ph:(617)492-2500

Directory. Annual. **Price:** Free to those included in listing; $3.00 per copy for other members.

200 ● Great Marques BMW
Book Sales, Inc.
110 Enterprise Ave.
Secaucus, NJ 070941995   Ph:(201)864-6341

Published 1989. **Price:** $10.98.

201 ● Roundel Magazine
BMW Car Club of America, Inc.
345 Harvard St.   Ph:(617)492-2500
Cambridge, MA 02138   Fax:(617)876-3424

Magazine for BMW enthusiasts; includes book reviews. Monthly. **Price:** $3.00.

202 ● Whispering Bomb
BMW Automobile Club of America, Los Angeles Region
P.O. Box 3828
City of Industry, CA 91744-0828   Ph:(714)595-6699

Contains information about the BMW (Bavarian Motor Works) automobile for owners and admirers. Covers news of new models, model changes, BMW racing results, factory developments, technical information, and Club activities. Monthly. **Editor(s):** James Tulk. **Price:** Available to members only.

ASSOCIATIONS

203 ● BMW Automobile Club of America
P.O. Box 3828
City of Industry, CA 91744-0828   Ph:(714)595-6699
Leif Anderberg, Pres.   Fax:(714)594-5178

Founded: 1970. **Membership:** 4280. Individuals who own a BMW (Bavarian Motor Works) automobile. Purposes are to further the BMW marque, to provide more enjoyment from the car, and to meet other owners of BMW automobiles. Sponsors two annual driving schools. Maintains library of factory manuals and related materials. Organizes competitions; bestows awards. Maintains charitable program. **Convention/Meeting:** Annual Oktoberfest - always September or October, Southern California; 1992 Lake Arrowhead.

204 ● BMW Car Club of America
345 Harvard St.
Cambridge, MA 02138   Ph:(617)492-2500
Mark L. Luckman, Exec.Dir.   Fax:(617)876-3424

Founded: 1969. **Membership:** 26,000. Owners of BMW (Bavarian Motor Works) automobiles and other interested persons. Promotes interest in BMW automobiles through technical, social, and competitive events; encourages the exchange of information among members. Club is independent of any commercial interests. **Convention/Meeting:** Annual Oktoberfest.

BMW 8-SERIES (1991-92)

Introduced in 1991 as part of BMW line; targeted at the high-performance grand-touring market. Introduction of the 1992 model to the U.S. was delayed due to an overabundance of 1991 model.

1991 BMW 850i

MAJOR FEATURES

● BMW 850i   has as 1992 standard equipment: 6-speed manual or 4-speed automatic transmission, anti-lock brake system, power steering, driver's side airbag, automatic climate control, leather interior, tilt steering wheel, power windows, remote locking and alarm, AM/FM stereo cassette/6-disc CD player, cellular phone, power sunroof, and cruise control.

PRICE HISTORY

The following new car prices reflect the approximate retail cost of the base model: **1991** - $77,700; **1992** - $77,700.

DIMENSIONS

Body Style	Years Avail	Wheel Base (in)	Lgth (in)	Ht (in)	Avg Wt (lbs)	Fuel Cap (gal)	Front Hdrm (in)	Front Legrm (in)
2d cpe	91-92	105.7	188.2	52.8	4,123	23.8	37.4	na

ENGINES

Type	Displace-ment (L)	Fuel Dly	HP @rpm	Torque @rpm (ft/lbs)	MPG Cty/Hwy	Years Avail
V-12	5.0	FI	296@5200	332@4100	12/19	91-92

KEY: I=in-line engine; V=V engine; F=flat engine; FI=fuel injection; bbl=barrel carburetor; T=turbo; D=diesel; HP=horsepower; MPG=estimated average miles per gallon.

EVALUATIONS, TESTS, AND RANKINGS

1991: "interior is typically BMW ... arguably the most technologically sophisticated and safest vehicle on the road." **Source:** "Autobahn Burner With Style," *Popular Mechanics*, November 1990, pp. 102, 104.

1991: "stands out as a kind of technological overachiever ... its conservative styling is likely to endure ... rear seats are little more than ceremonial window dressing." **Source:** "BMW 850i: The smartest kid in the class," *Road & Track*, June 1991, pp. 88-92.

1991: "a flashy, mind-boggling automobile ... sculpted spaceship shape ... this car has character." **Source:** "BMW coupe on a road all its own," *Detroit News*, April 24, 1991, pp. 1D-2D.

1991: "car's hunkered-down stance is enhanced by its long hood ... Steering is adequately quick, precise and has a good feel ... ride has a firm, solid feel, but comfortably so." **Source:** "BMW 850i shows smooth handling in traffic conditions of real world," *Flint Journal*, May 15, 1991.

1991: "Some of the high-tech gadgetry is pretty clever ... the driving experience itself ... is worth the price of admission ... the ultimate in ego gratification." **Source:** "BMW 850i is for grand touring," *Detroit Free Press*, April 18, 1991, p. 1D.

1991: "the kind of car that causes all of the drivers you pass to crane their eyes ... bristles with technological wonders ... new design is as aerodynamic as anything on the road." **Source:** "The Ultimate BMW Takes a Step Up," *New York Times*, March 3, 1991.

RECALLS

None to date.

REPAIR MANUALS

205 ● BMW 6 Cylinder
Peter Allen Video Productions
38-C Otis St.
West Babylon, NY 11704   Ph:(516)643-4372

How to tune-up, maintain, and pamper the entitled BMW engines. **Release date:** 1986. **Producer:** Peter Allen Productions. **Acquisition:** Purchase.

OTHER INFORMATION SOURCES

206 ● BMW Automobile Club of America—Journal
BMW Automobile Club of America (BMW-ACA)
P.O. Box 3828
City of Industry, CA 91744-0828   Ph:(714)595-6699

(in English and German), quarterly.

207 ● BMW Magazine
Marque Publications
P.O. Box 2791
Fullerton, CA 92633   Ph:(714)771-7126

Offers feature articles on BMW automobiles, new products, aftermarket accessories, and travel and lifestyles involving

BMW vehicles. Quarterly. **Editor(s):** Greg Pziuk, Publisher. **Price:** $12.50 per year; $3.95 per issue.

208 ● European Car
Argus Publishers Corp.
12100 Wilshire Blvd., Ste. 250   Ph:(213)820-3601
Los Angeles, CA 90025   Fax:(213)207-9388

Magazine covering Volkswagen, Porsche, Mercedes-Benz, Audi, Ferrari, Jaguar, and BMW automobiles. Bimonthly. **Editor(s):** Greg N. Brown. **Price:** $11.00 per year; $2.75 per issue.

209 ● Friends of BMW
BMW Car Club of America (BMWCCA)
345 Harvard St.
Cambridge, MA 02138   Ph:(617)492-2500

Directory. Annual. **Price:** Free to those included in listing; $3.00 per copy for other members.

210 ● Great Marques BMW
Book Sales, Inc.
110 Enterprise Ave.
Secaucus, NJ 070941995   Ph:(201)864-6341

Published 1989. **Price:** $10.98.

211 ● Roundel Magazine
BMW Car Club of America, Inc.
345 Harvard St.   Ph:(617)492-2500
Cambridge, MA 02138   Fax:(617)876-3424

Magazine for BMW enthusiasts; includes book reviews. Monthly. **Price:** $3.00.

212 ● Whispering Bomb
BMW Automobile Club of America, Los Angeles Region
P.O. Box 3828
City of Industry, CA 91744-0828   Ph:(714)595-6699

Contains information about the BMW (Bavarian Motor Works) automobile for owners and admirers. Covers news of new models, model changes, BMW racing results, factory developments, technical information, and Club activities. Monthly. **Editor(s):** James Tulk. **Price:** Available to members only.

ASSOCIATIONS

213 ● BMW Automobile Club of America
P.O. Box 3828
City of Industry, CA 91744-0828   Ph:(714)595-6699
Leif Anderberg, Pres.   Fax:(714)594-5178

Founded: 1970. **Membership:** 4280. Individuals who own a BMW (Bavarian Motor Works) automobile. Purposes are to further the BMW marque, to provide more enjoyment from the car, and to meet other owners of BMW automobiles. Sponsors two annual driving schools. Maintains library of factory manuals and related materials. Organizes competitions; bestows awards. Maintains charitable program. **Convention/Meeting:** Annual Oktoberfest - always September or October, Southern California; 1992 Lake Arrowhead.

214 ● BMW Car Club of America
345 Harvard St.
Cambridge, MA 02138   Ph:(617)492-2500
Mark L. Luckman, Exec.Dir.   Fax:(617)876-3424

Founded: 1969. **Membership:** 26,000. Owners of BMW (Bavarian Motor Works) automobiles and other interested persons. Promotes interest in BMW automobiles through

technical, social, and competitive events; encourages the exchange of information among members. Club is independent of any commercial interests. **Convention/Meeting:** Annual Oktoberfest.

BUICK CENTURY (1987-92)

Introduced as part of A car model line, along with corporate twins Oldsmobile Cutlass Ciera and Pontiac 6000. Named top domestic car in customer satisfaction in its class by J. D. Power and Associates. Named 1991 Safe Care of the Year by *Prevention* magazine. Produced at the General Motors plant in Ramos Arispe, Mexico.

1991 Buick Century Custom

MAJOR FEATURES

● Buick Century has as 1992 standard equipment: 3-speed automatic transmission, power rack-and-pinion steering, front disc/rear drum power brakes, front-wheel drive, air conditioning, and AM/FM stereo.

● Buick Century Custom adds as 1992 standard equipment: front seat with storage armrest, and split-folding rear seatback.

● Buick Century Limited adds as 1992 standard equipment: front seat with storage armrest, split-folding rear seatback, and trip odometer.

● Buick Century Custom and Limited Wagons add as 1992 standard equipment: split-folding rear seatback, lockable load area storage compartments and other exterior body stylings.

PRICE HISTORY

The following new car prices reflect the approximate retail cost of the base model: **1987** - $10,844; **1988** - $11,643; **1989** - $12,199; **1990** - $13,150; **1991** - $13,685; **1992** - $13,795.

DIMENSIONS

Body Style	Years Avail	Wheel Base (in)	Lgth (in)	Ht (in)	Avg Wt (lbs)	Fuel Cap (gal)	Front Hdrm (in)	Front Legrm (in)
2d cpe	87-92	104.9	189.1	53.7	2,862	15.7	38.6	42.1
4d sdn	88-92	104.9	189.1	54.2	2,914	15.7	38.6	42.1
5d wgn	87-92	104.9	190.9	54.2	3,054	15.7	38.6	42.1

ENGINES

Type	Displace-ment (L)	Fuel Dly	HP @rpm	Torque @rpm (ft/lbs)	MPG Cty/Hwy	Years Avail
I-4	2.5	FI	98@4800	135@3200	23/30	87-89
I-4	2.5	FI	110@5200	135@3200	22/31	88-92
V-6	2.8	2-bbl	112@4800	145@2100	na	87-87
V-6	2.8	FI	125@4800	160@3600	21/29	87-88
V-6	3.8	FI	165@5200	210@2000	19/29	88-88
V-6	3.8	FI	150@4400	200@2000	19/29	88-88
V-6	3.3	FI	160@5200	185@2000	19/30	89-92

KEY: I=in-line engine; V=V engine; F=flat engine; FI=fuel injection; bbl=barrel carburetor; T=turbo; D=diesel; HP=horsepower; MPG=estimated average miles per gallon.

EVALUATIONS, TESTS, AND RANKINGS

1991: "top domestic car in its class in the initial product quality according to the J. D. Power and Associates research firm." **Source:** "Special USA '91 Section," *Motor Trend*, October 1990, p. 52.

RECALLS

1988: (6,083 vehicles): Owners manual did not include statement on child restraint systems. Vehicles do not conform to FMVSS 210. **Corrective action:** Furnish owners with updated owners manuals that contain omitted instructions. *(NHTSA Campaign No. 88V007000.)*

1988: (27,369 passenger vehicles equipped with 2.8L V6 engine; includes several General Motors models): Fuel feed hose could leak at coupling on engine end of hose assembly. Fuel leakage into engine compartment could result in engine compartment fire that could spread to passenger compartment. **Corrective action:** Install new fuel feed hose assembly. *(NHTSA Campaign No. 88V164000.)*

SAFETY AND REPAIRS

1992: "GM Recalls '92 A-, W-Cars," *Automotive News*, December 2, 1991, p. 2. **Note:** Transmission problem could cause cars to remain in reverse when shifted into neutral.

1988: "Racing Century," *Popular Science*, May 1989, p. 71. **Note:** Buick Century with 3.8-liter V-6 engine races after starting.

1987: "Service Tips," *Popular Mechanics*, July 1987, p. 75. **Note:** Tip for 1985-87 2.8- and 3.8-liter engines that won't start.

REPAIR MANUALS

215 ● **Chilton's Buick Century and Regal, 1975-87**
Chilton Co.
Chilton Way
Radnor, PA 19089   Ph:(215)964-4000

Published 1988. **Price:** $15.95.

216 ● **Chilton's Chevrolet Celebrity, Buick Century, Olds Cutlass Ciera, Pontiac 6000, 1982-1988**
Chilton Co.
Chilton Way
Radnor, PA 19089   Ph:(215)964-4000

Also available in Spanish edition. Published 1988. **Price:** $15.95.

217 ● **Get Your Buick Fixed Right**
Consumer Reports Books
51 E. 42nd St., Ste. 800
New York, NY 10017   Ph:(212)682-9280

Published 1989. **Editor(s):** Mort Schultz. **Price:** $8.95.

218 ● **GM A-Cars Buick Century, Chevrolet Celebrity, Oldsmobile Cutlass Ciera, Pontiac 6000, 1982-87: Shop Manual**
Clymer Publications
P.O. Box 1209
Overland Park, KS 66212   Ph:(913)541-6694

Published 1987. **Price:** $14.95.

219 ● **Haynes Buick Mid-size Models Owners Workshop Manual No. 627: 1974-1987**
Haynes Publications, Inc.
861 Lawrence Dr.
Newbury Park, CA 91320   Ph:(818)889-5400

Editor(s): J.H. Haynes and Peter D. DuPre. **Price:** $15.95.

220 ● **Haynes General Motor A-Cars Owner's Workshop Manual, No. 829**
Haynes Publishing, Inc.
861 Lawrence Dr.
Newbury Park, CA 91320   Ph:(818)889-5400

Published 1982 through 1989. **Price:** $15.95.

OTHER INFORMATION SOURCES

221 ● **Bluegrass Buick News**
Buick Club of America, Bluegrass Chapter
2805 Heather Ln.
La Grange, KY 40031   Ph:(502)241-5529

Periodic.

222 ● **The Buick: A Complete History**
Auto Quarterly, Inc.
420 N. Park Rd., Ste. 200
Wyomissing, PA 19610   Ph:(215)375-8444

Price: $39.95.

223 ● **Buick Club of America—Membership Roster**
Buick Club of America
PO Box 898   Ph:(714)993-5645
Garden Grove, CA 92642-0898   Fax:(714)993-5645

Biennial.

224 ● **Buick Club of America, Nebraska Chapter— Newsletter**
Buick Club of America, Nebraska Chapter
9346 Monroe St.
Omaha, NE 68127   Ph:(402)339-0086

Quarterly.

225 ● **Buick Club of America, North Cascade Chapter— Newsletter [Washington state]**
Buick Club of America, North Cascade Chapter
13003 Third Ave., SE
Everett, WA 98204   Ph:(206)337-1264

Monthly.

**226 ● Buick Club of America, San Gabriel Valley Chapter—
        Newsletter [California]**
Buick Club of America, San Gabriel Valley Chapter—
Newsletter
P.O. Box 2355
Pasadena, CA 91102

Monthly.

**227 ● Buick Club of America, Southwestern Ohio Chapter—
        Newsletter**
Buick Club of America, Southwestern Ohio Chapter
10155 Andalusia Close
Cincinnati, OH 45241   Ph:(513)733-5313

Monthly.

228 ● Cream City Chronicle [Wisconsin]
Buick Club of America, Cream City Chapter
P.O. Box 27372
West Allis, WI 53227   Ph:(414)321-8377

Bimonthly.

229 ● Dyna's Chatter
Buick Club of America, Appalachian Chapter
233-1/2 W. Brady St.
Butler, PA 16001   Ph:(412)282-8109

Newsletter. Periodic.

230 ● Dyna's Chatter
Buick Club of America, Appalachian Chapter
233-1/2 W. Brady St.
Butler, PA 16001   Ph:(412)282-8109

Newsletter. Periodic.

231 ● Fireball Flash
Buick Club of America, Chicagoland Chapter
271 Terrace Pl.
Buffalo Grove, IL 60089   Ph:(708)537-7055

Monthly.

232 ● Fireball News
Buick Club of America, San Gabriel Valley Chapter
PO Box 2355
Pasadena, CA 91102

Monthly.

233 ● Jersey Shore Chapter News [New Jersey]
Buick Club of America, Jersey Shore Chapter
2425 Cedar St.
Manasquan, NJ 08736   Ph:(201)528-9409

Newsletter. Monthly.

234 ● The Limited
Buick Club of America, Puget Sound Chapter
2725 SW 347th St.
Federal Way, WA 98023   Ph:(206)874-4562

Monthly.

235 ● Pike Press
Buick Club of America, National Pike Chapter
71 Murtland Ave.
Washington, PA 15301   Ph:(412)222-0700

Periodic.

236 ● The Reflector
Buick Club of America, Glass City Chapter
109 Ashwood Ct.
Perrysburg, OH 43551   Ph:(419)874-2393

Monthly.

237 ● Running Board
Buick Club of America, Orange County Chapter
P.O. Box 5171
Fullerton, CA 92635   Ph:(213)925-3294

Monthly.

ASSOCIATIONS

238 ● Buick Club of America
P.O. Box 898
Garden Grove, CA 92642
Dale Osstyn, Pres.   Ph:(714)993-5645

Founded: 1966. **Membership:** 9400. Purposes are:
development, publication, and interchange of technical,
historical, and other information among members who are
interested in Buick automobiles; to promote fellowship among
members; to encourage the maintenance, restoration, and
preservation of all models of produced by the Buick Motor
Division of General Motors. Awards prizes at local, regional,
and national car shows; presents Senior Award for Buick
achieving the highest standards. Holds competitions; compiles
statistics; maintains small library. **Convention/Meeting:**
Annual display conference (with exhibits) - 1992 July, Olathe,
KS.

**239 ● Buick Club of America, Appalachian Chapter [South
        central Pennsylvania]**
233-1/2 W. Brady St.
Butler, PA 16001
Keith R. Bleakney, Dir.   Ph:(412)282-8109

Founded: 1974. **Membership:** 14. Individuals in south central
Pennsylvania interested in the preservation and restoration of
Buick automobiles. **Convention/Meeting:** Annual show.

240 ● Buick Club of America, Bluegrass Chapter [Kentucky]
2805 Heather Ln.
La Grange, KY 40031
Lawrence Ford, Pres.   Ph:(502)241-5529

Founded: 1985. **Membership:** 18. Individuals interested in the
history and preservation of the Buick automobile. Seeks to
further the image of the Buick marque through social events,
meets, tours, and public exhibitions.

241 ● Buick Club of America, Chicagoland Chapter [Illinois]
PO Box 863
Arlington Heights, IL 60006
Steven Kelly, Contact   Ph:(708)464-5933

Founded: 1967. **Membership:** 85. Enthusiasts of Buick
automobiles in the Chicago, IL metropolitan area. Serves as a
clearinghouse for the exchange of information on finding Buick
parts and Buick maintenance. **Convention/Meeting:** Monthly.

**242 ● Buick Club of America, Cream City Chapter
        [Wisconsin]**
P.O. Box 27372
West Allis, WI 53227
Jerry Whelan, Dir.   Ph:(414)321-8377

Founded: 1982. **Membership:** 100. Individuals in southeastern
Wisconsin interested in the maintenance, operation, and
restoration of Buick automobiles. Participates in car shows and
tours. **Convention/Meeting:** Monthly.

243 ● Buick Club of America, Glass City Chapter [Ohio]
138 E. 5th St.
Perrysburg, OH 43551
David S. Rex, Sec.-Treas.   Ph:(419)874-8903

Founded: 1972. **Membership:** 25. Individuals in northwestern Ohio and southern Michigan interested in the maintenance, operation, and restoration of Buick automobiles. Sponsors car shows.

244 ● Buick Club of America, Jersey Shore Chapter [New Jersey]
2425 Cedar St.
Manasquan, NJ 08736
Ronald H. Foerster, Dir.   Ph:(201)528-9409

Founded: 1979. **Membership:** 35. Antique automobile collectors. Promotes restoration, preservation, and enjoyment of Buick automobiles. **Convention/Meeting:** Annual All Buick Car Show - always September, Sea Girt, NJ. Also holds monthly meeting - always last Wednesday of the month.

245 ● Buick Club of America, Kansas Chapter
216 S. Chestnut
Olathe, KS 66061
Richard Sandberg, Exec. Officer   Ph:(913)764-0423

246 ● Buick Club of America, Lone Star Chapter [Texas]
14021 Stoneshire
Houston, TX 77060
Cecil Miles, Exec. Officer   Ph:(713)448-8196

247 ● Buick Club of America, National Pike Chapter [Pennsylvania]
71 Murtland Ave.
Washington, PA 15301
Joe Manfredi, Exec. Officer   Ph:(412)222-0700

Founded: 1986. **Membership:** 30. Automobile salespeople and dealers and other interested persons organized to restore and preserve the Buick marque.

248 ● Buick Club of America, Nebraska Chapter
9346 Monroe St.
Omaha, NE 68127
Larry D. Robb, Director   Ph:(402)339-0086

Founded: 1975. **Membership:** 20. Individuals in Nebraska and western Iowa interested in cars built by the Buick Division of General Motors. **Convention/Meeting:** Monthly.

249 ● Buick Club of America, North Texas Chapter
1614 Woodoak Dr.
Richardson, TX 75081
David G. Farmer, Exec. Officer   Ph:(214)699-9418

250 ● Buick Club of America, Puget Sound Chapter [Washington state]
2725 SW 347th St.
Federal Way, WA 98023
Tony Weiss, Exec. Officer   Ph:(206)874-4562

Founded: 1974. **Membership:** 72. Buick owners in the Puget Sound, WA area. Promotes the preservation and restoration of Buick automobiles. **Convention/Meeting:** Monthly - always the second Monday of the month.

251 ● Buick Club of America, San Gabriel Valley Chapter [California]
P.O. Box 2355
Pasadena, CA 91102
Lou Baiocco, Dir.

Founded: 1966. **Membership:** 70. Owners of Buick automobiles. Promotes the preservation and display of Buick cars. **Convention/Meeting:** Monthly.

252 ● Buick Club of America, Southwestern Ohio Chapter
8529 Clough Pk.
Cincinnati, OH 45244
Richard Kranpitz, Dir.   Ph:(513)474-0657

Founded: 1970. **Membership:** 35. Encourages the maintenance, restoration, and preservation of all models of Buick cars. Sponsors antique car show.

BUICK ELECTRA (1987-90)

Introduced as part of C car line, along with its corporate twins Buick Park Avenue, Cadillac Coupe De Ville, Cadillac Fleetwood, and Oldsmobile 98. In 1990 Buick Electra Estate Wagon was renamed the Buick Estate Wagon. Produced at the General Motors plant in Wentzville, Missouri. The Buick Electra T-Type was ranked as best overall value by *The Complete Car Cost Guide* in 1990. The entire model line was rated as having the highest repair cost in 1990 by the same publication.

MAJOR FEATURES

● Buick Electra Limited had as 1990 standard equipment: 4-speed automatic transmission, 4-wheel independent suspension, front disc/rear drum power brakes, power-assisted rack-and-pinion steering, power windows, power locks, cruise control, adjustable steering wheel, and air conditioning.

● Buick Electra T Type added as 1990 standard equipment: anti-lock braking system, Gran Touring suspension, and leather-wrapped steering wheel.

● Buick Electra Park Avenue added to base as 1990 standard equipment: cruise control, power locks and mirrors, and upgraded carpet and tires.

● Buick Electra Ultra added as 1990 standard equipment: anti-lock braking system, leather front seat with 20-way power adjustments, and alloy wheels.

● Buick Estate Wagon added as 1990 standard equipment: other exterior body stylings.

PRICE HISTORY

The following new car prices reflect the approximate retail cost of the base model: **1987** - $16,902; **1988** - $17,479; **1989** - $18,525; **1990** - $20,225.

DIMENSIONS

Body Style	Years Avail	Wheel Base (in)	Lgth (in)	Ht (in)	Avg Wt (lbs)	Fuel Cap (gal)	Front Hdrm (in)	Front Legrm (in)
4d sdn	87-90	110.8	196.9	55.7	3,307	18	39.3	42.4
5d wgn	87-90	115.9	220.5	59.3	4,339	22	39.6	42.2

ENGINES

Type	Displace-ment (L)	Fuel Dly	HP @rpm	Torque @rpm (ft/lbs)	MPG Cty/Hwy	Years Avail
V-6	3.8	FI	150@4400	200@2000	19/29	87-87
V-6	3.8	FI	165@5200	210@2000	19/29	88-88
V-6	3.8	FI	165@4800	210@2000	18/27	89-90
V-8	5.0	4-bbl	140@3200	255@2000	17/24	87-90

KEY: I=in-line engine; V=V engine; F=flat engine; FI=fuel injection; bbl=barrel carburetor; T=turbo; D=diesel; HP=horsepower; MPG=estimated average miles per gallon.

EVALUATIONS, TESTS, AND RANKINGS

1989: "headlamps remained strong when tested." **Source:** "Wagon Train: The last rear-drive wagons in America," *Motor Trend*, September 1988, pp. 86-90, 92, 94-95.

RECALLS

1990: (51,834 cars; includes other Buick models): Owner's manual does not fully explain how front shoulder belt comfort feature works. **Corrective action:** Insert sticker that provides missing information in owner's manual. *(NHTSA Campaign No. 90V112000.)*

1987: (479,715 cars; includes Pontiac, Oldsmobile, and Buick models): In line fusible link may melt down and ignite windshield washer fluid bottle bracket. **Corrective action:** Replace washer fluid bottle bracket. *(NHTSA Campaign No. 87V135000.)*

1987: (6,004 passenger cars with anti-lock brakes. Recall includes the Cadillac DeVille, Oldsmobile 98, Buick Electra, Buick LeSabre, and Pontiac 6000): Anti-lock brake system (ABS) pressure/warning switch may exhibit brake fluid seepage which can lead to loss of brake system hydraulic pump motor. Additionally, hydraulic pump motor of ABS electrical relays may have been exposed to water contamination during vehicle assembly. Can cause loss of hydraulic pump motor and/or loss of ABS function. Loss of hydraulic pump would result in loss of rear brakes as well as power to assist to front brakes. **Corrective action:** ABS and hydraulic pump motor electrical relays and 30 amp fuses will be replaced. Hydraulic pump motor assembly and pressure/warning switch will be inspected and, if required, replaced. *(NHTSA Campaign No. 87V093000.)*

1987: (35,057 passenger vehicles; includes several General Motors models): Excessive accelerator cable friction may restrict cables free movement between accelerator pedal and throttle body. This could prevent throttle from returning to closed (idle) position when accelerator pedal is released; thus, engine speed would not decrease, and loss of accelerator control could result in an accident. **Corrective action:** Replace accelerator cable. *(NHTSA Campaign No. 88V080000.)*

1987: (11,936 vehicles with 200 4R transmissions; includes Chevrolet, Pontiac, Oldsmobile, Buick, Cadillac, and GMC models): Manual valve link in transmission may have been improperly formed. **Corrective action:** Replace manual valve detent lever link. *(NHTSA Campaign No. 87V168000.)*

SAFETY AND REPAIRS

1987: "Car Clinic," *Popular Mechanics*, August 1990, p. 26. **Note:** Tip for clashing starter motor gears in 1987-88 General Motors 4.3, 5.0, and 5.7 liter engines.

REPAIR MANUALS

253 ● Buick-Olds-Pontiac Full-Size, 1975-87
Chilton Co.
Chilton Way
Radnor, PA 19089   Ph:(215)964-4000
Price: $14.95.

254 ● General Motors 8-Cylinder
Peter Allen Video Productions
38-C Otis St.
West Babylon, NY 11704   Ph:(516)643-4372

A program demonstrating basic maintenance and tune-up procedures for the entitled engine. **Release date:** 1986. **Producer:** Peter Allen Productions. **Acquisition:** Purchase.

255 ● Get Your Buick Fixed Right
Consumer Reports Books
51 E. 42nd St., Ste. 800
New York, NY 10017   Ph:(212)682-9280

Published 1989. **Editor(s):** Mort Schultz. **Price:** $8.95.

256 ● Haynes Buick, Olds, Pontiac, Full-Size Models: 1970-90
Haynes Publications, Inc.
861 Lawrence Dr.
Newbury Park, CA 91320   Ph:(818)889-5400

Published 1989. **Price:** $15.95.

OTHER INFORMATION SOURCES

257 ● Bluegrass Buick News
Buick Club of America, Bluegrass Chapter
2805 Heather Ln.
La Grange, KY 40031   Ph:(502)241-5529

Periodic.

258 ● The Buick: A Complete History
Auto Quarterly, Inc.
420 N. Park Rd., Ste. 200
Wyomissing, PA 19610   Ph:(215)375-8444

Price: $39.95.

259 ● Buick Club of America—Membership Roster
Buick Club of America
PO Box 898   Ph:(714)993-5645
Garden Grove, CA 92642-0898   Fax:(714)993-5645

Biennial.

260 ● Buick Club of America, Nebraska Chapter—Newsletter
Buick Club of America, Nebraska Chapter
9346 Monroe St.
Omaha, NE 68127   Ph:(402)339-0086

Quarterly.

261 ● Buick Club of America, North Cascade Chapter—Newsletter [Washington state]
Buick Club of America, North Cascade Chapter
13003 Third Ave., SE
Everett, WA 98204   Ph:(206)337-1264

Monthly.

**262 ● Buick Club of America, San Gabriel Valley Chapter—
    Newsletter [California]**
Buick Club of America, San Gabriel Valley Chapter—
Newsletter
P.O. Box 2355
Pasadena, CA 91102

Monthly.

**263 ● Buick Club of America, Southwestern Ohio Chapter—
    Newsletter**
Buick Club of America, Southwestern Ohio Chapter
10155 Andalusia Close
Cincinnati, OH 45241   Ph:(513)733-5313

Monthly.

264 ● Cream City Chronicle [Wisconsin]
Buick Club of America, Cream City Chapter
P.O. Box 27372
West Allis, WI 53227   Ph:(414)321-8377

Bimonthly.

265 ● Dyna's Chatter
Buick Club of America, Appalachian Chapter
233-1/2 W. Brady St.
Butler, PA 16001   Ph:(412)282-8109

Newsletter. Periodic.

266 ● Dyna's Chatter
Buick Club of America, Appalachian Chapter
233-1/2 W. Brady St.
Butler, PA 16001   Ph:(412)282-8109

Newsletter. Periodic.

267 ● Fireball Flash
Buick Club of America, Chicagoland Chapter
271 Terrace Pl.
Buffalo Grove, IL 60089   Ph:(708)537-7055

Monthly.

268 ● Fireball News
Buick Club of America, San Gabriel Valley Chapter
PO Box 2355
Pasadena, CA 91102

Monthly.

269 ● Jersey Shore Chapter News [New Jersey]
Buick Club of America, Jersey Shore Chapter
2425 Cedar St.
Manasquan, NJ 08736   Ph:(201)528-9409

Newsletter. Monthly.

270 ● The Limited
Buick Club of America, Puget Sound Chapter
2725 SW 347th St.
Federal Way, WA 98023   Ph:(206)874-4562

Monthly.

271 ● Pike Press
Buick Club of America, National Pike Chapter
71 Murtland Ave.
Washington, PA 15301   Ph:(412)222-0700

Periodic.

272 ● The Reflector
Buick Club of America, Glass City Chapter
109 Ashwood Ct.
Perrysburg, OH 43551   Ph:(419)874-2393

Monthly.

273 ● Running Board
Buick Club of America, Orange County Chapter
P.O. Box 5171
Fullerton, CA 92635   Ph:(213)925-3294

Monthly.

ASSOCIATIONS

274 ● Buick Club of America
P.O. Box 898
Garden Grove, CA 92642
Dale Osstyn, Pres.   Ph:(714)993-5645

Founded: 1966. **Membership:** 9400. Purposes are:
development, publication, and interchange of technical,
historical, and other information among members who are
interested in Buick automobiles; to promote fellowship among
members; to encourage the maintenance, restoration, and
preservation of all models of produced by the Buick Motor
Division of General Motors. Awards prizes at local, regional,
and national car shows; presents Senior Award for Buick
achieving the highest standards. Holds competitions; compiles
statistics; maintains small library. **Convention/Meeting:**
Annual display conference (with exhibits) - 1992 July, Olathe,
KS.

**275 ● Buick Club of America, Appalachian Chapter [South
    central Pennsylvania]**
233-1/2 W. Brady St.
Butler, PA 16001
Keith R. Bleakney, Dir.   Ph:(412)282-8109

Founded: 1974. **Membership:** 14. Individuals in south central
Pennsylvania interested in the preservation and restoration of
Buick automobiles. **Convention/Meeting:** Annual show.

276 ● Buick Club of America, Bluegrass Chapter [Kentucky]
2805 Heather Ln.
La Grange, KY 40031
Lawrence Ford, Pres.   Ph:(502)241-5529

Founded: 1985. **Membership:** 18. Individuals interested in the
history and preservation of the Buick automobile. Seeks to
further the image of the Buick marque through social events,
meets, tours, and public exhibitions.

277 ● Buick Club of America, Chicagoland Chapter [Illinois]
PO Box 863
Arlington Heights, IL 60006
Steven Kelly, Contact   Ph:(708)464-5933

Founded: 1967. **Membership:** 85. Enthusiasts of Buick
automobiles in the Chicago, IL metropolitan area. Serves as a
clearinghouse for the exchange of information on finding Buick
parts and Buick maintenance. **Convention/Meeting:** Monthly.

**278 ● Buick Club of America, Cream City Chapter
    [Wisconsin]**
P.O. Box 27372
West Allis, WI 53227
Jerry Whelan, Dir.   Ph:(414)321-8377

Founded: 1982. **Membership:** 100. Individuals in southeastern
Wisconsin interested in the maintenance, operation, and
restoration of Buick automobiles. Participates in car shows and
tours. **Convention/Meeting:** Monthly.

279 ● Buick Club of America, Glass City Chapter [Ohio]
138 E. 5th St.
Perrysburg, OH 43551
David S. Rex, Sec.-Treas.   Ph:(419)874-8903

Founded: 1972. **Membership:** 25. Individuals in northwestern Ohio and southern Michigan interested in the maintenance, operation, and restoration of Buick automobiles. Sponsors car shows.

280 ● Buick Club of America, Jersey Shore Chapter [New Jersey]
2425 Cedar St.
Manasquan, NJ 08736
Ronald H. Foerster, Dir.   Ph:(201)528-9409

Founded: 1979. **Membership:** 35. Antique automobile collectors. Promotes restoration, preservation, and enjoyment of Buick automobiles. **Convention/Meeting:** Annual All Buick Car Show - always September, Sea Girt, NJ. Also holds monthly meeting - always last Wednesday of the month.

281 ● Buick Club of America, Kansas Chapter
216 S. Chestnut
Olathe, KS 66061
Richard Sandberg, Exec. Officer   Ph:(913)764-0423

282 ● Buick Club of America, Lone Star Chapter [Texas]
14021 Stoneshire
Houston, TX 77060
Cecil Miles, Exec. Officer   Ph:(713)448-8196

283 ● Buick Club of America, National Pike Chapter [Pennsylvania]
71 Murtland Ave.
Washington, PA 15301
Joe Manfredi, Exec. Officer   Ph:(412)222-0700

Founded: 1986. **Membership:** 30. Automobile salespeople and dealers and other interested persons organized to restore and preserve the Buick marque.

284 ● Buick Club of America, Nebraska Chapter
9346 Monroe St.
Omaha, NE 68127
Larry D. Robb, Director   Ph:(402)339-0086

Founded: 1975. **Membership:** 20. Individuals in Nebraska and western Iowa interested in cars built by the Buick Division of General Motors. **Convention/Meeting:** Monthly.

285 ● Buick Club of America, North Texas Chapter
1614 Woodoak Dr.
Richardson, TX 75081
David G. Farmer, Exec. Officer   Ph:(214)699-9418

286 ● Buick Club of America, Puget Sound Chapter [Washington state]
2725 SW 347th St.
Federal Way, WA 98023
Tony Weiss, Exec. Officer   Ph:(206)874-4562

Founded: 1974. **Membership:** 72. Buick owners in the Puget Sound, WA area. Promotes the preservation and restoration of Buick automobiles. **Convention/Meeting:** Monthly - always the second Monday of the month.

287 ● Buick Club of America, San Gabriel Valley Chapter [California]
P.O. Box 2355
Pasadena, CA 91102
Lou Baiocco, Dir.

Founded: 1966. **Membership:** 70. Owners of Buick

automobiles. Promotes the preservation and display of Buick cars. **Convention/Meeting:** Monthly.

288 ● Buick Club of America, Southwestern Ohio Chapter
8529 Clough Pk.
Cincinnati, OH 45244
Richard Kranpitz, Dir.   Ph:(513)474-0657

Founded: 1970. **Membership:** 35. Encourages the maintenance, restoration, and preservation of all models of Buick cars. Sponsors antique car show.

BUICK LESABRE (1987-92)

Introduced as part of the General Motors H-car line, along with corporate twin Oldsmobile 88 Royale and Pontiac Bonneville. Produced at the General Motors plant in Flint, Michigan. Received a poor mark in *The Car Book's* 1991 Complaint Index. Ranked as very good in *The Car Book's* Occupant Injury History List in 1992 for the four-door model.

1992 Buick LeSabre Limited with Gran Touring Package

MAJOR FEATURES

● Buick LeSabre Custom 1992 standard equipment includes: 4-speed automatic transmission, power rack-and-pinion steering, front disc/rear drum power brakes, front-wheel drive, theft-deterrent system, air conditioning, and AM/FM stereo.

● Buick LeSabre Limited adds as 1992 standard equipment: anti-lock brakes, reclining front seats, electric rear-window defogger, and front storage armrest.

● Buick LaSabre Wagon had as 1989 standard equipment: 4-speed automatic transmission, power steering, power brakes, AM/FM stereo, and air conditioning.

PRICE HISTORY

The following new car prices reflect the approximate retail cost of the base model: **1987** - $13,438; **1988** - $14,405; **1989** - $15,330; **1990** - $16,050; **1991** - $17,080; **1992** - $18,695.

DIMENSIONS

Body Style	Years Avail	Wheel Base (in)	Lgth (in)	Ht (in)	Avg Wt (lbs)	Fuel Cap (gal)	Front Hdrm (in)	Front Legrm (in)
2d cpe	87-91	110.8	196.5	53.8	3,231	18	38.1	42.4
4d sdn	87-91	110.8	196.5	54.6	3,269	18	38.9	42.4
4d sdn	92-92	110.8	200.0	55.7	3,417	18	39.3	42.0
5d wgn	89-89	115.9	220.5	59.3	4,209	22.0	39.6	42.2

ENGINES

Type	Displacement (L)	Fuel Dly	HP @rpm	Torque @rpm (ft/lbs)	MPG Cty/Hwy	Years Avail
V-6	3.8	FI	150@4400	200@2000	19/29	87-88
V-6	3.8	FI	165@4800	210@2000	19/28	89-91
V-6	3.8	FI	170@4800	220@3200	18/28	92-92
V-8	5.0	4-bbl	140@3200	255@2000	17/24	89-90

KEY: I=in-line engine; V=V engine; F=flat engine; FI=fuel injection; bbl=barrel carburetor; T=turbo; D=diesel; HP=horsepower; MPG=estimated average miles per gallon.

EVALUATIONS, TESTS, AND RANKINGS

1992: "echoes the Park Avenue's sinuous lines ... optional Gran Touring Package ... adds a good dollop of driving character ... It stiffens the suspension feel a bit while still providing a comfortable ride." **Source:** "Buick turns out solid, strong performers," *The Flint Journal*, July 10, 1991, pp. D1-D2.

1991: "embodies the "sport" and "luxury" craved by buyers facing a double-identity crisis ... ride/handling combo wrong, wrong, wrong. Jiggles at speed but wallows all over ... performance improved rapidly with more miles." **Source:** "Life with LeSabre," *Car and Driver*, August, 1991, pp. 83-84, 87.

1991: "Buick's quality claims for the LeSabre—tops in the U.S.—are easy to believe ... strikes a very good balance between economy, acceptable performance, comfort and good handling." **Source:** "Buick LeSabre. Buick cashes in on quality," *Popular Mechanics*, June, 1991, pp. 39-41.

1990: "overall top-ranking domestic car in initial product quality, according to J. D. Power." **Source:** "LeSabre," *Motor Trend*, October 1990, p. 52.

1990: "the LeSabre's body is appealingly simple and angular ... "Traditional" is also the best way to describe the LeSabre's cabin ... suspension doesn't provide markedly improved body control." **Source:** "Buick LeSabre Limited," *Car and Driver*, September, 1990, pp. 96-97, 101.

RECALLS

1992: (20,765 passenger cars; includes Oldsmobile Ninety Eight, Oldsmobile Eighty Eight, Buick Park Avenue, Pontiac Bonneville, and Buick LeSabre): When applied, the parking brake lever assembly may release one or more teeth, reducing the cable load to the rear brakes. Depending on the extent of the lever release and road level, the parking brake may not hold the vehicle, allowing it to roll. Vehicle does not comply with FMVSS 105. **Corrective action:** Replace parking brake lever assembly. *(NHTSA Campaign No. 91V167000.)*

1989: (6 passenger cars; includes the Oldsmobile 88 and Buick LeSabre): Welds in left rear rocker panel area may break loose and cause excessive forward movement of the rear suspension. Could result in damage to fuel tanks or lines that could result in fuel leak during or after crash which would result in a fire. **Corrective action:** Install a reinforcement kit. *(NHTSA Campaign No. 89V188000.)*

1989: (6 passenger cars; includes the Oldsmobile 88 and Buick LeSabre): Welds in left rear rocker panel may break loose and cause excessive forward movement of the rear suspension. Increased deformation could cause left rear safety belt anchorage to not achieve load requirements of FMVSS 210. In event of vehicle crash, would increase likelihood of injury to seat occupant. **Corrective action:** Install reinforcement kit. *(NHTSA Campaign No. 89V188001.)*

1989: (1,655 passenger vehicles; includes several General Motors models): Fuel rollover valve assembly may not have been installed. In event of an accident in which vehicle becomes inverted missing valve could allow fuel spillage in excess of amount allowed by FMVSS 301 which could result in a fire. **Corrective action:** Replace fuel sender and pump assembly. *(NHTSA Campaign No. 88V143000.)*

1988: (34,574 vehicles): Owners manual did not include instructions on proper usage of rear seat safety belt systems. Vehicles do not conform to FMVSS 209. **Corrective action:** Furnish owners with updated owners manuals that contain omitted instructions. *(NHTSA Campaign No. 88V006000.)*

1987-88: (1,889 passenger vehicles equipped with anti-lock brake system): Low torque of brake hydraulic unit mounting bolts could cause increased brake pedal travel and/or poor pedal feel if attachment loosens. This condition could lead to separation of brake hydraulic unit from its mounting bracket and result in loss of brake function and an accident. **Corrective action:** Replace hydraulic unit mounting bolts. *(NHTSA Campaign No. 88V067000.)*

1987: (479,715 cars; includes Pontiac, Oldsmobile, and Buick models): In line fusible link may melt down and ignite windshield washer fluid bottle bracket. **Corrective action:** Replace washer fluid bottle bracket. *(NHTSA Campaign No. 87V135000.)*

1987: (1,755,897 vehicles equipped with cruise control and certain gasoline and diesel engines; includes several General Motors models; includes models made before 1987): Small nylon bushing in the cruise control servo bail may slip out of place, causing intermittent and unexpected increases in engine speed or dieseling (engine run on with ignition off). Servo rod assembly could catch on engine components and result in a stuck throttle with potential for a vehicle crash. **Corrective action:** Install a new bushing in cruise control servo bail. *(NHTSA Campaign No. 89V102000.)*

1987: (6,004 passenger cars with anti-lock brakes. Recall includes the Cadillac Deville, Oldsmobile 98, Buick Electra, Buick LeSabre, and Pontiac 6000): Anti-lock brake system (ABS) pressure/warning switch may exhibit brake fluid seepage which can lead to loss of brake system hydraulic pump motor. Additionally, hydraulic pump motor of ABS electrical relays may have been exposed to water contamination during vehicle assembly. Can cause loss of hydraulic pump motor and/or loss of ABS function. Loss of hydraulic pump would result in loss of rear brakes as well as power to assist to front brakes. **Corrective action:** ABS and hydraulic pump motor electrical relays and 30 amp fuses will be replaced. Hydraulic pump motor assembly and pressure/warning switch will be inspected and possibly replaced. *(NHTSA Campaign No. 87V093000.)*

SAFETY AND REPAIRS

1992: "GM Recalls Cars for Belt, Brake Ills," *Automotive News*, December 9, 1991, p. 43. **Note:** Parking brake may partially release after being set.

1987: "Unpowered steering," *Popular Science*, October 1989, p. 88. **Note:** Power steering stiff when cold in 1987 Buick LeSabre.

1987: "Car Clinic," *Popular Mechanics*, August 1990, p. 26. **Note:** Tip for clashing starter motor gears in 1987-88 General Motors 4.3, 5.0, and 5.7 liter engines.

REPAIR MANUALS

289 ● Buick-Olds-Pontiac Full-Size, 1975-87
Chilton Co.
Chilton Way
Radnor, PA 19089   Ph:(215)964-4000
Price: $14.95.

290 ● **General Motors 8-Cylinder**
Peter Allen Video Productions
38-C Otis St.
West Babylon, NY 11704   Ph:(516)643-4372

A program demonstrating basic maintenance and tune-up procedures for the entitled engine. **Release date:** 1986. **Producer:** Peter Allen Productions. **Acquisition:** Purchase.

291 ● **Get Your Buick Fixed Right**
Consumer Reports Books
51 E. 42nd St., Ste. 800
New York, NY 10017   Ph:(212)682-9280

Published 1989. **Editor(s):** Mort Schultz. **Price:** $8.95.

292 ● **Haynes Buick, Olds, Pontiac, Full-Size Models: 1970-90**
Haynes Publications, Inc.
861 Lawrence Dr.
Newbury Park, CA 91320   Ph:(818)889-5400

Published 1989. **Price:** $15.95.

OTHER INFORMATION SOURCES

293 ● **Bluegrass Buick News**
Buick Club of America, Bluegrass Chapter
2805 Heather Ln.
La Grange, KY 40031   Ph:(502)241-5529

Periodic.

294 ● **The Buick: A Complete History**
Auto Quarterly, Inc.
420 N. Park Rd., Ste. 200
Wyomissing, PA 19610   Ph:(215)375-8444

Price: $39.95.

295 ● **Buick Club of America—Membership Roster**
Buick Club of America
PO Box 898   Ph:(714)993-5645
Garden Grove, CA 92642-0898   Fax:(714)993-5645

Biennial.

296 ● **Buick Club of America, Nebraska Chapter—Newsletter**
Buick Club of America, Nebraska Chapter
9346 Monroe St.
Omaha, NE 68127   Ph:(402)339-0086

Quarterly.

297 ● **Buick Club of America, North Cascade Chapter—Newsletter [Washington state]**
Buick Club of America, North Cascade Chapter
13003 Third Ave., SE
Everett, WA 98204   Ph:(206)337-1264

Monthly.

298 ● **Buick Club of America, San Gabriel Valley Chapter—Newsletter [California]**
Buick Club of America, San Gabriel Valley Chapter—Newsletter
P.O. Box 2355
Pasadena, CA 91102

Monthly.

299 ● **Buick Club of America, Southwestern Ohio Chapter—Newsletter**
Buick Club of America, Southwestern Ohio Chapter
10155 Andalusia Close
Cincinnati, OH 45241   Ph:(513)733-5313

Monthly.

300 ● **Cream City Chronicle [Wisconsin]**
Buick Club of America, Cream City Chapter
P.O. Box 27372
West Allis, WI 53227   Ph:(414)321-8377

Bimonthly.

301 ● **Dyna's Chatter**
Buick Club of America, Appalachian Chapter
233-1/2 W. Brady St.
Butler, PA 16001   Ph:(412)282-8109

Newsletter. Periodic.

302 ● **Fireball Flash**
Buick Club of America, Chicagoland Chapter
271 Terrace Pl.
Buffalo Grove, IL 60089   Ph:(708)537-7055

Monthly.

303 ● **Fireball News**
Buick Club of America, San Gabriel Valley Chapter
PO Box 2355
Pasadena, CA 91102

Monthly.

304 ● **Jersey Shore Chapter News [New Jersey]**
Buick Club of America, Jersey Shore Chapter
2425 Cedar St.
Manasquan, NJ 08736   Ph:(201)528-9409

Newsletter. Monthly.

305 ● **The Limited**
Buick Club of America, Puget Sound Chapter
2725 SW 347th St.
Federal Way, WA 98023   Ph:(206)874-4562

Monthly.

306 ● **Pike Press**
Buick Club of America, National Pike Chapter
71 Murtland Ave.
Washington, PA 15301   Ph:(412)222-0700

Periodic.

307 ● **The Reflector**
Buick Club of America, Glass City Chapter
109 Ashwood Ct.
Perrysburg, OH 43551   Ph:(419)874-2393

Monthly.

308 ● **Running Board**
Buick Club of America, Orange County Chapter
P.O. Box 5171
Fullerton, CA 92635   Ph:(213)925-3294

Monthly.

ASSOCIATIONS

309 ● Buick Club of America
P.O. Box 898
Garden Grove, CA 92642
Dale Osstyn, Pres.   Ph:(714)993-5645

Founded: 1966. **Membership:** 9400. Purposes are: development, publication, and interchange of technical, historical, and other information among members who are interested in Buick automobiles; to promote fellowship among members; to encourage the maintenance, restoration, and preservation of all models of produced by the Buick Motor Division of General Motors. Awards prizes at local, regional, and national car shows; presents Senior Award for Buick achieving the highest standards. Holds competitions; compiles statistics; maintains small library. **Convention/Meeting:** Annual display conference (with exhibits) - 1992 July, Olathe, KS.

310 ● Buick Club of America, Appalachian Chapter [South central Pennsylvania]
233-1/2 W. Brady St.
Butler, PA 16001
Keith R. Bleakney, Dir.   Ph:(412)282-8109

Founded: 1974. **Membership:** 14. Individuals in south central Pennsylvania interested in the preservation and restoration of Buick automobiles. **Convention/Meeting:** Annual show.

311 ● Buick Club of America, Bluegrass Chapter [Kentucky]
2805 Heather Ln.
La Grange, KY 40031
Lawrence Ford, Pres.   Ph:(502)241-5529

Founded: 1985. **Membership:** 18. Individuals interested in the history and preservation of the Buick automobile. Seeks to further the image of the Buick marque through social events, meets, tours, and public exhibitions.

312 ● Buick Club of America, Chicagoland Chapter [Illinois]
PO Box 863
Arlington Heights, IL 60006
Steven Kelly, Contact   Ph:(708)464-5933

Founded: 1967. **Membership:** 85. Enthusiasts of Buick automobiles in the Chicago, IL metropolitan area. Serves as a clearinghouse for the exchange of information on finding Buick parts and Buick maintenance. **Convention/Meeting:** Monthly.

313 ● Buick Club of America, Cream City Chapter [Wisconsin]
P.O. Box 27372
West Allis, WI 53227
Jerry Whelan, Dir.   Ph:(414)321-8377

Founded: 1982. **Membership:** 100. Individuals in southeastern Wisconsin interested in the maintenance, operation, and restoration of Buick automobiles. Participates in car shows and tours. **Convention/Meeting:** Monthly.

314 ● Buick Club of America, Glass City Chapter [Ohio]
138 E. 5th St.
Perrysburg, OH 43551
David S. Rex, Sec.-Treas.   Ph:(419)874-8903

Founded: 1972. **Membership:** 25. Individuals in northwestern Ohio and southern Michigan interested in the maintenance, operation, and restoration of Buick automobiles. Sponsors car shows.

315 ● Buick Club of America, Jersey Shore Chapter [New Jersey]
2425 Cedar St.
Manasquan, NJ 08736
Ronald H. Foerster, Dir.   Ph:(201)528-9409

Founded: 1979. **Membership:** 35. Antique automobile collectors. Promotes restoration, preservation, and enjoyment of Buick automobiles. **Convention/Meeting:** Annual All Buick Car Show - always September, Sea Girt, NJ. Also holds monthly meeting - always last Wednesday of the month.

316 ● Buick Club of America, Kansas Chapter
216 S. Chestnut
Olathe, KS 66061
Richard Sandberg, Exec. Officer   Ph:(913)764-0423

317 ● Buick Club of America, Lone Star Chapter [Texas]
14021 Stoneshire
Houston, TX 77060
Cecil Miles, Exec. Officer   Ph:(713)448-8196

318 ● Buick Club of America, National Pike Chapter [Pennsylvania]
71 Murtland Ave.
Washington, PA 15301
Joe Manfredi, Exec. Officer   Ph:(412)222-0700

Founded: 1986. **Membership:** 30. Automobile salespeople and dealers and other interested persons organized to restore and preserve the Buick marque.

319 ● Buick Club of America, Nebraska Chapter
9346 Monroe St.
Omaha, NE 68127
Larry D. Robb, Director   Ph:(402)339-0086

Founded: 1975. **Membership:** 20. Individuals in Nebraska and western Iowa interested in cars built by the Buick Division of General Motors. **Convention/Meeting:** Monthly.

320 ● Buick Club of America, North Texas Chapter
1614 Woodoak Dr.
Richardson, TX 75081
David G. Farmer, Exec. Officer   Ph:(214)699-9418

321 ● Buick Club of America, Puget Sound Chapter [Washington state]
2725 SW 347th St.
Federal Way, WA 98023
Tony Weiss, Exec. Officer   Ph:(206)874-4562

Founded: 1974. **Membership:** 72. Buick owners in the Puget Sound, WA area. Promotes the preservation and restoration of Buick automobiles. **Convention/Meeting:** Monthly - always the second Monday of the month.

322 ● Buick Club of America, San Gabriel Valley Chapter [California]
P.O. Box 2355
Pasadena, CA 91102
Lou Baiocco, Dir.

Founded: 1966. **Membership:** 70. Owners of Buick automobiles. Promotes the preservation and display of Buick cars. **Convention/Meeting:** Monthly.

323 ● Buick Club of America, Southwestern Ohio Chapter
8529 Clough Pk.
Cincinnati, OH 45244
Richard Kranpitz, Dir.   Ph:(513)474-0657

Founded: 1970. **Membership:** 35. Encourages the maintenance, restoration, and preservation of all models of Buick cars. Sponsors antique car show.

BUICK PARK AVENUE (1991-92)

Introduced as a replacement for the Buick Electra in 1991. Produced at the General Motors plant in Wentzville, Missouri. Corporate twins are the Cadillac Coupe DeVille, Cadillac Fleetwood Coupe, and Oldsmobile 98 Regency. Nominated to the *Motor Trend* Car of the Year list in 1991.

1991 Buick Park Avenue

MAJOR FEATURES

● Buick Park Avenue 1992 standard equipment includes: 4-speed automatic transmission, power rack-and-pinion steering, front disc/rear drum power brakes, anti-lock brake system, front-wheel drive, driver's side airbag, theft-deterrent system, air conditioning, cruise control, solar control glass, AM/FM stereo cassette, and adjustable steering wheel.

● Buick Park Avenue Ultra adds as 1992 standard equipment: supercharged engine, climate control system, and upgraded interior.

PRICE HISTORY

The following new car prices reflect the approximate retail cost of the base model: **1991** - $24,385; **1992** - $25,285.

DIMENSIONS

Body Style	Years Avail	Wheel Base (in)	Lgth (in)	Ht (in)	Avg Wt (lbs)	Fuel Cap (gal)	Front Hdrm (in)	Front Legrm (in)
4d sdn	91-91	110.8	205.2	55.7	3,580	18	38.8	42
4d sdn	92-92	110.7	205.3	55.1	3,536	18	38.8	42

ENGINES

Type	Displacement (L)	Fuel Dly	HP @rpm	Torque @rpm (ft/lbs)	MPG Cty/Hwy	Years Avail
V-6	3.8	FI	170@4800	220@3200	18/27	91-92
V-6	3.8	FI	205@4400	260@2800	17/27	92-92

KEY: I=in-line engine; V=V engine; F=flat engine; FI=fuel injection; bbl=barrel carburetor; D=diesel; T=turbo; HP=horsepower; MPG=estimated average miles per gallon.

EVALUATIONS, TESTS, AND RANKINGS

1992: "supercharged engine is smooth . . . a silky powertrain . . . the power just builds rapidly and authoritatively." **Source:** "Buick turns out solid, strong performers," *The Flint Journal*, July 10, 1991.

1991: "the Ultra is the top of the Hill . . . muscular and aggressive, yet subtle and authoritative . . . Road feel is surprisingly constant over a wide range of surfaces." **Source:**

"Buick Park Avenue," *Motor Trend*, October 1990, pp. 98-100, 102.

1991: "[Park Avenue Ultra] . . . sleek, polished, full of high-tech and very pleasant indeed . . . ambient comfort has been given a lot of attention . . . silky ride." **Source:** "A Buick show car takes to the road," *The New York Times*, January 20, 1991.

1991: "mixed feelings prevail . . . lacks the charisma of a world-class car . . . not the ergonomic brilliance of an Acura Legend, but it is a good value." **Source:** "Buick Park Avenue Ultra," *Automobile Magazine*, September, 1991, p. 111.

RECALLS

1991: (51,834 vehicles; includes other Buick models): Owner's manual does not fully explain how front shoulder belt comfort feature works. **Corrective action:** Insert sticker that provides missing information in owner's manual. *(NHTSA Campaign No. 90V112000.)*

1991: (20,765 passenger cars; includes Oldsmobile Ninety Eight, Oldsmobile Eighty Eight, Buick Park Avenue, Pontiac Bonneville, and Buick LeSabre): When applied, the parking brake lever assembly may release one or more teeth, reducing the cable load to the rear brakes. Depending on the extent of the lever release and road level, the parking brake may not hold the vehicle, allowing it to roll. Vehicle does not comply with FMVSS 105. **Corrective action:** Replace parking brake lever assembly. *(NHTSA Campaign No. 91V167000.)*

SAFETY AND REPAIRS

1991: "GM Recalls Cars for Belt, Brake Ills," *Automotive News*, December 9, 1991, p. 43. **Note:** Parking brake may partially release after being set.

REPAIR MANUALS

324 ● **Get Your Buick Fixed Right**
Consumer Reports Books
51 E. 42nd St., Ste. 800
New York, NY 10017   Ph:(212)682-9280

Published 1989. **Editor(s):** Mort Schultz. **Price:** $8.95.

OTHER INFORMATION SOURCES

325 ● **Bluegrass Buick News**
Buick Club of America, Bluegrass Chapter
2805 Heather Ln.
La Grange, KY 40031   Ph:(502)241-5529

Periodic.

326 ● **The Buick: A Complete History**
Auto Quarterly, Inc.
420 N. Park Rd., Ste. 200
Wyomissing, PA 19610   Ph:(215)375-8444

Price: $39.95.

327 ● **Buick Club of America—Membership Roster**
Buick Club of America
PO Box 898   Ph:(714)993-5645
Garden Grove, CA 92642-0898   Fax:(714)993-5645

Biennial.

**328 ● Buick Club of America, Nebraska Chapter—
Newsletter**
Buick Club of America, Nebraska Chapter
9346 Monroe St.
Omaha, NE 68127   Ph:(402)339-0086

Quarterly.

**329 ● Buick Club of America, North Cascade Chapter—
Newsletter [Washington state]**
Buick Club of America, North Cascade Chapter
13003 Third Ave., SE
Everett, WA 98204   Ph:(206)337-1264

Monthly.

**330 ● Buick Club of America, San Gabriel Valley Chapter—
Newsletter [California]**
Buick Club of America, San Gabriel Valley Chapter—
Newsletter
P.O. Box 2355
Pasadena, CA 91102

Monthly.

**331 ● Buick Club of America, Southwestern Ohio Chapter—
Newsletter**
Buick Club of America, Southwestern Ohio Chapter
10155 Andalusia Close
Cincinnati, OH 45241   Ph:(513)733-5313

Monthly.

332 ● Cream City Chronicle [Wisconsin]
Buick Club of America, Cream City Chapter
P.O. Box 27372
West Allis, WI 53227   Ph:(414)321-8377

Bimonthly.

333 ● Dyna's Chatter
Buick Club of America, Appalachian Chapter
233-1/2 W. Brady St.
Butler, PA 16001   Ph:(412)282-8109

Newsletter. Periodic.

334 ● Dyna's Chatter
Buick Club of America, Appalachian Chapter
233-1/2 W. Brady St.
Butler, PA 16001   Ph:(412)282-8109

Newsletter. Periodic.

335 ● Fireball Flash
Buick Club of America, Chicagoland Chapter
271 Terrace Pl.
Buffalo Grove, IL 60089   Ph:(708)537-7055

Monthly.

336 ● Fireball News
Buick Club of America, San Gabriel Valley Chapter
PO Box 2355
Pasadena, CA 91102

Monthly.

337 ● Jersey Shore Chapter News [New Jersey]
Buick Club of America, Jersey Shore Chapter
2425 Cedar St.
Manasquan, NJ 08736   Ph:(201)528-9409

Newsletter. Monthly.

338 ● The Limited
Buick Club of America, Puget Sound Chapter
2725 SW 347th St.
Federal Way, WA 98023   Ph:(206)874-4562

Monthly.

339 ● Pike Press
Buick Club of America, National Pike Chapter
71 Murtland Ave.
Washington, PA 15301   Ph:(412)222-0700

Periodic.

340 ● The Reflector
Buick Club of America, Glass City Chapter
109 Ashwood Ct.
Perrysburg, OH 43551   Ph:(419)874-2393

Monthly.

341 ● Running Board
Buick Club of America, Orange County Chapter
P.O. Box 5171
Fullerton, CA 92635   Ph:(213)925-3294

Monthly.

ASSOCIATIONS

342 ● Buick Club of America
P.O. Box 898
Garden Grove, CA 92642
Dale Osstyn, Pres.   Ph:(714)993-5645

Founded: 1966. **Membership:** 9400. Purposes are:
development, publication, and interchange of technical,
historical, and other information among members who are
interested in Buick automobiles; to promote fellowship among
members; to encourage the maintenance, restoration, and
preservation of all models of produced by the Buick Motor
Division of General Motors. Awards prizes at local, regional,
and national car shows; presents Senior Award for Buick
achieving the highest standards. Holds competitions; compiles
statistics; maintains small library. **Convention/Meeting:**
Annual display conference (with exhibits) - 1992 July, Olathe,
KS.

**343 ● Buick Club of America, Appalachian Chapter [South
central Pennsylvania]**
233-1/2 W. Brady St.
Butler, PA 16001
Keith R. Bleakney, Dir.   Ph:(412)282-8109

Founded: 1974. **Membership:** 14. Individuals in south central
Pennsylvania interested in the preservation and restoration of
Buick automobiles. **Convention/Meeting:** Annual show.

344 ● Buick Club of America, Bluegrass Chapter [Kentucky]
2805 Heather Ln.
La Grange, KY 40031
Lawrence Ford, Pres.   Ph:(502)241-5529

Founded: 1985. **Membership:** 18. Individuals interested in the
history and preservation of the Buick automobile. Seeks to
further the image of the Buick marque through social events,
meets, tours, and public exhibitions.

345 ● Buick Club of America, Chicagoland Chapter [Illinois]
PO Box 863
Arlington Heights, IL 60006
Steven Kelly, Contact   Ph:(708)464-5933

Founded: 1967. **Membership:** 85. Enthusiasts of Buick automobiles in the Chicago, IL metropolitan area. Serves as a clearinghouse for the exchange of information on finding Buick parts and Buick maintenance. **Convention/Meeting:** Monthly.

346 ● Buick Club of America, Cream City Chapter [Wisconsin]
P.O. Box 27372
West Allis, WI 53227
Jerry Whelan, Dir.   Ph:(414)321-8377

Founded: 1982. **Membership:** 100. Individuals in southeastern Wisconsin interested in the maintenance, operation, and restoration of Buick automobiles. Participates in car shows and tours. **Convention/Meeting:** Monthly.

347 ● Buick Club of America, Glass City Chapter [Ohio]
138 E. 5th St.
Perrysburg, OH 43551
David S. Rex, Sec.-Treas.   Ph:(419)874-8903

Founded: 1972. **Membership:** 25. Individuals in northwestern Ohio and southern Michigan interested in the maintenance, operation, and restoration of Buick automobiles. Sponsors car shows.

348 ● Buick Club of America, Jersey Shore Chapter [New Jersey]
2425 Cedar St.
Manasquan, NJ 08736
Ronald H. Foerster, Dir.   Ph:(201)528-9409

Founded: 1979. **Membership:** 35. Antique automobile collectors. Promotes restoration, preservation, and enjoyment of Buick automobiles. **Convention/Meeting:** Annual All Buick Car Show - always September, Sea Girt, NJ. Also holds monthly meeting - always last Wednesday of the month.

349 ● Buick Club of America, Kansas Chapter
216 S. Chestnut
Olathe, KS 66061
Richard Sandberg, Exec. Officer   Ph:(913)764-0423

350 ● Buick Club of America, Lone Star Chapter [Texas]
14021 Stoneshire
Houston, TX 77060
Cecil Miles, Exec. Officer   Ph:(713)448-8196

351 ● Buick Club of America, National Pike Chapter [Pennsylvania]
71 Murtland Ave.
Washington, PA 15301
Joe Manfredi, Exec. Officer   Ph:(412)222-0700

Founded: 1986. **Membership:** 30. Automobile salespeople and dealers and other interested persons organized to restore and preserve the Buick marque.

352 ● Buick Club of America, Nebraska Chapter
9346 Monroe St.
Omaha, NE 68127
Larry D. Robb, Director   Ph:(402)339-0086

Founded: 1975. **Membership:** 20. Individuals in Nebraska and western Iowa interested in cars built by the Buick Division of General Motors. **Convention/Meeting:** Monthly.

353 ● Buick Club of America, North Texas Chapter
1614 Woodoak Dr.
Richardson, TX 75081
David G. Farmer, Exec. Officer   Ph:(214)699-9418

354 ● Buick Club of America, Puget Sound Chapter [Washington state]
2725 SW 347th St.
Federal Way, WA 98023
Tony Weiss, Exec. Officer   Ph:(206)874-4562

Founded: 1974. **Membership:** 72. Buick owners in the Puget Sound, WA area. Promotes the preservation and restoration of Buick automobiles. **Convention/Meeting:** Monthly - always the second Monday of the month.

355 ● Buick Club of America, San Gabriel Valley Chapter [California]
P.O. Box 2355
Pasadena, CA 91102
Lou Baiocco, Dir.

Founded: 1966. **Membership:** 70. Owners of Buick automobiles. Promotes the preservation and display of Buick cars. **Convention/Meeting:** Monthly.

356 ● Buick Club of America, Southwestern Ohio Chapter
8529 Clough Pk.
Cincinnati, OH 45244
Richard Kranpitz, Dir.   Ph:(513)474-0657

Founded: 1970. **Membership:** 35. Encourages the maintenance, restoration, and preservation of all models of Buick cars. Sponsors antique car show.

BUICK REATTA (1988-91)

Reatta Convertible named to *Car and Driver's* Ten Best Cars Nominees list of 1989. Produced at General Motors plant in Lansing, Michigan. Discontinued after 1991 model year.

1991 Buick Reatta

MAJOR FEATURES

● Buick Reatta 1991 standard equipment included: 4-speed automatic transmission, 4-wheel disc brakes with anti-lock braking system, power rack-and-pinion steering, driver's side airbag, air conditioning, power windows and locks, AM/FM stereo cassette with 6-speaker sound system, leather bucket seats, and security system.

PRICE HISTORY

The following new car prices reflect the approximate retail cost of the base model: **1988** - $25,000; **1989** - $26,700; **1990** - $28,335; **1991** - $29,300.

DIMENSIONS

Body Style	Years Avail	Wheel Base (in)	Lgth (in)	Ht (in)	Avg Wt (lbs)	Fuel Cap (gal)	Front Hdrm (in)	Front Legrm (in)
2d cpe	88-91	98.5	183.5	51.2	3,392	18.8	36.9	43.1
2d conv	90-91	98.5	183.5	51.2	3,593	18.8	36.9	43.1

ENGINES

Type	Displacement (L)	Fuel Dly	HP @rpm	Torque @rpm (ft/lbs)	MPG Cty/Hwy	Years Avail
V-6	3.8	FI	165@4800	210@2000	18/27	88-90
V-6	3.8	FI	170@4800	220@3200	18/27	91-91

KEY: I=in-line engine; V=V engine; F=flat engine; FI=fuel injection; bbl=barrel carburetor; T=turbo; D=diesel; HP=horsepower; MPG=estimated average miles per gallon.

EVALUATIONS, TESTS, AND RANKINGS

1990: "What detracts from the pleasure of cutting from corner to corner . . . is steering that suffers from insufficient on-center feel . . . its overall braking power was disappointing." **Source:** "Buick Reatta Convertible: When latter-day Thunderbirds are built, Buick will build them," *Road & Track,* October 1990, pp. 100-103.

1990: "Reatta rates as one of America's best convertible buys . . . avoids the stiff ride and cramped quarters of hard-edged sports cars . . . delivers sporty handling and a sense of partnership between car and driver." **Source:** "'Ragtops' rise again," *New Choices,* April, 1990, pp. 82, 84.

1990: "workmanship came in for a lot of positive comment, with no one rating the Reatta below the level of good . . . ride and handling got great marks . . . good-looking, dependable, enjoyable and no hassles at the dealership." **Source:** "Buick Reatta," *Popular Mechanics,* December, 1989, pp. 48-49.

1989: "Steering response is crisp . . . Acceleration is off a tick . . . Despite some minor cowl shake, the basic structure feels solid . . . The seats . . . proved a good deal longer on comfort than on lateral support." **Source:** "Buick Reatta Convertible: At long last, al fresco," *Motor Trend,* October 1989, pp. 61-62.

1989: "a gentleman's cruiser . . . sports-car style tempered with all the comfort and convenience of a sedan . . . a great body and an extra dash of soul." **Source:** "Buick Reatta Convertible: A Buick fit for the Riviera," *Car and Driver,* February, 1989, pp. 36-38.

RECALLS

1990: (857 vehicles): Incorrectly built forward sensor for air bag could delay deployment and increase severity of injury to unbelted driver in an accident. **Corrective action:** Replace forward discriminating sensor as necessary. *(NHTSA Campaign No. 90V031000.)*

1990: (10,166 vehicles; includes the Cadillac Eldorado, Cadillac Seville, Buick Riviera, and Buick Reatta models): Misaligned rear safety shoulder belt retractor assemblies could prevent engagement of inertia lock, increasing likelihood of injury to occupant in panic stop or accident. **Corrective action:** Realign rear shoulder belt retractor assembly. *(NHTSA Campaign No. 90V028000.)*

1990: (63,964 vehicles; includes Buick, Oldsmobile, and Cadillac models): Transaxle shift control cable may disengage from the floor shift control with loss of gear indicator reference and shift selector operation. Could result in unexpected vehicle movement and an accident. **Corrective action:** Install transaxle shift control cable retaining clip to prevent cable disengagement. *(NHTSA Campaign No. 90V164000.)*

1990: (18,904 passenger cars; includes Buick Reatta, and Buick Riviera): Brake indicator light may not light when ignition is in the "on" position, the parking brake is applied, and the shift selector is in the park or neutral gear range. Vehicles would not meet the requirements of FMVSS 101 and 105. **Corrective action:** Replace the prom in the body computer module. *(NHTSA Campaign No. 91V158000.)*

1989: (10,535 passenger cars equipped with 3800 V6 engines and anti-lock brakes; includes the Buick Riviera, Buick Reatta, and Oldsmobile Toronado): Left front brake pipe may contact the cruise control servo bracket. Brake line could wear through causing loss of brake fluid and partial loss of braking capability; could result in a vehicle crash. *(NHTSA Campaign No. 89V056000.)*

1988: (11,936 vehicles with 200 4R transmissions; includes Chevrolet, Pontiac, Oldsmobile, Buick, Cadillac, and GMC models): Manual valve link in transmission may have been improperly formed. **Corrective action:** Replace manual valve detent lever link. *(NHTSA Campaign No. 87V168000.)*

REPAIR MANUALS

357 ● **Get Your Buick Fixed Right**
Consumer Reports Books
51 E. 42nd St., Ste. 800
New York, NY 10017   Ph:(212)682-9280

Published 1989. **Editor(s):** Mort Schultz. **Price:** $8.95.

OTHER INFORMATION SOURCES

358 ● **Bluegrass Buick News**
Buick Club of America, Bluegrass Chapter
2805 Heather Ln.
La Grange, KY 40031   Ph:(502)241-5529

Periodic.

359 ● **The Buick: A Complete History**
Auto Quarterly, Inc.
420 N. Park Rd., Ste. 200
Wyomissing, PA 19610   Ph:(215)375-8444

Price: $39.95.

360 ● **Buick Club of America—Membership Roster**
Buick Club of America
PO Box 898   Ph:(714)993-5645
Garden Grove, CA 92642-0898   Fax:(714)993-5645

Biennial.

361 ● **Buick Club of America, Nebraska Chapter—Newsletter**
Buick Club of America, Nebraska Chapter
9346 Monroe St.
Omaha, NE 68127   Ph:(402)339-0086

Quarterly.

362 ● **Buick Club of America, North Cascade Chapter—Newsletter [Washington state]**
Buick Club of America, North Cascade Chapter
13003 Third Ave., SE
Everett, WA 98204   Ph:(206)337-1264

Monthly.

363 ● Buick Club of America, San Gabriel Valley Chapter—Newsletter [California]
Buick Club of America, San Gabriel Valley Chapter—
Newsletter
P.O. Box 2355
Pasadena, CA 91102

Monthly.

364 ● Buick Club of America, Southwestern Ohio Chapter—Newsletter
Buick Club of America, Southwestern Ohio Chapter
10155 Andalusia Close
Cincinnati, OH 45241   Ph:(513)733-5313

Monthly.

365 ● Cream City Chronicle [Wisconsin]
Buick Club of America, Cream City Chapter
P.O. Box 27372
West Allis, WI 53227   Ph:(414)321-8377

Bimonthly.

366 ● Dyna's Chatter
Buick Club of America, Appalachian Chapter
233-1/2 W. Brady St.
Butler, PA 16001   Ph:(412)282-8109

Newsletter. Periodic.

367 ● Dyna's Chatter
Buick Club of America, Appalachian Chapter
233-1/2 W. Brady St.
Butler, PA 16001   Ph:(412)282-8109

Newsletter. Periodic.

368 ● Fireball Flash
Buick Club of America, Chicagoland Chapter
271 Terrace Pl.
Buffalo Grove, IL 60089   Ph:(708)537-7055

Monthly.

369 ● Fireball News
Buick Club of America, San Gabriel Valley Chapter
PO Box 2355
Pasadena, CA 91102

Monthly.

370 ● GS Directory
Buick GS Club of America
1213 Gornto Rd.
Valdosta, GA 31601   Ph:(912)244-0577

About 3,800 owners of Buick Wildcats, Rivieras, Grand Nationals, Gran Sports, and other high performance Buick automobiles. Annual. **Editor(s):** Richard Lasseter, President. **Price:** Available to members only.

371 ● Jersey Shore Chapter News [New Jersey]
Buick Club of America, Jersey Shore Chapter
2425 Cedar St.
Manasquan, NJ 08736   Ph:(201)528-9409

Newsletter. Monthly.

372 ● The Limited
Buick Club of America, Puget Sound Chapter
2725 SW 347th St.
Federal Way, WA 98023   Ph:(206)874-4562

Monthly.

373 ● Pike Press
Buick Club of America, National Pike Chapter
71 Murtland Ave.
Washington, PA 15301   Ph:(412)222-0700

Periodic.

374 ● The Reflector
Buick Club of America, Glass City Chapter
109 Ashwood Ct.
Perrysburg, OH 43551   Ph:(419)874-2393

Monthly.

375 ● Running Board
Buick Club of America, Orange County Chapter
P.O. Box 5171
Fullerton, CA 92635   Ph:(213)925-3294

Monthly.

ASSOCIATIONS

376 ● Buick Club of America
P.O. Box 898
Garden Grove, CA 92642
Dale Osstyn, Pres.   Ph:(714)993-5645

Founded: 1966. **Membership:** 9400. Purposes are: development, publication, and interchange of technical, historical, and other information among members who are interested in Buick automobiles; to promote fellowship among members; to encourage the maintenance, restoration, and preservation of all models of produced by the Buick Motor Division of General Motors. Awards prizes at local, regional, and national car shows; presents Senior Award for Buick achieving the highest standards. Holds competitions; compiles statistics; maintains small library. **Convention/Meeting:** Annual display conference (with exhibits) - 1992 July, Olathe, KS.

377 ● Buick Club of America, Appalachian Chapter [South central Pennsylvania]
233-1/2 W. Brady St.
Butler, PA 16001
Keith R. Bleakney, Dir.   Ph:(412)282-8109

Founded: 1974. **Membership:** 14. Individuals in south central Pennsylvania interested in the preservation and restoration of Buick automobiles. **Convention/Meeting:** Annual show.

378 ● Buick Club of America, Bluegrass Chapter [Kentucky]
2805 Heather Ln.
La Grange, KY 40031
Lawrence Ford, Pres.   Ph:(502)241-5529

Founded: 1985. **Membership:** 18. Individuals interested in the history and preservation of the Buick automobile. Seeks to further the image of the Buick marque through social events, meets, tours, and public exhibitions.

379 ● Buick Club of America, Chicagoland Chapter [Illinois]
PO Box 863
Arlington Heights, IL 60006
Steven Kelly, Contact   Ph:(708)464-5933

Founded: 1967. **Membership:** 85. Enthusiasts of Buick

automobiles in the Chicago, IL metropolitan area. Serves as a clearinghouse for the exchange of information on finding Buick parts and Buick maintenance. **Convention/Meeting:** Monthly.

380 ● Buick Club of America, Cream City Chapter [Wisconsin]
P.O. Box 27372
West Allis, WI 53227
Jerry Whelan, Dir.　　　　　　　Ph:(414)321-8377

Founded: 1982. **Membership:** 100. Individuals in southeastern Wisconsin interested in the maintenance, operation, and restoration of Buick automobiles. Participates in car shows and tours. **Convention/Meeting:** Monthly.

381 ● Buick Club of America, Glass City Chapter [Ohio]
138 E. 5th St.
Perrysburg, OH 43551
David S. Rex, Sec.-Treas.　　　　　Ph:(419)874-8903

Founded: 1972. **Membership:** 25. Individuals in northwestern Ohio and southern Michigan interested in the maintenance, operation, and restoration of Buick automobiles. Sponsors car shows.

382 ● Buick Club of America, Jersey Shore Chapter [New Jersey]
2425 Cedar St.
Manasquan, NJ 08736
Ronald H. Foerster, Dir.　　　　　Ph:(201)528-9409

Founded: 1979. **Membership:** 35. Antique automobile collectors. Promotes restoration, preservation, and enjoyment of Buick automobiles. **Convention/Meeting:** Annual All Buick Car Show - always September, Sea Girt, NJ. Also holds monthly meeting - always last Wednesday of the month.

383 ● Buick Club of America, Kansas Chapter
216 S. Chestnut
Olathe, KS 66061
Richard Sandberg, Exec. Officer　　Ph:(913)764-0423

384 ● Buick Club of America, Lone Star Chapter [Texas]
14021 Stoneshire
Houston, TX 77060
Cecil Miles, Exec. Officer　　　　Ph:(713)448-8196

385 ● Buick Club of America, National Pike Chapter [Pennsylvania]
71 Murtland Ave.
Washington, PA 15301
Joe Manfredi, Exec. Officer　　　Ph:(412)222-0700

Founded: 1986. **Membership:** 30. Automobile salespeople and dealers and other interested persons organized to restore and preserve the Buick marque.

386 ● Buick Club of America, Nebraska Chapter
9346 Monroe St.
Omaha, NE 68127
Larry D. Robb, Director　　　　　Ph:(402)339-0086

Founded: 1975. **Membership:** 20. Individuals in Nebraska and western Iowa interested in cars built by the Buick Division of General Motors. **Convention/Meeting:** Monthly.

387 ● Buick Club of America, North Texas Chapter
1614 Woodoak Dr.
Richardson, TX 75081
David G. Farmer, Exec. Officer　　Ph:(214)699-9418

388 ● Buick Club of America, Puget Sound Chapter [Washington state]
2725 SW 347th St.
Federal Way, WA 98023
Tony Weiss, Exec. Officer　　　　Ph:(206)874-4562

Founded: 1974. **Membership:** 72. Buick owners in the Puget Sound, WA area. Promotes the preservation and restoration of Buick automobiles. **Convention/Meeting:** Monthly - always the second Monday of the month.

389 ● Buick Club of America, San Gabriel Valley Chapter [California]
P.O. Box 2355
Pasadena, CA 91102
Lou Baiocco, Dir.

Founded: 1966. **Membership:** 70. Owners of Buick automobiles. Promotes the preservation and display of Buick cars. **Convention/Meeting:** Monthly.

390 ● Buick Club of America, Southwestern Ohio Chapter
8529 Clough Pk.
Cincinnati, OH 45244
Richard Kranpitz, Dir.　　　　　Ph:(513)474-0657

Founded: 1970. **Membership:** 35. Encourages the maintenance, restoration, and preservation of all models of Buick cars. Sponsors antique car show.

BUICK REGAL CUSTOM (1987-92)

Introduced as part of General Motors W car line, along with corporate twins Chevrolet Lumina, Oldsmobile Cutlass Supreme, and Pontiac Grand Prix. Named to *Car and Driver's* Ten Best Cars Nominee list for 1989 and 1990 and *Motor Trend's* Car of the Year candidate list in 1990. Produced at General Motors in Oshawa, Ontario, Canada.

1991 Buick Regal Limited

MAJOR FEATURES

● Buick Regal Custom 1992 standard equipment includes: 4-speed automatic transmission, 4-wheel disc brakes, front-wheel drive, power rack-and-pinion steering, air conditioning, adjustable steering wheel, power door locks, and AM/FM stereo.

● Buick Regal Limited adds as 1992 standard equipment: analog instrumentation and anti-lock brake system.

● Buick Gran Sport adds as 1992 standard equipment: Gran

Touring suspension, upgraded interior, and other exterior body stylings.

● Regal Grand National was discontinued in 1988. It was the most powerful production car made in U.S. when it was produced.

PRICE HISTORY

The following new car prices reflect the approximate retail cost of the base model: **1987** - $11,562; **1988** - $12,449; **1989** - $14,614; **1990** - $15,200; **1991** - $15,690; **1992** - $16,610.

DIMENSIONS

Body Style	Years Avail	Wheel Base (in)	Lgth (in)	Ht (in)	Avg Wt (lbs)	Fuel Cap (gal)	Front Hdrm (in)	Front Legrm (in)
2d cpe	87-90	107.5	192.2	53	3,237	16.5	37.8	42.3
2d cpe	91-92	107.5	193.6	53	3,236	16.5	37.8	42.3
4d sdn	90-92	107.5	193.9	54.5	3,320	16.5	38.7	42.4

ENGINES

Type	Displace- ment (L)	Fuel Dly	HP @rpm	Torque @rpm (ft/lbs)	MPG Cty/Hwy	Years Avail
V-6	3.8	2-bbl	110@3800	190@1600	19/24	87-87
V-6	2.8	FI	125@4500	160@3600	20/29	88-88
V-6	2.8	FI	130@4500	170@3600	20/29	89-89
V-6	3.1	FI	135@4400	180@3600	19/30	90-90
V-6	3.8	FI	170@4800	220@3200	18/28	90-92
V-6	3.1	FI	140@4400	185@3200	19/29	91-92
V-6T	3.8	FI	200@na	na	17/25	87-87
V-8	5.0	4-bbl	140@na	na	18/25	87-87

KEY: I=in-line engine; V=V engine; F=flat engine; FI=fuel injection; bbl=barrel carburetor; T=turbo; D=diesel; HP=horsepower; MPG=estimated average miles per gallon.

EVALUATIONS, TESTS, AND RANKINGS

1991: "long-haul road comfort . . . odd instrument layout . . . provide the basics of family transportation with shadings of luxury or sport." **Source:** "Buick Regal GS: They should have called it the Revelation," *Car and Driver*, April 1991, pp. 119-121.

1991: "excellent low-speed response and quiet, effortless highway cruising . . . high levels of quality inside and out . . . analog instruments preferable to digital ones, but gauges positioned at odd angle." **Source:** "In Search of the Perfect 10," *Popular Science*, January, 1991, pp. 76-80, 94.

1990: "additional horsepower really wakes up the sedan . . . Handles quite well in the real world, while maintaining a quiet, comfortable ride . . . pillow-look adornment and video dash." **Source:** "Motor Trend's 1990 Car of the Year," *Motor Trend*, February 1990, pp. 54-57.

1989: "Buick Regal with special Gran Touring suspension package still exhibits a lot of body roll . . . includes stiffer springs and deflected-disc shock absorbers for ride control . . . the GM10 exercises are roomy, light, and efficient." **Source:** "Coupes," *Popular Science*, January 1989, pp. 42-44.

1989: "[Custom] . . . a very capable car . . . engineered for proper performance and patriotic fuel economy . . . styled with staying power." **Source:** "Long-Term Test," *Popular Mechanics*, January 1989, pp. 48, 50-51.

1988: "resolutely modern . . . interior is spacious and comfortable, dashboard is uncluttered . . . 125 horsepower, 2.8-liter V-6 provides ample muscle but is miserly in fuel consumption . . . fit and finish . . . were excellent . . . very comfortable, a pleasure to drive." **Source:** "GM has a lot riding

on new Buick Regal," *The Detroit News*, January 13, 1988, p. 1F.

1988: "Buick Regal Limited . . . a tasteful mix of modern sleekness and comfortable, familiar features . . . had the interior quiet of larger cars . . . The engine . . . worked smoothly . . . Fit and finish were admirable." **Source:** "Buick Regal does GM proud," *The Detroit News*, February 24, 1988, pp. 1F-2F.

1988: "The overall impression is more of a sophisticated 2-door sedan than a sports coupe . . . suspension tuned more for compliance than hard cornering . . . relatively sedate Regal will appeal to an older customer." **Source:** "American Flyers: Detroit's personal coupes square off in a home-grown hoedown," *Popular Mechanics*, June 1988, pp. 65-69, 109.

RECALLS

1990-91: (412,792 vehicles; includes Chevrolet Lumina, Pontiac Grand Prix, Buick Regal, and Oldsmobile Cutlass Supreme): Front shoulder safety belt webbing may separate at front belt upper guide loops on either side of front seat. **Corrective action:** Install controlled rotation bracket on driver and passenger side front seat belt guide loops. *(NHTSA Campaign No. 91V005000.)*

1990: (51,834 cars; includes other Buick models): Owner's manual does not fully explain how front shoulder belt comfort feature works. **Corrective action:** Insert sticker that provides missing information in owner's manual. *(NHTSA Campaign No. 90V112000.)*

1989-90: (476,422 vehicles; includes Buick, Chevrolet, Oldsmobile, and Pontiac models): Brake stoplamps may not illuminate or, in some cases, stoplamps will not stay illuminated all the time when brakes are applied due to a faulty stoplamp switch. **Corrective action:** Install an improved design stoplamp switch. *(NHTSA Campaign No. 90V185000.)*

1989: (3,784 passenger vehicles; includes Pontiac Grand Prix and Buick Regal): Fuel return lines could fracture and allow fuel to leak in area of fuel tank. In presence of ignition source, this condition could result in fire. **Corrective action:** Install new fuel return pipe assembly. *(NHTSA Campaign No. 88V188000.)*

1988-90: (673,000 passenger vehicles; includes the Pontiac Grand Prix, Buick Regal, Oldsmobile Cutlass Calais, and Chevrolet Lumina models): Front shoulder belt guide loop attachment fastener may pull through door mounted anchor plate. Seat belt may not properly restrain a passenger, resulting in increased risk of injury to occupant. **Corrective action:** Replace front shoulder belt guide loop attachment nuts and install new guide cover. *(NHTSA Campaign No. 90V054000.)*

1988: (9,661 passenger vehicles): Stop lamp switch may have loose electrical contact. Can overheat and melt surrounding plastic causing contact to stick open. Open contact would render brake lights inoperative whenbrake pedal is depressed. Also, transmission clutch control and cruise control contacts would remain closed. Results in cruise resume upon brake pedal release if cruise control is in on position. Either unexpected cruise resume or inoperative brake lights could result in vehicle crash. **Corrective action:** Rotary soplamp switch will be replaced on all involved vehicles. *(NHTSA Campaign No. 88V040000.)*

1988: (3,221 vehicles): Lower control arm to ball joint attachment can become loose. Also, certain cars could have tie rod ball stud nuts that were not properly torqued and could loosen. Continued operation of car with either condition could result in separation of that joint and possible loss of steering control and an accident. **Corrective action:** Replace both lower control arms; also, check tie rod ball stud nut torque. *(NHTSA Campaign No. 88V066000.)*

1988: (8,328 vehicles): Twisted components could allow left front brake hose to contact fender lining/rail area, over time brake hose could wear through. This could result in loss of brake fluid and partial loss of braking capability which could result in an accident. **Corrective action:** Inspect left front brake hose for proper installation and replace, as necessary. *(NHTSA Campaign No. 88V109000.)*

1988: (17,745 passenger vehicles; includes Pontiac Grand Prix and Buick Regal): Interference between transmission shift cable and bellcrank clip in steering column can result in disengagement of transmission cable. This condition could allow transmission to be in gear other than displayed by shift indicator. Vehicle could move in unexpected direction and cause vehicle crash without prior warning. **Corrective action:** Newly designed bellcrank clip will be installed. *(NHTSA Campaign No. 88V045000.)*

SAFETY AND REPAIRS

1992: "GM Recalls '92 A-, W-Cars," *Automotive News*, December 2, 1991, p. 2. **Note:** Transmission problem could cause cars to remain in reverse when shifted into neutral.

1991: "GM Recalls Cars for Belt Loops," *Automotive News*, February 10, 1992, p. 2. **Note:** May have cracked front-door shoulder belt guide loops.

1988: "Service Tips," *Popular Mechanics*, December 1989, p. 41. **Note:** Regal underhood lamp may be constantly on due to bad external switch.

1987: "Car Clinic," *Popular Mechanics*, August 1990, p. 26. **Note:** Tip for clashing starter motor gears in 1987-88 General Motors 4.3, 5.0, and 5.7 liter engines.

REPAIR MANUALS

391 ● Chilton's Buick Century and Regal, 1975-87
Chilton Co.
Chilton Way
Radnor, PA 19089   Ph:(215)964-4000

Published 1988. **Price:** $15.95.

392 ● General Motors 8-Cylinder
Peter Allen Video Productions
38-C Otis St.
West Babylon, NY 11704   Ph:(516)643-4372

A program demonstrating basic maintenance and tune-up procedures for the entitled engine. **Release date:** 1986. **Producer:** Peter Allen Productions. **Acquisition:** Purchase.

393 ● Get Your Buick Fixed Right
Consumer Reports Books
51 E. 42nd St., Ste. 800
New York, NY 10017   Ph:(212)682-9280

Published 1989. **Editor(s):** Mort Schultz. **Price:** $8.95.

394 ● Haynes Buick Mid-size Models Owners Workshop Manual No. 627: 1974-1987
Haynes Publications, Inc.
861 Lawrence Dr.
Newbury Park, CA 91320   Ph:(818)889-5400

Editor(s): J.H. Haynes and Peter D. DuPre. **Price:** $15.95.

395 ● Pontiac Grand Prix-Oldsmobile Cutlass-Buick Regal, 1988 Repair and Tune-up Guide
Chilton Co.
Chilton Way
Radnor, PA 19089   Ph:(215)964-4000

Published 1990. **Price:** $15.95.

OTHER INFORMATION SOURCES

396 ● Bluegrass Buick News
Buick Club of America, Bluegrass Chapter
2805 Heather Ln.
La Grange, KY 40031   Ph:(502)241-5529

Periodic.

397 ● The Buick: A Complete History
Auto Quarterly, Inc.
420 N. Park Rd., Ste. 200
Wyomissing, PA 19610   Ph:(215)375-8444

Price: $39.95.

398 ● Buick Club of America—Membership Roster
Buick Club of America
PO Box 898   Ph:(714)993-5645
Garden Grove, CA 92642-0898   Fax:(714)993-5645

Biennial.

399 ● Buick Club of America, Nebraska Chapter— Newsletter
Buick Club of America, Nebraska Chapter
9346 Monroe St.
Omaha, NE 68127   Ph:(402)339-0086

Quarterly.

400 ● Buick Club of America, North Cascade Chapter— Newsletter [Washington state]
Buick Club of America, North Cascade Chapter
13003 Third Ave., SE
Everett, WA 98204   Ph:(206)337-1264

Monthly.

401 ● Buick Club of America, San Gabriel Valley Chapter— Newsletter [California]
Buick Club of America, San Gabriel Valley Chapter— Newsletter
P.O. Box 2355
Pasadena, CA 91102

Monthly.

402 ● Buick Club of America, Southwestern Ohio Chapter— Newsletter
Buick Club of America, Southwestern Ohio Chapter
10155 Andalusia Close
Cincinnati, OH 45241   Ph:(513)733-5313

Monthly.

403 ● Buick GS Club of America—GS National Directory
Buick GS Club of America
1213 Gornto Rd.
Valdosta, GA 31602   Ph:(912)244-0577

Lists 3,900 owners and enthusiasts of the Buick Gran Sport automobile, manufactured from 1965 to 1973, and the Buick Grand National, manufactured in 1986 and 1987. Annual.

404 ● Buick GS Club of America, Indiana Chapter— Newsletter
Buick GS Club of America, Indiana Chapter
1029 Charlotte Ave.
Ft. Wayne, IN 46805   Ph:(219)484-7019

Newsletter. Bimonthly.

405 ● Cream City Chronicle [Wisconsin]
Buick Club of America, Cream City Chapter
P.O. Box 27372
West Allis, WI 53227   Ph:(414)321-8377

Bimonthly.

406 ● Dyna's Chatter
Buick Club of America, Appalachian Chapter
233-1/2 W. Brady St.
Butler, PA 16001   Ph:(412)282-8109

Newsletter. Periodic.

407 ● Dyna's Chatter
Buick Club of America, Appalachian Chapter
233-1/2 W. Brady St.
Butler, PA 16001   Ph:(412)282-8109

Newsletter. Periodic.

408 ● Fireball Flash
Buick Club of America, Chicagoland Chapter
271 Terrace Pl.
Buffalo Grove, IL 60089   Ph:(708)537-7055

Monthly.

409 ● Fireball News
Buick Club of America, San Gabriel Valley Chapter
PO Box 2355
Pasadena, CA 91102

Monthly.

410 ● GS Directory
Buick GS Club of America
1213 Gornto Rd.
Valdosta, GA 31601   Ph:(912)244-0577

About 3,800 owners of Buick Wildcats, Rivieras, Grand Nationals, Gran Sports, and other high performance Buick automobiles. Annual. **Editor(s):** Richard Lasseter, President. **Price:** Available to members only.

411 ● Jersey Shore Chapter News [New Jersey]
Buick Club of America, Jersey Shore Chapter
2425 Cedar St.
Manasquan, NJ 08736   Ph:(201)528-9409

Newsletter. Monthly.

412 ● The Limited
Buick Club of America, Puget Sound Chapter
2725 SW 347th St.
Federal Way, WA 98023   Ph:(206)874-4562

Monthly.

413 ● Pike Press
Buick Club of America, National Pike Chapter
71 Murtland Ave.
Washington, PA 15301   Ph:(412)222-0700

Periodic.

414 ● The Reflector
Buick Club of America, Glass City Chapter
109 Ashwood Ct.
Perrysburg, OH 43551   Ph:(419)874-2393

Monthly.

415 ● Running Board
Buick Club of America, Orange County Chapter
P.O. Box 5171
Fullerton, CA 92635   Ph:(213)925-3294

Monthly.

ASSOCIATIONS

416 ● Buick Club of America
P.O. Box 898
Garden Grove, CA 92642
Dale Osstyn, Pres.   Ph:(714)993-5645

Founded: 1966. **Membership:** 9400. Purposes are: development, publication, and interchange of technical, historical, and other information among members who are interested in Buick automobiles; to promote fellowship among members; to encourage the maintenance, restoration, and preservation of all models of produced by the Buick Motor Division of General Motors. Awards prizes at local, regional, and national car shows; presents Senior Award for Buick achieving the highest standards. Holds competitions; compiles statistics; maintains small library. **Convention/Meeting:** Annual display conference (with exhibits) - 1992 July, Olathe, KS.

417 ● Buick Club of America, Appalachian Chapter [South central Pennsylvania]
233-1/2 W. Brady St.
Butler, PA 16001
Keith R. Bleakney, Dir.   Ph:(412)282-8109

Founded: 1974. **Membership:** 14. Individuals in south central Pennsylvania interested in the preservation and restoration of Buick automobiles. **Convention/Meeting:** Annual show.

418 ● Buick Club of America, Bluegrass Chapter [Kentucky]
2805 Heather Ln.
La Grange, KY 40031
Lawrence Ford, Pres.   Ph:(502)241-5529

Founded: 1985. **Membership:** 18. Individuals interested in the history and preservation of the Buick automobile. Seeks to further the image of the Buick marque through social events, meets, tours, and public exhibitions.

419 ● Buick Club of America, Chicagoland Chapter [Illinois]
PO Box 863
Arlington Heights, IL 60006
Steven Kelly, Contact   Ph:(708)464-5933

Founded: 1967. **Membership:** 85. Enthusiasts of Buick automobiles in the Chicago, IL metropolitan area. Serves as a clearinghouse for the exchange of information on finding Buick parts and Buick maintenance. **Convention/Meeting:** Monthly.

420 ● Buick Club of America, Cream City Chapter [Wisconsin]
P.O. Box 27372
West Allis, WI 53227
Jerry Whelan, Dir.   Ph:(414)321-8377

Founded: 1982. **Membership:** 100. Individuals in southeastern Wisconsin interested in the maintenance, operation, and restoration of Buick automobiles. Participates in car shows and tours. **Convention/Meeting:** Monthly.

421 ● Buick Club of America, Glass City Chapter [Ohio]
138 E. 5th St.
Perrysburg, OH 43551
David S. Rex, Sec.-Treas.   Ph:(419)874-8903

Founded: 1972. **Membership:** 25. Individuals in northwestern

Ohio and southern Michigan interested in the maintenance, operation, and restoration of Buick automobiles. Sponsors car shows.

422 ● Buick Club of America, Jersey Shore Chapter [New Jersey]
2425 Cedar St.
Manasquan, NJ 08736
Ronald H. Foerster, Dir.   Ph:(201)528-9409

Founded: 1979. **Membership:** 35. Antique automobile collectors. Promotes restoration, preservation, and enjoyment of Buick automobiles. **Convention/Meeting:** Annual All Buick Car Show - always September, Sea Girt, NJ. Also holds monthly meeting - always last Wednesday of the month.

423 ● Buick Club of America, Kansas Chapter
216 S. Chestnut
Olathe, KS 66061
Richard Sandberg, Exec. Officer   Ph:(913)764-0423

424 ● Buick Club of America, Lone Star Chapter [Texas]
14021 Stoneshire
Houston, TX 77060
Cecil Miles, Exec. Officer   Ph:(713)448-8196

425 ● Buick Club of America, National Pike Chapter [Pennsylvania]
71 Murtland Ave.
Washington, PA 15301
Joe Manfredi, Exec. Officer   Ph:(412)222-0700

Founded: 1986. **Membership:** 30. Automobile salespeople and dealers and other interested persons organized to restore and preserve the Buick marque.

426 ● Buick Club of America, Nebraska Chapter
9346 Monroe St.
Omaha, NE 68127
Larry D. Robb, Director   Ph:(402)339-0086

Founded: 1975. **Membership:** 20. Individuals in Nebraska and western Iowa interested in cars built by the Buick Division of General Motors. **Convention/Meeting:** Monthly.

427 ● Buick Club of America, North Texas Chapter
1614 Woodoak Dr.
Richardson, TX 75081
David G. Farmer, Exec. Officer   Ph:(214)699-9418

428 ● Buick Club of America, Puget Sound Chapter [Washington state]
2725 SW 347th St.
Federal Way, WA 98023
Tony Weiss, Exec. Officer   Ph:(206)874-4562

Founded: 1974. **Membership:** 72. Buick owners in the Puget Sound, WA area. Promotes the preservation and restoration of Buick automobiles. **Convention/Meeting:** Monthly - always the second Monday of the month.

429 ● Buick Club of America, San Gabriel Valley Chapter [California]
P.O. Box 2355
Pasadena, CA 91102
Lou Baiocco, Dir.

Founded: 1966. **Membership:** 70. Owners of Buick automobiles. Promotes the preservation and display of Buick cars. **Convention/Meeting:** Monthly.

430 ● Buick Club of America, Southwestern Ohio Chapter
8529 Clough Pk.
Cincinnati, OH 45244
Richard Kranpitz, Dir.   Ph:(513)474-0657

Founded: 1970. **Membership:** 35. Encourages the maintenance, restoration, and preservation of all models of Buick cars. Sponsors antique car show.

431 ● Buick GS Club of America
1213 Gornto Rd.
Valdosta, GA 31602
Richard W. Lasseter, Founder & Pres.   Ph:(912)244-0577

Founded: 1982. **Membership:** 3,900. Owners and enthusiasts of the Buick Gran Sport automobile, manufactured from 1965 to 1973, and the Buick Grand National, manufactured in 1986 and 1987. Promotes the collectibility of the high-performance Gran Sport. Assists in the upkeep and maintenance of GS and GN automobiles. Provides parts sources and technical information. Sponsors drag racing competitions; bestows awards; maintains small library. **Convention/Meeting:** Annual car show and race, with exhibits and banquet - always first weekend in May, Bowling Green, KY.

BUICK RIVIERA (1987-92)

Introduced as part of the General Motors E car line, along with corporate twin Cadillac Eldorado. Listed as one of the "Best Bets of 1992" by *The Car Book*. Produced at the General Motors plant in Hamtramck, Michigan.

1991 Buick Riviera with Gran Touring Package

MAJOR FEATURES

● Buick Riviera 1992 standard equipment includes: 4-speed automatic transmission with overdrive, 4-wheel power disc brakes with anti-lock braking system, driver's side airbag, power rack-and-pinion steering, climate control system, cruise control, front-wheel drive, electronic instrumentation, and solar control glass.

PRICE HISTORY

The following new car prices reflect the approximate retail cost of the base model: **1987** - $20,337; **1988** - $21,615; **1989** - $22,540; **1990** - $23,040; **1991** - $24,560; **1992** - $25,415.

DIMENSIONS

Body Style	Years Avail	Wheel Base (in)	Lgth (in)	Ht (in)	Avg Wt (lbs)	Fuel Cap (gal)	Front Hdrm (in)	Front Legrm (in)
2d cpe	87-92	108.0	198.3	52.9	3,496	18.8	37.8	42.7

ENGINES

Type	Displace-ment (L)	Fuel Dly	HP @rpm	Torque @rpm (ft/lbs)	MPG Cty/Hwy	Years Avail
V-6	3.8	FI	150@4400	200@2000	19/29	87-87
V-6	3.8	FI	165@5200	210@2000	19/28	88-88
V-6	3.8	FI	165@4800	210@2000	18/27	89-90
V-6	3.8	FI	170@4800	220@3200	18/27	91-92

KEY: I=in-line engine; V=V engine; F=flat engine; FI=fuel injection; bbl=barrel carburetor; T=turbo; D=diesel; HP=horsepower; MPG=estimated average miles per gallon.

EVALUATIONS, TESTS, AND RANKINGS

1990: "one of America's cherished luxury coupes . . . ranked as the top domestic car and No. 2 among imports and domestic cars combined in a study by market researcher J. D. Power and Associates . . . Suspension and handling were not as mushy as you might expect." **Source:** "Riviera doesn't mess with new found success," *The Detroit News*, April 4, 1990, pp. 1C-2C.

RECALLS

1992: (2,371 passenger cars; includes Buick Riviera, Oldsmobile Toronado, Cadillac Eldorado, and Cadillac Seville): The intermediate shaft to steering rack lower coupling pinch bolt may be missing. If this condition exists and shaft disengagement occurs, loss of steering control will result. **Corrective action:** Install pinch bolt. *(NHTSA Campaign No. 91V157000.)*

1990: (10,166 passenger cars; includes the Buick Riviera, Cadillac Eldorado, Cadillac Seville, and Buick Reatta): Misaligned rear safety shoulder belt retractor assemblies could prevent engagement of inertia lock, increasing likelihood of injury to occupant in panic stop or accident. **Corrective action:** Realign rear shoulder belt retractor assembly. *(NHTSA Campaign No. 90V028000.)*

1990: (63,964 vehicles; includes Buick, Oldsmobile, and Cadillac models): Transaxle shift control cable may disengage from the floor shift control with loss of gear indicator reference and shift selector operation. Could result in unexpected vehicle movement and an accident. **Corrective action:** Install transaxle shift control cable retaining clip to prevent cable disengagement. *(NHTSA Campaign No. 90V164000.)*

1990: (18,904 passenger cars; includes Buick Reatta, and Buick Riviera): Brake indicator light may not light when ignition is in the "on" position, the parking brake is applied, and the shift selector is in the park or neutral gear range. Vehicles would not meet the requirements of FMVSS 101 and 105. **Corrective action:** Replace the prom in the body computer module. *(NHTSA Campaign No. 91V158000.)*

1989: (634 passenger cars equipped with anti-lock brakes; includes the Cadillac Seville, Cadillac Eldorado, Buick Riveria, and Oldsmobile Toronado): One or both ABS hydraulic unit mounting bolts may not be properly seated and could loosen. Could lead to separation of the ABS hydraulic unit from the mounting bracket and result in loss of brake function and a crash without prior warning. **Corrective action:** Replace both ABS hydraulic unit mounting bolts. *(NHTSA Campaign No. 89V055000.)*

1989: (10,535 passenger cars equipped with 3800 V6 engines and anti-lock brakes; includes the Buick Riviera, Buick Reatta, and Oldsmobile Toronado): Left front brake pipe may contact the cruise control servo bracket. Brake line could wear through causing loss of brake fluid and partial loss of braking capability; could result in a vehicle crash. *(NHTSA Campaign No. 89V056000.)*

1987: (65,136 passenger vehicles; includes Oldsmobile Tornado and Buick Riveria; includes models made before 1987):

Insufficient clearance between power steering pump pressure hose assembly and transmission governor/speed sensor connector could cause abrasion of hose. This could result in fluid leak, with potential for underhood fire. **Corrective action:** Replace power steering pump pressure hose. *(NHTSA Campaign No. 88V078000.)*

REPAIR MANUALS

432 ● Buick-Olds-Pontiac Full-Size, 1975-87
Chilton Co.
Chilton Way
Radnor, PA 19089   Ph:(215)964-4000

Price: $14.95.

433 ● Get Your Buick Fixed Right
Consumer Reports Books
51 E. 42nd St., Ste. 800
New York, NY 10017   Ph:(212)682-9280

Published 1989. **Editor(s):** Mort Schultz. **Price:** $8.95.

OTHER INFORMATION SOURCES

434 ● Bluegrass Buick News
Buick Club of America, Bluegrass Chapter
2805 Heather Ln.
La Grange, KY 40031   Ph:(502)241-5529

Periodic.

435 ● The Buick: A Complete History
Auto Quarterly, Inc.
420 N. Park Rd., Ste. 200
Wyomissing, PA 19610   Ph:(215)375-8444

Price: $39.95.

436 ● Buick Club of America—Membership Roster
Buick Club of America
PO Box 898   Ph:(714)993-5645
Garden Grove, CA 92642-0898   Fax:(714)993-5645

Biennial.

437 ● Buick Club of America, Nebraska Chapter—Newsletter
Buick Club of America, Nebraska Chapter
9346 Monroe St.
Omaha, NE 68127   Ph:(402)339-0086

Quarterly.

438 ● Buick Club of America, North Cascade Chapter—Newsletter [Washington state]
Buick Club of America, North Cascade Chapter
13003 Third Ave., SE
Everett, WA 98204   Ph:(206)337-1264

Monthly.

439 ● Buick Club of America, San Gabriel Valley Chapter—Newsletter [California]
Buick Club of America, San Gabriel Valley Chapter—Newsletter
P.O. Box 2355
Pasadena, CA 91102

Monthly.

440 ● Buick Club of America, Southwestern Ohio Chapter—Newsletter
Buick Club of America, Southwestern Ohio Chapter
10155 Andalusia Close
Cincinnati, OH 45241   Ph:(513)733-5313

Monthly.

441 ● Cream City Chronicle [Wisconsin]
Buick Club of America, Cream City Chapter
P.O. Box 27372
West Allis, WI 53227   Ph:(414)321-8377

Bimonthly.

442 ● Dyna's Chatter
Buick Club of America, Appalachian Chapter
233-1/2 W. Brady St.
Butler, PA 16001   Ph:(412)282-8109

Newsletter. Periodic.

443 ● Dyna's Chatter
Buick Club of America, Appalachian Chapter
233-1/2 W. Brady St.
Butler, PA 16001   Ph:(412)282-8109

Newsletter. Periodic.

444 ● Fireball Flash
Buick Club of America, Chicagoland Chapter
271 Terrace Pl.
Buffalo Grove, IL 60089   Ph:(708)537-7055

Monthly.

445 ● Fireball News
Buick Club of America, San Gabriel Valley Chapter
PO Box 2355
Pasadena, CA 91102

Monthly.

446 ● GS Directory
Buick GS Club of America
1213 Gornto Rd.
Valdosta, GA 31601   Ph:(912)244-0577

About 3,800 owners of Buick Wildcats, Rivieras, Grand Nationals, Gran Sports, and other high performance Buick automobiles. Annual. **Editor(s):** Richard Lasseter, President. **Price:** Available to members only.

447 ● Jersey Shore Chapter News [New Jersey]
Buick Club of America, Jersey Shore Chapter
2425 Cedar St.
Manasquan, NJ 08736   Ph:(201)528-9409

Newsletter. Monthly.

448 ● The Limited
Buick Club of America, Puget Sound Chapter
2725 SW 347th St.
Federal Way, WA 98023   Ph:(206)874-4562

Monthly.

449 ● Pike Press
Buick Club of America, National Pike Chapter
71 Murtland Ave.
Washington, PA 15301   Ph:(412)222-0700

Periodic.

450 ● The Reflector
Buick Club of America, Glass City Chapter
109 Ashwood Ct.
Perrysburg, OH 43551   Ph:(419)874-2393

Monthly.

451 ● Riviera Owners Association—Review
Riviera Owners Association
P.O. Box 26344
Lakewood, CO 80226   Ph:(303)987-3712

Features articles on members and their Buick Riviera automobiles. Offers tips on repair and restoration and provides reprints of "obsolete material." Bimonthly. **Editor(s):** Ray Knott and Virginia Knott. **Price:** Available to members only.

452 ● Running Board
Buick Club of America, Orange County Chapter
P.O. Box 5171
Fullerton, CA 92635   Ph:(213)925-3294

Monthly.

ASSOCIATIONS

453 ● Buick Club of America
P.O. Box 898
Garden Grove, CA 92642
Dale Osstyn, Pres.   Ph:(714)993-5645

Founded: 1966. **Membership:** 9400. Purposes are: development, publication, and interchange of technical, historical, and other information among members who are interested in Buick automobiles; to promote fellowship among members; to encourage the maintenance, restoration, and preservation of all models of produced by the Buick Motor Division of General Motors. Awards prizes at local, regional, and national car shows; presents Senior Award for Buick achieving the highest standards. Holds competitions; compiles statistics; maintains small library. **Convention/Meeting:** Annual display conference (with exhibits) - 1992 July, Olathe, KS.

454 ● Buick Club of America, Appalachian Chapter [South central Pennsylvania]
233-1/2 W. Brady St.
Butler, PA 16001
Keith R. Bleakney, Dir.   Ph:(412)282-8109

Founded: 1974. **Membership:** 14. Individuals in south central Pennsylvania interested in the preservation and restoration of Buick automobiles. **Convention/Meeting:** Annual show.

455 ● Buick Club of America, Bluegrass Chapter [Kentucky]
2805 Heather Ln.
La Grange, KY 40031
Lawrence Ford, Pres.   Ph:(502)241-5529

Founded: 1985. **Membership:** 18. Individuals interested in the history and preservation of the Buick automobile. Seeks to further the image of the Buick marque through social events, meets, tours, and public exhibitions.

456 ● Buick Club of America, Chicagoland Chapter [Illinois]
PO Box 863
Arlington Heights, IL 60006
Steven Kelly, Contact   Ph:(708)464-5933

Founded: 1967. **Membership:** 85. Enthusiasts of Buick automobiles in the Chicago, IL metropolitan area. Serves as a clearinghouse for the exchange of information on finding Buick parts and Buick maintenance. **Convention/Meeting:** Monthly.

457 ● Buick Club of America, Cream City Chapter [Wisconsin]
P.O. Box 27372
West Allis, WI 53227
Jerry Whelan, Dir. Ph:(414)321-8377

Founded: 1982. **Membership:** 100. Individuals in southeastern Wisconsin interested in the maintenance, operation, and restoration of Buick automobiles. Participates in car shows and tours. **Convention/Meeting:** Monthly.

458 ● Buick Club of America, Glass City Chapter [Ohio]
138 E. 5th St.
Perrysburg, OH 43551
David S. Rex, Sec.-Treas. Ph:(419)874-8903

Founded: 1972. **Membership:** 25. Individuals in northwestern Ohio and southern Michigan interested in the maintenance, operation, and restoration of Buick automobiles. Sponsors car shows.

459 ● Buick Club of America, Jersey Shore Chapter [New Jersey]
2425 Cedar St.
Manasquan, NJ 08736
Ronald H. Foerster, Dir. Ph:(201)528-9409

Founded: 1979. **Membership:** 35. Antique automobile collectors. Promotes restoration, preservation, and enjoyment of Buick automobiles. **Convention/Meeting:** Annual All Buick Car Show - always September, Sea Girt, NJ. Also holds monthly meeting - always last Wednesday of the month.

460 ● Buick Club of America, Kansas Chapter
216 S. Chestnut
Olathe, KS 66061
Richard Sandberg, Exec. Officer Ph:(913)764-0423

461 ● Buick Club of America, Lone Star Chapter [Texas]
14021 Stoneshire
Houston, TX 77060
Cecil Miles, Exec. Officer Ph:(713)448-8196

462 ● Buick Club of America, National Pike Chapter [Pennsylvania]
71 Murtland Ave.
Washington, PA 15301
Joe Manfredi, Exec. Officer Ph:(412)222-0700

Founded: 1986. **Membership:** 30. Automobile salespeople and dealers and other interested persons organized to restore and preserve the Buick marque.

463 ● Buick Club of America, Nebraska Chapter
9346 Monroe St.
Omaha, NE 68127
Larry D. Robb, Director Ph:(402)339-0086

Founded: 1975. **Membership:** 20. Individuals in Nebraska and western Iowa interested in cars built by the Buick Division of General Motors. **Convention/Meeting:** Monthly.

464 ● Buick Club of America, North Texas Chapter
1614 Woodoak Dr.
Richardson, TX 75081
David G. Farmer, Exec. Officer Ph:(214)699-9418

465 ● Buick Club of America, Puget Sound Chapter [Washington state]
2725 SW 347th St.
Federal Way, WA 98023
Tony Weiss, Exec. Officer Ph:(206)874-4562

Founded: 1974. **Membership:** 72. Buick owners in the Puget Sound, WA area. Promotes the preservation and restoration of Buick automobiles. **Convention/Meeting:** Monthly - always the second Monday of the month.

466 ● Buick Club of America, San Gabriel Valley Chapter [California]
P.O. Box 2355
Pasadena, CA 91102
Lou Baiocco, Dir.

Founded: 1966. **Membership:** 70. Owners of Buick automobiles. Promotes the preservation and display of Buick cars. **Convention/Meeting:** Monthly.

467 ● Buick Club of America, Southwestern Ohio Chapter
8529 Clough Pk.
Cincinnati, OH 45244
Richard Kranpitz, Dir. Ph:(513)474-0657

Founded: 1970. **Membership:** 35. Encourages the maintenance, restoration, and preservation of all models of Buick cars. Sponsors antique car show.

BUICK ROADMASTER (1991-92)

Roadmaster name returned in 1991 model year for the first time since 1958. Corporate twins are the Chevrolet Caprice and Oldsmobile Custom Cruiser.

1991 Buick Roadmaster Estate Wagon

MAJOR FEATURES

● Buick Roadmaster has as 1992 standard equipment: 4-speed automatic transmission with overdrive, independent front suspension, power front disc/rear drum brakes with anti-lock braking system, power steering, air conditioning, AM/FM stereo, tilt steering, and driver's side airbag.

● Buick Roadmaster Limited adds as 1992 standard equipment: electronic touch climate control, remote keyless entry with starter interrupt, six-way power seats (driver and passenger), and variable effort steering.

● Buick Roadmaster Estate Wagon adds as 1992 standard equipment: luggage rack, heavy-duty suspension, and an upgraded interior.

PRICE HISTORY

The following new car prices reflect the approximate retail cost of the base model: **1991** - $20,890; **1992** - $21,865.

DIMENSIONS

Body Style	Years Avail	Wheel Base (in)	Lgth (in)	Ht (in)	Avg Wt (lbs)	Fuel Cap (gal)	Front Hdrm (in)	Front Legrm (in)
4d sdn	92-92	115.9	215.8	55.9	4,073	23.0	39.2	42.2
5d wgn	91-91	115.9	217.5	60.1	4,415	22.0	39.7	42.2
5d wgn	92-92	115.9	217.7	60.3	4,468	na	39.6	42.2

ENGINES

Type	Displacement (L)	Fuel Dly	HP @rpm	Torque @rpm (ft/lbs)	MPG Cty/Hwy	Years Avail
V-8	5.0	FI	170@4200	255@2400	16/25	91-91
V-8	5.7	FI	180@4000	300@2400	16/25	92-92

KEY: I=in-line engine; V=V engine; F=flat engine; FI=fuel injection; bbl=barrel carburetor; T=turbo; D=diesel; HP=horsepower; MPG=estimated average miles per gallon.

EVALUATIONS, TESTS, AND RANKINGS

1992: "it's a return to the old standards that made the Buick name what it was . . . aerodynamically sleek . . . 5.7 liter V-8 powers this fat cat of the highway and carries it along with grace and aplomb." **Source:** "Buick Roadmaster Limited: Daddy Warbucks Rides Again," *Motor Trend*, November 1991, p. 105.

1992: "this car shines in a straight line with a gentle, almost surreal ride . . . during panic braking, the brake pedal's heavy, mushy feel makes the car feel ponderous . . . multiadjustable front seats and spacious rear seats make this car as comfortable as it is roomy." **Source:** "Buick Roadmaster Limited," *Car and Driver*, December 1991, pp. 123-125.

1992: "the Roadmaster sedan is a return to Buick in its most traditional sense as a big, frame-on chassis, front-engine, rear-wheel-drive car . . . a good car for just settling in and effortlessly gobbling up hours of expressway." **Source:** "Buick turns out solid, strong performers," *The Flint Journal*, July 10, 1991.

1992: "sheer size is not the problem here. It is the execution . . . it is the feel of the car that seems wrong . . . these big conventional sedans and wagons behave like the big conventional sedans and wagons of old." **Source:** "Buick Hunts The Future In Its Past," *The New York Times*, June 9, 1991.

1992: "quite a civilized beast . . . relatively conservative shape . . . rates as a "best buy" in the full-size segment." **Source:** "Roadmaster Makes 'Best Buy' List," *Detroit Free Press*, June 13, 1991, p. 7C.

1991: "rear-wheel-drive car is enormous . . . heavy at 4415 lb. of curb weight and decidedly un-trendy, with its floating ride and . . . woodgrain applique . . . Six passenger room . . . large trunk . . . and 5000-lb . . . towing capacity are . . . selling points." **Source:** "Buick Roadmaster/Estate Wagon," *Road & Track*, October 1990, p. 57.

1991: "seats are where this Buick really shines . . . Buick's Roadmaster is clearly slanted toward comfort . . . unusually smooth, supple ride." **Source:** "Genteel Wheels," *Home Mechanix*, September 1991, pp. 72-76, 84.

1991: "[Estate Wagon] . . . is good news for family towing . . . among the leaders in heavy hauling . . . the only test vehicle so equipped [with anti-lock brakes], and it clobbered the competition." **Source:** "Getting Hitched," *Popular Mechanics*, July 1991, pp. 39-42, 95.

1991: "This is the way they used to build them . . . Everything but the portholes." **Source:** "Big is beautiful," *Forbes*, May 27, 1991, pp. 342-343.

1991: "may be just the ticket for folks who still want a car that can haul a 5,000-pound trailer without fuss and be stylish enough for a night out . . . now mated to a 4-speed automatic, it ran flawlessly and delivered more than ample power . . . complaints are minor but irritating." **Source:** "Roadmaster wagon: Family room on wheels," *The Detroit News*, May 15, 1991, p. E1-2.

1991: "can hold a gaggle of grade-schoolers, scads of suitcases and still tow a 5,000-pound trailer . . . a smooth operator that also is the domestic prestige leader . . . delivers a comfortable ride under most conditions." **Source:** "Roadmaster wagon carries a bundle, lives up to billing," *The Flint Journal*, March 6, 1991, p. B1.

RECALLS

None to date.

REPAIR MANUALS

468 ● General Motors 8-Cylinder
Peter Allen Video Productions
38-C Otis St.
West Babylon, NY 11704   Ph:(516)643-4372

A program demonstrating basic maintenance and tune-up procedures for the entitled engine. **Release date:** 1986. **Producer:** Peter Allen Productions. **Acquisition:** Purchase.

469 ● Get Your Buick Fixed Right
Consumer Reports Books
51 E. 42nd St., Ste. 800
New York, NY 10017   Ph:(212)682-9280

Published 1989. **Editor(s):** Mort Schultz. **Price:** $8.95.

OTHER INFORMATION SOURCES

470 ● Bluegrass Buick News
Buick Club of America, Bluegrass Chapter
2805 Heather Ln.
La Grange, KY 40031   Ph:(502)241-5529

Periodic.

471 ● The Buick: A Complete History
Auto Quarterly, Inc.
420 N. Park Rd., Ste. 200
Wyomissing, PA 19610   Ph:(215)375-8444

Price: $39.95.

472 ● Buick Club of America—Membership Roster
Buick Club of America
PO Box 898   Ph:(714)993-5645
Garden Grove, CA 92642-0898   Fax:(714)993-5645

Biennial.

473 ● Buick Club of America, Nebraska Chapter—Newsletter
Buick Club of America, Nebraska Chapter
9346 Monroe St.
Omaha, NE 68127   Ph:(402)339-0086

Quarterly.

474 ● Buick Club of America, North Cascade Chapter—Newsletter [Washington state]
Buick Club of America, North Cascade Chapter
13003 Third Ave., SE
Everett, WA 98204   Ph:(206)337-1264
Monthly.

475 ● Buick Club of America, San Gabriel Valley Chapter—Newsletter [California]
Buick Club of America, San Gabriel Valley Chapter—Newsletter
P.O. Box 2355
Pasadena, CA 91102
Monthly.

476 ● Buick Club of America, Southwestern Ohio Chapter—Newsletter
Buick Club of America, Southwestern Ohio Chapter
10155 Andalusia Close
Cincinnati, OH 45241   Ph:(513)733-5313
Monthly.

477 ● Cream City Chronicle [Wisconsin]
Buick Club of America, Cream City Chapter
P.O. Box 27372
West Allis, WI 53227   Ph:(414)321-8377
Bimonthly.

478 ● Dyna's Chatter
Buick Club of America, Appalachian Chapter
233-1/2 W. Brady St.
Butler, PA 16001   Ph:(412)282-8109
Newsletter. Periodic.

479 ● Dyna's Chatter
Buick Club of America, Appalachian Chapter
233-1/2 W. Brady St.
Butler, PA 16001   Ph:(412)282-8109
Newsletter. Periodic.

480 ● Fireball Flash
Buick Club of America, Chicagoland Chapter
271 Terrace Pl.
Buffalo Grove, IL 60089   Ph:(708)537-7055
Monthly.

481 ● Fireball News
Buick Club of America, San Gabriel Valley Chapter
PO Box 2355
Pasadena, CA 91102
Monthly.

482 ● Jersey Shore Chapter News [New Jersey]
Buick Club of America, Jersey Shore Chapter
2425 Cedar St.
Manasquan, NJ 08736   Ph:(201)528-9409
Newsletter. Monthly.

483 ● The Limited
Buick Club of America, Puget Sound Chapter
2725 SW 347th St.
Federal Way, WA 98023   Ph:(206)874-4562
Monthly.

484 ● Pike Press
Buick Club of America, National Pike Chapter
71 Murtland Ave.
Washington, PA 15301   Ph:(412)222-0700
Periodic.

485 ● The Reflector
Buick Club of America, Glass City Chapter
109 Ashwood Ct.
Perrysburg, OH 43551   Ph:(419)874-2393
Monthly.

486 ● Running Board
Buick Club of America, Orange County Chapter
P.O. Box 5171
Fullerton, CA 92635   Ph:(213)925-3294
Monthly.

ASSOCIATIONS

487 ● Buick Club of America
P.O. Box 898
Garden Grove, CA 92642
Dale Osstyn, Pres.   Ph:(714)993-5645

Founded: 1966. **Membership:** 9400. Purposes are: development, publication, and interchange of technical, historical, and other information among members who are interested in Buick automobiles; to promote fellowship among members; to encourage the maintenance, restoration, and preservation of all models of produced by the Buick Motor Division of General Motors. Awards prizes at local, regional, and national car shows; presents Senior Award for Buick achieving the highest standards. Holds competitions; compiles statistics; maintains small library. **Convention/Meeting:** Annual display conference (with exhibits) - 1992 July, Olathe, KS.

488 ● Buick Club of America, Appalachian Chapter [South central Pennsylvania]
233-1/2 W. Brady St.
Butler, PA 16001
Keith R. Bleakney, Dir.   Ph:(412)282-8109

Founded: 1974. **Membership:** 14. Individuals in south central Pennsylvania interested in the preservation and restoration of Buick automobiles. **Convention/Meeting:** Annual show.

489 ● Buick Club of America, Bluegrass Chapter [Kentucky]
2805 Heather Ln.
La Grange, KY 40031
Lawrence Ford, Pres.   Ph:(502)241-5529

Founded: 1985. **Membership:** 18. Individuals interested in the history and preservation of the Buick automobile. Seeks to further the image of the Buick marque through social events, meets, tours, and public exhibitions.

490 ● Buick Club of America, Chicagoland Chapter [Illinois]
PO Box 863
Arlington Heights, IL 60006
Steven Kelly, Contact   Ph:(708)464-5933

Founded: 1967. **Membership:** 85. Enthusiasts of Buick automobiles in the Chicago, IL metropolitan area. Serves as a clearinghouse for the exchange of information on finding Buick parts and Buick maintenance. **Convention/Meeting:** Monthly.

491 ● Buick Club of America, Cream City Chapter [Wisconsin]
P.O. Box 27372
West Allis, WI 53227
Jerry Whelan, Dir.   Ph:(414)321-8377

Founded: 1982. **Membership:** 100. Individuals in southeastern Wisconsin interested in the maintenance, operation, and restoration of Buick automobiles. Participates in car shows and tours. **Convention/Meeting:** Monthly.

492 ● Buick Club of America, Glass City Chapter [Ohio]
138 E. 5th St.
Perrysburg, OH 43551
David S. Rex, Sec.-Treas.   Ph:(419)874-8903

Founded: 1972. **Membership:** 25. Individuals in northwestern Ohio and southern Michigan interested in the maintenance, operation, and restoration of Buick automobiles. Sponsors car shows.

493 ● Buick Club of America, Jersey Shore Chapter [New Jersey]
2425 Cedar St.
Manasquan, NJ 08736
Ronald H. Foerster, Dir.   Ph:(201)528-9409

Founded: 1979. **Membership:** 35. Antique automobile collectors. Promotes restoration, preservation, and enjoyment of Buick automobiles. **Convention/Meeting:** Annual All Buick Car Show - always September, Sea Girt, NJ. Also holds monthly meeting - always last Wednesday of the month.

494 ● Buick Club of America, Kansas Chapter
216 S. Chestnut
Olathe, KS 66061
Richard Sandberg, Exec. Officer   Ph:(913)764-0423

495 ● Buick Club of America, Lone Star Chapter [Texas]
14021 Stoneshire
Houston, TX 77060
Cecil Miles, Exec. Officer   Ph:(713)448-8196

496 ● Buick Club of America, National Pike Chapter [Pennsylvania]
71 Murtland Ave.
Washington, PA 15301
Joe Manfredi, Exec. Officer   Ph:(412)222-0700

Founded: 1986. **Membership:** 30. Automobile salespeople and dealers and other interested persons organized to restore and preserve the Buick marque.

497 ● Buick Club of America, Nebraska Chapter
9346 Monroe St.
Omaha, NE 68127
Larry D. Robb, Director   Ph:(402)339-0086

Founded: 1975. **Membership:** 20. Individuals in Nebraska and western Iowa interested in cars built by the Buick Division of General Motors. **Convention/Meeting:** Monthly.

498 ● Buick Club of America, North Texas Chapter
1614 Woodoak Dr.
Richardson, TX 75081
David G. Farmer, Exec. Officer   Ph:(214)699-9418

499 ● Buick Club of America, Puget Sound Chapter [Washington state]
2725 SW 347th St.
Federal Way, WA 98023
Tony Weiss, Exec. Officer   Ph:(206)874-4562

Founded: 1974. **Membership:** 72. Buick owners in the Puget Sound, WA area. Promotes the preservation and restoration of

Buick automobiles. **Convention/Meeting:** Monthly - always the second Monday of the month.

500 ● Buick Club of America, San Gabriel Valley Chapter [California]
P.O. Box 2355
Pasadena, CA 91102
Lou Baiocco, Dir.

Founded: 1966. **Membership:** 70. Owners of Buick automobiles. Promotes the preservation and display of Buick cars. **Convention/Meeting:** Monthly.

501 ● Buick Club of America, Southwestern Ohio Chapter
8529 Clough Pk.
Cincinnati, OH 45244
Richard Kranpitz, Dir.   Ph:(513)474-0657

Founded: 1970. **Membership:** 35. Encourages the maintenance, restoration, and preservation of all models of Buick cars. Sponsors antique car show.

BUICK SKYHAWK (1987-89)

Introduced as part of J car line, along with its corporate twins the Chevrolet Cavalier and Pontiac Sunbird. Produced until 1989 at General Motors plants in Leeds, Missouri and Janesville, Wisconsin. Ranked in 1989 as best among compact vehicles in a crash test rating index in *The Car Book*.

MAJOR FEATURES

● Buick Skyhawk had as 1989 standard equipment: 5-speed manual transmission, power rack-and-pinion steering, front disc/rear drum power brakes, 4-wheel independent suspension, and AM/FM stereo.

● Buick Skyhawk Wagon added as 1989 standard equipment: luggage rack and split folding rear seat.

PRICE HISTORY

The following new car prices reflect the approximate retail cost of the base model: **1987** - $8,522; **1988** - $8,884; **1989** - $9,285.

DIMENSIONS

Body Style	Years Avail	Wheel Base (in)	Lgth (in)	Ht (in)	Avg Wt (lbs)	Fuel Cap (gal)	Front Hdrm (in)	Front Legrm (in)
2d cpe	88-89	101.2	179.3	54	2,420	13.6	37.4	42.2
4d sdn	87-89	101.2	181.7	54	2,469	13.6	38.2	42.2
5d wgn	87-89	101.2	181.7	54.4	2,551	13.6	38.3	42.2

ENGINES

Type	Displace-ment (L)	Fuel Dly	HP @rpm	Torque @rpm (ft/lbs)	MPG Cty/Hwy	Years Avail
I-4	2.0	FI	96@4800	118@3600	27/38	87-88
I-4	2.0	FI	90@5600	108@3200	26/36	87-89
I-4T	2.0	FI	165@5600	175@4000	21/31	87-87

KEY: I=in-line engine; V=V engine; F=flat engine; FI=fuel injection; bbl=barrel carburetor; T=turbo; D=diesel; HP=horsepower; MPG=estimated average miles per gallon.

EVALUATIONS, TESTS, AND RANKINGS

1988: "reasonable road manners." **Source:** "Buick Skyhawk," *Car and Driver—Buyers Guide 1988*, 1988, p. 64.

RECALLS

1989: (13,095 passenger vehicles with 2.0L or 2.8L engines; includes several General Motors models): Fuel tank leak could occur due to small creases on tank underside cracking during pressure cycling which occurs during normal operation. In presence of ignition source, this condition could result in fire. **Corrective action:** Replace fuel tank. *(NHTSA Campaign No. 88V189000.)*

1987: (131,476 cars with 2.0 L engines; includes Buick, Pontiac, and Oldsmobile models): Fuel feed and/or return hose assemblies could crack, causing underhood fire. **Corrective action:** Replace fuel feed/return hoses and assemblies. *(NHTSA Campaign No. 87V184000.)*

SAFETY AND REPAIRS

1987: "Service Tips," *Popular Mechanics*, April 1988, p. 31. **Note:** Blistering paint on 1987 Skyhawk due to excessive primer.

REPAIR MANUALS

502 ● Chilton's Chevrolet Cavalier, Buick Skyhawk, Olds Firenza, Cadillac Cimarron, Pontiac 6000, 1982-88
Chilton Co.
Chilton Way
Radnor, PA 19089   Ph:(215)964-4000

Published 1988. **Price:** $15.95.

503 ● Get Your Buick Fixed Right
Consumer Reports Books
51 E. 42nd St., Ste. 800
New York, NY 10017   Ph:(212)682-9280

Published 1989. **Editor(s):** Mort Schultz. **Price:** $8.95.

504 ● GMC J Cars: Buick Skyhawk, Cadillac Cimarron, Chevrolet Cavalier, Oldsmobile Firenza, Pontiac J-2000, Sunbird Shop Manual, 1982-87
Clymer Publications
P.O. Box 1209
Overland Park, KS 66212   Ph:(913)541-6694

Published 1987. **Price:** $14.95.

505 ● Haynes General Motors J-Cars Owners Workshop Manual, No. 766: 1982-1989
Haynes Publishing, Inc.
861 Lawrence Dr.
Newbury Park, CA 91320   Ph:(818)889-5400

Published 1989. **Price:** $15.95.

OTHER INFORMATION SOURCES

506 ● Bluegrass Buick News
Buick Club of America, Bluegrass Chapter
2805 Heather Ln.
La Grange, KY 40031   Ph:(502)241-5529

Periodic.

507 ● The Buick: A Complete History
Auto Quarterly, Inc.
420 N. Park Rd., Ste. 200
Wyomissing, PA 19610   Ph:(215)375-8444

Price: $39.95.

508 ● Buick Club of America—Membership Roster
Buick Club of America
PO Box 898   Ph:(714)993-5645
Garden Grove, CA 92642-0898   Fax:(714)993-5645

Biennial.

509 ● Buick Club of America, Nebraska Chapter— Newsletter
Buick Club of America, Nebraska Chapter
9346 Monroe St.
Omaha, NE 68127   Ph:(402)339-0086

Quarterly.

510 ● Buick Club of America, North Cascade Chapter— Newsletter [Washington state]
Buick Club of America, North Cascade Chapter
13003 Third Ave., SE
Everett, WA 98204   Ph:(206)337-1264

Monthly.

511 ● Buick Club of America, San Gabriel Valley Chapter— Newsletter [California]
Buick Club of America, San Gabriel Valley Chapter—
Newsletter
P.O. Box 2355
Pasadena, CA 91102

Monthly.

512 ● Buick Club of America, Southwestern Ohio Chapter— Newsletter
Buick Club of America, Southwestern Ohio Chapter
10155 Andalusia Close
Cincinnati, OH 45241   Ph:(513)733-5313

Monthly.

513 ● Cream City Chronicle [Wisconsin]
Buick Club of America, Cream City Chapter
P.O. Box 27372
West Allis, WI 53227   Ph:(414)321-8377

Bimonthly.

514 ● Dyna's Chatter
Buick Club of America, Appalachian Chapter
233-1/2 W. Brady St.
Butler, PA 16001   Ph:(412)282-8109

Newsletter. Periodic.

515 ● Dyna's Chatter
Buick Club of America, Appalachian Chapter
233-1/2 W. Brady St.
Butler, PA 16001   Ph:(412)282-8109

Newsletter. Periodic.

516 ● Fireball Flash
Buick Club of America, Chicagoland Chapter
271 Terrace Pl.
Buffalo Grove, IL 60089   Ph:(708)537-7055

Monthly.

517 ● Fireball News
Buick Club of America, San Gabriel Valley Chapter
PO Box 2355
Pasadena, CA 91102

Monthly.

518 ● Jersey Shore Chapter News [New Jersey]
Buick Club of America, Jersey Shore Chapter
2425 Cedar St.
Manasquan, NJ 08736   Ph:(201)528-9409

Newsletter. Monthly.

519 ● The Limited
Buick Club of America, Puget Sound Chapter
2725 SW 347th St.
Federal Way, WA 98023   Ph:(206)874-4562

Monthly.

520 ● Pike Press
Buick Club of America, National Pike Chapter
71 Murtland Ave.
Washington, PA 15301   Ph:(412)222-0700

Periodic.

521 ● The Reflector
Buick Club of America, Glass City Chapter
109 Ashwood Ct.
Perrysburg, OH 43551   Ph:(419)874-2393

Monthly.

522 ● Running Board
Buick Club of America, Orange County Chapter
P.O. Box 5171
Fullerton, CA 92635   Ph:(213)925-3294

Monthly.

ASSOCIATIONS

523 ● Buick Club of America
P.O. Box 898
Garden Grove, CA 92642
Dale Osstyn, Pres.   Ph:(714)993-5645

Founded: 1966. **Membership:** 9400. Purposes are: development, publication, and interchange of technical, historical, and other information among members who are interested in Buick automobiles; to promote fellowship among members; to encourage the maintenance, restoration, and preservation of all models of produced by the Buick Motor Division of General Motors. Awards prizes at local, regional, and national car shows; presents Senior Award for Buick achieving the highest standards. Holds competitions; compiles statistics; maintains small library. **Convention/Meeting:** Annual display conference (with exhibits) - 1992 July, Olathe, KS.

524 ● Buick Club of America, Appalachian Chapter [South central Pennsylvania]
233-1/2 W. Brady St.
Butler, PA 16001
Keith R. Bleakney, Dir.   Ph:(412)282-8109

Founded: 1974. **Membership:** 14. Individuals in south central Pennsylvania interested in the preservation and restoration of Buick automobiles. **Convention/Meeting:** Annual show.

525 ● Buick Club of America, Bluegrass Chapter [Kentucky]
2805 Heather Ln.
La Grange, KY 40031
Lawrence Ford, Pres.   Ph:(502)241-5529

Founded: 1985. **Membership:** 18. Individuals interested in the history and preservation of the Buick automobile. Seeks to further the image of the Buick marque through social events, meets, tours, and public exhibitions.

526 ● Buick Club of America, Chicagoland Chapter [Illinois]
PO Box 863
Arlington Heights, IL 60006
Steven Kelly, Contact   Ph:(708)464-5933

Founded: 1967. **Membership:** 85. Enthusiasts of Buick automobiles in the Chicago, IL metropolitan area. Serves as a clearinghouse for the exchange of information on finding Buick parts and Buick maintenance. **Convention/Meeting:** Monthly.

527 ● Buick Club of America, Cream City Chapter [Wisconsin]
P.O. Box 27372
West Allis, WI 53227
Jerry Whelan, Dir.   Ph:(414)321-8377

Founded: 1982. **Membership:** 100. Individuals in southeastern Wisconsin interested in the maintenance, operation, and restoration of Buick automobiles. Participates in car shows and tours. **Convention/Meeting:** Monthly.

528 ● Buick Club of America, Glass City Chapter [Ohio]
138 E. 5th St.
Perrysburg, OH 43551
David S. Rex, Sec.-Treas.   Ph:(419)874-8903

Founded: 1972. **Membership:** 25. Individuals in northwestern Ohio and southern Michigan interested in the maintenance, operation, and restoration of Buick automobiles. Sponsors car shows.

529 ● Buick Club of America, Jersey Shore Chapter [New Jersey]
2425 Cedar St.
Manasquan, NJ 08736
Ronald H. Foerster, Dir.   Ph:(201)528-9409

Founded: 1979. **Membership:** 35. Antique automobile collectors. Promotes restoration, preservation, and enjoyment of Buick automobiles. **Convention/Meeting:** Annual All Buick Car Show - always September, Sea Girt, NJ. Also holds monthly meeting - always last Wednesday of the month.

530 ● Buick Club of America, Kansas Chapter
216 S. Chestnut
Olathe, KS 66061
Richard Sandberg, Exec. Officer   Ph:(913)764-0423

531 ● Buick Club of America, Lone Star Chapter [Texas]
14021 Stoneshire
Houston, TX 77060
Cecil Miles, Exec. Officer   Ph:(713)448-8196

532 ● Buick Club of America, National Pike Chapter [Pennsylvania]
71 Murtland Ave.
Washington, PA 15301
Joe Manfredi, Exec. Officer   Ph:(412)222-0700

Founded: 1986. **Membership:** 30. Automobile salespeople and dealers and other interested persons organized to restore and preserve the Buick marque.

533 ● Buick Club of America, Nebraska Chapter
9346 Monroe St.
Omaha, NE 68127
Larry D. Robb, Director   Ph:(402)339-0086

Founded: 1975. **Membership:** 20. Individuals in Nebraska and western Iowa interested in cars built by the Buick Division of General Motors. **Convention/Meeting:** Monthly.

534 ● Buick Club of America, North Texas Chapter
1614 Woodoak Dr.
Richardson, TX 75081
David G. Farmer, Exec. Officer   Ph:(214)699-9418

535 ● Buick Club of America, Puget Sound Chapter [Washington state]
2725 SW 347th St.
Federal Way, WA 98023
Tony Weiss, Exec. Officer   Ph:(206)874-4562

Founded: 1974. **Membership:** 72. Buick owners in the Puget Sound, WA area. Promotes the preservation and restoration of Buick automobiles. **Convention/Meeting:** Monthly - always the second Monday of the month.

536 ● Buick Club of America, San Gabriel Valley Chapter [California]
P.O. Box 2355
Pasadena, CA 91102
Lou Baiocco, Dir.

Founded: 1966. **Membership:** 70. Owners of Buick automobiles. Promotes the preservation and display of Buick cars. **Convention/Meeting:** Monthly.

537 ● Buick Club of America, Southwestern Ohio Chapter
8529 Clough Pk.
Cincinnati, OH 45244
Richard Kranpitz, Dir.   Ph:(513)474-0657

Founded: 1970. **Membership:** 35. Encourages the maintenance, restoration, and preservation of all models of Buick cars. Sponsors antique car show.

BUICK SKYLARK (1987-92)

Introduced as part of the N car line, along with the Oldsmobile Cutlass Supreme, and Pontiac Grand Am; the Oldsmobile Achieva was added to this line in 1992. Named in 1989 as a good choice among compact vehicles by *The Car Book*. Produced at General Motors plant in Lansing, Michigan.

1992 Buick Skylark Gran Sport

MAJOR FEATURES

● Buick Skylark has as 1992 standard equipment: 3-speed automatic transmission, power-assisted rack-and-pinion steering, front disc/rear drum power brakes with anti-lock system, and front-wheel drive.

● Buick Skylark Gran Sport adds as 1992 standard equipment: adjustable ride control suspension, leather/cloth bucket seats, and AM/FM stereo with cassette.

● Buick Skylark Custom and Luxury Edition added as 1991 standard equipment: upgraded interior and other exterior body stylings.

PRICE HISTORY

The following new car prices reflect the approximate retail cost of the base model: **1987** - $9,915; **1988** - $10,399; **1989** - $11,115; **1990** - $10,465; **1991** - $10,725; **1992** - $13,560.

DIMENSIONS

Body Style	Years Avail	Wheel Base (in)	Lgth (in)	Ht (in)	Avg Wt (lbs)	Fuel Cap (gal)	Front Hdrm (in)	Front Legrm (in)
2d cpe	88-91	103.4	180.0	52.1	2,593	13.6	37.7	42.9
2d cpe	92-92	103.4	189.2	52.2	2,782	15.2	37.8	43.3
4d sdn	87-91	103.4	180.0	52.1	2,654	13.6	37.7	42.9
4d sdn	92-92	103.4	189.2	52.2	2,846	15.2	37.8	43.3

ENGINES

Type	Displace-ment (L)	Fuel Dly	HP @rpm	Torque @rpm (ft/lbs)	MPG Cty/Hwy	Years Avail
I-4	2.5	FI	92@4400	134@2800	22/32	87-87
I-4	2.5	FI	98@4800	135@3200	23/33	88-88
I-4	2.3	FI	150@5200	160@4000	23/32	88-89
I-4	2.5	FI	110@5200	135@3200	22/31	89-91
I-4	2.3	FI	160@6200	155@5200	23/33	90-91
I-4	2.3	FI	120@5200	140@3200	na	92-92
V-6	3.0	FI	125@4900	150@2400	19/27	87-88
V-6	3.3	FI	160@5200	185@2000	19/29	89-92

KEY: I=in-line engine; V=V engine; F=flat engine; FI=fuel injection; bbl=barrel carburetor; T=turbo; D=diesel; HP=horsepower; MPG=estimated average miles per gallon.

EVALUATIONS, TESTS, AND RANKINGS

1992: "the most expressive version of the Skylark ... adjustable ride control provides a greater range of suspension response ... good seats and readable analog instruments." **Source:** "Buick Skylark GS," *Motor Trend*, October 1991, p. 83.

1991: "Of GM's three new compact cars, the Skylark has the softest ride ... entry-level to the big league of boulevard cruisers ... swoopy shape of new instrument panel." **Source:** "Buick Skylark," *Car and Driver*, October 1991, p. 55.

1990: "assembly feels good." **Source:** "Buick Skylark," *Car and Driver—Buyers Guide 1990*, 1989, p. 90.

1989: "Rear end occasionally gets unsettled during quick transient maneuvers ... interior looks like something straight out of the last decade ... peculiar mix of staid traditional styling and fully modern performance." **Source:** "Buick Skylark Custom: Buick puts more punch in its bantamweights," *Car and Driver*, April 1989, pp. 138-139.

RECALLS

1990: (3,202 cars; includes Buick and Oldsmobile models): Improperly torqued connection of front fuel feed and return hoses may loosen causing fuel leakage. **Corrective action:** Properly torque the front fuel feed and return hoses at the body rail lines to prevent fuel leakage. *(NHTSA Campaign No. 90V119000.)*

1988-89: (61,765 cars with Quad-4 engines; includes Buick, Pontiac, and Oldsmobile models): Cracking or separation of front fuel hose at coupling could allow fuel leakage and result in a fire. **Corrective action:** Replace front fuel feed hose assembly. *(NHTSA Campaign No. 90V042000.)*

1988: (101 cars with electronic digital instrument cluster): Loss of tail and side marker lamps. **Corrective action:** Replace headlight switch panel. *(NHTSA Campaign No. 87V169000.)*

1987: (22,300 passenger vehicles; includes Buick Skylark, Oldsmobile Calais, and Pontiac Grand Am): Fuel feed or fuel return hose at engine may rub against shift lever on 5 speed transaxle. In time a hole could be rubbed through hose and fuel could leak into engine compartment, possibly resulting in underhood fire. **Corrective action:** Replace fuel feed and return hose/pipe assemblies. *(NHTSA Campaign No. 88V032000.)*

REPAIR MANUALS

538 ● Get Your Buick Fixed Right
Consumer Reports Books
51 E. 42nd St., Ste. 800
New York, NY 10017   Ph:(212)682-9280

Published 1989. **Editor(s):** Mort Schultz. **Price:** $8.95.

OTHER INFORMATION SOURCES

539 ● Bluegrass Buick News
Buick Club of America, Bluegrass Chapter
2805 Heather Ln.
La Grange, KY 40031   Ph:(502)241-5529

Periodic.

540 ● The Buick: A Complete History
Auto Quarterly, Inc.
420 N. Park Rd., Ste. 200
Wyomissing, PA 19610   Ph:(215)375-8444

Price: $39.95.

541 ● Buick Club of America—Membership Roster
Buick Club of America
PO Box 898   Ph:(714)993-5645
Garden Grove, CA 92642-0898   Fax:(714)993-5645

Biennial.

542 ● Buick Club of America, Nebraska Chapter—Newsletter
Buick Club of America, Nebraska Chapter
9346 Monroe St.
Omaha, NE 68127   Ph:(402)339-0086

Quarterly.

543 ● Buick Club of America, North Cascade Chapter—Newsletter [Washington state]
Buick Club of America, North Cascade Chapter
13003 Third Ave., SE
Everett, WA 98204   Ph:(206)337-1264

Monthly.

544 ● Buick Club of America, San Gabriel Valley Chapter—Newsletter [California]
Buick Club of America, San Gabriel Valley Chapter—Newsletter
P.O. Box 2355
Pasadena, CA 91102

Monthly.

545 ● Buick Club of America, Southwestern Ohio Chapter—Newsletter
Buick Club of America, Southwestern Ohio Chapter
10155 Andalusia Close
Cincinnati, OH 45241   Ph:(513)733-5313

Monthly.

546 ● Buick GS Club of America, Indiana Chapter—Newsletter
Buick GS Club of America, Indiana Chapter
1029 Charlotte Ave.
Ft. Wayne, IN 46805   Ph:(219)484-7019

Newsletter. Bimonthly.

547 ● Cream City Chronicle [Wisconsin]
Buick Club of America, Cream City Chapter
P.O. Box 27372
West Allis, WI 53227   Ph:(414)321-8377

Bimonthly.

548 ● Dyna's Chatter
Buick Club of America, Appalachian Chapter
233-1/2 W. Brady St.
Butler, PA 16001   Ph:(412)282-8109

Newsletter. Periodic.

549 ● Dyna's Chatter
Buick Club of America, Appalachian Chapter
233-1/2 W. Brady St.
Butler, PA 16001   Ph:(412)282-8109

Newsletter. Periodic.

550 ● Fireball Flash
Buick Club of America, Chicagoland Chapter
271 Terrace Pl.
Buffalo Grove, IL 60089   Ph:(708)537-7055

Monthly.

551 ● Fireball News
Buick Club of America, San Gabriel Valley Chapter
PO Box 2355
Pasadena, CA 91102

Monthly.

552 ● GS Directory
Buick GS Club of America
1213 Gornto Rd.
Valdosta, GA 31601   Ph:(912)244-0577

About 3,800 owners of Buick Wildcats, Rivieras, Grand Nationals, Gran Sports, and other high performance Buick automobiles. Annual. **Editor(s):** Richard Lasseter, President. **Price:** Available to members only.

553 ● Jersey Shore Chapter News [New Jersey]
Buick Club of America, Jersey Shore Chapter
2425 Cedar St.
Manasquan, NJ 08736   Ph:(201)528-9409

Newsletter. Monthly.

554 ● The Limited
Buick Club of America, Puget Sound Chapter
2725 SW 347th St.
Federal Way, WA 98023   Ph:(206)874-4562

Monthly.

555 ● Pike Press
Buick Club of America, National Pike Chapter
71 Murtland Ave.
Washington, PA 15301   Ph:(412)222-0700

Periodic.

556 ● The Reflector
Buick Club of America, Glass City Chapter
109 Ashwood Ct.
Perrysburg, OH 43551   Ph:(419)874-2393

Monthly.

557 ● Running Board
Buick Club of America, Orange County Chapter
P.O. Box 5171
Fullerton, CA 92635   Ph:(213)925-3294

Monthly.

ASSOCIATIONS

558 ● Buick Club of America
P.O. Box 898
Garden Grove, CA 92642
Dale Osstyn, Pres.   Ph:(714)993-5645

Founded: 1966. **Membership:** 9400. Purposes are: development, publication, and interchange of technical, historical, and other information among members who are interested in Buick automobiles; to promote fellowship among members; to encourage the maintenance, restoration, and preservation of all models of produced by the Buick Motor Division of General Motors. Awards prizes at local, regional, and national car shows; presents Senior Award for Buick achieving the highest standards. Holds competitions; compiles statistics; maintains small library. **Convention/Meeting:** Annual display conference (with exhibits) - 1992 July, Olathe, KS.

559 ● Buick Club of America, Appalachian Chapter [South central Pennsylvania]
233-1/2 W. Brady St.
Butler, PA 16001
Keith R. Bleakney, Dir.   Ph:(412)282-8109

Founded: 1974. **Membership:** 14. Individuals in south central Pennsylvania interested in the preservation and restoration of Buick automobiles. **Convention/Meeting:** Annual show.

560 ● Buick Club of America, Bluegrass Chapter [Kentucky]
2805 Heather Ln.
La Grange, KY 40031
Lawrence Ford, Pres.   Ph:(502)241-5529

Founded: 1985. **Membership:** 18. Individuals interested in the history and preservation of the Buick automobile. Seeks to further the image of the Buick marque through social events, meets, tours, and public exhibitions.

561 ● Buick Club of America, Chicagoland Chapter [Illinois]
PO Box 863
Arlington Heights, IL 60006
Steven Kelly, Contact   Ph:(708)464-5933

Founded: 1967. **Membership:** 85. Enthusiasts of Buick automobiles in the Chicago, IL metropolitan area. Serves as a clearinghouse for the exchange of information on finding Buick parts and Buick maintenance. **Convention/Meeting:** Monthly.

562 ● Buick Club of America, Cream City Chapter [Wisconsin]
P.O. Box 27372
West Allis, WI 53227
Jerry Whelan, Dir.   Ph:(414)321-8377

Founded: 1982. **Membership:** 100. Individuals in southeastern Wisconsin interested in the maintenance, operation, and restoration of Buick automobiles. Participates in car shows and tours. **Convention/Meeting:** Monthly.

563 ● Buick Club of America, Glass City Chapter [Ohio]
138 E. 5th St.
Perrysburg, OH 43551
David S. Rex, Sec.-Treas.   Ph:(419)874-8903

Founded: 1972. **Membership:** 25. Individuals in northwestern Ohio and southern Michigan interested in the maintenance, operation, and restoration of Buick automobiles. Sponsors car shows.

564 ● Buick Club of America, Jersey Shore Chapter [New Jersey]
2425 Cedar St.
Manasquan, NJ 08736
Ronald H. Foerster, Dir.   Ph:(201)528-9409

Founded: 1979. **Membership:** 35. Antique automobile collectors. Promotes restoration, preservation, and enjoyment of Buick automobiles. **Convention/Meeting:** Annual All Buick Car Show - always September, Sea Girt, NJ. Also holds monthly meeting - always last Wednesday of the month.

565 ● Buick Club of America, Kansas Chapter
216 S. Chestnut
Olathe, KS 66061
Richard Sandberg, Exec. Officer   Ph:(913)764-0423

566 ● Buick Club of America, Lone Star Chapter [Texas]
14021 Stoneshire
Houston, TX 77060
Cecil Miles, Exec. Officer   Ph:(713)448-8196

567 ● Buick Club of America, National Pike Chapter [Pennsylvania]
71 Murtland Ave.
Washington, PA 15301
Joe Manfredi, Exec. Officer   Ph:(412)222-0700

Founded: 1986. **Membership:** 30. Automobile salespeople and dealers and other interested persons organized to restore and preserve the Buick marque.

568 ● Buick Club of America, Nebraska Chapter
9346 Monroe St.
Omaha, NE 68127
Larry D. Robb, Director   Ph:(402)339-0086

Founded: 1975. **Membership:** 20. Individuals in Nebraska and western Iowa interested in cars built by the Buick Division of General Motors. **Convention/Meeting:** Monthly.

569 ● Buick Club of America, North Texas Chapter
1614 Woodoak Dr.
Richardson, TX 75081
David G. Farmer, Exec. Officer   Ph:(214)699-9418

**570 ● Buick Club of America, Puget Sound Chapter
[Washington state]**
2725 SW 347th St.
Federal Way, WA 98023
Tony Weiss, Exec. Officer   Ph:(206)874-4562

Founded: 1974. **Membership:** 72. Buick owners in the Puget Sound, WA area. Promotes the preservation and restoration of Buick automobiles. **Convention/Meeting:** Monthly - always the second Monday of the month.

**571 ● Buick Club of America, San Gabriel Valley Chapter
[California]**
P.O. Box 2355
Pasadena, CA 91102
Lou Baiocco, Dir.

Founded: 1966. **Membership:** 70. Owners of Buick automobiles. Promotes the preservation and display of Buick cars. **Convention/Meeting:** Monthly.

572 ● Buick Club of America, Southwestern Ohio Chapter
8529 Clough Pk.
Cincinnati, OH 45244
Richard Kranpitz, Dir.   Ph:(513)474-0657

Founded: 1970. **Membership:** 35. Encourages the maintenance, restoration, and preservation of all models of Buick cars. Sponsors antique car show.

BUICK SOMERSET (1987)

Introduced as part of N car line, along with Buick Skylark, Oldsmobile Cutlass Calais, and Pontiac Grand Am. Replaced the X car line and was aimed at the young, urban professional market. Produced until 1987 at General Motors plant in Lansing, Michigan.

MAJOR FEATURES

● Buick Somerset had as 1987 standard equipment: 5-speed manual transmission, front independent/rear beam suspension, rack-and-pinion steering, front disc/rear drum brakes, air conditioning, and AM/FM stereo.

PRICE HISTORY

The following new car prices reflect the approximate retail cost of the base model: **1987 - $9,957.**

DIMENSIONS

Body Style	Years Avail	Wheel Base (in)	Lgth (in)	Ht (in)	Avg Wt (lbs)	Fuel Cap (gal)	Front Hdrm (in)	Front Legrm (in)
2d cpe	87-87	103.4	180	52.1	2,471	13.6	37.7	42.9

ENGINES

Type	Displacement (L)	Fuel Dly	HP @rpm	Torque @rpm (ft/lbs)	MPG Cty/Hwy	Years Avail
I-4	2.5	FI	92@4400	134@2800	22/32	87-87
V-6	3.0	FI	125@4900	150@2400	19/27	87-87

KEY: I=in-line engine; V=V engine; F=flat engine; FI=fuel injection; bbl=barrel carburetor; T=turbo; D=diesel; HP=horsepower; MPG=estimated average miles per gallon.

EVALUATIONS, TESTS, AND RANKINGS

1987: "redesigned center consoles." **Source:** "Pontiac Grand Am, Oldsmobile Calais, Buick Somerset," *Road & Track—Buyers Guide 1987*, 1986, p. 122.

RECALLS

None to date.

REPAIR MANUALS

573 ● Get Your Buick Fixed Right
Consumer Reports Books
51 E. 42nd St., Ste. 800
New York, NY 10017   Ph:(212)682-9280

Published 1989. **Editor(s):** Mort Schultz. **Price:** $8.95.

OTHER INFORMATION SOURCES

574 ● Bluegrass Buick News
Buick Club of America, Bluegrass Chapter
2805 Heather Ln.
La Grange, KY 40031   Ph:(502)241-5529

Periodic.

575 ● The Buick: A Complete History
Auto Quarterly, Inc.
420 N. Park Rd., Ste. 200
Wyomissing, PA 19610   Ph:(215)375-8444

Price: $39.95.

576 ● Buick Club of America—Membership Roster
Buick Club of America
PO Box 898   Ph:(714)993-5645
Garden Grove, CA 92642-0898   Fax:(714)993-5645

Biennial.

577 ● Buick Club of America, Nebraska Chapter—Newsletter
Buick Club of America, Nebraska Chapter
9346 Monroe St.
Omaha, NE 68127   Ph:(402)339-0086

Quarterly.

578 ● Buick Club of America, North Cascade Chapter—Newsletter [Washington state]
Buick Club of America, North Cascade Chapter
13003 Third Ave., SE
Everett, WA 98204   Ph:(206)337-1264

Monthly.

579 ● Buick Club of America, San Gabriel Valley Chapter—Newsletter [California]
Buick Club of America, San Gabriel Valley Chapter—Newsletter
P.O. Box 2355
Pasadena, CA 91102

Monthly.

580 ● Buick Club of America, Southwestern Ohio Chapter—Newsletter
Buick Club of America, Southwestern Ohio Chapter
10155 Andalusia Close
Cincinnati, OH 45241   Ph:(513)733-5313

Monthly.

581 ● Cream City Chronicle [Wisconsin]
Buick Club of America, Cream City Chapter
P.O. Box 27372
West Allis, WI 53227   Ph:(414)321-8377

Bimonthly.

582 ● Dyna's Chatter
Buick Club of America, Appalachian Chapter
233-1/2 W. Brady St.
Butler, PA 16001   Ph:(412)282-8109

Newsletter. Periodic.

583 ● Dyna's Chatter
Buick Club of America, Appalachian Chapter
233-1/2 W. Brady St.
Butler, PA 16001   Ph:(412)282-8109

Newsletter. Periodic.

584 ● Fireball Flash
Buick Club of America, Chicagoland Chapter
271 Terrace Pl.
Buffalo Grove, IL 60089   Ph:(708)537-7055

Monthly.

585 ● Fireball News
Buick Club of America, San Gabriel Valley Chapter
PO Box 2355
Pasadena, CA 91102

Monthly.

586 ● Jersey Shore Chapter News [New Jersey]
Buick Club of America, Jersey Shore Chapter
2425 Cedar St.
Manasquan, NJ 08736   Ph:(201)528-9409

Newsletter. Monthly.

587 ● The Limited
Buick Club of America, Puget Sound Chapter
2725 SW 347th St.
Federal Way, WA 98023   Ph:(206)874-4562

Monthly.

588 ● Pike Press
Buick Club of America, National Pike Chapter
71 Murtland Ave.
Washington, PA 15301   Ph:(412)222-0700

Periodic.

589 ● The Reflector
Buick Club of America, Glass City Chapter
109 Ashwood Ct.
Perrysburg, OH 43551   Ph:(419)874-2393

Monthly.

590 ● Running Board
Buick Club of America, Orange County Chapter
P.O. Box 5171
Fullerton, CA 92635   Ph:(213)925-3294

Monthly.

ASSOCIATIONS

591 ● Buick Club of America
P.O. Box 898
Garden Grove, CA 92642
Dale Osstyn, Pres.   Ph:(714)993-5645

Founded: 1966. **Membership:** 9400. Purposes are: development, publication, and interchange of technical, historical, and other information among members who are interested in Buick automobiles; to promote fellowship among members; to encourage the maintenance, restoration, and preservation of all models of produced by the Buick Motor Division of General Motors. Awards prizes at local, regional, and national car shows; presents Senior Award for Buick achieving the highest standards. Holds competitions; compiles statistics; maintains small library. **Convention/Meeting:** Annual display conference (with exhibits) - 1992 July, Olathe, KS.

592 ● Buick Club of America, Appalachian Chapter [South central Pennsylvania]
233-1/2 W. Brady St.
Butler, PA 16001
Keith R. Bleakney, Dir.   Ph:(412)282-8109

Founded: 1974. **Membership:** 14. Individuals in south central Pennsylvania interested in the preservation and restoration of Buick automobiles. **Convention/Meeting:** Annual show.

593 ● Buick Club of America, Bluegrass Chapter [Kentucky]
2805 Heather Ln.
La Grange, KY 40031
Lawrence Ford, Pres.   Ph:(502)241-5529

Founded: 1985. **Membership:** 18. Individuals interested in the history and preservation of the Buick automobile. Seeks to further the image of the Buick marque through social events, meets, tours, and public exhibitions.

594 ● Buick Club of America, Chicagoland Chapter [Illinois]
PO Box 863
Arlington Heights, IL 60006
Steven Kelly, Contact   Ph:(708)464-5933

Founded: 1967. **Membership:** 85. Enthusiasts of Buick automobiles in the Chicago, IL metropolitan area. Serves as a clearinghouse for the exchange of information on finding Buick parts and Buick maintenance. **Convention/Meeting:** Monthly.

595 ● Buick Club of America, Cream City Chapter [Wisconsin]
P.O. Box 27372
West Allis, WI 53227
Jerry Whelan, Dir.   Ph:(414)321-8377

Founded: 1982. **Membership:** 100. Individuals in southeastern Wisconsin interested in the maintenance, operation, and restoration of Buick automobiles. Participates in car shows and tours. **Convention/Meeting:** Monthly.

596 ● Buick Club of America, Glass City Chapter [Ohio]
138 E. 5th St.
Perrysburg, OH 43551
David S. Rex, Sec.-Treas.   Ph:(419)874-8903

Founded: 1972. **Membership:** 25. Individuals in northwestern Ohio and southern Michigan interested in the maintenance, operation, and restoration of Buick automobiles. Sponsors car shows.

597 ● Buick Club of America, Jersey Shore Chapter [New Jersey]
2425 Cedar St.
Manasquan, NJ 08736
Ronald H. Foerster, Dir.   Ph:(201)528-9409

Founded: 1979. **Membership:** 35. Antique automobile collectors. Promotes restoration, preservation, and enjoyment of Buick automobiles. **Convention/Meeting:** Annual All Buick Car Show - always September, Sea Girt, NJ. Also holds monthly meeting - always last Wednesday of the month.

598 ● Buick Club of America, Kansas Chapter
216 S. Chestnut
Olathe, KS 66061
Richard Sandberg, Exec. Officer   Ph:(913)764-0423

599 ● Buick Club of America, Lone Star Chapter [Texas]
14021 Stoneshire
Houston, TX 77060
Cecil Miles, Exec. Officer   Ph:(713)448-8196

600 ● Buick Club of America, National Pike Chapter [Pennsylvania]
71 Murtland Ave.
Washington, PA 15301
Joe Manfredi, Exec. Officer   Ph:(412)222-0700

Founded: 1986. **Membership:** 30. Automobile salespeople and dealers and other interested persons organized to restore and preserve the Buick marque.

601 ● Buick Club of America, Nebraska Chapter
9346 Monroe St.
Omaha, NE 68127
Larry D. Robb, Director   Ph:(402)339-0086

Founded: 1975. **Membership:** 20. Individuals in Nebraska and western Iowa interested in cars built by the Buick Division of General Motors. **Convention/Meeting:** Monthly.

602 ● Buick Club of America, North Texas Chapter
1614 Woodoak Dr.
Richardson, TX 75081
David G. Farmer, Exec. Officer   Ph:(214)699-9418

603 ● Buick Club of America, Puget Sound Chapter [Washington state]
2725 SW 347th St.
Federal Way, WA 98023
Tony Weiss, Exec. Officer   Ph:(206)874-4562

Founded: 1974. **Membership:** 72. Buick owners in the Puget Sound, WA area. Promotes the preservation and restoration of Buick automobiles. **Convention/Meeting:** Monthly - always the second Monday of the month.

604 ● Buick Club of America, San Gabriel Valley Chapter [California]
P.O. Box 2355
Pasadena, CA 91102
Lou Baiocco, Dir.

Founded: 1966. **Membership:** 70. Owners of Buick

automobiles. Promotes the preservation and display of Buick cars. **Convention/Meeting:** Monthly.

605 ● Buick Club of America, Southwestern Ohio Chapter
8529 Clough Pk.
Cincinnati, OH 45244
Richard Kranpitz, Dir.   Ph:(513)474-0657

Founded: 1970. **Membership:** 35. Encourages the maintenance, restoration, and preservation of all models of Buick cars. Sponsors antique car show.

CADILLAC ALLANTE (1987-92)

Introduced as a late 1987 model. The body styling is designed and handcrafted by Pininfarina in Italy. Produced at the Cadillac Motor Car Division plant in Hamtramck, Michigan.

1991 Cadillac Allante

MAJOR FEATURES

● Cadillac Allante has as 1992 standard equipment: 4-speed automatic transmission, power-assisted rack-and-pinion steering, independent four-wheel suspension system, folding convertible top or removable aluminum hardtop (convertible hardtop only), driver's side airbag, cruise control, 4-wheel disc brakes with anti-lock braking system, Traction-Control system, AM/FM stereo/cassette/compact disc player, power locks and windows, theft-deterrent system, electronic climate control system, rear window defogger, and electrically powered and heated rearview mirrors.

PRICE HISTORY

The following new car prices reflect the approximate retail cost of the base model: **1987** - $54,700; **1988** - $56,533; **1989** - $57,183; **1990** - $53,050; **1991** - $58,470; **1992** - $58,470.

DIMENSIONS

Body Style	Years Avail	Wheel Base (in)	Lgth (in)	Ht (in)	Avg Wt (lbs)	Fuel Cap (gal)	Front Hdrm (in)	Front Legrm (in)
2d conv	87-90	99.4	178.7	52.2	3,466	22	37.2	43.2
2d conv	91-92	99.4	178.7	51.2	3,552	22	37.2	43.2

ENGINES

Type	Displacement (L)	Fuel Dly	HP @rpm	Torque @rpm (ft/lbs)	MPG Cty/Hwy	Years Avail
V-8	4.1	FI	170@4300	230@3200	16/24	87-88
V-8	4.5	FI	200@4400	270@3200	15/22	89-92

KEY: I=in-line engine; V=V engine; F=flat engine; FI=fuel injection; bbl=barrel carburetor; T=turbo; D=diesel; HP=horsepower; MPG=estimated average miles per gallon.

EVALUATIONS, TESTS, AND RANKINGS

1991: "Stunning styling . . . Traction control makes the most of tire grip and allows exceptional low-end acceleration . . . Outstanding space and comfort." **Source:** "Cadillac Allante: Image Builder Needs A Better Image," *Autoweek's Autofile 1991 Edition,* 1990, pp. 16-20.

1990: "Transmission response is simply superb . . . ranks with the world's best in both performance and sophistication . . . manual soft-top is still more fiddly than it needs to be." **Source:** "Cadillac Allante," *Motor Trend,* January 1990, pp. 90-91, 94-95.

1990: "offers surprising performance, distinguished styling, and the creature comforts we've come to expect from Cadillac . . . also brings a slightly stiffer ride, button-happy ergonomics, and a frustrating convertible top . . . [reaches] 60 mph in 7.9 seconds." **Source:** "Cadillac Allante: High-Zoot Cruiser," *Motor Trend,* July 1991, p. 102.

1989: "Braking is excellent . . . steering . . . affords an unusually good level of feel . . . a veritable electronics warehouse." **Source:** "Cadillac Allante," *Road & Track,* 1988, p. 31.

1989: "quick, handles decently and is a delight to be in with the top down. Quality seems to be up to the level you'd expect." **Source:** "Cadillac Allante: Keeping the faith . . . and the faithful," *Road & Track,* May 1989, p. 138.

1989: "dashboard is still dotted with more than two dozen look-alike, feel-alike buttons that control everything from the lights to wipers to stereo . . . The roadster remained glued to the road at all times . . . Its ride is still on the harsh side, and its steering heavy under most conditions." **Source:** "World-class status eludes Allante," *The Detroit News,* April 19, 1989, pp. 1F-2F.

1987: "handsome car, but not striking; there are prettier cars. . .extremely comfortable, but Cadillacs are supposed to be . . . very American, even with its Pinifarina-designed body." **Source:** "Cadillac wins with Allante," *The Detroit News,* August 26, 1987, pp. 1F-2F.

RECALLS

1988: (538 cars): Pressure relief valve in fuel cap may stick during turn to vent function, causing valve to remain open. This could result in fuel spillage during and after collision and possibly a fire. Vehicles would not be in compliance with FMVSS 301. **Corrective action:** Install new fuel cap. *(NHTSA Campaign No. 88V072000.)*

REPAIR MANUALS

606 ● **Cadillac 1967-89 Repair and Tune-up Guide**
Chilton Co.
Chilton Way
Radnor, PA 19089   Ph:(215)964-4000

Published 1989. **Price:** $15.95.

607 ● **Get Your Cadillac Fixed Right**
Consumer Reports Books
51 E. 42nd St., Ste. 800
New York, NY 10017   Ph:(212)682-9280

Published 1990. **Editor(s):** Mort Schultz. **Price:** $8.95.

OTHER INFORMATION SOURCES

608 ● **Cadillac—American Luxury Car**
TAB Books, Inc.
Blue Ridge Summit, PA 17294-0850   Ph:(717)794-2191

Published 1988. **Editor(s):** Robert C. Ackerson. **Price:** $39.95.

609 ● **Cadillac Convertible Courier**
Cadillac Convertible Owners of America (CCOA)
P.O. Box 269
Ossining, NY 10562

Price: Three times per year.

610 ● **Cadillac Convertible Owners of America—Directory**
Cadillac Convertible Owners of America (CCOA)
P.O. Box 269
Ossining, NY 10562

Periodic.

611 ● **Cadillac-Lasalle Club—Directory**
Cadillac-LaSalle Club (CLC)
c/o Mary Lou Evans
3083 Howard Rd.
Petoskey, MI 49770   Ph:(616)347-4611

About 3,600 Cadillac and LaSalle automobile collectors. Biennial, odd years. **Editor(s):** Edith Childs. **Price:** Available to members only.

612 ● **Cadillac—LaSalle Club, Lake St. Clair Region— Membership Directory [Michigan]**
Cadillac—LaSalle Club, Lake St. Clair Region
38156 Southfarm Ct.
Northville, MI 48167   Ph:(313)477-9408

Annual.

613 ● **Cadillac-LaSalle Club, Lower Michigan Region— Newsletter**
Cadillac-LaSalle Club, Lower Michigan Region
229 Devon St.
Parchment, MI 49004   Ph:(616)342-2432

Semiannual.

614 ● **Cadillac Service Publication**
Humphries Publishing
1801 Opdyke
Auburn Hills, MI 48057   Ph:(313)373-8400

Bimonthly. **Editor(s):** J. Humphries.

615 ● **Cadillac: The Enduring Legend**
Smithmark Publishers, Inc.
112 Madison Ave.
New York, NY 10016   Ph:(212)532-6600

Published 1989. **Editor(s):** Nicky Wright. **Price:** $19.98.

616 ● **Cadillac the Heartbreak of America: Fifteen Years of Consumer Disillusionment**
Essential Information, Inc.
P.O. Box 19405
Washington, DC 20036   Ph:(202)387-8030

Published 1988. **Price:** $12.95.

617 ● Great Marques Cadillac
Book Sales, Inc.
110 Enterprise Ave.
Secaucus, NJ 07094-1995   Ph:(201)964-6341

Published 1989. **Editor(s):** Andrew Whyte. **Price:** $10.98.

618 ● Self Starter
Cadillac-LaSalle Club (CLC)
c/o Mary Lou Evans
3083 Howard Rd.
Petoskey, MI 49770-9504   Ph:(616)347-4611

Carries general and technical information about Cadillac and
LaSalle automobiles. Encourages enthusiasts to band together
for mutual interest in the preservation and restoration of these
vehicles. Monthly; also publishes an annual edition. **Editor(s):**
Edith Childs. **Price:** Included in membership dues.

619 ● The Standard
Cadillac—LaSalle Club, Lake St. Clair Region
38156 Southfarm Ct.
Northville, MI 48167   Ph:(313)477-9408

Monthly.

ASSOCIATIONS

620 ● Cadillac Convertible Owners of America
P.O. Box 269
Ossining, NY 10562
Roberta Lynn, V.Pres.

Founded: 1977. **Membership:** 300. Cadillac convertible
owners who wish to preserve and enhance the value of their
automobiles. Presents most beautiful car award. **Former
Name(s):** (1977) Eldorado Convertible Owners of America.
Convention/Meeting: Annual; also holds annual rally.

621 ● Cadillac-LaSalle Club
c/o Mary Lou Evans
3083 Howard Rd.
Petoskey, MI 49770
Mary Lou Evans, Membership Sec.   Ph:(616)347-4611

Founded: 1958. **Membership:** 4,200. Persons interested in
Cadillac or LaSalle automobiles. To preserve, restore, and enjoy
Cadillac and LaSalle cars of all models. **Convention/Meeting:**
Annual.

622 ● Cadillac-LaSalle Club, Lower Michigan Region
229 Devon St.
Parchment, MI 49004
William Wendel, Pres.   Ph:(616)342-2432

Founded: 1984. **Membership:** 25. Individuals from the western
lower peninsula of Michigan who own antique Cadillacs and
LaSalles. Sponsors summer picnic and fall color tour.
Convention/Meeting: Annual dinner meeting - always winter.

CADILLAC BROUGHAM (1987-92)

Cadillac's oldest and only rear-drive model. Brougham is the
only Cadillac that is not equipped with a standard driver's side
airbag. Produced at the Cadillac Motor Car Division plant in
Arlington, Texas.

1991 Cadillac Brougham

MAJOR FEATURES

● Cadillac Brougham has as 1992 standard equipment: 4-
speed automatic transmission, front disc/rear drum brakes
with anti-lock braking system, automatic climate control
system, cruise control, electronic variable assist power
steering, and electrically powered and heated rearview
mirrors.

● Cadillac d'Elegance adds as 1992 standard equipment:
upgraded interior stylings.

PRICE HISTORY

The following new car prices reflect the approximate retail cost
of the base model: **1987** - $22,637; **1988** - $23,846; **1989** -
$25,699; **1990** - $27,400; **1991** - $30,455; **1992** - $31,740.

DIMENSIONS

Body Style	Years Avail	Wheel Base (in)	Lgth (in)	Ht (in)	Avg Wt (lbs)	Fuel Cap (gal)	Front Hdrm (in)	Front Legrm (in)
4d sdn	87-90	121.5	221.0	56.7	4,283	25	39.0	42.0
4d sdn	91-92	121.5	221.0	57.4	4,277	25	39.0	42.0

ENGINES

Type	Displacement (L)	Fuel Dly	HP @rpm	Torque @rpm (ft/lbs)	MPG Cty/Hwy	Years Avail
V-8	5.0	4-bbl	140@3200	255@2000	17/24	87-90
V-8	5.7	FI	175@4200	400@2000	14/21	90-90
V-8	5.0	FI	170@4200	255@2400	17/25	91-92
V-8	5.7	FI	185@3800	300@2400	16/25	91-92

KEY: I=in-line engine; V=V engine; F=flat engine; FI=fuel injection;
bbl=barrel carburetor; T=turbo; D=diesel; HP=horsepower;
MPG=estimated average miles per gallon.

EVALUATIONS, TESTS, AND RANKINGS

1991: "On the open highway, the Brougham is at its best . . .
Caddy covers long stretches of road in a quiet, smooth,
comfortable manner . . . thoroughly American luxury car."
Source: "Cadillac Brougham: A Large Piece of Americana,"
Motor Trend, December 1990, pp. 88-90, 92.

1991: "suspension has been tightened up a bit. Take a sharp
turn and the body roll starts. . .then is held in check. . .can
make some moves without alarming one's. . .balance." **Source:**
"Big 1991 Cadillac Brougham is history on wheels," *The Flint
Journal,* December 19, 1990, pp. B1-B2.

RECALLS

1988: (5,234 cars): Rear seat belt shoulder retractor may not
lock. **Corrective action:** Replace rear seat belt shoulder
retractor assembly. *(NHTSA Campaign No. 87V185000.)*

1987-88: (1,755,897 vehicles equipped with cruise control and certain gasoline and diesel engines; includes several General Motors models; includes models made before 1987): Small nylon bushing in the cruise control servo bail may slip out of place, causing intermittent and unexpected increases in engine speed or dieseling (engine run on with ignition off). Servo rod assembly could catch on engine components and result in a stuck throttle with potential for a vehicle crash. **Corrective action:** Install a new bushing in cruise control servo bail. (NHTSA Campaign No. 89V102000.)

SAFETY AND REPAIRS

1987: "Car Clinic," *Popular Mechanics*, February 1990, p. 25. **Note:** Replacement accelerator cable for 1987-89 models.

1987: "Car Clinic," *Popular Mechanics*, August 1990, p. 26. **Note:** Tip for clashing starter motor gears in 1987-88 General Motors 4.3, 5.0, and 5.7 liter engines.

REPAIR MANUALS

623 ● Cadillac 1967-89 Repair and Tune-up Guide
Chilton Co.
Chilton Way
Radnor, PA 19089   Ph:(215)964-4000

Published 1989. **Price:** $15.95.

624 ● Get Your Cadillac Fixed Right
Consumer Reports Books
51 E. 42nd St., Ste. 800
New York, NY 10017   Ph:(212)682-9280

Published 1990. **Editor(s):** Mort Schultz. **Price:** $8.95.

OTHER INFORMATION SOURCES

625 ● Cadillac—American Luxury Car
TAB Books, Inc.
Blue Ridge Summit, PA 17294-0850   Ph:(717)794-2191

Published 1988. **Editor(s):** Robert C. Ackerson. **Price:** $39.95.

626 ● Cadillac-Lasalle Club—Directory
Cadillac-LaSalle Club (CLC)
c/o Mary Lou Evans
3083 Howard Rd.
Petoskey, MI 49770   Ph:(616)347-4611

About 3,600 Cadillac and LaSalle automobile collectors. Biennial, odd years. **Editor(s):** Edith Childs. **Price:** Available to members only.

627 ● Cadillac—LaSalle Club, Lake St. Clair Region—Membership Directory [Michigan]
Cadillac—LaSalle Club, Lake St. Clair Region
38156 Southfarm Ct.
Northville, MI 48167   Ph:(313)477-9408

Annual.

628 ● Cadillac-LaSalle Club, Lower Michigan Region—Newsletter
Cadillac-LaSalle Club, Lower Michigan Region
229 Devon St.
Parchment, MI 49004   Ph:(616)342-2432

Semiannual.

629 ● Cadillac Service Publication
Humphries Publishing
1801 Opdyke
Auburn Hills, MI 48057   Ph:(313)373-8400

Bimonthly. **Editor(s):** J. Humphries.

630 ● Cadillac: The Enduring Legend
Smithmark Publishers, Inc.
112 Madison Ave.
New York, NY 10016   Ph:(212)532-6600

Published 1989. **Editor(s):** Nicky Wright. **Price:** $19.98.

631 ● Cadillac the Heartbreak of America: Fifteen Years of Consumer Disillusionment
Essential Information, Inc.
P.O. Box 19405
Washington, DC 20036   Ph:(202)387-8030

Published 1988. **Price:** $12.95.

632 ● Great Marques Cadillac
Book Sales, Inc.
110 Enterprise Ave.
Secaucus, NJ 07094-1995   Ph:(201)964-6341

Published 1989. **Editor(s):** Andrew Whyte. **Price:** $10.98.

633 ● Self Starter
Cadillac-LaSalle Club (CLC)
c/o Mary Lou Evans
3083 Howard Rd.
Petoskey, MI 49770-9504   Ph:(616)347-4611

Carries general and technical information about Cadillac and LaSalle automobiles. Encourages enthusiasts to band together for mutual interest in the preservation and restoration of these vehicles. Monthly; also publishes an annual edition. **Editor(s):** Edith Childs. **Price:** Included in membership dues.

634 ● The Standard
Cadillac—LaSalle Club, Lake St. Clair Region
38156 Southfarm Ct.
Northville, MI 48167   Ph:(313)477-9408

Monthly.

ASSOCIATIONS

635 ● Cadillac-LaSalle Club
c/o Mary Lou Evans
3083 Howard Rd.
Petoskey, MI 49770
Mary Lou Evans, Membership Sec.   Ph:(616)347-4611

Founded: 1958. **Membership:** 4,200. Persons interested in Cadillac or LaSalle automobiles. To preserve, restore, and enjoy Cadillac and LaSalle cars of all models. **Convention/Meeting:** Annual.

636 ● Cadillac-LaSalle Club, Lower Michigan Region
229 Devon St.
Parchment, MI 49004
William Wendel, Pres.   Ph:(616)342-2432

Founded: 1984. **Membership:** 25. Individuals from the western lower peninsula of Michigan who own antique Cadillacs and LaSalles. Sponsors summer picnic and fall color tour. **Convention/Meeting:** Annual dinner meeting - always winter.

CADILLAC CIMARRON (1987-88)

Introduced as part of the J car line. Differs from Chevy Cavalier and Pontiac J2000 only in styling details and a longer list of standard equipment. Produced until 1988 at General Motors plant in Janesville, Wisconsin.

MAJOR FEATURES

● Cadillac Cimarron had as 1988 standard equipment: 5-speed manual transmission, front disc/rear drum brakes, 4-wheel independent suspension, and power-assisted rack-and-pinion steering.

PRICE HISTORY

The following new car prices reflect the approximate retail cost of the base model: **1987** - $15,032; **1988** - $16,071.

DIMENSIONS

Body Style	Years Avail	Wheel Base (in)	Lgth (in)	Ht (in)	Avg Wt (lbs)	Fuel Cap (gal)	Front Hdrm (in)	Front Legrm (in)
4d sdn	87-88	101.2	177.8	52.1	2,756	13.6	38.2	42.2

ENGINES

Type	Displacement (L)	Fuel Dly	HP @rpm	Torque @rpm (ft/lbs)	MPG Cty/Hwy	Years Avail
I-4	2.0	FI	90@5600	108@3200	25/34	87-87
V-6	2.8	FI	125@4500	160@3600	20/29	88-88

KEY: I=in-line engine; V=V engine; F=flat engine; FI=fuel injection; bbl=barrel carburetor; T=turbo; D=diesel; HP=horsepower; MPG=estimated average miles per gallon.

EVALUATIONS, TESTS, AND RANKINGS

1988: "dolled-up Chevy Cavalier." **Source:** "Cadillac Cimarron," *Car and Driver—Buyers Guide 1988*, 1988, p. 96.

RECALLS

None to date.

SAFETY AND REPAIRS

1987: "Cimarron stall," *Popular Science*, August 1989, p. 41. **Note:** 1987 Cimarron stalls after running 4 minutes regardless of weather conditions.

REPAIR MANUALS

637 ● **Cadillac 1967-89 Repair and Tune-up Guide**
Chilton Co.
Chilton Way
Radnor, PA 19089   Ph:(215)964-4000

Published 1989. **Price:** $15.95.

638 ● **Chilton's Chevrolet Cavalier, Buick Skyhawk, Olds Firenza, Cadillac Cimarron, Pontiac 6000, 1982-88**
Chilton Co.
Chilton Way
Radnor, PA 19089   Ph:(215)964-4000

Published 1988. **Price:** $15.95.

639 ● **Get Your Cadillac Fixed Right**
Consumer Reports Books
51 E. 42nd St., Ste. 800
New York, NY 10017   Ph:(212)682-9280

Published 1990. **Editor(s):** Mort Schultz. **Price:** $8.95.

640 ● **GMC J Cars: Buick Skyhawk, Cadillac Cimarron, Chevrolet Cavalier, Oldsmobile Firenza, Pontiac J-2000, Sunbird Shop Manual, 1982-87**
Clymer Publications
P.O. Box 1209
Overland Park, KS 66212   Ph:(913)541-6694

Published 1987. **Price:** $14.95.

OTHER INFORMATION SOURCES

641 ● **Cadillac—American Luxury Car**
TAB Books, Inc.
Blue Ridge Summit, PA 17294-0850   Ph:(717)794-2191

Published 1988. **Editor(s):** Robert C. Ackerson. **Price:** $39.95.

642 ● **Cadillac-Lasalle Club—Directory**
Cadillac-LaSalle Club (CLC)
c/o Mary Lou Evans
3083 Howard Rd.
Petoskey, MI 49770   Ph:(616)347-4611

About 3,600 Cadillac and LaSalle automobile collectors. Biennial, odd years. **Editor(s):** Edith Childs. **Price:** Available to members only.

643 ● **Cadillac—LaSalle Club, Lake St. Clair Region— Membership Directory [Michigan]**
Cadillac—LaSalle Club, Lake St. Clair Region
38156 Southfarm Ct.
Northville, MI 48167   Ph:(313)477-9408

Annual.

644 ● **Cadillac-LaSalle Club, Lower Michigan Region— Newsletter**
Cadillac-LaSalle Club, Lower Michigan Region
229 Devon St.
Parchment, MI 49004   Ph:(616)342-2432

Semiannual.

645 ● **Cadillac Service Publication**
Humphries Publishing
1801 Opdyke
Auburn Hills, MI 48057   Ph:(313)373-8400

Bimonthly. **Editor(s):** J. Humphries.

646 ● **Cadillac: The Enduring Legend**
Smithmark Publishers, Inc.
112 Madison Ave.
New York, NY 10016   Ph:(212)532-6600

Published 1989. **Editor(s):** Nicky Wright. **Price:** $19.98.

647 ● **Cadillac the Heartbreak of America: Fifteen Years of Consumer Disillusionment**
Essential Information, Inc.
P.O. Box 19405
Washington, DC 20036   Ph:(202)387-8030

Published 1988. **Price:** $12.95.

648 ● Great Marques Cadillac
Book Sales, Inc.
110 Enterprise Ave.
Secaucus, NJ 07094-1995   Ph:(201)964-6341

Published 1989. **Editor(s):** Andrew Whyte. **Price:** $10.98.

649 ● Self Starter
Cadillac-LaSalle Club (CLC)
c/o Mary Lou Evans
3083 Howard Rd.
Petoskey, MI 49770-9504   Ph:(616)347-4611

Carries general and technical information about Cadillac and
LaSalle automobiles. Encourages enthusiasts to band together
for mutual interest in the preservation and restoration of these
vehicles. Monthly; also publishes an annual edition. **Editor(s):**
Edith Childs. **Price:** Included in membership dues.

650 ● The Standard
Cadillac—LaSalle Club, Lake St. Clair Region
38156 Southfarm Ct.
Northville, MI 48167   Ph:(313)477-9408

Monthly.

ASSOCIATIONS

651 ● Cadillac-LaSalle Club
c/o Mary Lou Evans
3083 Howard Rd.
Petoskey, MI 49770
Mary Lou Evans, Membership Sec.   Ph:(616)347-4611

Founded: 1958. **Membership:** 4,200. Persons interested in
Cadillac or LaSalle automobiles. To preserve, restore, and enjoy
Cadillac and LaSalle cars of all models. **Convention/Meeting:**
Annual.

652 ● Cadillac-LaSalle Club, Lower Michigan Region
229 Devon St.
Parchment, MI 49004
William Wendel, Pres.   Ph:(616)342-2432

Founded: 1984. **Membership:** 25. Individuals from the western
lower peninsula of Michigan who own antique Cadillacs and
LaSalles. Sponsors summer picnic and fall color tour.
Convention/Meeting: Annual dinner meeting - always winter.

CADILLAC DE VILLE (1987-92)

Introduced as part of C car line, along with Buick Electra, Buick
Park Avenue, Cadillac Fleetwood, and Oldsmobile 98.
Produced at General Motors plant in Lake Orion, Michigan.
Named to *Motor Trend's* 1989 Top 10 New Domestic Car
Buys. Received a poor rating in *The Car Book's* complaint index
in 1991, while it received a very good rating on *The Car Book's*
occupant injury history list in 1992.

1991 Cadillac Sedan De Ville

MAJOR FEATURES

● Cadillac Coupe and Sedan De Ville have as 1992 standard
equipment: 4-speed automatic transmission, 4-wheel disc
brakes with anti-lock braking system, power-assisted rack-and-
pinion steering, driver's side airbag, cruise control, power locks
and windows, AM/FM stereo/cassette player, and tilt
steering.

● Cadillac De Ville Touring Sedan adds as 1992 standard
equipment: upgraded interior and other exterior body stylings.

PRICE HISTORY

The following new car prices reflect the approximate retail cost
of the base model: **1987** - $21,316; **1988** - $23,049; **1989** -
$24,960; **1990** - $26,960; **1991** - $30,455; **1992** - $31,740.

DIMENSIONS

Body Style	Years Avail	Wheel Base (in)	Lgth (in)	Ht (in)	Avg Wt (lbs)	Fuel Cap (gal)	Front Hdrm (in)	Front Legrm (in)
2d cpe	87-91	110.8	202.6	na	3,545	18	39.3	42.0
2d cpe	92-92	110.8	205.1	54.4	3,519	18	39.2	42.0
4d sdn	87-91	113.8	205.6	55.2	3,622	18	39.3	42.0
4d sdn	92-92	113.8	208.0	55.0	3,591	18	39.3	42.0

ENGINES

Type	Displacement (L)	Fuel Dly	HP @rpm	Torque @rpm (ft/lbs)	MPG Cty/Hwy	Years Avail
V-8	4.1	FI	130@4200	200@2200	17/25	87-87
V-8	4.5	FI	155@4000	240@2600	17/25	88-89
V-8	4.5	FI	180@4300	245@3000	16/25	90-90
V-8	4.9	FI	200@4100	275@3000	16/25	91-92

KEY: I=in-line engine; V=V engine; F=flat engine; FI=fuel injection;
bbl=barrel carburetor; T=turbo; D=diesel; HP=horsepower;
MPG=estimated average miles per gallon.

EVALUATIONS, TESTS, AND RANKINGS

1992: "looks crisper than the octogeneric de Villes . . . betters
other de Villes in the quarter-mile, too . . . a heckuva good
ride." **Source:** "Cadillac de Ville Touring Sedan," *Car and
Driver*, December 1991, p. 117.

1991: "In overall powertrain smoothness, Cadillac is now right
up there with BMW, Mercedes, Lexus . . . wish the rack-and-
pinion steering had a clearer sense of purpose . . . scores major
points . . . in its power delivery." **Source:** "Cadillac Sedan de
Ville," *Car and Driver*, March 1991, pp. 127-128.

1991: "it packs luxury, comfort and surprisingly high
technology into a hefty 17-foot-long package . . . drips chrome
. . . quiet and comfortable, despite its sporting nature." **Source:**
"High Technology on a Large Scale," *The New York Times*, July
28, 1991.

1990: "best luxury sedan buy offered by American car makers." **Source:** "Top 10 New Car Buys: Domestic," *Motor Trend,* November 1989, pp. 80-83, 86-89.

1990: "the best acceleration time of the group by a significant margin . . . softness of the suspension . . . conspires to hamper higher-speed handling snap . . . took overall top honors in the styling scoring." **Source:** "Land of the Giants: Cadillac Sedan de Ville versus Chrysler Imperial versus Lincoln Continental," *Motor Trend,* March 1990, pp. 100-104, 106, 108-109.

1989: "still light to handle and capable of speed . . . soft Caddy ride and suspension . . . summons the intimations of "mature" in all the doleful senses of the word." **Source:** "fins de siecle," *Vogue,* February 1989, p. 264.

RECALLS

1987: (6,004 passenger cars with anti-lock brakes. Recall includes the Cadillac DeVille, Oldsmobile 98, Buick Electra, Buick LeSabre, and Pontiac 6000): Anti-lock brake system (ABS) pressure/warning switch may exhibit brake fluid seepage which can lead to loss of brake system hydraulic pump motor. Additionally, hydraulic pump motor of ABS electrical relays may have been exposed to water contamination during vehicle assembly. Can cause loss of hydraulic pump motor and/or loss of ABS function. Loss of hydraulic pump would result in loss of rear brakes as well as power to assist to front brakes. **Corrective action:** ABS and hydraulic pump motor electrical relays and 30 amp fuses will be replaced. Hydraulic pump motor assembly and pressure/warning switch will be inspected and possibly replaced. (NHTSA Campaign No. 87V093000.)

SAFETY AND REPAIRS

1990: "Car Clinic," *Popular Mechanics,* July 1990, p. 25. **Note:** Tip for stalling in various early 1990 Cadillac models.

REPAIR MANUALS

653 ● Cadillac 1967-89 Repair and Tune-up Guide
Chilton Co.
Chilton Way
Radnor, PA 19089   Ph:(215)964-4000

Published 1989. **Price:** $15.95.

654 ● Get Your Cadillac Fixed Right
Consumer Reports Books
51 E. 42nd St., Ste. 800
New York, NY 10017   Ph:(212)682-9280

Published 1990. **Editor(s):** Mort Schultz. **Price:** $8.95.

OTHER INFORMATION SOURCES

655 ● Cadillac—American Luxury Car
TAB Books, Inc.
Blue Ridge Summit, PA 17294-0850   Ph:(717)794-2191

Published 1988. **Editor(s):** Robert C. Ackerson. **Price:** $39.95.

656 ● Cadillac-Lasalle Club—Directory
Cadillac-LaSalle Club (CLC)
c/o Mary Lou Evans
3083 Howard Rd.
Petoskey, MI 49770   Ph:(616)347-4611

About 3,600 Cadillac and LaSalle automobile collectors. Biennial, odd years. **Editor(s):** Edith Childs. **Price:** Available to members only.

657 ● Cadillac—LaSalle Club, Lake St. Clair Region— Membership Directory [Michigan]
Cadillac—LaSalle Club, Lake St. Clair Region
38156 Southfarm Ct.
Northville, MI 48167   Ph:(313)477-9408

Annual.

658 ● Cadillac-LaSalle Club, Lower Michigan Region— Newsletter
Cadillac-LaSalle Club, Lower Michigan Region
229 Devon St.
Parchment, MI 49004   Ph:(616)342-2432

Semiannual.

659 ● Cadillac Service Publication
Humphries Publishing
1801 Opdyke
Auburn Hills, MI 48057   Ph:(313)373-8400

Bimonthly. **Editor(s):** J. Humphries.

660 ● Cadillac: The Enduring Legend
Smithmark Publishers, Inc.
112 Madison Ave.
New York, NY 10016   Ph:(212)532-6600

Published 1989. **Editor(s):** Nicky Wright. **Price:** $19.98.

661 ● Cadillac the Heartbreak of America: Fifteen Years of Consumer Disillusionment
Essential Information, Inc.
P.O. Box 19405
Washington, DC 20036   Ph:(202)387-8030

Published 1988. **Price:** $12.95.

662 ● Great Marques Cadillac
Book Sales, Inc.
110 Enterprise Ave.
Secaucus, NJ 07094-1995   Ph:(201)964-6341

Published 1989. **Editor(s):** Andrew Whyte. **Price:** $10.98.

663 ● Self Starter
Cadillac-LaSalle Club (CLC)
c/o Mary Lou Evans
3083 Howard Rd.
Petoskey, MI 49770-9504   Ph:(616)347-4611

Carries general and technical information about Cadillac and LaSalle automobiles. Encourages enthusiasts to band together for mutual interest in the preservation and restoration of these vehicles. Monthly; also publishes an annual edition. **Editor(s):** Edith Childs. **Price:** Included in membership dues.

664 ● The Standard
Cadillac—LaSalle Club, Lake St. Clair Region
38156 Southfarm Ct.
Northville, MI 48167   Ph:(313)477-9408

Monthly.

ASSOCIATIONS

665 ● Cadillac-LaSalle Club
c/o Mary Lou Evans
3083 Howard Rd.
Petoskey, MI 49770
Mary Lou Evans, Membership Sec.   Ph:(616)347-4611

Founded: 1958. **Membership:** 4,200. Persons interested in

Cadillac or LaSalle automobiles. To preserve, restore, and enjoy Cadillac and LaSalle cars of all models. **Convention/Meeting:** Annual.

666 ● Cadillac-LaSalle Club, Lower Michigan Region
229 Devon St.
Parchment, MI 49004
William Wendel, Pres.   Ph:(616)342-2432

Founded: 1984. **Membership:** 25. Individuals from the western lower peninsula of Michigan who own antique Cadillacs and LaSalles. Sponsors summer picnic and fall color tour. **Convention/Meeting:** Annual dinner meeting - always winter.

CADILLAC ELDORADO (1987-92)

Introduced as part of E car line, along with Buick Riviera and Oldsmobile Toronado. Produced at the Cadillac Motor Car Division plant in Hamtramck, Michigan. Selected among large vehicles as a good choice by *The Car Book* in 1989. Named to *Car and Driver's* 1990 Ten Best Cars Nominees list.

1992 Cadillac Eldorado

MAJOR FEATURES

● Cadillac Eldorado has as 1992 standard equipment: 4-speed automatic transmission, front-wheel drive, 4-wheel disc brakes with anti-lock braking system, power-assisted rack-and-pinion steering, driver's side airbag, automatic climate control system, cruise control, rear window defogger with heated outside mirrors, and tilt steering.

● Cadillac Eldorado Touring Coupe adds as 1992 standard equipment: upgraded interior and other exterior body stylings.

PRICE HISTORY

The following new car prices reflect the approximate retail cost of the base model: **1987** - $23,740; **1988** - $24,891; **1989** - $26,738; **1990** - $28,855; **1991** - $31,495; **1992** - $32,470.

DIMENSIONS

Body Style	Years Avail	Wheel Base (in)	Lgth (in)	Ht (in)	Avg Wt (lbs)	Fuel Cap (gal)	Front Hdrm (in)	Front Legrm (in)
2d cpe	87-91	108	191.4	53.2	3,469	18.8	37.8	42.4
2d cpe	92-92	108	202.2	54.0	3,604	18.8	37.8	42.6

ENGINES

Type	Displacement (L)	Fuel Dly	HP @rpm	Torque @rpm (ft/lbs)	MPG Cty/Hwy	Years Avail
V-8	4.1	FI	130@4200	200@2200	17/25	87-87
V-8	4.5	FI	155@4000	240@2600	17/25	88-89
V-8	4.5	FI	180@4300	245@3000	16/25	90-90
V-8	4.9	FI	200@4100	275@3000	16/25	91-92

KEY: I=in-line engine; V=V engine; F=flat engine; FI=fuel injection; bbl=barrel carburetor; T=turbo; D=diesel; HP=horsepower; MPG=estimated average miles per gallon.

EVALUATIONS, TESTS, AND RANKINGS

1992: "smoother lines and are more performance-oriented." **Source:** "New Cadillacs Out," *New York Times*, August 29, 1991, p. D4.

1992: "Something is not quite right about the Eldo's shape . . . tightly clipped ride motions have been softened, and its handling is no longer as precise . . . can get everything the Eldorado Touring Coupe has to offer—and more—in a Seville." **Source:** "Cadillac Eldorado Touring Coupe," *Car and Driver*, October 1991, pp. 73-75, 79.

1992: "a pleasure to drive . . . Eldo gets a new cabin that is plush and roomy, yet considerably less gaudy . . . exterior design is at once contemporary and evocative." **Source:** "New Eldorado a Pleasure to Drive," *Detroit Free Press*, September 12, 1991, p. 1E.

1991: "Coupled with a revised electronic four-speed automatic, the fuel-injected V8 runs 0-60 in just over eight seconds flat, which is mighty quick by American luxury-car standards . . . Gas mileage is plain lousy." **Source:** "Eldorado Touring Coupe a winner," *Detroit Free Press*, September 27, 1990, p. 1F.

1990: "Eldorado shows a passing favoritism for the attractive Mercedes SL look." **Source:** "All-New '92 Cadillacs Won't Get Northstar V-8," *Motor Trend*, December 1991, p. 30.

RECALLS

1992: (2,371 passenger cars; includes Buick Riviera, Oldsmobile Toronado, Cadillac Eldorado, and Cadillac Seville): The intermediate shaft to steering rack lower coupling pinch bolt may be missing. If this condition exists and shaft disengagement occurs, loss of steering control will result. **Corrective action:** Install pinch bolt. *(NHTSA Campaign No. 91V157000.)*

1990: (10,166 passenger cars; includes the Buick Riviera, Cadillac Eldorado, Cadillac Seville, and Buick Reatta): Misaligned rear safety shoulder belt retractor assemblies could prevent engagement of inertia lock, increasing likelihood of injury to occupant in panic stop or accident. **Corrective action:** Realign rear shoulder belt retractor assembly. *(NHTSA Campaign No. 90V028000.)*

1990: (63,964 vehicles; includes Buick, Oldsmobile, and Cadillac models): Transaxle shift control cable may disengage from the floor shift control with loss of gear indicator reference and shift selector operation. Could result in unexpected vehicle movement and an accident. **Corrective action:** Install transaxle shift control cable retaining clip to prevent cable disengagement. *(NHTSA Campaign No. 90V164000.)*

1989: (634 passenger cars equipped with anti-lock brakes; includes the Cadillac Seville, Cadillac Eldorado, Buick Riveria, and Oldsmobile Toronado): One or both ABS hydraulic unit mounting bolts may not be properly seated and could loosen. Could lead to separation of the ABS hydraulic unit from the mounting bracket and result in loss of brake function and a crash without prior warning. **Corrective action:** Replace both

ABS hydraulic unit mounting bolts. *(NHTSA Campaign No. 89V055000.)*

1987: (56,783 cars; recall includes the Cadillac Eldorado and Cadillac Seville; includes models made before 1987): The twilight sentinel potentiometer (thumbwheel control) might have been manufactured with electrical contacts which could result in an intermittent headlight circuit. Could cause headlight and instrument panel lights to go out. Sudden loss of headlights could reduce driver visibility and might result in a vehicle crash without prior warning. **Corrective action:** Install a new part in one of the vehicle's control computers to prevent this condition from occuring. *(NHTSA Campaign No. 87V047000.)*

SAFETY AND REPAIRS

1990: "Car Clinic," *Popular Mechanics*, July 1990, p. 25. **Note:** Tip for stalling in various early 1990 Cadillac models.

REPAIR MANUALS

667 ● Cadillac 1967-89 Repair and Tune-up Guide
Chilton Co.
Chilton Way
Radnor, PA 19089   Ph:(215)964-4000

Published 1989. **Price:** $15.95.

668 ● Get Your Cadillac Fixed Right
Consumer Reports Books
51 E. 42nd St., Ste. 800
New York, NY 10017   Ph:(212)682-9280

Published 1990. **Editor(s):** Mort Schultz. **Price:** $8.95.

OTHER INFORMATION SOURCES

669 ● Cadillac—American Luxury Car
TAB Books, Inc.
Blue Ridge Summit, PA 17294-0850   Ph:(717)794-2191

Published 1988. **Editor(s):** Robert C. Ackerson. **Price:** $39.95.

670 ● Cadillac-Lasalle Club—Directory
Cadillac-LaSalle Club (CLC)
c/o Mary Lou Evans
3083 Howard Rd.
Petoskey, MI 49770   Ph:(616)347-4611

About 3,600 Cadillac and LaSalle automobile collectors. Biennial, odd years. **Editor(s):** Edith Childs. **Price:** Available to members only.

671 ● Cadillac—LaSalle Club, Lake St. Clair Region— Membership Directory [Michigan]
Cadillac—LaSalle Club, Lake St. Clair Region
38156 Southfarm Ct.
Northville, MI 48167   Ph:(313)477-9408

Annual.

672 ● Cadillac-LaSalle Club, Lower Michigan Region— Newsletter
Cadillac-LaSalle Club, Lower Michigan Region
229 Devon St.
Parchment, MI 49004   Ph:(616)342-2432

Semiannual.

673 ● Cadillac Service Publication
Humphries Publishing
1801 Opdyke
Auburn Hills, MI 48057   Ph:(313)373-8400

Bimonthly. **Editor(s):** J. Humphries.

674 ● Cadillac: The Enduring Legend
Smithmark Publishers, Inc.
112 Madison Ave.
New York, NY 10016   Ph:(212)532-6600

Published 1989. **Editor(s):** Nicky Wright. **Price:** $19.98.

675 ● Cadillac the Heartbreak of America: Fifteen Years of Consumer Disillusionment
Essential Information, Inc.
P.O. Box 19405
Washington, DC 20036   Ph:(202)387-8030

Published 1988. **Price:** $12.95.

676 ● Great Marques Cadillac
Book Sales, Inc.
110 Enterprise Ave.
Secaucus, NJ 07094-1995   Ph:(201)964-6341

Published 1989. **Editor(s):** Andrew Whyte. **Price:** $10.98.

677 ● Self Starter
Cadillac-LaSalle Club (CLC)
c/o Mary Lou Evans
3083 Howard Rd.
Petoskey, MI 49770-9504   Ph:(616)347-4611

Carries general and technical information about Cadillac and LaSalle automobiles. Encourages enthusiasts to band together for mutual interest in the preservation and restoration of these vehicles. Monthly; also publishes an annual edition. **Editor(s):** Edith Childs. **Price:** Included in membership dues.

678 ● The Standard
Cadillac—LaSalle Club, Lake St. Clair Region
38156 Southfarm Ct.
Northville, MI 48167   Ph:(313)477-9408

Monthly.

ASSOCIATIONS

679 ● Cadillac-LaSalle Club
c/o Mary Lou Evans
3083 Howard Rd.
Petoskey, MI 49770
Mary Lou Evans, Membership Sec.   Ph:(616)347-4611

Founded: 1958. **Membership:** 4,200. Persons interested in Cadillac or LaSalle automobiles. To preserve, restore, and enjoy Cadillac and LaSalle cars of all models. **Convention/Meeting:** Annual.

680 ● Cadillac-LaSalle Club, Lower Michigan Region
229 Devon St.
Parchment, MI 49004
William Wendel, Pres.   Ph:(616)342-2432

Founded: 1984. **Membership:** 25. Individuals from the western lower peninsula of Michigan who own antique Cadillacs and LaSalles. Sponsors summer picnic and fall color tour. **Convention/Meeting:** Annual dinner meeting - always winter.

CADILLAC FLEETWOOD (1987-92)

Introduced as part of C-car line, along with Buick Electra, Buick Park Avenue, Cadillac DeVille, and Oldsmobile 98. Produced at the Cadillac Motor Car Division plant in Arlington, Texas. The Fleetwood Sixty Special received an overall rating of worse than average by *The Complete Car Cost Guide* in 1990. The vehicle lineup was rated poor in the complaint index in 1991 and very good on the occupant injury history list in 1992 in *The Car Book*.

1991 Cadillac Fleetwood

MAJOR FEATURES

● Cadillac Fleetwood Coupe and Sedan have as 1992 standard equipment: 4.9L eight-cylinder engine, 4-speed automatic transmission, front wheel drive, front disc/rear drum brakes with anti-lock braking system, power-assisted rack-and-pinion steering, driver's side airbag, automatic climate control system, cruise control, rear window defogger with heated outside mirrors, Traction Control system, anti-theft system, and tilt steering.

● Cadillac Fleetwood Sixty Special adds as 1992 standard equipment: other exterior body stylings and an upgraded interior.

PRICE HISTORY

The following new car prices reflect the approximate retail cost of the base model: **1987** - $26,104; **1988** - $28,024; **1989** - $29,825; **1990** - $32,400; **1991** - $35,195; **1992** - $36,360.

DIMENSIONS

Body Style	Years Avail	Wheel Base (in)	Lgth (in)	Ht (in)	Avg Wt (lbs)	Fuel Cap (gal)	Front Hdrm (in)	Front Legrm (in)
2d cpe	89-91	110.8	202.6	54.9	3,593	18	39.3	42.0
2d cpe	92-92	110.8	205.1	54.4	3,566	18	39.2	42.0
4d sdn	87-91	113.8	205.6	55.2	3,675	18	39.3	42.0
4d sdn	92-92	113.8	208.0	55.0	3,642	18	39.3	42.0

ENGINES

Type	Displacement (L)	Fuel Dly	HP @rpm	Torque @rpm (ft/lbs)	MPG Cty/Hwy	Years Avail
V-8	4.1	FI	130@4200	200@2200	17/25	87-87
V-8	4.5	FI	155@4000	240@2600	17/25	88-89
V-8	4.5	FI	180@4300	245@3000	16/25	90-90
V-8	4.9	FI	200@4100	275@3000	16/25	91-92

KEY: I=in-line engine; V=V engine; F=flat engine; FI=fuel injection; bbl=barrel carburetor; T=turbo; D=diesel; HP=horsepower; MPG=estimated average miles per gallon.

EVALUATIONS, TESTS, AND RANKINGS

1990: "revives the grand, dominating appearance traditionally expected of a Cadillac ... Interior appointments pamper driver and passengers ... possibly the most impressive aspect of this car is the ride." **Source:** "Fleetwood Sedan: More Cadillac to love," *Design News*, October 2, 1989, p. 30.

1989: "ride is boulevard smooth and well hushed over most pavement ... There were no noticeable flaws in fit, finish, or operation." **Source:** "Cadillac's back with new Fleetwood," *The Detroit News*, March 1, 1989, pp. 1F, 2F.

1989: "battery of standard Cadillac comfort and convenience features." **Source:** "Cadillac De Ville & Fleetwood," *Road & Track—Buyer's Guide 1989*, 1988, p. 34.

RECALLS

1987-88: (223 cars; includes models made before 1987; includes other Lincoln models): Safety belts not installed for rear facing seats. (NHTSA Campaign No. 90V050000.)

1987-88: (223 cars; includes models made before 1987; includes other Lincoln models): Window film does not meet light transmission requirements. (NHTSA Campaign No. 90V049000.)

1987: (11,936 vehicles with 200 4R transmissions; includes Chevrolet, Pontiac, Oldsmobile, Buick, Cadillac, and GMC models): Manual valve link in transmission may have been improperly formed. **Corrective action:** Replace manual valve detent lever link. (NHTSA Campaign No. 87V168000.)

SAFETY AND REPAIRS

1990: "Car Clinic," *Popular Mechanics*, July 1990, p. 25. **Note:** Tip for stalling in various early 1990 Cadillac models.

REPAIR MANUALS

681 ● **Cadillac 1967-89 Repair and Tune-up Guide**
Chilton Co.
Chilton Way
Radnor, PA 19089   Ph:(215)964-4000

Published 1989. **Price:** $15.95.

682 ● **Get Your Cadillac Fixed Right**
Consumer Reports Books
51 E. 42nd St., Ste. 800
New York, NY 10017   Ph:(212)682-9280

Published 1990. **Editor(s):** Mort Schultz. **Price:** $8.95.

OTHER INFORMATION SOURCES

683 ● **Cadillac—American Luxury Car**
TAB Books, Inc.
Blue Ridge Summit, PA 17294-0850   Ph:(717)794-2191

Published 1988. **Editor(s):** Robert C. Ackerson. **Price:** $39.95.

684 ● **Cadillac-Lasalle Club—Directory**
Cadillac-LaSalle Club (CLC)
c/o Mary Lou Evans
3083 Howard Rd.
Petoskey, MI 49770   Ph:(616)347-4611

About 3,600 Cadillac and LaSalle automobile collectors. Biennial, odd years. **Editor(s):** Edith Childs. **Price:** Available to members only.

685 ● Cadillac—LaSalle Club, Lake St. Clair Region— Membership Directory [Michigan]
Cadillac—LaSalle Club, Lake St. Clair Region
38156 Southfarm Ct.
Northville, MI 48167   Ph:(313)477-9408

Annual.

686 ● Cadillac-LaSalle Club, Lower Michigan Region— Newsletter
Cadillac-LaSalle Club, Lower Michigan Region
229 Devon St.
Parchment, MI 49004   Ph:(616)342-2432

Semiannual.

687 ● Cadillac Service Publication
Humphries Publishing
1801 Opdyke
Auburn Hills, MI 48057   Ph:(313)373-8400

Bimonthly. **Editor(s):** J. Humphries.

688 ● Cadillac: The Enduring Legend
Smithmark Publishers, Inc.
112 Madison Ave.
New York, NY 10016   Ph:(212)532-6600

Published 1989. **Editor(s):** Nicky Wright. **Price:** $19.98.

689 ● Cadillac the Heartbreak of America: Fifteen Years of Consumer Disillusionment
Essential Information, Inc.
P.O. Box 19405
Washington, DC 20036   Ph:(202)387-8030

Published 1988. **Price:** $12.95.

690 ● Great Marques Cadillac
Book Sales, Inc.
110 Enterprise Ave.
Secaucus, NJ 07094-1995   Ph:(201)964-6341

Published 1989. **Editor(s):** Andrew Whyte. **Price:** $10.98.

691 ● Self Starter
Cadillac-LaSalle Club (CLC)
c/o Mary Lou Evans
3083 Howard Rd.
Petoskey, MI 49770-9504   Ph:(616)347-4611

Carries general and technical information about Cadillac and LaSalle automobiles. Encourages enthusiasts to band together for mutual interest in the preservation and restoration of these vehicles. Monthly; also publishes an annual edition. **Editor(s):** Edith Childs. **Price:** Included in membership dues.

692 ● The Standard
Cadillac—LaSalle Club, Lake St. Clair Region
38156 Southfarm Ct.
Northville, MI 48167   Ph:(313)477-9408

Monthly.

ASSOCIATIONS

693 ● Cadillac-LaSalle Club
c/o Mary Lou Evans
3083 Howard Rd.
Petoskey, MI 49770
Mary Lou Evans, Membership Sec.   Ph:(616)347-4611

Founded: 1958. **Membership:** 4,200. Persons interested in Cadillac or LaSalle automobiles. To preserve, restore, and enjoy Cadillac and LaSalle cars of all models. **Convention/Meeting:** Annual.

694 ● Cadillac-LaSalle Club, Lower Michigan Region
229 Devon St.
Parchment, MI 49004
William Wendel, Pres.   Ph:(616)342-2432

Founded: 1984. **Membership:** 25. Individuals from the western lower peninsula of Michigan who own antique Cadillacs and LaSalles. Sponsors summer picnic and fall color tour. **Convention/Meeting:** Annual dinner meeting - always winter.

CADILLAC SEVILLE (1987-92)

Basically a major revision of the Chevy Nova. Produced at the Cadillac Motor Car Division plant in Hamtramck, Michigan. Won the Malcolm Baldrige National Quality Award in 1990. The 1992 Cadillac Seville Touring Sedan was named Automobile of the Year by *Automobile Magazine*; also ranked as one of the Ten Best Cars by *Car and Driver*.

1992 Cadillac Seville Touring Sedan

MAJOR FEATURES

● Cadillac Seville Sedan has as 1992 standard equipment: 4-speed automatic transmission, 4-wheel disc brakes with anti-lock braking system, power-assisted rack-and-pinion steering, driver's side airbag, cruise control, power locks and windows, AM/FM stereo/cassette player, theft-deterrent system, and tilt steering.

● Cadillac Seville Touring Sedan, also known as the Cadillac STS, adds as 1992 standard equipment: all-leather interior, power lumbar support feature on driver and passenger seats, remote entry system, and touring suspension.

PRICE HISTORY

The following new car prices reflect the approximate retail cost of the base model: **1987** - $26,326; **1988** - $27,627; **1989** - $29,750; **1990** - $31,830; **1991** - $34,195; **1992** - $34,975.

DIMENSIONS

Body Style	Years Avail	Wheel Base (in)	Lgth (in)	Ht (in)	Avg Wt (lbs)	Fuel Cap (gal)	Front Hdrm (in)	Front Legrm (in)
4d sdn	87-91	108	190.8	53.2	3,512	18.8	37.8	42.5
4d sdn	92-92	111	203.9	54.0	3,648	18.8	37.6	42.8

ENGINES

Type	Displacement (L)	Fuel Dly	HP @rpm	Torque @rpm (ft/lbs)	MPG Cty/Hwy	Years Avail
V-8	4.1	FI	130@4200	200@2200	17/25	87-87
V-8	4.5	FI	155@4000	240@2600	17/25	88-89
V-8	4.5	FI	180@4300	245@3000	16/25	90-90
V-8	4.9	FI	200@4100	275@3000	16/25	91-92

KEY: I=in-line engine; V=V engine; F=flat engine; FI=fuel injection; bbl=barrel carburetor; T=turbo; D=diesel; HP=horsepower; MPG=estimated average miles per gallon.

EVALUATIONS, TESTS, AND RANKINGS

1992: "as good as the Cadillac STS is, it is not a perfect automobile ... Distinguished by its restraint ... proves that Detroit can build a tasteful American car that doesn't depend on BMW for its styling cues." **Source:** "Ten Best Cars," *Car and Driver*, January 1992, pp. 35-43.

1992: "longer hoodline, a sloping rear roofline, and a more massive appearance overall ... return[s] the next generation Seville to the position of prestige it once enjoyed." **Source:** "Cadillac heads back to the future," *Popular Mechanics*, April 1989, p. 49.

1992: "Styling is conservative ... quiet and sure-footed ... the strongest Cadillac sedan ever." **Source:** "1992 Cadillac Seville," *Road & Track*, May 1991, pp. 100-101.

1992: "Acceleration from a standing start is smooth, seamless, and extremely powerful ... took down 0-60 mph in a respectable 8.8 seconds ... going to be one of Cadillac's most precious gems." **Source:** "'92 Cadillac Seville STS," *Motor Trend*, May 1991, pp. 56-58.

1992: "the first serious American challenge to the Germans in the luxury class ... Sharp looks, European-style road handling." **Source:** "Big is beautiful," *Forbes*, May 27, 1991, pp. 342-343.

1992: "The STS has a stiffer suspension and tauter handling than the base model ... controls are logical, and the seats will hold you comfortably for a long-distance thruway cruise ... engine offers adequate acceleration and smooth high-speed performance." **Source:** "Cadillac aims twin Sevilles at 2 generations of drivers," *The Detroit News*, November 20, 1991, pp. D1, D5.

1992: "more rear-seat legroom. Improvements in the suspension significantly improve cornering and handling ... The Seville Touring Sedan offers crisper handling and more subdued styling." **Source:** "The road to comfort comes paved with high-tech gadgets," *The Detroit News*, October 6, 1991, p. 5D.

1992: "getting praise for offering one of the freshest designs since 1976 ... STS ... will have a more tightly wound ride ... corners better." **Source:** "Cadillac's Bid to Recapture Youth," *The New York Times*, May 7, 1991, pp. D1, D5.

1992: "offers luxury and looks *and* dynamic behavior ... control responses are quick and aggressive, and its ride is very much in the German tradition." **Source:** "Cadillac Seville Touring Sedan," *Automobile Magazine*, January 1992, pp. 62-63.

1992: "firm, yet comfortable and controlled ride ... bucket seats ... provide a snug, secure environment for hours of exuberant driving ... most advanced American luxury car yet built." **Source:** "Seville Touring Sedan to Challenge Lexus," *Detroit Free Press*, June 6, 1991, p. 1C.

1991: "willing 4.5-liter V8 makes 180 horsepower—more than enough to make any trip a memorable driving experience. Teamed up with the fat tires, responsive handling and leather

interior appointments." **Source:** "Long-Term Test Cars," *Popular Mechanics*, November 1990, pp. 56-59, 138.

1990: "beautifully finished ... probably would win its share of stop-light drag races ... excellent automatic heater and air conditioner." **Source:** "Driving in the lap of luxury," *U.S. News & World Report*, January 8, 1990.

1990: "exterior decor is restrained ... engine makes for a quick-reflex machine in the cut and thrust of city driving." **Source:** "Showdown," *Car and Driver*, December 1989, pp. 41-43, 46-50, 52, 54-56.

RECALLS

1992: (2,371 passenger cars; includes Buick Riviera, Oldsmobile Toronado, Cadillac Eldorado, and Cadillac Seville): The intermediate shaft to steering rack lower coupling pinch bolt may be missing. If this condition exists and shaft disengagement occurs, loss of steering control will result. **Corrective action:** Install pinch bolt. *(NHTSA Campaign No. 91V157000.)*

1990: (10,166 passenger cars; includes the Buick Riviera, Cadillac Eldorado, Cadillac Seville, and Buick Reatta): Misaligned rear safety shoulder belt retractor assemblies could prevent engagement of inertia lock, increasing likelihood of injury to occupant in panic stop or accident. **Corrective action:** Realign rear shoulder belt retractor assembly. *(NHTSA Campaign No. 90V028000.)*

1990: (63,964 vehicles; includes Buick, Oldsmobile, and Cadillac models): Transaxle shift control cable may disengage from the floor shift control with loss of gear indicator reference and shift selector operation. Could result in unexpected vehicle movement and an accident. **Corrective action:** Install transaxle shift control cable retaining clip to prevent cable disengagement. *(NHTSA Campaign No. 90V164000.)*

1989: (634 passenger cars equipped with anti-lock brakes; includes the Cadillac Seville, Cadillac Eldorado, Buick Riveria, and Oldsmobile Toronado): One or both ABS hydraulic unit mounting bolts may not be properly seated and could loosen. Could lead to separation of the ABS hydraulic unit from the mounting bracket and result in loss of brake function and a crash without prior warning. **Corrective action:** Replace both ABS hydraulic unit mounting bolts. *(NHTSA Campaign No. 89V055000.)*

1987: (56,783 cars; recall includes the Cadillac Eldorado and Cadillac Seville; includes models made before 1987): The twilight sentinel potentiometer (thumbwheel control) might have been manufactured with electrical contacts which could result in an intermittent headlight circuit. Could cause headlight and instrument panel lights to go out. Sudden loss of headlights could reduce driver visibility and might result in a vehicle crash without prior warning. **Corrective action:** Install a new part in one of the vehicle's control computers to prevent this condition from occuring. *(NHTSA Campaign No. 87V047000.)*

SAFETY AND REPAIRS

1990: "Car Clinic," *Popular Mechanics*, July 1990, p. 25. **Note:** Tip for stalling in various early 1990 Cadillac models.

REPAIR MANUALS

695 ● Cadillac 1967-89 Repair and Tune-up Guide
Chilton Co.
Chilton Way
Radnor, PA 19089   Ph:(215)964-4000

Published 1989. **Price:** $15.95.

696 ● Get Your Cadillac Fixed Right
Consumer Reports Books
51 E. 42nd St., Ste. 800
New York, NY 10017   Ph:(212)682-9280

Published 1990. **Editor(s):** Mort Schultz. **Price:** $8.95.

OTHER INFORMATION SOURCES

697 ● Cadillac—American Luxury Car
TAB Books, Inc.
Blue Ridge Summit, PA 17294-0850   Ph:(717)794-2191

Published 1988. **Editor(s):** Robert C. Ackerson. **Price:** $39.95.

698 ● Cadillac-Lasalle Club—Directory
Cadillac-LaSalle Club (CLC)
c/o Mary Lou Evans
3083 Howard Rd.
Petoskey, MI 49770   Ph:(616)347-4611

About 3,600 Cadillac and LaSalle automobile collectors.
Biennial, odd years. **Editor(s):** Edith Childs. **Price:** Available to
members only.

**699 ● Cadillac—LaSalle Club, Lake St. Clair Region—
    Membership Directory [Michigan]**
Cadillac—LaSalle Club, Lake St. Clair Region
38156 Southfarm Ct.
Northville, MI 48167   Ph:(313)477-9408

Annual.

**700 ● Cadillac-LaSalle Club, Lower Michigan Region—
    Newsletter**
Cadillac-LaSalle Club, Lower Michigan Region
229 Devon St.
Parchment, MI 49004   Ph:(616)342-2432

Semiannual.

701 ● Cadillac Service Publication
Humphries Publishing
1801 Opdyke
Auburn Hills, MI 48057   Ph:(313)373-8400

Bimonthly. **Editor(s):** J. Humphries.

702 ● Cadillac: The Enduring Legend
Smithmark Publishers, Inc.
112 Madison Ave.
New York, NY 10016   Ph:(212)532-6600

Published 1989. **Editor(s):** Nicky Wright. **Price:** $19.98.

**703 ● Cadillac the Heartbreak of America: Fifteen Years of
    Consumer Disillusionment**
Essential Information, Inc.
P.O. Box 19405
Washington, DC 20036   Ph:(202)387-8030

Published 1988. **Price:** $12.95.

704 ● Great Marques Cadillac
Book Sales, Inc.
110 Enterprise Ave.
Secaucus, NJ 07094-1995   Ph:(201)964-6341

Published 1989. **Editor(s):** Andrew Whyte. **Price:** $10.98.

705 ● Self Starter
Cadillac-LaSalle Club (CLC)
c/o Mary Lou Evans
3083 Howard Rd.
Petoskey, MI 49770-9504   Ph:(616)347-4611

Carries general and technical information about Cadillac and
LaSalle automobiles. Encourages enthusiasts to band together
for mutual interest in the preservation and restoration of these
vehicles. Monthly; also publishes an annual edition. **Editor(s):**
Edith Childs. **Price:** Included in membership dues.

706 ● The Standard
Cadillac—LaSalle Club, Lake St. Clair Region
38156 Southfarm Ct.
Northville, MI 48167   Ph:(313)477-9408

Monthly.

ASSOCIATIONS

707 ● Cadillac-LaSalle Club
c/o Mary Lou Evans
3083 Howard Rd.
Petoskey, MI 49770
Mary Lou Evans, Membership Sec.   Ph:(616)347-4611

Founded: 1958. **Membership:** 4,200. Persons interested in
Cadillac or LaSalle automobiles. To preserve, restore, and enjoy
Cadillac and LaSalle cars of all models. **Convention/Meeting:**
Annual.

708 ● Cadillac-LaSalle Club, Lower Michigan Region
229 Devon St.
Parchment, MI 49004
William Wendel, Pres.   Ph:(616)342-2432

Founded: 1984. **Membership:** 25. Individuals from the western
lower peninsula of Michigan who own antique Cadillacs and
LaSalles. Sponsors summer picnic and fall color tour.
Convention/Meeting: Annual dinner meeting - always winter.

CHEVROLET ASTRO (1987-92)

Corporate twin is the GMC Safari and similar to the Ford
Aerostar in design and construction. Produced at the General
Motors plant in Baltimore, Maryland. Astro LT named third
best minivan by *Car and Driver* in 1989.

MAJOR FEATURES

● Astro CS has as 1992 standard equipment: 4-speed
automatic transmission, front disc/rear drum brakes with anti-
lock braking system, and AM radio.

● Astro CL adds as 1992 standard equipment: rally wheels, air
conditioning, upgraded stereo system, tilt steering column,
and cruise control. The Chevy Astro CS is also offered in Sport
Group 1 or Sport Group 2 versions.

● Astro LT adds as 1992 standard equipment: CL Group plus
roof rack, upgraded tires, alloy wheels, and upgraded seating.

PRICE HISTORY

The following new car prices reflect the approximate retail cost
of the base model: **1987** - $8,797; **1988** - $10,696; **1989** -
$11,900; **1990** - $13,790; **1991** - $14,580; **1992** - $15,185.

DIMENSIONS

Body Style	Years Avail	Wheel Base (in)	Lgth (in)	Ht (in)	Avg Wt (lbs)	Fuel Cap (gal)	Front Hdrm (in)	Front Legrm (in)
5d van	87-88	111	176.8	74.5	4,404	17.0	na	na
5d van	89-89	111	176.8	74.9	5,000	17.0	na	na
5d van	90-91	111	176.8	74.9	5,000	27.0	na	na
5d van	92-92	111	176.8	76.2	5,700	27.0	na	na

ENGINES

Type	Displacement (L)	Fuel Dly	HP @rpm	Torque @rpm (ft/lbs)	MPG Cty/Hwy	Years Avail
V-6	4.3	FI	150@4000	230@2400	16/21	87-92

KEY: I=in-line engine; V=V engine; F=flat engine; FI=fuel injection; bbl=barrel carburetor; T=turbo; D=diesel; HP=horsepower; MPG=estimated average miles per gallon.

EVALUATIONS, TESTS, AND RANKINGS

1990: "a perfectly competent all-wheel-drive minivan ... nosier than the other vans in this group, and runs out of breath at relatively low rpm." **Source:** "Vans for all Seasons," *Popular Mechanics*, September 1990, pp. 24-27.

1990: "felt like a full-size truck ... visibility out the back was the worst of any van in the group ... the liveliest vehicle in the bunch to drive. The Engine was smooth and so was the transmission." **Source:** "Best of the Minivans," *Changing Times*, July 1990, pp. 41-45.

1989: "suffered from a trucklike feel. But ... it gains in likability if you consider it a civilized form of truck ... driving experience in the Astro was among the least pleasant of the group ... steering is completely numb ... split second seat is a handy, neat feature." **Source:** "Eeny, Meeny, Miney, Mini: We pick a winner from a field of eight minivans," *Car and Driver*, May 1989, pp. 62-63, 65, 67, 71, 75-77, 81.

RECALLS

None to date.

SAFETY AND REPAIRS

1987: "Car Clinic," *Popular Mechanics*, August 1990, p. 26. **Note:** Tip for clashing starter motor gears in 1987-88 General Motors 4.3, 5.0, and 5.7 liter engines.

REPAIR MANUALS

709 ● Chevrolet Astro and GMC Safari
Clymer Publications
P.O. Box 1209
Overland Park, KS 66212   Ph:(913)541-6694

Published 1988. **Price:** $14.00.

710 ● Chevrolet Astro-GMC Safari, 1985-1990
Chilton Co.
Chilton Way
Radnor, PA 19089   Ph:(215)964-4000

Published 1990. **Price:** $24.95.

711 ● Chilton's Chevrolet 1968-1988
Chilton Co.
Chilton Way
Radnor, PA 19089   Ph:(215)964-4000

Published 1989. **Price:** $15.95.

712 ● Get Your Chevrolet-GMC Fixed Right
Consumer Reports Books
51 E. 42nd St., Suite 800
New York, NY 10017   Ph:(212)682-9280

Editor(s): Mort Schultz. **Price:** $8.95.

OTHER INFORMATION SOURCES

713 ● All Chevy
McMullen Publishing, Inc.
2145 W. La Palma Ave.   Ph:(714)635-9040
Anaheim, CA 92801-1785   Fax:(714)533-9999

Auto magazine for Chevrolet car enthusiasts. Quarterly. **Editor(s):** Thomas M. McMullen, Publisher.

714 ● Friends Magazine
Ceco Publishing
3221 W. Big Beaver, Ste. 110
Troy, MI 48084   Ph:(313)575-9400

Offers articles on Chevrolet automobiles. Monthly. **Editor(s):** Michael Brudenell. **Price:** Free.

715 ● Standard Catalog of Chevrolet
Krause Publications, Inc.
700 E. State St.
Iola, WI 54990   Ph:(715)445-2214

Published 1990. **Price:** $19.95.

CHEVROLET BERETTA (1987-92)

Introduced with the Chevrolet Corsica in March 1987; first editions went to rental agencies rather than dealerships. Produced at the General Motors plant in Wilmington, Delaware. Named to *Car and Driver's* 1990 Ten Best Cars Nominee list. Ranked second among compact cars in crash test performance by *The Car Book* in 1992.

1988 Chevrolet Beretta

MAJOR FEATURES

● Chevrolet Beretta has as 1992 standard equipment: 5-speed manual transmission, front-wheel drive, power rack-and-pinion steering, front disc/rear drum brakes with anti-lock braking system, driver's side airbag, and AM/FM stereo.

● Chevrolet Beretta GT adds as 1992 standard equipment: split-folding rear seat, Level III sport suspension, and 15-inch cast aluminum wheels.

● Chevrolet Beretta GTZ adds as 1992 standard equipment: leather-wrapped steering wheel, Level IV sport suspension, upgraded tires, and 16-inch cast aluminum wheels.

● Chevrolet Beretta GTU was a modification of the GT package done by Cars & Concepts. It offered in 1989 as standard features: front and rear spoilers, performance handling package, and other exterior body stylings.

PRICE HISTORY

The following new car prices reflect the approximate retail cost of the base model: **1988** - $10,135; **1989** - $10,575; **1990** - $10,320; **1991** - $10,365; **1992** - $10,999.

DIMENSIONS

Body Style	Years Avail	Wheel Base (in)	Lgth (in)	Ht (in)	Avg Wt (lbs)	Fuel Cap (gal)	Front Hdrm (in)	Front Legrm (in)
2d cpe	87-90	103.4	187.2	52.9	2,637	15.6	38	43.4
2d cpe	91-92	103.4	183.4	56.2	2,649	15.6	38.1	43.4
2d conv	90-90	103.4	187.2	53.1	2,745	15.6	40	43.4

ENGINES

Type	Displacement (L)	Fuel Dly	HP @rpm	Torque @rpm (ft/lbs)	MPG Cty/Hwy	Years Avail
I-4	2.0	FI	90@5600	108@3200	24/34	87-89
I-4	2.2	FI	95@5200	120@3200	24/33	90-91
I-4	2.3	FI	180@6200	160@5200	22/31	90-92
I-4	2.2	FI	110@5200	130@3200	25/34	92-92
V-6	2.8	FI	125@4500	160@3600	20/29	87-88
V-6	2.8	FI	130@4700	160@3600	18/29	89-89
V-6	3.1	FI	135@4200	180@3600	19/28	90-90
V-6	3.1	FI	140@4200	185@3200	19/28	91-92

KEY: I=in-line engine; V=V engine; F=flat engine; FI=fuel injection; bbl=barrel carburetor; T=turbo; D=diesel; HP=horsepower; MPG=estimated average miles per gallon.

EVALUATIONS, TESTS, AND RANKINGS

1991: "[GTZ] received decent marks for comfort and instrumentation . . . criticisms for the details . . . fast, however, its buzzy engine note was not appreciated." **Source:** "Cheap Thrills," *July 1991, pp. 42-48, 51-53*, Motor Trend.

1990: "Almost everyone likes the way Chevy's lean and clean Beretta looks;. . .doesn't drive very lean or clean unless you're just tooling down the highway . . . suspension goes sloppy and nasty on roads . . . Despite good test-track numbers, the Beretta is a low-excitement . . . low-aspirations car." **Source:** "Eleven for Thirteen: Sportsters, $13,000 and under, that you can actually enjoy," *Car and Driver*, June 1990, pp. 46-50, 52, 61, 63, 64, 64, 66-69.

1990: "[GTZ] an extremely well-balanced front wheel drive performance car . . . straight-line performance of the car is respectable even though you have to flog the engine to get it . . . provides a fun, forgiving ride that's easy and enjoyable to drive hard." **Source:** "GeTting Zerious," *Hot Rod*, March 1990, pp. 104-106.

1989: "[GTU] handling is very good with understeer tending towardneutral . . . poor choice of interior materials . . . needs more detail development to be really competitive." **Source:** "Coupes de Grace," *Popular Mechanics*, May 1989, pp. 120-124, 212, 214.

1988: "base model's four-banger is an abomination, but the six adds sufficient brio to make the car a solid contender in this group. . .Beretta's interior is comfortable for four adults." **Source:** "Hitting for High Average," *Car and Driver*, August 1988, pp. 58-69.

1987: "Beretta GT two-door coupe . . . is fast . . . It's efficient . . . it's attractive . . . steering wheel is set cockeyed to the dash . . . bucket seats are the best GM has ever made, very

supporting and comfortable." **Source:** "Chevy Muscle: Beretta GT seems a good bet to quicken America's heartbeat," *The Detroit News*, February 11, 1987, pp. 1F-2F.

RECALLS

1991: (36,364 passenger cars; includes the Chevrolet Beretta and Chevrolet Corsica): Nut attaching steering wheel may not have been properly tightened during installation, causing the steering wheel to separate from steering column, resulting in loss of vehicle control. **Corrective action:** Tighten the nut to the proper torque as necessary. *(NHTSA Campaign No. 91V083000.)*

1990: (26,464 cars; includes other Chevrolet models): Rear center seat belt information omitted from owner's manual. **Corrective action:** Insert missing information into owner's manual. *(NHTSA Campaign No. 90V065000.)*

1989: (29,951 cars; includes Chevrolet Corsica and Chevrolet Beretta): Front seat belt latch plates may not engage the buckle assemblies. In an event of an accident, unbelted or improperly belted occupants are more at risk to injury than if belts are properly buckled. **Corrective action:** Replace improperly functioning buckle assemblies. *(NHTSA Campaign No. 89V034000.)*

1989: (642 cars; includes the Chevrolet Corsica and Chevrolet Beretta): Front seat frame assembly may contain an improper, missing and/or mislocated weld that could fracture. Could cause unexpected seat movement and result in personal injury and/or loss of control of the car. **Corrective action:** Replace both front seat assemblies. *(NHTSA Campaign No. 89V087000.)*

1989: (13,095 passenger vehicles with 2.0L or 2.8L engines; includes several General Motors models): Fuel tank leak could occur due to small creases on tank underside cracking during pressure cycling which occurs during normal operation. In presence of ignition source, this condition could result in fire. **Corrective action:** Replace fuel tank. *(NHTSA Campaign No. 88V189000.)*

1987-88: (170,769 passenger cars; includes Chevrolet Beretta nad Chevrolet Corsica): Door hinge (upper or lower) may break while opening or closing door making it difficult to reposition and close properly. Hinge separation may reduce structural integrity of side of car and increase risk of injury in certain types of accidents. **Corrective action:** Replace door hinges on both doors. *(NHTSA Campaign No. 89V225000.)*

1987-88: (282,052 passenger vehicles; includes Chevrolet Corsica and Beretta): Secondary hood latch assembly may not have been properly adjusted in latch becoming bent. Bent secondary hood latch could cause primary latch to malfunction. If this occured hood could unexpectedly open. If this happened while vehicle is in motion, reduction of forward visibility could cause vehicle crash without prior warning. **Corrective action:** Inspect and replace secondary hood latch assemblies as required. *(NHTSA Campaign No. 88V039000.)*

1987: (2,020 cars; recall includes the Chevrolet Corsica and Chevrolet Beretta): Loss of skid plate could lead to disengagement of both secondary and primary hood latches. Hood could open unexpectantly; if vehicle were in motion, the hood could contact the windshield, reduce the drivers vision area, and a crash could occur without prior warning. **Corrective action:** Install a secondary latch skid plate and/or secondary latch skid plate retaining screws. *(NHTSA Campaign No. 87V062000.)*

SAFETY AND REPAIRS

1990: "GM Recalls Cars for Belt, Brake Ills," *Automotive News*, December 9, 1991, p. 43. **Note:** 1989-90 Berettas have faulty shoulder belt retractors.

REPAIR MANUALS

716 ● Chilton's Chevrolet 1968-1988
Chilton Co.
Chilton Way
Radnor, PA 19089   Ph:(215)964-4000

Published 1989. **Price:** $15.95.

717 ● Chilton's Chevrolet Corsica and Beretta 1988
Chilton Co.
Chilton Way
Radnor, PA 19089   Ph:(215)964-4000

Published 1989. **Price:** $15.95.

718 ● Get Your Chevrolet-GMC Fixed Right
Consumer Reports Books
51 E. 42nd St., Suite 800
New York, NY 10017   Ph:(212)682-9280

Editor(s): Mort Schultz. **Price:** $8.95.

OTHER INFORMATION SOURCES

719 ● All Chevy
McMullen Publishing, Inc.
2145 W. La Palma Ave.   Ph:(714)635-9040
Anaheim, CA 92801-1785   Fax:(714)533-9999

Auto magazine for Chevrolet car enthusiasts. Quarterly.
Editor(s): Thomas M. McMullen, Publisher.

720 ● Chevrolet High Performance
Peterson Publishing Co.
6725 Sunset Blvd.
Los Angeles, CA 90028   Ph:(213)854-2222

Explains how to repair, restore, and improve performance of
specific Chevrolet models. Bimonthly. **Editor(s):** Isaac Martin.
Price: $11.95 per year; $2.95 per issue.

721 ● Chevy Power
Engledrum Publishing Corp.
153 Asharoken Ave.
Northport, NY 11768   Ph:(516)261-5260

Bimonthly. **Price:** $2.95 per issue.

722 ● Friends Magazine
Ceco Publishing
3221 W. Big Beaver, Ste. 110
Troy, MI 48084   Ph:(313)575-9400

Offers articles on Chevrolet automobiles. Monthly. **Editor(s):**
Michael Brudenell. **Price:** Free.

723 ● Standard Catalog of Chevrolet
Krause Publications, Inc.
700 E. State St.
Iola, WI 54990   Ph:(715)445-2214

Published 1990. **Price:** $19.95.

724 ● Super Chevy
Argus Publishers Corp.
12100 Wilshire Blvd., Ste. 250
Los Angeles, CA 90025   Ph:(213)820-3601
          Fax:(213)207-9388

Automotive magazine. Monthly. **Editor(s):** Bruce Hampson.
Price: $16.00.

CHEVROLET BLAZER (1987-92)

Corporate twins are the GMC Jimmy and Oldsmobile Bravada.
Produced at the General Motors plants in Flint and Pontiac,
Michigan. S-10 Blazer 4-door in 2WD and 4WD (with 107-
inch wheelbase was added to the Blazer line in 1991).

1990 Chevrolet Blazer

MAJOR FEATURES

● Chevrolet Blazer, 2-door and 4-door, have as 1992 standard
equipment: 5-speed manual transmission, front disc/rear drum
brakes with anti-lock braking system, power steering, and AM
radio.

● Chevrolet S-10 Blazer, a full-size sport-utility vehicle, adds as
1992 standard equipment: heavy-duty suspension, four-wheel
drive, tinted glass, high-back bucket seats, and other exterior
body stylings.

● Chevrolet S-10 Blazer Tahoe LT adds as 1992 standard
equipment: other exterior body stylings and an upgraded
interior.

PRICE HISTORY

The following new car prices reflect the approximate retail cost
of the base model: **1988** - $10,505; **1989** - $11,680; **1990** -
$12,966; **1991** - $13,845.

DIMENSIONS

Body Style	Years Avail	Wheel Base (in)	Lgth (in)	Ht (in)	Avg Wt (lbs)	Fuel Cap (gal)	Front Hdrm (in)	Front Legrm (in)
utl wgn	87-88	100.5	170.3	64.7	3,894	13.2	na	na
utl wgn	89-92	100.5	170.3	64.1	4,350	20	39.1	42.5

ENGINES

Type	Displacement (L)	Fuel Dly	HP @rpm	Torque @rpm (ft/lbs)	MPG Cty/Hwy	Years Avail
I-4	2.5	FI	na	na	22/28	87-88
V-6	2.8	FI	na	na	18/25	87-89
V-6	4.3	FI	160@4000	230@2800	17/22	89-92

KEY: I=in-line engine; V=V engine; F=flat engine; FI=fuel injection;
bbl=barrel carburetor; T=turbo; D=diesel; HP=horsepower;
MPG=estimated average miles per gallon.

EVALUATIONS, TESTS, AND RANKINGS

1992: "Its new profile is more contemporary ... longer
wheelbase and improved suspension ... rugged nature is
further enhanced with a maximum tow rating of 7000

pounds." **Source:** "Truck of the Year," *Motor Trend*, December 1991, pp. 104-105.

1991: "The Blazer still requires a twist of the hips to get in the back seat, especially when entering on the driver's side . . . Ramcharger delivered a better ride than the heavier Blazer. But the latter had much better engine performance." **Source:** "Selecting a Full-Size 4x4," *Sports Afield*, January 1991, pp. 36.

1991: "few stand up to hard use any better . . . performance has improved with the miles . . . impressed with the S-10 Blazer's appetite for hard work and its all-around durability." **Source:** "Long-Term Test," *Popular Mechanics*, June 1991, pp. 32-33.

1989: "disappointed at the lack of engine performance. . .interior is nicely stated. . .but. . .ergonomics are not well thought out." **Source:** "Dirt Rods: An expert torture test for the cream of the compact SUV crop," *Popular Mechanics*, March 1989, pp. 113-116, 120.

RECALLS

1991: (181 trucks; includes GMC and Chevrolet models): Improper primer could allow windshield and side windows to loosen. *(NHTSA Campaign No. 90V107000.)*

1991: (181 pickup trucks; includes several GMC and Chevrolet truck models): Use of improper primer on metal surfaces of windshield and side window openings could cause low adhesion to metal surface and would not provide retention required by FMVSS 212. Would not prevent the ejection of vehicle occupants during a crash. **Corrective action:** Remove and reinstall glass using proper primer. *(NHTSA Campaign No. 90V107000.)*

1991: (102,885 light trucks and multi-purpose vehicles; includes the GMC Jimmy, Chevrolet S-10 Pickup, Chevrolet Blazer, and Oldsmobile Bravada): Vehicles have been shipped with the fuel tank sender seal out of position. In the event of a rollover accident, an out of position seal could allow fuel spillage in excess of the amount prescribed by FMVSS 301. Spilled fuel could ignite near an ignition source. **Corrective action:** Replace sender seals. *(NHTSA Campaign No. 91V108000.)*

1987: (60 trucks; recall includes the GMC S15 and Chevrolet S10): Inner tie rod to relay rod nuts on steering linkage may be improperly torqued and not crimped. Loss of one or both nuts could lead to inner tie rod disengagement, which could result in loss of steering control and a truck crash. **Corrective action:** Replace steering linkage assembly. *(NHTSA Campaign No. 87V021000.)*

SAFETY AND REPAIRS

1987: "Car Clinic," *Popular Mechanics*, August 1990, p. 26. **Note:** Tip for clashing starter motor gears in 1987-88 General Motors 4.3, 5.0, and 5.7 liter engines.

REPAIR MANUALS

725 ● Chevrolet and GMC 4-Wheel Drive Tune-Up: 1967-1987
Clymer Publications
P.O. Box 1209
Overland Park, KS 66212   Ph:(913)541-6694

With Illustrations. Published 1983. **Editor(s):** Jeff Robinson. **Price:** $14.99.

726 ● Chevy and GMC Two-Wheel Drive Mid-Size S- and T-Pickups, Blazers, and Jimmy, 1982-1988 (Gas and Diesel)
Clymer Publications
P.O. Box 1209
Overland Park, KS 66212   Ph:(913)541-6694

Published 1987. **Price:** $26.95.

727 ● Chilton's Chevrolet 1968-1988
Chilton Co.
Chilton Way
Radnor, PA 19089   Ph:(215)964-4000

Published 1989. **Price:** $15.95.

728 ● Get Your Chevrolet-GMC Fixed Right
Consumer Reports Books
51 E. 42nd St., Suite 800
New York, NY 10017   Ph:(212)682-9280

Editor(s): Mort Schultz. **Price:** $8.95.

OTHER INFORMATION SOURCES

729 ● All Chevy
McMullen Publishing, Inc.
2145 W. La Palma Ave.   Ph:(714)635-9040
Anaheim, CA 92801-1785   Fax:(714)533-9999

Auto magazine for Chevrolet car enthusiasts. Quarterly. **Editor(s):** Thomas M. McMullen, Publisher.

730 ● Chevrolet S-10 Blazer, GMC S-15, and Olds Bravada, 1982-1990
Chilton Co.
Chilton Way
Radnor, PA 19089   Ph:(215)964-4000

Published 1991. **Price:** $19.95.

731 ● Chevy Outdoors
The Aegis Group
30400 Van Dyke   Ph:(313)574-9100
Warren, MI 48093   Fax:(313)575-9535

Quarterly. **Editor(s):** Michael Brudenell. **Price:** $8.00.

732 ● Friends Magazine
Ceco Publishing
3221 W. Big Beaver, Ste. 110
Troy, MI 48084   Ph:(313)575-9400

Offers articles on Chevrolet automobiles. Monthly. **Editor(s):** Michael Brudenell. **Price:** Free.

733 ● Standard Catalog of Chevrolet
Krause Publications, Inc.
700 E. State St.
Iola, WI 54990   Ph:(715)445-2214

Published 1990. **Price:** $19.95.

CHEVROLET CAMARO (1987-92)

Introduced as part of F-car line along with Pontiac Firebird. Produced at the General Motors plant in Van Nuys, California. Z-28 replaced IROC-Z on performance coupe and convertible in 1991. Ranked in 1992 as one of the best intermediate-sized cars in crash test performance by *The Car Book*.

1992 Chevrolet Camaro Z28 Coupe

MAJOR FEATURES

● Camaro RS Coupe and RS Convertible have as 1992 standard equipment: 5-speed manual transmission, power steering, power front disc/rear drum brakes, front independent suspension/rear axle, driver's side airbag, security system, AM/FM stereo, and 25th Anniversary emblem on instrument panel.

● Camaro Z28 Coupe and Z28 Convertible add as 1992 standard equipment: 5.0-liter V-8 engine, limited-slip differential, fog lamps, and upgraded tires.

● Camaro Heritage Edition is a special exterior package offered in 1992 that commemorates the 25th anniversary of the Chevrolet Camaro.

● Camaro IROC-Z had as 1990 standard equipment: 5.0-liter V-8 engine. Discontinued after Camaro's participation in the International Race of Champions ended.

PRICE HISTORY

The following new car prices reflect the approximate retail cost of the base model: **1987** - $9,995; **1988** - $10,995; **1989** - $11,495; **1990** - $10,995; **1991** - $12,180; **1992** - $12,075.

DIMENSIONS

Body Style	Years Avail	Wheel Base (in)	Lgth (in)	Ht (in)	Avg Wt (lbs)	Fuel Cap (gal)	Front Hdrm (in)	Front Legrm (in)
3d cpe	87-92	101	192.6	50.4	3,105	15.5	37	43
2d conv	90-91	101	192.6	51.1	3,203	15.5	37.1	42.9
2d conv	92-92	101	192.6	51.5	3,220	15.5	37.2	43

ENGINES

Type	Displacement (L)	Fuel Dly	HP @rpm	Torque @rpm (ft/lbs)	MPG Cty/Hwy	Years Avail
V-6	2.8	FI	135@4900	160@3900	18/27	87-89
V-6	3.1	FI	140@4400	180@3600	17/27	90-92
V-8	5.0	4-bbl	170@4400	250@2800	16/25	87-87
V-8	5.0	4-bbl	165@4400	245@2800	16/25	87-87
V-8	5.0	FI	190@4000	295@2800	16/25	87-87
V-8	5.7	FI	225@4400	330@2800	16/25	87-87
V-8	5.0	FI	215@4400	295@3200	17/25	87-90
V-8	5.7	FI	230@4400	330@3200	17/25	88-89
V-8	5.0	FI	170@4000	255@2400	16/26	88-92
V-8	5.0	FI	230@4400	300@3200	17/26	90-92
V-8	5.7	FI	245@4400	345@3200	17/25	90-92

KEY: I=in-line engine; V=V engine; F=flat engine; FI=fuel injection; bbl=barrel carburetor; T=turbo; D=diesel; HP=horsepower; MPG=estimated average miles per gallon.

EVALUATIONS, TESTS, AND RANKINGS

1991: "ideal car for high-profilers and young-minded V-8 adherents who want a cruisemobile . . . excessive rear lockup and poor modulation of the brake pedal . . . road and drivertrain noise permeate the cockpit, especially in the rear seats." **Source:** "Chevrolet Camaro Z28," *Car and Driver*, July 1990, pp. 157, 159.

1990: "IROC-Z Convertible suffered on the road course due to its automatic transmission. . .tranny seemed to be at a loss at times as to what to do in answer to the driver's commands . . . feel could be better, and the brakes are slow to release after locking." **Source:** "Bang for the Buck," *Motor Trend*, November 1989, pp. 42-46, 48, 52-55, 58-59, 62, 64, 66-68, 72, 76.

1989: "one of the most beautiful cars made in America . . . faster and more nimble than any of its predecessors, and it does all this with superb driveability . . . third-generation Camaro has nearly reached its full potential." **Source:** "Roc Solid '89 IROC-Z: Performance You Can Count On," *Hot Rod*, May 1989, pp. 100-102.

1988: "IROC-Z stopped the radar gun at 148 mph and was the highest-placed automatic in the field . . . had a distinctly noticeable wind rumble . . . was quite happy at speed and was easy to keep pointed in the correct direction." **Source:** "Top-Speed 10: Indulging our go-fast fetish again," *Motor Trend*, September 1988, pp. 32-39, 42, 44.

1987: "At steady highway speeds. . .coughed and bucked strongly . . . there was a problem with the on-board computer . . . Chevrolet decided not to put a power top on its convertible . . . once you practice the folding procedure a few times, top-flopping by hand is a snap." **Source:** "Performance Ragtops," *Popular Science*, August 1987, pp. 26-27, 32, 36, 38.

RECALLS

1991: (21 vehicles): Poor bond adhesion between windshield glass and mounting, which could allow the windshield to separate from vehicle during a collision. **Corrective action:** Remove all sealer from windshield and mounting; apply new bonding and sealant material, and reinstall windshield. *(NHTSA Campaign No. 91V031000.)*

1991: (40,696 coupes and convertibles; includes the Chevrolet Camaro and Pontiac Firebird): Metal latchplates may not engage the safety belt buckle assemblies. Movement of the seat occupant in this situation could cause latchplate release from the buckle subjecting the occupant to increased risk of injury in the event of a sudden stop or accident. **Corrective action:** Replace the retractor assembly for the safety belt (front and rear in coupes, and front only in convertibles). *(NHTSA Campaign No. 91V067000.)*

1991: (173 passenger cars): Front seat upper hinge cover screws are too long, and interfere with the seat back inertia lock. This prevents the seat back from locking properly. An unlocked seat back would increase the risk of injury to the seat occupant in the event of a sudden stop or vehicle impact. **Corrective action:** Replace screws securing upper hinge trim cover with correct length screws. *(NHTSA Campaign No. 91V074000.)*

1990: (10,297 cars with 5.0L and 5.7L V8 engines; includes Chevrolet and Pontiac models): Fuel feed hoses may pull out of crimped coupling at engine allowing fuel leakage. **Corrective action:** Install a properly crimped fuel return hose. *(NHTSA Campaign No. 90V114000.)*

1989: (34 convertible top passenger vehicles): Webbing on buckle portion of rear lap/shoulder belts may be too long. In event of severe vehicle crash, effectiveness of lap/shoulder belt may be reduced. **Corrective action:** Replace rear inboard seat belts with belts of proper length. *(NHTSA Campaign No. 88V191000.)*

1988-89: (29,331 cars with 2.8L V6 engines; includes Chevrolet and Pontiac models): Fuel feed hoses may pull out of crimped coupling at engine allowing fuel leakage. **Corrective action:** Install a redesigned fuel feed hose. *(NHTSA Campaign No. 90V115000.)*

1987-90: (1,600,000 cars; includes Chevrolet and Pontiac models; includes models made before 1987): Lack of ultraviolet stabilizer in plastic components of safety belt buckle assemblies could allow sunlight to weaken components. **Corrective action:** Replace or repair seat belt buckle. *(NHTSA Campaign No. 90V105000.)*

SAFETY AND REPAIRS

1987: "Car Clinic," *Popular Mechanics,* August 1990, p. 26. **Note:** Tip for clashing starter motor gears in 1987-88 General Motors 4.3, 5.0, and 5.7 liter engines.

REPAIR MANUALS

734 ● Camaro 228 and Firebird Trans Am Shop Manual, 1982-1987
Clymer Publications
P.O. Box 1209
Overland Park, KS 66212   Ph:(913)541-6694

Published 1989. **Editor(s):** Kalton C. Lahue. **Price:** $14.95.

735 ● Camaro and Firebird, 1982-1987: Super Shop Manual
Clymer Publications
P.O. Box 1209
Overland Park, KS 66212   Ph:(913)541-6694

Published 1988. **Editor(s):** Alan Ahlstrand. **Price:** $26.95.

736 ● Chilton's Camaro 1982-1988
Chilton Co.
Chilton Way
Radnor, PA 19089   Ph:(215)964-4000

Published 1988. **Price:** $15.95.

737 ● Chilton's Chevrolet 1968-1988
Chilton Co.
Chilton Way
Radnor, PA 19089   Ph:(215)964-4000

Published 1989. **Price:** $15.95.

738 ● General Motors 8-Cylinder
Peter Allen Video Productions
38-C Otis St.
West Babylon, NY 11704   Ph:(516)643-4372

A program demonstrating basic maintenance and tune-up procedures for the entitled engine. **Release date:** 1986. **Producer:** Peter Allen Productions. **Acquisition:** Purchase.

739 ● Get Your Chevrolet-GMC Fixed Right
Consumer Reports Books
51 E. 42nd St., Suite 800
New York, NY 10017   Ph:(212)682-9280

Editor(s): Mort Schultz. **Price:** $8.95.

740 ● Haynes Chevrolet Camaro Owners Workshop Manual, No. 866: 1982-1990
Haynes Publications, Inc.
861 Lawrence Dr.
Newbury Park, CA 91320   Ph:(818)889-5400

Editor(s): J. H. Haynes and John B. Raffa. **Price:** $15.95

OTHER INFORMATION SOURCES

741 ● All Chevy
McMullen Publishing, Inc.
2145 W. La Palma Ave.   Ph:(714)635-9040
Anaheim, CA 92801-1785   Fax:(714)533-9999

Auto magazine for Chevrolet car enthusiasts. Quarterly. **Editor(s):** Thomas M. McMullen, Publisher.

742 ● Camaro America
Camaro Owners of America (COA)
701 N. Keyser Ave.
Scranton, PA 18508   Ph:(717)346-7495

Bimonthly.

743 ● Camaro Corral
United States Camaro Club
3944 Indian Ripple Rd.
Dayton, OH 45440   Ph:(513)426-6494

Magazine. Bimonthly. **Price:** Included in membership dues.

744 ● Camaro White Book 1967-1987
Motorbooks International
729 Prospect Ave.
Osceola, WI 54020   Ph:(715)294-3345

Published 1987. **Editor(s):** Michael Antonick. **Price:** $9.95.

745 ● Chevrolet High Performance
Peterson Publishing Co.
6725 Sunset Blvd.
Los Angeles, CA 90028   Ph:(213)854-2222

Explains how to repair, restore, and improve performance of specific Chevrolet models. Bimonthly. **Editor(s):** Isaac Martin. **Price:** $11.95 per year; $2.95 per issue.

746 ● Chevy Power
Engledrum Publishing Corp.
153 Asharoken Ave.
Northport, NY 11768   Ph:(516)261-5260

Bimonthly. **Price:** $2.95 per issue.

747 ● Friends Magazine
Ceco Publishing
3221 W. Big Beaver, Ste. 110
Troy, MI 48084   Ph:(313)575-9400

Offers articles on Chevrolet automobiles. Monthly. **Editor(s):** Michael Brudenell. **Price:** Free.

748 ● Illustrated Camaro Buyer's Guide
Motorbooks International, Pubs. & Wholesalers, Inc.
729 Prospect Ave.
Osceola, WI 54020   Ph:(715)294-3345

Published 1987. **Author(s):** Michael Antonick. **Price:** $16.95.

749 ● In the Fast Lane
International Camaro Club
2001 Pittston Ave.
Scranton, PA 18505   Ph:(717)347-5839

Newsletter; provides technical data, calendar of events, regional news, and classified ads listing Camaro cars and parts. Bimonthly. **Price:** Included in membership dues.

750 ● Standard Catalog of Chevrolet
Krause Publications, Inc.
700 E. State St.
Iola, WI 54990 | Ph:(715)445-2214

Published 1990. **Price:** $19.95.

751 ● The Story of Camaro
Simitar Entertainment
3850 Annapolis Ln. | Ph:(612)559-6660
Plymouth, MN 55447 | Fax:(612)559-0210

Footage of the Camaro in action shows why its speed and handling have made it such a popular car. **Release date:** 1988. **Producer:** Simitar Entertainment. **Price:** $9.95.

752 ● Super Chevy
Argus Publishers Corp.
12100 Wilshire Blvd., Ste. 250 | Ph:(213)820-3601
Los Angeles, CA 90025 | Fax:(213)207-9388

Automotive magazine. Monthly. **Editor(s):** Bruce Hampson. **Price:** $16.00.

753 ● A to Z Camaro Parts Directory
Camaro Owners of America (COA)
701 N. Keyser Ave.
Scranton, PA 18508 | Ph:(717)346-7495

Periodic.

ASSOCIATIONS

754 ● Camaro Owners of America
701 N. Keyser Ave.
Scranton, PA 18508
A. M. Koveleski, Pres. | Ph:(717)346-7495

Founded: 1981. **Membership:** 1,500. Owners and enthusiasts of the Chevrolet Camaro automobile. Provides information on the upkeep, maintenance, restoration, and general knowledge of the Camaro. Services include coupons and discounts on selected merchandise and a classified ad section for buying, selling, and trading cars, parts, and accessories. Maintains library collection of articles and books on Camaros. Sponsors Camaro photo and drawing contests and annual national Camaro 500 meet. **Convention/Meeting:** Annual.

755 ● International Camaro Club
2001 Pittston Ave.
Scranton, PA 18505
Bob Clifford, Pres. | Ph:(717)347-5839

Founded: 1984. **Membership:** 2,500. Chevrolet Camaro enthusiasts and local Camaro clubs. Provides a forum for the exchange of information and parts; sponsors shows and rallies; presents awards. Operates Trim Tag ID Project, which compiles codes for trim tags that appear on the Camaro; these codes are used to aid in restorations and purchasing of cars. Maintains a pace car registry and library. Bestows Member of the Year Award. **Convention/Meeting:** Semiannual car meet (with exhibits) - always June, Oshawa, ON, Canada and August, Pocono Mountains, PA.

756 ● United States Camaro Club
3944 Indian Ripple Rd.
Dayton, OH 45440 | Ph:(513)426-6494
Erlene Jordan, Marketing Dir. | Fax:(513)429-5392

Founded: 1984. **Membership:** 9,800. Owners and enthusiasts interested in Camaro automobiles built between 1967 and 1989. Works with technicians and car dealers on writing educational and technical information concerning the Camaro. Holds swap meets, car shows, and other programs including

trim tag code research and cruise-ins. Provides discount cards on parts and services from advertisers. Sponsors competitions and bestows awards; compiles statistics. Maintains 1500 volume library of automobile magazines and mechanical and dealer books. Plans to create museum. **Convention/Meeting:** Annual car show (with exhibits), usually July or August.

CHEVROLET CAPRICE (1987-92)

Introduced as part of B-car line, along with Buick Estate Wagon, Oldsmobile Custom Cruiser, and Pontiac Safari. Produced at the General Motors plants in Arlington, Texas and Ypsilanti, Michigan (Ypsilanti plant parts data: domestic parts - 98%, imported parts - 2%, *Federal Trade Zone Board*, 1989). Caprice Classic LTZ was named 1991 Car of the Year by *Motor Trend*. Listed as one of the Best Bets of 1992 by *The Car Book*.

1991 Chevrolet Caprice Wagon

MAJOR FEATURES

● Chevrolet Caprice and Caprice Classic have as 1992 standard equipment: 4-speed automatic transmission, power steering, power front disc/rear drum brakes with anti-lock braking system, driver's side airbag, air conditioning, and AM/FM stereo.

● Chevrolet Caprice Classic LTZ adds as 1992 standard equipment: heavy-duty full-frame, 15-inch aluminum wheels, and upgraded tires.

● Chevrolet Caprice Wagon adds as 1992 standard equipment: luggage rack, rear wiper/washer, and upgraded tires.

PRICE HISTORY

The following new car prices reflect the approximate retail cost of the base model: **1987** - $10,995; **1988** - $12,030; **1989** - $13,865; **1990** - $15,995; **1991** - $16,515; **1992** - $17,300.

DIMENSIONS

Body Style	Years Avail	Wheel Base (in)	Lgth (in)	Ht (in)	Avg Wt (lbs)	Fuel Cap (gal)	Front Hdrm (in)	Front Legrm (in)
2d cpe	87-87	116	212.8	56.4	3,527	24.5	38.5	42.2
4d sdn	87-92	116	214.1	56.7	3,907	23.0	39.3	42.2
5d wgn	87-90	116	215.7	58.2	4,324	22	39.6	42.2
5d wgn	91-92	116	217.3	60.9	4,354	22	39.7	42.2

ENGINES

Type	Displace-ment (L)	Fuel Dly	HP @rpm	Torque @rpm (ft/lbs)	MPG Cty/Hwy	Years Avail
V-6	4.3	FI	140@4200	225@2000	19/27	87-88
V-8	5.0	4-bbl	170@4400	250@2800	16/24	87-88
V-8	5.0	4-bbl	140@3200	255@2000	na	88-90
V-8	5.0	FI	170@4200	225@2400	17/26	89-92
V-8	5.7	FI	180@4000	300@2400	16/25	92-92

KEY: I=in-line engine; V=V engine; F=flat engine; FI=fuel injection; bbl=barrel carburetor; T=turbo; D=diesel; HP=horsepower; MPG=estimated average miles per gallon.

EVALUATIONS, TESTS, AND RANKINGS

1992: "rides tauter and with less chop, has firm-feel power steering, and handles more precisely than a base sedan . . . though weighing in at 4066 pounds, the LTZ has a sporty, light-on-its-feet feeling." **Source:** "Ford Crown Victoria LX vs. Chevrolet Caprice Classic LTZ: Uptown Showdown," *Motor Trend*, December 1991, pp. 68-72.

1991: "If you like big, comfortable cars, there's a good chance you could love this one . . . The spacious interior has enough leg, elbow, shoulder and every other kind of room to make 900-mile trips a breeze . . . enormous trunk." **Source:** "Long-Term Test Cars," *Popular Mechanics*, March 1991, pp. 44-46.

1991: "LTZ feels far more sure-footed than traditional American sedans. . .doesn't sacrifice much in terms of ride quality to achieve such high levels of handling prowess." **Source:** "Car of the Year," *Motor Trend*, February 1991, pp. 41-52.

1991: "Handling. . .is adequate . . . there's not a lot of feedback to the driver through steering . . . It's a good freeway cruiser, the only off-note being that at highway speeds there is a somewhat bothersome wind noise." **Source:** "Chevrolet Caprice Wagon all you need for toting, towing," *Flint Journal*, January 10, 1991, p. B2.

1991: "handled tight corners and bending freeway ramps surprisingly well." **Source:** "Chevy follows Classic philosophy," *Detroit News*, January 9, 1991, pp. F1-F2.

1991: "In high-speed driving. . .hunkers down like a freight train when pushed into curves, and does it without rocking and rolling. Responds well to drver input and there is feedback through the steering and seat." **Source:** "LTZ version of Caprice Classic can boogie," *Flint Journal*, February 20, 1991, pp. B1-B2.

1991: "with the important exception of standard ABS braking, the 1991 Caprice is not a better car than the one it replaces." **Source:** "Civil War II," *Popular Mechanics*, July 1990, pp. 56-59.

1990: "well suited to long-distance travels . . . the live axle out back acts up over one-side bumps, producing a distressing case of lateral jitterbugging." **Source:** "Chevrolet Caprice Classic," *Car and Driver*, August 1990, pp. 113-116.

1989: "engine has been around in several versions for many years and is relatively unsophisticated . . . ride quality is excellent . . . personal room in all dimensions is generous, front and rear." **Source:** "Ford LTD Crown Victoria and Chevrolet Caprice Classic Brougham LS: Icons of the American Family Car," *Motor Trend*, August 1989, pp. 88-92, 94.

RECALLS

1990: (21,415 vehicles): Plastic fuel filter assemblies may develop leaks due to static charge buildups found in the plastic fuel lines and filter, which may act as an ignition source. **Corrective action:** Replace plastic assembly with metal fuel filter and bracket. *(NHTSA Campaign No. 90V096000.)*

1987-88: (1,755,897 vehicles equipped with cruise control and certain gasoline and diesel engines; includes several General Motors models; includes models made before 1987): Small nylon bushing in the cruise control servo bail may slip out of place, causing intermittent and unexpected increases in engine speed or dieseling (engine run on with ignition off). Servo rod assembly could catch on engine components and result in a stuck throttle with potential for a vehicle crash. **Corrective action:** Install a new bushing in cruise control servo bail. *(NHTSA Campaign No. 89V102000.)*

1987: (11,936 vehicles with 200 4R transmissions; includes Chevrolet, Pontiac, Oldsmobile, Buick, Cadillac, and GMC models): Manual valve link in transmission may have been improperly formed. **Corrective action:** Replace manual valve detent lever link. *(NHTSA Campaign No. 87V168000.)*

SAFETY AND REPAIRS

1987: "Car Clinic," *Popular Mechanics*, August 1990, p. 26. **Note:** Tip for clashing starter motor gears in 1987-88 General Motors 4.3, 5.0, and 5.7 liter engines.

REPAIR MANUALS

757 ● Chilton's Chevrolet 1968-1988
Chilton Co.
Chilton Way
Radnor, PA 19089   Ph:(215)964-4000

Published 1989. **Price:** $15.95.

758 ● General Motors 8-Cylinder
Peter Allen Video Productions
38-C Otis St.
West Babylon, NY 11704   Ph:(516)643-4372

A program demonstrating basic maintenance and tune-up procedures for the entitled engine. **Release date:** 1986. **Producer:** Peter Allen Productions. **Acquisition:** Purchase.

759 ● Get Your Chevrolet-GMC Fixed Right
Consumer Reports Books
51 E. 42nd St., Suite 800
New York, NY 10017   Ph:(212)682-9280

Editor(s): Mort Schultz. **Price:** $8.95.

760 ● Haynes Chevrolet Full-Size Sedans Owners Workshop Manual, No. 704: 1969-1990
Haynes Publications, Inc.
861 Lawrence Dr.
Newbury Park, CA 91320   Ph:(818)889-5400

Published 1983. **Editor(s):** J.H. Haynes and Curt Choate. **Price:** $15.95.

OTHER INFORMATION SOURCES

761 ● All Chevy
McMullen Publishing, Inc.
2145 W. La Palma Ave.   Ph:(714)635-9040
Anaheim, CA 92801-1785   Fax:(714)533-9999

Auto magazine for Chevrolet car enthusiasts. Quarterly. **Editor(s):** Thomas M. McMullen, Publisher.

762 ● Friends Magazine
Ceco Publishing
3221 W. Big Beaver, Ste. 110
Troy, MI 48084   Ph:(313)575-9400

Offers articles on Chevrolet automobiles. Monthly. **Editor(s):** Michael Brudenell. **Price:** Free.

763 ● **Standard Catalog of Chevrolet**
Krause Publications, Inc.
700 E. State St.
Iola, WI 54990

Ph:(715)445-2214

Published 1990. **Price:** $19.95.

CHEVROLET CAVALIER (1987-92)

Introduced as part of J-car line, along with Buick Skyhawk and Pontiac Sunbird. Listed as one of the Best Bets of 1992 by *The Car Book*. The Chevrolet Cavalier VL was rated as having the lowest insurance cost among vehicles in the compact wagon class in 1990 by *The Complete Car Cost Guide*. Produced at the General Motors plant in Lordstown, Ohio.

1992 Chevrolet Cavalier Z24 Convertible

MAJOR FEATURES

● Chevrolet Cavalier VL Sedan and Cavalier VL Coupe have as 1992 standard equipment: 2.2 liter I-4 engine, 5-speed manual transmission, power rack-and-pinion steering, and front disc/rear drum brakes.

● Chevrolet Cavalier RS Coupe, Cavalier RS Sedan, and Cavalier RS Convertible have as 1992 standard equipment: anti-lock brakes, tinted glass, and AM/FM radio.

● Cavalier VL and RS Wagons have as 1992 standard equipment: 3-speed automatic transmission, and anti-lock brakes.

● Chevrolet Cavalier Z24 Coupe and Convertible add as 1992 standard equipment: 3.1 liter V6 engine, anti-lock brakes, 15-inch aluminum wheels and deck lid spoiler.

● Chevrolet Cavalier Z51, only available with the Cavalier RS, added as 1991 standard equipment: upgraded suspension, rally cluster with tachometer, and touring tires.

PRICE HISTORY

The following new car prices reflect the approximate retail cost of the base model: **1987** - $7,255; **1988** - $6,995; **1989** - $7,375; **1990** - $7,577; **1991** - $7,995; **1992** - $8,899.

DIMENSIONS

Body Style	Years Avail	Wheel Base (in)	Lgth (in)	Ht (in)	Avg Wt (lbs)	Fuel Cap (gal)	Front Hdrm (in)	Front Legrm (in)
2d cpe	87-90	101.2	178.6	52.0	2,465	13.6	37.8	42.9
2d cpe	91-91	101.3	182.3	52.0	2,480	13.6	37.8	42.9
2d cpe	92-92	101.3	182.3	52.0	2,509	15.2	37.8	42.6
2d conv	87-88	101.2	178.7	52.7	2,665	13.6	39.1	42.9
2d conv	92-92	101.3	182.3	52.0	2,672	15.2	37.8	42.2
4d sdn	87-90	101.2	178.6	53.6	2,471	13.6	39.1	42.2
4d sdn	91-91	101.3	182.3	53.6	2,491	13.6	38.6	42.2
4d sdn	92-92	101.3	182.3	53.6	2,520	15.2	39.1	42.1
5d wgn	87-87	101.2	174.5	52.8	2,401	13.6	38.3	42.2
5d wgn	88-89	101.2	177.9	54.3	2,450	13.6	38.3	42.2
5d wgn	90-90	101.2	178.0	54.1	2,529	13.6	38.9	42.2
5d wgn	91-91	101.3	181.1	52.0	2,587	13.6	38.3	42.2
5d wgn	92-92	101.3	181.1	52.0	2,617	15.2	38.9	42.1

ENGINES

Type	Displacement (L)	Fuel Dly	HP @rpm	Torque @rpm (ft/lbs)	MPG Cty/Hwy	Years Avail
I-4	2.0	FI	90@5600	110@2400	25/34	87-87
I-4	2.0	FI	90@5600	108@3200	26/36	88-89
I-4	2.2	FI	95@5200	120@3200	24/35	90-91
I-4	2.2	FI	110@5200	130@3200	25/36	92-92
V-6	2.8	FI	125@4500	160@3600	18/29	87-89
V-6	3.1	FI	140@4500	185@3600	19/28	90-91
V-6	3.1	FI	140@4200	185@3200	19/28	92-92

KEY: I=in-line engine; V=V engine; F=flat engine; FI=fuel injection; bbl=barrel carburetor; T=turbo; D=diesel; HP=horsepower; MPG=estimated average miles per gallon.

EVALUATIONS, TESTS, AND RANKINGS

1991: "[Convertible] quivers only over the harshest bumps . . . engine generates a lot of fan noise, however, and its power delivery is a bit jerky at light throttle . . . dashboard styling is overwrought." **Source:** "Chevrolet Cavalier RS," *Car and Driver,* August, 1991, p. 54.

1991: "relatively low levels of wind buffeting . . . sporting performance and good handling . . . slight case of cowl shake and steering column jitters when traversing potholes or train tracks." **Source:** "Top-Down Showdown: We test the hottest cars under the sun," *Motor Trend,* June 1991, pp. 49-59, 62-63.

1990: "Z24 seems well past its prime—if it ever really had one. . .Still. . .the Cavalier Z24 plants its big tires resolutely as long as you don't fling it around too quickly on challenging roads." **Source:** "Eleven for Thirteen: Sportsters, $13,000 and under, that you can actually enjoy," *Car and Driver,* June 1990, p. 50.

1989: "Cavalier RS delivers a good but unimpressive blend of ride, braking and handling . . . the motor on the test car stalled or stuttered at least once after nearly every cold start. Access to. . .serviced items under the hood is only fair." **Source:** "Cavalier sports new safety features," *Detroit News,* February 15, 1989, p. 2F.

RECALLS

1992: (3,212 passenger cars; includes Chevrolet Cavalier, and Pontiac Sunbird): The secondary hood latch spring is improperly installed or missing. If this latch is not engaged, and the primary hood latch is also not engaged, the hood could open unexpectedly, possibly when the vehicle is in motion. **Corrective action:** Inspect hood latch assemblies and install a new secondary hood latch spring where necessary. (NHTSA Campaign No. 91V166000.)

1991: (41,718 passenger vehicles; includes Chevrolet Cavalier, and Pontiac Sunbird): Front door interlock striker may fail, causing door frame collapse and insufficient strength for the shoulder belt anchorage. Vehicle does not comply with FMVSS 210. **Corrective action:** Replace the passive restraint interlock striker studs on front doors. *(NHTSA Campaign No. 91V165000.)*

1989: (13,095 passenger vehicles with 2.0L or 2.8L engines; includes several General Motors models): Fuel tank leak could occur due to small creases on tank underside cracking during pressure cycling which occurs during normal operation. In presence of ignition source, this condition could result in fire. **Corrective action:** Replace fuel tank. *(NHTSA Campaign No. 88V189000.)*

1988: (14,840 coupe and convertible passenger vehicles; includes Chevrolet Cavalier and Pontiac Sunbird): Rear lamp wiring harness may contain open or intermittent circuits affecting back up lamp or license plate lamp operation. Lamps would flash or be inoperative; cars would not comply with FMVSS 108. **Corrective action:** Install new wiring harness. *(NHTSA Campaign No. 88V095000.)*

1988: (33 passenger vehicles; includes Chevrolet Cavalier and Pontiac Sunbird): There may be poor bond adhesion between windshield glass and mounting. Windshield could separate during a 30 mph frontal barrier test required by FMVSS 212. Such separation during an accident could result in unbelted occupant being ejected and injured. **Corrective action:** Reinstall windshield assuring proper adhesion. *(NHTSA Campaign No. 88V121000.)*

1987: (65,594 passenger vehicles equipped with 2.0 liter engines): Accelerator control cable may contain water which could freeze while vehicle is parked causing travel of accelerator control cable to become restricted when throttle is initially opened. Engine speed may not decrease which could result in loss of accelerator control and a crash without prior warning. **Corrective action:** Replace accelerator control cable. *(NHTSA Campaign No. 87V011000.)*

SAFETY AND REPAIRS

1991: "GM Recalls Cars for Belt Loops," *Automotive News,* February 10, 1992, p. 2. **Note:** May have cracked front-door shoulder belt guide loops.

1991: "GM Recalls Cars for Belt, Brake Ills," *Automotive News,* December 9, 1991, p. 43. **Note:** Substandard front door striker studs.

1988: "Piecemeal," *Popular Mechanics,* November 1989, p. 43. **Note:** 1988 Cavalier has problems with stalling and cruise control.

REPAIR MANUALS

764 ● Chilton's Chevrolet 1968-1988
Chilton Co.
Chilton Way
Radnor, PA 19089   Ph:(215)964-4000

Published 1989. **Price:** $15.95.

765 ● Chilton's Chevrolet Cavalier, Buick Skyhawk, Olds Firenza, Cadillac Cimarron, Pontiac 6000, 1982-88
Chilton Co.
Chilton Way
Radnor, PA 19089   Ph:(215)964-4000

Published 1988. **Price:** $15.95.

766 ● Get Your Chevrolet-GMC Fixed Right
Consumer Reports Books
51 E. 42nd St., Suite 800
New York, NY 10017   Ph:(212)682-9280

Editor(s): Mort Schultz. **Price:** $8.95.

767 ● GMC J Cars: Buick Skyhawk, Cadillac Cimarron, Chevrolet Cavalier, Oldsmobile Firenza, Pontiac J-2000, Sunbird Shop Manual, 1982-87
Clymer Publications
P.O. Box 1209
Overland Park, KS 66212   Ph:(913)541-6694

Published 1987. **Price:** $14.95.

768 ● Haynes Chevrolet Full-Size Sedans Owners Workshop Manual, No. 704: 1969-1990
Haynes Publications, Inc.
861 Lawrence Dr.
Newbury Park, CA 91320   Ph:(818)889-5400

Published 1983. **Editor(s):** J.H. Haynes and Curt Choate. **Price:** $15.95.

769 ● Haynes General Motors J-Cars Owners Workshop Manual, No. 766: 1982-1989
Haynes Publishing, Inc.
861 Lawrence Dr.
Newbury Park, CA 91320   Ph:(818)889-5400

Published 1989. **Price:** $15.95.

770 ● Haynes General Motors J-Cars Owners Workshop Manual, No. 766: 1982-1989
Haynes Publishing, Inc.
861 Lawrence Dr.
Newbury Park, CA 91320   Ph:(818)889-5400

Published 1989. **Price:** $15.95.

OTHER INFORMATION SOURCES

771 ● All Chevy
McMullen Publishing, Inc.
2145 W. La Palma Ave.   Ph:(714)635-9040
Anaheim, CA 92801-1785   Fax:(714)533-9999

Auto magazine for Chevrolet car enthusiasts. Quarterly. **Editor(s):** Thomas M. McMullen, Publisher.

772 ● Chevrolet High Performance
Peterson Publishing Co.
6725 Sunset Blvd.
Los Angeles, CA 90028   Ph:(213)854-2222

Explains how to repair, restore, and improve performance of specific Chevrolet models. Bimonthly. **Editor(s):** Isaac Martin. **Price:** $11.95 per year; $2.95 per issue.

773 ● Chevy Power
Engledrum Publishing Corp.
153 Asharoken Ave.
Northport, NY 11768   Ph:(516)261-5260

Bimonthly. **Price:** $2.95 per issue.

774 ● Friends Magazine
Ceco Publishing
3221 W. Big Beaver, Ste. 110
Troy, MI 48084 Ph:(313)575-9400

Offers articles on Chevrolet automobiles. Monthly. **Editor(s):**
Michael Brudenell. **Price:** Free.

775 ● Standard Catalog of Chevrolet
Krause Publications, Inc.
700 E. State St.
Iola, WI 54990 Ph:(715)445-2214

Published 1990. **Price:** $19.95.

776 ● Super Chevy
Argus Publishers Corp.
12100 Wilshire Blvd., Ste. 250 Ph:(213)820-3601
Los Angeles, CA 90025 Fax:(213)207-9388

Automotive magazine. Monthly. **Editor(s):** Bruce Hampson.
Price: $16.00.

CHEVROLET CELEBRITY (1987-90)

Introduced as part of A-car line, along with Buick Century, Oldsmobile Cutlass Ciera, and Pontiac 6000. Celebrity Wagon produced until 1990 at the General Motors plant in Ste. Therese, Quebec, Canada. All other models discontinued after 1989 and replaced by the Lumina in 1990.

1987 Chevrolet Celebrity

MAJOR FEATURES

● Chevrolet Celebrity Wagon had as 1990 standard equipment: 3-speed manual transmission, front independent suspension, power-assisted rack-and-pinion steering, and power front disc/rear drumbrakes.

● Celebrity had as 1989 standard equipment: 3-speed automatic transmission, power rack-and-pinion steering, front disc/rear drum brakes, cloth upholstery.

● Celebrity CL, Celebrity Eurosport, and Celebrity Classic added as 1989 standard equipment: upgraded interior and additional exterior body stylings. The wagons were also offered in the Eurosport and Estate versions.

PRICE HISTORY

The following new car prices reflect the approximate retail cost of the base model: **1987** - $9,995; **1988** - $10,585; **1989** - $11,495; **1990** - $12,395.

DIMENSIONS

Body Style	Years Avail	Wheel Base (in)	Lgth (in)	Ht (in)	Avg Wt (lbs)	Fuel Cap (gal)	Front Hdrm (in)	Front Legrm (in)
2d cpe	87-88	104.9	188.3	54.1	2,685	15.7	38.6	42.1
4d sdn	87-89	104.9	188.3	54.1	2,751	15.7	38.6	42.1
5d wgn	87-90	104.9	190.8	54.3	2,847	15.7	38.6	42.1

ENGINES

Type	Displacement (L)	Fuel Dly	HP @rpm	Torque @rpm (ft/lbs)	MPG Cty/Hwy	Years Avail
I-4	2.5	FI	98@4800	135@3200	23/30	87-89
I-4	2.5	FI	110@5200	135@3200	na	90-90
V-6	2.8	FI	125@4500	160@3600	20/29	87-89
V-6	3.1	FI	135@4400	180@3600	na	90-90

KEY: I=in-line engine; V=V engine; F=flat engine; FI=fuel injection; bbl=barrel carburetor; T=turbo; D=diesel; HP=horsepower; MPG=estimated average miles per gallon.

EVALUATIONS, TESTS, AND RANKINGS

1987: "attractive, versatile, and contemporary." **Source:** "Chevrolet Celebrity," *Road & Track—Buyer's Guide 1987*, 1986, p. 38.

RECALLS

1988: (27,369 passenger vehicles equipped with 2.8L V6 engine; includes several General Motors models): Fuel feed hose could leak at coupling on engine end of hose assembly. Fuel leakage into engine compartment could result in engine compartment fire that could spread to passenger compartment. **Corrective action:** Install new fuel feed hose assembly. *(NHTSA Campaign No. 88V164000.)*

SAFETY AND REPAIRS

1988: "NHTSA Upgrades Probe of Brakes on Ford Trucks," *Automotive News*, December 9, 1991, p. 40. **Note:** 1987-88 CelebrITys could have loose steering wheels.

REPAIR MANUALS

777 ● Chilton's Chevrolet 1968-1988
Chilton Co.
Chilton Way
Radnor, PA 19089 Ph:(215)964-4000

Published 1989. **Price:** $15.95.

778 ● Chilton's Chevrolet Celebrity, Buick Century, Olds Cutlass Ciera, Pontiac 6000, 1982-1988
Chilton Co.
Chilton Way
Radnor, PA 19089 Ph:(215)964-4000

Also available in Spanish edition. Published 1988. **Price:** $15.95.

779 ● Get Your Chevrolet-GMC Fixed Right
Consumer Reports Books
51 E. 42nd St., Suite 800
New York, NY 10017 Ph:(212)682-9280

Editor(s): Mort Schultz. **Price:** $8.95.

780 ● GM A-Cars Buick Century, Chevrolet Celebrity, Oldsmobile Cutlass Ciera, Pontiac 6000, 1982-87: Shop Manual
Clymer Publications
P.O. Box 1209
Overland Park, KS 66212   Ph:(913)541-6694

Published 1987. **Price:** $14.95.

781 ● Haynes General Motor A-Cars Owner's Workshop Manual, No. 829
Haynes Publishing, Inc.
861 Lawrence Dr.
Newbury Park, CA 91320   Ph:(818)889-5400

Published 1982 through 1989. **Price:** $15.95.

OTHER INFORMATION SOURCES

782 ● All Chevy
McMullen Publishing, Inc.
2145 W. La Palma Ave.   Ph:(714)635-9040
Anaheim, CA 92801-1785   Fax:(714)533-9999

Auto magazine for Chevrolet car enthusiasts. Quarterly.
Editor(s): Thomas M. McMullen, Publisher.

783 ● Friends Magazine
Ceco Publishing
3221 W. Big Beaver, Ste. 110
Troy, MI 48084   Ph:(313)575-9400

Offers articles on Chevrolet automobiles. Monthly. **Editor(s):**
Michael Brudenell. **Price:** Free.

784 ● Standard Catalog of Chevrolet
Krause Publications, Inc.
700 E. State St.
Iola, WI 54990   Ph:(715)445-2214

Published 1990. **Price:** $19.95.

CHEVROLET CHEVETTE (1987)

A rear-drive subcompact based on the GM T-car design from
Opel in Germany. Had a reputation for oil burning and valve-
cover leaks, though parts and service proved easy to locate.
Produced until 1987 at the General Motors plant in Lakewood,
Georgia.

1987 Chevrolet Chevette

MAJOR FEATURES

● Chevrolet Chevette and Chevette CS had as 1987 standard
equipment: automatic transmission, rack-and-pinion steering,
front disc/rear drum brakes, and power windows.

PRICE HISTORY

The following new car prices reflect the approximate retail cost
of the base model: **1987** - $4,995.

DIMENSIONS

Body Style	Years Avail	Wheel Base (in)	Lgth (in)	Ht (in)	Avg Wt (lbs)	Fuel Cap (gal)	Front Hdrm (in)	Front Legrm (in)
3d sdn	87-87	94.3	161.9	52.8	2,078	12.2	37.8	41.7
5d sdn	87-87	97.3	164.9	52.8	2,137	12.2	37.9	41.7

ENGINES

Type	Displacement (L)	Fuel Dly	HP @rpm	Torque @rpm (ft/lbs)	MPG Cty/Hwy	Years Avail
I-4	1.6	2-bbl	65@5200	80@3200	27/35	87-87

KEY: I=in-line engine; V=V engine; F=flat engine; FI=fuel injection;
bbl=barrel carburetor; T=turbo; D=diesel; HP=horsepower;
MPG=estimated average miles per gallon.

EVALUATIONS, TESTS, AND RANKINGS

1987: ''ride (mediocre), interior space (limited).'' **Source:**
''Chevrolet Chevette, Pontiac 1000,'' *Road & Track—Buyers
Guide 1987*, 1986, p. 39.

RECALLS

None to date.

REPAIR MANUALS

785 ● Chevrolet Chevette and Pontiac T 1000 Service Repair Handbook: All Models 1976-1987
Clymer Publications
P.O. Box 1209
Overland Park, KS 66212   Ph:(913)541-6694

Price: $14.95.

786 ● Chilton's Chevette and Pontiac T1000 1976-1988
Chilton Co.
Chilton Way
Radnor, PA 19089   Ph:(215)964-4000

Published 1989. **Price:** $15.95.

787 ● Chilton's Chevrolet 1968-1988
Chilton Co.
Chilton Way
Radnor, PA 19089   Ph:(215)964-4000

Published 1989. **Price:** $15.95.

788 ● Get Your Chevrolet-GMC Fixed Right
Consumer Reports Books
51 E. 42nd St., Suite 800
New York, NY 10017   Ph:(212)682-9280

Editor(s): Mort Schultz. **Price:** $8.95.

789 ● Haynes Chevrolet Chevette-Pontiac T1000 Owners Workshop Manuals, No. 449: 1976-1987
Haynes Publications, Inc.
861 Lawrence Dr.
Newbury Park, CA 91320   Ph:(818)889-5400

Editor(s): J.H. Haynes and R.G. Hawes. **Price:** $15.95.

OTHER INFORMATION SOURCES

790 ● All Chevy
McMullen Publishing, Inc.
2145 W. La Palma Ave.
Anaheim, CA 92801-1785
Ph:(714)635-9040
Fax:(714)533-9999

Auto magazine for Chevrolet car enthusiasts. Quarterly.
Editor(s): Thomas M. McMullen, Publisher.

791 ● Friends Magazine
Ceco Publishing
3221 W. Big Beaver, Ste. 110
Troy, MI 48084
Ph:(313)575-9400

Offers articles on Chevrolet automobiles. Monthly. **Editor(s):**
Michael Brudenell. **Price:** Free.

792 ● Standard Catalog of Chevrolet
Krause Publications, Inc.
700 E. State St.
Iola, WI 54990
Ph:(715)445-2214

Published 1990. **Price:** $19.95.

CHEVROLET CORSICA (1987-92)

Introduced in March 1987; first editions went to rental agencies rather than dealerships. It is essentially similar to the Chevrolet Beretta. Corsica LTZ was discontinued after 1990. Received an overall rating of average from *The Complete Car Cost Guide* in 1990. Listed as one of the Best Bets of 1992 by *The Car Book*. Produced at the General Motors plant in Wilmington, Delaware.

1988 Chevrolet Corsica

MAJOR FEATURES

● Chevrolet Corsica LT has as 1992 standard equipment: 2.2 liter I-4 engine, 5-speed manual transmission, rack-and-pinion power steering, front disc/rear drum brakes with anti-lock, and driver's side airbag.

● Corsica Z52 added as 1991 standard equipment: uplevel console, compact disc player, aluminum wheels, and touring tires. Available in either a four-door hatchback or sedan.

● Corsica LTZ added as 1990 standard equipment: 3.1 liter V-6 fuel-injected engine, air conditioning, sport suspension, luggage rack, and upgraded interior. Only available as a four-door sedan.

● Corsica VFV (variable-fueled vehicle) runs on 85 percent methanol and 15 percent premium unleaded gasoline. It is part of the California Energy Commission's methanol demonstration program and adds as 1992 standard equipment: 2.8 liter V-6 engine.

PRICE HISTORY

The following new car prices reflect the approximate retail cost of the base model: **1987** - $8,995; **1988** - $9,555; **1989** - $9,985; **1990** - $9,495; **1991** - $10,070; **1992** - $10,999.

DIMENSIONS

Body Style	Years Avail	Wheel Base (in)	Lgth (in)	Ht (in)	Avg Wt (lbs)	Fuel Cap (gal)	Front Hdrm (in)	Front Legrm (in)
4d sdn	87-87	103.4	183.4	52.7	2,491	13.6	38.9	43.4
4d sdn	88-89	103.4	183.4	52.7	2,595	13.6	38.1	43.4
4d sdn	90-90	103.4	183.4	53.8	2,635	13.6	38.1	43.4
4d sdn	91-92	103.4	183.4	56.2	2,638	15.6	38.1	43.4

ENGINES

Type	Displace-ment (L)	Fuel Dly	HP @rpm	Torque @rpm (ft/lbs)	MPG Cty/Hwy	Years Avail
I-4	2.0	FI	90@5600	108@3200	24/34	87-89
I-4	2.2	FI	95@5200	120@3200	24/33	90-91
I-4	2.2	FI	110@5200	130@3200	25/34	92-92
V-6	2.8	FI	130@4700	160@3600	18/29	87-89
V-6	3.1	FI	135@4200	180@3600	19/28	90-90
V-6	3.1	FI	140@4200	185@3200	19/28	91-92

KEY: I=in-line engine; V=V engine; F=flat engine; FI=fuel injection; bbl=barrel carburetor; T=turbo; D=diesel; HP=horsepower; MPG=estimated average miles per gallon.

EVALUATIONS, TESTS, AND RANKINGS

1990: "a bit quicker than the gasoline-fed Corsica LTZ ... burns its fuel more efficiently, but alcohol fuel has less energy per gallon than regular gasoline ... when methanol combustion occurs, there's a significant amount of formaldehyde produced." **Source:** "Chevrolet Corsica VFV: Working toward cleaner air," *Motor Trend*, April 1990, pp. 106-107.

1989: "interior doesn't measure up to its exterior ... an excellent, attractive platform from which Chevrolet could build a great family sedan." **Source:** "Best Sellers: A 13-car pitched battle for small sedan supremacy," *Popular Mechanics*, July 1989, pp. 60-63, 120-122.

1989: "attractive, shapely, and fun to be with ... power-assisted rack-and-pinion steering is a tad light but quite precise ... simply a Corsica with only a little extra personality." **Source:** "Chevrolet Corsica LTZ," *Motor Trend*, April 1989, pp. 93-96.

1989: "sporty handling ... for commuting with pizazz, but a heavy dose of practicality ... ride is comfortable, although a section of rough road will start it wallowing and pitching." **Source:** "Go to Work in Style," *Home Mechanix*, January 1989, pp. 64-67.

1988: "relaxing to drive ... drives with an easy viscosity ... The Corsica may not stop as quickly or hold up as well over the long haul as ... its foes." **Source:** "Hitting for High Average: We pick the One Best Sedan your $14,000 will buy," *Car and Driver*, August 1988, pp. 58-69.

RECALLS

1991: (36,364 passenger cars; includes the Chevrolet Beretta and Chevrolet Corsica): Nut attaching steering wheel may not have been properly tightened during installation, causing the steering wheel to separate from steering column, resulting in loss of vehicle control. **Corrective action:** Tighten the nut to the proper torque as necessary. (*NHTSA Campaign No. 91V083000.*)

1990: (26,464 cars; includes other Chevrolet models): Rear center seat belt information omitted from owner's manual. **Corrective action:** Insert missing information into owner's manual. *(NHTSA Campaign No. 90V065000.)*

1989: (29,951 cars; includes Chevrolet Corsica and Chevrolet Beretta): Front seat belt latch plates may not engage the buckle assemblies. In an event of an accident, unbelted or improperly belted occupants are more at risk to injury than if belts are properly buckled. **Corrective action:** Replace improperly functioning buckle assemblies. *(NHTSA Campaign No. 89V034000.)*

1989: (642 cars; includes the Chevrolet Corsica and Chevrolet Beretta): Front seat frame assembly may contain an improper, missing and/or mislocated weld that could fracture. Could cause unexpected seat movement and result in personal injury and/or loss of control of the car. **Corrective action:** Replace both front seat assemblies. *(NHTSA Campaign No. 89V087000.)*

1989: (13,095 passenger vehicles with 2.0L or 2.8L engines; includes several General Motors models): Fuel tank leak could occur due to small creases on tank underside cracking during pressure cycling which occurs during normal operation. In presence of ignition source, this condition could result in fire. **Corrective action:** Replace fuel tank. *(NHTSA Campaign No. 88V189000.)*

1987-88: (170,769 passenger cars; includes Chevrolet Beretta and Chevrolet Corsica): Door hinge (upper or lower) may break while opening or closing door making it difficult to reposition and close properly. Hinge separation may reduce structural integrity of side of car and increase risk of injury in certain types of accidents. **Corrective action:** Replace door hinges on both doors. *(NHTSA Campaign No. 89V225000.)*

1987-88: (282,052 passenger vehicles; includes Chevrolet Corsica and Beretta): Secondary hood latch assembly may not have been properly adjusted in latch becoming bent. Bent secondary hood latch could cause primary latch to malfunction. If this occured hood could unexpectantly open. If this happened while vehicle is in motion, reduction of forward visibility could cause vehicle crash without prior warning. **Corrective action:** Inspect and replace secondary hood latch assemblies as required. *(NHTSA Campaign No. 88V039000.)*

1987: (2,020 cars; recall includes the Chevrolet Corsica and Chevrolet Beretta): Loss of skid plate could lead to disengagement of both secondary and primary hood latches. Hood could open unexpectantly; if vehicle were in motion, the hood could contact the windshield, reduce the drivers vision area, and a crash could occur without prior warning. **Corrective action:** Install a secondary latch skid plate and/or secondary latch skid plate retaining screws. *(NHTSA Campaign No. 87V062000.)*

SAFETY AND REPAIRS

1990: "GM Recalls Cars for Belt, Brake Ills," *Automotive News,* December 9, 1991, p.43. **Note:** 1989-90 Corsicas have faulty shoulder belt retractors.

1989: "GM Recalls Cars, Trucks," *Automotive News,* January 27, 1992, p.2. **Note:** Cracks may develop at outer edges of the wheel spokes causing them to separate from the rim.

REPAIR MANUALS

793 ● Chilton's Chevrolet 1968-1988
Chilton Co.
Chilton Way
Radnor, PA 19089   Ph:(215)964-4000

Published 1989. **Price:** $15.95.

794 ● Chilton's Chevrolet Corsica and Beretta 1988
Chilton Co.
Chilton Way
Radnor, PA 19089   Ph:(215)964-4000

Published 1989. **Price:** $15.95.

795 ● Get Your Chevrolet-GMC Fixed Right
Consumer Reports Books
51 E. 42nd St., Suite 800
New York, NY 10017   Ph:(212)682-9280

Editor(s): Mort Schultz. **Price:** $8.95.

OTHER INFORMATION SOURCES

796 ● All Chevy
McMullen Publishing, Inc.
2145 W. La Palma Ave.   Ph:(714)635-9040
Anaheim, CA 92801-1785   Fax:(714)533-9999

Auto magazine for Chevrolet car enthusiasts. Quarterly. **Editor(s):** Thomas M. McMullen, Publisher.

797 ● Chevrolet High Performance
Peterson Publishing Co.
6725 Sunset Blvd.
Los Angeles, CA 90028   Ph:(213)854-2222

Explains how to repair, restore, and improve performance of specific Chevrolet models. Bimonthly. **Editor(s):** Isaac Martin. **Price:** $11.95 per year; $2.95 per issue.

798 ● Chevy Power
Engledrum Publishing Corp.
153 Asharoken Ave.
Northport, NY 11768   Ph:(516)261-5260

Bimonthly. **Price:** $2.95 per issue.

799 ● Friends Magazine
Ceco Publishing
3221 W. Big Beaver, Ste. 110
Troy, MI 48084   Ph:(313)575-9400

Offers articles on Chevrolet automobiles. Monthly. **Editor(s):** Michael Brudenell. **Price:** Free.

800 ● Standard Catalog of Chevrolet
Krause Publications, Inc.
700 E. State St.
Iola, WI 54990   Ph:(715)445-2214

Published 1990. **Price:** $19.95.

801 ● Super Chevy
Argus Publishers Corp.
12100 Wilshire Blvd., Ste. 250   Ph:(213)820-3601
Los Angeles, CA 90025   Fax:(213)207-9388

Automotive magazine. Monthly. **Editor(s):** Bruce Hampson. **Price:** $16.00.

CHEVROLET CORVETTE (1987-92)

Produced at the General Motors plant in Bowling Green, Kentucky. Made *Car and Driver's* Ten Best Cars List in 1987 and 1988. Named to *Car and Driver's* 1989 Ten Best Performers list for quickest 0-60 mph acceleration (4.5 seconds), quarter-mile (12.8 seconds), top speed (175 mph), quickest 70-0 mph braking (157 feet), and roadholding (0.89 g).

Placed in *Motor Trend's* 1989 Top 10 New Cars Buys: Domestic. Corvette ZR-1 chosen by *RAT* as one of the Ten Best Cars in the World in 1991.

1991 Chevrolet Corvette Coupe

MAJOR FEATURES

● Corvette Coupe and Convertible has as 1992 standard equipment: 6-speed manual transmission, 4-wheel power disc brakes with anti-lock braking system, power rack-and-pinion steering, cruise control, driver's side airbag, security system, air conditioning, rear defogger, power windows and door locks, and AM/FM stereo cassette.

● Corvette ZR-1 adds as 1992 standard equipment: supercharged engine, upgraded tires, solar glass, and high performance stereo system.

PRICE HISTORY

The following new car prices reflect the approximate retail cost of the base model: **1987** - $27,999; **1988** - $29,480; **1989** - $31,545; **1990** - $31,979; **1991** - $32,455; **1992** - $33,635.

DIMENSIONS

Body Style	Years Avail	Wheel Base (in)	Lgth (in)	Ht (in)	Avg Wt (lbs)	Fuel Cap (gal)	Front Hdrm (in)	Front Legrm (in)
2d cpe	87-90	96.2	176.5	46.7	3,255	20	36.5	42.6
2d cpe	91-92	96.2	178.5	46.3	3,223	20	36.4	42.0
2d conv	89-90	96.2	176.5	46.4	3,301	20	36.5	42.6
2d conv	91-92	96.2	178.5	47.3	3,269	20	36.4	42.0

ENGINES

Type	Displacement (L)	Fuel Dly	HP @rpm	Torque @rpm (ft/lbs)	MPG Cty/Hwy	Years Avail
V-8	5.7	FI	240@4000	345@3200	16/25	87-90
V-8	5.7	FI	250@4400	350@3200	16/25	90-90
V-8	5.7	FI	245@4000	340@3200	16/26	91-91
V-8	5.7	FI	375@5800	370@4800	16/25	91-92
V-8	5.7	FI	300@5000	330@4000	17/25	92-92

KEY: I=in-line engine; V=V engine; F=flat engine; FI=fuel injection; bbl=barrel carburetor; T=turbo; D=diesel; HP=horsepower; MPG=estimated average miles per gallon.

EVALUATIONS, TESTS, AND RANKINGS

1992: "there are important changes, adding up to profound improvements to the Corvette's dynamic repertoire ... best sense of structural integrity the cars have ever had ... the '92 models are the consummate Corvettes in the history of the line." **Source:** "Chevrolet Corvette LT1," *Automobile Magazine*, October 1991, pp. 102-103.

1992: "fuel economy on the city cycle is better ... may well

possess the best ride of any sports car ... on its way to becoming a sophiscated, all-weather, long-distance touring machine." **Source:** "Chevrolet Corvette," *Car and Driver*, October 1991, p. 71.

1992: "will probably go down in history books as a watershed model for the breed ... improved ride and compliance on the road ... drivers can now venture fearlessly into the snow and sleet, even with all that horsepower." **Source:** "New For '92," *Road & Track*, November 1991, p. 92.

1992: "this is a all-season Corvette, as docile on the slippery stuff as most front-drivers ... offers a quieter, more comfortable ride." **Source:** "Chevrolet Corvette LT1," *Motor Trend*, October 1991, pp. 46-49.

1992: "howls with more power than ever ... massive and bulky feel, peculiar instrument cluster ... delivers a surprisingly good ride." **Source:** "Chevrolet Corvette," *Car and Driver*, December 1991, pp. 77-79.

1992: "not a slick sports car but a brutish howler ... not unpleasant at touring speeds ... whole package is simply delightful." **Source:** "Chevrolet Corvette LT1," *Automobile Magazine*, January 1992.

1992: "will be a benchmark in Corvette history ... overall ride quality is of grand tourer caliber ... excellent engineering." **Source:** "Chevrolet Corvette LT1," *Road & Track*, January 1992, pp. 63-66.

1991: "Torque flows as sweetly as maple syrup. . .close-ratio transmission does an excellent job of spreading the motor's deliciousness ... delivers impressive performance without taxing the driver." **Source:** "Chevrolet Corvette L98 Coupe," *Motor Trend*, February 1991, pp. 76-80.

1991: "all comes together now in a sophisticated and satisfying performance package." **Source:** "Chevrolet Corvette L98," *Automobile*, January 1991, p. 54.

1991: "Cargo space is limited in size and shape and it's hard to reach ... Drive the Corvette, though, and quibbles about storage fade ... practical? Not very. . .fun? You bet." **Source:** "Corvette Convertible: Slick, Quick and a Kick to Drive," *Autoweek's Autofile 1991 Edition*, 1990, pp. 108-109.

1991: "fiberglass contoured body is impressive ... built for high-speed cruising ... roof can be difficult to remove." **Source:** "The ZR-1: Right on Track," *Design News*, October 1, 1990, pp. 222-223.

1991: "tight-fitting fabric top ... seals out wind and water superbly ... Rear visibility isn't too good ... rather high interior noise levels." **Source:** "Top-Down Showdown: We test the hottest cars under the sun," *Motor Trend*, June 1991, pp. 49-59, 62-63.

1990: "'90 Corvette is the best car it's ever been, the performance equal of a Ferrari for literally 50% of a Ferrari's price ... But fundamental to the Corvette's appeal is that it's American, a thoroughbred domestic sports car among the world's best." **Source:** "Top 10 New Car Buys: Domestic," *Motor Trend*, November 1989, pp. 80-83, 86-89.

1990: "neutral chassis worked its wide Goodyears to maximum advantage. . .easy to drive at the limit, and it stuck phenomenally well." **Source:** "Bang for the Buck," *Motor Trend*, November 1989, pp. 42-46, 48, 52-55, 58-59, 62, 64, 66-68, 72, 76.

1990: "unrefined ... the ride ... was stiff. Steering was heavy ... holds the road tenaciously." **Source:** "Still King of the Hill," *Changing Times*, July 1990, p. 88.

1989: "just gets better and better, and it gets more civilized in the bargain ... 0 to 60 mph in under six seconds and a top speed of more than 150 mph ... performance envelope is rounded out by equally impressive braking and handling." **Source:** "Ten Best Cars: And picking them wasn't easy," *Car and Driver*, January 1989, pp. 30-35.

1989: "high-speed manners remain impeccable; it's absolutely stable ... and even at top speed, it feels like it's loafing." **Source:** "Top-Speed 10: Indulging our go-fast fetish again," *Motor Trend*, September 1988, pp. 32-39, 42, 44.

1989: "a giant step ahead of any production sports car ever built in this country ... combines everyday good manners with performance potentials that equal or surpass the world's most exalted thoroughbreds ... this car is a rocket." **Source:** "Chevrolet Corvette ZR-1," *Popular Mechanics*, June 1989, pp. 79, 104-105.

1987: "the Chevrolet Corvette is one of the most controversial automobiles ever to grace the C/D parking lot. Certain staff members find plenty of fault with this car, while others lust after the bolide from Bowling Green with a fervor that surpasses all dissension." **Source:** "Ten Best Cars: Fun work, but somebody's got to do it," *Car and Driver*, January 1987, pp. 36-41.

RECALLS

1990: (213 passenger cars with LT5 engines): Cracking of fuel feed and return line ends could allow fuel to leak that may result in an engine compartment fire. **Corrective action:** Install new fuel lines with correct end flare configuration. *(NHTSA Campaign No. 90V008000.)*

1988-89: (45,969 vehicles): Fracture in rear wheel tie rod assembly could result in loss of control and a crash without prior warning. **Corrective action:** Replace faulty tie rod assemblies. *(NHTSA Campaign No. 90V032000.)*

1988: (4,901 passenger vehicles equipped with 17 inch wheels): Missing weld that attaches wheel center to rim could allow wheel center to separate from rim. This could result in partial loss of steering control and brakes, loss of tire air pressure, and sudden change in vehicle direction, which could result in crash without prior warning. **Corrective action:** Replace wheels with missing welds. *(NHTSA Campaign No. 88V017000.)*

1987-91: (231,833 passenger cars; includes models made before 1987): Under certain vehicle operations and occupant usage conditions, the safety belts can lock up or jam in the safety belt retractor. If lock-up occurs, it is impossible to pull belt out of the retractor, rendering it useless. **Corrective action:** Replace the safety belts if lock-up occurs. *(NHTSA Campaign No. 91V143000.)*

SAFETY AND REPAIRS

1988: "High performance = snow performance," *Road & Track*, May 1988, p. 172. **Note:** Reasons why the Chevrolet Corvette is not a good all-weather performer.

1987: "Car Clinic," *Popular Mechanics*, August 1990, p. 26. **Note:** Tip for clashing starter motor gears in 1987-88 General Motors 4.3, 5.0, and 5.7 liter engines.

REPAIR MANUALS

802 ● Chilton's Chevrolet 1968-1988
Chilton Co.
Chilton Way
Radnor, PA 19089   Ph:(215)964-4000

Published 1989. **Price:** $15.95.

803 ● General Motors 8-Cylinder
Peter Allen Video Productions
38-C Otis St.
West Babylon, NY 11704   Ph:(516)643-4372

A program demonstrating basic maintenance and tune-up procedures for the entitled engine. **Release date:** 1986. **Producer:** Peter Allen Productions. **Acquisition:** Purchase.

804 ● Get Your Chevrolet-GMC Fixed Right
Consumer Reports Books
51 E. 42nd St., Suite 800
New York, NY 10017   Ph:(212)682-9280

Editor(s): Mort Schultz. **Price:** $8.95.

805 ● Haynes Corvette Owners Workshop Manual, No. 1336: All Models 1984-1989
Haynes Publications, Inc.
861 Lawrence Dr.
Newbury Park, CA 91320   Ph:(818)889-5400

Published 1987. **Editor(s):** J. H. Haynes. **Price:** 15.95.

OTHER INFORMATION SOURCES

806 ● All Chevy
McMullen Publishing, Inc.
2145 W. La Palma Ave.   Ph:(714)635-9040
Anaheim, CA 92801-1785   Fax:(714)533-9999

Auto magazine for Chevrolet car enthusiasts. Quarterly. **Editor(s):** Thomas M. McMullen, Publisher.

807 ● Chevrolet High Performance
Peterson Publishing Co.
6725 Sunset Blvd.
Los Angeles, CA 90028   Ph:(213)854-2222

Explains how to repair, restore, and improve performance of specific Chevrolet models. Bimonthly. **Editor(s):** Isaac Martin. **Price:** $11.95 per year; $2.95 per issue.

808 ● Chevy Power
Engledrum Publishing Corp.
153 Asharoken Ave.
Northport, NY 11768   Ph:(516)261-5260

Bimonthly. **Price:** $2.95 per issue.

809 ● Corvette
Petersen Publishing Co.
7750 Sunset Blvd.
Los Angeles, CA 90046   Ph:(213)854-2222

Automotive magazine. Five times/year. (January, April, August, October, and November). **Editor(s):** Ron Cogan.

810 ● Corvette: A Complete Story
Smithmark Publishers, Inc.
112 Madison Ave.
New York, NY 10016   Ph:(212)532-6600

Published 1988. **Editor(s):** Thomas Bonsall. **Price:** $9.98.

811 ● Corvette: America's Sports Car Legend
Publications International, Ltd.
7373 N. Cicero Ave.
Lincolnwood, IL 60646   Ph:(312)676-3470

Published 1989. **Price:** $49.95.

812 ● Corvette: America's Supercar
Running Press Book Publishers
125 S. 22nd St.
Philadelphia, PA 19103   Ph:(215)567-5080

Published 1990. **Price:** $14.98.

813 ● The Corvette Black Book: 1953-92
Motorbooks International
729 Prospect Ave.
Osceola, WI 54020   Ph:(715)294-3345

Published 1991. **Editor(s):** Michael Antonick. **Price:** $9.95.

814 ● Corvette Driver-Owner Guide for 1953-1988 Models: Maximizing Your Corvette's Potential
Motorbooks International
729 Prospect Ave.
Osceola, WI 54020   Ph:(715)294-3345

Published 1987. **Price:** $13.95.

815 ● Corvette Fever—Directory of Corvette-Related Businesses Issue
Dobbs Publishing Group
P.O. Box 7157
Lakeland, FL 33807   Ph:(813)644-0449

List of manufacturers and suppliers of parts, services, and accessories for the Chevrolet Corvette automobile. Annual, April. **Editor(s):** Patricia Stevens. **Price:** $2.75.

816 ● Corvette Fever Magazine
Dobbs Publications
3816 Industry Blvd.   Ph:(813)646-5743
Lakeland, FL 33811   Fax:(813)644-8373

Magazine for Corvette enthusiasts. Monthly. **Editor(s):** Paul Zazarine, Editorial Dir. **Price:** $23.97/year.

817 ● Corvette Illustrated
Ceco Publishing
3221 W. Big Beaver, Ste. 110
Troy, MI 48084   Ph:(313)634-9040

Quarterly. **Price:** $3.50.

818 ● Corvette: Portrait of a Legend
Smithmark Publishers, Inc.
112 Madison Ave.
New York, NY 10016   Ph:(212)532-6600

Published 1989. **Price:** $39.98.

819 ● Corvette Quarterly
The Aegis Group
30400 Van Dyke   Ph:(313)574-9100
Warren, MI 48093   Fax:(313)575-9535

Magazine for Corvette enthusiasts. Quarterly. **Editor(s):** Jerry Burton. **Price:** $8.00/year; $2.00 per single issue.

820 ● Corvette: The Legend Lives On
Automobile Quarterly, Inc.
420 N. Park Rd., Ste. 200
Wyomissing, PA 19610-2918   Ph:(215)375-8444

Published 1987. **Editor(s):** Roy D. Query. **Price:** $49.95.

821 ● For Vetts Only
National Corvette Owner's Association
P.O. Box 777-A
Falls Church, VA 22046   Ph:(703)533-7222

Newsletter. Promotes the enjoyment and popularity of Corvette automobiles. Provides technical reports and carries information on interior products, auto parts discount benefits, and Chevrolet dealers; includes calendar of events. Monthly. **Price:** Included in membership dues; $18.00/year for nonmembers.

822 ● Four for the Road: Corvette, Ferrari, Mercedes-Benz, Porsche—The Greatest of the Survivors Series
Motorbooks International
729 Prospect Ave.
Osceola, WI 54020   Ph:(715)294-3345

Published 1989. **Editor(s):** Henry Rasmussen. **Price:** $19.95.

823 ● Friends Magazine
Ceco Publishing
3221 W. Big Beaver, Ste. 110
Troy, MI 48084   Ph:(313)575-9400

Offers articles on Chevrolet automobiles. Monthly. **Editor(s):** Michael Brudenell. **Price:** Free.

824 ● Illustrated Corvette Buyer's Guide
Motorbooks International
729 Prospect Ave.
Osceola, WI 54020   Ph:(715)294-3345

Pubished 1987. **Price:** $15.95.

825 ● Keepin' Track of Vettes
NSR Communications Corp.
P.O. Box 48   Ph:(914)425-2649
Spring Valley, NY 10977   Fax:(914)638-3864

Covers Corvette hobby, technical, restoration, how-to, club, racing, and mechanical information; also offers classified ads and national Corvette event listings. Monthly. **Editor(s):** Shelli Finkel. **Price:** $21.95 per year; $2.95 per issue.

826 ● Mississippi Valley Corvette Association—Newsletter
Mississippi Valley Corvette Association
c/o Merle Hazelwonder
5212 Airport Rd.
Godfrey, IL 62035   Ph:(618)466-6548

Periodic.

827 ● National Council of Corvette Clubs—Handbook
National Council of Corvette Clubs (NCCC)
P.O. Box 813
Adams Basin, NY 14410

Annual.

828 ● Secrets of Corvette Detailing
Motorbooks International
729 Prospect Ave.
Osceola, WI 54020   Ph:(715)294-3345

Published 1988. **Price:** $14.95.

829 ● Standard Catalog of Chevrolet
Krause Publications, Inc.
700 E. State St.
Iola, WI 54990   Ph:(715)445-2214

Published 1990. **Price:** $19.95.

830 ● The Story of Corvette
Simitar Entertainment
3850 Annapolis Ln.   Ph:(612)559-6660
Plymouth, MN 55447   Fax:(612)559-0210

The story behind Chevy's classic American sports car is told from the beginning. **Release date:** 1988. **Producer:** Simitar Entertainment. **Price:** $9.95.

831 ● Super Chevy
Argus Publishers Corp.
12100 Wilshire Blvd., Ste. 250   Ph:(213)820-3601
Los Angeles, CA 90025   Fax:(213)207-9388

Automotive magazine. Monthly. **Editor(s):** Bruce Hampson. **Price:** $16.00.

832 ● Valley Vettes Corvette Club—Newsletter
Valley Vettes Corvette Club
P.O. Box 2373
Yakima, WA 98907   Ph:(509)248-1931

Monthly.

833 ● Vette
CSK Publishing Co., Inc.
299 Market St.   Ph:(201)712-9300
Saddle Brook, NJ 07662   Fax:(201)712-9899

Magazine devoted to Corvette enthusiasts, featuring restored, customized, modified, and classic models. Includes coverage of national events and large regionals. Monthly. **Editor(s):** D. Randy Riggs. **Price:** $24.00/year; $3.50 per single issue.

834 ● Vette Vues
Vette Vues
5064 Roswell Rd., Ste. B-102
Atlanta, GA 30342   Ph:(404)252-2575

Contains articles of interest to Chevrolet Corvette enthusiasts. Monthly. **Editor(s):** James Prather, Publisher. **Price:** $20.00 per year; $3.00 per issue.

835 ● Vetten USA
Vetten USA
1074 Center St.
P.O. Box 179
Ludlow, MA 01056

Monthly. **Price:** $8.00.

ASSOCIATIONS

836 ● National Corvette Owners Association
P.O. Box 777-A
Falls Church, VA 22046   Ph:(703)533-7222
Robert J. Salta, Membership Dir.   Fax:(703)553-1153

Founded: 1975. **Membership:** 12,000. Corvette owners and enthusiasts united to encourage and increase the enjoyment and popularity of Corvette automobiles. Provides members with benefits such as insurance, interior discounts, and auto supply discounts. Maintains reference book collection.

837 ● National Council of Corvette Clubs
P.O. Box 813
Adams Basin, NY 14410

Founded: 1960. **Membership:** 10,000. Federation of clubs of owners of Corvette automobiles. Sponsors amateur competition; compiles statistics; bestows awards. **Convention/Meeting:** Annual (with exhibits). **Additional Numbers:** Toll-free: 800-245-VETT.

CHEVROLET LUMINA (1990-92)

Introduced in 1989 as a '90 model, the Lumina is currently produced at the General Motors plant in Oshawa, Ontario, Canada. Two-door rated as good, and the four-door rated as poor in crash test performance by *The Car Book*.

1992 Chevrolet Lumina Euro Sedan

MAJOR FEATURES

● Lumina Sedan and Coupe have as 1992 standard equipment: 3-speed automatic transmission, 4-wheel power disc brakes, power rack-and-pinion steering, and AM/FM stereo.

● Lumina Euro adds as 1992 standard equipment: anti-lock brakes, upgraded suspension, and 15-inch aluminum wheels, and decklid spoiler.

● Lumina Euro 3.4 adds as 1992 standard equipment: 3.4 liter V-6 engine, four-speed automatic transmission, and upgraded tires.

● Lumina Z34 sport coupe has a slightly longer wheelbase than the base Lumina and adds as 1992 standard equipment: 5-speed manual transmission, sport suspension, rear spoiler, air conditioning, AM/FM stereo cassette system, and 16-inch aluminum wheels.

PRICE HISTORY

The following new car prices reflect the approximate retail cost of the base model: **1990** - $12,140; **1991** - $12,670; **1992** - $13,200.

DIMENSIONS

Body Style	Years Avail	Wheel Base (in)	Lgth (in)	Ht (in)	Avg Wt (lbs)	Fuel Cap (gal)	Front Hdrm (in)	Front Legrm (in)
2d cpe	90-92	107.5	198.3	53.3	3,115	17.1	37.6	42.4
4d sdn	90-92	107.5	198.3	53.6	3,220	17.1	38.8	42.4

ENGINES

Type	Displacement (L)	Fuel Dly	HP @rpm	Torque @rpm (ft/lbs)	MPG Cty/Hwy	Years Avail
I-4	2.5	FI	110@5200	135@3200	21/27	90-90
I-4	2.5	FI	105@4800	135@3200	21/28	91-92
V-6	3.1	FI	135@4400	180@3600	19/30	90-90
V-6	3.4	FI	210@5200	215@4000	17/27	91-92
V-6	3.1	FI	140@4200	185@3200	19/29	91-92

KEY: I=in-line engine; V=V engine; F=flat engine; FI=fuel injection; bbl=barrel carburetor; T=turbo; D=diesel; HP=horsepower; MPG=estimated average miles per gallon.

EVALUATIONS, TESTS, AND RANKINGS

1991: "slalom handling was consistent and predictable, if not speedy ... The interior has been this car's weak suit ... the Lumina coupe suffers from heavy-door syndrome ... The bottom line is that the Z34 is a laudable accomplishment." **Source:** "Chevrolet Lumina Z34," *Motor Trend*, October 1990, pp. 42-46, 48.

1991: "Fail-safe handling. . .nails the essentials." **Source:** "Yankee Clippers," *Car and Driver*, March 1991, pp. 40, 42-45, 48-50.

1991: "a stout workhorse with the potential for a long, reliable life span ... represents an excellent value ... found the [interior]fairly cheap and the instrumentation disorganized and undersized by any standard." **Source:** "In Search of the Perfect 10," *Popular Science*, January 1991, pp. 76-80, 94.

1991: "midsize, quick, comfortable and pleasant to drive ... a good balance between ride and handling ... Fit and finish were good inside and out." **Source:** "Chevy's latest Z-car pleasant to drive if not that exciting," *The Flint Journal*, July 17, 1991, pp. E1-E2.

1991: "redefines performance parameters for the '90s ... amply equipped for either families or would-be street racers ... appropriate sporting hardware is all there." **Source:** "Sporty Lumina Is Dual Performer," *Detroit Free Press*, August 29, 1991, p. 1C.

1990: "Seating. . .was respectable. Legroom in the rear was good with the front seats moved up, and still adequate with the seats moved back. . .Fuel economy was decent." **Source:** "GM's mid-size hopes ride on Lumina," *The Detroit News*, June 21, 1989, pp. 1F-2F.

1990: "[Lumina Euro Sedan] gets slightly better grades [than Ford Taurus] for visibility, thanks to its more generous greenhouse ... sporty feel and superior road handling." **Source:** "Civil War," *Popular Mechanics*, December, 1989, pp. 57-59.

1990: "a car that's relatively trouble-free ... Handling also came in for considerable praise ... economical and snappy." **Source:** "Chevrolet Lumina," *Popular Mechanics*, April 1990, pp. 77-79.

RECALLS

1990: (412,792 vehicles; includes Chevrolet Lumina, Pontiac Grand Prix, Buick Regal, and Oldsmobile Cutlass Supreme): Front shoulder safety belt webbing may separate at front belt upper guide loops on either side of front seat. **Corrective action:** Install controlled rotation bracket on driver and passenger side front seat belt guide loops. *(NHTSA Campaign No. 91V005000.)*

1990: (673,000 passenger vehicles; includes the Pontiac Grand Prix, Buick Regal, Oldsmobile Cutlass Calais, and Chevrolet Lumina models): Front shoulder belt guide loop attachment fastener may pull through door mounted anchor plate. Seat belt may not properly restrain a passenger, resulting in increased risk of injury to occupant. **Corrective action:** Replace front shoulder belt guide loop attachment nuts and install new guide cover. *(NHTSA Campaign No. 90V054000.)*

1990: (476,422 vehicles; includes Buick, Chevrolet, Oldsmobile, and Pontiac models): Brake stoplamps may not illuminate or, in some cases, stoplamps will not stay illuminated all the time when brakes are applied due to a faulty stoplamp switch. **Corrective action:** Install an improved design stoplamp switch. *(NHTSA Campaign No. 90V185000.)*

SAFETY AND REPAIRS

1992: "GM Recalls '92 A-, W-Cars," *Automotive News*, December 2, 1991, p. 2. **Note:** Transmission problem could cause cars to remain in reverse when shifted into neutral.

1991: "GM Recalls Cars for Belt Loops," *Automotive News*, February 10, 1992, p. 2. **Note:** May have cracked front-door shoulder belt guide loops.

1990: ""Say, Smokey—," *Popular Science*, July 1990, p. 96. **Note:** '90 Lumina with rotten egg odor.

REPAIR MANUALS

838 ● Get Your Chevrolet-GMC Fixed Right
Consumer Reports Books
51 E. 42nd St., Suite 800
New York, NY 10017   Ph:(212)682-9280

Editor(s): Mort Schultz. **Price:** $8.95.

839 ● Haynes Chevrolet Full-Size Sedans Owners Workshop Manual, No. 704: 1969-1990
Haynes Publications, Inc.
861 Lawrence Dr.
Newbury Park, CA 91320   Ph:(818)889-5400

Published 1983. **Editor(s):** J.H. Haynes and Curt Choate. **Price:** $15.95.

OTHER INFORMATION SOURCES

840 ● All Chevy
McMullen Publishing, Inc.
2145 W. La Palma Ave.   Ph:(714)635-9040
Anaheim, CA 92801-1785   Fax:(714)533-9999

Auto magazine for Chevrolet car enthusiasts. Quarterly. **Editor(s):** Thomas M. McMullen, Publisher.

841 ● Chevrolet High Performance
Peterson Publishing Co.
6725 Sunset Blvd.
Los Angeles, CA 90028   Ph:(213)854-2222

Explains how to repair, restore, and improve performance of specific Chevrolet models. Bimonthly. **Editor(s):** Isaac Martin. **Price:** $11.95 per year; $2.95 per issue.

842 ● Chevy Power
Engledrum Publishing Corp.
153 Asharoken Ave.
Northport, NY 11768   Ph:(516)261-5260

Bimonthly. **Price:** $2.95 per issue.

843 ● Friends Magazine
Ceco Publishing
3221 W. Big Beaver, Ste. 110
Troy, MI 48084   Ph:(313)575-9400

Offers articles on Chevrolet automobiles. Monthly. **Editor(s):** Michael Brudenell. **Price:** Free.

844 ● Standard Catalog of Chevrolet
Krause Publications, Inc.
700 E. State St.
Iola, WI 54990   Ph:(715)445-2214

Published 1990. **Price:** $19.95.

845 ● **Super Chevy**
Argus Publishers Corp.
12100 Wilshire Blvd., Ste. 250   Ph:(213)820-3601
Los Angeles, CA 90025   Fax:(213)207-9388

Automotive magazine. Monthly. **Editor(s):** Bruce Hampson.
Price: $16.00.

CHEVROLET LUMINA APV (1990-92)

Produced at the General Motors plant in Tarrytown, New
York. Similar to the Oldsmobile Silhouette and Pontiac Trans
Sport. Listed as one of the "Best Bets of 1992" and ranked as
one of the best among minivans in crash test performance by
The Car Book.

1990 Chevrolet Lumina APV

MAJOR FEATURES

● Chevrolet Lumina APV has as 1992 standard equipment: 3-
speed automatic transmission, power rack-and-pinion steering,
power front disc/rear drum brakes with anti-lock, front
independent suspension/rear rigid axle, rear window
wiper/washer, and AM/FM stereo.

● Chevrolet Lumina APV CL adds as 1992 standard
equipment: air conditioning and tilt steering.

PRICE HISTORY

The following new car prices reflect the approximate retail cost
of the base model: **1990** - $13,995; **1991** - $14,730; **1992** -
$15,570.

DIMENSIONS

Body Style	Years Avail	Wheel Base (in)	Lgth (in)	Ht (in)	Avg Wt (lbs)	Fuel Cap (gal)	Front Hdrm (in)	Front Legrm (in)
mvan	90-92	109.8	194.2	65.7	3,462	20.0	35.7	40.7

ENGINES

Type	Displacement (L)	Fuel Dly	HP @rpm	Torque @rpm (ft/lbs)	MPG Cty/Hwy	Years Avail
V-6	3.1	FI	120@4400	175@2200	18/23	90-92
V-6	3.8	FI	165@4300	220@3200	17/24	92-92

KEY: I=in-line engine; V=V engine; F=flat engine; FI=fuel injection;
bbl=barrel carburetor; T=turbo; D=diesel; HP=horsepower;
MPG=estimated average miles per gallon.

EVALUATIONS, TESTS, AND RANKINGS

1991: "comfortable and distinctive looking ... the most
enduring feature is the ease with which the seats can be
removed to create cargo space ... engine is no better than
tepid." **Source:** "Meet the New Minivans," *New Choices for
the Best Years,* October, 1990, pp. 86-87.

1990: "minivan is versatile." **Source:** "Vans and Minivans,"
Car and Driver—Buyers Guide 1990, 1989, p. 176.

1990: "capable of easily handling long loads ... The light-
weight pop-out rear seats in ... Lumina are a unique feature
... problems with visivility in the APV." **Source:** "The Wedge
vs. The Box," *Popular Science,* August 1990, pp. 76-79, 81.

1990: "high expectations for these new vans magnified a
number of detail disappointments ... Clambering into the rear
seats is a chore." **Source:** "The Light Vantastics," *Popular
Mechanics,* February 1990, pp. 62-67.

RECALLS

1990: (343 multipurpose passenger vehicles; includes the
Chevrolet Lumina APV, Pontiac Trans Sport, and Oldsmobile
Silhouette): Rear modular seat frame hold-down hooks may not
meet the required pull force at the rear set anchorage.
Corrective action: Replace rear hold-down hooks and pivot
rivets with heat treated hardware. *(NHTSA Campaign No.
89V164000.)*

1990: (400 passenger vans with grey interiors; includes
Chevrolet Lumina APV, Oldsmobile Silhouette, and Pontiac
Trans Sport models): Right hand seat/shoulder belt retractor
may have been installed in the second row left hand seat
position. Incorrect retractor may cause belts to lock up if van is
parked on a steep grade. **Corrective action:** Replace shoulder
belt assembly. *(NHTSA Campaign No. 91V046000.)*

REPAIR MANUALS

846 ● **Get Your Chevrolet-GMC Fixed Right**
Consumer Reports Books
51 E. 42nd St., Suite 800
New York, NY 10017   Ph:(212)682-9280

Editor(s): Mort Schultz. **Price:** $8.95.

OTHER INFORMATION SOURCES

847 ● **All Chevy**
McMullen Publishing, Inc.
2145 W. La Palma Ave.   Ph:(714)635-9040
Anaheim, CA 92801-1785   Fax:(714)533-9999

Auto magazine for Chevrolet car enthusiasts. Quarterly.
Editor(s): Thomas M. McMullen, Publisher.

848 ● **Chevrolet Lumina—Pontiac Transport Olds Silhouette,
1988-90**
Chilton Co.
Chilton Way
Radnor, PA 19089   Ph:(215)964-4000

Published March 1991. **Price:** $15.95.

849 ● **Chevy Outdoors**
The Aegis Group
30400 Van Dyke   Ph:(313)574-9100
Warren, MI 48093   Fax:(313)575-9535

Quarterly. **Editor(s):** Michael Brudenell. **Price:** $8.00.

850 ● **Friends Magazine**
Ceco Publishing
3221 W. Big Beaver, Ste. 110
Troy, MI 48084   Ph:(313)575-9400

Offers articles on Chevrolet automobiles. Monthly. **Editor(s):**
Michael Brudenell. **Price:** Free.

851 ● **Standard Catalog of Chevrolet**
Krause Publications, Inc.
700 E. State St.
Iola, WI 54990   Ph:(715)445-2214

Published 1990. **Price:** $19.95.

CHEVROLET MONTE CARLO (1987-88)

Produced until 1988 at the General Motors plant in Pontiac,
Michigan; replaced by the Chevrolet Lumina. Basic design is
shared by G-Body Pontiac Grand Prix, Buick Regal and Olds
Cutlass Supreme.

1987 Chevrolet Monte Carlo

MAJOR FEATURES

● Monte Carlo had as 1988 standard equipment: 4-speed
automatic transmission, front disc/rear drum brakes, front
independent suspension/rear rigid axle, power steering, and
cruise control.

PRICE HISTORY

The following new car prices reflect the approximate retail cost
of the base model: **1987** - $11,306; **1988** - $12,330.

DIMENSIONS

Body Style	Years Avail	Wheel Base (in)	Lgth (in)	Ht (in)	Avg Wt (lbs)	Fuel Cap (gal)	Front Hdrm (in)	Front Legrm (in)
2d cpe	87-88	108	200.4	54.4	3,211	17.6	37.9	42.8

ENGINES

Type	Displacement (L)	Fuel Dlvy	HP @rpm	Torque @rpm (ft/lbs)	MPG Cty/Hwy	Years Avail
V-6	4.3	FI	145@4200	225@2000	19/27	87-88
V-8	5.0	4-bbl	150@4000	240@2000	17/24	87-88
V-8	5.0	4-bbl	180@4800	225@3200	17/24	87-88

KEY: I=in-line engine; V=V engine; F=flat engine; FI=fuel injection;
bbl=barrel carburetor; T=turbo; D=diesel; HP=horsepower;
MPG=estimated average miles per gallon.

EVALUATIONS, TESTS, AND RANKINGS

1988: "wholly unspectacular. . ." **Source:** "Chevrolet Monte
Carlo," *Car and Driver—Buyers Guide 1988*, 1988, p. 86.

RECALLS

1987: (11,936 vehicles with 200 4R transmissions; includes
Chevrolet, Pontiac, Oldsmobile, Buick, Cadillac, and GMC
models): Manual valve link in transmission may have been
improperly formed. **Corrective action:** Replace manual valve
detent lever link. *(NHTSA Campaign No. 87V168000.)*

SAFETY AND REPAIRS

1987: "Car Clinic," *Popular Mechanics,* August 1990, p. 26.
Note: Tip for clashing starter motor gears in 1987-88 General
Motors 4.3, 5.0, and 5.7 liter engines.

REPAIR MANUALS

852 ● **Chilton's Chevrolet 1968-1988**
Chilton Co.
Chilton Way
Radnor, PA 19089   Ph:(215)964-4000

Published 1989. **Price:** $15.95.

853 ● **General Motors 8-Cylinder**
Peter Allen Video Productions
38-C Otis St.
West Babylon, NY 11704   Ph:(516)643-4372

A program demonstrating basic maintenance and tune-up
procedures for the entitled engine. **Release date:** 1986.
Producer: Peter Allen Productions. **Acquisition:** Purchase.

854 ● **Get Your Chevrolet-GMC Fixed Right**
Consumer Reports Books
51 E. 42nd St., Suite 800
New York, NY 10017   Ph:(212)682-9280

Editor(s): Mort Schultz. **Price:** $8.95.

855 ● **Haynes Chevrolet Monte Carlo Owner's Manual, No.
626: 1970-1988**
Haynes Publications, Inc.
861 Lawrence Dr.
Newbury Park, CA 91320   Ph:(818)889-5400

Price: $15.95.

OTHER INFORMATION SOURCES

856 ● **All Chevy**
McMullen Publishing, Inc.
2145 W. La Palma Ave.   Ph:(714)635-9040
Anaheim, CA 92801-1785   Fax:(714)533-9999

Auto magazine for Chevrolet car enthusiasts. Quarterly.
Editor(s): Thomas M. McMullen, Publisher.

857 ● **Chevrolet High Performance**
Peterson Publishing Co.
6725 Sunset Blvd.
Los Angeles, CA 90028   Ph:(213)854-2222

Explains how to repair, restore, and improve performance of
specific Chevrolet models. Bimonthly. **Editor(s):** Isaac Martin.
Price: $11.95 per year; $2.95 per issue.

858 ● Chevy Power
Engledrum Publishing Corp.
153 Asharoken Ave.
Northport, NY 11768   Ph:(516)261-5260

Bimonthly. **Price:** $2.95 per issue.

859 ● The Class of Monte Carlo
National Monte Carlo Owners Association
c/o Larry Ashcraft
P.O. Box 187
Independence, KY 41051   Ph:(606)491-2378

Monthly.

860 ● Friends Magazine
Ceco Publishing
3221 W. Big Beaver, Ste. 110
Troy, MI 48084   Ph:(313)575-9400

Offers articles on Chevrolet automobiles. Monthly. **Editor(s):**
Michael Brudenell. **Price:** Free.

861 ● Standard Catalog of Chevrolet
Krause Publications, Inc.
700 E. State St.
Iola, WI 54990   Ph:(715)445-2214

Published 1990. **Price:** $19.95.

862 ● Super Chevy
Argus Publishers Corp.
12100 Wilshire Blvd., Ste. 250   Ph:(213)820-3601
Los Angeles, CA 90025   Fax:(213)207-9388

Automotive magazine. Monthly. **Editor(s):** Bruce Hampson.
Price: $16.00.

CHEVROLET NOVA (1987-88)

Similar to the Toyota Corolla, the Chevrolet Nova was jointly
produced by General Motors and Toyota at the New United
Motor Mfg. Inc. plant in Fremont, California, until discontinued
in 1988.

1987 Chevrolet Nova

MAJOR FEATURES

● Nova had as 1988 standard equipment: 5-speed manual
transmission, 4-wheel independent suspension, rack-and-
pinion steering, and front disc/rear drum brakes.

PRICE HISTORY

The following new car prices reflect the approximate retail cost
of the base model: **1987** - $8,258; **1988** - $8,795.

DIMENSIONS

Body Style	Years Avail	Wheel Base (in)	Lgth (in)	Ht (in)	Avg Wt (lbs)	Fuel Cap (gal)	Front Hdrm (in)	Front Legrm (in)
5d lbk	87-88	95.7	166.3	52.8	2,204	13.2	na	na
4d sdn	87-88	95.7	166.3	53	2,162	13.2	na	na

ENGINES

Type	Displacement (L)	Fuel Dly	HP @rpm	Torque @rpm (ft/lbs)	MPG Cty/Hwy	Years Avail
I-4	1.6	2-bbl	na	na	30/37	87-88
I-4	1.6	FI	110@na	na	25/29	88-88

KEY: I=in-line engine; V=V engine; F=flat engine; FI=fuel injection;
bbl=barrel carburetor; T=turbo; D=diesel; HP=horsepower;
MPG=estimated average miles per gallon.

EVALUATIONS, TESTS, AND RANKINGS

1987: "₉perfect for what it is—totally competent family
transportation, totally generic, totally dull' . . . straightforward,
dependable, surprisingly comfortable sedan, with no rude
surprises." **Source:** "Asian Invasion," *Popular Mechanics,* July
1987, pp. 90-94, 148.

RECALLS

None to date.

REPAIR MANUALS

863 ● Chevrolet Nova 1985-1989 Repair and Tune-up Guide
Chilton Co.
Chilton Way
Radnor, PA 19089   Ph:(215)964-4000

Published 1989. **Price:** $15.95.

864 ● Chilton's Chevrolet 1968-1988
Chilton Co.
Chilton Way
Radnor, PA 19089   Ph:(215)964-4000

Published 1989. **Price:** $15.95.

865 ● Get Your Chevrolet-GMC Fixed Right
Consumer Reports Books
51 E. 42nd St., Suite 800
New York, NY 10017   Ph:(212)682-9280

Editor(s): Mort Schultz. **Price:** $8.95.

OTHER INFORMATION SOURCES

866 ● All Chevy
McMullen Publishing, Inc.
2145 W. La Palma Ave.   Ph:(714)635-9040
Anaheim, CA 92801-1785   Fax:(714)533-9999

Auto magazine for Chevrolet car enthusiasts. Quarterly.
Editor(s): Thomas M. McMullen, Publisher.

867 ● Friends Magazine
Ceco Publishing
3221 W. Big Beaver, Ste. 110
Troy, MI 48084   Ph:(313)575-9400

Offers articles on Chevrolet automobiles. Monthly. **Editor(s):**
Michael Brudenell. **Price:** Free.

868 ● **Standard Catalog of Chevrolet**
Krause Publications, Inc.
700 E. State St.
Iola, WI 54990

Ph:(715)445-2214

Published 1990. **Price:** $19.95.

CHEVROLET S10 PICKUP (1987-92)

Produced at the General Motors plants in Moraine, Ohio and Shreveport, Louisiana.

1991 Chevrolet S10 Pickup

MAJOR FEATURES

● S10 Pickup has as 1992 standard equipment: 5-speed manual transmission, front disc/rear drum brakes with anti-lock braking system, power steering, side-view mirrors, and AM radio.

● S10 4WD EL adds as 1992 standard equipment: four-wheel drive, upgraded interior, and self-aligning steering wheel.

Dimension data that follows is for the S-10 2WD. Dimensions of other pickups in series may vary.

PRICE HISTORY

The following new car prices reflect the approximate retail cost of the base model: **1987** - $6,595; **1988** - $6,795; **1989** - $7,474; **1990** - $7,995; **1991** - $8,369.

DIMENSIONS

Body Style	Years Avail	Wheel Base (in)	Lgth (in)	Ht (in)	Avg Wt (lbs)	Fuel Cap (gal)	Front Hdrm (in)	Front Legrm (in)
trk	87-88	108.3	178.2	61.3	3,570	13.2	na	na
trk	89-91	108.3	178.2	61.3	4,200	20.0	na	na
trk	92-92	108.3	178.2	63.1	4,200	20.0	na	na

ENGINES

Type	Displacement (L)	Fuel Dly	HP @rpm	Torque @rpm (ft/lbs)	MPG Cty/Hwy	Years Avail
I-4	2.5	FI	98@na	na	23/29	87-87
I-4	2.5	FI	92@na	na	23/27	88-89
I-4	2.5	FI	105@4800	135@3200	23/27	90-92
V-6	2.8	FI	na	na	18/24	87-87
V-6	2.8	FI	125@na	na	19/25	88-92
V-6	4.3	FI	160@4000	230@2800	17/22	89-92

KEY: I=in-line engine; V=V engine; F=flat engine; FI=fuel injection; bbl=barrel carburetor; T=turbo; D=diesel; HP=horsepower; MPG=estimated average miles per gallon.

EVALUATIONS, TESTS, AND RANKINGS

1990: "an enlightening experience ... exceptional acceleration in all gears ... steering ... is very responsive." **Source:** "Compact Pickups With New Power," *Sports Afield*, July 1990, p. 32.

1989: "finished mid-pack in most tests, although it showed a strong aptitude for passing acceleration in comparison with the manual-transmission-equipped ... did fine in the slalom test ... it should serve the serious off-roader well." **Source:** "Mudders," *Popular Science*, July 1989, pp. 33-34, 38-40, 42, 44.

RECALLS

1991: (181 pickup trucks; includes several GMC and Chevrolet truck models): Use of improper primer on metal surfaces of windshield and side window openings could cause low adhesion to metal surface and would not provide retention required by FMVSS 212. Would not prevent the ejection of vehicle occupants during a crash. **Corrective action:** Remove and reinstall glass using proper primer. (NHTSA Campaign No. 90V107000.)

1991: (102,885 light trucks and multi-purpose vehicles; includes the GMC Jimmy, Chevrolet S-10 Pickup, Chevrolet Blazer, and Oldsmobile Bravada): Vehicles have been shipped with the fuel tank sender seal out of position. In the event of a rollover accident, an out of position seal could allow fuel spillage in excess of the amount prescribed by FMVSS 301. Spilled fuel could ignite near an ignition source. **Corrective action:** Replace sender seals. (NHTSA Campaign No. 91V108000.)

SAFETY AND REPAIRS

1987: "Car Clinic," *Popular Mechanics*, August 1990, p. 26. **Note:** Tip for clashing starter motor gears in 1987-88 General Motors 4.3, 5.0, and 5.7 liter engines.

REPAIR MANUALS

869 ● **Chevrolet and GMC 4-Wheel Drive Tune-Up: 1967-1987**
Clymer Publications
P.O. Box 1209
Overland Park, KS 66212

Ph:(913)541-6694

With Illustrations. Published 1983. **Editor(s):** Jeff Robinson. **Price:** $14.99.

870 ● **Chevrolet GMC Trucks, 1988-90**
Chilton Co.
Chilton Way
Radnor, PA 19089

Ph:(215)964-4000

Published 1990. **Price:** $19.95.

871 ● **Chevrolet S-10, GMC S-15 Pickups 1982—90**
Chilton Co.
Chilton Way
Radnor, PA 19089

Ph:(215)964-4000

Total car care service. Published 1991. **Price:** $19.95.

872 ● **Chevy and GMC Two-Wheel Drive Mid-Size S- and T-Pickups, Blazers, and Jimmy, 1982-1988 (Gas and Diesel)**
Clymer Publications
P.O. Box 1209
Overland Park, KS 66212

Ph:(913)541-6694

Published 1987. **Price:** $26.95.

873 ● Chilton's Chevrolet 1968-1988
Chilton Co.
Chilton Way
Radnor, PA 19089   Ph:(215)964-4000

Published 1989. **Price:** $15.95.

874 ● Chilton's Chevrolet/GMC Pick-ups and Suburban 1970-1987
Chilton Co.
Chilton Way
Radnor, PA 19089   Ph:(215)964-4000

Published 1988. **Price:** $15.95.

875 ● Get Your Chevrolet-GMC Fixed Right
Consumer Reports Books
51 E. 42nd St., Suite 800
New York, NY 10017   Ph:(212)682-9280

Editor(s): Mort Schultz. **Price:** $8.95.

876 ● Haynes Chevrolet and GMC Pick-Ups Owners Workshop Manual, No. 420: 1967-1987
Haynes Publications, Inc.
861 Lawrence Dr.
Newbury Park, CA 91320   Ph:(818)889-5400

Published 1988. **Price:** $15.95.

877 ● Haynes Chevy GMC Pickups, 1988-90
Haynes Publications, Inc.
861 Lawrence Dr.
Newbury Park, CA 91320   Ph:(818)889-5400

Published 1990. **Price:** $15.95.

OTHER INFORMATION SOURCES

878 ● All Chevy
McMullen Publishing, Inc.
2145 W. La Palma Ave.   Ph:(714)635-9040
Anaheim, CA 92801-1785   Fax:(714)533-9999

Auto magazine for Chevrolet car enthusiasts. Quarterly.
Editor(s): Thomas M. McMullen, Publisher.

879 ● Chevy Outdoors
The Aegis Group
30400 Van Dyke   Ph:(313)574-9100
Warren, MI 48093   Fax:(313)575-9535

Quarterly. **Editor(s):** Michael Brudenell. **Price:** $8.00.

880 ● Friends Magazine
Ceco Publishing
3221 W. Big Beaver, Ste. 110
Troy, MI 48084   Ph:(313)575-9400

Offers articles on Chevrolet automobiles. Monthly. **Editor(s):**
Michael Brudenell. **Price:** Free.

881 ● Standard Catalog of Chevrolet
Krause Publications, Inc.
700 E. State St.
Iola, WI 54990   Ph:(715)445-2214

Published 1990. **Price:** $19.95.

CHEVROLET SPECTRUM (1987-88)

Produced in Japan by Isuzu until it was renamed the Geo Spectrum in 1989, trimmed to a single price series, and the turbo-charged engine was dropped. The performance and handling of the early versions were considered barely adequate.

1987 Chevrolet Spectrum

MAJOR FEATURES

● Spectrum and Spectrum Turbo had as 1988 standard equipment: 5-speed manual transmission, rack-and-pinion steering, 4-wheel independent suspension, and front disc/rear drums.

PRICE HISTORY

The following new car prices reflect the approximate retail cost of the base model: **1987** - $7,412; **1988** - $6,495.

DIMENSIONS

Body Style	Years Avail	Wheel Base (in)	Lgth (in)	Ht (in)	Avg Wt (lbs)	Fuel Cap (gal)	Front Hdrm (in)	Front Legrm (in)
3d lbk	87-88	94.5	157.4	52.0	1,962	11.1	38.0	41.7
4d sdn	88-88	94.5	160.2	52.0	2,185	11.1	37.7	41.7

ENGINES

Type	Displacement (L)	Fuel Dly	HP @rpm	Torque @rpm (ft/lbs)	MPG Cty/Hwy	Years Avail
I-4	1.5	2-bbl	70@5400	87@3400	37/41	87-88
I-4T	1.5	FI	110@5400	120@3400	28/36	88-88

KEY: I=in-line engine; V=V engine; F=flat engine; FI=fuel injection; bbl=barrel carburetor; T=turbo; D=diesel; HP=horsepower; MPG=estimated average miles per gallon.

EVALUATIONS, TESTS, AND RANKINGS

1987: "poor track performance. . .looked smart and traditional'. . . yet another Japanese economy car that I can't get excited about." **Source:** "Asian Invasion," *Popular Mechanics*, July 1987, pp. 90-94, 148.

RECALLS

1987-88: (7,665 vehicles): Perforation of fuel tank or attached fuel feed pipe due to corrosion of tank or fuel feed pipe materials. This condition could allow fuel to leak from fuel tank and ultimately result in fire without prior warning. Such a fire could spread to passenger compartment. **Corrective action:** Fuel tank will be replaced on all involved vehicles. *(NHTSA Campaign No. 88V036000.)*

1987-88: (8,238 vehicles): Positive crankcase ventilation valve may provide inadequate air flow under low engine load conditions. Can allow water/oil mixture to build up in hose from oil separator to air inlet duct. After engine is stopped, water/oil mixture can, freeze and completely block oil separator oil duct hose. Results in increase pressure within crankcase. Causes oil leaks, if sufficient quantity of oil came in contact with hot exhausst system engine compartment fire could result. **Corrective action:** PCV valve will be replaced with new valve. (NHTSA Campaign No. 88V046000.)

SAFETY AND REPAIRS

1987: "Chevy and Isuzu Recall 100,000 Spectrum Types," *Automotive News,* November 11, 1991, p. 2. **Note:** '87 Spectrums have excessive emissions of carbon monoxide.

REPAIR MANUALS

882 ● **Chilton's Chevrolet 1968-1988**
Chilton Co.
Chilton Way
Radnor, PA 19089   Ph:(215)964-4000

Published 1989. **Price:** $15.95.

883 ● **Get Your Chevrolet-GMC Fixed Right**
Consumer Reports Books
51 E. 42nd St., Suite 800
New York, NY 10017   Ph:(212)682-9280

Editor(s): Mort Schultz. **Price:** $8.95.

OTHER INFORMATION SOURCES

884 ● **All Chevy**
McMullen Publishing, Inc.
2145 W. La Palma Ave.   Ph:(714)635-9040
Anaheim, CA 92801-1785   Fax:(714)533-9999

Auto magazine for Chevrolet car enthusiasts. Quarterly. **Editor(s):** Thomas M. McMullen, Publisher.

885 ● **Chevrolet High Performance**
Peterson Publishing Co.
6725 Sunset Blvd.
Los Angeles, CA 90028   Ph:(213)854-2222

Explains how to repair, restore, and improve performance of specific Chevrolet models. Bimonthly. **Editor(s):** Isaac Martin. **Price:** $11.95 per year; $2.95 per issue.

886 ● **Chevy Power**
Engledrum Publishing Corp.
153 Asharoken Ave.
Northport, NY 11768   Ph:(516)261-5260

Bimonthly. **Price:** $2.95 per issue.

887 ● **Friends Magazine**
Ceco Publishing
3221 W. Big Beaver, Ste. 110
Troy, MI 48084   Ph:(313)575-9400

Offers articles on Chevrolet automobiles. Monthly. **Editor(s):** Michael Brudenell. **Price:** Free.

888 ● **Standard Catalog of Chevrolet**
Krause Publications, Inc.
700 E. State St.
Iola, WI 54990   Ph:(715)445-2214

Published 1990. **Price:** $19.95.

889 ● **Super Chevy**
Argus Publishers Corp.
12100 Wilshire Blvd., Ste. 250   Ph:(213)820-3601
Los Angeles, CA 90025   Fax:(213)207-9388

Automotive magazine. Monthly. **Editor(s):** Bruce Hampson. **Price:** $16.00.

CHEVROLET SPORTVAN (1987-92)

Considered a full-size van, the Sportvan series gained throttle body fuel injection in 1987. In 1990, rear wheel anti-lock brakes and the new extended model on G30s were added to the line.

1987 Chevrolet Beauville Sportvan

MAJOR FEATURES

● G10 Sportvan 1992 standard equipment includes: 4-speed automatic transmission, front disc/rear drum brakes with anti-lock braking system, AM radio, trip odometer, and dome lamps.

● G20 Sportvan adds standard equipment: 33 gallon gas tank.

● G30 Sportvan 1992 comes with a 5.7-liter V8 engine as standard.

Dimensions below are for the G10 Sportvan. Others in series have longer wheelbases and overall length in addition to other dimension variations. Engine horsepower output also varies slightly within the Sportvan line.

PRICE HISTORY

The following new car prices reflect the approximate retail cost of the base model: **1988** - $11,922; **1989** - $12,638; **1990** - $14,565; **1991** - $15,340.

DIMENSIONS

Body Style	Years Avail	Wheel Base (in)	Lgth (in)	Ht (in)	Avg Wt (lbs)	Fuel Cap (gal)	Front Hdrm (in)	Front Legrm (in)
van	87-91	110	178.2	79.1	5,600	22	na	na
van	92-92	110	178.2	79.5	4,900	22	na	na

ENGINES

Type	Displace-ment (L)	Fuel Dly	HP @rpm	Torque @rpm (ft/lbs)	MPG Cty/Hwy	Years Avail
V-6	4.3	FI	150@4000	230@2400	15/19	87-92
V-8	5.7	FI	190@4000	300@2400	14/19	87-91
V-8	5.0	FI	170@na	na	13/17	87-92
V-8	7.4	FI	230@na	na	na	89-92
V-8	5.7	FI	195@na	na	13/17	92-92
V-8D	6.2	na	145@3600	260@1900	16/22	87-92

KEY: I=in-line engine; V=V engine; F=flat engine; FI=fuel injection; bbl=barrel carburetor; T=turbo; D=diesel; HP=horsepower; MPG=estimated average miles per gallon.

EVALUATIONS, TESTS, AND RANKINGS

1991: "the extended-length, full-size van's bulk slowed down performance . . . the lengthy wheelbase gave it superb stability at highway speeds . . . For serious towing, we suggest an upgrade to the 7.4-liter engine." **Source:** "Getting Hitched," *Popular Mechanics,* July 1991, pp. 39-42, 95.

1988: "can be dressed in several combinations." **Source:** "Chevrolet Van/Sportvan," *Car and Driver—Buyers Guide 1988,* 1988, p. 148.

RECALLS

1990: (242 trucks; includes other GMC and Chevrolet models): Improperly torqued tie rod clamp fasteners could allow tie rods to loosen and separate. **Corrective action:** Properly torque tie rod clamps and readjust toe-in as necessary. *(NHTSA Campaign No. 90V074000.)*

1989-91: (25,807 vans; includes GMC Rally, Chevrolet Sportvan, and other GMC models): Seat back of rear bench may break away from seat cushion in an accident. **Corrective action:** Install reinforcement that runs from side of seat back frame assembly to seat cushion frame assembly, strengthening seat back. *(NHTSA Campaign No. 91V040000.)*

1987: (463 vans; includes Chevrolet Sportvan and GMC Rally): Fuel tank lower filler pipe may contain small holes at some spot welds used to attach mounting bracket. Fuel could leak from pipe during refueling or turning and spill fuel in excess of amount prescribed by FMVSS 301. **Corrective action:** Replace fuel tank lower filler pipe. *(NHTSA Campaign No. 88V016000.)*

SAFETY AND REPAIRS

1987: "Car Clinic," *Popular Mechanics,* August 1990, p. 26. **Note:** Tip for clashing starter motor gears in 1987-88 General Motors 4.3, 5.0, and 5.7 liter engines.

REPAIR MANUALS

890 ● **Chilton's Chevrolet 1968-1988**
Chilton Co.
Chilton Way
Radnor, PA 19089   Ph:(215)964-4000

Published 1989. **Price:** $15.95.

891 ● **General Motors 8-Cylinder**
Peter Allen Video Productions
38-C Otis St.
West Babylon, NY 11704   Ph:(516)643-4372

A program demonstrating basic maintenance and tune-up procedures for the entitled engine. **Release date:** 1986. **Producer:** Peter Allen Productions. **Acquisition:** Purchase.

892 ● **Get Your Chevrolet-GMC Fixed Right**
Consumer Reports Books
51 E. 42nd St., Suite 800
New York, NY 10017   Ph:(212)682-9280

Editor(s): Mort Schultz. **Price:** $8.95.

893 ● **Haynes Chevrolet V-8 Vans Owners Workshop Manual No. 345, 1968-1989**
Haynes Publications, Inc.
861 Lawrence Dr.
Newbury Park, CA 91320   Ph:(818)889-5400

Published 1983. **Editor(s):** J.H. Haynes and P.G. Strasman. **Price:** $15.95.

OTHER INFORMATION SOURCES

894 ● **All Chevy**
McMullen Publishing, Inc.
2145 W. La Palma Ave.   Ph:(714)635-9040
Anaheim, CA 92801-1785   Fax:(714)533-9999

Auto magazine for Chevrolet car enthusiasts. Quarterly. **Editor(s):** Thomas M. McMullen, Publisher.

895 ● **Chevy Outdoors**
The Aegis Group
30400 Van Dyke   Ph:(313)574-9100
Warren, MI 48093   Fax:(313)575-9535

Quarterly. **Editor(s):** Michael Brudenell. **Price:** $8.00.

896 ● **Friends Magazine**
Ceco Publishing
3221 W. Big Beaver, Ste. 110
Troy, MI 48084   Ph:(313)575-9400

Offers articles on Chevrolet automobiles. Monthly. **Editor(s):** Michael Brudenell. **Price:** Free.

897 ● **Standard Catalog of Chevrolet**
Krause Publications, Inc.
700 E. State St.
Iola, WI 54990   Ph:(715)445-2214

Published 1990. **Price:** $19.95.

CHEVROLET SPRINT (1987-88)

Produced by Suzuki of Japan, the Chevrolet Sprint debuted as the lightest production car sold in the U.S. In 1989, it was restyled and sold under the Geo Metro name through Chevrolet dealers.

1987 Chevrolet Sprint

MAJOR FEATURES

● Sprint and Sprint ER had as 1988 standard equipment: 5-speed manual transmission, front independent suspension/rear rigid axle, rack-and-pinion steering, and front disc/rear drum brakes.

● Sprint Turbo added as 1988 standard equipment: turbocharged engine, air conditioning, and AM/FM stereo.

PRICE HISTORY

The following new car prices reflect the approximate retail cost of the base model: **1987** - $5,995; **1988** - $5,495.

DIMENSIONS

Body Style	Years Avail	Wheel Base (in)	Lgth (in)	Ht (in)	Avg Wt (lbs)	Fuel Cap (gal)	Front Hdrm (in)	Front Legrm (in)
3d lbk	87-88	88.4	144.5	53.1	1,565	8.7	36	42
5d lbk	87-88	92.3	148.2	53.1	1,620	8.7	36	42

ENGINES

Type	Displacement (L)	Fuel Dly	HP @rpm	Torque @rpm (ft/lbs)	MPG Cty/Hwy	Years Avail
I-3	1.0	2-bbl	48@5100	77@3200	44/49	87-88
I-3T	1.0	FI	70@5500	107@3500	37/43	88-88
I-4T	1.4	FI	110@5400	120@3400	na	88-88

KEY: I=in-line engine; V=V engine; F=flat engine; FI=fuel injection; bbl=barrel carburetor; T=turbo; D=diesel; HP=horsepower; MPG=estimated average miles per gallon.

EVALUATIONS, TESTS, AND RANKINGS

1988: "steering feels a little vague, its brakes a little grabby, its clutch a little flimsy, 5th gear out in right field . . . acceleration was also in the middle of the three . . . provides excellent accommodation for this class.can deliver more than 50 mpg consistently." **Source:** "3X3: Nine cylinders of basic transportation: Chevrolet Sprint/Daihatsu Charade/Subaru Justy," *Road & Track*, July 1988, pp. 66-70, 74.

1988: "materials are obviously inexpensive, but assembly quality and finish are excellent . . . was underwhelming in the corners and in our handling tests . . . blast to throw around for a few miles, but you soon tire of the rather choppy ride, buzzy engine and chassis vibration." **Source:** "Econo Commandos: The world's top pocket rockets in a fight to the finish," *Popular Mechanics*, July 1988, pp. 51-55.

1987: "impressed with the standard Sprint, despite some obvious shortcomings. . .typical comments were loud, slow, flimsy and too much fun!; noisy, tinny, full of vibrations. I love it." **Source:** "Asian Invasion," *Popular Mechanics*, July 1987, pp. 90-94, 148.

RECALLS

None to date.

REPAIR MANUALS

898 ● **Chilton's Chevrolet 1968-1988**
Chilton Co.
Chilton Way
Radnor, PA 19089   Ph:(215)964-4000

Published 1989. **Price:** $15.95.

899 ● **Get Your Chevrolet-GMC Fixed Right**
Consumer Reports Books
51 E. 42nd St., Suite 800
New York, NY 10017   Ph:(212)682-9280

Editor(s): Mort Schultz. **Price:** $8.95.

OTHER INFORMATION SOURCES

900 ● **All Chevy**
McMullen Publishing, Inc.
2145 W. La Palma Ave.   Ph:(714)635-9040
Anaheim, CA 92801-1785   Fax:(714)533-9999

Auto magazine for Chevrolet car enthusiasts. Quarterly. **Editor(s):** Thomas M. McMullen, Publisher.

901 ● **Chevrolet High Performance**
Peterson Publishing Co.
6725 Sunset Blvd.
Los Angeles, CA 90028   Ph:(213)854-2222

Explains how to repair, restore, and improve performance of specific Chevrolet models. Bimonthly. **Editor(s):** Isaac Martin. **Price:** $11.95 per year; $2.95 per issue.

902 ● **Chevy Power**
Engledrum Publishing Corp.
153 Asharoken Ave.
Northport, NY 11768   Ph:(516)261-5260

Bimonthly. **Price:** $2.95 per issue.

903 ● **Friends Magazine**
Ceco Publishing
3221 W. Big Beaver, Ste. 110
Troy, MI 48084   Ph:(313)575-9400

Offers articles on Chevrolet automobiles. Monthly. **Editor(s):** Michael Brudenell. **Price:** Free.

904 ● **Standard Catalog of Chevrolet**
Krause Publications, Inc.
700 E. State St.
Iola, WI 54990   Ph:(715)445-2214

Published 1990. **Price:** $19.95.

905 ● **Super Chevy**
Argus Publishers Corp.
12100 Wilshire Blvd., Ste. 250   Ph:(213)820-3601
Los Angeles, CA 90025   Fax:(213)207-9388

Automotive magazine. Monthly. **Editor(s):** Bruce Hampson. **Price:** $16.00.

CHEVROLET SUBURBAN (1987-92)

Corporate twin is the GMC Suburban. Produced at General Motors plant in Flint, Michigan.

1990 Chevrolet Suburban

MAJOR FEATURES

• Chevrolet Suburban standard equipment for 1992 includes: 4-speed automatic transmission, heavy-duty suspension, front disc/rear drum power brakes with anti-lock braking system, power steering, and upgraded interior

• Chevrolet R10/1500 and R20/2500 Suburban standard equipment for 1992 includes: 4-speed automatic transmission, front independent suspension/rear rigid axle, front disc/rear drum power brakes with anti-lock braking system, power steering, and trip odometer.

• Chevrolet V10/V1500 and V20/V2500 add as 1992 standard equipment: 4-wheel drive.

Dimensions in chart that follows contains information on the R10 Suburban. Other Suburbans in the series have higher weights, greater fuel capacity, and other variations, including a decreased/increased horsepower output with engine options.

PRICE HISTORY

The following new car prices reflect the approximate retail cost of the base model: **1988** - $13,945; **1989** - $14,545; **1990** - $15,615; **1991** - $16,560.

DIMENSIONS

Body Style	Years Avail	Wheel Base (in)	Lgth (in)	Ht (in)	Avg Wt (lbs)	Fuel Cap (gal)	Front Hdrm (in)	Front Legrm (in)
5d wgn	87-88	129.5	219.1	72	6,100	25	na	na
5d wgn	89-89	129.5	219.1	72	6,100	31	na	na
5d wgn	90-91	129.5	219.1	72	6,100	37	na	na
5d wgn	92-92	131.5	219.5	74.9	7,200	40	na	na

ENGINES

Type	Displacement (L)	Fuel Dly	HP @rpm	Torque @rpm (ft/lbs)	MPG Cty/Hwy	Years Avail
V-8	5.0	FI	na	na	14/18	87-87
V-8	5.7	4-bbl	na	na	13/17	87-87
V-8	5.7	FI	210@4000	300@2800	13/17	88-92
V-8	7.4	FI	230@na	na	na	92-92
V-8D	6.2	FI	145@3600	260@1900	16/22	87-91

KEY: I=in-line engine; V=V engine; F=flat engine; FI=fuel injection; bbl=barrel carburetor; T=turbo; D=diesel; HP=horsepower; MPG=estimated average miles per gallon.

EVALUATIONS, TESTS, AND RANKINGS

1992: "The layout is spacious though not very clever . . . more comfortable inside than it used to be . . . smoother-shaped, quieter, and as heavy-duty as ever." **Source:** "Chevy Suburban 1500 4x4 Silverado," *Car and Driver*, December 1991, p. 120.

1992: "offers a sleeker look . . . styling more in tune with the '90s . . . additional 1000 pounds of towing capacity, four-wheel ABS, improved suspension." **Source:** "Preview 1992 Motor Trend Truck of the Year," *Motor Trend*, December 1991, pp. 104-105.

1990: "can go anywhere and tow anything with the best of the big pickups. Inside, there's room for a Little League team's starting lineup . . . as tough and dependable as they come." **Source:** "Lifetime of Versatility," *Home Mechanix*, February 1990, p. 69.

1989: "three bench seats will accommodate nine adults, with plenty of leg, elbow and head room to spare . . . handles like a pickup truck, rides like a pickup truck and guzzles gasoline like a pickup truck." **Source:** "Versatile Vehicles: Three cars built for work—and play," *Home Mechanix*, July 1989, pp. 64-70.

1989: "ample room inside . . . supportive front seats are perfect for long trips . . . can be outfitted as a bare bones utility vehicle, a super luxury 4WD station wagon/tow vehicle or anything in between." **Source:** "Pickups for Gardeners," *Organic Gardening*, September 1989, pp. 61-67.

RECALLS

1988: (277 van type passenger vehicle equipped with bucket seats and gray interior trim; includes Chevrolet and GMC Surburbans): Driver's seat and/or shoulder belt locking mechanism may not operate. In a crash, affected belts would not lock, thereby increasing the possibility of injury to the seat occupant. **Corrective action:** Install a new driver's seat belt assembly. (NHTSA Campaign No. 89V010000.)

SAFETY AND REPAIRS

1987: "Car Clinic," *Popular Mechanics*, August 1990, p. 26. **Note:** Tip for clashing starter motor gears in 1987-88 General Motors 4.3, 5.0, and 5.7 liter engines.

REPAIR MANUALS

906 ● Chevrolet and GMC 4-Wheel Drive Tune-Up: 1967-1987
Clymer Publications
P.O. Box 1209
Overland Park, KS 66212   Ph:(913)541-6694

With Illustrations. Published 1983. **Editor(s):** Jeff Robinson. **Price:** $14.99.

907 ● Chevy and GMC C-Series, Pickups, and Suburbans: 1967-1987: Includes Suburbans Shop Manual
Clymer Publications
P.O. Box 1209
Overland Park, KS 66212   Ph:(913)541-6694

With illustrations. **Price:** $14.95.

908 ● Chevy and GMC Two Wheel Drive C and R-Series Pickups, Suburbans, and Vans, 1970-1987 (Gas and Diesel)
Clymer Publications
P.O. Box 1209
Overland Park, KS 66212   Ph:(913)541-6694

With illustrations. Published 1990. **Price:** $26.95.

909 ● Chilton's Chevrolet 1968-1988
Chilton Co.
Chilton Way
Radnor, PA 19089   Ph:(215)964-4000

Published 1989. **Price:** $15.95.

910 ● Chilton's Chevrolet/GMC Pick-ups and Suburban 1970-1987
Chilton Co.
Chilton Way
Radnor, PA 19089   Ph:(215)964-4000

Published 1988. **Price:** $15.95.

911 ● General Motors 8-Cylinder
Peter Allen Video Productions
38-C Otis St.
West Babylon, NY 11704   Ph:(516)643-4372

A program demonstrating basic maintenance and tune-up procedures for the entitled engine. **Release date:** 1986. **Producer:** Peter Allen Productions. **Acquisition:** Purchase.

912 ● Get Your Chevrolet-GMC Fixed Right
Consumer Reports Books
51 E. 42nd St., Suite 800
New York, NY 10017   Ph:(212)682-9280

Editor(s): Mort Schultz. **Price:** $8.95.

OTHER INFORMATION SOURCES

913 ● All Chevy
McMullen Publishing, Inc.
2145 W. La Palma Ave.   Ph:(714)635-9040
Anaheim, CA 92801-1785   Fax:(714)533-9999

Auto magazine for Chevrolet car enthusiasts. Quarterly. **Editor(s):** Thomas M. McMullen, Publisher.

914 ● Chevy Outdoors
The Aegis Group
30400 Van Dyke   Ph:(313)574-9100
Warren, MI 48093   Fax:(313)575-9535

Quarterly. **Editor(s):** Michael Brudenell. **Price:** $8.00.

915 ● Friends Magazine
Ceco Publishing
3221 W. Big Beaver, Ste. 110
Troy, MI 48084   Ph:(313)575-9400

Offers articles on Chevrolet automobiles. Monthly. **Editor(s):** Michael Brudenell. **Price:** Free.

916 ● Standard Catalog of Chevrolet
Krause Publications, Inc.
700 E. State St.
Iola, WI 54990   Ph:(715)445-2214

Published 1990. **Price:** $19.95.

CHRYSLER CONQUEST (1987-89)

Chrysler Conquest and its corporate cousin, the Mitsubishi Starion, were produced until 1989 by Mitsubishi Motors in Japan. The Chrysler Conquest was imported and sold by Dodge and Plymouth dealers. In 1989, *The Car Book* rated its crash performance as good and its repair cost as medium.

MAJOR FEATURES

● Chrysler Conquest TSi (turbocharged sports intercooled) had as 1989 standard equipment: turbo sohc inline-4 engine, 5-speed manual transmission, independent front and rear suspension, four-wheel disc brakes with anti-lock rear brakes, recirculating ball power steering, Yokohama high-performance radials in dual size, air-conditioning, bucket seats, alarm system, and rear-window washer/wiper with heavy-duty defroster.

PRICE HISTORY

The following new car prices reflect the approximate retail cost of the base model: **1987** - $14,417; **1988** - $18,683; **1989** - $18,974.

DIMENSIONS

Body Style	Years Avail	Wheel Base (in)	Lgth (in)	Ht (in)	Avg Wt (lbs)	Fuel Cap (gal)	Front Hdrm (in)	Front Legrm (in)
3d cpe	87-89	95.9	173.2	50.2	3,031	19.8	36.6	40.7

ENGINES

Type	Displacement (L)	Fuel Dly	HP @rpm	Torque @rpm (ft/lbs)	MPG Cty/Hwy	Years Avail
I-4T	2.6	FI	188@5000	234@2500	18/22	87-89

KEY: I=in-line engine; V=V engine; F=flat engine; FI=fuel injection; bbl=barrel carburetor; T=turbo; D=diesel; HP=horsepower; MPG=estimated average miles per gallon.

EVALUATIONS, TESTS, AND RANKINGS

1987: "TSi has the performance to back up its muscular looks. . .Top speed is over 130 mph. . .Four-wheel disc brakes with rear anti-skid provide breath-taking deceleration capability." **Source:** "Chrysler's TSi: the secret is out," *The Detroit News*, August 20, 1986, pp. F1-F2.

RECALLS

None to date.

REPAIR MANUALS

917 ● Chilton's Colt/Challenger/Conquest/Vista, 1971-1988: Repair and Tune-Up Guide
Chilton Co.
Chilton Way
Radnor, PA 19089   Ph:(215)964-4000

Published 1989. **Price:** $15.95.

918 ● Chilton's Guide to Chassis Electronics and Power Accessories, 1988-1991 Ford/Chrysler/Jeep/Eagle
Chilton Co.
Chilton Way
Radnor, PA 19089   Ph:(215)964-4000

Published March 1991. **Price:** $19.95.

919 ● Chrysler, Dodge, Plymouth: 1972-1987 Rear Wheel Drive Tune-up Maintenance
Clymer Publications
P.O. Box 1209
Overland Park, KS 66212   Ph:(913)541-6694

Published 1987. **Price:** $14.95.

920 ● Motor Auto Repair 1983-1989 Chrysler
Hearst Bks.
105 Madison Ave.
New York, NY 10016   Ph:(212)889-3050

Published 1989. **Price:** $13.95.

OTHER INFORMATION SOURCES

921 ● Chrysler Performance Parts Association Newsletter
Chrysler Performance Parts Association (CPPA)
Box 1210
Azusa, CA 91702   Ph:(818)303-6220

Bimonthly. **Price:** Included in membership dues.

922 ● Chrysler Power Magazine
Chrysler Performance Parts Association (CPPA)
P.O. Box 1210
Azusa, CA 91702   Ph:(818)303-6220

Bimonthly. **Price:** Included in membership dues.

923 ● High Performance Mopar
CSK Publishing Co., Inc.
299 Market St.   Ph:(201)712-9300
Saddle Brook, NJ 07662   Fax:(201)712-9899

Magazine on old and new Chrysler performance cars featuring road tests on both old and new cars. Bimonthly. **Editor(s):** Steve Collison. **Price:** $15.00/year; $3.25 per single issue.

924 ● How to Build Chrysler, Dodge, Plymouth
Motorbooks International, Pubs. & Wholesalers, Inc.
729 Prospect Ave.
Osceola, WI 54020   Ph:(715)294-3345

Published 1990. **Editor(s):** Geoff Carter. **Price:** $17.95.

925 ● Mighty Mopars
MOPAR Scat Pack Club
PO Box 2303
Dearborn, MI 48123   Ph:(313)563-5974

Collects and publishes information for individuals dedicated to the preservation and restoration of Chrysler high-performance cars. Deals with technical matters, parts, and car history. Recurring features include restoration tips, news of members, and announcements of shows, swap meets, and races sponsored by the Club. Bimonthly. **Price:** Available to members only; $12.00/year or $2.00 per issue for nonmembers.

926 ● MOPAR
JHS Publishers, Inc.
175 Hudson St.
Hackensack, NJ 07601-6826   Ph:(201)488-7171

Annual. **Editor(s):** Cliff Gromer. **Price:** $2.95.

927 ● Mopar Muscle
Dobbs Publications
3816 Industry Blvd.   Ph:(813)646-5743
Lakeland, FL 33811   Fax:(813)644-8373

Automotive magazine. Bimonthly. **Price:** $3.50 per single issue.

928 ● MoPerformance
MoPerformance
1580 Hampton Rd.
Bensalem, PA 19020   Ph:(215)639-4456

Features articles of interest to owners and enthusiasts of Chrysler performance cars. Bimonthly. **Editor(s):** Robert Oskiera, Editor and Publisher. **Price:** $15.00/yr.; $3.00/issue.

929 ● Standard Catalog of Chrysler 1924-1990
Krause Pubns., Inc.
700 E. State St.
Iola, WI 54990   Ph:(715)445-2214

Published 1990. **Price:** $19.95.

930 ● Torsion Bar
Chrysler Product Owners Club
806 Winhall Way
Silver Spring, MD 20904

Promotes the collection, preservation, restoration, maintenance, exhibition, and enjoyment of Chrysler product cars, trucks, and other vehicles. Includes technical advice on the restoration of Chalmers, Chrysler, DeSoto, Dodge, Imperial, Maxwell, and Plymouth vehicles. Monthly. **Price:** Available to members only.

ASSOCIATIONS

931 ● Chrysler Performance Parts Association
Box 1210
Azusa, CA 91702   Ph:(818)303-6220
Roland Osborne, Chm.   Fax:(818)303-2481

Founded: 1976. **Membership:** 5,000. Clearinghouse for information on from whom, where, and how to obtain vintage, muscle, and high-tech Chrysler performance parts. **Former Name(s):** (1979) National HEMI Owners; (1980) MOPAR Muscle Club. **Convention/Meeting:** Annual national meet.

932 ● Chrysler Product Owners Club
5203 Edmondson Ave.
Baltimore, MD 21229
Brian K. Scott, Exec. Officer

Founded: 1978. **Membership:** 210. Collectors and restorers of Chrysler-product automobiles. Promotes the collection, preservation, restoration, maintenance, exhibition, and enjoyment of all Chrysler product cars, trucks, and other vehicles, including Chrysler, DeSoto, Dodge, Imperial, and Plymouth. Offers technical advice; provides list of cars, parts, and services. Maintains library of service and parts manuals from the 1930s to 1989. **Convention/Meeting:** Annual.

933 ● Special Interest Auto Club
P.O. Box 681
Centreville, VA 22020
Stephen L. DiGiulian, Pres.   Ph:(703)631-0018

Founded: 1978. **Membership:** 2,000. Owners and enthusiasts of Chrysler high-performance automobiles manufactured from 1964 to the present including Dodge Challengers and Plymouth Barracudas. Purpose is to help restore and preserve Chrysler high-performance cars. Maintains merchandise department and parts program listing cars and parts wanted and for sale. Sponsors national and regional shows and meets; compiles statistics; maintains biographical archives and speakers' bureau. **Former Name(s):** (1981) T/A-AAR Special Interest Auto Club. **Convention/Meeting:** Annual (with exhibits) - always July, midwestern U.S.

934 ● WPC Club
P.O. Box 3504
Kalamazoo, MI 49003-3504
Ralph Kendall, Pres.   Ph:(616)372-1067

Founded: 1969. **Membership:** 4,850. Individuals dedicated to the preservation, restoration, and enjoyment of Chrysler product cars. Conducts social activities; houses library. Awards annual trophies at national meets. **Convention/Meeting:** Annual; also sponsors International Winter Photo Meet.

CHRYSLER FIFTH AVENUE (1987-89)

Along with the Dodge Diplomat and Plymouth Gran Fury, the Fifth Avenue is a variation on the rear-wheel drive design that originated with the Dodge Aspen/Plymouth Volare. Produced until 1989 at the Chrysler Motors plant in Kenosha, Wisconsin. Emerged in 1990 as part of the New Yorker lineup on the same platform as the Chrysler Imperial.

MAJOR FEATURES

- Fifth Avenue had as 1989 standard equipment: rear-drive, three-speed, TorqueFlite automatic transmission, power steering, independent front suspension, front vented disc brakes, rear drum brakes, and air-conditioning.

PRICE HISTORY

The following new car prices reflect the approximate retail cost of the base model: **1987** - $15,966; **1988** - $17,243; **1989** - $18,345.

DIMENSIONS

Body Style	Years Avail	Wheel Base (in)	Lgth (in)	Ht (in)	Avg Wt (lbs)	Fuel Cap (gal)	Front Hdrm (in)	Front Legrm (in)
4d sdn	87-89	112.7	206.7	55.1	3,770	18	39.3	42.5

ENGINES

Type	Displacement (L)	Fuel Dly	HP @rpm	Torque @rpm (ft/lbs)	MPG Cty/Hwy	Years Avail
V-8	5.2	2-bbl	140@3600	265@2000	16/22	87-89

KEY: I=in-line engine; V=V engine; F=flat engine; FI=fuel injection; bbl=barrel carburetor; T=turbo; D=diesel; HP=horsepower; MPG=estimated average miles per gallon.

EVALUATIONS, TESTS, AND RANKINGS

1988: "traditional rear-drive sedans that sell quite well." **Source:** "Chrysler Fifth Avenue," *Car and Driver—Buyers Guide 1988*, 1988, p. 100.

RECALLS

1988: (12,000 passenger cars equipped with automatic speed control. Recall includes the Chrysler Fifth Avenue, Plymouth Fury, Dodge Diplomat): Engine compartment wiring harness fusible link wires may be trapped under the speed control servo bracket. Trapped wires may eventually cause a high resistance electrical short that can result in an underhood fire. **Corrective action:** Free any trapped wiring; then secure wiring with a tie strap to keep away from speed control bracket. (NHTSA Campaign No. 87V164000.)

REPAIR MANUALS

935 ● **Chilton's Guide to Chassis Electronics and Power Accessories, 1988-1991 Ford/Chrysler/Jeep/Eagle**
Chilton Co.
Chilton Way
Radnor, PA 19089   Ph:(215)964-4000

Published March 1991. **Price:** $19.95.

936 ● **Chrysler, Dodge, Plymouth: 1972-1987 Rear Wheel Drive Tune-up Maintenance**
Clymer Publications
P.O. Box 1209
Overland Park, KS 66212   Ph:(913)541-6694

Published 1987. **Price:** $14.95.

937 ● **Motor Auto Repair 1983-1989 Chrysler**
Hearst Bks.
105 Madison Ave.
New York, NY 10016   Ph:(212)889-3050

Published 1989. **Price:** $13.95.

OTHER INFORMATION SOURCES

938 ● **How to Build Chrysler, Dodge, Plymouth**
Motorbooks International, Pubs. & Wholesalers, Inc.
729 Prospect Ave.
Osceola, WI 54020   Ph:(715)294-3345

Published 1990. **Editor(s):** Geoff Carter. **Price:** $17.95.

939 ● **Standard Catalog of Chrysler 1924-1990**
Krause Pubns., Inc.
700 E. State St.
Iola, WI 54990   Ph:(715)445-2214

Published 1990. **Price:** $19.95.

940 ● **Torsion Bar**
Chrysler Product Owners Club
806 Winhall Way
Silver Spring, MD 20904

Promotes the collection, preservation, restoration, maintenance, exhibition, and enjoyment of Chrysler product cars, trucks, and other vehicles. Includes technical advice on the restoration of Chalmers, Chrysler, DeSoto, Dodge, Imperial, Maxwell, and Plymouth vehicles. Monthly. **Price:** Available to members only.

ASSOCIATIONS

941 ● **Chrysler Product Owners Club**
5203 Edmondson Ave.
Baltimore, MD 21229
Brian K. Scott, Exec. Officer

Founded: 1978. **Membership:** 210. Collectors and restorers of Chrysler-product automobiles. Promotes the collection, preservation, restoration, maintenance, exhibition, and enjoyment of all Chrysler product cars, trucks, and other vehicles, including Chrysler, DeSoto, Dodge, Imperial, and Plymouth. Offers technical advice; provides list of cars, parts, and services. Maintains library of service and parts manuals from the 1930s to 1989. **Convention/Meeting:** Annual.

942 ● **WPC Club**
P.O. Box 3504
Kalamazoo, MI 49003-3504
Ralph Kendall, Pres.   Ph:(616)372-1067

Founded: 1969. **Membership:** 4,850. Individuals dedicated to the preservation, restoration, and enjoyment of Chrysler product cars. Conducts social activities; houses library. Awards annual trophies at national meets. **Convention/Meeting:** Annual; also sponsors International Winter Photo Meet.

CHRYSLER IMPERIAL (1990-92)

Based on the New Yorker platform. Classified in the full-size vehicle class. Produced at the Chrysler Motors plant in Belvidere, Illinois. Graded as having the lowest maintenance cost, the highest insurance cost, and the lowest repair cost among mid-size vehicles by *The Complete Car Cost Guide* in 1990. Received poor crash test and low repair cost ratings from the *The Car Book* in 1991 and 1992.

1992 Chrysler Imperial

MAJOR FEATURES

● Imperial has as 1992 standard equipment: 4-speed automatic, Ultradrive transmission, Iso-strut front suspension, power rack-and-pinion steering, four-wheel disc, anti-lock brakes, air conditioning, electric rear window defroster, driver air bag, electronic speed control, and tilt steering column.

PRICE HISTORY

The following new car prices reflect the approximate retail cost of the base model: **1990** - $25,495; **1991** - $26,978; **1992** - $28,453.

DIMENSIONS

Body Style	Years Avail	Wheel Base (in)	Lgth (in)	Ht (in)	Avg Wt (lbs)	Fuel Cap (gal)	Front Hdrm (in)	Front Legrm (in)
4d sdn	90-92	109.3	203	55.3	3,534	16	38.4	43

ENGINES

Type	Displace-ment (L)	Fuel Dly	HP @rpm	Torque @rpm (ft/lbs)	MPG Cty/Hwy	Years Avail
V-6	3.3	FI	150@5000	185@3600	18/25	90-90
V-6	3.8	FI	150@4400	203@3200	18/25	91-92

KEY: I=in-line engine; V=V engine; F=flat engine; FI=fuel injection; bbl=barrel carburetor; T=turbo; D=diesel; HP=horsepower; MPG=estimated average miles per gallon.

EVALUATIONS, TESTS, AND RANKINGS

1990: "ride was cushioned, even on harsh bumps, because of an air suspension system that automatically regulates air volume in the car's springs. . .trunk was flat and huge. . .premium stereo offered good sound." **Source:** "Imperial returns Chrysler to traditional luxury market," *The Detroit News*, January 10, 1990, pp. C3-C4.

1990: "of the C-body theme, except that it revives the more-expensive Imperial nameplate in the pecking order above existing Chrysler sedans. . .comfortable Chrysler seating. . .extremely cushy and lustily aromatic for the real-world drive."

Source: "Land of the Giants," *Motor Trend*, March 1990, pp. 100-104, 106, 108-109.

1990: "delivered decent handling . . . favorably impressed by the Imperial's engine performance . . . excessive induction noise at full throttle." **Source:** "The Big Three," *Popular Mechanics*, March 1990, pp. 61-65.

1990: "the Imperial's mechanicals. . .offer enough power for freeway merging and passing as well as a soft ride and reasonably good handling . . . interior is spacious, even sumptuous . . . well designed for its intended market segment." **Source:** "Imperial Rates a Royal Salute," *Design News*, October 1990, pp. 234-235.

RECALLS

1991: (130,000 passenger vehicles; includes Chrysler Imperial, Chrysler Fifth Avenue, Chrysler Salon, Chrysler LeBaron, Dodge Dynasty, Dodge Spirit, and Plymouth Acclaim): Front outboard safety belt may become difficult to latch or unlatch due to a webbing stiffener entering the buckle housing and dislodging the buckle latch guide. latch may open during an accident or sudden stop. **Corrective action:** Replace buckle latch engagement. *(NHTSA Campaign No. 91V122000.)*

REPAIR MANUALS

943 ● **Chilton's Guide to Chassis Electronics and Power Accessories, 1988-1991 Ford/Chrysler/Jeep/Eagle**
Chilton Co.
Chilton Way
Radnor, PA 19089   Ph:(215)964-4000

Published March 1991. **Price:** $19.95.

OTHER INFORMATION SOURCES

944 ● **How to Build Chrysler, Dodge, Plymouth**
Motorbooks International, Pubs. & Wholesalers, Inc.
729 Prospect Ave.
Osceola, WI 54020   Ph:(715)294-3345

Published 1990. **Editor(s):** Geoff Carter. **Price:** $17.95.

945 ● **Slant 6 News**
Slant 6 Club of America
PO Box 4414
Salem, OR 97302   Ph:(503)581-2230

Club magazine containing technical articles and advisory information on maintenance and restoration of Chrysler Corp. vehicles powered by slant 6 engines. Quarterly. **Editor(s):** Jack Poehler, Editor/Advertising Mgr. **Price:** $18.00.

946 ● **Standard Catalog of Chrysler 1924-1990**
Krause Pubns., Inc.
700 E. State St.
Iola, WI 54990   Ph:(715)445-2214

Published 1990. **Price:** $19.95.

947 ● **Torsion Bar**
Chrysler Product Owners Club
806 Winhall Way
Silver Spring, MD 20904

Promotes the collection, preservation, restoration, maintenance, exhibition, and enjoyment of Chrysler product cars, trucks, and other vehicles. Includes technical advice on the restoration of Chalmers, Chrysler, DeSoto, Dodge, Imperial, Maxwell, and Plymouth vehicles. Monthly. **Price:** Available to members only.

ASSOCIATIONS

948 ● Chrysler Product Owners Club
5203 Edmondson Ave.
Baltimore, MD 21229
Brian K. Scott, Exec. Officer

Founded: 1978. **Membership:** 210. Collectors and restorers of Chrysler-product automobiles. Promotes the collection, preservation, restoration, maintenance, exhibition, and enjoyment of all Chrysler product cars, trucks, and other vehicles, including Chrysler, DeSoto, Dodge, Imperial, and Plymouth. Offers technical advice; provides list of cars, parts, and services. Maintains library of service and parts manuals from the 1930s to 1989. **Convention/Meeting:** Annual.

949 ● Slant 6 Club of America
PO Box 4414
Salem, OR 97302   Ph:(503)581-2230

Founded: 1980. Owners and enthusiasts of Chrysler automobiles with V-6 engines.

950 ● WPC Club
P.O. Box 3504
Kalamazoo, MI 49003-3504
Ralph Kendall, Pres.   Ph:(616)372-1067

Founded: 1969. **Membership:** 4,850. Individuals dedicated to the preservation, restoration, and enjoyment of Chrysler product cars. Conducts social activities; houses library. Awards annual trophies at national meets. **Convention/Meeting:** Annual; also sponsors International Winter Photo Meet.

CHRYSLER LEBARON COUPE/CONVERTIBLE (1987-92)

The LeBaron Coupe is categorized in the EPA compact vehicle class. Nominated to *Motor Trend's* 1987 Car of the Year class. Produced since 1987 at the Chrysler Motors plants in Newark, Delaware and Toluca, Mexico. The LeBaron Convertible is categorized in the EPA subcompact vehicle class. Appeals to upscale, affluent buyers, a high percentage of whom are women. Both vehicles replaced the older LeBaron J Coupe and Convertible, which were built on the K-car chassis. Both the LeBaron Coupe and Convertible were rated average in occupant injury history by *The Car Book* in 1992.

1992 Chrysler LeBaron Premium Convertible LX

MAJOR FEATURES

● LeBaron Highline Coupe and LeBaron Highline Convertible have as 1992 standard equipment: 2.5 liter engine, three-speed automatic transmission, Iso-strut front suspension, power rack-and-pinion steering, front power disc brakes, rear window electric defroster, restraint system with driver air bag,

14-inch lace wheelcovers, and a power operated convertible top (LeBaron Highline Convertible only).

● LeBaron Premium Coupe LX and LeBaron Premium Convertible 1992 standard features: 3.0 liter, V-6 engine, four-speed automatic Ultradrive transmission, air conditioning, 15-inch luxury wheelcovers, an assortment of interior accessories, and a power operated convertible top (LeBaron Premium Convertible only).

● LeBaron Premium Coupe GTC and LeBaron Premium Convertible GTC 1992 standard equipment: five-speed manual transmission, tilt steering column, sport handling suspension, 15-inch aluminum wheelcovers, electronic speed control, additional interior accessories, and a power operated convertible top (LeBaron Premium Convertible GTC only).

The following base prices are for the LeBaron Coupe only.

PRICE HISTORY

The following new car prices reflect the approximate retail cost of the base model: **1987** - $11,295; **1988** - $10,995; **1989** - $11,495; **1990** - $12,495; **1991** - $12,995; **1992** - $13,488.

DIMENSIONS

Body Style	Years Avail	Wheel Base (in)	Lgth (in)	Ht (in)	Avg Wt (lbs)	Fuel Cap (gal)	Front Hdrm (in)	Front Legrm (in)
2d cpe	87-91	100.3	184.9	51.0	2,853	14.0	37.6	42.4
2d cpe	92-92	100.5	184.8	53.3	2,863	14.0	37.6	42.4
2d conv	87-92	100.5	184.8	52.4	3,010	14.0	38.3	42.4

ENGINES

Type	Displacement (L)	Fuel Dly	HP @rpm	Torque @rpm (ft/lbs)	MPG Cty/Hwy	Years Avail
I-4	2.5	FI	100@4800	135@2800	22/28	87-92
I-4T	2.2	FI	146@5200	171@3600	20/29	87-87
I-4T	2.2	FI	146@5200	170@3600	21/29	88-88
I-4T	2.5	FI	150@4800	180@2000	20/29	89-90
I-4T	2.2	FI	174@5200	210@2400	20/28	90-90
I-4T	2.5	FI	152@4800	211@2800	21/27	91-92
V-6	3.0	FI	141@5000	171@2800	18/27	90-91
V-6	3.0	FI	141@5000	167@3600	18/27	92-92

KEY: I=in-line engine; V=V engine; F=flat engine; FI=fuel injection; bbl=barrel carburetor; T=turbo; D=diesel; HP=horsepower; MPG=estimated average miles per gallon.

EVALUATIONS, TESTS, AND RANKINGS

1991: "too much chrome, but exterior styling is still handsome . . . Rear seat room is outstanding . . . Interior design. . .form overshadows function." **Source:** "Chrysler Le Baron Coupe: Return to Glory will have to Wait," *Autoweek's Autofile 1991 Edition,* 1990, pp. 67-71.

1991: "a mixed bag of good and bad features . . . Top up, the LeBaron is a champ . . . Top down, it's a mobile wind tunnel." **Source:** "Top-Down Showdown: We test the hottest cars under the sun," *Motor Trend,* June 1991, pp. 49-59, 62-63.

1990: "While not rip-roaring, it offered plenty of zip. . .easy to maneuver. . .flat, nicely carpeted truck. . .front bucket seats felt fine. The back seat, however, would be a tight squeeze for three." **Source:** "LeBaron dresses up: GT coupe refines interior, adds power," *The Detroit News,* February 7, 1990, pp. 1B, 7B.

1989: "a potent performer . . . though the suspension feels soft, it does apoor job filtering out small bumps and pavement irregularities . . . attention grabbing shape." **Source:** "Chrysler LeBaron GTC: Lookin' good, lookin' back," *Car and Driver,* July 1989, pp. 121-123.

1988: "ride is harsh. . .seats are quite comfortable. . .very handsome car." **Source:** "Chrysler LeBaron Coupe," *Home Mechanix,* February 1988, pp. 76-77.

1987: "beautiful to look at and is very slick and smooth. . .ride is suprisingly firm and the steering is tight and gives just the right amount of resistance." **Source:** "The new LeBaron: A slick, smoooth pile of electronic toys," *The Detroit News,* January 28, 1987, pp. 1F-2F.

1987: "an absolute knock-out. . .smooth, contemporary, and thoughtfully integrated. . .[LeBaron convertible is] one of the better performers in this group." **Source:** "Ragtop Fever: Born-again convertibles bring back driving fun," *Popular Mechanics,* June 1987, pp. 71-75, 123.

RECALLS

1991: (398 passenger cars): The two air bag system front impact sensors may not be secured to their mounting brackets. Air bag will not deploy in a frontal collision if the front impact sensors are not attached. **Corrective action:** Repair to assure proper attachment of front impact sensors to brackets. *(NHTSA Campaign No. 90V194000.)*

1991: (18,000 passenger cars; includes several Chrysler, Dodge, and Plymouth models): Front disc brake caliper guide pin bolts may not have been adequately torqued and could loosen. This could cause reduced braking effectiveness and could result in an accident. **Corrective action:** Properly torque front brake caliper guide pin bolts to 250 lbs. *(NHTSA Campaign No. 90V162000.)*

1991: (90 passenger cars; includes the Chrysler LeBaron Coupe/Convertible and Dodge Daytona): Mismatched parking brake cable lengths to the rear wheels reduce braking ability of one of the rear wheels, in violation of FMVSS 105. Insufficient braking ability could result in inadvertent vehicle rollaway. **Corrective action:** Replace mismatched parking brake cable with one of correct length. *(NHTSA Campaign No. 91V078000.)*

1990: (257 passenger cars with grey interior; includes Chrysler and Dodge models): Air bag inflator modules may not contain diffuser holes between the ignitor and propellant chambers. Air bags would not deploy in an impact situation, which could lead to driver injury. **Corrective action:** Replace air bag inflator modules with properly machined modules. *(NHTSA Campaign No. 90V080000.)*

1989-90: (625,000 cars; includes several Plymouth, Dodge, and Chrysler vehicles): Engine valve cover gasket may dislocate and allow an engine oil leak at the gasket. Leakage of oil in the engine compartment could cause a fire. **Corrective action:** Replace gasket cover with revised cover, and RTV sealant will be applied in place of a gasket. *(NHTSA Campaign No. 89V237000.)*

1987: (4,400 vehicles): Driver's floormat mispositioned such as to interfere with accelerator pedal. Floormat may restrict return of accelerator pedal to the idle position. **Corrective action:** Floormat will be replaced with a redesigned mat to eliminate the interference. *(NHTSA Campaign No. 87V107000.)*

1987: (580,000 vehicles equipped with 2.2L turbocharged engine; includes models made before 1987; includes Chrysler, Dodge, and Plymouth models): Fuel leakage may occur in low ambient temperature operation at connections of an engine compartment fuel supply hose to the pressure regulator and to the fuel rail. In the presence of an ignition source, fuel leakage could result in a fire. **Corrective action:** Relocate pressure regulator; replace fuel supply with formed hose with revised routing configuration to ensure sealing integrity. *(NHTSA Campaign No. 88V105000.)*

REPAIR MANUALS

951 ● **Chilton's Chrysler Front Wheel Drive 1981-1988**
Chilton Co.
Chilton Way
Radnor, PA 19089   Ph:(215)964-4000

Published 1988. **Price:** $15.95.

952 ● **Chilton's Guide to Chassis Electronics and Power Accessories, 1988-1991 Ford/Chrysler/Jeep/Eagle**
Chilton Co.
Chilton Way
Radnor, PA 19089   Ph:(215)964-4000

Published March 1991. **Price:** $19.95.

953 ● **Haynes Chrysler Mid-Size Cars Owners Workshop Manual, 1982-1989**
Haynes Publications, Inc.
861 Lawrence Dr.
Newbury Park, CA 91320   Ph:(818)889-5400

Published 1987. **Editor(s):** J.H.Haynes. **Price:** $15.95.

954 ● **Motor Auto Repair 1983-1989 Chrysler**
Hearst Bks.
105 Madison Ave.
New York, NY 10016   Ph:(212)889-3050

Published 1989. **Price:** $13.95.

OTHER INFORMATION SOURCES

955 ● **Chrysler Performance Parts Association Newsletter**
Chrysler Performance Parts Association (CPPA)
Box 1210
Azusa, CA 91702   Ph:(818)303-6220

Bimonthly. **Price:** Included in membership dues.

956 ● **Chrysler Power Magazine**
Chrysler Performance Parts Association (CPPA)
P.O. Box 1210
Azusa, CA 91702   Ph:(818)303-6220

Bimonthly. **Price:** Included in membership dues.

957 ● **High Performance Mopar**
CSK Publishing Co., Inc.
299 Market St.   Ph:(201)712-9300
Saddle Brook, NJ 07662   Fax:(201)712-9899

Magazine on old and new Chrysler performance cars featuring road tests on both old and new cars. Bimonthly. **Editor(s):** Steve Collison. **Price:** $15.00/year; $3.25 per single issue.

958 ● **How to Build Chrysler, Dodge, Plymouth**
Motorbooks International, Pubs. & Wholesalers, Inc.
729 Prospect Ave.
Osceola, WI 54020   Ph:(715)294-3345

Published 1990. **Editor(s):** Geoff Carter. **Price:** $17.95.

959 ● **Mighty Mopars**
MOPAR Scat Pack Club
PO Box 2303
Dearborn, MI 48123   Ph:(313)563-5974

Collects and publishes information for individuals dedicated to the preservation and restoration of Chrysler high-performance cars. Deals with technical matters, parts, and car history. Recurring features include restoration tips, news of members, and announcements of shows, swap meets, and races sponsored by the Club. Bimonthly. **Price:** Available to members only; $12.00/year or $2.00 per issue for nonmembers.

960 ● MOPAR
JHS Publishers, Inc.
175 Hudson St.
Hackensack, NJ 07601-6826   Ph:(201)488-7171

Annual. **Editor(s):** Cliff Gromer. **Price:** $2.95.

961 ● Mopar Muscle
Dobbs Publications
3816 Industry Blvd.   Ph:(813)646-5743
Lakeland, FL 33811   Fax:(813)644-8373

Automotive magazine. Bimonthly. **Price:** $3.50 per single issue.

962 ● MoPerformance
MoPerformance
1580 Hampton Rd.
Bensalem, PA 19020   Ph:(215)639-4456

Features articles of interest to owners and enthusiasts of Chrysler performance cars. Bimonthly. **Editor(s):** Robert Oskiera, Editor and Publisher. **Price:** $15.00/yr.; $3.00/issue.

963 ● Slant 6 News
Slant 6 Club of America
PO Box 4414
Salem, OR 97302   Ph:(503)581-2230

Club magazine containing technical articles and advisory information on maintenance and restoration of Chrysler Corp. vehicles powered by slant 6 engines. Quarterly. **Editor(s):** Jack Poehler, Editor/Advertising Mgr. **Price:** $18.00.

964 ● Standard Catalog of Chrysler 1924-1990
Krause Pubns., Inc.
700 E. State St.
Iola, WI 54990   Ph:(715)445-2214

Published 1990. **Price:** $19.95.

965 ● Torsion Bar
Chrysler Product Owners Club
806 Winhall Way
Silver Spring, MD 20904

Promotes the collection, preservation, restoration, maintenance, exhibition, and enjoyment of Chrysler product cars, trucks, and other vehicles. Includes technical advice on the restoration of Chalmers, Chrysler, DeSoto, Dodge, Imperial, Maxwell, and Plymouth vehicles. Monthly. **Price:** Available to members only.

ASSOCIATIONS

966 ● Chrysler Performance Parts Association
Box 1210
Azusa, CA 91702   Ph:(818)303-6220
Roland Osborne, Chm.   Fax:(818)303-2481

Founded: 1976. **Membership:** 5,000. Clearinghouse for information on from whom, where, and how to obtain vintage, muscle, and high-tech Chrysler performance parts. **Former Name(s):** (1979) National HEMI Owners; (1980) MOPAR Muscle Club. **Convention/Meeting:** Annual national meet.

967 ● Chrysler Product Owners Club
5203 Edmondson Ave.
Baltimore, MD 21229
Brian K. Scott, Exec. Officer

Founded: 1978. **Membership:** 210. Collectors and restorers of Chrysler-product automobiles. Promotes the collection, preservation, restoration, maintenance, exhibition, and enjoyment of all Chrysler product cars, trucks, and other vehicles, including Chrysler, DeSoto, Dodge, Imperial, and Plymouth. Offers technical advice; provides list of cars, parts, and services. Maintains library of service and parts manuals from the 1930s to 1989. **Convention/Meeting:** Annual.

968 ● Slant 6 Club of America
PO Box 4414
Salem, OR 97302   Ph:(503)581-2230

Founded: 1980. Owners and enthusiasts of Chrysler automobiles with V-6 engines.

969 ● Special Interest Auto Club
P.O. Box 681
Centreville, VA 22020
Stephen L. DiGiulian, Pres.   Ph:(703)631-0018

Founded: 1978. **Membership:** 2,000. Owners and enthusiasts of Chrysler high-performance automobiles manufactured from 1964 to the present including Dodge Challengers and Plymouth Barracudas. Purpose is to help restore and preserve Chrysler high-performance cars. Maintains merchandise department and parts program listing cars and parts wanted and for sale. Sponsors national and regional shows and meets; compiles statistics; maintains biographical archives and speakers' bureau. **Former Name(s):** (1981) T/A-AAR Special Interest Auto Club. **Convention/Meeting:** Annual (with exhibits) - always July, midwestern U.S.

970 ● WPC Club
P.O. Box 3504
Kalamazoo, MI 49003-3504
Ralph Kendall, Pres.   Ph:(616)372-1067

Founded: 1969. **Membership:** 4,850. Individuals dedicated to the preservation, restoration, and enjoyment of Chrysler product cars. Conducts social activities; houses library. Awards annual trophies at national meets. **Convention/Meeting:** Annual; also sponsors International Winter Photo Meet.

CHRYSLER LEBARON SEDAN (1987-92)

Originally introduced as first of several versions of the compact front-drive K-car line. The older model LeBaron and Town & Country were discontinued after 1988; LeBaron Highline, LeBaron Premium, and LeBaron GTS ended production after 1989. LeBaron Sedan, which is built on the Dodge Spirit/Plymouth Acclaim A-body platform, was introduced in 1990. The Landau and LX models were introduced in 1992. The older generation LeBarons were built at the Chrysler Motors plant in Sterling Heights, Michigan; the LeBaron Sedan is produced in Toluca, Mexico and Newark, Delaware.

1992 Chrysler LeBaron Sedan

MAJOR FEATURES

● LeBaron Sedan offers as 1992 standard equipment: 2.5 liter, I-4 engine, three-speed automatic transmission, Iso-strut suspension, power rack-and-pinion steering, power disc brakes, electric rear window defroster, message center, driver's side air bag, electronic speed control, and tilt steering column.

● LeBaron Landau adds as 1992 standard equipment: 3.0 liter, V-6 engine, four-speed automatic transmission, air conditioning, AM/FM stereo/cassette, landau roof, and additional trim.

● LeBaron LX adds as 1992 standard equipment: fog lamps, deck lid luggage rack, trip computer, and 15-inch wheels and tires.

● LeBaron Highline had as 1989 standard equipment: five-speed manual transmission, independent front suspension, front disc brakes, and rack-and-pinion power steering.

● LeBaron Premium added as 1989 standard equipment: additional trim and accessories.

● LeBaron GTS added as 1989 standard equipment: 2.5 liter turbocharged engine, also known as the Turbo II, high performance suspension system, and an assortment of trim and accessories.

● LeBaron had as 1988 standard features: 3-speed automatic transmission, independent front suspension, front disc brakes, rack-and-pinion steering, and electronic instrument clusters.

● Town & Country Wagon added as 1988 standard equipment: wood panel moldings, and various accessories.

PRICE HISTORY

The following new car prices reflect the approximate retail cost of the base model: **1987** - $10,707; **1988** - $11,286; **1989** - $13,495; **1990** - $15,995; **1991** - $16,501; **1992** - $13,998.

DIMENSIONS

Body Style	Years Avail	Wheel Base (in)	Lgth (in)	Ht (in)	Avg Wt (lbs)	Fuel Cap (gal)	Front Hdrm (in)	Front Legrm (in)
4d lbk	87-89	103.1	180.4	53.0	2,926	14.0	38.3	41.1
4d sdn	87-89	100.3	180.4	53.0	2,714	14.0	38.3	41.1
4d sdn	90-91	103.3	181.2	53.7	3,040	16.0	38.4	41.9
4d sdn	92-92	103.5	182.7	53.7	2,972	16.0	38.4	41.9
wgn	87-88	100.4	179.0	53.2	2,759	14.0	38.5	42.2

ENGINES

Type	Displacement (L)	Fuel Dly	HP @rpm	Torque @rpm (ft/lbs)	MPG Cty/Hwy	Years Avail
I-4	2.2	FI	97@5600	122@3200	24/32	87-87
I-4	2.5	FI	100@4800	136@2800	24/34	87-89
I-4	2.2	FI	96@4400	133@2800	25/34	88-88
I-4	2.2	FI	100@5200	133@3200	na	88-88
I-4	2.2	FI	93@4800	122@3200	na	88-89
I-4	2.5	FI	100@4800	135@2800	23/27	92-92
I-4T	2.2	FI	146@5200	170@3600	21/29	87-88
I-4T	2.5	FI	150@4800	180@2000	20/29	89-89
I-4T	2.2	FI	174@5200	200@2400	20/28	89-89
V-6	3.0	FI	141@5000	171@2800	19/29	90-91
V-6	3.0	FI	141@5000	167@3600	20/28	92-92

KEY: I=in-line engine; V=V engine; F=flat engine; FI=fuel injection; bbl=barrel carburetor; T=turbo; D=diesel; HP=horsepower; MPG=estimated average miles per gallon.

EVALUATIONS, TESTS, AND RANKINGS

1991: "the 60-degree, V-6 is a willing partner in the LeBaron's quest for comfort and serenity . . . the motor scoots the car along with something resembling alacrity . . . Chrysler's fired an important salvo into the under $20,000 segment." **Source:** "Chrysler LeBaron Sedan: What's in a Name, Anyway," *Motor Trend,* November 1990, pp. 104-108.

1990: "handsomely redesigned interior." **Source:** "Chrysler LeBaron," *Car and Driver—Buyers Guide 1990,* 1989, p. 23.

1987: "Nearly 45 percent of the owners. . .surveyed ranked handling as the Lancer/GTS's best liked feature. . .Interior roominess and comfort received excellent marks overall." **Source:** "Chrysler LeBaron GTS and Dodge Lancer," *Popular Mechanics,* March 1987, pp. 67, 130, 138.

RECALLS

1991: (398 passenger cars): The two air bag system front impact sensors may not be secured to their mounting brackets. Air bag will not deploy in a frontal collision if the front impact sensors are not attached. **Corrective action:** Repair to assure proper attachment of front impact sensors to brackets. *(NHTSA Campaign No. 90V194000.)*

1991: (18,000 passenger cars; includes several Chrysler, Dodge, and Plymouth models): Front disc brake caliper guide pin bolts may not have been adequately torqued and could loosen. This could cause reduced braking effectiveness and could result in an accident. **Corrective action:** Properly torque front brake caliper guide pin bolts to 250 lbs. *(NHTSA Campaign No. 90V162000.)*

1991: (130,000 passenger vehicles; includes Chrysler Imperial, Chrysler Fifth Avenue, Chrysler Salon, Chrysler LeBaron, Dodge Dynasty, Dodge Spirit, and Plymouth Acclaim): Front outboard safety belt may become difficult to latch or unlatch due to a webbing stiffener entering the buckle housing and dislodging the buckle latch guide. Latch may open during an accident or sudden stop. **Corrective action:** Replace buckle latch engagement. *(NHTSA Campaign No. 91V122000.)*

1990: (257 passenger cars with grey interior; includes Chrysler and Dodge models): Air bag inflator modules may not contain diffuser holes between the ignitor and propellant chambers. Air bags would not deploy in an impact situation, which could lead to driver injury. **Corrective action:** Replace air bag inflator modules with properly machined modules. *(NHTSA Campaign No. 90V080000.)*

1989-90: (625,000 cars; includes several Plymouth, Dodge, and Chrysler vehicles): Engine valve cover gasket may dislocate and allow an engine oil leak at the gasket. Leakage of oil in the engine compartment could cause a fire. **Corrective action:**

Replace gasket cover with revised cover, and RTV sealant will be applied in place of a gasket. *(NHTSA Campaign No. 89V237000.)*

1987: (4,400 vehicles): Driver's floormat mispositioned such as to interfere with accelerator pedal. Floormat may restrict return of accelerator pedal to the idle position. **Corrective action:** Floormat will be replaced with a redesigned mat to eliminate the interference. *(NHTSA Campaign No. 87V107000.)*

1987: (580,000 vehicles equipped with 2.2L turbocharged engine; includes models made before 1987; includes Chrysler, Dodge, and Plymouth models): Fuel leakage may occur in low ambient temperature operation at connections of an engine compartment fuel supply hose to the pressure regulator and to the fuel rail. In the presence of an ignition source, fuel leakage could result in a fire. **Corrective action:** Relocate pressure regulator; replace fuel supply with formed hose with revised routing configuration to ensure sealing integrity. *(NHTSA Campaign No. 88V105000.)*

REPAIR MANUALS

971 ● Chilton's Chrysler Front Wheel Drive 1981-1988
Chilton Co.
Chilton Way
Radnor, PA 19089   Ph:(215)964-4000

Published 1988. **Price:** $15.95.

972 ● Chilton's Guide to Chassis Electronics and Power Accessories, 1988-1991 Ford/Chrysler/Jeep/Eagle
Chilton Co.
Chilton Way
Radnor, PA 19089   Ph:(215)964-4000

Published March 1991. **Price:** $19.95.

973 ● Haynes Chrysler Mid-Size Cars Owners Workshop Manual, 1982-1989
Haynes Publications, Inc.
861 Lawrence Dr.
Newbury Park, CA 91320   Ph:(818)889-5400

Published 1987. **Editor(s):** J.H.Haynes. **Price:** $15.95.

974 ● Motor Auto Repair 1983-1989 Chrysler
Hearst Bks.
105 Madison Ave.
New York, NY 10016   Ph:(212)889-3050

Published 1989. **Price:** $13.95.

OTHER INFORMATION SOURCES

975 ● Chrysler Performance Parts Association Newsletter
Chrysler Performance Parts Association (CPPA)
Box 1210
Azusa, CA 91702   Ph:(818)303-6220

Bimonthly. **Price:** Included in membership dues.

976 ● Chrysler Power Magazine
Chrysler Performance Parts Association (CPPA)
P.O. Box 1210
Azusa, CA 91702   Ph:(818)303-6220

Bimonthly. **Price:** Included in membership dues.

977 ● High Performance Mopar
CSK Publishing Co., Inc.
299 Market St.   Ph:(201)712-9300
Saddle Brook, NJ 07662   Fax:(201)712-9899

Magazine on old and new Chrysler performance cars featuring road tests on both old and new cars. Bimonthly. **Editor(s):** Steve Collison. **Price:** $15.00/year; $3.25 per single issue.

978 ● How to Build Chrysler, Dodge, Plymouth
Motorbooks International, Pubs. & Wholesalers, Inc.
729 Prospect Ave.
Osceola, WI 54020   Ph:(715)294-3345

Published 1990. **Editor(s):** Geoff Carter. **Price:** $17.95.

979 ● Mighty Mopars
MOPAR Scat Pack Club
PO Box 2303
Dearborn, MI 48123   Ph:(313)563-5974

Collects and publishes information for individuals dedicated to the preservation and restoration of Chrysler high-performance cars. Deals with technical matters, parts, and car history. Recurring features include restoration tips, news of members, and announcements of shows, swap meets, and races sponsored by the Club. Bimonthly. **Price:** Available to members only; $12.00/year or $2.00 per issue for nonmembers.

980 ● MOPAR
JHS Publishers, Inc.
175 Hudson St.
Hackensack, NJ 07601-6826   Ph:(201)488-7171

Annual. **Editor(s):** Cliff Gromer. **Price:** $2.95.

981 ● Mopar Muscle
Dobbs Publications
3816 Industry Blvd.   Ph:(813)646-5743
Lakeland, FL 33811   Fax:(813)644-8373

Automotive magazine. Bimonthly. **Price:** $3.50 per single issue.

982 ● MoPerformance
MoPerformance
1580 Hampton Rd.
Bensalem, PA 19020   Ph:(215)639-4456

Features articles of interest to owners and enthusiasts of Chrysler performance cars. Bimonthly. **Editor(s):** Robert Oskiera, Editor and Publisher. **Price:** $15.00/yr.; $3.00/issue.

983 ● Slant 6 News
Slant 6 Club of America
PO Box 4414
Salem, OR 97302   Ph:(503)581-2230

Club magazine containing technical articles and advisory information on maintenance and restoration of Chrysler Corp. vehicles powered by slant 6 engines. Quarterly. **Editor(s):** Jack Poehler, Editor/Advertising Mgr. **Price:** $18.00.

984 ● Standard Catalog of Chrysler 1924-1990
Krause Pubns., Inc.
700 E. State St.
Iola, WI 54990   Ph:(715)445-2214

Published 1990. **Price:** $19.95.

985 ● Torsion Bar
Chrysler Product Owners Club
806 Winhall Way
Silver Spring, MD 20904

Promotes the collection, preservation, restoration, maintenance, exhibition, and enjoyment of Chrysler product cars, trucks, and other vehicles. Includes technical advice on the restoration of Chalmers, Chrysler, DeSoto, Dodge, Imperial, Maxwell, and Plymouth vehicles. Monthly. **Price:** Available to members only.

ASSOCIATIONS

986 ● Chrysler Performance Parts Association
Box 1210
Azusa, CA 91702   Ph:(818)303-6220
Roland Osborne, Chm.   Fax:(818)303-2481

Founded: 1976. **Membership:** 5,000. Clearinghouse for information on from whom, where, and how to obtain vintage, muscle, and high-tech Chrysler performance parts. **Former Name(s):** (1979) National HEMI Owners; (1980) MOPAR Muscle Club. **Convention/Meeting:** Annual national meet.

987 ● Chrysler Product Owners Club
5203 Edmondson Ave.
Baltimore, MD 21229
Brian K. Scott, Exec. Officer

Founded: 1978. **Membership:** 210. Collectors and restorers of Chrysler-product automobiles. Promotes the collection, preservation, restoration, maintenance, exhibition, and enjoyment of all Chrysler product cars, trucks, and other vehicles, including Chrysler, DeSoto, Dodge, Imperial, and Plymouth. Offers technical advice; provides list of cars, parts, and services. Maintains library of service and parts manuals from the 1930s to 1989. **Convention/Meeting:** Annual.

988 ● Slant 6 Club of America
PO Box 4414
Salem, OR 97302   Ph:(503)581-2230

Founded: 1980. Owners and enthusiasts of Chrysler automobiles with V-6 engines.

989 ● Special Interest Auto Club
P.O. Box 681
Centreville, VA 22020
Stephen L. DiGiulian, Pres.   Ph:(703)631-0018

Founded: 1978. **Membership:** 2,000. Owners and enthusiasts of Chrysler high-performance automobiles manufactured from 1964 to the present including Dodge Challengers and Plymouth Barracudas. Purpose is to help restore and preserve Chrysler high-performance cars. Maintains merchandise department and parts program listing cars and parts wanted and for sale. Sponsors national and regional shows and meets; compiles statistics; maintains biographical archives and speakers' bureau. **Former Name(s):** (1981) T/A-AAR Special Interest Auto Club. **Convention/Meeting:** Annual (with exhibits) - always July, midwestern U.S.

990 ● WPC Club
P.O. Box 3504
Kalamazoo, MI 49003-3504
Ralph Kendall, Pres.   Ph:(616)372-1067

Founded: 1969. **Membership:** 4,850. Individuals dedicated to the preservation, restoration, and enjoyment of Chrysler product cars. Conducts social activities; houses library. Awards annual trophies at national meets. **Convention/Meeting:** Annual; also sponsors International Winter Photo Meet.

CHRYSLER NEW YORKER (1987-92)

A full-size four-door sedan derived from the K-car platform. The base model Chrysler New Yorker was produced until 1990. The 3.0 liter, V-6 engine was a collaboration between Chrysler and Mitsubishi Motors. Through 1990, it was also offered in the New Yorker Landau version. Currently, it is continued in the New Yorker Fifth Avenue and the New Yorker Salon trim. The New Yorker was produced at the Chrysler Motors plant in Detroit, Michigan, and Belvidere, Illinois; the New Yorker Landau was made in Belvidere, Illinois; and the New Yorker Salon and the New Yorker Fifth Avenue are produced in Belvidere, Illinois. Listed in *The Complete Car Cost Guide* in 1990 as having the lowest maintenance cost among midsize vehicles.

1992 Chrysler New Yorker Salon

MAJOR FEATURES

● New Yorker Fifth Avenue, similar to the longer Chrysler Imperial, has as 1992 standard equipment: 3.3 liter, V-6, multi-port injection engine, front-drive, 4-speed automatic electronic transmission, Iso-strut suspension, power rack-and-pinion steering, front power disc brakes, power rear drum brakes, air conditioning, electric rear window defroster, message center, security features, electronic speed control, driver's side air bag, and an assortment of interior styling features.

● New Yorker Salon adds as 1992 standard equipment: smaller body dimensions/capacities, four-speed automatic Ultradrive transmission, and an assortment of interior styling features.

● New Yorker had as 1990 standard equipment: 3.0 liter SOHC V-6 engine, front-drive, 4-speed automatic transmission, independent front suspension, front vented disc brakes.

● New Yorker Landau added as 1990 standard equipment: Landau vinyl body color roof, air-conditioning, and additional accessories.

PRICE HISTORY

The following new car prices reflect the approximate retail cost of the base model: **1987** - $14,396; **1988** - $17,373; **1989** - $17,416; **1990** - $16,342; **1991** - $17,971; **1992** - $18,849.

DIMENSIONS

Body Style	Years Avail	Wheel Base (in)	Lgth (in)	Ht (in)	Avg Wt (lbs)	Fuel Cap (gal)	Front Hdrm (in)	Front Legrm (in)
4d sdn	87-87	103.3	187.2	53.1	2,757	14	38.7	42.2
4d sdn	88-88	103.3	187.2	53.1	2,826	14	38.7	42.2
4d sdn	88-92	109.5	198.6	55.1	3,425	16	38.4	43.0
4d sdn	89-90	104.3	193.6	54.8	3,214	16	38.3	41.9
4d sdn	91-92	104.5	193.6	53.6	3,346	16	38.3	41.9

ENGINES

Type	Displace-ment (L)	Fuel Dly	HP @rpm	Torque @rpm (ft/lbs)	MPG Cty/Hwy	Years Avail
I-4	2.5	FI	100@4800	133@2800	22/27	87-87
I-4T	2.2	FI	146@5200	170@2400	19/24	87-88
V-6	3.0	FI	141@5000	171@2800	18/26	88-89
V-6	3.3	FI	147@4800	183@3600	19/25	90-92
V-6	3.8	FI	150@4400	203@3200	17/25	91-92

KEY: I=in-line engine; V=V engine; F=flat engine; FI=fuel injection; bbl=barrel carburetor; T=turbo; D=diesel; HP=horsepower; MPG=estimated average miles per gallon.

EVALUATIONS, TESTS, AND RANKINGS

1990: "While. . .suspension system doesn't get high marks for creativity. . .it does get good marks for the way it works. . .It feels big, as in spaciousness, but it doesn't feel *big*, as in intimidatingly large." **Source:** "Chrysler New Yorker Fifth Avenue," *Motor Trend*, January 1990, pp. 40-43.

1989: "the New Yorker combines a reliable—if not racy—engine with brakes that react fast without grabbing . . . well-appointed interior . . . high-tech sedan with the big car feel of a Sixties gas guzzler." **Source:** "Yesteryear's Luxury in a Cushy New Chrysler," *Business Week*, January 9, 1989, p. 134.

1988: "instrumented testing returned only 10.91 sec between 0-60, but. . .never felt the car lacked authority in hard accel modes. . .smoothly decisive braking action. . .interior comfort is. . .comfy." **Source:** "Chrysler New Yorker: Spelling chrome with a K," *Motor Trend*, September 1988, pp. 68-70.

RECALLS

1991: (18,000 passenger cars; includes several Chrysler, Dodge, and Plymouth models): Front disc brake caliper guide pin bolts may not have been adequately torqued and could loosen. This could cause reduced braking effectiveness and could result in an accident. **Corrective action:** Properly torque front brake caliper guide pin bolts to 250 lbs. (NHTSA Campaign No. 90V162000.)

1991: (130,000 passenger vehicles; includes Chrysler Imperial, Chrysler Fifth Avenue, Chrysler Salon, Chrysler LeBaron, Dodge Dynasty, Dodge Spirit, and Plymouth Acclaim): Front outboard safety belt may become difficult to latch or unlatch due to a webbing stiffener entering the buckle housing and dislodging the buckle latch guide. Latch may open during an accident or sudden stop. **Corrective action:** Replace buckle latch engagement. (NHTSA Campaign No. 91V122000.)

1990: (257 cars with grey interior; includes Chrysler and Dodge models): Lack of diffuser holes in airbag inflator modules between igniter and propellant chambers could prevent deployment, which could lead to driver injury. **Corrective action:** Replace air bag inflator modules with properly machined modules. (NHTSA Campaign No. 90V080000.)

1987: (580,000 vehicles equipped with 2.2L turbocharged engine; includes models made before 1987; includes Chrysler, Dodge, and Plymouth models): Fuel leakage may occur in low ambient temperature operation at connections of an engine compartment fuel supply hose to the pressure regulator and to the fuel rail. In the presence of an ignition source, fuel leakage could result in a fire. **Corrective action:** Relocate pressure regulator; replace fuel supply with formed hose with revised routing configuration to ensure sealing integrity. (NHTSA Campaign No. 88V105000.)

REPAIR MANUALS

991 ● **Chilton's Guide to Chassis Electronics and Power Accessories, 1988-1991 Ford/Chrysler/Jeep/Eagle**
Chilton Co.
Chilton Way
Radnor, PA 19089   Ph:(215)964-4000

Published March 1991. **Price:** $19.95.

992 ● **Chrysler, Dodge, Plymouth: 1972-1987 Rear Wheel Drive Tune-up Maintenance**
Clymer Publications
P.O. Box 1209
Overland Park, KS 66212   Ph:(913)541-6694

Published 1987. **Price:** $14.95.

993 ● **Haynes Chrysler Mid-Size Cars Owners Workshop Manual, 1982-1989**
Haynes Publications, Inc.
861 Lawrence Dr.
Newbury Park, CA 91320   Ph:(818)889-5400

Published 1987. **Editor(s):** J.H.Haynes. **Price:** $15.95.

994 ● **Motor Auto Repair 1983-1989 Chrysler**
Hearst Bks.
105 Madison Ave.
New York, NY 10016   Ph:(212)889-3050

Published 1989. **Price:** $13.95.

OTHER INFORMATION SOURCES

995 ● **How to Build Chrysler, Dodge, Plymouth**
Motorbooks International, Pubs. & Wholesalers, Inc.
729 Prospect Ave.
Osceola, WI 54020   Ph:(715)294-3345

Published 1990. **Editor(s):** Geoff Carter. **Price:** $17.95.

996 ● **Slant 6 News**
Slant 6 Club of America
PO Box 4414
Salem, OR 97302   Ph:(503)581-2230

Club magazine containing technical articles and advisory information on maintenance and restoration of Chrysler Corp. vehicles powered by slant 6 engines. Quarterly. **Editor(s):** Jack Poehler, Editor/Advertising Mgr. **Price:** $18.00.

997 ● **Standard Catalog of Chrysler 1924-1990**
Krause Pubns., Inc.
700 E. State St.
Iola, WI 54990   Ph:(715)445-2214

Published 1990. **Price:** $19.95.

998 ● **Torsion Bar**
Chrysler Product Owners Club
806 Winhall Way
Silver Spring, MD 20904

Promotes the collection, preservation, restoration, maintenance, exhibition, and enjoyment of Chrysler product cars, trucks, and other vehicles. Includes technical advice on the restoration of Chalmers, Chrysler, DeSoto, Dodge, Imperial, Maxwell, and Plymouth vehicles. Monthly. **Price:** Available to members only.

ASSOCIATIONS

999 ● Chrysler Product Owners Club
5203 Edmondson Ave.
Baltimore, MD 21229
Brian K. Scott, Exec. Officer

Founded: 1978. **Membership:** 210. Collectors and restorers of Chrysler-product automobiles. Promotes the collection, preservation, restoration, maintenance, exhibition, and enjoyment of all Chrysler product cars, trucks, and other vehicles, including Chrysler, DeSoto, Dodge, Imperial, and Plymouth. Offers technical advice; provides list of cars, parts, and services. Maintains library of service and parts manuals from the 1930s to 1989. **Convention/Meeting:** Annual.

1000 ● Slant 6 Club of America
PO Box 4414
Salem, OR 97302   Ph:(503)581-2230

Founded: 1980. Owners and enthusiasts of Chrysler automobiles with V-6 engines.

1001 ● WPC Club
P.O. Box 3504
Kalamazoo, MI 49003-3504
Ralph Kendall, Pres.   Ph:(616)372-1067

Founded: 1969. **Membership:** 4,850. Individuals dedicated to the preservation, restoration, and enjoyment of Chrysler product cars. Conducts social activities; houses library. Awards annual trophies at national meets. **Convention/Meeting:** Annual; also sponsors International Winter Photo Meet.

CHRYSLER TC BY MASERATI (1989-91)

A two-door luxury sport convertible categorized in the subcompact vehicle class. Only about 500 vehicles equipped with the 2.2 liter turbocharged engine and five-speed manual transmission were exported to the U.S. Built at the Maserati Automobiles plant in Milan, Italy until 1991.

1991 Chrysler TC by Maserati

MAJOR FEATURES

● TC by Maserati had as 1991 standard equipment: 3.0 liter, multi-port fuel injection, V-6 engine, four-speed automatic transmission, Iso-strut front suspension, power rack-and-pinion steering, all-wheel power disc brakes with anti-lock system, cast aluminum wheels, air-conditioning, automatic speed control, Infinity II sound system, molded hardtop, leather interior, tinted glass, tilt steering wheel, and tonneau cover.

PRICE HISTORY

The following new car prices reflect the approximate retail cost of the base model: **1989** - $33,000; **1990** - $35,500; **1991** - $37,000.

DIMENSIONS

Body Style	Years Avail	Wheel Base (in)	Lgth (in)	Ht (in)	Avg Wt (lbs)	Fuel Cap (gal)	Front Hdrm (in)	Front Legrm (in)
2d conv	89-91	93.0	175.8	51.9	3,276	14.0	37.4	42.4

ENGINES

Type	Displace-ment (L)	Fuel Dly	HP @rpm	Torque @rpm (ft/lbs)	MPG Cty/Hwy	Years Avail
I-4T	2.2	FI	174@5200	200@2400	18/22	89-89
I-4T	2.2	FI	200@5500	220@3400	18/25	89-90
V-6	3.0	FI	141@5000	171@2800	18/24	90-91

KEY: I=in-line engine; V=V engine; F=flat engine; FI=fuel injection; bbl=barrel carburetor; T=turbo; D=diesel; HP=horsepower; MPG=estimated average miles per gallon.

EVALUATIONS, TESTS, AND RANKINGS

1990: "one of the brightest spots of this late-to-market convertible is the way both large and small American fit inside." **Source:** "Chrysler's TC by Maserati," *Car and Driver—Buyers Guide 1990*, 1989, pp. 140-141.

1989: "The interior of the TC is luxurious. . .premium stopping ability." **Source:** "Chrysler's TC by Maserati," *Road & Track—Buyer's Guide 1989*, 1988, p. 48.

RECALLS

None to date.

REPAIR MANUALS

1002 ● Chilton's Guide to Chassis Electronics and Power Accessories, 1988-1991 Ford/Chrysler/Jeep/Eagle
Chilton Co.
Chilton Way
Radnor, PA 19089   Ph:(215)964-4000

Published March 1991. **Price:** $19.95.

1003 ● Motor Auto Repair 1983-1989 Chrysler
Hearst Bks.
105 Madison Ave.
New York, NY 10016   Ph:(212)889-3050

Published 1989. **Price:** $13.95.

OTHER INFORMATION SOURCES

1004 ● Chrysler Performance Parts Association Newsletter
Chrysler Performance Parts Association (CPPA)
Box 1210
Azusa, CA 91702   Ph:(818)303-6220

Bimonthly. **Price:** Included in membership dues.

1005 ● Chrysler Power Magazine
Chrysler Performance Parts Association (CPPA)
P.O. Box 1210
Azusa, CA 91702   Ph:(818)303-6220

Bimonthly. **Price:** Included in membership dues.

1006 ● High Performance Mopar
CSK Publishing Co., Inc.
299 Market St.
Saddle Brook, NJ 07662

Ph:(201)712-9300
Fax:(201)712-9899

Magazine on old and new Chrysler performance cars featuring road tests on both old and new cars. Bimonthly. **Editor(s):** Steve Collison. **Price:** $15.00/year; $3.25 per single issue.

1007 ● Mighty Mopars
MOPAR Scat Pack Club
PO Box 2303
Dearborn, MI 48123

Ph:(313)563-5974

Collects and publishes information for individuals dedicated to the preservation and restoration of Chrysler high-performance cars. Deals with technical matters, parts, and car history. Recurring features include restoration tips, news of members, and announcements of shows, swap meets, and races sponsored by the Club. Bimonthly. **Price:** Available to members only; $12.00/year or $2.00 per issue for nonmembers.

1008 ● MOPAR
JHS Publishers, Inc.
175 Hudson St.
Hackensack, NJ 07601-6826

Ph:(201)488-7171

Annual. **Editor(s):** Cliff Gromer. **Price:** $2.95.

1009 ● Mopar Muscle
Dobbs Publications
3816 Industry Blvd.
Lakeland, FL 33811

Ph:(813)646-5743
Fax:(813)644-8373

Automotive magazine. Bimonthly. **Price:** $3.50 per single issue.

1010 ● MoPerformance
MoPerformance
1580 Hampton Rd.
Bensalem, PA 19020

Ph:(215)639-4456

Features articles of interest to owners and enthusiasts of Chrysler performance cars. Bimonthly. **Editor(s):** Robert Oskiera, Editor and Publisher. **Price:** $15.00/yr.; $3.00/issue.

1011 ● Slant 6 News
Slant 6 Club of America
PO Box 4414
Salem, OR 97302

Ph:(503)581-2230

Club magazine containing technical articles and advisory information on maintenance and restoration of Chrysler Corp. vehicles powered by slant 6 engines. Quarterly. **Editor(s):** Jack Poehler, Editor/Advertising Mgr. **Price:** $18.00.

1012 ● Standard Catalog of Chrysler 1924-1990
Krause Pubns., Inc.
700 E. State St.
Iola, WI 54990

Ph:(715)445-2214

Published 1990. **Price:** $19.95.

1013 ● Torsion Bar
Chrysler Product Owners Club
806 Winhall Way
Silver Spring, MD 20904

Promotes the collection, preservation, restoration, maintenance, exhibition, and enjoyment of Chrysler product cars, trucks, and other vehicles. Includes technical advice on the restoration of Chalmers, Chrysler, DeSoto, Dodge, Imperial, Maxwell, and Plymouth vehicles. Monthly. **Price:** Available to members only.

ASSOCIATIONS

1014 ● Chrysler Performance Parts Association
Box 1210
Azusa, CA 91702
Roland Osborne, Chm.

Ph:(818)303-6220
Fax:(818)303-2481

Founded: 1976. **Membership:** 5,000. Clearinghouse for information on from whom, where, and how to obtain vintage, muscle, and high-tech Chrysler performance parts. **Former Name(s):** (1979) National HEMI Owners; (1980) MOPAR Muscle Club. **Convention/Meeting:** Annual national meet.

1015 ● Chrysler Product Owners Club
5203 Edmondson Ave.
Baltimore, MD 21229
Brian K. Scott, Exec. Officer

Founded: 1978. **Membership:** 210. Collectors and restorers of Chrysler-product automobiles. Promotes the collection, preservation, restoration, maintenance, exhibition, and enjoyment of all Chrysler product cars, trucks, and other vehicles, including Chrysler, DeSoto, Dodge, Imperial, and Plymouth. Offers technical advice; provides list of cars, parts, and services. Maintains library of service and parts manuals from the 1930s to 1989. **Convention/Meeting:** Annual.

1016 ● Slant 6 Club of America
PO Box 4414
Salem, OR 97302

Ph:(503)581-2230

Founded: 1980. Owners and enthusiasts of Chrysler automobiles with V-6 engines.

1017 ● Special Interest Auto Club
P.O. Box 681
Centreville, VA 22020
Stephen L. DiGiulian, Pres.

Ph:(703)631-0018

Founded: 1978. **Membership:** 2,000. Owners and enthusiasts of Chrysler high-performance automobiles manufactured from 1964 to the present including Dodge Challengers and Plymouth Barracudas. Purpose is to help restore and preserve Chrysler high-performance cars. Maintains merchandise department and parts program listing cars and parts wanted and for sale. Sponsors national and regional shows and meets; compiles statistics; maintains biographical archives and speakers' bureau. **Former Name(s):** (1981) T/A-AAR Special Interest Auto Club. **Convention/Meeting:** Annual (with exhibits) - always July, midwestern U.S.

1018 ● WPC Club
P.O. Box 3504
Kalamazoo, MI 49003-3504
Ralph Kendall, Pres.

Ph:(616)372-1067

Founded: 1969. **Membership:** 4,850. Individuals dedicated to the preservation, restoration, and enjoyment of Chrysler product cars. Conducts social activities; houses library. Awards annual trophies at national meets. **Convention/Meeting:** Annual; also sponsors International Winter Photo Meet.

CHRYSLER TOWN & COUNTRY (1990-92)

Introduced in 1990 as the upscale version of the Dodge Caravan and Plymouth Voyager. Targeted toward mature buyers and buyers with families who seek larger, more comfortable, well-equipped vehicles as an alternative sedan and station wagon. This seven-passenger mini-wagon is categorized in the special purpose vehicle class. Graded as one of the best in a crash test performance among minivans by The

Car Book in 1992. Produced at the Chrysler Motors plant in St. Louis, Missouri.

1992 Chrysler Town & Country

MAJOR FEATURES

● Town & Country has as 1992 standard equipment: 4-speed automatic, front-wheel drive, electronic transmission, Iso-strut front suspension, power rack-and-pinion steering, four-wheel anti-lock brakes, air-conditioning, rear window defroster, tinted glass, luggage rack, electronic speed control, tilt steering column, and numerous storage compartments.

PRICE HISTORY

The following new car prices reflect the approximate retail cost of the base model: **1990** - $23,500; **1991** - $23,956; **1992** - $24,621.

DIMENSIONS

Body Style	Years Avail	Wheel Base (in)	Lgth (in)	Ht (in)	Avg Wt (lbs)	Fuel Cap (gal)	Front Hdrm (in)	Front Legrm (in)
4d mvan	90-91	119.3	192.4	66.4	3,817	20.0	37.3	38.2
4d mvan	92-92	119.3	192.8	68.8	na	20.0	na	na

ENGINES

Type	Displace-ment (L)	Fuel Dly	HP @rpm	Torque @rpm (ft/lbs)	MPG Cty/Hwy	Years Avail
V-6	3.3	FI	150@4800	185@3600	17/23	90-92

KEY: I=in-line engine; V=V engine; F=flat engine; FI=fuel injection; bbl=barrel carburetor; T=turbo; D=diesel; HP=horsepower; MPG=estimated average miles per gallon.

EVALUATIONS, TESTS, AND RANKINGS

1991: "softened grille design, smaller headlights, and more glass all around. . .new instrument panel and an overall design." **Source:** "A New Look (Sort of) for Chrysler's Van," *New York Times*, November 18, 1990.

1991: "sleeker, rounder, more aerodynamic. . .marked improvement in steering feel and response, cornering and ride. . .an especially nice engine." **Source:** "1991 Chrysler Minivans: Good things get better," *Road & Track*, November 1990, 154-155.

1991: "the interior . . . has a solid upscale environment, made with durable materials . . . handling . . . is predictable and responsive . . . steering is positive and accurate but—although power assisted—may feel heavy." **Source:** "Town & Country changes subtle, worthwhile," *Flint Journal*, April 24, 1991, pp. D1-D2.

1990: "great outward visibility, easy entry and exit and lots of space to transport people and things . . . smooth and easy

boulevard ride." **Source:** "Motor Trend's 1990 Guide to Chrysler Town & Country," *Motor Trend*, January 1990, pp. 54-57.

1990: "approached most highway bumps with a harshness . . . it excels with steering that is predictable and tracks straight . . . ease of parking, entry and egress, and loading and unloading are part of the basic architecture of the Chrysler minivan." **Source:** "The Wedge vs. The Box," *Popular Science*, August 1990, pp. 76-79, 81.

RECALLS

1990: (640,000 passenger vans; includes the Chrysler Town & Country, Dodge Caravan, and Plymouth Voyager): Inboard front seatbelt assembly straps can suffer fatigue failure of the strap near its anchor position resulting in increased likelihood of injury to seat occupant. **Corrective action:** Replace fatigued straps or retrofit straps with a reinforcement plate and removal of an anti-rotation tab to prevent fatigue failure. (*NHTSA Campaign No. 91V053000.*)

REPAIR MANUALS

1019 ● **Chilton's Guide to Chassis Electronics and Power Accessories, 1988-1991 Ford/Chrysler/Jeep/Eagle**
Chilton Co.
Chilton Way
Radnor, PA 19089   Ph:(215)964-4000

Published March 1991. **Price:** $19.95.

OTHER INFORMATION SOURCES

1020 ● **How to Build Chrysler, Dodge, Plymouth**
Motorbooks International, Pubs. & Wholesalers, Inc.
729 Prospect Ave.
Osceola, WI 54020   Ph:(715)294-3345

Published 1990. **Editor(s):** Geoff Carter. **Price:** $17.95.

1021 ● **Slant 6 News**
Slant 6 Club of America
PO Box 4414
Salem, OR 97302   Ph:(503)581-2230

Club magazine containing technical articles and advisory information on maintenance and restoration of Chrysler Corp. vehicles powered by slant 6 engines. Quarterly. **Editor(s):** Jack Poehler, Editor/Advertising Mgr. **Price:** $18.00.

1022 ● **Standard Catalog of Chrysler 1924-1990**
Krause Pubns., Inc.
700 E. State St.
Iola, WI 54990   Ph:(715)445-2214

Published 1990. **Price:** $19.95.

1023 ● **Torsion Bar**
Chrysler Product Owners Club
806 Winhall Way
Silver Spring, MD 20904

Promotes the collection, preservation, restoration, maintenance, exhibition, and enjoyment of Chrysler product cars, trucks, and other vehicles. Includes technical advice on the restoration of Chalmers, Chrysler, DeSoto, Dodge, Imperial, Maxwell, and Plymouth vehicles. Monthly. **Price:** Available to members only.

ASSOCIATIONS

1024 ● Chrysler Product Owners Club
5203 Edmondson Ave.
Baltimore, MD 21229
Brian K. Scott, Exec. Officer

Founded: 1978. **Membership:** 210. Collectors and restorers of Chrysler-product automobiles. Promotes the collection, preservation, restoration, maintenance, exhibition, and enjoyment of all Chrysler product cars, trucks, and other vehicles, including Chrysler, DeSoto, Dodge, Imperial, and Plymouth. Offers technical advice; provides list of cars, parts, and services. Maintains library of service and parts manuals from the 1930s to 1989. **Convention/Meeting:** Annual.

1025 ● Slant 6 Club of America
PO Box 4414
Salem, OR 97302   Ph:(503)581-2230

Founded: 1980. Owners and enthusiasts of Chrysler automobiles with V-6 engines.

1026 ● WPC Club
P.O. Box 3504
Kalamazoo, MI 49003-3504
Ralph Kendall, Pres.   Ph:(616)372-1067

Founded: 1969. **Membership:** 4,850. Individuals dedicated to the preservation, restoration, and enjoyment of Chrysler product cars. Conducts social activities; houses library. Awards annual trophies at national meets. **Convention/Meeting:** Annual; also sponsors International Winter Photo Meet.

DAIHATSU CHARADE (1988-1992)

Ranked top of its class in crashworthiness by the National Highway Traffic Safety Administration in past years. Ranked top of its class for new-car owner satisfaction in 1989, second only to the Porsche, according to J.D. Power and Associates' Initial Quality Survey. Won the Group A Class 1 and Class 3 championships of the Kenya Safari Rally, a six-day, 2,606 mile endurance race. Listed as one of the Best Bets of 1992, and ranked among the best subcompact cars in crash test performance by *The Car Book*. Currently produced in Osaka, Japan.

1990 Daihatsu Charade Sedan

MAJOR FEATURES

● Charade hatchback with base SE trim level has as 1992 standard equipment: 5-speed manual or 3-speed automatic transmission, multi-port electronic fuel injection system, 4-wheel independent suspension, front-wheel drive, rack-and-pinion steering, power assisted front disc/rear drum brakes, reclining front bucket seats, and electric rear window defogger.

● Charade sedan SE has as 1992 standard equipment: same equipment as the hatchback as well as upgraded passenger restraint system, remote trunk release, remote fuel filler door release, and other interior acessories.

● Charade sedan SX adds as 1992 standard features: power steering, radial tires, premium wheel covers, other exterior body stylings, and an upgraded interior.

● Charade CLX added as 1989 standard features: air conditioning, 4-speaker stereo system, and 70-series tires on alloy wheels.

● Charade CES added as 1989 standard features: full instrumentation, remote control mirrors, and fold-down arm seats.

● Charade CLS added as 1989 standard features: same as the Charade CES and included a rear window wiper-washer and larger wheels and tires.

PRICE HISTORY

The following new car prices reflect the approximate retail cost of the base model: **1988** - $6,397; **1989** - $6,197; **1990** - $6,597; **1991** - $6,397; **1992** - $6,797.

DIMENSIONS

Body Style	Years Avail	Wheel Base (in)	Lgth (in)	Ht (in)	Avg Wt (lbs)	Fuel Cap (gal)	Front Hdrm (in)	Front Legrm (in)
3d lbk	88-92	92.1	144.9	54.5	1,820	10.6	37.5	41.1
sdn	90-92	92.1	159.6	54.5	2,050	10.6	38.6	37.7

ENGINES

Type	Displace-ment (L)	Fuel Dly	HP @rpm	Torque @rpm (ft/lbs)	MPG Cty/Hwy	Years Avail
I-3	1.0	FI	53@5200	58@3600	38/42	88-92
I-4	1.3	FI	80@6000	74@4400	35/38	90-92

KEY: I=in-line engine; V=V engine; F=flat engine; FI=fuel injection; bbl=barrel carburetor; T=turbo; D=diesel; HP=horsepower; MPG=estimated average miles per gallon.

EVALUATIONS, TESTS, AND RANKINGS

1990: ``fresh good looks, excellent controls, and a very sporty feel. . .As expected, its steep-grade performance [was also weak].'' **Source:** ``3x3,'' *Road & Track*, July 1988, pp. 66-70, 74.

1990: ``thrifty and as game as ever.'' **Source:** ``Daihatsu Charade,'' *Road & Track*, October 1990, p. 64.

1989: ``the new four pours out its power in a much more refined manner . . . The bad news is that Daihatsu has reduced the size of the Charade's tires . . . has softened the suspension a bit for 1989—dramatically improving ride quality.'' **Source:** ``Daihatsu Charade CLS,'' *Car and Driver*, September 1989, pp. 127-129.

RECALLS

1990: (33 vehicles): Primary side brake cup within the master cylinder may fail causing loss of brake fluid line pressure in one-half of the dual braking system. This would cause reduced braking effectiveness and increased stopping distances that result in an accident. **Corrective action:** Replace master cylinder. *(NHTSA Campaign No. 89V213000.)*

DAIHATSU ROCKY (1990-92)

Medium-sized rough terrain vehicle. Competes against the Chevrolet Suburban, Dodge Ramcharger, Ford Bronco, and Ford Bronco II. Currently produced in Osaka, Japan.

1990 Daihatsu Rocky

MAJOR FEATURES

● Rocky SE has as 1992 standard equipment: five-speed manual transmission, independent front double wishbone suspension, four-wheel drive, power-assisted front disc brakes, sunroof, detachable hard top or retractable soft top, and reclining front bucket seats.

● Rocky SX adds as 1992 standard features: automatic locking hubs, rear window defogger, rear window wiper/washer, remote back door release, and tilt steering wheel.

● Daihatsu Rocky is also available in several equipment packages: SE Off-Road Package, SE/SX Preferred Package, SX Convenience Package, and the SX Plus Package.

PRICE HISTORY

The following new car prices reflect the approximate retail cost of the base model: **1990** - $10,897; **1991** - $11,297.

DIMENSIONS

Body Style	Years Avail	Wheel Base (in)	Lgth (in)	Ht (in)	Avg Wt (lbs)	Fuel Cap (gal)	Front Hdrm (in)	Front Legrm (in)
utl wgn	90-92	85.6	148.2	67.7	2,778	15.9	na	na

ENGINES

Type	Displace-ment (L)	Fuel Dly	HP @rpm	Torque @rpm (ft/lbs)	MPG Cty/Hwy	Years Avail
I-4	1.6	FI	94@5700	94@3200	23/23	90-92

KEY: I=in-line engine; V=V engine; F=flat engine; FI=fuel injection; bbl=barrel carburetor; T=turbo; D=diesel; HP=horsepower; MPG=estimated average miles per gallon.

EVALUATIONS, TESTS, AND RANKINGS

1991: "[the engine] doesn't turn out to be much. . .rides comfortably." **Source:** "Dirty Little Devils," *Automobile Magazine*, February 1991, pp. 81-82, 85.

1991: "does boast a wide track . . . providing a better ride and less danger of rollover . . . added stability both on and off road . . . 94 hp and 94 foot-pounds of torque—not exceptional, but enough to handle the vehicle's 3600 pounds." **Source:** "Testing the new mini 4x4s," *Sports Afield*, October 1990, pp. 110-112, 114-116.

1991: "Off-the-line acceleration and passing quickness are average, but the engine strains climbing hills . . . ride is still choppy, and there's too much sway in stiff crosswinds . . . sturdy enough to withstand a pounding over bumpy roads." **Source:** "Your Car: Roadwork with the Rocky," *Changing Times*, October 1990, pp. 99-100.

1991: "most memorable characteristics are its versatility and wide, 57.9-inch track . . . One thing you don't get with the Rocky is a tight turning radius . . . wasn't a barn-burner and worked diligently to get up to speed quickly in two-wheel drive." **Source:** "Rocky cuts wide swath in off-road market," *The Detroit News*, May 29, 1991, pp. 1D-2D.

1990: "better in many categories than the Sidekick. . .a bit more stable-feeling." **Source:** "Invasion of the Space Cadets," *Motor Trend*, April 1990, pp. 115-124, 118, 123-4.

RECALLS

None to date.

DODGE 600 (1987-88)

Corporate twin of the Chrysler New Yorker and Plymouth Caravelle, the Dodge 600 was produced until 1988 at, among other sites, the Chrysler Motors plants in Detroit, Michigan, and St. Louis, Missouri. It was considered a stretched version of the K-car.

MAJOR FEATURES

● Dodge 600 version had as 1988 standard equipment: independent suspension, vented front disc brakes, rear drum brakes, and rack & pinion steering.

● Dodge 600 SE had as 1988 standard equipment: independent suspension, vented front disc brakes, rear drum brakes, and rack & pinion steering.

PRICE HISTORY

The following new car prices reflect the approximate retail cost of the base model: **1987** - $10,010; **1988** - $10,659.

DIMENSIONS

Body Style	Years Avail	Wheel Base (in)	Lgth (in)	Ht (in)	Avg Wt (lbs)	Fuel Cap (gal)	Front Hdrm (in)	Front Legrm (in)
4d sdn	87-87	103.3	179.2	53.1	2,594	14.0	38.7	42.2
4d sdn	88-88	103.3	185.1	50.8	2,604	14.0	38.6	42.2

ENGINES

Type	Displace-ment (L)	Fuel Dly	HP @rpm	Torque @rpm (ft/lbs)	MPG Cty/Hwy	Years Avail
I-4	2.2	FI	97@5200	122@3200	23/26	87-87
I-4	2.5	FI	100@4800	133@2800	23/28	87-88
I-4	2.2	FI	93@4800	165@3200	23/28	88-88
I-4T	2.2	FI	146@5200	170@3600	20/25	87-88

KEY: I=in-line engine; V=V engine; F=flat engine; FI=fuel injection; bbl=barrel carburetor; T=turbo; D=diesel; HP=horsepower; MPG=estimated average miles per gallon.

EVALUATIONS, TESTS, AND RANKINGS

1988: "sensible, commodious, down-to-earth." **Source:**

"Dodge 600," *Car and Driver—Buyers Guide 1988*, 1988, p. 74.

RECALLS

1987: (580,000 vehicles equipped with 2.2L turbocharged engine; includes models made before 1987; includes Chrysler, Dodge, and Plymouth models): Fuel leakage may occur in low ambient temperature operation at connections of an engine compartment fuel supply hose to the pressure regulator and to the fuel rail. In the presence of an ignition source, fuel leakage could result in a fire. **Corrective action:** Relocate pressure regulator; replace fuel supply with formed hose with revised routing configuration to ensure sealing integrity. *(NHTSA Campaign No. 88V105000.)*

SAFETY AND REPAIRS

1987: "Pure Logic," *Popular Mechanics*, June 1988, pp. 40-41. **Note:** rough idle when in neutral with air conditioning on.

OTHER INFORMATION SOURCES

1027 ● **How to Build Chrysler, Dodge, Plymouth**
Motorbooks International, Pubs. & Wholesalers, Inc.
729 Prospect Ave.
Osceola, WI 54020   Ph:(715)294-3345

Published 1990. **Editor(s):** Geoff Carter. **Price:** $17.95.

1028 ● **Torsion Bar**
Chrysler Product Owners Club
806 Winhall Way
Silver Spring, MD 20904

Promotes the collection, preservation, restoration, maintenance, exhibition, and enjoyment of Chrysler product cars, trucks, and other vehicles. Includes technical advice on the restoration of Chalmers, Chrysler, DeSoto, Dodge, Imperial, Maxwell, and Plymouth vehicles. Monthly. **Price:** Available to members only.

ASSOCIATIONS

1029 ● **Chrysler Product Owners Club**
5203 Edmondson Ave.
Baltimore, MD 21229
Brian K. Scott, Exec. Officer

Founded: 1978. **Membership:** 210. Collectors and restorers of Chrysler-product automobiles. Promotes the collection, preservation, restoration, maintenance, exhibition, and enjoyment of all Chrysler product cars, trucks, and other vehicles, including Chrysler, DeSoto, Dodge, Imperial, and Plymouth. Offers technical advice; provides list of cars, parts, and services. Maintains library of service and parts manuals from the 1930s to 1989. **Convention/Meeting:** Annual.

1030 ● **WPC Club**
P.O. Box 3504
Kalamazoo, MI 49003-3504
Ralph Kendall, Pres.   Ph:(616)372-1067

Founded: 1969. **Membership:** 4,850. Individuals dedicated to the preservation, restoration, and enjoyment of Chrysler product cars. Conducts social activities; houses library. Awards annual trophies at national meets. **Convention/Meeting:** Annual; also sponsors International Winter Photo Meet.

DODGE ARIES (1987-89)

Introduced as part of the K-car model line, along with its corporate twin the Plymouth Reliant. Produced until 1989 at, among other locations, the Chrysler Motors plants in Detroit, Michigan (Jefferson plant), St. Louis, Missouri, Newark, Delaware, and Toluca, Mexico.

MAJOR FEATURES

● Dodge Aries had as 1989 standard equipment: 5-speed manual transmission, power brakes, reclining front bucket seats and upgraded interior, intermittent wipers, and 185/70R13 SBR tires.

● Aries America was offered through 1989 as part of a cost-cutting program to reduce manufacturing and retail costs by offering a single trim level with most options grouped into packages.

● Dodge Aries LE added as 1989 standard equipment: 3-speed automatic transmission, tinted glass, dual remote side view mirrors, power steering, AM/FM stereo radio, other exterior body stylings, special sound insulation, extra trim for the trunk, 14-inch wheels and tires, and wheel covers.

● Dodge Aries LE wagon added as 1989 standard equipment: a special tonneau cover.

PRICE HISTORY

The following new car prices reflect the approximate retail cost of the base model: **1987** - $7,879; **1988** - $6,995; **1989** - $7,595.

DIMENSIONS

Body Style	Years Avail	Wheel Base (in)	Lgth (in)	Ht (in)	Avg Wt (lbs)	Fuel Cap (gal)	Front Hdrm (in)	Front Legrm (in)
2d sdn	87-89	100.3	178.6	52.5	2,424	14.0	38.2	42.2
4d sdn	87-89	100.3	178.6	52.9	2,450	14.0	38.2	42.2
5d wgn	87-89	100.4	178.5	53.2	2,500	14.0	38.2	42.2

ENGINES

Type	Displacement (L)	Fuel Dly	HP @rpm	Torque @rpm (ft/lbs)	MPG Cty/Hwy	Years Avail
I-4	2.2	FI	97@5200	122@3200	na	87-87
I-4	2.5	FI	100@4800	133@2800	23/28	87-89
I-4	2.2	FI	93@4800	122@3200	25/34	87-89

KEY: I=in-line engine; V=V engine; F=flat engine; FI=fuel injection; bbl=barrel carburetor; T=turbo; D=diesel; HP=horsepower; MPG=estimated average miles per gallon.

EVALUATIONS, TESTS, AND RANKINGS

1989: "Plain, simple, and affordable transportation." **Source:** "Dodge Aries, Plymouth Reliant," *Road & Track—Buyer's Guide 1989*, 1988, p. 52.

RECALLS

1989-89: (625,000 cars; includes several Plymouth, Dodge and Chrysler vehicles): Engine valve cover gasket may dislocate and allow an engine oil leak at the gasket. Leakage of oil in the engine compartment could cause a fire. **Corrective action:** Replace gasket cover with revised cover, and RTV sealant will be applied in place of a gasket. *(NHTSA Campaign No. 89V237000.)*

REPAIR MANUALS

**1031 ● Haynes Dodge Aries and Plymouth Reliant Owners
Workshop Manual, 1981-1988**
Haynes Publications, Inc.
861 Lawrence Dr.
Newbury Park, CA 91320   Ph:(818)889-5400

Editor(s): J. H. Haynes and Larry Warren. **Price:** $15.95.

OTHER INFORMATION SOURCES

1032 ● How to Build Chrysler, Dodge, Plymouth
Motorbooks International, Pubs. & Wholesalers, Inc.
729 Prospect Ave.
Osceola, WI 54020   Ph:(715)294-3345

Published 1990. **Editor(s):** Geoff Carter. **Price:** $17.95.

1033 ● Torsion Bar
Chrysler Product Owners Club
806 Winhall Way
Silver Spring, MD 20904

Promotes the collection, preservation, restoration, maintenance, exhibition, and enjoyment of Chrysler product cars, trucks, and other vehicles. Includes technical advice on the restoration of Chalmers, Chrysler, DeSoto, Dodge, Imperial, Maxwell, and Plymouth vehicles. Monthly. **Price:** Available to members only.

ASSOCIATIONS

1034 ● Chrysler Product Owners Club
5203 Edmondson Ave.
Baltimore, MD 21229
Brian K. Scott, Exec. Officer

Founded: 1978. **Membership:** 210. Collectors and restorers of Chrysler-product automobiles. Promotes the collection, preservation, restoration, maintenance, exhibition, and enjoyment of all Chrysler product cars, trucks, and other vehicles, including Chrysler, DeSoto, Dodge, Imperial, and Plymouth. Offers technical advice; provides list of cars, parts, and services. Maintains library of service and parts manuals from the 1930s to 1989. **Convention/Meeting:** Annual.

1035 ● WPC Club
P.O. Box 3504
Kalamazoo, MI 49003-3504
Ralph Kendall, Pres.   Ph:(616)372-1067

Founded: 1969. **Membership:** 4,850. Individuals dedicated to the preservation, restoration, and enjoyment of Chrysler product cars. Conducts social activities; houses library. Awards annual trophies at national meets. **Convention/Meeting:** Annual; also sponsors International Winter Photo Meet.

DODGE CARAVAN (1987-92)

Along with its corporate twins, the Plymouth Voyager and Chrysler Town & Country, the Caravan was the first compact van made by an American auto manufacturer. Multi-award winning vehicle, including *Motor Trend's* Top Ten Domestic New Car Buys in 1989 and 1991, was selected an "All-Star" in 1991 by *Automobile* magazine, and was called "Most Versatile Vehicle of the Year" by *Home Mechanix* in 1991. Nominated as one of *Car and Driver's* Ten Best Cars in 1990. Built at the Chrysler Motors plants in St. Louis, Missouri (No. 2), and Windsor, Ontario, Canada. The front-wheel drive Caravan is offered in 1992 with a 2.5 liter 4-cylinder engine with 5-speed

manual transmission; the Caravan SE adds a 3-speed automatic transmission as a standard feature. Caravan LE and Grand Caravan have a 3.0 liter V-6 engine built by Mitsubishi Motors Corporation. Grand Caravan SE and Grand Caravan LE are offered with a 3.3 liter V-6 engine with 4-speed automatic transmission. Caravan SE/LE and Grand Caravan SE/LE are also offered with all-wheel drive.

1992 Dodge Caravan SE

MAJOR FEATURES

● Caravan has as 1992 standard equipment: Iso-strut front suspension, power-assisted rack-and-pinion steering, front power-assisted disc brakes, and 5-passenger seating arrangement.

● Caravan SE and Grand Caravan SE add as 1992 standard features: 7-passenger seating arrangement, power liftgate release, power fold away mirrors, rear trim panel storage and cupholders, and sport wheel covers.

● Caravan LE and Grand Caravan LE add as 1992 standard features: front air conditioning, cruise control, deluxe body sound insulation, styled steel wheels, remote fuel filler door release, heated mirrors, and floor mats.

● Mini Ram Van added as 1991 standard equipment: front bucket seats.

● Caravan PES Turbo added as 1990 standard features: inline-4, turbo-charged engine.

PRICE HISTORY

The following new car prices reflect the approximate retail cost of the base model: **1988** - $10,887; **1989** - $10,592; **1990** - $11,215; **1991** - $12,337; **1992** - $13,406.

DIMENSIONS

Body Style	Years Avail	Wheel Base (in)	Lgth (in)	Ht (in)	Avg Wt (lbs)	Fuel Cap (gal)	Front Hdrm (in)	Front Legrm (in)
mvan	87-88	112	175.9	64.4	4,060	15	na	na
mvan	89-91	112.3	175.9	64.6	4,070	20	39.0	38.2
mvan	92-92	112.3	178.1	66.0	na	20	na	na

ENGINES

Type	Displace-ment (L)	Fuel Dly	HP @rpm	Torque @rpm (ft/lbs)	MPG Cty/Hwy	Years Avail
I-4	2.2	2-bbl	95@na	na	22/29	87-87
I-4	2.6	2-bbl	104@na	na	19/22	87-87
I-4	2.5	FI	100@4800	135@2800	21/24	87-92
I-4T	2.5	FI	150@na	na	18/26	89-90
V-6	3.0	FI	141@5000	171@2800	19/24	87-91
V-6	3.3	FI	150@4800	185@3600	17/23	90-92
V-6	3.0	FI	142@5000	173@2400	19/24	92-92

KEY: I=in-line engine; V=V engine; F=flat engine; FI=fuel injection; bbl=barrel carburetor; T=turbo; D=diesel; HP=horsepower; MPG=estimated average miles per gallon.

EVALUATIONS, TESTS, AND RANKINGS

1991: "[Grand Caravan LE] cabin's layout was superb . . . the most functional and efficient designs among the domestic minivans." **Source:** "Parents love minivan's touches," *Detroit Free Press*, August 2, 1990, p. C1.

1991: "Exterior changes have resulted in new sheet metal, but the vans remain the same in size and dimension. . .noticeable changes come inside, with a new instrument panel and an overall design that Chrysler likes to call friendlier, meaning rounded corners and smoothly blended surfaces." **Source:** "A New Look (Sort Of) for Chrysler's Van," *New York Times*, November 18, 1990.

1991: "clear evolution of the original. . .same basic dimensions have been retained, but the styling is softer and more car-like. . .Front suspension and steering revisions. . .result in handling and steering-like improvements." **Source:** "Chrysler Mini-Vans," *Motor Trend*, October 1990, pp. 70-72.

1991: "Not a single competitive vehicle can handle the wide variety of tasks required of a minivan with the same equanimity as Chrysler's. . .formerly clunky interior is now first-rate." **Source:** "Dodge Caravan/Plymouth Voyager," *Automobile Magazine*, January 1991, p. 55.

1990: "best minivan you can buy in America." **Source:** "Top 10 New Car Buys Domestic," *Motor Trend*, November 1989, p. 82.

1990: "[Grand Caravan] scored it tops among the bigger minivans in the test . . . front-wheel-drive chassis enhances this vehicle's basic car-like feeling . . . the six analog gages, 3-spoke steering wheel and logically located controls are a vast improvement." **Source:** "The Light Vantastics," *Popular Mechanics*, February 1990, pp. 62-67.

1990: "refined four-speed automatic transmission shifts more smoothly than previous version . . . lines are crisp, simple and functional . . . dashboard has a tacky, old-fashioned look." **Source:** "MiniVanguard," *Home Mechanix*, March 1990, pp. 56-60.

1989: "driveline provided smooth, steady power and got good grades from from everyone . . . low marks for its styling." **Source:** "Eeny, Meeny, Miney, Mini," *Car and Driver*, May 1989, pp. 62-63, 65, 67, 71, 75-77, 81.

1989: "interior is as innocuous as elevator music . . . After 20,207 miles of hauling . . . Dodge Caravan was as trouble-free as we could possibly have asked." **Source:** "Long-Term Test: Pontiac 6000 STE AWD, Ford Festiva LX, and Dodge Caravan SE," *Popular Mechanics*, June 1989, pp. 120, 123, 125.

1989: "Grand Caravan excelled in 50-to-70 mph testing . . . showed significant brake fade after multiple stops . . . recommend waiting until Chrysler engineers fine tune its operation before buying a vehicle equipped with an Ultradrive transmission." **Source:** "Space Machines," *Popular Science*, May 1989, pp. 40-42, 44-46, 48.

1987: "outstanding driveability, fuel economy, and ergonomics . . . newly robust horsepower and torque . . . drawbacks are . . . poor instrument visability, and handling acuity that's not up to the high standard personified by the rest of the vehicle." **Source:** "High-Performance Family Vans; The American people-movers: Chevy Astro/GMC Safari. Dodge Caravan/Plymouth Voyager, Ford Aerostar," *Motor Trend*, June 1987, pp. 70-76.

RECALLS

1991: (1,300 mini-vans): Incorrect turn signal flasher installed inhibits indication of signal lamp outage. Vehicle does not comply with FMVSS 108. **Corrective action:** Replace turn signal flasher with proper flasher. *(NHTSA Campaign No. 91V041000.)*

1990: (100 minivans; includes Dodge Caravan and Plymouth Voyager models): Incorrect screws may have been used in installing the load sensing brake proportioning valve to its bracket causing the clamping load to be less than intended. Could result in inconsistent front to rear brake balance with potential for rear brake skid under heavy braking conditions. **Corrective action:** Replace proportioning valve to bracket screws with proper length screws. *(NHTSA Campaign No. 90V145000.)*

1989-90: (625,000 cars; includes several Plymouth, Dodge, and Chrysler vehicles): Engine valve cover gasket may dislocate and allow an engine oil leak at the gasket. Leakage of oil in the engine compartment could cause a fire. **Corrective action:** Replace gasket cover with revised cover, and RTV sealant will be applied in place of a gasket. *(NHTSA Campaign No. 89V237000.)*

1989-90: (640,000 passenger vans; includes the Chrysler Town & Country, Dodge Caravan, and Plymouth Voyager): Inboard front seat belt assembly straps can suffer fatigue failure of the strap near its anchor position resulting in increased likelihood of injury to seat occupant. **Corrective action:** Replace fatigued straps or retrofit straps with a reinforcement plate and removal of an anti-rotation tab to prevent fatigue failure. *(NHTSA Campaign No. 91V053000.)*

1988: (4,000 cars; includes Plymouth and Dodge models): Fuel tanks may be constructed of improper material. Fuel could leak at the tank seam which, in presence of an ignition source, could result in a fire. **Corrective action:** Replace suspect fuel tanks. *(NHTSA Campaign No. 88V107000.)*

1988: (375 vans): Fuel tanks may have been damaged during tank manufacture, which may result in fuel leakage with the potential for a fire. **Corrective action:** Replace fuel tanks as necessary. *(NHTSA Campaign No. 88V010000.)*

SAFETY AND REPAIRS

1987: "Car Clinic," *Popular Mechanics*, June 1990, p. 49. **Note:** Tip for throttle plate sticking on 1987-88 Chrysler fwd cars and vans with 3.0-liter Mitsubishi engines.

REPAIR MANUALS

1036 ● **Chilton's Dodge Caravan-Plymouth Voyager, 1984-1988: Repair and Tune-Up Guide**
Chilton Co.
Chilton Way
Radnor, PA 19089   Ph:(215)964-4000

Published 1989. **Price:** $15.95.

1037 ● Chilton's Dodge/Plymouth Vans 1967-1988
Chilton Co.
Chilton Way
Radnor, PA 19089   Ph:(215)964-4000

Published 1989. **Price:** $15.95.

1038 ● Dodge Caravan, Mini Ram Van, Plymouth Voyager, 1984-1987
Clymer Publications
P.O. Box 1209
Overland Park, KS 66212   Ph:(913)541-6694

Published 1986. **Price:** $14.95.

1039 ● Haynes Dodge and Plymouth Vans Owners Workshop Manual, No. 349: 1971-1991
Haynes Publications, Inc.
861 Lawrence Dr.
Newbury Park, CA 91320   Ph:(818)889-5400

Published 1983. **Editor(s):** J. H. Haynes and P. Ward. **Price:** $15.95.

OTHER INFORMATION SOURCES

1040 ● How to Build Chrysler, Dodge, Plymouth
Motorbooks International, Pubs. & Wholesalers, Inc.
729 Prospect Ave.
Osceola, WI 54020   Ph:(715)294-3345

Published 1990. **Editor(s):** Geoff Carter. **Price:** $17.95.

1041 ● Torsion Bar
Chrysler Product Owners Club
806 Winhall Way
Silver Spring, MD 20904

Promotes the collection, preservation, restoration, maintenance, exhibition, and enjoyment of Chrysler product cars, trucks, and other vehicles. Includes technical advice on the restoration of Chalmers, Chrysler, DeSoto, Dodge, Imperial, Maxwell, and Plymouth vehicles. Monthly. **Price:** Available to members only.

ASSOCIATIONS

1042 ● Chrysler Product Owners Club
5203 Edmondson Ave.
Baltimore, MD 21229
Brian K. Scott, Exec. Officer

Founded: 1978. **Membership:** 210. Collectors and restorers of Chrysler-product automobiles. Promotes the collection, preservation, restoration, maintenance, exhibition, and enjoyment of all Chrysler product cars, trucks, and other vehicles, including Chrysler, DeSoto, Dodge, Imperial, and Plymouth. Offers technical advice; provides list of cars, parts, and services. Maintains library of service and parts manuals from the 1930s to 1989. **Convention/Meeting:** Annual.

1043 ● WPC Club
P.O. Box 3504
Kalamazoo, MI 49003-3504
Ralph Kendall, Pres.   Ph:(616)372-1067

Founded: 1969. **Membership:** 4,850. Individuals dedicated to the preservation, restoration, and enjoyment of Chrysler product cars. Conducts social activities; houses library. Awards annual trophies at national meets. **Convention/Meeting:** Annual; also sponsors International Winter Photo Meet.

DODGE CHARGER (1987)

Corporate twin of the Plymouth Turismo. Produced until 1987 at, among other locations, the Chrysler motor plant in Belvidere, IL. Dropped after 1987 as production shifted to Omni and Horizon sedans.

MAJOR FEATURES

● Dodge Charger had as 1987 standard equipment: 5-speed manual transmission, rear-window heater, 13-inch styled steel wheels, and a rallye instrument panel consisting of coolant temperature, oil pressure, voltage gauges, and tachometer.

● Shelby Charger GLH-S had as 1987 standard equipment: 15-inch cast alloy wheels, P205/50VR-15 Goodyear radial tires, various other exterior body stylings, and removable glass sunroof.

PRICE HISTORY

The following new car prices reflect the approximate retail cost of the base model: **1987 - $7,199.**

DIMENSIONS

Body Style	Years Avail	Wheel Base (in)	Lgth (in)	Ht (in)	Avg Wt (lbs)	Fuel Cap (gal)	Front Hdrm (in)	Front Legrm (in)
3d cpe	87-87	96.6	174.8	50.8	2,290	13.0	37.2	42.5

ENGINES

Type	Displace-ment (L)	Fuel Dly	HP @rpm	Torque @rpm (ft/lbs)	MPG Cty/Hwy	Years Avail
I-4	2.2	2-bbl	96@5200	119@3200	25/35	87-87
I-4T	2.2	na	146@na	na	19/28	87-87

KEY: I=in-line engine; V=V engine; F=flat engine; FI=fuel injection; bbl=barrel carburetor; T=turbo; D=diesel; HP=horsepower; MPG=estimated average miles per gallon.

EVALUATIONS, TESTS, AND RANKINGS

1987: "fun-to-drive affordable sports coupe." **Source:** "Shelby Charger GLH-S," *Road & Track—Buyer's Guide 1987 Issue,* 1986, p. 138.

RECALLS

1987: (580,000 vehicles equipped with 2.2L turbocharged engine; includes models made before 1987; includes Chrysler, Dodge, and Plymouth models): Fuel leakage may occur in low ambient temperature operation at connections of an engine compartment fuel supply hose to the pressure regulator and to the fuel rail. In the presence of an ignition source, fuel leakage could result in a fire. **Corrective action:** Relocate pressure regulator; replace fuel supply with formed hose with revised routing configuration to ensure sealing integrity. *(NHTSA Campaign No. 88V105000.)*

1987: (95,000 passenger vehicles; includes Plymouth Horizon, Plymouth Turismo, Dodge Omni, and Dodge Charger): Pressure regulator installed in the fuel supply plumbing system leaks fuel into the engine compartment possibly resulting in fire. **Corrective action:** The fuel supply pressure regulator assembly will be replaced with a new assembly. *(NHTSA Campaign No. 91V132000.)*

REPAIR MANUALS

1044 ● Dodge Omni, 024, Charger, Rampage, and Plymouth Horizon, TC3, Turismo and Scamp 1978-1987: Shop Manual
Clymer Publications
P.O. Box 1209
Overland Park, KS 66212   Ph:(913)541-6694

Published 1987. **Price:** $14.95.

OTHER INFORMATION SOURCES

1045 ● How to Build Chrysler, Dodge, Plymouth
Motorbooks International, Pubs. & Wholesalers, Inc.
729 Prospect Ave.
Osceola, WI 54020   Ph:(715)294-3345

Published 1990. **Editor(s):** Geoff Carter. **Price:** $17.95.

1046 ● Shelby Times
Shelby Dodge Automobile Club
P.O. Box 759
West Redding, CT 06896   Ph:(203)438-7370

Magazine. Quarterly.

1047 ● Torsion Bar
Chrysler Product Owners Club
806 Winhall Way
Silver Spring, MD 20904

Promotes the collection, preservation, restoration, maintenance, exhibition, and enjoyment of Chrysler product cars, trucks, and other vehicles. Includes technical advice on the restoration of Chalmers, Chrysler, DeSoto, Dodge, Imperial, Maxwell, and Plymouth vehicles. Monthly. **Price:** Available to members only.

ASSOCIATIONS

1048 ● Chrysler Performance Parts Association
Box 1210
Azusa, CA 91702   Ph:(818)303-6220
Roland Osborne, Chm.   Fax:(818)303-2481

Founded: 1976. **Membership:** 5,000. Clearinghouse for information on from whom, where, and how to obtain vintage, muscle, and high-tech Chrysler performance parts. **Former Name(s):** (1979) National HEMI Owners; (1980) MOPAR Muscle Club. **Convention/Meeting:** Annual national meet.

1049 ● Chrysler Product Owners Club
5203 Edmondson Ave.
Baltimore, MD 21229
Brian K. Scott, Exec. Officer

Founded: 1978. **Membership:** 210. Collectors and restorers of Chrysler-product automobiles. Promotes the collection, preservation, restoration, maintenance, exhibition, and enjoyment of all Chrysler product cars, trucks, and other vehicles, including Chrysler, DeSoto, Dodge, Imperial, and Plymouth. Offers technical advice; provides list of cars, parts, and services. Maintains library of service and parts manuals from the 1930s to 1989. **Convention/Meeting:** Annual.

1050 ● Shelby Dodge Automobile Club
PO Box 759
West Redding, CT 06896
Kenneth A. Eber, Dir.   Ph:(203)438-7370

Founded: 1983. **Membership:** 2500. Owners and enthusiasts of Shelby Dodge automobiles. Purposes are to: provide information on Shelby Dodges; sponsor events related to the cars. **Convention/Meeting:** Annual - always summer.

1051 ● Special Interest Auto Club
P.O. Box 681
Centreville, VA 22020
Stephen L. DiGiulian, Pres.   Ph:(703)631-0018

Founded: 1978. **Membership:** 2,000. Owners and enthusiasts of Chrysler high-performance automobiles manufactured from 1964 to the present including Dodge Challengers and Plymouth Barracudas. Purpose is to help restore and preserve Chrysler high-performance cars. Maintains merchandise department and parts program listing cars and parts wanted and for sale. Sponsors national and regional shows and meets; compiles statistics; maintains biographical archives and speakers' bureau. **Former Name(s):** (1981) T/A-AAR Special Interest Auto Club. **Convention/Meeting:** Annual (with exhibits) - always July, midwestern U.S.

1052 ● WPC Club
P.O. Box 3504
Kalamazoo, MI 49003-3504
Ralph Kendall, Pres.   Ph:(616)372-1067

Founded: 1969. **Membership:** 4,850. Individuals dedicated to the preservation, restoration, and enjoyment of Chrysler product cars. Conducts social activities; houses library. Awards annual trophies at national meets. **Convention/Meeting:** Annual; also sponsors International Winter Photo Meet.

DODGE COLT (1987-92)

An entry-level subcompact hatchback that competes against the Toyota Tercel, Nissan Sentra, Honda Civic, and Mazda 323. Corporate twin of the Plymouth Colt and American cousin of the Mitsubishi Mirage. Named as the best buy among 11 sports cars by *Car and Driver* in 1990. Currently produced at the Mitsubishi plants in Mizushima and Okazaki, Japan, and sold under separate Dodge and Plymouth names. The Colt Vista Wagon was discontinued under the Dodge nameplate after the 1991 model year.

1991 Dodge Colt GT

MAJOR FEATURES

● Colt 1992 standard equipment: 4-speed manual transmission, front independent strut suspension, rear 3-link torsion axle suspension, rack & pinion steering, front power disc brakes, rear power drum brakes, and automatic passive restraint.

● Colt GL adds as 1992 standard equipment: 5-speed manual transmission, upgraded tires, and outside dual manual remote mirrors.

● Colt Vista 2WD Wagon added as 1991 standard equipment:

5-speed manual transmission, independent full-trailing arm suspension, front-wheel drive, reclining bucket seats, center and rear fold-down split seats, liftgate window defroster, rear seat heat ducts, and front mud guards.

● Colt Vista 4WD Wagon added as 1991 standard equipment: *on demand* 4WD, independent semi-trailing arm suspension, power rack & pinion steering, upgraded tires, and rear mud guards.

● Colt GT had as 1990 standard equipment: 5-speed manual transmission, independent strut front suspension, anti-roll bar, rigid rear axle integral suspension, vented front disc brakes, rear disc brakes, and radial tires.

● Colt DL and Colt DL Wagon had as 1990 standard equipment: front or four-wheel drive, 5-speed manual transmission, independent front suspension, rigid axle rear suspension, vented front disc brakes, and rear drum brakes.

● Colt E had as 1989 standard features: 4-speed manual transmission, power brakes, and aero-style halogen headlamps.

● Colt Turbo had as 1989 standard equipment: front wheel drive and 5-speed manual transmission.

● Colt Premier had as 1987 standard features: 5-speed manual transmission and aero-style halogen headlamps.

PRICE HISTORY

The following new car prices reflect the approximate retail cost of the base model: **1987** - $5,949; **1988** - $5,998; **1989** - $6,678; **1990** - $6,851; **1991** - $7,067; **1992** - $7,302.

DIMENSIONS

Body Style	Years Avail	Wheel Base (in)	Lgth (in)	Ht (in)	Avg Wt (lbs)	Fuel Cap (gal)	Front Hdrm (in)	Front Legrm (in)
2d lbk	89-92	93.9	158.7	51.9	2,205	13.2	38.3	41.9
3d sdn	87-88	93.7	157.3	50.8	1,876	11.9	na	na
4d sdn	87-88	93.7	169.1	50.8	1,989	11.9	na	na
5d sdn	87-88	93.7	157.3	53.5	1,966	11.9	na	na
5d wgn	89-90	103.3	176.6	57.3	2,634	13.2	38.3	38.8
5d wgn	89-90	93.7	169.0	53.7	2,271	12.4	37.7	40.6
5d wgn	91-91	103.3	176.6	59.8	2,667	13.2	38.3	38.8
5d wgn	91-91	103.5	176.6	62.4	2,965	14.5	38.3	38.8

ENGINES

Type	Displace-ment (L)	Fuel Dly	HP @rpm	Torque @rpm (ft/lbs)	MPG Cty/Hwy	Years Avail
I-4	1.5	FI	81@5500	91@3000	31/36	87-90
I-4	2.0	FI	99@5000	116@4000	23/29	89-89
I-4	1.5	FI	75@5500	87@2500	29/35	89-91
I-4	1.6	FI	123@6500	101@5000	23/28	90-90
I-4	2.0	FI	96@5000	113@3500	22/29	90-91
I-4	1.5	FI	92@6000	93@3000	31/36	91-92
I-4T	1.6	FI	135@6000	141@3000	23/29	87-89

KEY: I=in-line engine; V=V engine; F=flat engine; FI=fuel injection; bbl=barrel carburetor; T=turbo; D=diesel; HP=horsepower; MPG=estimated average miles per gallon.

EVALUATIONS, TESTS, AND RANKINGS

1990: "[Colt GT] a delight to drive ... superior slalom prowess, excellent braking." **Source**: "Eleven for Thirteen," *Car and Driver*, June 1990, pp. 46-52, 61-69.

1989: "Dodge Colt Turbo ... excellent performance." **Source**: "Ten Best Cars," *Car and Driver*, January 1989, pp. 30-35.

1987: "100,000 miles with nothing more than new tires and oil changes seems to be a common experience." **Source**: "Asian Invasion," *Popular Mechanics*, July 1987, pp. 90-94, 148.

1987: "hot performance, superior handling and a surprising degree of luxury and comfort." **Source**: "Underestimated Colt surprising, as always," *The Detroit News*, December 3, 1986, pp. 1F, 2F.

RECALLS

None to date.

REPAIR MANUALS

1053 ● **Chilton's Colt/Challenger/Conquest/Vista, 1971-1988: Repair and Tune-Up Guide**
Chilton Co.
Chilton Way
Radnor, PA 19089   Ph:(215)964-4000

Published 1989. **Price:** $15.95.

1054 ● **Haynes Dodge Colt-Plymouth Champ FWD Owners Workshop Manual, No. 610: 1978-1987**
Haynes Publications, Inc.
861 Lawrence Dr.
Newbury Park, CA 91320   Ph:(818)889-5400

Editor(s): P. G. Strasman **Price:** $15.95.

OTHER INFORMATION SOURCES

1055 ● **How to Build Chrysler, Dodge, Plymouth**
Motorbooks International, Pubs. & Wholesalers, Inc.
729 Prospect Ave.
Osceola, WI 54020   Ph:(715)294-3345

Published 1990. **Editor(s):** Geoff Carter. **Price:** $17.95.

1056 ● **Torsion Bar**
Chrysler Product Owners Club
806 Winhall Way
Silver Spring, MD 20904

Promotes the collection, preservation, restoration, maintenance, exhibition, and enjoyment of Chrysler product cars, trucks, and other vehicles. Includes technical advice on the restoration of Chalmers, Chrysler, DeSoto, Dodge, Imperial, Maxwell, and Plymouth vehicles. Monthly. **Price:** Available to members only.

ASSOCIATIONS

1057 ● **Chrysler Performance Parts Association**
Box 1210
Azusa, CA 91702   Ph:(818)303-6220
Roland Osborne, Chm.   Fax:(818)303-2481

Founded: 1976. **Membership:** 5,000. Clearinghouse for information on from whom, where, and how to obtain vintage, muscle, and high-tech Chrysler performance parts. **Former Name(s):** (1979) National HEMI Owners; (1980) MOPAR Muscle Club. **Convention/Meeting:** Annual national meet.

1058 ● **Chrysler Product Owners Club**
5203 Edmondson Ave.
Baltimore, MD 21229
Brian K. Scott, Exec. Officer

Founded: 1978. **Membership:** 210. Collectors and restorers of Chrysler-product automobiles. Promotes the collection, preservation, restoration, maintenance, exhibition, and enjoyment of all Chrysler product cars, trucks, and other vehicles, including Chrysler, DeSoto, Dodge, Imperial, and Plymouth. Offers technical advice; provides list of cars, parts, and services. Maintains library of service and parts manuals from the 1930s to 1989. **Convention/Meeting:** Annual.

1059 ● Special Interest Auto Club
P.O. Box 681
Centreville, VA 22020
Stephen L. DiGiulian, Pres.   Ph:(703)631-0018

Founded: 1978. **Membership:** 2,000. Owners and enthusiasts of Chrysler high-performance automobiles manufactured from 1964 to the present including Dodge Challengers and Plymouth Barracudas. Purpose is to help restore and preserve Chrysler high-performance cars. Maintains merchandise department and parts program listing cars and parts wanted and for sale. Sponsors national and regional shows and meets; compiles statistics; maintains biographical archives and speakers' bureau. **Former Name(s):** (1981) T/A-AAR Special Interest Auto Club. **Convention/Meeting:** Annual (with exhibits) - always July, midwestern U.S.

1060 ● WPC Club
P.O. Box 3504
Kalamazoo, MI 49003-3504
Ralph Kendall, Pres.   Ph:(616)372-1067

Founded: 1969. **Membership:** 4,850. Individuals dedicated to the preservation, restoration, and enjoyment of Chrysler product cars. Conducts social activities; houses library. Awards annual trophies at national meets. **Convention/Meeting:** Annual; also sponsors International Winter Photo Meet.

DODGE DAKOTA (1987-92)

Dodge Dakota, comes in a variety of configurations, transmissions, and trim levels. Dakota 2WD and 4WD are both offered in five trim levels: S, Sport, Base, Special LE, and Super LE. In addition to multiple trim levels, the Dakota 2WD comes in three body configurations: Standard, Club Cab, and Cab Chassis. The Dakota 4WD is only offered in the Standard and Club Cab configurations.

1992 Dodge Dakota Sport

MAJOR FEATURES

● Dakota S has as 1992 standard equipment: 2.5L 4-cylinder engine (2WD), 3.9L 6-cylinder engine (4WD), manual rack-and-pinion steering (2WD), power recirculating ball steering (4WD), power front disc/rear drum brakes with ABS, two-speed windshield wipers, removable tailgate, and locking glove box.

● Dakota Sport adds as 1992 standard equipment: flip out rear

quarter windows, intermittent windshield wipers, stabilizer bar (4WD), and AM/FM cassette stereo system with 4 speakers.

● Dakota Base has as 1992 standard equipment: AM/FM stereo with 2 speakers, removable tailgate, and locking glove box.

● Dakota Special LE adds as 1992 standard equipment: 22 gallon fuel tank, and an upgraded interior.

● Dakota Super LE adds as 1992 standard equipment: air conditioning and tilt steering column.

PRICE HISTORY

The following new car prices reflect the approximate retail cost of the base model: **1988** - $6,875; **1989** - $7,497; **1990** - $7,995; **1991** - $8,483.

DIMENSIONS

Body Style	Years Avail	Wheel Base (in)	Lgth (in)	Ht (in)	Avg Wt (lbs)	Fuel Cap (gal)	Front Hdrm (in)	Front Legrm (in)
trk	87-92	112.0	184.2	64.2	4,250	15.0	na	na

ENGINES

Type	Displacement (L)	Fuel Dly	HP @rpm	Torque @rpm (ft/lbs)	MPG Cty/Hwy	Years Avail
I-4	2.2	2-bbl	93@na	na	23/28	87-88
I-4	2.5	FI	117@5250	139@3500	21/27	89-92
V-6	3.9	FI	125@na	na	17/23	87-88
V-6	3.9	na	180@4800	225@3200	16/22	88-92
V-6	3.9	FI	125@na	na	15/20	89-91

KEY: I=in-line engine; V=V engine; F=flat engine; FI=fuel injection; bbl=barrel carburetor; T=turbo; D=diesel; HP=horsepower; MPG=estimated average miles per gallon.

RECALLS

1991: (3,500 Pickup trucks equipped with four-speed automatic transmissions): Steel braided fuel hose routing may allow contact between the base and transmission wiring harness. Could cause hose damage and fuel leakage that, in the presence of an ignition source, could result in a fire. **Corrective action:** Install a tie strap to secure the transmission wiring away from the fuel hose. (NHTSA Campaign No. 90V176000.)

REPAIR MANUALS

1061 ● Chilton's Dodge/Plymouth Trucks 1967-1988
Chilton Co.
Chilton Way
Radnor, PA 19089   Ph:(215)964-4000

With illustrations. Published 1989. **Price:** $15.95.

1062 ● Haynes Dodge Pick-ups Owner's Workshop Manuals, No. 912: 1974-1990
Haynes Publications, Inc.
861 Lawrence Dr.
Newbury Park, CA 91320   Ph:(818)889-5400

Editor(s): J. H. Haynes and David Hayden. **Price:** $15.95.

OTHER INFORMATION SOURCES

1063 • How to Build Chrysler, Dodge, Plymouth
Motorbooks International, Pubs. & Wholesalers, Inc.
729 Prospect Ave.
Osceola, WI 54020   Ph:(715)294-3345

Published 1990. **Editor(s):** Geoff Carter. **Price:** $17.95.

1064 • Torsion Bar
Chrysler Product Owners Club
806 Winhall Way
Silver Spring, MD 20904

Promotes the collection, preservation, restoration, maintenance, exhibition, and enjoyment of Chrysler product cars, trucks, and other vehicles. Includes technical advice on the restoration of Chalmers, Chrysler, DeSoto, Dodge, Imperial, Maxwell, and Plymouth vehicles. Monthly. **Price:** Available to members only.

ASSOCIATIONS

1065 • Chrysler Product Owners Club
5203 Edmondson Ave.
Baltimore, MD 21229
Brian K. Scott, Exec. Officer

Founded: 1978. **Membership:** 210. Collectors and restorers of Chrysler-product automobiles. Promotes the collection, preservation, restoration, maintenance, exhibition, and enjoyment of all Chrysler product cars, trucks, and other vehicles, including Chrysler, DeSoto, Dodge, Imperial, and Plymouth. Offers technical advice; provides list of cars, parts, and services. Maintains library of service and parts manuals from the 1930s to 1989. **Convention/Meeting:** Annual.

1066 • WPC Club
P.O. Box 3504
Kalamazoo, MI 49003-3504
Ralph Kendall, Pres.   Ph:(616)372-1067

Founded: 1969. **Membership:** 4,850. Individuals dedicated to the preservation, restoration, and enjoyment of Chrysler product cars. Conducts social activities; houses library. Awards annual trophies at national meets. **Convention/Meeting:** Annual; also sponsors International Winter Photo Meet.

DODGE DAYTONA (1987-92)

Originally built from the Chrysler K-car sedan platform. Produced at the Chrysler Motors No. 1 plant in St. Louis, MO, and Sterling Heights, MI. (plant parts data: domestic parts - 85%, imported parts - 15%, *Federal Trade Zone Board*, 1989). Appeals to single, younger buyers looking for an affordable small sports car. The Daytona IROC and Daytona IROC R/T are added for the 1992 model year.

1992 Dodge Daytona ES

MAJOR FEATURES

• Daytona 1992 standard features: 5-speed manual transmission, Iso-strut front suspension, power rack & pinion steering, front disc brakes, message center (car graphic display bar for: low washer fluid, liftgate ajar, door ajar), and driver side air bag.

• Daytona ES adds as 1992 standard features: fog lights, rear spoiler, and Turbostar aluminum road wheels.

• Daytona IROC adds as 1992 standard features: 3.0 liter, V-6 engine, five-speed manual transmission, performance tuned shocks, struts, springs, and large diameter sway bars, and aluminum "Ninja" wheels.

• Daytona IROC R/T adds as 1992 standard features: 2.2 liter, 16-valve turbo III engine.

• Daytona ES Turbo had as 1991 standard features: a turbo-charged engine.

• Daytona Shelby had as 1991 standard features: 5-speed manual high-output manual transmission, power-assisted four wheel high performance disc brakes, fog lights, rear spoiler, performance tuned sport suspension, and cast aluminum wheels.

• Daytona CS had as 1989 standard features: 2.2 liter, V-8 turbo II engine, five-speed manual transmission, and power-assisted rack-and-pinion steering.

• Daytona Shelby Z had as 1988 standard features: turbo-charged engine, 5-speed manual transmission, Iso strut suspension, and power-assisted steering.

• Daytona Pacifica had as 1988 standard features: front-wheel drive, 5-speed manual transmission, turbo-charged engine, and upgraded interior.

PRICE HISTORY

The following new car prices reflect the approximate retail cost of the base model: **1987** - $9,799; **1988** - $8,995; **1989** - $9,295; **1990** - $9,745; **1991** - $10,500; **1992** - $10,469.

DIMENSIONS

Body Style	Years Avail	Wheel Base (in)	Lgth (in)	Ht (in)	Avg Wt (lbs)	Fuel Cap (gal)	Front Hdrm (in)	Front Legrm (in)
2d lbk	89-89	97.0	178.4	50.6	2,951	14.0	37.1	42.4
2d lbk	89-91	97.0	179.2	50.1	2,777	14.0	37.1	42.4
2d lbk	92-92	97.2	179.8	51.8	2,779	14.0	37.1	42.5
3d cpe	87-87	97.0	179.3	50.1	2,676	14.0	37.1	42.4
3d cpe	87-87	97.0	179.3	51.3	2,862	14.0	37.1	42.4
3d cpe	88-88	97.0	175.0	50.3	2,698	14.0	37.1	42.4
3d cpe	88-88	97.0	175.9	50.8	2,841	14.0	37.1	42.4

ENGINES

Type	Displace-ment (L)	Fuel Dly	HP @rpm	Torque @rpm (ft/lbs)	MPG Cty/Hwy	Years Avail
I-4	2.5	FI	100@4800	135@2800	23/31	87-92
I-4T	2.2	FI	146@5200	170@2400	21/29	87-88
I-4T	2.2	FI	174@5200	210@2400	20/28	87-90
I-4T	2.5	FI	150@4800	180@2000	20/29	89-90
I-4T	2.5	FI	152@4800	211@2800	21/27	91-92
I-4T	2.2	FI	224@6000	217@2800	19/27	92-92
V-6	3.0	FI	141@5000	171@2800	19/27	90-91
V-6	3.0	FI	141@5000	167@3600	19/28	92-92

KEY: I=in-line engine; V=V engine; F=flat engine; FI=fuel injection; bbl=barrel carburetor; T=turbo; D=diesel; HP=horsepower; MPG=estimated average miles per gallon.

EVALUATIONS, TESTS, AND RANKINGS

1992: "At the test track, it will perform magical feats . . . hates every bump it encounters in the real world . . . On smooth pavement, the Daytona R/T is impressive." **Source:** "Dodge Daytona IROC R/T," *Motor Trend,* October 1991, p. 58.

1992: "[Dodge Daytona IROC] has the spirit of a race car with its feisty turbo engine . . . Lag is minimal, and balance shafts quell much of the boom and vibration that plagued earlier shaftless 2.2-liter engines . . . downright jiggly on public roads." **Source:** "Driving Impressions: New or '92," *Road & Track,* November 1991, pp. 92-94.

1992: "quite handsome, admirable, youthful-for-its-age . . . a single bump still reverberates through the floorpan to feel like many . . . engine is the main attraction." **Source:** "Dodge Daytona IROC R/T," *Car and Driver,* October 1991, p. 59.

1991: "Performance is good, with minimal lag." **Source:** "Dodge Daytona," *Road & Track,* October 1990, p.64.

1990: "exhibits a newfound polish and sophistication . . . suspension strides over most sections of broken pavement with ease . . . when traveling fast over bumpy pavement, the suspension lacks body control." **Source:** "Dodge Daytona ES," *Car & Driver,* August 1990, pp. 123-125.

1990: "[Dodge Daytona ES] has received many worthwhile upgrades . . . interior's basic architecture hearkens back to an age when designing airy cabins wasn't the high priority . . . drivetrain . . . is the sweetest part of the deal." **Source:** "Six-Packs To Go," *Road & Track,* May 1990, pp. 130-131, 135, 137, 139-141.

1989: "accelerates passionately . . . as much a real sports car as you'll ever see . . . interior is equal parts comfort and efficiency." **Source:** "Dodge Daytona CS," *Motor Trend,* August 1989, pp. 67-70.

1988: "Dodge Daytona Shelby Z . . . was the only close runner-up to the Probe . . . in raw acceleration . . . basic harshness only partially offset by excellent performance in . . . acceleration and braking." **Source:** "6 Quick Coupes," *Popular Science,* September 1988, pp. 32-34, 36, 40-41.

1988: "very attractive and comfortable appointments, beautiful exterior finishes and high performance which is smooth and sophisticated . . . ride is very steady and comfortable." **Source:** "Color purple enhances hot Daytona Pacifica," *The Detroit News,* December 23, 1987, pp. 1E-2E.

1987: "Dodge Daytona Z . . . came in with a solid 135.39 mph . . . Wind noise was quite noticeable." **Source:** "Domestic Dynamite," *Motor Trend,* August 1987, pp. 44-51.

1987: "ride is comfortably firm without being unduly harsh." **Source:** "Dodge Daytona Shelby Z: The new G-body sports bullet," *Motor Trend,* July 1987, pp. 96-98.

RECALLS

1991: (300 passenger cars): Incorrect tire pressure placard was installed on cars; does not comply with FMVSS 110. Could result in excessive wear and damage. **Corrective action:** Install correct placard containing proper pressure information. (NHTSA Campaign No. 90V169000.)

1991: (18,000 passenger cars; includes several Chrysler, Dodge, and Plymouth models): Front disc brake caliper guide pin bolts may not have been adequately torqued and could loosen. This could cause reduced braking effectiveness and could result in an accident. **Corrective action:** Properly torque front brake caliper guide pin bolts to 250 lbs. (NHTSA Campaign No. 90V162000.)

1991: (90 passenger cars; includes the Chrysler LeBaron Coupe/Convertible and Dodge Daytona): Mismatched parking brake cable lengths to the rear wheels reduce braking ability of one of the rear wheels, in violation of FMVSS 105. Insufficient braking ability could result in inadvertent vehicle rollaway. **Corrective action:** Replace mismatched parking brake cable with one of correct length. (NHTSA Campaign No. 91V078000.)

1990: (257 passenger cars with grey interior; includes Chrysler and Dodge models): Air bag inflator modules may not contain diffuser holes between the ignitor and propellant chambers. Air bags would not deploy in an impact situation, which could lead to driver injury. **Corrective action:** Replace air bag inflator modules with properly machined modules. (NHTSA Campaign No. 90V080000.)

1989-90: (625,000 cars; includes several Plymouth, Dodge, and Chrysler models): Engine valve cover gasket may dislocate and allow an engine oil leak at the gasket. Leakage of oil in the engine compartment could cause a fire. **Corrective action:** Replace gasket cover with revised cover, and RTV sealant will be applied in place of a gasket. (NHTSA Campaign No. 89V237000.)

1987: (580,000 vehicles equipped with 2.2L turbocharged engine; includes models made before 1987; includes Chrysler, Dodge, and Plymouth models): Fuel leakage may occur in low ambient temperature operation at connections of an engine compartment fuel supply hose to the pressure regulator and to the fuel rail. In presence of ignition source, fuel leakage could result in a fire. **Corrective action:** Relocate pressure regulator; replace fuel supply with formed hose with revised routing configuration to ensure sealing. (NHTSA Campaign No. 88V105000.)

1987: (1,550 vehicles; includes the Dodge Lancer and Dodge Shadow): Parking brake mechanism component may disengage. Could result in loss of parking brake function; also, loose component could jam in parking brake assembly. **Corrective action:** Replace parking brake assembly. (NHTSA Campaign No. 89V038000.)

REPAIR MANUALS

1067 ● **Haynes Dodge Daytona and Chrysler Laser Owners Workshop Manual, No. 1140: 1984-1989**
Haynes Publications, Inc.
861 Lawrence Dr.
Newbury Park, CA 91320   Ph:(818)889-5400

Published 1988. **Editor(s):** J. H. Haynes and Larry Warren. **Price:** $15.95.

OTHER INFORMATION SOURCES

1068 ● How to Build Chrysler, Dodge, Plymouth
Motorbooks International, Pubs. & Wholesalers, Inc.
729 Prospect Ave.
Osceola, WI 54020   Ph:(715)294-3345

Published 1990. **Editor(s):** Geoff Carter. **Price:** $17.95.

1069 ● Shelby Times
Shelby Dodge Automobile Club
P.O. Box 759
West Redding, CT 06896   Ph:(203)438-7370

Magazine. Quarterly.

1070 ● Torsion Bar
Chrysler Product Owners Club
806 Winhall Way
Silver Spring, MD 20904

Promotes the collection, preservation, restoration, maintenance, exhibition, and enjoyment of Chrysler product cars, trucks, and other vehicles. Includes technical advice on the restoration of Chalmers, Chrysler, DeSoto, Dodge, Imperial, Maxwell, and Plymouth vehicles. Monthly. **Price:** Available to members only.

ASSOCIATIONS

1071 ● Chrysler Performance Parts Association
Box 1210
Azusa, CA 91702   Ph:(818)303-6220
Roland Osborne, Chm.   Fax:(818)303-2481

Founded: 1976. **Membership:** 5,000. Clearinghouse for information on from whom, where, and how to obtain vintage, muscle, and high-tech Chrysler performance parts. **Former Name(s):** (1979) National HEMI Owners; (1980) MOPAR Muscle Club. **Convention/Meeting:** Annual national meet.

1072 ● Chrysler Product Owners Club
5203 Edmondson Ave.
Baltimore, MD 21229
Brian K. Scott, Exec. Officer

Founded: 1978. **Membership:** 210. Collectors and restorers of Chrysler-product automobiles. Promotes the collection, preservation, restoration, maintenance, exhibition, and enjoyment of all Chrysler product cars, trucks, and other vehicles, including Chrysler, DeSoto, Dodge, Imperial, and Plymouth. Offers technical advice; provides list of cars, parts, and services. Maintains library of service and parts manuals from the 1930s to 1989. **Convention/Meeting:** Annual.

1073 ● Shelby Dodge Automobile Club
PO Box 759
West Redding, CT 06896
Kenneth A. Eber, Dir.   Ph:(203)438-7370

Founded: 1983. **Membership:** 2500. Owners and enthusiasts of Shelby Dodge automobiles. Purposes are to: provide information on Shelby Dodges; sponsor events related to the cars. **Convention/Meeting:** Annual - always summer.

1074 ● Special Interest Auto Club
P.O. Box 681
Centreville, VA 22020
Stephen L. DiGiulian, Pres.   Ph:(703)631-0018

Founded: 1978. **Membership:** 2,000. Owners and enthusiasts of Chrysler high-performance automobiles manufactured from 1964 to the present including Dodge Challengers and

Plymouth Barracudas. Purpose is to help restore and preserve Chrysler high-performance cars. Maintains merchandise department and parts program listing cars and parts wanted and for sale. Sponsors national and regional shows and meets; compiles statistics; maintains biographical archives and speakers' bureau. **Former Name(s):** (1981) T/A-AAR Special Interest Auto Club. **Convention/Meeting:** Annual (with exhibits) - always July, midwestern U.S.

1075 ● WPC Club
P.O. Box 3504
Kalamazoo, MI 49003-3504
Ralph Kendall, Pres.   Ph:(616)372-1067

Founded: 1969. **Membership:** 4,850. Individuals dedicated to the preservation, restoration, and enjoyment of Chrysler product cars. Conducts social activities; houses library. Awards annual trophies at national meets. **Convention/Meeting:** Annual; also sponsors International Winter Photo Meet.

DODGE DIPLOMAT (1987-89)

Corporate twin of the Chrysler Fifth Avenue and the Plymouth Gran Fury. Variation on the rear-wheel drive design that started as the late Dodge Aspen/Plymouth Volare. Popular mainly as police cars and taxis. Produced until 1989 at the closed Chrysler Motors plant in Kenosha, WI.

MAJOR FEATURES

● Diplomat had as 1989 standard features: 3-speed Torqueflite automatic transmission, rear-wheel drive design, independent front suspension, vented front disc brakes.

● Diplomat SE added as 1989 standard features: distinctive grille and outside trim.

PRICE HISTORY

The following new car prices reflect the approximate retail cost of the base model: **1987** - $10,598; **1988** - $11,407; **1989** - $11,995.

DIMENSIONS

Body Style	Years Avail	Wheel Base (in)	Lgth (in)	Ht (in)	Avg Wt (lbs)	Fuel Cap (gal)	Front Hdrm (in)	Front Legrm (in)
4d sdn	87-89	112.7	204.6	55.3	3,566	18.0	39.3	42.5

ENGINES

Type	Displacement (L)	Fuel Dly	HP @rpm	Torque @rpm (ft/lbs)	MPG Cty/Hwy	Years Avail
V-8	5.2	2-bbl	140@3600	265@2000	16/22	87-89

KEY: I=in-line engine; V=V engine; F=flat engine; FI=fuel injection; bbl=barrel carburetor; T=turbo; D=diesel; HP=horsepower; MPG=estimated average miles per gallon.

RECALLS

1988-89: (12,000 passenger cars equipped with air bags; includes the Plymouth Gran Fury and Dodge Diplomat): Steering wheel may crack at its hub weld attachment because of fatigue loading and eventually separate from the hub, resulting in loss of steering control. **Corrective action:** Replace steering wheels with revised wheel with arc welds added at the wheel stamping-to-hub attachment. *(NHTSA Campaign No. 91V051000.)*

1988: (12,000 passenger cars equipped with automatic speed control. Recall includes the Chrysler Fifth Avenue, Plymouth Fury, Dodge Diplomat): Engine compartment wiring harness fusible link wires may be trapped under the speed control servo bracket. Trapped wires may eventually cause a high resistance electrical short that can result in an underhood fire. **Corrective action:** Free any trapped wiring; then secure wiring with a tie strap to keep away from speed control bracket. *(NHTSA Campaign No. 87V164000.)*

SAFETY AND REPAIRS

1987: "Undiplomatic Gesture," *Popular Mechanics*, December 1987, p. 8. **Note:** Tip for V-8 Diplomat with rumbling noise at the transmission housing extension.

REPAIR MANUALS

1076 ● **Chrysler, Dodge, Plymouth: 1972-1987 Rear Wheel Drive Tune-up Maintenance**
Clymer Publications
P.O. Box 1209
Overland Park, KS 66212   Ph:(913)541-6694

Published 1987. **Price:** $14.95.

OTHER INFORMATION SOURCES

1077 ● **How to Build Chrysler, Dodge, Plymouth**
Motorbooks International, Pubs. & Wholesalers, Inc.
729 Prospect Ave.
Osceola, WI 54020   Ph:(715)294-3345

Published 1990. **Editor(s):** Geoff Carter. **Price:** $17.95.

1078 ● **Torsion Bar**
Chrysler Product Owners Club
806 Winhall Way
Silver Spring, MD 20904

Promotes the collection, preservation, restoration, maintenance, exhibition, and enjoyment of Chrysler product cars, trucks, and other vehicles. Includes technical advice on the restoration of Chalmers, Chrysler, DeSoto, Dodge, Imperial, Maxwell, and Plymouth vehicles. Monthly. **Price:** Available to members only.

ASSOCIATIONS

1079 ● **Chrysler Product Owners Club**
5203 Edmondson Ave.
Baltimore, MD 21229
Brian K. Scott, Exec. Officer

Founded: 1978. **Membership:** 210. Collectors and restorers of Chrysler-product automobiles. Promotes the collection, preservation, restoration, maintenance, exhibition, and enjoyment of all Chrysler product cars, trucks, and other vehicles, including Chrysler, DeSoto, Dodge, Imperial, and Plymouth. Offers technical advice; provides list of cars, parts, and services. Maintains library of service and parts manuals from the 1930s to 1989. **Convention/Meeting:** Annual.

1080 ● **WPC Club**
P.O. Box 3504
Kalamazoo, MI 49003-3504
Ralph Kendall, Pres.   Ph:(616)372-1067

Founded: 1969. **Membership:** 4,850. Individuals dedicated to the preservation, restoration, and enjoyment of Chrysler product cars. Conducts social activities; houses library. Awards annual trophies at national meets. **Convention/Meeting:** Annual; also sponsors International Winter Photo Meet.

DODGE DYNASTY (1988-92)

Introduced in 1988, along with its corporate cousin the Chrysler New Yorker, as a mid-size sedan with appointments that appeal to families. Competes in the midsize segment against the Chevrolet Lumina, Ford Taurus, and Pontiac Grand Prix. C-platform is assembled at the Chrysler Motors plant in Belvidere, IL.

1991 Dodge Dynasty

MAJOR FEATURES

● Dynasty 1992 standard equipment: 3-speed automatic transmission, Iso strut front suspension, power rack-and-pinion steering, power front disc/rear drum brakes, and passive restraint system.

● Dynasty LE adds as 1992 standard equipment: upgraded engine, 4-speed automatic transmission, and message center (door ajar, deck lid jar, low washer fluid).

PRICE HISTORY

The following new car prices reflect the approximate retail cost of the base model: **1988** - $11,666; **1989** - $12,295; **1990** - $12,995; **1991** - $13,697; **1992** - $14,277.

DIMENSIONS

Body Style	Years Avail	Wheel Base (in)	Lgth (in)	Ht (in)	Avg Wt (lbs)	Fuel Cap (gal)	Front Hdrm (in)	Front Legrm (in)
4d sdn	88-91	104.3	192.0	53.5	2,996	16.0	38.3	41.9
4d sdn	92-92	104.5	192.0	55.7	3,026	16.0	38.3	41.9

ENGINES

Type	Displace-ment (L)	Fuel Dly	HP @rpm	Torque @rpm (ft/lbs)	MPG Cty/Hwy	Years Avail
I-4	2.5	FI	100@4800	135@2800	22/28	88-92
V-6	3.0	FI	136@4800	168@2800	19/26	88-88
V-6	3.0	FI	141@5000	171@2800	20/27	89-92
V-6	3.3	FI	147@4800	183@3600	19/25	90-92

KEY: I=in-line engine; V=V engine; F=flat engine; FI=fuel injection; bbl=barrel carburetor; T=turbo; D=diesel; HP=horsepower; MPG=estimated average miles per gallon.

EVALUATIONS, TESTS, AND RANKINGS

1990: "a practical 4-door family sedan with a touch of class . . . buyers cited the Dynasty's styling as the one big feature that won them over . . . looks good, performs well, gets decent fuel economy." **Source:** "Dodge Dynasty," *Popular Mechanics*, February 1990, pp. 53-55.

1989: "first-rate ride." **Source:** "Chrysler New Yorker, Dodge Dynasty," *Road & Track—Buyer's Guide 1989*, 1988, p. 46.

1988: "vintage Dodge: a roomy, comfortable car that looks more expensive than it is." **Source:** "New Yorker, Dynasty: Variations on a theme," *The Detroit News*, October 21, 1987, p. 1F-2F.

RECALLS

1991: (18,000 passenger cars; includes several Chrysler, Dodge, and Plymouth models): Front disc brake caliper guide pin bolts may not have been adequately torqued and could loosen. This could cause reduced braking effectiveness and could result in an accident. **Corrective action:** Properly torque front brake caliper guide pin bolts to 250 lbs. *(NHTSA Campaign No. 90V162000.)*

1991: (130,000 passenger vehicles; includes Chrysler Imperial, Chrysler Fifth Avenue, Chrysler Salon, Chrysler LeBaron, Dodge Dynasty, Dodge Spirit, and Plymouth Acclaim): Front outboard safety belt may become difficult to latch or unlatch due to a webbing stiffener entering the buckle housing and dislodging the buckle latch guide. Latch may open during an accident or sudden stop. **Corrective action:** Replace buckle latch engagement. *(NHTSA Campaign No. 91V122000.)*

1990: (257 passenger cars with grey interior; incudes Chrysler and Dodge models): Air bag inflator modules may not contain diffuser holes between the ignitor and propellant chambers. Air bags would not deploy in an impact situation, which could lead to driver injury. **Corrective action:** Replace air bag inflator modules with properly machined modules. *(NHTSA Campaign No. 90V080000.)*

1989-90: (625,000 cars; includes several Plymouth, Dodge, and Chrysler vehicles): Engine valve cover gasket may dislocate and allow an engine oil leak at the gasket. Leakage of oil in the engine compartment could cause a fire. **Corrective action:** Replace gasket cover with revised cover, and RTV sealant will be applied in place of a gasket. *(NHTSA Campaign No. 89V237000.)*

OTHER INFORMATION SOURCES

1081 ● How to Build Chrysler, Dodge, Plymouth
Motorbooks International, Pubs. & Wholesalers, Inc.
729 Prospect Ave.
Osceola, WI 54020   Ph:(715)294-3345

Published 1990. **Editor(s):** Geoff Carter. **Price:** $17.95.

1082 ● Torsion Bar
Chrysler Product Owners Club
806 Winhall Way
Silver Spring, MD 20904

Promotes the collection, preservation, restoration, maintenance, exhibition, and enjoyment of Chrysler product cars, trucks, and other vehicles. Includes technical advice on the restoration of Chalmers, Chrysler, DeSoto, Dodge, Imperial, Maxwell, and Plymouth vehicles. Monthly. **Price:** Available to members only.

ASSOCIATIONS

1083 ● Chrysler Product Owners Club
5203 Edmondson Ave.
Baltimore, MD 21229
Brian K. Scott, Exec. Officer

Founded: 1978. **Membership:** 210. Collectors and restorers of Chrysler-product automobiles. Promotes the collection, preservation, restoration, maintenance, exhibition, and enjoyment of all Chrysler product cars, trucks, and other

vehicles, including Chrysler, DeSoto, Dodge, Imperial, and Plymouth. Offers technical advice; provides list of cars, parts, and services. Maintains library of service and parts manuals from the 1930s to 1989. **Convention/Meeting:** Annual.

1084 ● WPC Club
P.O. Box 3504
Kalamazoo, MI 49003-3504
Ralph Kendall, Pres.   Ph:(616)372-1067

Founded: 1969. **Membership:** 4,850. Individuals dedicated to the preservation, restoration, and enjoyment of Chrysler product cars. Conducts social activities; houses library. Awards annual trophies at national meets. **Convention/Meeting:** Annual; also sponsors International Winter Photo Meet.

DODGE LANCER (1987-89)

Originally assembled on the K-car platform, along with its corporate twin, the Chrysler LeBaron GTS. Produced through March 1989 at the Chrysler Motors plant in Sterling Heights, MI. Replaced in 1990 by the Dodge Spirit/Plymouth Acclaim, with a new chassis and body.

MAJOR FEATURES

● Lancer had as 1989 standard features: 5-speed manual transmission, power steering and brakes, message center with warning lights, and several interior appointments.

● Lancer ES added as 1989 standard features: turbo-charged engine, air conditioning, alloy wheels.

● Lancer Shelby added as 1989 standard equipment: Turbo II engine, monochrome exterior treatment, fog lights, and stereo sound package.

PRICE HISTORY

The following new car prices reflect the approximate retail cost of the base model: **1987** - $9,852; **1988** - $10,482; **1989** - $11,195.

DIMENSIONS

Body Style	Years Avail	Wheel Base (in)	Lgth (in)	Ht (in)	Avg Wt (lbs)	Fuel Cap (gal)	Front Hdrm (in)	Front Legrm (in)
4d lbk	87-89	103.1	180.4	53.0	2,643	14.0	38.3	41.1

ENGINES

Type	Displace-ment (L)	Fuel Dly	HP @rpm	Torque @rpm (ft/lbs)	MPG Cty/Hwy	Years Avail
I-4	2.2	FI	93@4800	122@3200	24/34	87-89
I-4	2.5	FI	100@4800	135@2800	24/34	87-89
I-4T	2.2	FI	146@5200	170@3600	20/29	87-87
I-4T	2.2	FI	146@5200	170@2400	21/29	88-88
I-4T	2.2	FI	174@5200	200@2400	20/28	88-89
I-4T	2.5	FI	150@4800	180@2000	20/29	89-89

KEY: I=in-line engine; V=V engine; F=flat engine; FI=fuel injection; bbl=barrel carburetor; T=turbo; D=diesel; HP=horsepower; MPG=estimated average miles per gallon.

EVALUATIONS, TESTS, AND RANKINGS

1987: "Nearly 45 percent of owners . . . ranked handling as . . . best liked feature . . . Fuel mileage pleased . . . Customer satisfaction ran high." **Source:** "Chrysler LeBaron GTS and Dodge Lancer," *Popular Mechanics*, March 1987, p. 67.

1987: "Zero to 60 takes 7.7 seconds . . . top speed is.135 mph . . . sumptous leather interior . . . accelerated smoothly . . . substandard shifter." **Source:** "Mom loves this Shelby," *The Detroit News*, April 1, 1987, p. 1F-2F.

RECALLS

1989: (625,000 cars; includes several Plymouth, Dodge, and Chrysler models): Engine valve cover gasket may dislocate and allow an engine oil leak at the gasket. Leakage of oil in the engine compartment could cause a fire. **Corrective action:** Replace gasket cover with revised cover, and RTV sealant will be applied in place of a gasket. *(NHTSA Campaign No. 89V237000.)*

1987: (580,000 vehicles equipped with 2.2L turbocharged engine; includes models made before 1987; includes Chrysler, Dodge, and Plymouth models): Fuel leakage may occur in low ambient temperature operation at connections of an engine compartment fuel supply hose to the pressure regulator and to the fuel rail. In the presence of an ignition source, fuel leakage could result in a fire. **Corrective action:** Relocate pressure regulator; replace fuel supply with formed hose with revised routing configuration to ensure sealing integrity. *(NHTSA Campaign No. 88V105000.)*

1987: (1,550 cars; includes the Dodge Lancer, Dodge Shelby, and Dodge Shadow): Parking brake mechanism component may disengage. Could result in loss of parking brake function; also, loose component could jam in parking brake assembly. **Corrective action:** Replace parking brake assembly. *(NHTSA Campaign No. 89V038000.)*

OTHER INFORMATION SOURCES

1085 ● How to Build Chrysler, Dodge, Plymouth
Motorbooks International, Pubs. & Wholesalers, Inc.
729 Prospect Ave.
Osceola, WI 54020   Ph:(715)294-3345

Published 1990. **Editor(s):** Geoff Carter. **Price:** $17.95.

1086 ● Shelby Times
Shelby Dodge Automobile Club
P.O. Box 759
West Redding, CT 06896   Ph:(203)438-7370

Magazine. Quarterly.

1087 ● Torsion Bar
Chrysler Product Owners Club
806 Winhall Way
Silver Spring, MD 20904

Promotes the collection, preservation, restoration, maintenance, exhibition, and enjoyment of Chrysler product cars, trucks, and other vehicles. Includes technical advice on the restoration of Chalmers, Chrysler, DeSoto, Dodge, Imperial, Maxwell, and Plymouth vehicles. Monthly. **Price:** Available to members only.

ASSOCIATIONS

1088 ● Chrysler Performance Parts Association
Box 1210
Azusa, CA 91702   Ph:(818)303-6220
Roland Osborne, Chm.   Fax:(818)303-2481

Founded: 1976. **Membership:** 5,000. Clearinghouse for information on from whom, where, and how to obtain vintage, muscle, and high-tech Chrysler performance parts. **Former Name(s):** (1979) National HEMI Owners; (1980) MOPAR Muscle Club. **Convention/Meeting:** Annual national meet.

1089 ● Chrysler Product Owners Club
5203 Edmondson Ave.
Baltimore, MD 21229
Brian K. Scott, Exec. Officer

Founded: 1978. **Membership:** 210. Collectors and restorers of Chrysler-product automobiles. Promotes the collection, preservation, restoration, maintenance, exhibition, and enjoyment of all Chrysler product cars, trucks, and other vehicles, including Chrysler, DeSoto, Dodge, Imperial, and Plymouth. Offers technical advice; provides list of cars, parts, and services. Maintains library of service and parts manuals from the 1930s to 1989. **Convention/Meeting:** Annual.

1090 ● Shelby Dodge Automobile Club
PO Box 759
West Redding, CT 06896
Kenneth A. Eber, Dir.   Ph:(203)438-7370

Founded: 1983. **Membership:** 2500. Owners and enthusiasts of Shelby Dodge automobiles. Purposes are to: provide information on Shelby Dodges; sponsor events related to the cars. **Convention/Meeting:** Annual - always summer.

1091 ● Special Interest Auto Club
P.O. Box 681
Centreville, VA 22020
Stephen L. DiGiulian, Pres.   Ph:(703)631-0018

Founded: 1978. **Membership:** 2,000. Owners and enthusiasts of Chrysler high-performance automobiles manufactured from 1964 to the present including Dodge Challengers and Plymouth Barracudas. Purpose is to help restore and preserve Chrysler high-performance cars. Maintains merchandise department and parts program listing cars and parts wanted and for sale. Sponsors national and regional shows and meets; compiles statistics; maintains biographical archives and speakers' bureau. **Former Name(s):** (1981) T/A-AAR Special Interest Auto Club. **Convention/Meeting:** Annual (with exhibits) - always July, midwestern U.S.

1092 ● WPC Club
P.O. Box 3504
Kalamazoo, MI 49003-3504
Ralph Kendall, Pres.   Ph:(616)372-1067

Founded: 1969. **Membership:** 4,850. Individuals dedicated to the preservation, restoration, and enjoyment of Chrysler product cars. Conducts social activities; houses library. Awards annual trophies at national meets. **Convention/Meeting:** Annual; also sponsors International Winter Photo Meet.

DODGE MONACO (1990-92)

Corporate twin of the Eagle Premier. Introduced in 1990 to compete against the Ford Taurus, Mercury Sable, Chevrolet Lumina, Toyota Cressida, and Pontiac Grand Prix. Built at the Chrysler Motors plant in Bramalea, Ontario, Canada.

1991 Dodge Monaco ES

MAJOR FEATURES

● Monaco LE has as standard 1992 features: 4-speed automatic transmission with overdrive, Macpherson strut front suspension, power rack and pinion steering, power front disc brakes, power rear drum brakes, passive restraint seatbelt system, and Venturi wheel covers.

● Monaco ES adds as 1992 standard features: Touring front suspension, air conditioning system, body color grille, upgraded stereo package, and polycast Eurosport wheels and other exterior body stylings.

PRICE HISTORY

The following new car prices reflect the approximate retail cost of the base model: **1990** - $14,995; **1991** - $13,747; **1992** - $14,354.

DIMENSIONS

Body Style	Years Avail	Wheel Base (in)	Lgth (in)	Ht (in)	Avg Wt (lbs)	Fuel Cap (gal)	Front Hdrm (in)	Front Legrm (in)
4d sdn	90-91	106	192.8	54.7	2,983	16.0	38.5	43.8
4d sdn	92-92	106	192.8	53.3	2,991	16.0	38.5	43.8

ENGINES

Type	Displacement (L)	Fuel Dly	HP @rpm	Torque @rpm (ft/lbs)	MPG Cty/Hwy	Years Avail
V-6	3.0	FI	150@5000	171@3600	18/26	90-92

KEY: I=in-line engine; V=V engine; F=flat engine; FI=fuel injection; bbl=barrel carburetor; T=turbo; D=diesel; HP=horsepower; MPG=estimated average miles per gallon.

EVALUATIONS, TESTS, AND RANKINGS

1991: "comfort and space at a reasonable price." **Source:** "Dodge Monaco ES," *Road & Track,* November 1990, p. 83.

1990: "classy and . . . formal exterior with aerodynamic competence . . . interior textures and colors don't blend cohesively . . . Ergonomics are the Monaco's shortfall . . . In the ride-quality segment, . . . [received] highest honors." **Source:** "Sun, Sand, & Sedans," *Motor Trend,* June 1990, p. 96-99, 102-104, 106.

RECALLS

1991: (5,500 vehicles): Routing of battery main feed wiring may allow it to contact air cleaner bracket and continued contact may lead to an electrical short circuit. **Corrective action:** Main feed on all involved vehicles will be rerouted and secured with tie straps away from air cleaner bracket. *(NHTSA Campaign No. 91V042000.)*

1990-91: (76,000 vehicles; includes Eagle Premier and Dodge Monaco models): Rear brake tube routing is contacted by fuel tank heat shield when suspension is in full jounce position. Damages brake fluid tube. Loss of brake fluid affects braking capability, which could result in an accident. **Corrective action:** Modify heat shield to eliminate potential for shield contacting brake tube. *(NHTSA Campaign No. 91V027000.)*

1990: (12,500 cars; includes other Eagle models): Separation of lower intermediate steering shaft at rubber isolator coupling could result in loss of control. *(NHTSA Campaign No. 90V058000.)*

1990: (97,500 passenger cars; includes Eagle Premier and Dodge Monaco models): Routing of the front brake hose may cause excessive hose flexing resulting in premature fatigue cracking of the outer hose cover. This could lead to hose failure and loss of brake fluid reducing braking effectiveness. **Corrective action:** Replace front brake hoses with hoses redesigned to provide a modified routing configuration. *(NHTSA Campaign No. 90V205000.)*

OTHER INFORMATION SOURCES

1093 ● How to Build Chrysler, Dodge, Plymouth
Motorbooks International, Pubs. & Wholesalers, Inc.
729 Prospect Ave.
Osceola, WI 54020   Ph:(715)294-3345

Published 1990. **Editor(s):** Geoff Carter. **Price:** $17.95.

1094 ● Torsion Bar
Chrysler Product Owners Club
806 Winhall Way
Silver Spring, MD 20904

Promotes the collection, preservation, restoration, maintenance, exhibition, and enjoyment of Chrysler product cars, trucks, and other vehicles. Includes technical advice on the restoration of Chalmers, Chrysler, DeSoto, Dodge, Imperial, Maxwell, and Plymouth vehicles. Monthly. **Price:** Available to members only.

ASSOCIATIONS

1095 ● Chrysler Product Owners Club
5203 Edmondson Ave.
Baltimore, MD 21229
Brian K. Scott, Exec. Officer

Founded: 1978. **Membership:** 210. Collectors and restorers of Chrysler-product automobiles. Promotes the collection, preservation, restoration, maintenance, exhibition, and enjoyment of all Chrysler product cars, trucks, and other vehicles, including Chrysler, DeSoto, Dodge, Imperial, and Plymouth. Offers technical advice; provides list of cars, parts, and services. Maintains library of service and parts manuals from the 1930s to 1989. **Convention/Meeting:** Annual.

1096 ● WPC Club
P.O. Box 3504
Kalamazoo, MI 49003-3504
Ralph Kendall, Pres.   Ph:(616)372-1067

Founded: 1969. **Membership:** 4,850. Individuals dedicated to the preservation, restoration, and enjoyment of Chrysler product cars. Conducts social activities; houses library. Awards annual trophies at national meets. **Convention/Meeting:** Annual; also sponsors International Winter Photo Meet.

DODGE OMNI (1987-90)

Along with its corporate twin the Plymouth Horizon, the Dodge Omni was the first U.S.-made front-drive subcompact. Produced until 1990 at the Chrysler Motors plants in Belvidere, IL, Kenosha, WI, and the Jefferson plant in Detroit, MI.

MAJOR FEATURES

● Omni had as standard 1990 equipment: front-wheel drive, 5-speed manual transmission, independent front strut suspension, power-assisted rack-and-pinion steering, and front disc brakes.

● Omni America was offered in 1989 as part of a cost-cutting program to reduce manufacturing and retail costs by offering a single trim level with most options grouped into packages.

● Omni GLH-S added as 1987 standard features: turbocharged engine, modified intake manifold, alloy wheels, and Goodyear Gatorback tires.

PRICE HISTORY

The following new car prices reflect the approximate retail cost of the base model: **1987** - $5,799; **1988** - $5,995; **1989** - $6,595; **1990** - $6,995.

DIMENSIONS

Body Style	Years Avail	Wheel Base (in)	Lgth (in)	Ht (in)	Avg Wt (lbs)	Fuel Cap (gal)	Front Hdrm (in)	Front Legrm (in)
4d lbk	87-90	99.1	163.2	53.0	2,237	13.0	38.1	42.1

ENGINES

Type	Displacement (L)	Fuel Dly	HP @rpm	Torque @rpm (ft/lbs)	MPG Cty/Hwy	Years Avail
I-4	2.2	2-bbl	96@5200	119@3200	25/34	87-87
I-4	2.2	FI	93@4800	122@3200	26/35	88-90

KEY: I=in-line engine; V=V engine; F=flat engine; FI=fuel injection; bbl=barrel carburetor; T=turbo; D=diesel; HP=horsepower; MPG=estimated average miles per gallon.

EVALUATIONS, TESTS, AND RANKINGS

1990: "After a dozen years of fussing, the bugs are out." **Source:** "Dodge Omni," *Motor Trend—1990 New Car Buyer's Guide,* 1990, p. 89.

1988: "one of the least expensive cars sold in the States." **Source:** "Dodge Omni," *Car and Driver—Buyers Guide 1988,* 1988, p. 22.

1987: "very good ride." **Source:** "Dodge Omni, Plymouth Horizon," *Road & Track—Buyers Guide 1987,* 1986, p. 58.

RECALLS

1989-90: (625,000 cars; includes several Plymouth, Dodge and Chrysler vehicles): Engine valve cover gasket may dislocate and allow an engine oil leak at the gasket. Leakage of oil in the engine compartment could cause a fire. **Corrective action:** Replace gasket cover with revised cover, and RTV sealant will be applied in place of a gasket. *(NHTSA Campaign No. 89V237000.)*

1988: (120,000 cars; includes the Plymouth Horizon and Dodge Omni): Steering wheel horn pads do not contain the horn symbol display as required by FMVSS 101. Vehicles do not comply with FMVSS 101, controls and displays. **Corrective**

action: Send notification postcard to owners to assist any future owners who might be unsure of horn location. *(NHTSA Campaign No. 89V091000.)*

1987: (580,000 vehicles equipped with 2.2L turbocharged engine; includes models made before 1987; includes Chrysler, Dodge, and Plymouth models): Fuel leakage may occur in low ambient temperature operation at connections of an engine compartment fuel supply hose to the pressure regulator and to the fuel rail. In the presence of an ignition source, fuel leakage could result in a fire. **Corrective action:** Relocate pressure regulator; replace fuel supply with formed hose with revised routing configuration to ensure sealing integrity. *(NHTSA Campaign No. 88V105000.)*

1987: (95,000 passenger vehicles; includes Plymouth Horizon, Plymouth Turismo, Dodge Omni, and Dodge Charger): Pressure regulator installed in the fuel supply plumbing system leaks fuel into the engine compartment possibly resulting in fire. **Corrective action:** The fuel supply pressure regulator assembly will be replaced with new assembly. *(NHTSA Campaign No. 91V132000.)*

SAFETY AND REPAIRS

1989: "Service Tips," *Popular Mechanics,* October 1989, p. 41. **Note:** Tip for removing water from a/c housing on 1987-89 Omnis.

REPAIR MANUALS

1097 ● **Dodge Omni, 024, Charger, Rampage, and Plymouth Horizon, TC3, Turismo and Scamp 1978-1987: Shop Manual**
Clymer Publications
P.O. Box 1209
Overland Park, KS 66212   Ph:(913)541-6694

Published 1987. **Price:** $14.95.

OTHER INFORMATION SOURCES

1098 ● **How to Build Chrysler, Dodge, Plymouth**
Motorbooks International, Pubs. & Wholesalers, Inc.
729 Prospect Ave.
Osceola, WI 54020   Ph:(715)294-3345

Published 1990. **Editor(s):** Geoff Carter. **Price:** $17.95.

1099 ● **Shelby Times**
Shelby Dodge Automobile Club
P.O. Box 759
West Redding, CT 06896   Ph:(203)438-7370

Magazine. Quarterly.

1100 ● **Torsion Bar**
Chrysler Product Owners Club
806 Winhall Way
Silver Spring, MD 20904

Promotes the collection, preservation, restoration, maintenance, exhibition, and enjoyment of Chrysler product cars, trucks, and other vehicles. Includes technical advice on the restoration of Chalmers, Chrysler, DeSoto, Dodge, Imperial, Maxwell, and Plymouth vehicles. Monthly. **Price:** Available to members only.

ASSOCIATIONS

1101 ● Chrysler Performance Parts Association
Box 1210
Azusa, CA 91702   Ph:(818)303-6220
Roland Osborne, Chm.   Fax:(818)303-2481

Founded: 1976. **Membership:** 5,000. Clearinghouse for information on from whom, where, and how to obtain vintage, muscle, and high-tech Chrysler performance parts. **Former Name(s):** (1979) National HEMI Owners; (1980) MOPAR Muscle Club. **Convention/Meeting:** Annual national meet.

1102 ● Chrysler Product Owners Club
5203 Edmondson Ave.
Baltimore, MD 21229
Brian K. Scott, Exec. Officer

Founded: 1978. **Membership:** 210. Collectors and restorers of Chrysler-product automobiles. Promotes the collection, preservation, restoration, maintenance, exhibition, and enjoyment of all Chrysler product cars, trucks, and other vehicles, including Chrysler, DeSoto, Dodge, Imperial, and Plymouth. Offers technical advice; provides list of cars, parts, and services. Maintains library of service and parts manuals from the 1930s to 1989. **Convention/Meeting:** Annual.

1103 ● Shelby Dodge Automobile Club
PO Box 759
West Redding, CT 06896
Kenneth A. Eber, Dir.   Ph:(203)438-7370

Founded: 1983. **Membership:** 2500. Owners and enthusiasts of Shelby Dodge automobiles. Purposes are to: provide information on Shelby Dodges; sponsor events related to the cars. **Convention/Meeting:** Annual - always summer.

1104 ● Special Interest Auto Club
P.O. Box 681
Centreville, VA 22020
Stephen L. DiGiulian, Pres.   Ph:(703)631-0018

Founded: 1978. **Membership:** 2,000. Owners and enthusiasts of Chrysler high-performance automobiles manufactured from 1964 to the present including Dodge Challengers and Plymouth Barracudas. Purpose is to help restore and preserve Chrysler high-performance cars. Maintains merchandise department and parts program listing cars and parts wanted and for sale. Sponsors national and regional shows and meets; compiles statistics; maintains biographical archives and speakers' bureau. **Former Name(s):** (1981) T/A-AAR Special Interest Auto Club. **Convention/Meeting:** Annual (with exhibits) - always July, midwestern U.S.

1105 ● WPC Club
P.O. Box 3504
Kalamazoo, MI 49003-3504
Ralph Kendall, Pres.   Ph:(616)372-1067

Founded: 1969. **Membership:** 4,850. Individuals dedicated to the preservation, restoration, and enjoyment of Chrysler product cars. Conducts social activities; houses library. Awards annual trophies at national meets. **Convention/Meeting:** Annual; also sponsors International Winter Photo Meet.

DODGE RAIDER (1987-89)

Corporate cousin of the Mitsubishi Montero. Produced in Japan by Mitsubishi and offered by Chrysler Motors until 1989.

MAJOR FEATURES

● Dodge Raider had as 1989 standard equipment: 3.0 liter V-6 engine, four-wheel drive, 5-speed manual transmission, power recirculating ball steering, vented front disc brakes, rear drum brakes, automatic locking front hubs, tailgate-mounted spare tire, tilt steering wheel, and tinted glass.

PRICE HISTORY

The following new car prices reflect the approximate retail cost of the base model: **1987** - $10,317; **1988** - $11,702; **1989** - $12,550.

DIMENSIONS

Body Style	Years Avail	Wheel Base (in)	Lgth (in)	Ht (in)	Avg Wt (lbs)	Fuel Cap (gal)	Front Hdrm (in)	Front Legrm (in)
utl wgn	87-89	92.5	157.3	72.8	4,165	15.9	na	na

ENGINES

Type	Displace- ment (L)	Fuel Dly	HP @rpm	Torque @rpm (ft/lbs)	MPG Cty/Hwy	Years Avail
I-4	2.6	2-bbl	na	na	16/19	87-89
V-6	3.0	FI	na	na	15/18	89-89

KEY: I=in-line engine; V=V engine; F=flat engine; FI=fuel injection; bbl=barrel carburetor; T=turbo; D=diesel; HP=horsepower; MPG=estimated average miles per gallon.

EVALUATIONS, TESTS, AND RANKINGS

1989: "engine performance is very good . . . ride is very harsh because the wheelbase is very short." **Source:** "Dirt Rods," *Popular Mechanics*, March 1989, pp. 113-116, 120.

1987: "has enough to get by, but none to spare . . . hobbyhorses over most bumps." **Source:** "Dodge Raider," *Car and Driver*, June 1987, p. 131-132.

1987: "one of the sweeter-running big fours." **Source:** "Dodge Raider, Mitsubishi Montero," *Road & Track—Buyer's Guide 1987*, 1986, p. 174.

RECALLS

None to date.

OTHER INFORMATION SOURCES

1106 ● How to Build Chrysler, Dodge, Plymouth
Motorbooks International, Pubs. & Wholesalers, Inc.
729 Prospect Ave.
Osceola, WI 54020   Ph:(715)294-3345

Published 1990. **Editor(s):** Geoff Carter. **Price:** $17.95.

1107 ● Torsion Bar
Chrysler Product Owners Club
806 Winhall Way
Silver Spring, MD 20904

Promotes the collection, preservation, restoration, maintenance, exhibition, and enjoyment of Chrysler product cars, trucks, and other vehicles. Includes technical advice on the restoration of Chalmers, Chrysler, DeSoto, Dodge, Imperial, Maxwell, and Plymouth vehicles. Monthly. **Price:** Available to members only.

ASSOCIATIONS

1108 ● Chrysler Product Owners Club
5203 Edmondson Ave.
Baltimore, MD 21229
Brian K. Scott, Exec. Officer

Founded: 1978. **Membership:** 210. Collectors and restorers of Chrysler-product automobiles. Promotes the collection, preservation, restoration, maintenance, exhibition, and enjoyment of all Chrysler product cars, trucks, and other vehicles, including Chrysler, DeSoto, Dodge, Imperial, and Plymouth. Offers technical advice; provides list of cars, parts, and services. Maintains library of service and parts manuals from the 1930s to 1989. **Convention/Meeting:** Annual.

1109 ● WPC Club
P.O. Box 3504
Kalamazoo, MI 49003-3504
Ralph Kendall, Pres.   Ph:(616)372-1067

Founded: 1969. **Membership:** 4,850. Individuals dedicated to the preservation, restoration, and enjoyment of Chrysler product cars. Conducts social activities; houses library. Awards annual trophies at national meets. **Convention/Meeting:** Annual; also sponsors International Winter Photo Meet.

DODGE RAM 50 (1987-92)

Introduced in the 1987 model year and positioned for the entry level, compact truck market. Produced in Okazaki, Japan by Mitsubishi.

1991 Dodge Ram 50

MAJOR FEATURES

● Ram 50 has as 1992 standard features: 2-wheel drive, 5-speed manual transmission, power front disc/rear drum brakes, double wall cargo box, adjustable steering column, and styled stamped argent wheels with center cap.

● Ram 50 SE adds as 1992 standard equipment: upgraded interior and exterior features.

● Power Ram 50 has as 1992 standard features: 4-wheel drive, 5-speed manual transmission, painted, wide-spoked wheels, and upgraded interior styling.

● Ram 50 Sports Cab offers as 1992 standard features: an extended cab, extra inside room behind seats for storage and a cloth and vinyl split-back bench with recliners.

● Ram 50 LE had as 1991 standard equipment: two-wheel drive, five-speed manual transmission, power front disc/rear drum brakes, rear-wheel anti-lock braking system, double wall cargo box, adjustable steering column, and upgraded interior and exterior features.

● Power Ram 50 SE and Power Ram 50 LE added larger fuel tanks and upgraded interiors and exteriors as 1991 standard features. Power Ram 50 LE also added a rear-wheel anti-lock brake system.

● Power Ram 50 SE and LE Sports Cab offered as 1991 standard features: an extended cab, extra inside room behind the seats for storage, and a cloth and vinyl split-back bench with recliners.

PRICE HISTORY

The following new car prices reflect the approximate retail cost of the base model: **1987** - $6,434; **1988** - $7,053; **1989** - $7,664; **1990** - $7,787; **1991** - $7,787.

DIMENSIONS

Body Style	Years Avail	Wheel Base (in)	Lgth (in)	Ht (in)	Avg Wt (lbs)	Fuel Cap (gal)	Front Hdrm (in)	Front Legrm (in)
trk	87-92	105.1	176.9	60.8	4,165	13.7	na	na

ENGINES

Type	Displace-ment (L)	Fuel Dly	HP @rpm	Torque @rpm (ft/lbs)	MPG Cty/Hwy	Years Avail
I-4	2.6	2-bbl	109@na	na	20/25	87-89
I-4	2.0	2-bbl	90@na	na	23/28	87-89
I-4	2.4	FI	116@5000	136@3500	19/24	90-92
V-6	3.0	FI	143@5000	168@2500	17/22	90-91

KEY: I=in-line engine; V=V engine; F=flat engine; FI=fuel injection; bbl=barrel carburetor; T=turbo; D=diesel; HP=horsepower; MPG=estimated average miles per gallon.

EVALUATIONS, TESTS, AND RANKINGS

1990: "a gutsy little machine that handles comfortably on the highway and is both sturdy and maneuverable in off-road situations ... interior trim is carlike, with easy-to-read instruments." **Source:** "Compact Pickups with New Power," *Sports Afield,* July 1990, p. 32.

1988: "no shortage of fancy fixings." **Source:** "Dodge Ram 50," *Car and Driver—Buyers Guide 1988,* 1988, p. 127.

1987: "now more attractive than ever." **Source:** "Dodge Ram, Mitsubishi Pickups," *Road & Track—Buyer's Guide 1987,* 1986, p. 175.

RECALLS

None to date.

REPAIR MANUALS

1110 ● Chilton's Dodge/Plymouth Trucks 1967-1988
Chilton Co.
Chilton Way
Radnor, PA 19089   Ph:(215)964-4000

With illustrations. Published 1989. **Price:** $15.95.

1111 ● Haynes Dodge and Plymouth Vans Owners Workshop Manual, No. 349: 1971-1991
Haynes Publications, Inc.
861 Lawrence Dr.
Newbury Park, CA 91320   Ph:(818)889-5400

Published 1983. **Editor(s):** J. H. Haynes and P. Ward. **Price:** $15.95.

1112 ● Haynes Dodge D-50 and Plymouth Arrow and Mitsubishi Pick-ups Owner's Workshop Manual, No. 556: 1979-1988
Haynes Publications, Inc.
861 Lawrence Dr.
Newbury Park, CA 91320   Ph:(818)889-5400

Editor(s): J. H. Haynes and Curt Choate. **Price:** $15.95.

1113 ● Haynes Dodge Pick-ups Owner's Workshop Manuals, No. 912: 1974-1990
Haynes Publications, Inc.
861 Lawrence Dr.
Newbury Park, CA 91320   Ph:(818)889-5400

Editor(s): J. H. Haynes and David Hayden. **Price:** $15.95.

OTHER INFORMATION SOURCES

1114 ● How to Build Chrysler, Dodge, Plymouth
Motorbooks International, Pubs. & Wholesalers, Inc.
729 Prospect Ave.
Osceola, WI 54020   Ph:(715)294-3345

Published 1990. **Editor(s):** Geoff Carter. **Price:** $17.95.

1115 ● Torsion Bar
Chrysler Product Owners Club
806 Winhall Way
Silver Spring, MD 20904

Promotes the collection, preservation, restoration, maintenance, exhibition, and enjoyment of Chrysler product cars, trucks, and other vehicles. Includes technical advice on the restoration of Chalmers, Chrysler, DeSoto, Dodge, Imperial, Maxwell, and Plymouth vehicles. Monthly. **Price:** Available to members only.

ASSOCIATIONS

1116 ● Chrysler Product Owners Club
5203 Edmondson Ave.
Baltimore, MD 21229
Brian K. Scott, Exec. Officer

Founded: 1978. **Membership:** 210. Collectors and restorers of Chrysler-product automobiles. Promotes the collection, preservation, restoration, maintenance, exhibition, and enjoyment of all Chrysler product cars, trucks, and other vehicles, including Chrysler, DeSoto, Dodge, Imperial, and Plymouth. Offers technical advice; provides list of cars, parts, and services. Maintains library of service and parts manuals from the 1930s to 1989. **Convention/Meeting:** Annual.

1117 ● WPC Club
P.O. Box 3504
Kalamazoo, MI 49003-3504
Ralph Kendall, Pres.   Ph:(616)372-1067

Founded: 1969. **Membership:** 4,850. Individuals dedicated to the preservation, restoration, and enjoyment of Chrysler product cars. Conducts social activities; houses library. Awards annual trophies at national meets. **Convention/Meeting:** Annual; also sponsors International Winter Photo Meet.

DODGE RAM VAN/WAGON (1987-92)

The Ram Van and Ram Wagon are positioned in the standard wagon segment and purchased by commercial and personal recreational use buyers. Produced at the Chrysler Motors plant in Windsor, Ontario, Canada. The Ram Wagon is targeted at families and service-oriented businesses needing a roomy vehicle that can carry five to 15 people.

1992 Dodge B250 Ram Wagon

MAJOR FEATURES

● Ram B150 Van has as standard 1992 equipment: 3.9 liter, fuel-injected engine, rear-wheel drive, 5-speed overdrive manual transmission, independent front suspension, power recirculating ball steering, power front disc brakes, 5,000 lbs. GVW payload package, and unibelt restraint system.

● Ram B250 Van adds as standard 1992 equipment: 6,010 lbs. GVW payload package.

● Ram B350 Van adds as 1992 standard equipment: 5.2 liter, fuel-injected engine, 7,500 lbs. GVW payload package, axle type jack.

● Ram B150 Wagon has as standard 1992 equipment: 3.9 liter, fuel-injected engine, rear-wheel drive, 5-speed overdrive manual transmission, 5,300 lbs. GVW payload package, solid axle front suspension, power recirculating ball steering, power front disc brakes, and unibelt restraint system.

Ram B250 Wagon adds as 1992 standard equipment: 6,010 lbs. GVW payload package.

● Ram B350 Wagon adds as 1992 standard equipment: 5.2 liter, fuel-injected engine, 7,500 lbs. GVW payload package, 4,500 lbs. cap, axle type jack.

The following base prices are for the Dodge Ram Van only.

PRICE HISTORY

The following new car prices reflect the approximate retail cost of the base model: **1988** - $10,839; **1989** - $11,430; **1990** - $12,345; **1991** - $13,088.

DIMENSIONS

Body Style	Years Avail	Wheel Base (in)	Lgth (in)	Ht (in)	Avg Wt (lbs)	Fuel Cap (gal)	Front Hdrm (in)	Front Legrm (in)
van	87-88	112.0	175.9	64.2	4,060	15.0	na	na
van	87-91	109.6	178.9	79.6	5,300	22	na	na
van	92-92	109.6	180.7	na	5,300	22	na	na

ENGINES

Type	Displacement (L)	Fuel Dly	HP @rpm	Torque @rpm (ft/lbs)	MPG Cty/Hwy	Years Avail
I-6	3.7	1-bbl	125@na	na	16/20	87-87
V-6	5.2	FI	140@na	na	13/16	87-89
V-6	3.9	FI	125@4000	195@2000	13/18	88-91
V-6	3.9	FI	180@4800	225@3200	14/18	92-92
V-8	5.9	FI	190@4000	292@2400	11/14	87-92
V-8	5.9	FI	205@4400	305@2000	11/13	90-91
V-8	5.2	FI	170@4000	260@2500	na	90-91
V-8	5.2	FI	230@4800	280@3200	12/16	92-92

KEY: I=in-line engine; V=V engine; F=flat engine; FI=fuel injection; bbl=barrel carburetor; T=turbo; D=diesel; HP=horsepower; MPG=estimated average miles per gallon.

EVALUATIONS, TESTS, AND RANKINGS

1990: "born to haul." **Source:** "Dodge Ram Van/Ram Wagon," *Car and Driver—Buyers Guide 1990,* 1989, pp. 178-179.

RECALLS

1988: (3,500 vehicles including the Dodge B150 Wagon, Dodge B250 Wagon, and Dodge B350 Wagon): Automatic transmission may contain a park sprag rod assembly that may stick. Could allow the vehicle to roll with the gear shift lever in park position. **Corrective action:** Vehicles will have park sprag rod assemblies replaced. *(NHTSA Campaign No. 87V194000.)*

1988: (2,200 vans equipped with a 700 amp battery): Battery may interfere with hood inner panel at the front three cell vent cap of the battery. Such interference may dislodge cap and allow hydrogen gas to escape and cause a fire hazard. **Corrective action:** Replace three cell cap with individual battery cell caps. *(NHTSA Campaign No. 88V073000.)*

1988: (4,000 vehicles; includes Plymouth and Dodge models): Fuel tanks may be constructed of improper material. Fuel could leak at the tank seam which, in presence of an ignition source, could result in a fire. **Corrective action:** Replace suspect fuel tanks. *(NHTSA Campaign No. 88V107000.)*

1988: (375 vans): Fuel tanks may have been damaged during tank manufacture, which may result in fuel leakage with the potential for a fire. **Corrective action:** Replace fuel tanks as necessary. *(NHTSA Campaign No. 88V010000.)*

1987: (1,083 wagons equipped with 9 1/4 in. rear axle. Recall includes the Dodge B150 Wagon, Dodge B250 Wagon, and Dodge B350 Wagon): Rear axle shafts may contain brake drum/wheel studs that are not centered with the drum pilot diameter. Could prevent full seating of the drum to the shaft flange, which may result in wheel stud nut loosening. **Corrective action:** Replace axle shafts as necessary. *(NHTSA Campaign No. 87V094000.)*

REPAIR MANUALS

1118 ● **Chilton's Dodge/Plymouth Vans 1967-1988**
Chilton Co.
Chilton Way
Radnor, PA 19089   Ph:(215)964-4000

Published 1989. **Price:** $15.95.

1119 ● **Haynes Dodge and Plymouth Vans Owners Workshop Manual, No. 349: 1971-1991**
Haynes Publications, Inc.
861 Lawrence Dr.
Newbury Park, CA 91320   Ph:(818)889-5400

Published 1983. **Editor(s):** J. H. Haynes and P. Ward. **Price:** $15.95.

OTHER INFORMATION SOURCES

1120 ● **How to Build Chrysler, Dodge, Plymouth**
Motorbooks International, Pubs. & Wholesalers, Inc.
729 Prospect Ave.
Osceola, WI 54020   Ph:(715)294-3345

Published 1990. **Editor(s):** Geoff Carter. **Price:** $17.95.

1121 ● **Torsion Bar**
Chrysler Product Owners Club
806 Winhall Way
Silver Spring, MD 20904

Promotes the collection, preservation, restoration, maintenance, exhibition, and enjoyment of Chrysler product cars, trucks, and other vehicles. Includes technical advice on the restoration of Chalmers, Chrysler, DeSoto, Dodge, Imperial, Maxwell, and Plymouth vehicles. Monthly. **Price:** Available to members only.

ASSOCIATIONS

1122 ● **Chrysler Product Owners Club**
5203 Edmondson Ave.
Baltimore, MD 21229
Brian K. Scott, Exec. Officer

Founded: 1978. **Membership:** 210. Collectors and restorers of Chrysler-product automobiles. Promotes the collection, preservation, restoration, maintenance, exhibition, and enjoyment of all Chrysler product cars, trucks, and other vehicles, including Chrysler, DeSoto, Dodge, Imperial, and Plymouth. Offers technical advice; provides list of cars, parts, and services. Maintains library of service and parts manuals from the 1930s to 1989. **Convention/Meeting:** Annual.

1123 ● **WPC Club**
P.O. Box 3504
Kalamazoo, MI 49003-3504
Ralph Kendall, Pres.   Ph:(616)372-1067

Founded: 1969. **Membership:** 4,850. Individuals dedicated to the preservation, restoration, and enjoyment of Chrysler product cars. Conducts social activities; houses library. Awards annual trophies at national meets. **Convention/Meeting:** Annual; also sponsors International Winter Photo Meet.

DODGE RAMCHARGER (1987-92)

Dodge 4x4 Ramcharger, a 2-door sport utility wagon, is targeted to outdoor enthusiasts who want a full-size, personal use off-road vehicle. The 4x2 model offers additional towing capability with a V-8 engine. Produced at the Chrysler Motors plant in Lago Alberto, Mexico.

1991 Dodge Ramcharger

MAJOR FEATURES

● 4x4 Ramcharger S has as standard 1992 equipment: four-wheel drive, 4-speed manual transmission, 6,000 lbs. GVW payload package, 3-leaf single-stage semi-elliptic front suspension, integral power steering, front power disc brakes, and unibelt restraint system with tension reliever and automatic retract.

● 4x2 Ramcharger S offers as 1992 standard equipment: two-wheel drive, 4-speed automatic transmission, 5,600 lbs. GVW payload package, coil front suspension, integral front suspension, front power disc brakes, and unibelt restraint system with tension reliever and automatic retract.

● 4x4 Ramcharger STD and 4x2 Ramcharger STD add as 1992 standard equipment: upgraded interior.

● 4x4 Ramcharger LE and Canyon Sport and 4x2 Ramcharger LE and Canyon Sport add as 1992 standard equipment: additional exterior and interior body moldings, upgraded instrument panel and front seating, air conditioning, front bumper guards, and rear window electric defroster.

PRICE HISTORY

The following new car prices reflect the approximate retail cost of the base model: **1988** - $11,776; **1989** - $12,785; **1990** - $14,275; **1991** - $15,172.

DIMENSIONS

Body Style	Years Avail	Wheel Base (in)	Lgth (in)	Ht (in)	Avg Wt (lbs)	Fuel Cap (gal)	Front Hdrm (in)	Front Legrm (in)
utl wgn	87-90	106.0	184.6	69.7	5,600	35.0	na	na
utl wgn	91-92	106.0	188.8	69.7	5,600	34.0	na	na

ENGINES

Type	Displacement (L)	Fuel Dly	HP @rpm	Torque @rpm (ft/lbs)	MPG Cty/Hwy	Years Avail
V-8	5.2	2-bbl	na	na	13/15	87-87
V-8	5.9	4-bbl	na	na	11/13	87-88
V-8	5.2	FI	170@4000	260@2500	13/16	88-91
V-8	5.9	FI	190@4000	292@2400	11/14	89-92
V-8	5.2	FI	230@4800	280@3200	13/16	92-92

KEY: I=in-line engine; V=V engine; F=flat engine; FI=fuel injection; bbl=barrel carburetor; T=turbo; D=diesel; HP=horsepower; MPG=estimated average miles per gallon.

EVALUATIONS, TESTS, AND RANKINGS

1991: "As for ride comfort, the Ramcharger has made the greatest strides ... seats and suspension are almost on par with those of the Bronco ... big side windows and door glass area in the Dodge virtually eliminate the closed-in feeling prevalent with the Bronco and Blazer." **Source:** "Selecting a full-size 4x4," *Sports Afield*, January 1991, p. 36.

1990: "big, heavy truck with the aerodynamics of a billboard." **Source:** "Dodge Ramcharger," *Car and Driver—Buyers Guide 1990*, 1989, pp. 164-65.

RECALLS

None to date.

REPAIR MANUALS

1124 ● **Chilton's Dodge/Plymouth Trucks 1967-1988**
Chilton Co.
Chilton Way
Radnor, PA 19089   Ph:(215)964-4000

With illustrations. Published 1989. **Price:** $15.95.

OTHER INFORMATION SOURCES

1125 ● **How to Build Chrysler, Dodge, Plymouth**
Motorbooks International, Pubs. & Wholesalers, Inc.
729 Prospect Ave.
Osceola, WI 54020   Ph:(715)294-3345

Published 1990. **Editor(s):** Geoff Carter. **Price:** $17.95.

1126 ● **Torsion Bar**
Chrysler Product Owners Club
806 Winhall Way
Silver Spring, MD 20904

Promotes the collection, preservation, restoration, maintenance, exhibition, and enjoyment of Chrysler product cars, trucks, and other vehicles. Includes technical advice on the restoration of Chalmers, Chrysler, DeSoto, Dodge, Imperial, Maxwell, and Plymouth vehicles. Monthly. **Price:** Available to members only.

ASSOCIATIONS

1127 ● **Chrysler Product Owners Club**
5203 Edmondson Ave.
Baltimore, MD 21229
Brian K. Scott, Exec. Officer

Founded: 1978. **Membership:** 210. Collectors and restorers of Chrysler-product automobiles. Promotes the collection, preservation, restoration, maintenance, exhibition, and enjoyment of all Chrysler product cars, trucks, and other vehicles, including Chrysler, DeSoto, Dodge, Imperial, and Plymouth. Offers technical advice; provides list of cars, parts, and services. Maintains library of service and parts manuals from the 1930s to 1989. **Convention/Meeting:** Annual.

1128 ● **WPC Club**
P.O. Box 3504
Kalamazoo, MI 49003-3504
Ralph Kendall, Pres.   Ph:(616)372-1067

Founded: 1969. **Membership:** 4,850. Individuals dedicated to the preservation, restoration, and enjoyment of Chrysler product cars. Conducts social activities; houses library. Awards annual trophies at national meets. **Convention/Meeting:** Annual; also sponsors International Winter Photo Meet.

DODGE SHADOW (1987-92)

Originally designed as a replacement for the Dodge Omni/Plymouth Horizon in 1987, along with its corporate twin the Plymouth Sundance. Instead, it was elevated to the upscale small-car class. Produced at the Chrysler Motors plant at Sterling Heights, Michigan, and Toluca, Mexico (convertible versions only). Named as *Motor Trend's* 1989 Best Domestic Econosport model. Listed as one of the Best Bets of 1992 by *The Car Book*.

1992 Dodge Shadow Convertible

MAJOR FEATURES

● Shadow offers as 1992 standard equipment: 2.2-liter engine, 5-speed manual transmission, front-wheel drive, Iso-strut front suspension, power rack-and-pinion steering, power front disc brakes, passive restraint seatbelt system with driver's side air bag.

● Shadow America is offered in 1992 as part of a cost-cutting program to reduce manufacturing and retail costs by offering a single trim level with most options grouped into packages.

● Shadow Convertible adds as 1992 standard equipment: dual outside remote control mirrors, and upgraded interior.

● Shadow ES and Shadow Convertible ES add as 1992 standard features: fog lights, sport suspension, aluminum wheels, tachometer, intermittent windshield wiper/washer, and other exterior body stylings.

● Shelby CSX offered as 1989 features: turbo-charged engine with a Garrett Variable Nozzle Turbo (VNT), Monroe Formula GP shocks, larger disc front brakes, rear drum brakes, rear deck wing, front air dam, and ground-effect rocker panels.

PRICE HISTORY

The following new car prices reflect the approximate retail cost of the base model: **1987** - $7,699; **1988** - $7,995; **1989** - $8,595; **1990** - $8,785; **1991** - $7,699; **1992** - $7,984.

DIMENSIONS

Body Style	Years Avail	Wheel Base (in)	Lgth (in)	Ht (in)	Avg Wt (lbs)	Fuel Cap (gal)	Front Hdrm (in)	Front Legrm (in)
2d lbk	87-88	97.0	171.7	52.7	2,520	14.0	38.3	41.5
2d lbk	89-92	97.0	171.7	52.7	2,615	14.0	38.3	41.5
4d lbk	87-88	97.0	171.1	52.7	2,558	14.0	38.2	42.2
4d lbk	89-92	97.0	171.7	52.7	2,652	14.0	38.3	41.5
conv	91-92	97.0	171.7	52.6	2,910	14.0	38.3	41.5

ENGINES

Type	Displacement (L)	Fuel Dly	HP @rpm	Torque @rpm (ft/lbs)	MPG Cty/Hwy	Years Avail
I-4	2.2	FI	100@5200	133@3200	25/33	87-88
I-4	2.5	FI	96@4400	133@2800	23/31	88-88
I-4	2.2	FI	93@4800	122@3200	26/32	89-92
I-4	2.5	FI	100@4800	135@2800	23/31	89-92
I-4T	2.2	FI	146@5200	170@2400	21/29	87-88
I-4T	2.5	FI	150@4800	180@2000	21/29	89-90
I-4T	2.5	FI	174@5200	210@2400	20/28	90-90
I-4T	2.5	na	152@4800	210@2400	20/26	92-92

KEY: I=in-line engine; V=V engine; F=flat engine; FI=fuel injection; bbl=barrel carburetor; T=turbo; D=diesel; HP=horsepower; MPG=estimated average miles per gallon.

EVALUATIONS, TESTS, AND RANKINGS

1991: "rear-seat room, which is not bad for a small convertible . . . raising the manual top is simple . . . pleasingly finished, with a few glaring exceptions." **Source:** "Dodge Shadow ES," *Car and Driver*, August 1991, p. 64.

1990: "dated interior . . . engine supplies brisk acceleration." **Source:** "Dodge Shadow ES Convertible," *Road & Track*, November 1990, pp. 142-143.

1990: "economical high-performance magic." **Source:** "Econosport: Dodge Shadow ES," *Motor Trend*, November 1989, p. 82.

1989: "raw performance numbers . . . near the top of . . . list." **Source:** "Coupes de Grace," *Popular Mechanics*, May 1989, p. 120-124, 212, 214.

1989: "a very one-dimensional vehicle, and a questionable choice for your only car . . . smooth, twisty canyon roads, which is where the CSX suspension really shines . . . we vote it most fun/dollar." **Source:** "Motown Muscle: Dodge Shelby CSX—love it or hate it," *Popular Mechanics*, January 1989, pp. 53-57, 116.

1987: "aimed at young singles and newly married couples . . . slightly bigger and more plush than most subcompacts and will put Chrysler in direct competition with . . . Chevrolet Cavalier and Pontiac Sunbird and sporty subcompacts imported from Japan." **Source:** "Shadow, Sundance roll at Chrysler," *The Detroit News*, September 11, 1986, p. 1C-2C.

1987: "workmanship and overall quality of the Sundance/Shadow brought out some of the best marks." **Source:** "Ask the Man Who Owns One," *Popular Mechanics*, August 1987, pp. 62, 91.

RECALLS

1991: (398 passenger cars): The two air bag system front impact sensors may not be secured to their mounting brackets. Air bag will not deploy in a frontal collision if the front impact sensors are not attached. **Corrective action:** Repair to assure proper attachment of front impact sensors to brackets. *(NHTSA Campaign No. 90V194000.)*

1991: (18,000 passenger cars; includes several Chrysler, Dodge, and Plymouth models): Front disc brake caliper guide pin bolts may not have been adequately torqued and could loosen. This could cause reduced braking effectiveness and could result in an accident. **Corrective action:** Properly torque front brake caliper guide pin bolts to 250 lbs. *(NHTSA Campaign No. 90V162000.)*

1989-90: (625,000 cars; includes several Plymouth, Dodge and Chrysler vehicles): Engine valve cover gasket may dislocate and allow an engine oil leak at the gasket. Leakage of oil in the engine compartment could cause a fire. **Corrective action:** Replace gasket cover with revised cover, and RTV sealant will be applied in place of a gasket. *(NHTSA Campaign No. 89V237000.)*

1988: (6,500 cars; includes Plymouth and Dodge models): Front passenger seat lap belt retractor, which incorporates a child seat belt locking feature, may malfunction. Seat belt lock would extract and child seat may move out of its restrained position. **Corrective action:** Redesign retractor. *(NHTSA Campaign No. 88V129000.)*

1987: (580,000 vehicles equipped with 2.2L turbocharged engine; includes models made before 1987; includes Chrysler, Dodge, and Plymouth models): Fuel leakage may occur in low ambient temperature operation at connections of an engine compartment fuel supply hose to the pressure regulator and to the fuel rail. In the presence of an ignition soruce, fuel leakage could result in a fire. **Corrective action:** Relocate pressure regulator; replace fuel supply with formed hose with revised routing configuration to ensure sealing integrity. *(NHTSA Campaign No. 88V105000.)*

1987: (1,550 cars; includes the Dodge Lancer, Dodge Shelby, and Dodge Shadow): Parking brake mechanism component may disengage. Could result in loss of parking brake function; also, loose component could jam in parking brake assembly. **Corrective action:** Replace parking brake assembly. *(NHTSA Campaign No. 89V038000.)*

SAFETY AND REPAIRS

1987: "Shimmying Shadow," *Home Mechanix,* February 1989, p. 86. **Note:** 1987 Shadow with front end shimmy and vibration.

OTHER INFORMATION SOURCES

1129 ● How to Build Chrysler, Dodge, Plymouth
Motorbooks International, Pubs. & Wholesalers, Inc.
729 Prospect Ave.
Osceola, WI 54020   Ph:(715)294-3345

Published 1990. **Editor(s):** Geoff Carter. **Price:** $17.95.

1130 ● Shelby Times
Shelby Dodge Automobile Club
P.O. Box 759
West Redding, CT 06896   Ph:(203)438-7370

Magazine. Quarterly.

1131 ● Torsion Bar
Chrysler Product Owners Club
806 Winhall Way
Silver Spring, MD 20904

Promotes the collection, preservation, restoration, maintenance, exhibition, and enjoyment of Chrysler product cars, trucks, and other vehicles. Includes technical advice on the restoration of Chalmers, Chrysler, DeSoto, Dodge, Imperial, Maxwell, and Plymouth vehicles. Monthly. **Price:** Available to members only.

ASSOCIATIONS

1132 ● Chrysler Performance Parts Association
Box 1210
Azusa, CA 91702   Ph:(818)303-6220
Roland Osborne, Chm.   Fax:(818)303-2481

Founded: 1976. **Membership:** 5,000. Clearinghouse for information on from whom, where, and how to obtain vintage, muscle, and high-tech Chrysler performance parts. **Former Name(s):** (1979) National HEMI Owners; (1980) MOPAR Muscle Club. **Convention/Meeting:** Annual national meet.

1133 ● Chrysler Product Owners Club
5203 Edmondson Ave.
Baltimore, MD 21229
Brian K. Scott, Exec. Officer

Founded: 1978. **Membership:** 210. Collectors and restorers of Chrysler-product automobiles. Promotes the collection, preservation, restoration, maintenance, exhibition, and enjoyment of all Chrysler product cars, trucks, and other vehicles, including Chrysler, DeSoto, Dodge, Imperial, and Plymouth. Offers technical advice; provides list of cars, parts, and services. Maintains library of service and parts manuals from the 1930s to 1989. **Convention/Meeting:** Annual.

1134 ● Shelby Dodge Automobile Club
PO Box 759
West Redding, CT 06896
Kenneth A. Eber, Dir.   Ph:(203)438-7370

Founded: 1983. **Membership:** 2500. Owners and enthusiasts of Shelby Dodge automobiles. Purposes are to: provide information on Shelby Dodges; sponsor events related to the cars. **Convention/Meeting:** Annual - always summer.

1135 ● Special Interest Auto Club
P.O. Box 681
Centreville, VA 22020
Stephen L. DiGiulian, Pres.   Ph:(703)631-0018

Founded: 1978. **Membership:** 2,000. Owners and enthusiasts of Chrysler high-performance automobiles manufactured from 1964 to the present including Dodge Challengers and Plymouth Barracudas. Purpose is to help restore and preserve Chrysler high-performance cars. Maintains merchandise department and parts program listing cars and parts wanted and for sale. Sponsors national and regional shows and meets; compiles statistics; maintains biographical archives and speakers' bureau. **Former Name(s):** (1981) T/A-AAR Special Interest Auto Club. **Convention/Meeting:** Annual (with exhibits) - always July, midwestern U.S.

1136 ● WPC Club
P.O. Box 3504
Kalamazoo, MI 49003-3504
Ralph Kendall, Pres.   Ph:(616)372-1067

Founded: 1969. **Membership:** 4,850. Individuals dedicated to the preservation, restoration, and enjoyment of Chrysler product cars. Conducts social activities; houses library. Awards annual trophies at national meets. **Convention/Meeting:** Annual; also sponsors International Winter Photo Meet.

DODGE SPIRIT (1989-92)

Introduced in mid-1989 as a larger-sized replacement for the Dodge Aries/Plymouth Reliant, along with its corporate twin the Plymouth Acclaim. The mid-sized car is produced at the Chrysler Motors plants in Newark, Delaware, and Toluca, Mexico (Dodge Spirit R/T version only). Ranked sixth in *Popular Mechanics* Best Sellers list for 1989. Listed as one of the Best Bets of 1992 by *The Car Book.*

1992 Dodge Spirit R/T

MAJOR FEATURES

● Spirit has as 1992 standard features: 2.5 liter engine, 5-speed manual transmission, Iso-strut front suspension, power rack-and-pinion steering, power front disc brakes, restraint system with passive driver airbag, and Venturi wheelcovers.

● Spirit LE adds as 1992 standard equipment: 3-speed

automatic transmission, electric rear window defroster, Fascia integral fog lamps, premium sound insulation, electronic speed control, tilt steering column, and Atlas wheelcovers.

● Spirit ES adds as 1992 standard features: 2.5 liter turbo engine, 5-speed manual transmission, four-wheel disc brakes, trip computer, and steel/cast aluminum European wheels.

● Spirit R/T adds as standard 1992 equipment: 2.5 liter, 16-valve turbo-charged engine, rear deck spoiler, and air conditioning.

PRICE HISTORY

The following new car prices reflect the approximate retail cost of the base model: **1989** - $9,995; **1990** - $10,495; **1991** - $10,976; **1992** - $11,470.

DIMENSIONS

Body Style	Years Avail	Wheel Base (in)	Lgth (in)	Ht (in)	Avg Wt (lbs)	Fuel Cap (gal)	Front Hdrm (in)	Front Legrm (in)
4d sdn	89-92	103.5	181.2	53.5	2,788	16.0	38.4	41.9

ENGINES

Type	Displacement (L)	Fuel Dly	HP @rpm	Torque @rpm (ft/lbs)	MPG Cty/Hwy	Years Avail
I-4	2.5	FI	100@4800	135@2800	23/31	89-92
I-4T	2.5	FI	150@4800	180@2000	21/29	89-90
I-4T	2.5	FI	152@4800	210@2400	23/31	91-92
I-4T	2.2	FI	224@6000	217@2800	19/26	91-92
V-6	3.0	FI	141@5000	171@2800	20/27	89-92

KEY: I=in-line engine; V=V engine; F=flat engine; FI=fuel injection; bbl=barrel carburetor; T=turbo; D=diesel; HP=horsepower; MPG=estimated average miles per gallon.

EVALUATIONS, TESTS, AND RANKINGS

1991: ''engine adds a generous dose of performance ... subdued exterior styling is answered in kind with an understated but well-defined interior.'' **Source:** ''Dodge has the proper Spirit [Spirit R/T],'' *The Detroit News*, November 7, 1990, pp. 1D-2D.

1991: ''one of the most refined turbos around ... steering response seemed better than on previous Spirits.'' **Source:** ''Dodge Spirit R/T,'' *Car and Driver*, October 1990, pp. 107-108.

1991: ''[Dodge Spirit R/T] ... actually got one 0-60 mph run of less than 6 seconds ... the interior ... was more comfortable and quieter than ... anticipated ... engine is a trifle peaky.'' **Source:** ''Fast Four Doors,'' *Popular Mechanics*, January 1991, p. 31.

1991: ''a flat-out quick car ... 2.2-liter is now smoother, quieter, and more powerful ... shifter is still a little balky, but ... better than the one in the Ford Taurus SHO and easier to use.'' **Source:** ''Dodge Spirit R/T: Mopar performance rides again,'' *Motor Trend*, October 1990, pp. 76-77.

1991: ''Lotus-modified engine ... transforms the Spirit into a serious contender in the domestic sport-sedan segment.'' **Source:** ''Dodge Spirit R/T a gutsy sedan,'' *Detroit Free Press*, December 20, 1990, p. 1C.

1991: ''Performance is brisk ... Chassis refinements increase on-center steering feel.'' **Source:** ''Dodge Spirit,'' *Road & Track*, January 1991, p. 64.

1990: ''If you have heard that [Dodge Spirit ES Turbo]is the roomiest and most refined of the family, you heard right ... a

very nice car, comfortable, and easy to drive.'' **Source:** ''Two From Chrysler,'' *Design News*, October 2, 1989, p. 45.

1989: ''[Dodge Spirit ES] is probably the best sedan Chrysler has ever built.'' **Source:** ''Best Sellers,'' *Popular Mechanics*, July 1989, pp. 60-63, 120-122.

1989: ''Spirit has one of the few four-cylinder engines we've tested in medium-priced domenstic cars with smoothness comparable to a V6 ... superior performance, crisp handling, and a reasonable ride ... major drawbacks are the dated-looking interior and lack of chassis stiffness.'' **Source:** ''New Spirit in Family Cars,'' *Popular Science*, June 1989, pp. 48-54.

1989: ''no sedan in this mid-size price class does its job nearly as well as the new Dodge ... All voters expressed pleasant surprise at the Spirit's spirit ... The Dodge Spirit ES makes its competition—foreign or domenstic—look poorly thought-out.'' **Source:** ''1989 Car of the Year,'' *Motor Trend*, February 1989, pp. 48-58.

RECALLS

1991: (398 passenger cars): The two air bag system front impact sensors may not be secured to their mounting brackets. Air bag will not deploy in a frontal collision if the front impact sensors are not attached. **Corrective action:** Repair to assure proper attachment of front impact sensors to brackets. *(NHTSA Campaign No. 90V194000.)*

1991: (18,000 passenger cars; includes several Chrysler, Dodge, and Plymouth models): Front disc brake caliper guide pin bolts may not have been adequately torqued and could loosen. This could cause reduced braking effectiveness and could result in an accident. **Corrective action:** Properly torque front brake caliper guide pin bolts to 250 lbs. *(NHTSA Campaign No. 90V162000.)*

1991: (130,000 passenger vehicles; includes Chrysler Imperial, Chrysler Fifth Avenue, Chrysler Salon, Chrysler LeBaron, Dodge Dynasty, Dodge Spirit, and Plymouth Acclaim): Front outboard safety belt may become difficult to latch or unlatch due to a webbing stiffener entering the buckle housing and dislodging the buckle latch guide. Latch may open during an accident or sudden stop. **Corrective action:** Replace buckle latch engagement. *(NHTSA Campaign No. 91V122000.)*

1989-90: (625,000 cars; includes several Plymouth, Dodge and Chrysler vehicles): Engine valve cover gasket may dislocate and allow an engine oil leak at the gasket. Leakage of oil in the engine compartment could cause a fire. **Corrective action:** Replace gasket cover with revised cover, and RTV sealant will be applied in place of a gasket. *(NHTSA Campaign No. 89V237000.)*

OTHER INFORMATION SOURCES

1137 ● **How to Build Chrysler, Dodge, Plymouth**
Motorbooks International, Pubs. & Wholesalers, Inc.
729 Prospect Ave.
Osceola, WI 54020   Ph:(715)294-3345

Published 1990. **Editor(s):** Geoff Carter. **Price:** $17.95.

1138 ● **Torsion Bar**
Chrysler Product Owners Club
806 Winhall Way
Silver Spring, MD 20904

Promotes the collection, preservation, restoration, maintenance, exhibition, and enjoyment of Chrysler product cars, trucks, and other vehicles. Includes technical advice on the restoration of Chalmers, Chrysler, DeSoto, Dodge, Imperial, Maxwell, and Plymouth vehicles. Monthly. **Price:** Available to members only.

ASSOCIATIONS

1139 ● Chrysler Performance Parts Association
Box 1210
Azusa, CA 91702   Ph:(818)303-6220
Roland Osborne, Chm.   Fax:(818)303-2481

Founded: 1976. **Membership:** 5,000. Clearinghouse for information on from whom, where, and how to obtain vintage, muscle, and high-tech Chrysler performance parts. **Former Name(s):** (1979) National HEMI Owners; (1980) MOPAR Muscle Club. **Convention/Meeting:** Annual national meet.

1140 ● Chrysler Product Owners Club
5203 Edmondson Ave.
Baltimore, MD 21229
Brian K. Scott, Exec. Officer

Founded: 1978. **Membership:** 210. Collectors and restorers of Chrysler-product automobiles. Promotes the collection, preservation, restoration, maintenance, exhibition, and enjoyment of all Chrysler product cars, trucks, and other vehicles, including Chrysler, DeSoto, Dodge, Imperial, and Plymouth. Offers technical advice; provides list of cars, parts, and services. Maintains library of service and parts manuals from the 1930s to 1989. **Convention/Meeting:** Annual.

1141 ● Special Interest Auto Club
P.O. Box 681
Centreville, VA 22020
Stephen L. DiGiulian, Pres.   Ph:(703)631-0018

Founded: 1978. **Membership:** 2,000. Owners and enthusiasts of Chrysler high-performance automobiles manufactured from 1964 to the present including Dodge Challengers and Plymouth Barracudas. Purpose is to help restore and preserve Chrysler high-performance cars. Maintains merchandise department and parts program listing cars and parts wanted and for sale. Sponsors national and regional shows and meets; compiles statistics; maintains biographical archives and speakers' bureau. **Former Name(s):** (1981) T/A-AAR Special Interest Auto Club. **Convention/Meeting:** Annual (with exhibits) - always July, midwestern U.S.

1142 ● WPC Club
P.O. Box 3504
Kalamazoo, MI 49003-3504
Ralph Kendall, Pres.   Ph:(616)372-1067

Founded: 1969. **Membership:** 4,850. Individuals dedicated to the preservation, restoration, and enjoyment of Chrysler product cars. Conducts social activities; houses library. Awards annual trophies at national meets. **Convention/Meeting:** Annual; also sponsors International Winter Photo Meet.

DODGE STEALTH (1991-1992)

The Sports Coupe is designed by Chrysler and engineered by Mitsubishi, and is the corporate cousin of the Mitsubishi 3000 GT VR-4. Competes in both the middle and high-end sports specialty markets, alongside the Pontiac Firebird, Nissan 300ZX, Mazda RX-7, and Toyota Supra. Called the "Star of the 1991 Model Year" by *Car and Driver* Magazine. Produced at the Mitsubishi Motors plant in Nagoya, Japan.

1992 Dodge Stealth ES

MAJOR FEATURES

● Stealth has as 1992 standard equipment: 3.0 liter, 12-valve SOHC V-6 engine, 5-speed manual transmission, McPherson strut front suspension, power rack-and-pinion steering, vented power front disc brakes, polycast wheels, electric rear defroster, pop-up halogen headlamps, and passive restraint system with driver's side air bag.

● Stealth ES, formerly cited as Stealth Sport, adds as 1992 standard equipment: 3.0 liter, 24-valve DOHC V-6 engine, fog lamps, upgraded tires, and cast aluminum wheels.

● Stealth R/T adds as 1992 standard equipment: air conditioning, anti-lock brakes, additional console accessories, ultimate sound stereo, rear spoiler, and sport suspension.

● Stealth R/T Turbo adds as 1992 standard equipment: 3.0 liter 24-valve DOHC twin intercooled turbo V-6 engine, styled aluminum wheels, and 4-wheel steering hydraulic control.

PRICE HISTORY

The following new car prices reflect the approximate retail cost of the base model: **1991** - $16,619; **1992** - $17,155.

DIMENSIONS

Body Style	Years Avail	Wheel Base (in)	Lgth (in)	Ht (in)	Avg Wt (lbs)	Fuel Cap (gal)	Front Hdrm (in)	Front Legrm (in)
2d cpe	91-92	97.2	179.1	49.1	3,086	19.8	37.1	44.2

ENGINES

Type	Displace-ment (L)	Fuel Dly	HP @rpm	Torque @rpm (ft/lbs)	MPG Cty/Hwy	Years Avail
V-6	3.0	FI	164@5500	185@4000	19/24	91-92
V-6	3.0	FI	222@6000	201@4500	18/24	91-92
V-6T	3.0	FI	300@6000	307@2500	18/24	91-92

KEY: I=in-line engine; V=V engine; F=flat engine; FI=fuel injection; bbl=barrel carburetor; T=turbo; D=diesel; HP=horsepower; MPG=estimated average miles per gallon.

EVALUATIONS, TESTS, AND RANKINGS

1991: "genuine head turner . . . zero to 60 in six seconds." **Source:** "The Dodge Stealth Roars Into View," *New York Times*, November 25, 1990.

1991: "back seat, as diminutive as it is, is significant to many buyers . . . incredibly easy to drive at the limit . . . ergonomics are strangely offbeat." **Source:** "Dodge Stealth R/T Turbo," *Motor Trend*, October 1990, pp. 106-109, 112.

1991: "quiet interior and isolated, but precise, ride and handling . . . shifter is balky when hurried." **Source:** "Dodge Stealth," *Road & Track*, January 1991, p. 65.

1991: "so much technostuff for so little money." **Source:** "Fast Five: A Glucose Tolerance Test for Car Crazies," *Motor Trend,* December 1990, p. 38-45.

1991: "magnificent hybrid of American styling and Japanese engineering." **Source:** "Stealth Turbo sets hearts racing," *Detroit Free Press,* October 25, 1990, p. 1D.

1991: "neck-snapping acceleration, uncanny cornering, and skid-free stops ... take sharp, bumpy corners serenely ... Inside, the cars are a bit disappointing ... switches aren't always easy to find." **Source:** "A Pair of Techno-Whiz Speedsters," *Business Week,* May 13, 1991, p. 116.

1991: "packs more technology than the competitors ... top speed is projected to be around 160 miles per hour. It'll zip from zero to 60 mph in 5.4 seconds." **Source:** "Innovation: Dodge Stealth," *Fortune,* February 26, 1990, p. 110.

RECALLS

None to date.

OTHER INFORMATION SOURCES

1143 ● Torsion Bar
Chrysler Product Owners Club
806 Winhall Way
Silver Spring, MD 20904

Promotes the collection, preservation, restoration, maintenance, exhibition, and enjoyment of Chrysler product cars, trucks, and other vehicles. Includes technical advice on the restoration of Chalmers, Chrysler, DeSoto, Dodge, Imperial, Maxwell, and Plymouth vehicles. Monthly. **Price:** Available to members only.

1144 ● Chrysler Performance Parts Association Newsletter
Chrysler Performance Parts Association (CPPA)
Box 1210
Azusa, CA 91702   Ph:(818)303-6220

Bimonthly. **Price:** Included in membership dues.

1145 ● Chrysler Power Magazine
Chrysler Performance Parts Association (CPPA)
P.O. Box 1210
Azusa, CA 91702   Ph:(818)303-6220

Bimonthly. **Price:** Included in membership dues.

1146 ● Slant 6 News
Slant 6 Club of America
PO Box 4414
Salem, OR 97302   Ph:(503)581-2230

Club magazine containing technical articles and advisory information on maintenance and restoration of Chrysler Corp. vehicles powered by slant 6 engines. Quarterly. **Editor(s):** Jack Poehler, Editor/Advertising Mgr. **Price:** $18.00.

ASSOCIATIONS

1147 ● Chrysler Performance Parts Association
Box 1210
Azusa, CA 91702   Ph:(818)303-6220
Roland Osborne, Chm.   Fax:(818)303-2481

Founded: 1976. **Membership:** 5,000. Clearinghouse for information on from whom, where, and how to obtain vintage, muscle, and high-tech Chrysler performance parts. **Former Name(s):** (1979) National HEMI Owners; (1980) MOPAR Muscle Club. **Convention/Meeting:** Annual national meet.

1148 ● Chrysler Product Owners Club
5203 Edmondson Ave.
Baltimore, MD 21229
Brian K. Scott, Exec. Officer

Founded: 1978. **Membership:** 210. Collectors and restorers of Chrysler-product automobiles. Promotes the collection, preservation, restoration, maintenance, exhibition, and enjoyment of all Chrysler product cars, trucks, and other vehicles, including Chrysler, DeSoto, Dodge, Imperial, and Plymouth. Offers technical advice; provides list of cars, parts, and services. Maintains library of service and parts manuals from the 1930s to 1989. **Convention/Meeting:** Annual.

1149 ● Special Interest Auto Club
P.O. Box 681
Centreville, VA 22020
Stephen L. DiGiulian, Pres.   Ph:(703)631-0018

Founded: 1978. **Membership:** 2,000. Owners and enthusiasts of Chrysler high-performance automobiles manufactured from 1964 to the present including Dodge Challengers and Plymouth Barracudas. Purpose is to help restore and preserve Chrysler high-performance cars. Maintains merchandise department and parts program listing cars and parts wanted and for sale. Sponsors national and regional shows and meets; compiles statistics; maintains biographical archives and speakers' bureau. **Former Name(s):** (1981) T/A-AAR Special Interest Auto Club. **Convention/Meeting:** Annual (with exhibits) - always July, midwestern U.S.

1150 ● WPC Club
P.O. Box 3504
Kalamazoo, MI 49003-3504
Ralph Kendall, Pres.   Ph:(616)372-1067

Founded: 1969. **Membership:** 4,850. Individuals dedicated to the preservation, restoration, and enjoyment of Chrysler product cars. Conducts social activities; houses library. Awards annual trophies at national meets. **Convention/Meeting:** Annual; also sponsors International Winter Photo Meet.

1151 ● Slant 6 Club of America
PO Box 4414
Salem, OR 97302   Ph:(503)581-2230

Founded: 1980. Owners and enthusiasts of Chrysler automobiles with V-6 engines.

DODGE VIPER (1992)

Introduced in 1992, Dodge Viper is a two-passenger, rear-wheel drive limited production car assembled by hand at the New Mack Development Center facility in Detroit, Michigan. Inspiration for the Viper was the 400-horsepower Ford Cobra, built in the mid-1960s. Viper is constructed of fiberglass-reinforced plastic, lacks windows and outside door handles, and has an open cockpit. Special features include an all-aluminum engine, and structural urethane foam interior trim. Named in 1991 by *Popular Science* as one of the year's greatest achievements in science and technology. Listed as one of the Products of the Year by *Forbes* in 1991. Viper earned this recognition by progressing from a concept car to production in less than three years with a budget of $70 million.

MAJOR FEATURES

● Dodge Viper has as 1992 standard equipment: 6-speed manual transmission, 4-wheel independent suspension with anti-roll bars, power-assisted 4-wheel disc brakes, power-assisted rack-and-pinion steering, full analog instrumentation including 180-mph speedometer, front bucket seats, door-mounted 3-point safety belts, tilt steering wheel, red exterior paint, and AM/FM-stereo radio/cassette with six speakers.

PRICE HISTORY

The following new car prices reflect the approximate retail cost of the base model: **1992** - $50,000.

DIMENSIONS

Body Style	Years Avail	Wheel Base (in)	Lgth (in)	Ht (in)	Avg Wt (lbs)	Fuel Cap (gal)	Front Hdrm (in)	Front Legrm (in)
2d conv	92-92	96.2	175.1	44.0	3450	22.0	na	na

ENGINES

Type	Displacement (L)	Fuel Dly	HP @rpm	Torque @rpm (ft/lbs)	MPG Cty/Hwy	Years Avail
V-10	8.0	FI	400@4600	450@3600	14/19	92-92

KEY: I=in-line engine; V=V engine; F=flat engine; FI=fuel injection; bbl=barrel carburetor; T=turbo; D=diesel; HP=horsepower; MPG=estimated average miles per gallon.

EVALUATIONS, TESTS, AND RANKINGS

1992: "Light on the accouterments, heavy on the performance hardware . . . explosive locomotion and the power to blast to 100 or 150 mph at will . . . It has rekindled passions for an all-conquering, brawny-engine, front-midships roadster." **Source:** "Snake Bitten," *Road & Track*, February 1992, pp. 50-55.

1992: "lone vehicle in a new automotive micro-niche that could be called "retro muscle" . . . engine's torque curve is so flat the V-10 hardly seems to be working . . . Wind noise and buffeting are surprisingly low, and the side exhausts are actually almost quiet at idle and in cruising situations." **Source:** "Dodge Viper," *Motor Trend*, September 1991, pp. 36-43.

1992: "intended to go fast, stop hard, hang onto corners . . . oddly difficult to see out of . . . felt solid, secure, and predictable for the most part. It is nicely balanced, with a little polite understeer most of the time." **Source:** "Dodge Viper RT/10," *Car and Driver*, March 1992, pp. 38-43.

1992: "Torque turns into velocity in a heartbeat . . . looks like a show car and drives like sex on wheels . . . special-purpose automobile that maximizes driving enjoyment by eliminating extraneous baggage." **Source:** "Dodge Viper: Dancing with Snakes," *Motor Trend*, November 1991, pp. 80-82.

RECALLS

None to date.

OTHER INFORMATION SOURCES

1152 ● **How to Build Chrysler, Dodge, Plymouth**
Motorbooks International, Pubs. & Wholesalers, Inc.
729 Prospect Ave.
Osceola, WI 54020   Ph:(715)294-3345

Published 1990. **Editor(s):** Geoff Carter. **Price:** $17.95.

1153 ● **Torsion Bar**
Chrysler Product Owners Club
806 Winhall Way
Silver Spring, MD 20904

Promotes the collection, preservation, restoration, maintenance, exhibition, and enjoyment of Chrysler product cars, trucks, and other vehicles. Includes technical advice on

the restoration of Chalmers, Chrysler, DeSoto, Dodge, Imperial, Maxwell, and Plymouth vehicles. Monthly. **Price:** Available to members only.

ASSOCIATIONS

1154 ● **Chrysler Performance Parts Association**
Box 1210
Azusa, CA 91702   Ph:(818)303-6220
Roland Osborne, Chm.   Fax:(818)303-2481

Founded: 1976. **Membership:** 5,000. Clearinghouse for information on from whom, where, and how to obtain vintage, muscle, and high-tech Chrysler performance parts. **Former Name(s):** (1979) National HEMI Owners; (1980) MOPAR Muscle Club. **Convention/Meeting:** Annual national meet.

1155 ● **Chrysler Product Owners Club**
5203 Edmondson Ave.
Baltimore, MD 21229
Brian K. Scott, Exec. Officer

Founded: 1978. **Membership:** 210. Collectors and restorers of Chrysler-product automobiles. Promotes the collection, preservation, restoration, maintenance, exhibition, and enjoyment of all Chrysler product cars, trucks, and other vehicles, including Chrysler, DeSoto, Dodge, Imperial, and Plymouth. Offers technical advice; provides list of cars, parts, and services. Maintains library of service and parts manuals from the 1930s to 1989. **Convention/Meeting:** Annual.

1156 ● **Special Interest Auto Club**
P.O. Box 681
Centreville, VA 22020
Stephen L. DiGiulian, Pres.   Ph:(703)631-0018

Founded: 1978. **Membership:** 2,000. Owners and enthusiasts of Chrysler high-performance automobiles manufactured from 1964 to the present including Dodge Challengers and Plymouth Barracudas. Purpose is to help restore and preserve Chrysler high-performance cars. Maintains merchandise department and parts program listing cars and parts wanted and for sale. Sponsors national and regional shows and meets; compiles statistics; maintains biographical archives and speakers' bureau. **Former Name(s):** (1981) T/A-AAR Special Interest Auto Club. **Convention/Meeting:** Annual (with exhibits) - always July, midwestern U.S.

1157 ● **WPC Club**
P.O. Box 3504
Kalamazoo, MI 49003-3504
Ralph Kendall, Pres.   Ph:(616)372-1067

Founded: 1969. **Membership:** 4,850. Individuals dedicated to the preservation, restoration, and enjoyment of Chrysler product cars. Conducts social activities; houses library. Awards annual trophies at national meets. **Convention/Meeting:** Annual; also sponsors International Winter Photo Meet.

EAGLE MEDALLION (1988-89)

Originally introduced in Europe as the Renault 21. Renault Medallion became the Eagle Medallion when the Chrysler Corporation purchased American Motors Corporation. Produced in France by Renault under the Eagle name until the model was discontinued in 1989. Made *The Car Book* Worst Crash Test List in 1989.

MAJOR FEATURES

● Medallion had as 1989 standard equipment: 2.2 liter, 4-cylinder engine, five-speed manual transmission, power steering, power-assisted brakes, independent front strut suspension, and vented front disc brakes.

● Medallion DL added as 1989 standard equipment: tilt steering column, tinted glass, rear-window defroster, and remoted-controlled outside mirrors.

● Medallion DL Wagon added as 1989 standard equipment: 3-speed automatic transmission and a third bench seat.

● Medallion LX added as 1989 standard equipment: additional exterior and interior accessories.

● Medallion LX Wagon added as 1989 standard equipment: 3-speed automatic transmission, a third bench seat, and additional exterior and interior accessories.

PRICE HISTORY

The following new car prices reflect the approximate retail cost of the base model: **1988** - $10,405; **1989** - $10,405.

DIMENSIONS

Body Style	Years Avail	Wheel Base (in)	Lgth (in)	Ht (in)	Avg Wt (lbs)	Fuel Cap (gal)	Front Hdrm (in)	Front Legrm (in)
4d sdn	88-89	102.4	183.2	52.8	2,650	17.4	38	43
5d wgn	88-89	108.3	189.7	53.1	2,809	17.4	38	43

ENGINES

Type	Displace-ment (L)	Fuel Dly	HP @rpm	Torque @rpm (ft/lbs)	MPG Cty/Hwy	Years Avail
I-4	2.2	FI	103@5500	124@3000	23/31	88-89
V-6	3.0	FI	150@5000	171@3600	17/21	89-89

KEY: I=in-line engine; V=V engine; F=flat engine; FI=fuel injection; bbl=barrel carburetor; T=turbo; D=diesel; HP=horsepower; MPG=estimated average miles per gallon.

EVALUATIONS, TESTS, AND RANKINGS

1989: "When it's running well, it's actually a terrific small sedan. . ." **Source:** "Long Term Test: Oldsmobile Calais, Mazda 626 4WS Turbo, Buick Regal Custom, Dodge Caravan SE, Ford Festiva LX, Eagle Medallion," *Popular Mechanics*, January 1989, pp. 48-51.

1989: "The most delightful aspect about this car is its ride and handling. . .only caution concerns the car's track record." **Source:** "Eagle Medallion," *Road & Track—Buyer's Guide 1989*, 1988, p. 62.

RECALLS

1988-89: (30,000 vehicles; includes Renault Medallion and Eagle Medallion models): Fuse block wiring terminals may not adequately clamp the positive electrical connection of heater blower motor fuse blades. Increases electrical resistance that could overheat and ignite fuse block and terminal wiring. **Corrective action:** Modify fuse block terminal to ensure adequate retention clamp load on heater blower fuse blades. *(NHTSA Campaign No. 91V037000.)*

SAFETY AND REPAIRS

1988: "Car Clinic," *Popular Mechanics*, January 1990, p. 41. **Note:** Tip for howling brake noise.

REPAIR MANUALS

1158 ● **Chilton's Guide to Chassis Electronics and Power Accessories, 1988-1991 Ford/Chrysler/Jeep/Eagle**
Chilton Co.
Chilton Way
Radnor, PA 19089   Ph:(215)964-4000

Published March 1991. **Price:** $19.95.

ASSOCIATIONS

1159 ● **Chrysler Product Owners Club**
5203 Edmondson Ave.
Baltimore, MD 21229
Brian K. Scott, Exec. Officer

Founded: 1978. **Membership:** 210. Collectors and restorers of Chrysler-product automobiles. Promotes the collection, preservation, restoration, maintenance, exhibition, and enjoyment of all Chrysler product cars, trucks, and other vehicles, including Chrysler, DeSoto, Dodge, Imperial, and Plymouth. Offers technical advice; provides list of cars, parts, and services. Maintains library of service and parts manuals from the 1930s to 1989. **Convention/Meeting:** Annual.

1160 ● **WPC Club**
P.O. Box 3504
Kalamazoo, MI 49003-3504
Ralph Kendall, Pres.   Ph:(616)372-1067

Founded: 1969. **Membership:** 4,850. Individuals dedicated to the preservation, restoration, and enjoyment of Chrysler product cars. Conducts social activities; houses library. Awards annual trophies at national meets. **Convention/Meeting:** Annual; also sponsors International Winter Photo Meet.

EAGLE PREMIER (1988-92)

Originally designed by Renault and American Motors Corporation. Became the Eagle Premier when the Chrysler Corporation purchased American Motors Corporation in 1987; corporate twin of the Dodge Monaco. Contemporary aerodynamic styling credited to Italian designer, Giorgetto Giugiaro, who also has done design work in the past for Maserati. Nominated to the *Car and Driver* Ten Best Cars List in 1990. Received a poor mark in *The Car Book's* complaint index in 1992. Produced at the Chrysler Motors plant in Bramalea, Ontario, Canada.

1992 Eagle Premier LX

MAJOR FEATURES

● Premier LX has as 1992 standard equipment: 4-speed automatic transmission with overdrive, Macpherson strut front suspension, power rack-and-pinion steering, four-wheel power disc brakes, steel wheels, air conditioning system, and tinted windows.

● Premier ES adds as 1992 standard equipment: polycast wheels, upgraded exterior and interior body stylings, and speed control.

● Premier ES Limited adds as 1992 standard equipment: anti-locking brake systems, aluminum wheels, speed control, premium audio system, and upgraded exterior and interior body stylings.

PRICE HISTORY

The following new car prices reflect the approximate retail cost of the base model: **1988** - $12,474; **1989** - $13,576; **1990** - $15,350; **1991** - $15,051; **1992** - $15,716.

DIMENSIONS

Body Style	Years Avail	Wheel Base (in)	Lgth (in)	Ht (in)	Avg Wt (lbs)	Fuel Cap (gal)	Front Hdrm (in)	Front Legrm (in)
4d sdn	88-92	106	192.8	54.7	3,039	16	38.5	43.8

ENGINES

Type	Displace-ment (L)	Fuel Dly	HP @rpm	Torque @rpm (ft/lbs)	MPG Cty/Hwy	Years Avail
I-4	2.5	FI	111@4750	142@2500	22/31	88-89
V-6	3.0	FI	150@5000	171@3600	18/26	88-92

KEY: I=in-line engine; V=V engine; F=flat engine; FI=fuel injection; bbl=barrel carburetor; T=turbo; D=diesel; HP=horsepower; MPG=estimated average miles per gallon.

EVALUATIONS, TESTS, AND RANKINGS

1991: "Reasonable performance." **Source:** "Eagle Premier," *Road & Track,* October 1990, p. 65.

1990: "somewhat generic in design. . .Positive aspects. . .comfortable and supportive seats and an interior that feels spacious." **Source:** "Eagle Premier," *Car and Driver—Buyers Guide 1990,* 1989, pp. 96-97.

1989: "remains one of the best-behaved sedans on the road . . . compliant ride . . . reveals an absence of added harshness but improved bump absorption . . . plastic dash and console. They glare inexpensively amid the mostly classy fittings." **Source:** "Eagle Premier ES Limited," *Car and Driver,* June 1989, pp. 133-134.

1988: "Eagle Premier breathes class. Its aerodynamic design combines European style with high tech. . .Another point for Chrysler. . .primary and secondary seals. . .shut out wind and road noise." **Source:** "Eagle Premier Takes Off Fast," *Design News,* October 3, 1988, pp. 226-227.

RECALLS

1991: (5,500 vehicles): Routing of battery main feed wiring may allow it to contact air cleaner bracket and continued contact may lead to an electrical short circuit. **Corrective action:** Main feed on all involved vehicles will be rerouted and secured with tie straps away from air cleaner bracket. *(NHTSA Campaign No. 91V042000.)*

1990: (12,500 cars; includes other Dodge models): Separation of lower intermediate steering shaft at rubber isolator coupling could result in loss of control. *(NHTSA Campaign No. 90V058000.)*

1989-91: (76,000 vehicles; includes Eagle Premier and Dodge Monaco models): Rear brake tube routing is contacted by fuel tank heat shield when suspension is in full jounce position. Damages brake fluid tube. Loss of brake fluid affects braking capability, which could result in an accident. **Corrective action:** Modify heat shield to eliminate potential for shield contacting brake tube. *(NHTSA Campaign No. 91V027000.)*

1988-90: (97,500 passenger cars; includes Eagle Premier and Dodge Monaco models): Routing of the front brake hose may cause excessive hose flexing resulting in premature fatigue cracking of the outer hose cover. This could lead to hose failure and loss of brake fluid reducing braking effectiveness. **Corrective action:** Replace front brake hoses with hoses redesigned to provide a modified routing configuration. *(NHTSA Campaign No. 90V205000.)*

1988: (95 vehicles with four cylinder engine): Automatic transmissions experienced endurance failures of park mechanism components during severe testing. Vehicles would be subject to transmission failures. **Corrective action:** Retrofit transmission. *(NHTSA Campaign No. 88V128000.)*

1988: (5,000 cars): Master cylinder may have been misassembled causing a blocked hydraulic fluid outlet port and restricted fluid flow. Results in increased brake pedal travel and partial loss of braking capability. **Corrective action:** Replace master brake cylinder. *(NHTSA Campaign No. 88V002000.)*

REPAIR MANUALS

1161 ● **Chilton's Guide to Chassis Electronics and Power Accessories, 1988-1991 Ford/Chrysler/Jeep/Eagle**
Chilton Co.
Chilton Way
Radnor, PA 19089   Ph:(215)964-4000

Published March 1991. **Price:** $19.95.

ASSOCIATIONS

1162 ● **Chrysler Product Owners Club**
5203 Edmondson Ave.
Baltimore, MD 21229
Brian K. Scott, Exec. Officer

Founded: 1978. **Membership:** 210. Collectors and restorers of Chrysler-product automobiles. Promotes the collection, preservation, restoration, maintenance, exhibition, and enjoyment of all Chrysler product cars, trucks, and other vehicles, including Chrysler, DeSoto, Dodge, Imperial, and Plymouth. Offers technical advice; provides list of cars, parts, and services. Maintains library of service and parts manuals from the 1930s to 1989. **Convention/Meeting:** Annual.

1163 ● **WPC Club**
P.O. Box 3504
Kalamazoo, MI 49003-3504
Ralph Kendall, Pres.   Ph:(616)372-1067

Founded: 1969. **Membership:** 4,850. Individuals dedicated to the preservation, restoration, and enjoyment of Chrysler product cars. Conducts social activities; houses library. Awards annual trophies at national meets. **Convention/Meeting:** Annual; also sponsors International Winter Photo Meet.

EAGLE SUMMIT (1989-92)

Compact/subcompact vehicle was introduced in 1989, the 3-dr. hatchback model was introduced in 1991, and the wagon model introduced in 1992. Essentially similar to the Dodge/Plymouth Colt and the Mitsubishi Mirage. Produced at the Diamond-Star Motors plant in Normal, Illinois (4-dr. sedan), and the Mitsubishi Motors plants in Mizushima, Japan (3-dr. hatchback), and Okazaki, Japan (wagon).

1992 Eagle Summit Wagon AWD

MAJOR FEATURES

● Summit 4-Door has as 1992 standard equipment: 5-speed manual transmission, independent strut front suspension, front wheel drive, manual rack-and-pinion steering, front power disc brakes, steel disc wheels, and side window demister.

● Summit 4-Door ES adds as 1992 standard equipment: rear window defroster, power-assisted rack-and-pinion steering, tilt steering wheel, and various exterior and interior accessories.

● Summit 3-Door has as 1992 standard equipment: 4-speed manual transmission, independent strut front suspension, front wheel drive, manual rack-and-pinion steering, front power disc brakes, steel disc wheels, and side window demister.

● Summit 3-Door ES 1992 standard equipment: 5-speed manual transmission, and various exterior and interior accessories.

● Summit Wagon DL has as 1992 standard equipment: 5-speed manual transmission, MacPherson strut front suspension and independent rear suspension, power rack-and-pinion steering, power front disc, rear drum brakes, and front-wheel drive.

● Summit Wagon LX adds as 1992 standard equipment: tinted windows, rear seating area heat ducts, dual electric outside mirrors, and other exterior body stylings.

● Summit Wagon AWD has as 1992 standard equipment: all-wheel drive, rear seating area heat ducts, dual electric outside mirrors, front and rear mudguards, and other exterior body stylings.

● Summit DL had as 1990 standard equipment: 4-speed automatic transmission and upgraded exterior and interior body stylings.

● Summit LX 1990 had as standard equipment: 4-speed automatic transmission and an assortment of exterior body moldings and interior accessories.

PRICE HISTORY

The following new car prices reflect the approximate retail cost of the base model: **1989** - $9,347; **1990** - $8,895; **1991** - $8,618; **1992** - $7,302.

DIMENSIONS

Body Style	Years Avail	Wheel Base (in)	Lgth (in)	Ht (in)	Avg Wt (lbs)	Fuel Cap (gal)	Front Hdrm (in)	Front Legrm (in)
3d lbk	91-92	93.9	158.7	51.9	2,205	13.2	38.3	41.9
4d sdn	89-92	96.7	170.1	52.8	2,271	13.2	39.1	41.9
5d wgn	92-92	99.2	168.5	64.4	2,701	14.5	40.0	40.8

ENGINES

Type	Displace-ment (L)	Fuel Dly	HP @rpm	Torque @rpm (ft/lbs)	MPG Cty/Hwy	Years Avail
I-4	1.6	FI	113@6500	99@5000	23/28	89-89
I-4	1.5	FI	81@5500	91@3000	28/34	89-90
I-4	1.6	FI	123@6500	137@5000	23/28	90-90
I-4	1.5	FI	92@6000	93@3000	29/35	91-92
I-4	1.8	FI	113@6,000	116@4,500	23/29	92-92
I-4	2.4	FI	116@5,000	136@3,500	19/24	92-92

KEY: I=in-line engine; V=V engine; F=flat engine; FI=fuel injection; bbl=barrel carburetor; T=turbo; D=diesel; HP=horsepower; MPG=estimated average miles per gallon.

EVALUATIONS, TESTS, AND RANKINGS

1992: "economical engine with more than enough torque. . .interior is a cloth-and-vinyl joy. . .rear bench offers more-than-usual legroom." **Source**: "Chrysler's Wee Hauler Named Summit," *New York Times*, December 29, 1991.

1991: "pleasant econobox." **Source**: "Eagle Summit," *Road & Track*, October 1990, p. 65.

1991: "Summit ES models use a high-revving 1.6-liter power plant that seems to know no upper limit . . . clearly superior on the track and road . . . emerges as the most wholesome of the four, winning points for overall driving pleasure, ride, comfort, and handling." **Source**: "Global Designs For Compact Sedans," *Popular Science*, November 1990, pp. 91-95.

1991: "Compared to the Corolla/Prizm . . . the Mirage/Summit was definitelysecond rank." **Source**: "Blind Taste Test," *Popular Mechanics*, November 1990, pp. 43-47, 124-125.

1989: "Resculpted for 1989. . .drivers have a better view in all directions. . .new, larger instruments easier to read." **Source**: "Dodge/Plymouth Colt, Eagle Summit," *Road & Track— Buyer's Guide 1989*, 1988, p. 53.

1989: "The five-speed manual gearbox is a joy . . . steering is accurate, and the suspension dances through the twisties with modest understeer . . . A high-g run through a choppy bend can produce some pretty unsavory body motions." **Source**: "Eagle Summit LX," *Car and Driver*, August 1989, pp. 130-131, 134-135.

RECALLS

None to date.

REPAIR MANUALS

1164 ● **Chilton's Guide to Chassis Electronics and Power Accessories, 1988-1991 Ford/Chrysler/Jeep/Eagle**
Chilton Co.
Chilton Way
Radnor, PA 19089   Ph:(215)964-4000

Published March 1991. **Price**: $19.95.

ASSOCIATIONS

1165 ● **Chrysler Product Owners Club**
5203 Edmondson Ave.
Baltimore, MD 21229
Brian K. Scott, Exec. Officer

Founded: 1978. **Membership**: 210. Collectors and restorers of Chrysler-product automobiles. Promotes the collection, preservation, restoration, maintenance, exhibition, and enjoyment of all Chrysler product cars, trucks, and other vehicles, including Chrysler, DeSoto, Dodge, Imperial, and Plymouth. Offers technical advice; provides list of cars, parts, and services. Maintains library of service and parts manuals from the 1930s to 1989. **Convention/Meeting:** Annual.

1166 ● WPC Club
P.O. Box 3504
Kalamazoo, MI 49003-3504
Ralph Kendall, Pres.   Ph:(616)372-1067

Founded: 1969. **Membership:** 4,850. Individuals dedicated to the preservation, restoration, and enjoyment of Chrysler product cars. Conducts social activities; houses library. Awards annual trophies at national meets. **Convention/Meeting:** Annual; also sponsors International Winter Photo Meet.

EAGLE TALON (1990-92)

Two-door sports coupe listed in the EPA small specialty vehicle class. Produced since 1990 at the Diamond-Star Motors plant in Normal, Illinois (plant parts data: domestic parts - 35%, imported parts - 65%; *Federal Trade Zone Board*, 1989). The Talon TSi was named to *Car and Driver's* Ten Best Cars list in 1990, 1991, and 1992, and *Automobile Magazine* named Talon to its 1990 All-Stars Team. Both Motorweek (PBS-TV) and the Automobile Journalists' Association of Canada named it "Best Sports Coupe of the Year" in 1990. Corporate twin of the Plymouth Laser and corporate cousin of the Mitsubishi Eclipse.

1992 Eagle Talon TSi AWD

MAJOR FEATURES

● Talon FWD has as 1992 standard equipment: 5-speed manual overdrive transmission, front-wheel drive, independent, MacPherson-type struts suspension, power-assisted, hydraulic rack-and-pinion steering, four-wheel power disc brakes, polycast wheels, rear window defroster, sport instrumentation, and a spoiler.

● Talon TSi FWD adds as 1992 standard equipment: intercooled turbocharged engine, performance fascias and lower bodyside aero effects, and additional interior stylings.

● Talon TSi AWD adds as 1992 standard equipment: intercooled turbocharged engine, all-wheel drive, alloy wheels, performance fascias and lower bodyside aero effects; performance enthusiast suspension with upgraded springs, struts, and stabilizer bars, and independent, double wishbone rear design; and additional interior stylings.

PRICE HISTORY

The following new car prices reflect the approximate retail cost of the base model: **1990** - $12,995; **1991** - $12,990; **1992** - $13,862.

DIMENSIONS

Body Style	Years Avail	Wheel Base (in)	Lgth (in)	Ht (in)	Avg Wt (lbs)	Fuel Cap (gal)	Front Hdrm (in)	Front Legrm (in)
2d cpe	90-91	97.2	170.5	51.4	2,711	15.8	37.9	43.9
2d cpe	92-92	97.2	172.4	51.4	2,712	15.8	37.9	43.9

ENGINES

Type	Displacement (L)	Fuel Dly	HP @rpm	Torque @rpm (ft/lbs)	MPG Cty/Hwy	Years Avail
I-4	2.0	FI	135@6000	125@5000	22/29	90-92
I-4T	2.0	FI	190@6000	203@3000	21/28	90-91
I-4T	2.0	FI	195@6000	203@3000	20/25	90-92

KEY: I=in-line engine; V=V engine; F=flat engine; FI=fuel injection; bbl=barrel carburetor; T=turbo; D=diesel; HP=horsepower; MPG=estimated average miles per gallon.

EVALUATIONS, TESTS, AND RANKINGS

1991: "really does have claws with its turbocharged, 203-bhp engine. . ." **Source:** "Eagle Talon," *Road & Track*, October 1991.

1991: "Outstanding value for the money. . .stunning acceleration. . .Brake performance is in the top rank of non-ABS systems. . .[non] all-wheel drive versions torque steer can be a nuisance. . .Rear seat room is abysmal, possibly the worst in the class." **Source:** "Diamond-Star Coupes: An All-Star Play," *Autoweek AutoFile Annual*, 1991, pp. 34-38.

1991: "Strong point: an incredible propensity to make mass quantities of real estate disappear in the rearview mirror. . .The only disappointment has been mediocre gas mileage. . .few cars can decelerate this hard." **Source:** "Long-Term Test Cars; Eagle Talon TSi," *Popular Mechanics*, November 1990, pp. 57-59, 138.

1991: "a splendid, high-performance coupe . . . interior is logical and comfortable . . . instruments are easy to see and get top marks for being simple and easy to use." **Source:** "Talon's power enough 'go' for most drivers," *The Flint Journal*, May 8, 1991, pp. E1, E2.

1990: "one of the best performance-car deals of the year." **Source:** "Eagle Talon," *Motor Trend—1990 New Car Buyer's Guide*, 1990, p. 92.

1990: "an affordable approach to high-performance in all-wheel drive. . .thoughtful construction and meaningful details." **Source:** "New Car Highlights; Eagle Talon TSi AWD," *Motor Trend—1990 Buyer's Guide*, 1990, pp. 38-39.

1990: "Full-time all-wheel drive system designed to increase overall highway performance and boost traction on slippery surfaces." **Source:** "Eagle expects to gain foothold with Talon," *The Detroit News*, September 28, 1989, pp. E1-E2.

RECALLS

1990: (210 passenger cars; includes Mitsubishi Eclipse, Eagle Talon, and Plymouth Laser models. NHTSA Campaign Nos. 90V106001 and 90V106002 address same defect): Diluted primer may have been used on the windshield opening flanges prior to windshield glass installation which would not provide the retention required by FMVSS 212. Windshields would not prevent ejection of vehicle occupants during a vehicle crash, which causes serious injuries and fatalities. **Corrective action:** Replace windshields, associated parts, and primer. *(NHTSA Campaign No. 90V106000.)*

1990: (632 passenger cars equipped with Diamond-Star Motors sunroofs; includes Eagle Talon, Mitsubishi Eclipse, and Plymouth Laser models. NHTSA Campaign Nos. 90V056001 and 90V056002 address same defect): Operation of sunroof in non-standard manner may cause male hinge disengagement from the roof hinge receiver. Sunroof glass could detach fromthe roof and result in injury to occupants or persons in the vicinity. **Corrective action:** Replace male hinge with a modified version to increase roof hinge receiver retention ability. *(NHTSA Campaign No. 90V056000.)*

REPAIR MANUALS

1167 ● **Chilton's Guide to Chassis Electronics and Power Accessories, 1988-1991 Ford/Chrysler/Jeep/Eagle**
Chilton Co.
Chilton Way
Radnor, PA 19089   Ph:(215)964-4000

Published March 1991. **Price:** $19.95.

ASSOCIATIONS

1168 ● **Chrysler Performance Parts Association**
Box 1210
Azusa, CA 91702   Ph:(818)303-6220
Roland Osborne, Chm.   Fax:(818)303-2481

Founded: 1976. **Membership:** 5,000. Clearinghouse for information on from whom, where, and how to obtain vintage, muscle, and high-tech Chrysler performance parts. **Former Name(s):** (1979) National HEMI Owners; (1980) MOPAR Muscle Club. **Convention/Meeting:** Annual national meet.

1169 ● **Chrysler Product Owners Club**
5203 Edmondson Ave.
Baltimore, MD 21229
Brian K. Scott, Exec. Officer

Founded: 1978. **Membership:** 210. Collectors and restorers of Chrysler-product automobiles. Promotes the collection, preservation, restoration, maintenance, exhibition, and enjoyment of all Chrysler product cars, trucks, and other vehicles, including Chrysler, DeSoto, Dodge, Imperial, and Plymouth. Offers technical advice; provides list of cars, parts, and services. Maintains library of service and parts manuals from the 1930s to 1989. **Convention/Meeting:** Annual.

1170 ● **Special Interest Auto Club**
P.O. Box 681
Centreville, VA 22020
Stephen L. DiGiulian, Pres.   Ph:(703)631-0018

Founded: 1978. **Membership:** 2,000. Owners and enthusiasts of Chrysler high-performance automobiles manufactured from 1964 to the present including Dodge Challengers and Plymouth Barracudas. Purpose is to help restore and preserve Chrysler high-performance cars. Maintains merchandise department and parts program listing cars and parts wanted and for sale. Sponsors national and regional shows and meets; compiles statistics; maintains biographical archives and speakers' bureau. **Former Name(s):** (1981) T/A-AAR Special Interest Auto Club. **Convention/Meeting:** Annual (with exhibits) - always July, midwestern U.S.

1171 ● **WPC Club**
P.O. Box 3504
Kalamazoo, MI 49003-3504
Ralph Kendall, Pres.   Ph:(616)372-1067

Founded: 1969. **Membership:** 4,850. Individuals dedicated to the preservation, restoration, and enjoyment of Chrysler product cars. Conducts social activities; houses library. Awards annual trophies at national meets. **Convention/Meeting:** Annual; also sponsors International Winter Photo Meet.

FERRARI 328 (1987-89)

Luxury sports car competes with the Ford Corvette ZR-1 and the 300ZX Turbo. Produced in Modena, Italy until 1989, the Ferrari 328 replaced the 308.

MAJOR FEATURES

● Ferrari 328 had as 1989 standard equipment: leather interior, electric windows, front and rear disc brakes, 5-speed manual transmission, and air conditioning.

● Ferrari 328 GTE added as 1989 standard equipment: targa roof.

● Ferrari 328 GTS added as standard equipment: coupe trim, tube shocks, and anti-roll bar.

● Ferrari 328 Quattrovalvole added as standard equipment: front and rear independent suspensions, and handcrafted coachwork.

PRICE HISTORY

The following new car prices reflect the approximate retail cost of the base model: **1987** - $64,500; **1988** - $71,900; **1989** - $77,900.

DIMENSIONS

Body Style	Years Avail	Wheel Base (in)	Lgth (in)	Ht (in)	Avg Wt (lbs)	Fuel Cap (gal)	Front Hdrm (in)	Front Legrm (in)
2d cpe	87-89	92.5	168.7	40.1	3,140	18.5	34.5	na
2d trga	87-89	92.5	168.7	40.1	3,140	18.5	34.5	na

ENGINES

Type	Displacement (L)	Fuel Dly	HP @rpm	Torque @rpm (ft/lbs)	MPG Cty/Hwy	Years Avail
V-8	3.2	FI	260@7000	214@5500	13/18	87-89

KEY: I=in-line engine; V=V engine; F=flat engine; FI=fuel injection; bbl=barrel carburetor; T=turbo; D=diesel; HP=horsepower; MPG=estimated average miles per gallon.

EVALUATIONS, TESTS, AND RANKINGS

1989: "sleek, snarky, and downright low . . . steering wheel is still in the Italian position. . .engine noise is a constant. . .Ferrari has built an excellent vehicle." **Source:** "Ferrari Fun in the Florida Sun," *Motor Trend*, September 1989, pp. 70-2, 74-5.

1989: "U.S. regulation has russled a lot of the horses out of Ferrari's corral." **Source:** "Ferrari 328GTE and 328GTS," *Road & Track—Buyer's Guide 1989*, 1988, p. 67.

1989: "sleeker and more agile than the larger, more expensive Testarossa." **Source:** "2 for the Road," *Regardie's Magazine*, September 1989, pp. 169-170, 172-180, 182.

1988: "[328 GTS] didn't differ remarkably from the one we evaluated in May 1986. . .displayed its *pur sang* in feeling rock solid up to its top speed." **Source:** "Five Exotic Convertibles: Whining through the gears in California's Napa and Sonoma," *Road & Track*, July 1988, pp. 52-9.

RECALLS

1987-88: (1,331 vehicles; includes models made before 1987): Front lower suspension arm forks could deform after substantial impacts, such as in an accident, possibly resulting in eventual collapse of the suspension arm with impaired handling, which could result in an accident. **Corrective action:** Replace four front lower suspension arm forks of a greater thickness. *(NHTSA Campaign No. 89V111000.)*

OTHER INFORMATION SOURCES

1172 ● The Complete Book of Ferrari
Publications International Ltd.
7373 N. Cicero Ave.
Lincolnwood, IL 60646   Ph:(312)676-3470

Published 1989. **Price:** $15.95.

1173 ● European Car
Argus Publishers Corp.
12100 Wilshire Blvd., Ste. 250   Ph:(213)820-3601
Los Angeles, CA 90025   Fax:(213)207-9388

Magazine covering Volkswagen, Porsche, Mercedes-Benz, Audi, Ferrari, Jaguar, and BMW automobiles. Bimonthly. **Editor(s):** Greg N. Brown. **Price:** $11.00 per year; $2.75 per issue.

1174 ● Exotic Cars of the World: Fabulous Ferraris
Pools & Crew Communications
922 NW 50th St.
Seattle, WA 98107   Ph:(206)782-5755

The most sought after cars on the market are introduced here in the collection of one man. A plethora of models line the garage of this Ferrari fanatic. **Acquisition:** Purchase.

1175 ● Fantasy Cars
Increase Video
6860 Canby Ave., Ste. 117-118   Ph:(818)342-2880
Reseda, CA 91335   Fax:(818)342-4029

A Lamborghini, Ferrari, and Porsche are taken for a test drive. **Release date:** 1989. **Producer:** Increase Video. **Price:** $29.95.

1176 ● Ferrari Club Magazine
Ferrari Owners Club
1708 Seabright Ave.
Long Beach, CA 90813   Ph:(213)432-9607

Magazine for Ferrari owners.

1177 ● Ferrari Club of America—Bulletin
Ferrari Club of America (FCA)
9632 SE City View Dr.
Portland, OR 97266   Ph:(503)777-1240

Monthly.

1178 ● Ferrari Club of America—Membership Roster
Ferrari Club of America (FCA)
9632 SE City View Dr.
Portland, OR 97266   Ph:(503)777-1240

Biennial.

1179 ● Ferrari: Forty Years on the Road
Motorbooks International
729 Prospect Ave.
Osceola, WI 54020   Ph:(715)294-3345

Published 1989. **Editor(s):** Stanley Nowak. **Price:** $59.95.

1180 ● Ferrari: Guide to Performance
Motorbooks International
729 Prospect Ave.
Osceola, WI 54020   Ph:(715)294-3345

Published 1987. **Editor(s):** Allen Bishop-Faulkner. **Price:** $14.95.

1181 ● Ferrari Index
Ferrari Data Bank (FDB)
Rte. 3, PO Box 425
Jasper, FL 32052   Ph:(904)792-2480

Annual.

1182 ● Ferrari Journal
Ferrari Data Bank
Rte. 3
P.O. Box 425
Jasper, FL 32052   Ph:(904)792-2480

Contains articles on Ferrari as well as classified ads for Ferrari automobiles. Monthly. **Editor(s):** Robert Marvin. **Price:** $24.00 per year; $3.00 per copy.

1183 ● Ferrari Owners Club—Directory and Yearbook
Ferrari Owners Club (FOC)
1708 Seabright Ave.
Long Beach, CA 90813   Ph:(213)432-9607

Annual.

1184 ● Ferrari Owners Club—Newsletter
Ferrari Owners Club (FOC)
1708 Seabright Ave.
Long Beach, CA 90813   Ph:(213)432-9607

Monthly.

1185 ● Ferrari Register
Ferrari Data Bank (FDB)
Rte. 3, PO Box 425
Jasper, FL 32052   Ph:(904)792-2480

Annual.

1186 ● Ferrari: The Road Cars
Haynes Publications, Inc.
861 Lawrence Dr.
Newbury Park, CA 91320   Ph:(818)889-5400

Published 1988. **Editor(s):** Antoine Prunet. **Price:** $45.00.

1187 ● Four for the Road: Corvette, Ferrari, Mercedes-Benz, Porsche—The Greatest of the Survivors Series
Motorbooks International
729 Prospect Ave.
Osceola, WI 54020   Ph:(715)294-3345

Published 1989. **Editor(s):** Henry Rasmussen. **Price:** $19.95.

1188 ● Great Marques Ferrari
Book Sales, Inc.
110 Enterprise Ave.
Secaucus, NJ 07094-1995   Ph:(201)864-6341

Published 1989. **Price:** $10.98.

1189 ● Inside Ferrari
Motorbooks International
729 Prospect Ave.
Osceola, WI 54020   Ph:(715)294-3345

Published 1990. **Editor(s):** Michael Dregni. **Price:** $29.95.

1190 ● Prancing Horse
Ferrari Club of America (FCA)
9632 SE City View Dr.
Portland, OR 97266   Ph:(503)777-1240

Quarterly.

ASSOCIATIONS

1191 ● Ferrari Club of America
9632 SE City View Dr.
Portland, OR 97266-6903   Ph:(503)777-1240
Tom Williamson Jr.,, Pres.   Fax:(303)777-1240

Founded: 1962. **Membership:** 3,500. Individuals and firms having an interest in Ferrari automobiles. Purposes are: to inspire ownership, operation, restoration, and preservation of Ferrari automobiles; to serve members as a source of information regarding Ferrari history and technical data; to organize meets and exhibits; to assist members in locating Ferrari automobiles and parts. Conducts technical seminars; sponsors competitions and bestows awards; maintains biographical archives. **Convention/Meeting:** Annual meet (with exhibits).

1192 ● Ferrari Club of America, Northwest Region
18515 SE 287th St.
Kent, WA 98042
Bruce Patzmann, Exec. Officer   Ph:(206)630-2286

1193 ● Ferrari Data Bank
Rte. 3, P.O. Box 425
Jasper, FL 32052
Dr. Robert B. Marvin, Curator   Ph:(904)792-2480

Founded: 1980. **Membership:** 7,800. Owners, clubs, dealers, and enthusiasts of Ferrari automobiles manufactured from 1948 to the present. Collects and publishes data on individual Ferrari cars. Acts as an information resource; maintains biographical archives and 5000 volume library of books, letters, and photographs on automobiles and related subjects. Compiles statistics; maintains museum.

1194 ● Ferrari Owners Club
1708 Seabright Ave.
Long Beach, CA 90813   Ph:(213)432-9607
Pat Benz, Mgr.   Fax:(213)983-1430

Founded: 1961. **Membership:** 1,700. Ferrari owners and enthusiasts. Promotes and seeks to further the enjoyment of the Ferrari automobile. Sponsors competitions and special events; bestows awards. Holds monthly gathering which includes rallies, tours, time trials, and dinner. **Convention/Meeting:** Holds annual West Coast Ferrari Literature and Model Meet (with exhibits).

FERRARI 348 (1990-92)

Introduced in 1990 model year, this transverse mounted mid-engine sports car replaced the Ferrari 328 series. Competes with the Chevrolet Corvette ZR-1. Named among the Ten Best Cars in the World in 1991 by *Road & Track*. Named to the 1991 *Automobile Magazine* All-Star Team. The Ferrari 348 is currently built in Modena, Italy.

MAJOR FEATURES

● 348 1992 standard equipment: 5-speed manual transmission, anti-roll bars, vented front and rear disc-brakes, rack and pinion steering, feul injection, and independent front and rear suspension.

● 348ts 1992 added standard equipment: targa top, gearbox mounted transversale, adjustable steering wheel, and various interior adjustments.

● 348tb added as 1992 added standard equipment: rear wheel drive coupe and various body style adjustments.

PRICE HISTORY

The following new car prices reflect the approximate retail cost of the base model: **1990** - $100,000; **1991** - $103,500.

DIMENSIONS

Body Style	Years Avail	Wheel Base (in)	Lgth (in)	Ht (in)	Avg Wt (lbs)	Fuel Cap (gal)	Front Hdrm (in)	Front Legrm (in)
2d cpe	90-92	96.5	166.7	46.1	3,223	23.2	na	na
2d trga	90-92	96.5	166.7	46.1	3,223	23.2	na	na

ENGINES

Type	Displacement (L)	Fuel Dly	HP @rpm	Torque @rpm (ft/lbs)	MPG Cty/Hwy	Years Avail
V-8T	3.4	FI	300@7000	228@4000	13/18	90-92

KEY: I=in-line engine; V=V engine; F=flat engine; FI=fuel injection; bbl=barrel carburetor; T=turbo; D=diesel; HP=horsepower; MPG=estimated average miles per gallon.

EVALUATIONS, TESTS, AND RANKINGS

1991: "may well be the best engineered Ferrari yet developed for road use." **Source:** "Ferrari 348tb & ts," *Road & Track*, December 1990.

1991: "exciting, balanced performance . . . benchmark for all followers and pretenders." **Source:** "Ferrari 348tb," *Automobile Magazine*, January 1991, p. 56.

1990: "looks potent and imposing on the road . . . suspension is stiff, but there's little harshness over small imperfections." **Source:** "Ferrari 348tb," *Car and Driver*, December 1989, pp. 33-35, 37.

1990: "It looks good, and it goes superbly, but it doesn't sound like a V-8 . . . It's simply an efficient device, to be used to the fullest." **Source:** "Ferrari 348: It's more attractive than it looks," *Motor Trend*, March 1990, pp. 94-96, 98, 141.

RECALLS

None to date.

OTHER INFORMATION SOURCES

1195 ● The Complete Book of Ferrari
Publications International Ltd.
7373 N. Cicero Ave.
Lincolnwood, IL 60646   Ph:(312)676-3470

Published 1989. **Price:** $15.95.

1196 ● European Car
Argus Publishers Corp.
12100 Wilshire Blvd., Ste. 250   Ph:(213)820-3601
Los Angeles, CA 90025   Fax:(213)207-9388

Magazine covering Volkswagen, Porsche, Mercedes-Benz, Audi, Ferrari, Jaguar, and BMW automobiles. Bimonthly. **Editor(s):** Greg N. Brown. **Price:** $11.00 per year; $2.75 per issue.

1197 ● Exotic Cars of the World: Fabulous Ferraris
Pools & Crew Communications
922 NW 50th St.
Seattle, WA 98107   Ph:(206)782-5755

The most sought after cars on the market are introduced here in the collection of one man. A plethora of models line the garage of this Ferrari fanatic. **Acquisition:** Purchase.

1198 ● Fantasy Cars
Increase Video
6860 Canby Ave., Ste. 117-118   Ph:(818)342-2880
Reseda, CA 91335   Fax:(818)342-4029

A Lamborghini, Ferrari, and Porsche are taken for a test drive. **Release date:** 1989. **Producer:** Increase Video. **Price:** $29.95.

1199 ● Ferrari Club Magazine
Ferrari Owners Club
1708 Seabright Ave.
Long Beach, CA 90813   Ph:(213)432-9607

Magazine for Ferrari owners.

1200 ● Ferrari Club of America—Bulletin
Ferrari Club of America (FCA)
9632 SE City View Dr.
Portland, OR 97266   Ph:(503)777-1240

Monthly.

1201 ● Ferrari Club of America—Membership Roster
Ferrari Club of America (FCA)
9632 SE City View Dr.
Portland, OR 97266   Ph:(503)777-1240

Biennial.

1202 ● Ferrari: Forty Years on the Road
Motorbooks International
729 Prospect Ave.
Osceola, WI 54020   Ph:(715)294-3345

Published 1989. **Editor(s):** Stanley Nowak. **Price:** $59.95.

1203 ● Ferrari: Guide to Performance
Motorbooks International
729 Prospect Ave.
Osceola, WI 54020   Ph:(715)294-3345

Published 1987. **Editor(s):** Allen Bishop-Faulkner. **Price:** $14.95.

1204 ● Ferrari Index
Ferrari Data Bank (FDB)
Rte. 3, PO Box 425
Jasper, FL 32052   Ph:(904)792-2480

Annual.

1205 ● Ferrari Journal
Ferrari Data Bank
Rte. 3
P.O. Box 425
Jasper, FL 32052   Ph:(904)792-2480

Contains articles on Ferrari as well as classified ads for Ferrari automobiles. Monthly. **Editor(s):** Robert Marvin. **Price:** $24.00 per year; $3.00 per copy.

1206 ● Ferrari Owners Club—Directory and Yearbook
Ferrari Owners Club (FOC)
1708 Seabright Ave.
Long Beach, CA 90813   Ph:(213)432-9607

Annual.

1207 ● Ferrari Owners Club—Newsletter
Ferrari Owners Club (FOC)
1708 Seabright Ave.
Long Beach, CA 90813   Ph:(213)432-9607

Monthly.

1208 ● Ferrari Register
Ferrari Data Bank (FDB)
Rte. 3, PO Box 425
Jasper, FL 32052   Ph:(904)792-2480

Annual.

1209 ● Ferrari: The Road Cars
Haynes Publications, Inc.
861 Lawrence Dr.
Newbury Park, CA 91320   Ph:(818)889-5400

Published 1988. **Editor(s):** Antoine Prunet. **Price:** $45.00.

1210 ● Four for the Road: Corvette, Ferrari, Mercedes-Benz, Porsche—The Greatest of the Survivors Series
Motorbooks International
729 Prospect Ave.
Osceola, WI 54020   Ph:(715)294-3345

Published 1989. **Editor(s):** Henry Rasmussen. **Price:** $19.95.

1211 ● Great Marques Ferrari
Book Sales, Inc.
110 Enterprise Ave.
Secaucus, NJ 07094-1995   Ph:(201)864-6341

Published 1989. **Price:** $10.98.

1212 ● Inside Ferrari
Motorbooks International
729 Prospect Ave.
Osceola, WI 54020   Ph:(715)294-3345

Published 1990. **Editor(s):** Michael Dregni. **Price:** $29.95.

1213 ● Prancing Horse
Ferrari Club of America (FCA)
9632 SE City View Dr.
Portland, OR 97266   Ph:(503)777-1240

Quarterly.

ASSOCIATIONS

1214 ● Ferrari Club of America
9632 SE City View Dr.
Portland, OR 97266-6903   Ph:(503)777-1240
Tom Williamson Jr.,, Pres.   Fax:(303)777-1240

Founded: 1962. **Membership:** 3,500. Individuals and firms having an interest in Ferrari automobiles. Purposes are: to inspire ownership, operation, restoration, and preservation of Ferrari automobiles; to serve members as a source of information regarding Ferrari history and technical data; to organize meets and exhibits; to assist members in locating Ferrari automobiles and parts. Conducts technical seminars; sponsors competitions and bestows awards; maintains biographical archives. **Convention/Meeting:** Annual meet (with exhibits).

1215 ● Ferrari Club of America, Northwest Region
18515 SE 287th St.
Kent, WA 98042
Bruce Patzmann, Exec. Officer   Ph:(206)630-2286

1216 ● Ferrari Data Bank
Rte. 3, P.O. Box 425
Jasper, FL 32052
Dr. Robert B. Marvin, Curator   Ph:(904)792-2480

Founded: 1980. **Membership:** 7,800. Owners, clubs, dealers, and enthusiasts of Ferrari automobiles manufactured from 1948 to the present. Collects and publishes data on individual Ferrari cars. Acts as an information resource; maintains biographical archives and 5000 volume library of books, letters, and photographs on automobiles and related subjects. Compiles statistics; maintains museum.

1217 ● Ferrari Owners Club
1708 Seabright Ave.
Long Beach, CA 90813   Ph:(213)432-9607
Pat Benz, Mgr.   Fax:(213)983-1430

Founded: 1961. **Membership:** 1,700. Ferrari owners and enthusiasts. Promotes and seeks to further the enjoyment of the Ferrari automobile. Sponsors competitions and special events; bestows awards. Holds monthly gathering which includes rallies, tours, time trials, and dinner. **Convention/Meeting:** Holds annual West Coast Ferrari Literature and Model Meet (with exhibits).

FERRARI F40 (1990-92)

Built in Modena, Italy, the Ferrari F40 is a competition sports car converted to street use.

MAJOR FEATURES

● Ferrari F40 1992 standard equipment: fuel injection, anti-roll bars, front and rear vented disc brakes, plastic windows that do not roll down, 2 turbos, 5-speed manual transmission.

PRICE HISTORY

The following new car prices reflect the approximate retail cost of the base model: **1990** - $300,000; **1991** - $415,000; **1992** - $450,000.

DIMENSIONS

Body Style	Years Avail	Wheel Base (in)	Lgth (in)	Ht (in)	Avg Wt (lbs)	Fuel Cap (gal)	Front Hdrm (in)	Front Legrm (in)
2d cpe	90-92	96.5	171.3	44.3	2,980	26.4	na	na

ENGINES

Type	Displacement (L)	Fuel Dly	HP @rpm	Torque @rpm (ft/lbs)	MPG Cty/Hwy	Years Avail
V-8	2.9	FI	478@7000	425@4000	12/17	90-92

KEY: I=in-line engine; V=V engine; F=flat engine; FI=fuel injection; bbl=barrel carburetor; T=turbo; D=diesel; HP=horsepower; MPG=estimated average miles per gallon.

EVALUATIONS, TESTS, AND RANKINGS

1991: "entire car quivers with readiness." **Source:** "Ferrari F40," *Road & Track—The Complete Car Buyer's Guide 1991,* 1990, p. 91.

1991: "Flat out, it goes 197. You have our word . . . It growls, it whooshes, it whirs." **Source:** "Ferrari F40," *Car and Driver,* February 1991, pp. 33-37.

1991: "true to the contemporary exotic-car formula of performance first and practicality last." **Source:** "Ferrari F40," *Road & Track,* October 1991, pp. 86-90.

1990: "it catapults from 0 to 60 mph in 3.9 sec . . . and runs on to 201 mph." **Source:** "Reigning Champions," *Motor Trend,* July 1990, pp. 44-50, 52.

RECALLS

None to date.

OTHER INFORMATION SOURCES

1218 ● The Complete Book of Ferrari
Publications International Ltd.
7373 N. Cicero Ave.
Lincolnwood, IL 60646   Ph:(312)676-3470

Published 1989. **Price:** $15.95.

1219 ● European Car
Argus Publishers Corp.
12100 Wilshire Blvd., Ste. 250
Los Angeles, CA 90025   Ph:(213)820-3601
                                              Fax:(213)207-9388

Magazine covering Volkswagen, Porsche, Mercedes-Benz, Audi, Ferrari, Jaguar, and BMW automobiles. Bimonthly. **Editor(s):** Greg N. Brown. **Price:** $11.00 per year; $2.75 per issue.

1220 ● Exotic Cars of the World: Fabulous Ferraris
Pools & Crew Communications
922 NW 50th St.
Seattle, WA 98107   Ph:(206)782-5755

The most sought after cars on the market are introduced here in the collection of one man. A plethora of models line the garage of this Ferrari fanatic. **Acquisition:** Purchase.

1221 ● Fantasy Cars
Increase Video
6860 Canby Ave., Ste. 117-118
Reseda, CA 91335   Ph:(818)342-2880
                                              Fax:(818)342-4029

A Lamborghini, Ferrari, and Porsche are taken for a test drive. **Release date:** 1989. **Producer:** Increase Video. **Price:** $29.95.

1222 ● Ferrari Club Magazine
Ferrari Owners Club
1708 Seabright Ave.
Long Beach, CA 90813   Ph:(213)432-9607

Magazine for Ferrari owners.

1223 ● Ferrari Club of America—Bulletin
Ferrari Club of America (FCA)
9632 SE City View Dr.
Portland, OR 97266   Ph:(503)777-1240

Monthly.

1224 ● Ferrari Club of America—Membership Roster
Ferrari Club of America (FCA)
9632 SE City View Dr.
Portland, OR 97266   Ph:(503)777-1240

Biennial.

1225 ● Ferrari: Forty Years on the Road
Motorbooks International
729 Prospect Ave.
Osceola, WI 54020   Ph:(715)294-3345

Published 1989. **Editor(s):** Stanley Nowak. **Price:** $59.95.

1226 ● Ferrari: Guide to Performance
Motorbooks International
729 Prospect Ave.
Osceola, WI 54020   Ph:(715)294-3345

Published 1987. **Editor(s):** Allen Bishop-Faulkner. **Price:** $14.95.

1227 ● Ferrari Index
Ferrari Data Bank (FDB)
Rte. 3, PO Box 425
Jasper, FL 32052   Ph:(904)792-2480

Annual.

1228 ● Ferrari Journal
Ferrari Data Bank
Rte. 3
P.O. Box 425
Jasper, FL 32052   Ph:(904)792-2480

Contains articles on Ferrari as well as classified ads for Ferrari automobiles. Monthly. **Editor(s):** Robert Marvin. **Price:** $24.00 per year; $3.00 per copy.

1229 ● Ferrari Owners Club—Directory and Yearbook
Ferrari Owners Club (FOC)
1708 Seabright Ave.
Long Beach, CA 90813   Ph:(213)432-9607

Annual.

1230 ● Ferrari Owners Club—Newsletter
Ferrari Owners Club (FOC)
1708 Seabright Ave.
Long Beach, CA 90813   Ph:(213)432-9607

Monthly.

1231 ● Ferrari Register
Ferrari Data Bank (FDB)
Rte. 3, PO Box 425
Jasper, FL 32052   Ph:(904)792-2480

Annual.

1232 ● Ferrari: The Road Cars
Haynes Publications, Inc.
861 Lawrence Dr.
Newbury Park, CA 91320   Ph:(818)889-5400

Published 1988. **Editor(s):** Antoine Prunet. **Price:** $45.00.

1233 ● Four for the Road: Corvette, Ferrari, Mercedes-Benz, Porsche—The Greatest of the Survivors Series
Motorbooks International
729 Prospect Ave.
Osceola, WI 54020   Ph:(715)294-3345

Published 1989. **Editor(s):** Henry Rasmussen. **Price:** $19.95.

1234 ● Great Marques Ferrari
Book Sales, Inc.
110 Enterprise Ave.
Secaucus, NJ 07094-1995   Ph:(201)864-6341

Published 1989. **Price:** $10.98.

1235 ● Inside Ferrari
Motorbooks International
729 Prospect Ave.
Osceola, WI 54020   Ph:(715)294-3345

Published 1990. **Editor(s):** Michael Dregni. **Price:** $29.95.

1236 ● Prancing Horse
Ferrari Club of America (FCA)
9632 SE City View Dr.
Portland, OR 97266   Ph:(503)777-1240

Quarterly.

ASSOCIATIONS

1237 ● Ferrari Club of America
9632 SE City View Dr.
Portland, OR 97266-6903   Ph:(503)777-1240
Tom Williamson Jr.,, Pres.   Fax:(303)777-1240

Founded: 1962. **Membership:** 3,500. Individuals and firms having an interest in Ferrari automobiles. Purposes are: to inspire ownership, operation, restoration, and preservation of Ferrari automobiles; to serve members as a source of information regarding Ferrari history and technical data; to organize meets and exhibits; to assist members in locating Ferrari automobiles and parts. Conducts technical seminars; sponsors competitions and bestows awards; maintains biographical archives. **Convention/Meeting:** Annual meet (with exhibits).

1238 ● Ferrari Club of America, Northwest Region
18515 SE 287th St.
Kent, WA 98042
Bruce Patzmann, Exec. Officer   Ph:(206)630-2286

1239 ● Ferrari Data Bank
Rte. 3, P.O. Box 425
Jasper, FL 32052
Dr. Robert B. Marvin, Curator   Ph:(904)792-2480

Founded: 1980. **Membership:** 7,800. Owners, clubs, dealers, and enthusiasts of Ferrari automobiles manufactured from 1948 to the present. Collects and publishes data on individual Ferrari cars. Acts as an information resource; maintains biographical archives and 5000 volume library of books, letters, and photographs on automobiles and related subjects. Compiles statistics; maintains museum.

1240 ● Ferrari Owners Club
1708 Seabright Ave.
Long Beach, CA 90813   Ph:(213)432-9607
Pat Benz, Mgr.   Fax:(213)983-1430

Founded: 1961. **Membership:** 1,700. Ferrari owners and enthusiasts. Promotes and seeks to further the enjoyment of the Ferrari automobile. Sponsors competitions and special events; bestows awards. Holds monthly gathering which includes rallies, tours, time trials, and dinner. **Convention/Meeting:** Holds annual West Coast Ferrari Literature and Model Meet (with exhibits).

FERRARI MONDIAL (1987-92)

Built in Modena, Italy, this luxury sports car is in competition with the Jaguar XJ-S, BMW 750iL, and Ford Mustang GT.

MAJOR FEATURES

● Ferrari Mondial t coupe 1992 standard equipment: fuel injected 5-speed manual transmission, rack and pinion steering, independent front and rear suspension, and anti-lock brakes, power windows, locks, sunroof, tilt steering wheel, four seats, and rear defroster.

● Mondial Cabriolet (convertible) 1992 standard equipment: anti-roll bar, vented rear and front disc brakes, and removable targa roof, air conditioning, various interior adjustments.

PRICE HISTORY

The following new car prices reflect the approximate retail cost of the base model: **1987** - $68,300; **1988** - $76,400; **1989** - $76,400; **1990** - $83,100; **1991** - $101,200; **1992** - $101,200.

DIMENSIONS

Body Style	Years Avail	Wheel Base (in)	Lgth (in)	Ht (in)	Avg Wt (lbs)	Fuel Cap (gal)	Front Hdrm (in)	Front Legrm (in)
2d cpe	87-87	104.3	178.5	48.6	3,426	18.5	38.5	33.5
2d cpe	88-91	104.3	182.7	49.6	3,400	18.5	38.5	33.5
2d conv	87-89	104.3	178.5	48.6	3,640	18.5	38.5	33.5
2d conv	90-92	104.3	178.5	49.8	3,462	18.5	38.5	33.5

ENGINES

Type	Displacement (L)	Fuel Dly	HP @rpm	Torque @rpm (ft/lbs)	MPG Cty/Hwy	Years Avail
V-8	3.2	FI	260@7000	213@5500	13/18	87-89
V-8	3.4	FI	300@7000	228@4000	13/17	90-92

KEY: I=in-line engine; V=V engine; F=flat engine; FI=fuel injection; bbl=barrel carburetor; T=turbo; D=diesel; HP=horsepower; MPG=estimated average miles per gallon.

EVALUATIONS, TESTS, AND RANKINGS

1991: "second pair of seats is for occasional use at best. . .power-assisted steering ... actually improves what was already one of the world's better." **Source:** "Ferrari Mondial t Cabriolet: Maranello's most practical product," *Road & Track*, January 1991, pp. 90-94.

1990: "leather-clad seats look like a million bucks, but they don't feel that way. . .steering is sensitive enough to give the driver the feeling that he's shaking hands with the front tires." **Source:** "Ferrari Mondial 3.2," *Car and Driver*, October 1989, p. 109, 111.

1987: "handling very predictable, particularly in high-speed

corners. . .added horsepower makes it easier to drive with the throttle at all speeds." **Source:** "Ferrari Mondial and Mondial Cabriolet," *Road & Track—Buyer's Guide*, 1986, p. 60.

RECALLS

None to date.

OTHER INFORMATION SOURCES

1241 ● The Complete Book of Ferrari
Publications International Ltd.
7373 N. Cicero Ave.
Lincolnwood, IL 60646   Ph:(312)676-3470

Published 1989. **Price:** $15.95.

1242 ● European Car
Argus Publishers Corp.
12100 Wilshire Blvd., Ste. 250   Ph:(213)820-3601
Los Angeles, CA 90025   Fax:(213)207-9388

Magazine covering Volkswagen, Porsche, Mercedes-Benz, Audi, Ferrari, Jaguar, and BMW automobiles. Bimonthly. **Editor(s):** Greg N. Brown. **Price:** $11.00 per year; $2.75 per issue.

1243 ● Exotic Cars of the World: Fabulous Ferraris
Pools & Crew Communications
922 NW 50th St.
Seattle, WA 98107   Ph:(206)782-5755

The most sought after cars on the market are introduced here in the collection of one man. A plethora of models line the garage of this Ferrari fanatic. **Acquisition:** Purchase.

1244 ● Fantasy Cars
Increase Video
6860 Canby Ave., Ste. 117-118   Ph:(818)342-2880
Reseda, CA 91335   Fax:(818)342-4029

A Lamborghini, Ferrari, and Porsche are taken for a test drive. **Release date:** 1989. **Producer:** Increase Video. **Price:** $29.95.

1245 ● Ferrari Club Magazine
Ferrari Owners Club
1708 Seabright Ave.
Long Beach, CA 90813   Ph:(213)432-9607

Magazine for Ferrari owners.

1246 ● Ferrari Club of America—Bulletin
Ferrari Club of America (FCA)
9632 SE City View Dr.
Portland, OR 97266   Ph:(503)777-1240

Monthly.

1247 ● Ferrari Club of America—Membership Roster
Ferrari Club of America (FCA)
9632 SE City View Dr.
Portland, OR 97266   Ph:(503)777-1240

Biennial.

1248 ● Ferrari: Forty Years on the Road
Motorbooks International
729 Prospect Ave.
Osceola, WI 54020   Ph:(715)294-3345

Published 1989. **Editor(s):** Stanley Nowak. **Price:** $59.95.

1249 ● Ferrari: Guide to Performance
Motorbooks International
729 Prospect Ave.
Osceola, WI 54020   Ph:(715)294-3345

Published 1987. **Editor(s):** Allen Bishop-Faulkner. **Price:**
$14.95.

1250 ● Ferrari Index
Ferrari Data Bank (FDB)
Rte. 3, PO Box 425
Jasper, FL 32052   Ph:(904)792-2480

Annual.

1251 ● Ferrari Journal
Ferrari Data Bank
Rte. 3
P.O. Box 425
Jasper, FL 32052   Ph:(904)792-2480

Contains articles on Ferrari as well as classified ads for Ferrari
automobiles. Monthly. **Editor(s):** Robert Marvin. **Price:** $24.00
per year; $3.00 per copy.

1252 ● Ferrari Owners Club—Directory and Yearbook
Ferrari Owners Club (FOC)
1708 Seabright Ave.
Long Beach, CA 90813   Ph:(213)432-9607

Annual.

1253 ● Ferrari Owners Club—Newsletter
Ferrari Owners Club (FOC)
1708 Seabright Ave.
Long Beach, CA 90813   Ph:(213)432-9607

Monthly.

1254 ● Ferrari Register
Ferrari Data Bank (FDB)
Rte. 3, PO Box 425
Jasper, FL 32052   Ph:(904)792-2480

Annual.

1255 ● Ferrari: The Road Cars
Haynes Publications, Inc.
861 Lawrence Dr.
Newbury Park, CA 91320   Ph:(818)889-5400

Published 1988. **Editor(s):** Antoine Prunet. **Price:** $45.00.

1256 ● Four for the Road: Corvette, Ferrari, Mercedes-Benz,
Porsche—The Greatest of the Survivors Series
Motorbooks International
729 Prospect Ave.
Osceola, WI 54020   Ph:(715)294-3345

Published 1989. **Editor(s):** Henry Rasmussen. **Price:** $19.95.

1257 ● Great Marques Ferrari
Book Sales, Inc.
110 Enterprise Ave.
Secaucus, NJ 07094-1995   Ph:(201)864-6341

Published 1989. **Price:** $10.98.

1258 ● Inside Ferrari
Motorbooks International
729 Prospect Ave.
Osceola, WI 54020   Ph:(715)294-3345

Published 1990. **Editor(s):** Michael Dregni. **Price:** $29.95.

1259 ● Prancing Horse
Ferrari Club of America (FCA)
9632 SE City View Dr.
Portland, OR 97266   Ph:(503)777-1240

Quarterly.

ASSOCIATIONS

1260 ● Ferrari Club of America
9632 SE City View Dr.
Portland, OR 97266-6903   Ph:(503)777-1240
Tom Williamson Jr.,, Pres.   Fax:(303)777-1240

Founded: 1962. **Membership:** 3,500. Individuals and firms
having an interest in Ferrari automobiles. Purposes are: to
inspire ownership, operation, restoration, and preservation of
Ferrari automobiles; to serve members as a source of
information regarding Ferrari history and technical data; to
organize meets and exhibits; to assist members in locating
Ferrari automobiles and parts. Conducts technical seminars;
sponsors competitions and bestows awards; maintains
biographical archives. **Convention/Meeting:** Annual meet
(with exhibits).

1261 ● Ferrari Club of America, Northwest Region
18515 SE 287th St.
Kent, WA 98042
Bruce Patzmann, Exec. Officer   Ph:(206)630-2286

1262 ● Ferrari Data Bank
Rte. 3, P.O. Box 425
Jasper, FL 32052
Dr. Robert B. Marvin, Curator   Ph:(904)792-2480

Founded: 1980. **Membership:** 7,800. Owners, clubs, dealers,
and enthusiasts of Ferrari automobiles manufactured from
1948 to the present. Collects and publishes data on individual
Ferrari cars. Acts as an information resource; maintains
biographical archives and 5000 volume library of books, letters,
and photographs on automobiles and related subjects.
Compiles statistics; maintains museum.

1263 ● Ferrari Owners Club
1708 Seabright Ave.
Long Beach, CA 90813   Ph:(213)432-9607
Pat Benz, Mgr.   Fax:(213)983-1430

Founded: 1961. **Membership:** 1,700. Ferrari owners and
enthusiasts. Promotes and seeks to further the enjoyment of
the Ferrari automobile. Sponsors competitions and special
events; bestows awards. Holds monthly gathering which
includes rallies, tours, time trials, and dinner.
Convention/Meeting: Holds annual West Coast Ferrari
Literature and Model Meet (with exhibits).

FERRARI TESTAROSSA (1987-92)

Produced in Modena, Italy, this high performance coupe
competes with the Corvette, Porsche, Lotus Espirit Turbo, and
Lamborghini Countach. Named one of the Top 10 Exoticars by
Motor Trend in 1988. Awarded the 1987 Ten Best Performers
in top speed category by *Car and Driver* Buyers Guide 1988.

MAJOR FEATURES

● Testarossa 1992 standard equipment: fuel injection, 4-wheel disc brakes, electric windows, 5-speed manual transmission, independent suspension, front and rear anti-roll bar, and air conditioning.

PRICE HISTORY

The following new car prices reflect the approximate retail cost of the base model: **1987** - $109,700; **1988** - $134,000; **1989** - $140,700; **1990** - $161,600; **1991** - $169,000; **1992** - $174,800.

DIMENSIONS

Body Style	Years Avail	Wheel Base (in)	Lgth (in)	Ht (in)	Avg Wt (lbs)	Fuel Cap (gal)	Front Hdrm (in)	Front Legrm (in)
2d cpe	87-92	100.4	176.6	44.5	3,660	26.5	36	na

ENGINES

Type	Displace-ment (L)	Fuel Dly	HP @rpm	Torque @rpm (ft/lbs)	MPG Cty/Hwy	Years Avail
V-12	4.9	FI	380@5750	354@4500	10/15	87-91
H-12	4.9	FI	380@5750	354@4500	11/16	89-92

KEY: I=in-line engine; V=V engine; F=flat engine; FI=fuel injection; bbl=barrel carburetor; T=turbo; D=diesel; HP=horsepower; MPG=estimated average miles per gallon.

EVALUATIONS, TESTS, AND RANKINGS

1989: "succeeded in outdoing [Lamborghini] in pure down-the-road performance." **Source:** "Ferrari Testarossa," *Road & Track—Buyer's Guide 1989*, 1988, p. 66.

1989: "car wasn't as stable as we've come to expect of Ferraris and was decidedly nervous at its top speed. . .the big flat-12 was perfectly in its element, sounding wonderfully Ferrariesque." **Source:** "Top-Speed 10: Indulging our go-fast fetish again," *Motor Trend*, September 1988, pp. 32-9, 42, 44.

1989: "goes from 0 to 60 mph in 6.2 seconds . . . air conditioning works extremely well . . . a very wide car . . . prudent drivers had better look before they leap into another lane." **Source:** "Ferrari Testarossa," *Road & Track*, October 1989, pp. 66-67, 69, 71.

1988: "are faster, more comfortable, and handle better than their predecessors." **Source:** "Top Ten Exoticars," *Motor Trend*, March 1988, pp. 33-9, 42-3, 46-9.

1987: "handling dynamics. . .seemed tailor-made to such high speeds. . .all pressures and temperatures were stable and in the green, and the engine was loafing at 6500rpm." **Source:** "Europe's Fastest of the Fast: Three redheads and a blonde," *Motor Trend*, January 1987, pp. 28-31, 34-5.

1987: "swoopiest styling in the known universe." **Source:** "Ferrari Testarosa Quad Turbo," *Motor Trend*, June 1987, pp. 57-9, 62, 64.

RECALLS

1987-88: (468 vehicles): Automatic passive restraint system may not operate due to payout motor defect in safety belt retractor assembly. Automatic operation of passive restraint system would become intermittent or completely inoperative. **Corrective action:** Replace seat belt assembly. *(NHTSA Campaign No. 88V186000.)*

OTHER INFORMATION SOURCES

1264 ● The Complete Book of Ferrari
Publications International Ltd.
7373 N. Cicero Ave.
Lincolnwood, IL 60646   Ph:(312)676-3470

Published 1989. **Price:** $15.95.

1265 ● European Car
Argus Publishers Corp.
12100 Wilshire Blvd., Ste. 250   Ph:(213)820-3601
Los Angeles, CA 90025   Fax:(213)207-9388

Magazine covering Volkswagen, Porsche, Mercedes-Benz, Audi, Ferrari, Jaguar, and BMW automobiles. Bimonthly. **Editor(s):** Greg N. Brown. **Price:** $11.00 per year; $2.75 per issue.

1266 ● Exotic Cars of the World: Fabulous Ferraris
Pools & Crew Communications
922 NW 50th St.
Seattle, WA 98107   Ph:(206)782-5755

The most sought after cars on the market are introduced here in the collection of one man. A plethora of models line the garage of this Ferrari fanatic. **Acquisition:** Purchase.

1267 ● Fantasy Cars
Increase Video
6860 Canby Ave., Ste. 117-118   Ph:(818)342-2880
Reseda, CA 91335   Fax:(818)342-4029

A Lamborghini, Ferrari, and Porsche are taken for a test drive. **Release date:** 1989. **Producer:** Increase Video. **Price:** $29.95.

1268 ● Ferrari Club Magazine
Ferrari Owners Club
1708 Seabright Ave.
Long Beach, CA 90813   Ph:(213)432-9607

Magazine for Ferrari owners.

1269 ● Ferrari Club of America—Bulletin
Ferrari Club of America (FCA)
9632 SE City View Dr.
Portland, OR 97266   Ph:(503)777-1240

Monthly.

1270 ● Ferrari Club of America—Membership Roster
Ferrari Club of America (FCA)
9632 SE City View Dr.
Portland, OR 97266   Ph:(503)777-1240

Biennial.

1271 ● Ferrari: Forty Years on the Road
Motorbooks International
729 Prospect Ave.
Osceola, WI 54020   Ph:(715)294-3345

Published 1989. **Editor(s):** Stanley Nowak. **Price:** $59.95.

1272 ● Ferrari: Guide to Performance
Motorbooks International
729 Prospect Ave.
Osceola, WI 54020   Ph:(715)294-3345

Published 1987. **Editor(s):** Allen Bishop-Faulkner. **Price:** $14.95.

1273 ● Ferrari Index
Ferrari Data Bank (FDB)
Rte. 3, PO Box 425
Jasper, FL 32052   Ph:(904)792-2480

Annual.

1274 ● Ferrari Journal
Ferrari Data Bank
Rte. 3
P.O. Box 425
Jasper, FL 32052   Ph:(904)792-2480

Contains articles on Ferrari as well as classified ads for Ferrari automobiles. Monthly. **Editor(s):** Robert Marvin. **Price:** $24.00 per year; $3.00 per copy.

1275 ● Ferrari Owners Club—Directory and Yearbook
Ferrari Owners Club (FOC)
1708 Seabright Ave.
Long Beach, CA 90813   Ph:(213)432-9607

Annual.

1276 ● Ferrari Owners Club—Newsletter
Ferrari Owners Club (FOC)
1708 Seabright Ave.
Long Beach, CA 90813   Ph:(213)432-9607

Monthly.

1277 ● Ferrari Register
Ferrari Data Bank (FDB)
Rte. 3, PO Box 425
Jasper, FL 32052   Ph:(904)792-2480

Annual.

1278 ● Ferrari Testarossa
Motorbooks International
112 Madison Ave.
New York, NY 10016   Ph:(212)532-6600

Published 1990. **Editor(s):** Philip Porter. **Price:** $19.95.

1279 ● Ferrari: The Road Cars
Haynes Publications, Inc.
861 Lawrence Dr.
Newbury Park, CA 91320   Ph:(818)889-5400

Published 1988. **Editor(s):** Antoine Prunet. **Price:** $45.00.

1280 ● Four for the Road: Corvette, Ferrari, Mercedes-Benz, Porsche—The Greatest of the Survivors Series
Motorbooks International
729 Prospect Ave.
Osceola, WI 54020   Ph:(715)294-3345

Published 1989. **Editor(s):** Henry Rasmussen. **Price:** $19.95.

1281 ● Great Marques Ferrari
Book Sales, Inc.
110 Enterprise Ave.
Secaucus, NJ 07094-1995   Ph:(201)864-6341

Published 1989. **Price:** $10.98.

1282 ● Inside Ferrari
Motorbooks International
729 Prospect Ave.
Osceola, WI 54020   Ph:(715)294-3345

Published 1990. **Editor(s):** Michael Dregni. **Price:** $29.95.

1283 ● Prancing Horse
Ferrari Club of America (FCA)
9632 SE City View Dr.
Portland, OR 97266   Ph:(503)777-1240

Quarterly.

1284 ● Supercar Showdown
Simitar Entertainment
3850 Annapolis Ln.   Ph:(612)559-6660
Plymouth, MN 55447   Fax:(612)559-0210

A Porsche 911 Turbo, Ferrari Testarossa, and Lamborghini Countach are compared. **Release date:** 1988. **Producer:** Simitar Entertainment. **Price:** $9.95.

ASSOCIATIONS

1285 ● Ferrari Club of America
9632 SE City View Dr.
Portland, OR 97266-6903   Ph:(503)777-1240
Tom Williamson Jr.,, Pres.   Fax:(303)777-1240

Founded: 1962. **Membership:** 3,500. Individuals and firms having an interest in Ferrari automobiles. Purposes are: to inspire ownership, operation, restoration, and preservation of Ferrari automobiles; to serve members as a source of information regarding Ferrari history and technical data; to organize meets and exhibits; to assist members in locating Ferrari automobiles and parts. Conducts technical seminars; sponsors competitions and bestows awards; maintains biographical archives. **Convention/Meeting:** Annual meet (with exhibits).

1286 ● Ferrari Club of America, Northwest Region
18515 SE 287th St.
Kent, WA 98042
Bruce Patzmann, Exec. Officer   Ph:(206)630-2286

1287 ● Ferrari Data Bank
Rte. 3, P.O. Box 425
Jasper, FL 32052
Dr. Robert B. Marvin, Curator   Ph:(904)792-2480

Founded: 1980. **Membership:** 7,800. Owners, clubs, dealers, and enthusiasts of Ferrari automobiles manufactured from 1948 to the present. Collects and publishes data on individual Ferrari cars. Acts as an information resource; maintains biographical archives and 5000 volume library of books, letters, and photographs on automobiles and related subjects. Compiles statistics; maintains museum.

1288 ● Ferrari Owners Club
1708 Seabright Ave.
Long Beach, CA 90813   Ph:(213)432-9607
Pat Benz, Mgr.   Fax:(213)983-1430

Founded: 1961. **Membership:** 1,700. Ferrari owners and enthusiasts. Promotes and seeks to further the enjoyment of the Ferrari automobile. Sponsors competitions and special events; bestows awards. Holds monthly gathering which includes rallies, tours, time trials, and dinner. **Convention/Meeting:** Holds annual West Coast Ferrari Literature and Model Meet (with exhibits).

FORD AEROSTAR (1987-92)

Produced in St. Louis, Missouri, the Ford Aerostar was the first domestic minivan available with both four-wheel drive and a extended-length body configuration. Received a poor mark in a complaint index in *The Car Book* in 1991.

1991 Ford Aerostar

MAJOR FEATURES

● Aerostar XL and XL Plus 1992 standard equipment: 3.0 liter V-6 engine, 5-speed manual transmission (2WD; 4WD models have 4.0-liter V-6 with 4-speed automatic transmission), power front disc/rear drum brakes with anti-lock rear system, power-assisted rack-and-pinion steering, front independent/rear live axle suspension, and driver's-side air bag.

● Aerostar XLT adds as 1992 standard equipment: front air conditioning, cloth front captain's chairs, 2-passenger middle and 3-passenger rear bench seats, liftgate convenience net, and leather-wrapped steering wheel. The Aerostar XLT has an extended length of 190.3 inches.

● Aerostar Eddie Bauer adds as 1992 standard equipment: high capacity air-conditioning, rear heater, rear seat/bed, upgraded upholstery, luggage rack, rear defogger, Super Sound System, and forged alloy wheels.

PRICE HISTORY

The following new car prices reflect the approximate retail cost of the base model: **1988** - $10,924; **1989** - $11,745; **1990** - $12,267; **1991** - $13,018; **1992** - $13,739.

DIMENSIONS

Body Style	Years Avail	Wheel Base (in)	Lgth (in)	Ht (in)	Avg Wt (lbs)	Fuel Cap (gal)	Front Hdrm (in)	Front Legrm (in)
4d van	87-88	118.9	174.9	72.9	4,120	17.0	39.5	41.5
4d van	89-92	118.9	174.9	72.9	4,900	21.0	39.5	41.4

ENGINES

Type	Displace-ment (L)	Fuel Dly	HP @rpm	Torque @rpm (ft/lbs)	MPG Cty/Hwy	Years Avail
I-4	2.3	FI	88@na	na	22/26	87-87
V-6	3.0	FI	145@4800	165@3600	17/23	87-92
V-6	4.0	FI	155@4000	230@2400	16/21	90-92

KEY: I=in-line engine; V=V engine; F=flat engine; FI=fuel injection; bbl=barrel carburetor; T=turbo; D=diesel; HP=horsepower; MPG=estimated average miles per gallon.

EVALUATIONS, TESTS, AND RANKINGS

1991: "Ride quality is on the stiff side, but long-haul comfort is surprisingly good . . . Aerostar's V-6 engine is its strong suit. Its all-around performance is spirited." **Source:** "Meet the new minivans," *New Choices for the Best Years,* October 1990, pp. 86-87.

1990: "slant-nosed aero styling and well-rounded versatility." **Source:** "Invasion of the Space Cadets," *Motor Trend,* April 1990, pp. 115-124.

1990: "impressive power." **Source:** "The Light Vantastics," *Popular Mechanics,* February 1990, pp. 62-64, 66-67.

1990: "The ride is firm, in a no-nonsense, pleasant way . . . The Aerostar's real appeal is in its distinctly untrucklike appearance and appointments." **Source:** "Mini vanguard: Four futuristic small vans that offer old-fashioned punctuality," *Home Mechanix,* March 1990, pp. 56-60.

1990: "built like a truck . . . handled and rode like one, too . . . sound system was extraordinary." **Source:** "The Best of the Minivans," *Changing Times,* July 1990, pp. 41-45.

1989: "steering felt dead . . . handled decently enough." **Source:** "Eeny, Meeny, Miney, Mini," *Car and Driver,* May 1989, pp. 62-63, 65, 67, 71, 75-77, 81.

1989: "*Ford Aerostar Eddie Bauer Edition* interior is nice blend of tasteful design and good ergonomics . . . Best compromise between car and trucklike feel and ride . . . Inconveniently sized rear cargo area." **Source:** "Minivans: Similarities are only skin deep," *Home Mechanix,* December 1988, pp. 68-71, 87.

1989: "back two benches . . . are readily removable . . . takes hauling honors . . . V6 engine is an underachiever." **Source:** "Space Machines," *Popular Science,* May 1989, pp. 40-42, 44-46, 48.

1987: "extra-cushy extra-passenger seating arrangements . . . under-hood access to engine is incredibly tight . . . suffers a wide B-pillar that sharply decreases the view over the driver's left shoulder." **Source:** "High Performance Family Vans," *Motor Trend,* June 1987, pp. 70-76.

RECALLS

1990: (30,000 vehicles): Inability to maintain pressure in the secondary system of the master cylinder could increase brake pedal travel and reduce brake performance at temperatures less than 40 degrees. Would cause reduced braking effectiveness and increased stopping distance that could result in a crash or collision. **Corrective action:** Install new design master cylinder incorporating a redesigned seal. *(NHTSA Campaign No. 89V223000.)*

1989-90: (14,300 vans equipped with quad captain's chairs): Second row right hand seat assembly has a tilt forward function. A latch retains seat in normal ride position and may release under severe frontal impact conditions, allowing seat to pivot forward. In event of accident, the risk of injury to occupant is increased. **Corrective action:** Replace seat pawl assembly with a revised design assembly. *(NHTSA Campaign No. 90V144000.)*

1987-88: (60,000 multi purpose vehicle van, equipped with optional trailer tow package; includes models made before 1987): Vehicles equipped with trailer tow package have trailer taillight relay assembly that contains wires of smaller gauge than fuse link which protects circuit. Should a short circuit occur in wiring within relay or if water intrusion occurs smaller gauge wire in relay will function as fuse link and overheat. Possibility exists for fire if wires are exposed to combustible materials. **Corrective action:** Installation of relay with wires of gauge adequate to protect circuit. *(NHTSA Campaign No. 88V091000.)*

1987-88: (112,000 vans built at the St. Louis assembly plant): Some liftgate gas cylinder-to-body attachment ball studs may fracture in either the open or closed position causing the liftgate to close suddenly, possibly resulting in bodily injury. **Corrective action:** Replace the gas cylinder-to-body attachment ball studs. *(NHTSA Campaign No. 91V136000.)*

1987: (118,787 vans equipped with captain's chairs): Vans produced without plastic cover designed to cover outboard seat back pivot hinge allowing webbing of front passenger-side safety belts to become abraded or cut due to contact with exposed hinge. Damage to belt webbing could weaken belts to point of failure increasing risk of injury in an accident or sudden stop. **Corrective action:** Install plastic pivot cover; replace belts as necessary. *(NHTSA Campaign No. 89V226000.)*

1987: (3,600,000 passenger cars and light trucks equipped with fuel injection. Recall includes several Ford, Mercury, and Lincoln models; includes models made before 1987): Spring lock fuel line coupling may not be properly engaged. Coupling could disengage due to fuel pressure, vibration, and engine movements; this would cause loss of fuel which, in presence of an ignition source, creates a fire risk. **Corrective action:** Install retainer clips over the couplings to prevent coupling separation and fuel leakage. *(NHTSA Campaign No. 87V139000.)*

SAFETY AND REPAIRS

1991: "Transmission Defect Baffles Ford; 788,796 Trucks Have It," *Automotive News,* October 28, 1991, p. 47. **Note:** 1990-91 Aerostars with automatic transmissions may have safety defect in parking gear that could allow vehicles to roll.

1991: "Ford Recalls 641,562 Units," *Automotive News,* December 2, 1991, p. 2. **Note:** 1990-91 Aerostar minivans with 3.0 liter engines will have throttle position sensors replaced.

1988: "1984-88 Mercedes 190s and 1987-88 Aerostars Recalled," *Automotive News,* October 28, 1991, p. 29. **Note:** Ball studs on rear liftgates may break.

REPAIR MANUALS

1289 ● Chilton's Ford Aerostar, 1985-1990
Chilton Co.
Chilton Way
Radnor, PA 19089   Ph:(215)964-4000

Published 1990. **Price:** $19.95.

1290 ● Chilton's Ford Repair Manual 1980-1987
Chilton Co.
Chilton Way
Radnor, PA 19089   Ph:(215)964-4000

Published 1987. **Price:** $19.95.

1291 ● Chilton's Ford Vans, 1961-1988
Chilton Co.
Chilton Way
Radnor, PA 19089   Ph:(215)964-4000

Published 1988. **Price:** $15.95.

1292 ● Chilton's Guide to Chassis Electronics and Power Accessories, 1988-1991 Ford/Chrysler/Jeep/Eagle
Chilton Co.
Chilton Way
Radnor, PA 19089   Ph:(215)964-4000

Published March 1991. **Price:** $19.95.

1293 ● Ford, Lincoln, Mercury Car Repair and Tune-Up Guide: 1972-1987
Clymer Publications
P.O. Box 1209
Overland Park, KS 66212   Ph:(913)541-6694

Published 1987. **Price:** 14.95.

1294 ● Haynes Ford Aerostar Mini-Vans Owners Workshop Manual, No. 1476: 1986-1990
Haynes Publications, Inc.
861 Lawrence Dr.
Newbury Park, CA 91320   Ph:(818)889-5400

Editor(s): J. H. Haynes and Larry Warren. **Price:** $15.95.

1295 ● Motor Auto Repair 1983-1989 Ford
Hearst Books
105 Madison Ave.
New York, NY 10016   Ph:(212)889-3050

Published 1989. **Price:** $14.95.

OTHER INFORMATION SOURCES

1296 ● FOMOCO Owners Club—Newsletter
FOMOCO Owners Club
3804 Conifer Dr.
Loveland, CO 80538   Ph:(303)669-8767

Monthly.

1297 ● Ford-Lincoln-Mercury Club of Florida—Newsletter
Ford-Lincoln-Mercury Club of Florida
P.O. Box 13514
Tampa, FL 33681   Ph:(813)839-0241

Monthly.

1298 ● Ford-O-Gram
Performance Ford Club of America
13155 U.S. Rte. 23
Ashville, OH 43103   Ph:(614)983-2273

Carries information on past and present Ford powered products for car collectors and restorers, race car enthusiasts, and truck and tractor pullers. Recurring features include reports on Club competitions and educational programs, news of members, and calendar of events. Bimonthly. **Price:** Available to members only.

1299 ● Standard Catalog of Ford 1896-1990
Krause Publications, Inc.
700 E. State St.
Iola, WI 54990   Ph:(715)445-2214

Published 1990. **Price:** $19.95.

1300 ● Your Ford: Including Lincoln-Mercury: Essential Service Information for Owners and Mechanics
Consumer Reports Books
51 E. 42nd St., Ste. 800
New York, NY 10017   Ph:(212)682-9280

Based on technical service bulletins issued to Ford and Lincoln-Mercury dealers from 1985 through 1987. Published 1988. **Editor(s):** Mort J. Schultz. **Price:** $8.00.

ASSOCIATIONS

1301 ● FOMOCO Owners Club
3633 Akron Ct.
Loveland, CO 80538
Barry Abels, Exec. Ofc.   Ph:(303)669-8767

Founded: 1985. **Membership:** 250. Individuals dedicated to the exhibition, preservation, and restoration of Edsel, Ford, Lincoln, and Mercury automobiles. Conducts charitable activities; sponsors educational programs. Bestows awards. **Convention/Meeting:** Annual (with exhibits) - 1991 September, Lakewood, CO.

FORD BRONCO (1987-92)

Large, 4-wheel drive utility vehicle based on Ford's full-sized pick-up truck. Produced at the Michigan Truck Plant in Wayne, Michigan.

1991 Ford Silver Anniversary Bronco

MAJOR FEATURES

● Bronco Custom 1992 standard equipment: 4-wheel drive, 5-speed manual transmission, power front disc/rear drum brakes with computerized anti-lock system, power steering, front independent/rear live axle suspension, automatic hublocks.

● Bronco XLT adds as 1992 standard equipment: color-keyed instrument panel appliques and an upgraded interior.

● Bronco Eddie Bauer adds as 1992 standard equipment: E40D transmission, ''Touch Drive'' electric shift transfer case, deep-dish forged-aluminum wheels, all-terrain tires, air conditioning, outside swing-away spare tire carrier, and floormats.

● The 1991 Silver Anniversary Bronco commemorated the 25th anniversary of the Bronco model. It was essentially an Eddie Bauer Bronco with trim upgrades and red accents, paint, and black leather seats.

PRICE HISTORY

The following new car prices reflect the approximate retail cost of the base model: **1988** - $12,279; **1989** - $15,909; **1990** - $16,795; **1991** - $17,639.

DIMENSIONS

Body Style	Years Avail	Wheel Base (in)	Lgth (in)	Ht (in)	Avg Wt (lbs)	Fuel Cap (gal)	Front Hdrm (in)	Front Legrm (in)
utl wgn	87-91	104.7	180.5	74.5	6,050	32.0	41.2	41.1
utl wgn	92-92	104.7	183.6	74.5	na	32.0	41.2	41.1

ENGINES

Type	Displacement (L)	Fuel Dly	HP @rpm	Torque @rpm (ft/lbs)	MPG Cty/Hwy	Years Avail
I-6	4.9	FI	145@3400	265@2000	14/17	87-92
V-8	5.8	4-bbl	na	na	11/12	87-87
V-8	5.0	FI	185@3800	265@2400	13/17	87-92
V-8	5.8	FI	200@3800	300@2800	12/16	88-92

KEY: I=in-line engine; V=V engine; F=flat engine; FI=fuel injection; bbl=barrel carburetor; T=turbo; D=diesel; HP=horsepower; MPG=estimated average miles per gallon.

EVALUATIONS, TESTS, AND RANKINGS

1991: ''Four-wheel drive allowed me to climb over everything, though the off-road ride was quite bouncy . . . rear anti-lock brakes worked wonderfully.'' **Source:** ''Ford's Bronco Marks its 25th Year,'' *The Detroit News*, November 21, 1990, pp.1D-2D.

1991: ''with the tip-and-slide front bucket seats, offers the easiest access . . . Off-pavement performance in rugged terrain found the Bronco the champ.'' **Source:** ''Selecting a Full-Size 4x4,'' *Sports Afield*, January 1991, p.36.

RECALLS

None to date.

REPAIR MANUALS

1302 ● **Chilton's Ford Repair Manual 1980-1987**
Chilton Co.
Chilton Way
Radnor, PA 19089   Ph:(215)964-4000

Published 1987. **Price:** $19.95.

1303 ● **Chilton's Guide to Chassis Electronics and Power Accessories, 1988-1991 Ford/Chrysler/Jeep/Eagle**
Chilton Co.
Chilton Way
Radnor, PA 19089   Ph:(215)964-4000

Published March 1991. **Price:** $19.95.

1304 ● **Chilton's Professional Electronics Diagnostic Manual Ford Cars and Trucks 1984-1988: Motor-Age Professional Mechanic's Edition**
Chilton Co.
Chilton Way
Radnor, PA 19089   Ph:(215)964-4000

Published 1988. **Price:** $52.00

1305 ● **Ford Four-Wheel Drive Bronco and F-Series Pickups, 1969-1987**
Clymer Publications
P.O. Box 1209
Overland Park, KS 66212   Ph:(913)541-6694

Published 1987. **Price:** $26.95.

1306 ● **Ford, Lincoln, Mercury Car Repair and Tune-Up Guide: 1972-1987**
Clymer Publications
P.O. Box 1209
Overland Park, KS 66212   Ph:(913)541-6694

Published 1987. **Price:** 14.95.

1307 ● **Ford Pickups and Bronco 1987-1990**
Chilton Co.
Chilton Way
Radnor, PA 19089   Ph:(215)964-4000

Total car care service. February 1990. **Price:** $19.95.

1308 ● **Haynes Ford Pick-Ups and Bronco Owners Workshop Manual, No. 880**
Haynes Publications, Inc.
861 Lawrence Dr.
Newbury Park, CA 91320   Ph:(818)889-5400

Editor(s): J. H. Haynes and John B. Raffa. **Price:** $15.95.

1309 ● Motor Auto Repair 1983-1989 Ford
Hearst Books
105 Madison Ave.
New York, NY 10016   Ph:(212)889-3050

Published 1989. **Price:** $14.95.

OTHER INFORMATION SOURCES

1310 ● FOMOCO Owners Club—Newsletter
FOMOCO Owners Club
3804 Conifer Dr.
Loveland, CO 80538   Ph:(303)669-8767

Monthly.

1311 ● Ford-Lincoln-Mercury Club of Florida—Newsletter
Ford-Lincoln-Mercury Club of Florida
P.O. Box 13514
Tampa, FL 33681   Ph:(813)839-0241

Monthly.

1312 ● Ford-O-Gram
Performance Ford Club of America
13155 U.S. Rte. 23
Ashville, OH 43103   Ph:(614)983-2273

Carries information on past and present Ford powered products for car collectors and restorers, race car enthusiasts, and truck and tractor pullers. Recurring features include reports on Club competitions and educational programs, news of members, and calendar of events. Bimonthly. **Price:** Available to members only.

1313 ● Standard Catalog of Ford 1896-1990
Krause Publications, Inc.
700 E. State St.
Iola, WI 54990   Ph:(715)445-2214

Published 1990. **Price:** $19.95.

**1314 ● Your Ford: Including Lincoln-Mercury: Essential
      Service Information for Owners and Mechanics**
Consumer Reports Books
51 E. 42nd St., Ste. 800
New York, NY 10017   Ph:(212)682-9280

Based on technical service bulletins issued to Ford and Lincoln-Mercury dealers from 1985 through 1987. Published 1988. **Editor(s):** Mort J. Schultz. **Price:** $8.00.

ASSOCIATIONS

1315 ● FOMOCO Owners Club
3633 Akron Ct.
Loveland, CO 80538
Barry Abels, Exec. Ofc.   Ph:(303)669-8767

Founded: 1985. **Membership:** 250. Individuals dedicated to the exhibition, preservation, and restoration of Edsel, Ford, Lincoln, and Mercury automobiles. Conducts charitable activities; sponsors educational programs. Bestows awards. **Convention/Meeting:** Annual (with exhibits) - 1991 September, Lakewood, CO.

FORD BRONCO II (1987-90)

Compact sport utility vehicle that was available in a 3-door body style in 2- or 4-wheel drive. Patterned after bigger Ford

Bronco 4x4, the Ford Bronco II was produced in Louisville, Kentucky until it was replaced in 1991 by the Ford Explorer.

MAJOR FEATURES

● Bronco II XL had as 1990 standard equipment: 5-speed manual transmission, front disc/rear drum brakes, front independent/rear live axle suspension, power steering, and anti-lock rear brakes.

● Bronco II XLT added as 1990 standard equipment: color-keyed instrument panel appliques.

● Bronco II Eddie Bauer added as 1990 standard equipment: upgraded floormats and an upgraded interior.

● Bronco II 4WD added as 1990 standard equipment: four-wheel drive system and manual locking front hubs.

PRICE HISTORY

The following new car prices reflect the approximate retail cost of the base model: **1988** - $11,707; **1989** - $12,405; **1990** - $13,001.

DIMENSIONS

Body Style	Years Avail	Wheel Base (in)	Lgth (in)	Ht (in)	Avg Wt (lbs)	Fuel Cap (gal)	Front Hdrm (in)	Front Legrm (in)
utl wgn	87-88	94	158.3	68.2	3,770	23	na	na
utl wgn	89-90	94	161.9	69.9	4,040	23	na	na

ENGINES

Type	Displace-ment (L)	Fuel Dly	HP @rpm	Torque @rpm (ft/lbs)	MPG Cty/Hwy	Years Avail
V-6	2.9	FI	na	na	17/22	87-90

KEY: I=in-line engine; V=V engine; F=flat engine; FI=fuel injection; bbl=barrel carburetor; T=turbo; D=diesel; HP=horsepower; MPG=estimated average miles per gallon.

EVALUATIONS, TESTS, AND RANKINGS

1989: "'engine feels strong with lots of midrange torque, the styling is pleasantly boxy and it seems well put together ... Steering wheel: too high. Seats: not enough support ... suspension is too soft." **Source:** "Dirt Rods," *Popular Mechanics*, March 1989, pp. 113-116, 120.

1989: "offers easy driveability, economical operation, good looks ... Kneeroom for extra-tall back-seat passengers could be an issue ... The engine fires up easily, purrs with a silky-smooth idle and pulls well through its power band." **Source:** "Bronco II: Ford's versatile, compact sport-utility vehicle gets a facelift and a 4900-pound tow rating," *Trailer Life*, June 1989, pp. 57-59, 111-112.

1988: "one of the new breed of smaller but brawny off-road trucks." **Source:** "Ford Bronco II," *Car and Driver—Buyer's Guide 1988*, 1988, p. 139.

RECALLS

1989: (25,000 4x4 multipurpose vehicles equipped with front axle automatic locking hubs; recall includes the Ford Ranger and Ford Bronco II): Front wheel bearing adjusting nut retaining keys may be missing from front axle assemblies, allowing the nut to loosen. Could result in detachment of wheel and hub assembly from the axle, loss of vehicle control, and an accident. **Corrective action:** Install retaining keys in front wheel hub assemblies where missing. *(NHTSA Campaign No. 89V109000.)*

1987: (3,600,000 passenger cars and light trucks equipped with fuel injection. Recall includes several Ford, Mercury, and Lincoln models; includes models made before 1987): Spring lock fuel line coupling may not be properly engaged. Coupling could disengage due to fuel pressure, vibration, and engine movements; this would cause loss of fuel which, in presence of an ignition source, creates a fire risk. **Corrective action:** Install retainer clips over the couplings to prevent coupling separation and fuel leakage. *(NHTSA Campaign No. 87V139000.)*

1987: (17,420 multi-purpose 4x4 passenger vehicles. Recall includes the Ford Bronco and Ford Ranger): Stickers concerning handling and maneuverability which are affixed to driver's sun visor sleeves do not meet criteria for permanent adhesion. Vehicles do not meet formats specified by parts 573 and 579 of 49CFR. **Corrective action:** Owners will be mailed new sun visor sleeves with all applicable decal information permanently affixed. *(NHTSA Campaign No. 87V070000.)*

SAFETY AND REPAIRS

1987: "Service Tips," *Popular Mechanics*, November 1989, p.43. **Note:** '87 Ford Rangers and Bronco IIs may experience throttle-plate sticking.

REPAIR MANUALS

1316 ● **Chilton's Ford Repair Manual 1980-1987**
Chilton Co.
Chilton Way
Radnor, PA 19089   Ph:(215)964-4000

Published 1987. **Price:** $19.95.

1317 ● **Chilton's Guide to Chassis Electronics and Power Accessories, 1988-1991 Ford/Chrysler/Jeep/Eagle**
Chilton Co.
Chilton Way
Radnor, PA 19089   Ph:(215)964-4000

Published March 1991. **Price:** $19.95.

1318 ● **Chilton's Professional Electronics Diagnostic Manual Ford Cars and Trucks 1984-1988: Motor-Age Professional Mechanic's Edition**
Chilton Co.
Chilton Way
Radnor, PA 19089   Ph:(215)964-4000

Published 1988. **Price:** $52.00

1319 ● **Ford Four-Wheel Drive Bronco and F-Series Pickups, 1969-1987**
Clymer Publications
P.O. Box 1209
Overland Park, KS 66212   Ph:(913)541-6694

Published 1987. **Price:** $26.95.

1320 ● **Ford, Lincoln, Mercury Car Repair and Tune-Up Guide: 1972-1987**
Clymer Publications
P.O. Box 1209
Overland Park, KS 66212   Ph:(913)541-6694

Published 1987. **Price:** 14.95.

1321 ● **Ford Ranger and Bronco II 1983-1988: Includes Diesel and Four-Wheel Drive Shop Manual**
Clymer Publications
P.O. Box 1209
Overland Park, KS 66212   Ph:(913)541-6694

Editor(s): Kalton C. Lahue. **Price:** $14.95.

1322 ● **Haynes Ford Ranger and Bronco II Owners Workshop Manual, No. 1026: 1983-1989**
Haynes Publications, Inc.
861 Lawrence Dr.
Newbury Park, CA 91320   Ph:(818)889-5400

Price: $15.95.

1323 ● **Motor Auto Repair 1983-1989 Ford**
Hearst Books
105 Madison Ave.
New York, NY 10016   Ph:(212)889-3050

Published 1989. **Price:** $14.95.

1324 ● **Ranger-Bronco II 1983-1988: Repair and Tune-Up Guide**
Chilton Co.
Chilton Way
Radnor, PA 19089   Ph:(215)964-4000

Published 1989. **Price:** $15.95.

OTHER INFORMATION SOURCES

1325 ● **FOMOCO Owners Club—Newsletter**
FOMOCO Owners Club
3804 Conifer Dr.
Loveland, CO 80538   Ph:(303)669-8767

Monthly.

1326 ● **Ford-Lincoln-Mercury Club of Florida—Newsletter**
Ford-Lincoln-Mercury Club of Florida
P.O. Box 13514
Tampa, FL 33681   Ph:(813)839-0241

Monthly.

1327 ● **Ford-O-Gram**
Performance Ford Club of America
13155 U.S. Rte. 23
Ashville, OH 43103   Ph:(614)983-2273

Carries information on past and present Ford powered products for car collectors and restorers, race car enthusiasts, and truck and tractor pullers. Recurring features include reports on Club competitions and educational programs, news of members, and calendar of events. Bimonthly. **Price:** Available to members only.

1328 ● **Standard Catalog of Ford 1896-1990**
Krause Publications, Inc.
700 E. State St.
Iola, WI 54990   Ph:(715)445-2214

Published 1990. **Price:** $19.95.

1329 ● **Your Ford: Including Lincoln-Mercury: Essential Service Information for Owners and Mechanics**
Consumer Reports Books
51 E. 42nd St., Ste. 800
New York, NY 10017   Ph:(212)682-9280

Based on technical service bulletins issued to Ford and Lincoln-

Mercury dealers from 1985 through 1987. Published 1988.
Editor(s): Mort J. Schultz. **Price:** $8.00.

ASSOCIATIONS

1330 ● **FOMOCO Owners Club**
3633 Akron Ct.
Loveland, CO 80538
Barry Abels, Exec. Ofc.   Ph:(303)669-8767

Founded: 1985. **Membership:** 250. Individuals dedicated to
the exhibition, preservation, and restoration of Edsel, Ford,
Lincoln, and Mercury automobiles. Conducts charitable
activities; sponsors educational programs. Bestows awards.
Convention/Meeting: Annual (with exhibits) - 1991
September, Lakewood, CO.

FORD CLUB WAGON (1987-92)

A full-size passenger wagon similar to the Econoline van, the
Ford Club Wagon is the largest passenger vehicle
manufactured by Ford Motor Co. Produced in Lorain, Ohio
(plant parts data: domestic parts - 79%, imported parts - 21%;
Federal Trade Zone Board, 1989).

1992 Ford Econoline Club Wagon

MAJOR FEATURES

● Club Wagon Custom has as 1992 standard equipment: 4.9-
liter inline 6-cylinder engine, 4-speed electronic over-drive
transmission, front independent/rear live axle suspension,
power steering, power front disc/rear drum brakes with anti-
lock rear system, and aerodynamic exterior body stylings.

● Club Wagon XLT for 1992 offers added length.

● Club Wagon Chateau for 1992 adds: four captain's chairs
and a seat bed.

PRICE HISTORY

The following new car prices reflect the approximate retail cost
of the base model: **1988** - $14,621; **1989** - $15,241; **1990** -
$16,596; **1991** - $16,557.

DIMENSIONS

Body Style	Years Avail	Wheel Base (in)	Lgth (in)	Ht (in)	Avg Wt (lbs)	Fuel Cap (gal)	Front Hdrm (in)	Front Legrm (in)
van	87-89	124.0	186.6	79.2	5,500	18.0	na	na
van	90-91	138.0	206.8	80.9	na	22.0	na	na
van	92-92	138.0	211.8	79.5	na	35.0	41.5	39.5

ENGINES

Type	Displace- ment (L)	Fuel Dly	HP @rpm	Torque @rpm (ft/lbs)	MPG Cty/Hwy	Years Avail
I-6	4.9	FI	145@3400	265@2000	14/17	87-92
I-6	4.9	FI	150@na	na	na	92-92
V-8	5.8	4-bbl	na	na	11/13	87-87
V-8	5.8	FI	210@na	na	11/14	87-91
V-8	5.0	FI	185@3800	265@2800	13/17	87-92
V-8	7.5	FI	230@na	na	na	89-92
V-8	5.8	FI	200@3800	300@2800	11/15	92-92
V-8D	7.3	na	180@na	na	na	89-92

KEY: I=in-line engine; V=V engine; F=flat engine; FI=fuel injection;
bbl=barrel carburetor; T=turbo; D=diesel; HP=horsepower;
MPG=estimated average miles per gallon.

EVALUATIONS, TESTS, AND RANKINGS

1992: ''one of the friendliest van interiors this side of a
conversion shop ... reworked instrument panel ... is
attractive and functional ... fresh, new look and car-like
amenities.'' **Source:** ''Ford Club Wagon Chateau: The Full-Size
Van Enters the '90s,'' *Motor Trend,* November 1991, pp. 95-
96.

1992: ''aerodynamic styling ... Car-like amenities ... smoothly
contoured dash.'' **Source:** ''Preview: 1992 Motor Trend Truck
of the Year,'' *Motor Trend,* December 1991, pp. 104-105.

1992: ''softer lines, with more rounded corners ... marked
improvement in ride comfort and control ... ranks at the top of
its class as a premium people mover.'' **Source:** ''Club Wagon
Sets the Standard,'' *Detroit Free Press,* August 15, 1991, p. 1E.

1991: ''body lines are sleek and its interior is luxurious ...
definite aura of sophistication ... excellent piece of work.''
Source: ''Ford Club Wagon,'' *Trailer Life,* September 1991, pp.
55-58, 98, 101.

1990: ''comes with gas-filled shocks for a better ride.'' **Source:**
''Ford Econoline/Club Wagon,'' *Car and Driver—Buyer's
Guide 1990,* 1989, pp. 178-179.

1989: ''design is beginning to get a bit dated ... ages shows in
the lack of amenities ... big, rugged van, tall, stiffly sprung for
heavy loads.'' **Source:** ''Long Haulers,'' *Popular Mechanics,*
September 1989, pp. 62-64, 99.

RECALLS

1989-90: (111,000 4 x 2 light trucks and vans equipped with
one-piece driveshaft and an E40D transmission; includes
several other Ford models): Snap ring that locates the park
gear on the output shaft of the transmission may fracture. Park
gear would not engage, allowing the vehicle to roll freely,
resulting in an accident. **Corrective action:** Install improved
snap ring and revised transmission extension housing. *(NHTSA
Campaign No. 90V101000.)*

1987: (188,000 Club Wagons equipped with 7.5 liter and 5.8
liter engines; includes several other Ford vehicles; includes
models made before 1987): Vehicles are subject to excessive
underhood temperatures and fuel system pressures in severe
duty applications. Creates potential for fuel expulsion from the
fuel filler pipe which in the presence of an ignition source,
could result in a fire. **Corrective action:** Install modification kits
to minimize possibility of fuel expulsion and to shield
underbody components from exhaust system heat. *(NHTSA
Campaign No. 87V144000.)*

SAFETY AND REPAIRS

1991: ''Ford Recalls Vans, Town Car,'' *Automotive News,*
December 23, 1991, p. 2. **Note:** 1989-91 models may have

malfunctioning fuel tank selector valve that could lead to over-filling fuel tank.

REPAIR MANUALS

1331 ● Chilton's Ford Repair Manual 1980-1987
Chilton Co.
Chilton Way
Radnor, PA 19089   Ph:(215)964-4000

Published 1987. **Price:** $19.95.

1332 ● Chilton's Guide to Chassis Electronics and Power Accessories, 1988-1991 Ford/Chrysler/Jeep/Eagle
Chilton Co.
Chilton Way
Radnor, PA 19089   Ph:(215)964-4000

Published March 1991. **Price:** $19.95.

1333 ● Chilton's Professional Electronics Diagnostic Manual Ford Cars and Trucks 1984-1988: Motor-Age Professional Mechanic's Edition
Chilton Co.
Chilton Way
Radnor, PA 19089   Ph:(215)964-4000

Published 1988. **Price:** $52.00

1334 ● Ford, Lincoln, Mercury Car Repair and Tune-Up Guide: 1972-1987
Clymer Publications
P.O. Box 1209
Overland Park, KS 66212   Ph:(913)541-6694

Published 1987. **Price:** 14.95.

1335 ● Motor Auto Repair 1983-1989 Ford
Hearst Books
105 Madison Ave.
New York, NY 10016   Ph:(212)889-3050

Published 1989. **Price:** $14.95.

OTHER INFORMATION SOURCES

1336 ● FOMOCO Owners Club—Newsletter
FOMOCO Owners Club
3804 Conifer Dr.
Loveland, CO 80538   Ph:(303)669-8767

Monthly.

1337 ● Ford-Lincoln-Mercury Club of Florida—Newsletter
Ford-Lincoln-Mercury Club of Florida
P.O. Box 13514
Tampa, FL 33681   Ph:(813)839-0241

Monthly.

1338 ● Ford-O-Gram
Performance Ford Club of America
13155 U.S. Rte. 23
Ashville, OH 43103   Ph:(614)983-2273

Carries information on past and present Ford powered products for car collectors and restorers, race car enthusiasts, and truck and tractor pullers. Recurring features include reports on Club competitions and educational programs, news of members, and calendar of events. Bimonthly. **Price:** Available to members only.

1339 ● Standard Catalog of Ford 1896-1990
Krause Publications, Inc.
700 E. State St.
Iola, WI 54990   Ph:(715)445-2214

Published 1990. **Price:** $19.95.

1340 ● Your Ford: Including Lincoln-Mercury: Essential Service Information for Owners and Mechanics
Consumer Reports Books
51 E. 42nd St., Ste. 800
New York, NY 10017   Ph:(212)682-9280

Based on technical service bulletins issued to Ford and Lincoln-Mercury dealers from 1985 through 1987. Published 1988. **Editor(s):** Mort J. Schultz. **Price:** $8.00.

ASSOCIATIONS

1341 ● FOMOCO Owners Club
3633 Akron Ct.
Loveland, CO 80538
Barry Abels, Exec. Ofc.   Ph:(303)669-8767

Founded: 1985. **Membership:** 250. Individuals dedicated to the exhibition, preservation, and restoration of Edsel, Ford, Lincoln, and Mercury automobiles. Conducts charitable activities; sponsors educational programs. Bestows awards. **Convention/Meeting:** Annual (with exhibits) - 1991 September, Lakewood, CO.

FORD ESCORT (1987-92)

Subcompact created to replace the Ford Pinto, the Escort was redesigned significantly for the first time in 1991. Now based on the Mazda 323, Escort comes in four lines, Escort Pony (two-door hatchback), LX (two-and four-door hatchbacks, four-door sedan and four-door wagon), LX-E (four-door sedan), and the GT (three-door coupe). Produced in Wayne, Michigan and Hermosillo, Mexico, the Escort was America's best-selling car in the 1980s. Chosen by *The Complete Car Cost Guide* in 1990 as a subcompact wagon (Escort LX) with the one of the lowest maintenance, fuel, and insurance costs, but with one of the highest repair costs and lowest resale values. The same publication also selected the subcompact (Escort LX) for one of the lowest insurance costs and the subcompact (Escort Pony) for one of the lowest resale values.

1991 Ford Escort LX

MAJOR FEATURES

● Escort Pony, has as 1991 standard equipment: 1.9-liter I-4 engine, 5-speed manual transmission, rack-and-pinion steering, cloth and vinyl reclining bucket seats, one-piece folding rear seatback, and tinted glass.

● Escort LX adds as 1992 standard equipment: upgraded

upholstery, 60/40 split rear seatback, bodyside molding, and full wheel covers.

● Escort Sedan adds as 1992 standard equipment: tachometer, intermittent wipers, and upgraded tires.

● Escort GT and LX-E add as 1992 standard equipment: Mazda-built 1.8-liter 16-valve engine, power steering, 4-wheel disc brakes, sport suspension, Light Group, fog lights, rear spoiler, rocker panel cladding, and alloy wheels.

● Escort EXP, a two-seat sport coupe, was introduced just prior to the 1987 model year and was discontinued after the 1988 model year. It had as 1988 standard equipment: 5-speed manual transmission, 4-wheel independent suspension, front disc/rear drum brakes, fully integrated headlamp and bumper systems, aerodynamic arches around the wheel, and dark taillamp lenses.

PRICE HISTORY

The following new car prices reflect the approximate retail cost of the base model: **1987** - $6,586; **1988** - $6,586; **1989** - $6,964; **1990** - $7,402; **1991** - $8,016; **1992** - $8,355.

DIMENSIONS

Body Style	Years Avail	Wheel Base (in)	Lgth (in)	Ht (in)	Avg Wt (lbs)	Fuel Cap (gal)	Front Hdrm (in)	Front Legrm (in)
2d lbk	87-87	94.2	166.9	53.7	2,180	13	37.9	41.5
2d lbk	88-90	94.2	169.4	53.7	2,242	11.5	38.1	41.5
2d lbk	91-91	98.4	170.9	52.5	2,321	13.2	38.4	41.7
2d lbk	92-92	98.4	170.0	52.5	2,312	11.9	38.4	41.7
4d lbk	87-90	94.2	166.4	53.7	2,310	13	38.1	41.5
4d lbk	91-91	98.4	170.9	52.5	2,361	13.2	38.4	41.7
4d lbk	92-92	98.4	170.0	52.5	2,355	11.9	38.4	41.7
3d cpe	87-88	94.2	168.4	51	2,340	13	36.5	41.9
4d sdn	92-92	98.4	170.9	52.7	2,364	11.9	38.4	41.7
5d wgn	87-90	94.2	169.4	53.4	2,313	13	38.1	41.5
5d wgn	91-91	98.4	171.3	53.6	2,446	13.2	38.4	41.7
5d wgn	92-92	98.4	171.3	53.6	2,411	11.9	38.4	41.7

ENGINES

Type	Displacement (L)	Fuel Dly	HP @rpm	Torque @rpm (ft/lbs)	MPG Cty/Hwy	Years Avail
I-4	1.9	FI	115@5200	120@4400	25/34	87-87
I-4	1.9	FI	90@4600	106@3400	24/30	87-90
I-4	1.9	FI	110@5400	115@4200	25/32	88-89
I-4	1.9	FI	88@4400	108@3800	30/37	91-92
I-4	1.8	FI	127@6500	114@4500	26/31	91-92
I-4D	2.0	FI	58@3600	84@3000	37/45	87-87

KEY: I=in-line engine; V=V engine; F=flat engine; FI=fuel injection; bbl=barrel carburetor; T=turbo; D=diesel; HP=horsepower; MPG=estimated average miles per gallon.

EVALUATIONS, TESTS, AND RANKINGS

1991: "1991 model offers better aerodynamics, more room, more power and even more mongrelization . . . does look an awful lot like an Acura Legend . . . handling is stable and reassuring." **Source:** "Escort Evolves into Mainstay," *New York Times*, May 1990, p. 4S.

1991: "handling was outstanding . . . short on hype, long on value." **Source:** "Long-Term Test Cars," *Popular Mechanics*, March 1991, pp. 44-46.

1991: "cruise control . . . was easiest to use . . . seats also offer plenty of side support . . . [engine] felt surprisingly smooth and powerful off the line." **Source:** "Station to Station: HM tests four new-for-1991 family wagons," *Home Mechanix*, June 1991, pp. 78-83.

1990: "LX version is the way to get the most value for your hard-earned dollar." **Source:** "Top Ten New Car Buys," *Motor Trend*, November 1989, p. 80-83, 86-89.

1990: "cars are considerably larger . . . claustrophobic cockpit feel of the old models . . . new GT snaps to at speeds that would leave the old 1.9-liter H.O. gasping for air." **Source:** "Ford Escort: Dearborn takes its biggest gamble yet," *Motor Trend*, March 1990, 86-88, 140.

1989: "Peppy performance . . . Good handling . . . Lack of engine choice." **Source:** "Go to Work in Style," *Home Mechanix*, January 1989, pp. 64-67.

1988: "overall feel [of GT] is very high-tech and modern . . . big and roomy inside . . . engine is also very noisy and thirsty." **Source:** "Econo Commandos," *Popular Mechanics*, July 1988, pp. 51-55, 119.

1988: "revelation how well the Escort handled the zigzags and switchbacks . . . excellent job of filtering road irregularities." **Source:** "There is Plenty to Like About Ford's Escort GT," *The Detroit News*, July 20, 1988, pp. 1F-2F.

RECALLS

1991: (6,000 vehicles): Fuel line that secures bolt may interfere with accelerator pedal causing it to stick at wide open throttle. **Corrective action:** Cut off extra length of bolt that protrudes above surface of weld nut to prevent interference. *(NHTSA Campaign No. 90V076000.)*

1990: (3,300 cars; includes the Ford Escort and Ford Escort EXP): Special primer that promotes the bonding of a urethane adhesive to the glass was not applied to the windshields before installation. Could cause the windshield not to be properly adhered to body, and vehicle would not comply with FMVSS 212. **Corrective action:** Remove and properly install windshield using special primer. *(NHTSA Campaign No. 89V174000.)*

1987-88: (3,600,000 passenger cars and light trucks equipped with fuel injection. Recall includes several Ford, Mercury, and Lincoln models; includes models made before 1987): Spring lock fuel line coupling may not be properly engaged. Coupling could disengage due to fuel pressure, vibration, and engine movements; this would cause loss of fuel which, in presence of an ignition source, creates a fire risk. **Corrective action:** Install retainer clips over the couplings to prevent coupling separation and fuel leakage. *(NHTSA Campaign No. 87V139000.)*

1987: (350 passenger cars equipped with stainless steel decorative lug nuts included with styled steel polycast, and cast aluminum wheels. Includes Ford Escort, Ford Tempo, and Mercury Lynx): Lug nuts could gall and possibly seize on the wheel studs without providing adequate clamping load on the wheels. Wheel studs could fracture creating a risk of a wheel separating with little forewarning. **Corrective action:** Replace wheel lug nuts and if necessary, replace wheels and wheel studs. *(NHTSA Campaign No. 87V060000.)*

1987: (1,367,500 cars; includes the Ford Escort and Mercury Lynx; includes models made before 1987): Forward outboard pedestal of the seat track of driver's seat may be susceptible to fatigue fracture. Could result in limited degree of rocking motion of driver's seat assembly upon acceleration or deceleration, which could cause an accident. **Corrective action:** Install a reinforcement of all models and a new seat track as necessary. *(NHTSA Campaign No. 89V170000.)*

SAFETY AND REPAIRS

1987: "Car Clinic," *Popular Mechanics*, December 1987, p.11. **Note:** Tip for hard-starting '87 Escort, EXP, or Lynx.

1987: "Cover Story," *Popular Mechanics*, November 1988, p.51. **Note:** Noise coming from the rear of a 1987 Escort or Lynx.

1987: "Car Clinic," *Popular Mechanics,* July 1988, p.30. **Note:** Emulsion build-up and tailpipe waterdrips in the 1987 Escort.

1987: "Car Clinic," *Popular Mechanics,* October 1990, p. 107. **Note:** Tip for clicking noise from front brakes in 87-88 Escort, Mercury Topaz, and Mercury Lynx.

REPAIR MANUALS

1342 ● Chilton Ford-Mercury Front Wheel Drive 1981-1987
Chilton Co.
Chilton Way
Radnor, PA 19089   Ph:(215)964-4000

Published 1987. **Price:** $14.95.

1343 ● Chilton's Ford Repair Manual 1980-1987
Chilton Co.
Chilton Way
Radnor, PA 19089   Ph:(215)964-4000

Published 1987. **Price:** $19.95.

1344 ● Chilton's Guide to Chassis Electronics and Power Accessories, 1988-1991 Ford/Chrysler/Jeep/Eagle
Chilton Co.
Chilton Way
Radnor, PA 19089   Ph:(215)964-4000

Published March 1991. **Price:** $19.95.

1345 ● Chilton's Professional Electronics Diagnostic Manual Ford Cars and Trucks 1984-1988: Motor-Age Professional Mechanic's Edition
Chilton Co.
Chilton Way
Radnor, PA 19089   Ph:(215)964-4000

Published 1988. **Price:** $52.00

1346 ● Ford Escort-EXP and Mercury Lynx-LN7, 1981-1989: Shop Manual
Clymer Publications
P.O. Box 1209
Overland Park, KS 66212   Ph:(913)541-6694

Published 1989. **Price:** $14.95.

1347 ● Ford, Lincoln, Mercury Car Repair and Tune-Up Guide: 1972-1987
Clymer Publications
P.O. Box 1209
Overland Park, KS 66212   Ph:(913)541-6694

Published 1987. **Price:** 14.95.

1348 ● Haynes Ford Escort and Mercury Lynx Owners Manual Workshop Manual, No. 789: 1981-1988
Haynes Publications, Inc.
861 Lawrence Dr.
Newbury Park, CA 91320   Ph:(818)889-5400

Price: $15.95.

1349 ● Motor Auto Repair 1983-1989 Ford
Hearst Books
105 Madison Ave.
New York, NY 10016   Ph:(212)889-3050

Published 1989. **Price:** $14.95.

OTHER INFORMATION SOURCES

1350 ● FOMOCO Owners Club—Newsletter
FOMOCO Owners Club
3804 Conifer Dr.
Loveland, CO 80538   Ph:(303)669-8767

Monthly.

1351 ● Ford Enthusiast Magazine
Performance Ford Club of America
PO Box 32
Ashville, OH 43103   Ph:(614)983-4777

Provides information of high performance Ford models. Bimonthly. **Editor(s):** France Crites, Publisher and Editor. **Price:** $20.00 per year; $3.50 per issue.

1352 ● Ford-Lincoln-Mercury Club of Florida—Newsletter
Ford-Lincoln-Mercury Club of Florida
P.O. Box 13514
Tampa, FL 33681   Ph:(813)839-0241

Monthly.

1353 ● Ford-O-Gram
Performance Ford Club of America
13155 U.S. Rte. 23
Ashville, OH 43103   Ph:(614)983-2273

Carries information on past and present Ford powered products for car collectors and restorers, race car enthusiasts, and truck and tractor pullers. Recurring features include reports on Club competitions and educational programs, news of members, and calendar of events. Bimonthly. **Price:** Available to members only.

1354 ● Standard Catalog of Ford 1896-1990
Krause Publications, Inc.
700 E. State St.
Iola, WI 54990   Ph:(715)445-2214

Published 1990. **Price:** $19.95.

1355 ● Super Ford
Dobbs Publications, Inc.
3816 Industry Blvd.   Ph:(813)646-5743
Lakeland, FL 33811   Fax:(813)644-8373

Magazine for owners of high performance Fords. Monthly. **Editor(s):** Tom Wilson. **Price:** $23.97/year; $3.50 per single issue.

1356 ● Your Ford: Including Lincoln-Mercury: Essential Service Information for Owners and Mechanics
Consumer Reports Books
51 E. 42nd St., Ste. 800
New York, NY 10017   Ph:(212)682-9280

Based on technical service bulletins issued to Ford and Lincoln-Mercury dealers from 1985 through 1987. Published 1988. **Editor(s):** Mort J. Schultz. **Price:** $8.00.

ASSOCIATIONS

1357 ● FOMOCO Owners Club
3633 Akron Ct.
Loveland, CO 80538
Barry Abels, Exec. Ofc.   Ph:(303)669-8767

Founded: 1985. **Membership:** 250. Individuals dedicated to the exhibition, preservation, and restoration of Edsel, Ford, Lincoln, and Mercury automobiles. Conducts charitable activities; sponsors educational programs. Bestows awards. **Convention/Meeting:** Annual (with exhibits) - 1991 September, Lakewood, CO.

1358 ● Performance Ford Club of America, Inc.
13155 U.S. Rt. 23
Ashville, OH 43103
Charles Crites, Pres.   Ph:(614)983-2273

Founded: 1981. **Membership:** 6,000. Car collectors and restorers, race car enthusiasts, and truck and tractor pullers. Provides restoration, promotion, and maintenance Ford-powered products. Conducts research on past and present products. Sponsors specialized education; holds competitions and bestows awards. **Convention/Meeting:** Annual national show (with exhibits) - 1992 Sept. 5-6, Xenia, OH.

FORD EXPLORER (1991-92)

Replaced the Bronco II in 1991. *Four Wheeler* magazine named the 4-door Explorer 4x4 "Four Wheeler of the Year" in 1990 and selected the 2-door 4x4 model for the same honor in 1991.

1991 Ford Explorer

MAJOR FEATURES

● Explorer XL has as 1992 standard equipment: 5-speed manual transmission, power front disc/rear drum brakes with computerized rear anti-lock system, power steering, Touch Drive electronic shift (4WD), and flip-open opera windows (3-door).

● Explorer Sport adds as 1992 standard equipment: rear wiper, washer, and defroster, rear quarter privacy glass, Light Group, load floor tiedown net, leather-wrapped steering wheel, and alloy wheels.

● Explorer XLT adds as 1992 standard equipment: cloth captain's chairs; power windows, mirrors, and locks; tilt steering column, cruise control, and an upgraded interior.

● Explorer Eddie Bauer adds to Sport as 1992 standard equipment: premium captains' chairs; power windows, mirrors, and locks; cruise control, tilt steering column, roof rack, upgraded door panels with pockets, duffle bag, and garment bag.

PRICE HISTORY

The following new car prices reflect the approximate retail cost of the base model: **1991** - $14,586; **1992** - $15,854.

DIMENSIONS

Body Style	Years Avail	Wheel Base (in)	Lgth (in)	Ht (in)	Avg Wt (lbs)	Fuel Cap (gal)	Front Hdrm (in)	Front Legrm (in)
3d wgn	91-92	102.1	174.4	67.5	3675	19.0	39.9	42.1
5d wgn	91-92	111.9	184.3	67.3	3854	19.0	39.9	42.1

ENGINES

Type	Displacement (L)	Fuel Dly	HP @rpm	Torque @rpm (ft/lbs)	MPG Cty/Hwy	Years Avail
V-6	4.0	FI	155@4200	220@2400	17/21	91-92

KEY: I=in-line engine; V=V engine; F=flat engine; FI=fuel injection; bbl=barrel carburetor; T=turbo; D=diesel; HP=horsepower; MPG=estimated average miles per gallon.

EVALUATIONS, TESTS, AND RANKINGS

1991: "sums up all the things we like about sport-utes . . . makes those things relevant and affordable." **Source:** "Ford Explorer," *Automobile Magazine*, January 1991, p. 57.

1991: "long wheelbase comprises off-road performance . . . a deserving successor to the Bronco II." **Source:** "Worth the Wait," *Field and Stream*, December 1990, pp. 78, 80, 83.

1991: "sets new standards of comfort and refinement . . . driver's seat has a commanding view of the road . . . highway ride is excellent." **Source:** "Strong and Sporty: These stylish vehicles are still trucks under the skin," *Organic Gardening*, November 1990, pp. 58-61.

1991: "[Ford Explorer Eddie Bauer offer] the best seats in any vehicle anywhere . . . represents a perfect middle point between a minivan and a station wagon." **Source:** "Ford Explorer: Four seasons test," *Automobile Magazine*, December 1991, pp. 100-102, 106, 108, 109.

1991: "solid comfort and quietness . . . Controls are convenient and logically laid out . . . functionally well-rounded." **Source:** "Long-term Wrapup: Ford Explorer XLT," *Road & Track*, January 1992, p. 88.

1991: "a sleeker, more aerodynamic appearance . . . than that of the Bronco II . . . Controls in the carlike interior are within easy reach of the driver." **Source:** "4-Door off-Roaders," *Sports Afield*, March 1990, pp. 120-122, 143-145.

1991: "improves rear seat access, and is our choice as a tow vehicle . . . runs smooth and strong." **Source:** "Tow Test: Ford Explorer," *Boating*, March 1991, p. 30.

1991: "enabled us to make the rugged adventure in sophisticated style . . . the one thing I wouldn't change is the vehicle." **Source:** "Death Valley to Pikes Peak," *Popular Mechanics*, September 1990, pp. 38-42.

RECALLS

1991: (2,500 multi-purpose passenger four-door vehicles with sunroofs): Removal and reinstallation of sunroof glass by operator with hinge assemblies accidentally improperly mated could allow sunroof to detach while vehicle is being driven, with risk of injury to following vehicles or people in the vicinity, or to vehicle occupants if the glass should fall into the cabin. **Corrective action:** Install revised sunroof hinges that will adequately retain sunroof assembly. *(NHTSA Campaign No. 90V098000.)*

1991: (220,000 multi-purpose vehicles): Rear bumper reinforcement may be subject to fatigue cracking under extended trailer tow service when using a bumper-mounted trailer hitch ball and could separate from vehicle. **Corrective action:** Install two brackets to reinforce bumper. Bumper mounted trailer hitch ball assembly should not be used until repair procedure is completed. *(NHTSA Campaign No. 91V026000.)*

1991: (18,000 multi-purpose vehicles): Hot plate weld which attaches vapor vent valve carrier to plastic fuel tank may partially fracture, allowing vapor of fuel to escape or fuel to leak. Could cause a fire. **Corrective action:** Fuel tank will be removed and inspected for weld integrity. Fuel tanks with inadequate welds will be replaced. *(NHTSA Campaign No. 91V025000.)*

1991: (25,000 multi-purpose vehicles): Front heat shield may contact the front of plastic fuel tank, causing cuts or other damage to extent of penetration. Causes vapors to escape and possibly fuel to spill, which could catch fire. **Corrective action:** Relocate heat shield; inspect and replace damaged fuel tanks. *(NHTSA Campaign No. 91V024000.)*

SAFETY AND REPAIRS

1991: ``Transmission Defect Baffles Ford; 788,796 Trucks Have It,'' *Automotive News,* October 28, 1991, p. 47. **Note:** Safety defect in the parking gear of automatic transmissions could allow trucks to roll.

REPAIR MANUALS

1359 ● **Chilton's Guide to Chassis Electronics and Power Accessories, 1988-1991 Ford/Chrysler/Jeep/Eagle**
Chilton Co.
Chilton Way
Radnor, PA 19089   Ph:(215)964-4000

Published March 1991. **Price:** $19.95.

OTHER INFORMATION SOURCES

1360 ● **FOMOCO Owners Club—Newsletter**
FOMOCO Owners Club
3804 Conifer Dr.
Loveland, CO 80538   Ph:(303)669-8767

Monthly.

1361 ● **Ford-Lincoln-Mercury Club of Florida—Newsletter**
Ford-Lincoln-Mercury Club of Florida
P.O. Box 13514
Tampa, FL 33681   Ph:(813)839-0241

Monthly.

1362 ● **Ford-O-Gram**
Performance Ford Club of America
13155 U.S. Rte. 23
Ashville, OH 43103   Ph:(614)983-2273

Carries information on past and present Ford powered products for car collectors and restorers, race car enthusiasts, and truck and tractor pullers. Recurring features include reports on Club competitions and educational programs, news of members, and calendar of events. Bimonthly. **Price:** Available to members only.

1363 ● **Standard Catalog of Ford 1896-1990**
Krause Publications, Inc.
700 E. State St.
Iola, WI 54990   Ph:(715)445-2214

Published 1990. **Price:** $19.95.

ASSOCIATIONS

1364 ● **FOMOCO Owners Club**
3633 Akron Ct.
Loveland, CO 80538
Barry Abels, Exec. Ofc.   Ph:(303)669-8767

Founded: 1985. **Membership:** 250. Individuals dedicated to the exhibition, preservation, and restoration of Edsel, Ford, Lincoln, and Mercury automobiles. Conducts charitable activities; sponsors educational programs. Bestows awards. **Convention/Meeting:** Annual (with exhibits) - 1991 September, Lakewood, CO.

FORD FESTIVA (1988-92)

Introduced in 1987 as a 1988 model, the Ford Festiva is based on a design by Mazda and built for Ford in South Korea by Kia Motors. Chosen by *The Complete Car Cost Guide* in 1990 as a subcompact (Festiva L) with one of the lowest maintenance costs and by *Car and Driver—Buyer's Guide 1988* as one of the Ten Best Performers for observed fuel economy (Festiva LX).

1991 Ford Festiva L

MAJOR FEATURES

● Festiva L has as 1992 standard equipment: 5-speed manual transmission, front disc/rear drum brakes, independent suspension, cloth and vinyl reclining bucket seats.

● Festiva GL (combined and replaced L Plus and LX models) adds as 1992 standard equipment: AM/FM radio, rear wiper/washer, cargo cover, alloy wheels, other exterior body stylings, and an upgraded interior.

● Festiva L Plus added as 1990 equipment: wide bodyside moldings, door pockets, tachometer and trip odometer, rear defogger, and AM/FM radio.

● Festiva LX added as 1990 equipment: tilt steering column, soft-feel steering wheel, upgraded seats with see-through head restraints, and upgraded sound insulation.

PRICE HISTORY

The following new car prices reflect the approximate retail cost of the base model: **1988** - $5,595; **1989** - $6,073; **1990** - $6,319; **1991** - $6,648; **1992** - $6,941.

DIMENSIONS

Body Style	Years Avail	Wheel Base (in)	Lgth (in)	Ht (in)	Avg Wt (lbs)	Fuel Cap (gal)	Front Hdrm (in)	Front Legrm (in)
2d lbk	88-92	90.2	140.5	55.3	1,797	10	38.6	40.6

ENGINES

Type	Displace-ment (L)	Fuel Dly	HP @rpm	Torque @rpm (ft/lbs)	MPG Cty/Hwy	Years Avail
I-4	1.3	2-bbl	58@5000	75@3500	39/43	88-89
I-4	1.3	FI	63@5000	73@3000	35/41	90-92

KEY: I=in-line engine; V=V engine; F=flat engine; FI=fuel injection; bbl=barrel carburetor; T=turbo; D=diesel; HP=horsepower; MPG=estimated average miles per gallon.

EVALUATIONS, TESTS, AND RANKINGS

1989: ''ergonomic layout and attention to detail give it a competitive edge ... suspension provides a ride that is surprisingly reasonable.'' **Source:** ''Eight for Ten,'' *Car and Driver*, December 1988, pp.54-58, 60, 63-66, 68.

1989: ''unusually balky response at part throttle ... delightful little car ... quiet, peppy enough to keep pace, comfortable, roomy and inexpensive.'' **Source:** ''Long-Term Test,'' *Popular Mechanics*, June 1989, pp. 120, 123, 125.

1988: ''able to accomodate four rationally sized adults in reasonable comfort ... done at the cost of some style ... nicely equipped in base form.'' **Source:** ''Ford Festiva: What's Tall and Short and Costs Less Than $6000,'' *Motor Trend*, May 1987, pp.74-76.

1988: ''a blast to drive.'' **Source:** ''Asian Invasion,'' *Popular Mechanics*, July 1987, pp.90-94, 148.

1988: ''admirable job of packaging ... visibility all around the driver is excellent ... Most impressive were the smoothness of the engine and transmission and the relative quiet of the car.'' **Source:** ''Ford Festiva's a Minicar Americans Can Live With,'' *The Detroit News*, June 10, 1987, pp.1F-2F.

RECALLS

1990: (268 vehicles): Fasten seat belt warning light may not work in cold temperatures. Occupants would not receive this warning to use safety belts and cars would not comply with FMVSS 208. **Corrective action:** Replace instrument clusters in the affected cars. *(NHTSA Campaign No. 90V045000.)*

REPAIR MANUALS

1365 ● Chilton's Guide to Chassis Electronics and Power Accessories, 1988-1991 Ford/Chrysler/Jeep/Eagle
Chilton Co.
Chilton Way
Radnor, PA 19089   Ph:(215)964-4000

Published March 1991. **Price:** $19.95.

1366 ● Chilton's Professional Electronics Diagnostic Manual Ford Cars and Trucks 1984-1988: Motor-Age Professional Mechanic's Edition
Chilton Co.
Chilton Way
Radnor, PA 19089   Ph:(215)964-4000

Published 1988. **Price:** $52.00.

1367 ● Motor Auto Repair 1983-1989 Ford
Hearst Books
105 Madison Ave.
New York, NY 10016   Ph:(212)889-3050

Published 1989. **Price:** $14.95.

OTHER INFORMATION SOURCES

1368 ● FOMOCO Owners Club—Newsletter
FOMOCO Owners Club
3804 Conifer Dr.
Loveland, CO 80538   Ph:(303)669-8767

Monthly.

1369 ● Ford-Lincoln-Mercury Club of Florida—Newsletter
Ford-Lincoln-Mercury Club of Florida
P.O. Box 13514
Tampa, FL 33681   Ph:(813)839-0241

Monthly.

1370 ● Ford-O-Gram
Performance Ford Club of America
13155 U.S. Rte. 23
Ashville, OH 43103   Ph:(614)983-2273

Carries information on past and present Ford powered products for car collectors and restorers, race car enthusiasts, and truck and tractor pullers. Recurring features include reports on Club competitions and educational programs, news of members, and calendar of events. Bimonthly. **Price:** Available to members only.

1371 ● Standard Catalog of Ford 1896-1990
Krause Publications, Inc.
700 E. State St.
Iola, WI 54990   Ph:(715)445-2214

Published 1990. **Price:** $19.95.

1372 ● Your Ford: Including Lincoln-Mercury: Essential Service Information for Owners and Mechanics
Consumer Reports Books
51 E. 42nd St., Ste. 800
New York, NY 10017   Ph:(212)682-9280

Based on technical service bulletins issued to Ford and Lincoln-Mercury dealers from 1985 through 1987. Published 1988. **Editor(s):** Mort J. Schultz. **Price:** $8.00.

ASSOCIATIONS

1373 ● FOMOCO Owners Club
3633 Akron Ct.
Loveland, CO 80538
Barry Abels, Exec. Ofc.   Ph:(303)669-8767

Founded: 1985. **Membership:** 250. Individuals dedicated to the exhibition, preservation, and restoration of Edsel, Ford, Lincoln, and Mercury automobiles. Conducts charitable activities; sponsors educational programs. Bestows awards. **Convention/Meeting:** Annual (with exhibits) - 1991 September, Lakewood, CO.

FORD LTD CROWN VICTORIA (1987-92)

Corporate twin of the Mercury Grand Marquis, the Ford LTD Crown Victoria is available in LTD Crown Victoria, LTD Crown Victoria LX, LTD Country Squire Wagon, and Touring Sedan models. The vehicle has undergone its first major redesign since 1979. Chosen by *The Complete Car Cost Guide* as having the best overall value for a large auto in 1990. Produced in St. Thomas, Ontario, Canada.

1992 Ford LTD Crown Victoria

MAJOR FEATURES

● LTD Crown Victoria 1992 standard equipment includes: 4-speed automatic transmission, front independent suspension, four-wheel disc brakes, power steering, air conditioning, power windows, stereo system, driver's-side airbag, tilt steering column, and tinted glass.

● LTD Crown Victoria LX adds as 1992 standard equipment: Light Decor Group, and upgraded trim interior.

● Country Squire Wagon 1992 standard equipment includes: luggage rack, 3-way tailgate with power window, and simulated woodgrain. Country Squire LX adds dual-facing rear seats as standard.

● Touring Sedan adds as 1992 standard equipment a more efficient, 4.6-liter, 210-horsepower engine, anti-lock brakes, sport suspension, alloy wheels, other exterior body stylings, and cruise control.

PRICE HISTORY

The following new car prices reflect the approximate retail cost of the base model: **1987** - $14,315; **1988** - $14,010; **1989** - $15,851; **1990** - $17,251; **1991** - $18,728; **1992** - $19,563.

DIMENSIONS

Body Style	Years Avail	Wheel Base (in)	Lgth (in)	Ht (in)	Avg Wt (lbs)	Fuel Cap (gal)	Front Hdrm (in)	Front Legrm (in)
2d sdn	87-87	114.3	211	55.3	3,724	18	37.9	43.5
4d sdn	87-91	114.3	211	55.6	3,822	18	38.3	42.5
4d sdn	92-92	114.4	212.4	56.7	3,748	20	39.4	42.5
5d wgn	87-91	114.3	215.7	56.5	3,978	18	39.2	42.5

ENGINES

Type	Displacement (L)	Fuel Dly	HP @rpm	Torque @rpm (ft/lbs)	MPG Cty/Hwy	Years Avail
V-8	5.0	FI	150@3200	270@2000	17/24	87-91
V-8	4.6	FI	190@4200	260@3200	18/25	92-92
V-8	4.6	FI	210@4600	270@3400	na	92-92

KEY: I=in-line engine; V=V engine; F=flat engine; FI=fuel injection; bbl=barrel carburetor; T=turbo; D=diesel; HP=horsepower; MPG=estimated average miles per gallon.

EVALUATIONS, TESTS, AND RANKINGS

1992: "The long, slab-like instrument panel still looks a bit stodgy . . . elegant looks and smooth ride." **Source:** "New look, old comforts in '92 Crown Victoria," *The Detroit News*, May 8, 1991, p. D1.

1992: "Skydome-sized cars . . . posts an 8.8-second 0-to-60 time . . . speed-sensitive steering . . . still too numb at post-50-

mph speeds." **Source:** "Ford Crown Victoria LX," *Car and Driver*, November 1991, p. 154.

1992: "puzzled transmission pounds out of and back into overdrive as if punishing you for indecision . . . changes made to the Crown Victoria LX are both dramatic and effective." **Source:** "Uptown Showdown: Ford Crown Victoria LX vs. Chevrolet Caprice Classic LTZ," *Motor Trend*, December 1991, pp. 68-72.

1992: "styling is svelte and elegant . . . something of a rubbery feel as the car whips from side to side." **Source:** "Restyled Crown Victoria keeps traits of tradition," *The Flint Journal*, June 12, 1991, pp. E1-E2.

1991: "long-time favorite." **Source:** "Special USA '91 Section," *Motor Trend*, October 1990, p. 62.

1989: "Fuel economy is respectable . . . handles well . . . the design—both interior and exterior—is dated." **Source:** "When Dependability Counts," *Home Mechanix*, February 1989, pp. 78-81, 85.

RECALLS

1991: (6,800 vehicles with automatic overdrive transmission; includes Ford LTD Crown Victoria, Ford Mustang, Ford Thunderbird, Mercury Cougar, and Mercury Grand Marquis): Park rod assembly contains park cam with inadequate surface hardness, which could lead to park disengagement. **Corrective action:** Replace park rod assembly on automatic transmission. *(NHTSA Campaign No. 91V048000.)*

1989: (225 flexible fuel vehicles with fuel systems modified to operate with gasoline, methanol, or combinations of the two fuels): Glass element that separates electronic circuitry from pressurized fuel may loosen and create an opening that could allow pressurized fuel to enter body of optical sensor. This could cause a fuel leak which, in the presence of a source of ignition, could result in a fire. **Corrective action:** Install new optical sensors. *(NHTSA Campaign No. 90V151000.)*

1987-88: (21,200 station wagons equipped with optional dual facing rear seats; includes Ford and Mercury models): Automatic retractor for seat belts for dual facing rear seats may be installed in an improper location. Seat belt could bind between seat cushion and seat back, causing the retractor to be sluggish or unable to take up excess belt slack. **Corrective action:** Remove and properly install the right auxillary seat belts. *(NHTSA Campaign No. 88V028000.)*

1987: (3,600,000 passenger cars and light trucks equipped with fuel injection. Recall includes several Ford, Mercury, and Lincoln models; includes models made before 1987): Spring lock fuel line coupling may not be properly engaged. Coupling could disengage due to fuel pressure, vibration, and engine movements; this would cause loss of fuel which, in presence of an ignition source, creates a fire risk. **Corrective action:** Install retainer clips over the couplings to prevent coupling separation and fuel leakage. *(NHTSA Campaign No. 87V139000.)*

1987: (11,119 passenger cars equipped with 5.0 liter fuel injected engines. Recall includes Ford Crown Victoria, Mercury Grand Marquis, and Lincoln Town Car): Fuel rails may be bent so that No. 5 injector cups are out of design position. Could cause a fuel leak, which in presence of an ignition source could result in an engine fire. **Corrective action:** Replace fuel rail assemblies as necessary. *(NHTSA Campaign No. 87V131000.)*

1987: (29,600 passenger vehicles with 5.0 liter engines. Recall includes the Ford LTD Crown Victoria, Mercury Grand Marquis, and Lincoln Town Car): Steering centerlinks may break at a bend location. Steering control would be diminished, with reduced control of left wheel only and considerable steering wheel free play. **Corrective action:**

Replace steering centerlink. *(NHTSA Campaign No. 87V012000.)*

REPAIR MANUALS

1374 • Chilton's Ford-Lincoln-Mercury Full-Size, 1968-1988
Chilton Co.
Chilton Way
Radnor, PA 19089   Ph:(215)964-4000

Published 1989. **Price:** $15.95.

1375 • Chilton's Ford Repair Manual 1980-1987
Chilton Co.
Chilton Way
Radnor, PA 19089   Ph:(215)964-4000

Published 1987. **Price:** $19.95.

1376 • Chilton's Guide to Chassis Electronics and Power Accessories, 1988-1991 Ford/Chrysler/Jeep/Eagle
Chilton Co.
Chilton Way
Radnor, PA 19089   Ph:(215)964-4000

Published March 1991. **Price:** $19.95.

1377 • Chilton's Professional Electronics Diagnostic Manual Ford Cars and Trucks 1984-1988: Motor-Age Professional Mechanic's Edition
Chilton Co.
Chilton Way
Radnor, PA 19089   Ph:(215)964-4000

Published 1988. **Price:** $52.00

1378 • Ford, Lincoln, Mercury Car Repair and Tune-Up Guide: 1972-1987
Clymer Publications
P.O. Box 1209
Overland Park, KS 66212   Ph:(913)541-6694

Published 1987. **Price:** 14.95.

1379 • Haynes Ford and Mercury Full-Size Owners Workshop Manual, No. 754: 1975-1987
Haynes Publications, Inc.
861 Lawrence Dr.
Newbury Park, CA 91320   Ph:(818)889-5400

Published 1988. **Editor(s):** J. H. Haynes and Chaun Muir. **Price:** $15.95.

1380 • Motor Auto Repair 1983-1989 Ford
Hearst Books
105 Madison Ave.
New York, NY 10016   Ph:(212)889-3050

Published 1989. **Price:** $14.95.

OTHER INFORMATION SOURCES

1381 • FOMOCO Owners Club—Newsletter
FOMOCO Owners Club
3804 Conifer Dr.
Loveland, CO 80538   Ph:(303)669-8767

Monthly.

1382 • Ford-Lincoln-Mercury Club of Florida—Newsletter
Ford-Lincoln-Mercury Club of Florida
P.O. Box 13514
Tampa, FL 33681   Ph:(813)839-0241

Monthly.

1383 • Ford-O-Gram
Performance Ford Club of America
13155 U.S. Rte. 23
Ashville, OH 43103   Ph:(614)983-2273

Carries information on past and present Ford powered products for car collectors and restorers, race car enthusiasts, and truck and tractor pullers. Recurring features include reports on Club competitions and educational programs, news of members, and calendar of events. Bimonthly. **Price:** Available to members only.

1384 • Standard Catalog of Ford 1896-1990
Krause Publications, Inc.
700 E. State St.
Iola, WI 54990   Ph:(715)445-2214

Published 1990. **Price:** $19.95.

1385 • Your Ford: Including Lincoln-Mercury: Essential Service Information for Owners and Mechanics
Consumer Reports Books
51 E. 42nd St., Ste. 800
New York, NY 10017   Ph:(212)682-9280

Based on technical service bulletins issued to Ford and Lincoln-Mercury dealers from 1985 through 1987. Published 1988. **Editor(s):** Mort J. Schultz. **Price:** $8.00.

ASSOCIATIONS

1386 • FOMOCO Owners Club
3633 Akron Ct.
Loveland, CO 80538
Barry Abels, Exec. Ofc.   Ph:(303)669-8767

Founded: 1985. **Membership:** 250. Individuals dedicated to the exhibition, preservation, and restoration of Edsel, Ford, Lincoln, and Mercury automobiles. Conducts charitable activities; sponsors educational programs. Bestows awards. **Convention/Meeting:** Annual (with exhibits) - 1991 September, Lakewood, CO.

FORD MUSTANG (1987-92)

Produced in Dearborn, Michigan, the Ford Mustang(plant parts data: domestic parts - 80%, imported parts - 25%; *Federal Trade Zone Board*, 1989) celebrated its 25th anniversary in 1989 with dashboard emblems in all 1989 model Mustangs. Rated among the best in crash test performance for compact vehicles by *The Car Book*. Chosen by *The Complete Car Cost Guide* in 1990 as having the best overall value and lowest insurance cost for a sport car (Mustang LX 5.0 Sport) and the lowest maintenance cost (Mustang LX Series). Selected as best 4-seat high performance car (Mustang GT 5.0) in the price range of $12,500-$17,500 by *Road & Track*.

1991 Ford Mustang GT

MAJOR FEATURES

● Mustang LX has as 1992 standard equipment: 5-speed manual transmission, front independent suspension with rear live axle, front disc/rear drum brakes, power-assisted rack-and-pinion steering, driver's-side airbag, and cloth reclining front bucket seats; convertibles have power windows, doors, and locks.

● Mustang LX 5.0L adds as 1992 standard equipment: 5.0-liter V-8 engine with dual exhaust, Traction-Lok axle, handling suspension, articulated sport seats with power lumbar adjustment, leather-wrapped steering wheel, all-season performance tires on five-spoke aluminum wheels.

● Mustang GT adds as 1992 standard equipment: front air dam with fog lamps, rear spoiler, and sill extensions.

PRICE HISTORY

The following new car prices reflect the approximate retail cost of the base model: **1987** - $8,271; **1988** - $8,835; **1989** - $9,050; **1990** - $9,456; **1991** - $10,215; **1992** - $10,215.

DIMENSIONS

Body Style	Years Avail	Wheel Base (in)	Lgth (in)	Ht (in)	Avg Wt (lbs)	Fuel Cap (gal)	Front Hdrm (in)	Front Legrm (in)
2d lbk	87-92	100.5	179.6	52.1	2,834	15.4	37	41.7
2d cpe	87-92	100.5	179.6	52.1	2,775	15.4	37	41.7
2d conv	87-91	100.5	179.6	52.1	2,996	15.4	37.6	41.7

ENGINES

Type	Displacement (L)	Fuel Dly	HP @rpm	Torque @rpm (ft/lbs)	MPG Cty/Hwy	Years Avail
I-4	2.3	FI	90@3800	130@2800	25/30	87-88
I-4	2.3	FI	88@4000	132@2600	23/29	89-90
I-4	2.3	FI	105@4600	135@2600	22/30	91-92
V-8	5.0	FI	225@4200	300@3200	17/24	87-92

KEY: I=in-line engine; V=V engine; F=flat engine; FI=fuel injection; bbl=barrel carburetor; T=turbo; D=diesel; HP=horsepower; MPG=estimated average miles per gallon.

EVALUATIONS, TESTS, AND RANKINGS

1991: "above-average handling . . . high fun factor . . . a lot of shake, rattle and body roll." **Source:** "Ford Mustang GT Convertible: Fun If You Forget the Shake, Rattle and Roll," *Autofile*, 1991, pp. 14-15.

1991: "installation of the boot is not exactly an exercise in simplicity . . . top up, the Mustang is a relatively quiet cruiser . . . Wind buffeting is high once the lid is lowered." **Source:** "Top-Down Showdown: We test the hottest cars under the sun," *Motor Trend*, June 1991, pp. 49-59, 62-63.

1990: "Mustang LX, was remarkable under braking—remarkably bad . . . limitless supply of rich, creamy torque at any rpm." **Source:** "Bang for the Buck," *Motor Trend*, November 1989, pp. 42-46, 48, 52-55, 58-59, 62, 64, 66-68, 72, 76.

1990: "best American GT for the money yet devised by man." **Source:** "Top 10 New Car Buys," *Motor Trend*, November 1989, pp. 80-83, 86-89.

1989: "surprisingly comfortable . . . the Cartech Mustang GT at just a hair more than $25,000, turned out to be the second fastest and second quickest (second to a car costing six times as much)." **Source:** "High-Bank Scrimmage," *Road & Track*, August 1988, pp. 46-52, 57.

1989: "[Mustang LX 5.0] delivers more power per buck than anything else in this competition . . . any dog-armed mechanic with a room-temperature IQ could fix it while drunk." **Source:** "Hitting for High Average," *Car and Driver*, August 1988, pp. 58-69.

1989: "offers some of the most driving fun for the money." **Source:** "Power Coupes," *Popular Science*, April 1989, pp. 28-29, 32-34.

1988: "exceptional engine . . . strong performances in every test except braking." **Source:** "Performance Ragtops," *Popular Science*, August 1987, pp. 26-27, 32, 36, 38.

1987: "Enjoyment for Mustang GT fans is feeling a violent surge of power tearing at the rear wheels in first gear when you thought you were only nudging it . . . only one major complaint—the rear roof pillars are so wide that over-the-shoulder visibility in the rear quarters is severely limited." **Source:** "'87 Mustang GT is Closest Thing to a Muscle Car," *The Detroit News*, January 14, 1987, pp. 1F-2F.

1987: "engine is a tower of power . . . more than enough torque here to wind the speedometer needle like a clock." **Source:** "Cars: Fun Work, But Somebody's Got To Do It," *Car and Driver*, January 1987, pp. 36-41.

RECALLS

1991: (6,800 vehicles with automatic overdrive transmission; includes Ford LTD Crown Victoria, Ford Mustang, Ford Thunderbird, Mercury Cougar, and Mercury Grand Marquis): Park rod assembly contains park cam with inadequate surface hardness, which could lead to park disengagement. **Corrective action:** Replace park rod assembly on automatic transmission. *(NHTSA Campaign No. 91V048000.)*

1987: (3,600,000 passenger cars and light trucks equipped with fuel injection. Recall includes several Ford, Mercury, and Lincoln models; includes models made before 1987): Spring lock fuel line coupling may not be properly engaged. Coupling could disengage due to fuel pressure, vibration, and engine movements; this would cause loss of fuel which, in presence of an ignition source, creates a fire risk. **Corrective action:** Install retainer clips over the couplings to prevent coupling separation and fuel leakage. *(NHTSA Campaign No. 87V139000.)*

SAFETY AND REPAIRS

1991: "NHTSA Upgrades Probe of Brakes on Ford Trucks," *Automotive News*, December 9, 1991, p. 40. **Note:** 1987-91 Mustangs may experience hood latch failures.

1987: "Tip for more power in 1987 5 liter engine," *Car Review*, July 1987, p. 50. **Note:** Re: Ford Mustang.

REPAIR MANUALS

1387 ● Chilton's Ford Repair Manual 1980-1987
Chilton Co.
Chilton Way
Radnor, PA 19089   Ph:(215)964-4000

Published 1987. **Price:** $19.95.

1388 ● Chilton's Guide to Chassis Electronics and Power Accessories, 1988-1991 Ford/Chrysler/Jeep/Eagle
Chilton Co.
Chilton Way
Radnor, PA 19089   Ph:(215)964-4000

Published March 1991. **Price:** $19.95.

1389 ● Chilton's Mustang-Capri-Merkur 1979-1988
Chilton Co.
Chilton Way
Radnor, PA 19089   Ph:(215)964-4000

Published 1989. **Price:** $15.95.

1390 ● Chilton's Professional Electronics Diagnostic Manual Ford Cars and Trucks 1984-1988: Motor-Age Professional Mechanic's Edition
Chilton Co.
Chilton Way
Radnor, PA 19089   Ph:(215)964-4000

Published 1988. **Price:** $52.00

1391 ● Ford, Lincoln, Mercury Car Repair and Tune-Up Guide: 1972-1987
Clymer Publications
P.O. Box 1209
Overland Park, KS 66212   Ph:(913)541-6694

Published 1987. **Price:** 14.95.

1392 ● Ford Mustang and Mercury Capri 1979-1987: Includes Turbo Shop Manual
Clymer Publications
P.O. Box 1209
Overland Park, KS 66212   Ph:(913)541-6694

Published 1986. **Editor(s):** Ron Wright. **Price:** $14.95.

1393 ● Haynes Ford Mustang and Mercury Capri (In-Line) Owners Workshop Manual, No. 654: 1979-1990
Haynes Publications, Inc.
861 Lawrence Dr.
Newbury Park, CA 91320   Ph:(818)889-5400

Editor(s): J. H. Haynes and Larry Warren. **Price:** $15.95.

1394 ● Haynes Ford Mustang and Mercury Capri (V-6 and V-8) Owners Workshop Manual, No. 558: 1979-1989
Haynes Publications, Inc.
861 Lawrence Dr.
Newbury Park, CA 91320   Ph:(818)889-5400

Price: $15.95.

1395 ● Motor Auto Repair 1983-1989 Ford
Hearst Books
105 Madison Ave.
New York, NY 10016   Ph:(212)889-3050

Published 1989. **Price:** $14.95.

1396 ● Mustang and Capri, 1979-1987: Super Shop Manual
Clymer Publications
P.O. Box 1209
Overland Park, KS 66212   Ph:(913)541-6694

Published 1988. **Price:** $26.95.

OTHER INFORMATION SOURCES

1397 ● Adirondack Shelby-Mustang Regional Club—Newsletter
Adirondack Shelby-Mustang Regional Club
P.O. Box 4427
Halfmoon, NY 12065

Provides information for enthusiasts of Ford Mustang and Shelby automobiles. Monthly.

1398 ● The Complete Book of Mustang
Publications International Ltd.
7373 N. Cicero Ave.
Lincolnwood, IL 60646   Ph:(312)676-3470

Published 1989. **Price:** $15.98.

1399 ● Fabulous Mustangs and Exotic Fords
Argus Publishers Corp.
12100 Wilshire Blvd., Ste. 250
Los Angeles, CA 90025   Ph:(213)820-3601

Bimonthly. **Editor(s):** Jeff Tann. **Price:** $15.00 per year; $2.95 per copy.

1400 ● FOMOCO Owners Club—Newsletter
FOMOCO Owners Club
3804 Conifer Dr.
Loveland, CO 80538   Ph:(303)669-8767

Monthly.

1401 ● Ford Enthusiast Magazine
Performance Ford Club of America
PO Box 32
Ashville, OH 43103   Ph:(614)983-4777

Provides information of high performance Ford models. Bimonthly. **Editor(s):** France Crites, Publisher and Editor. **Price:** $20.00 per year; $3.50 per issue.

1402 ● Ford Legends
Simitar Entertainment
3850 Annapolis Ln.   Ph:(612)559-6660
Plymouth, MN 55447   Fax:(612)559-0210

Ride in a Cobra, Shelby, Mustang, and GT-40 in this video of Ford's fastest cars. **Producer:** Simitar Entertainment. **Price:** $9.95.

1403 ● Ford-Lincoln-Mercury Club of Florida—Newsletter
Ford-Lincoln-Mercury Club of Florida
P.O. Box 13514
Tampa, FL 33681   Ph:(813)839-0241

Monthly.

1404 ● Ford/Mustang Buyer's Guide
Ford/Mustang Buyer's Guide
203 N. Main St., Ste. 400
Bloomington, IN 61701

Monthly. **Editor(s):** C.P. Meyer, Publisher. **Price:** $18.00 per year; $1.75 per issue.

1405 ● **Ford-O-Gram**
Performance Ford Club of America
13155 U.S. Rte. 23
Ashville, OH 43103   Ph:(614)983-2273

Carries information on past and present Ford powered products for car collectors and restorers, race car enthusiasts, and truck and tractor pullers. Recurring features include reports on Club competitions and educational programs, news of members, and calendar of events. Bimonthly. **Price:** Available to members only.

1406 ● **Hoosier Mustang Club News [Indiana]**
Hoosier Mustang Club
P.O. Box 2065
Columbus, IN 47202   Ph:(812)376-8971

Newsletter. Monthly.

1407 ● **Illustrated Mustang Buyer's Guide**
Motorbooks International, Publishers & Wholesalers, Inc.
729 Prospect Ave.
Osceola, WI 54020   Ph:(715)294-3345

Published 1989. **Editor(s):** Peter Sessler. **Price:** $16.95.

1408 ● **Michiana Mustangs—Newsletter [Indiana, Michigan]**
Michiana Mustangs
c/o Charlie Cobb
3222 Burr Oak Ave.
Elkhart, IN 46517   Ph:(219)293-2802

Bimonthly.

1409 ● **Mustang**
Petersen Publishing Co.
8490 Sunset Blvd.   Ph:(213)854-2222
Los Angeles, CA 90069   Fax:(213)854-2263

Magazine featuring a variety of Mustang events and other car-related activities across the country. Bimonthly. **Editor(s):** Bruce Caldwell. **Price:** $9.95/year; $2.95 per single issue.

1410 ● **Mustang**
Running Press Book Publishers
125 S. 22nd St.
Philadelphia, PA 19103   Ph:(215)567-5080

Published 1991. **Editor(s):** Roger Hicks. **Price:** $14.98.

1411 ● **Mustang, 1965-1989 GT-MACH One Guide**
Tab Books, Inc.
Blue Ridge Summit, PA 172940850   Ph:(717)794-2191

Published 1989. **Editor(s):** Jim Smart. **Price:** $24.95.

1412 ● **Mustang: A Living Legend**
Motorbooks International
729 Prospect Ave.
Osceola, WI 54020   Ph:(715)294-3345

Published 1987. **Editor(s):** Michael O'Leary. **Price:** $15.95.

1413 ● **Mustang Annual**
Motorbooks International
729 Prospect Ave.
Osceola, WI 54020   Ph:(715)294-3345

Annual. **Price:** $6.95.

1414 ● **Mustang Club of America, Northeastern Ohio Regional Group—Newsletter**
Mustang Club of America, Northeastern Ohio Regional Group
287 Wallace Dr.
Berea, OH 44017   Ph:(216)234-5146

Monthly.

1415 ● **Mustang Illustrated**
McMullen Publishing, Inc.
2145 W. La Palma Ave.   Ph:(714)635-9040
Anaheim, CA 92801-1785   Fax:(714)533-9979

Magazine for Mustang car enthusiasts. Quarterly. **Editor(s):** Bob McClurg. **Price:** $7.99/year; $3.50 per single issue.

1416 ● **Mustang Monthly**
Dobbs Publications, Inc.
3816 Industry Blvd.   Ph:(813)646-5743
Lakeland, FL 33811   Fax:(813)644-8373

Magazine for Mustang enthusiasts. Monthly. **Editor(s):** Bob McClurg. **Price:** $23.97/year; $2.95 per single issue.

1417 ● **Mustang Owners Club of Southeastern Michigan—Newsletter**
Mustang Owners Club of Southeastern Michigan
P.O. Box 39088
Redford, MI 48239

Monthly.

1418 ● **Mustang Red Book, 1965-1990**
Motorbooks International
729 Prospect Ave.
Osceola, WI 54020   Ph:(715)294-3345

Published 1990. **Editor(s):** Peter Sessler. **Price:** $9.95.

1419 ● **Mustang: The 25th Silver Anniversary**
NAC Home Video
1300 Quail, Ste. 201
Newport Beach, CA 92660   Ph:(213)876-9946

A celebration of the one car that has truly become a piece of Americana. Included are rare clips of original prototypes and blueprints and a special look at the glory of the muscle years. **Release date:** 1989. **Producer:** Ford Motor Co. **Price:** $12.98.

1420 ● **Mustang: The Enduring Legend**
Smithmark Publishers, Inc.
112 Madison Ave.
New York, NY 10016   Ph:(212)532-6600

Published 1991. **Editor(s):** Nicky Wright. **Price:** $19.98.

1421 ● **Mustang Times**
Mustang Club of America (MCA)
P.O. Box 447
Lithonia, GA 30058   Ph:(404)482-4822

Includes association news, information on new members, and calendar of events. Monthly. **Price:** Included in membership dues.

1422 ● **Mustang Times Magazine [South Carolina]**
Central Savannah River Area Mustang Club
P.O. Box 296
Graniteville, SC 29829   Ph:(803)663-7938

Periodic.

1423 ● The Pony Express
Mustang Owners Club International
2720 Tennessee, N.E.
Albuquerque, NM 87110   Ph:(505)296-2554

Intended for enthusiasts of the Ford Mustang (includes all models, 1964-Present). Publishes articles on Mustang history, restoration information, valuation, racing reports, and events around the world. Monthly. **Editor(s):** Paul G. McLaughlin. **Price:** Available to members only.

1424 ● Standard Catalog of Ford 1896-1990
Krause Publications, Inc.
700 E. State St.
Iola, WI 54990   Ph:(715)445-2214

Published 1990. **Price:** $19.95.

1425 ● The Story of Mustang
Simitar Entertainment
3850 Annapolis Ln.   Ph:(612)559-6660
Plymouth, MN 55447   Fax:(612)559-0210

Shows the history of this classic American automobile. **Release date:** 1988. **Producer:** Simitar Entertainment. **Price:** $9.95.

1426 ● Super Ford
Dobbs Publications, Inc.
3816 Industry Blvd.   Ph:(813)646-5743
Lakeland, FL 33811   Fax:(813)644-8373

Magazine for owners of high performance Fords. Monthly. **Editor(s):** Tom Wilson. **Price:** $23.97/year; $3.50 per single issue.

1427 ● Your Ford: Including Lincoln-Mercury: Essential Service Information for Owners and Mechanics
Consumer Reports Books
51 E. 42nd St., Ste. 800
New York, NY 10017   Ph:(212)682-9280

Based on technical service bulletins issued to Ford and Lincoln-Mercury dealers from 1985 through 1987. Published 1988. **Editor(s):** Mort J. Schultz. **Price:** $8.00.

ASSOCIATIONS

1428 ● FOMOCO Owners Club
3633 Akron Ct.
Loveland, CO 80538
Barry Abels, Exec. Ofc.   Ph:(303)669-8767

Founded: 1985. **Membership:** 250. Individuals dedicated to the exhibition, preservation, and restoration of Edsel, Ford, Lincoln, and Mercury automobiles. Conducts charitable activities; sponsors educational programs. Bestows awards. **Convention/Meeting:** Annual (with exhibits) - 1991 September, Lakewood, CO.

1429 ● Mustang Club of America
P.O. Box 447
Lithonia, GA 30058
Bill Dillard, Pres.   Ph:(404)482-4822

Founded: 1976. **Membership:** 5,500. Owners and enthusiasts of Ford Mustang and Shelby automobiles produced since 1964. Purpose is to preserve and maintain Ford Mustang and Shelby cars and to serve as an accurate technical source of information concerning these automobiles. Offers restoration and maintenance advice. Sponsors tours, rallies, picnics, campouts, and other group events; holds a buy-sell-swap forum. Bestows awards; operates charitable program. **Convention/Meeting:** 2-4 shows/swap meets/year (with exhibits).

1430 ● Mustang Owners Club International
2720 Tennessee, NE
Albuquerque, NM 87110
Paul G. McLaughlin, Pres.   Ph:(505)296-2554

Founded: 1975. **Membership:** 650. Owners and enthusiasts with an interest in the preservation and promotion of Ford Mustangs produced since 1965. Sponsors regional and national meets, shows, picnics, tours, and seminars. Maintains 500 volume library of books, catalogs, and magazines. **Former Name(s):** (1983) Mustang Owners Club. **Convention/Meeting:** Annual.

1431 ● Performance Ford Club of America, Inc.
13155 U.S. Rt. 23
Ashville, OH 43103
Charles Crites, Pres.   Ph:(614)983-2273

Founded: 1981. **Membership:** 6,000. Car collectors and restorers, race car enthusiasts, and truck and tractor pullers. Provides restoration, promotion, and maintenance Ford-powered products. Conducts research on past and present products. Sponsors specialized education; holds competitions and bestows awards. **Convention/Meeting:** Annual national show (with exhibits) - 1992 Sept. 5-6, Xenia, OH.

FORD PROBE (1989-92)

Originally intended to replace the rear-drive Mustang, Probe was introduced in May 1988 as a 1989 model. Probe shares similar components with the Mazda MX-6 and is produced at the Mazda plant in Flat Rock, Michigan (plant parts data: domestic parts - 42%, imported parts - 58%; *Federal Trade Zone Board*, 1989). Selected by *Autoweek* to make its list of ''The Best and Brightest'' 1989 cars and featured among the best products of 1988 by *Business Week*. It was named to the Ten Best Cars Nominees list by *Car and Driver—Buyer's Guide 1990*.

1991 Ford Probe GT

MAJOR FEATURES

● Probe GL has as 1992 standard equipment: 2.2-liter I-4 engine, 5-speed manual transmission, front-wheel drive, four-wheel independent suspension, power front disc/rear drum brakes, 50/50 split rear seats, AM/FM stereo, power steering, motorized front seat belts, and cloth reclining front bucket seats.

● Probe LX adds as 1992 standard equipment: 3.0-liter V-6 engine, 4-wheel disc brakes, tilt steering column and instrument cluster, and tinted glass.

● Probe LX Sport adds as 1992 standard equipment: rear-deck spoiler, performance tires, and 15-inch aluminum wheels.

● Probe GT adds as 1992 standard equipment: 2.2-liter

turbocharged engine, handling suspension, automatic adjusting suspension, variable power-assist speed-sensitive steering, front air dam with foglamps, rear spoiler, sill extensions, and an upgraded interior.

PRICE HISTORY

The following new car prices reflect the approximate retail cost of the base model: **1989** - $10,943; **1990** - $11,470; **1991** - $11,743; **1992** - $12,257.

DIMENSIONS

Body Style	Years Avail	Wheel Base (in)	Lgth (in)	Ht (in)	Avg Wt (lbs)	Fuel Cap (gal)	Front Hdrm (in)	Front Legrm (in)
2d cpe	89-92	99	177	51.8	2,730	15.1	37.3	42.5

ENGINES

Type	Displacement (L)	Fuel Dly	HP @rpm	Torque @rpm (ft/lbs)	MPG Cty/Hwy	Years Avail
I-4	2.2	FI	110@4700	130@3000	24/31	89-92
I-4T	2.2	FI	145@4300	190@3500	21/27	89-92
V-6	3.0	FI	140@4800	160@3000	19/26	90-90
V-6	3.0	FI	145@4800	165@3400	19/26	91-92

KEY: I=in-line engine; V=V engine; F=flat engine; FI=fuel injection; bbl=barrel carburetor; T=turbo; D=diesel; HP=horsepower; MPG=estimated average miles per gallon.

EVALUATIONS, TESTS, AND RANKINGS

1991: "LX's V6 is smooth, gutsy ... Tilt cluster keeps instruments from being blocked by wheel ... Cargo capacity (rear seat down) is immense for sport coupe." **Source**: "Ford Probe: Something for Almost Everyone," *Autofile*, 1991, pp. 54-58.

1990: "GT's turbo motor generates a good turn of speed and has a broad, useful powerband." **Source**: "Bang for the Buck," *Motor Trend*, November 1989, pp. 42-46, 48, 52-55, 58-59, 62, 64, 66-68, 72, 76.

1990: "has all the right moves ... eye-catching modern exterior design ... supple-yet-competent suspension makes for the best roadholding." **Source**: "Six-Packs to Go; Chevy Beretta, Dodge Daytona and Ford Probe: best American sports coupes," *Road & Track*, May 1990, pp. 130-131, 135, 137, 139-141.

1990: "practically limousinelike in its comportment ... the metabolism of a cruiser rather than a charger ... ride motions feel excessively jouncy over reasonably good pavement." **Source**: "Coupes Du Jour," *Popular Science*, February 1990, pp. 50-52, 56-57.

1989: "chassis is virtually identical to that of the MX-6 coupe ... turbo lag is virtually nonexistent ... stiffened the suspension slightly to reduce body roll in corners ... at some expense in ride harshness." **Source**: "Ford's Probe: Made in Michigan—by Mazda," *Popular Science*, May 1988, p. 85.

1989: "boulevard ride is good, and high-speed handling on the track (especially the GT) is balanced and solid." **Source**: "1989 Ford Probe," *Popular Mechanics*, March 1988, p. 129.

1989: "more stable, more predictable and less limited by understeer than the Mazda version." **Source**: "6 Quick Coupes," *Popular Science*, September 1988, pp. 32-34, 36, 40-41.

1989: "[GT] ... engine has outstanding low- and midrange torque ... brakes are excellent." **Source**: "Coupes De Grace," *Popular Mechanics*, May 1989, pp. 120-124, 212, 214.

1989: "GT looks and feels like the sports coupe it is." **Source**: "Ten Best Cars," *Car and Driver*, January 1989, pp. 30-35.

RECALLS

1991: (7,700 Probe GL models): Brackets mounting automatic shoulder belt retractor assembly may have an understrength spot weld. Shoulder belt could fail in a collision. **Corrective action:** Install two bolts in the brackets to prevent shoulder belt failure. *(NHTSA Campaign No. 91V016000.)*

1990: (2,900 cars): Throttle levers may have been bent during assembly. Throttle may stick and not return fully to idle position. **Corrective action:** Place affected vehicles on delivery hold until repaired. *(NHTSA Campaign No. 89V159000.)*

SAFETY AND REPAIRS

1989: "Ford Covers Mufflers," *Automotive News*, February 10, 1992, p. 128. **Note:** Extended warranty coverage provided for mufflers.

REPAIR MANUALS

1432 ● Chilton's Guide to Chassis Electronics and Power Accessories, 1988-1991 Ford/Chrysler/Jeep/Eagle
Chilton Co.
Chilton Way
Radnor, PA 19089   Ph:(215)964-4000

Published March 1991. **Price:** $19.95.

1433 ● Motor Auto Repair 1983-1989 Ford
Hearst Books
105 Madison Ave.
New York, NY 10016   Ph:(212)889-3050

Published 1989. **Price:** $14.95.

OTHER INFORMATION SOURCES

1434 ● FOMOCO Owners Club—Newsletter
FOMOCO Owners Club
3804 Conifer Dr.
Loveland, CO 80538   Ph:(303)669-8767

Monthly.

1435 ● Ford Enthusiast Magazine
Performance Ford Club of America
PO Box 32
Ashville, OH 43103   Ph:(614)983-4777

Provides information of high performance Ford models. Bimonthly. **Editor(s):** France Crites, Publisher and Editor. **Price:** $20.00 per year; $3.50 per issue.

1436 ● Ford-Lincoln-Mercury Club of Florida—Newsletter
Ford-Lincoln-Mercury Club of Florida
P.O. Box 13514
Tampa, FL 33681   Ph:(813)839-0241

Monthly.

1437 ● Ford-O-Gram
Performance Ford Club of America
13155 U.S. Rte. 23
Ashville, OH 43103   Ph:(614)983-2273

Carries information on past and present Ford powered products for car collectors and restorers, race car enthusiasts, and truck and tractor pullers. Recurring features include reports on Club competitions and educational programs, news of members, and calendar of events. Bimonthly. **Price:** Available to members only.

1438 ● Standard Catalog of Ford 1896-1990
Krause Publications, Inc.
700 E. State St.
Iola, WI 54990   Ph:(715)445-2214

Published 1990. **Price:** $19.95.

1439 ● Super Ford
Dobbs Publications, Inc.
3816 Industry Blvd.   Ph:(813)646-5743
Lakeland, FL 33811   Fax:(813)644-8373

Magazine for owners of high performance Fords. Monthly.
Editor(s): Tom Wilson. **Price:** $23.97/year; $3.50 per single issue.

ASSOCIATIONS

1440 ● FOMOCO Owners Club
3633 Akron Ct.
Loveland, CO 80538
Barry Abels, Exec. Ofc.   Ph:(303)669-8767

Founded: 1985. **Membership:** 250. Individuals dedicated to the exhibition, preservation, and restoration of Edsel, Ford, Lincoln, and Mercury automobiles. Conducts charitable activities; sponsors educational programs. Bestows awards. **Convention/Meeting:** Annual (with exhibits) - 1991 September, Lakewood, CO.

1441 ● Performance Ford Club of America, Inc.
13155 U.S. Rt. 23
Ashville, OH 43103
Charles Crites, Pres.   Ph:(614)983-2273

Founded: 1981. **Membership:** 6,000. Car collectors and restorers, race car enthusiasts, and truck and tractor pullers. Provides restoration, promotion, and maintenance Ford-powered products. Conducts research on past and present products. Sponsors specialized education; holds competitions and bestows awards. **Convention/Meeting:** Annual national show (with exhibits) - 1992 Sept. 5-6, Xenia, OH.

FORD RANGER (1987-92)

Compact truck that comes in 4x2 and 4x4 drive systems, Regular Cab, or Supercab body configurations, S, XLT, STX, Sport, and Custom trim levels, and a variety of engines. All except the Regular Cab 4 x 2 model are equipped with power steering. All except the ''S'' model can be fitted with optional sport and rally packages. Produced at the Ford plant in Louisville, Kentucky. (Note: The dimension chart provides information for the Ford Ranger Regular Cab version.)

1992 Ford Ranger

MAJOR FEATURES

● Ranger S has as 1992 standard equipment: 5-speed manual transmission, power front disc/rear drum brakes with computerized anti-lock rear system, front independent/rear live suspension, and gas-pressurized shock absorbers.

● Ranger XLT model comes with an upgraded interior and has an overall body length of 193.7 in 1992.

● Ranger STX and Sport add as 1992 standard equipment: fog lamps, bumper guards, power steering, electronic AM/FM stereo radio with cassette player and clock, leather-wrapped steering wheel, and deep-dish cast aluminum wheels.

● Ranger Custom adds as 1992 standard equipment: 3-passenger vinyl bench seat.

PRICE HISTORY

The following new car prices reflect the approximate retail cost of the base model: **1988** - $7,093; **1989** - $7,693; **1990** - $7,856; **1991** - $8,374.

DIMENSIONS

Body Style	Years Avail	Wheel Base (in)	Lgth (in)	Ht (in)	Avg Wt (lbs)	Fuel Cap (gal)	Front Hdrm (in)	Front Legrm (in)
trk	87-88	107.9	175.6	64.0	3,900	15.2	39.2	42.4
trk	89-92	107.9	176.5	63.7	4,080	16.3	39.2	42.4

ENGINES

Type	Displace- ment (L)	Fuel Dly	HP @rpm	Torque @rpm (ft/lbs)	MPG Cty/Hwy	Years Avail
I-4	2.3	FI	90@na	na	22/27	87-88
I-4	2.0	2-bbl	na	na	22/26	88-88
I-4	2.3	FI	100@4600	133@2600	23/28	89-92
I-4TD	2.3	na	na	na	28/30	87-87
V-6	2.9	FI	140@4600	170@2600	18/22	87-92
V-6	4.0	FI	160@4200	225@2400	18/23	90-92
V-6	3.0	FI	145@4800	170@3600	20/25	91-92

KEY: I=in-line engine; V=V engine; F=flat engine; FI=fuel injection; bbl=barrel carburetor; T=turbo; D=diesel; HP=horsepower; MPG=estimated average miles per gallon.

EVALUATIONS, TESTS, AND RANKINGS

1991: ''Ford Ranger Sport was comparatively opulent with trim ... racy wheels ... adds character ... Lousy unladen weight distribution handicaps pickup trucks in tests of cornering grips.'' **Source:** ''The Econobox Quandry,'' *Car and Driver*, September 1991, pp. 51-54.

1990: ''high-spirited.'' **Source:** ''Ford Ranger,'' *Car and Driver—Buyer's Guide*, 1989, pp. 184-185.

1990: "STX Ranger pickup has all the creature comforts of a modern sedan . . . rough, tough off-road capability . . . engine easily kept up with expressway traffic." **Source:** "Compact Pickups With New Power," *Sports Afield,* July 1990, p. 32.

1989: "great fun to drive . . . lots of pep . . . solid, stable feeling under all conditions." **Source:** "Compact Commandos," *Popular Mechanics,* February 1989, pp. 51-55, 122.

1989: "Controls are user-friendly . . . high-quality paint finish and rattle-free construction . . . outstanding value for the money." **Source:** "Pickups for Gardeners," *Organic Gardening,* September 1989, pp. 61-64, 66-67.

1989: "excellent ground clearance . . . one of those trucks that rides better off-road than on . . . smooth power train is the Ranger's most endearing feature." **Source:** "Mudders," *Popular Science,* July 1989, pp. 33-34, 38-40, 42, 44.

RECALLS

1990: (4,000 vehicles): Throttle lever may contact throttle body air inlet tube, with the potential for throttle remaining open following release of accelerator pedal from full-throttle position in trucks with 4.0 liter engines. Uncontrolled acceleration could create lack of control and cause an accident. **Corrective action:** Replace air inlet tube with newly designed replacement with an increased throttle lever-to-inlet tube clearance. *(NHTSA Campaign No. 89V234000.)*

1990: (4,000 trucks with 4.0 engines): Uncontrolled acceleration possible due to contact between throttle lever and body. **Corrective action:** Replace air inlet with newly designed replacement. *(NHTSA Campaign No. 90V044000.)*

1989: (25,000 4x4 multipurpose vehicles equipped with front axle automatic locking hubs; recall includes the Ford Ranger and Ford Bronco II): Front wheel bearing adjusting nut retaining keys may be missing from front axle assemblies, allowing the nut to loosen. Could result in detachment of wheel and hub assembly from the axle, loss of vehicle control, and an accident. **Corrective action:** Install retaining keys in front wheel hub assemblies where missing. *(NHTSA Campaign No. 89V109000.)*

1988: (141 regular cab pickup trucks equipped with limited slip rear axles; includes other Ford models): Trucks were built with incorrect rear brake assemblies. Tendency for rear brake lockup would exist particularly during heavy brake application with a lightly loaded truck. Increased stopping distance would be required. **Corrective action:** Replace rear brake assemblies. *(NHTSA Campaign No. 87V141000.)*

1987: (3,600,000 passenger cars and light trucks equipped with fuel injection. Recall includes several Ford, Mercury, and Lincoln models; includes models made before 1987): Spring lock fuel line coupling may not be properly engaged. Coupling could disengage due to fuel pressure, vibration, and engine movements; this would cause loss of fuel which, in presence of an ignition source, creates a fire risk. **Corrective action:** Install retainer clips over the couplings to prevent coupling separation and fuel leakage. *(NHTSA Campaign No. 87V139000.)*

1987: (13,430 vehicles): Buckle portion of the seatbelt assembly may not have been properly anchored to the floor. Seatbelt assembly would not withstand a substantial impact load and would be a potential for personal injury. **Corrective action:** Inspect and make proper installation of seatbelt and buckle anchor bolts, if necessary. *(NHTSA Campaign No. 87V075000.)*

1987: (17,420 multi-purpose 4x4 passenger vehicles. Recall includes the Ford Bronco and Ford Ranger): Stickers concerning handling and maneuverability which are affixed to driver's sun visor sleeves do not meet criteria for permanent adhesion. Vehicles do not meet formats specified by parts 573 and 579 of 49CFR. **Corrective action:** Owners will be mailed new sun visor sleeves with all applicable decal information permanently affixed. *(NHTSA Campaign No. 87V070000.)*

1987: (1,220 pickup trucks modified into Bigfoot Cruisers by Scherer Truck Equipment, Inc): Wheel lug nut cone angles do not match lug nut seating angles. Nuts could loosen in service creating potential for wheels to separate from truck. **Corrective action:** Repair to prevent loosening of lug nuts. *(NHTSA Campaign No. 87V140000.)*

SAFETY AND REPAIRS

1990: "Transmission Defect Baffles Ford; 788,796 Trucks Have It," *Automotive News,* **Note:** Safety defect in parking brake of automatic transmissions could allow vehicles to roll.

1987: "Service Tips," *Popular Mechanics,* November 1989, p. 43. **Note:** '87 Ford Rangers and Bronco IIs may experience throttle-plate sticking.

REPAIR MANUALS

1442 ● Chilton's Ford Repair Manual 1980-1987
Chilton Co.
Chilton Way
Radnor, PA 19089   Ph:(215)964-4000

Published 1987. **Price:** $19.95.

1443 ● Chilton's Guide to Chassis Electronics and Power Accessories, 1988-1991 Ford/Chrysler/Jeep/Eagle
Chilton Co.
Chilton Way
Radnor, PA 19089   Ph:(215)964-4000

Published March 1991. **Price:** $19.95.

1444 ● Chilton's Professional Electronics Diagnostic Manual Ford Cars and Trucks 1984-1988: Motor-Age Professional Mechanic's Edition
Chilton Co.
Chilton Way
Radnor, PA 19089   Ph:(215)964-4000

Published 1988. **Price:** $52.00

1445 ● Ford Pickups: 1969-1987 Shop Manual
Clymer Publications
P.O. Box 1209
Overland Park, KS 66212   Ph:(913)541-6694

With illustrations. Published 1986. **Price:** $14.95.

1446 ● Ford Pickups and Bronco 1987-1990
Chilton Co.
Chilton Way
Radnor, PA 19089   Ph:(215)964-4000

Total car care service. February 1990. **Price:** $19.95.

1447 ● Ford Ranger and Bronco II 1983-1988: Includes Diesel and Four-Wheel Drive Shop Manual
Clymer Publications
P.O. Box 1209
Overland Park, KS 66212   Ph:(913)541-6694

Editor(s): Kalton C. Lahue. **Price:** $14.95.

1448 ● Haynes Ford Pick-Ups and Bronco Owners Workshop Manual, No. 880
Haynes Publications, Inc.
861 Lawrence Dr.
Newbury Park, CA 91320   Ph:(818)889-5400

Editor(s): J. H. Haynes and John B. Raffa. **Price:** $15.95.

1449 ● Haynes Ford Ranger and Bronco II Owners Workshop Manual, No. 1026: 1983-1989
Haynes Publications, Inc.
861 Lawrence Dr.
Newbury Park, CA 91320   Ph:(818)889-5400

Price: $15.95.

1450 ● Motor Auto Repair 1983-1989 Ford
Hearst Books
105 Madison Ave.
New York, NY 10016   Ph:(212)889-3050

Published 1989. **Price:** $14.95.

1451 ● Ranger-Bronco II 1983-1988: Repair and Tune-Up Guide
Chilton Co.
Chilton Way
Radnor, PA 19089   Ph:(215)964-4000

Published 1989. **Price:** $15.95.

OTHER INFORMATION SOURCES

1452 ● FOMOCO Owners Club—Newsletter
FOMOCO Owners Club
3804 Conifer Dr.
Loveland, CO 80538   Ph:(303)669-8767

Monthly.

1453 ● Ford Enthusiast Magazine
Performance Ford Club of America
PO Box 32
Ashville, OH 43103   Ph:(614)983-4777

Provides information of high performance Ford models. Bimonthly. **Editor(s):** France Crites, Publisher and Editor. **Price:** $20.00 per year; $3.50 per issue.

1454 ● Ford-Lincoln-Mercury Club of Florida—Newsletter
Ford-Lincoln-Mercury Club of Florida
P.O. Box 13514
Tampa, FL 33681   Ph:(813)839-0241

Monthly.

1455 ● Ford-O-Gram
Performance Ford Club of America
13155 U.S. Rte. 23
Ashville, OH 43103   Ph:(614)983-2273

Carries information on past and present Ford powered products for car collectors and restorers, race car enthusiasts, and truck and tractor pullers. Recurring features include reports on Club competitions and educational programs, news of members, and calendar of events. Bimonthly. **Price:** Available to members only.

1456 ● Standard Catalog of Ford 1896-1990
Krause Publications, Inc.
700 E. State St.
Iola, WI 54990   Ph:(715)445-2214

Published 1990. **Price:** $19.95.

1457 ● Super Ford
Dobbs Publications, Inc.
3816 Industry Blvd.   Ph:(813)646-5743
Lakeland, FL 33811   Fax:(813)644-8373

Magazine for owners of high performance Fords. Monthly. **Editor(s):** Tom Wilson. **Price:** $23.97/year; $3.50 per single issue.

1458 ● Your Ford: Including Lincoln-Mercury: Essential Service Information for Owners and Mechanics
Consumer Reports Books
51 E. 42nd St., Ste. 800
New York, NY 10017   Ph:(212)682-9280

Based on technical service bulletins issued to Ford and Lincoln-Mercury dealers from 1985 through 1987. Published 1988. **Editor(s):** Mort J. Schultz. **Price:** $8.00.

ASSOCIATIONS

1459 ● FOMOCO Owners Club
3633 Akron Ct.
Loveland, CO 80538
Barry Abels, Exec. Ofc.   Ph:(303)669-8767

Founded: 1985. **Membership:** 250. Individuals dedicated to the exhibition, preservation, and restoration of Edsel, Ford, Lincoln, and Mercury automobiles. Conducts charitable activities; sponsors educational programs. Bestows awards. **Convention/Meeting:** Annual (with exhibits) - 1991 September, Lakewood, CO.

FORD TAURUS (1987-92)

Corporate twin of the Mercury Sable, Taurus is produced in Chicago, Illinois and Atlanta, Georgia (Atlanta plant parts data: domestic parts - 96%, imported parts - 4%, *Federal Trade Zone Board*, 1989). In 1990, chosen by *The Complete Car Cost Guide* as having one of the best overall values for a compact car (Taurus L) and compact wagon (Taurus GL); the highest fuel cost (Taurus LX); and highest repair cost (Taurus Series). Selected by *Car and Driver—Buyer's Guide 1990* as a "Ten Best Cars" nominee and the best sedan in the $12,500-$17,500 range by Road & Track in the same year. Chosen as one of *The Car Book*'s Best Bets of 1992. Nominated to the *Car and Driver* Ten Best list in 1992.

1991 Ford Taurus SHO

MAJOR FEATURES

● Taurus L and L Wagon have as 1992 standard equipment: 3.0-liter V-6 engine, 4-speed automatic transmission, power steering, driver's side airbag, tilt steering column, tinted glass, 4-wheel disc brakes, and 4-wheel independent suspension. New for 1992 are numerous design changes including nine new colors and new aluminum wheels and wheel covers.

● Taurus GL and GL Wagon add as 1992 standard equipment: numerous exterior body stylings and interior accessories.

● Taurus LX and LX Wagon add as 1992 standard equipment: variable-assist power steering, air conditioning, Convenience Kit, Light Group, and alloy wheels.

● Taurus LX Wagon adds as 1992 standard equipment: 3.8-liter V-6 engine.

● Taurus SHO adds as 1992 standard equipment: 3.0-liter DOHC 24-valve engine with dual exhaust, anti-lock 4-wheel disc brakes, fog lamps, rear defogger, cruise control, high-level audio system, cassette player, an upgraded interior, and performance tires on alloy wheels.

● Taurus L-Plus had as 1991 standard equipment: 2.5 liter I4 automatic engine and an automatic transmission.

PRICE HISTORY

The following new car prices reflect the approximate retail cost of the base model: **1987** - $10,650; **1988** - $11,380; **1989** - $11,778; **1990** - $12,640; **1991** - $13,934; **1992** - $14,980.

DIMENSIONS

Body Style	Years Avail	Wheel Base (in)	Lgth (in)	Ht (in)	Avg Wt (lbs)	Fuel Cap (gal)	Front Hdrm (in)	Front Legrm (in)
4d sdn	87-90	106	188.4	54.6	2,872	16.0	38.3	41.7
4d sdn	89-89	106	188.4	54.6	3,078	18.6	38.3	41.7
4d sdn	91-91	106	188.4	54.1	3,049	16.0	38.3	41.7
4d sdn	92-92	106	192.0	54.1	3,131	16.0	38.3	41.7
5d wgn	87-91	106	191.9	55.4	3,276	16.0	38.6	41.7
5d wgn	92-92	106	193.1	55.5	3,294	16.0	38.6	41.7

ENGINES

Type	Displacement (L)	Fuel Dly	HP @rpm	Torque @rpm (ft/lbs)	MPG Cty/Hwy	Years Avail
I-4	2.5	FI	90@4400	130@2600	20/26	87-90
I-4	2.5	FI	105@4400	140@2400	na	91-91
V-6	3.0	FI	140@4800	160@3000	20/29	87-92
V-6	3.8	FI	140@3800	215@2200	18/28	88-92
V-6	3.0	FI	220@6200	200@4800	18/26	89-92

KEY: I=in-line engine; V=V engine; F=flat engine; FI=fuel injection; bbl=barrel carburetor; T=turbo; D=diesel; HP=horsepower; MPG=estimated average miles per gallon.

EVALUATIONS, TESTS, AND RANKINGS

1992: "archetypal American muscle car . . . still quick, muscular, and fun to throw around corners . . . new-found structural integrity." **Source:** "Ford Taurus SHO: One of America's best is now even better," *Automobile Magazine*, October 1991, pp. 58, 63.

1992: "a well-behaved car . . . adequate power under-foot to hustle down the road . . . new interior is a big step forward." **Source:** "Ford Taurus LX Station Wagon: Mini-van withdrawal therapy," *Motor Trend*, October 1991, pp. 86-88.

1992: "significantly refined and upgraded . . . greatest improvement . . . is its overall feel on the road . . . moves a step

closer to best-in-class." **Source:** "Taurus changes for the better," *Detroit Free Press*, October 17, 1991, p. 1D.

1992: "Radio controls are larger and easier to use . . . model is nearly four inches longer, adding space in the trunk." **Source:** "Changes to 1992 Taurus are evolutionary, not revolutionary," *The Detroit News*, September 5, 1991, p. E2.

1991: "four-cylinders just won't overwhelm you with energy . . . Taurus/Sable line still provides the best range of family sedans." **Source:** "Ford Taurus/Mercury Sable," *Car and Driver*, January 1991, p. 41.

1991: "SHO was about as well-equipped as any modern American luxury car, with the added bonus of plenty of smooth horsepower and handling to match. . .all sorts of storage space and even more space for people." **Source:** "Fast Fourdoors: Detroit's new breed of super sedans makes high performance a family affair," *Popular Mechanics*, January 1991, pp. 28-29.

1991: "powerful yet tractable under virtually all conditions, but the gearshift is balky enough to dilute the pleasure the engine can deliver. . .one of the more resonable automobiles to insure." **Source:** "Ford Taurus SHO: Predator Lying in Wait," *Autofile*, 1991, pp. 130-134.

1991: "ride is excellent, striking a nice balance between softness and control. . .Wind, road, and mechanical noise are suppressed to the point of insignificance. . .If the SHO has. . .vulnerabilty, it is the transmission." **Source:** "Ford Taurus SHO," *Automobile*, January 1991, p. 58.

1991: "unflappable handling. . .SHO's interior is in a class by itself." **Source:** "Yankee Clippers," *Car and Driver*, March 1991, pp. 40, 42-45, 48-50.

1990: "the best American-built sport sedan in the nation. . .retains surprisingly supple ride quality." **Source:** "Top Ten New Car Buys: Domestic," *Motor Trend*, November 1989, pp. 80-83, 86-89.

1990: "continues to set the pace in the 1990s . . . the once groundbreaking appearance is beginning to wear at the edges . . . a little clunky compared to some of the sleek, graceful shapes of other cars." **Source:** "Not-So-Sedate Sedans: Three all-American family four-doors," *Home Mechanix*, June 1990, pp. 104-107.

1990: "SHO's strong suit is its performance . . . Quick response and ease of handling . . . a powerful car, but one that leaves the driver in control." **Source:** "Performance and Practicality," *Design News*, October 2, 1989, pp. 138-139.

1989: "Taurus SHO is maximum capability with minimum recognition." **Source:** "Weenie with a Black Belt," *Esquire*, March 1989, p. 60.

1989: "serious performance in a demure wrapper . . . as much as anyone's bolted into a front-drive car . . . Braking . . . could be better." **Source:** "Motown Muscle: Ford Taurus SHO—the new Q-ship," *Popular Mechanics*, January 1989, pp. 53-57, 116.

1988: "car performed admirably, and it was easy to see why the Taurus is so popular." **Source:** "Ford's Taurus gamble pays off," *The Detroit News*, March 1988, pp. F1-F2.

1988: "driving experience undiminished by its cargo capacity . . . More inspiring by far is the car's sure-footedness." **Source:** "Ford Taurus LX Wagon," *Car and Driver*, August 1987, pp. 101, 103, 105-106.

1987: "steering is surprisingly direct. . .road manners are confidence-inspiring. . .interior looks and feels like the inside of a modern automobile." **Source:** "Cars: Fun Work, But

Somebody's Got To Do It,'' *Car and Driver,* January 1987, pp. 36-41.

RECALLS

1992: (1,300 passenger cars): The secondary portion of the liftgate latch may not function. If the latch is not in the primary latch position, the liftgate could open unexpectedly, possibly while the vehicle is moving. **Corrective action:** Replace malfunctioning liftgate latches. *(NHTSA Campaign No. 91V145000.)*

1990: (2,900 passenger cars with autolamp headlamp control system; recall includes Ford Taurus and Mercury Sable): Incorrect transistor may cause autolamp system light sensor module malfunction. Headlamps could turn off while vehicle is being driven or remain on after vehicle is parked. Loss of headlights while driving at night could be hazardous to the driver and other traffic. **Corrective action:** Replace light sensor modules. *(NHTSA Campaign No. 89V171000.)*

1990: (1,212 passenger cars equipped with police vehicle option package and 14 x 5.5'' heavy-duty steel wheel): Wheels may contain cracks that could propogate in raised portion of wheel center. Under severe duty, this could result in separation of wheel rim from center with loss of control and possibly a collision. **Corrective action:** Replace wheels with wheels of a revised design. *(NHTSA Campaign No. 90V159000.)*

1988-89: (278,000 vehicles; includes Ford Taurus and Mercury Sable models): Power seat switch wiring is routed over rather than under front seat support brace, allowing dammage by seat cushion spring ends. May result in an electrical short and a fire in seat cushion material. **Corrective action:** Revise routing of power seat wiring to prevent damage from seat cushion spring contact. *(NHTSA Campaign No. 91V036000.)*

1987: (3,600,000 passenger cars and light trucks equipped with fuel injection. Recall includes several Ford, Mercury, and Lincoln models; includes models made before 1987): Spring lock fuel line coupling may not be properly engaged. Coupling could disengage due to fuel pressure, vibration, and engine movements; this would cause loss of fuel which, in presence of an ignition source, creates a fire risk. **Corrective action:** Install retainer clips over the couplings to prevent coupling separation and fuel leakage. *(NHTSA Campaign No. 87V139000.)*

1987: (28,000 station wagons equipped with optional rear window wiper motors. Recall includes the Ford Taurus Wagon and Mercury Sable Wagon; includes models made before 1987): Road salt-induced erosion of the wiper motor conductor strips could cause localized thermal stress within the glass. Glass could fracture while station wagon is being driven or parked, creating a risk of injury to occupants or sudden distraction to the driver. **Corrective action:** Apply sealant to conductor strips and protective tape to lower backlites. *(NHTSA Campaign No. 87V017000.)*

1987: (325,000 passenger vehicles sold or registered in the following states: CT, IL, IN, ME, MA, MI, NH, NJ, NY, OH, PA, RI, VT, and WI; includes models made before 1987): Front disc brake rotors may experience severe corrosion if operated in areas where calcium chloride and sodium chloride are used extensively. Severely corroded rotors may fracture or separate near the inner edges of the brake discs causing reduced braking effectiveness, possibly resulting in an accident. **Corrective action:** Replace front brake rotors with full cast front brake rotors. *(NHTSA Campaign No. 91V134000.)*

SAFETY AND REPAIRS

1991: "Taurus Cargo Bin Probed After Child Suffocates," *Automotive News,* October 7, 1991, p. 2. **Note:** NHTSA has received four reports of children getting stuck inside a rear

storage compartment of Ford Taurus and Mercury Sable wagons built since 1986.

1990: "Cures for the altitude blues," *Road & Track,* December 1989, pp. 162-163. **Note:** Power loss at high altitudes.

1989: "NHTSA Investigating Taurus Start Switches," *Automotive News,* November 4, 1991, p. 52. **Note:** Ignition switches could overheat in 1986-89 models.

REPAIR MANUALS

1460 ● **Chilton's Ford Repair Manual 1980-1987**
Chilton Co.
Chilton Way
Radnor, PA 19089   Ph:(215)964-4000

Published 1987. **Price:** $19.95.

1461 ● **Chilton's Guide to Chassis Electronics and Power Accessories, 1988-1991 Ford/Chrysler/Jeep/Eagle**
Chilton Co.
Chilton Way
Radnor, PA 19089   Ph:(215)964-4000

Published March 1991. **Price:** $19.95.

1462 ● **Chilton's Professional Electronics Diagnostic Manual Ford Cars and Trucks 1984-1988: Motor-Age Professional Mechanic's Edition**
Chilton Co.
Chilton Way
Radnor, PA 19089   Ph:(215)964-4000

Published 1988. **Price:** $52.00.

1463 ● **Ford, Lincoln, Mercury Car Repair and Tune-Up Guide: 1972-1987**
Clymer Publications
P.O. Box 1209
Overland Park, KS 66212   Ph:(913)541-6694

Published 1987. **Price:** 14.95.

1464 ● **Haynes Ford Taurus and Mercury Sable Owners Workshop Manual, No. 1421: 1986-1990**
Haynes Publications, Inc.
861 Lawrence Dr.
Newbury Park, CA 91320   Ph:(818)889-5400

Editor(s): J. H. Haynes and Bob Henderson. **Price:** $15.95.

1465 ● **Motor Auto Repair 1983-1989 Ford**
Hearst Books
105 Madison Ave.
New York, NY 10016   Ph:(212)889-3050

Published 1989. **Price:** $14.95.

OTHER INFORMATION SOURCES

1466 ● **FOMOCO Owners Club—Newsletter**
FOMOCO Owners Club
3804 Conifer Dr.
Loveland, CO 80538   Ph:(303)669-8767

Monthly.

1467 ● **Ford Enthusiast Magazine**
Performance Ford Club of America
PO Box 32
Ashville, OH 43103   Ph:(614)983-4777

Provides information of high performance Ford models.

Bimonthly. **Editor(s):** France Crites, Publisher and Editor. **Price:** $20.00 per year; $3.50 per issue.

1468 ● Ford-Lincoln-Mercury Club of Florida—Newsletter
Ford-Lincoln-Mercury Club of Florida
P.O. Box 13514
Tampa, FL 33681   Ph:(813)839-0241

Monthly.

1469 ● Ford-O-Gram
Performance Ford Club of America
13155 U.S. Rte. 23
Ashville, OH 43103   Ph:(614)983-2273

Carries information on past and present Ford powered products for car collectors and restorers, race car enthusiasts, and truck and tractor pullers. Recurring features include reports on Club competitions and educational programs, news of members, and calendar of events. Bimonthly. **Price:** Available to members only.

1470 ● Standard Catalog of Ford 1896-1990
Krause Publications, Inc.
700 E. State St.
Iola, WI 54990   Ph:(715)445-2214

Published 1990. **Price:** $19.95.

1471 ● Super Ford
Dobbs Publications, Inc.
3816 Industry Blvd.   Ph:(813)646-5743
Lakeland, FL 33811   Fax:(813)644-8373

Magazine for owners of high performance Fords. Monthly. **Editor(s):** Tom Wilson. **Price:** $23.97/year; $3.50 per single issue.

1472 ● Taurus: The Making of the Car That Saved Ford
NAL/Dutton
1633 Broadway
New York, NY 10019   Ph:(212)397-8000

Published 1991. **Editor(s):** Eric Taub. **Price:** $21.95.

1473 ● Your Ford: Including Lincoln-Mercury: Essential Service Information for Owners and Mechanics
Consumer Reports Books
51 E. 42nd St., Ste. 800
New York, NY 10017   Ph:(212)682-9280

Based on technical service bulletins issued to Ford and Lincoln-Mercury dealers from 1985 through 1987. Published 1988. **Editor(s):** Mort J. Schultz. **Price:** $8.00.

ASSOCIATIONS

1474 ● FOMOCO Owners Club
3633 Akron Ct.
Loveland, CO 80538
Barry Abels, Exec. Ofc.   Ph:(303)669-8767

Founded: 1985. **Membership:** 250. Individuals dedicated to the exhibition, preservation, and restoration of Edsel, Ford, Lincoln, and Mercury automobiles. Conducts charitable activities; sponsors educational programs. Bestows awards. **Convention/Meeting:** Annual (with exhibits) - 1991 September, Lakewood, CO.

1475 ● Performance Ford Club of America, Inc.
13155 U.S. Rt. 23
Ashville, OH 43103
Charles Crites, Pres.   Ph:(614)983-2273

Founded: 1981. **Membership:** 6,000. Car collectors and restorers, race car enthusiasts, and truck and tractor pullers. Provides restoration, promotion, and maintenance Ford-powered products. Conducts research on past and present products. Sponsors specialized education; holds competitions and bestows awards. **Convention/Meeting:** Annual national show (with exhibits) - 1992 Sept. 5-6, Xenia, OH.

FORD TEMPO (1987-92)

Corporate twin is the Mercury Topaz. Produced in Oakville, Ontario, Canada and Kansas City, Missouri (Missouri plant parts data: domestic parts - 92%, imported parts - 8%; *Federal Trade Zone Board*, 1989). Chosen by *The Complete Car Cost Guide* in 1990 as having one of the lowest resale values for a compact (Tempo LX).

1991 Ford Tempo GL

MAJOR FEATURES

● Tempo GL has as 1992 standard equipment: 2.3-liter I-4 engine, 5-speed manual transmission, power steering, 4-wheel independent suspension, front disc/rear drum brakes and tinted glass.

● Tempo GLS adds as 1992 standard equipment: 3.0-liter V-6 engine with sequential electronic fuel injection (SEFI), sport suspension, rear spoiler, fog lamps, performance tires, alloy wheels, performance front seats with power lumbar supports, Light Group, and cassette player.

● Tempo LX adds to GL as 1992 standard equipment: touring suspension, tilt steering column, and power mirrors and locks.

● Tempo Four Wheel Drive added to GL as 1991 standard equipment: higher-output engine, four-wheel drive system, and upgraded interior.

PRICE HISTORY

The following new car prices reflect the approximate retail cost of the base model: **1987** - $8,160; **1988** - $8,658; **1989** - $9,057; **1990** - $9,483; **1991** - $8,350; **1992** - $9,987.

DIMENSIONS

Body Style	Years Avail	Wheel Base (in)	Lgth (in)	Ht (in)	Avg Wt (lbs)	Fuel Cap (gal)	Front Hdrm (in)	Front Legrm (in)
2d cpe	87-92	99.9	176.7	52.8	2,532	15.9	37.5	41.5
4d sdn	87-92	99.9	177.0	52.9	2,600	15.9	37.5	41.5
4d sdn	89-90	99.9	177.0	52.9	2,808	14.2	37.5	41.5

ENGINES

Type	Displace-ment (L)	Fuel Dly	HP @rpm	Torque @rpm (ft/lbs)	MPG Cty/Hwy	Years Avail
I-4	2.3	FI	86@3800	120@3200	22/30	87-87
I-4	2.3	FI	94@4000	126@3200	22/30	87-87
I-4	2.3	FI	98@4400	124@2200	21/29	88-91
I-4	2.3	FI	100@4400	130@2600	22/32	88-91
I-4	2.3	FI	96@4400	128@2600	23/33	92-92
V-6	3.0	FI	135@5500	150@3250	21/28	92-92

KEY: I=in-line engine; V=V engine; F=flat engine; FI=fuel injection; bbl=barrel carburetor; T=turbo; D=diesel; HP=horsepower; MPG=estimated average miles per gallon.

EVALUATIONS, TESTS, AND RANKINGS

1992: "steering is refreshingly sure and precise ... gets a bit floaty over rough or uneven surfaces ... delivers an impressively high level of utility along with a healthy dose of genuine sportiness." **Source:** "Ford Tempo GLS," *Motor Trend,* December 1991, p. 92.

1989: "[GLS] did just fine in most of our standardized tests ... gear-shift is a notchy cable shifter, the engine is noisy and there's a lot of wind buffeting around the windshield." **Source:** "Best Sellers," *Popular Mechanics,* July 1989, pp. 60-63, 120-122.

1989: "fuel-injection system ... boosted output to a respectable level and improved driveability ... recurring tendency to stumble and a persistent engine buzz at all engine speeds." **Source:** "New Spirit in Family Cars," *Popular Science,* June 1989, pp. 48-50, 52, 54.

1988: "meeting the needs of buyers interested primarily in reasonably priced day-to-day transportation. . .HSO engine is unresponsive and noisy." **Source:** "Ford Tempo All Wheel Drive," *Car and Driver,* September 1987, pp. 103, 105.

1988: "GLS model we tested, the engine is called the 2300 HSO ... It puts out a rather ho-hum 100 horsepower ... steering, brakes and suspension all feel squishy." **Source:** "Restyled Ford Tempo Skips a Beat," *The Detroit News,* July 1988, pp. 1F-2F.

RECALLS

1988: (91,000 vehicles with 2.3L engines; includes Ford and Mercury models): Two attachment screws for the throttle position sensors could loosen and back out. If both screws come out, sensors could disengage from the throttle shaft, preventing return of the throttle from mid position. **Corrective action:** Replace attachment screws with screws pre-applied adhesive that will be tightened to a higher torque specification. *(NHTSA Campaign No. 88V024000.)*

1987: (350 passenger cars equipped with stainless steel decorative lug nuts included with styled steel polycast, and cast aluminum wheels. Includes Ford Escort, Ford Tempo, and Mercury Lynx): Lug nuts could gall and possibly seize on the wheel studs without providing adequate clamping load on the wheels. Wheel studs could fracture creating a risk of a wheel separating with little forewarning. **Corrective action:** Replace wheel lug nuts and if necessary, replace wheels and wheel studs. *(NHTSA Campaign No. 87V060000.)*

SAFETY AND REPAIRS

1991: "Ford Recalls 641,562 Units," *Automotive News,* December 2, 1991, p. 2. **Note:** 1990-91 Tempo models with 2.3 liter engines will have throttle position sensors replaced.

1989: "Ford puts 5/50 on Fuel Pumps," *Automotive News,* November 25, 1991, p. 2. **Note:** 1988-89 Tempos have extended warranty coverage on fuel pumps, which may have a weak internal seal.

1987: "Auto Q & A," *Home Mechanix,* August 1990, p. 88. **Note:** '87 Tempo with intermittent high idle and surging problem.

REPAIR MANUALS

1476 ● Chilton Ford-Mercury Front Wheel Drive 1981-1987
Chilton Co.
Chilton Way
Radnor, PA 19089   Ph:(215)964-4000

Published 1987. **Price:** $14.95.

1477 ● Chilton's Ford Repair Manual 1980-1987
Chilton Co.
Chilton Way
Radnor, PA 19089   Ph:(215)964-4000

Published 1987. **Price:** $19.95.

1478 ● Chilton's Guide to Chassis Electronics and Power Accessories, 1988-1991 Ford/Chrysler/Jeep/Eagle
Chilton Co.
Chilton Way
Radnor, PA 19089   Ph:(215)964-4000

Published March 1991. **Price:** $19.95.

1479 ● Chilton's Professional Electronics Diagnostic Manual Ford Cars and Trucks 1984-1988: Motor-Age Professional Mechanic's Edition
Chilton Co.
Chilton Way
Radnor, PA 19089   Ph:(215)964-4000

Published 1988. **Price:** $52.00.

1480 ● Ford, Lincoln, Mercury Car Repair and Tune-Up Guide: 1972-1987
Clymer Publications
P.O. Box 1209
Overland Park, KS 66212   Ph:(913)541-6694

Published 1987. **Price:** 14.95.

1481 ● Ford Tempo and Mercury Topaz, 1984-1987
Clymer Publications
P.O. Box 1209
Overland Park, KS 66212   Ph:(913)541-6694

Published 1987. **Price:** $14.95.

1482 ● Haynes Ford Tempo-Mercury Topaz Owners Workshop Manual, No. 1418: 1984-1989
Haynes Publications, Inc.
861 Lawrence Dr.
Newbury Park, CA 91320   Ph:(818)889-5400

Published 1988. **Price:** $15.95.

1483 ● Motor Auto Repair 1983-1989 Ford
Hearst Books
105 Madison Ave.
New York, NY 10016   Ph:(212)889-3050

Published 1989. **Price:** $14.95.

OTHER INFORMATION SOURCES

1484 ● FOMOCO Owners Club—Newsletter
FOMOCO Owners Club
3804 Conifer Dr.
Loveland, CO 80538   Ph:(303)669-8767

Monthly.

1485 ● Ford-Lincoln-Mercury Club of Florida—Newsletter
Ford-Lincoln-Mercury Club of Florida
P.O. Box 13514
Tampa, FL 33681   Ph:(813)839-0241

Monthly.

1486 ● Ford-O-Gram
Performance Ford Club of America
13155 U.S. Rte. 23
Ashville, OH 43103   Ph:(614)983-2273

Carries information on past and present Ford powered products for car collectors and restorers, race car enthusiasts, and truck and tractor pullers. Recurring features include reports on Club competitions and educational programs, news of members, and calendar of events. Bimonthly. **Price:** Available to members only.

1487 ● Standard Catalog of Ford 1896-1990
Krause Publications, Inc.
700 E. State St.
Iola, WI 54990   Ph:(715)445-2214

Published 1990. **Price:** $19.95.

1488 ● Your Ford: Including Lincoln-Mercury: Essential Service Information for Owners and Mechanics
Consumer Reports Books
51 E. 42nd St., Ste. 800
New York, NY 10017   Ph:(212)682-9280

Based on technical service bulletins issued to Ford and Lincoln-Mercury dealers from 1985 through 1987. Published 1988. **Editor(s):** Mort J. Schultz. **Price:** $8.00.

ASSOCIATIONS

1489 ● FOMOCO Owners Club
3633 Akron Ct.
Loveland, CO 80538
Barry Abels, Exec. Ofc.   Ph:(303)669-8767

Founded: 1985. **Membership:** 250. Individuals dedicated to the exhibition, preservation, and restoration of Edsel, Ford, Lincoln, and Mercury automobiles. Conducts charitable activities; sponsors educational programs. Bestows awards. **Convention/Meeting:** Annual (with exhibits) - 1991 September, Lakewood, CO.

FORD THUNDERBIRD (1987-92)

Produced in Lorain, Ohio, the Ford Thunderbird is the corporate twin of the Mercury Cougar. (plant parts data: domestic parts - 79%, imported parts - 21%; *Federal Trade Zone Board*, 1989). In 1990, chosen by *The Complete Car Cost Guide* as having one of the lowest fuel and maintenance costs and highest resale values for a large car; the lowest repair costs (Thunderbird Series); and the highest fuel and insurance costs (Thunderbird Super Coupe). Selected as ''Car of the Year'' by *Motor Trend* in 1987 and 1989, and as a ''Ten Best Cars Nominee'' by *Car and Driver—Buyer's Guide 1990*. Rated

among the best in crash test performance by *The Car Book* in 1992.

1992 Ford Thunderbird LX

MAJOR FEATURES

● Thunderbird has as 1992 standard equipment: 4-speed automatic transmission, rack-and-pinion power steering, motorized front seat belts, 4-wheel independent suspension, air conditioning, power front disc brakes, and tinted glass.

● Thunderbird LX adds as 1992 standard equipment: variable power-assist speed-sensitive steering, electronic AM/FM stereo with cassette, Power Lock Group, leather-wrapped steering wheel, and cloth leather/vinyl seat trim.

● Thunderbird Super Coupe adds to base 1992 standard equipment: 3.8-liter supercharged V-6 engine, 5-speed manual transmission, anti-lock 4-wheel disc brakes, adjustable sport suspension, speed-sensitive power steering, fog lights, upgraded tires on alloy wheels, and an upgraded sport interior trim.

● Thunderbird Sport has as 1992 standard equipment: 5.0L High Output V-8 engine, cruise control, tilt steering column, variable-assist power steering, fog lights, Handling Package, and upgraded handling tires on alloy wheels.

● Thunderbird Turbo Coupe was a limited edition version and had as 1988 standard equipment: turbo-charged engine.

PRICE HISTORY

The following new car prices reflect the approximate retail cost of the base model: **1987** - $13,028; **1988** - $13,495; **1989** - $14,612; **1990** - $14,980; **1991** - $15,385; **1992** - $16,345.

DIMENSIONS

Body Style	Years Avail	Wheel Base (in)	Lgth (in)	Ht (in)	Avg Wt (lbs)	Fuel Cap (gal)	Front Hdrm (in)	Front Legrm (in)
2d cpe	87-88	104.2	202.1	53.4	3,215	22.1	37.7	42
2d cpe	89-92	113	198.7	52.7	3,550	18	38.1	42.5

ENGINES

Type	Displacement (L)	Fuel Dly	HP @rpm	Torque @rpm (ft/lbs)	MPG Cty/Hwy	Years Avail
I-4T	2.3	FI	190@4600	240@3400	18/27	87-88
V-6	3.8	FI	120@3600	205@1600	17/22	87-87
V-6	3.8	FI	140@3800	215@2400	20/27	88-92
V-6	3.8	FI	210@4000	315@2600	17/24	89-92
V-8	5.0	FI	155@3400	265@2200	18/27	87-88
V-8	5.0	FI	200@4000	275@3000	17/24	91-92

KEY: I=in-line engine; V=V engine; F=flat engine; FI=fuel injection; bbl=barrel carburetor; T=turbo; D=diesel; HP=horsepower; MPG=estimated average miles per gallon.

EVALUATIONS, TESTS, AND RANKINGS

1991: "Ride quality and handling are good, a middle ground between comfort and performance. . .surprisingly noisy at legal-limit speeds for a luxury car. . .Instrumentation was excellent." **Source:** "Ford Brings Back V-8 for the Purists," *The Detroit News*, October 31, 1990, pp. E1-E2.

1991: "idle is smooth—smoother than the Mustang GT's—and levels of noise, vibration, and harshness are commendably low. . .offers a worthwhile improvement in passing power." **Source:** "Ford Thunderbird V-8: Thirty-three percent more cylinders, but not as much more fun," *Car and Driver*, October 1990, pp. 91-92.

1991: "Steering. . .provides good road feedback at highway speeds, yet allows easy low-speed maneuvering for parking. . .a blast to drive." **Source:** "Ford Thunderbird V-8: A T-Bird with the heart of a Mustang," *Motor Trend*, October 1990, pp. 80-81.

1991: "Super Coupe lives up to its name in acceleration, braking, and handling. . .also offers generous room for passengers and cargo." **Source:** "Ford Thunderbird SC: Flawed—But Still Fabulous—Flier," *Autoweek's Autofile 1991 Edition*, 1991, pp. 78-82.

1991: "actual performance was intimately manageable, perhaps surprisingly so." **Source:** "American Power," *Motor Trend*, January 1991, pp. 30-39.

1991: "Styling is a graceful sweep of lines with a European flavor . . . keeps its footing well over smooth and rough surfaces . . . steering effort is a bit too light at high speeds." **Source:** "Optional V-8 gives Thunderbird power it needs to spread wings," *The Flint Journal*, April 10, 1991, p. D2.

1990: "Traction is a problem . . . [T-Bird Super Coupe] needed every last scrap of pavement to make the bend without lifting the throttle or ending up in the ravine. . .car feels heavier than it is." **Source:** "Bang for the Buck," *Motor Trend*, November 1989, pp. 42-46, 48, 52-55, 58-59, 62, 64, 66-68, 72, 76.

1990: "absolute authority and first class style." **Source:** "Top Ten New Car Buys," *Motor Trend*, November 1989, pp. 80-83, 86-89.

1989: "roomier interior, excellent road balance. . .quick and agile in accelerating onto freeways." **Source:** "A Super New Coupe: Powerful Thunderbird runs away from competition," *The Detroit News*, January 4, 1989, pp. F1-F2.

1989: "a rear-drive mid-size sporty coupe that defies direct comparison . . . almost feels like a muscle car at times." **Source:** "Coupes," *Popular Science*, January 1989, pp. 42-44.

1989: "Super Coupe version . . . does zero to 60 in about 7.5 seconds. That's quick." **Source:** "The People's Choice," *Regardie's*, July 1989, pp. 125-130.

1988: "Turbo coupe blends upscale Eurocar-type handling and zip in an American package. . .Turbo coupe's seats are still comfortable after hours of driving." **Source:** "The Thunderbird Soars: Fast, tight, precise '88 Turbo fulfills the promise of decades," *The Detroit News*, November 25, 1987, pp. D1-D2.

RECALLS

1991: (6,800 vehicles with automatic overdrive transmission; includes Ford LTD Crown Victoria, Ford Mustang, Ford Thunderbird, Mercury Cougar, and Mercury Grand Marquis): Park rod assembly contains park cam with inadequate surface hardness, which could lead to park disengagement. **Corrective action:** Replace park rod assembly on automatic transmission. *(NHTSA Campaign No. 91V048000.)*

1990-91: (125,000 passenger cars; includes the Ford

Thunderbird and Mercury Cougar): The nuts that hold windshield wiper motor to the wiper module may not have been sufficiently tightened and may loosen or come off causing changed wiper pattern, or the wipers may jam if two of the three nuts come off resulting in reduced driver visibility in inclement weather conditions. **Corrective action:** Apply torque retention material to wiper motor studs and nuts and retorque. *(NHTSA Campaign No. 91V076000.)*

1990: (72 passenger cars with 3.8 liter engines; includes the Ford Thunderbird and Mercury Cougar): Excessive length of battery-to-starter cables could allow contact with engine damper pulley resulting in cable damage, an electrical short and possibly an underhood fire. **Corrective action:** Replace battery to starter cable with correct length cable. *(NHTSA Campaign No. 90V026000.)*

1989: (113,200 cars; includes Ford Thunderbird and Mercury Cougar models): Due to contact between the brake caliper of the inboard front wheel and the front stabilizer bar, there may be increased brake pedal travel following low speed turning manuevers. Could cause a reduction in brake performance that could result in an accident. **Corrective action:** Install acorn type front suspension strut nuts to eliminate stabilizer bar to brake caliper contact. *(NHTSA Campaign No. 89V081000.)*

1989: (10,600 cars; includes Ford Thunderbird and Mercury Cougar models): Improperly heat treated rear suspension knuckles could experience high mileage fatigue cracks and eventual fracture. Could result in rear suspension failure at the affected wheel with an adverse affect on control of car. **Corrective action:** Replace knuckles that have affected lot codes. *(NHTSA Campaign No. 89V080000.)*

1989: (124 passenger vehicles; includes Mercury Cougar and Ford Thunderbird): Plastic rollover valve mounting plate may not be properly sealed to plastic fuel tank. Fuel or vapor could leak, which could result in vehicle fire. **Corrective action:** Replace fuel tank. *(NHTSA Campaign No. 88V165000.)*

1988: (682 vehicles): Interference between rear axle shaft flanges and disc brake rotor, preventing proper seating of the rotor. An improperly seated rotor could result in a reduction of the clamping forces of the wheel studs, possibly leading to fractured studs and rear wheel separation. **Corrective action:** Inspection of vehicles and, where necessary, replace rear axle shafts and rear brake rotors. *(NHTSA Campaign No. 88V033000.)*

1987: (3,600,000 passenger cars and light trucks equipped with fuel injection. Recall includes several Ford, Mercury, and Lincoln models; includes models made before 1987): Spring lock fuel line coupling may not be properly engaged. Coupling could disengage due to fuel pressure, vibration, and engine movements; this would cause loss of fuel which, in presence of an ignition source, creates a fire risk. **Corrective action:** Install retainer clips over the couplings to prevent coupling separation and fuel leakage. *(NHTSA Campaign No. 87V139000.)*

SAFETY AND REPAIRS

1989: "Car Clinic," *Popular Mechanics*, February 1990, p. 22. **Note:** 1989 Cougar (Thunderbirds are mechanically identical) with clanking and squealing noise from rear.

REPAIR MANUALS

1490 ● **Chilton's Ford-Lincoln-Mercury Full-Size, 1968-1988** Chilton Co.
Chilton Way
Radnor, PA 19089   Ph:(215)964-4000

Published 1989. **Price:** $15.95.

1491 ● Chilton's Ford Repair Manual 1980-1987
Chilton Co.
Chilton Way
Radnor, PA 19089   Ph:(215)964-4000

Published 1987. **Price:** $19.95.

1492 ● Chilton's Ford Thunderbird, Mercury Cougar, Lincoln Continental-Mark VII, 1980-1987
Chilton Co.
Chilton Way
Radnor, PA 19089   Ph:(215)964-4000

Published 1988. **Price:** $15.95.

1493 ● Chilton's Guide to Chassis Electronics and Power Accessories, 1988-1991 Ford/Chrysler/Jeep/Eagle
Chilton Co.
Chilton Way
Radnor, PA 19089   Ph:(215)964-4000

Published March 1991. **Price:** $19.95.

1494 ● Chilton's Professional Electronics Diagnostic Manual Ford Cars and Trucks 1984-1988: Motor-Age Professional Mechanic's Edition
Chilton Co.
Chilton Way
Radnor, PA 19089   Ph:(215)964-4000

Published 1988. **Price:** $52.00.

1495 ● Ford, Lincoln, Mercury Car Repair and Tune-Up Guide: 1972-1987
Clymer Publications
P.O. Box 1209
Overland Park, KS 66212   Ph:(913)541-6694

Published 1987. **Price:** 14.95.

1496 ● Haynes Ford and Mercury Full-Size Owners Workshop Manual, No. 754: 1975-1987
Haynes Publications, Inc.
861 Lawrence Dr.
Newbury Park, CA 91320   Ph:(818)889-5400

Published 1988. **Editor(s):** J. H. Haynes and Chaun Muir. **Price:** $15.95.

1497 ● Haynes Ford Thunderbird and Mercury Cougar, No. 1338: 1983-1988
Haynes Publications, Inc.
861 Lawrence Dr.
Newbury Park, CA 91320   Ph:(818)889-5400

Editor(s): J. H. Haynes and Mike Stubblefield. **Price:** $15.95.

1498 ● Motor Auto Repair 1983-1989 Ford
Hearst Books
105 Madison Ave.
New York, NY 10016   Ph:(212)889-3050

Published 1989. **Price:** $14.95.

OTHER INFORMATION SOURCES

1499 ● Big Bird
Thunderbirds of America
PO Box 2766
Cedar Rapids, IA 52406   Ph:(319)364-6859

Acts as a medium for the exchange of ideas, information, and parts to assist owners with the restoration and preservation of

1967 to present model Ford Thunderbird automobiles. Carries historical and technical articles. Recurring features include updates on club activities, news of members and their automobiles, and a calendar of events. Bimonthly. **Price:** Available to members only.

1500 ● FOMOCO Owners Club—Newsletter
FOMOCO Owners Club
3804 Conifer Dr.
Loveland, CO 80538   Ph:(303)669-8767

Monthly.

1501 ● Ford Enthusiast Magazine
Performance Ford Club of America
PO Box 32
Ashville, OH 43103   Ph:(614)983-4777

Provides information of high performance Ford models. Bimonthly. **Editor(s):** France Crites, Publisher and Editor. **Price:** $20.00 per year; $3.50 per issue.

1502 ● Ford-Lincoln-Mercury Club of Florida—Newsletter
Ford-Lincoln-Mercury Club of Florida
P.O. Box 13514
Tampa, FL 33681   Ph:(813)839-0241

Monthly.

1503 ● Ford-O-Gram
Performance Ford Club of America
13155 U.S. Rte. 23
Ashville, OH 43103   Ph:(614)983-2273

Carries information on past and present Ford powered products for car collectors and restorers, race car enthusiasts, and truck and tractor pullers. Recurring features include reports on Club competitions and educational programs, news of members, and calendar of events. Bimonthly. **Price:** Available to members only.

1504 ● Standard Catalog of Ford 1896-1990
Krause Publications, Inc.
700 E. State St.
Iola, WI 54990   Ph:(715)445-2214

Published 1990. **Price:** $19.95.

1505 ● Super Ford
Dobbs Publications, Inc.
3816 Industry Blvd.   Ph:(813)646-5743
Lakeland, FL 33811   Fax:(813)644-8373

Magazine for owners of high performance Fords. Monthly. **Editor(s):** Tom Wilson. **Price:** $23.97/year; $3.50 per single issue.

1506 ● Your Ford: Including Lincoln-Mercury: Essential Service Information for Owners and Mechanics
Consumer Reports Books
51 E. 42nd St., Ste. 800
New York, NY 10017   Ph:(212)682-9280

Based on technical service bulletins issued to Ford and Lincoln-Mercury dealers from 1985 through 1987. Published 1988. **Editor(s):** Mort J. Schultz. **Price:** $8.00.

ASSOCIATIONS

1507 ● FOMOCO Owners Club
3633 Akron Ct.
Loveland, CO 80538
Barry Abels, Exec. Ofc.   Ph:(303)669-8767

Founded: 1985. **Membership:** 250. Individuals dedicated to the exhibition, preservation, and restoration of Edsel, Ford, Lincoln, and Mercury automobiles. Conducts charitable activities; sponsors educational programs. Bestows awards. **Convention/Meeting:** Annual (with exhibits) - 1991 September, Lakewood, CO.

1508 ● Performance Ford Club of America, Inc.
13155 U.S. Rt. 23
Ashville, OH 43103
Charles Crites, Pres.   Ph:(614)983-2273

Founded: 1981. **Membership:** 6,000. Car collectors and restorers, race car enthusiasts, and truck and tractor pullers. Provides restoration, promotion, and maintenance Ford-powered products. Conducts research on past and present products. Sponsors specialized education; holds competitions and bestows awards. **Convention/Meeting:** Annual national show (with exhibits) - 1992 Sept. 5-6, Xenia, OH.

GEO METRO (1989-92)

Formerly the Chevrolet Sprint, the Geo Metro is built in Ingersoll, Ontario, Canada as a joint venture between General Motors and Suzuki. The convertible, however, is manufactured in Japan. Metro LSi named to 1989 *Car and Driver's* Ten Best Performers List for road horsepower at 50 mph (10 hp), EPA city fuel economy (46 mpg), and observed fuel economy (35 mpg).

1990 Geo Metro

MAJOR FEATURES

● Geo Metro base model has as 1992 standard equipment: 5-speed manual transmission, rack-and-pinion steering, 4-wheel independent suspension, front disc/rear drum power brakes, and rear seat shoulder belts.

● Geo Metro XFI adds to 1992 standard equipment: left remote and right manual mirrors and wheel covers.

● Geo Metro LSi adds as 1992 standard equipment: cloth upholstery, trip odometer, rear defogger, driver's side airbag (convertible), tachometer, visor vanity mirrors for the driver and passenger, and a locking glove box.

PRICE HISTORY

The following new car prices reflect the approximate retail cost

of the base model: **1989** - $5,995; **1990** - $5,995; **1991** - $6,795; **1992** - $6,999.

DIMENSIONS

Body Style	Years Avail	Wheel Base (in)	Lgth (in)	Ht (in)	Avg Wt (lbs)	Fuel Cap (gal)	Front Hdrm (in)	Front Legrm (in)
2d lbk	89-89	89.2	146.1	52.4	1,585	10.6	38	41.7
2d cpe	89-89	89.2	146.1	52.4	1,591	10.6	38	41.7
2d cpe	90-91	89.2	146.1	51.9	1,620	10.6	39.7	42.5
2d cpe	92-92	89.2	147.4	52.4	1,650	10.6	37.8	42.5
2d conv	90-91	89.2	146.1	51.9	1,753	10.6	39.7	42.4
2d conv	92-92	89.2	147.4	52.0	1,753	10.6	39.6	42.4
5d wgn	89-91	93.1	150.0	53.5	1,693	10.6	38.8	42.5
5d wgn	92-92	93.1	151.4	53.5	1,694	10.6	38.8	42.5

ENGINES

Type	Displacement (L)	Fuel Dly	HP @rpm	Torque @rpm (ft/lbs)	MPG Cty/Hwy	Years Avail
I-3	1.0	FI	49@4700	58@3300	53/58	89-92
I-3	1.0	FI	52@5700	58@3300	46/50	90-92

KEY: I=in-line engine; V=V engine; F=flat engine; FI=fuel injection; bbl=barrel carburetor; T=turbo; D=diesel; HP=horsepower; MPG=estimated average miles per gallon.

EVALUATIONS, TESTS, AND RANKINGS

1991: "designed to appeal to single female buyers looking for a high mileage, high excitement, and low maintenance at a low price . . . what Geo claims is a back seat is up for debate . . . Handling is about what you'd expect from a small . . . car . . . unimpressive road-holding ability." **Source:** "Geo Metro LSi Convertible: Home-court advantage," *Motor Trend*, January 1991, pp. 74-76.

1991: "steering is light but lifeless, most likely due to budget tires and soft springs . . . roadster version continues the Metro's minimalist theme . . . A ride in the Metro convertible is anything but boring . . . it is probably the most fun you can have in an economy car." **Source:** "Geo Metro LSi Convertible: Cuteness, Chapter 2," *Car and Driver*, January 1991, pp. 136, 139-140.

1991: "rear seat too uncomfortable for long rides . . . operation of the top is a complicated trial . . . relatively little wind buffeting at highway speeds." **Source:** "Top-Down Showdown: We test the hottest cars under the sun," *Motor Trend*, June 1991, pp. 49-59, 62-63.

1990: "Sporty, chic and available in a variety of loud and lively colours . . . a fuel-efficient minicar." **Source:** "The heartbeat of America is imported," *The Economist*, September 8, 1990, p. 81.

1989: "problem lies primarily with the engine . . . motorcycles have bigger and more powerful engines. . .lack of power actually isn't the biggest problem; it's the noise and vibration that we find most annoying." **Source:** "Geo Metro LSi: What you see is what you get," *Car and Driver*, June 1989, pp. 187, 189.

RECALLS

None to date.

GEO PRIZM (1990-92)

Formerly the Chevrolet Nova, the Prizm is the corporate cousin of the Toyota Corolla. Produced at New United Motor Mfg. Inc. plant in Fremont, California as a joint venture between General Motors and Toyota. (plant parts data: domestic parts - 33%, imported parts - 67%; *Federal Trade Zone Board,* 1989). Geo Prizm GSi named to *Car and Driver's* 1990 Ten Best Cars Nominee list. The 5-door model, available in 1990 and 1991, has been discontinued.

1990 Geo Prizm

MAJOR FEATURES

● Geo Prizm has as 1992 standard equipment: 5-speed manual transmission, front disc/rear drum power brakes, 4-wheel independent suspension, rack-and-pinion steering, and cloth bucket seats.

● Geo Prizm GSi adds as 1992 standard equipment: higher output engine, 4-wheel disc brakes, power steering, upgraded suspension, air conditioning, tilt steering column, rear spoiler, rear defogger, and AM/FM stereo.

● Geo Prizm LSi adds as 1992 standard equipment: upgraded interior.

PRICE HISTORY

The following new car prices reflect the approximate retail cost of the base model: **1990** - $10,125; **1991** - $9,680; **1992** - $10,125.

DIMENSIONS

Body Style	Years Avail	Wheel Base (in)	Lgth (in)	Ht (in)	Avg Wt (lbs)	Fuel Cap (gal)	Front Hdrm (in)	Front Legrm (in)
4d sdn	90-92	95.7	170.7	52.4	2,435	13.2	38.3	40.9
5d sdn	90-91	95.7	170.7	52.4	2,413	13.2	38.3	40.9

ENGINES

Type	Displacement (L)	Fuel Dly	HP @rpm	Torque @rpm (ft/lbs)	MPG Cty/Hwy	Years Avail
I-4	1.6	FI	102@5800	101@4800	28/33	90-92
I-4	1.6	FI	130@6800	105@6000	25/31	90-92

KEY: I=in-line engine; V=V engine; F=flat engine; FI=fuel injection; bbl=barrel carburetor; T=turbo; D=diesel; HP=horsepower; MPG=estimated average miles per gallon.

EVALUATIONS, TESTS, AND RANKINGS

1991: "difficulty in controlling the car near its limit . . . lack the controls over suspension geometry necessary to prevent unwanted changes of wheel positon under hard cornering or when there are large variations in rear-seat loading." **Source:** "Global Designs for Compact Sedans," *Popular Science,* November 1990, pp. 91-95.

1991: "capable of delivering big servings of fun . . . operation of the top is a complicated trial . . . relatively little wind buffeting at highway speeds." **Source:** "Top-Down Showdown: We test the hottest cars under the sun," *Motor Trend,* June 1991, pp. 49-59, 62-63.

1990: "three-speed automatic transmission . . . worked up to speed in a smooth, timely manner. . .were no jerks or whines. . .dashboard gauges were large and easy to read. . .plenty of room up front, but it might be a close fit for three adults in back." **Source:** "Geo Prizm balances small size with comfort," *The Detroit News,* May 3, 1989, pp. 1F-2F.

1990: "acceleration is brisk and sporty, responsive and full of eager life . . . the car displayed premature brake lockup . . . enjoyed driving the Prizm GSi . . . acceleration is in the first rank of the class." **Source:** "Geo Prizm GSi: A fresh, new color in the import rainbow," *Motor Trend,* January 1990, pp. 66, 68-69.

1990: "won't electrify you with high-g performance or dazzle you with fancy moves . . . what it will do is charm you . . . designed to perform with a maximum of utility and a minimum of fuss. . .all put together well. . .won't find a buzz or rattle within ten miles of this car." **Source:** "Geo Prizm LSi: Think of it as the J-car that never was," *Car and Driver,* April 1989, pp. 81-85.

1990: "Engine performance is the car's most outstanding feature . . . Other than the unforgiving seats, the interior is typical of small Japanese economy cars . . . offers excellent value and a heritage of superb reliability for your money." **Source:** "When Dependability Counts," *Home Mechanix,* February 1989, pp. 78-81, 85.

RECALLS

1991: (654 vehicles): Lug nuts that retain wheels and wheel covers may have been torqued to lower than recommended specifications, which could result in a loose wheel that could fall off with potential for loss of control and an accident. **Corrective action:** Remove original wheel cover, torque lug nut to specification, and install full wheel covers that are retained by spring clips. *(NHTSA Campaign No. 90V191000.)*

GEO SPECTRUM (1989)

Formerly the Chevrolet Spectrum, the Geo Spectrum was the corporate cousin of the Isuzu I-Mark. Produced until 1989 in Japan as a joint venture between General Motors and Isuzu; it was sold through Chevrolet dealerships. In 1990, it was redesigned and replaced by the Geo Storm. Rated as poor in crash test performance and high in repair cost by *The Car Book* in 1989.

1989 Geo Spectrum

MAJOR FEATURES

● Geo Spectrum had as 1989 standard equipment: 5-speed manual transmission, rack-and-pinion steering, front independent/rear beam suspension, and power front disc/rear drum brakes.

PRICE HISTORY

The following new car prices reflect the approximate retail cost of the base model: **1989** - $7,295.

DIMENSIONS

Body Style	Years Avail	Wheel Base (in)	Lgth (in)	Ht (in)	Avg Wt (lbs)	Fuel Cap (gal)	Front Hdrm (in)	Front Legrm (in)
3d sdn	89-89	94.5	157.4	52	1,962	11.1	38	41.7
4d sdn	89-89	94.5	160.2	52	1,989	11.1	37.7	41.7

ENGINES

Type	Displace- ment (L)	Fuel Dly	HP @rpm	Torque @rpm (ft/lbs)	MPG Cty/Hwy	Years Avail
I-4	1.5	2-bbl	70@5400	87@3400	37/41	89-89

KEY: I=in-line engine; V=V engine; F=flat engine; FI=fuel injection; bbl=barrel carburetor; T=turbo; D=diesel; HP=horsepower; MPG=estimated average miles per gallon.

EVALUATIONS, TESTS, AND RANKINGS

1989: "honest, reliable service." **Source:** "Geo Spectrum," *Road & Track—Buyer's Guide 1989*, 1988, p. 79.

RECALLS

None to date.

GEO STORM (1990-92)

The Storm is manufactured in Fujisama, Japan and is the corporate cousin of Isuzu Impulse. Produced as a joint venture between Isuzu and General Motors. Named to *The Car Book's* Best Bets of 1992 among subcompacts.

1992 Geo Storm

MAJOR FEATURES

● Geo Storm has as 1992 standard equipment: 5-speed manual transmission, power rack-and-pinion steering, front disc/rear drum brakes, driver's side airbag, AM/FM stereo, and rear defogger.

● Geo Storm GSi adds as 1992 standard equipment: a new 1.8L MPFI 16-valve 4-cylinder engine, sport suspension, rocker extensions, and rear spoiler.

● Geo Storm Hatchback adds: detachable rear quarter windows, and rear loadspace cover.

PRICE HISTORY

The following new car prices reflect the approximate retail cost of the base model: **1990** - $10,390; **1991** - $10,670; **1992** - $11,330.

DIMENSIONS

Body Style	Years Avail	Wheel Base (in)	Lgth (in)	Ht (in)	Avg Wt (lbs)	Fuel Cap (gal)	Front Hdrm (in)	Front Legrm (in)
2d cpe	90-92	96.5	164	51.1	2,292	12.4	37.5	43.8

ENGINES

Type	Displace- ment (L)	Fuel Dly	HP @rpm	Torque @rpm (ft/lbs)	MPG Cty/Hwy	Years Avail
I-4	1.6	FI	130@7000	102@5800	25/33	90-91
I-4	1.6	FI	95@5800	97@4800	30/36	90-92
I-4	1.8	FI	140@6400	120@4600	23/31	92-92

KEY: I=in-line engine; V=V engine; F=flat engine; FI=fuel injection; bbl=barrel carburetor; T=turbo; D=diesel; HP=horsepower; MPG=estimated average miles per gallon.

EVALUATIONS, TESTS, AND RANKINGS

1992: "it's noisy, nervous, and feels a little cheap . . . You have to concentrate to drive smoothly . . . Think of the rear-seat area as a first-class cabin for your grocery bags and you'll never be disappointed." **Source:** "The Bonsai GTs: Japan shrinks the American pony car and a new class is born," *Car and Driver,* November 1991, pp. 112-114, 116, 118-119, 122.

1991: "good performer . . . good looking, with styling that makes a statement . . . in many ways the Storm emphasized the cheap rather than the inexpensive." **Source:** "Geo Storm: Slick, quick and inexpensive," *Autoweek's Autofile 1991 Edition,* 1990, pp. 30-31.

1991: "practical interior space, good fuel economy, and sport handling." *The Flint Journal,* January 30, 1991, pp. E1-E2.

1991: "the Storm is a style setter in its own right . . . the instrument panel is a deeply tunneled information display and a marvel of ergonomics . . . As always on a good Japanese coupe, there are plenty of places to stash small items." **Source:** "Getaway Coupes," *Popular Science,* July 1991, pp. 76-80.

1991: "The new Storm certainly has none of that utilitarian look about it . . . its plastic trim and cloth seats give the hatchback's cabin a decidedly low buck look . . . an engine that while ambitious, is just plain too loud." **Source:** "Geo Storm: A hatchback with style," *Detroit News,* March 6, 1991, p. 2F.

1990: "The shapes and forms, both inside and out, are original and strong . . . space-capsulish." **Source:** "Eleven for Thirteen: Sportsters, $13,000 and under, that you can actually enjoy," *Car and Driver,* June 1990, p. 61.

1990: "nifty little runner. . .The engine sounds less smooth above 5000 rpm." **Source:** "Geo Storm," *Car and Driver— Buyers Guide 1990,* 1989, p. 72.

1990: "potent little engine. . .revs like a chain saw. . .ride is firm, and body motions are well controlled." **Source:** "Geo Storm GSi: Not exactly Hurricane Hugo, but definitely a full-fledged nor'wester," *Car and Driver,* May 1990, pp. 62-63.

RECALLS

1990: (15,200 vehicles): When using front seatback release levers to tip front seatback forward to gain entry to, or exit from, the rear seat, it is possible to insert a finger into the seatback hinge mechanism. Could result in finger being pinched and possibly seriously injured. **Corrective action:** Repair to prevent condition that would permit finger injury. *(NHTSA Campaign No. 89V203000.)*

GEO TRACKER (1989-92)

A lower-priced 4x4 built from the same design as the Suzuki Sidekick and manufactured in Ingersoll, Ontario, Canada, by CAMI, a Suzuki/General Motors of Canada joint venture. The Tracker lineup constists of 2WD convertible, a 4WD convertible, and a 4WD hardtop. Named to *Motor Trend's* 1989 Top 10 New Car Buys import list.

1991 Geo Tracker

MAJOR FEATURES

● Geo Tracker 1992 standard equipment includes: 5-speed manual transmission, front disc/rear drum brakes with anti-lock braking system, manual locking fronthubs, recirculating ball manual steering, cloth seats, and rear seat shoulder belts.

● Geo Tracker LSi adds as 1992 standard equipment: on-demand, part-time 4WD, automatic locking front hubs, upgraded seats, rear bucket seats, and styled wheels.

PRICE HISTORY

The following new car prices reflect the approximate retail cost of the base model: **1989** - $10,395; **1990** - $10,725; **1991** - $8,999; **1992** - $9,695.

DIMENSIONS

Body Style	Years Avail	Wheel Base (in)	Lgth (in)	Ht (in)	Avg Wt (lbs)	Fuel Cap (gal)	Front Hdrm (in)	Front Legrm (in)
utl wgn	89-92	86.6	142.5	65.6	2,238	11.1	39.5	42.1

ENGINES

Type	Displacement (L)	Fuel Dly	HP @rpm	Torque @rpm (ft/lbs)	MPG Cty/Hwy	Years Avail
I-4	1.6	FI	80@5400	94@3000	25/27	89-92

KEY: I=in-line engine; V=V engine; F=flat engine; FI=fuel injection; bbl=barrel carburetor; T=turbo; D=diesel; HP=horsepower; MPG=estimated average miles per gallon.

EVALUATIONS, TESTS, AND RANKINGS

1991: "more an expedition vehicle than an off-road-racing truck . . . What the Tracker does better than the Jeep is handle the tough stuff without hammering its occupants into hamburger . . . more civilized in civilian use as well, without sacrificing much of its muscle." **Source:** "Dirty Little Devils," *Automobile Magazine,* February 1991, pp. 78-85.

1991: "the vehicle does maintain highway speeds with little difficulty and has more than enough muscle for its weight to move through most off-road challenges." **Source:** "Testing the New Mini 4x4," *Sports Afield,* October 1990, pp. 110-112, 114-116.

1991: "strong points are interior finish and appointments . . . Short wheelbase and a suspension setup . . . add up to a choppy freeway ride." **Source:** "Beach Bandits," *Popular Mechanics,* July 1991, pp. 21-25.

1990: "has a pronounced tendency to understeer . . . struggles most of the time, whining at high rpm in low gears off the road and barely keeping up with traffic on the expressway . . . appealing, but so toylike it would be left behind by the likes of Wrangler, either off or on the road." **Source:** "Pocket 4X4s: Over the hills and through the mud to test the mettle of Jeep's competitors," *Popular Science,* May 1990, pp. 102-105.

1990: "Sitting behind the wheel of a Tracker, you quickly learn it is a simple, straightforward, singularly fun vehicle . . . feels solid and competent . . . radio and ventilation controls are up high, where they are visible and accessible." **Source:** "Dustbustersl Four small sport-utilities and four dusty editors tame the Mojave Road," *Car and Driver,* November 1989, pp. 136-140, 142, 146, 148, 152-153, 156, 158.

1990: "parking was a pain, and required great physical effort . . . the only brutal lack was luggage space: There was none . . . it's so high inside that only basketball players need to duck." **Source:** "Tracker Meets the Challenge: This 4WD had plenty of charisma on highways—and off-road," *Design News,* October 2, 1989, pp. 158-159.

1989: "soak up road shock with . . . sophiscated independent front suspension (IFS) system up front . . . Interior leg and headroom . . . is much greater than that of the Samurai." **Source:** "Intruders in the Dust," *Popular Mechanics,* March 1989, pp. 122, 124, 127.

RECALLS

None to date.

GMC JIMMY (1987-92)

Formerly named the S-10 Jimmy, the GMC Jimmy is the corporate twin of the Chevrolet Blazer. Produced at the General Motors plants in Shreveport, Louisiana and Flint, Michigan. GMC Jimmy is available in 2-door and 4-door body styles, and 2-wheel and 4-wheel drive.

1991 GMC Jimmy

MAJOR FEATURES

● GMC Jimmy SL has as 1992 standard equipment: 5-speed manual overdrive transmission, front independent suspension, front disc/rear drum brakes with anti-lock braking system, power steering, high-back vinyl front bucket seats, steel wheels, and AM/FM stereo.

● GMC Jimmy SLS adds as 1992 standard equipment: cast aluminum wheels, upgraded interior and other exterior body stylings.

● GMC Jimmy SLE adds as 1992 standard equipment: Rally wheels with black center inserts, upgraded interior, and other exterior body stylings.

● GMC Jimmy SLT adds as 1992 standard equipment: power locks and windows, folding rear bench seat, cast aluminum wheels, softride suspension, electric shift transfer case, digital instrumentation with tachometer, and other exterior body stylings.

● GMC Typhoon has as 1992 standard equipment: turbocharged engine (same as GMC Syclone), four-speed automatic transmission, full-time four-wheel drive, 4-wheel anti-lock braking system, sports suspension, cruise control, aluminum wheels, AM/FM cassette stereo, air conditioning, other exterior body stylings, and an upgraded interior.

Dimensions that follow are for the GMC two-door model.

PRICE HISTORY

The following new car prices reflect the approximate retail cost of the base model: **1988** - $10,552; **1989** - $11,738; **1990** - $12,698; **1991** - $14,060.

DIMENSIONS

Body Style	Years Avail	Wheel Base (in)	Lgth (in)	Ht (in)	Avg Wt (lbs)	Fuel Cap (gal)	Front Hdrm (in)	Front Legrm (in)
utl wgn	87-88	100.5	170.3	64.7	3,894	13.2	na	na
utl wgn	89-92	100.5	170.3	64.1	4,350	20.0	na	na

ENGINES

Type	Displacement (L)	Fuel Dly	HP @rpm	Torque @rpm (ft/lbs)	MPG Cty/Hwy	Years Avail
I-4	2.5	FI	98@na	na	17/25	87-88
I-4	2.5	FI	125@na	na	na	89-89
V-6	2.8	FI	na	na	18/25	87-89
V-6	4.3	FI	160@4000	230@2800	17/23	89-91
V-6	4.3	FI	195@na	na	na	92-92
V-6	4.3	FI	160@4200	225@2400	17/22	92-92

KEY: I=in-line engine; V=V engine; F=flat engine; FI=fuel injection; bbl=barrel carburetor; T=turbo; D=diesel; HP=horsepower; MPG=estimated average miles per gallon.

EVALUATIONS, TESTS, AND RANKINGS

1992: "ground-effects styling . . . offers a variety of niceties." **Source:** "Preview 1992 Motor Trend Truck of the Year," *Motor Trend,* December 1991, pp. 104-105.

1992: "one of the fastest vehicles, period, in a straight line . . . produces lots of body roll . . . inherent design disadvantages, including the loss of off-road utility, no trailer towing." **Source:** "GMC Typhoon," *Road & Track,* February 1992, pp. 73-75.

1992: "Typhoon has come out of the closet . . . superb turbocharged engine . . . lack of an exclusive instrument panel." **Source:** "Typhoon is for Hard Driving," *Detroit Free Press,* October 10, 1991, Section C.

1992: "slalom speeds . . . quicker than most of the BMWs we've tested . . . few rough edges . . . a ride that's jiggly over bad pavement." **Source:** "GMC Typhoon," *Motor Trend,* October 1991, pp. 74-76.

1992: "wheelbase helps give the Typhoon quick responses . . . little better balance in the corners than the Syclone." **Source:** "GMC Typhoon," *Automobile Magazine,* December 1991, p. 28.

1992: "aggresive stance, swoopy aero moldings and rich leather interior . . . meant to be driven hard . . . turbocharged engine packs the punch of a much-larger V8." **Source:** "Typhoon Is For Hard Driving," *Detroit Free Press,* October 10, 1991, p. 1C.

1990: "Seventh place . . . it still doesn't feel finished to us . . . it's a rough son of a gun that manages to be unobtrusive only at light-throttle cruise. Any other time . . . it feels and sounds like a V-8 with two plug wires pulled . . . the seats are too flat and uncushioned." **Source:** "Desert Sports: Seven sport-utility vehicles show us their stuff," *Car and Driver,* April, 1990, pp. 38-43, 48-49, 52-55.

RECALLS

1991: (181 trucks; includes GMC and Chevrolet models): Improper primer could allow windshield and side windows to loosen. **Corrective action:** Remove and reinstall glass using proper primer. *(NHTSA Campaign No. 90V107000.)*

1991: (237 light duty trucks; includes GMC Jimmy and GMC Sonoma models): Nuts used to attach lower control arms, rear spring and shackle, and rear shock absorbers do not meet specifications and could strip, which could allow the arm to detach, resulting in loss of vehicle control and an accident. **Corrective action:** Replace lower control arm attachment nuts as well as rear spring and shackle, and rear shock absorber nuts. *(NHTSA Campaign No. 90V193000.)*

1991: (181 pickup trucks; includes several GMC and Chevrolet truck models): Use of improper primer on metal surfaces of windshield and side window openings could cause low adhesion to metal surface and would not provide retention required by FMVSS 212. Would not prevent the ejection of vehicle occupants during a crash. **Corrective action:** Remove and reinstall glass using proper primer. *(NHTSA Campaign No. 90V107000.)*

1991: (102,885 light trucks and multi-purpose vehicles; includes the GMC Jimmy, Chevrolet S-10 Pickup, Chevrolet Blazer, and Oldsmobile Bravada): Vehicles have been shipped with the fuel tank sender seal out of position. In the event of a rollover accident, an out of position seal could allow fuel spillage in excess of the amount prescribed by FMVSS 301. Spilled fuel could ignite near an ignition source. **Corrective action:** Replace sender seals. *(NHTSA Campaign No. 91V108000.)*

1987: (60 trucks; recall includes the GMC Jimmy and Chevrolet S10 models): Inner tie rod to relay rod nuts on steering linkage may be improperly torqued and not crimped. Loss of one or both nuts could lead to inner tie rod disengagement, which could result in loss of steering control and a truck crash. **Corrective action:** Replace steering linkage assembly. *(NHTSA Campaign No. 87V021000.)*

SAFETY AND REPAIRS

1987: "Car Clinic," *Popular Mechanics*, August 1990, p. 26. **Note:** Tip for clashing starter motor gears in 1987-88 General Motors 4.3, 5.0, and 5.7 liter engines.

1992: "GMC Typhoon Hit by Recall," *Automotive News*, December 2, 1991, p. 2. **Note:** 1992 Typhoons have potential for rear brake pipe failure.

REPAIR MANUALS

1509 ● **Chevrolet and GMC 4-Wheel Drive Tune-Up: 1967-1987**
Clymer Publications
P.O. Box 1209
Overland Park, KS 66212   Ph:(913)541-6694

With Illustrations. Published 1983. **Editor(s):** Jeff Robinson. **Price:** $14.99.

1510 ● **Chevy and GMC Two-Wheel Drive Mid-Size S- and T-Pickups, Blazers, and Jimmy, 1982-1988 (Gas and Diesel)**
Clymer Publications
P.O. Box 1209
Overland Park, KS 66212   Ph:(913)541-6694

Published 1987. **Price:** $26.95.

1511 ● **Get Your Chevrolet-GMC Fixed Right**
Consumer Reports Books
51 E. 42nd St., Suite 800
New York, NY 10017   Ph:(212)682-9280

Editor(s): Mort Schultz. **Price:** $8.95.

1512 ● **Haynes Chevrolet and GMC Pick-Ups Owners Workshop Manual, No. 420: 1967-1987**
Haynes Publications, Inc.
861 Lawrence Dr.
Newbury Park, CA 91320   Ph:(818)889-5400

Published 1988. **Price:** $15.95.

1513 ● **Haynes Chevy GMC Pickups, 1988-90**
Haynes Publications, Inc.
861 Lawrence Dr.
Newbury Park, CA 91320   Ph:(818)889-5400

Published 1990. **Price:** $15.95.

OTHER INFORMATION SOURCES

1514 ● **Chevrolet S-10 Blazer, GMC S-15, and Olds Bravada, 1982-1990**
Chilton Co.
Chilton Way
Radnor, PA 19089   Ph:(215)964-4000

Published 1991. **Price:** $19.95.

GMC RALLY (1987-92)

Passenger van line of GMC.

1991 GMC Rally Extended Passenger Van

MAJOR FEATURES

● GMC G-1500 Rally has as 1992 standard equipment: V6 engine with electronic fuel injection, 4-speed automatic overdrive transmission, front disc/rear drum power brakes with rear wheel anti-lock braking system, power steering, analog instrument cluster, tinted glass, side window defoggers, and AM/FM stereo.

● GMC G-2500 and G-3500 Rallys have as 1992 standard equipment: upgraded payloads and tire sizes. G-3500 has a 5.7 liter V8 engine

● GMC Rally STX adds as 1992 standard equipment: 7.4 L V-8 engine, sport styled steering wheel, and an upgraded interior.

Dimensions that follow are for the smaller wheelbase 1500. Other Rally vans have longer wheelbases, among other variations in their dimensions.

PRICE HISTORY

The following new car prices reflect the approximate retail cost of the base model: **1988** - $11,973; **1989** - $12,698; **1990** - $14,163; **1991** - $15,510.

DIMENSIONS

Body Style	Years Avail	Wheel Base (in)	Lgth (in)	Ht (in)	Avg Wt (lbs)	Fuel Cap (gal)	Front Hdrm (in)	Front Legrm (in)
4d van	87-92	110.0	178.2	79.4	5,600	22.0	na	na

ENGINES

Type	Displace-ment (L)	Fuel Dly	HP @rpm	Torque @rpm (ft/lbs)	MPG Cty/Hwy	Years Avail
V-6	4.3	FI	170@na	na	na	87-87
V-6	4.3	FI	150@4000	230@2400	15/19	88-92
V-8	5.0	4-bbl	na	na	na	87-87
V-8	5.0	FI	170@4000	255@2400	14/18	88-91
V-8	5.0	FI	190@4000	300@2400	14/19	89-91
V-8	7.4	FI	230@3600	385@1600	na	89-92
V-8	5.7	FI	155@na	na	13/17	92-92
V-8	5.7	FI	195@na	na	13/17	92-92
V-8	5.7	FI	190@na	na	13/17	92-92
V-8D	6.2	FI	145@3600	260@1900	16/22	89-92
V-8D	6.2	FI	155@3500	285@2000	na	90-92

KEY: I=in-line engine; V=V engine; F=flat engine; FI=fuel injection; bbl=barrel carburetor; T=turbo; D=diesel; HP=horsepower; MPG=estimated average miles per gallon.

EVALUATIONS, TESTS, AND RANKINGS

1990: "towed our 29-foot Alfa well under most driving conditions, yet an uncomfortable amount of trailer sway (yaw) could be created ... Ride quality while towing suffered modestly from freeway hop ... interior spaciousness makes it especially versatile." **Source:** "GMC Rally STX," *Trailer Life*, February 1990, pp. 80-82, 132, 134.

1989: "Towing the Alfa trailer. . .was no trouble at all ... always up to the task of climbing mountain grades and snaking along twisting roads ... Engine-oil and coolant temperatures remained within the safe zone. . .over demanding desert grades in 90-degree F weather." **Source:** "GMC Rally Van," *Trailer Life*, December 1988, pp. 53-55, 123.

RECALLS

1990: (242 trucks; includes other GMC and Chevrolet models): Improperly torqued tie rod clamp fasteners could allow tie rods to loosen and separate. **Corrective action:** Properly torque tie rod clamps and readjust toe-in as necessary. (NHTSA Campaign No. 90V074000.)

1989-91: (25,807 vans; includes GMC Rally, Chevrolet Sportvan, and other GMC models): Seat back of rear bench may break away from seat cushion in an accident. **Corrective action:** Install reinforcement that runs from side of seat back frame assembly to seat cushion frame assembly, strengthening seat back. (NHTSA Campaign No. 91V040000.)

1987: (463 vans; includes Chevrolet Sportvan and GMC Rally): Fuel tank lower filler pipe may contain small holes at some spot welds used to attach mounting bracket. Fuel could leak from pipe during refueling or turning and spill fuel in excess of amount prescribed by FMVSS 301. **Corrective action:** Replace fuel tank lower filler pipe. (NHTSA Campaign No. 88V016000.)

SAFETY AND REPAIRS

1987: "Car Clinic," *Popular Mechanics*, August 1990, p. 26. **Note:** Tip for clashing starter motor gears in 1987-88 General Motors 4.3, 5.0, and 5.7 liter engines.

REPAIR MANUALS

1515 ● General Motors 8-Cylinder
Peter Allen Video Productions
38-C Otis St.
West Babylon, NY 11704   Ph:(516)643-4372

A program demonstrating basic maintenance and tune-up procedures for the entitled engine. **Release date:** 1986. **Producer:** Peter Allen Productions. **Acquisition:** Purchase.

1516 ● Get Your Chevrolet-GMC Fixed Right
Consumer Reports Books
51 E. 42nd St., Suite 800
New York, NY 10017   Ph:(212)682-9280

Editor(s): Mort Schultz. **Price:** $8.95.

GMC SAFARI (1987-92)

Produced at the General Motors plant in Baltimore, Maryland. The Safari is offered in two- and four-wheel drive models, and regular or extended body styles.

1991 GMC Safari Mid-Size Passenger Van

MAJOR FEATURES

● GMC Safari SLX 1992 standard equipment includes: 4.3L six-cylinder engine, 4-speed automatic transmission, front disc/rear drum brakes with anti-lock braking system, power steering, and AM/FM stereo.

● GMC Safari SLE adds as 1992 standard equipment: custom steering wheel, sunshades, and gauge instrument cluster with trip odometer.

● GMC Safari SLT adds as 1992 standard equipment: other exterior body stylings and upgraded interior.

PRICE HISTORY

The following new car prices reflect the approximate retail cost of the base model: **1988** - $10,745; **1989** - $11,957; **1990** - $13,503; **1991** - $14,815; **1992** - $15,404.

DIMENSIONS

Body Style	Years Avail	Wheel Base (in)	Lgth (in)	Ht (in)	Avg Wt (lbs)	Fuel Cap (gal)	Front Hdrm (in)	Front Legrm (in)
4d van	87-88	111	176.8	74.5	4,404	17	na	na
4d van	89-92	111	176.8	74.5	5,000	27	na	na

ENGINES

Type	Displace-ment (L)	Fuel Dly	HP @rpm	Torque @rpm (ft/lbs)	MPG Cty/Hwy	Years Avail
V-6	4.3	FI	150@4000	230@2400	15/20	87-92
V-6	4.3	FI	170@4600	225@2800	19/20	90-91

KEY: I=in-line engine; V=V engine; F=flat engine; FI=fuel injection; bbl=barrel carburetor; T=turbo; D=diesel; HP=horsepower; MPG=estimated average miles per gallon.

EVALUATIONS, TESTS, AND RANKINGS

1990: "Utility and function have always been this GMC's

strong suit." **Source:** "Motor Trend's 1990 Truck of the Year," *Motor Trend,* April 1990, pp. 120-121.

1990: "has good power, a smooth drive system, adequate handling . . . basic concept, nevertheless, is somewhat flawed . . . The 5-passenger model is far more useful." **Source:** "Vans for All Seasons," *Popular Mechanics,* September 1990, pp. 24-27.

1989: "handled well. The ride was smooth and quiet, the van accelerated nicely . . . sometimes a bit sluggish (and noisy) going up hills . . . the plush interior of the Safari passenger van reminded me of a first-class airline section." **Source:** "GM Safari: Comfort for the long haul," *Design News,* August 21, 1989, p. 26.

1989: "a distinct improvement over earlier models . . . good looks, new safety features and a versatile interior . . . excellent vehicle for an active family." **Source:** "A Van for All Reasons," *Organic Gardening,* July/August 1989, p. 18.

1988: "All Safaris boast fine aerodynamic-drag coefficients." **Source:** "GMC Safari," *Car and Driver—Buyers Guide 1988,* 1988, p. 146.

RECALLS

None to date.

SAFETY AND REPAIRS

1987: "Car Clinic," *Popular Mechanics,* August 1990, p. 26. **Note:** Tip for clashing starter motor gears in 1987-88 General Motors 4.3, 5.0, and 5.7 liter engines.

REPAIR MANUALS

1517 ● **Chevrolet and GMC 4-Wheel Drive Tune-Up: 1967-1987**
Clymer Publications
P.O. Box 1209
Overland Park, KS 66212   Ph:(913)541-6694

With Illustrations. Published 1983. **Editor(s):** Jeff Robinson. **Price:** $14.99.

1518 ● **Chevrolet Astro and GMC Safari**
Clymer Publications
P.O. Box 1209
Overland Park, KS 66212   Ph:(913)541-6694

Published 1988. **Price:** $14.00.

1519 ● **Chevrolet Astro-GMC Safari, 1985-1990**
Chilton Co.
Chilton Way
Radnor, PA 19089   Ph:(215)964-4000

Published 1990. **Price:** $24.95.

1520 ● **Get Your Chevrolet-GMC Fixed Right**
Consumer Reports Books
51 E. 42nd St., Suite 800
New York, NY 10017   Ph:(212)682-9280

Editor(s): Mort Schultz. **Price:** $8.95.

GMC SONOMA (1987-92)

Formerly the GMC S15 Pickup, the GMC Sonoma is produced at the General Motors plants in Pontiac, Michigan, and Shreveport, Louisiana. Available in 2WD, 4WD, and All Wheel

drive types and in Regular Cab and Club Coupe body configurations.

1991 GMC Sonoma

MAJOR FEATURES

● Sonoma SL has as 1992 standard equipment: 5-speed manual transmission, hydraulic front disc/rear drum brakes with rear-wheel anti-lock braking system, manual recirculating ball steering, AM/FM stereo, and folding back front bench seats with head restraints.

● Sonoma SLS adds as 1992 standard equipment: upgraded interior and other exterior body stylings.

● Sonoma SLE adds as 1992 standard equipment: dual outside, below-eyeline black mirrors, and exterior moldings and trim.

● Sonoma GT adds as 1992 standard equipment: high performance engine, automatic transmission, sport chassis, sport suspension, limited-slip positraction rear wheel drive, and air conditioning.

● GMC Syclone adds as 1992 standard equipment: turbocharged engine, all-wheel drive, 4-speed automatic transmission, 4-wheel anti-lock braking system, cruise control, sport suspension, leather-wrapped steering wheel, upgraded stereo system, air conditioning, and tinted windows.

● S-15 Pickup offered as 1989 standard equipment: 4-speed automatic overdrive transmission, independent front suspension, power-assisted recirculating ball steering, and power-assisted front disc/rear drum brakes. The GMC S-15 Pickup was offered in three trim levels: Sierra, High Sierra, and the top-of-the-line Sierra Classic.

Dimensions in the chart that follows reflect short wheelbase, regular cab pickup. Other pickups in the series may vary.

PRICE HISTORY

The following new car prices reflect the approximate retail cost of the base model: **1988** - $6,840; **1989** - $7,527; **1990** - $7,637; **1991** - $8,466.

DIMENSIONS

Body Style	Years Avail	Wheel Base (in)	Lgth (in)	Ht (in)	Avg Wt (lbs)	Fuel Cap (gal)	Front Hdrm (in)	Front Legrm (in)
trk	87-88	108.3	178.2	61.3	3,570	13.2	na	na
trk	89-89	108.3	178.2	61.3	3,662	20.0	na	na
trk	90-92	108.3	178.2	61.6	4,200	20.0	na	na

ENGINES

Type	Displace-ment (L)	Fuel Dly	HP @rpm	Torque @rpm (ft/lbs)	MPG Cty/Hwy	Years Avail
I-4	2.5	FI	98@na	na	23/29	87-87
I-4	2.5	FI	92@na	na	23/27	88-89
I-4	2.5	FI	105@4800	135@3200	23/27	90-92
V-6	2.8	FI	125@4800	150@2400	19/25	87-92
V-6	4.3	FI	160@4000	230@2800	17/23	89-92

KEY: I=in-line engine; V=V engine; F=flat engine; FI=fuel injection; bbl=barrel carburetor; T=turbo; D=diesel; HP=horsepower; MPG=estimated average miles per gallon.

EVALUATIONS, TESTS, AND RANKINGS

1991: "reaches 30 mph in just 1.4 seconds—quicker than any production vehicle we have ever tested. It reaches 40 mph in only 2.2 seconds . . . 60 mph takes a mere 4.3 seconds . . . well suited to everyday driving situations . . . one of the wildest, most affordable supertoys in the automotive kingdom." **Source:** "GMC Truck Syclone: Zero to 60 in 4.6 seconds. In the rain," *Car and Driver*, November 1990, pp. 143-145.

1991: "After a day of flogging. . .really needed a fresh Wheaties injection to optimize its flagging spirit. It flat died before shifting out of second gear . . . Ride quality . . . was just fine." **Source:** "GMC Syclone: Teenage Mutant Ninja Turbo," *Motor Trend*, December 1990, pp. 76, 78.

1991: "understeer is pronounced during hard cornering . . . provides a confidence-inspiring level of stability during most driving conditions . . . one fast machine." **Source:** "GMC Syclone," *Road & Track*, March 1991, pp. 101-102.

1991: "wickedly fast . . . lacks socially redeemable virtues. It's expensive, gulps gasoline, doesn't haul much weight and only has two seats . . . most expensive compact pickup on the market." **Source:** "Syclone packs enough power for muscle car ranks," *The Flint Journal*, July 10, 1991, pp. D1, D2.

1989: "provided plenty of smooth power on crowded city streets or on the open road . . . a bit sluggish when I floored the accelerator to obtain passing speed . . . much impressed with the electronic instrument cluster." **Source:** "GMC S-15 4 x 4: Pickup with punch," *Design News*, September 18, 1989.

1989: "[GMC S-15 Sierra Classic] the 4.3-liter V6 . . . has great power and bottomless torque . . . inherently good chassis, heavy-duty suspension . . . Good looking, powerful, fun to drive and moderately priced." **Source:** "Compact Commandos," *Popular Mechanics*, February 1989, pp. 51-55, 122.

1989: "packs a potent 160-horsepower wallop . . . a snappy street performer . . . rides, corners, and stops with equal competence." **Source:** "Light Hauler: GMC's 4.3L, 160-HP S-15 is glowing with potential," *Hot Rod*, August 1989, pp. 116-119.

RECALLS

1991: (181 trucks; includes GMC and Chevrolet models): Improper primer could allow windshield and side windows to loosen. **Corrective action:** Remove and reinstall glass using proper primer. (NHTSA Campaign No. 90V107000.)

1991: (181 pickup trucks; includes several GMC and Chevrolet truck models): Use of improper primer on metal surfaces of windshield and side window openings could cause low adhesion to metal surface and would not provide retention required by FMVSS 212. Would not prevent the ejection of vehicle occupants during a crash. **Corrective action:** Remove and reinstall glass using proper primer. (NHTSA Campaign No. 90V107000.)

1991: (237 light duty trucks; includes GMC Jimmy and GMC

Sonoma models): Nuts used to attach lower control arms, rear spring and shackle, and rear shock absorbers do not meet specifications and could strip, which could allow the arm to detach, resulting in loss of vehicle control and an accident. **Corrective action:** Replace lower control arm attachment nuts as well as rear spring and shackle, and rear shock absorber nuts. (NHTSA Campaign No. 90V193000.)

SAFETY AND REPAIRS

1987: "Car Clinic," *Popular Mechanics*, August 1990, p. 26. **Note:** Tip for clashing starter motor gears in 1987-88 General Motors 4.3, 5.0, and 5.7 liter engines.

REPAIR MANUALS

1521 ● **Chevrolet GMC Trucks, 1988-90**
Chilton Co.
Chilton Way
Radnor, PA 19089   Ph:(215)964-4000

Published 1990. **Price:** $19.95.

1522 ● **Chevrolet S-10, GMC S-15 Pickups 1982—90**
Chilton Co.
Chilton Way
Radnor, PA 19089   Ph:(215)964-4000

Total car care service. Published 1991. **Price:** $19.95.

1523 ● **Chevy and GMC Two-Wheel Drive Mid-Size S- and T-Pickups, Blazers, and Jimmy, 1982-1988 (Gas and Diesel)**
Clymer Publications
P.O. Box 1209
Overland Park, KS 66212   Ph:(913)541-6694

Published 1987. **Price:** $26.95.

1524 ● **Chilton's Chevrolet/GMC Pick-ups and Suburban 1970-1987**
Chilton Co.
Chilton Way
Radnor, PA 19089   Ph:(215)964-4000

Published 1988. **Price:** $15.95.

1525 ● **General Motors 8-Cylinder**
Peter Allen Video Productions
38-C Otis St.
West Babylon, NY 11704   Ph:(516)643-4372

A program demonstrating basic maintenance and tune-up procedures for the entitled engine. **Release date:** 1986. **Producer:** Peter Allen Productions. **Acquisition:** Purchase.

1526 ● **Get Your Chevrolet-GMC Fixed Right**
Consumer Reports Books
51 E. 42nd St., Suite 800
New York, NY 10017   Ph:(212)682-9280

Editor(s): Mort Schultz. **Price:** $8.95.

1527 ● **Haynes Chevrolet and GMC Pick-Ups Owners Workshop Manual, No. 420: 1967-1987**
Haynes Publications, Inc.
861 Lawrence Dr.
Newbury Park, CA 91320   Ph:(818)889-5400

Published 1988. **Price:** $15.95.

1528 ● **Haynes Chevy GMC Pickups, 1988-90**
Haynes Publications, Inc.
861 Lawrence Dr.
Newbury Park, CA 91320   Ph:(818)889-5400

Published 1990. **Price:** $15.95.

GMC SUBURBAN (1987-92)

Corporate twin is the Chevrolet Suburban. Produced at the General Motors plant in Flint, Michigan. 1992 models have a longer wheelbase than previous models and are available in two-wheel drive (C) and four-wheel drive (K) versions and different trim levels.

1991 GMC Suburban

MAJOR FEATURES

● GMC Suburban with base SL trim level has as 1992 standard equipment: heavy-duty V8 engine, independent front suspension, 4-speed automatic overdrive transmission, front disc/rear drum brakes with anti-lock braking system, power steering, and AM/FM radio.

● GMC Suburban with SLE trim level adds as 1992 standard equipment: dual cloth front bucket seats, wall-to-wall carpeting, overhead console containing dual map reading lamps and storage compartments.

● GMC R-1500 and R-2500 Suburban have as 1992 standard equipment: 4-speed automatic transmission, front disc/rear drum brakes with anti-lock braking system, power steering, and AM/FM radio.

● GMC V-1500 and V-2500 Suburban 1992 standard equipment includes: 4-wheel drive.

Dimensions that follow are for the R-1500 GMC Suburban. Others in the series may vary.

PRICE HISTORY

The following new car prices reflect the approximate retail cost of the base model: **1988** - $13,997; **1989** - $14,605; **1990** - $15,198; **1991** - $16,775.

DIMENSIONS

Body Style	Years Avail	Wheel Base (in)	Lgth (in)	Ht (in)	Avg Wt (lbs)	Fuel Cap (gal)	Front Hdrm (in)	Front Legrm (in)
5d wgn	87-88	129.5	219.1	72	6,100	25	na	na
5d wgn	89-89	129.5	219.1	72	6,100	31	na	na
5d wgn	90-91	129.5	219.1	72	6,100	37	na	na
5d wgn	92-92	131.5	218.9	68.8	6,800	42	na	na

ENGINES

Type	Displace-ment (L)	Fuel Dly	HP @rpm	Torque @rpm (ft/lbs)	MPG Cty/Hwy	Years Avail
V-8	5.7	4-bbl	210@na	na	13/17	87-87
V-8	5.0	FI	170@na	na	14/18	87-87
V-8	5.7	FI	210@4000	na	13/17	88-92
V-8D	6.2	FI	145@3600	na	16/22	87-91

KEY: I=in-line engine; V=V engine; F=flat engine; FI=fuel injection; bbl=barrel carburetor; T=turbo; D=diesel; HP=horsepower; MPG=estimated average miles per gallon.

EVALUATIONS, TESTS, AND RANKINGS

1990: "job is to haul lots of stuff ... 4wd is handy for life among the dunes ... considerable attention [given] to improving efficiency and performance." **Source:** "GMC Suburban," *Car and Driver—Buyers Guide 1990*, 1989, pp. 168-169.

RECALLS

1988: (277 van type passenger vehicle equipped with bucket seats and gray interior trim; includes Chevrolet and GMC Surburbans): Driver's seat and/or shoulder belt locking mechanism may not operate. In a crash, affected belts would not lock, thereby increasing the possibility of injury to the seat occupant. **Corrective action:** Install a new driver's seat belt assembly. (NHTSA Campaign No. 89V010000.)

SAFETY AND REPAIRS

1987: "Car Clinic," *Popular Mechanics*, August 1990, p. 26. **Note:** Tip for clashing starter motor gears in 1987-88 General Motors 4.3, 5.0, and 5.7 liter engines.

REPAIR MANUALS

1529 ● **Chevrolet and GMC 4-Wheel Drive Tune-Up: 1967-1987**
Clymer Publications
P.O. Box 1209
Overland Park, KS 66212   Ph:(913)541-6694

With Illustrations. Published 1983. **Editor(s):** Jeff Robinson. **Price:** $14.99.

1530 ● **Chevy and GMC C-Series, Pickups, and Suburbans: 1967-1987: Includes Suburbans Shop Manual**
Clymer Publications
P.O. Box 1209
Overland Park, KS 66212   Ph:(913)541-6694

With illustrations. **Price:** $14.95.

1531 ● **Chevy and GMC Two Wheel Drive C and R-Series Pickups, Suburbans, and Vans, 1970-1987 (Gas and Diesel)**
Clymer Publications
P.O. Box 1209
Overland Park, KS 66212   Ph:(913)541-6694

With illustrations. Published 1990. **Price:** $26.95.

1532 ● **Chilton's Chevrolet/GMC Pick-ups and Suburban 1970-1987**
Chilton Co.
Chilton Way
Radnor, PA 19089   Ph:(215)964-4000

Published 1988. **Price:** $15.95.

1533 ● General Motors 8-Cylinder
Peter Allen Video Productions
38-C Otis St.
West Babylon, NY 11704   Ph:(516)643-4372

A program demonstrating basic maintenance and tune-up procedures for the entitled engine. **Release date:** 1986. **Producer:** Peter Allen Productions. **Acquisition:** Purchase.

HONDA ACCORD (1987-92)

Mid-range car that competes with the Toyota Camry, Nissan Stanza GXE, Subaru Legacy LS, Pontiac Grand Am LE, Acura Integra LS, Chevrolet Beretta GT, Chevrolet Corsica, Ford Mustang LX 5.0, Ford Taurus, and Cadillac Seville. Awarded one of the Top Ten New Car Buys in 1989 by *Motor Trend*. Listed on *Car and Driver* Ten Best Cars lists in 1987, 88, 89, and 90. Awarded Best Coupe/Sedan in 1990 by *Road & Track*. The 1992 *Car Book* rates the Honda Accord among the worst in Warranty Coverage, among the best in Resale Value, and rates the Honda Accord Wagon among the best in its class in Crash Test Performance. Currently produced in Marysville, Ohio and Saitama, Japan. (plant parts data: domestic parts - 73%, imported parts - 27%; *Federal Trade Zone Board*, 1989).

1992 Honda Accord EX Coupe

MAJOR FEATURES

● Accord Coupe and Sedan DX has 1992 standard equipment: 5-speed manual transmission or 4-speed automatic transmissions, power steering, rear defogger, tinted glass, intermittent wipers, and driver's side airbag with Supplemental Restraint System (SRS).

● Accord Coupe and Sedan LX adds as 1992 standard equipment: air conditioning, cruise control, AM/FM stereo cassette, and driver's seat armrest.

● Accord Coupe and Sedan EX adds as 1992 standard equipment: 140 horsepower engine, anti-lock braking (ABS) system, power sunroof, alloy wheels, sport suspension, front spoiler, and upgraded tires.

● Accord Wagon LX adds as 1992 standard equipment: cargo cover and upgraded tires.

● Accord Wagon EX adds as 1992 standard equipment: remote keyless entry system.

● Accord Coupe and Sedan LXi added as 1991 standard equipment: electric moon roof, electronic fuel injection, locking lid for fuel filter, and driver's seat lumbar support.

● Accord Coupe and Sedan SE added as 1991 standard equipment: bronze-tinted glass, anti-lock brakes, 4-wheel disc brakes, and leather-wrapped steering wheel.

PRICE HISTORY

The following new car prices reflect the approximate retail cost of the base model: **1987** - $10,120; **1988** - $11,040; **1989** - $11,230; **1990** - $12,145; **1991** - $12,525; **1992** - $13,025.

DIMENSIONS

Body Style	Years Avail	Wheel Base (in)	Lgth (in)	Ht (in)	Avg Wt (lbs)	Fuel Cap (gal)	Front Hdrm (in)	Front Legrm (in)
3d lbk	87-89	102.4	174.8	52.6	2,513	15.9	38.0	42.8
2d cpe	88-88	102.4	179.1	52.6	2,493	15.9	37.9	42.9
2d cpe	89-89	102.4	179.7	52.7	2,493	15.9	37.9	42.9
2d cpe	90-90	107.1	184.8	53.9	2,738	17.0	38.8	42.9
2d cpe	91-91	107.1	184.8	52.2	2,738	17.0	38.8	42.9
2d cpe	92-92	107.1	185.2	54.1	2,738	17.0	38.8	42.9
4d sdn	87-87	102.4	178.5	53.4	2,421	15.9	38.7	42.8
4d sdn	88-88	102.4	179.1	53.4	2,500	15.9	38.7	42.8
4d sdn	88-89	102.4	179.7	53.4	2,579	15.9	38.7	42.8
4d sdn	90-90	107.1	184.8	54.7	2,733	17.0	38.9	42.6
4d sdn	91-91	107.1	184.8	52.8	2,733	17.0	38.9	42.6
4d sdn	92-92	107.1	185.2	54.7	2,733	17.0	38.9	42.6
5d wgn	92-92	107.1	186.8	55.1	3,139	17.0	39.0	42.7

ENGINES

Type	Displacement (L)	Fuel Dly	HP @rpm	Torque @rpm (ft/lbs)	MPG Cty/Hwy	Years Avail
I-4	2.0	FI	110@5500	114@3500	27/34	87-88
I-4	2.0	2-bbl	98@5500	109@3500	27/34	87-88
I-4	2.0	FI	120@5800	122@4000	25/30	88-89
I-4	2.2	FI	130@5200	142@4000	24/30	90-91
I-4	2.2	FI	125@5200	137@4000	24/30	90-92
I-4	2.2	FI	140@5600	142@4500	na	92-92

KEY: I=in-line engine; V=V engine; F=flat engine; FI=fuel injection; bbl=barrel carburetor; T=turbo; D=diesel; HP=horsepower; MPG=estimated average miles per gallon.

EVALUATIONS, TESTS, AND RANKINGS

1991: "impressed with the Accord's comfort and roominess. . .mechanical bits profit from design subtleties as well. . .Even little things like heat/ventilation controls exhibit thoughtful refinement." **Source:** "Honda Accord EX," *Road & Track*, December 1990, p. 55.

1991: "this sedan has a kind of European instinct for arrowing straight down the road." **Source:** "Honda Accord EX," *Car and Driver*, December 1990, pp. 48-9.

1991: "good road manners. . .electronically controlled 4-speed gets a C-plus here- kickdowns are abrupt, and seem to be long in coming. . .plenty of acceleration. . .fair amount of noise to go along with the power. . .even space for skis. . .certainly dependable, civilized transportation, devoid of bad habits." **Source:** "Long-Term Test Cars," *Popular Mechanics*, March 1991, pp. 44-46.

1991: "console is clean, clear, and easy to use . . . has get-up-and-go to spare . . . front seat seems a trifle short on legroom." **Source:** "Welcome Wagon: Honda's new Accord station wagon greets growing families," *House and Garden*, July 1991, p. 40.

1991: "logical instrument cluster arranged neatly in the driver's line of sight . . . plenty of wheelspin during fast takeoffs . . . powerful engine and well-appointed interior." **Source:** "Station to Station: HM tests four new-for-1991 family wagons," *Home Mechanix*, June 1991, pp. 78-83.

1990: "more interior space. . .double wishbone suspension delivers a supple ride with excellent handling." **Source:** "Top

Ten New Car Buys- Import,'' *Motor Trend,* November 1989, pp. 80-3, 86-9.

1990: ''more than just style. . .[engines]sure are smooth. . .Lots of other Accord characteristics have been carried over, though hardly a component exists that hasn't been reengineered in the interest of refinement.'' **Source:** ''1990 Honda Accord,'' *Road & Track,* November 1989, pp. 151, 153, 155.

1990: ''better-than-adequate ride and handling. . .pleased with the increase in headroom. . .very good stability under all conditions and very good grip almost to the limit. . .would have liked an armrest between the (front) seats.'' **Source:** ''Honda Accord: A Conservative With A Cause,'' *Autoweek's Autofile 1991 Edition,* 1990, pp. 124-28.

1990: ''plenty of areas where the car could still stand some improvement. . .car feels underpowered. . .doesn't like being driven hard. It likes to loaf along, which it does without a fuss. . .upholstery seems like it will last forever. . .a safe, stable feel. . .automatic shoulder belt that jams about once a week.'' **Source:** ''Long-Term Test Cars,'' *Popular Mechanics,* November 1990, pp. 56-9, 138.

1990: ''certainly doesn't win any accolades for gas mileage . . . strong point remains a sense of style and purpose . . . performance remains balanced and lively enough.'' **Source:** ''Compact Sedans Grow Up,'' *Popular Science,* April 1990, pp. 80-84.

1989: ''a testimony to Honda's ceaseless effort to stay ahead of prevailing trends and technology. . .perfectly arranged pedals, the effortless shifter, and speed-sensitive power steering. . .produce a driving experience we can't get enough of.'' **Source:** ''Ten Best Cars,'' *Car and Driver,* January 1989, pp. 30-5.

1989: ''one of the most sophisticated small sedans ever built. . .feels terrific. . .steering is firm and positive, the handling is neutral. . .Even the trunk is well finished off. . .ergonomics are excellent, with controls and gauges that put you at ease immediately.'' **Source:** ''Best Sellers,'' *Popular Mechanics,* July 1989, pp. 60-3, 120-2.

1989: ''model of efficiency and practicality. . .the standard by which all other compact sedans are judged. . .High quality is an essential attribute of this car.'' **Source:** ''Hitting for High Average,'' *Car and Driver,* August 1988, p. 58-69.

1989: ''same well-designed dashboard as the other models, providing unobstructed and legible instrumentation. . .highest blends of power, ride, comfort, and handling of any car in its class. . .gets top marks in braking and simulation evasive maneuvers.'' **Source:** ''U.S. made Accord coupe hits target,'' *The Detroit News,* April 12, 1989; pp. 1F-2F.

1989: ''best family sedan in the world . . . the perfect package: good looks, comfortable ride, and pleasing performance . . . quick, classy, comfortable, and unfortunately expensive.'' **Source:** ''The People's Choice,'' *Regardie's Magazine,* July 1989, pp. 125-130.

1988: ''feels right to both import and domestic buyers. . .simply has a lot of carefully planned features. . .small rear seat. . .have been complaints of sudden acceleration.'' **Source:** ''Honda's Accord earns praise,'' *The Detroit News,* March 16, 1988; pp. 1F-2F.

1987: ''glides through life with superb aerodynamics, an efficient engine, and a chassis that should be eligible for an honorary Weight Watchers degree. Part sports car, part limousine, part econobox.'' **Source:** ''Cars: Fun Work, But Somebody's Got To Do It,'' *Car and Driver,* January 1987, pp. 36-41.

RECALLS

1987-88: (99,088 cars; includes Acura and Honda models): Sections 6A and 6B were omitted from owner's manual. **Corrective action:** Insert corrective pages. *(NHTSA Campaign No. 87V171000.)*

SAFETY AND REPAIRS

1992: ''Honda to Fix Bad Oil Switch,'' *Automotive News,* January 27, 1992, p. 2.

1991: ''Accord Wagons Recalled to Repair Cargo Light,'' *Automotive News,* November 11, 1991, p. 2.

1989: ''Car Clinic,'' *Popular Mechanics,* July 1990, p. 25. **Note:** Tip for rattling noise in '89 Accords.

1988: ''Car Clinic,'' *Popular Mechanics,* February 1990, p. 25. **Note:** Tip for floppy sun visors on 1988-89 Honda Accord and Prelude.

REPAIR MANUALS

1534 ● Chilton's Honda, 1973-1988
Chilton Co.
Chilton Way
Radnor, PA 19089   Ph:(215)964-4000

Published 1989. **Price:** $15.95.

1535 ● Honda Accord
Peter Allen Video Productions
38-C Otis St.
West Babylon, NY 11704   Ph:(516)643-4372

How to tune-up, maintain, and perform minor repairs on the Honda. **Release date:** 1986. **Producer:** Peter Allen Productions. **Acquisition:** Purchase.

1536 ● Mitchell Glove Compartment Companion for Your Honda
Harcourt Brace Jovanovich, Inc.
6277 Sea Harbor Dr.
Orlando, FL 32821   Ph:(407)345-2000

Published 1988.

OTHER INFORMATION SOURCES

1537 ● Honda Car Club Newsletter
Honda Car Club
P.O. Box 4383
North Hollywood, CA 91607   Ph:(818)982-3419

Monthly.

1538 ● Hondacar
Hondacar International
P.O. Box 5242
Deptford, NJ 08096

Newsletter. Bimonthly. **Price:** Included in membership dues.

ASSOCIATIONS

1539 ● Honda Car Club
P.O. Box 4383
North Hollywood, CA 91607
Miroslav Kefurt, Pres.   Ph:(818)982-3419

Founded: 1969. **Membership:** 3,520. Owners of Honda automobiles. Provides information and technical advice; arranges parts discounts for members; promotes the

restoration of older Honda cars. Sponsors rallies.
Convention/Meeting: Annual.

1540 ● Hondacar International
P.O. Box 5242
Deptford, NJ 08096
John Blair, Pres.

Founded: 1976. **Membership:** 1,700. Persons interested in any model of the Honda or Acura automobile. Purpose is to inform owners of both the pleasures of and potential problems with their cars, and to suggest ways to avoid such problems. **Former Name(s):** Honda Civic Club.

HONDA CIVIC (1987-92)

Sub-compact that competes against the Saab 9000 Turbo, Acura Legend Coupe, Volkswagen GTI, Chevrolet Beretta GT, Pontiac LeMans GSE, Nissan Sentra, and the Suzuki Swift GT. Hatchback named in the Best Sedan under $7,500 list in 1987 by *Road & Track*. Named as an Econo Commando by *Popular Mechanics* in 1988. Voted one of the Eight Best Econosedans in 1988 by *Car and Driver*. Named Top 10 New Car Buys-Domestic, Imports by *Road & Track* in 1989. Selected by *Car and Driver* in 1989 as one of the Top Ten Cars. Nominated in *Car and Driver's* Ten Best Cars List in 1990. Rated among the best in fuel economy by the 1992 *Car Book*. Currently produced in Alliston, Ontario, Canada; Marysville, Ohio; (plant parts data: domestic parts - 73%, imported parts - 27%, *Federal Trade Zone Board*, 1989) and East Liberty, Ohio.

1992 Honda Civic DX Hatchback

MAJOR FEATURES

● Civic CX Hatchback has as 1992 standard equipment: 5-speed manual transmission, double wishbone suspension, front anti-roll bar, tinted windows, rear defogger, rack-and-pinion steering, and powered disc/drum brakes.

● Civic DX Hatchback and Sedan adds as 1992 standard equipment: power steering (Sedans; hatchback with automatic transmission only) rear wiper/washer window, tilt steering column, cargo cover (hatchback), and various interior adjustments.

● Civic LX Sedan 1992 standard equipment adds to DX 4-door: cruise control, power windows, mirrors, and locks, and wheel covers.

● Civic EX Sedan adds as 1992 standard equipment: 1.6 liter, 16-valve engine, power-assisted, 4-wheel anti-lock disc brakes, power moonroof, and upgraded interior trim.

● Civic VX Hatchback 1992 standard equipment: 1.5 liter, 16-valve VTEC-E engine and alloy wheels.

● Civic Si Sedan 1992 standard equipment: 1.6 liter, 16-valve

engine, 4-wheel disc brakes, power steering, power moonroof with tilt feature, sport seats, cruise control, wheel covers, and upgraded tires.

● Civic 2wd Wagon added as 1991 standard equipment: digital clock and tachometer.

● Civic 4wd Wagon added as 1991 standard equipment: 6-speed manual or 4-speed automatic transmission and permanent four-wheel drive.

PRICE HISTORY

The following new car prices reflect the approximate retail cost of the base model: **1987** - $8,580; **1988** - $6,285; **1989** - $6,385; **1990** - $6,635; **1991** - $6,995; **1992** - $7,900.

DIMENSIONS

Body Style	Years Avail	Wheel Base (in)	Lgth (in)	Ht (in)	Avg Wt (lbs)	Fuel Cap (gal)	Front Hdrm (in)	Front Legrm (in)
3d lbk	89-89	98.4	156.1	52.5	2,013	11.9	38.2	43.3
3d lbk	90-91	98.4	157.1	52.5	2,127	11.9	38.2	43.3
3d lbk	92-92	101.3	160.2	53.0	2,094	11.9	38.6	42.5
4d sdn	87-87	96.5	163.4	54.5	1,940	12.1	38.1	40.3
4d sdn	88-89	98.4	166.5	53.5	2,138	11.9	38.5	43.1
4d sdn	90-91	98.4	168.8	53.5	2,255	11.9	38.5	43.1
4d sdn	92-92	103.2	173.0	54.1	2,275	11.9	37.2	42.5
5d wgn	87-87	96.5	158.7	58.3	2,304	12.1	39.2	38.9
5d wgn	88-89	98.4	161.7	57.9	2,262	11.9	39.4	41.2
5d wgn	90-91	98.4	161.7	56.1	2,328	11.9	39.4	41.2

ENGINES

Type	Displace-ment (L)	Fuel Dly	HP @rpm	Torque @rpm (ft/lbs)	MPG Cty/Hwy	Years Avail
I-4	1.5	3-bbl	76@6000	84@3500	30/33	87-87
I-4	1.3	3-bbl	60@5500	73@3500	37/43	87-87
I-4	1.5	FI	92@6000	89@3500	33/37	88-88
I-4	1.6	FI	108@6000	100@5000	28/32	88-91
I-4	1.5	FI	70@5500	83@3000	33/37	89-91
I-4	1.5	FI	92@6000	89@4500	31/35	89-91
I-4	1.6	FI	125@6600	106@5200	29/36	92-92
I-4	1.5	FI	70@5500	91@2000	42/48	92-92
I-4	1.5	FI	102@5900	98@5000	35/40	92-92
I-4	1.5	FI	92@5500	97@4500	40/47	92-92

KEY: I=in-line engine; V=V engine; F=flat engine; FI=fuel injection; bbl=barrel carburetor; T=turbo; D=diesel; HP=horsepower; MPG=estimated average miles per gallon.

EVALUATIONS, TESTS, AND RANKINGS

1992: "high-efficiency engine's use of VTEC is remarkable . . . chassis is remarkably rigid . . . exceptional ride quality over poor surfaces." **Source:** "New For '92," *Road & Track*, December 1991, pp. 90, 92, 190, 192, 194.

1992: "smoother, longer, and more rigid . . . these new models are economical only in their consumption of fuel and road space . . . In sophistication and technology, they're downright lavish." **Source:** "1992 Import Cars: Honda Civic," *Car and Driver*, November 1991, pp. 71-72, 75.

1992: "improved acceleration and economy . . . much quieter than previous Civics . . . Safe, economical, comfortable, and fun to drive." **Source:** "Honda Civic: It's the world's best small car. What did you expect," *Automobile Magazine*, November 1991, pp. 108-109, 112-113.

1992: "a refined maturity, some muscle, and even more economy." **Source:** "Honda Civic Si: More than double your pleasure," *Motor Trend*, December 1991, pp. 60-62, 64.

1992: "strict emission standards . . . cut the engine's fuel econmy by 7% . . . will boast 48 mpg in town, 55 on the highway . . . with little trade-off in performance or weight." **Source:** "55 Miles Per Gallon: How Honda Did It [Civic VX]," *Business Week,* September 23, 1991, pp. 82-83.

1992: "Civic's VTEC-E engine . . . more powerful than the power plants found in many comparably sized cars." **Source:** "A Fuel-Efficient Grab for Power," *New York Times,* September 20, 1991, pp. D1, D3.

1991: "continues to amaze us and the buying public. . .driving pleasure, quality, and value." **Source:** "Honda Civic," *Car and Driver,* January 1991, p. 43.

1991: "one of the most synergistic blends of economy and sportiness to be found anywhere . . . offers budget-bound buyers a most palatable option." **Source:** "Top Ten Import New Car Buys [Honda Civic Si]," *Motor Trend,* November 1990, pp. 61-63.

1990: "economical and reliable. . .bespeaks engineering competence. . .smooth, free revving." **Source:** "Eleven for Thirteen: Sportsters, $13,000 and under, that you can actually enjoy," *Car and Driver,* June 1990, p. 46-50, 52, 61, 63, 64, 66-9.

1990: "practical, roomy interior, fresh exterior, and build quality that rivals Mercedes-Benz." **Source:** "Top Ten New Car Buys- Domestic, Import," *Motor Trend,* November 1989, pp. 80-83, 86-89.

1990: "passenger compartment provides a comfortable and ergonomically sound haven . . . serious rival for any competitor on the market today . . . offers an outstanding alternative for those people who need a small yet spacious sedan." **Source:** "Honda Civic EX," *Motor Trend,* May 1990, pp. 96-98, 100.

1989: "best average-priced sedan in the world. . .smaller on the outside, bigger on the inside. . .doesn't know how to be boring. . .drivetrain is slicker than Oil of Olay. . .athletic agility and sports-car steering. . .spacious interior." **Source:** "Hitting for High Average," *Car and Driver,* August 1988, pp. 58-69.

1989: "offers the best combination of performance, versatility, and good looks. . .offers more value than just about any car on the market. . .is less claustrophobic than its predecessors. . .pleasing, distinctive appearance." **Source:** "Eight for Ten," *Car and Driver,* December 1988, p. 54-8, 60, 63, 64-6, 68.

1989: "amazes us to see a car conceived as low-cost transportation turn out to be so much fun to drive." **Source:** "Ten Best Cars," *Car and Driver,* January 1989, pp. 30-5.

1988: "unique detail." **Source:** "Best Cars: By Value and Passion," *Road & Track,* December 1987, p. 46-57.

1988: "unadorned econobox. . .graceful, clean and modern. . .best interior ergonomics this side of Mercedes-Benz." **Source:** "Econo Commandos," *Popular Mechanics,* July 1988, pp. 51-5, 119.

1988: "powered by the most potent engines ever offered. . .strongest unibody for any Civic ever built. . .cut down on interior noise levels. . .most aerodynamic Hondas ever produced. . .nicer for rear seat passengers." **Source:** "Honda's Civic Pride: How do you make the best better," *Motor Trend,* November 1987, pp. 62-6, 70.

RECALLS

1990: (18 DX and LX sedans with automatic transmissions): Due to improperly machined internal shaft in the transmission, the pawl mechanism may not fully engage when transmission is in park position, which could result in a crash. **Corrective action:** Install an improved parking pawl shaft. *(NHTSA Campaign No. 90V163000.)*

1990: (65 DX and LX sedans): Poor adhesion may occur between paint layers in the windshield mounting area due to defective paint batches or overspraying. Paint separation and loss of windshield retention ability could cause windshield to separate from vehicle and harm occupants and others in the vicinity. **Corrective action:** Reinstall windshield to insure proper retention. *(NHTSA Campaign No. 90V126000.)*

1988: (4,514 cars with automatic transmissions): Increased idle while car is stopped in gear due to electronic fuel injection control unit. **Corrective action:** Replace electronic fuel injection control unit. *(NHTSA Campaign No. 87V173000.)*

1987-88: (99,088 cars; includes Acura and Honda models): Sections 6A and 6B were omitted from owner's manual. **Corrective action:** Insert corrective pages. *(NHTSA Campaign No. 87V171000.)*

1987: (360,198 passenger vehicles; includes Honda Civic and Acura Integra; includes models made before 1987): Under high ambient temperatures front windshield wiper contact unit could loosen and become dislodged. This could result in windshield wiper failure and would affect driver visibility. **Corrective action:** Install contact unit holder that would prevent loosening. *(NHTSA Campaign No. 88V180000.)*

SAFETY AND REPAIRS

1992: "Honda to Fix Bad Oil Switch," *Automotive News,* January 27, 1992, p. 2.

REPAIR MANUALS

1541 ● **Chilton's Honda, 1973-1988**
Chilton Co.
Chilton Way
Radnor, PA 19089   Ph:(215)964-4000

Published 1989. **Price:** $15.95.

1542 ● **Mitchell Glove Compartment Companion for Your Honda**
Harcourt Brace Jovanovich, Inc.
6277 Sea Harbor Dr.
Orlando, FL 32821   Ph:(407)345-2000

Published 1988.

OTHER INFORMATION SOURCES

1543 ● **Honda Car Club Newsletter**
Honda Car Club
P.O. Box 4383
North Hollywood, CA 91607   Ph:(818)982-3419

Monthly.

1544 ● **Hondacar**
Hondacar International
P.O. Box 5242
Deptford, NJ 08096

Newsletter. Bimonthly. **Price:** Included in membership dues.

ASSOCIATIONS

1545 ● **Honda Car Club**
P.O. Box 4383
North Hollywood, CA 91607
Miroslav Kefurt, Pres.   Ph:(818)982-3419

Founded: 1969. **Membership:** 3,520. Owners of Honda automobiles. Provides information and technical advice; arranges parts discounts for members; promotes the restoration of older Honda cars. Sponsors rallies. **Convention/Meeting:** Annual.

1546 ● Hondacar International
P.O. Box 5242
Deptford, NJ 08096
John Blair, Pres.

Founded: 1976. **Membership:** 1,700. Persons interested in any model of the Honda or Acura automobile. Purpose is to inform owners of both the pleasures of and potential problems with their cars, and to suggest ways to avoid such problems. **Former Name(s):** Honda Civic Club.

HONDA CRX (1987-92)

A hatchback made in Japan and related to the Honda Civic subcompact. Competed against Pontiac Fiero, Acura Integra, Mazda MX-5 Miata, Lexus LS400, GEO Storm, Beretta GT, and Dodge Colt GT. Awarded one of the Ten Best Performers in 1987 by Car and Driver. Awarded Best High Performance Car Under $12,500 by Road & Track in 1987. Awarded Top Ten New Car Buy, Domestic, Import in 1989 by Motor Trend. Awarded Best Sports/GT less than $13,000 by Road & Track in 1990. A replacement for the Honda CRX is scheduled to debut in late 1992.

1991 Honda CRX HF

MAJOR FEATURES

● CRX 1992 standard equipment: Five-speed manual transmission, four-wheel double wishbone suspension, power disc/drum brakes, rack-and-pinion steering, tilt-wheel steering, and remote controlled outside mirrors.

● CRX Si added as 1992 standard equipment: power sunroof, rear wiper/washer, and 1.6 liter, 16V engine.

● CRX HF Sedan added as 1992 standard equipment: 1.5 liter, 8-valve engine, tachometer, remote fuel filler door and hatch release, and rear window defroster.

PRICE HISTORY

The following new car prices reflect the approximate retail cost of the base model: **1987** - $7,759; **1988** - $8,755; **1989** - $8,895; **1990** - $9,145; **1991** - $9,325.

DIMENSIONS

Body Style	Years Avail	Wheel Base (in)	Lgth (in)	Ht (in)	Avg Wt (lbs)	Fuel Cap (gal)	Front Hdrm (in)	Front Legrm (in)
2d cpe	87-87	86.6	144.7	50.8	1,713	10.0	37.6	42.7
2d cpe	87-87	86.6	147.8	50.8	1,978	11.9	37.6	42.7
2d cpe	88-88	90.6	147.8	50.0	1,922	11.9	37.0	43.9
2d cpe	89-90	90.6	147.8	50.1	2,048	11.9	37.0	40.8
2d cpe	91-92	90.6	148.5	50.1	1,967	10.6	37.0	40.8

ENGINES

Type	Displacement (L)	Fuel Dly	HP @rpm	Torque @rpm (ft/lbs)	MPG Cty/Hwy	Years Avail
I-4	1.5	3-bbl	58@4500	79@2500	45/50	87-87
I-4	1.5	FI	91@5500	93@4500	na	87-87
I-4	1.5	FI	92@6000	89@4500	32/36	88-92
I-4	1.6	FI	108@6000	100@5000	28/33	88-92
I-4	1.5	FI	62@6000	90@2000	43/49	88-92

KEY: I=in-line engine; V=V engine; F=flat engine; FI=fuel injection; bbl=barrel carburetor; T=turbo; D=diesel; HP=horsepower; MPG=estimated average miles per gallon.

EVALUATIONS, TESTS, AND RANKINGS

1991: "six-foot-one is about the greatest practical height for driving the CRX. . .fine ergonomics. . .quick, nibble, and controllable." **Source:** "Honda CRX Si: A good thing in a small package," Autofile, 1991, pp. 23-7.

1990: "CRX Si rivals a pair of World Series tickets as one of your best entertainment values." **Source:** "Top Ten New Car Buys- Domestic, Import," Motor Trend, November 1990, pp. 80-3, 86-9.

1990: "[CRX Si is] refined. . .sophisticated. . .well engineered. . .fun to drive." **Source:** "Eleven For Thirteen," Car and Driver, June 1990, pp. 46-50, 52, 61, 63-4, 66-9.

1988: "the handling and performance is greatly enhanced. . .transmission was smooth. . .crisp steering becomes a little tough at slow speeds . . . interior is spacious for such a small car. . .huge blind spot and poor rear vision in genral." **Source:** "Honda CRX Si Coupe," The Detroit News, December 2, 1987; pp. F1, F2.

1988: "[CRX Si is] slicker-than-ever." **Source:** "10 Best Cars," Road & Track, December 1987, pp. 46-57.

1988: "racked up the highest repair bill among 31 small two-door cars." **Source:** "Honda CRX costs most after crash: Small 2-door cars rated for protection in 5-mph collisions," The Detroit News, February 2, 1988; p. A 3.

RECALLS

None to date.

REPAIR MANUALS

1547 ● Chilton's Honda, 1973-1988
Chilton Co.
Chilton Way
Radnor, PA 19089   Ph:(215)964-4000

Published 1989. **Price:** $15.95.

1548 ● Honda CRX Shop Manual, 1983-1987
Motorbooks International
729 Prospect Ave.
Osceola, WI 54020   Ph:(715)294-3345

Published 1988. **Editor(s):** R. M. Clarke. **Price:** $15.95.

1549 ● Mitchell Glove Compartment Companion for Your Honda
Harcourt Brace Jovanovich, Inc.
6277 Sea Harbor Dr.
Orlando, FL 32821   Ph:(407)345-2000

Published 1988.

OTHER INFORMATION SOURCES

1550 ● Honda Car Club Newsletter
Honda Car Club
P.O. Box 4383
North Hollywood, CA 91607   Ph:(818)982-3419

Monthly.

1551 ● Hondacar
Hondacar International
P.O. Box 5242
Deptford, NJ 08096

Newsletter. Bimonthly. **Price:** Included in membership dues.

ASSOCIATIONS

1552 ● Honda Car Club
P.O. Box 4383
North Hollywood, CA 91607
Miroslav Kefurt, Pres.   Ph:(818)982-3419

Founded: 1969. **Membership:** 3,520. Owners of Honda automobiles. Provides information and technical advice; arranges parts discounts for members; promotes the restoration of older Honda cars. Sponsors rallies. **Convention/Meeting:** Annual.

1553 ● Hondacar International
P.O. Box 5242
Deptford, NJ 08096
John Blair, Pres.

Founded: 1976. **Membership:** 1,700. Persons interested in any model of the Honda or Acura automobile. Purpose is to inform owners of both the pleasures of and potential problems with their cars, and to suggest ways to avoid such problems. **Former Name(s):** Honda Civic Club.

HONDA PRELUDE (1987-92)

A two-door coupe that has been redesigned for 1992. Competes against Ford Probe, Mazda 626 Turbo, Isuzu Impulse Turbo, Mazda MX-6 GT, Mitsubishi Cordia Turbo, Nissan 200SX SE, Subaru XT6, and Toyota Celica GT-S. Made in Sayama, Japan.

1992 Honda Prelude Si

MAJOR FEATURES

● Prelude S has as 1992 standard equipment: 5-speed manual transmission, power-assisted 4-wheel disc brakes, driver's side airbag with Supplemental Restraint System (SRS), cruise control, power sunroof, rear defoggers, tinted glass, folding rear seatback, power steering, and anti-roll bar.

● Prelude Si adds as 1992 standard equipment: anti-lock braking system (ABS), alloy wheels, chin spoiler and air conditioning.

PRICE HISTORY

The following new car prices reflect the approximate retail cost of the base model: **1987** - $12,230; **1988** - $13,640; **1989** - $13,945; **1990** - $13,495; **1991** - $15,095; **1992** - $16,250.

DIMENSIONS

Body Style	Years Avail	Wheel Base (in)	Lgth (in)	Ht (in)	Avg Wt (lbs)	Fuel Cap (gal)	Front Hdrm (in)	Front Legrm (in)
2d cpe	87-87	96.5	172.0	48.6	2,379	15.8	37.3	43.2
2d cpe	88-88	101.0	175.6	49.2	2,665	15.9	36.9	43.1
2d cpe	89-91	101.0	177.6	49.2	2,639	15.9	36.9	43.1
2d cpe	92-92	100.4	174.8	50.8	2,765	15.9	38.0	35.1

ENGINES

Type	Displacement (L)	Fuel Dly	HP @rpm	Torque @rpm (ft/lbs)	MPG Cty/Hwy	Years Avail
I-4	1.8	2x1 bbl	110@na	na	25/31	87-87
I-4	2.0	FI	110@5500	114@4500	25/31	87-87
I-4	2.0	2-bbl	104@5800	111@4000	22/27	88-90
I-4	2.0	FI	135@6200	127@4000	22/27	88-91
I-4	2.1	FI	140@5800	135@5000	22/26	90-91
I-4	2.2	FI	135@5200	196@4000	na	92-92
I-4	2.2	FI	160@5800	156@4500	na	92-92

KEY: I=in-line engine; V=V engine; F=flat engine; FI=fuel injection; bbl=barrel carburetor; T=turbo; D=diesel; HP=horsepower; MPG=estimated average miles per gallon.

EVALUATIONS, TESTS, AND RANKINGS

1992: "softer yet more massive presence." **Source:** "Ten Best Cars," *Car and Driver*, January 1992, pp. 35-43.

1992: "sports-car handling, a strong engine, and audacious styling . . . sheds its previous rational, somewhat conservative personality." **Source:** "Honda Prelude Si 4WS: Hitting the seam in the zone," *Motor Trend*, November 1991, pp. 84-85, 88-89.

1992: "generally it's a very simple car to drive quickly . . . strikes an interesting balance of luxury, style and competent performance." **Source:** "Honda Prelude Si-4WS: Honda re-creates its sports coupe," *Road & Track*, November 1991, pp. 64-68.

1992: "design of the rear end is particularly daring . . . driving position is excellent, the seats are comfortable . . . instruments are properly visible." **Source:** "Honda Prelude: Desperately seeking excitement," *Car and Driver*, November 1991, pp. 50-53.

1992: "a sharp step upward from the previous car . . . higher performance, a smoother ride, better handling . . . new Prelude is strongly biased toward sportiness." **Source:** "Honda Prelude Si 4WS," *Automobile Magazine*, November 1991, pp. 116-117.

1992: "a bit surprised by the plastic trim piece that fell off the rear-view mirror. . .loves to squirt around hairpin corners and sprint away from stoplights without muscle-car obtrusiveness." **Source:** "Prelude upgraded for 1992," *Detroit Free Press*, February 6, 1992, p. C1.

1990: "if technical razzle-dazzle counts for anything, the Si is worth the price." **Source:** "Honda Prelude Si: Technical tour de force," *Road & Track*, July 1990, p. 108.

1989: "fastest and easiest to drive in the slalom. . .engine is a pleasure to live with." **Source:** "Coupes de Grace: The small, the quick and the slick in a high desert shootout," *Popular Mechanics*, May 1989, pp. 120-4, 212, 214.

1989: "engine is considerably smoother and noticeably happier at high rpm . . . behavior is totally predictable . . . a pleasing and useful interior." **Source:** "Two Times Four Equals Great," *Car and Driver*, July 1989, pp. 36-39, 41, 56-57, 59.

1988: "4ws Prelude performed better in the dry and worse in the wet than the 2ws Prelude—not a worthwhile trade-off." **Source:** "Turning Points: A hard Look at four-wheel steering," *Car and Driver*, December 1987, pp. 75-7, 79-80, 83.

1988: "an aim-it-where-you-want-it car . . . striking exterior." **Source:** "Catalina Pony Express: Riding the roads in the Japanese sporty cars," *Motor Trend*, May 1988, pp. 54-8, 61, 64-6.

RECALLS

1988: (7,893 cars): Coolant seepage may occur with residue accumulating on throttle valve. **Corrective action:** Replace throttle body assembly. *(NHTSA Campaign No. 87V122000.)*

1988: (99,088 cars; includes Acura and Honda models): Sections 6A and 6B were omitted from owner's manual. **Corrective action:** Insert corrective pages. *(NHTSA Campaign No. 87V171000.)*

1988: (76,973 cars): Accelerator pedal stopper may be bent when excessive downward force is applied after pedal has contacted stopper. Could result in loss of accelerator control should pedal be caught. **Corrective action:** Install support to prevent stopper from bending. *(NHTSA Campaign No. 89V097000.)*

1988: (25,252 cars): Rear inboard seat anchorage bracket for front seats may not withstand the force required by FMVSS 207. Bracket failure could result in seat becoming loose. **Corrective action:** Install reinforcing plate to rear inboard seat anchorage bracket for each front seat. *(NHTSA Campaign No. 89V093000.)*

1988: (66,239 cars): Vibration and high underhood temperatures could cause power steering supply hose at connector clamp seal to develop fluid leak. If fluid contacts hot exhaust manifold, it may cause smoke and possibly underhood fire. **Corrective action:** Install improved power steering supply hose assembly. *(NHTSA Campaign No. 88V059000.)*

SAFETY AND REPAIRS

1988: "Car Clinic," *Popular Mechanics*, February 1990, p. 25. **Note:** Tip for floppy sun visor on 1988-89 Honda Accord and Prelude.

REPAIR MANUALS

1554 ● Chilton's Honda, 1973-1988
Chilton Co.
Chilton Way
Radnor, PA 19089   Ph:(215)964-4000
Published 1989. **Price:** $15.95.

1555 ● Haynes Honda Prelude CVCC Owners Workshop Manuals, No 601: 1979-1989
Haynes Publications, Inc.
861 Lawrence Dr.
Newbury Park, CA 91320   Ph:(818)889-5400

Editor(s): Ray M. Jones. **Price:** $15.95.

1556 ● Mitchell Glove Compartment Companion for Your Honda
Harcourt Brace Jovanovich, Inc.
6277 Sea Harbor Dr.
Orlando, FL 32821   Ph:(407)345-2000
Published 1988.

OTHER INFORMATION SOURCES

1557 ● Honda Car Club Newsletter
Honda Car Club
P.O. Box 4383
North Hollywood, CA 91607   Ph:(818)982-3419
Monthly.

1558 ● Hondacar
Hondacar International
P.O. Box 5242
Deptford, NJ 08096

Newsletter. Bimonthly. **Price:** Included in membership dues.

ASSOCIATIONS

1559 ● Honda Car Club
P.O. Box 4383
North Hollywood, CA 91607
Miroslav Kefurt, Pres.   Ph:(818)982-3419

Founded: 1969. **Membership:** 3,520. Owners of Honda automobiles. Provides information and technical advice; arranges parts discounts for members; promotes the restoration of older Honda cars. Sponsors rallies. **Convention/Meeting:** Annual.

1560 ● Hondacar International
P.O. Box 5242
Deptford, NJ 08096
John Blair, Pres.

Founded: 1976. **Membership:** 1,700. Persons interested in any model of the Honda or Acura automobile. Purpose is to inform owners of both the pleasures of and potential problems with their cars, and to suggest ways to avoid such problems. **Former Name(s):** Honda Civic Club.

HYUNDAI ELANTRA (1992)

A high-end subcompact sedan positioned between the Excel and the Sonata. Featuring a high level of standard equipment, the Elantra competes with the Toyota Corolla, Nissan Sentra, and Ford Escort. Currently produced in Ulfan, South Korea, the Hyundai Elantra is available in base model and GLS trim.

1992 Hyundai Elantra

MAJOR FEATURES

● Elantra has as 1992 standard equipment: 1.6-liter 4-cylinder engine, 5-speed manual transmission, power steering, front disc/rear drum power brakes, rear defogger, and variable-intermittent wipers.

● Elantra GLS adds as 1992 standard equipment: 6-way adjustable driver's seat, upgraded upholstery, power mirrors, windows and locks, and tilt steering.

PRICE HISTORY

The following new car prices reflect the approximate retail cost of the base model: **1992 - $8,995.**

DIMENSIONS

Body Style	Years Avail	Wheel Base (in)	Lgth (in)	Ht (in)	Avg Wt (lbs)	Fuel Cap (gal)	Front Hdrm (in)	Front Legrm (in)
4d sdn	92-92	98.4	171.6	54.5	2,452	13.7	38.4	42.6

ENGINES

Type	Displacement (L)	Fuel Dly	HP @rpm	Torque @rpm (ft/lbs)	MPG Cty/Hwy	Years Avail
I-4	1.6	FI	113@6000	102@5000	22/29	92-92

KEY: I=in-line engine; V=V engine; F=flat engine; FI=fuel injection; bbl=barrel carburetor; T=turbo; D=diesel; HP=horsepower; MPG=estimated average miles per gallon.

EVALUATIONS, TESTS, AND RANKINGS

1992: "nice blend of comfort, style, and sporting muscle . . . Comfy seats, nice stereo, and cool breeze of air conditioning are fine . . . smoothly predictable and well balanced." **Source:** "Hyundai Elantra: Cooking with Korea's Newest Tomato," *Motor Trend,* September 1991, pp. 86-87.

1992: "surprising roominess and a clean, simple interior layout . . . too much roll softness in front for the truly enthusiastic . . . newfound splash of sportiness and style." **Source:** "Hyundai Elantra: South Korea's bid for the prime time," *Road & Track,* September 1991, p. 96.

1992: "styling is tidy and modern, if a little conservative . . . pleasant to drive. Its steering is quick and accurate . . . steering wheel['s] . . . banana-shaped hub molding is less than elegant." **Source:** "The Elantra Mantra: Hyundai's fourth U.S. car looks to be its best," *Automobile Magazine,* October 1991, pp. 115-116.

RECALLS

None to date.

HYUNDAI EXCEL (1987-92)

Currently produced in South Korea, Excel is a sub-compact car competing against Chevrolet Nova, Chevrolet Spectrum, Mercury Tracer, Pontiac Lemans, and Chevrolet Sprint. Rated a Best Bet of 1992 and selected among the best in a 1992 crash test performance by *The Car Book.* The five-door model was discontinued after the 1991 model year.

1991 Hyundai Excel GS

MAJOR FEATURES

● Excel has as 1992 standard equipment: 4-speed manual transmission, front and rear stabilizer bars, four-wheel independent suspension, power-assisted front disc/rear drum brakes, rack-and-pinion steering, other exterior body stylings, front bucket seats, front passive restraint system, and other interior features.

● Excel GL adds as 1992 standard equipment: 5-speed manual transmission, upgraded exterior trim, tinted glass, AM/FM ETR cassette with two speakers, and additional interior features.

● Excel GS adds as 1992 standard equipment: bodycolor rear spoiler, all-season radial tires, tachometer, and sportier interior trim.

● Excel GLS added as 1991 standard equipment: power steering, AM/FM cassette, and velour upholstery.

PRICE HISTORY

The following new car prices reflect the approximate retail cost of the base model: **1987 - $5,195; 1988 - $5,395; 1989 - $5,724; 1990 - $5,899; 1991 - $6,375; 1992 - $6,595.**

DIMENSIONS

Body Style	Years Avail	Wheel Base (in)	Lgth (in)	Ht (in)	Avg Wt (lbs)	Fuel Cap (gal)	Front Hdrm (in)	Front Legrm (in)
3d lbk	87-88	93.7	161.0	54.1	2,156	10.6	37.5	40.9
3d lbk	89-89	93.7	160.9	54.1	2,156	10.6	37.5	40.9
3d lbk	90-92	93.8	161.4	54.5	2,040	11.9	37.8	41.7
5d lbk	89-89	93.7	160.9	54.1	2,178	10.6	37.5	40.9
5d lbk	90-91	93.8	161.4	54.5	2,040	11.9	37.8	41.7
4d sdn	89-89	93.7	168.0	54.1	2,178	10.6	37.5	40.9
4d sdn	90-92	93.8	168.3	54.5	2,202	11.9	37.8	41.7

ENGINES

Type	Displace-ment (L)	Fuel Dly	HP @rpm	Torque @rpm (ft/lbs)	MPG Cty/Hwy	Years Avail
I-4	1.5	2-bbl	68@5500	82@3500	28/37	87-89
I-4	1.5	FI	81@5500	91@3000	29/36	90-92

KEY: I=in-line engine; V=V engine; F=flat engine; FI=fuel injection; bbl=barrel carburetor; T=turbo; D=diesel; HP=horsepower; MPG=estimated average miles per gallon.

EVALUATIONS, TESTS, AND RANKINGS

1990: "reasonably quick around town . . . interior . . . not the least bit stylish, but it gets the job done . . . does everything this sort of car ought to do." **Source:** "Hyundai Excel GLS: Bigger, better, and more expensive," *Car and Driver,* December 1989, pp. 109-113.

1989: "had been a fine cruiser . . . needed more power for climbing steep grades . . . air conditioning strained the engine noticeably . . . door locks are so easy to disable that a cross-eyed baby could break into it . . . trouble getting a clean shift to fifth gear." **Source:** "Life with a Hyundai Excel," *Car and Driver,* February 1989, pp. 111-113.

1987: "was inferior to the mechanically identical Colt . . . interior's poor fit and finish . . . "twitchy" handling." **Source:** "Asian Invasion," *Popular Mechanics,* July 1987, pp. 90-94, 148.

1987: " . . . biggest gripe had to do with horsepower." **Source:** "Hyundai Excel: More than a million owner-driven miles bring lots of smiles. The price of this Korean car makes buyers happy, too," *Popular Mechanics,* May 1987, pp. 186, 188-9, 192.

RECALLS

1990: (2,281 cars; includes Mitsubishi Precis models): Improperly heat treated lock washer could crack causing wheel bearing damage. **Corrective action:** Replace lock washer on each front wheel and repair area around lock washer as necessary. *(NHTSA Campaign No. 90V053000.)*

1987-89: (8,550 passenger vehicles with specific cruise systems; includes models made before 1987): If cruise control switch is in on position when starting engine system may be affected by a short duration voltage drop. **Corrective action:** Replace electronic control module. *(NHTSA Campaign No. 89V100000.)*

1987: (321,000 cars with automatic and 4 or 5 speed transmissions; includes models made before 1987; includes Hyundai and Mitsubishi models): Possible loss of braking efficiency during repeated hard applications. **Corrective action:** Replace front brake pads. *(NHTSA Campaign No. 87V180000.)*

SAFETY AND REPAIRS

1989: "Hyundai Dealer Dials up Disaster," *Automotive News,* February 10, 1992, p. 2. **Note:** 1986-89 Excels may have corroding valves.

1989: "NHTSA Steps Up Excel Belt Inquiry," *Automotive News,* January 20, 1992, p. 39. **Note:** 1987-89 Excel models may experience shoulder belt failure.

1989: "Hyundai Recalls Subcompacts," *Automotive News,* January 6, 1992, p. 2. **Note:** 1986-1989 Excel models may have a defective reed valve subassembly that could ultimately result in engine fire.

REPAIR MANUALS

1561 ● Chilton's Hyundai 1985-1987
Chilton Co.
Chilton Way
Radnor, PA 19089   Ph:(215)964-4000

Published 1987. **Price:** $14.95.

1562 ● Haynes Hyundai Excel: 1986-1989
Haynes Publications, Inc.
861 Lawrence Dr.
Newbury Park, CA 91320   Ph:(818)889-5400

Published 1989. **Price:** $15.95.

HYUNDAI SCOUPE (1991-92)

Currently produced in Ulsan, South Korea, the Hyundai Scoupe is a 2-door notchback sports coupe that competes against the Honda CRX, GEO Storm, Ford Mustang, Toyota Tercel, and Mazda 323. Appeals to young and value-conscious buyers.

1991 Hyundai Scoupe

MAJOR FEATURES

● Scoupe has as 1992 standard equipment: 1.5 liter SOHC 4-cylinder MPI engine, 5-speed manual transmission, power front disc/rear drum brakes, front and rear stabilizer bars, intermittent wipers, rear-window defroster, bucket seats, passive restraint system, and various other interior features.

● Scoupe LS adds as 1992 standard equipment: powering steering with tilt wheel, wider radial tires, power windows, 6-way adjustable driver's seat, and an upgraded interior.

PRICE HISTORY

The following new car prices reflect the approximate retail cost of the base model: **1991** - $8,495; **1992** - $8,799.

DIMENSIONS

Body Style	Years Avail	Wheel Base (in)	Lgth (in)	Ht (in)	Avg Wt (lbs)	Fuel Cap (gal)	Front Hdrm (in)	Front Legrm (in)
2d cpe	91-92	93.8	165.9	50.0	2,119	11.9	38.1	42.8

ENGINES

Type	Displace-ment (L)	Fuel Dly	HP @rpm	Torque @rpm (ft/lbs)	MPG Cty/Hwy	Years Avail
I-4	1.5	FI	81@5500	91@3000	26/34	91-92

KEY: I=in-line engine; V=V engine; F=flat engine; FI=fuel injection; bbl=barrel carburetor; T=turbo; D=diesel; HP=horsepower; MPG=estimated average miles per gallon.

EVALUATIONS, TESTS, AND RANKINGS

1991: "a sportier version of Hyudai's subcompact Excel . . . suspension is on the spongy side . . . acceleration that is only adequate with just the driver aboard . . . one of the slickest five-speeds available." **Source:** "Economy ride, with good looks," *The Detroit News*, December 19, 1990, pp. F1-F2.

1991: "has two main attractions . . . low sticker price . . . and a three year, bumper-to-bumper warranty . . . interior trim . . . is impressive, except for the steering wheel." **Source:** "Scoupe is strictly standard issue," *Detroit Free Press*, November 15, 1990, p. C1.

1991: "amazing amount of stuff at the price . . . should you put passengers in the back seat, you can expect them not to ride with you ever again." **Source:** "Hyundai's Scoupe Fills a Sensible Niche," *New York Times*, November 4, 1990.

1991: "very competitive pricing." **Source:** "Hyundai Scoupe," *Road & Track*, October 1990, p. 73.

1991: "fresher and more spirited than . . . previous efforts . . . a squishy-soft, Excel-like ride . . . good performance and good quality." **Source:** "Hyundai Scoupe LS," *Automobile Magazine*, December 1990.

1991: "low sticker price is central to understanding the Scoupe . . . a decent, honest little car that delivers." **Source:** "Hyundai Soupe LS: Basic transportation with a little flair-just don't forget the price," *Car and Driver*, November 1990, pp. 69-70.

1991: "clean, swoopy, and devoid of ornamentation . . . inside? Comfortable and generous . . . value for the buck." **Source:** "Hyundai Scoupe," *Motor Trend*, December 1990, pp. 104-106.

1991: "sassy little car . . . fair amount of handling . . . feels tight and solid . . . corners with little body roll and keeps its footing well on various surfaces." **Source:** "Hyundai hopes buyers scoop up bright idea: Sporty Scoupe offers spirit for less cost," *Flint Journal*, January 2, 1991, pp. D1-D2.

1991: "engine is noisy . . . handsome, if a trifle unadorned . . . needs more power." **Source:** "Getaway Coupes," *Popular Science*, July 1991, pp. 76-80.

RECALLS

None to date.

HYUNDAI SONATA (1989-92)

Mid-sized car that competes against the Dodge Spirit, Ford Tempo, Toyota Camry, Mazda 626, Mitsubishi Galant, and Plymouth Acclaim. Named in *Popular Mechanics's* Best Seller list in 1989. Nominated Ten Best Cars by *Car and Driver* in 1990. Currently built in Korea and Bromont, Quebec, Canada.

1992 Hyundai Sonata

MAJOR FEATURES

● Sonata has as 1992 standard equipment: 2.0L DOHC 16-valve, 4-cylinder engine, 5-speed manual transmission, independent front and rear suspension, power-assisted front disc/rear drum brakes, anti-lock braking system, power-assisted rack-and-pinion steering, tilt steering column, rear window defogger, tinted glass, and an assortment of exterior and interior features.

● Sonata GLS adds as 1992 standard equipment: 4-speed automatic transmission with overdrive, cruise control, air conditioning, upgraded stereo/cassette system, and various interior refinements.

PRICE HISTORY

The following new car prices reflect the approximate retail cost of the base model: **1989** - $9,695; **1990** - $9,999; **1991** - $10,900; **1992** - $11,150.

DIMENSIONS

Body Style	Years Avail	Wheel Base (in)	Lgth (in)	Ht (in)	Avg Wt (lbs)	Fuel Cap (gal)	Front Hdrm (in)	Front Legrm (in)
4d sdn	89-92	104.3	184.3	55.4	2,723	15.9	38.5	42.4

ENGINES

Type	Displace-ment (L)	Fuel Dly	HP @rpm	Torque @rpm (ft/lbs)	MPG Cty/Hwy	Years Avail
I-4	2.4	FI	110@4500	138@3500	20/25	89-89
I-4	2.4	FI	116@4500	142@3500	21/28	90-91
I-4	2.0	FI	128@6000	121@5000	20/27	92-92
V-6	3.0	FI	142@5000	168@2500	18/24	90-92

KEY: I=in-line engine; V=V engine; F=flat engine; FI=fuel injection; bbl=barrel carburetor; T=turbo; D=diesel; HP=horsepower; MPG=estimated average miles per gallon.

EVALUATIONS, TESTS, AND RANKINGS

1992: "attention to fluid and harmonious design . . . interior appointments . . . generally handsome and sensible . . . a mainstream offering for the family sedan buyer." **Source:** "Hyundai Sonata: You can afford to be stylish," *Motor Trend*, October 1991, p. 90.

1992: "surprising legroom in the back seat . . . interior is well and sensibly put together . . . acceleration and highway performance are good." **Source:** "Humming Along with Hyundai's Sonata," *New York Times*, November 10, 1991.

1990: "more powerful, smooth." **Source:** "Hyundai Sonata," *Road & Track*, October 1990, p. 73.

1990: "Highway driving is smooth and quiet . . . What the Sonata lacks in wow, it makes up for in comfort . . . a solid car in which you can comfortably fit your family." **Source:** "Korea Sends Us Low-Cost Sedan," *Design News*, October 2, 1989, pp. 162-163.

1990: "loads of interior space . . . while the Hyundai provides a lot of car for the money, it dosesn't measure up to the competition." **Source:** "Compact Sedans Grow Up," *Popular Science*, April 1990, pp. 80-84.

1989: "Inexpensive, sturdy, workable . . . roomier than any of its competitors . . . comfortable four-adult car . . . one of the most powerful cars in its class." **Source:** "Hyundai Sonata," *Road & Track*, July 1989, pp. 85-6.

1989: "has come a long way in a short time . . . roomy interior borrows many of the same Mercedes 300 E styling cues used on Mazda's 626 . . . dash in particular is very European . . . ride and handling are better than average." **Source:** "Best Sellers," *Popular Mechanics*, July 1989, pp. 60-3, 120-22.

1989: "lot of car for the money . . . isn't an exciting car, but wasn't designed to be exciting . . . designed to be practical, sensible . . . very liveable . . . performed well at more than mile-high elevations . . . begs for a better driver's seat." **Source:** "Hyundai Sonata: More of a good thing," *Motor Trend*, June 1989, pp. 93-6, 98.

1989: "more powerful and best equipped cars in its class- all at an affordable price . . . Head and leg room is indeed generous throughout, especially in the rear where even tall adults will find ample room . . . engine a bit loud for a car this size." **Source:** "Sonata sedan offers room to grow," *The Detroit News*, March 15, 1989, pp. F1, F2.

1989: "just what you wouldn't expect—a big car from Korea . . . surprisingly effective package." **Source:** "1989 offers an 8-pack of memorable cars," *The Detroit News*, July 2, 1989, p. H1.

1989: "pluses are the many standard interior amenities . . . hardly a race car around the turns . . . family-car supple, even on rough roads." **Source:** "Style For a Song," *Home Mechanix*, August 1989, p. 76.

RECALLS

1989-90: (39,361 cars): Hood could open due to binding of safety catch on secondary hood latch striker. **Corrective action:** Replace hood latch striker assembly. *(NHTSA Campaign No. 90V038000.)*

1989-90: (43,590 cars with 2.5L engines): Damage to fuel supply hose could allow fuel leakage into engine and could result in a fire. **Corrective action:** Rotate spring clamp to prevent contact with fuel hose; replace damaged hoses. *(NHTSA Campaign No. 90V037000.)*

INFINITI G20 (1991-92)

A front-drive 4-door luxury-sport sedan that competes against BMW 318is, Audi 80/90, and Mercedes-Benz 190. Currently produced in Oppama, Japan, by Nissan's upscale Infiniti division.

1991 Infiniti G20

MAJOR FEATURES

● G20 has as 1992 standard equipment: all-independent suspension with front and rear stabilizer bars, power steering, anti-lock four-wheel disc brakes, air conditioning, cruise control, tilt steering, theft deterrent system, and five-speed manual transmission.

PRICE HISTORY

The following new car prices reflect the approximate retail cost of the base model: **1991** - $17,750; **1992** - $18,300.

DIMENSIONS

Body Style	Years Avail	Wheel Base (in)	Lgth (in)	Ht (in)	Avg Wt (lbs)	Fuel Cap (gal)	Front Hdrm (in)	Front Legrm (in)
4d sdn	91-92	100.4	175.0	54.9	2,535	15.9	38.8	42.0

ENGINES

Type	Displace-ment (L)	Fuel Dly	HP @rpm	Torque @rpm (ft/lbs)	MPG Cty/Hwy	Years Avail
I-4	2.0	FI	140@6400	132@4800	24/32	91-92

KEY: I=in-line engine; V=V engine; F=flat engine; FI=fuel injection; bbl=barrel carburetor; T=turbo; D=diesel; HP=horsepower; MPG=estimated average miles per gallon.

EVALUATIONS, TESTS, AND RANKINGS

1991: "Attention yuppies. . .sleek, wind tunnel-honed look. . .ride quality is excellent." **Source:** "New Infiniti rivals BMW 318is," *Detroit Free Press*, October 18, 1990, p. 1F.

1991: "styling is clean and fresh. . .interior is a pleasant, efficient environment. . .the bigger-car feel doesn't mean sluggish in performance or handling." **Source:** "Infiniti gives ride you don't want to end," *The Flint Journal*, Wednesday February 13, 1991, pp. E1-2.

1991: "well-equipped." **Source:** "Infiniti G20," *Road & Track*, October 1990, p. 73.

1991: "only comes one way: loaded. . .tidy enough appearance. . .when the going gets hilly, expect to do a fair amount of downshifting." **Source:** "Infiniti G20: When a little means a lot," *Motor Trend*, January 1991, p. 60-3.

1991: "a sleek, comfortable, nimble, sedan with decent performance. . .an unusually roomy cabin. . .pleasing contoured instrument panel." **Source:** "Infiniti G20: Cheap luxury? Affordable exclusivity? A low-end/high-line strategy creates some curious marketing but a fine $20,000 sedan," *Car and Driver*, November 1990, pp. 93-6.

1991: "breaks new ground in several areas, including chassis design . . . tremendous fun to drive quickly . . . sculpted, curvy instrument panel." **Source:** "Entry-Level Luxury," *Popular Science*, April 1991, pp. 76-80, 96.

RECALLS

None to date.

INFINITI M30 (1990-92)

A 2-door luxury coupe and convertible, manufactured by Infiniti in Oppama, Japan. The convertible version is assembled by American Sunroof Corporation in California. Competes against the Acura Legend, BMW 325i, and Ford Thunderbird Super Coupe. Rated among the best in its class by *The Car Book* in a 1992 crash test performance.

1991 Infiniti M30

MAJOR FEATURES

● M30 has as 1992 standard equipment: 4-speed automatic transmission, 4-wheel anti-lock disc brakes, power rack-and-pinion steering, independent suspension, driver's side airbag, cruise control, power sunroof, leather seats, sound system, climate control, tinted glass, power windows and locks, tilt steering, intermittent wipers, and theft deterrent system.

PRICE HISTORY

The following new car prices reflect the approximate retail cost of the base model: **1990** - $23,500; **1991** - $24,500; **1992** - $25,000.

DIMENSIONS

Body Style	Years Avail	Wheel Base (in)	Lgth (in)	Ht (in)	Avg Wt (lbs)	Fuel Cap (gal)	Front Hdrm (in)	Front Legrm (in)
2d cpe	90-92	103.0	188.8	54.3	3,333	17.2	36.8	42.2
2d conv	90-92	103.0	188.8	54.3	3,576	17.2	35.0	42.2

ENGINES

Type	Displacement (L)	Fuel Dly	HP @rpm	Torque @rpm (ft/lbs)	MPG Cty/Hwy	Years Avail
V-6	3.0	FI	162@5200	180@3600	19/25	90-92

KEY: I=in-line engine; V=V engine; F=flat engine; FI=fuel injection; bbl=barrel carburetor; D=diesel; HP=horsepower; MPG=estimated average miles per gallon.

EVALUATIONS, TESTS, AND RANKINGS

1991: "less squat, dive, and wallowing would make the M30 just that much more fun on the curves . . . Open up your trick-

or-treat bags, because the M30's gonna fill 'em up with standards." **Source:** "Infiniti M30 Convertible: Everything under the sun," *Motor Trend*, August 1991, pp. 59-60.

1991: "M30 isn't the perfect convertible. But, boy, it's close . . . mature design and painless convertibility make it a classic ragtop." **Source:** "Infiniti M30: The one-finger convertible," *Car and Driver*, August 1991, pp. 56-57.

1991: "same as its sports coupe counterpart . . . top is a one-touch pushbutton operation." **Source:** "Automobiles: New Cars," *Popular Mechanics*, June 1991, pp. 98-102.

1990: "there are ergonomic flaws that have no place in any car. . .engine is growlish if not outright tinny . . . fit and finish level second to none." **Source:** "Simply put, Infiniti M30 falls short," *The Detroit News*, February 28, 1990, pp. 8D-9D.

1990: "convertible. . .broadens the appeal." **Source:** "Infiniti M30," *Road & Track*, October 1990, p. 73.

1990: "a confidence-builder on a twisty byway . . . no noteworthy bad habits in the handling department." **Source:** "Fall Firsts," *Popular Mechanics*, September 1989, pp. 105-106.

RECALLS

None to date.

INFINITI Q45 (1990-92)

A luxury sedan that competes against Lexus LS400, Mitsubishi Galant GS, Mercedes-Benz 300E, BMW 535i, and Jaguar XJ6. Awarded one of the Ten Best Cars in the World in 1991 by *Road & Track*. Currently produced in Tochigi, Japan.

1991 Infiniti Q45

MAJOR FEATURES

● Q45 has as 1992 standard equipment: 4-speed automatic transmission, 4-wheel anti-lock disc brakes, power steering, driver's side air bag, cruise control, automatic climate control, computer-controlled automatic suspension, power sunroof, tinted glass, power windows and locks, power driver's seat with two-position memory, heated power mirrors, intermittent wipers, and theft deterrent system.

PRICE HISTORY

The following new car prices reflect the approximate retail cost of the base model: **1990** - $38,000; **1991** - $40,000; **1992** - $42,000.

DIMENSIONS

Body Style	Years Avail	Wheel Base (in)	Lgth (in)	Ht (in)	Avg Wt (lbs)	Fuel Cap (gal)	Front Hdrm (in)	Front Legrm (in)
4d sdn	90-92	113.2	199.8	56.3	3,950	22.5	38.2	43.9

ENGINES

Type	Displace-ment (L)	Fuel Dly	HP @rpm	Torque @rpm (ft/lbs)	MPG Cty/Hwy	Years Avail
V-8	4.5	FI	278@6000	292@4000	16/22	90-92

KEY: I=in-line engine; V=V engine; F=flat engine; FI=fuel injection; bbl=barrel carburetor; T=turbo; D=diesel; HP=horsepower; MPG=estimated average miles per gallon.

EVALUATIONS, TESTS, AND RANKINGS

1991: ``sends the pavement spinning rearward beneath its wheels. . .handling is also progressive and smooth.'' **Source:** ``Infiniti Q45: Clashing Symbolism,'' *Autoweek's AutoFile 1991 Edition*, 1990, pp. 147-151.

1991: ``blazing performance at a good price . . . inexplicably light on its feet . . . averaged 19 mpg and ate no oil.'' **Source:** ``Life with Infiniti Q45: Clockwork lightning,'' *Car and Driver*, December 1990, pp. 129-130, 133.

1990: ``seductive . . . so smooth, so quiet, so wonderfully powerful, driving it is a . . . truly pleasurable personal experience.'' **Source:** ``Luxurious Q45 offers plain pleasure,'' *The Detroit News*, January 24, 1990, pp. 5B-6B.

1990: ``is going to shoulder its way into the fancy-car party and sit down at the head table . . . Germans will no longer have a monopoly on autobahn performance . . . was remarkably easy to enter and exit.'' **Source:** ``Infiniti Q-Series: Another reason to be rich,'' *Car and Driver*, January 1989, pp. 112-13, 115-16, 118.

1990: ``autobahn-class performance.'' **Source:** ``Top Ten New Car Buys, Domestic, Import,'' *Motor Trend*, November 1989, pp. 80-3, 86-9.

1990: ``handsome, elegant and conservative . . . adequate room for three adults in the rear . . . engine is smooth, quiet, powerful, torquey, flexible . . . spectacular.'' **Source:** ``Infiniti Q45,'' *Road & Track*, September 1989, pp. 105-107, 109.

1990: ``From some angles it's radical . . . And from some angles the Q45 is simply beautiful . . . The profile will win a parking space in front of the snootiest hotel in the land.'' **Source:** ``What's in a Nameplate,'' *Esquire*, January 1990, p. 18.

RECALLS

None to date.

ISUZU AMIGO (1989-92)

A two-seater split hardtop/softtop leisure jeep in competition against Jeep Wrangler, Dodge Dakota Sport Convertible, Ford Ranger Supercab STX, Toyota Xtracab SR5 V-6, Geo Tracker, and Mitsubishi Montero LS 4-Door V-6. Named in *Motor Trend's* 1989 Truck of the Year list. Voted First Place in a Comparison Test by *Car and Driver* in 1989. Voted Third Place in a Comparison Test by *Automobile Magazine* in 1991.

1991 Isuzu Amigo

MAJOR FEATURES

● Amigo has as 1992 standard equipment: 5-speed manual transmission, power steering, ventilated power front disc/rear drum brakes, rear-wheel anti-lock brake system, all-terrain tires, two passenger cabin, independent double wishbone front suspension, and anti-roll bar.

● Amigo S 2.3 adds as 1992 standard equipment: 2.3-liter SOHC 4-cylinder engine and various interior features.

● Amigo S 2.6 adds as 1992 standard equipment: 2.6-liter SOHC 4-cylinder engine.

● Amigo XS adds as 1992 standard equipment: four wheel power-assisted disc brakes, tilt steering, intermittent wipers, and various interior adjustments.

● Amigo S 4wd adds as 1992 standard equipment: power steering, skid plates, and 4-wheel drive.

● Amigo XS 4wd adds as 1992 standard equipment: alloy wheels and 4-wheel drive.

PRICE HISTORY

The following new car prices reflect the approximate retail cost of the base model: **1989** - $8,999; **1990** - $9,459; **1991** - $9,799.

DIMENSIONS

Body Style	Years Avail	Wheel Base (in)	Lgth (in)	Ht (in)	Avg Wt (lbs)	Fuel Cap (gal)	Front Hdrm (in)	Front Legrm (in)
utl wgn	89-92	91.7	164.2	65.2	3,750	21.9	38.0	42.5

ENGINES

Type	Displace-ment (L)	Fuel Dly	HP @rpm	Torque @rpm (ft/lbs)	MPG Cty/Hwy	Years Avail
I-4	2.3	2-bbl	96@4600	123@2600	19/21	89-92
I-4	2.6	FI	120@5000	146@2600	17/20	89-92

KEY: I=in-line engine; V=V engine; F=flat engine; FI=fuel injection; bbl=barrel carburetor; T=turbo; D=diesel; HP=horsepower; MPG=estimated average miles per gallon.

EVALUATIONS, TESTS, AND RANKINGS

1991: ``heavy, ponderous . . . every bit a truck in the dirt. . .interior was one of our favorites.'' **Source:** ``Dirty Little Devils,'' *Automobile Magazine*, February 1991, pp. 79-85.

1991: ``power steering made parking and turning maneuvers quite carlike . . . interior has comfortable, well-padded front bucket seats . . . instrument panel has large readable guages.'' **Source:** ``Testing The New Mini 4x4s,'' *Sports Afield*, October 1990, pp. 110-112, 114-116.

1991: "What this one lacks in cargo space, it makes up in open air fun . . . just asks to be tossed around corners and driven hard . . . convertible top is a mixture of romance and inconvenience." **Source:** "California Dive Wagons: Isuzu's sport utility vehicles for shoreline access," *Skin Diver*, June 1991, pp. 8-10, 227-231.

1990: "the most desirable of the "cheap Jeeps". . .interior looks clean and modern, the seats are comfortable." **Source:** "Dustbusters," *Car and Driver*, November 1989, pp. 136-40, 142, 146, 148, 152-53, 156, 159.

1990: "will climb hills and turn heads whereever it goes." **Source:** "Best Of The Rough Country 4x4s," *Sports Afield*, January 1990, pp. 36, 122.

1990: "adequate off-road performance, superior on-highway characteristics, and considerable flexibility because of its unique body design." **Source:** "Pocket 4x4s," *Popular Science*, May 1990, pp. 102-105.

1989: "emphasizes the serious sport side of the market and adds something fresh to the styling of 4-wheel drives. . .innovative bodywork." **Source:** "Intruders in the Desert," *Popular Mechanics*, March 1989.

1989: "[Truck of the Year contender Amigo] drives like a luxury car. . .nice looks, but you could hide half of Orange County in the blind spots." **Source:** "Motor Trend's 1989 Truck of the Year: Out of the barn and into the bistro," *Motor Trend*, April 1989, pp. 108-12, 114-16.

1989: "Top down, the Amigo resembles nothing more accurately than a pickup squashed end-to-end . . . interior appointment, though basic, promote a feel of luxury . . . a respectable alternative to the others in its class." **Source:** "User Friendly 4x4," *Outdoor Life*, September 1989, pp. 36, 40.

1989: "makes a strong statement of purpose, utility and fun . . . It's in the dirt that the Amigo really shines . . . represents a wind-in-the-face, back to nature approach." **Source:** "Isuzu Amigo: A dive wagon you can take to the water's edge," *Skin Diver*, August 1989, pp. 46-48, 56.

RECALLS

None to date.

ISUZU I-MARK (1987-89)

A sub-compact car that competed against Ford Escort, Mercury Tracer, Mazda 323, Volkswagon Fox, Yugo GV, and Plymouth Horizon. Japanese cousin of the Geo Spectrum.

MAJOR FEATURES

● I-Mark S had as 1989 standard equipment: 5-speed manual transmission, independent front and semi-independent rear suspension, power-assisted rack-and-pinion steering, and anti-roll bar, rear defogger, and tinted glass.

● I-Mark RS DOHC added as 1989 standard equipment: AM/FM cassette, various interior and exterior adjustments, and 1.6-liter 16-valve PFI 4-cylinder engine.

● I-Mark XS added as 1989 standard equipment: 1.5-liter inline-4 70 bhp engine, power steering, power mirrors, and rear wiper/washer.

● I-Mark LS Turbo added as 1989 standard equipment: revised

Lotus suspension, 1.5-liter 110 bhp engine, and removable sunroof.

PRICE HISTORY

The following new car prices reflect the approximate retail cost of the base model: **1987** - $7,119; **1988** - $7,659; **1989** - $7,779.

DIMENSIONS

Body Style	Years Avail	Wheel Base (in)	Lgth (in)	Ht (in)	Avg Wt (lbs)	Fuel Cap (gal)	Front Hdrm (in)	Front Legrm (in)
3d lbk	87-89	94.5	157.4	54.1	1,923	11.1	38.0	41.7
4d sdn	88-89	94.5	160.2	54.1	2,024	11.1	37.7	41.7

ENGINES

Type	Displace-ment (L)	Fuel Dly	HP @rpm	Torque @rpm (ft/lbs)	MPG Cty/Hwy	Years Avail
I-4	1.5	2-bbl	70@5400	87@3400	37/41	87-89
I-4	1.5	2-bbl	110@5400	120@3500	33/39	89-89
I-4	1.6	FI	125@6800	102@5400	24/32	89-89
I-4T	1.5	FI	110@5400	120@3500	26/34	88-89

KEY: I=in-line engine; V=V engine; F=flat engine; FI=fuel injection; bbl=barrel carburetor; T=turbo; D=diesel; HP=horsepower; MPG=estimated average miles per gallon.

EVALUATIONS, TESTS, AND RANKINGS

1989: "[RS Turbo] produces a steady surge of power. . .runs out of breath at high revs." **Source:** "Four Fun Fours," *Road & Track*, September 1988, pp. 92-6, 99-101.

1989: "front and rear suspension. . .improve road feel and cornering ability." **Source:** "Lotus helps out," *The Detroit News*, January 8, 1989, p. C10.

1989: "falls somewhat short of magic, but it's certainly not a sow's ear either. . .engine is loud. . .is a delight to drive on the racetrack or smooth roads, but on the typically broken pavement you find everywhere in the snow belt the ride is tough and choppy." **Source:** "Isuzu I-Mark RS," *Car and Driver*, March 1989, pp. 123-5.

1989: "it's fast, handles well. . .real nice inside, comfy, cloth-covers seats. . .it's a steal." **Source:** "Isuzu I-Mark RS," *Motor Trend*, January 1989, pp. 58-60.

1988: "well built, attractively designed subcompact. . .brakes have also been upgraded with addition of larger ventilated discs up front rather than solid units. . .translates into crisp handling. . .seats four adults comfortably." **Source:** "Isuzu I-Mark Turbo," *Motor Trend*, August 1987, pp. 87-90.

RECALLS

1987-88: (2,090 cars): Perforation fuel tank attached fuel feed pipe due to corrosion of tank or fuel feed pipe materials. This condition could allow fuel to leak from fuel tank and ultimately result in fire without prior warning. Such fire could spread to passenger compartment. **Corrective action:** Replace gas tank with new corrosion resistant tank. *(NHTSA Campaign No. 88V041000.)*

1987-88: (2,483 cars): Positive crankcase ventilation valve may provide inadequate air flow under low engine load conditions. Allows water/oil mixture to build up in hose from oil separator to air inlet duct. After engine is stopped, this water/oil mixture can, freeze and completely block oil separator air duct hose. Results in increased pressure within crankcase. Causes oil leaks. If sufficient quantity of oil came in contact with hot exhaust system engine compartment, fire could result. **Corrective**

action: PCV valve will be replaced with new valve. *(NHTSA Campaign No. 88V042000.)*

SAFETY AND REPAIRS

1987: "Chevy and Isuzu Recall 100,000 Spectrum Types," *Automotive News,* November 11, 1991, p. 2. **Note:** '87 I-Marks have excessive emissions of carbon monoxide.

ISUZU IMPULSE (1987-92)

A sports coupe that competes against the Mitsubishi Eclipse, Plymouth Laser, Ford Mustang, Eagle Talon, and Toyota Corolla GT-S coupe. Japanese twin of the Geo Storm GSi. Named 1990 Import Car of the Year by *Car and Driver* and 1991 Import Car of the Year by *Motor Trend.* Currently produced in Fujesaiwa, Japan. A 3-door hatchback-style model was added to the 1991 model lineup.

1991 Isuzu Impulse XS

MAJOR FEATURES

● Impulse XS has as 1992 standard equipment: AM/FM stereo power-assisted rack-and-pinion steering, four-wheel disc brakes, driver's side air bag, and five-speed manual or four-speed automatic transmission.

● 1992 Impulse RS adds as standard equipment: turbocharged engine, permanant four-wheel drive, four-wheel independent suspension, air conditioning, sunroof, and other interior and exterior adjustments.

PRICE HISTORY

The following new car prices reflect the approximate retail cost of the base model: **1987** - $14,639; **1988** - $14,109; **1989** - $14,329; **1990** - $11,999; **1991** - $12,049; **1992** - $12,499.

DIMENSIONS

Body Style	Years Avail	Wheel Base (in)	Lgth (in)	Ht (in)	Avg Wt (lbs)	Fuel Cap (gal)	Front Hdrm (in)	Front Legrm (in)
3d lbk	91-91	96.5	163.6	52.4	2,367	12.4	37.4	43.8
3d lbk	92-92	96.5	164.1	52.3	2,645	12.4	37.4	43.8
2d cpe	87-89	96.1	172.6	51.4	2,727	15.1	36.9	41.9
2d cpe	90-90	96.5	166.0	51.1	2,411	12.4	37.4	43.8
2d cpe	91-92	96.5	166.1	51.8	2,451	12.4	37.4	43.8

ENGINES

Type	Displacement (L)	Fuel Dly	HP @rpm	Torque @rpm (ft/lbs)	MPG Cty/Hwy	Years Avail
I-4	1.9	FI	90@5000	146@3000	na	87-87
I-4	2.3	FI	110@5000	127@3000	20/26	88-89
I-4	1.6	FI	130@6800	102@4600	26/33	90-91
I-4	1.8	FI	140@6400	120@4600	23/32	92-92
I-4T	1.9	FI	140@5400	166@3000	na	87-87
I-4T	2.0	FI	140@5400	166@3000	21/27	88-89
I-4T	1.6	FI	160@6600	150@4800	22/28	90-92

KEY: I=in-line engine; V=V engine; F=flat engine; FI=fuel injection; bbl=barrel carburetor; T=turbo; D=diesel; HP=horsepower; MPG=estimated average miles per gallon.

EVALUATIONS, TESTS, AND RANKINGS

1991: "engine noise intrudes. . .into the cabin." **Source:** "Isuzu Impulse," *Road & Track,* October 1990, p. 75.

1991: "has been built to a modest price. . .found it lively, exceptionally well balanced, and pleasingly reactive to steering and throttle inputs during hard cornering." **Source:** "Isuzu Impulse RS: Turbo-boosted, four-wheel-driven, and maybe a smidgen too affordable for its own kind," *Car and Driver,* November 1990, pp. 75, 77.

1991: "engine acts so rough and buzzy above 6000. . .straight-line acceleration is not this car's bragging point. . .carves up a curvy section with ease." **Source:** "Isuzu Impulse XS," *Motor Trend,* December 1990, pp. 82-5.

1991: "fun-spirited car. . .engine is raucous. . .also noted assorted squeaks and rattles. . .seats are comfortable." **Source:** "1991 Import Car of the Year," *Motor Trend,* March 1991, pp. 34-50.

1990: "[The XS is] a competent little sports car with a high fun quotient. . .powered by a zippy twin-cam engine. . .sleek exterior design." **Source:** "Sporty charm propels the Impulse," *Detroit Free Press,* Thursday July 19, 1990, p. D1.

1990: "suspension is slightly stiff, yet capable . . . sporty feel and taut handling . . . Solid, lively and fun to drive." **Source:** "Isuzu Impulse XS: As Impulse or Storm, it augurs well for the decade," *Road & Track,* July 1990, pp. 85, 87, 89, 91.

1989: "feels soft and supple, while providing the driver with a solid feel. . .extremely fluid." **Source:** "Power Coupes," *Popular Science,* April 1989, pp. 28-9, 32-4.

1989: "commendably stable at speed. . .only fair in lateral acceleration." **Source:** "Coupes de Grace," *Popular Mechanics,* May 1989, pp. 120-24, 212, 214.

1987: "wants to be driven smoothly. . .RS edition doesn't elevate the Impulse to superstar status." **Source:** "Isuzu Impulse Turbo RS: Inching closer to center stage," *Car and Driver,* June 1987, pp. 137-9.

1987: "an ergonomically excellent driving position. . .taller types may find head room somewhat limited. . .worthy contender in its class." **Source:** "Isuzu Impulse Turbo RS: A little white magic from the land of the rising sun," *Motor Trend,* April 1987, pp. 70-2, 74.

RECALLS

None to date.

ISUZU PICKUP (1987-92)

Currently produced in Lafayette, Indiana, the Isuzu Pickup competes with the Toyota SR-5 V6, Ford Ranger STX, Jeep Comanche Pioneer, GMC S-15 Sierra Classic, and Shelby Dakota V8. Previously named the P'UP before 1987. The Pickups are available in standard, longbed, and Spacecab bodies, in two- or four-wheel drive, as well as in S or LS trim levels.

1991 Isuzu Pickup

MAJOR FEATURES

● Pickup has as 1992 standard equipment: 2.3L SOHC four-cylinder engine, five-speed manual transmission, anti-roll bar, rear wheel drive, independent suspension, front vented disc brakes, and rear disc or drum brakes with anti-lock brake system.

● The four-wheel drive models include a 2.6L four-cylinder fuel-injected engine; the LS two-wheel drive includes automatic transmission; and the Spacecab has an extended cab with two forward-facing rear jump seats.

● Pickup XS had as 1991 standard equipment: 2.3L engine and two-wheel drive.

PRICE HISTORY

The following new car prices reflect the approximate retail cost of the base model: **1988** - $7,199; **1989** - $7,649; **1990** - $7,779; **1991** - $7,999.

DIMENSIONS

Body Style	Years Avail	Wheel Base (in)	Lgth (in)	Ht (in)	Avg Wt (lbs)	Fuel Cap (gal)	Front Hdrm (in)	Front Legrm (in)
trk	87-87	104.3	174.4	59.3	3,550	13.2	na	na
trk	88-92	105.6	177.3	62.3	4,300	14.0	na	na

ENGINES

Type	Displacement (L)	Fuel Dly	HP @rpm	Torque @rpm (ft/lbs)	MPG Cty/Hwy	Years Avail
I-4	1.9	2-bbl	82@na	na	25/31	87-87
I-4	2.3	2-bbl	96@na	na	22/24	87-91
I-4	2.6	FI	120@5000	146@2600	19/24	88-92
I-4	2.3	FI	96@4600	123@2600	22/24	92-92
I-4D	2.2	na	na	na	32/35	87-87
I-4TD	2.2	na	na	na	31/33	87-87
V-6	3.1	FI	120@4400	165@2800	15/19	92-92

KEY: I=in-line engine; V=V engine; F=flat engine; FI=fuel injection; bbl=barrel carburetor; T=turbo; D=diesel; HP=horsepower; MPG=estimated average miles per gallon.

EVALUATIONS, TESTS, AND RANKINGS

1990: "surprising acceleration and reasonable load-carrying muscle on or off-road." **Source:** "Practical Pickups For Sportsmen," *Sports Afield*, May 1990, pp. 90-93, 100-101.

1990: "engine feels strained when ascending steep grades . . . thick-rimmed steering wheel offers comfortable driving . . . can get a bit bouncy off-road." **Source:** "Loadin' Up," *Organic Gardening*, April 1990, pp. 55-58.

1989: "overall effect is modern, pleasant and clean. . .superior aerodynamics. . .poor brakes and handling. . .notchy shifter." **Source:** "Compact Commandos," *Popular Mechanics*, February 1989, pp. 51-55, 122.

1987: "better-than-average fuel economy. . .well engineered package." **Source:** "Isuzu P'UP," *Road & Track—Buyer's Guide 1987*, 1986, p. 179.

RECALLS

None to date.

ISUZU RODEO (1991-92)

A sports utility vehicle that competes with Dodge Dakota V-8, GMC Syclone, Mazda Navajo, Oldsmobile Bravado, and Jeep's Wrangler Renegade. Named 1991 Truck of the Year by *Motor Trend*. Currently produced in Lafayette, Indiana, by Subaru-Isuzu Automotive, a joint venture that also builds the Subaru Legacy.

1991 Isuzu Rodeo

MAJOR FEATURES

● Rodeo S has as 1992 standard equipment: 2.6 liter four-cylinder engine, fuel injection, five-speed manual transmission, front double wishbone suspension, tinted glass, rear wheel anti-lock brakes, power assisted front disc brakes, and child-safe rear doors.

● Rodeo S 3.1 adds as 1992 standard equipment: 3.1-liter V-6 engine and four-wheel drive.

● Rodeo XS adds to the Rodeo S 3.1: five-speed manual or four-speed automatic transmission (automatic transmission features three driving modes: power, economy, and winter start that limits wheelspin), various interior adjustments, and four-wheel drive.

● Rodeo LS adds to the Rodeo S 3.1: various interior adjustments, rear wiper/washer, AM/FM stereo cassette, and four-wheel drive.

PRICE HISTORY

The following new car prices reflect the approximate retail cost of the base model: **1991** - $12,499.

DIMENSIONS

Body Style	Years Avail	Wheel Base (in)	Lgth (in)	Ht (in)	Avg Wt (lbs)	Fuel Cap (gal)	Front Hdrm (in)	Front Legrm (in)
utl wgn	91-92	108.7	176.4	65.4	na	21.9	38.2	42.5

ENGINES

Type	Displacement (L)	Fuel Dly	HP @rpm	Torque @rpm (ft/lbs)	MPG Cty/Hwy	Years Avail
I-4	2.3	FI	120@5000	146@2600	18/22	91-92
V-6	3.1	FI	120@4400	165@2800	15/19	91-92

KEY: I=in-line engine; V=V engine; F=flat engine; FI=fuel injection; bbl=barrel carburetor; T=turbo; D=diesel; HP=horsepower; MPG=estimated average miles per gallon.

EVALUATIONS, TESTS, AND RANKINGS

1991: "body has a massive look. . .macho exterior is belied by extremely civil behavior on the highway. . .comfortable and thoughtfully engineered." **Source:** "From Indiana, A Banzai Buckaroo," *New York Times*, January 13, 1991.

1991: "family recreation vehicle. . .rode extremely well. . .also shrugged off the licks from the dirt roads. . .good highway manners." **Source:** "Isuzu Rodeo XS," *Automobile Magazine*, December 1990, p. 22.

1991: "muscularly handsome. . .attractively finished, well-appointed and comfortable interior. . .makes better use of available space than either Toyota or Nissan." **Source:** "Isuzu Rodeo: A North American exclusive," *Road & Track*, November 1990, p. 98.

1991: "[Nominee vehicle Rodeo] interior room is superior. . .fit and finish good. . .power seemed adequate for normal street driving." **Source:** "1991 Truck of the Year: The new and improved," *Motor Trend*, January 1991, pp. 79-85.

1991: "just the ticket to transport our family. . .high degree of comfort and utility, and the fringe benefit of being American-built. . .a combination that's tough to beat." **Source:** "Smooth Isuzu Rodeo saves bucks," *Detroit Free Press*, Thusday August 30, 1990, p. C1.

1991: "comfortable for errands or driving to work. Yet it has the brawn to tackle rugged terrair . . . coddles you with amenities . . . the back seat easily holds adults." **Source:** "Isuzu offers smooth ride in Rodeo," *The Detroit News*, April 3, 1991, pp. D1-D2.

1991: "excellent fit and finish . . . a sizable number of standard features . . . styling is aerodynamic." **Source:** "Range Rodeo," *Outdoor Life*, November 1990, pp. 50, 53.

1991: "displays the flair, style and dash of the '90s . . . feels more like a luxury car than a truck . . . Its sleek looks disguise the Rodeo's practicality." **Source:** "California Dive Wagons: Isuzu's sport utility vehicles for shoreline access," *Skin Diver*, June 1991, pp. 8-10, 227-231.

1991: "will lure plenty of buyers with its refinement and low price . . . drives as nicely as it looks, offering smooth power delivery, a well-isolated ride, and effortless steering." **Source:** "Update: Sport-Utility Vehicles," *U.S. News and World Report*, May 13, 1991, pp. A4-A6, A8-A10, A12, A14-A15.

RECALLS

1991: (3,023 multi-purpose passenger vehicles with V6 engines and automatic transmission): The transmission fluid level gauges (dip sticks) are not to designed specifications. The gauge indicates that transmission fluid should be added when it is at the correct level. Adding excess transmission fluid will cause the fluid to leak as the engine temperature rises, creating the potential for a fire. **Corrective action:** Replace oil level gauge and notify owners to use only the specified amount of automatic transmission fluid. *(NHTSA Campaign No. 91V118000.)*

ISUZU STYLUS (1990-92)

A four-door sedan that replaced the I-Mark series competes with Nissan Sentra SE-R, Honda Civic Si, and Ford Escort. Shares its front-drive chassis with the Isuzu Impulse. Isuzu builds moderately different hatchbacks which are sold as the Geo Storm. Awarded 1991 Import Car of the Year by *Motor Trend*.

1991 Isuzu Stylus XS

MAJOR FEATURES

● Stylus S has as 1992 standard equipment: 1.6 liter 12-valve engine, 5-speed manual or 3-speed automatic transmission, independent suspension, vented front disc/rear drum brakes, child-proof rear door locks, driver side airbag, and tinted glass.

● Stylus RS adds as 1992 standard equipment: 1.8 liter, 16-valve engine, power-assisted four-wheel disc brakes, power rack-and-pinion steering, AM/FM stereo, and other various interior adjustments, and rear spoiler.

● Stylus XS added as 1991 standard equipment: DOHC 16-valve engine, power steering, sport suspension, power mirrors, and various interior adjustments.

PRICE HISTORY

The following new car prices reflect the approximate retail cost of the base model: **1991** - $9,199; **1992** - $9,249.

DIMENSIONS

Body Style	Years Avail	Wheel Base (in)	Lgth (in)	Ht (in)	Avg Wt (lbs)	Fuel Cap (gal)	Front Hdrm (in)	Front Legrm (in)
4d sdn	90-91	96.5	165.1	54.0	2,261	12.4	39.0	43.3
4d sdn	92-92	96.5	165.1	54.7	2,253	12.4	38.4	43.3

ENGINES

Type	Displacement (L)	Fuel Dly	HP @rpm	Torque @rpm (ft/lbs)	MPG Cty/Hwy	Years Avail
I-4	1.6	FI	130@6800	102@4600	26/33	90-91
I-4	1.6	FI	96@5800	97@3400	31/37	90-92
I-4	1.8	FI	140@6400	120@4600	23/31	92-92

KEY: I=in-line engine; V=V engine; F=flat engine; FI=fuel injection; bbl=barrel carburetor; T=turbo; D=diesel; HP=horsepower; MPG=estimated average miles per gallon.

EVALUATIONS, TESTS, AND RANKINGS

1991: "aggressive countenance. . .lack of visual balance doesn't affect the Stylus' handling. . .all in all, good driving fun." **Source:** "Isuzu Stylus," *Road & Track*, October 1990, p. 75.

1991: "spacious interior and aerodynamic exterior." **Source:** "Preview: 1991 Import Car of the Year," *Motor Trend*, February 1991, pp. 96-97.

1991: "has a sportier nature than your average little sedan. . .handling edge over the Honda. . .general noisiness were significant. . .comfortable, well-sculpted seating." **Source:** "1991 Import Car of the Year," *Motor Trend*, March 1991, pp. 33-50.

1991: "eye-catching body. . .rear, head, and knee room are adequate. . .[engine] produces unpleasant sound waves." **Source:** "Isuzu Stylus XS," *Car and Driver*, March 1991, pp. 121-3.

1991: "an avant-garde small-car design . . . fabric selections, plastics, and color matchings are pretty good . . . didn't perform particularly well at the proving grounds." **Source:** "No Frills," *Popular Science*, August 1991, pp. 60-63, 86-87.

1991: "corners flattest in sharp turns . . . flip side of this sporting nature is a rough ride, little steering feel and lots of wheelspin during fast starts." **Source:** "Fuel-Efficient Family Cars for 1991," *Home Mechanix*, March 1991, pp. 69-73.

RECALLS

None to date.

ISUZU TROOPER (1987-92)

The Isuzu Trooper, redesigned in 1992, is a rough terrain vehicle that competes with the Mitsubishi Montero and Ford Explorer. The earlier Trooper design received a sixth place vote in a comparison test of seven off-road vehicles by *Car and Driver* in 1990. A smaller version of this Trooper, the Isuzu Trooper II, was an off-road vehicle that competed against the Mitsubishi Montero, Jeep Wrangler, and Suzuki Samurai. It was discontinued after the 1989 model. The newly designed Trooper, scheduled to go on sale in March of 1992, is bigger and has more powerful engine options than the previous vehicle under this nameplate.

1991 Isuzu Trooper

MAJOR FEATURES

● Trooper S, the entry-level Trooper, and the 1992 LS model have as 1992 standard equipment: two-speed, part-time, four-wheel-drive, automatic locking hub, enhanced independent suspension, anti-roll bar, power brakes, five-speed manual transmission, electronic fuel injection, and power steering.

● Trooper XS added as 1991 standard equipment: rear wiper/washer, alloy wheels, and an upgraded interior.

● Trooper XS added as 1991 standard equipment: intermittent wipers and an upgraded interior.

● Trooper S V6 added as 1991 standard equipment: 2.8 liter TBI V-6 engine.

● Trooper II Deluxe had as 1989 standard equipment: fuel injection, four-wheel drive, 5-speed manual transmission, vented disc/drum brakes, tilt steering, tinted windows, and various interior features.

● Trooper II LS added as 1989 standard equipment: air conditioning, independent wishbone suspension, air conditioning, rear seat heat, and various interior adjustments.

Dimensions that appear in the chart below are for the larger wheelbase Trooper.

PRICE HISTORY

The following new car prices reflect the approximate retail cost of the base model: **1987** - $10,809; **1988** - $11,909; **1989** - $13,149; **1990** - $13,499; **1991** - $13,999.

DIMENSIONS

Body Style	Years Avail	Wheel Base (in)	Lgth (in)	Ht (in)	Avg Wt (lbs)	Fuel Cap (gal)	Front Hdrm (in)	Front Legrm (in)
utl wgn	87-87	104.3	175.2	71.7	4,740	21.9	na	na
utl wgn	88-91	104.3	176.0	71.7	4,740	21.9	na	na
utl wgn	92-92	108.7	178.9	72.8	4,155	na	na	na

ENGINES

Type	Displacement (L)	Fuel Dly	HP @rpm	Torque @rpm (ft/lbs)	MPG Cty/Hwy	Years Avail
I-4	2.6	FI	120@na	na	16/18	88-91
I-4TD	2.2	2-bbl	96@na	na	25/25	87-87
V-6	2.8	FI	120@na	na	15/18	89-91
V-6	3.2	FI	175@5200	188@4000	16/18	92-92
V-6	3.2	FI	190@5600	195@3800	15/17	92-92

KEY: I=in-line engine; V=V engine; F=flat engine; FI=fuel injection; bbl=barrel carburetor; T=turbo; D=diesel; HP=horsepower; MPG=estimated average miles per gallon.

EVALUATIONS, TESTS, AND RANKINGS

1991: "rugged, reliable transport . . . razor-edged, quasi-military styling projects a homely, no nonsense attitude . . . plenty of carrying capacity." **Source:** "California Dive Wagons: Isuzu's sport utility vehicles for shoreline access," *Skin Diver*, June 1991, pp. 8-10, 227-231.

1990: "generous in the headroom department. . .tough and capable off-roader that seems more and more at home as the terrain grows rougher. . .pavement ride is a little stiff." **Source:** "Desert Sports: Seven sport-utility vehicles show us their stuff," *Car and Driver*, April 1990, pp. 38-44, 46, 48-49, 52-55.

1990: "good road manners and can handle any kind of footing . . . fun to drive wherever you go." **Source:** "4-Doors For all Seasons," *New Choices*, December 1989, pp. 84, 86-87.

1990: "Fine on-road handling . . . bouncy, banging off-road ride . . . aerodynamics is not Trooper's really strong point." **Source:** "Trooper II To Go," *Outdoor Life*, December 1989, pp. 50, 53.

1989: "dashboard design may be the best available in the field . . . Suspension and ride on-road is just OK . . . off-road . . . seems to smooth out into an exceptional ride over the rough spots." **Source:** "Personal Pick," *Outdoor Life*, June 1989, pp. 20, 24-25.

1988: "will hammer down rough trails with less thump, bump, and pitch. . .poor showing in the lane change and its extra length. . .passable comfort." **Source:** "No Frills Four Wheel Drive," *Popular Mechanics*, January 1988, pp. 26-8, 32, 34, 36.

1987: "truck-tough underneath the fancy interior. . .jouncing the passengers as you travel. . .don't plan to tow a trailer or a boat." **Source:** "Isuzu Trooper II," *Motor Trend*, July 1987, pp. 67, 115.

RECALLS

1990-91: (17,048 multi-purpose vehicles with V-6 engines and only automatic transmission vehicles): Putting in more transmission oil than specified can cause oil to bleed through air groove on to exhaust manifold if oil temperature rises, which could ignite rubber hoses and result in a fire. **Corrective action:** Replace oil level gauge and notify owners to use only the specified amount of automatic transmission fluid. *(NHTSA Campaign No. 90V167000.)*

1990-91: (12,222 multi-purpose vehicles with V-6 engines): Improperly installed hose on the oil cooler could come in contact with exhaust manifold and could melt. Engine oil could leak out and result in fire. **Corrective action:** Properly install cooler hose clip to prevent contact with exhaust manifold. *(NHTSA Campaign No. 90V166000.)*

1988: (22,591 Trooper II vehicles): Guide pin on rear disc brake caliper support could have loosened during transport and would no longer hold caliper in correct position. This could result in brake drag, premature brake pad wear and partial loss of braking power with potential for an accident. **Corrective action:** Install brake caliper guide pin kit. *(NHTSA Campaign No. 88V062000.)*

1987-88: (463 Trooper and Trooper II vehicles with rear heater): Pipe rupture and fuel leakage may occur due to engine design. **Corrective action:** Install new lines and clip. *(NHTSA Campaign No. 89V001000.)*

1987: (2,349 Trooper II vehicles): Two piece aluminum wheels may not have been welded at point where press fitted onto rim. Wheel could separate from rim. **Corrective action:** Replace wheels. *(NHTSA Campaign No. 87V057000.)*

JAGUAR XJ-6 (1987-92)

A high performance sports car that competes against the BMW 735, Mercedes-Benz 420SEL, Audi 5000CS Quattro, and Lamborghini series. Rated in the highest resale value and highest repair costs categories for a luxury car by *The Complete Car Cost Guide* in 1990. Named one of the 10 Best Cars in 1988 by *Car and Driver*. Currently produced in Coventry, England.

1991 Jaguar XJ-6

MAJOR FEATURES

● XJ-6 has as 1992 standard equipment: 4.0L six-cylinder engine, four-speed automatic transmission, four-wheel anti-lock disc brakes, power steering, power windows and locks, cruise control, trip computer, tilt steering column, rear defogger, AM/FM stereo cassette with CB channel 19 monitor.

● XJ-6 Sovereign adds as 1992 standard equipment: hydraulic ride leveling, power sunroof, additional exterior chrome trim, and interior veneer stylings.

● XJ-6 Vanden Plas adds as 1992 standard equipment: headlight washer/wipers with heated nozzles, burl walnut picnic tables attached to front seatbacks, and various interior adjustments.

● XJ-6 Vanden Plas Majestic, discontinued in 1990, has been reintroduced in 1992. In addition to Vanden Plas features, the Majestic features: an alarm system, leather upholstery and trim, and sheepskin mats.

PRICE HISTORY

The following new car prices reflect the approximate retail cost of the base model: **1987** - $37,500; **1988** - $43,500; **1989** - $44,000; **1990** - $39,700; **1991** - $43,000; **1992** - $44,500.

DIMENSIONS

Body Style	Years Avail	Wheel Base (in)	Lgth (in)	Ht (in)	Avg Wt (lbs)	Fuel Cap (gal)	Front Hdrm (in)	Front Legrm (in)
4d sdn	87-87	113.0	199.6	52.8	4,057	23.8	38.1	39.3
4d sdn	88-92	113.0	196.4	54.3	3,935	23.2	36.6	41.7

ENGINES

Type	Displace-ment (L)	Fuel Dly	HP @rpm	Torque @rpm (ft/lbs)	MPG Cty/Hwy	Years Avail
I-6	4.2	FI	176@4750	219@2500	15/19	87-87
I-6	3.6	FI	181@4750	221@3750	18/25	88-88
I-6	3.6	FI	195@5000	232@4000	17/23	89-89
I-6	4.0	FI	223@4750	278@3650	17/22	90-92

KEY: I=in-line engine; V=V engine; F=flat engine; FI=fuel injection; bbl=barrel carburetor; T=turbo; D=diesel; HP=horsepower; MPG=estimated average miles per gallon.

EVALUATIONS, TESTS, AND RANKINGS

1991: "the most handsome 4-door sedan. . .is capable of high-speed road work while comforting its occupants in chapel-like tranquility." **Source:** "Jaguar XJ-6 1985-1988," *Road & Track*, January 1991, 112-17.

1991: "the Sovereign feels as if it weighs only an ounce or two less than a barge . . . Pleasant enough ride and handling, but you feel the weight in the wheel in corners and turns." **Source:** "Sovereign gives one a stately ride," *Detroit Free Press*, June 24, 1991, p. 18F.

1990: "later upshifts and quicker downshifts, delivering better performance. . .limited leg room. . .unnoticed are any quivers or quakes from the chassis in hard driving." **Source:** "Jaguar XJ-6: Vanden Plas: A bigger six sharpens the Cat's claws," *Road & Track*, March 1990, pp. 66-8, 69.

1990: "offers nearly Cadillac-like ride quality at the sacrifice of some sporting capabilities. . .baffling climate controls." **Source:** "Jaguar XJ-6 Sovereign: Gearing for action in the luxury wars," *Motor Trend*, April 1990, pp. 103-5.

1989: "climate-control panel is nearly indecipherable. . .touch of sportiness." **Source:** "Jaguar XJ-6," *Motor Trend*, May 1989, pp. 154-6, 159.

1989: "The big sedan remains elegant, eccentric, evolutionary, and every inch a Jaguar motorcar . . . continues to be among the better driving experiences the luxury-car world offers." **Source:** "Jaguar Vanden Plas: More power for old money," *Car and Driver*, August 1989, pp. 83, 85, 87.

1988: "beautiful coachwork and interior trim. . .attention to detail. . .some tire noise at highway speeds." **Source:** "Jaguar XJ-6 3.6: A winner is refined," *Motor Trend*, September 1987, pp. 81-6.

1987: "remains a pretty zingy sedan. . .offers a worthwhile aerodynamic improvement. . .magnificent ride. . .steering is still light. . .soft suspension. . .headroom comes up short." **Source:** "Jaguar XJ-6: Jaguar's new combat cat hops out of the box and under the gun," *Car and Driver*, June 1987, pp. 117, 118-23, 125.

RECALLS

1990: (1,284 cars; includes other Jaguar models): Head of rear caliper fixing bolt may break off, resulting in an increase in stopping distance. **Corrective action:** Replace bolt. *(NHTSA Campaign No. 89V235000.)*

1988-89: (29,000 passenger cars; includes Jaguar XJ-6 and Jaguar XJ-6 Vanden Plas, and Jaguar XJ-G Vanden Plas Majestic models): Leaking of brake accumulator switch near electrical wiring could result in electrical power interruption and fluid loss could lead to loss of power assistance to braking system. **Corrective action:** Replace brake accumulator switches with revised seals. *(NHTSA Campaign No. 90V024000.)*

1988-89: (38,315 passenger cars; includes the Jaguar XJ-6, Jaguar XJ-6 Vanden Plas, and Jaguar XJ-6 Vanden Plas Majestic models): Rupture of high pressure fluid supply hose could cause loss of brake power assist which could result in loss of control and an accident; also, fluid could cause an engine compartment fire. **Corrective action:** Install new power hydraulic hose of a different specification. *(NHTSA Campaign No. 90V023000.)*

1988: (3,500 cars; includes several Jaguar models): Cruise control may fail to disengage and rear brake lamps may fail due to brake lamp microswitch assembly. **Corrective action:** Install modified microswitch. *(NHTSA Campaign No. 87V105000.)*

1988: (16,000 four door sedans; includes Jaguar XJ-6 and Jaguar XJ-6 Vanden Plas models): Certain front suspension lower spring pan fixings may fail due to stress corrosion. This may allow cars front suspension to settle onto bump stop on one side. **Corrective action:** Install revised specification front suspension spring pan fixings. *(NHTSA Campaign No. 88V018000.)*

REPAIR MANUALS

1563 ● **Jaguar 6 Cylinder**
Peter Allen Video Productions
38-C Otis St.
West Babylon, NY 11704   Ph:(516)643-4372

How to tune-up and maintain the larger Jaguar engines. **Release date:** 1986. **Producer:** Peter Allen Productions. **Acquisition:** Purchase.

1564 ● **Jaguar XJ-6 and XJ-12 Series 3**
Robert Bentley Publishing, Inc.
1000 Massachusetts Ave.
Cambridge, MA 02138   Ph:(617)547-4170

Price: $80.00.

1565 ● **The Jaguar XJ-6 Series 1, 2.8, and 4.2 Litre Workshop Manual**
Robert Bentley Publishing, Inc.
1000 Massachusetts Ave.
Cambridge, MA 02138   Ph:(617)547-4170

Price: $80.00.

1566 ● **Jaguar XJ-6 Series 2**
Robert Bentley Publishing, Inc.
1000 Massachusetts Ave.
Cambridge, MA 02138   Ph:(671)547-4170

Price: $80.00.

OTHER INFORMATION SOURCES

1567 ● **Classic Jaguar Association—News and Technical Bulletin**
Classic Jaguar Association (CJA)
c/o Jack Hilton
26045 Rotunda Dr.
Carmel, CA 93923   Ph:(408)625-6476

Bimonthly.

1568 ● **Ejag News Magazine**
Ejag Publications
PO Box J
Carlisle, MA 01741   Ph:(617)369-5531

Covers Jaguar and Daimier automobiles. Monthly. **Editor(s):** Lori Toepel.

1569 ● European Car
Argus Publishers Corp.
12100 Wilshire Blvd., Ste. 250   Ph:(213)820-3601
Los Angeles, CA 90025   Fax:(213)207-9388

Magazine covering Volkswagen, Porsche, Mercedes-Benz, Audi, Ferrari, Jaguar, and BMW automobiles. Bimonthly. **Editor(s):** Greg N. Brown. **Price:** $11.00 per year; $2.75 per issue.

1570 ● Great Marques Jaguar
Book Sales, Inc.
110 Enterprise Ave.
Secaucus, NJ 07094-1995   Ph:(201)864-6341

Published 1989. **Price:** $10.98.

1571 ● Heart of America Jaguar Club—Newsletter
Heart of America Jaguar Club
7211 W. 98th Terrace, Ste. 100
Overland Park, KS 66212   Ph:(913)381-8211

Monthly.

1572 ● Illustrated Jaguar Buyer's Guide
Motorbooks International
729 Prospect Ave.
Osceola, WI 54020   Ph:(715)294-3345

Published 1987. **Editor(s):** James Hoehn. **Price:** $16.95.

1573 ● Jaguar Journal
Jaguar Clubs of North America
555 MacArthur Blvd.
Mahwah, NJ 07430   Ph:(201)818-8148

Bimonthly.

1574 ● Jaguar: Roaring to Victory
Simitar Entertainment
3850 Annapolis Ln.   Ph:(612)559-6660
Plymouth, MN 55447   Fax:(612)559-0210

A look at the exciting British automobile at the track and on the open road. **Producer:** Simitar Entertainment. **Price:** $9.95.

1575 ● The Jaguar Scrapbook
Motorbooks International
729 Prospect Ave.
Osceda, WI 54020   Ph:(715)294-3345

1990. **Editor(s):** Philip Porter. **Price:** $29.95.

1576 ● Jaguar Sports Cars
Haynes Publications, Inc.
861 Lawrence Dr.
Newbury Park, CA 91320   Ph:(818)889-5400

Editor(s): Paul Skilleter. **Price:** $49.95.

1577 ● The Jaguar XJ-6 Series 3 Driver's Handbook
Robert Bentley Publishing, Inc.
1000 Massachusetts Ave.
Cambridge, MA 02138   Ph:(617)547-4170

1990. **Price:** $16.00.

ASSOCIATIONS

1578 ● Classic Jaguar Association
c/o Jack Hilton
26045 Rotunda Dr.
Carmel, CA 93923
Jack Hilton, Pres.   Ph:(408)625-6476

Founded: 1961. **Membership:** 500. International organization of owners or enthusiasts of pre-war SS cars and post-war models of Jaguar; also accepts membership of later model Jaguar owners. Promotes ownership and operation of these automobiles. Conducts technical and historical research. Maintain spare parts coordination worldwide. Maintains biographical archives and library of 200 technical articles, books, and historical publications. **Convention/Meeting:** Quarterly, with swap meet and exhibits.

1579 ● Heart of America Jaguar Club [Kansas]
7211 W. 98th Terrace, Ste. 100
Overland Park, KS 66212
Barry Greenstein, Chm.   Ph:(913)381-8211

Founded: 1968. **Membership:** 75. Owners of Jaguar automobiles. Conducts social activities. Holds annual concours. **Convention/Meeting:** Monthly.

1580 ● Jaguar Clubs of North America
Jaguar Cars Inc.
555 MacArthur Blvd.
Mahwah, NJ 07430   Ph:(201)818-8144
Michael L. Cook, V.Pres.   Fax:(201)818-0281

Founded: 1954. **Membership:** 50. Jaguar clubs in the U.S. and Canada representing a combined membership of 5,200. Works to: foster and encourage a spirit of mutual interest and assistance for Jaguar automobile enthusiasts; promote public interest in motoring and motor sports; develop road safety; encourage an improved understanding of traffic laws; promote social and motoring events. Sponsors competitions, including National Concours d'Elegance car show and rally championships; presents awards. **Convention/Meeting:** Annual conference - always March; 1993— Seattle, WA. Also holds biennial meet - always New York City metro area.

JAGUAR XJ-S (1987-92)

A high performance sports car that competes against the Cadillac Fleetwood, Lexus LS400, Infiniti Q45, Mercedes-Benz 300E, and BMW 535i. Rated by *The Complete Car Cost Guide* in the highest fuel cost, highest insurance costs, and highest repair costs categories in the luxury car class for 1990. Currently produced in Conventry, England, the Jaguar XJ-S has gone through extensive revisions in 1992.

1991 Jaguar XJ-S Classic Collection Convertible

MAJOR FEATURES

● XJ-S Coupe has as 1992 standard equipment: 5.3 twelve-cylinder engine, three-speed automatic transmission, power rack-and-pinion steering, four-wheel anti-lock brakes, driver side airbag, automatic climate control, power lock and windows, cruise control, tilt steering column, heated power mirrors, heated windshield washer nozzles, heated rear window, power headlamp washers, full leather interior trim, and various interior features.

● XJ-S Convertible (Spyder) adds as 1992 standard equipment: convertible top and various interior adjustments.

● XJ-S Classic Collection Convertible added as 1991 standard equipment: polished alloy wheels, leather-wrapped steering wheel, Alpine sound system, and other interior enhancements.

● XJ-S Collection Rouge was discontinued in 1990. It featured a red exterior, gold side stripes, and red spoke wheels.

PRICE HISTORY

The following new car prices reflect the approximate retail cost of the base model: **1987** - $39,700; **1988** - $47,000; **1989** - $48,000; **1990** - $48,000; **1991** - $53,000; **1992** - $60,500.

DIMENSIONS

Body Style	Years Avail	Wheel Base (in)	Lgth (in)	Ht (in)	Avg Wt (lbs)	Fuel Cap (gal)	Front Hdrm (in)	Front Legrm (in)
2d cpe	87-91	102.0	191.7	47.8	4,050	24.0	36.1	41.3
2d cpe	92-92	102.0	191.2	48.6	3,970	24.0	36.1	41.3
2d conv	87-91	102.0	191.7	47.8	4,250	21.6	36.1	41.3
2d conv	92-92	102.0	191.2	48.6	4,194	21.6	36.1	41.3

ENGINES

Type	Displacement (L)	Fuel Dly	HP @rpm	Torque @rpm (ft/lbs)	MPG Cty/Hwy	Years Avail
V-12	5.3	FI	262@5000	290@5000	13/18	87-91
V-12	5.3	FI	263@5350	288@3200	13/18	92-92

KEY: I=in-line engine; V=V engine; F=flat engine; FI=fuel injection; bbl=barrel carburetor; T=turbo; D=diesel; HP=horsepower; MPG=estimated average miles per gallon.

EVALUATIONS, TESTS, AND RANKINGS

1992: "handling, though not the stuff of records, is respectable and eminently predictable . . . its a car that loves to cruise fast . . . In the cabin, comfort and quietness reign." **Source:** "New for '92," *Road & Track,* November 1991, pp. 92-94.

1992: "updated XJ-S embodies a more contemporary feel . . . trademark rear sail panels have been delicately resculpted . . . engine has been tweaked for more punch and better driveability." **Source:** "Reskinning the Sport Cat," *Motor Trend,* August 1991, p. 15.

1992: "car incorporates 1,200 new or modified parts . . . fuel-delivery system has been improved for easier starting . . . Ford's research has been a boon." **Source:** "The Jag Rag: Happy Birthday Sweet 16," *New York Times,* August 11, 1991.

1991: "more roundly contoured than before . . . elegant interior in the British manner has become far more modern in character . . . On the freeway, the XJS cruises effortlessly." **Source:** "Jaguar XJS: A new way to re-skin a cat," *Car and Driver,* July 1991, pp. 123-124, 127.

1991: "It's a pleasant driving and comfortable riding touring car, not a fast, nimble sports car." **Source:** "Jaguar is no longer

in its prime but can still offer touch of class," *The Flint Journal,* August 14, 1991, pp. E4-E5.

1991: "creamy leather interior and glossy elm trim bespoke bags of luxury . . . Driving position . . . leaves a lot to be desired . . . storage is more than ample." **Source:** "Jaguar's XJ-S: Sunshine and Power," *New York Times,* May 5, 1991, p. S14.

1990: "like nothing else on the road. . .sleek. . .front seats are supportive and comfortable." **Source:** "Jaguar still not a 'me-too' car," *The Detroit News,* Wednesday November 28, 1990, pp. 1E-2E.

1990: "built for comfortable, high-speed motoring, not drag racing . . . steering light and responsive but well-controlled . . . not tricky to drive, and covers the miles in a most civilized manner." **Source:** "Jaguar XJS: Luxury Fun-Car," *Design News,* October 2, 1989, pp. 170-171.

1989: "oozes tradition. . .confidently, tastefully opulent." **Source:** "Jaguar XJ-S: More evidence that Jaguar's finest tradition is tradition itself," *Car and Driver,* February 1989, p. 55.

1989: "well-appointed leather-and-walnut interior is a work of art . . . convertible may be a gorgeous car for sports, but it's no sports car." **Source:** "2 for the Road," *Regardie's,* September 1989, pp. 169-170, 172, 180, 182.

1988: "pampers its two occupants. . .engine has a relaxed manner. . .free of sqeaks and rattles, and felt tight and precise." **Source:** "Because you can never be too rich or to tanned," *Motor Trend,* August 1988, pp. 97-9, 102.

RECALLS

1992: (700 passenger cars; coupes and convertibles): The engine harness may come in contact with the air conditioning expansion valve protection plate, causing chafing of the harness. This may result in short circuits of the electrical wiring and possible vehicle stalling. **Corrective action:** Reposition the air conditioning expansion valve protection plate to preclude possibility of contact with the electrical harness. *(NHTSA Campaign No. 91V155000.)*

1987-90: (31,835 cars; includes models made before 1987; includes other Jaguar models): Dirt in cruise control valves could prevent disengagement, which could result in loss of control and an accident. **Corrective action:** Replace cruise control actuator and install additional vacuum dump valve. *(NHTSA Campaign No. 90V035000.)*

1987-90: (35,000 two-door coupes, cabriolets, and convertibles; includes models made before 1987): Excessive fuel vapor pressure can occur that, after prolonged cycling, could weaken fuel tank structure causing fuel leaks, which could result in a fire. **Corrective action:** Install a revised fuel purge system which eliminates excessive vapor pressure build-up. *(NHTSA Campaign No. 90V123000.)*

1987-88: (1,994 convertible passenger cars; includes models made before 1987): Excessive fuel vapor pressure can occur which creates fuel odors and after prolonged cycling could cause weakening of fuel tank structure, which could result in fuel tank leaks. If source of ignition is present, fire could result. **Corrective action:** Install revised purge system components. *(NHTSA Campaign No. 89V168000.)*

REPAIR MANUALS

1581 ● **Jaguar 6 Cylinder**
Peter Allen Video Productions
38-C Otis St.
West Babylon, NY 11704   Ph:(516)643-4372

How to tune-up and maintain the larger Jaguar engines.

Release date: 1986. **Producer:** Peter Allen Productions. **Acquisition:** Purchase.

1582 ● Jaguar XJ-S Workshop Manual
Robert Bentley Publishing, Inc.
1000 Massachusetts Ave.
Cambridge, MA 02138   Ph:(617)547-4170

Price: $80.00.

OTHER INFORMATION SOURCES

1583 ● Classic Jaguar Association—News and Technical Bulletin
Classic Jaguar Association (CJA)
c/o Jack Hilton
26045 Rotunda Dr.
Carmel, CA 93923   Ph:(408)625-6476

Bimonthly.

1584 ● Ejag News Magazine
Ejag Publications
PO Box J
Carlisle, MA 01741   Ph:(617)369-5531

Covers Jaguar and Daimier automobiles. Monthly. **Editor(s):** Lori Toepel.

1585 ● European Car
Argus Publishers Corp.
12100 Wilshire Blvd., Ste. 250   Ph:(213)820-3601
Los Angeles, CA 90025   Fax:(213)207-9388

Magazine covering Volkswagen, Porsche, Mercedes-Benz, Audi, Ferrari, Jaguar, and BMW automobiles. Bimonthly. **Editor(s):** Greg N. Brown. **Price:** $11.00 per year; $2.75 per issue.

1586 ● Great Marques Jaguar
Book Sales, Inc.
110 Enterprise Ave.
Secaucus, NJ 07094-1995   Ph:(201)864-6341

Published 1989. **Price:** $10.98.

1587 ● Heart of America Jaguar Club—Newsletter
Heart of America Jaguar Club
7211 W. 98th Terrace, Ste. 100
Overland Park, KS 66212   Ph:(913)381-8211

Monthly.

1588 ● Illustrated Jaguar Buyer's Guide
Motorbooks International
729 Prospect Ave.
Osceola, WI 54020   Ph:(715)294-3345

Published 1987. **Editor(s):** James Hoehn. **Price:** $16.95.

1589 ● Jaguar Journal
Jaguar Clubs of North America
555 MacArthur Blvd.
Mahwah, NJ 07430   Ph:(201)818-8148

Bimonthly.

1590 ● Jaguar: Roaring to Victory
Simitar Entertainment
3850 Annapolis Ln.   Ph:(612)559-6660
Plymouth, MN 55447   Fax:(612)559-0210

A look at the exciting British automobile at the track and on the open road. **Producer:** Simitar Entertainment. **Price:** $9.95.

1591 ● The Jaguar Scrapbook
Motorbooks International
729 Prospect Ave.
Osceda, WI 54020   Ph:(715)294-3345

1990. **Editor(s):** Philip Porter. **Price:** $29.95.

1592 ● Jaguar Sports Cars
Haynes Publications, Inc.
861 Lawrence Dr.
Newbury Park, CA 91320   Ph:(818)889-5400

Editor(s): Paul Skilleter. **Price:** $49.95.

ASSOCIATIONS

1593 ● Classic Jaguar Association
c/o Jack Hilton
26045 Rotunda Dr.
Carmel, CA 93923
Jack Hilton, Pres.   Ph:(408)625-6476

Founded: 1961. **Membership:** 500. International organization of owners or enthusiasts of pre-war SS cars and post-war models of Jaguar; also accepts membership of later model Jaguar owners. Promotes ownership and operation of these automobiles. Conducts technical and historical research. Maintain spare parts coordination worldwide. Maintains biographical archives and library of 200 technical articles, books, and historical publications. **Convention/Meeting:** Quarterly, with swap meet and exhibits.

1594 ● Heart of America Jaguar Club [Kansas]
7211 W. 98th Terrace, Ste. 100
Overland Park, KS 66212
Barry Greenstein, Chm.   Ph:(913)381-8211

Founded: 1968. **Membership:** 75. Owners of Jaguar automobiles. Conducts social activities. Holds annual concours. **Convention/Meeting:** Monthly.

1595 ● Jaguar Clubs of North America
Jaguar Cars Inc.
555 MacArthur Blvd.
Mahwah, NJ 07430   Ph:(201)818-8144
Michael L. Cook, V.Pres.   Fax:(201)818-0281

Founded: 1954. **Membership:** 50. Jaguar clubs in the U.S. and Canada representing a combined membership of 5,200. Works to: foster and encourage a spirit of mutual interest and assistance for Jaguar automobile enthusiasts; promote public interest in motoring and motor sports; develop road safety; encourage an improved understanding of traffic laws; promote social and motoring events. Sponsors competitions, including National Concours d'Elegance car show and rally championships; presents awards. **Convention/Meeting:** Annual conference - always March; 1993— Seattle, WA. Also holds biennial meet - always New York City metro area.

JEEP CHEROKEE (1987-92)

Classified as a multi-purpose vehicle by the EPA. Received several awards since its introduction, including the 4x4 of the

Year title from *4 Wheel & Off-Road, Four Wheeler* and *Off Road* magazines. In addition, the 1990 Cherokee was presented with *4 WHEEL's* Best of the Best, after beating 1990 versions of all past winners of the magazines 4x4 of the Year award. In 1991, the Jeep Wagoneer model was replaced by the Cherokee Briarwood, while the Jeep Pioneer was replaced by the five-door Jeep Cherokee Sport. The Jeep Cherokee Laredo and Jeep Cherokee Limited remained unchanged, except for their engines. Produced at the Jeep-Eagle plant in Toledo, Ohio.

1992 Jeep 4WD Cherokee Limited

MAJOR FEATURES

● Jeep Cherokee has as 1992 standard equipment: Two- or four-wheel drive in two-door and four-door versions, 2.5 liter, four-cylinder engine, five-speed manual overdrive transmission, front coil spring suspension, rear leaf spring suspension mounted above axle, power recirculating ball steering, front power disc brakes, rear power drum brakes, restraint system with front and rear three-point lap and shoulder belts, and steel wheels.

● Jeep Cherokee Sport adds as 1992 standard features: Two- or four-wheel drive in two- and four-door versions, 4.0 liter, six-cylinder engine, five-speed manual overdrive transmission, aluminum wheels, and additional exterior and interior body stylings.

● Jeep Cherokee Laredo adds as 1992 standard features: Two-wheel drive in four-door version and four-wheel drive in two- and four-door version, tachometer, roof rack, spoke aluminum wheels with bright hubs, rear window wiper/washer, and additional body stylings.

● Jeep Cherokee Limited adds as 1992 standard equipment: Four-wheel drive in four-door version, four-speed automatic overdrive transmission, air conditioning system, cruise control, rear window defroster, tilting steering column, aluminum crosswire wheels, color keyed wheels, and a variety of accessories.

● Jeep Cherokee Briarwood adds as 1992 standard equipment: Four-wheel drive in four-door version, aluminum crosswire wheels with dark silver, exterior woodgrain bodyside and liftgate, and an assortment of exterior and interior accessories.

PRICE HISTORY

The following new car prices reflect the approximate retail cost of the base model: **1988** - $11,186; **1989** - $12,374; **1990** - $13,295; **1991** - $13,060; **1992** - $14,346.

DIMENSIONS

Body Style	Years Avail	Wheel Base (in)	Lgth (in)	Ht (in)	Avg Wt (lbs)	Fuel Cap (gal)	Front Hdrm (in)	Front Legrm (in)
utl wgn	87-87	101.4	165.3	63.3	4,393	13.5	na	na
utl wgn	88-88	101.4	165.3	63.3	4,657	13.5	na	na
utl wgn	89-91	101.4	165.3	63.3	4,550	20.2	38.3	41.0
utl wgn	92-92	101.4	168.8	63.3	na	20.2	38.3	41.0

ENGINES

Type	Displacement (L)	Fuel Dly	HP @rpm	Torque @rpm (ft/lbs)	MPG Cty/Hwy	Years Avail
I-4	2.5	FI	121@na	na	19/24	87-90
I-4	2.5	FI	130@5250	149@3250	19/24	91-92
I-6	4.0	FI	177@na	na	17/22	87-90
I-6	4.0	FI	190@4750	225@4000	18/22	91-92

KEY: I=in-line engine; V=V engine; F=flat engine; FI=fuel injection; bbl=barrel carburetor; T=turbo; D=diesel; HP=horsepower; MPG=estimated average miles per gallon.

EVALUATIONS, TESTS, AND RANKINGS

1991: "classic . . . propelled by the most potent engine in its class . . . crisp shape is as timeless as they come." **Source:** "Update: Sport-Utility Vehicles," *U.S. News and World Report [reprinted from Car and Driver]*, May 13, 1991, pp. A4-A6, A8-A10, A12, A14-A15.

1991: "remains the standard for compact sport utility vehicles . . . It does show its age, however, in the amount of usable space inside . . . Jeep has surpassed the competition with its full-time Selec-Trac 4WD system." **Source:** "Strong and Sporty," *Organic Gardening*, November 1990, p. 58-61.

1990: "ruggedly attractive styling." **Source:** "Top 10 New Car Buys Domestic; Sport/Utility: Jeep Cherokee 4-liter," *Motor Trend*, November 1989, p. 83.

1990: "still have a good running start on the new introductions . . . technology and styling improving each year . . . console extends rearward, providing additional reading lights for second-seat passengers." **Source:** "4-Door Off-Roaders," *Sports Afield*, March 1990, pp. 120-122, 143-145.

1990: "continues to be one of . . . the hottest seller in the class . . . its various models can handle rough roads . . . without compromising on everyday street-going comfort . . . lone domestic offering—and the market leader." **Source:** "4-Doors For All Seasons," *New Choices for the Best Years*, December 1989, pp. 84, 86-87.

1990: "a solid package, with several undeniable strengths . . . standout items on the 1990 model are the engine, the four-wheel-drive system, and an innovative anti-lock brake system . . . The key area where Jeep loses ground is the suspension. Newer vehicles in this class feature more sophisticated systems." **Source:** "Pioneer Spirit," *Field and Stream*, April 1990, pp. 84, 86.

1989: "[Cherokee Ltd] can go anywhere, is less expensive at $ 26,000, and still boasts interior sophistication with leather seats and digital panels." **Source:** "Driving," *Vogue*, August 1989, p. 248.

1989: "[engine is]the best available in any downsized utility or pickup truck . . . five-speed manual is a real joy to drive—smooth and crisp . . . cruise control became erratic." **Source:** "Personal Pick," *Outdoor Life*, June 1989, pp. 20, 24-25.

1988: "performed superbly off road. . .bouncy, jostling ride on pavement, especially at highway speeds." **Source:** "Jeep Cherokee Limited has European flair," *The Detroit News*, April 13, 1988, pp. F1-F2.

1988: "ground clearance is said to be best in class." **Source:** "Jeep Cherokee/Wagoneer," *Car and Driver—Buyers Guide 1988,* 1988, p. 138.

RECALLS

1991: (425 multi-purpose vehicles equipped with anti-lock brake system): Improperly installed brake fluid tube may allow tube to contact steering intermediate shaft, resulting in brake fluid leakage and loss of braking capability. **Corrective action:** Reposition brake tube to avoid contact with steering shaft; also, replace any damaged brake tubes. *(NHTSA Campaign No. 91V023000.)*

1991: (160 multi-purpose four-wheel drive vehicles): Suspension jounce bumper could contact left rear wheel brake tube when suspension is at full jounce (bounce). Contact at full jounce may cause the brake tube to collapse and restrict the hydraulic brake fluid pressure to the left rear brake which affects the braking capability of the vehicle. **Corrective action:** Replace left rear brake tube designed to eliminate contact with bumper. *(NHTSA Campaign No. 90V206000.)*

1990: (17,000 multipurpose passenger vehicles; includes the Jeep Wagoneer and Jeep Cherokee): Improper insertion/fitting of the hose-to-end fittings of the high pressure hose on the anti-lock brake system can cause detachment of the hose from the ABS System, and discharge of hydraulic fluid. Causes the loss of the ABS function and hydraulic brake assist, leaving only manual brakes and decreasing stopping ability. Discharge of hydraulic fluid could result in an engine compartment fire. **Corrective action:** Replace the ABS high pressure hose. *(NHTSA Campaign No. 91V063000.)*

1989-90: (33,000 multi-purpose vehicles equipped with anti-lock brake system; includes Jeep Cherokee and Jeep Wagoneer models): May be hydraulic fluid contamination from condensation formation that can cause malfunctioning of anti-lock brake system. **Corrective action:** Replace ABS low pressure hose; rebuild master brake cylinder; inspect, service interference problems, and replace front brake hose as necessary. *(NHTSA Campaign No. 91V003000.)*

1989-90: (165,000 multi-purpose vehicles equipped with 4.0 liter engine and automatic transmission; includes Jeep Cherokee, Jeep Comanche, and Jeep Wagoneer models): Malfunction of fuel injection system throttle position sensor could cause intermittent high engine idle speed immediately after starting engine. Could result in unexpected acceleration. **Corrective action:** Replace throttle position sensors with sensors that would send correct signals to the fuel injection system. *(NHTSA Campaign No. 90V177000.)*

1987: (3,996 multipurpose vehicles with cruise control. Recall includes Jeep Cherokee, Jeep Wrangler, and Jeep Grand Wagoneer): Cruise control module could have inconsistent cruise control operation. Could result in loss of control and an accident. **Corrective action:** Replace module, as necessary. *(NHTSA Campaign No. 87V022000.)*

1987: (20,439 multi-purpose vehicles equipped with 4.0 liter engines. Recall includes the Jeep Wagoneer and Jeep Cherokee): Vehicle may contain an out of tolerance throttle body. Could prevent the accelerator from returning to idle when released. **Corrective action:** Replace suspect throttle bodies. *(NHTSA Campaign No. 87V035000.)*

1987: (1,600 vehicles equipped with 2.1L turbo diesel engine; includes models made before 1987): Brake booster vacuum reservoir canisters may develop leaks due to bumper impact, resulting in loss of power brake assist and an increase in stopping distance. **Corrective action:** Replace brake booster vacuum canisters with new type canisters; also install a restriction orifice to ensure sufficient vacuum in event canister leakage occurs. *(NHTSA Campaign No. 88V106000.)*

SAFETY AND REPAIRS

1987: "Car Clinic," *Popular Mechanics,* April 1990, p. 27. **Note:** Tip for high idle and poor acceleration in 1987-88 2.5 and 4.0 models.

REPAIR MANUALS

1596 ● **Chilton's Guide to Chassis Electronics and Power Accessories, 1988-1991 Ford/Chrysler/Jeep/Eagle**
Chilton Co.
Chilton Way
Radnor, PA 19089   Ph:(215)964-4000

Published March 1991. **Price:** $19.95.

1597 ● **Haynes Jeep Cherokee, 1984-1989**
Haynes Publications, Inc.
861 Lawrence Dr.
Newbury Park, CA 91320   Ph:(818)889-5400

Published 1989. **Price:** $15.95.

1598 ● **Jeep 6-Cylinder**
Peter Allen Video Productions
38-C Otis St.
West Babylon, NY 11704   Ph:(516)643-4372

How to tune-up and maintain the Jeep engine. **Release date:** 1986. **Producer:** Peter Allen Productions. **Acquisition:** Purchase.

1599 ● **Jeep Wagoneer-Comanche-Cherokee 1984-1991**
Chilton Co.
Chilton Way
Radnor, PA 19089   Ph:(215)964-4000

Published August 1991. **Price:** $15.95.

OTHER INFORMATION SOURCES

1600 ● **Illustrated Jeep Buyer's Guide**
Motorbooks International
729 Prospect Ave
Osceola, WI 54020   Ph:(715)294-3345

Published 1987. **Editor(s):** Pete Sessler. **Price:** $16.95.

1601 ● **Jeep: Mechanical Mule to People's Plaything**
Motorbooks International
729 Prospect Ave.
Osceola, WI 54020   Ph:(715)294-3345

Published 1987. **Editor(s):** Henry Rasmussen. **Price:** $24.95.

ASSOCIATIONS

1602 ● **Chrysler Product Owners Club**
5203 Edmondson Ave.
Baltimore, MD 21229
Brian K. Scott, Exec. Officer

Founded: 1978. **Membership:** 210. Collectors and restorers of Chrysler-product automobiles. Promotes the collection, preservation, restoration, maintenance, exhibition, and enjoyment of all Chrysler product cars, trucks, and other vehicles, including Chrysler, DeSoto, Dodge, Imperial, and Plymouth. Offers technical advice; provides list of cars, parts, and services. Maintains library of service and parts manuals from the 1930s to 1989. **Convention/Meeting:** Annual.

1603 ● **WPC Club**
P.O. Box 3504
Kalamazoo, MI 49003-3504
Ralph Kendall, Pres.   Ph:(616)372-1067

Founded: 1969. **Membership:** 4,850. Individuals dedicated to the preservation, restoration, and enjoyment of Chrysler product cars. Conducts social activities; houses library. Awards annual trophies at national meets. **Convention/Meeting:** Annual; also sponsors International Winter Photo Meet.

1604 ● **Yakima Ridgerunners Jeep Club [Washington state]**
PO Box 2403
Yakima, WA 98907
Greg Anderson, Contact   Ph:(509)248-8531

Founded: 1947. **Membership:** 30. Service organization. **Convention/Meeting:** Monthly.

JEEP COMANCHE (1987-92)

Categorized in the EPA standard pickup vehicle class. Target audience includes younger, independent, outdoor-oriented buyers who like to drive. Selected by *Four Wheeler* as a ''Ten Best Buys'' designate in 1991. Built at the Jeep-Eagle production site in Toledo, Ohio. The three-passenger Comanche is available in two-wheel-drive or four-wheel-drive, with a long wheelbase or short wheelbase.

1992 Jeep Comanche Eliminator

MAJOR FEATURES

● Comanche Base and Sport models have as 1992 standard equipment: 2.5 liter, four-cylinder engine, 4-speed manual transmission, two-wheel drive, coil spring, live axle, quadralink front suspension with track bar, power recirculating ball steering, front-power disc brakes, rear-power drum brakes and steel disc wheels.

● Comanche Pioneer adds as 1992 standard equipment: 4.0-liter, six-cylinder engine, five-speed manual transmission, cab back trim panel, and a number of interior accessories.

● Comanche Eliminator adds as 1992 standard equipment: 4.0 liter, six-cylinder engine, five-speed manual transmission, fog lamps, aluminum wheels, rear sliding window, and an assortment of body stylings.

PRICE HISTORY

The following new car prices reflect the approximate retail cost of the base model: **1988** - $7,114; **1989** - $8,585; **1990** - $8,095; **1991** - $8,767.

DIMENSIONS

Body Style	Years Avail	Wheel Base (in)	Lgth (in)	Ht (in)	Avg Wt (lbs)	Fuel Cap (gal)	Front Hdrm (in)	Front Legrm (in)
trk	87-88	113.0	179.2	63.7	4,477	16.0	na	na
trk	89-91	113.1	179.2	64.7	4,650	18.0	39.4	43.0
trk	92-92	113.1	179.3	64.6	4,650	18.0	38.3	41.1

ENGINES

Type	Displacement (L)	Fuel Dly	HP @rpm	Torque @rpm (ft/lbs)	MPG Cty/Hwy	Years Avail
I-4	2.5	FI	121@na	na	18/24	87-90
I-4	2.5	FI	130@5250	149@3250	19/24	91-92
I-4T	2.1	FI	126@na	na	28/30	87-87
I-6	4.0	FI	177@na	na	16/20	87-90
I-6	4.0	FI	190@4750	225@4000	18/22	91-92

KEY: I=in-line engine; V=V engine; F=flat engine; FI=fuel injection; bbl=barrel carburetor; T=turbo; D=diesel; HP=horsepower; MPG=estimated average miles per gallon.

EVALUATIONS, TESTS, AND RANKINGS

1990: ''Driven sensibly, it will go nearly everywhere a 4x4 can . . . one of the largest trucks in this price range . . . has a wide stance and feels solid and sure-footed on tight turns.'' **Source:** ''Practical Pickups for Sportsmen,'' *Sports Afield*, May 1990, pp. 90-93, 100-101.

1989: ''handsome bodywork.'' **Source:** ''Jeep Comanche,'' *Road & Track—Buyer's Guide 1989*, 1988, p. 193.

1989: ''a muscle truck . . . it's a handful to drive fast. Steering feel is too light, and there's a lot of roll in hard cornering . . . poor ergonomics.'' **Source:** ''Compact Commandos,'' *Popular Mechanics*, February 1989, pp. 51-55, 112.

1989: ''Despite its outstanding track performance, the Comanche's design seems crude and outdated . . . poorest ride quality of the group . . . in dire need of a thorough updating.'' **Source:** ''Mudders,'' *Popular Science*, July 1989, pp. 33-34, 38-40, 42, 44.

RECALLS

1989-90: (165,000 multi-purpose vehicles equipped with 4.0 liter engine and automatic transmission; includes Jeep Cherokee, Jeep Comanche, and Jeep Wagoneer models): Malfunction of fuel injection system throttle position sensor could cause intermittent high engine idle speed immediately after starting engine. Could result in unexpected acceleration. **Corrective action:** Replace throttle position sensors with sensors that would send correct signals to the fuel injection system. *(NHTSA Campaign No. 90V177000.)*

1987: (1,600 vehicles equipped with 2.1 liter turbo diesel engine; includes Jeep Wagoneer, Cherokee, and Comanche models; includes models made before 1987): Brake booster vacuum reservoir canisters may develop leaks due to bumper impact. This would result in loss of power brake assist and an increase in stopping distance. **Corrective action:** Replace brake booster vacuum canisters with new type canisters; also, install a restriction orifice to ensure sufficient vacuum in event canister leakage occurs. *(NHTSA Campaign No. 88V106000.)*

1987: (3,996 multipurpose vehicles with cruise control; includes the Jeep Wagoneer, Jeep Cherokee, Jeep Comanche, Jeep Grand Wagoneer, and Jeep Wrangler): Cruise control module could have inconsistent cruise control operation. Inconsistent cruise control operation could result in loss of control and an accident. **Corrective action:** Replace module, as necessary. *(NHTSA Campaign No. 87V022000.)*

1987: (20,439 multipurpose vehicles equipped with 4.0 liter engines; includes the Jeep Comanche, Jeep Wagoneer, and Jeep Cherokee): Vehicle may contain an out of tolerance throttle body. This could prevent the accelerator from returning to idle when released. **Corrective action:** Replace suspect throttle bodies. (NHTSA Campaign No. 87VO35000.)

SAFETY AND REPAIRS

1987: "Auto Q & A," *Home Mechanix*, January 1990, p. 83. **Note:** Tip for cold weather stalling in 87-89 4 cylinder.

1987: "Car Clinic," *Popular Mechanics*, April 1990, p. 27. **Note:** Tip for high idle and poor acceleration in 1987-88 2.5 and 4.0 models.

REPAIR MANUALS

1605 ● Chilton's Guide to Chassis Electronics and Power Accessories, 1988-1991 Ford/Chrysler/Jeep/Eagle
Chilton Co.
Chilton Way
Radnor, PA 19089   Ph:(215)964-4000

Published March 1991. **Price:** $19.95.

1606 ● Jeep 6-Cylinder
Peter Allen Video Productions
38-C Otis St.
West Babylon, NY 11704   Ph:(516)643-4372

How to tune-up and maintain the Jeep engine. **Release date:** 1986. **Producer:** Peter Allen Productions. **Acquisition:** Purchase.

1607 ● Jeep Wagoneer-Comanche-Cherokee 1984-1991
Chilton Co.
Chilton Way
Radnor, PA 19089   Ph:(215)964-4000

Published August 1991. **Price:** $15.95.

OTHER INFORMATION SOURCES

1608 ● Illustrated Jeep Buyer's Guide
Motorbooks International
729 Prospect Ave
Osceola, WI 54020   Ph:(715)294-3345

Published 1987. **Editor(s):** Pete Sessler. **Price:** $16.95.

1609 ● Jeep: Mechanical Mule to People's Plaything
Motorbooks International
729 Prospect Ave.
Osceola, WI 54020   Ph:(715)294-3345

Published 1987. **Editor(s):** Henry Rasmussen. **Price:** $24.95.

ASSOCIATIONS

1610 ● Chrysler Product Owners Club
5203 Edmondson Ave.
Baltimore, MD 21229
Brian K. Scott, Exec. Officer

Founded: 1978. **Membership:** 210. Collectors and restorers of Chrysler-product automobiles. Promotes the collection, preservation, restoration, maintenance, exhibition, and enjoyment of all Chrysler product cars, trucks, and other vehicles, including Chrysler, DeSoto, Dodge, Imperial, and Plymouth. Offers technical advice; provides list of cars, parts, and services. Maintains library of service and parts manuals from the 1930s to 1989. **Convention/Meeting:** Annual.

1611 ● WPC Club
P.O. Box 3504
Kalamazoo, MI 49003-3504
Ralph Kendall, Pres.   Ph:(616)372-1067

Founded: 1969. **Membership:** 4,850. Individuals dedicated to the preservation, restoration, and enjoyment of Chrysler product cars. Conducts social activities; houses library. Awards annual trophies at national meets. **Convention/Meeting:** Annual; also sponsors International Winter Photo Meet.

1612 ● Yakima Ridgerunners Jeep Club [Washington state]
PO Box 2403
Yakima, WA 98907
Greg Anderson, Contact   Ph:(509)248-8531

Founded: 1947. **Membership:** 30. Service organization. **Convention/Meeting:** Monthly.

JEEP GRAND WAGONEER (1987-91)

A multi-purpose vehicle targeted at men and women in their late 40s who are professionals or entrepreneurs. Received grades of medium, poor, and average in repair cost, warranty rating, and complaint index, respectively, from *The Car Book* in 1991. Manufactured through the 1991 model at the Jeep-Eagle Corporation production site in Toledo, Ohio.

1991 Jeep Grand Wagoneer

MAJOR FEATURES

● Jeep Wagoneer had as 1991 standard equipment: 5.9 liter V-8 engine, full-time 4WD, leaf spring front suspension mounted below with track bar, recirculating ball power steering, power disc brakes, power rear drum brakes, aluminum wheels, air conditioning system, cruise control, rear window defroster, fog lamps, restraint system consisting of front lap and shoulder belts (center lap belt), and rear lap belts, roof rack, tilting steering column, woodgrain exterior bodysides and liftgate, and a number of interior accessories.

PRICE HISTORY

The following new car prices reflect the approximate retail cost of the base model: **1988** - $24,623; **1989** - $26,639; **1990** - $27,795; **1991** - $29,241.

DIMENSIONS

Body Style	Years Avail	Wheel Base (in)	Lgth (in)	Ht (in)	Avg Wt (lbs)	Fuel Cap (gal)	Front Hdrm (in)	Front Legrm (in)
utl wgn	87-91	108.7	186.4	66.4	5,975	20.3	37.1	40.5

ENGINES

Type	Displace- ment (L)	Fuel Dly	HP @rpm	Torque @rpm (ft/lbs)	MPG Cty/Hwy	Years Avail
I-6	4.2	2-bbl	121@na	na	14/19	87-87
V-8	5.9	2-bbl	144@3200	280@1500	11/13	87-91

KEY: I=in-line engine; V=V engine; F=flat engine; FI=fuel injection; bbl=barrel carburetor; T=turbo; D=diesel; HP=horsepower; MPG=estimated average miles per gallon.

EVALUATIONS, TESTS, AND RANKINGS

1990: "It provides first-class luxury, convenience, and prestige." **Source:** "Jeep Grand Wagoneer," *Car and Driver—Buyers Guide 1990*, 1989, p. 170.

1990: "Jeep's live axles jump and bounce over washboard surfaces far more than those in the Range Rover or the Land Cruiser . . . The cabin's ergonomics leave much to wish for . . . displays confident, balanced handling on the skidpad and on the road." **Source:** "Roughing it," *Car and Driver*, August 1990, pp. 98-101, 104, 107-108.

RECALLS

1987-88: (180,000 multipurpose vehicles equipped with a power tailgate window; includes other Jeep models; includes models made before 1987): Key-operated tailgate window will continue to close if the spring-loaded key does not return to off position when released. Window could close on a child or others resulting in personal injury. **Corrective action:** Owners should not leave key in tailgate of unattended vehicle. Repair mechanism to assure proper key return operation. *(NHTSA Campaign No. 87V178000.)*

1987: (3,996 multipurpose vehicles with cruise control. Recall includes Jeep Cherokee, Jeep Wrangler, and Jeep Grand Wagoneer): Cruise control module could have inconsistent cruise control operation. Could result in loss of control and an accident. **Corrective action:** Replace module, as necessary. *(NHTSA Campaign No. 87V022000.)*

SAFETY AND REPAIRS

1989: "Car Clinic," *Popular Mechanics*, January 1990, p. 41. **Note:** Tip for correct front wheel toe-in.

1987: "Car Clinic," *Popular Mechanics*, April 1990, p. 27. **Note:** Tip for high idle and poor acceleration in 1987-88 2.5 and 4.0 models.

1987: "Car Clinic," *Popular Mechanics*, October 1990, p. 107. **Note:** Correct oil filter for 1987 and later models with Jeep/Eagle 4.2-liter engines.

REPAIR MANUALS

1613 ● **Chilton's Guide to Chassis Electronics and Power Accessories, 1988-1991 Ford/Chrysler/Jeep/Eagle**
Chilton Co.
Chilton Way
Radnor, PA 19089   Ph:(215)964-4000

Published March 1991. **Price:** $19.95.

1614 ● **Jeep 6-Cylinder**
Peter Allen Video Productions
38-C Otis St.
West Babylon, NY 11704   Ph:(516)643-4372

How to tune-up and maintain the Jeep engine. **Release date:** 1986. **Producer:** Peter Allen Productions. **Acquisition:** Purchase.

1615 ● **Jeep Wagoneer-Comanche-Cherokee 1984-1991**
Chilton Co.
Chilton Way
Radnor, PA 19089   Ph:(215)964-4000

Published August 1991. **Price:** $15.95.

OTHER INFORMATION SOURCES

1616 ● **Illustrated Jeep Buyer's Guide**
Motorbooks International
729 Prospect Ave
Osceola, WI 54020   Ph:(715)294-3345

Published 1987. **Editor(s):** Pete Sessler. **Price:** $16.95.

1617 ● **Jeep: Mechanical Mule to People's Plaything**
Motorbooks International
729 Prospect Ave.
Osceola, WI 54020   Ph:(715)294-3345

Published 1987. **Editor(s):** Henry Rasmussen. **Price:** $24.95.

ASSOCIATIONS

1618 ● **Chrysler Product Owners Club**
5203 Edmondson Ave.
Baltimore, MD 21229
Brian K. Scott, Exec. Officer

Founded: 1978. **Membership:** 210. Collectors and restorers of Chrysler-product automobiles. Promotes the collection, preservation, restoration, maintenance, exhibition, and enjoyment of all Chrysler product cars, trucks, and other vehicles, including Chrysler, DeSoto, Dodge, Imperial, and Plymouth. Offers technical advice; provides list of cars, parts, and services. Maintains library of service and parts manuals from the 1930s to 1989. **Convention/Meeting:** Annual.

1619 ● **WPC Club**
P.O. Box 3504
Kalamazoo, MI 49003-3504
Ralph Kendall, Pres.   Ph:(616)372-1067

Founded: 1969. **Membership:** 4,850. Individuals dedicated to the preservation, restoration, and enjoyment of Chrysler product cars. Conducts social activities; houses library. Awards annual trophies at national meets. **Convention/Meeting:** Annual; also sponsors International Winter Photo Meet.

1620 ● **Yakima Ridgerunners Jeep Club [Washington state]**
PO Box 2403
Yakima, WA 98907
Greg Anderson, Contact   Ph:(509)248-8531

Founded: 1947. **Membership:** 30. Service organization. **Convention/Meeting:** Monthly.

JEEP WAGONEER (1987-90)

A smaller model of the Jeep Grand Wagoneer, it was produced until 1990. In 1991, it was replaced by the Jeep Cherokee Briarwood. Produced at the Jeep-Eagle Corporation production site in Toledo, Ohio.

MAJOR FEATURES

● Wagoneer had as 1990 standard equipment: 2.5 liter inline-four engine, full- and part-time four wheel drive system, four wheel anti-lock brake system, five-speed manual transmission, front disc brakes, recirculating ball power steering.

● Wagoneer Limited added as 1990 standard equipment: four-speed automatic transmission with lockup, air conditioning system, tilt steering, rear window defroster, and various interior accessories.

PRICE HISTORY

The following new car prices reflect the approximate retail cost of the base model: **1988** - $21,926; **1989** - $23,455; **1990** - $24,795.

DIMENSIONS

Body Style	Years Avail	Wheel Base (in)	Lgth (in)	Ht (in)	Avg Wt (lbs)	Fuel Cap (gal)	Front Hdrm (in)	Front Legrm (in)
utl wgn	87-88	101.4	165.3	63.3	4,657	13.5	na	na
utl wgn	89-90	101.4	165.3	63.3	4,550	20.2	na	na

ENGINES

Type	Displace-ment (L)	Fuel Dly	HP @rpm	Torque @rpm (ft/lbs)	MPG Cty/Hwy	Years Avail
I-4	2.5	FI	121@na	na	19/24	87-89
I-4T	2.1	FI	na	na	28/29	87-87
I-6	4.0	FI	177@na	na	16/20	87-90

KEY: I=in-line engine; V=V engine; F=flat engine; FI=fuel injection; bbl=barrel carburetor; T=turbo; D=diesel; HP=horsepower; MPG=estimated average miles per gallon.

EVALUATIONS, TESTS, AND RANKINGS

1989: "benchmarks of the U.S. sport utility market." **Source:** "Jeep Cherokee & Wagoneer," *Road & Track—Buyer's Guide 1989*, 1988, p. 192.

1987: "If you want a comfortable and capable multipurpose machine that also happens to be *fast*, the new Wagoneer is hard to beat." **Source:** "Jeep Wagoneer Limited: Still civilized, now dynamized," *Car and Driver*, July 1987, pp. 125-126, 128.

RECALLS

1990: (17,000 multipurpose passenger vehicles; includes the Jeep Wagoneer and Jeep Cherokee): Improper insertion/fitting of the hose-to-end fittings of the high pressure hose on the anti-lock brake system can cause detachment of the hose from the ABS System, and discharge of hydraulic fluid. Causes the loss of the ABS function and hydraulic brake assist, leaving only manual brakes and decreasing stopping ability. Discharge of hydraulic fluid could result in an engine compartment fire. **Corrective action:** Replace the ABS high pressure hose. *(NHTSA Campaign No. 91V063000.)*

1989-90: (33,000 multi-purpose vehicles equipped with anti-lock brake system; includes Jeep Cherokee and Jeep Wagoneer models): May be hydraulic fluid contamination from condensation formation that can cause malfunctioning of anti-lock brake system. **Corrective action:** Replace ABS low pressure hose; rebuild master brake cylinder; inspect, service interference problems, and replace front brake hose as necessary. *(NHTSA Campaign No. 91V003000.)*

1989-90: (165,000 multi-purpose vehicles equipped with 4.0 liter engine and automatic transmission; includes Jeep Cherokee, Jeep Comanche, and Jeep Wagoneer models): Malfunction of fuel injection system throttle position sensor could cause intermittent high engine idle speed immediately after starting engine. Could result in unexpected acceleration. **Corrective action:** Replace throttle position sensors with

sensors that would send correct signals to the fuel injection system. *(NHTSA Campaign No. 90V177000.)*

1987: (3,996 multipurpose vehicles with cruise control; includes the Jeep Wagoneer, Jeep Cherokee, Jeep Comanche, Jeep Grand Wagoneer, Jeep J10, Jeep Wrangler): Cruise control module could have inconsistent cruise control operation. Could result in loss of control and an accident. **Corrective action:** Replace module, as necessary. *(NHTSA Campaign No. 87V022000.)*

1987: (20,439 multipurpose vehicles equipped with 4.0 liter engines. Recall includes the Jeep Wagoneer and Jeep Cherokee): Vehicle may contain an out of tolerance throttle body. Could prevent the accelerator from returning to idle when released. **Corrective action:** Replace suspect throttle bodies. *(NHTSA Campaign No. 87V035000.)*

1987: (1,600 vehicles equipped with 2.1L turbo diesel engine; includes models made before 1987): Brake booster vacuum reservoir canisters may develop leaks due to bumper impact, resulting in loss of power brake assist and an increase in stopping distance. **Corrective action:** Replace brake booster vacuum canisters with new type canisters; also install a restriction orifice to ensure sufficient vacuum in event canister leakage occurs. *(NHTSA Campaign No. 88V106000.)*

1987: (11 vehicles): Tire reserve load label may not have been installed. **Corrective action:** Install proper label. *(NHTSA Campaign No. 89V219000.)*

SAFETY AND REPAIRS

1987: "Rotten Eggs Revisited," *Home Mechanix*, July 1988, p. 78. **Note:** Jeep Wagoneer with rotten egg odor from engine.

1987: "Car Clinic," *Popular Mechanics*, April 1990, p. 27. **Note:** Tip for high idle and poor acceleration in 1987-88 2.5 and 4.0 models.

REPAIR MANUALS

1621 ● **Chilton's Guide to Chassis Electronics and Power Accessories, 1988-1991 Ford/Chrysler/Jeep/Eagle**
Chilton Co.
Chilton Way
Radnor, PA 19089   Ph:(215)964-4000

Published March 1991. **Price:** $19.95.

1622 ● **Jeep 6-Cylinder**
Peter Allen Video Productions
38-C Otis St.
West Babylon, NY 11704   Ph:(516)643-4372

How to tune-up and maintain the Jeep engine. **Release date:** 1986. **Producer:** Peter Allen Productions. **Acquisition:** Purchase.

1623 ● **Jeep Wagoneer-Comanche-Cherokee 1984-1991**
Chilton Co.
Chilton Way
Radnor, PA 19089   Ph:(215)964-4000

Published August 1991. **Price:** $15.95.

OTHER INFORMATION SOURCES

1624 ● **Illustrated Jeep Buyer's Guide**
Motorbooks International
729 Prospect Ave
Osceola, WI 54020   Ph:(715)294-3345

Published 1987. **Editor(s):** Pete Sessler. **Price:** $16.95.

1625 ● Jeep: Mechanical Mule to People's Plaything
Motorbooks International
729 Prospect Ave.
Osceola, WI 54020   Ph:(715)294-3345

Published 1987. **Editor(s):** Henry Rasmussen. **Price:** $24.95.

1626 ● Jeep: The Fifty Year History
Motorbooks International
729 Prospect Ave.
Osceola, WI 54020   Ph:(715)294-3345

Published 1988. **Editor(s):** Robert C. Akerson. **Price:** $49.95.

ASSOCIATIONS

1627 ● Chrysler Product Owners Club
5203 Edmondson Ave.
Baltimore, MD 21229
Brian K. Scott, Exec. Officer

Founded: 1978. **Membership:** 210. Collectors and restorers of Chrysler-product automobiles. Promotes the collection, preservation, restoration, maintenance, exhibition, and enjoyment of all Chrysler product cars, trucks, and other vehicles, including Chrysler, DeSoto, Dodge, Imperial, and Plymouth. Offers technical advice; provides list of cars, parts, and services. Maintains library of service and parts manuals from the 1930s to 1989. **Convention/Meeting:** Annual.

1628 ● WPC Club
P.O. Box 3504
Kalamazoo, MI 49003-3504
Ralph Kendall, Pres.   Ph:(616)372-1067

Founded: 1969. **Membership:** 4,850. Individuals dedicated to the preservation, restoration, and enjoyment of Chrysler product cars. Conducts social activities; houses library. Awards annual trophies at national meets. **Convention/Meeting:** Annual; also sponsors International Winter Photo Meet.

1629 ● Yakima Ridgerunners Jeep Club [Washington state]
PO Box 2403
Yakima, WA 98907
Greg Anderson, Contact   Ph:(509)248-8531

Founded: 1947. **Membership:** 30. Service organization. **Convention/Meeting:** Monthly.

JEEP WRANGLER (1987-92)

Classified in the EPA multi-purpose vehicle class. Appeals to the youngest sport utility buyers who are adventurous, image-conscious, outdoor people. Included as Ten Best Buys in the sport utility category by both *Four Wheeler* and *4Wheel & Off-Road* magazines in 1991. Manufactured since 1987 at the Jeep-Eagle production facility in Brampton, Ontario, Canada.

1991 Jeep Wrangler S

MAJOR FEATURES

● Wrangler has as 1992 standard equipment: 2.5 liter, 4-cylinder engine, part-time four-wheel drive, 5-speed manual transmission with overdrive, and an assortment of exterior body stylings and interior accessories.

● Wrangler S adds as 1992 standard equipment: front bucket seats and styled steel argent wheels (actually offered below the base model, since it has fewer options).

● Wrangler Islander adds as 1992 standard equipment: 4.0-liter, 6-cylinder engine, styled steel silver wheels and a variety of body accessories.

● Wrangler Sahara adds as 1992 standard equipment: 4.0-liter, 6-cylinder engine, fog lamps, power steering, styled steel sand metallic wheels, and additional body accessories.

● Wrangler Renegade adds as 1992 standard equipment: 4.0 liter, six-cylinder engine, five-speed manual overdrive transmission, part-time four-wheel drive, aluminum five spoke wheels, and numerous body accessories.

● Wrangler Sports Decor had as 1987 standard equipment: 2.5 liter, inline-4 engine, five-speed manual transmission, part-time and full-time four wheel drive systems, fabric top, and accessories.

● Wrangler Laredo added as 1987 equipment: fiberglass hardtop, runningboards, and other accessories.

PRICE HISTORY

The following new car prices reflect the approximate retail cost of the base model: **1988** - $8,995; **1989** - $8,995; **1990** - $9,393; **1991** - $9,910; **1992** - $10,393.

DIMENSIONS

Body Style	Years Avail	Wheel Base (in)	Lgth (in)	Ht (in)	Avg Wt (lbs)	Fuel Cap (gal)	Front Hdrm (in)	Front Legrm (in)
utl wgn	87-88	93.4	152.0	72.0	3,702	15.0	na	na
utl wgn	89-92	93.4	153.0	72.0	4,350	15.0	41.4	39.4

ENGINES

Type	Displace-ment (L)	Fuel Dly	HP @rpm	Torque @rpm (ft/lbs)	MPG Cty/Hwy	Years Avail
I-4	2.5	FI	117@na	na	16/20	87-90
I-4	2.5	na	123@5250	139@3250	18/20	91-92
I-6	4.2	2-bbl	112@na	na	16/20	87-89
I-6	4.2	4-bbl	112@na	na	16/20	90-90
I-6	4.0	na	180@4750	220@4000	17/21	91-92

KEY: I=in-line engine; V=V engine; F=flat engine; FI=fuel injection; bbl=barrel carburetor; T=turbo; D=diesel; HP=horsepower; MPG=estimated average miles per gallon.

EVALUATIONS, TESTS, AND RANKINGS

1991: "Ride motions are civilized when the road surface is calm. . .In the dirt,. . .became a runaway freight train." **Source:** "Dirty Little Devils," *Automobile Magazine,* February 1991, pp. 79-85.

1991: "enough muscle at the low end to move you through and over most difficult situations . . . Back trails were handled with ease . . . only noticeable fault was that some of the instrument gauges spread along the dash were difficult to read from the driver's seat." **Source:** "Testing the New Mini 4x4s," *Sports Afield,* October 1991, pp. 110-112, 114-116.

1991: "disproportionate rollover rate . . . ride was surprisingly good . . . much to complain about in terms of ergonomics." **Source:** "Jeep Marks 50 Years of 4-Wheel Drive," *The New York Times,* March 17, 1991.

1990: "handling is much improved. . .uncomfortably crude when it is driven on the road. . ." **Source:** "Pocket 4x4s: Over the hills and through the mud to test the mettle of Jeep's competitors," *Popular Science,* May 1990, pp. 102-105.

1990: "it remains leather-strap tough . . . improved chassis tuning . . . the entire wheel/tire/chassis combination works reassuringly well." **Source:** "Jeep Wrangler Sahara," *Car and Driver,* June 1990, pp. 157, 159.

1989: "With a ground clearance of 8.1 inches and a relatively short wheelbase, the Jeep feels unstoppable." **Source:** "Dustbusters! Four small sport-utilities and four dusty editors tame the Mojave Road," *Car and Driver,* November 1989, pp. 136-140, 142, 146, 148, 152-53, 156, 158.

1988: "stands out as the original, and still best, of the basic soft-top four-wheel-drive utilities." **Source:** "No-Frills Four-Wheel Drive," *Popular Science,* January 1988, pp. 26-28, 32, 34, 36.

RECALLS

1991: (2,800 multi-purpose passenger vehicle): Certification label does not contain required tire and wheel information. Does not comply with FMVSS 120. **Corrective action:** Install supplemental tire information labels adjacent to certification labels. *(NHTSA Campaign No. 90V178000.)*

1989: (75 vehicles equipped with metal fuel tanks): In a rear impact collision, fuel tank may leak fuel in excess of amount allowed by FMVSS 301 because of misbuilt fuel tank skid plates. In the presence of an ignition source, this could result in fire. Vehicle would not comply with FMVSS 301. **Corrective action:** Install flange on fuel tank skid plate. *(NHTSA Campaign No. 90V168000.)*

1987-88: (75,000 vehicles): Windshield frame metal may crack at the wiper arm pivot mountings due to metal stress during wiper operation, resulting in dislocation and binding of the wiper system linkage. **Corrective action:** Retrofit windshield frame reinforcement at wiper pivot locations and redesigned linkage components to reduce stress at pivot mountings. *(NHTSA Campaign No. 88V155000.)*

1987: (3,996 multipurpose vehicles with cruise control. Recall includes Jeep Cherokee, Jeep Wrangler, Jeep Grand Wagoneer): Cruise control module could have inconsistent cruise control operation. Could result in loss of control and an accident. **Corrective action:** Replace module, as necessary. *(NHTSA Campaign No. 87V022000.)*

SAFETY AND REPAIRS

1987: "Car Clinic," *Popular Mechanics,* April 1990, p. 27. **Note:** Tip for high idle and poor acceleration in 1987-88 2.5 and 4.0 models.

REPAIR MANUALS

1630 ● **Chilton's Guide to Chassis Electronics and Power Accessories, 1988-1991 Ford/Chrysler/Jeep/Eagle**
Chilton Co.
Chilton Way
Radnor, PA 19089   Ph:(215)964-4000

Published March 1991. **Price:** $19.95.

1631 ● **Chilton's Jeep CJ 1945-1987**
Chilton Co.
Chilton Way
Radnor, PA 19089   Ph:(215)964-4000

Published 1987. **Price:** $15.95.

1632 ● **Jeep 6-Cylinder**
Peter Allen Video Productions
38-C Otis St.
West Babylon, NY 11704   Ph:(516)643-4372

How to tune-up and maintain the Jeep engine. **Release date:** 1986. **Producer:** Peter Allen Productions. **Acquisition:** Purchase.

OTHER INFORMATION SOURCES

1633 ● **Illustrated Jeep Buyer's Guide**
Motorbooks International
729 Prospect Ave
Osceola, WI 54020   Ph:(715)294-3345

Published 1987. **Editor(s):** Pete Sessler. **Price:** $16.95.

1634 ● **Jeep: Mechanical Mule to People's Plaything**
Motorbooks International
729 Prospect Ave
Osceola, WI 54020   Ph:(715)294-3345

Published 1987. **Editor(s):** Henry Rasmussen. **Price:** $24.95.

1635 ● **Jeep: The Fifty Year History**
Motorbooks International
729 Prospect Ave.
Osceola, WI 54020   Ph:(715)294-3345

Published 1988. **Editor(s):** Robert C. Akerson. **Price:** $49.95.

ASSOCIATIONS

1636 ● **Chrysler Product Owners Club**
5203 Edmondson Ave.
Baltimore, MD 21229
Brian K. Scott, Exec. Officer

Founded: 1978. **Membership:** 210. Collectors and restorers of Chrysler-product automobiles. Promotes the collection, preservation, restoration, maintenance, exhibition, and enjoyment of all Chrysler product cars, trucks, and other vehicles, including Chrysler, DeSoto, Dodge, Imperial, and Plymouth. Offers technical advice; provides list of cars, parts, and services. Maintains library of service and parts manuals from the 1930s to 1989. **Convention/Meeting:** Annual.

1637 ● **WPC Club**
P.O. Box 3504
Kalamazoo, MI 49003-3504
Ralph Kendall, Pres.   Ph:(616)372-1067

Founded: 1969. **Membership:** 4,850. Individuals dedicated to the preservation, restoration, and enjoyment of Chrysler product cars. Conducts social activities; houses library. Awards annual trophies at national meets. **Convention/Meeting:** Annual; also sponsors International Winter Photo Meet.

1638 ● **Yakima Ridgerunners Jeep Club [Washington state]**
PO Box 2403
Yakima, WA 98907
Greg Anderson, Contact   Ph:(509)248-8531

Founded: 1947. **Membership:** 30. Service organization. **Convention/Meeting:** Monthly.

LAFORZA (1989-90)

A luxury sports/utility truck that competed against the Isuzu Trooper II, Range Rover, Jeep Cherokee, and Jeep Wrangler. Interior was produced in Turin, Italy, then shipped to Brighton, Michigan for the engine and final assembly. In August 1990, Laforza Automobiles, Inc. filed for bankruptcy, effectively ending production of the Laforza vehicle.

MAJOR FEATURES

● Laforza had as 1990 standard equipment: four-speed manual transmission, front independent suspension, power assisted front disc and rear drum brakes, power assisted rack and pinion steering, and fuel injection.

PRICE HISTORY

The following new car prices reflect the approximate retail cost of the base model: **1989** - $43,850; **1990** - $44,000.

DIMENSIONS

Body Style	Years Avail	Wheel Base (in)	Lgth (in)	Ht (in)	Avg Wt (lbs)	Fuel Cap (gal)	Front Hdrm (in)	Front Legrm (in)
utl wgn	89-90	106.2	179.9	72.6	5,250	27.5	na	na

ENGINES

Type	Displace-ment (L)	Fuel Dly	HP @rpm	Torque @rpm (ft/lbs)	MPG Cty/Hwy	Years Avail
V-8	5.0	na	185@na	na	na	89-90

KEY: I=in-line engine; V=V engine; F=flat engine; FI=fuel injection; bbl=barrel carburetor; T=turbo; D=diesel; HP=horsepower; MPG=estimated average miles per gallon.

EVALUATIONS, TESTS, AND RANKINGS

1990: "Exterior design is decidedly European ... A large number of luxury touches are added ... LaForza is possibly a look into the future." **Source:** "4x4 First Class," *Outdoor Life*, July 1990, pp. 46,50.

1989: "prestige, ruggedness and luxury." **Source:** "Laforza," *Road & Track—Buyer's Guide 1989*, 1988, p. 194.

1989: "a brute of an SUV ... leather-lined machomobile." **Source:** "Intruders in the Dust: More new ways to ride in the rough," *Popular Mechanics*, March 1989, pp. 122, 124, 127.

RECALLS

1989-90: (268 vehicles): Brake pedal to push rod pivot bolts could work loose and detach the pedal assembly from brake booster reaction rod; this would disable hydraulic brake system. **Corrective action:** Replace pivot bolt and nut with upgraded bolt and nut lock. *(NHTSA Campaign No. 90V019000.)*

1989-90: (188 vehicles): Tire inflation pressure recommended for rear tire will not support gross axle weight rating/FMVSS 120. **Corrective action:** Provide tire inflation information on a new combined certification-tire information label, and stamp wheel rims with dot. *(NHTSA Campaign No. 90V013000.)*

1989-90: (323 multi-purpose passenger vehicles): Design defect of the sealing grommet causes inadequate sealing of fuel filler neck at the fuel tank, which may result in fuel leakage. Could catch fire if an ignition source is present. **Corrective action:** Install replacement fuel tank and hardware. *(NHTSA Campaign No. 90V127000.)*

1989: (189 vehicles): Incorrect bolt and nut arrangement and size was used to install both front and rear drive shaft assemblies at differential pinion flanges. Could cause driveshaft to loosen, vibrate and may result in driveshaft detaching potential for loss of control and an accident. **Corrective action:** Install correct attaching bolts and torque to proper specifications. *(NHTSA Campaign No. 89V181000.)*

LAMBORGHINI COUNTACH (1987-90)

Lamborghini was absorbed by the Chrysler Corporation in 1987. Named one of Top 10 Exoticars by *Motor Trend* in 1988. Manufactured in Modena, Italy, the Lamborghini Countach ceased production after 1990 model year.

MAJOR FEATURES

● Countach had as 1990 standard equipment: independent front and rear suspension, front and rear disc brakes, vaccuum assisted rack and pinion steering, five-speed manual transmission, power windows, and various interior and exterior features.

● Countach 5000S added as 1987 standard equipment: DOHC 48-valve V12 engine and various interior adjustments.

● Countach 5000S Quattrovalvole added as 1988 standard equipment: DOHC 5.2-liter engine and various interior adjustments.

● Countach II added as 1989 standard equipment: lighter weight by 250 pounds and various interior and exterior adjustments.

PRICE HISTORY

The following new car prices reflect the approximate retail cost of the base model: **1987** - $125,000; **1988** - $138,500; **1989** - $145,000.

DIMENSIONS

Body Style	Years Avail	Wheel Base (in)	Lgth (in)	Ht (in)	Avg Wt (lbs)	Fuel Cap (gal)	Front Hdrm (in)	Front Legrm (in)
2d cpe	87-87	96.5	163.0	42.1	3,278	31.8	na	na
2d cpe	88-90	102.0	163.0	42.1	3,280	31.8	na	na

ENGINES

Type	Displace-ment (L)	Fuel Dly	HP @rpm	Torque @rpm (ft/lbs)	MPG Cty/Hwy	Years Avail
V-12	5.3	FI	420@7000	340@5000	6/10	87-87
V-12	5.2	FI	455@7000	369@5200	6/10	88-90

KEY: I=in-line engine; V=V engine; F=flat engine; FI=fuel injection; bbl=barrel carburetor; T=turbo; D=diesel; HP=horsepower; MPG=estimated average miles per gallon.

EVALUATIONS, TESTS, AND RANKINGS

1989: ''overheating. . .was a constant problem. . .side windows. . .still open less than 3 inches. . .racing-car spirit.'' **Source:** ''Lamborghini Countach: The legendary supercar benefits from money injection,'' *Road & Track,* October 1988, pp. 46-50.

1989: ''seats are significantly improved.'' **Source:** ''25th Anniversary: Lamborghini Countach,'' *Motor Trend,* December 1988, pp. 104-5.

1988: ''it's fast. . .racing experience. . .vision is awful other than straight ahead.'' **Source:** ''Top 10 Exoticars,'' *Motor Trend,* March 1988, pp. 35-9, 42-3, 46-9.

RECALLS

None to date.

OTHER INFORMATION SOURCES

1639 ● The Complete Lamborghini
Publications International, Ltd.
7373 N. Cicero Ave.
Lincolnwood, IL 60646   Ph:(312)767-3470

Published 1988. **Editor(s):** Pete Lyons. **Price:** $29.95.

1640 ● Fantasy Cars
Increase Video
6860 Canby Ave., Ste. 117-118   Ph:(818)342-2880
Reseda, CA 91335   Fax:(818)342-4029

A Lamborghini, Ferrari, and Porsche are taken for a test drive. **Release date:** 1989. **Producer:** Increase Video. **Price:** $29.95.

1641 ● Illustrated Lamborghini Buyer's Guide
Motorbooks International, Pubs. & Wholesalers, Inc.
729 Prospect Ave.
Osceola, WI 54020   Ph:(715)294-3345

Published 1983. **Editor(s):** De La Rive Box. **Price:** $16.95.

1642 ● Lamborghini
W. H. Smith Publishing, Inc.
112 Madison Ave.
New York, NY 10016   Ph:(212)532-6600

Published 1988. **Editor(s):** Thomas E. Bonsall. **Price:** $9.98.

1643 ● Lamborghini Club Magazine
Lamborghini Club of America
4 Sol Brae Way
Orinda, CA 94563   Ph:(415)254-2107

Magazine for Lamborghini owners that contains technical articles, want ads, and calendar of events. Quarterly. **Price:** Free to qualified subscribers; $50.00.

1644 ● Lamborghini Countach: Super Profile
Haynes Publications, Inc.
861 Lawrence Dr.
Newbury Park, CA 91320   Ph:(818)889-5400

Published 1987. **Editor(s):** Paul Clark. **Price:** $11.95.

1645 ● Supercar Showdown
Simitar Entertainment
3850 Annapolis Ln.   Ph:(612)559-6660
Plymouth, MN 55447   Fax:(612)559-0210

A Porsche 911 Turbo, Ferrari Testarossa, and Lamborghini Countach are compared. **Release date:** 1988. **Producer:** Simitar Entertainment. **Price:** $9.95.

ASSOCIATIONS

1646 ● Lamborghini Club America
170 Monte Vista Rd.
Orinda, CA 94563-1613
James Heady, Pres.   Ph:(415)254-2107

Founded: 1978. **Membership:** 1,500. Lamborghini automobile owners and enthusiasts. Provides assistance in locating parts and reputable service facilities. Disseminates information; sponsors social gatherings. **Former Name(s):** (1989) Nuova Lamborghini Club. **Convention/Meeting:** Bimonthly (with exhibits).

LAMBORGHINI DIABLO (1990-92)

Replacement for the Lamborghini Countach. Competes with the Jaguar XJ-S and the Ferrari Testarossa. Currently produced in Modena, Italy.

1991 Lamborghini Diablo

MAJOR FEATURES

● Diablo had as 1992 standard equipment: 5.7L twelve-cylinder engine, multipoint electronic fuel injection, five-speed manual transmission, four wheel independent four-wheel steering, compact disc player, A-arm front and rear suspension, vented disc brakes, spoilers, tilt wheel steering, power windows, power mirrors, automatic climate control, and various interior features.

PRICE HISTORY

The following new car prices reflect the approximate retail cost of the base model: **1991** - $239,000; **1992** - $239,000.

DIMENSIONS

Body Style	Years Avail	Wheel Base (in)	Lgth (in)	Ht (in)	Avg Wt (lbs)	Fuel Cap (gal)	Front Hdrm (in)	Front Legrm (in)
2d cpe	90-92	104.3	175.6	43.5	3,640	26.4	na	na

ENGINES

Type	Displace-ment (L)	Fuel Dly	HP @rpm	Torque @rpm (ft/lbs)	MPG Cty/Hwy	Years Avail
V-12	5.7	FI	485@7000	428@5200	9/14	90-92

KEY: I=in-line engine; V=V engine; F=flat engine; FI=fuel injection; bbl=barrel carburetor; T=turbo; D=diesel; HP=horsepower; MPG=estimated average miles per gallon.

EVALUATIONS, TESTS, AND RANKINGS

1991: "capable of speeds in excess of 200 mph—under ideal circumstances. . .is brutish and, thus physically demanding. . .cockpit becomes the world's fastest sauna." **Source:** "Lamborghini Diablo: Bullish when it needs to be, docile when it doesn't, it's devilishly fast," *Road & Track*, December 1990, p. 79.

1991: "surges forward with pure authority. . .ultimate supercar. . .leaves little room for the passengers." **Source:** "Lamborghini Diablo: The beasty boy from Sant'Agata still reigns over the wild bunch," *Car and Driver*, December 1990, pp. 74-8.

1991: "feels solid and perfectly natural. . .late braking was ill-advised. . .refinement isn't on the Diablo's list of strengths, and neither is slavish attention to detail design." **Source:** "Lamborgini Diablo: Satanic Worship," *Motor Trend*, December 1990, pp. 48-53.

1991: "a car not to be trifled with. . .terribly cramped in the cockpit. . .view ahead is excellent." **Source:** "Running of the Bull: On the road with Lamborghini's Diablo," *Automobile Magazine*, January 1991, pp. 90-6.

1990: "world's fastest production car." **Source:** "Diablo earns respect with hot engine, sleek lines," *The Detroit News*, March 5, 1990, pp. E1, E3.

1990: "reaches 62 mph in 4.1 seconds . . . cabin is roomier than the Countach's, or even a Testarossa's." **Source:** "Lamborghini Diablo," *Car and Driver*, March 1990, pp. 38-42.

1990: "It looks as if you should fly it, not drive it." **Source:** "The World's Fastest Car is Now . . . A Chrysler," *Business Week*, February 12, 1990, p. 44.

RECALLS

None to date.

OTHER INFORMATION SOURCES

1647 ● **The Complete Lamborghini**
Publications International, Ltd.
7373 N. Cicero Ave.
Lincolnwood, IL 60646   Ph:(312)767-3470

Published 1988. **Editor(s):** Pete Lyons. **Price:** $29.95.

1648 ● **Fantasy Cars**
Increase Video
6860 Canby Ave., Ste. 117-118   Ph:(818)342-2880
Reseda, CA 91335   Fax:(818)342-4029

A Lamborghini, Ferrari, and Porsche are taken for a test drive. **Release date:** 1989. **Producer:** Increase Video. **Price:** $29.95.

1649 ● **Illustrated Lamborghini Buyer's Guide**
Motorbooks International, Pubs. & Wholesalers, Inc.
729 Prospect Ave.
Osceola, WI 54020   Ph:(715)294-3345

Published 1983. **Editor(s):** De La Rive Box. **Price:** $16.95.

1650 ● **Lamborghini**
W. H. Smith Publishing, Inc.
112 Madison Ave.
New York, NY 10016   Ph:(212)532-6600

Published 1988. **Editor(s):** Thomas E. Bonsall. **Price:** $9.98.

1651 ● **Lamborghini Club Magazine**
Lamborghini Club of America
4 Sol Brae Way
Orinda, CA 94563   Ph:(415)254-2107

Magazine for Lamborghini owners that contains technical articles, want ads, and calendar of events. Quarterly. **Price:** Free to qualified subscribers; $50.00.

ASSOCIATIONS

1652 ● **Lamborghini Club America**
170 Monte Vista Rd.
Orinda, CA 94563-1613
James Heady, Pres.   Ph:(415)254-2107

Founded: 1978. **Membership:** 1,500. Lamborghini automobile owners and enthusiasts. Provides assistance in locating parts and reputable service facilities. Disseminates information; sponsors social gatherings. **Former Name(s):** (1989) Nuova Lamborghini Club. **Convention/Meeting:** Bimonthly (with exhibits).

LAMBORGHINI LM002 (1988-91)

An all-terrain sport utility vehicle that competed primarily against the Range Rover. The fuel tank of the LM002 was moved from under the rear seat and reduced in size in 1991. The Lamborghini LM002 ceased production after the 1991 model year.

MAJOR FEATURES

● LM002 had as 1991 standard equipment: 5.2L twelve-cylinder engine, four-wheel drive, vented front disc brakes, five-speed manual and cross country reduction transmission, front A-arm and rear control-arm suspension, and power assisted recirculating ball steering, and 325/65 VR17 tires.

PRICE HISTORY

The following new car prices reflect the approximate retail cost of the base model: **1989** - $126,000; **1990** - $145,500; **1991** - $158,000.

DIMENSIONS

Body Style	Years Avail	Wheel Base (in)	Lgth (in)	Ht (in)	Avg Wt (lbs)	Fuel Cap (gal)	Front Hdrm (in)	Front Legrm (in)
utl wgn	88-88	122.4	192.9	72.5	5,720	60.8	na	na
utl wgn	89-90	122.4	193.0	72.8	5,720	73.0	na	na
utl wgn	91-91	118.1	193.0	72.8	6,850	45.0	na	na

ENGINES

Type	Displace-ment (L)	Fuel Dly	HP @rpm	Torque @rpm (ft/lbs)	MPG Cty/Hwy	Years Avail
V-12	5.2	6x2 bbl	450@na	na	na	88-91

KEY: I=in-line engine; V=V engine; F=flat engine; FI=fuel injection; bbl=barrel carburetor; T=turbo; D=diesel; HP=horsepower; MPG=estimated average miles per gallon.

EVALUATIONS, TESTS, AND RANKINGS

1990: "for rough duty driving." **Source:** "Lamborghini LM002," *Car and Driver—Buyers Guide 1990*, 1989, pp. 172-3.

1989: "enough propulsion on hand to give the LM002 a top speed of 125 mph on pavement." **Source:** "Back-Country Brute," *Popular Mechanics*, September 1989, p. 42.

1989: "can cover great distances ... —and in luxury ... serious off-road vehicle." **Source:** "Anytime ... Anywhere," *Home Mechanix*, July 1989, p. 68.

RECALLS

None to date.

OTHER INFORMATION SOURCES

1653 ● The Complete Lamborghini
Publications International, Ltd.
7373 N. Cicero Ave.
Lincolnwood, IL 60646   Ph:(312)767-3470

Published 1988. **Editor(s):** Pete Lyons. **Price:** $29.95.

1654 ● Fantasy Cars
Increase Video
6860 Canby Ave., Ste. 117-118   Ph:(818)342-2880
Reseda, CA 91335   Fax:(818)342-4029

A Lamborghini, Ferrari, and Porsche are taken for a test drive. **Release date:** 1989. **Producer:** Increase Video. **Price:** $29.95.

1655 ● Illustrated Lamborghini Buyer's Guide
Motorbooks International, Pubs. & Wholesalers, Inc.
729 Prospect Ave.
Osceola, WI 54020   Ph:(715)294-3345

Published 1983. **Editor(s):** De La Rive Box. **Price:** $16.95.

1656 ● Lamborghini
W. H. Smith Publishing, Inc.
112 Madison Ave.
New York, NY 10016   Ph:(212)532-6600

Published 1988. **Editor(s):** Thomas E. Bonsall. **Price:** $9.98.

1657 ● Lamborghini Club Magazine
Lamborghini Club of America
4 Sol Brae Way
Orinda, CA 94563   Ph:(415)254-2107

Magazine for Lamborghini owners that contains technical articles, want ads, and calendar of events. Quarterly. **Price:** Free to qualified subscribers; $50.00.

ASSOCIATIONS

1658 ● Lamborghini Club America
170 Monte Vista Rd.
Orinda, CA 94563-1613
James Heady, Pres.   Ph:(415)254-2107

Founded: 1978. **Membership:** 1,500. Lamborghini automobile owners and enthusiasts. Provides assistance in locating parts and reputable service facilities. Disseminates information; sponsors social gatherings. **Former Name(s):** (1989) Nuova Lamborghini Club. **Convention/Meeting:** Bimonthly (with exhibits).

LEXUS ES 250 (1989-91)

Lexus is a division of Toyota Motor Sales, U.S.A. The ES 250 was derived from the same design as the Toyota Camry. Competed against the Ford Taurus SHO, Nissan Maxima SE, BMW 318i, Infiniti G20, and Mazda 929. It was produced in Tsutsumi, Japan through 1991 and was replaced by the Lexus ES 300.

1991 Lexus ES 250

MAJOR FEATURES

● ES 250 had as 1991 standard equipment: 2.5L six-cylinder engine, five-speed manual transmission, four-wheel anti-lock disc brakes, power steering, driver's side airbag, air conditioning, power windows and locks, alloy wheels, theft deterrent system, and various interior features.

PRICE HISTORY

The following new car prices reflect the approximate retail cost of the base model: **1990** - $21,050; **1991** - $21,500.

DIMENSIONS

Body Style	Years Avail	Wheel Base (in)	Lgth (in)	Ht (in)	Avg Wt (lbs)	Fuel Cap (gal)	Front Hdrm (in)	Front Legrm (in)
4d sdn	89-91	102.4	183.1	53.1	3,163	15.9	37.8	42.9

ENGINES

Type	Displace-ment (L)	Fuel Dly	HP @rpm	Torque @rpm (ft/lbs)	MPG Cty/Hwy	Years Avail
V-6	2.5	FI	156@5600	160@4400	19/25	89-91

KEY: I=in-line engine; V=V engine; F=flat engine; FI=fuel injection; bbl=barrel carburetor; T=turbo; D=diesel; HP=horsepower; MPG=estimated average miles per gallon.

EVALUATIONS, TESTS, AND RANKINGS

1991: "the archetypal entry-level luxury car ... extraordinarily solid and quiet ... ride is posh, not soft." **Source:** "Entry-Level Luxury," *Popular Science*, April 1991, pp. 76-80, 96.

1990: "elements of both sportiness and luxury. . .embodies a high degree of user-friendliness. . .merits a solid B grade." **Source:** "Lexus ES 250," *Motor Trend*, February 1990, pp. 90-3.

1990: "uncanny lack of engine and road noise. . .clear gauges, well-designed controls, and an attractive design. . .uncommonly smooth and silky." **Source:** "Lexus ES 250," *Car and Driver*, May 1990, pp. 91-6.

1990: "an extremely quiet car ... suspension is typically Japanese—supple and refined ... interior ... is conservative and tasteful." **Source:** "Fall Firsts," *Popular Mechanics*, September 1989, p. 53.

1990: "interior seems up to speed in terms of luxury appointments." **Source:** "Lexus ES 250 & LS 400: Doing the Europeans one better," *Motor Trend*, January 1989, pp. 69-71, 113.

RECALLS

1990: (8,301 vehicles): Cruise control actuator may not release, resulting in increased stopping distances. **Corrective action:** Replace cruise control actuator. *(NHTSA Campaign No. 89V211000.)*

LEXUS ES 300 (1992)

Introduced in 1992, the Lexus ES 300 is a front-engine, front-wheel-drive, five passenger luxury sport sedan that replaces the ES 250 as the entry-level Lexus. Currently assembled in Tsutumi, Japan, the ES 300 competes against Acura Vigor and Mitsubishi Diamante.

1992 Lexus ES 300

MAJOR FEATURES

● ES 300 has as 1992 standard equipment: 3.0-liter, 24-valve V6 engine, 5-speed manual transmission, 4-wheel power disc brakes with ABS, driver's side airbag, fully independent MacPherson strut suspension, power windows and door locks, power steering, tilt steering column, cruise control, automatic climate control, remote-entry system, and AM/FM cassette stereo system.

PRICE HISTORY

The following new car prices reflect the approximate retail cost of the base model: **1992** - $25,250.

DIMENSIONS

Body Style	Years Avail	Wheel Base (in)	Lgth (in)	Ht (in)	Avg Wt (lbs)	Fuel Cap (gal)	Front Hdrm (in)	Front Legrm (in)
4d nbk	92-92	103.1	187.8	53.9	3,362	18.5	37.8	43.5

ENGINES

Type	Displace-ment (L)	Fuel Dly	HP @rpm	Torque @rpm (ft/lbs)	MPG Cty/Hwy	Years Avail
V-6	3.0	FI	185@5200	195@4400	19/26	92-92

KEY: I=in-line engine; V=V engine; F=flat engine; FI=fuel injection; bbl=barrel carburetor; T=turbo; D=diesel; HP=horsepower; MPG=estimated average miles per gallon.

EVALUATIONS, TESTS, AND RANKINGS

1992: "steering is crisp and precise . . . nothing ruffles the suspension . . . pleasantly quiet car . . . extremely able machine in every way." **Source:** "New Cars: Lexus ES Update," *Popular Mechanics*, September 1991, pp. 96-98.

1992: "sleeker, sportier, less family-sedanish look . . . carefully balanced blend of sporty performance and spoiling comfort . . . on-center feel at highway speeds was vague and wishy-washy." **Source:** "Lexus ES 300: Out of the shadow and into the limelight," *Motor Trend*, September 1991, pp. 67-69.

1992: "Roomier, more powerful, more comfortable, quieter, and more handsome than the ES250 it replaces . . . sureness of purpose, a sophistication, and a quiet flair." **Source:** "Lexus ES300: Fleshing out the formidable Lexus line," *Automobile Magazine*, October 1991, pp. 112-114.

1992: "luxury abounds in the spacious cabin . . . has the makings of a great soldier . . . European-sedan feel." **Source:** "1992 Lexus ES 300," *Road & Track*, October 1991, p. 40.

1992: "design is smooth and flowing . . . a notably light and agile look . . . steering a bit light and overly fussy on-center." **Source:** "1992 Import Cars—Lexus ES300: The Camry clone gets the broom," *Car and Driver*, November 1991, p. 108.

1992: "ride tends toward feeling firm but comfortable . . . Handling is predictable and controlled . . . Exterior styling is softly rounded and swept back . . . interior styling flows in a pleasant, contemporary fashion." **Source:** "Lexus adds to its luxury lineup with the all-new ES 300 sedan," *The Flint Journal*, November 13, 1991, p. E2.

1992: "Operation of the clutch was unforgivably clumsy . . . moderately spirited, well-balanced, extremely quiet, comfortable and well-made . . . interior design was simple, with a sculpted elegance." **Source:** "'Baby Lexus' a pleasant addition to family," *The Detroit News*, September 4, 1991, pp. 1D, 2D.

1992: "rear-seat passengers may have to do a tuck if their front-seat hosts are long-legged . . . engine feels quick and responsive . . . Impressively quiet, even at speed." **Source:** "Lexus ES 300: Like father, like son," *Road & Track*, January 1992, pp. 68-71.

1992: "artful concept, flawless execution, and silken behavior . . . Handling is flat and completely predictable . . . ride is solid and quiet." **Source:** "Lexus ES300: Make that three in a row for the folks from Nagoya," *Automobile Magazine*, January 1992, p. 51.

1992: "established new standards for quality and performance in the near-luxury segment . . . superb road car, with impeccable manners, invigorating performance and lavish appointments . . . impressive acceleration with respectable fuel economy." **Source:** "New Lexus ES300 Set Standards," *Detroit Free Press*, September 19, 1991, p. 1E.

RECALLS

None to date.

LEXUS LS 400 (1990-92)

Lexus is a division of Toyota Motor Sales, U.S.A. Voted Top 10 New Car Buys, Import by *Motor Trend* in 1989. Voted one of the Ten Best Cars by *Car and Driver* in 1990. Voted third place in a *Car and Driver* Best Sedan comparison test in 1990. Ranked as the top nameplate in J.D. Power and Associates's Initial Quality Study Customer Satisfaction Index in 1990. Named the Import Car of the Year by the Motoring Press Association in 1990. Currently produced in Tahara, Japan.

1991 Lexus LS 400

MAJOR FEATURES

● Lexus LS 400 has as 1992 standard equipment: 4.0L eight-cylinder engine, four-speed automatic transmission, four-wheel anti-lock disc brakes, power steering, driver's side air bag, automatic climate control, cruise control, alloy wheels, front and rear anti-roll bar, and various interior features.

PRICE HISTORY

The following new car prices reflect the approximate retail cost of the base model: **1990** - $36,000; **1991** - $39,000; **1992** - $42,200.

DIMENSIONS

Body Style	Years Avail	Wheel Base (in)	Lgth (in)	Ht (in)	Avg Wt (lbs)	Fuel Cap (gal)	Front Hdrm (in)	Front Legrm (in)
4d sdn	90-92	110.8	196.7	55.3	3,759	22.5	38.6	43.8

ENGINES

Type	Displacement (L)	Fuel Dly	HP @rpm	Torque @rpm (ft/lbs)	MPG Cty/Hwy	Years Avail
V-8	4.0	FI	250@5600	260@4400	18/23	90-92

KEY: I=in-line engine; V=V engine; F=flat engine; FI=fuel injection; bbl=barrel carburetor; T=turbo; D=diesel; HP=horsepower; MPG=estimated average miles per gallon.

EVALUATIONS, TESTS, AND RANKINGS

1991: "smoothness, speed, overall silkiness, outstanding value." **Source:** "Finding the Best Sedan in the World," *Car and Driver*, November 1990, pp. 113-28.

1991: "a paragon of detail. . .instrument panel is so artfully laid out and easy to use." **Source:** "Lexus LS 400," *Automobile Magazine*, January 1991, p. 59.

1991: "interior of this vehicle imparts a true feeling of luxury . . . a first-class piece of work . . . combines luxury, style, and distinguished engineering all in one delightful package." **Source:** "Japan's Winning Entry in the Luxury Race," *Design News*, October 1, 1990, pp. 230-231.

1990: "road-holding is excellent. . .all is quiet, smooth, and competent. . .roomy, comfortable, and uncluttered." **Source:** "Lexus delivers low-cost luxury," *The Detroit News*, August 9, 1989, pp. 1F, 2F.

1990: "crisp steering, but could use more aggressive tires. . .feels taut and tidy." **Source:** "Motor Trend's 1990 Import car of the Year," *Motor Trend*, March 1990, pp. 44-63.

1990: "an exquisite automobile . . . quiet almost to the point of sensory deprivation . . . a vaguely robotlike quality." **Source:**

"Driving in the Lap of Luxury," *U.S. News & World Report*, January 8, 1990, pp. 59-62.

1990: "unexpected smoothness . . . slips through the air with less resistance than any other luxury car on the market . . . more refined, with a voice of silken serenity." **Source:** "What's in a Nameplate," *Esquire*, January 1990, p. 18.

1990: "the first car audio systems that sounded as well balanced while sitting in the rear as they did up front." **Source:** "Super Sonics Car," *Audio*, October 1989, pp. 123-124.

1989: "technological tour de force . . . positively reeks of breeding and careful development." **Source:** "Lexus ES250 and LS400," *Car and Driver*, January 1989, pp. 138-140.

RECALLS

1990: (8,577 vehicles): Lamp housing of center high mounted stop lamp may become distorted after prolonged illumination and high temperatures. **Corrective action:** Replace lamp housing with one of higher temperature resistance. *(NHTSA Campaign No. 89V212000.)*

1990: (8,301 vehicles): Cruise control actuator may not release, resulting in increased stopping distances. **Corrective action:** Replace cruise control actuator. *(NHTSA Campaign No. 89V211000.)*

LEXUS SC 300/400 (1992)

The SC 300, a luxury sport coupe went on sale in the fall of 1991 and the rear-drive SC 400 2-door coupe went on sale in June of 1991. The SC 400 was designed by Toyota's U.S. styling center, Calty Design Research, Inc., in Newport Beach, Calif. Both vehicles are assembled in Tsutsumi, Japan, and compete with the more expensive German luxury coupes. The Lexus SC 400 was named the Import Car of the Year by *Motor Trend* in 1992. It was also selected to the *Automobile Magazine* All-Stars list and the *Car and Driver* Ten Best Cars nominees list in 1992.

1992 Lexus SC 400

MAJOR FEATURES

● SC 300 1992 standard equipment: 3.0-liter I-6 engine, 5-speed manual transmission, 4-wheel ventilated disc brakes with ABS, driver's-side airbag, double wishbone suspension, alloy wheels, multi-adjustable front seats, power tilt/telescopic steering, automatic climate control, rear defogger, cruise control, AM/FM/cassette sound system, and remote entry.

● SC 400 adds as 1992 standard equipment: 4.0-liter V-8 engine, 4-speed automatic transmission, and leather upholstery.

PRICE HISTORY

The following new car prices reflect the approximate retail cost of the base model: **1992** - $31,100; **1992** - $37,500.

DIMENSIONS

Body Style	Years Avail	Wheel Base (in)	Lgth (in)	Ht (in)	Avg Wt (lbs)	Fuel Cap (gal)	Front Hdrm (in)	Front Legrm (in)
2d cpe	92-92	105.9	191.1	52.4	3,494	20.6	38.3	44.1
2d cpe	92-92	105.9	191.1	52.6	3,575	20.6	38.3	44.1

ENGINES

Type	Displacement (L)	Fuel Dly	HP @rpm	Torque @rpm (ft/lbs)	MPG Cty/Hwy	Years Avail
I-6	3.0	FI	225@6,000	210@4,800	18/22	92-92
V-8	4.0	FI	250@5,600	260@4,400	18/22	92-92

KEY: I=in-line engine; V=V engine; F=flat engine; FI=fuel injection; bbl=barrel carburetor; T=turbo; D=diesel; HP=horsepower; MPG=estimated average miles per gallon.

EVALUATIONS, TESTS, AND RANKINGS

1992: "a car built for drivers ... styling ... exhibits enough beauty of line to supply most of the world's auto industry ... as handsome as they come." **Source:** "Ten Best Cars: And a glimpse into the future, too," *Car and Driver*, January 1992, pp. 35-43.

1992: "has nearly every amenity imaginable ... Rear passenger room is good for a coupe ... a new blend of style, comfort, balance, quality, smoothness and power." **Source:** "Lexus luxury coupe may set new standard," *The Detroit News*, June 19, 1991, pp. 1D-2D.

1992: "glossy paintwork, lovely leather, and fine trim ... suspension proves generally firm yet smooth and absorbent ... hard braking brings more nose-dive." **Source:** "Lexus SC400: Okay, kids, can you say "ballistic," *Car and Driver*, October 1991, pp. 109-112.

1992: "swift, assuringly agile, svelte of style, solidly built and a pleasure to drive ... well-balanced, nicely tailored, quality package ... Interior styling is clean, flowing and functional." **Source:** "Lexus puts one swell sport coupe on the road," *The Flint Journal*, September 25, 1991, p, D3.

1992: "boasts a rounded, aerodynamic look ... futuristic wraparound instrument panel." **Source:** "The road to comfort comes paved with high-tech gadgets," *The Detroit News*, October 6, 1991, p. 5D.

1992: "a car to mortgage your sweet mother's future for ... aerodynamic and fast and quiet and comfortable ... Legroom is sorely limited, as is trunk space." **Source:** "From Lexus, a Coupe to Make Your Own," *New York Times*, July 14, 1991.

1992: "sportiness, luxury and reliability ... opulent leather-trimmed interior ... a car that seems to have it all." **Source:** "Lexus SC 400: Elegance—with a sporting edge," *Road & Track*, January 1992, p. 90.

1992: "has the respect of engineers everywhere ... Noise, vibration, and harshness levels are ... among the best in the industry ... equipped with every imaginable convenience." **Source:** "Lexus SC400: God still lives in the details," *Automobile Magazine*, January 1992, p. 52.

RECALLS

None to date.

LINCOLN CONTINENTAL (1987-92)

A mid-size sedan built to rival the Cadillac Seville. A number of modifications, such as front wheel drive, lighter curb weight, increased length, and increased interior space and trunk size, were implemented in 1988. In 1989, it was the first U.S. car with airbags standard for both the driver and front-seat passenger. Produced in Wixom, Michigan (plant parts data: domestic parts - 82%, imported parts - 18%, *Federal Trade Zone Board*, 1989).

1991 Lincoln Continental

MAJOR FEATURES

● Continental Executive Series has as 1992 standard equipment: 4-speed automatic transmission, 4-wheel-disc anti-lock brakes, driver-side and passenger-side air-bag supplemental restraint systems, cruise control, speed-sensitive, variable-assist power steering, computer-controlled air suspension, automatic climate control with sunload sensor, tilt steering wheel column, rear defogger, and tinted glass.

● Continental Signature Series adds as 1992 standard equipment: keyless entry system, power decklid pulldown, automatic headlamp control convenience group, power passenger seat, and alloy wheels.

PRICE HISTORY

The following new car prices reflect the approximate retail cost of the base model: **1987** - $25,484; **1988** - $26,078; **1989** - $28,430; **1990** - $29,422; **1991** - $30,335; **1992** - $32,263.

DIMENSIONS

Body Style	Years Avail	Wheel Base (in)	Lgth (in)	Ht (in)	Avg Wt (lbs)	Fuel Cap (gal)	Front Hdrm (in)	Front Legrm (in)
4d sdn	87-87	108.5	200.7	55.6	3,799	20.3	38.5	42.0
4d sdn	88-92	109.0	205.1	55.6	3,628	18.4	38.7	41.7

ENGINES

Type	Displacement (L)	Fuel Dly	HP @rpm	Torque @rpm (ft/lbs)	MPG Cty/Hwy	Years Avail
V-6	3.8	FI	140@3800	215@2200	18/25	88-90
V-6	3.8	FI	155@4000	220@2200	na	91-91
V-6	3.8	FI	160@4400	225@3000	17/25	92-92
V-8	5.0	FI	150@3200	270@2000	17/27	87-87

KEY: I=in-line engine; V=V engine; F=flat engine; FI=fuel injection; bbl=barrel carburetor; T=turbo; D=diesel; HP=horsepower; MPG=estimated average miles per gallon.

EVALUATIONS, TESTS, AND RANKINGS

1991: "good room, but lack of storage is a surprising problem." **Source:** "A 50th Birthday for Edsel Ford's Continental," *New York Times*, October 14, 1990, p.31.

1990: "a very smooth ride and remarkably good, though not sporty, handling." **Source:** "Driving in the Lap of Luxury," *U.S. News & World Report*, January 8, 1990, pp. 59, 62.

1990: "slips over the highway as if it were riding on a cloud . . . remarkably good, though not sporty, handling . . . on twisting back roads it rocked and rolled too much." **Source:** "Driving in the lap of luxury," *U.S. News & World Report*, January 8, 1990, pp. 59-62.

1989: "A pillowy ride with surprisingly capable handling. . .sensibly sized, luxuriously fitted, and well-engineered." **Source:** "Ten Best Cars," *Car and Driver*, January 1989, pp. 30-35.

1988: "User-friendly design prevails throughout and. . .puts some vaunted European marques to shame. . .disappointed by the near total lack of interior storage bins and boxes." **Source:** "1988 Lincoln Continental," *Motor Trend*, October 1987, pp. 62-63, 66.

1988: "first and foremost a car with a plush ride. . .roomier, more contemporary looking and better handling than their last one, with no sacrifice." **Source:** "Lincoln Continental: A trimmer craft with tighter rigging," *Road & Track*, April 1988, pp. 94-96.

1988: "cushy ride hard when it's necessary to control body roll, and the car remains amazingly level and stable in turns and evasive maneuvers." **Source:** "New 'down-sized' Continental a big winner," *The Detroit News*, April 20, 1988, pp. F1-F2.

RECALLS

1989: (750 vehicles): Left side, rear seatbelt retractor assembly may be improperly secured and could pull free of its mounting location. Occupant, though still restrained by the lap portion of the belt, would not have upper body protection. **Corrective action:** Reinstall the retractor attachment bolt. *(NHTSA Campaign No. 89V048000.)*

1988: (8,848 vehicles): Two torsion springs attached to rear suspension control arms may fracture and rub against a rear tire, resulting in sudden loss of tire inflation pressure with potential for an accident. **Corrective action:** Install torsion spring seats to restrict the springs from contacting the tire if they should fracture. *(NHTSA Campaign No. 88V030000.)*

1988: (4,500 vehicles): Driver and right front passenger inboard seat belts may be improperly anchored due to loose nuts that could back off. Belt anchor could disengage the stud; an unattached belt assembly would not withstand an impact load. **Corrective action:** Inboard seat belt anchorages will be corrected to prevent loosening. *(NHTSA Campaign No. 88V027000.)*

1988: (22,893 vehicles): Transmission shift cables may not meet Ford's pull out load specifications for swivel tube portion of cable, which could allow swivel tube to separate from shift cable assembly. Operator would not be able to shift from one of the drive gears into park position. **Corrective action:** Replace shift cable. *(NHTSA Campaign No. 88V101000.)*

1988: (26,000 vehicles): Nylon shielded wiring harness, located in engine compartment, is susceptible to heat damage and melting of nylon material in 100 degree plus weather. Melted nylon shield could drip onto exhaust manifold and result in underhood fire. **Corrective action:** Wrap wiring harness with heat resistant fiberglass tape. *(NHTSA Campaign No. 88V114000.)*

1988: (28,000 vehicles): Electrical circuit that controls current to brake pump motor relay, heater and air conditioning blower motor, turn signals, and electronic message center may overheat due to inability of ignition circuit wiring connections to dissipate heat generated by electrical loads. Brake pump motor will not operate, substantially reducing braking capability; brake warning light will appear. **Corrective action:** Replace ignition switch and modify switch wiring. *(NHTSA Campaign No. 88V118000.)*

1987: (3,600,000 passenger cars and light trucks equipped with fuel injection. Recall includes several Ford, Mercury, and Lincoln models; includes models made before 1987): Spring lock fuel line coupling may not be properly engaged. Coupling could disengage due to fuel pressure, vibration, and engine movements; this would cause loss of fuel which, in presence of an ignition source, creates a fire risk. **Corrective action:** Install retainer clips over the couplings to prevent coupling separation and fuel leakage. *(NHTSA Campaign No. 87V139000.)*

REPAIR MANUALS

1659 ● **Chilton's Ford-Lincoln-Mercury Full-Size, 1968-1988**
Chilton Co.
Chilton Way
Radnor, PA 19089   Ph:(215)964-4000

Published 1989. **Price:** $15.95.

1660 ● **Chilton's Ford Thunderbird, Mercury Cougar, Lincoln Continental-Mark VII, 1980-1987**
Chilton Co.
Chilton Way
Radnor, PA 19089   Ph:(215)964-4000

Published 1988. **Price:** $15.95.

1661 ● **Ford, Lincoln, Mercury Car Repair and Tune-Up Guide: 1972-1987**
Clymer Publications
P.O. Box 1209
Overland Park, KS 66212   Ph:(913)541-6694

Published 1987. **Price:** 14.95.

OTHER INFORMATION SOURCES

1662 ● **Cars of Lincoln-Mercury**
Crestline Publishing Co.
1251 N. Jefferson Ave.
Sarasota, FL 34237   Ph:(813)955-8080

Published 1987. **Editor(s):** George H. Dammann and James K. Wagner. **Price:** $34.95.

1663 ● **Continental Bulletin**
Lincoln and Continental Owners Club (LCOC)
712 1st Ave.
Seaside, OR 97138   Ph:(503)738-5247

Bimonthly.

1664 ● **Continental Comments**
Lincoln and Continental Owners Club, Texas Gulf Coast Region
c/o Ron Stein
2480 Times Blvd., No. 203-A
Houston, TX 77005   Ph:(713)521-3450

Newsletter.

1665 ● Continental Comments
Lincoln and Continental Owners Club (LCOC)
712 First Ave.
Seaside, OR 97138   Ph:(503)738-5247

Includes annual meet issue. Quarterly.

1666 ● FOMOCO Owners Club—Newsletter
FOMOCO Owners Club
3804 Conifer Dr.
Loveland, CO 80538   Ph:(303)669-8767

Monthly.

1667 ● Ford-Lincoln-Mercury Club of Florida—Newsletter
Ford-Lincoln-Mercury Club of Florida
P.O. Box 13514
Tampa, FL 33681   Ph:(813)839-0241

Monthly.

1668 ● Lincoln and Continental Owners Club—Authenticity Manual
Lincoln and Continental Owners Club (LCOC)
712 1st Ave.
Seaside, OR 97138   Ph:(503)738-5247

1669 ● Lincoln and Continental Owners Club—Directory
Lincoln and Continental Owners Club (LCOC)
712 1st Ave.
Seaside, OR 97138   Ph:(503)738-5247

Annual.

1670 ● Lincoln and Continental Owners Club, Southern Region—Bulletin
Lincoln and Continental Owners Club, Southern Region
535 Kent Rd.
Roswell, GA 30075   Ph:(404)642-8988

Periodic.

1671 ● Lincoln and Continental Owners Club, Southern Region—Comments
Lincoln and Continental Owners Club, Southern Region
535 Kent Rd.
Roswell, GA 30075   Ph:(404)642-8988

Periodic.

1672 ● Your Ford: Including Lincoln-Mercury: Essential Service Information for Owners and Mechanics
Consumer Reports Books
51 E. 42nd St., Ste. 800
New York, NY 10017   Ph:(212)682-9280

Based on technical service bulletins issued to Ford and Lincoln-Mercury dealers from 1985 through 1987. Published 1988. **Editor(s):** Mort J. Schultz. **Price:** $8.00.

ASSOCIATIONS

1673 ● FOMOCO Owners Club
3633 Akron Ct.
Loveland, CO 80538
Barry Abels, Exec. Ofc.   Ph:(303)669-8767

Founded: 1985. **Membership:** 250. Individuals dedicated to the exhibition, preservation, and restoration of Edsel, Ford, Lincoln, and Mercury automobiles. Conducts charitable activities; sponsors educational programs. Bestows awards. **Convention/Meeting:** Annual (with exhibits) - 1991 September, Lakewood, CO.

1674 ● Lincoln and Continental Owners Club
712 First Ave.
Seaside, OR 97138
Russ Lende, Membership Sec.   Ph:(503)738-5247

Founded: 1953. **Membership:** 4,000. Persons interested in preserving and restoring Lincolns and Continentals. Provides information on location and exchange of replacement parts and restoration service. Bestows awards. **Former Name(s):** (1988) Lincoln Continental Owners Club. **Convention/Meeting:** Annual national meet held in each region.

LINCOLN MARK VII (1987-92)

Produced in Wixom, Michigan along with the Lincoln Continental and Town Car models (plant parts data: domestic parts - 82%, imported parts - 18%, *Federal Trade Zone Board*, 1989). Chosen by *The Complete Car Cost Guide* in 1990 as having one of the lowest maintenance costs for a luxury car. For 1992, both series of the Mark VII receive upgraded interior trim and exterior improvements, including a new style grille.

1991 Lincoln Mark VII

MAJOR FEATURES

● Mark VII Bill Blass Series has as 1992 standard equipment: 4-speed automatic transmission, anti-lock 4-wheel disc brakes, power steering, driver's side airbag, electronic air suspension with automatic level control, illuminated and keyless entry system, automatic climate control, leather upholstery, cruise control, rear defogger, tinted glass, tilt steering wheel column, and several interior accessories.

● Mark VII LSC (Luxury Sports Coupe) adds as 1992 standard equipment: articulated sports seats, analog instruments including tachometer and coolant temperature gauge, and fog lights.

PRICE HISTORY

The following new car prices reflect the approximate retail cost of the base model: **1987** - $25,016; **1988** - $26,380; **1989** - $27,569; **1990** - $29,246; **1991** - $30,362; **1992** - $32,032.

DIMENSIONS

Body Style	Years Avail	Wheel Base (in)	Lgth (in)	Ht (in)	Avg Wt (lbs)	Fuel Cap (gal)	Front Hdrm (in)	Front Legrm (in)
2d cpe	87-90	108.5	202.8	54.2	3,722	22.1	37.8	42.0
2d cpe	91-92	108.5	202.8	54.2	3,782	21.0	37.8	42.0

ENGINES

Type	Displace-ment (L)	Fuel Dly	HP @rpm	Torque @rpm (ft/lbs)	MPG Cty/Hwy	Years Avail
V-8	5.0	FI	200@4000	285@3000	na	87-87
V-8	5.0	FI	150@3200	270@2000	17/27	87-87
V-8	5.0	FI	225@4000	300@3200	17/24	88-88
V-8	5.0	FI	225@4200	300@3200	17/24	89-92

KEY: I=in-line engine; V=V engine; F=flat engine; FI=fuel injection; bbl=barrel carburetor; T=turbo; D=diesel; HP=horsepower; MPG=estimated average miles per gallon.

EVALUATIONS, TESTS, AND RANKINGS

1991: "gives a ride one would expect from a sporty, low-slung, two-seater . . . Highway driving provided a smooth, powerful ride . . . General handling of the LSC was a joy." **Source:** "Mark VII LSC combines luxury with sportiness," *Design News,* March 25, 1991, p. 46.

1987: "reasonable in size, if a bit on the heavy side. Its styling artfully combines old-fashioned elegance with modern aerodynamic lines . . . driveline produced annoying vibrations." **Source:** "Lincoln Mark VII LSC: Dearborn keeps polishing its crown jewel," *Car and Driver,* July 1987, pp. 43-48.

RECALLS

1987-88: (3,600,000 passenger cars and light trucks equipped with fuel injection. Recall includes several Ford, Mercury, and Lincoln models; includes models made before 1987): Spring lock fuel line coupling may not be properly engaged. Coupling could disengage due to fuel pressure, vibration, and engine movements; this would cause loss of fuel which, in presence of an ignition source, creates a fire risk. **Corrective action:** Install retainer clips over the couplings to prevent coupling separation and fuel leakage. (*NHTSA Campaign No. 87V139000.*)

SAFETY AND REPAIRS

1988: "Moaning Metallic Brakes," *Road & Track,* February 1990, p. 141. **Note:** '88 Continental with moaning brake noise.

REPAIR MANUALS

1675 ● Chilton's Ford-Lincoln-Mercury Full-Size, 1968-1988
Chilton Co.
Chilton Way
Radnor, PA 19089   Ph:(215)964-4000

Published 1989. **Price:** $15.95.

1676 ● Chilton's Ford Thunderbird, Mercury Cougar, Lincoln Continental-Mark VII, 1980-1987
Chilton Co.
Chilton Way
Radnor, PA 19089   Ph:(215)964-4000

Published 1988. **Price:** $15.95.

1677 ● Ford, Lincoln, Mercury Car Repair and Tune-Up Guide: 1972-1987
Clymer Publications
P.O. Box 1209
Overland Park, KS 66212   Ph:(913)541-6694

Published 1987. **Price:** 14.95.

OTHER INFORMATION SOURCES

1678 ● Cars of Lincoln-Mercury
Crestline Publishing Co.
1251 N. Jefferson Ave.
Sarasota, FL 34237   Ph:(813)955-8080

Published 1987. **Editor(s):** George H. Dammann and James K. Wagner. **Price:** $34.95.

1679 ● FOMOCO Owners Club—Newsletter
FOMOCO Owners Club
3804 Conifer Dr.
Loveland, CO 80538   Ph:(303)669-8767

Monthly.

1680 ● Ford-Lincoln-Mercury Club of Florida—Newsletter
Ford-Lincoln-Mercury Club of Florida
P.O. Box 13514
Tampa, FL 33681   Ph:(813)839-0241

Monthly.

1681 ● Lincoln and Continental Owners Club—Authenticity Manual
Lincoln and Continental Owners Club (LCOC)
712 1st Ave.
Seaside, OR 97138   Ph:(503)738-5247

1682 ● Lincoln and Continental Owners Club—Directory
Lincoln and Continental Owners Club (LCOC)
712 1st Ave.
Seaside, OR 97138   Ph:(503)738-5247

Annual.

1683 ● Lincoln and Continental Owners Club, Southern Region—Bulletin
Lincoln and Continental Owners Club, Southern Region
535 Kent Rd.
Roswell, GA 30075   Ph:(404)642-8988

Periodic.

1684 ● Lincoln and Continental Owners Club, Southern Region—Comments
Lincoln and Continental Owners Club, Southern Region
535 Kent Rd.
Roswell, GA 30075   Ph:(404)642-8988

Periodic.

1685 ● Your Ford: Including Lincoln-Mercury: Essential Service Information for Owners and Mechanics
Consumer Reports Books
51 E. 42nd St., Ste. 800
New York, NY 10017   Ph:(212)682-9280

Based on technical service bulletins issued to Ford and Lincoln-Mercury dealers from 1985 through 1987. Published 1988. **Editor(s):** Mort J. Schultz. **Price:** $8.00.

ASSOCIATIONS

1686 ● FOMOCO Owners Club
3633 Akron Ct.
Loveland, CO 80538
Barry Abels, Exec. Ofc.   Ph:(303)669-8767

Founded: 1985. **Membership:** 250. Individuals dedicated to the exhibition, preservation, and restoration of Edsel, Ford, Lincoln, and Mercury automobiles. Conducts charitable activities; sponsors educational programs. Bestows awards. **Convention/Meeting:** Annual (with exhibits) - 1991 September, Lakewood, CO.

1687 • Lincoln and Continental Owners Club
712 First Ave.
Seaside, OR 97138
Russ Lende, Membership Sec.   Ph:(503)738-5247

Founded: 1953. **Membership:** 4,000. Persons interested in preserving and restoring Lincolns and Continentals. Provides information on location and exchange of replacement parts and restoration service. Bestows awards. **Former Name(s):** (1988) Lincoln Continental Owners Club. **Convention/Meeting:** Annual national meet held in each region.

LINCOLN TOWN CAR (1987-92)

Produced in Wixom, Michigan (plant parts data: domestic parts - 82%, imported parts - 18%, *Federal Trade Zone Board,* 1989). Chosen by *The Complete Car Cost Guide* as having one of the lowest insurance costs (Town Car) and the lowest maintenance costs (Town Car Series) for a luxury car. Also selected by *Motor Trend* Magazine as "1990 Car of the Year."

1991 Lincoln Town Car

MAJOR FEATURES

● Town Car Executive Series has as 1992 standard equipment: electronically assisted automatic 4-speed overdrive transmission; 4-wheel disc brakes; front independent/rear four-bar link suspension; speed-sensitive, variable assist power steering; driver's-side and passenger-side airbag; tilt steering column; analog instrumentation; and power driver's seat.

● Town Car Signature Series adds as 1992 standard equipment: electronic instruments, Autolamp system, and upgraded interior.

● Town Car Cartier Designer Series adds as 1992 standard equipment: cloth and leather seat with position memory and power lumbar support, power recliners, and Ford JBL audio system.

PRICE HISTORY

The following new car prices reflect the approximate retail cost of the base model: **1987** - $23,126; **1988** - $24,373; **1989** - $25,562; **1990** - $27,986; **1991** - $29,581; **1992** - $31,211.

DIMENSIONS

Body Style	Years Avail	Wheel Base (in)	Lgth (in)	Ht (in)	Avg Wt (lbs)	Fuel Cap (gal)	Front Hdrm (in)	Front Legrm (in)
4d sdn	87-89	117.3	219.0	55.9	4,051	18.0	39.0	43.5
4d sdn	90-90	117.4	220.2	56.7	4,025	18.0	39.0	42.5
4d sdn	91-92	117.4	218.9	56.9	4,024	20.0	39.0	42.5

ENGINES

Type	Displacement (L)	Fuel Dly	HP @rpm	Torque @rpm (ft/lbs)	MPG Cty/Hwy	Years Avail
V-8	5.0	FI	150@3200	270@2000	17/24	87-90
V-8	5.0	FI	160@3400	280@2200	na	87-90
V-8	4.6	FI	190@4200	260@3600	17/23	91-92
V-8	4.6	FI	210@4600	270@3400	na	91-92

KEY: I=in-line engine; V=V engine; F=flat engine; FI=fuel injection; bbl=barrel carburetor; T=turbo; D=diesel; HP=horsepower; MPG=estimated average miles per gallon.

EVALUATIONS, TESTS, AND RANKINGS

1991: "front suspension geometry has been revised to improve tracking and minimize body roll. The rear air springs still contribute to a willowy ride. . .perhaps the best of its breed." **Source:** "'91 Town Car offers better ride," *Detroit Free Press,* November 8, 1990, p. 1E.

1991: "the new 4.6-liter engine may be the best V-8 America ever produced." **Source:** "1991 Lincoln Town Car: The most modern American V-8 lives here," *Car and Driver,* October 1990, pp. 103-104.

1990: "seats offer excellent back and thigh cushioning, though lateral support, as you'd expect, is a bit lacking . . . rest of the interior fits with the Lincoln definition of luxury . . . engine and transmission don't reach the level set by the rest of the car." **Source:** "Lincoln Town Car," *Motor Trend,* October 1989, pp. 85-87.

1990: "new rounded exterior design is much more efficient than the previous model . . . Interior passenger space is increased . . . numerous safety improvements." **Source:** "Town Car tradition carries on," *The Detroit News,* September 13, 1989, pp. 61-62.

1990: "Inside it seems only slightly smaller than a rural county . . . ample exterior dimensions can make parking a chore . . . brisk acceleration in town and smooth bursts of power for highway passing." **Source:** "Luxury In the American Sedan," *New Choices for the Best Years,* March 1990, pp. 82-83.

1990: "roomy, comfortable, quiet . . . touted as the quietest automobile in the world . . . proves that bigger is sometimes better." **Source:** "Talk of the Town Car: A redesigned Lincoln brings new urbanity to luxury driving," *House and Garden,* September 1989, p. 232.

1990: "Seating is cavernous and comfortable, performance and handling are adequate . . . quiet as the reading room at the local library." **Source:** "Land Yachts," *Popular Science,* January 1990, pp. 64-68.

1988: "seats. . .were terrible leather marshmallows with no discernable means of support . . . worst criticism was reserved for the Lincoln's vague steering. . .uncomfortable table to drive at highway speeds." **Source:** "Battle of the Behemoths," *Popular Mechanics,* September 1987, pp. 53-55, 98.

1988: "big, heavy monster still with the basic design it had in the late 1970s, practically drove itself . . . fill-up can be costly . . . somewhat mushy suspension." **Source:** "The Lincoln Town Car is long on luxury," *The Detroit News,* March 30, 1988, pp. 1F-2F.

1987: ''no fuel miser, but for a luxury car its efficiency is at least respectable . . . most imported luxo-cruisers can easily put the Town Car's performance to shame. In its favor, the Lincoln does provide impeccable drivability.'' **Source:** ''Lincoln Town Car: One dinosaur that's a long way from extinction,'' *Car and Driver*, April 1987, pp. 99, 101-102, 104, 107.

RECALLS

1991: (26,000 vehicles): Distorted fuel lines in engine compartment may contact steering column universal joint and cause damage to fuel line. Fuel leakage could result in a fire. **Corrective action:** Reposition fuel line to prevent contact with universal joint; if fuel lines are already damaged, repair or replace fuel lines. (NHTSA Campaign No. 91V008000.)

1991: (72,000 passenger cars): The secondary hood latch may not engage when the hood is closed. If the vehicle is in motion when the latch releases, the hood could fly up. **Corrective action:** Install a new hood latching assembly. (NHTSA Campaign No. 91V147000.)

1987-89: (223 cars; includes models made before 1987; includes other Cadillac models): Safety belts not installed for rear facing seats. (NHTSA Campaign No. 90V050000.)

1987-89: (223 cars; includes models made before 1987; includes other Cadillac models): Window film does not meet light transmission requirements. (NHTSA Campaign No. 90V049000.)

1987-88: (3,600,000 passenger cars and light trucks equipped with fuel injection. Recall includes several Ford, Mercury, and Lincoln models; includes models made before 1987): Spring lock fuel line coupling may not be properly engaged. Coupling could disengage due to fuel pressure, vibration, and engine movements; this would cause loss of fuel which, in presence of an ignition source, creates a fire risk. **Corrective action:** Install retainer clips over the couplings to prevent coupling separation and fuel leakage. (NHTSA Campaign No. 87V139000.)

1987: (11,119 passenger cars equipped with 5.0 liter fuel injected engines. Recall includes Ford Crown Victoria, Mercury Grand Marquis, and Lincoln Town Car): Fuel rails may be bent so that No. 5 injector cups are out of design position. Could cause a fuel leak, which in presence of an ignition source could result in an engine fire. **Corrective action:** Replace fuel rail assemblies as necessary. (NHTSA Campaign No. 87V131000.)

1987: (1,200 vehicles): Idler arm brackets may fracture at the threaded shafts due to improper heat treatment. Driver would experience a clunking noise on turns and a loose feeling in the steering wheel; steering control would be maintained. **Corrective action:** Replace idler arm assembly. (NHTSA Campaign No. 87V018000.)

1987: (29,600 passenger vehicles with 5.0 liter engines. Recall includes the Ford LTD Crown Victoria, Mercury Grand Marquis, and Lincoln Town Car): Steering centerlinks may break at a bend location. Steering control would be diminished, with reduced control of left wheel only and considerable steering wheel free play. **Corrective action:** Replace steering centerlink. (NHTSA Campaign No. 87V012000.)

SAFETY AND REPAIRS

1991: ''Ford Recalls Vans, Town Car,'' *Automotive News*, December 23, 1991, p. 2. **Note:** Defective hood latch assembly.

REPAIR MANUALS

1688 ● **Chilton's Ford-Lincoln-Mercury Full-Size, 1968-1988**
Chilton Co.
Chilton Way
Radnor, PA 19089   Ph:(215)964-4000

Published 1989. **Price:** $15.95.

1689 ● **Ford, Lincoln, Mercury Car Repair and Tune-Up Guide: 1972-1987**
Clymer Publications
P.O. Box 1209
Overland Park, KS 66212   Ph:(913)541-6694

Published 1987. **Price:** 14.95.

OTHER INFORMATION SOURCES

1690 ● **Cars of Lincoln-Mercury**
Crestline Publishing Co.
1251 N. Jefferson Ave.
Sarasota, FL 34237   Ph:(813)955-8080

Published 1987. **Editor(s):** George H. Dammann and James K. Wagner. **Price:** $34.95.

1691 ● **FOMOCO Owners Club—Newsletter**
FOMOCO Owners Club
3804 Conifer Dr.
Loveland, CO 80538   Ph:(303)669-8767

Monthly.

1692 ● **Ford-Lincoln-Mercury Club of Florida—Newsletter**
Ford-Lincoln-Mercury Club of Florida
P.O. Box 13514
Tampa, FL 33681   Ph:(813)839-0241

Monthly.

1693 ● **Lincoln and Continental Owners Club—Authenticity Manual**
Lincoln and Continental Owners Club (LCOC)
712 1st Ave.
Seaside, OR 97138   Ph:(503)738-5247

1694 ● **Lincoln and Continental Owners Club—Directory**
Lincoln and Continental Owners Club (LCOC)
712 1st Ave.
Seaside, OR 97138   Ph:(503)738-5247

Annual.

1695 ● **Lincoln and Continental Owners Club, Southern Region—Bulletin**
Lincoln and Continental Owners Club, Southern Region
535 Kent Rd.
Roswell, GA 30075   Ph:(404)642-8988

Periodic.

1696 ● **Lincoln and Continental Owners Club, Southern Region—Comments**
Lincoln and Continental Owners Club, Southern Region
535 Kent Rd.
Roswell, GA 30075   Ph:(404)642-8988

Periodic.

1697 ● Your Ford: Including Lincoln-Mercury: Essential Service Information for Owners and Mechanics
Consumer Reports Books
51 E. 42nd St., Ste. 800
New York, NY 10017   Ph:(212)682-9280

Based on technical service bulletins issued to Ford and Lincoln-Mercury dealers from 1985 through 1987. Published 1988. **Editor(s):** Mort J. Schultz. **Price:** $8.00.

ASSOCIATIONS

1698 ● FOMOCO Owners Club
3633 Akron Ct.
Loveland, CO 80538
Barry Abels, Exec. Ofc.   Ph:(303)669-8767

Founded: 1985. **Membership:** 250. Individuals dedicated to the exhibition, preservation, and restoration of Edsel, Ford, Lincoln, and Mercury automobiles. Conducts charitable activities; sponsors educational programs. Bestows awards. **Convention/Meeting:** Annual (with exhibits) - 1991 September, Lakewood, CO.

1699 ● Lincoln and Continental Owners Club
712 First Ave.
Seaside, OR 97138
Russ Lende, Membership Sec.   Ph:(503)738-5247

Founded: 1953. **Membership:** 4,000. Persons interested in preserving and restoring Lincolns and Continentals. Provides information on location and exchange of replacement parts and restoration service. Bestows awards. **Former Name(s):** (1988) Lincoln Continental Owners Club. **Convention/Meeting:** Annual national meet held in each region.

LOTUS ELAN (1991, 1993)

Production of 1991 Elan 2-seater convertible for U.S. markets, also known as the the Elan SE, began in November 1990. Produced in England, only 800 were imported to the U.S. during 1991 calendar year. Lotus Cars USA will not market 1992 models in the U.S. However, 1993 models will be brought to market during the second quarter of 1992; vehicle information was unavailable at the time of publication.

1991 Lotus Elan

MAJOR FEATURES

● Elan had as 1991 standard equipment: Isuzu-Lotus 1.6L four-cylinder turbocharged engine, five-speed manual transmission, front vented disc brakes, rear disc brakes, driver's side supplemental inflatable restraint system, alloy wheels, air conditioning; power mirrors, doors, and windows; and various interior features.

PRICE HISTORY

The following new car prices reflect the approximate retail cost of the base model: **1991** - $39,040.

DIMENSIONS

Body Style	Years Avail	Wheel Base (in)	Lgth (in)	Ht (in)	Avg Wt (lbs)	Fuel Cap (gal)	Front Hdrm (in)	Front Legrm (in)
2d conv	91-91	88.6	152.2	48.4	2,340	10.2	37.0	41.0

ENGINES

Type	Displacement (L)	Fuel Dly	HP @rpm	Torque @rpm (ft/lbs)	MPG Cty/Hwy	Years Avail
I-4T	1.6	na	162@6600	148@4200	na	91-91

KEY: I=in-line engine; V=V engine; F=flat engine; FI=fuel injection; bbl=barrel carburetor; T=turbo; D=diesel; HP=horsepower; MPG=estimated average miles per gallon.

EVALUATIONS, TESTS, AND RANKINGS

1991: "large persons can get in and out of it with ease. . .civilized, eminently enjoyable roadster that is a joy to occupy and a joy to drive . . .comfortably spacious cabin." **Source:** "Lotus Elan: An honored name blossoms anew. At a price," *Car and Driver*, March 1991, pp. 76-80.

1991: "the first Lotus that comes close to being a daily driver . . . lacks a certain character and urgency . . . a surprisingly good long-distance cruiser." **Source:** "Mrs. Peel's Wheels: Diana Rigg takes a spin in the new Lotus Elan, a high-tech version of her *Avengers* sportster," *Vanity Fair*, March 1991, pp. 192, 194.

1991: "can't quite cut it against the best-handling cars available in America . . . steering is numb to the touch—an unforgivable sin." **Source:** "The World's Best-Handling Cars," *Motor Trend*, May 1991, pp. 38-48, 50.

RECALLS

None to date.

REPAIR MANUALS

1700 ● Lotus Twin-Cam Engine
Motorbooks International
729 Prospect Ave.
Osceola, WI 54020   Ph:(715)294-3345

Published 1988. **Editor(s):** Miles Wilkins. **Price:** $39.95.

OTHER INFORMATION SOURCES

1701 ● Lotus Elan: The Complete Story
Motorbooks Intl.
729 Prospect Ave.
Osceola, WI 54020   Ph:(715)294-3345

Published 1991. **Editor(s):** Mike Taylor. **Price:** $29.95.

1702 ● Lotus—Membership Roster
Lotus
P.O. Box L
College Park, MD 20740

Annual.

1703 ● Lotus Remarque
Lotus Ltd.
Box L
College Park, MD 20741

Magazine for Lotus car owners; includes book reviews, calendar of events, and technical articles. Monthly. **Editor(s):** M.S. Winston. **Price:** $20.00.

1704 ● Lotus: The Elan, Cortina, and Europa
TAB Books, Inc.
Box 40
Blue Ridge Summit, PA 17214   Ph:(717)794-2191

Lists of Lotus sports car clubs and sources for parts and service. Published October 1985. **Editor(s):** Richard Newton and Raymond Psulkowski. **Price:** $19.95.

1705 ● Lotus West—Directory
Lotus West (LW)
P.O. Box 75972
Los Angeles, CA 90005   Ph:(213)492-1556

Annual.

1706 ● Stress Cracks
Lotus West (LW)
P.O. Box 75972
Los Angeles, CA 90005   Ph:(213)492-1556

Newsletter; includes technical and social event information. Monthly. **Price:** Included in membership dues.

1707 ● Super Profile: Lotus Elan
Haynes Publications, Inc.
861 Lawrence Dr.
Newbury Park, CA 91320   Ph:(818)889-5400

Editor(s): Graham Armour. **Price:** $11.95.

ASSOCIATIONS

1708 ● Lotus
P.O. Box L
College Park, MD 20741
C. A. Gregorie, Sec.

Founded: 1973. **Membership:** 1,750. Owners and enthusiasts of Lotus automobiles (ownership not required for membership). Objective is to provide and exchange information on Lotus cars. **Convention/Meeting:** Annual meet and conference (with exhibits).

1709 ● Lotus West
P.O. Box 75972
Los Angeles, CA 90005
Steve Griffin, Pres.   Ph:(213)492-1556

Founded: 1968. **Membership:** 200. Owners and enthusiasts of the Lotus automobile. Collects and disseminates information on the Lotus; sponsors racing and slaloming events and social activities. **Convention/Meeting:** Annual West Coast meet; also holds monthly meeting - always first Thursday of the month. **Additional Numbers:** Toll-free: 800-825-4159.

LOTUS ESPRIT (1987-91, 1993)

A sports coupe that competed against the Porsche 911 Turbo, Mercedes-Benz 560SL, Ford GT-40, Lamborghini Countach, and Ford Mustang. Voted among the Top 10 Exoticars by *Motor Trend* in 1988. Produced in England, only 800 were

imported to the U.S. in 1991. Lotus Cars USA will not market 1992 models in the U.S., but 1993 models will be brought to market during the second quarter of 1992; new vehicle information unavailable at time of publication.

1991 Lotus Esprit Turbo SE

MAJOR FEATURES

● Esprit had as 1991 standard equipment: 2.2L four-cylinder engine, five-speed manual transmission, independent front and rear suspension, front anti-roll bar, power rear and front ventilated disc brakes, and various interior features.

● Esprit Turbo had as 1991 standard equipment: turbocharged water-cooled engine, power windows, air conditioning, rear defroster, various interior appointments, and tinted glass.

● Esprit Turbo SE added the following standard equipment for 1991: four-wheel anti-lock disc brakes, and various exterior accessories.

PRICE HISTORY

The following new car prices reflect the approximate retail cost of the base model: **1987** - $56,991; **1988** - $62,500; **1989** - $67,500; **1990** - $81,950; **1991** - $86,750.

DIMENSIONS

Body Style	Years Avail	Wheel Base (in)	Lgth (in)	Ht (in)	Avg Wt (lbs)	Fuel Cap (gal)	Front Hdrm (in)	Front Legrm (in)
2d cpe	87-87	96.0	169.0	44.5	2,700	20.1	37.0	31.0
2d cpe	88-88	97.8	170.2	45.7	2,946	20.8	37.0	31.0
2d cpe	89-91	96.0	170.5	45.3	2,820	18.5	37.0	31.0

ENGINES

Type	Displace- ment (L)	Fuel Dly	HP @rpm	Torque @rpm (ft/lbs)	MPG Cty/Hwy	Years Avail
I-4T	2.2	FI	215@6250	194@5000	na	87-88
I-4T	2.2	FI	228@6500	218@4000	17/27	89-90
I-4T	2.2	FI	264@6500	261@3900	na	90-91

KEY: I=in-line engine; V=V engine; F=flat engine; FI=fuel injection; bbl=barrel carburetor; T=turbo; D=diesel; HP=horsepower; MPG=estimated average miles per gallon.

EVALUATIONS, TESTS, AND RANKINGS

1990: "shows its Grand Prix heritage in handling . . . interior is plush . . . built for the long run." **Source:** "Top Ten Exoticars," *Motor Trend*, March 1988, pp. 35-9, 42-3, 46-9.

1990: "you can't see much of anything through the Esprit's Lilliputian backlight . . . Upon start-up, the engine shakes like a wet springer spaniel . . . an addictive speed buzz." **Source:** "Lotus Esprit Turbo SE: Fast, but will it last," *Car and Driver*, December 1989, pp. 86-87, 89, 92.

1989: ''high-performance competence ... seats uniformly uncomfortable ... reduced rear and sideview sightlines.'' **Source:** ''Two Turbos, No Waiting,'' *Motor Trend*, December 1988, pp. 38-43, 46.

1989: ''You sit in most cars, but you wear the Lotus Esprit ... superexotic machinery ... will outperform darn near anything else on the road.'' **Source:** ''2 for the road,'' *Regardies*, September 1989, pp. 169-170, 172-180, 182.

1988: ''instruments could be made a little larger ... powerplant is responsive ... an exotic by any standards, offering high performance.'' **Source:** ''Lotus Esprit Turbo,'' *Road & Track*, January 1988, pp. 81, 84.

1988: ''seriously fast car ... footwells are ... cramped ... steering, slow and heavy in traffic, becomes lighter and more precise at speed.'' **Source:** ''Lotus Esprit Turbo,'' *Car and Driver*, June 1988, pp 40-6.

RECALLS

None to date.

REPAIR MANUALS

1710 ● **Lotus Twin-Cam Engine**
Motorbooks International
729 Prospect Ave.
Osceola, WI 54020   Ph:(715)294-3345

Published 1988. **Editor(s):** Miles Wilkins. **Price:** $39.95.

OTHER INFORMATION SOURCES

1711 ● **Lotus—Membership Roster**
Lotus
P.O. Box L
College Park, MD 20740

Annual.

1712 ● **Lotus Remarque**
Lotus Ltd.
Box L
College Park, MD 20741

Magazine for Lotus car owners; includes book reviews, calendar of events, and technical articles. Monthly. **Editor(s):** M.S. Winston. **Price:** $20.00.

1713 ● **Lotus West—Directory**
Lotus West (LW)
P.O. Box 75972
Los Angeles, CA 90005   Ph:(213)492-1556

Annual.

1714 ● **Stress Cracks**
Lotus West (LW)
P.O. Box 75972
Los Angeles, CA 90005   Ph:(213)492-1556

Newsletter; includes technical and social event information. Monthly. **Price:** Included in membership dues.

ASSOCIATIONS

1715 ● **Lotus**
P.O. Box L
College Park, MD 20741
C. A. Gregorie, Sec.

Founded: 1973. **Membership:** 1,750. Owners and enthusiasts

of Lotus automobiles (ownership not required for membership). Objective is to provide and exchange information on Lotus cars. **Convention/Meeting:** Annual meet and conference (with exhibits).

1716 ● **Lotus West**
P.O. Box 75972
Los Angeles, CA 90005
Steve Griffin, Pres.   Ph:(213)492-1556

Founded: 1968. **Membership:** 200. Owners and enthusiasts of the Lotus automobile. Collects and disseminates information on the Lotus; sponsors racing and slaloming events and social activities. **Convention/Meeting:** Annual West Coast meet; also holds monthly meeting - always first Thursday of the month. **Additional Numbers:** Toll-free: 800-825-4159.

MASERATI 222 (1990)

A two-door luxury sports coupe that competed against the Lamborghini Diablo, Ferrari Mondial t, Cadillac Allante, Nissan 300ZX, Toyota Supra, BMW 5-series, Porsche 944, Jaguar XJ-S, and Aston Martin Virage. Produced in Modena, Italy through 1990.

MAJOR FEATURES

● Maserati 222 had as 1990 standard equipment: all-around independent suspension, five-speed manual transmission, power-assisted front ventilated and rear disc brakes, automatic climate control, power windows, and various luxury features.

● Maserati 222E added as 1990 standard equipment: 2.8-liter V6 Turbo 222hp engine.

DIMENSIONS

Body Style	Years Avail	Wheel Base (in)	Lgth (in)	Ht (in)	Avg Wt (lbs)	Fuel Cap (gal)	Front Hdrm (in)	Front Legrm (in)
2d cpe	90-90	98.1	162.0	51.0	2,590	na	na	na

ENGINES

Type	Displacement (L)	Fuel Dly	HP @rpm	Torque @rpm (ft/lbs)	MPG Cty/Hwy	Years Avail
V-6	2.8	FI	222@na	na	na	90-90

KEY: I=in-line engine; V=V engine; F=flat engine; FI=fuel injection; bbl=barrel carburetor; T=turbo; D=diesel; HP=horsepower; MPG=estimated average miles per gallon.

RECALLS

None to date.

OTHER INFORMATION SOURCES

1717 ● **Maserati Market Letter**
Maserati Club International, MIE, Inc.
P.O. Box 772   Ph:(206)455-4449
Mercer Island, WA 98040   Fax:(206)646-5458

Provides members with information and technical assistance regarding Maserati automobiles, including all models from 1926 to the present. Helps members locate new and used parts through the Exchange's extensive inventory. Recurring features include technical articles, concourse exhibitions, and rallies conducted by the Exchange and of accessories available. Every six weeks. **Editor(s):** Francis G. Mandarano. **Price:** Available to members only.

1718 ● Maserati Owners Club of North America Quarterly
Maserati Owners Club of America
Box 6554
Orange, CA 92667

Provides news of interest on Maserati sports car. **Editor(s):** Ken Olson. **Price:** $30.00/year, U.S.; $40.00 elsewhere.

1719 ● Viale Ciro Menotti
Maserati Information Exchange (MIE)
Box 772   Ph:(206)455-4449
Mercer Island, WA 98040   Fax:(206)646-5458

Magazine that contains information of interest to Maserati enthusiasts. Quarterly. **Editor(s):** Francis Mandarano, Publisher. **Price:** $50.00 per year; $15.00 per issue.

ASSOCIATIONS

1720 ● Maserati Information Exchange
Box 772
Mercer Island, WA 98040
Francis G. Mandarano, Exec. Officer   Ph:(206)455-4449

Founded: 1976. **Membership:** 3,000. Owners and enthusiasts of Maserati sports automobiles, manufactured in Italy from 1926 to the present. Provides members with information and technical assistance and conducts meets. Maintains extensive inventory of new and used parts. Conducts four-day events with technical sessions, concourse exhibitions, and rallies. Presents awards; sells accessories. Maintains a service and restoration facility. **Convention/Meeting:** Annual meet - usually August.

1721 ● Maserati Owners Club of North America
Box 6554
Orange, CA 92667
Bill LeMasters, Pres.

Founded: 1978. **Membership:** 350. Owners and enthusiasts of Maseratis. Provides forum for social contact between members. Disseminates technical information. **Convention/Meeting:** Social and technical meetings (with exhibits), every 6 weeks.

MASERATI 228 (1989-90)

Produced in Modena, Italy through 1990.

MAJOR FEATURES

● Maserati 228 had as 1990 standard equipment: 2.8L six-cylinder engine, fuel injection, all-around independent suspension, five-speed manual transmission, power-assisted four-wheel disc brakes, power-assisted rack-and-pinion steering, automatic climate control, power windows, and various interior features.

PRICE HISTORY

The following new car prices reflect the approximate retail cost of the base model: **1989** - $55,835; **1990** - $57,540.

DIMENSIONS

Body Style	Years Avail	Wheel Base (in)	Lgth (in)	Ht (in)	Avg Wt (lbs)	Fuel Cap (gal)	Front Hdrm (in)	Front Legrm (in)
2d cpe	89-90	102.4	175.6	52.4	3,100	17.4	na	na

ENGINES

Type	Displace-ment (L)	Fuel Dly	HP @rpm	Torque @rpm (ft/lbs)	MPG Cty/Hwy	Years Avail
V-6T	2.8	FI	225@5600	246@3500	14/19	89-90

KEY: I=in-line engine; V=V engine; F=flat engine; FI=fuel injection; bbl=barrel carburetor; T=turbo; D=diesel; HP=horsepower; MPG=estimated average miles per gallon.

EVALUATIONS, TESTS, AND RANKINGS

1990: "a personality. . .power is readily available. . .turbo "lag" is almost nonexistent. . .gearbox also was a bit balky." **Source:** "Powerful personality," *The Detroit News*, January 25, 1990, pp 1F-2F.

1989: "performed flawlessly." **Source:** "Maserati has done a lot of growing up lately," *Detroit Free Press*, Monday Febuary 6, 1989, p. 10C.

RECALLS

None to date.

OTHER INFORMATION SOURCES

1722 ● Illustrated Maserati Buyer's Guide
Motorbooks International
729 Prospect Ave
Osceola, WI 54020   Ph:(715)294-3345

Published 1989. **Editor(s):** Richard Crump. **Price:** $16.95.

1723 ● Maserati Market Letter
Maserati Club International, MIE, Inc.
P.O. Box 772   Ph:(206)455-4449
Mercer Island, WA 98040   Fax:(206)646-5458

Provides members with information and technical assistance regarding Maserati automobiles, including all models from 1926 to the present. Helps members locate new and used parts through the Exchange's extensive inventory. Recurring features include technical articles, concourse exhibitions, and rallies conducted by the Exchange and of accessories available. Every six weeks. **Editor(s):** Francis G. Mandarano. **Price:** Available to members only.

1724 ● Maserati Owners Club of North America Quarterly
Maserati Owners Club of America
Box 6554
Orange, CA 92667

Provides news of interest on Maserati sports car. **Editor(s):** Ken Olson. **Price:** $30.00/year, U.S.; $40.00 elsewhere.

1725 ● Viale Ciro Menotti
Maserati Information Exchange (MIE)
Box 772   Ph:(206)455-4449
Mercer Island, WA 98040   Fax:(206)646-5458

Magazine that contains information of interest to Maserati enthusiasts. Quarterly. **Editor(s):** Francis Mandarano, Publisher. **Price:** $50.00 per year; $15.00 per issue.

ASSOCIATIONS

1726 ● Maserati Information Exchange
Box 772
Mercer Island, WA 98040
Francis G. Mandarano, Exec. Officer   Ph:(206)455-4449

Founded: 1976. **Membership:** 3,000. Owners and enthusiasts of Maserati sports automobiles, manufactured in Italy from 1926 to the present. Provides members with information and technical assistance and conducts meets. Maintains extensive inventory of new and used parts. Conducts four-day events with technical sessions, concourse exhibitions, and rallies. Presents awards; sells accessories. Maintains a service and restoration facility. **Convention/Meeting:** Annual meet - usually August.

1727 ● Maserati Owners Club of North America
Box 6554
Orange, CA 92667
Bill LeMasters, Pres.

Founded: 1978. **Membership:** 350. Owners and enthusiasts of Maseratis. Provides forum for social contact between members. Disseminates technical information. **Convention/Meeting:** Social and technical meetings (with exhibits), every 6 weeks.

MASERATI 425 (1987-88)

Known as the Maserati Biturbo 425 before 1987. Produced in Modena, Italy through 1988.

MAJOR FEATURES

● Maserati 425 had as 1988 standard equipment: 2.5L six-cylinder turbocharged engine, five-speed manual transmission, electronic fuel injection, all-independent suspension, four-wheel disc brakes, and upgraded interior.

PRICE HISTORY

The following new car prices reflect the approximate retail cost of the base model: **1988 - $34,975.**

DIMENSIONS

Body Style	Years Avail	Wheel Base (in)	Lgth (in)	Ht (in)	Avg Wt (lbs)	Fuel Cap (gal)	Front Hdrm (in)	Front Legrm (in)
4d sdn	87-88	102.4	173.2	53.5	2,780	20.0	na	na

ENGINES

Type	Displace-ment (L)	Fuel Dly	HP @rpm	Torque @rpm (ft/lbs)	MPG Cty/Hwy	Years Avail
V-6T	2.5	FI	188@5500	208@3000	13/15	87-88

KEY: I=in-line engine; V=V engine; F=flat engine; FI=fuel injection; bbl=barrel carburetor; T=turbo; D=diesel; HP=horsepower; MPG=estimated average miles per gallon.

EVALUATIONS, TESTS, AND RANKINGS

1988: "remarkably plush accomodations." **Source:** "Maserati Biturbo/425/Spyder," *Car and Driver—Buyers guide 1988,* 1988, p. 117.

RECALLS

None to date.

OTHER INFORMATION SOURCES

1728 ● Illustrated Maserati Buyer's Guide
Motorbooks International
729 Prospect Ave
Osceola, WI 54020   Ph:(715)294-3345

Published 1989. **Editor(s):** Richard Crump. **Price:** $16.95.

1729 ● Maserati Market Letter
Maserati Club International, MIE, Inc.
P.O. Box 772   Ph:(206)455-4449
Mercer Island, WA 98040   Fax:(206)646-5458

Provides members with information and technical assistance regarding Maserati automobiles, including all models from 1926 to the present. Helps members locate new and used parts through the Exchange's extensive inventory. Recurring features include technical articles, concourse exhibitions, and rallies conducted by the Exchange and of accessories available. Every six weeks. **Editor(s):** Francis G. Mandarano. **Price:** Available to members only.

1730 ● Maserati Owners Club of North America Quarterly
Maserati Owners Club of America
Box 6554
Orange, CA 92667

Provides news of interest on Maserati sports car. **Editor(s):** Ken Olson. **Price:** $30.00/year, U.S.; $40.00 elsewhere.

1731 ● Viale Ciro Menotti
Maserati Information Exchange (MIE)
Box 772   Ph:(206)455-4449
Mercer Island, WA 98040   Fax:(206)646-5458

Magazine that contains information of interest to Maserati enthusiasts. Quarterly. **Editor(s):** Francis Mandarano, Publisher. **Price:** $50.00 per year; $15.00 per issue.

ASSOCIATIONS

1732 ● Maserati Information Exchange
Box 772
Mercer Island, WA 98040
Francis G. Mandarano, Exec. Officer   Ph:(206)455-4449

Founded: 1976. **Membership:** 3,000. Owners and enthusiasts of Maserati sports automobiles, manufactured in Italy from 1926 to the present. Provides members with information and technical assistance and conducts meets. Maintains extensive inventory of new and used parts. Conducts four-day events with technical sessions, concourse exhibitions, and rallies. Presents awards; sells accessories. Maintains a service and restoration facility. **Convention/Meeting:** Annual meet - usually August.

1733 ● Maserati Owners Club of North America
Box 6554
Orange, CA 92667
Bill LeMasters, Pres.

Founded: 1978. **Membership:** 350. Owners and enthusiasts of Maseratis. Provides forum for social contact between members. Disseminates technical information. **Convention/Meeting:** Social and technical meetings (with exhibits), every 6 weeks.

MASERATI 430 (1988-92)

Currently produced in Modena, Italy, the Maserati 430 was known as Biturbo 430 before 1989.

MAJOR FEATURES

● 430 has as 1992 standard equipment: 2.8L, six-cylinder turbocharged engine, five-speed manual transmission, power windows and mirrors, power-assisted rack-and-pinion steering, all-around independent suspension, dual exhaust, four-wheel disc brakes, tilt steering wheel, automatic seat belts, tinted glass, rear-window defogger, air conditioning, automatic climate control, and various interior features.

PRICE HISTORY

The following new car prices reflect the approximate retail cost of the base model: **1989** - $44,320; **1990** - $46,025; **1991** - $48,000.

DIMENSIONS

Body Style	Years Avail	Wheel Base (in)	Lgth (in)	Ht (in)	Avg Wt (lbs)	Fuel Cap (gal)	Front Hdrm (in)	Front Legrm (in)
4d sdn	88-92	102.4	173.2	53.5	3,035	20.0	na	na

ENGINES

Type	Displacement (L)	Fuel Dly	HP @rpm	Torque @rpm (ft/lbs)	MPG Cty/Hwy	Years Avail
V-6T	2.8	FI	225@5600	246@3500	15/18	88-92

KEY: I=in-line engine; V=V engine; F=flat engine; FI=fuel injection; bbl=barrel carburetor; T=turbo; D=diesel; HP=horsepower; MPG=estimated average miles per gallon.

EVALUATIONS, TESTS, AND RANKINGS

1989: "handsomely crafted leather seats. . .vibrates a good deal at idle. . .comfortable, handsome." **Source:** "Maserati 430," *Road & Track,* February 1989, pp. 84-86.

1989: "sports fine coachwork ... This is a *fast* car ... performance that's flashier than many low-slung exotics." **Source:** "Imports: Hot Rides in Rear-Wheel Drive," *Popular Mechanics,* April 1989, p. 30.

1988: "lavish interior. . .smooth engine. . .inspiring performance. . .faster, tighter, and more refined than its predecessor." **Source:** "Maserati 430: Sharpening the trident," *Car and Driver,* May 1988, p. 35.

RECALLS

None to date.

OTHER INFORMATION SOURCES

1734 ● Illustrated Maserati Buyer's Guide
Motorbooks International
729 Prospect Ave
Osceola, WI 54020   Ph:(715)294-3345

Published 1989. **Editor(s):** Richard Crump. **Price:** $16.95.

1735 ● Maserati Market Letter
Maserati Club International, MIE, Inc.
P.O. Box 772   Ph:(206)455-4449
Mercer Island, WA 98040   Fax:(206)646-5458

Provides members with information and technical assistance regarding Maserati automobiles, including all models from 1926 to the present. Helps members locate new and used parts through the Exchange's extensive inventory. Recurring features include technical articles, concourse exhibitions, and rallies conducted by the Exchange and of accessories available. Every six weeks. **Editor(s):** Francis G. Mandarano. **Price:** Available to members only.

1736 ● Maserati Owners Club of North America Quarterly
Maserati Owners Club of America
Box 6554
Orange, CA 92667

Provides news of interest on Maserati sports car. **Editor(s):** Ken Olson. **Price:** $30.00/year, U.S.; $40.00 elsewhere.

1737 ● Viale Ciro Menotti
Maserati Information Exchange (MIE)
Box 772   Ph:(206)455-4449
Mercer Island, WA 98040   Fax:(206)646-5458

Magazine that contains information of interest to Maserati enthusiasts. Quarterly. **Editor(s):** Francis Mandarano, Publisher. **Price:** $50.00 per year; $15.00 per issue.

ASSOCIATIONS

1738 ● Maserati Information Exchange
Box 772
Mercer Island, WA 98040
Francis G. Mandarano, Exec. Officer   Ph:(206)455-4449

Founded: 1976. **Membership:** 3,000. Owners and enthusiasts of Maserati sports automobiles, manufactured in Italy from 1926 to the present. Provides members with information and technical assistance and conducts meets. Maintains extensive inventory of new and used parts. Conducts four-day events with technical sessions, concourse exhibitions, and rallies. Presents awards; sells accessories. Maintains a service and restoration facility. **Convention/Meeting:** Annual meet - usually August.

1739 ● Maserati Owners Club of North America
Box 6554
Orange, CA 92667
Bill LeMasters, Pres.

Founded: 1978. **Membership:** 350. Owners and enthusiasts of Maseratis. Provides forum for social contact between members. Disseminates technical information. **Convention/Meeting:** Social and technical meetings (with exhibits), every 6 weeks.

MASERATI KARIF (1989-90)

A high performance two-door coupe produced in Modena, Italy through 1990.

MAJOR FEATURES

● Maserati Karif had as 1990 standard equipment: 2.8L six-cylinder turbocharged engine, five-speed manual transmission, all-around independent suspension, power-assisted rack-and-pinion steering, fuel injection, front anti-roll bar, power front ventilated and rear disc brake, and various interior features.

DIMENSIONS

Body Style	Years Avail	Wheel Base (in)	Lgth (in)	Ht (in)	Avg Wt (lbs)	Fuel Cap (gal)	Front Hdrm (in)	Front Legrm (in)
2d cpe	89-90	94.5	159.2	51.6	2,820	21.7	na	na

ENGINES

Type	Displacement (L)	Fuel Dly	HP @rpm	Torque @rpm (ft/lbs)	MPG Cty/Hwy	Years Avail
V-6	2.8	FI	285@6000	318@4000	na	89-90

KEY: I=in-line engine; V=V engine; F=flat engine; FI=fuel injection; bbl=barrel carburetor; T=turbo; D=diesel; HP=horsepower; MPG=estimated average miles per gallon.

EVALUATIONS, TESTS, AND RANKINGS

1990: "supple leather. . .plenty of head and shoulder room. . .wonderfully opulent driving position." **Source:** "Maserati Karif," *Road & Track,* August 1988, pp. 92, 94-5.

RECALLS

None to date.

OTHER INFORMATION SOURCES

1740 ● Illustrated Maserati Buyer's Guide
Motorbooks International
729 Prospect Ave
Osceola, WI 54020   Ph:(715)294-3345

Published 1989. **Editor(s):** Richard Crump. **Price:** $16.95.

1741 ● Maserati Market Letter
Maserati Club International, MIE, Inc.
P.O. Box 772   Ph:(206)455-4449
Mercer Island, WA 98040   Fax:(206)646-5458

Provides members with information and technical assistance
regarding Maserati automobiles, including all models from 1926
to the present. Helps members locate new and used parts
through the Exchange's extensive inventory. Recurring
features include technical articles, concourse exhibitions, and
rallies conducted by the Exchange and of accessories available.
Every six weeks. **Editor(s):** Francis G. Mandarano. **Price:**
Available to members only.

1742 ● Maserati Owners Club of North America Quarterly
Maserati Owners Club of America
Box 6554
Orange, CA 92667

Provides news of interest on Maserati sports car. **Editor(s):** Ken
Olson. **Price:** $30.00/year, U.S.; $40.00 elsewhere.

1743 ● Viale Ciro Menotti
Maserati Information Exchange (MIE)
Box 772   Ph:(206)455-4449
Mercer Island, WA 98040   Fax:(206)646-5458

Magazine that contains information of interest to Maserati
enthusiasts. Quarterly. **Editor(s):** Francis Mandarano,
Publisher. **Price:** $50.00 per year; $15.00 per issue.

ASSOCIATIONS

1744 ● Maserati Information Exchange
Box 772
Mercer Island, WA 98040
Francis G. Mandarano, Exec. Officer   Ph:(206)455-4449

Founded: 1976. **Membership:** 3,000. Owners and enthusiasts
of Maserati sports automobiles, manufactured in Italy from
1926 to the present. Provides members with information and
technical assistance and conducts meets. Maintains extensive
inventory of new and used parts. Conducts four-day events
with technical sessions, concourse exhibitions, and rallies.
Presents awards; sells accessories. Maintains a service and
restoration facility. **Convention/Meeting:** Annual meet -
usually August.

1745 ● Maserati Owners Club of North America
Box 6554
Orange, CA 92667
Bill LeMasters, Pres.

Founded: 1978. **Membership:** 350. Owners and enthusiasts of
Maseratis. Provides forum for social contact between members.
Disseminates technical information. **Convention/Meeting:**
Social and technical meetings (with exhibits), every 6 weeks.

MASERATI SHAMAL (1991-92)

Currently produced in Modena, Italy, the Maserati Shamal is a
two-seater coupe designed in a joint effort between the
Maserati styling department and Marcello Gandini, the Italian
designer who created both the Countach and Diablo for
Lamborghini. It is capable of reaching speeds in excess of 165
mph.

1992 Maserati Shamal

MAJOR FEATURES

● Shamal has as 1992 standard equipment: V-8 engine, six-
speed manual transmission, electronically adjustable
suspension system, anti-roll bar, power-assisted rack-and-
pinion steering, power front disc brakes, rear handbrake,
tinted glass, power windows, and various interior and exterior
features.

PRICE HISTORY

The following new car prices reflect the approximate retail cost
of the base model: **1991** - $85,000; **1992** - $85,000.

DIMENSIONS

Body Style	Years Avail	Wheel Base (in)	Lgth (in)	Ht (in)	Avg Wt (lbs)	Fuel Cap (gal)	Front Hdrm (in)	Front Legrm (in)
2d cpe	91-92	94.5	161.5	50.0	2,844	18.0	na	na

ENGINES

Type	Displace- ment (L)	Fuel Dly	HP @rpm	Torque @rpm (ft/lbs)	MPG Cty/Hwy	Years Avail
V-8T	3.2	FI	325@6000	320@3000	na	91-92

KEY: I=in-line engine; V=V engine; F=flat engine; FI=fuel injection;
bbl=barrel carburetor; T=turbo; D=diesel; HP=horsepower;
MPG=estimated average miles per gallon.

EVALUATIONS, TESTS, AND RANKINGS

1991: "resemblance in the bodies of the Biturbo and Shamal."
Source: "Maserati Shamal," *Road & Track—Buyer's Guide
1991*, 1991, p. 189.

RECALLS

None to date.

OTHER INFORMATION SOURCES

1746 ● Maserati Market Letter

Maserati Club International, MIE, Inc.
P.O. Box 772   Ph:(206)455-4449
Mercer Island, WA 98040   Fax:(206)646-5458

Provides members with information and technical assistance regarding Maserati automobiles, including all models from 1926 to the present. Helps members locate new and used parts through the Exchange's extensive inventory. Recurring features include technical articles, concourse exhibitions, and rallies conducted by the Exchange and of accessories available. Every six weeks. **Editor(s):** Francis G. Mandarano. **Price:** Available to members only.

1747 ● Maserati Owners Club of North America Quarterly

Maserati Owners Club of America
Box 6554
Orange, CA 92667

Provides news of interest on Maserati sports car. **Editor(s):** Ken Olson. **Price:** $30.00/year, U.S.; $40.00 elsewhere.

1748 ● Viale Ciro Menotti

Maserati Information Exchange (MIE)
Box 772   Ph:(206)455-4449
Mercer Island, WA 98040   Fax:(206)646-5458

Magazine that contains information of interest to Maserati enthusiasts. Quarterly. **Editor(s):** Francis Mandarano, Publisher. **Price:** $50.00 per year; $15.00 per issue.

ASSOCIATIONS

1749 ● Maserati Owners Club of North America

Box 6554
Orange, CA 92667
Bill LeMasters, Pres.

Founded: 1978. **Membership:** 350. Owners and enthusiasts of Maseratis. Provides forum for social contact between members. Disseminates technical information. **Convention/Meeting:** Social and technical meetings (with exhibits), every 6 weeks.

MASERATI SPYDER (1987-92)

A two-door luxury convertible of the Maserati line. Ranked highest fuel cost and highest maintenance cost sports car in 1990 by *Complete Car Cost Guide*. Currently produced in Modena, Italy, it was known as the Biturbo Spyder before 1989.

1991 Maserati Spyder

MAJOR FEATURES

● 1992 Spyder standard equipment includes: 2.8L six-cylinder twin-turbocharged engine, five-speed manual transmission, all-around independent suspension, power-assisted rack-and-pinion steering, four-wheel disc brakes, power windows, tinted windows, convertible roof, automatic climate control, and various interior features.

PRICE HISTORY

The following new car prices reflect the approximate retail cost of the base model: **1987** - $38,695; **1988** - $39,975; **1989** - $46,310; **1990** - $48,015; **1991** - $50,375; **1992** - $51,000.

DIMENSIONS

Body Style	Years Avail	Wheel Base (in)	Lgth (in)	Ht (in)	Avg Wt (lbs)	Fuel Cap (gal)	Front Hdrm (in)	Front Legrm (in)
2d conv	87-92	94.5	159.2	51.6	2,925	18.0	na	na

ENGINES

Type	Displacement (L)	Fuel Dly	HP @rpm	Torque @rpm (ft/lbs)	MPG Cty/Hwy	Years Avail
V-6T	2.8	FI	225@5600	246@3500	15/20	87-92

KEY: I=in-line engine; V=V engine; F=flat engine; FI=fuel injection; bbl=barrel carburetor; T=turbo; D=diesel; HP=horsepower; MPG=estimated average miles per gallon.

EVALUATIONS, TESTS, AND RANKINGS

1988: "raising or lowering the top is a piece of cake; it seals tightly around the windshield. . .suspension and brakes are also quite capable. . .its handling dynamics are the equal of all but the most exotic." **Source:** "Maserati Biturbo i Spyder," *Motor Trend*, October 1987, pp. 49-50.

1988: "cozy cockpit. . .[seats] powder-puff appeareance and soft. . .provide excellent support." **Source:** "Maserati Biturbo i Spyder," *Car and Driver*, September 1987, pp. 51-3, 55.

1987: "very responsive with its computer-controlled electronic fuel injection and ignition systems. . .not primarily a muscle car, it is a thing of beauty. . .unusual sense of total control at any speed and in any situation." **Source:** "Maserati's everyday exotic," *The Detroit News*, June 24, 1987, pp. 1F-2F.

RECALLS

None to date.

OTHER INFORMATION SOURCES

1750 ● Illustrated Maserati Buyer's Guide

Motorbooks International
729 Prospect Ave
Osceola, WI 54020   Ph:(715)294-3345

Published 1989. **Editor(s):** Richard Crump. **Price:** $16.95.

1751 ● Maserati Market Letter

Maserati Club International, MIE, Inc.
P.O. Box 772   Ph:(206)455-4449
Mercer Island, WA 98040   Fax:(206)646-5458

Provides members with information and technical assistance regarding Maserati automobiles, including all models from 1926 to the present. Helps members locate new and used parts through the Exchange's extensive inventory. Recurring features include technical articles, concourse exhibitions, and rallies conducted by the Exchange and of accessories available.

Every six weeks. **Editor(s):** Francis G. Mandarano. **Price:** Available to members only.

1752 ● Maserati Owners Club of North America Quarterly
Maserati Owners Club of America
Box 6554
Orange, CA 92667

Provides news of interest on Maserati sports car. **Editor(s):** Ken Olson. **Price:** $30.00/year, U.S.; $40.00 elsewhere.

1753 ● Viale Ciro Menotti
Maserati Information Exchange (MIE)
Box 772   Ph:(206)455-4449
Mercer Island, WA 98040   Fax:(206)646-5458

Magazine that contains information of interest to Maserati enthusiasts. Quarterly. **Editor(s):** Francis Mandarano, Publisher. **Price:** $50.00 per year; $15.00 per issue.

ASSOCIATIONS

1754 ● Maserati Information Exchange
Box 772
Mercer Island, WA 98040
Francis G. Mandarano, Exec. Officer   Ph:(206)455-4449

Founded: 1976. **Membership:** 3,000. Owners and enthusiasts of Maserati sports automobiles, manufactured in Italy from 1926 to the present. Provides members with information and technical assistance and conducts meets. Maintains extensive inventory of new and used parts. Conducts four-day events with technical sessions, concourse exhibitions, and rallies. Presents awards; sells accessories. Maintains a service and restoration facility. **Convention/Meeting:** Annual meet - usually August.

1755 ● Maserati Owners Club of North America
Box 6554
Orange, CA 92667
Bill LeMasters, Pres.

Founded: 1978. **Membership:** 350. Owners and enthusiasts of Maseratis. Provides forum for social contact between members. Disseminates technical information. **Convention/Meeting:** Social and technical meetings (with exhibits), every 6 weeks.

MAZDA 323/PROTEGE (1987-92)

The Mazda 323 has been offered as a three-door hatchback since 1990; the Mazda Protege is offered as a four-door sedan. Named to the *Car and Driver* Ten Best Cars Nominees list (323 Protege) in 1990.

1991 Mazda 323

MAJOR FEATURES

● 323 has as 1992 standard features: 1.6-liter 4-cylinder engine, 5-speed manual transmission, four-wheel independent suspension, front disc/rear drum brakes, rack-and-pinion power steering, power-assisted brakes, reclining front bucket seats, full carpeting, rear window defogger, and redesigned taillight panel.

● 323 SE adds as 1992 standard equipment: full wheel covers, bodyside mouldings, dual remote mirrors, tinted glass, tweed cloth upholstery, and split fold-down rear seatback.

● Protege DX version has as 1992 standard features: 1.8-liter 16-valve 4-cylinder engine, 5-speed manual transmission with overdrive, lock-up torque converter and hold, hydraulic valve lash adjusters, tinted glass, cloth seating, door panel inserts, rear defoggers, full wheel covers, front disc/rear drum brakes and redesigned taillight panel.

● Protege LX adds as 1992 standard features: upgraded engine, 4-wheel disc brakes, velour upholstery, AM/FM stereo with cassette player, cruise control; and power windows, door locks, and mirrors, and 14-inch full wheel covers.

● Protege 4WD had as 1991 standard features: 60/40 folding rear seatback or a trunklid that extends to bumper height, and full-time system four-wheel drive with locking center differential.

● 323 GTX version had as 1988 standard features: 4-wheel drive and alloy wheels.

● 323 GT version had as 1988 standard features: upgraded engine.

● 323 Wagon had as 1988 standard equipment: other exterior body stylings.

PRICE HISTORY

The following new car prices reflect the approximate retail cost of the base model: **1987** - $6,099; **1988** - $5,999; **1989** - $6,449; **1990** - $5,599; **1991** - $6,949; **1992** - $6,999.

DIMENSIONS

Body Style	Years Avail	Wheel Base (in)	Lgth (in)	Ht (in)	Avg Wt (lbs)	Fuel Cap (gal)	Front Hdrm (in)	Front Legrm (in)
3d lbk	87-87	94.5	161.8	54.7	2,060	11.9	38.4	41.5
3d lbk	88-89	94.5	161.8	54.7	2,100	12.7	38.3	41.5
3d lbk	90-92	96.5	163.6	54.3	2,238	13.2	38.6	42.2
4d sdn	87-89	94.5	169.7	54.7	2,150	12.7	38.3	41.5
4d sdn	90-92	98.4	171.5	54.1	2,359	14.5	38.4	42.2
5d wgn	87-88	94.5	169.7	56.3	2,230	12.7	38.2	41.5

ENGINES

Type	Displace-ment (L)	Fuel Dly	HP @rpm	Torque @rpm (ft/lbs)	MPG Cty/Hwy	Years Avail
I-4	1.6	FI	82@5000	92@2500	29/37	87-92
I-4	1.8	FI	125@6500	114@4500	25/30	90-92
I-4	1.8	FI	103@5500	111@4000	28/36	90-92
I-4T	1.6	FI	132@6000	136@3000	22/27	88-89

KEY: I=in-line engine; V=V engine; F=flat engine; FI=fuel injection; bbl=barrel carburetor; T=turbo; D=diesel; HP=horsepower; MPG=estimated average miles per gallon.

EVALUATIONS, TESTS, AND RANKINGS

1991: ``excellent accommodations for a subcompact . . . body is 80 percent sturdier than the old 323 sedan's because of computer-aided design . . . body's resistance to flex coupled with good suspension damping and generous travel kept driver and passengers comfortable and made it easy to control.'' **Source:** ''Mazda Protege: Greater than the Sum of its Parts,'' *Autoweek's AutoFile 1991 Edition,* 1990, pp.112 -116.

1990: ''partly due to more power. . .chassis transfers less road noise even though it's considerably stiffer . . . translates into confidence . . . truly fun to drive, and you quickly forget you're in a 4-door economy sedan . . . it's bigger, looks good, and is competitively priced.'' **Source:** ''Mazda 323 Protege LX,'' *Motor Trend,* December 1989, p.122, 124-125.

1989: ''slips through heavy traffic like soap through a bather's fingers . . . as predictable and confidence-inspiring as you could ask . . . there's nothing inside the car to intrude on fast driving.'' **Source:** ''Mazda 323 GTX,'' *Motor Trend,* March 1989, pp. 106, 108, 141.

1988: ''performance car whose traction and agility and sheer alacrity across country most rivals are unable to match . . . steering is swift and direct . . . whole vehicle turns into corners sharply, with confidence and good balance . . . gear stick can be rowed back and forth with great haste.'' **Source:** ''Mazda 323 GTX,'' *Motor Trend,* June 1988, pp.75-76.

1988: ''sporty, yet soft when the road isn't. . .Distinctively, but not distastefully styled.'' **Source:** ''Four Fun Fours: Turbos, 16 valves and 4wd lend excitement to this confrontation,'' *Road & Track,* September 1988, pp.92-96, 99-101.

1988: ''323 still put up the best quarter-mile numbers, and did 0 to 60 in a zippy 7.4 seconds . . . joy to drive at normal highway speeds . . . too much roll in the corners, hints of torque steer under acceleration . . . difficult car to drive fast and not as much fun as you'd expect.'' **Source:** ''Econo Commandos: the world's top pocket rockets in a fight to the finish,'' *Popular Mechanics,* July 1988, pp.51-55, 119.

1988: ''fast, nimble, comfortable . . . offers an impressive blend of performance, efficiency, and solidity at an affordable price . . . the 323 GT combines the best attributes of a family sedan and a sports car at a bargain price.'' **Source:** ''Hitting for High Average: we pick the One Best Sedan your $14,000 will buy,'' *Car and Driver,* August 1988, pp.58-69.

RECALLS

None to date.

REPAIR MANUALS

1756 ● **Mazda 1971-1989 Repair and Tune-Up Guide**
Chilton Co.
Chilton Way
Radnor, PA 19089   Ph:(215)964-4000

Published 1989. **Price:** $15.95.

MAZDA 626 (1987-92)

In 1988, the Mazda 626 lineup was revised to include four-door sedans and five-door liftbacks. In the fall of 1989, U.S. production of the 626 four-door sedan began at Mazda's plant in Flat Rock, Michigan. The 1990 models featured revised interior and exterior styling, while several new option packages were added to the Mazda 626 car line in 1991. In 1992, the five-door liftback has been dropped. While many 626 components will continue to be produced overseas, all 1992 Mazda 626 sedans will be assembled in the U.S.

1991 Mazda 626 LX

MAJOR FEATURES

● 626 DX has as 1992 standard features: 5-speed manual transmission, front independent suspension, power-assisted rack-and-pinion steering, and front disc/rear drum brakes.

● 626 LX adds as 1992 standard features: power windows, door locks, and mirrors, AM/FM cassette stereo system, cruise control, and an upgraded interior.

● 626 Coupe was offered in DX and LX trim in 1987. It was replaced by the Mazda MX-6 the following year.

PRICE HISTORY

The following new car prices reflect the approximate retail cost of the base model: **1987** - $9,899; **1988** - $10,999; **1989** - $11,449; **1990** - $12,459; **1991** - $12,825; **1992** - $13,225.

DIMENSIONS

Body Style	Years Avail	Wheel Base (in)	Lgth (in)	Ht (in)	Avg Wt (lbs)	Fuel Cap (gal)	Front Hdrm (in)	Front Legrm (in)
5d lbk	89-91	101.4	179.3	54.1	2,680	15.9	38.7	43.6
2d cpe	87-87	98.8	177.8	53.7	2,385	15.8	38.9	41.4
4d sdn	87-87	98.8	177.8	55.5	2,450	15.8	38.9	41.4
4d sdn	88-92	101.4	179.3	55.5	2,610	15.9	39.0	43.7

ENGINES

Type	Displace-ment (L)	Fuel Dly	HP @rpm	Torque @rpm (ft/lbs)	MPG Cty/Hwy	Years Avail
I-4	2.0	FI	93@5000	115@2500	26/32	87-87
I-4	2.2	FI	110@4700	130@3000	24/31	88-92
I-4T	2.0	FI	120@5000	150@3000	22/28	87-87
I-4T	2.2	FI	145@4300	190@3500	21/28	88-92

KEY: I=in-line engine; V=V engine; F=flat engine; FI=fuel injection; bbl=barrel carburetor; T=turbo; D=diesel; HP=horsepower; MPG=estimated average miles per gallon.

EVALUATIONS, TESTS, AND RANKINGS

1990: ''Riding and handling of the LX model was smooth, balanced and well insulated over a wide variety of road surfaces.'' **Source:** ''Mazda 626: ₉Made in U.S.A,'' *The Detroit News,* May 16, 1990, pp. D1-D2.

1989: ''very well put together using premium materials.'' **Source:** ''Mazda 626 LX,'' *Popular Mechanics,* July 1989, pp. 60-63, 120-122.

1989: ''a tempting combination of speed, room, and reasonable price . . . delivers much of the performance of the European purebreds - without the cost.'' **Source:** ''Life with Mazda 626,'' *Car and Driver,* March 1989, p. 113, 115, 119.

1988: ''engineered to make the rear wheels think for

themselves.'' **Source:** ''Mazda 626/MX-6: Steering is by all Fours on the Third-Generation 626,'' *Popular Mechanics,* October 1987, pp. 120, 122-124.

1988: ''good visibility outward . . . Thin pillars all around contribute to the airy feel . . . clean, well-executed designs.'' **Source:** ''1988 Mazda 626,'' *Motor Trend,* December 1987, p. 102-104, 106.

RECALLS

1988: (33,868 cars; includes other Mazda models): Fuel tank fixing band may rub against fuel tank due to vehicle vibrations. May result in fuel tank hole. **Corrective action:** Repair fuel fixing band by installing rubber sheet. *(NHTSA Campaign No. 87V186000.)*

1988: (400 cars; includes other Mazda models): Floor mat could interfere with release of accelerator pedal due to shape of mat. **Corrective action:** Replace with redesigned mat. *(NHTSA Campaign No. 87V149000.)*

1988: (14,807 cars): Brake shoe may separate from wheel brake cylinder piston in rear brake drums, damaging wheel brake cylinder dust boot. **Corrective action:** Replace wheel brake cylinder dust boot. *(NHTSA Campaign No. 87V196000.)*

1988: (72,883 vehicles; includes Mazda 626 and Mazda MX6): At ambient temperatures below 0 degree Farenheit, frost may accumulate within throttle body under extended constant speed operation. Frost accumulation on the throttle valve may prevent valve from returning smoothly. **Corrective action:** Install new type thermostat designed to raise coolant temperature and warm throttle body to level above freezing. *(NHTSA Campaign No. 88V022000.)*

1988: (42,810 passenger cars with automatic shoulder belt): Drive spring that drives automatic belt may break. Would prevent full forward movement of seat belt anchorage from lock position when door is opened. **Corrective action:** Replace automatic shoulder belt. *(NHTSA Campaign No. 88V063000.)*

1987: (102,548 cars; includes models made before 1987): Malfunction of ignition switch terminal could result in failure of windshield wipers and washer, engine cooling fan, heater blower, and air conditioning compressor. **Corrective action:** Replace ignition switches. *(NHTSA Campaign No. 90V118000.)*

REPAIR MANUALS

1757 ● **Mazda 626, 1983-1988**
Clymer Publications
P. O. Box 1209
Overland Park, KS 66212   Ph:(913)541-6694

Published 1989. **Price:** $14.95.

1758 ● **Mazda 1971-1989 Repair and Tune-Up Guide**
Chilton Co.
Chilton Way
Radnor, PA 19089   Ph:(215)964-4000

Published 1989. **Price:** $15.95.

1759 ● **Mazda GLC, 626, RX 7**
Peter Allen Video Productions
38-C Otis St.
West Babylon, NY 11704   Ph:(516)643-4372

Three tapes on how to maintain and tune-up the three Mazda engines. **Release date:** 1986. **Producer:** Peter Allen Productions. **Acquisition:** Purchase.

MAZDA 929 (1988-92)

The Mazda 929 was introduced in 1987 as a 1988 model. The 929 S was added in 1990, with both models received exterior and interior revisions. For 1991, two new option packages were offered, and the forged alloy wheels from the 929 S became standard. For 1992, the 929 has been completely restyled utilizing such technological innovations as solar ventilation and ''fuzzy logic'' cruise-control systems. The model line is assembled in Hiroshima, Japan.

1992 Mazda 929

MAJOR FEATURES

● 929 has as 1992 standard features: 3.0-liter 24 valve V6 engine, 4-speed automatic transmission, power steering, dual front air bags, power-assisted 4-wheel disc brakes, with anti-lock brake system, automatic climate control system, cruise control, rear defogger, and power sunroof.

● The 1991 929 S added as standard features: anti-lock brake system (ABS).

PRICE HISTORY

The following new car prices reflect the approximate retail cost of the base model: **1988** - $19,850; **1989** - $22,900; **1990** - $23,300; **1991** - $23,850; **1992** - $27,800.

DIMENSIONS

Body Style	Years Avail	Wheel Base (in)	Lgth (in)	Ht (in)	Avg Wt (lbs)	Fuel Cap (gal)	Front Hdrm (in)	Front Legrm (in)
4d sdn	88-88	106.7	193.1	54.5	3,282	18.5	38.8	43.3
4d sdn	89-89	106.7	193.1	54.5	3,373	18.5	37.8	43.3
4d sdn	90-91	106.7	194.1	54.5	3,477	18.5	37.8	43.3
4d sdn	92-92	112.2	193.7	54.9	3,596	18.5	37.4	43.4

ENGINES

Type	Displacement (L)	Fuel Dly	HP @rpm	Torque @rpm (ft/lbs)	MPG Cty/Hwy	Years Avail
V-6	3.0	FI	158@5500	170@4000	19/23	88-91
V-6	3.0	FI	190@5600	191@4500	18/22	90-91
V-6	3.0	FI	195@5700	200@3500	19/24	92-92

KEY: I=in-line engine; V=V engine; F=flat engine; FI=fuel injection; bbl=barrel carburetor; T=turbo; D=diesel; HP=horsepower; MPG=estimated average miles per gallon.

EVALUATIONS, TESTS, AND RANKINGS

1992: ''The look is long, low and elegant . . . interior looks much less rigid and much more comforting than before . . . newfound style makes it a considerably more attractive and legitimate player." **Source:** "1992 Mazda 929," *Road & Track*, October 1991, p. 44.

1992: "sheer pleasure to drive . . . looks, personality, and poise . . . artful styling, spacious, well-appointed interior, excellent highway performance, and sporty cornering." **Source:** "Mazda 929: Moving into the High-Rent District," *Motor Trend*, November 1991, pp. 98-100.

1992: "the only four-door you may mistake for a coupe . . . usefully boxy trunk . . . proves small for a 3600-pound sedan . . . steering felt touchy just off center." **Source:** "Mazda 929: No longer built like the box it came in," *Car and Driver*, November 1991, pp. 55-57.

1992: "graceful exterior, comfortable interior and competent performance . . . solid improvement over the car it replaces . . . stylish, well-equipped sedan." **Source:** "New Mazda is stylish, solid but still part of the crowd," *The Detroit News*, October 9, 1991, pp. 1E, 5E.

1992: "first thing you notice about the new Mazda 929 is its shape . . . ride . . . is luxury soft, yet well-controlled, without becoming floaty." **Source:** "Real World 101," *Road & Track*, February 1992, pp. 59-67, 69.

1992: "interior is . . . at once warm and modern . . . dash area looks as if it had been sculpted by running water . . . looks a little better than it really is." **Source:** "Mazda 929," *Automobile Magazine*, December 1991, pp. 65-66, 68.

1991: "exterior styling is a little tired . . . interior . . . is less than modern . . . continues to be a car with good driving feel, decent performance and lots of comfort and convenience." **Source:** "As luxury car, Mazda 929 S is a bit old hat," *Flint Journal*, July 24, 1991, pp. E1, E2.

1990: "mechanical improvements given the 929S add up to measurable gains in power and handling . . . suspension retains a smooth boulevard ride, but adds a degree of stiffness on winding roads . . . dull styling." **Source:** "Mazda Adds Power to Luxury Sedan," *The Detroit News*, January 17, 1990, pp. B1, B6.

1990: "a comfortable cruising machine, not a sport sedan . . . competent, well-thought-out . . . Never dazzling, but never disappointing." **Source:** "Mazda 929 S: Clark Kent gets pumped up," *Motor Trend*, January 1990, pp. 99-101.

1989: "its ride . . . is supple without being sloppy. . .supremely quiet." **Source:** "Mazda 929," *Road & Track—Buyer's Guide 1989*, 1988, p. 103.

1989: "dashboard instruments were arrayed impressively over two-thirds of the dash but were clearly marked and easy to read . . . maneuvered as easily as some smaller cars in tight spaces . . . ranked third last year in having the least number of complaints from new buyers." **Source:** "Mazda's Flagship Sails Along Smoothly," *The Detroit News*, February 22, 1989, pp. F1-F2.

1988: "ride is smooth and well controlled. . .doesn't lack sportiness." **Source:** "Mazda 929," *Road & Track*, April 1988, p. 142.

1988: "somewhat bland but nice-driving." **Source:** "Mazda 929," *Car and Driver—Buyer's Guide 1988*, 1988, p. 105.

1988: "offers plenty of legroom even for backseat passengers . . . nearly optimal control of lockup at each corner . . . efficient rear-drive layout." **Source:** "Mazda 929," *Car and Driver*, March 1988, pp. 97-99, 101.

1988: "stunning craftsmanship . . . all-around excellent ride . . . Acceleration is adequate in urban traffic, superior on the open road." **Source:** "Mazda 929 Betrays its Sedate Look," *The Detroit News*, May 25, 1988, pp. F1-F2.

RECALLS

None to date.

REPAIR MANUALS

1760 ● **Mazda 1971-1989 Repair and Tune-Up Guide**
Chilton Co.
Chilton Way
Radnor, PA 19089   Ph:(215)964-4000

Published 1989. **Price:** $15.95.

MAZDA B2000 SERIES (1987-92)

As of 1992, Mazda pickup trucks have been ranked highest in the compact pickup segment of the J.D. Power and Associates Light Duty Truck Customer Satisfaction Index (CSI) four of the past five years, and have been ranked highest in the Power New Truck Initial Quality Study (IQS) for the past two years. The B2000 Series is available in short or long bed, regular cab or Cab Plus, and sporty SE-5 or Luxury LE-5 trim levels. While the B2200 Truck is only available in 2WD version, the B2600 Truck is available in both 2WD and 4WD versions.

1991 Mazda B2600i 4WD

MAJOR FEATURES

● Mazda B2200 2WD and B2600 2WD have as 1992 standard features: 2.2L four-cylinder engine, 5-speed manual transmission, front disc/rear drum brakes, and rear wheel anti-lock braking system.

● Mazda B2600i 4WD adds as 1992 standard features: 2.6-liter 12-valve engine, fender flares, and automatic-locking front hubs.

● Mazda B2200 LX had as 1989 standard equipment: 2.2L, four-cyclinder engine, five-speed manual transmision, and upgraded interior.

Dimensions that follow are for the short bed version of the series.

PRICE HISTORY

The following new car prices reflect the approximate retail cost of the base model: **1987** - $6,595; **1988** - $7,549; **1989** - $7,799; **1990** - $7,949; **1991** - $8,449; **1992** - $9,120.

DIMENSIONS

Body Style	Years Avail	Wheel Base (in)	Lgth (in)	Ht (in)	Avg Wt (lbs)	Fuel Cap (gal)	Front Hdrm (in)	Front Legrm (in)
trk	87-92	108.7	177.6	61.8	4,460	14.8	na	na

ENGINES

Type	Displace-ment (L)	Fuel Dly	HP @rpm	Torque @rpm (ft/lbs)	MPG Cty/Hwy	Years Avail
I-4	2.6	2-bbl	102@na	na	18/24	87-88
I-4	2.2	2-bbl	85@4500	118@2500	21/26	87-92
I-4	2.6	FI	121@4600	149@3500	19/23	89-92

KEY: I=in-line engine; V=V engine; F=flat engine; FI=fuel injection; bbl=barrel carburetor; T=turbo; D=diesel; HP=horsepower; MPG=estimated average miles per gallon.

EVALUATIONS, TESTS, AND RANKINGS

1990: "still manages to look and perform on par with the newest trucks ... ride is good, even on rutted roads ... ground clearance should be more than adequate on off-road trips." **Source:** "Loadin' Up," *Organic Gardening*, April 1990, pp. 55-58.

1990: "quick response in traffic ... load-toting muscle for backcountry camping ... Despite a smallish engine, it's a snappy performer." **Source:** "Practical Pickups For Sportsmen," *Sports Afield*, May 1990, pp. 90-93, 100-101.

1989: "Engine aside, the B2200 is a fine truck ... interior cuts a very good line between car-like luxury and truck toughness ... ergonomics are excellent ... mediocre performer not only in acceleration ... but [also] in braking." **Source:** "Compact Commandos," *Popular Mechanics*, February 1989, pp.51-55, 122.

1988: "Mazda realizes that most contemporary mini-trucks provide plenty of utility and comfort, so it has appealed to your pocketbook by pricing its trucks low ... B-series has enough room and cargo capacity for a couple of dirt bikes in back, or the equivalent in wood, camping gear." **Source:** "Mazda B2200/B2600," *Car and Driver—Buyer's Guide, 1988*, 1988, pp.129.

RECALLS

None to date.

REPAIR MANUALS

1761 ● Haynes Mazda B-Series Pick-ups Owners Workshop Manual, No. 267: 1972-1990
Haynes Publications, Inc.
861 Lawrence Dr.
Newbury Park, CA 91320   Ph:(818)889-5400

Editor(s): J. H. Haynes and P. Ward. **Price:** $15.95.

1762 ● Mazda 1971-1989 Repair and Tune-Up Guide
Chilton Co.
Chilton Way
Radnor, PA 19089   Ph:(215)964-4000

Published 1989. **Price:** $15.95.

1763 ● Mazda Pick-Ups 1971-1989: Repair and Tune-Up Guide
Chilton Co.
Chilton Way
Radnor, PA 19089   Ph:(215)964-4000

Published 1989. **Price:** $15.95.

1764 ● Mazda Pickups, 1972-1988
Haynes Publications, Inc.
861 Lawrence Dr.
Newbury Park, CA 91320   Ph:(818)889-5400

Published 1989. **Price:** $15.95.

1765 ● Mazda Pickups Two and Four Wheel Drive, 1979-1989
Clymer Publications
P. O. Box 1209
Overland Park, KS 66212   Ph:(913)541-6694

Published 1990. **Price:** $26.95.

MAZDA MPV (1989-92)

Introduced in 1988 as a 1989 model the MPV became the best-selling import vehicle in its class and received several awards from the automotive media, including being named "Best Minivan" by the *Motorweek* television automotive magazine. *Car and Driver* magazine named the MPV as one of its 10 Best Vehicles for 1990 and as the "Best Buy" in its class. In addition, the MPV has been ranked highest in its class in the J.D. Power and Associates Initial Quality Study in past years. Produced in Hiroshima, Japan.

1991 Mazda MPV

MAJOR FEATURES

● MPV 5-passenger wagon/van has as 1992 standard equipment: 2.6-liter I-4 engine, 4-speed automatic transmission, power-assisted rack-and-pinion steering, rear-wheel anti-lock brake system, front disc/rear drum brakes, swing-out rear side door with child-safety lock, tilt steering column, AM/FM/cassette stereo sound system, rear defogger, and rear window wiper/washer.

● MPV 7-passenger wagon adds as 1992 standard equipment: 2.6-liter or 3.0-liter V-6 engine, 5-speed manual transmission and redesigned alloy wheels.

● MPV 7-passenger 4WD wagon 1992 standard equipment: selectable four-wheel drive system.

PRICE HISTORY

The following new car prices reflect the approximate retail cost of the base model: **1989** - $13,199; **1990** - $13,699; **1991** - $14,135; **1992** - $15,665.

DIMENSIONS

Body Style	Years Avail	Wheel Base (in)	Lgth (in)	Ht (in)	Avg Wt (lbs)	Fuel Cap (gal)	Front Hdrm (in)	Front Legrm (in)
4d van	89-92	110.4	175.8	68.1	3,459	15.9	40.0	40.6

ENGINES

Type	Displace-ment (L)	Fuel Dly	HP @rpm	Torque @rpm (ft/lbs)	MPG Cty/Hwy	Years Avail
I-4	2.6	FI	121@4600	149@3500	20/25	89-91
I-4	2.6	FI	126@na	na	18/24	92-92
V-6	3.0	FI	150@5000	165@4000	17/22	89-92

KEY: I=in-line engine; V=V engine; F=flat engine; FI=fuel injection; bbl=barrel carburetor; T=turbo; D=diesel; HP=horsepower; MPG=estimated average miles per gallon.

EVALUATIONS, TESTS, AND RANKINGS

1991: "easy to use, pleasant to look at, and a joy to drive down the road." **Source:** "Ten Best Cars," *Car and Driver*, January 1991, p.44.

1991: "rides and handles like a car. . .responds accurately and predictably enough to satisfy even a demanding driver under most conditions. . ." **Source:** "Mazda MPV: Still a winner even with four cylinders," *Car and Driver*, December 1990, pp.42-43.

1991: "mechanical reliability was outstanding. . .call it a winner." **Source:** "Mazda MPV 4WD," *Automobile*, November 1990, pp.117-118, 120.

1991: "only real complaint about the MPV is the transmission, starting with the mushiest, vaguest column shifter in the industry." **Source:** "Long-Term Test Cars," *Popular Mechanics*, November 1990.

1991: "ride quality is remarkably like a contemporary sedan . . . engine offers lively performance . . . MPV's maneuverability makes it a pleasure to handle in everyday traffic." **Source:** "Meet The New Minivans: Cars for the long haul," *New Choices for the Best Years*, October 1990, pp. 86-87.

1990: "luxury class parts serve it well." **Source:** "Top Ten New Car Buys; Import," *Motor Trend*, November 1989, pp.80-83, 86-89.

1990: "seats were comfortable, and visibility was excellent all around . . . came the closest to performing like a car . . . little room inside to walk easily from front to back." **Source:** "Best of the Minivans: A 200-mile trek on city and country roads separates the winners from the pack," *Changing Times*, July 1990, pp. 41-45.

1990: "ingratiating level of carlike handling . . . overall quiet ride, precise steering, and predictable balance . . . road-worthy performance." **Source:** "The Wedge vs. The Box," *Popular Science*, August 1990, pp. 76-79, 81.

1989: "[design is] clean, pleasant, unforced. . .interior is comfortably accomodating to a driver/passenger pair, with excellent outward visibility. . .dash, its instruments, and controls are rationally and handsomely arranged, though the shift lever is almost comically oversize." **Source:** "Mazda MPV: A 4-door sedan for the Millenium, here and now," *Road & Track*, October 1988, pp.60-62.

1989: "offers distinctive styling . . . entry into the MPV is easier than dropping a letter into a mailbox . . . how does it drive? Quite well thank you . . . jumps instantly to the top of the list of imported mini-vans." **Source:** "Mazda MPV: Coming on strong in the mini-van race," *Motor Trend*, November 1988, pp.95-97.

1989: "terrific-looking piece . . . ride quality and handling rank right up there with the Chrysler twins . . . engines run smoothly to their redlines." **Source:** "Mazda MPV: A late starter—but worth the wait," *Car and Driver*, November 1988, pp.99-100.

1989: "the new 'Best in Class,' with the emphasis on class."

Source: "Eeny, Meeny, Miney, Mini," *Car and Driver*, May 1989, pp.62-63, 65, 67, 71, 75-77, 81.

1989: "firm-handling, extremely comfortable road machine . . . can provide extra grip on the highway . . . excellent cargo capacity." **Source:** "Four-By-Four By Van," *Outdoor Life*, April 1989, pp. 59, 63.

RECALLS

1989: (10,587 passenger vans): Attachment hardware brackets for third seat safety belt may not withstand specified tensile load. **Corrective action:** Replace safety belt assembly. *(NHTSA Campaign No. 89V194000.)*

1989: (6,680 multi-purpose vehicles): When vehicle is exposed to temperatures below 5 degrees Fahrenheit, the neutral detergent used as an assembly lubricant may stick to check valve, preventing valve from functioning. Could cause an inoperative brake power assist which decreases braking ability. **Corrective action:** Replace vacuum hose assembly. *(NHTSA Campaign No. 91V013000.)*

1989: (29,824 multi-purpose vehicles): When applying the foot (service) brake in the low vehicle speed condition, the braking power produced may be more than expected. This could result in rear brake lock-up and the vehicle becoming difficult to control. **Corrective action:** Replace brake shoe assembly with improved assembly. *(NHTSA Campaign No. 91V161000.)*

SAFETY AND REPAIRS

1991: "NHTSA Upgrades Probe of Brakes on Ford Trucks," *Automotive News*, December 9, 1991, p. 40. **Note:** 1990-91 Mazda MPV minivans with anti-lock brake systems could experience inconsistent brake performance.

REPAIR MANUALS

1766 ● **Mazda 1971-1989 Repair and Tune-Up Guide**
Chilton Co.
Chilton Way
Radnor, PA 19089   Ph:(215)964-4000

Published 1989. **Price:** $15.95.

MAZDA MX-3 (1992)

Introduced in 1991 as a 1992 model, the Mazda MX-3 sport coupe rounds out Mazda's line of sporty cars, which includes the RX-7 and MX-5 Miata. The front-wheel drive, four passenger MX-3 competes against the Nissan NX 1600/2000, Geo Storm, and Toyota Paseo. A 3-door hatchback coupe, the MX-3 is based on the subcompact Mazda 323 platform. It is available in two versions: a base version and a more upscale GS. The MX-3 is currently produced in Hiroshima, Japan.

1992 Mazda MX-3 GS

MAJOR FEATURES

● MX-3 has as 1992 standard equipment: 1.6-liter 4-cylinder engine, 5-speed manual transmission, power steering, front disc/rear drum brakes, cloth reclining bucket seats, and rear defogger.

● MX-3 GS adds as 1992 standard equipment: 1.8-liter V-6 engine, 4-wheel disc brakes, tilt steering column, rear wiper/washer, front and rear spoilers, and alloy wheels.

PRICE HISTORY

The following new car prices reflect the approximate retail cost of the base model: **1992** - $11,000.

DIMENSIONS

Body Style	Years Avail	Wheel Base (in)	Lgth (in)	Ht (in)	Avg Wt (lbs)	Fuel Cap (gal)	Front Hdrm (in)	Front Legrm (in)
3d cpe	92-92	96.3	165.7	51.6	2,332	13.2	38.2	42.6
3d cpe	92-92	96.3	165.7	51.6	2,541	13.2	38.2	42.6

ENGINES

Type	Displace-ment (L)	Fuel Dly	HP @rpm	Torque @rpm (ft/lbs)	MPG Cty/Hwy	Years Avail
I-4	1.6	FI	88@5000	98@4000	25/32	92-92
V-6	1.8	FI	130@6500	115@4500	20/27	92-92

KEY: I=in-line engine; V=V engine; F=flat engine; FI=fuel injection; bbl=barrel carburetor; T=turbo; D=diesel; HP=horsepower; MPG=estimated average miles per gallon.

EVALUATIONS, TESTS, AND RANKINGS

1992: "offers the distinction of the only V6 engine available in cars of this class ... V6 should be smoother than any powerplant offered in this class." **Source:** "New Cars: Mazda MX-3," *Popular Mechanics*, June 1991, pp. 48-102.

RECALLS

None to date.

MAZDA MX-5 MIATA (1990-92)

Introduced in mid-1989 as a 1990 model, the Mazda MX-5 Miata is produced in Hiroshima, Japan. Also known as the Mazda Miata, it was named "Automobile of the Year" by *Automobile Magazine* and *Road & Track* magazine hailed it as one of the five "World's Best Cars." Named the "most trouble-free" sports car in the 1990 J.D. Power and Associates New Car Initial Quality Study. Named a Best Bet by *The Car Book* in 1992.

1991 Mazda MX-5 Miata

MAJOR FEATURES

● MX-5 Miata has as 1992 standard equipment: 1.6-liter 16-valve I-4 engine, 5-speed manual transmission, rear-wheel drive, 4-wheel independent suspension, rack-and-pinion power steering, power-assisted 4-wheel disc brakes, retractable halogen headlights, driver's side airbag, and rear defroster for detachable hardtop.

PRICE HISTORY

The following new car prices reflect the approximate retail cost of the base model: **1990** - $13,800; **1991** - $14,300; **1992** - $14,800.

DIMENSIONS

Body Style	Years Avail	Wheel Base (in)	Lgth (in)	Ht (in)	Avg Wt (lbs)	Fuel Cap (gal)	Front Hdrm (in)	Front Legrm (in)
2d cpe	90-92	89.2	155.4	48.2	2,216	11.9	37.1	42.7

ENGINES

Type	Displace-ment (L)	Fuel Dly	HP @rpm	Torque @rpm (ft/lbs)	MPG Cty/Hwy	Years Avail
I-4	1.6	FI	116@6500	100@5500	24/30	90-92

KEY: I=in-line engine; V=V engine; F=flat engine; FI=fuel injection; bbl=barrel carburetor; T=turbo; D=diesel; HP=horsepower; MPG=estimated average miles per gallon.

EVALUATIONS, TESTS, AND RANKINGS

1992: "everyone's secret automotive heartthrob ... sounds good ... performance is stout enough to reward the driver with smiles." **Source:** "Ten Best Cars," *Car and Driver*, January 1992, pp. 35-43.

1992: "driving experience in the Miata is still basic and vital ... Road inputs are easily read ... engine-speed-sensitive steering is tight and precise." **Source:** "Mazda MX-5 Miata," *Automobile Magazine*, January 1992, p. 53.

1991: "slickest shifter this side of a race car ... shy on cargo capacity." **Source:** "Mazda MX-5 Miata: Finding Fun in Toyland," *Autofile*, 1991, pp. 7-11.

1991: "quick steering, willing engine, short-throw gearbox, taut suspension and fits-like-glove driving position give it a feeling of instantaneous response." **Source:** "Carrying the Torch," *Road & Track*, November 1990, pp. 44-52, 55-56.

1991: "just as fault-free and fun to drive as it was on day one ... excellent all-around fuel economy performance of 28.2 mpg ... service has been superb." **Source:** "Long-Term Test Cars," *Popular Mechanics*, November 1990, pp. 56-59, 138.

1991: "responsive, quick, wonderful car to drive ... Miata is a

bit stubborn in the cold.'' **Source:** ``Mazda MX-5 Miata,''
Automobile, January 1991, pp. 117-121.

1991: ``has its own unique character . . . Miata . . . a generic
name for a sexy, fun, little sports car.'' **Source:** ``Design of
Miata proves it works: Sales success retains status quo,'' *The
Flint Journal*, May 22, 1991, pp. B1, B2.

1991: ``No ragtop is sexier.'' **Source:** ``What's Next: Spring
showers bring May ragtops,'' *USA Weekend*, May 17-19,
1991, p. 18.

1990: ``5-speed is indeed remarkable, offering the kind of gear
changing previously available only in an Indy car . . . good grip
and linear steering provide a large helping of driving
confidence, and the car's near-perfect 48/52% weight
distribution and high-speed cornering effectiveness support
you fully.'' **Source:** ``Motor Trend's 1990 Import Car of the
Year,'' *Motor Trend*, March 1990, pp. 44-63.

1990: ``Upon cold start, the engine has a hesitation at low rpm
that goes away in 10-15 seconds . . . brakes are a mite grabby
in their first few applications, before they heat up and settle
down to their usual reassuring predictability . . . [the top]
certainly won't last the life of the car.'' **Source:** ``Long-Term
Update,'' *Road & Track*, February 1990, p. 126.

1990: ``features air bags and an engine which is less powerful
than that of a ``pure'' sports car.'' **Source:** ``Mazda's Miata
Faces an Uphill Battle for Sales,'' *The Detroit News*, June 16,
1989, pp. F1-F2.

1990: ``so cute you want to take it home and keep it as a pet
. . . all curves and soft lines . . . an out-and-out sports car.''
Source: ``Return of the roadster: the free-spirited Mazda Miata
seduces America and David Barry,'' *Vogue*, March 1990, p.
386B.

1990: ``embodies the virtues of the old British roadsters . . .
simplicity, low weight, agile handling, wind in the hair . . .
modern engine technology, quality construction, general all-
around reliabilty.'' **Source:** ``Sports car then and now,'' *New
Choices for the Best Years*, July 1990, pp. 86-87.

1990: ``one of the most elegantly designed cars, of any kind, to
come along in years . . . voluptuosly curvy body . . . refreshing
lack of ornamentation.'' **Source:** ``Two for the Road: The
Mazda Miata puts a new spin on the roadster,'' *House and
Garden*, August 1989, p. 44.

1990: ``Cute and handsome at the same time . . . beautifully
built, yet reliable and nearly flawless in performance . . . the
best sports car buy ever. Period.'' **Source:** ``2 for the Road,''
Regardie's, September 1989, pp. 169-170, 172-180, 182.

RECALLS

1991: (300 passenger vehicles with anti-lock brake systems): A
return fluid line of the front brake system is poorly connected
to a rear brake fluid return. Total loss of fluid in the front brake
system leads to increased stopping distance, and could result in
vehicle collision. **Corrective action:** Replace defective ABS
systems. *(NHTSA Campaign No. 91V079000.)*

OTHER INFORMATION SOURCES

1767 ● Guide to Mazda Miata MX-5
Motorbooks International
729 Prospect Ave.
Osceola, WI 54020   Ph:(715)294-3345

Published 1990. **Editor(s):** Jay W. Lamb. **Price:** $15.95.

MAZDA MX-6 (1988-92)

Introduced in 1987 as a 1988 model, it replaced the Mazda
626 coupe. In September of 1987, the MX-6 was the first
vehicle to roll off Mazda's assembly line at Mazda Motor
Manufacturing (USA) Corp. (MMUC) in Flat Rock, Michigan.
For 1992, all MX-6 models will be produced in the U.S. (plant
parts data: domestic parts - 42%, imported parts - 58%).

1991 Mazda MX-6 GT

MAJOR FEATURES

● Mazda MX-6 DX has as 1992 standard equipment: 2.2-liter
I-4 engine, 5-speed manual transmission, front independent
suspension, power-assisted rack-and-pinion steering, and
front disc/rear drum brakes.

● Mazda MX-6 LX adds as 1992 standard equipment: power
windows, door locks, and mirrors, AM/FM cassette stereo
system, cruise control, and an upgraded interior.

● Mazda MX-6 GT adds as standard 1992 equipment:
turbocharged engine, four-wheel disc brakes, fog lights, rear
spoiler, upraded tires, and alloy wheels.

PRICE HISTORY

The following new car prices reflect the approximate retail cost
of the base model: **1988** - $11,099; **1989** - $11,399; **1990** -
$12,279; **1991** - $12,625; **1992** - $13,465.

DIMENSIONS

Body Style	Years Avail	Wheel Base (in)	Lgth (in)	Ht (in)	Avg Wt (lbs)	Fuel Cap (gal)	Front Hdrm (in)	Front Legrm (in)
2d cpe	88-92	99.0	177.0	53.5	2,560	15.9	38.4	43.6

ENGINES

Type	Displace- ment (L)	Fuel Dly	HP @rpm	Torque @rpm (ft/lbs)	MPG Cty/Hwy	Years Avail
I-4	2.2	FI	110@4700	130@3000	24/31	88-92
I-4T	2.2	FI	145@4300	190@3500	21/28	88-92

KEY: I=in-line engine; V=V engine; F=flat engine; FI=fuel injection;
bbl=barrel carburetor; T=turbo; D=diesel; HP=horsepower;
MPG=estimated average miles per gallon.

EVALUATIONS, TESTS, AND RANKINGS

1990: ``likes to understeer . . . brakes go away in a few laps and
return to good health only after a cool-down period.'' **Source:**
``Bang for the Buck,'' *Motor Trend*, November 1989, pp. 42-
46, 48, 52-55, 58-59, 62, 64, 66-68, 72, 76.

1989: ``can be a handful in wet weather . . . Boost comes on with a bang, resulting in unwanted wheelspin and torque steer." **Source:** "Coupes De Grace," *Popular Mechanics,* May 1989, pp. 120-124, 212, 214.

1988: "[MX-6 GT] can really wail out the horsepower and, more particularly, the torque." **Source:** "Catalina Pony Express," *Motor Trend,* May 1988, pp. 54-58, 61, 64-66.

RECALLS

1988: (33,868 cars; includes other Mazda models): Fuel tank fixing band may rub against fuel tank due to vehicle vibrations. May result in fuel tank hole. **Corrective action:** Repair fuel fixing band by installing rubber sheet. *(NHTSA Campaign No. 87V186000.)*

1988: (400 cars; includes other Mazda models): Floor mat could interfere with release of accelerator pedal due to shape of mat. **Corrective action:** Replace with redesigned mat. *(NHTSA Campaign No. 87V149000.)*

1988: (14,807 vehicles): Brake shoe may separate from wheel brake cylinder piston in rear brake drums, damaging wheel brake cylinder dust boot. **Corrective action:** Replace wheel brake cylinder dust boot. *(NHTSA Campaign No. 87V196000.)*

1988: (72,883 vehicles; includes Mazda 626 and Mazda MX6): At ambient temperatures below 0 degree Farenheit, frost may accumulate within throttle body under extended constant speed operation. Frost accumulation on the throttle valve may prevent valve from returning smoothly. **Corrective action:** Install new type thermostat designed to raise coolant temperature and warm throttle body to level above freezing. *(NHTSA Campaign No. 88V022000.)*

REPAIR MANUALS

1768 ● **Mazda 1971-1989 Repair and Tune-Up Guide**
Chilton Co.
Chilton Way
Radnor, PA 19089   Ph:(215)964-4000

Published 1989. **Price:** $15.95.

MAZDA NAVAJO (1991-92)

1991 was the first year for the Mazda Navajo, the company's first entry into the sport utility segment. Designed and engineered by the Ford Motor Co. with developmental input from Mazda. Produced for Mazda by Ford in its Louisville, Kentucky assembly plant. Except for minor appearance differences and interior trim, the Mazda Navajo is identical to the Ford Explorer.

1992 Mazda Navajo LX 4x4

MAJOR FEATURES

● Navajo DX 4x4 and 4x2 have as 1992 standard equipment:

4.0L six-cylinder engine, 5-speed manual transmission, 4-wheel drive with shift-on-the-fly, front disc/rear drum brakes, rear-wheel anti-lock brake system, front independent/rear live axle suspension, power-assisted steering, AM/FM stereo sound system, and tinted glass.

● Navajo LX 4x4 and 4x2 add as 1992 standard equipment: alloy wheels, and other exterior body stylings power windows and door locks, and an upgraded interior.

PRICE HISTORY

The following new car prices reflect the approximate retail cost of the base model: **1991** - $17,835; **1992** - $15,795.

DIMENSIONS

Body Style	Years Avail	Wheel Base (in)	Lgth (in)	Ht (in)	Avg Wt (lbs)	Fuel Cap (gal)	Front Hdrm (in)	Front Legrm (in)
utl wgn	91-92	102.1	175.3	68.1	3,851	19.3	39.9	42.4

ENGINES

Type	Displacement (L)	Fuel Dly	HP @rpm	Torque @rpm (ft/lbs)	MPG Cty/Hwy	Years Avail
V-6	4.0	FI	155@4200	220@2400	17/22	91-92

KEY: I=in-line engine; V=V engine; F=flat engine; FI=fuel injection; bbl=barrel carburetor; T=turbo; D=diesel; HP=horsepower; MPG=estimated average miles per gallon.

EVALUATIONS, TESTS, AND RANKINGS

1991: "road behavior is first-class . . . big, simple, positive, hand-filling controls." **Source:** "Navajo in Eskimoland," *Automobile magazine,* December 1990, pp. 102-104.

1991: "Driver and passenger comfort is this Mazda's hallmark . . . 'interior is accomodating and well designed'. . .reasonable performance." **Source:** "The New and the Improved," *Motor Trend,* January 1991, pp. 79-84.

1991: "shorter span causes it to pitch more on bumps . . . interior adhered to our idea of handsomeness . . . sports easy and convenient shifting." **Source:** "Mazda Navajo LX: Hey, Mom, they're making sushi in Kentucky," *Car and Driver,* June 1991, pp. 38-40, 42, 45.

1991: "neat, sporty appearance . . . Off-the-line response is exemplary . . . highway cruising is hushed . . . overall comfort is excellent." **Source:** "Update: Sport-Utility Vehicles," *U.S. News and World Report,* May 13, 1991, pp. A4, A6, A8-A10, A12, A14-A15.

1991: "absence of a second set of doors is inconvenient . . . fuel economy . . . is nothing to brag about . . . car-like cabin . . . roomy, comfortable and well-equipped." **Source:** "Navajo is Tribute to Ford Explorer," *Detroit Free Press,* June 27, 1991, p. 6D.

RECALLS

1991: (10,000 light-duty trucks): Rear bumper may be susceptible to fatigue cracking under extended trailer tow service when using a bumper mounted trailer hitch, resulting in bumper detachment. **Corrective action:** Install two additional brackets, one additional bar, and associated fasteners to prevent bumper separation. *(NHTSA Campaign No. 91V028000.)*

1991: (6,424 light-duty trucks): Front heat shield extension may contact upper front corner of fuel tank damaging or puncturing fuel tank. **Corrective action:** Relocate heat shield;

replace fuel tank if damaged or punctured. (NHTSA Campaign No. 91V020000.)

SAFETY AND REPAIRS

1991: "Transmission Defect Baffles Ford; 788,796 Trucks Have It," *Automotive News*, October 28, 1991, p. 47. **Note:** Safety defect in the parking gear of automatic transmissions could allow vehicles to roll.

MAZDA RX-7 (1987-91, 1993)

In 1987, the Mazda RX-7 received several awards, including: best high-performance car by *Road & Track*; the *Motor Trend* Import Car of the Year award; and named to the Ten Best list by *Car and Driver*. In 1988, a factory-built convertible version was added to the RX-7 line. A restyled RX-7 is scheduled to debut in mid-1992 as a 1993 model; vehicle information unavailable at time of publication.

1991 Mazda RX-7

MAJOR FEATURES

● RX-7 Coupe GTU had as 1991 standard equipment: 5-speed manual transmission, independent suspension with rear dynamic tracking suspension, aluminum alloy wheels, racing-inspired 4-wheel disc brakes, power-assisted rack-and-pinion steering, power windows and door locks, anti-theft alarm system, air conditioning, leather-wrapped steering wheel and shift knob, and AM/FM stereo with auto-reverse cassette.

● RX-7 GXL   added as 1991 standard equipment: cruise control, tilt steering wheel column, tinted glass, and rear window defroster.

● RX-7 Turbo 1991 standard equipment included: turbocharged engine and an anti-lock brake system (ABS).

● RX-7 Convertible 1991 standard equipment added: driver's side airbag and a compact disc player.

● RX-7 Turbo II 1990 standard equipment: a turbocharged engine offering less horsepower than the turbocharged engine in the RX-7 Turbo model.

PRICE HISTORY

The following new car prices reflect the approximate retail cost of the base model: **1987** - $14,199; **1988** - $16,150; **1989** - $17,300; **1990** - $17,880; **1991** - $20,000.

DIMENSIONS

Body Style	Years Avail	Wheel Base (in)	Lgth (in)	Ht (in)	Avg Wt (lbs)	Fuel Cap (gal)	Front Hdrm (in)	Front Legrm (in)
2d cpe	87-88	95.7	168.9	49.8	2,625	16.6	37.2	43.7
2d cpe	89-91	95.7	169.9	49.8	2,787	18.5	37.2	43.8
2d conv	88-91	95.7	168.9	49.8	3,003	16.6	37.2	43.8

ENGINES

Type	Displace-ment (L)	Fuel Dly	HP @rpm	Torque @rpm (ft/lbs)	MPG Cty/Hwy	Years Avail
R Wkl	1.3	FI	146@6500	138@3500	17/24	87-88
R Wkl	1.3	FI	160@7000	140@4000	17/25	89-91
R WklT	1.3	FI	182@6500	183@3500	17/23	87-88
R WklT	1.3	FI	200@6500	196@3500	16/24	89-91

KEY: I=in-line engine; V=V engine; F=flat engine; FI=fuel injection; bbl=barrel carburetor; T=turbo; D=diesel; HP=horsepower; MPG=estimated average miles per gallon.

EVALUATIONS, TESTS, AND RANKINGS

1991: "not adrenalin-pumping fast or eye-poppingly styled . . . sexy enough to attract favorable comments . . . ride . . . can get harsh on rough washboard roads." **Source:** "Mazda RX-7 eager, feels good to drive," *The Flint Journal*, June 5, 1991, pp. D1, D2.

1991: "top features a glass rear window plus a headliner . . . wind buffeting . . . so insignificant as to be practically unnoticeable." **Source:** "Top-Down Showdown: We test the hottest cars under the sun," *Motor Trend*, June 1991, pp. 49-59, 62-63.

1990: "low, organic shape is perfect for pop-topping . . . bodywork is wide and smooth . . . asphalt is where the rotary powerplant and the all-independent suspension and the four-wheel disc brakes bring heat of their own . . . interior remains inviting." **Source:** "Mazda RX-7," *Car and Driver—Buyer's Guide 1990*, 1989, p.142-143.

1990: "has the power and handling to keep up with the best in its class." **Source:** "Carrying the Torch," *Road & Track*, November 1990, pp.44-53, 56.

1989: "revisions to the rear suspension . . . produce significant gain in handling . . . engineers have been inside the RX-7's rotary engine . . . net is a bump in output." **Source:** "The Rites of Spring," *Popular Mechanics*, March 1989, pp.61-64, 134.

1989: "turbocharged rotary engine is delightfully progressive and responsive. Braking is exceptional." **Source:** "Bang for the Buck," *Motor Trend*, November 1989, pp.42-46, 48, 52-55, 58-59, 62, 64, 66-68, 72, 76.

1989: "no torque steer under hard acceleration as there is in so many front-drive sporty cars . . . ventilation system was powerful . . . shoulder belts . . . were the most sensitive and comforting." **Source:** "RX-7 Evolves into Stylish Sports Car," *The Detroit News*, August 16, 1989, pp. 1F-2F.

1988: "interior is still one of the best in a sports car . . . seats, Recaro-like, offer good support . . . shifter works . . . just a bit stiff when cold." **Source:** "Mazda RX-7: The First Decade," *Road & Track*, August 1988, pp.68-69, 72-73, 76.

1988: "power delivery is smooth . . . convertible top mechanism seems needlessly complex . . . space-capsule feeling . . . impression is of confinement." **Source:** "Sea Cruise," *Motor Trend*, August 1988, pp.36-39, 41-43, 128, 130.

1988: "In a packed field . . . a close but clear winner." **Source:** "10 Best Cars," *Road & Track*, December 1987, pp.46-57.

1988: "crammed bumper-to-bumper with high-tech sophistication." **Source:** "Mazda Convertible Breezes Along," *The Detroit News,* May 4, 1988, pp.1F-2F.

1987: "182-horsepower RX-7 Turbo an attention grabber." **Source:** "Cars: Fun Work, But Somebody's Got To Do It," *Car and Driver,* January 1987, pp.36-41.

RECALLS

1987: (17,850 cars; includes models made before 1987): Road salt may accumulate on front brake calipers, causing disc pad corrosion. **Corrective action:** Repair front brake calipers to prevent road salt accumulation. *(NHTSA Campaign No. 87V160000.)*

REPAIR MANUALS

1769 ● **Haynes Mazda RX-7 Owners Workshop Manual, No. 1419: 1986-1989**
Haynes Publications, Inc.
861 Lawrence Dr.
Newbury Park, CA 91320   Ph:(818)889-5400

Published 1989. **Editor(s):** J. H. Haynes. **Price:** $15.95.

1770 ● **Mazda 1971-1989 Repair and Tune-Up Guide**
Chilton Co.
Chilton Way
Radnor, PA 19089   Ph:(215)964-4000

Published 1989. **Price:** $15.95.

1771 ● **Mazda GLC, 626, RX 7**
Peter Allen Video Productions
38-C Otis St.
West Babylon, NY 11704   Ph:(516)643-4372

Three tapes on how to maintain and tune-up the three Mazda engines. **Release date:** 1986. **Producer:** Peter Allen Productions. **Acquisition:** Purchase.

OTHER INFORMATION SOURCES

1772 ● **Rotary Review**
Mazda RX-7 Club
1774 S. Alvira
Los Angeles, CA 90035   Ph:(213)933-6993

Magazine for Mazda RX-7 owners. Quarterly. **Price:** $30.00.

1773 ● **Rotary Rocket**
RX-7 Club of America
904 Silver Spur Rd., No. 418
Palos Verdes Estates, CA 90274-3802 Ph:(213)544-0822

Magazine for owners of Mazda Rx-7. Quarterly. **Editor(s):** Curtis L. May, Publisher. **Price:** $30.00, included in membership.

1774 ● **RX-7 Report**
RX-7 Club of America
4020 Palos Verdes Dr. N., Ste. 108
Rolling Hills, CA 90274   Ph:(213)544-0822

Newsletter. Quarterly.

MERCEDES-BENZ 190 (1987-1992)

The smallest Mercedes sedans, the 190 series dropped the 2.3-liter 4-cylinder engine from its vehicles in 1989, replacing it

with the 2.6-liter 6-cylinder engine, which had been available as an option since 1987; the 2.3 reappeared in the 190 line-up in 1991. A 2.5-liter 5-cylinder diesel engine (Mercedes 190D 2.5; 190D 2.5 Turbo) was also available, but not in California.

1991 Mercedes-Benz 190E 2.6

MAJOR FEATURES

● 190E 2.3 1992 standard equipment includes 5-speed manual or 4-speed automatic transmission, 2.3 liter in-line 4-cylinder fuel injected engine, front and rear independent suspension, anti-lock braking system, power steering, cruise control, stereo cassette, climate control, power windows, Supplemental Restraint System (including driver's side air bag), and alloy wheels.

● 190E 2.6 adds as 1992 standard equipment: 2.6 liter 6-cylinder fuel injected engine, and electrically adjustable front bucket seats and head restraints.

● 190E 2.5-16 Evolution II, the longer, wider, lower, and more powerful version of the 190 had standard equipment that included a 16-valve 232 hp engine, hydropneumatic self-leveling control system, flared wheel arches, skirts and air dams, and "race car" styled rear wing.

PRICE HISTORY

The following new car prices reflect the approximate retail cost of the base model: **1987** - $27,430; **1988** - $29,190; **1989** - $30,980; **1990** - $31,600; **1991** - $28,350; **1992** - $28,950.

DIMENSIONS

Body Style	Years Avail	Wheel Base (in)	Lgth (in)	Ht (in)	Avg Wt (lbs)	Fuel Cap (gal)	Front Hdrm (in)	Front Legrm (in)
4d sdn	87-89	104.9	175.1	54.7	2,955	14.5	36.9	41.9
4d sdn	90-92	104.9	175.1	54.1	2,955	14.5	36.9	41.9

ENGINES

Type	Displace-ment (L)	Fuel Dly	HP @rpm	Torque @rpm (ft/lbs)	MPG Cty/Hwy	Years Avail
I-4	2.3	FI	167@5800	162@4750	na	87-87
I-4	2.3	FI	130@5100	146@3500	21/29	87-88
I-4	2.3	FI	130@5100	146@3500	20/28	91-92
I-5D	2.5	FI	93@4600	122@2800	30/34	87-88
I-5D	2.5	FI	90@4600	117@2800	28/33	89-89
I-6	2.6	FI	158@5800	146@3500	18/26	88-88
I-6	2.6	FI	158@5800	162@4600	19/27	88-92

KEY: I=in-line engine; V=V engine; F=flat engine; FI=fuel injection; bbl=barrel carburetor; T=turbo; D=diesel; HP=horsepower; MPG=estimated average miles per gallon.

EVALUATIONS, TESTS, AND RANKINGS

1991: "much of the magic rests squarely within the . . . engine bay . . . foremost was the car's balance and stability . . . handling characteristics were gratifying." **Source:** "Mercedes-Benz 190E 2.5-16 Evolution II," *Road & Track,* November 1990, p.90, 94.

1990: "small inside and out . . . so equipped it is fun and very rewarding to drive briskly . . . suspension, like every Mercedes', will roll over the ugliest of potholes without upsetting the car or its occupants . . . a bit harsher and noiseir than the lesser-priced sedans." **Source:** "Mercedes-Benz 190," *Car and Driver—Buyer's Guide 1990,* 1989, pp.128-129.

1989: "excellent steering, superbly controlled ride, comfortable seats and vaultlike doors." **Source:** "Mercedes Benz 190 E 2.6," *Road & Track,* May 1989, pp.48-50, 52.

1988: "It laughs at potholes . . . strong cruiser." **Source:** "Mercedes Benz 190E 2.3," *Car and Driver,* December 1987, pp.123, 125.

RECALLS

1987-88: (96,541 passenger cars; includes models made before 1987): The design of the parking brake grip makes it possible to distort the grip and pinch the brake release knob. If the release knob sticks in a partial engage/release position, the lever may release unintentionally, causing reduction in parking brake force that would lead to vehicle rollaway. **Corrective action:** Replace the parking brake grip with a new grip type. *(NHTSA Campaign No. 91V137000.)*

1987: (283 cars with airbags; includes models made before 1987; includes Mercedes-Benz models): Push/pull forces of electrical connection between airbag and steering wheel are not within specifications. Could result in airbag failure. **Corrective action:** Replace airbag unit. *(NHTSA Campaign No. 87V073000.)*

SAFETY AND REPAIRS

1988: "1984-88 Mercedes 190s and 1987-88 Aerostars Recalled," *Automotive News,* October 28, 1991, p. 29. **Note:** Parking brake may unintentionally be released.

REPAIR MANUALS

1775 ● Mercedes Diesel
Peter Allen Video Productions
38-C Otis St.
West Babylon, NY 11704   Ph:(516)643-4372

How to maintain, tune-up, and care for the diesel Benz engines. **Release date:** 1986. **Producer:** Peter Allen Productions. **Acquisition:** Purchase.

OTHER INFORMATION SOURCES

1776 ● European Car
Argus Publishers Corp.
12100 Wilshire Blvd., Ste. 250   Ph:(213)820-3601
Los Angeles, CA 90025   Fax:(213)207-9388

Magazine covering Volkswagen, Porsche, Mercedes-Benz, Audi, Ferrari, Jaguar, and BMW automobiles. Bimonthly. **Editor(s):** Greg N. Brown. **Price:** $11.00 per year; $2.75 per issue.

1777 ● Four for the Road: Corvette, Ferrari, Mercedes-Benz, Porsche—The Greatest of the Survivors Series
Motorbooks International
729 Prospect Ave.
Osceola, WI 54020   Ph:(715)294-3345

Published 1989. **Editor(s):** Henry Rasmussen. **Price:** $19.95.

1778 ● Great Marques Mercedes-Benz
Book Sales, Inc.
110 Enterprise Ave.
Secaucus, NJ 07094-1995   Ph:(201)864-6341

Published 1989. **Editor(s):** Roger Bell. **Price:** $10.98.

1779 ● Mercedes-Benz Star
Mercedes-Benz Club of America
1235 Pierce St.   Ph:(303)235-0116
Lakewood, CO 80214   Fax:(303)237-6080

Magazine covering the history, new models, events, and news about Mercedes-Benz autos; including technical information on maintenance, operation, and restoration. Bimonthly. **Editor(s):** Frank Barrett, Editor and Publisher. **Price:** $30.00.

1780 ● Mercedes Magazine
Marque Publishers
P.O. Box 2791
Fullerton, CA 92633   Ph:(714)771-7126

Covers upscale travel, lifestyles, new products and aftermarket accessories for Mercedes-Benz vehicles and their owners. Quarterly. **Editor(s):** R. Janis. **Price:** $12.00 per year; $3.95 per issue.

ASSOCIATIONS

1781 ● Mercedes-Benz Club of America
1907 Lelaray St.
Colorado Springs, CO 80909   Ph:(719)633-6427
Nancy Stith, Mgr.   Fax:(719)633-9283

Founded: 1956. **Membership:** 22,000. Owners and others interested in Mercedes-Benz cars. Sponsors four regional events and local section rallies, concours d'elegance, and gymkhanas. Provides technical information on maintenance and parts. Conducts educational and research programs; sponsors charitable activities; bestows awards. **Convention/Meeting:** Annual - always November. Also holds semiannual meeting. **Additional Numbers:** Toll-free: 800-637-2360.

1782 ● Mercedes-Benz Club of Ft. Worth [Texas]
c/o Gerry M. Goodman
3633 W. 7th
Ft. Worth, TX 76107
Gerry M. Goodman, Pres.   Ph:(817)735-9333

Founded: 1980. **Membership:** 200. Mercedes Benz owners organized to promote and enjoy the automobile. Sponsors annual Concours d'Elegance. **Convention/Meeting:** Bimonthly.

MERCEDES-BENZ 260E (1988-89)

Discontinued after 1989. Part of Mercedes' mid-sized sedan series, the 260E was a lower-priced sister of the 300E with less standard equipment.

MAJOR FEATURES

● 260E 1989 standard equipment includes: 4-speed automatic transmission, power steering, anti-lock braking system, 4-wheel disc brakes, Supplemental Restraint System (SRS), and front/rear independent suspension.

PRICE HISTORY

The following new car prices reflect the approximate retail cost of the base model: **1988** - $37,845; **1989** - $39,200.

DIMENSIONS

Body Style	Years Avail	Wheel Base (in)	Lgth (in)	Ht (in)	Avg Wt (lbs)	Fuel Cap (gal)	Front Hdrm (in)	Front Legrm (in)
4d sdn	88-88	110.2	187.2	56.9	3,175	14.5	36.9	41.7
4d sdn	89-89	110.2	187.2	56.9	3,210	18.5	36.9	41.7

ENGINES

Type	Displacement (L)	Fuel Dly	HP @rpm	Torque @rpm (ft/lbs)	MPG Cty/Hwy	Years Avail
I-6	2.6	FI	158@5800	162@4600	20/24	88-89

KEY: I=in-line engine; V=V engine; F=flat engine; FI=fuel injection; bbl=barrel carburetor; T=turbo; D=diesel; HP=horsepower; MPG=estimated average miles per gallon.

EVALUATIONS, TESTS, AND RANKINGS

1989: "tidy unitized body featuring a high rear deck that tapers slightly for aerodynamic advantage ... impeccably tailored ... driving experience is somewhat anesthetized by the power-assisted recirculating-ball steering." **Source:** "Mercedes-Benz 260E: A sedan like vanilla Haagen-Dazs," *Motor Trend*, November 1988, pp.77-79.

1989: "safety is simply one facet that makes these Mercedes so valued." **Source:** "Mercedes-Benz 260E, 300E & 300TE," *Road & Track—Buyer's Guide 1989*, 1988, p.105.

RECALLS

1988: (283 cars with airbags; includes models made before 1987; includes Mercedes-Benz models): Push/pull forces of electrical connection between airbag and steering wheel are not within specifications. Could result in airbag failure. **Corrective action:** Replace airbag unit. *(NHTSA Campaign No. 87V073000.)*

OTHER INFORMATION SOURCES

1783 ● European Car
Argus Publishers Corp.
12100 Wilshire Blvd., Ste. 250   Ph:(213)820-3601
Los Angeles, CA 90025   Fax:(213)207-9388

Magazine covering Volkswagen, Porsche, Mercedes-Benz, Audi, Ferrari, Jaguar, and BMW automobiles. Bimonthly. **Editor(s):** Greg N. Brown. **Price:** $11.00 per year; $2.75 per issue.

1784 ● Four for the Road: Corvette, Ferrari, Mercedes-Benz, Porsche—The Greatest of the Survivors Series
Motorbooks International
729 Prospect Ave.
Osceola, WI 54020   Ph:(715)294-3345

Published 1989. **Editor(s):** Henry Rasmussen. **Price:** $19.95.

1785 ● Great Marques Mercedes-Benz
Book Sales, Inc.
110 Enterprise Ave.
Secaucus, NJ 07094-1995   Ph:(201)864-6341

Published 1989. **Editor(s):** Roger Bell. **Price:** $10.98.

1786 ● Mercedes-Benz Star
Mercedes-Benz Club of America
1235 Pierce St.   Ph:(303)235-0116
Lakewood, CO 80214   Fax:(303)237-6080

Magazine covering the history, new models, events, and news about Mercedes-Benz autos; including technical information on maintenance, operation, and restoration. Bimonthly. **Editor(s):** Frank Barrett, Editor and Publisher. **Price:** $30.00.

1787 ● Mercedes Magazine
Marque Publishers
P.O. Box 2791
Fullerton, CA 92633   Ph:(714)771-7126

Covers upscale travel, lifestyles, new products and aftermarket accessories for Mercedes-Benz vehicles and their owners. Quarterly. **Editor(s):** R. Janis. **Price:** $12.00 per year; $3.95 per issue.

ASSOCIATIONS

1788 ● Mercedes-Benz Club of America
1907 Lelaray St.
Colorado Springs, CO 80909   Ph:(719)633-6427
Nancy Stith, Mgr.   Fax:(719)633-9283

Founded: 1956. **Membership:** 22,000. Owners and others interested in Mercedes-Benz cars. Sponsors four regional events and local section rallies, concours d'elegance, and gymkhanas. Provides technical information on maintenance and parts. Conducts educational and research programs; sponsors charitable activities; bestows awards. **Convention/Meeting:** Annual - always November. Also holds semiannual meeting. **Additional Numbers:** Toll-free: 800-637-2360.

1789 ● Mercedes-Benz Club of Ft. Worth [Texas]
c/o Gerry M. Goodman
3633 W. 7th
Ft. Worth, TX 76107
Gerry M. Goodman, Pres.   Ph:(817)735-9333

Founded: 1980. **Membership:** 200. Mercedes Benz owners organized to promote and enjoy the automobile. Sponsors annual Concours d'Elegance. **Convention/Meeting:** Bimonthly.

MERCEDES-BENZ 300 (1987-92)

300 series is Mercedes-Benz's mid-size vehicle class of coupes, sedans, and wagons. Assembled in Germany. The 300E was chosen as one of the Ten Best Cars in the World, 1991 by *Road & Track*.

1991 Mercedes-Benz 300E 4MATIC

MAJOR FEATURES

● Standard equipment for the 300 series includes: 3.0 liter six-cylinder engine, 4-speed automatic transmission, front/rear independent suspension, power-assisted steering, anti-lock braking system, Supplemental Restraint System, heated power mirrors, tachometer, auto temperature control, memory seats, ride leveling, power windows, sound system, central locking system, and leather-wrapped steering wheel.

● 300D 2.5 Turbo is a mid-size, turbodiesel sedan with a 2.5 liter, five cylinder engine. Other diesel models available are the 3.5 liter, six-cylinder 300SD Turbo and formerly the 350SDL Turbo. The 300SD is one of five new 1992 S-Class luxury sedans featuring a steel body structure and many interior accessories. It is essentially the diesel version of the 300SE described below. The SDL was the roomier, larger wheelbase version used for the 300SEL.

● 300E is a 5-passenger sedan; the "E" abbreviates *einspritzung*, the German term approximating "fuel injected." The 300E 2.6 sedan is a slightly less powerful version of the 300E, with 2.6 liter displacement instead of the standard 3.0 in other 300 models.

● 300E 4MATIC, first introduced in Geneva in 1987 and available in the U.S. since 1989, comes with automatic all wheel drive.

● 300TE wagons come with hydropneumatic self-leveling rear suspension. A 300TE 4MATIC is also available.

● 300CE, introduced in Geneva in 1987, is a shorter wheelbase coupe design of the 300E.

● 300SE is one of five 1992 S-Class luxury sedans. 300SE standard equipment for 1992 adds: steel body structure, driver and front passenger airbags, two-zone climate control, 12-way power seats with three position memory, double-paned side window glass, 11-speaker Bose Beta sound system, and integrated cellular phone antenna and prewiring. (The 300SEL was identical to the former 300SE, except for a longer wheelbase). Mercedes-Benz's 300SL convertible coupe/roadster crops almost a foot off the wheelbase dimensions of the base 300E and comes with a DOHC 3.0 liter six-cylinder engine and five-link rear suspension. Introduced in Geneva in 1989 for the 1990 model year.

● The 4-door specifications below are for the 300E; the 2-door specifications are for the 300SL coupe; the wagon specifications are for the 300 TE.

PRICE HISTORY

The following new car prices reflect the approximate retail cost of the base model: **1987** - $35,850; **1988** - $43,365; **1989** - $44,850; **1990** - $39,700; **1991** - $41,400; **1992** - $42,950.

DIMENSIONS

Body Style	Years Avail	Wheel Base (in)	Lgth (in)	Ht (in)	Avg Wt (lbs)	Fuel Cap (gal)	Front Hdrm (in)	Front Legrm (in)
2d cpe	90-91	99.0	176.0	50.7	4,010	21.1	37.1	42.4
2d cpe	92-92	106.9	183.9	54.9	3,505	18.5	36.0	41.9
4d sdn	87-92	110.2	187.2	56.3	3,365	18.5	36.9	41.9
5d wgn	87-92	110.2	188.2	59.8	3,590	19.0	37.4	41.7

ENGINES

Type	Displacement (L)	Fuel Dly	HP @rpm	Torque @rpm (ft/lbs)	MPG Cty/Hwy	Years Avail
I-5TD	2.5	FI	121@4600	165@2400	26/31	90-92
I-6	3.0	FI	177@5700	188@4400	18/23	87-92
I-6	3.0	FI	228@6300	201@4600	16/22	90-91
I-6	3.5	FI	134@4000	229@2000	22/25	90-91
I-6	3.0	FI	217@6400	195@4600	18/23	90-92
I-6	2.6	FI	158@5800	162@4600	20/25	90-92
I-6	3.2	FI	228@5800	229@4100	na	92-92
I-6TD	3.0	FI	143@4600	195@2400	23/27	87-87
I-6TD	3.5	FI	134@4000	229@2000	22/25	91-91
I-6TD	3.5	FI	148@4000	229@2200	na	92-92

KEY: I=in-line engine; V=V engine; F=flat engine; FI=fuel injection; bbl=barrel carburetor; T=turbo; D=diesel; HP=horsepower; MPG=estimated average miles per gallon.

EVALUATIONS, TESTS, AND RANKINGS

1992: "Its interior, like its engineering, is tough . . . class with a low profile . . . The car simply does what you ask it to do." **Source:** "Class, in a Garden-Variety Wagon," *The New York Times*, September 22, 1991.

1991: "performance feels lovely . . . engine is silky smooth . . . steering response is rather abrupt, making it somewhat difficult to turn in to a curve with optimum fluency." **Source:** "Mercedes Benz 300E: Appeal Endures Despite Competition," *Autofile*, 1991, pp.159-163.

1991: "is Mercedes-Benz's most capable car." **Source:** "Mercedes-Benz 300E 4Matic," *Automobile Magazine*, January 1991, pp.113-114.

1991: "when 4Matic is in action-and also when it's not . . . the hardware shines." **Source:** "Driving Impressions; Mercedes-Benz 300TE 4Matic," *Road & Track*, November 1990, p.84.

1991: "big, impressive, impeccably trimmed . . . will perform with surprising power and ease . . . will carry three large adults in comfort." **Source:** "Mercedes-Benz 350SDL Turbo: A diesel worthy of a Rockefeller," *Car and Driver*, December 1990, pp.40-41.

1990: "silent operation, solid feel, and impeccable . . . smooth highway performance . . . brakes . . . to a stop without fanfare." **Source:** "Mercedes offers smooth luxury coupe: 300CE combines style, comfort, power," *The Detroit News*, August 22, 1990, pp.1D-2D.

1990: "Cleaner, quieter, more powerful, and more fuel efficient than their predecessors . . . total lack of a traditional diesel personality . . . While neither vehicle falls into the road-rocket category, both are more than capable of keeping on top of any traffic situation." **Source:** "Mercedes-Benz 350SDL Turbo/300D 2.5 Turbo," *Motor Trend*, July 1990, pp. 104-107.

1990: "The doors, windshield pillars, cowl, and floorpan all have been massively overengineered to ensure maximum security . . . exceptional refinement . . . it would be tough to find a sounder long-term investment. For our money, the 500SL stands as the far more enjoyable of the two." **Source:**

"Mercedes/Benz 300SL & 500SL," *Motor Trend*, December 1989, pp. 54-57, 60, 62.

1989: "most thoroughly thought-through 4-door sedan in the world . . . superb mix of willingness and authority." **Source:** "World's Best Cars," *Road & Track*, July 1989, pp.40, 47.

1988: "300TE, almost three times the cost of our least expensive car . . . however, the Mercedes is probably three times the car." **Source:** "Wagon Train: The last rear-drive wagons in America," *Motor Trend*, September 1988, pp.86-90, 92, 94-95.

1988: "smooth, quiet and understated, but with an air of indestructibility . . . concentrates on solid comforts." **Source:** "Mercedes 300SEL has quiet quality," *The Detroit News*, 1988, pp.1F-2F.

1987: "most versatile all-around performer . . . on the hills, the flats and in everyday traffic." **Source:** "Topping 100 in a 300E," *The Detroit News*, June 10, 1987, pp.1F-2F.

RECALLS

1990: (1,584 cars; includes other Mercedes-Benz models): Plastic cover of preresistor for auxiliary fan may melt, possibly igniting the preresistor and resulting in an underhood fire. **Corrective action:** Replace the preresistor with version having a metal cover. Until the preresistor is changed, the climate control system should be operated in the EC mode. *(NHTSA Campaign No. 90V068000.)*

1990: (594 passenger cars; includes the BMW 300, 420, and 500 models): Bolts used for brake strut support do not meet specifications and may break, which could result in loss of control and an accident. **Corrective action:** Replace hex nut bolts with bolts that meet specifications. *(NHTSA Campaign No. 90V033000.)*

1990: (278 cars; includes other Mercedes-Benz models): Left front and rear tires damaged by worn chain drive of conveyor system, which could result in loss of control and an accident. **Corrective action:** Replaced damaged tires with tires of the same brand name. *(NHTSA Campaign No. 90V062000.)*

1987: (283 cars with airbags; includes models made before 1987; includes Mercedes-Benz models): Push/pull forces of electrical connection between airbag and steering wheel are not within specifications. Could result in airbag failure. **Corrective action:** Replace airbag unit. *(NHTSA Campaign No. 87V073000.)*

1987: (230 cars with airbags; includes other Mercedes-Benz models): Airbag gas generator may not ignite at low ambient temperatures. **Corrective action:** Replace airbag unit. *(NHTSA Campaign No. 87V132000.)*

REPAIR MANUALS

1790 ● Mercedes Diesel
Peter Allen Video Productions
38-C Otis St.
West Babylon, NY 11704   Ph:(516)643-4372

How to maintain, tune-up, and care for the diesel Benz engines. **Release date:** 1986. **Producer:** Peter Allen Productions. **Acquisition:** Purchase.

OTHER INFORMATION SOURCES

1791 ● European Car
Argus Publishers Corp.
12100 Wilshire Blvd., Ste. 250   Ph:(213)820-3601
Los Angeles, CA 90025   Fax:(213)207-9388

Magazine covering Volkswagen, Porsche, Mercedes-Benz,

Audi, Ferrari, Jaguar, and BMW automobiles. Bimonthly. **Editor(s):** Greg N. Brown. **Price:** $11.00 per year; $2.75 per issue.

1792 ● Four for the Road: Corvette, Ferrari, Mercedes-Benz, Porsche—The Greatest of the Survivors Series
Motorbooks International
729 Prospect Ave.
Osceola, WI 54020   Ph:(715)294-3345

Published 1989. **Editor(s):** Henry Rasmussen. **Price:** $19.95.

1793 ● Great Marques Mercedes-Benz
Book Sales, Inc.
110 Enterprise Ave.
Secaucus, NJ 07094-1995   Ph:(201)864-6341

Published 1989. **Editor(s):** Roger Bell. **Price:** $10.98.

1794 ● Mercedes-Benz Star
Mercedes-Benz Club of America
1235 Pierce St.   Ph:(303)235-0116
Lakewood, CO 80214   Fax:(303)237-6080

Magazine covering the history, new models, events, and news about Mercedes-Benz autos; including technical information on maintenance, operation, and restoration. Bimonthly. **Editor(s):** Frank Barrett, Editor and Publisher. **Price:** $30.00.

1795 ● Mercedes Magazine
Marque Publishers
P.O. Box 2791
Fullerton, CA 92633   Ph:(714)771-7126

Covers upscale travel, lifestyles, new products and aftermarket accessories for Mercedes-Benz vehicles and their owners. Quarterly. **Editor(s):** R. Janis. **Price:** $12.00 per year; $3.95 per issue.

ASSOCIATIONS

1796 ● Mercedes-Benz Club of America
1907 Lelaray St.
Colorado Springs, CO 80909   Ph:(719)633-6427
Nancy Stith, Mgr.   Fax:(719)633-9283

Founded: 1956. **Membership:** 22,000. Owners and others interested in Mercedes-Benz cars. Sponsors four regional events and local section rallies, concours d'elegance, and gymkhanas. Provides technical information on maintenance and parts. Conducts educational and research programs; sponsors charitable activities; bestows awards. **Convention/Meeting:** Annual - always November. Also holds semiannual meeting. **Additional Numbers:** Toll-free: 800-637-2360.

1797 ● Mercedes-Benz Club of Ft. Worth [Texas]
c/o Gerry M. Goodman
3633 W. 7th
Ft. Worth, TX 76107
Gerry M. Goodman, Pres.   Ph:(817)735-9333

Founded: 1980. **Membership:** 200. Mercedes Benz owners organized to promote and enjoy the automobile. Sponsors annual Concours d'Elegance. **Convention/Meeting:** Bimonthly.

MERCEDES-BENZ 400 (1987-92)

Part of the Mercedes-Benz S Class, the 400SEL was chosen by

The Complete Car Cost Guide as one of the best overall values in luxury cars and one of the lowest in the area of repair costs.

1992 Mercedes-Benz 400SE

MAJOR FEATURES

● 400E (midsize sedan similar in exterior style to the 300E), introduced in 1992, has as standard equipment: 8 cylinder, multivalve 4.2 liter engine, independent suspension, 4-speed automatic transmission, anti-lock braking system, power-assisted steering, cruise control, Supplemental Restraint System, light alloy wheels, high-performance sound system, leather upholstery, and anti-theft alarm system.

● 400SE is one of five new 1992 S-Class luxury sedans. 400SE standard equipment for 1992 adds: steel body structure, two-zone climate control system, driver and front passenger airbags, 11-speaker Bose Beta sound system, rear reading lamps, front seat backs with lumbar support, integrated cellular phone antenna and prewiring, and fuel economy indicator.

● 420SEL, replaced by the 400SE for 1992, had as 1991 standard equipment: 4-speed automatic transmission, front/rear independent suspension, power-assisted steering, 4-wheel disc brakes, Antilock Braking System, light alloy wheels, AM/FM stereo with cassette player, electrically telescopic steering column, and Supplemental Restraint System.

The base prices below are for Mercedes-Benz 420SEL (1987-1991) and 400SE (1992).

PRICE HISTORY

The following new car prices reflect the approximate retail cost of the base model: **1987** - $54,050; **1988** - $59,080; **1989** - $61,210; **1990** - $62,500; **1991** - $63,600; **1992** - $77,900.

DIMENSIONS

Body Style	Years Avail	Wheel Base (in)	Lgth (in)	Ht (in)	Avg Wt (lbs)	Fuel Cap (gal)	Front Hdrm (in)	Front Legrm (in)
4d sdn	87-91	121.1	208.1	56.7	3,915	23.8	37.3	41.9
4d sdn	92-92	110.2	187.2	56.3	3,660	18.5	36.9	41.7
4d sdn	92-92	119.7	201.3	58.9	4,720	26.4	38.0	41.3

ENGINES

Type	Displace-ment (L)	Fuel Dly	HP @rpm	Torque @rpm (ft/lbs)	MPG Cty/Hwy	Years Avail
V-8	4.2	FI	201@5200	228@3600	15/19	87-91
V-8	4.2	FI	268@5700	295@3900	na	92-92
V-8	4.2	FI	282@5700	302@3900	na	92-92

KEY: I=in-line engine; V=V engine; F=flat engine; FI=fuel injection; bbl=barrel carburetor; T=turbo; D=diesel; HP=horsepower; MPG=estimated average miles per gallon.

EVALUATIONS, TESTS, AND RANKINGS

1992: "Mercedes' response to the luxury-car buyers who seek V-8 torque in a midsize luxury package . . . Ride quality and handling . . . medium-soft springing, excellent damping, with a very precise feel . . . an impressive performer and fleshes out the 300-class lineup quite nicely." **Source:** "Mercedes-Benz 400E," *Road & Track,* December 1991, p. 94.

1992: "The mildness of personality is completely forgotten . . . unquestionably leaves the commoners behind . . . a barely noticeable change, until you step on the gas." **Source:** "Mercedes-Benz 400E," *Car and Driver,* November 1991, pp. 103, 105.

1992: "Cruising the highways in the 400SE is a sublime pleasure . . . Superb and silent ride, and a sense of invulnerability . . . Excessive size, weight, and cost." **Source:** "Mercedes-Benz 400SE," *Car and Driver,* December 1991, pp. 87-89.

1992: "[400SE] a steel unit-body that whispers through the wind . . . most amazing thing is the hush of all that performance . . . The ride is, as always, stiff but thoroughly comfortable." **Source:** "Something New Under the Sun," *The New York Times,* October 27, 1991.

1992: "a superb all-around tourer . . . suspension . . . allows a fair amount of body roll . . . comfortable, formidable, and at worst, a thoroughly competent handler." **Source:** "Mercedes-Benz 400E," *Motor Trend,* December, 1991, pp. 80-82.

1992: "handles exceptionally well across a wide range of roads . . . power delivery and braking are especially good . . . U.S. and Asian competitors offer noticeably more interior space." **Source:** "Mercedes-Benz 400E," *Automobile Magazine,* p. 27.

1990: "feels ponderous . . . capable when it's time to hurry. The suspension is well disciplined . . . obsolete." **Source:** "Showdown [Mercedes-Benz 420SEL]," *Car and Driver,* December 1989, pp. 41-43, 46-50, 52, 54-56.

1988: "world's best-built big sedans." **Source:** "Mercedes-Benz 300SEL/420SEL/560SEC/SEL," *Car and Driver—Buyer's Guide 1988,* 1987, p. 119.

1987: "finest workmanship in the industry; the best fit and finish; a reputation for safety, reliability, solidity and dealer service second to none." **Source:** "Mercedes-Benz 420SEL," *Road & Track,* September 1987, pp. 60-62.

RECALLS

1990: (594 passenger cars; includes the BMW 300, 420, and 500 models): Bolts used for brake strut support do not meet specifications and may break, which could result in loss of control and an accident. **Corrective action:** Replace hex nut bolts with bolts that meet specifications. *(NHTSA Campaign No. 90V033000.)*

1987: (230 cars with airbags; includes other Mercedes-Benz models): Airbag gas generator may not ignite at low ambient temperatures. **Corrective action:** Replace airbag unit. *(NHTSA Campaign No. 87V132000.)*

REPAIR MANUALS

1798 ● **Mercedes 8-Cylinder**
Peter Allen Video Productions
38-C Otis St.
West Babylon, NY 11704   Ph:(516)643-4372

How to tune-up and maintain the classic Benz engine. **Release date:** 1986. **Producer:** Peter Allen Productions. **Acquisition:** Purchase.

OTHER INFORMATION SOURCES

1799 ● European Car
Argus Publishers Corp.
12100 Wilshire Blvd., Ste. 250   Ph:(213)820-3601
Los Angeles, CA 90025   Fax:(213)207-9388

Magazine covering Volkswagen, Porsche, Mercedes-Benz, Audi, Ferrari, Jaguar, and BMW automobiles. Bimonthly. **Editor(s):** Greg N. Brown. **Price:** $11.00 per year; $2.75 per issue.

1800 ● Four for the Road: Corvette, Ferrari, Mercedes-Benz, Porsche—The Greatest of the Survivors Series
Motorbooks International
729 Prospect Ave.
Osceola, WI 54020   Ph:(715)294-3345

Published 1989. **Editor(s):** Henry Rasmussen. **Price:** $19.95.

1801 ● Great Marques Mercedes-Benz
Book Sales, Inc.
110 Enterprise Ave.
Secaucus, NJ 07094-1995   Ph:(201)864-6341

Published 1989. **Editor(s):** Roger Bell. **Price:** $10.98.

1802 ● Mercedes-Benz Star
Mercedes-Benz Club of America
1235 Pierce St.   Ph:(303)235-0116
Lakewood, CO 80214   Fax:(303)237-6080

Magazine covering the history, new models, events, and news about Mercedes-Benz autos; including technical information on maintenance, operation, and restoration. Bimonthly. **Editor(s):** Frank Barrett, Editor and Publisher. **Price:** $30.00.

1803 ● Mercedes Magazine
Marque Publishers
P.O. Box 2791
Fullerton, CA 92633   Ph:(714)771-7126

Covers upscale travel, lifestyles, new products and aftermarket accessories for Mercedes-Benz vehicles and their owners. Quarterly. **Editor(s):** R. Janis. **Price:** $12.00 per year; $3.95 per issue.

ASSOCIATIONS

1804 ● Mercedes-Benz Club of America
1907 Lelaray St.
Colorado Springs, CO 80909   Ph:(719)633-6427
Nancy Stith, Mgr.   Fax:(719)633-9283

Founded: 1956. **Membership:** 22,000. Owners and others interested in Mercedes-Benz cars. Sponsors four regional events and local section rallies, concours d'elegance, and gymkhanas. Provides technical information on maintenance and parts. Conducts educational and research programs; sponsors charitable activities; bestows awards. **Convention/Meeting:** Annual - always November. Also holds semiannual meeting. **Additional Numbers:** Toll-free: 800-637-2360.

1805 ● Mercedes-Benz Club of Ft. Worth [Texas]
c/o Gerry M. Goodman
3633 W. 7th
Ft. Worth, TX 76107
Gerry M. Goodman, Pres.   Ph:(817)735-9333

Founded: 1980. **Membership:** 200. Mercedes Benz owners organized to promote and enjoy the automobile. Sponsors annual Concours d'Elegance. **Convention/Meeting:** Bimonthly.

MERCEDES-BENZ 500 (1990-92)

Introduced in 1990 to be the successor to the 560, the 500 now comes as a convertible and sedan. Named by *Road & Track* as one of the Ten Best Cars in the World, 1991. Chosen by *The Complete Car Cost Guide* as having one of the highest insurance costs but one of the lowest repair costs for luxury cars.

1991 Mercedes-Benz 500SL

MAJOR FEATURES

● 500SL (sports convertible) 1992 standard equipment: V-type, 8-cylinder, multivalve, 5.0 liter engine, 4-speed automatic transmission, independent suspension, power-assisted steering, antilock braking system, Supplemental Restraint System (SRS), cruise control, antitheft alarm system, high-performance sound system, wind deflector, and infrared remote control locking system.

● 500E (midsize sedan) adds as 1992 standard equipment: rear axle hydropneumatic level control, and electrically heated front seats. It does not add: wind deflector, and infrared remote control locking system.

● 500SEL is one of five 1992 S-Class luxury sedans. 500SEL standard equipment for 1992 adds: steel body structure, active charcoal climate control filter, driver and front passenger airbags, 12-way power seats with three-position memory, double-paned side window glass, 11-speaker Bose Beta sound system, and integrated cellular phone antenna and prewiring.

● 500SEC added as 1991 standard equipment: coupe body style.

PRICE HISTORY

The following new car prices reflect the approximate retail cost of the base model: **1990** - $83,500; **1991** - $92,700; **1992** - $97,500.

DIMENSIONS

Body Style	Years Avail	Wheel Base (in)	Lgth (in)	Ht (in)	Avg Wt (lbs)	Fuel Cap (gal)	Front Hdrm (in)	Front Legrm (in)
2d cpe	90-92	99.0	176.0	50.7	4,145	21.1	37.1	42.4
4d sdn	92-92	110.2	187.2	55.4	3,750	23.8	na	na
4d sdn	92-92	123.6	205.2	58.9	4,740	26.4	na	na

ENGINES

Type	Displace-ment (L)	Fuel Dly	HP @rpm	Torque @rpm (ft/lbs)	MPG Cty/Hwy	Years Avail
V-8	5.0	FI	322@5500	332@4000	14/18	90-91
V-8	5.0	FI	322@5700	354@3900	14/18	92-92

KEY: I=in-line engine; V=V engine; F=flat engine; FI=fuel injection; bbl=barrel carburetor; T=turbo; D=diesel; HP=horsepower; MPG=estimated average miles per gallon.

EVALUATIONS, TESTS, AND RANKINGS

1992: "Ride quality is superb . . . Steering feel has been improved over the slow, rather lethargic feel of the old car's . . . Can a car, no matter how brilliantly executed, be too big, too thirsty and too expensive." **Source:** "Mercedes-Benz 500SEL," *Road & Track*, December 1991, pp. 64-67.

1991: "one fine driver's car." **Source:** "Mercedes-Benz 500SL," *Road & Track*, December 1990, p.53.

1991: "delightfully sporty mid-size sedan with the taut, muscular feel of a powerful sports car . . . firm but supple suspension settings, responsive steering, and incredibly strong brakes." **Source:** "500E: Blitzen Benz," *Automobile Magazine*, December 1990, pp.61-62.

1991: "car rides tautly, is quick-steering, and feels bull-powerful." **Source:** "Mercedes-Benz 500E," *Car and Driver*, December 1990, pp.101-102, 104, 106, 108, 111.

1991: "[500SL] a symphony of the car builder's art . . . as solid as they come . . . Teutonic stiffness in the car's mien." **Source:** "Mercedes by the Numbers (and Letters)," *The New York Times*, August 18, 1991.

1991: "powerful, stable, and full of more technology than the Museum of Science and Industry . . . inability to seal out some minor leaks that resulted from our carwash test . . . ventilation system is beyond reproach." **Source:** "Top-Down Showdown: We test the hottest cars under the sun," *Motor Trend*, June 1991, pp. 49-59, 62-63.

1990: "[500SL] state of the art . . . Despite the high horsepower, acceleration isn't really startling . . . gives you a feeling of solidity, stability and supreme confidence." **Source:** "Fall Firsts," *Popular Mechanics*, September 1989, 51-53, 105.

1990: "[500SL] the new "must have" wheels for film industry hotshots." **Source:** "Car of the Stars," *Forbes*, May 28, 1990 p. 13.

1990: "[500SL] good-looking, in a brutish sort of way. And it feels taut and responsive, even though it weighs 4,200 pounds . . . Hands down, this must be the safest sports car ever built." **Source:** "2 for the Road," *Regardie's Magazine*, September 1989, pp. 169-170, 172-180, 182.

RECALLS

1990: (594 passenger cars; includes the BMW 300, 420, and 500 models): Bolts used for brake strut support do not meet specifications and may break, which could result in loss of control and an accident. **Corrective action:** Replace hex nut bolts with bolts that meet specifications. *(NHTSA Campaign No. 90V033000.)*

1990: (278 cars; includes other Mercedes-Benz models): Left front and rear tires damaged by worn chain drive of conveyor system, which could result in an accident. **Corrective action:** Replace damaged tires with tires of the same brand name. *(NHTSA Campaign No. 90V062000.)*

REPAIR MANUALS

1806 ● **Mercedes 8-Cylinder**
Peter Allen Video Productions
38-C Otis St.
West Babylon, NY 11704　　　　Ph:(516)643-4372

How to tune-up and maintain the classic Benz engine. **Release date:** 1986. **Producer:** Peter Allen Productions. **Acquisition:** Purchase.

OTHER INFORMATION SOURCES

1807 ● **European Car**
Argus Publishers Corp.
12100 Wilshire Blvd., Ste. 250　　Ph:(213)820-3601
Los Angeles, CA 90025　　　　　　Fax:(213)207-9388

Magazine covering Volkswagen, Porsche, Mercedes-Benz, Audi, Ferrari, Jaguar, and BMW automobiles. Bimonthly. **Editor(s):** Greg N. Brown. **Price:** $11.00 per year; $2.75 per issue.

1808 ● **Four for the Road: Corvette, Ferrari, Mercedes-Benz, Porsche—The Greatest of the Survivors Series**
Motorbooks International
729 Prospect Ave.
Osceola, WI 54020　　　　　　　Ph:(715)294-3345

Published 1989. **Editor(s):** Henry Rasmussen. **Price:** $19.95.

1809 ● **Great Marques Mercedes-Benz**
Book Sales, Inc.
110 Enterprise Ave.
Secaucus, NJ 07094-1995　　　　Ph:(201)864-6341

Published 1989. **Editor(s):** Roger Bell. **Price:** $10.98.

1810 ● **Mercedes-Benz Star**
Mercedes-Benz Club of America
1235 Pierce St.　　　　　　　　Ph:(303)235-0116
Lakewood, CO 80214　　　　　　Fax:(303)237-6080

Magazine covering the history, new models, events, and news about Mercedes-Benz autos; including technical information on maintenance, operation, and restoration. Bimonthly. **Editor(s):** Frank Barrett, Editor and Publisher. **Price:** $30.00.

1811 ● **Mercedes Magazine**
Marque Publishers
P.O. Box 2791
Fullerton, CA 92633　　　　　　Ph:(714)771-7126

Covers upscale travel, lifestyles, new products and aftermarket accessories for Mercedes-Benz vehicles and their owners. Quarterly. **Editor(s):** R. Janis. **Price:** $12.00 per year; $3.95 per issue.

ASSOCIATIONS

1812 ● **Mercedes-Benz Club of America**
1907 Lelaray St.
Colorado Springs, CO 80909　　Ph:(719)633-6427
Nancy Stith, Mgr.　　　　　　　Fax:(719)633-9283

Founded: 1956. **Membership:** 22,000. Owners and others interested in Mercedes-Benz cars. Sponsors four regional events and local section rallies, concours d'elegance, and gymkhanas. Provides technical information on maintenance and parts. Conducts educational and research programs; sponsors charitable activities; bestows awards. **Convention/Meeting:** Annual - always November. Also holds semiannual meeting. **Additional Numbers:** Toll-free: 800-637-2360.

1813 ● **Mercedes-Benz Club of Ft. Worth [Texas]**
c/o Gerry M. Goodman
3633 W. 7th
Ft. Worth, TX 76107
Gerry M. Goodman, Pres.   Ph:(817)735-9333

Founded: 1980. **Membership:** 200. Mercedes Benz owners organized to promote and enjoy the automobile. Sponsors annual Concours d'Elegance. **Convention/Meeting:** Bimonthly.

MERCEDES-BENZ 560 (1987-91)

Replaced in the Mercedes line-up by the 500 and 600SEL in 1992, the 560 was chosen by *Car and Driver* as one of the ten best performers in 1987 for interior sound level at 70 mph.

MAJOR FEATURES

● 560SL 1991 standard equipment included: 4-speed automatic transmission, independent suspension, power-assisted rack-and-pinion steering, anti-lock braking system, front/rear disc brakes, leather upholstery, electrically telescopic steering column, infrared remote control locking system, and Supplemental Restraint System (SRS).

● 560SEL added as 1991 standard equipment: rear axle hydropneumatic level control, limited-slip differential, electric sliding sunroof with rear pop-up feature, and electrically heated front seats.

● 560SEC added as 1991 standard equipment: automatic front seat belt extenders.

PRICE HISTORY

The following new car prices reflect the approximate retail cost of the base model: **1987** - $57,450; **1988** - $62,110; **1989** - $64,230; **1990** - $73,800; **1991** - $75,100.

DIMENSIONS

Body Style	Years Avail	Wheel Base (in)	Lgth (in)	Ht (in)	Avg Wt (lbs)	Fuel Cap (gal)	Front Hdrm (in)	Front Legrm (in)
2d cpe	87-87	96.7	180.3	51.5	3,705	22.5	36.7	42.2
2d cpe	87-91	112.2	199.2	55.0	3,915	23.8	36.8	41.9
2d cpe	88-89	96.7	180.3	51.1	3,705	22.5	36.7	42.2
4d sdn	87-87	120.9	208.1	56.3	4,035	23.8	37.3	41.9
4d sdn	88-91	121.1	208.1	56.3	4,100	23.8	37.3	41.9

ENGINES

Type	Displacement (L)	Fuel Dly	HP @rpm	Torque @rpm (ft/lbs)	MPG Cty/Hwy	Years Avail
V-8	5.6	FI	227@4750	279@3250	14/17	87-89
V-8	5.6	FI	238@4800	287@3500	14/17	87-91

KEY: I=in-line engine; V=V engine; F=flat engine; FI=fuel injection; bbl=barrel carburetor; T=turbo; D=diesel; HP=horsepower; MPG=estimated average miles per gallon.

EVALUATIONS, TESTS, AND RANKINGS

1991: "steering felt unnecessarily heavy but wasn't uncomfortable." **Source:** "Finding the Best Sedan in the World," *Car and Driver*, November 1990, pp. 113-115, 118, 122, 124-128.

1991: "astonishing acceleration ... supremely comfortable cruiser over virtually any road surface ... state of the art in luxury sedans." **Source:** "Mercedes 560SEL a comfy cruiser," *The Detroit News*, July 4, 1991, p. 1C.

1991: "supremely comfortable cruiser ... cabin is exceptionally roomy and quiet ... remains the state of the art in luxury sedans." **Source:** "Mercedes 560SEL A Comfy Cruiser," *Detroit Free Press*, July 4, 1991, p. 1C.

1990: "felt somewhat clumsy, lacked in grip, and was prone to heavy understeer ... feels rich and accommodating ... center position in the back seat is invariably comfortable." **Source:** "East vs. West," *Popular Science*, December 1989, pp. 78-83, 102-104.

1990: "relatively simple and unadorned cockpit ... impressive blend of advanced materials." **Source:** "Mercedes Holds Hidden Treasures," *The Detroit News*, May 9, 1990, pp. 1F-2F.

1989: "feels a bit ponderous ... throttle moves a long way before anything happens ... shocks feel floaty over the bumps ... Its reflexes are slow ... cockpit comfort." **Source:** "Cadillac Allante versus Mercedes 560SL," *Car and Driver*, February 1989, pp. 46-51.

1989: "[560SL] handling isn't up to the Mercedes standards of the 1980s ... just doesn't seem fast ... tall drivers will find that the seat doesn't go back far enough." **Source:** "The People's Choice," *Regardie's*, July 1989, pp. 125-130.

1987: "Coupe handles well, is fairly quick, is handsomely styled, and stops on a dime ... quiet, comfortable, and practical." **Source:** "Mercedes-Benz 560SEC AMG," *Motor Trend*, August 1987, pp. 65-66.

1987: "fit and finish are nothing short of extraordinary." **Source:** "Mercedes-Benz 560SEL," *Car and Driver*, July 1987, pp. 121, 123.

RECALLS

1987: (283 cars with airbags; includes models made before 1987; includes Mercedes-Benz models): Push/pull forces of electrical connection between airbag and steering wheel are not within specifications. Could result in airbag failure. **Corrective action:** Replace airbag unit. *(NHTSA Campaign No. 87V073000.)*

1987: (230 cars with airbags; includes other Mercedes-Benz models): Airbag gas generator may not ignite at low ambient temperatures. **Corrective action:** Replace airbag unit. *(NHTSA Campaign No. 87V132000.)*

REPAIR MANUALS

1814 ● **Mercedes 8-Cylinder**
Peter Allen Video Productions
38-C Otis St.
West Babylon, NY 11704   Ph:(516)643-4372

How to tune-up and maintain the classic Benz engine. **Release date:** 1986. **Producer:** Peter Allen Productions. **Acquisition:** Purchase.

OTHER INFORMATION SOURCES

1815 ● **European Car**
Argus Publishers Corp.
12100 Wilshire Blvd., Ste. 250   Ph:(213)820-3601
Los Angeles, CA 90025   Fax:(213)207-9388

Magazine covering Volkswagen, Porsche, Mercedes-Benz, Audi, Ferrari, Jaguar, and BMW automobiles. Bimonthly. **Editor(s):** Greg N. Brown. **Price:** $11.00 per year; $2.75 per issue.

1816 ● **Four for the Road: Corvette, Ferrari, Mercedes-Benz, Porsche—The Greatest of the Survivors Series**
Motorbooks International
729 Prospect Ave.
Osceola, WI 54020   Ph:(715)294-3345

Published 1989. **Editor(s):** Henry Rasmussen. **Price:** $19.95.

1817 ● **Great Marques Mercedes-Benz**
Book Sales, Inc.
110 Enterprise Ave.
Secaucus, NJ 07094-1995   Ph:(201)864-6341

Published 1989. **Editor(s):** Roger Bell. **Price:** $10.98.

1818 ● **Mercedes-Benz Star**
Mercedes-Benz Club of America
1235 Pierce St.   Ph:(303)235-0116
Lakewood, CO 80214   Fax:(303)237-6080

Magazine covering the history, new models, events, and news about Mercedes-Benz autos; including technical information on maintenance, operation, and restoration. Bimonthly. **Editor(s):** Frank Barrett, Editor and Publisher. **Price:** $30.00.

1819 ● **Mercedes Magazine**
Marque Publishers
P.O. Box 2791
Fullerton, CA 92633   Ph:(714)771-7126

Covers upscale travel, lifestyles, new products and aftermarket accessories for Mercedes-Benz vehicles and their owners. Quarterly. **Editor(s):** R. Janis. **Price:** $12.00 per year; $3.95 per issue.

ASSOCIATIONS

1820 ● **Mercedes-Benz Club of America**
1907 Lelaray St.
Colorado Springs, CO 80909   Ph:(719)633-6427
Nancy Stith, Mgr.   Fax:(719)633-9283

Founded: 1956. **Membership:** 22,000. Owners and others interested in Mercedes-Benz cars. Sponsors four regional events and local section rallies, concours d'elegance, and gymkhanas. Provides technical information on maintenance and parts. Conducts educational and research programs; sponsors charitable activities; bestows awards. **Convention/Meeting:** Annual - always November. Also holds semiannual meeting. **Additional Numbers:** Toll-free: 800-637-2360.

1821 ● **Mercedes-Benz Club of Ft. Worth [Texas]**
c/o Gerry M. Goodman
3633 W. 7th
Ft. Worth, TX 76107
Gerry M. Goodman, Pres.   Ph:(817)735-9333

Founded: 1980. **Membership:** 200. Mercedes Benz owners organized to promote and enjoy the automobile. Sponsors annual Concours d'Elegance. **Convention/Meeting:** Bimonthly.

MERCEDES-BENZ 600SEL (1992)

Introduced as the new Mercedes flagship in 1992, the 600SEL is the first Mercedes production V12. It replaces the 560SEL and is one of five new S-Class luxury sedans featuring a steel body structure to provide a higher level of safety, as well as double-paned side windows to resist fogging, two-zone climate control system, driver and front passenger airbags, 12-

way power seats with three-position memory, 11 speaker Bose Beta sound system, antitheft alarm system, and integrated cellular phone antenna and prewiring.

1992 Mercedes-Benz 600SEL

MAJOR FEATURES

● 600SEL 1992 standard equipment also includes: 12 cylinder, multivalve, 6.0 liter electronic fuel injected engine, 4-speed automatic transmission, power-assisted 4-wheel disc brakes with anti-lock braking system, power assisted steering, rear axle hydropneumatic level control, Automatic Slip Control, Adaptive Damping System, active charcoal climate control filter, electrically heated front seats, cruise control, ten-disc CD changer, electrically operated sunroof, and electrically operated rear window sunshade.

PRICE HISTORY

The following new car prices reflect the approximate retail cost of the base model: **1992** - $127,800.

DIMENSIONS

Body Style	Years Avail	Wheel Base (in)	Lgth (in)	Ht (in)	Avg Wt (lbs)	Fuel Cap (gal)	Front Hdrm (in)	Front Legrm (in)
4d sdn	92-92	123.6	205.2	58.7	4,985	26.4	38.0	41.3

ENGINES

Type	Displacement (L)	Fuel Dly	HP @rpm	Torque @rpm (ft/lbs)	MPG Cty/Hwy	Years Avail
V-12	6.0	FI	402@5200	428@3800	na	92-92

KEY: I=in-line engine; V=V engine; F=flat engine; FI=fuel injection; bbl=barrel carburetor; T=turbo; D=diesel; HP=horsepower; MPG=estimated average miles per gallon.

EVALUATIONS, TESTS, AND RANKINGS

1992: "has come in for criticism as a result of its inflated size and weight . . . a new dollop of techno-goodies." **Source:** "Mercedes by the Numbers (and Letters)," *The New York Times*, August 18, 1991.

RECALLS

None to date.

OTHER INFORMATION SOURCES

1822 ● **European Car**
Argus Publishers Corp.
12100 Wilshire Blvd., Ste. 250   Ph:(213)820-3601
Los Angeles, CA 90025   Fax:(213)207-9388

Magazine covering Volkswagen, Porsche, Mercedes-Benz,

Audi, Ferrari, Jaguar, and BMW automobiles. Bimonthly.
Editor(s): Greg N. Brown. **Price:** $11.00 per year; $2.75 per issue.

1823 ● Mercedes-Benz Star
Mercedes-Benz Club of America
1235 Pierce St.   Ph:(303)235-0116
Lakewood, CO 80214   Fax:(303)237-6080

Magazine covering the history, new models, events, and news about Mercedes-Benz autos; including technical information on maintenance, operation, and restoration. Bimonthly.
Editor(s): Frank Barrett, Editor and Publisher. **Price:** $30.00.

1824 ● Mercedes Magazine
Marque Publishers
P.O. Box 2791
Fullerton, CA 92633   Ph:(714)771-7126

Covers upscale travel, lifestyles, new products and aftermarket accessories for Mercedes-Benz vehicles and their owners. Quarterly. **Editor(s):** R. Janis. **Price:** $12.00 per year; $3.95 per issue.

ASSOCIATIONS

1825 ● Mercedes-Benz Club of America
1907 Lelaray St.
Colorado Springs, CO 80909   Ph:(719)633-6427
Nancy Stith, Mgr.   Fax:(719)633-9283

Founded: 1956. **Membership:** 22,000. Owners and others interested in Mercedes-Benz cars. Sponsors four regional events and local section rallies, concours d'elegance, and gymkhanas. Provides technical information on maintenance and parts. Conducts educational and research programs; sponsors charitable activities; bestows awards. **Convention/Meeting:** Annual - always November. Also holds semiannual meeting. **Additional Numbers:** Toll-free: 800-637-2360.

1826 ● Mercedes-Benz Club of Ft. Worth [Texas]
c/o Gerry M. Goodman
3633 W. 7th
Ft. Worth, TX 76107
Gerry M. Goodman, Pres.   Ph:(817)735-9333

Founded: 1980. **Membership:** 200. Mercedes Benz owners organized to promote and enjoy the automobile. Sponsors annual Concours d'Elegance. **Convention/Meeting:** Bimonthly.

MERCURY CAPRI (1991-92)

Introduced as a 1991 model, Ford's Ghia Studios in Italy styled the Mercury Capri's exterior, while the interior design was done by Italdesign SpA. of Turin, Italy. The powertrain and chassis were developed in conjunction with Mazda, in which Ford Motor Company has a 25 percent equity. Ford of Australia is building the Capri at its assembly plant in Broadmeadows, outside of Melbourne.

1991 Mercury Capri XR2

MAJOR FEATURES

● Capri has as 1992 standard equipment: 5-speed manual transmission, front-wheel drive, power-assisted rack-and-pinion steering, driver-side airbag, four-wheel independent suspension, four-wheel power disc brakes, leather-wrapped steering wheel, and tinted glass.

● Capri XR2 adds as 1992 standard equipment: turbocharged, intercooled engine with boost gauge, air conditioning, cruise control, AM/FM stereo with cassette player, rear spoiler, fog lights, and aluminum wheels.

PRICE HISTORY

The following new car prices reflect the approximate retail cost of the base model: **1990** - $12,588; **1991** - $13,690; **1992** - $14,452.

DIMENSIONS

Body Style	Years Avail	Wheel Base (in)	Lgth (in)	Ht (in)	Avg Wt (lbs)	Fuel Cap (gal)	Front Hdrm (in)	Front Legrm (in)
2d conv	91-92	94.7	166.1	50.2	2,404	11.1	37.8	41.2

ENGINES

Type	Displacement (L)	Fuel Dly	HP @rpm	Torque @rpm (ft/lbs)	MPG Cty/Hwy	Years Avail
I-4	1.6	FI	100@5750	95@5500	25/31	91-92
I-4T	1.6	FI	132@6000	136@3000	23/28	91-92

KEY: I=in-line engine; V=V engine; F=flat engine; FI=fuel injection; bbl=barrel carburetor; T=turbo; D=diesel; HP=horsepower; MPG=estimated average miles per gallon.

EVALUATIONS, TESTS, AND RANKINGS

1991: "good cargo space, cushy ride, blowered brawn . . . dubious rigidity, dull handling, unexciting body . . . terrific job of dissipating impacts . . . strong suit is the way it tracks down the interstate . . . most glaring flaw is cowl shake." **Source:** "Mercury Capri XR2," *Car and Driver*, January 1991, pp. 125-127, 129, 132, 134.

1991: "a no-hassle, trouble-free, easy-to-use, top-down sportster." **Source:** "Mercury Capri," *Popular Mechanics*, December 1990, pp. 25.

1991: "good alternative for buyers who are interested in convertible fun, but still need the utility of a small back seat and a reasonably sized trunk . . . swift, straight-line sprints and plush ride quality are . . . forte." **Source:** "Import Car of the Year," *Motor Trend*, March 1991, pp. 33-35, 37-46, 48, 50.

1991: "sporty car with predictable cornering manners and average handling . . . thinly padded rear bench will accommodate two . . . passenger compartment has an open feel ... powerwise, there's a lot to like." **Source:** "Mercury Capri XR2 Turbo," *Motor Trend,* June 1990, pp. 54, 56-61.

1991: "Capri takes dead aim at the Miata." **Source:** "Top Down, Hopes Up," *Time,* June 25, 1990, p. 49.

RECALLS

1991: (4,200 vehicles): Rubber tube that connects transmission to transmission oil cooler in the radiator may disconnect causing discharge of fluid. **Corrective action:** Install revised line and clamps to improve line retention to transmission. *(NHTSA Campaign No. 91V009000.)*

OTHER INFORMATION SOURCES

1827 ● **FOMOCO Owners Club—Newsletter**
FOMOCO Owners Club
3804 Conifer Dr.
Loveland, CO 80538   Ph:(303)669-8767

Monthly.

1828 ● **Ford-Lincoln-Mercury Club of Florida—Newsletter**
Ford-Lincoln-Mercury Club of Florida
P.O. Box 13514
Tampa, FL 33681   Ph:(813)839-0241

Monthly.

1829 ● **The Sporting Fords [Mercury Capri]**
Motorbooks International
729 Prospect Ave.
Osceola, WI 54020   Ph:(715)294-3345

Published 1990. **Editor(s):** Jeremy Walton. **Price:** $24.95.

ASSOCIATIONS

1830 ● **FOMOCO Owners Club**
3633 Akron Ct.
Loveland, CO 80538
Barry Abels, Exec. Ofc.   Ph:(303)669-8767

Founded: 1985. **Membership:** 250. Individuals dedicated to the exhibition, preservation, and restoration of Edsel, Ford, Lincoln, and Mercury automobiles. Conducts charitable activities; sponsors educational programs. Bestows awards. **Convention/Meeting:** Annual (with exhibits) - 1991 September, Lakewood, CO.

1831 ● **Mercury Club**
702 Center St.
McKeesport, PA 15132
Keith Waltower, Pres.   Ph:(412)751-9409

Founded: 1984. Ford Mercury automobile enthusiasts dedicated to the preservation and enjoyment of Mercury automobiles manufactured from 1939 to the present. Maintains registry; provides sources for parts and services.

MERCURY COUGAR (1987-92)

A corporate twin of the Ford Thunderbird, the Mercury Cougar is produced in Lorain, Ohio. Rated among the best in its class in "Crash Test Performance" by *The Car Book* in 1992.

1991 Mercury Cougar XR7

MAJOR FEATURES

● Cougar LS 1992 standard equipment: 3.8-liter V-6 engine, 4-speed automatic transmission, power-assisted rack-and-pinion steering. air conditioning, tinted glass, and AM/FM radio.

● Cougar XR7 adds as 1992 standard equipment: 5.0-liter V-8 engine, four-wheel anti-lock disc brakes, adjustable handling suspension, sports seats, fog lamps, and alloy wheels.

● Cougar Silver Anniversary will be introduced in mid-1992 model year as a special edition LS model that features a 5.0-liter V-8 engine, a monochromatic color scheme, BBS aluminum wheels, and special interior and exterior trim.

PRICE HISTORY

The following new car prices reflect the approximate retail cost of the base model: **1987** - $15,660; **1988** - $14,026; **1989** - $15,448; **1990** - $15,816; **1991** - $15,696; **1992** - $16,460.

DIMENSIONS

Body Style	Years Avail	Wheel Base (in)	Lgth (in)	Ht (in)	Avg Wt (lbs)	Fuel Cap (gal)	Front Hdrm (in)	Front Legrm (in)
2d cpe	87-88	104.2	200.8	53.8	3,237	22.1	37.7	42
2d cpe	89-90	113	198.7	52.7	3,608	19	38.1	42.5
2d cpe	91-91	113	199.9	52.7	3,587	19	38.1	42.5
2d cpe	92-92	113	199.9	52.7	3,587	18	38.1	42.5

ENGINES

Type	Displace-ment (L)	Fuel Dly	HP @rpm	Torque @rpm (ft/lbs)	MPG Cty/Hwy	Years Avail
V-6	3.8	FI	120@3600	205@1600	21/27	87-87
V-6	3.8	FI	140@3800	215@2400	20/27	88-92
V-6	3.8	FI	210@4000	315@2600	17/24	89-90
V-8	5.0	FI	150@3200	270@2000	18/27	87-87
V-8	5.0	FI	155@3400	265@2200	18/25	88-88
V-8	5.0	FI	200@4000	275@3000	17/24	91-92

KEY: I=in-line engine; V=V engine; F=flat engine; FI=fuel injection; bbl=barrel carburetor; T=turbo; D=diesel; HP=horsepower; MPG=estimated average miles per gallon.

EVALUATIONS, TESTS, AND RANKINGS

1991: "More engine in less space . . . long sloping windshield, while it looks elegant, offers a limited vertical view . . . Considering its size, the XR7 is surprisingly nimble." **Source:** "Cougar XR7 delivers roomy thrills," *Design News,* April 8, 1991, pp. 26, 29.

1989: "aero-look sleekness . . . capable of quickly attaining high speed. The reduction of power assist improves road feel." **Source:** "'89 Mercury Cougar XR7," *Motor Trend,* January 1989, pp. 46-50.

1987: "good behavior in transient maneuvers ... Stopping power was ... strong point ... isolation from wind and road noise was excellent ... balance of luxury and performance." **Source:** "Mercury Cougar," *Motor Trend*, September 1987, pp. 48-51.

RECALLS

1991: (6,800 vehicles with automatic overdrive transmission; includes Ford LTD Crown Victoria, Ford Mustang, Ford Thunderbird, Mercury Cougar, and Mercury Grand Marquis): Park rod assembly contains park cam with inadequate surface hardness, which could lead to park disengagement. **Corrective action:** Replace park rod assembly on automatic transmission. *(NHTSA Campaign No. 91V048000.)*

1990-91: (125,000 passenger cars; includes the Ford Thunderbird and Mercury Cougar): The nuts that hold windshield wiper motor to the wiper module may not have been sufficiently tightened and may loosen or come off causing changed wiper pattern, or the wipers may jam if two of the three nuts come off resulting in reduced driver visibility in inclement weather conditions. **Corrective action:** Apply torque retention material to wiper motor studs and nuts and retorque. *(NHTSA Campaign No. 91V076000.)*

1990: (72 passenger cars with 3.8 liter engines; includes the Ford Thunderbird and Mercury Cougar): Excessive length of battery-to-starter cables could allow contact with engine damper pulley resulting in cable damage, an electrical short and possibly an underhood fire. **Corrective action:** Replace battery to starter cable with correct length cable. *(NHTSA Campaign No. 90V026000.)*

1989: (113,200 cars; includes Ford Thunderbird and Mercury Cougar models): Due to contact between the brake caliper of the inboard front wheel and the front stabilizer bar, there may be increased brake pedal travel following low speed turning maneuvers. Could cause a reduction in brake performance that could result in an accident. **Corrective action:** Install acorn type front suspension strut nuts to eliminate stabilizer bar to brake caliper contact. *(NHTSA Campaign No. 89V081000.)*

1989: (10,600 cars; includes Ford Thunderbird and Mercury Cougar models): Improperly heat treated rear suspension knuckles could experience high mileage fatigue cracks and eventual fracture. Could result in rear suspension failure at the affected wheel with an adverse affect on control of car. **Corrective action:** Replace knuckles that have affected lot codes. *(NHTSA Campaign No. 89V080000.)*

1989: (124 passenger vehicles; includes Mercury Cougar and Ford Thunderbird): Plastic rollover valve mounting plate may not be properly sealed to plastic fuel tank. Fuel or vapor could leak, which could result in vehicle fire. **Corrective action:** Replace fuel tank. *(NHTSA Campaign No. 88V165000.)*

1987: (3,600,000 passenger cars and light trucks equipped with fuel injection. Recall includes several Ford, Mercury, and Lincoln models; includes models made before 1987): Spring lock fuel line coupling may not be properly engaged. Coupling could disengage due to fuel pressure, vibration, and engine movements; this would cause loss of fuel which, in presence of an ignition source, creates a fire risk. **Corrective action:** Install retainer clips over the couplings to prevent coupling separation and fuel leakage. *(NHTSA Campaign No. 87V139000.)*

SAFETY AND REPAIRS

1989: "Car Clinic," *Popular Mechanics*, February 1990, p. 22. **Note:** '89 Cougar with clanking and squealing noise from rear.

REPAIR MANUALS

1832 ● Chilton's Ford-Lincoln-Mercury Full-Size, 1968-1988
Chilton Co.
Chilton Way
Radnor, PA 19089   Ph:(215)964-4000

Published 1989. **Price:** $15.95.

1833 ● Chilton's Ford Thunderbird, Mercury Cougar, Lincoln Continental-Mark VII, 1980-1987
Chilton Co.
Chilton Way
Radnor, PA 19089   Ph:(215)964-4000

Published 1988. **Price:** $15.95.

1834 ● Ford, Lincoln, Mercury Car Repair and Tune-Up Guide: 1972-1987
Clymer Publications
P.O. Box 1209
Overland Park, KS 66212   Ph:(913)541-6694

Published 1987. **Price:** 14.95.

1835 ● Haynes Ford and Mercury Full-Size Owners Workshop Manual, No. 754: 1975-1987
Haynes Publications, Inc.
861 Lawrence Dr.
Newbury Park, CA 91320   Ph:(818)889-5400

Published 1988. **Editor(s):** J. H. Haynes and Chaun Muir. **Price:** $15.95.

OTHER INFORMATION SOURCES

1836 ● Cars of Lincoln-Mercury
Crestline Publishing Co.
1251 N. Jefferson Ave.
Sarasota, FL 34237   Ph:(813)955-8080

Published 1987. **Editor(s):** George H. Dammann and James K. Wagner. **Price:** $34.95.

1837 ● FOMOCO Owners Club—Newsletter
FOMOCO Owners Club
3804 Conifer Dr.
Loveland, CO 80538   Ph:(303)669-8767

Monthly.

1838 ● Ford-Lincoln-Mercury Club of Florida—Newsletter
Ford-Lincoln-Mercury Club of Florida
P.O. Box 13514
Tampa, FL 33681   Ph:(813)839-0241

Monthly.

1839 ● Your Ford: Including Lincoln-Mercury: Essential Service Information for Owners and Mechanics
Consumer Reports Books
51 E. 42nd St., Ste. 800
New York, NY 10017   Ph:(212)682-9280

Based on technical service bulletins issued to Ford and Lincoln-Mercury dealers from 1985 through 1987. Published 1988. **Editor(s):** Mort J. Schultz. **Price:** $8.00.

ASSOCIATIONS

1840 ● FOMOCO Owners Club
3633 Akron Ct.
Loveland, CO 80538
Barry Abels, Exec. Ofc.   Ph:(303)669-8767

Founded: 1985. **Membership:** 250. Individuals dedicated to the exhibition, preservation, and restoration of Edsel, Ford, Lincoln, and Mercury automobiles. Conducts charitable activities; sponsors educational programs. Bestows awards. **Convention/Meeting:** Annual (with exhibits) - 1991 September, Lakewood, CO.

1841 ● Mercury Club
702 Center St.
McKeesport, PA 15132
Keith Waltower, Pres.   Ph:(412)751-9409

Founded: 1984. Ford Mercury automobile enthusiasts dedicated to the preservation and enjoyment of Mercury automobiles manufactured from 1939 to the present. Maintains registry; provides sources for parts and services.

MERCURY GRAND MARQUIS (1987-92)

Corporate twin is the Ford LTD Crown Victoria, the Mercury Grand Marquis two-door model was discontinued in 1988.

1992 Mercury Grand Marquis

MAJOR FEATURES

● Grand Marquis GS 1992 standard equipment: 4.6-liter V-8 engine coupled with 4-speed automatic transmission, four-wheel disc brakes, front independent/rear four-bar link suspension, driver's side airbag, rear shoulder belts, autolamp system, and half vinyl roof.

● Grand Marquis LS 1992 standard equipment: rear armrest, front seatback map pockets, and upscale trim.

● Colony Park GS added as 1991 standard equipment: vinyl trim, power 3-way tailgate, lockable storage compartments, and simulated woodgrain exterior applique.

● Colony Park LS added as 1991 standard equipment: map and engine compartment lights.

PRICE HISTORY

The following new car prices reflect the approximate retail cost of the base model: **1987** - $15,163; **1988** - $16,079; **1989** - $16,701; **1990** - $17,784; **1991** - $19,316; **1992** - $20,216.

DIMENSIONS

Body Style	Years Avail	Wheel Base (in)	Lgth (in)	Ht (in)	Avg Wt (lbs)	Fuel Cap (gal)	Front Hdrm (in)	Front Legrm (in)
2d sdn	87-87	114.3	214.0	55.5	3,757	18.0	37.9	43.5
4d sdn	87-91	114.3	213.6	55.5	3,836	18.0	38.3	42.5
4d sdn	92-92	114.4	212.4	56.9	3,768	20.0	39.4	42.5
5d wgn	87-91	114.3	218.0	56.5	4,032	18.0	39.2	42.5

ENGINES

Type	Displacement (L)	Fuel Dly	HP @rpm	Torque @rpm (ft/lbs)	MPG Cty/Hwy	Years Avail
V-8	5.0	FI	150@3200	270@2000	17/24	87-91
V-8	5.0	FI	160@3400	280@2200	na	89-91
V-8	4.6	FI	190@4200	260@3200	18/25	92-92
V-8	4.6	FI	210@4600	270@3400	na	92-92

KEY: I=in-line engine; V=V engine; F=flat engine; FI=fuel injection; bbl=barrel carburetor; T=turbo; D=diesel; HP=horsepower; MPG=estimated average miles per gallon.

EVALUATIONS, TESTS, AND RANKINGS

1992: "4.6-liter V8 . . . is smooth . . . more rounded, and aerodynamics have improved . . . low nose is complemented by a high and cavernous trunk." **Source:** "Mercury Applies Conventional Wisdom," *The New York Times,* April 28, 1991.

1991: "best-handling large American sedan built today . . . attractive alternative to any import car in its price range." **Source:** "Genteel Wheels," *Home Mechanix,* September 1991, pp. 72-76, 84.

1991: "simply looks more expensive than it is . . . handsome exterior skin . . . cabin is a little bland . . . well-equipped luxury car masquerading as a family sedan." **Source:** "Grand Marquis has the Juice," *Detroit Free Press,* August 1, 1991, p. 1E.

1990: "same characteristics pervade the Grand Marquis, which strives for nothing if not nearness to, and yet not quite equality with (dare it be said?), the big Lincolns . . . provide[s] . . . a certain emotional distance from the world, partly through long-accepted styling cues." **Source:** "Mercury Grand Marquis," *Car and Driver—Buyers Guide 1990,* 1989, p. 101.

1990: "[Grand Marquis Wagon] . . . carrying capacity is . . . forte. This is megaMarquisness." **Source:** "Mercury Grand Marquis," *Car and Driver—Buyer's Guide 1990,* 1989, pp. 154-155.

RECALLS

1991: (6,800 vehicles with automatic overdrive transmission; includes Ford LTD Crown Victoria, Ford Mustang, Ford Thunderbird, Mercury Cougar, and Mercury Grand Marquis): Park rod assembly contains park cam with inadequate surface hardness, which could lead to park disengagement. **Corrective action:** Replace park rod assembly on automatic transmission. *(NHTSA Campaign No. 91V048000.)*

1987-88: (21,200 station wagons equipped with optional dual facing rear seats; includes Ford and Mercury models): Automatic retractor for seat belts for dual facing rear seats may be installed in an improper location. Seat belt could bind between seat cushion and seat back, causing the retractor to be sluggish or unable to take up excess belt slack. **Corrective action:** Remove and properly install the right auxiliary seat belts. *(NHTSA Campaign No. 88V028000.)*

1987: (11,119 passenger cars equipped with 5.0 liter fuel injected engines. Recall includes Ford Crown Victoria, Mercury Grand Marquis, and Lincoln Town Car): Fuel rails may be bent so that No. 5 injector cups are out of design position. Could cause a fuel leak, which in presence of an ignition source could result in an engine fire. **Corrective action:** Replace fuel rail assemblies as necessary. *(NHTSA Campaign No. 87V131000.)*

1987: (29,600 passenger vehicles with 5.0 liter engines. Recall includes the Ford LTD Crown Victoria, Mercury Grand Marquis, and Lincoln Town Car): Steering centerlinks may break at a bend location. Steering control would be diminished, with reduced control of left wheel only and considerable steering wheel free play. **Corrective action:** Replace steering centerlink. *(NHTSA Campaign No. 87V012000.)*

REPAIR MANUALS

1842 ● Chilton's Ford-Lincoln-Mercury Full-Size, 1968-1988
Chilton Co.
Chilton Way
Radnor, PA 19089   Ph:(215)964-4000

Published 1989. **Price:** $15.95.

1843 ● Ford, Lincoln, Mercury Car Repair and Tune-Up Guide: 1972-1987
Clymer Publications
P.O. Box 1209
Overland Park, KS 66212   Ph:(913)541-6694

Published 1987. **Price:** 14.95.

1844 ● Haynes Ford and Mercury Full-Size Owners Workshop Manual, No. 754: 1975-1987
Haynes Publications, Inc.
861 Lawrence Dr.
Newbury Park, CA 91320   Ph:(818)889-5400

Published 1988. **Editor(s):** J. H. Haynes and Chaun Muir. **Price:** $15.95.

OTHER INFORMATION SOURCES

1845 ● Cars of Lincoln-Mercury
Crestline Publishing Co.
1251 N. Jefferson Ave.
Sarasota, FL 34237   Ph:(813)955-8080

Published 1987. **Editor(s):** George H. Dammann and James K. Wagner. **Price:** $34.95.

1846 ● Ford-Lincoln-Mercury Club of Florida—Newsletter
Ford-Lincoln-Mercury Club of Florida
P.O. Box 13514
Tampa, FL 33681   Ph:(813)839-0241

Monthly.

1847 ● Your Ford: Including Lincoln-Mercury: Essential Service Information for Owners and Mechanics
Consumer Reports Books
51 E. 42nd St., Ste. 800
New York, NY 10017   Ph:(212)682-9280

Based on technical service bulletins issued to Ford and Lincoln-Mercury dealers from 1985 through 1987. Published 1988. **Editor(s):** Mort J. Schultz. **Price:** $8.00.

ASSOCIATIONS

1848 ● FOMOCO Owners Club
3633 Akron Ct.
Loveland, CO 80538
Barry Abels, Exec. Ofc.   Ph:(303)669-8767

Founded: 1985. **Membership:** 250. Individuals dedicated to

the exhibition, preservation, and restoration of Edsel, Ford, Lincoln, and Mercury automobiles. Conducts charitable activities; sponsors educational programs. Bestows awards. **Convention/Meeting:** Annual (with exhibits) - 1991 September, Lakewood, CO.

1849 ● Mercury Club
702 Center St.
McKeesport, PA 15132
Keith Waltower, Pres.   Ph:(412)751-9409

Founded: 1984. Ford Mercury automobile enthusiasts dedicated to the preservation and enjoyment of Mercury automobiles manufactured from 1939 to the present. Maintains registry; provides sources for parts and services.

MERCURY LYNX (1987)

The Mercury Lynx was the corporate twin of the Ford Escort. Produced in Wayne, Michigan and Edison, New Jersey until it was discontinued in 1987.

1987 Mercury Lynx XR3

MAJOR FEATURES

● Lynx L 1987 standard equipment: 5-speed manual transmission, front/rear independent suspension, front disc/rear drum brakes, and rack-and-pinion steering.

● Lynx GS added as 1987 standard equipment: wheel hub covers and lug nuts.

● Lynx XR3 added as 1987 standard equipment: asymmetrical grille, air dam, spoiler, and wheel spats.

PRICE HISTORY

The following new car prices reflect the approximate retail cost of the base model: **1987** - $6,716.

DIMENSIONS

Body Style	Years Avail	Wheel Base (in)	Lgth (in)	Ht (in)	Avg Wt (lbs)	Fuel Cap (gal)	Front Hdrm (in)	Front Legrm (in)
3d sdn	87-87	94.2	166.9	53.3	2,183	13	37.9	41.5
5d sdn	87-87	94.2	166.9	53.5	2,258	13	37.9	41.5
5d wgn	87-87	94.2	168	53.5	2,277	13	37.9	41.5

ENGINES

Type	Displace-ment (L)	Fuel Dly	HP @rpm	Torque @rpm (ft/lbs)	MPG Cty/Hwy	Years Avail
I-4	1.9	2-bbl	90@4600	106@3400	25/34	87-87
I-4	1.9	FI	115@5200	120@4400	22/26	87-87
I-4D	2.0	FI	58@3600	84@3000	37/45	87-87

KEY: I=in-line engine; V=V engine; F=flat engine; FI=fuel injection; bbl=barrel carburetor; T=turbo; D=diesel; HP=horsepower; MPG=estimated average miles per gallon.

RECALLS

1987: (3,600,000 passenger cars and light trucks equipped with fuel injection. Recall includes several Ford, Mercury, and Lincoln models; includes models made before 1987): Spring lock fuel line coupling may not be properly engaged. Coupling could disengage due to fuel pressure, vibration, and engine movements; this would cause loss of fuel which, in presence of an ignition source, creates a fire risk. **Corrective action:** Install retainer clips over the couplings to prevent coupling separation and fuel leakage. (NHTSA Campaign No. 87V139000.)

1987: (350 passenger cars equipped with stainless steel decorative lug nuts included with styled steel polycast, and cast aluminum wheels. Includes Ford Escort, Ford Tempo, and Mercury Lynx): Lug nuts could gall and possibly seize on the wheel studs without providing adequate clamping load on the wheels. Wheel studs could fracture creating a risk of a wheel separating with little forewarning. **Corrective action:** Replace wheel lug nuts and if necessary, replace wheels and wheel studs. (NHTSA Campaign No. 87V060000.)

1987: (1,367,500 cars; includes the Ford Escort and Mercury Lynx; includes models made before 1987): Forward outboard pedestal of the seat track of driver's seat may be susceptible to fatigue fracture. Could result in limited degree of rocking motion of driver's seat assembly upon acceleration or deceleration, which could cause an accident. **Corrective action:** Install a reinforcement of all models and a new seat track as necessary. (NHTSA Campaign No. 89V170000.)

SAFETY AND REPAIRS

1987: "Cover Story," *Popular Mechanics,* November 1988, p.51. **Note:** 1987 Escort (and Lynx) with noise from rear of car.

1987: "Car Clinic," *Popular Mechanics,* October 1990, p. 107. **Note:** Tip for clicking noise from front brakes in 87-88 Escort, Mercury Topaz, and Mercury Lynx.

REPAIR MANUALS

1850 ● **Chilton Ford-Mercury Front Wheel Drive 1981-1987**
Chilton Co.
Chilton Way
Radnor, PA 19089   Ph:(215)964-4000

Published 1987. **Price:** $14.95.

1851 ● **Ford Escort-EXP and Mercury Lynx-LN7, 1981-1989: Shop Manual**
Clymer Publications
P.O. Box 1209
Overland Park, KS 66212   Ph:(913)541-6694

Published 1989. **Price:** $14.95.

1852 ● **Ford, Lincoln, Mercury Car Repair and Tune-Up Guide: 1972-1987**
Clymer Publications
P.O. Box 1209
Overland Park, KS 66212   Ph:(913)541-6694

Published 1987. **Price:** 14.95.

1853 ● **Haynes Ford Escort and Mercury Lynx Owners Manual Workshop Manual, No. 789: 1981-1988**
Haynes Publications, Inc.
861 Lawrence Dr.
Newbury Park, CA 91320   Ph:(818)889-5400

Price: $15.95.

OTHER INFORMATION SOURCES

1854 ● **Cars of Lincoln-Mercury**
Crestline Publishing Co.
1251 N. Jefferson Ave.
Sarasota, FL 34237   Ph:(813)955-8080

Published 1987. **Editor(s):** George H. Dammann and James K. Wagner. **Price:** $34.95.

1855 ● **FOMOCO Owners Club—Newsletter**
FOMOCO Owners Club
3804 Conifer Dr.
Loveland, CO 80538   Ph:(303)669-8767

Monthly.

1856 ● **Ford-Lincoln-Mercury Club of Florida—Newsletter**
Ford-Lincoln-Mercury Club of Florida
P.O. Box 13514
Tampa, FL 33681   Ph:(813)839-0241

Monthly.

1857 ● **Your Ford: Including Lincoln-Mercury: Essential Service Information for Owners and Mechanics**
Consumer Reports Books
51 E. 42nd St., Ste. 800
New York, NY 10017   Ph:(212)682-9280

Based on technical service bulletins issued to Ford and Lincoln-Mercury dealers from 1985 through 1987. Published 1988. **Editor(s):** Mort J. Schultz. **Price:** $8.00.

ASSOCIATIONS

1858 ● **FOMOCO Owners Club**
3633 Akron Ct.
Loveland, CO 80538
Barry Abels, Exec. Ofc.   Ph:(303)669-8767

Founded: 1985. **Membership:** 250. Individuals dedicated to the exhibition, preservation, and restoration of Edsel, Ford, Lincoln, and Mercury automobiles. Conducts charitable activities; sponsors educational programs. Bestows awards. **Convention/Meeting:** Annual (with exhibits) - 1991 September, Lakewood, CO.

1859 ● **Mercury Club**
702 Center St.
McKeesport, PA 15132
Keith Waltower, Pres.   Ph:(412)751-9409

Founded: 1984. Ford Mercury automobile enthusiasts dedicated to the preservation and enjoyment of Mercury automobiles manufactured from 1939 to the present. Maintains registry; provides sources for parts and services.

MERCURY SABLE (1987-92)

Corporate twin of the Ford Taurus, the Mercury Sable is produced in Chicago, Illinois and Atlanta, Georgia (Atlanta plant parts data: domestic parts - 96%, imported parts - 4%, *Federal Trade Zone Board*, 1989). Remained in fifth place on *Car and Driver-Buyer's Guide 1990* Ten Best Cars List. Listed in *The Complete Car Cost Guide* in 1990 as a midsize car with one of the highest repair costs (Sable Series, including the GS), lowest insurance costs (Sable GS), lowest fuel costs (Sable), lowest maintenance cost (Sable Series, including the GS), and the best overall value (Sable LS and GS). Rated a "Best Bet of 1992" in the intermediate class by *The Car Book*.

1992 Mercury Sable

MAJOR FEATURES

● Sable GS Sedan and Wagon 1992 standard equipment includes: 4-speed automatic transmission, 4-wheel independent suspension, power steering, tilt steering column, driver-side air bag, and front disc/rear drum brakes; wagon has 60/40 folding rear seat, tiedown hooks, and luggage racks. In addition, Sable features all-new sheet metal on every exterior panel except the roof.

● Sable LS Sedan and Wagon add as 1992 standard equipment: power windows, automatic parking brake release, Light Group, other exterior body stylings, upgraded upholstery, and interior trim.

PRICE HISTORY

The following new car prices reflect the approximate retail cost of the base model: **1987** - $12,340; **1988** - $13,772; **1989** - $14,101; **1990** - $15,065; **1991** - $15,372; **1992** - $16,418.

DIMENSIONS

Body Style	Years Avail	Wheel Base (in)	Lgth (in)	Ht (in)	Avg Wt (lbs)	Fuel Cap (gal)	Front Hdrm (in)	Front Legrm (in)
4d sdn	87-88	106.0	190.9	54.3	3,097	16.0	38.3	41.7
4d sdn	89-92	106.0	192.2	54.4	3,147	16.0	38.3	41.7
5d wgn	87-89	106.0	191.9	55.1	3,228	16.0	38.6	41.7
5d wgn	90-90	106.0	192.2	55.1	3,260	16.0	38.6	41.7
5d wgn	91-92	106.0	193.3	55.1	3,292	16.0	38.6	41.7

ENGINES

Type	Displace- ment (L)	Fuel Dly	HP @rpm	Torque @rpm (ft/lbs)	MPG Cty/Hwy	Years Avail
V-6	3.0	FI	140@4800	160@3000	20/29	87-92
V-6	3.8	FI	140@3800	215@2200	18/28	88-92

KEY: I=in-line engine; V=V engine; F=flat engine; FI=fuel injection; bbl=barrel carburetor; T=turbo; D=diesel; HP=horsepower; MPG=estimated average miles per gallon.

EVALUATIONS, TESTS, AND RANKINGS

1992: "safety-oriented, solid and sensible, but not very sexy ... styling is clean and the silhouette is a bit trimmer ... Interior styling is more adventuresome, but far from heart-pounding." **Source:** "Sable still a solid, sensible choice," *The Flint Journal*, November 20, 1991, pp. E1-E2.

1992: "Taurus/Sable twins are surprisingly nimble for their size ... Taurus/Sable siblings have certainly been improved ... they're both well-mannered, refined, spacious family sedans." **Source:** "Ford Taurus LX, Mercury Sable LS: Better, different but less distinctive," *Road & Track*, January 1992, pp. 57-60.

1992: "Sleeker interior ... external changes are minor." **Source:** "New Taurus, New Sable, Old Blueprint," *Business Week*, September 9, 1991, p. 43.

1990: "Sable's shape, five years old, perseveres as fresh as new money ... offers a fully modern design treatment inside and out ... Forethought ripples throughout the entire car." **Source:** "Sun, Sand, & Sedans," *Motor Trend*, June 1990, pp. 96-99, 102-104, 106.

1990: "sleek shape surrounds a comfy and cozy cabin ... blessed with a wonderful chassis ... superb family sedan that looks and drives like a much more expensive car." **Source:** "Mercury Sable LS: The Taurus's twin takes its turn," *Car and Driver*, February 1990, p. 111.

1988: "fully independent rear end, was second softest in the front seat cushion ... precise steering, stability, and sure-footedness ... fine combination of modern interior and exterior design, solid handling, and adequate, if not spectacular, performance." **Source:** "Luxury for Less," *Popular Science*, July 1988, pp.28-30, 32.

RECALLS

1990: (2,900 passenger cars with autolamp headlamp control system; recall includes Ford Taurus and Mercury Sable): Incorrect transistor may cause autolamp system light sensor module malfunction. Headlamps could turn off while vehicle is being driven or remain on after vehicle is parked. Loss of headlights while driving at night could be hazardous to the driver and other traffic. **Corrective action:** Replace light sensor modules. *(NHTSA Campaign No. 89V171000.)*

1989: (22,000 cars): Front side marker lamps were unintentionally equipped with clear bulbs, instead of amber colored bulbs as specified in FMVSS 108. Vehicles would not comply with standards. **Corrective action:** Replace clear bulbs with amber colored bulbs. *(NHTSA Campaign No. 88V190000.)*

1988-89: (278,000 vehicles; includes Ford Taurus and Mercury Sable models): Power seat switch wiring is routed over rather than under front seat support brace, allowing damage by seat cushion spring ends. May result in an electrical short and a fire in seat cushion material. **Corrective action:** Revise routing of power seat wiring to prevent damage from seat cushion spring contact. *(NHTSA Campaign No. 91V036000.)*

1987: (3,600,000 passenger cars and light trucks equipped with fuel injection. Recall includes several Ford, Mercury, and Lincoln models; includes models made before 1987): Spring lock fuel line coupling may not be properly engaged. Coupling could disengage due to fuel pressure, vibration, and engine movements; this would cause loss of fuel which, in presence of an ignition source, creates a fire risk. **Corrective action:** Install retainer clips over the couplings to prevent coupling separation and fuel leakage. *(NHTSA Campaign No. 87V139000.)*

1987: (28,000 station wagons equipped with optional rear window wiper motors. Recall includes the Ford Taurus Wagon and Mercury Sable Wagon; includes models made before 1987): Road salt-induced erosion of the wiper motor conductor strips could cause localized thermal stress within the glass. Glass could fracture while station wagon is being driven or parked, creating a risk or injury to occupants or sudden distraction to the driver. **Corrective action:** Apply sealant to conductor strips and protective tape to lower backlites. *(NHTSA Campaign No. 87V017000.)*

1987: (325,000 passenger vehicles sold or registered in the following states: CT, IL, IN, ME, MA, MI, NH, NJ, NY, OH, PA, RI, VT, and WI; includes models made before 1987): Front disc brake rotors may experience severe corrosion if operated in areas where calcium chloride and sodium chloride are used extensively. Severely corroded rotors may fracture or separate near the inner edges of the brake discs causing reduced braking effectiveness, possibly resulting in an accident. **Corrective action:** Replace front brake rotors with full cast front brake rotors. *(NHTSA Campaign No. 91V134000.)*

SAFETY AND REPAIRS

1991: ''Taurus Cargo Bin Probed After Child Suffocates,'' *Automotive News,* October 7, 1991, p. 2. **Note:** NHTSA has received four reports of children getting stuck inside a rear storage compartment of Ford Taurus and Mercury Sable wagons built since 1986.

1989: ''NHTSA Investigating Taurus Start Switches,'' *Automotive News,* November 4, 1991, p. 52. **Note:** Ignition switches could overheat in 1986-89 Sable models.

REPAIR MANUALS

1860 ● **Ford, Lincoln, Mercury Car Repair and Tune-Up Guide: 1972-1987**
Clymer Publications
P.O. Box 1209
Overland Park, KS 66212   Ph:(913)541-6694

Published 1987. **Price:** 14.95.

1861 ● **Haynes Ford Taurus and Mercury Sable Owners Workshop Manual, No. 1421: 1986-1990**
Haynes Publications, Inc.
861 Lawrence Dr.
Newbury Park, CA 91320   Ph:(818)889-5400

Editor(s): J. H. Haynes and Bob Henderson. **Price:** $15.95.

OTHER INFORMATION SOURCES

1862 ● **Cars of Lincoln-Mercury**
Crestline Publishing Co.
1251 N. Jefferson Ave.
Sarasota, FL 34237   Ph:(813)955-8080

Published 1987. **Editor(s):** George H. Dammann and James K. Wagner. **Price:** $34.95.

1863 ● **FOMOCO Owners Club—Newsletter**
FOMOCO Owners Club
3804 Conifer Dr.
Loveland, CO 80538   Ph:(303)669-8767

Monthly.

1864 ● **Ford-Lincoln-Mercury Club of Florida—Newsletter**
Ford-Lincoln-Mercury Club of Florida
P.O. Box 13514
Tampa, FL 33681   Ph:(813)839-0241

Monthly.

1865 ● **Your Ford: Including Lincoln-Mercury: Essential Service Information for Owners and Mechanics**
Consumer Reports Books
51 E. 42nd St., Ste. 800
New York, NY 10017   Ph:(212)682-9280

Based on technical service bulletins issued to Ford and Lincoln-Mercury dealers from 1985 through 1987. Published 1988. **Editor(s):** Mort J. Schultz. **Price:** $8.00.

ASSOCIATIONS

1866 ● **FOMOCO Owners Club**
3633 Akron Ct.
Loveland, CO 80538
Barry Abels, Exec. Ofc.   Ph:(303)669-8767

Founded: 1985. **Membership:** 250. Individuals dedicated to the exhibition, preservation, and restoration of Edsel, Ford, Lincoln, and Mercury automobiles. Conducts charitable activities; sponsors educational programs. Bestows awards. **Convention/Meeting:** Annual (with exhibits) - 1991 September, Lakewood, CO.

1867 ● **Mercury Club**
702 Center St.
McKeesport, PA 15132
Keith Waltower, Pres.   Ph:(412)751-9409

Founded: 1984. Ford Mercury automobile enthusiasts dedicated to the preservation and enjoyment of Mercury automobiles manufactured from 1939 to the present. Maintains registry; provides sources for parts and services.

MERCURY TOPAZ (1987-92)

Corporate twin of the Ford Tempo, the Mercury Topaz is produced in Kansas City, Missouri.

1988 Mercury Topaz

MAJOR FEATURES

● Topaz GS 1992 standard equipment includes: 2.3-liter I-4 engine, 5-speed manual transmission, 4-wheel independent suspension, power-assisted rack-and-pinion steering, front-wheel drive, and tinted glass.

● Topaz LS adds as 1992 standard equipment: sport suspension, performance tires, rear defogger, cruise control, Light Group, AM/FM stereo cassette, and tilt steering column.

● Topaz LTS adds to LS as 1992 standard equipment: 3.0-liter V-6 engine, performance axle ratio, air conditioning, power driver's seat, alloy wheels, leather-wrapped steering wheel, premium sound system, and sport seats.

● Topaz XR5 adds to GS as 1992 standard equipment:

upgraded 3.0-liter V-6 engine, sport suspension, performance tires on alloy wheels, rear defogger, Light Group, AM/FM stereo cassette, tilt steering column, and sport seats.

PRICE HISTORY

The following new car prices reflect the approximate retail cost of the base model: **1987** - $8,664; **1988** - $9,166; **1989** - $9,577; **1990** - $10,007; **1991** - $10,112; **1992** - $10,512.

DIMENSIONS

Body Style	Years Avail	Wheel Base (in)	Lgth (in)	Ht (in)	Avg Wt (lbs)	Fuel Cap (gal)	Front Hdrm (in)	Front Legrm (in)
2d sdn	87-92	99.9	176.7	52.8	2,546	15.9	37.5	41.5
4d sdn	87-92	99.9	177.0	52.9	2,602	15.9	37.5	41.5

ENGINES

Type	Displacement (L)	Fuel Dly	HP @rpm	Torque @rpm (ft/lbs)	MPG Cty/Hwy	Years Avail
I-4	2.3	FI	86@3800	120@3200	25/34	87-87
I-4	2.3	FI	94@4000	120@3200	22/30	87-87
I-4	2.3	FI	98@4400	124@2200	22/32	88-91
I-4	2.3	FI	100@4400	130@2600	21/29	88-91
I-4	2.3	FI	96@4400	128@2600	23/33	92-92
V-6	3.0	FI	140@5500	151@4250	21/28	92-92

KEY: I=in-line engine; V=V engine; F=flat engine; FI=fuel injection; bbl=barrel carburetor; T=turbo; D=diesel; HP=horsepower; MPG=estimated average miles per gallon.

EVALUATIONS, TESTS, AND RANKINGS

1989: "offers sensible, day-to-day transportation. Don't look for excitement . . . sluggish increase in speed . . . There was lots of room in the trunk." **Source:** "Topaz Loses the Jelly Bean Look," *The Detroit News*, February 1, 1989, pp.1F-2F.

RECALLS

1988: (91,000 vehicles with 2.3L engines; includes Ford and Mercury models): Two attachment screws for the throttle position sensors could loosen and back out. If both screws come out, sensors could disengage from the throttle shaft, preventing return of the throttle from mid position. **Corrective action:** Replace attachment screws with screws pre-applied adhesive that will be tightened to a higher torque specification. *(NHTSA Campaign No. 88V024000.)*

SAFETY AND REPAIRS

1991: "Ford Recalls 641,562 Units," *Automotive News*, December 2, 1991, p. 2. **Note:** 1990-91 Topaz models with 2.3 liter engines will have throttle position sensors replaced.

1989: "Ford Puts 5/50 on Fuel Pumps," *Automotive News*, November 25, 1991, p. 2. **Note:** 1988-89 Topaz models get extended warranty on fuel pump, which may have a weak internal seal.

1987: "Car Clinic," *Popular Mechanics*, October 1990, p. 107. **Note:** Tip for clicking noise from front brakes in 87-88 Escort, Mercury Topaz, and Mercury Lynx.

REPAIR MANUALS

1868 ● **Chilton Ford-Mercury Front Wheel Drive 1981-1987**
Chilton Co.
Chilton Way
Radnor, PA 19089   Ph:(215)964-4000

Published 1987. **Price:** $14.95.

1869 ● **Ford, Lincoln, Mercury Car Repair and Tune-Up Guide: 1972-1987**
Clymer Publications
P.O. Box 1209
Overland Park, KS 66212   Ph:(913)541-6694

Published 1987. **Price:** 14.95.

1870 ● **Ford Tempo and Mercury Topaz, 1984-1987**
Clymer Publications
P.O. Box 1209
Overland Park, KS 66212   Ph:(913)541-6694

Published 1987. **Price:** $14.95.

1871 ● **Haynes Ford Tempo-Mercury Topaz Owners Workshop Manual, No. 1418: 1984-1989**
Haynes Publications, Inc.
861 Lawrence Dr.
Newbury Park, CA 91320   Ph:(818)889-5400

Published 1988. **Price:** $15.95.

OTHER INFORMATION SOURCES

1872 ● **Cars of Lincoln-Mercury**
Crestline Publishing Co.
1251 N. Jefferson Ave.
Sarasota, FL 34237   Ph:(813)955-8080

Published 1987. **Editor(s):** George H. Dammann and James K. Wagner. **Price:** $34.95.

1873 ● **FOMOCO Owners Club—Newsletter**
FOMOCO Owners Club
3804 Conifer Dr.
Loveland, CO 80538   Ph:(303)669-8767

Monthly.

1874 ● **Ford-Lincoln-Mercury Club of Florida—Newsletter**
Ford-Lincoln-Mercury Club of Florida
P.O. Box 13514
Tampa, FL 33681   Ph:(813)839-0241

Monthly.

1875 ● **Your Ford: Including Lincoln-Mercury: Essential Service Information for Owners and Mechanics**
Consumer Reports Books
51 E. 42nd St., Ste. 800
New York, NY 10017   Ph:(212)682-9280

Based on technical service bulletins issued to Ford and Lincoln-Mercury dealers from 1985 through 1987. Published 1988. **Editor(s):** Mort J. Schultz. **Price:** $8.00.

ASSOCIATIONS

1876 ● **FOMOCO Owners Club**
3633 Akron Ct.
Loveland, CO 80538
Barry Abels, Exec. Ofc.   Ph:(303)669-8767

Founded: 1985. **Membership:** 250. Individuals dedicated to the exhibition, preservation, and restoration of Edsel, Ford, Lincoln, and Mercury automobiles. Conducts charitable activities; sponsors educational programs. Bestows awards. **Convention/Meeting:** Annual (with exhibits) - 1991 September, Lakewood, CO.

1877 ● Mercury Club
702 Center St.
McKeesport, PA 15132
Keith Waltower, Pres.   Ph:(412)751-9409

Founded: 1984. Ford Mercury automobile enthusiasts dedicated to the preservation and enjoyment of Mercury automobiles manufactured from 1939 to the present. Maintains registry; provides sources for parts and services.

MERCURY TRACER (1988-92)

Introduced in March 1987 as an 1988 model, Tracer is built in Hermosillo, Mexico. Marketed as an upscale replacement for the Lynx, which was the Mercury version of the Ford Escort.

1991 Mercury Tracer LTS

MAJOR FEATURES

● Tracer Notchback and Wagon 1992 standard equipment includes: 1.9-liter I-4 engine, 5-speed manual transmission, four-wheel independent suspension, power-assisted rack-and-pinion steering, front disc/rear drum brakes, AM/FM radio, and tinted glass. Wagon adds: power steering, rear defogger, cargo cover, rear wiper/washer, and full wheel covers.

● Tracer LTS adds as 1992 standard equipment: 1.8-liter 16-valve engine, 4-wheel disc brakes, sport suspension, cruise control, AM/FM stereo with cassette, tilt steering column, and alloy wheels.

PRICE HISTORY

The following new car prices reflect the approximate retail cost of the base model: **1988** - $8,216; **1989** - $8,672; **1990** - $8,969; **1991** - $9,427; **1992** - $9,773.

DIMENSIONS

Body Style	Years Avail	Wheel Base (in)	Lgth (in)	Ht (in)	Avg Wt (lbs)	Fuel Cap (gal)	Front Hdrm (in)	Front Legrm (in)
3d sdn	88-90	94.7	162.0	53.0	2,205	11.9	38.3	41.5
4d sdn	88-90	94.7	162.0	53.0	2,240	11.9	38.3	41.5
4d sdn	91-92	98.4	170.9	52.7	2,356	11.9	38.4	41.7
5d wgn	88-89	94.7	162.0	53.0	2,240	11.9	38.3	41.5
5d wgn	90-90	94.7	169.7	53.7	2,335	11.9	38.2	41.5
5d wgn	91-92	98.4	171.3	53.6	2,468	11.9	38.4	41.7

ENGINES

Type	Displace-ment (L)	Fuel Dly	HP @rpm	Torque @rpm (ft/lbs)	MPG Cty/Hwy	Years Avail
I-4	1.6	FI	82@5000	92@2500	29/36	88-90
I-4	1.9	FI	88@4400	108@3800	30/37	91-92
I-4	1.8	FI	127@6500	114@4500	26/31	91-92

KEY: I=in-line engine; V=V engine; F=flat engine; FI=fuel injection; bbl=barrel carburetor; T=turbo; D=diesel; HP=horsepower; MPG=estimated average miles per gallon.

EVALUATIONS, TESTS, AND RANKINGS

1991: "has ample back-seat room . . . interior fit and finish complements the exterior quite well . . . aerodynamic design, along with its low, aggresive stance dimensions, make this economical." **Source:** "Mercury Tracer LTS," *Motor Trend,* December 1990, pp. 57-59.

1991: "one of the most appealing small sedans on the market . . . screwed together with admirable precision, resulting in a machine with excellent fit and finish." **Source:** "Mercury Tracer LTS," *Car and Driver,* March 1991.

1991: "enough handling prowess here to deal with aggressive street driving . . . seats are firm but not harsh." **Source:** "The Motor Trend Car of the Year," *Motor Trend,* February 1991, pp. 41-47, 50-52.

1991: "excellent fit and finish, enough room, a reasonable price . . . drivers will profit nicely, however, from the pleasures delivered by this quick, crisp sports sedan." **Source:** "Mercury Tracer LTS," *Car and Driver,* January 1991, p. 44.

1991: "a pleasant compromise between handling and comfortable ride . . . Fit and finish generally were good inside and out . . . controls are driver oriented." **Source:** "Curves, turns no problem for Tracer LTS," *The Flint Journal,* April 3, 1991, pp. B1-B2.

1989: "technically sophisticated and roomy package, and a bargain price." **Source:** "Eight for Ten," *Car and Driver,* December 1988, pp. 54-58, 60, 63-66, 68.

1988: "fabric seats are a nice luxury in this price range . . . testers impressed by the chassis." **Source:** "Asian Invasion," *Popular Mechanics,* July 1987, pp. 90-94, 148.

1988: "comfortable to drive under most city-type conditions . . . has a decent engine." **Source:** "Mercury Tracer," *Motor Trend,* March 1987, pp. 45-47.

RECALLS

1988: (66,300 cars): Some lap shoulder belt retractors were built with certain out of tolerance components. Retractors may lock at low belt pullout rates, this could discourage seatbelt usage. **Corrective action:** Replace front lap shoulder belt assemblies, as necessary. *(NHTSA Campaign No. 89V085000.)*

1988: (191 cars): Incorrect fuel filler neck attachment screws were used to attach the neck to the rear quarter panels. Could cause a rattle between the fuel filler pipe and the surrounding body structure. **Corrective action:** Replace incorrect screws with new bolt/washer assemblies. *(NHTSA Campaign No. 87V092000.)*

REPAIR MANUALS

1878 ● Ford, Lincoln, Mercury Car Repair and Tune-Up Guide: 1972-1987
Clymer Publications
P.O. Box 1209
Overland Park, KS 66212   Ph:(913)541-6694

Published 1987. **Price:** 14.95.

OTHER INFORMATION SOURCES

1879 ● Cars of Lincoln-Mercury
Crestline Publishing Co.
1251 N. Jefferson Ave.
Sarasota, FL 34237   Ph:(813)955-8080

Published 1987. **Editor(s):** George H. Dammann and James K. Wagner. **Price:** $34.95.

1880 ● FOMOCO Owners Club—Newsletter
FOMOCO Owners Club
3804 Conifer Dr.
Loveland, CO 80538   Ph:(303)669-8767

Monthly.

1881 ● Ford-Lincoln-Mercury Club of Florida—Newsletter
Ford-Lincoln-Mercury Club of Florida
P.O. Box 13514
Tampa, FL 33681   Ph:(813)839-0241

Monthly.

1882 ● Your Ford: Including Lincoln-Mercury: Essential Service Information for Owners and Mechanics
Consumer Reports Books
51 E. 42nd St., Ste. 800
New York, NY 10017   Ph:(212)682-9280

Based on technical service bulletins issued to Ford and Lincoln-Mercury dealers from 1985 through 1987. Published 1988. **Editor(s):** Mort J. Schultz. **Price:** $8.00.

ASSOCIATIONS

1883 ● FOMOCO Owners Club
3633 Akron Ct.
Loveland, CO 80538
Barry Abels, Exec. Ofc.   Ph:(303)669-8767

Founded: 1985. **Membership:** 250. Individuals dedicated to the exhibition, preservation, and restoration of Edsel, Ford, Lincoln, and Mercury automobiles. Conducts charitable activities; sponsors educational programs. Bestows awards. **Convention/Meeting:** Annual (with exhibits) - 1991 September, Lakewood, CO.

1884 ● Mercury Club
702 Center St.
McKeesport, PA 15132
Keith Waltower, Pres.   Ph:(412)751-9409

Founded: 1984. Ford Mercury automobile enthusiasts dedicated to the preservation and enjoyment of Mercury automobiles manufactured from 1939 to the present. Maintains registry; provides sources for parts and services.

MERKUR SCORPIO (1988-89)

Imported from Ford of Germany and sold through Lincoln-Mercury dealers with Merkur franchises. Brought to the U.S. in May 1987 as an 1988 model, but discontinued in the U.S. after 1989. Chosen by *Road & Track* as the best value sedan in the $22,500-$27,500 range in the 10 Best Competition.

1989 Scorpio

MAJOR FEATURES

● Scorpio had as 1989 standard equipment: 2.9L six-cylinder engine, 5-speed manual transmission, power steering, 4-wheel disc brakes, anti-lock braking system, automatic climate control, cruise control, and tilt telescopic steering column.

PRICE HISTORY

The following new car prices reflect the approximate retail cost of the base model: **1988** - $24,048; **1989** - $25,052.

DIMENSIONS

Body Style	Years Avail	Wheel Base (in)	Lgth (in)	Ht (in)	Avg Wt (lbs)	Fuel Cap (gal)	Front Hdrm (in)	Front Legrm (in)
5d lbk	88-89	108.7	186.4	69.5	3,241	16.9	38.0	41.3

ENGINES

Type	Displace-ment (L)	Fuel Dly	HP @rpm	Torque @rpm (ft/lbs)	MPG Cty/Hwy	Years Avail
V-6	2.9	FI	144@5500	162@3000	17/23	88-89

KEY: I=in-line engine; V=V engine; F=flat engine; FI=fuel injection; bbl=barrel carburetor; T=turbo; D=diesel; HP=horsepower; MPG=estimated average miles per gallon.

EVALUATIONS, TESTS, AND RANKINGS

1988: "passenger compartment is generous . . . controls feel good . . . seats are excellent." **Source:** "Merkur Scorpio," *Road & Track*, June 1987, pp. 226-230.

1988: "roomy, upscale environment. . .loses some serious points in the handling department." **Source:** "Merkur Scorpio," *Motor Trend*, June 1988, pp. 94-95, 97-98.

1988: "One of the most driveable, controlled and safe vehicles on the market." **Source:** "Autobahn or interstate, Ford Scorpio is a star," *The Detroit News*, February 10, 1988, pp. 1F-2F.

RECALLS

1988: (176 cars): Transmission linkage was adjusted improperly during production. If this condition exists, there is potential that transmission parking pawl may not fully engage parking gear when transmission selector lever is placed in park. **Corrective action:** Inspect all vehicles and adjust transmission linkage properly. *(NHTSA Campaign No. 88V084000.)*

REPAIR MANUALS

1885 ● Chilton's Mustang-Capri-Merkur 1979-1988
Chilton Co.
Chilton Way
Radnor, PA 19089   Ph:(215)964-4000

Published 1989. **Price:** $15.95.

OTHER INFORMATION SOURCES

1886 ● FOMOCO Owners Club—Newsletter
FOMOCO Owners Club
3804 Conifer Dr.
Loveland, CO 80538   Ph:(303)669-8767

Monthly.

1887 ● Ford-Lincoln-Mercury Club of Florida—Newsletter
Ford-Lincoln-Mercury Club of Florida
P.O. Box 13514
Tampa, FL 33681   Ph:(813)839-0241

Monthly.

ASSOCIATIONS

1888 ● FOMOCO Owners Club
3633 Akron Ct.
Loveland, CO 80538
Barry Abels, Exec. Ofc.   Ph:(303)669-8767

Founded: 1985. **Membership:** 250. Individuals dedicated to the exhibition, preservation, and restoration of Edsel, Ford, Lincoln, and Mercury automobiles. Conducts charitable activities; sponsors educational programs. Bestows awards. **Convention/Meeting:** Annual (with exhibits) - 1991 September, Lakewood, CO.

MERKUR XR4TI (1987-89)

Based directly on Ford of Germany's Sierra, the XR4Ti was built in Germany and sold through Lincoln-Mercury dealers. Discontinued after 1989.

1988 Merkur XR4Ti

MAJOR FEATURES

● XR4Ti had as 1989 standard equipment: 2.3 liter, four-cylinder engine, 5-speed manual transmission, front/rear independent transmission, front disc/rear drum brakes, power-assisted rack-and-pinion steering, and cast aluminum wheels.

PRICE HISTORY

The following new car prices reflect the approximate retail cost of the base model: **1987** - $17,832; **1988** - $19,142; **1989** - $19,759.

DIMENSIONS

Body Style	Years Avail	Wheel Base (in)	Lgth (in)	Ht (in)	Avg Wt (lbs)	Fuel Cap (gal)	Front Hdrm (in)	Front Legrm (in)
3d lbk	87-89	102.7	178.4	53.8	2,920	15.0	38.5	41.0

ENGINES

Type	Displacement (L)	Fuel Dly	HP @rpm	Torque @rpm (ft/lbs)	MPG Cty/Hwy	Years Avail
I-4T	2.3	FI	145@4400	180@3000	18/21	87-89
I-4T	2.3	FI	175@5000	200@3000	19/25	87-89

KEY: I=in-line engine; V=V engine; F=flat engine; FI=fuel injection; bbl=barrel carburetor; T=turbo; D=diesel; HP=horsepower; MPG=estimated average miles per gallon.

EVALUATIONS, TESTS, AND RANKINGS

1989: ``front has a clean aero look.'' **Source:** ``Merkur XR4Ti,'' *Road & Track—Buyer's Guide 1989*, 1988, p. 89.

1988: ``suspension sponges up large bumps. . .steering is sharp . . . only annoying habit is a strong sensitivity to crosswinds.'' **Source:** ``Merkur XR4Ti,'' *Car and Driver*, June 1988, p. 145.

1987: ``Good power and handling. . .It handles and rides almost as well fully loaded, a rare trait.'' **Source:** ``Merkur XR4Ti,'' *Popular Mechanics*, March 1987, pp. 71, 116-117.

1987: ``courageous styling, remarkably good road manners and Teutonic interior opulence.'' **Source:** ``Merkur XR4Ti,'' *Road & Track—Buyer's Guide 1987*, 1986, p. 98.

RECALLS

None to date.

REPAIR MANUALS

1889 ● Chilton's Mustang-Capri-Merkur 1979-1988
Chilton Co.
Chilton Way
Radnor, PA 19089   Ph:(215)964-4000

Published 1989. **Price:** $15.95.

OTHER INFORMATION SOURCES

1890 ● FOMOCO Owners Club—Newsletter
FOMOCO Owners Club
3804 Conifer Dr.
Loveland, CO 80538   Ph:(303)669-8767

Monthly.

1891 ● Ford-Lincoln-Mercury Club of Florida—Newsletter
Ford-Lincoln-Mercury Club of Florida
P.O. Box 13514
Tampa, FL 33681   Ph:(813)839-0241

Monthly.

ASSOCIATIONS

1892 ● FOMOCO Owners Club
3633 Akron Ct.
Loveland, CO 80538
Barry Abels, Exec. Ofc.   Ph:(303)669-8767

Founded: 1985. **Membership:** 250. Individuals dedicated to the exhibition, preservation, and restoration of Edsel, Ford, Lincoln, and Mercury automobiles. Conducts charitable activities; sponsors educational programs. Bestows awards. **Convention/Meeting:** Annual (with exhibits) - 1991 September, Lakewood, CO.

MITSUBISHI 3000GT (1991-92)

Asian cousin of the Dodge Stealth, the Mitsubishi 3000GT is produced in Nagoya, Japan. One of the first cars introduced in America that combined all-wheel drive and four-wheel steering. The Mitsubishi 3000GT VR-4 was named the *Motor Trend* Import Car of the Year in 1991.

1991 Mitsubishi 3000GT SL

MAJOR FEATURES

● 3000GT has as 1992 standard equipment: 3.0L six-cylinder engine, 5-speed manual transmission, 4-wheel power disc brakes, 4-wheel independent suspension, rack-and-pinion power steering, driver's-side airbag, keyless door locking, AM/FM cassette with four speakers, tilt steering column, rear defogger, leather-wrapped steering wheel, automatic headlamp shut-off system, and tinted glass.

● 3000GT SL adds as 1992 standard equipment: anti-lock brakes, electronically controlled suspension, rear wiper/washer, automatic climate control, upgraded audio system, and anti-theft system.

● 3000GT VR-4 adds as 1992 standard equipment: turbocharged engine, Getrag 5-speed manual overdrive transmission, permanent 4-wheel drive, 4-wheel steering, limited-slip rear differential, Active Aero System featuring a front air dam and rear spoiler, and Active Exhaust system, and an upgraded interior.

PRICE HISTORY

The following new car prices reflect the approximate retail cost of the base model: **1991** - $19,439; **1992** - $20,049.

DIMENSIONS

Body Style	Years Avail	Wheel Base (in)	Lgth (in)	Ht (in)	Avg Wt (lbs)	Fuel Cap (gal)	Front Hdrm (in)	Front Legrm (in)
3d lbk	91-92	97.2	179.1	50.6	3,207	20	37.1	44.2

ENGINES

Type	Displace-ment (L)	Fuel Dly	HP @rpm	Torque @rpm (ft/lbs)	MPG Cty/Hwy	Years Avail
V-6	3.0	FI	222@6000	201@4500	19/24	91-92
V-6T	3.0	FI	300@6000	307@2500	18/24	91-92

KEY: I=in-line engine; V=V engine; F=flat engine; FI=fuel injection; bbl=barrel carburetor; T=turbo; D=diesel; HP=horsepower; MPG=estimated average miles per gallon.

EVALUATIONS, TESTS, AND RANKINGS

1991: "industry's first 'active exhaust' system which, as described in a company release, 'permits the driver to select a quiet suburban setting (or) a throatier, more assertive sound' ... chock full of advanced automotive technology ... well-instrumented cockpit is comfortable enough for two." **Source:** "Compact Sportster is High-Tech Toy," *Detroit Free Press,* December 27, 1990, p. 1D.

1991: "all-wheel-drive platform is stable without ever feeling ponderous, in spite of its substantial weight. The car is responsive, too ... easy to drive at the limit ... automatically adjustable suspension is never at a loss, and regardless of the situation, the car feels firmly nailed down." **Source:** "Dodge Stealth R/T Turbo—Mitsubishi 3000GT VR-4," *Motor Trend,* October 1990, pp. 106-109, 112.

1991: "unquestionably the most hardware packed entry in its class ... interior is noteworthy, too: a mostly successful blend of easy-to-reach controls and appealing materials ... doesn't rank with the Z's in style and efficiency." **Source:** "Driving Impression: Mitsubishi 3000GT VR-4," *Car and Driver,* November 1990, pp. 36-37, 39.

1991: "features active aerodynamics above 50 mph, the front airdam automatically lowers and the rear spoiler raises." **Source:** "Fast Five," *Motor Trend,* December 1990, pp. 38-45.

RECALLS

None to date.

MITSUBISHI CORDIA (1987-88)

Produced by Mitsubishi Motor Corporation in Tokyo, Japan through 1988. Based on the discontinued Mitsubishi Tredia's front-drive chassis, which was a derivation of the layout supplied to Chrysler in the form of the Colt.

MAJOR FEATURES

● Cordia L had as 1988 standard equipment: 5-speed manual transmission, 4-wheel independent suspension, front disc/rear drum brakes, and rack-and-pinion steering.

● Cordia Turbo had as 1988 standard equipment: turbocharged engine, alloy wheels, front air dam, and rear spoiler.

PRICE HISTORY

The following new car prices reflect the approximate retail cost of the base model: **1987** - $9,859; **1988** - $10,829.

DIMENSIONS

Body Style	Years Avail	Wheel Base (in)	Lgth (in)	Ht (in)	Avg Wt (lbs)	Fuel Cap (gal)	Front Hdrm (in)	Front Legrm (in)
3d lbk	87-88	96.3	173.0	49.4	2,337	12.8	36.8	41.3

ENGINES

Type	Displace-ment (L)	Fuel Dly	HP @rpm	Torque @rpm (ft/lbs)	MPG Cty/Hwy	Years Avail
I-4	2.0	2-bbl	88@5000	108@3500	24/31	87-88
I-4T	1.8	FI	116@5500	129@3000	22/28	87-88

KEY: I=in-line engine; V=V engine; F=flat engine; FI=fuel injection; bbl=barrel carburetor; T=turbo; D=diesel; HP=horsepower; MPG=estimated average miles per gallon.

EVALUATIONS, TESTS, AND RANKINGS

1988: "the Cordia does provide a great deal of performance per dollar spent." **Source:** "Catalina Pony Express," *Motor Trend,* May 1988, pp. 54-58, 61, 64-66.

RECALLS

None to date.

MITSUBISHI DIAMANTE (1992)

Introduced in 1992, the Diamante replaces the Sigma as Mitsubishi's luxury sedan. It is designed and built by Mitsubishi Motors Corp. in Oye, Japan.

1992 Mitsubishi Diamante LS

MAJOR FEATURES

● Mitsubishi Diamante has as 1992 standard equipment: 4-speed automatic transmission, MacPherson strut front independent multi-link rear suspension, 4-wheel disc brakes, power-assisted rack-and-pinion steering, front-wheel drive, driver's side air bag; power windows, mirrors, and door locks; air conditioning, rear defogger, anti-theft system, tilt steering wheel, cruise control, seven-way adjustable driver's seat, woodgrain instrument panel and door accents, cloth seats, and AM/FM stereo cassette.

● Mitsubishi Diamante LS adds as 1992 standard equipment: higher output engine, 4-wheel anti-lock disc brakes, 5-spoke alloy wheels, premium sound system, and an upgraded interior.

PRICE HISTORY

The following new car prices reflect the approximate retail cost of the base model: **1992 - $19,939.**

DIMENSIONS

Body Style	Years Avail	Wheel Base (in)	Lgth (in)	Ht (in)	Avg Wt (lbs)	Fuel Cap (gal)	Front Hdrm (in)	Front Legrm (in)
4d sdn	92-92	107.1	190.2	55.5	3,428	19.0	38.6	43.9

ENGINES

Type	Displace-ment (L)	Fuel Dly	HP @rpm	Torque @rpm (ft/lbs)	MPG Cty/Hwy	Years Avail
V-6	3.0	FI	175@5500	185@3000	18/24	92-92
V-6	3.0	FI	202@6000	199@3000	18/25	92-92

KEY: I=in-line engine; V=V engine; F=flat engine; FI=fuel injection; bbl=barrel carburetor; T=turbo; D=diesel; HP=horsepower; MPG=estimated average miles per gallon.

EVALUATIONS, TESTS, AND RANKINGS

1992: "Cornering is nicely controlled and the ride is really superb . . . enthusiasts with more finely honed driving skills . . . may find Trace Control intrusive . . . squarely in the ballpark with the BMW 5-Series and a notch down from its Japanese performance luxury-sedan competitors." **Source:** "Mitsubishi Diamante LS," *Road & Track,* June 1991, pp. 114-118.

1992: "laden with buttons, switches, and systems that people will take for technology . . . performance is quite spritely . . . electronic adjustments—why not just make the car work right instead of making it adjustable." **Source:** "Mitsubishi Diamante LS," *Car and Driver,* September 1991, pp. 87-90.

1992: "loaded model is stuffed with electronics to smooth shifting, suspension, wheel spin and cornering." **Source:** "Big is Beautiful," *Forbes,* May, 27, 1991, p. 342, 343.

1992: "less interior space than the domestic sedans . . . able to hold the road nearly as well as the Legend . . . engine and transmission response at low speeds isn't what it should be." **Source:** "Genteel Wheels," *Home Mechanix,* September 1991, pp. 72-76, 84.

1992: "distinctive lines, particularly at the front . . . may well be one of the best buys in its class . . . Ride quality is as good as the best, and not much noise finds its way into the nicely designed interior." **Source:** "New Cars: Mitsubishi Diamante," *Popular Mechanics,* May 1991, p. 113.

1992: "will fare well in the new environment because it is priced well below comparable European import rivals." **Source:** "Mitsubishi aims for luxury market," *The Detroit News,* January 8, 1991, p. 9D.

1992: "upscale Diamante features traction control, trace control and electronic suspension." **Source:** "The road to comfort comes paved with high-tech gadgets," *The Detroit News,* October 6, 1991, p. 5D.

1992: "too much technology . . . solid and well finished . . . hushed and economical performance." **Source:** "Diamante: New Facets for High Tech," *The New York Times,* June 23, 1991.

1992: "engine, which was the smoothest of the low-side-sedan trio, had little to give in the lower rev range . . . 4-speed automatic transmission in the Diamante was a model of smooth shifting . . . on the handling course . . . car was not only under-engined, but also under-tired and hard to control."

Source: "Real World 101," *Road & Track*, February 1992, pp. 59-69.

1992: "has fine roadholding . . . steering is comfortably weighted and accurate . . . designers have done an even better job, housing the extensive gadgetry in remarkably good taste." **Source:** "Mitsubishi Diamante 30R," *Automobile Magazine*, November 1990, p. 34.

RECALLS

None to date.

MITSUBISHI ECLIPSE (1990-92)

Introduced in January 1990, the Mitsubishi Eclipse is produced at the Diamond Star Motors plant in Normal, Illinois, that Mitsubishi operates with Chrysler (plant parts data: domestic parts - 35%, imported parts - 65%, *Federal Trade Zone Board*, 1989). Shares basic components with Eagle Talon and Plymouth Laser. Chosen by *The Complete Car Cost Guide* as having one of the highest repair costs for a subcompact in 1991. Selected to the *Car and Driver* Ten Best Cars list in 1992.

1992 Mitsubishi Eclipse GS

MAJOR FEATURES

● Eclipse has as 1992 standard equipment: 1.8L four-cylinder engine, 5-speed manual transmission, 4-wheel disc brakes, front independent/rear 3-link suspension, automatic headlamp shut-off system, and tilt steering column.

● Eclipse GS adds as 1992 standard equipment: rack-and-pinion power-assisted steering, electric rear window defroster, upgraded stereo system, center console with storage areas, full wheel covers, and rear cargo cover.

● Eclipse GS DOHC 16 adds as 1992 standard equipment: 2.0-liter DOHC 16-valve engine, sport suspension, power antenna, and hood with power bulge.

● Eclipse GS Turbo adds as 1992 standard equipment: turbocharged engine, rear wiper/washer, anti-lock braking system, engine oil cooler, air dam and rear spoiler, sill extensions, 6-way front sport seats, cruise control, air conditioning, power antenna, and alloy wheels.

● Eclipse GSX adds as 1992 standard equipment: permanent 4-wheel drive, limited-slip differential, 4-wheel independent suspension, ABS in combination with standard limited-slip differential, dual exhaust, and driving lamps.

PRICE HISTORY

The following new car prices reflect the approximate retail cost

of the base model: **1990** - $10,819; **1991** - $11,139; **1992** - $11,259.

DIMENSIONS

Body Style	Years Avail	Wheel Base (in)	Lgth (in)	Ht (in)	Avg Wt (lbs)	Fuel Cap (gal)	Front Hdrm (in)	Front Legrm (in)
2d cpe	90-91	97.2	170.5	51.4	2,524	15.9	37.9	43.9
2d cpe	92-92	97.2	172.8	51.4	2,524	15.9	37.9	43.9

ENGINES

Type	Displace-ment (L)	Fuel Dly	HP @rpm	Torque @rpm (ft/lbs)	MPG Cty/Hwy	Years Avail
I-4	1.8	FI	92@5000	105@3500	23/32	90-92
I-4	2.0	FI	135@6000	125@6000	22/29	90-92
I-4T	2.0	FI	190@6000	203@3000	21/28	90-92
I-4T	2.0	FI	195@6000	203@3000	20/25	90-92
I-4T	2.0	FI	180@5500	195@3000	na	92-92

KEY: I=in-line engine; V=V engine; F=flat engine; FI=fuel injection; bbl=barrel carburetor; T=turbo; D=diesel; HP=horsepower; MPG=estimated average miles per gallon.

EVALUATIONS, TESTS, AND RANKINGS

1992: "styling remains contemporary and aggressive . . . even in the worst traction conditions, the GSX is stable and predictable . . . one of the all-time great buys in a performance sport coupe." **Source:** "Mitsubishi Eclipse GSX," *Motor Trend*, October 1991, pp. 60-62a.

1992: "Combination of value, good looks, and tummy-tightening performance." **Source:** "Ten Best Cars," *Car and Driver*, January 1992, pp. 35-43.

1991: "ideal blend of economy and speed . . . cabin is equally appealing . . . Fine controls lie within easy reach. Well-positioned pedals await serious heel-and-toe work." **Source:** "Mitsubishi Eclipse GSX," *Car and Driver*, December 1990, pp. 46-47.

1991: "some torque steer tugging at the front wheels. Not cheap, but it offers a good bit of sports car performance for the money . . . steering is power-assisted but retains enough resistance to help give the driver good feel of the road . . . driver's cockpit is very user friendly. Controls are well-placed." **Source:** "Mitsubishi Eclipse GS Turbo offers snug, spirited ride," *The Flint Journal*, January 16, 1991, pp. D1-D2.

1990: "exhibits neutral handling in most situations . . . feels noticeably better balanced than the 2wd Laser . . . in slower corners, the awd car will lapse into understeer, but it continues to get its power to the ground more effectively." **Source:** "Bang for the Buck," *Motor Trend*, November 1989, pp. 42-46, 48, 52-55, 58-59, 62, 64, 66-68, 72, 76.

1990: "good aerodynamics and plenty of power produced the highest top speed in the basic test group . . . Interior layout is generally good but the instrument panel styling draws attention to itself with odd diagonal placement of part of the layout . . . Seating is not the strongest suit for these . . . cars." **Source:** "Coupes de Grace," *Popular Mechanics*, May 1989, pp. 120-124, 212, 214.

1990: "modern styling, agile handling, and raw power." **Source:** "Power Coupes," *Popular Science*, April 1989, pp. 28-29, 32-34.

RECALLS

1990: (5,510 cars; includes Plymouth Laser and Mitsubishi Eclipse vehicles): Wiring harness for the headlamps may break due to the stress created by the headlamp pop-up devices.

Causes loss of headlamp illumination which have a potential for an accident. **Corrective action:** Headlamp wiring harness routing will be modified and damaged wires repaired. *(NHTSA Campaign No. 89V128000.)*

1990: (210 passenger cars; includes Eagle Talon, Mitsubishi Eclipse, and Plymouth Laser models. NHTSA Campaign Nos. 90V106001 and 90V106002 address same defect): Diluted primer may have been used on the windshield opening flanges prior to windshield glass installation which would not provide the retention required by FMVSS 212. Windshields would not prevent ejection of vehicle occupants during a vehicle crash, which causes serious injuries and fatalities. **Corrective action:** Replace windshields, associated parts, and primer. *(NHTSA Campaign No. 90V106000.)*

1990: (632 passenger cars equipped with Diamond-Star Motors sunroofs; includes Eagle Talon, Mitsubishi Eclipse, and Plymouth Laser models. NHTSA Campaign Nos. 90V056001 and 90V056002 address same defect): Operation of sunroof in non-standard manner may cause male hinge disengagement from the roof hinge receiver. Sunroof glass could detach from the roof and result in injury to occupants or persons in the vicinity. **Corrective action:** Replace male hinge with a modified version to increase roof hinge receiver retention ability. *(NHTSA Campaign No. 90V056000.)*

SAFETY AND REPAIRS

1990: "Car Clinic," *Popular Mechanics*, July 1990, p. 25. **Note:** Tip for wheel vibration in early Eclipses.

MITSUBISHI EXPO LRV (1992)

Introduced in 1992, the Mitsubishi Expo LRV (light recreation vehicle) and Expo are classified as compact sport wagons. They are similar to the Eagle Summit Wagon and Plymouth Colt Vista. Expo LRV has a 4-door body style with sliding rear passenger door and rear liftgate, 5-passenger seating capacity, and a slightly smaller engine than the Expo. Expo has a 5-door body style with four hinged doors and a rear liftback, and 7-passenger seating capacity. All models are available with a 5-speed manual or 4-speed automatic transmission. Produced in Okazaki, Japan.

1992 Mitsubishi Expo LRV

MAJOR FEATURES

● Expo LRV has as 1992 standard equipment: 1.8-liter I-4 engine, 5-speed manual transmission, front disc/rear drum brakes, power-assisted rack-and-pinion steering, strut-type independent front suspension, high-back front bucket seats, folding/tumbling rear bench seat, cloth upholstery, and tilt steering column.

● Expo LRV Sport adds as 1992 standard equipment: full wheel

covers, lowback front bucket seats, rear window defogger, and an upgraded interior.

● Expo LRV Sport AWD adds as 1992 standard equipment: full-time all-wheel drive, front mudguards, rear stabilizer bar and other exterior body stylings.

● Expo has as 1992 standard equipment: 2.4-liter I-4 engine, 5-speed manual transmission, 4-wheel independent suspension, power-assisted rack-and-pinion steering, front disc/rear drum brakes, low-back front bucket seats, second and third seats with outboard headrests and 50/50 folding/reclining seatbacks, cloth upholstery, tilt steering column, rear window defogger, and rear wiper/washer.

● Expo SP adds as 1992 standard equipment: ETR AM/FM/casette with four speakers, and an upgraded interior.

● Expo SP AWD adds as 1992 standard equipment: full-time all-wheel drive.

Price information and dimensions below are for the base model Expo LRV and base model Expo.

PRICE HISTORY

The following new car prices reflect the approximate retail cost of the base model: **1992** - $11,169; **1992** - $13,549.

DIMENSIONS

Body Style	Years Avail	Wheel Base (in)	Lgth (in)	Ht (in)	Avg Wt (lbs)	Fuel Cap (gal)	Front Hdrm (in)	Front Legrm (in)
wgn	92-92	99.2	168.6	64.4	2,701	14.5	40.0	40.8
wgn	92-92	107.1	177.4	62.6	2,942	15.8	39.3	40.5

ENGINES

Type	Displace-ment (L)	Fuel Dly	HP @rpm	Torque @rpm (ft/lbs)	MPG Cty/Hwy	Years Avail
I-4	1.8	FI	113@6000	116@4500	23/29	92-92
I-4	2.4	FI	116@5000	136@3500	21/27	92-92

KEY: I=in-line engine; V=V engine; F=flat engine; FI=fuel injection; bbl=barrel carburetor; T=turbo; D=diesel; HP=horsepower; MPG=estimated average miles per gallon.

EVALUATIONS, TESTS, AND RANKINGS

1992: "space inside is used both interestingly and effectively . . . Expos trade off some of the handling benefits that go with a low center of gravity . . . feel a little tippy in emergency maneuvers." **Source:** "Mitsubishi Expo Lineup Alters Minivan Definition," *Popular Mechanics*, August 1991, p. 90.

1992: "rear provides decent legroom . . . interior is generally well thought out . . . vehicles are quiet and comfortable, and both engines afford sufficient power." **Source:** "When is a Van not a Van? When it's an Expo," *The New York Times*, September 8, 1991, Section 8, p. 16.

1992: "LRV's shape grows on you . . . LRV's steering is slower than in most small sedans. Also, both body roll and understeer come sooner and are more exaggerated . . . Rear-seat leg room is not cavernous, but it's no worse than in a small sedan." **Source:** "Mitsubishi Expo LRV Sport," *Car and Driver*, November 1991, pp. 134-135, 137.

RECALLS

None to date.

MITSUBISHI GALANT (1987-92)

A front-drive compact that competes against the Honda Accord, Mazda 626, and the Toyota Camry. Chosen by *The Complete Car Cost Guide* as having one of the highest repair costs for a subcompact in 1990. The Galant GSX was replaced by the Galant VR-4 in 1992.

1991 Galant GSR

MAJOR FEATURES

● Galant has as 1992 standard equipment: 2.0L four-cylinder engine, 5-speed manual or 4-speed automatic transmission, power-assisted rack-and-pinion steering, front disc/rear drum brakes, tilt steering column, tinted glass, rear window defogger, and various exterior and interior enhancements.

● Galant LS adds as 1992 standard equipment: 4-speed automatic transmission; power windows, locks, and mirrors, AM/FM cassette with power antenna; velour upholstery, cruise control, wheel covers, and an upgraded interior.

● Galant GS adds as 1992 standard equipment: DOHC 16-valve engine, 4-wheel disc brakes, sports tweed upholstery, anti-theft system, and upgraded tires.

● Galant GSR adds as 1992 standard equipment: anti-lock brakes, electronically controlled suspension, rear spoiler, and alloy wheels.

● Galant VR-4 adds as 1992 standard equipment: turbocharged engine, anti-lock brakes, 4-wheel steering, air conditioning, leather upholstery, anti-theft system, and rear spoiler.

● Galant GSX had as 1991 standard equipment: permanent 4-wheel drive and fully independent automatic suspension.

PRICE HISTORY

The following new car prices reflect the approximate retail cost of the base model: **1987** - $14,139; **1988** - $16,129; **1989** - $10,971; **1990** - $10,989; **1991** - $11,439; **1992** - $11,699.

DIMENSIONS

Body Style	Years Avail	Wheel Base (in)	Lgth (in)	Ht (in)	Avg Wt (lbs)	Fuel Cap (gal)	Front Hdrm (in)	Front Legrm (in)
4d sdn	87-87	102.4	183.1	51.6	2,811	15.9	38.3	40.3
4d sdn	88-92	102.4	183.9	53.5	2,667	15.9	38.6	41.9

ENGINES

Type	Displace-ment (L)	Fuel Dly	HP @rpm	Torque @rpm (ft/lbs)	MPG Cty/Hwy	Years Avail
I-4	2.4	FI	110@4500	138@3500	20/27	87-87
I-4	2.0	FI	102@5000	116@4500	23/30	88-92
I-4	2.0	FI	135@6000	125@5000	20/23	89-91
I-4	2.0	FI	144@6000	134@4500	20/25	92-92
I-4T	2.0	FI	195@6000	203@3000	19/25	91-92

KEY: I=in-line engine; V=V engine; F=flat engine; FI=fuel injection; bbl=barrel carburetor; T=turbo; D=diesel; HP=horsepower; MPG=estimated average miles per gallon.

EVALUATIONS, TESTS, AND RANKINGS

1991: "biggest advantage lies in the Galant's chassis . . . Suspension control and feel are superior . . . Not so perfect is the shifter of the five-speed manual in the GS and GSX." **Source:** "Mitsubishi Galant: Nimble Sedan Marks Time," *Autofile,* 1991, pp. 117-121.

1991: "shifter, unfortunately, is less impressive . . . presents 4-wheel steering's best argument to date." **Source:** "Mitsubishi Galant VR-4," *Road & Track,* November 1990, pp. 76-77, 79-80.

1991: "engine is a buttery delight: smooth, powerful, responsive, silky . . . exhibits a certain crispness in its action . . . leaning toward the sport side of luxury, is more eager, but requests more involvement." **Source:** "Mitsubishi Galant VR-4 vs. Subaru Legacy Sport Sedan," *Motor Trend,* February 1991, pp. 70-73.

1990: "nice balance and agility provided by four-wheel drive . . . performance is spirited, mainly because of the engine's smoothness at high rpm . . . front seats have a wide range of adjustments for comfort and support . . . trunk is spacious." **Source:** "Sensible Galant Packs Sports Punch," *The Detroit News,* January 31, 1990, pp. 5B-6B.

1990: "solid transportation with a dash of style . . . superb control on wet or snow-covered roads . . . engine is quiet and smooth." **Source:** "Foreign Affairs," *Home Mechanix,* September 1990, pp. 74-76.

1990: "high-sided and lumpy, with a piecemeal instrument panel . . . sits you down in living-room comfort . . . good visibility and considerable interior space." **Source:** "Compact Sedans Grow Up," *Popular Science,* April 1990, pp. 80-84.

1989: "Galant GS . . . a bargain as well as a top-notch performer." **Source:** "Top New Car Buys," *Motor Trend,* November 1989, pp. 80-83, 86-89.

1989: "not a true 'active' suspension, but certainly one of the most high-tech suspension designs of any sedan currently in production. The Galant shines at the track . . . This is a real sports sedan, with a staggering list of high-tech features." **Source:** "Best Sellers," *Popular Mechanics,* July 1989, pp. 60-63, 120-122.

1988: "minimized degrees of roll, dive and squat in response to cornering, braking and acceleration." **Source:** "Will the Real Galant Please Stand Out," *Road & Track,* March 1988, p. 69.

1987: "partly compensates for its lack of punch with good low-down lugging ability. There's no frustrating hesitancy in low revs throttle response, no tiresome drivetrain snatch, no mid-range hiccups." **Source:** "Mitsubishi Galant," *Motor Trend,* March 1987, pp. 85-87.

RECALLS

None to date.

MITSUBISHI MIGHTY MAX (1987-92)

A relatively new nameplate in America, but its trucks have been sold for several years by Chrysler under the names Dodge Ram 50 and, formerly, Plymouth Arrow. Named "Pickup Truck of the Year" in 1990, by *Four Wheeler* magazine.

1991 Mitsubishi Mighty Max 4WD

MAJOR FEATURES

● Mighty Max has as 1992 standard equipment: 5-speed manual transmission, front vented power disc/rear drum brakes with load sensing proportioning, tilt steering wheel, one-touch tailgate release, double-wall cargo box, and cargo tie-down hooks.

● Mighty Max Macrocab adds as 1992 standard equipment: extended cab, split-back 60/40 reclining seat, rear-cab cargo straps, and under-floor storage.

● Mighty Max One Ton adds as 1992 standard equipment: welded double-wall cargo box, one-ton payload rating, and power-assisted steering.

● Mighty Max 4WD adds as 1992 equipment: 3.0-liter, 151-hp V-6 engine, part-time 4-wheel-drive, five-speed manual overdrive transmission, rear wheel anti-lock brakes, two-speed transfer case, auto-lock front hubs, and various exterior additions.

PRICE HISTORY

The following new car prices reflect the approximate retail cost of the base model: **1987** - $6,499; **1988** - $6,999; **1989** - $7,599; **1990** - $7,689; **1991** - $7,879; **1992** - $8,079.

DIMENSIONS

Body Style	Years Avail	Wheel Base (in)	Lgth (in)	Ht (in)	Avg Wt (lbs)	Fuel Cap (gal)	Front Hdrm (in)	Front Legrm (in)
trk	87-92	105.1	177.2	58.3	4,165	13.7	na	na

ENGINES

Type	Displace-ment (L)	Fuel Dly	HP @rpm	Torque @rpm (ft/lbs)	MPG Cty/Hwy	Years Avail
I-4	2.0	2-bbl	90@na	na	na	87-89
I-4	2.6	2-bbl	109@na	na	na	87-89
I-4	2.4	FI	116@5000	136@3500	23/27	90-92
V-6	3.0	FI	151@5000	174@4000	19/23	90-92

KEY: I=in-line engine; V=V engine; F=flat engine; FI=fuel injection; bbl=barrel carburetor; T=turbo; D=diesel; HP=horsepower; MPG=estimated average miles per gallon.

EVALUATIONS, TESTS, AND RANKINGS

1990: "small storage space behind the seat. . .isn't very comfortable or supportive even for short drives. . .service points on the engine all are easily accessible. . .ride unloaded is harsh." **Source:** "Loadin' Up," *Organic Gardening*, April 1990, pp. 55-58.

1988: "among the quickest." **Source:** "Mitsubishi Pickup," *Car and Driver—Buyers Guide 1988*, 1988, p. 127.

RECALLS

None to date.

MITSUBISHI MIRAGE (1987-92)

American cousins are the Dodge and Plymouth Colt. The 4-door Mirage is produced at the Diamond-Star Motors plant in Normal, Illinois; the 3-door Mirage is imported from Mizushima, Japan.

1991 Mitsubishi Mirage

MAJOR FEATURES

● Mirage VL 1992 standard equipment: 1.5-liter 4-cylinder engine, 4-speed manual transmission, power-assisted front disc/rear drum brakes, and reclining front bucket seats.

● Mirage Base adds as 1992 standard equipment: 5-speed manual or 3-speed automatic transmission and rear defogger (3-door).

● Mirage Sedan adds as 1992 standard equipment: 4-speed automatic transmission and tinted glass.

● Mirage LS adds as 1992 standard equipment: wheel covers, upgraded tires, and an upgraded interior.

● Mirage GS DOHC adds as 1992 standard equipment: 1.6-liter DOHC 16-valve engine, 4-wheel disc brakes, power steering, tilt-telescopic steering wheel, sport seats, and full wheel covers.

● Mirage Cyborg 16V-T added as 1990 standard equipment: turbocharged and intercooled engine and front wheel drive.

PRICE HISTORY

The following new car prices reflect the approximate retail cost of the base model: **1987** - $5,969; **1988** - $8,619; **1989** - $8,859; **1990** - $6,929; **1991** - $7,149; **1992** - $7,319.

DIMENSIONS

Body Style	Years Avail	Wheel Base (in)	Lgth (in)	Ht (in)	Avg Wt (lbs)	Fuel Cap (gal)	Front Hdrm (in)	Front Legrm (in)
3d sdn	87-88	93.7	157.3	53.5	1,984	11.9	37.7	40.6
3d sdn	89-92	93.9	158.7	52.0	2,205	13.2	38.3	41.9
4d sdn	89-92	96.7	170.1	52.8	2,271	13.2	39.1	41.9

ENGINES

Type	Displace-ment (L)	Fuel Dly	HP @rpm	Torque @rpm (ft/lbs)	MPG Cty/Hwy	Years Avail
I-4	1.5	2-bbl	68@5500	85@3500	32/37	87-87
I-4	1.5	FI	81@5500	91@3000	28/34	89-90
I-4	1.5	FI	92@6000	93@3000	29/35	91-92
I-4	1.6	FI	123@6500	101@5000	23/28	91-92
I-4T	1.6	FI	105@5500	122@3500	25/31	87-88
I-4T	1.6	FI	135@6000	141@3000	23/29	89-90

KEY: I=in-line engine; V=V engine; F=flat engine; FI=fuel injection; bbl=barrel carburetor; T=turbo; D=diesel; HP=horsepower; MPG=estimated average miles per gallon.

EVALUATIONS, TESTS, AND RANKINGS

1991: "Delivers a smooth cruise with effective stopping . . . steering is pleasantly balanced, and the suspension ideally tuned for even motoring." **Source:** "Mitsubishi Mirage is Nice, But," *The Detroit News*, February 13, 1991, pp. 1D-2D.

1991: "a small car with a bit of flare . . . There is actual legroom in back . . . shows what can be done with relatively little space." **Source:** "In a Small World, Mirage Is an Oasis," *New York Times*, July 21, 1991, Sect. 8, p. 12.

1989: "excellent performance." **Source:** "Ten Best Cars," *Car and Driver*, January 1989, pp. 30-35.

1989: "dazzling performance for a car of this (small) caliber . . . Ergonomically correct and supremely comfortable, the cockpit is user-friendly." **Source:** "Four Fun Fours," *Road & Track*, September 1988, pp. 92-96, 99-101.

1989: "handling may be a wee bit squirelly in hard driving over tricky roads." **Source:** "Eight for Ten," *Car and Driver*, December 1988, pp. 54-58, 60, 63-66, 68.

1988: "suspension does its best to handle the considerable power, but neither of its settings is ideal for sporty driving . . . handles predictably." **Source:** "Mitsubishi Mirage Cyborg 16 V-T," *Car and Driver*, April 1988, p. 35.

1987: "useful transportation, sensible and practical." **Source:** "Servings of Sensible, Flights of Fancy," *Road & Track*, March 1987, p. 95.

RECALLS

None to date.

MITSUBISHI MONTERO (1987-92)

Completely redesigned in 1992, the Montero nearly equals the Toyota 4-Runner in all-out acceleration and climbing ability. Dropped 3-door version in 1990.

1992 Mitsubishi Montero

MAJOR FEATURES

● Montero has as 1992 standard equipment: 5-speed manual transmission, "shift-on-the-fly" 2-wheel to 4-wheel drive and use of 4-wheel drive on any surface, 4-wheel power disc brakes, front independent suspension/rear live axle, power steering, tilt steering column, and cloth reclining front bucket seats.

● Montero RS adds as 1992 standard equipment: 4-speed automatic transmission, rear wiper/washer, bodyside molding, and reclining rear seat.

● Montero LS adds as 1992 standard equipment: 5-speed manual or 4-speed automatic transmission, multi-mode anti-lock braking system, three-mode adjustable rate shock absorber system, cruise control, limited-slip differential, suspended driver's seat, power windows and locks, AM/FM cassette, sport mirrors, and mud guards.

● Montero SR adds as 1992 standard equipment: larger all-terrain steel-belted radial tires and various interior enhancements.

PRICE HISTORY

The following new car prices reflect the approximate retail cost of the base model: **1987** - $9,889; **1988** - $11,929; **1989** - $12,299; **1990** - $13,949; **1991** - $15,789.

DIMENSIONS

Body Style	Years Avail	Wheel Base (in)	Lgth (in)	Ht (in)	Avg Wt (lbs)	Fuel Cap (gal)	Front Hdrm (in)	Front Legrm (in)
utl wgn	87-87	92.5	157.3	72.4	4,310	15.9	na	na
utl wgn	88-88	92.5	157.3	72.4	4,165	15.9	na	na
utl wgn	89-89	92.5	153.5	72.4	4,210	15.8	na	na
utl wgn	89-92	106.1	181.7	74.4	5,291	24.3	40.6	39.6

ENGINES

Type	Displace-ment (L)	Fuel Dly	HP @rpm	Torque @rpm (ft/lbs)	MPG Cty/Hwy	Years Avail
I-4	2.6	2-bbl	109@na	na	16/19	87-90
V-6	3.0	FI	143@5000	168@2500	15/18	89-92

KEY: I=in-line engine; V=V engine; F=flat engine; FI=fuel injection; bbl=barrel carburetor; T=turbo; D=diesel; HP=horsepower; MPG=estimated average miles per gallon.

EVALUATIONS, TESTS, AND RANKINGS

1992: "variety of upscale features and a contemporary look . . . interior is designed for the active sport/utility enthusiast." **Source:** "Preview 1992 Motor Trend Truck of the Year [Mitsubishi Montero SR]," *Motor Trend*, December 1991, pp. 104-105.

1992: "creeps up any slope in relaxed fashion . . . gives excellent, everyday all-weather grip . . . nothing can keep you from treading on." **Source:** "1992 Mitsubishi Montero," *Road & Track*, January 1992, p. 32.

1992: "new model is longer, wider and taller than its predecessor. . .Inside, the Montero lives up to its billing as a luxury cruiser." **Source:** "After 10 Years, an All-New Montero," *New York Times*, January 19, 1992.

1991: "an admirable cruiser . . . nary an intrusion from the engine compartment or the road.large glass panes and thin roof pillars provide excellent visibility." **Source:** "Update: Sport-Utility Vehicles," *U.S News & World Report*, May 13, 1991, pp. A4-A6, A8-A10, A12, A14-A15.

1990: "comfortable and quiet . . . in freeway cruising . . . sure-footed off the pavement as well." **Source:** "Desert Sports," *Car and Driver*, April 1990, pp. 38-44, 46, 48-49, 52-55.

1990: "good road manners . . . fun to drive wherever you go." **Source:** "4-Doors For all Seasons," *New Choices for the Best Years*, December 1989, pp. 84, 86-87.

1990: "more agricultural than the competition . . . right at home hauling hunters across the Alaskan outback . . . finished as well as any of its competitors." **Source:** "Suburban Chic," *Popular Mechanics*, August 1990, pp. 55-59, 109.

1989: "Head room was impressive . . . Leg room in front was also good . . . steering was quick and responsive." **Source:** "Montero 4-Door LS," *Motor Trend*, November 1988, pp. 117, 120-121, 124.

1989: "comfortable family wagon, a go-anywhere adventure vehicle, an economical runabout and a fine tow rig." **Source:** "Montero Four-Door 4x4," *Trailer Life*, February 1989, pp. 52-54, 140-141.

1989: "it's the added space and doors that really broaden the Montero's appeal." **Source:** "Import Report: Six, Four and Four," *Home Mechanix*, April 1989, pp. 84-86, 103-105.

1989: "certain offroad handling characteristics . . . sacrificed to get a smoother-riding, comfortable vehicle . . . interior is top drawer . . . engineered with comfort and convenience in mind." **Source:** "Smooth Operator: When the going gets tough, comfort and convenience can really help smooth the way," *Field and Stream*, March 1989, pp. 72, 93-94.

1987: "reasonably comfortable ride . . . maneuvers well in traffic and . . . parallel parking . . . provides adequate but far from roomy seating space for two." **Source:** "Four-Wheelers From Afar," *Money*, April 1987, pp. 62-64,66, 68, 70.

RECALLS

1989: (7500 cars with V-6 engines): Engine subject to throttle valve icing, not allowing it to return to idle. **Corrective action:** Install heated adapter plate. *(NHTSA Campaign No. 89V030000.)*

MITSUBISHI PRECIS (1987-1992)

Essentially similar to Hyundai Excel, the Mitsubishi Precis is built in Korea for Mistubishi to sell in the U.S. Chosen by *The Complete Car Cost Guide* as having one of the lowest insurance and maintenance costs for a subcompact in 1990. Hyundai discontinued the 5-door version after the 1990 model year.

MAJOR FEATURES

● Precis 1992 standard equipment: 4-speed manual transmission, rack-and-pinion steering, front disc/rear drum brakes, 4-wheel independent suspension, upgraded cloth material for seats and door inserts, and rear defogger.

● Precis RS added as 1991 standard equipment: 5-speed manual transmission, cloth trim, remote fuel door and hatch releases, rear wiper/washer, and tinted glass.

● Precis LS added as 1990 standard equipment: 5-speed manual or 3-speed automatic transmission, upgraded steering wheel, AM/FM cassette stereo system, and wheel covers.

PRICE HISTORY

The following new car prices reflect the approximate retail cost of the base model: **1987** - $5,195; **1988** - $5,395; **1989** - $5,724; **1990** - $5,899; **1991** - $6,469; **1992** - $6,579.

DIMENSIONS

Body Style	Years Avail	Wheel Base (in)	Lgth (in)	Ht (in)	Avg Wt (lbs)	Fuel Cap (gal)	Front Hdrm (in)	Front Legrm (in)
3d lbk	87-89	93.7	160.9	54.1	2,161	10.6	37.5	40.9
3d lbk	90-92	93.8	161.4	54.5	2,380	11.9	37.8	41.9
5d lbk	87-90	93.7	160.9	54.1	2,161	10.6	37.5	40.9

ENGINES

Type	Displacement (L)	Fuel Dly	HP @rpm	Torque @rpm (ft/lbs)	MPG Cty/Hwy	Years Avail
I-4	1.5	2-bbl	68@5500	82@3500	28/37	87-89
I-4	1.5	FI	76@5500	87@2500	27/28	90-90
I-4	1.5	FI	81@5500	91@3000	29/36	91-92

KEY: I=in-line engine; V=V engine; F=flat engine; FI=fuel injection; bbl=barrel carburetor; T=turbo; D=diesel; HP=horsepower; MPG=estimated average miles per gallon.

EVALUATIONS, TESTS, AND RANKINGS

1990: "comfortable ride." **Source:** "Mitsubishi Precis," *Car and Driver—Buyer's Guide 1990*, 1990, p. 56-57.

RECALLS

1990: (2,281 cars; includes Hyundai Excel models): Improperly heat treated lock washer could crack causing wheel bearing damage. **Corrective action:** Replace lock washer on each front wheel and repair area around lock washer as necessary. *(NHTSA Campaign No. 90V053000.)*

1987: (321,000 cars with automatic and 4 or 5 speed transmissions; includes Hyundai and Mitsubishi models): Possible loss of braking efficiency during repeated hard applications. **Corrective action:** Replace front brake pads. *(NHTSA Campaign No. 87V180000.)*

SAFETY AND REPAIRS

1989: "Hyundai Recalls Subcompacts," *Automotive News*, January 6, 1992, p. 2. **Note:** 1987-1989 models may have a defective reed valve subassembly that could ultimately result in engine fire.

MITSUBISHI SIGMA (1988-90)

Based on an earlier Mitsubishi Galant, it was introduced to North America in 1988 as the Galant Sigma in a model makeover. In 1989, the name was changed simply to Sigma to avoid confusion with the new Galant. Though discontinued in 1990, the Mitsubishi Sigma was chosen by *The Complete Car Cost Guide* as having one of the highest fuel and repair costs for a compact in the same year.

MAJOR FEATURES

● Sigma had as 1990 equipment: 4-speed automatic transmission, power steering, front independent suspension/rear rigid axle, 4-wheel disc brakes, driver's side airbag, automatic climate control, 8-way adjustable driver's seat, tilt steering column, AM/FM cassette with EQ, leather-wrapped steering wheel, theft-deterrent system, and alloy wheels.

PRICE HISTORY

The following new car prices reflect the approximate retail cost of the base model: **1988** - $16,129; **1989** - $17,069; **1990** - $17,879.

DIMENSIONS

Body Style	Years Avail	Wheel Base (in)	Lgth (in)	Ht (in)	Avg Wt (lbs)	Fuel Cap (gal)	Front Hdrm (in)	Front Legrm (in)
4d sdn	88-90	102.4	185.8	51.6	3,108	15.9	37.5	40.3

ENGINES

Type	Displacement (L)	Fuel Dly	HP @rpm	Torque @rpm (ft/lbs)	MPG Cty/Hwy	Years Avail
I-4	2.4	FI	102@5000	116@4500	21/27	88-90
V-6	3.0	FI	142@5000	168@2500	18/22	88-90

KEY: I=in-line engine; V=V engine; F=flat engine; FI=fuel injection; bbl=barrel carburetor; T=turbo; D=diesel; HP=horsepower; MPG=estimated average miles per gallon.

EVALUATIONS, TESTS, AND RANKINGS

1989: "Ride ... is excellent." **Source:** "Mitsubishi Sigma," *Road & Track—Buyer's Guide 1989*, 1988, p.119.

RECALLS

None to date.

MITSUBISHI STARION (1987-89)

Japanese cousin of the Chrysler Conquest, the Mitsubishi Starion was produced until 1989 by Mitsubishi Motors in Japan. Rated good in crash test performance and rated high for repair costs by *The Car Book* in 1989.

MAJOR FEATURES

● Starion had as 1989 standard equipment: turbocharged, intercooled 4-cylinder engine; 5-speed manual transmission; power steering; power 4-wheel disc brakes; anti-lock rear brakes; limited slip differential; rear defogger and wiper/washer; bronze-tinted glass; leather-wrapped steering

wheel; AM/FM stereo cassette with/EQ; theft protection device; and alloy wheels.

PRICE HISTORY

The following new car prices reflect the approximate retail cost of the base model: **1987** - $15,649; **1988** - $17,129; **1989** - $19,859.

DIMENSIONS

Body Style	Years Avail	Wheel Base (in)	Lgth (in)	Ht (in)	Avg Wt (lbs)	Fuel Cap (gal)	Front Hdrm (in)	Front Legrm (in)
3d lbk	87-89	95.9	173.2	50.2	3,036	19.8	36.6	40.8

ENGINES

Type	Displacement (L)	Fuel Dly	HP @rpm	Torque @rpm (ft/lbs)	MPG Cty/Hwy	Years Avail
I-4T	2.6	FI	176@5000	223@2500	18/23	87-87
I-4T	2.6	FI	145@5000	185@2500	18/23	87-87
I-4T	2.6	FI	188@5000	234@2500	18/22	88-89

KEY: I=in-line engine; V=V engine; F=flat engine; FI=fuel injection; bbl=barrel carburetor; T=turbo; D=diesel; HP=horsepower; MPG=estimated average miles per gallon.

EVALUATIONS, TESTS, AND RANKINGS

1989: "Power is good, but the transmission has a stiff, truck-like feel ... stable, trustworthy feel." **Source:** "Bang for the Buck," *Motor Trend,* November 1989, pp.42-46, 48, 52-55, 58-59, 62, 64, 66-68, 72, 76.

1987: "five best features owners found: fun to drive, handling, performance, reliability, styling ... five worst features owners found: interior, fuel consumption, service, economy of operation, and reliability." **Source:** "Mitsubishi Starion/Chrysler Conquest, Nissan 300ZX and Toyota Supra," *Road & Track*, May 1987, pp. 154-158, 160.

RECALLS

None to date.

MITSUBISHI TREDIA (1987-88)

Similar to the Mitsubishi Cordia, the Mitsubishi Tredia was discontinued in 1988. Though the Tredia had generally good repair records, it rated as among the worst for insurance claims, according to industry statistics.

MAJOR FEATURES

● Tredia L had as 1988 standard equipment: 5-speed manual transmission, 4-wheel independent suspension, front disc/rear drum brakes, rack-and-pinion steering, and AM/FM stereo with cassette and four speakers.

● Tredia Turbo added as 1988 standard equipment: turbocharged engine and cast alloy wheels.

● Tredia LS added as 1988 standard equipment: 3-speed electronically controlled automatic transmission, power-assisted steering, and power brakes.

PRICE HISTORY

The following new car prices reflect the approximate retail cost of the base model: **1987** - $9,559.

DIMENSIONS

Body Style	Years Avail	Wheel Base (in)	Lgth (in)	Ht (in)	Avg Wt (lbs)	Fuel Cap (gal)	Front Hdrm (in)	Front Legrm (in)
4d sdn	87-88	96.3	172.4	51.6	2,370	12.8	37.6	40.9

ENGINES

Type	Displacement (L)	Fuel Dly	HP @rpm	Torque @rpm (ft/lbs)	MPG Cty/Hwy	Years Avail
I-4	2.0	2-bbl	88@5000	108@3500	24/31	87-88
I-4T	1.8	FI	116@5500	129@3000	22/29	87-88

KEY: I=in-line engine; V=V engine; F=flat engine; FI=fuel injection; bbl=barrel carburetor; T=turbo; D=diesel; HP=horsepower; MPG=estimated average miles per gallon.

EVALUATIONS, TESTS, AND RANKINGS

1987: "an inexpensive, sedate-looking 4-door sedan that is a real sleeper on the open road. . .metallic paint has held up well and looks as good as new. . .interior also has held up well with no major problems." **Source:** "Mitsubishi Tredia Turbo at 50,000 Miles," *Road & Track*, April 1987, p.136, 138.

RECALLS

None to date.

MITSUBISHI VAN (1987-90)

The Mitsubishi Van, which used a similar mid-engine layout on rear-drive chassis as Toyota, was discontinued after the 1990 model year.

MAJOR FEATURES

● Van had as 1990 standard equipment: 4-speed automatic transmission, front independent suspension/rear live axle, front disc/rear drum brakes, rear defogger and wiper/washer, velour upholstery, third fold-down, removable bench seat, and tilt steering column.

● Van LS added as 1990 standard equipment: power steering, power mirrors and windows, cruise control, bronze tinted glass, bodyside molding, and AM/FM cassette stereo system.

PRICE HISTORY

The following new car prices reflect the approximate retail cost of the base model: **1987** - $9,839; **1988** - $10,189; **1990** - $11,229.

DIMENSIONS

Body Style	Years Avail	Wheel Base (in)	Lgth (in)	Ht (in)	Avg Wt (lbs)	Fuel Cap (gal)	Front Hdrm (in)	Front Legrm (in)
5d van	87-87	88.0	175.2	71.3	4,795	14.2	na	na
5d van	88-90	88.0	171.7	71.3	4,861	14.2	na	na

ENGINES

Type	Displacement (L)	Fuel Dly	HP @rpm	Torque @rpm (ft/lbs)	MPG Cty/Hwy	Years Avail
I-4	2.4	FI	107@na	na	18/21	87-90

KEY: I=in-line engine; V=V engine; F=flat engine; FI=fuel injection; bbl=barrel carburetor; T=turbo; D=diesel; HP=horsepower; MPG=estimated average miles per gallon.

EVALUATIONS, TESTS, AND RANKINGS

1990: "driving position awkward, engine maintenance difficult . . . Compared to more modern minivans . . . feels dated." **Source:** "The Light Vantastics," *Popular Mechanics*, February 1990, pp. 62-67.

1988: "Braking was most assuredly the weakest point . . . entry was judged the best handler, and its engine delivered the most accessible torque." **Source:** "Mini-Vans: Maxi Versatility," *Motor Trend*, July 1987, pp. 86-91, 94-95.

1987: "produced adequate pep for climbing even the steepest hills." **Source:** "Versatile Van from Japan," *Popular Science*, May 1987, p. 33.

1987: "one of the better buys in the field for all-around comfort, driveability and utility . . . Acceleration is okay . . . serious trailer pulling is out." **Source:** "Mitsubishi Vans," *Popular Mechanics*, April 1987, pp. 158, 160.

RECALLS

None to date.

MITSUBISHI WAGON (1987-91)

The Mitsubishi Wagon, which used mid-engine layouts on rear-drive chassis similar to Toyota, was discontinued at end of 1991.

MAJOR FEATURES

● Wagon had as 1991 standard equipment: 2.4L four-cylinder engine, 4-speed automatic transmission, front independent suspension/rear rigid axle, front disc/rear drum brakes, tilt steering column, velour upholstery, two recline/swivel/slide middle seats, third fold-down, removable bench seat, and tilt steering column.

● Wagon LS added as 1991 standard equipment: cruise control, power steering, power mirrors, bronze tinted glass, bodyside molding, and AM/FM cassette stereo system.

PRICE HISTORY

The following new car prices reflect the approximate retail cost of the base model: **1987** - $12,789; **1988** - $14,269; **1989** - $14,929; **1990** - $14,929.

DIMENSIONS

Body Style	Years Avail	Wheel Base (in)	Lgth (in)	Ht (in)	Avg Wt (lbs)	Fuel Cap (gal)	Front Hdrm (in)	Front Legrm (in)
5d wgn	87-87	88.0	175.2	71.3	4,795	14.2	na	na
5d wgn	88-91	88.0	171.7	71.3	4,861	14.2	na	na

ENGINES

Type	Displace-ment (L)	Fuel Dly	HP @rpm	Torque @rpm (ft/lbs)	MPG Cty/Hwy	Years Avail
I-4	2.4	FI	107@na	na	18/21	87-91

KEY: I=in-line engine; V=V engine; F=flat engine; FI=fuel injection; bbl=barrel carburetor; T=turbo; D=diesel; HP=horsepower; MPG=estimated average miles per gallon.

EVALUATIONS, TESTS, AND RANKINGS

1990: "handled adequately . . . Noise made talking and hearing difficult . . . hard to get into." **Source:** "Best of the Minivans," *Changing Times*, July 1990, pp. 41-45.

1989: "driver-ahead-of-engine interior layout . . . prevents front-seat passengers from gaining access to the rear once inside . . . comfortable driving position." **Source:** "Eeny, Meeny, Miney, Mini: We pick a winner from a field of eight minivans," *Car and Driver*, May 1989, pp. 62-63, 65, 67, 71, 75-77, 81.

1987: "flexible seating . . . Efficiency does suffer with a sprawled-out powertrain and a high floor . . . has a perfectly level load floor at the liftgate, so cargo can readily be slid in or out . . . Crosswinds tend to blow it all over the highway." **Source:** "Mitsubishi Wagon LS," *Car and Driver*, March 1987, pp. 93, 95, 97-98.

1987: "Front seating is good, visibility is excellent, and the requisite switches and controls are all within easy reach. . .Ride comfort is generally good." **Source:** "Motor Trend's 1987 Import Car of the Year," *Motor Trend*, April 1987, p. 35, 37-39, 41-42, 44, 46-47, 51.

RECALLS

None to date.

NISSAN 200SX (1987-88)

A sports-coupe that competed against the Subaru XT6, Honda Prelude Si, Isuzu Impulse Turbo, Merkur XR4Ti, and Celica GT-S. Produced in Kyushu, Japan, until 1988, when it was replaced by the Nissan 240SX.

MAJOR FEATURES

• 200SX has as 1988 standard equipment: five-speed manual transmission, four-wheel disc brakes, 2.0-liter 4-cylinder 102-bhp engine, all around independent suspension, anti-roll bar, and various interior features.

• 200SX SE adds as 1988 standard equipment: 3.0 liter V-6 engine, power steering, power-assisted brakes, anti-theft system, alloy wheels, power windows and locks, and various interior adjustments.

PRICE HISTORY

The following new car prices reflect the approximate retail cost of the base model: **1987** - $11,199; **1988** - $12,449.

DIMENSIONS

Body Style	Years Avail	Wheel Base (in)	Lgth (in)	Ht (in)	Avg Wt (lbs)	Fuel Cap (gal)	Front Hdrm (in)	Front Legrm (in)
2d cpe	87-88	95.5	174.4	52.4	2,645	14.5	38.1	44.4
3d cpe	87-88	95.5	175.6	52.4	2,590	14.5	37.8	44.4

ENGINES

Type	Displace-ment (L)	Fuel Dly	HP @rpm	Torque @rpm (ft/lbs)	MPG Cty/Hwy	Years Avail
I-4	2.0	FI	102@5200	116@3200	22/28	87-87
I-4	2.0	FI	99@5200	116@2800	23/28	88-88
V-6	3.0	FI	160@5200	174@4000	19/26	87-87
V-6	3.0	FI	165@5200	168@3200	19/26	88-88

KEY: I=in-line engine; V=V engine; F=flat engine; FI=fuel injection; bbl=barrel carburetor; T=turbo; D=diesel; HP=horsepower; MPG=estimated average miles per gallon.

EVALUATIONS, TESTS, AND RANKINGS

1988: "[200SX SE] ride comfort is good. . .quiet is in the middle of the road." **Source:** "Catalina Pony Express: Riding the roads in the Japanese sporty cars," *Motor Trend*, May 1988, pp. 54-8, 61, 64-6.

1987: "suspect a lazy engine. . .joy level is strictly average. . .trying hard, but lacking that elusive spark of brilliance." **Source:** "Nissan 200SX SE: Three years, two cylinders, and 200 pounds later," *Car and Driver*, March 1987, pp. 123-24.

1987: "sassy enough shape. . .a car with potential. . .sharp throttle response. . .makes a wonderful cruiser. . .a comfy long-haul ride. . .good cruise control, good sound system. . .massive understeer. . .seriously in need of some suspension work. . .steering needs help." **Source:** "Nissan 200SX SE: A big mac from Tokyo," *Motor Trend*, July 1987, pp. 58, 60-2.

RECALLS

None to date.

REPAIR MANUALS

1893 • **Mitchell Glove Compartment Companion for Your Nissan**
Harcourt Brace Jovanovich, Inc.
6277 Sea Harbor Dr.
Orlando, FL 32821   Ph:(407)345-2000

Published 1988.

OTHER INFORMATION SOURCES

1894 • **Z Club Bulletin**
Z Club of America
550 Lexington Ave.
Clifton, NJ 07011   Ph:(201)546-9200

Newsletter providing technical information on Datsun/Nissan automobiles. Contains new product reviews. Bimonthly. **Price:** Included in membership dues.

NISSAN 240SX (1989-92)

A sports/specialty coupe that competes against the Shelby CSX, Mitsubishi Eclipse GS, Mazda MX-6 GT, Toyota Celica GT-S, and Ford Probe GT. Replaced the Nissan 200SX. The base-trim model was known as the Nissan 240SX XE until replaced by the 240SX LE for the 1992 model year. A convertible version of the 240SX is planned for later in 1992. Voted one of the top six coupes by *Popular Mechanics* in 1988. Competed in *Motor Trend's* 1989 Import Car of the Year competition. Named in the highest insurance cost list for a subcompact car by *The Complete Car Cost Guide* in 1990. Nominated Ten Best Cars in 1990 by *Car and Driver*. Voted 1991 Import Car of the Year by *Car and Driver*. Rated among the best in its class in Crash Test Performance for 1992 by the *Car Book*. Currently produced in Yokosuka, Japan.

1991 Nissan 240SX

MAJOR FEATURES

● 240SX has as 1992 standard equipment: five-speed manual transmission, four-wheel disc brakes, rear wheel drive, 4-wheel independent suspension, power steering, power antenna, tilt steering column, rear defogger, tinted glass, power mirrors, front and rear anti-roll bars, and various interior and exterior features.

● 240SX SE adds as 1992 standard equipment: power windows and locks, cruise control, rear window wiper/washer in three-door hatchback, front air dam, rear spoiler, alloy wheels, and various interior enhancements.

● 240SX LE adds as 1992 standard equipment: leather upholstery and air conditioning.

PRICE HISTORY

The following new car prices reflect the approximate retail cost of the base model: **1989** - $13,249; **1990** - $13,249; **1991** - $14,095; **1992** - $14,515.

DIMENSIONS

Body Style	Years Avail	Wheel Base (in)	Lgth (in)	Ht (in)	Avg Wt (lbs)	Fuel Cap (gal)	Front Hdrm (in)	Front Legrm (in)
3d lbk	89-92	97.4	178.0	50.8	2,690	15.9	37.8	42.0
2d cpe	89-92	97.4	178.0	50.8	2,669	15.9	37.8	42.0

ENGINES

Type	Displace- ment (L)	Fuel Dly	HP @rpm	Torque @rpm (ft/lbs)	MPG Cty/Hwy	Years Avail
I-4	2.4	FI	140@5600	152@4400	20/27	89-90
I-4	2.4	FI	155@5600	160@4400	22/27	91-92

KEY: I=in-line engine; V=V engine; F=flat engine; FI=fuel injection; bbl=barrel carburetor; T=turbo; D=diesel; HP=horsepower; MPG=estimated average miles per gallon.

EVALUATIONS, TESTS, AND RANKINGS

1991: "steering. . .bit on the light side. . .highlight of this Nissan is the suspension. . .brakes struck us as unexceptional. . .in winter it's absolutely undriveable. . .pedal positioning results in insufficient thigh support." **Source:** "Nissan 240SX: Appeal lies in feel, rear-wheel drive," *Autoweek's Autofile 1991 Edition,* 1990, pp. 41-4.

1991: "Handling tends to be more fun at the dry limit when the rear wheels are driving. . .engine vibrations are probably there, but they remain below the threshold of notice. . .*too much* headroom. . .[power steering] feels so transparent and honest that you keep forgetting it's power." **Source:** "1991

Import Cars: Nissan 240SX: A smooth looker gets smoother still," *Car and Driver,* November 1990, pp. 80, 88.

1991: "engine is also fairly frugal. . .one of the best-handling cars on the road today. . .Anti-roll bars fore and aft dutifully minimize body roll. . .more precise vehicle turn-in. . .rear quarters are decidedly sized for kids of modest proportions." **Source:** "Nissan 240SX SE: Operation pick-me-up," *Motor Trend,* December 1990, pp. 62-3, 66, 68.

1991: "rear seats that are as useful as fool's gold. . .seats. . .fit the driver and passenger as comfortably as an old pair of sweat pants. . .loaf easily around town. . .accelerate quickly onto the highways." **Source:** "New-fashioned Nissans: a golden Sentra and a gilded 240SX," *Road & Track,* November 1990, pp. 145, 149.

1991: "sweet, stylish, and extremely responsive. . .wonderful feel on the road. . .doesn't have tremendous amount of power. . .a devoted understeer. . .for both aggressive and passive drivers. . .*Huge* button controls can be operated without taking one's eyes from the road." **Source:** "Nissan 240SX SE: A well-rounded performer sporting serious style," *Automobile Magazine,* January 1991, pp. 61-3.

1990: "paragon of reliability . . . 240SX's chassis never met a road surface it didn't like . . . seats . . . hold you in place." **Source:** "Nissan 240SX SE: Bid farewell to our back-road Baryshnikov," *Road & Track,* March 1990, pp. 80-81.

1989: "best subjective handling of the entire group. . .agility and predictability won the hearts of the entire test crew. . .gearbox is pure pleasure. . .roomy, with good seats. . .Exterior styling is slick." **Source:** "Coupes de Grace: The small, the quick and the slick in a high desert shootout," *Popular Mechanics,* May 1989, pp. 120-4, 212, 214.

1989: "proved to be quick, stable, positive, and comfortable. . .a bit cramped inside. . .on the weak side in power." **Source:** "6 Quick Coupes," *Popular Mechanics,* September 1988, pp. 32-4, 36, 40-1.

1989: "has all the good stuff . . . ride could be less jarring . . . engine could be more willing at higher speeds." **Source:** "2 For the Road," *Regardie's,* September 1989, pp. 169-170, 172-180, 182.

1989: "a practical car for young families . . . a ball to drive, too." **Source:** "Import Report," *Home Mechanix,* April 1989, pp. 84-86, 103-105.

1989: "reaches 60 mph in 8.8 seconds . . . dashboard buttons are hard to find . . . wins for that glued-to-the-road feel of the true sports car." **Source:** "Sizzling Performance—Without Sticker Shock," *Business Week,* February 6, 1989, p. 105.

RECALLS

None to date.

REPAIR MANUALS

1895 ● **Mitchell Glove Compartment Companion for Your Nissan**
Harcourt Brace Jovanovich, Inc.
6277 Sea Harbor Dr.
Orlando, FL 32821   Ph:(407)345-2000
Published 1988.

OTHER INFORMATION SOURCES

1896 ● **Z Club Bulletin**
Z Club of America
550 Lexington Ave.
Clifton, NJ 07011   Ph:(201)546-9200

Newsletter providing technical information on Datsun/Nissan automobiles. Contains new product reviews. Bimonthly. **Price:** Included in membership dues.

NISSAN 300ZX (1987-92)

A sports/GT car that competes against the Mitsubishi 3000GT, Dodge Stealth, Porsche 944, Toyota MR2, Mazda RX-7, Mazda Miata, and Corvette. Placed fourth place in *Motor Trend's* Top-Speed Ten competition in 1988. Ranked in *Car and Driver's* 1989 Top 10 Performance Coupes list. Rated Best Sports/GT priced at $32,000 to $50,000 by *Road & Track* in 1990. Rated Best Sports/GT priced at $21,000 to $32,000 in 1990 *Road & Track*. Placed in the highest insurance cost and highest resale value for a sports car in 1990 by *The Complete Car Cost Guide.* One of the Ten Best Cars in the World in 1991 according to *Road and Track*. Nominated for the Ten Best Car list by *Car and Driver* in 1990, 1991, and 1992. Currently built in Hiratsuka, Japan.

1991 Nissan 300ZX

MAJOR FEATURES

● Nissan 300ZX has as 1992 standard equipment: five-speed manual or four-speed automatic transmission, (T-bar roof models only), anti-lock four-wheel disc brakes, power steering, driver's-side air bag, automatic climate control, power windows and locks, cruise control, theft-deterrent system, rear defogger, rear window wiper/washer, cloth seat upholstery, and alloy wheels.

● Nissan 300ZX 2+2 adds as 1992 standard equipment: 2+2 seating configuration.

● Nissan 300ZX Turbo adds as 1992 standard equipment: turbo-charged engine, four-wheel steering, adjustable shock absorbers, rear spoiler, and side window defrosters.

PRICE HISTORY

The following new car prices reflect the approximate retail cost of the base model: **1987** - $18,849; **1988** - $21,699; **1989** - $24,649; **1990** - $27,900; **1991** - $28,175; **1992** - $29,120.

DIMENSIONS

Body Style	Years Avail	Wheel Base (in)	Lgth (in)	Ht (in)	Avg Wt (lbs)	Fuel Cap (gal)	Front Hdrm (in)	Front Legrm (in)
2d cpe	87-89	99.2	178.5	49.8	3,265	19.0	37.2	43.6
2d cpe	90-92	101.2	178.0	49.4	3,313	19.0	37.1	43.0
3d cpe	87-89	91.3	173.7	49.7	3,164	19.0	36.6	43.6
3d cpe	90-92	96.5	169.5	49.2	3,186	19.0	36.8	43.0

ENGINES

Type	Displacement (L)	Fuel Dly	HP @rpm	Torque @rpm (ft/lbs)	MPG Cty/Hwy	Years Avail
V-6	3.0	FI	165@5200	174@4000	17/25	87-89
V-6	3.0	FI	222@6400	198@4800	18/24	90-92
V-6T	3.0	FI	205@5200	227@3600	17/25	87-89
V-6T	3.0	FI	280@6400	283@3600	18/24	90-91
V-6T	3.0	FI	300@6400	283@3600	18/24	90-92

KEY: I=in-line engine; V=V engine; F=flat engine; FI=fuel injection; bbl=barrel carburetor; T=turbo; D=diesel; HP=horsepower; MPG=estimated average miles per gallon.

EVALUATIONS, TESTS, AND RANKINGS

1992: "brings a new feel to touring in the grand manner." **Source:** "Ten Best Cars," *Car and Driver,* January 1992, pp. 35-43.

1992: "innovative styling, superb handling, and exhilarating performance . . . rear seat works better as luggage space." **Source:** "Nissan 300ZX,"   *Car and Driver,* October 1991, p. 116.

1992: "better than its predecessors . . . as good as anything anywhere . . . go-kart-quick steering." **Source:** "Nissan 300ZX Turbo," *Automobile Magazine,* January 1992, p. 55.

1991: "dependable. . .outstanding acceleration and amazingly forgiving handling. . .some problems with the brakes." **Source:** "Nissan 300ZX Turbo: Twelve months: Despite twenty-seven days out of service, we loved our Z-car enough to award it five stars," *Automobile Magazine,* February 1991, pp. 49-53.

1991: "comfort and quietness. . .great sense of stability. . .solid, strong." **Source:** "Carrying the Torch: A look at the naturally aspirated, base-level (sometimes affordable) sports cars that define the genre for the nineties: Mazda Miata, Mazda RX-7, Nissan 300ZX, Porsche 944, Toyota MR2," *Road & Track,* November 1990, pp. 45-56.

1991: "extra length causes no loss in eye appeal . . . overall balance feels good . . . solid, responsive, predictable and forgiving." **Source:** "Nothing sacrificed in stretching Nissan 300ZX into a two-seater," *The Flint Journal,* June 19, 1991, p. E2.

1990: "pleasant ride, blistering acceleration." **Source:** "Straman 300ZX Convertible: More flash and dash per unit cash," *Car and Driver,* October 1990, p. 152.

1990: "in a league with the world's best . . . head turner and ego booster . . . fun, fleetness of foot, sleekness of styling and all-around even temper." **Source:** "Nissan 300ZX: Does everything it's supposed to—and more," *Popular Mechanics,* June 1990, pp. 65-67.

1989: "manual gearbox is easy to operate, braking and steering effort are hefty but not taxing." **Source:** "1989 offers an 8-pack of memorable cars," *The Detroit News,* July 2, 1989, p. H1.

1989: "distinct harsh, jiggly feeling. . .was predictably stable on the banking." **Source:** "Top-speed 10: Indulging our go-fast fetish again," *Motor Trend,* September 1988, pp. 32-4, 42, 44.

1989: "can feel ponderous, especially in city driving . . . wide, racy, and low-slung . . . ride is extremely smooth." **Source:** "Nissan's New 'Z-Car' Gets An A For Acceleration," *Business Week*, April 10, 1989, p. 100.

1989: "real high-performance sports car . . . looks as terrific as it drives . . . looks much better in the metal than it does in photographs." **Source:** "2 for the road," *Regardie's*, September 1989, pp. 169-170, 172-180, 182.

1989: "an excellent ride with enthralling handling and good speed . . . raw sex appeal . . . draws a crowd better than a county fair kissing booth." **Source:** "Two-Seat Heat," *Popular Science*, September 1989, pp. 38-40, 42, 44, 48.

RECALLS

1987: (183,519 cars with automatic transmissions; includes models made before 1987; includes Datsun and Nissan models): Unintended acceleration. **Corrective action:** Install shift interlock system. *(NHTSA Campaign No. 87V098000.)*

REPAIR MANUALS

1897 ● **Mitchell Glove Compartment Companion for Your Nissan**
Harcourt Brace Jovanovich, Inc.
6277 Sea Harbor Dr.
Orlando, FL 32821   Ph:(407)345-2000

Published 1988.

OTHER INFORMATION SOURCES

1898 ● **Z Club Bulletin**
Z Club of America
550 Lexington Ave.
Clifton, NJ 07011   Ph:(201)546-9200

Newsletter providing technical information on Datsun/Nissan automobiles. Contains new product reviews. Bimonthly. **Price:** Included in membership dues.

NISSAN AXXESS (1990)

A mini-van that competed against the Chevrolet Astro LT, Dodge Caravan LE, Ford Aerostar Eddie Bauer Edition, Mazda MPV V6, and Toyota Van LE. Placed third out of eight mini-vans in a 1989 comparison test by *Car and Driver*. Produced in Japan; discontinued importing after 1990.

MAJOR FEATURES

● Nissan Axxess XE had as 1990 standard equipment: five-speed manual transmission, front and rear independent suspension, power steering, power disc/drum brakes, sway bars, power door locks, and rear window wiper.

● Nissan Axxess SE added as 1990 standard equipment: seven seating configuration and various interior adjustments.

● Nissan Axxess XE and Axxess SE 4WD added as 1990 standard equipment: four-wheel drive.

PRICE HISTORY

The following new car prices reflect the approximate retail cost of the base model: **1990 - $13,949.**

DIMENSIONS

Body Style	Years Avail	Wheel Base (in)	Lgth (in)	Ht (in)	Avg Wt (lbs)	Fuel Cap (gal)	Front Hdrm (in)	Front Legrm (in)
5d wgn	90-90	102.8	171.9	64.6	2,877	17.2	39.7	38.6

ENGINES

Type	Displacement (L)	Fuel Dly	HP @rpm	Torque @rpm (ft/lbs)	MPG Cty/Hwy	Years Avail
I-4	2.4	FI	138@5600	148@4400	21/26	90-90

KEY: I=in-line engine; V=V engine; F=flat engine; FI=fuel injection; bbl=barrel carburetor; T=turbo; D=diesel; HP=horsepower; MPG=estimated average miles per gallon.

EVALUATIONS, TESTS, AND RANKINGS

1990: "excellent for access. . .limited luggage room. . .ride is superior." **Source:** "Nissan Axxess: A people-mover with panache," *Road & Track*, May 1989, p. 146.

1990: "doesn't seem very vanlike. . .little lower to the ground and a lot smaller. . .steering is sharp, with good feel and feedback." **Source:** "Eeny, Meeny, Miney, Mini: We pick a winner from a field of eight minivans," *Car and Driver*, May 1989, pp. 62-3, 67, 71, 75-7, 81.

1990: "it'll perform so many functions you might think you have a garageful of cars at your disposals. . .smooth, car-like ride and reasonably car-like handling." **Source:** "Nissan Axxess: The class of a new class," *Motor Trend*, April 1989, pp. 79-82.

1990: "rides, handles and feels like a passenger car, a very sporty passenger car . . . quick, fast machine." **Source:** "New-Look Nissan Axxess AWD," *Outdoor Life*, November 1989, pp. 58, 60.

1990: "more a raised station wagon than a small van . . . more useful than the common station wagon . . . engine performs roughly and noisily." **Source:** "Versatile Vehicles: Three cars built for work-and play," *Home Mechanix*, July 1989, pp. 64-70.

1990: "offers superior access . . . consistently solid road manners . . . can seat six in good comfort." **Source:** "Space Machines: Front drive vs. rear drive vs. all-wheel drive," *Popular Science*, May 1989, pp. 40-42, 44-46, 48.

RECALLS

None to date.

REPAIR MANUALS

1899 ● **Mitchell Glove Compartment Companion for Your Nissan**
Harcourt Brace Jovanovich, Inc.
6277 Sea Harbor Dr.
Orlando, FL 32821   Ph:(407)345-2000

Published 1988.

OTHER INFORMATION SOURCES

1900 ● **Z Club Bulletin**
Z Club of America
550 Lexington Ave.
Clifton, NJ 07011   Ph:(201)546-9200

Newsletter providing technical information on Datsun/Nissan automobiles. Contains new product reviews. Bimonthly. **Price:** Included in membership dues.

NISSAN MAXIMA (1987-1992)

A sports sedan that competes against the Toyota Cressida, Ford Taurus, and Acura Legend. Station wagon model ceased production in 1988. Named the *Home Mechanix* Car of the Year in 1989. Placed in highest maintenance cost category for a compact car by *The Complete Car Cost Guide* in 1990. Chosen Best Coupe/Sedan $17,000 to $28,000 range by *Road & Track* in 1990. Voted one of the Ten Best Cars by *Car and Driver* in 1990. Selected to the *Road & Track* Ten Best Cars in the World list in 1991. The Nissan Maxima is currently produced in Yokosuka, Japan.

1991 Nissan Maxima GXE

MAJOR FEATURES

● Nissan Maxima GXE has as 1992 standard equipment: four-speed automatic transmission, tilt steering column, power windows and locks with keyless entry, AM/FM cassette stereo system, cruise control, theft deterrent system, rear defogger, and alloy wheels.

● Nissan Maxima SE adds as 1992 standard equipment: 24-valve 3.0-liter V6 engine, five-speed manual transmission, four-wheel disc brakes, sports suspension, fog lights, power sunroof, electric trunk release, and rear spoiler.

● Nissan Maxima Station Wagon and Wagon SE added as 1988 standard equipment: air conditioning.

PRICE HISTORY

The following new car prices reflect the approximate retail cost of the base model: **1987** - $16,649; **1988** - $17,499; **1989** - $17,499; **1990** - $17,899; **1991** - $19,375; **1992** - $19,695.

DIMENSIONS

Body Style	Years Avail	Wheel Base (in)	Lgth (in)	Ht (in)	Avg Wt (lbs)	Fuel Cap (gal)	Front Hdrm (in)	Front Legrm (in)
4d sdn	87-87	100.4	181.5	55.1	3,040	15.9	37.0	42.0
4d sdn	88-88	100.4	181.4	54.7	3,120	17.2	37.0	42.0
4d sdn	89-92	104.3	187.6	55.1	3,129	18.5	39.5	43.7
5d wgn	87-88	100.4	184.8	55.7	3,280	15.9	37.0	42.0

ENGINES

Type	Displace- ment (L)	Fuel Dly	HP @rpm	Torque @rpm (ft/lbs)	MPG Cty/Hwy	Years Avail
I-6	3.0	FI	152@5200	167@3600	18/26	87-87
V-6	3.0	FI	157@5200	168@3600	18/26	88-88
V-6	3.0	FI	160@5200	182@2800	21/26	89-92
V-6	3.0	FI	190@5600	190@4000	na	92-92

KEY: I=in-line engine; V=V engine; F=flat engine; FI=fuel injection; bbl=barrel carburetor; T=turbo; D=diesel; HP=horsepower; MPG=estimated average miles per gallon.

EVALUATIONS, TESTS, AND RANKINGS

1992: "a suave, together ride . . . smooth good looks . . . enough performance to keep you interested." **Source:** "Nissan Maxima SE: Somebody just raised the bar," *Car and Driver*, November 1991, pp. 151-152.

1992: "likes to be driven hard . . . doubles as a nifty midsize luxury sedan . . . SE package . . . is still a pleasure to experience." **Source:** "Maxima gets a power boost," *Detroit Free Press*, December 12, 1991, p. 1C.

1992: "Pedal modulation was good, stops were straight . . . exceptionally nice tourer." **Source:** "Warning: Magnum Load on Board," *Motor Trend*, October 1991, pp. 80-81.

1991: "real sense of spaciousness in the cockpit . . . noisy motorized shoulder belts . . . excess body roll and underdamped ride." **Source:** "Six-Pack To Go," *Car and Driver*, September 1991, pp. 58-60, 62, 64-67, 68-70, 72, 74, 77.

1991: "160-bhp V-6 . . . is certainly powerful, responsive and refined . . . exterior and interior shapes are handsome and tasteful." **Source:** "The 10 Best Cars in the World 1991," *Road & Track*, December 1990, pp. 46-58.

1990: "attractively styled automobile . . . very good performance, sure-footed handling and lots of comfort . . . ergonomics are excellent." **Source:** "Nissan Maxima," *Design News*, October 2, 1989, pp. 174-175.

1990: "supremely comfortable, thoroughly refined sports sedan . . . offers the best mix of quality, space, performance and value." **Source:** "Best Buys, 1990," *Car and Driver*, May 1990, pp. 37, 42-43.

1989: "pleasant environment for both driver and passenger. . .rearseat kneeroom is outstanding." **Source:** "Nissan 240SX and Maxima: Two nicely rounded rounds incoming," *Car and Driver*, September 1988, pp. 62-5, 67, 71.

1989: "excellent ergonomics, intelligent use of space and flowing, organic form interiors. . .succeeds at making the driver feel cozy, but not claustrophobic." **Source:** "Nissan Maxima SE: Sensuously packaged sports sedan," *Road & Track*, April 1989, pp. 146-50.

1989: "designed-in serviceability . . . ignition system layout is as good as it gets . . . factory-service manual is worthy of special praise." **Source:** "Maximum Performance: Serviceability makes the Nissan Maxima our choice for Car of the Year," *Home Mechanix*, May 1989, pp. 58-61, 84.

1988: "sonar suspension is admirable. . .steering, though too light at speed, is surprisingly direct and precise. . .adequately insulated from the noisy world outside." **Source:** "Nissan Maxima GXE: Now *this* is smooth talkin'," *Motor Trend*, January 1988, pp. 64-6.

RECALLS

None to date.

REPAIR MANUALS

1901 ● Mitchell Glove Compartment Companion for Your Nissan
Harcourt Brace Jovanovich, Inc.
6277 Sea Harbor Dr.
Orlando, FL 32821   Ph:(407)345-2000

Published 1988.

1902 ● Nissan Maxima 1985-1989
Motorbooks International
729 Prospect Ave.
Osceola, WI 54020   Ph:(715)294-3345

Price: $15.95.

OTHER INFORMATION SOURCES

1903 ● Z Club Bulletin
Z Club of America
550 Lexington Ave.
Clifton, NJ 07011   Ph:(201)546-9200

Newsletter providing technical information on Datsun/Nissan automobiles. Contains new product reviews. Bimonthly. **Price:** Included in membership dues.

NISSAN NX 1600/2000 (1987-92)

A sports coupe that competes against the Acura Integra, Dodge Colt Turbo, Honda CRX si, Toyota Corolla GT-S, Volkswagon GTI, Geo Storm, and Toyota Celica. Awarded the Import Car of the Year by *Motor Trend* in 1987 and 1991. Known as the Pulsar before 1988 and the Pulsar NX before 1990. Also known as the NX Coupe, the NX 1600/2000 is currently produced in Zama, Japan.

1992 Nissan NX 2000 Coupe

MAJOR FEATURES

● NX 1600 Coupe has as 1992 standard equipment: 1.6-liter DOHC 16-valve 110hp engine, driver's side airbag, fuel injection, front and rear independent suspension, power rack-and-pinion steering, power front disc brakes, and five-speed manual transmission.

● NX 2000 Coupe adds as 1992 standard equipment: 140-horsepower 2.0-liter DOHC 16-valve four cylinder engine, four-wheel disc brakes, front and rear anti-roll bars, T-top body style, fog lights, front airdam, rear spoiler, alloy wheels, stereo system, and an upgraded interior.

● Pulsar NX XE had as 1990 standard equipment: power brakes, power steering, front and rear stabilizer bars, T-bar roof with removable panels, dual power mirrors, rear spoiler, and tilt wheel steering.

● Pulsar NX SE added to the 1990 Pulsar NX XE standard equipment: 1.8-liter DOHC engine, four-wheel disc brakes, rear sway bar, front spoiler, and alloy wheels.

● Pulsar XE had as 1988 standard equipment: SOHC inline-4 70bhp engine and five-speed manual or three-speed automatic transmission.

● Pulsar SE added to 1988 Pulsar XE standard equipment: 16-valve 113 bhp engine.

PRICE HISTORY

The following new car prices reflect the approximate retail cost of the base model: **1987** - $11,049; **1988** - $11,749; **1989** - $11,999; **1990** - $12,249; **1991** - $11,090; **1992** - $11,300.

DIMENSIONS

Body Style	Years Avail	Wheel Base (in)	Lgth (in)	Ht (in)	Avg Wt (lbs)	Fuel Cap (gal)	Front Hdrm (in)	Front Legrm (in)
3d cpe	87-90	95.7	166.5	51.0	2,365	13.2	38.0	42.0
3d cpe	90-90	95.7	166.5	51.0	2,566	13.2	38.0	42.0
3d cpe	91-91	95.7	162.4	51.8	2,516	13.2	38.0	42.0
3d cpe	92-92	95.7	162.4	51.4	2,350	13.2	37.3	41.6

ENGINES

Type	Displacement (L)	Fuel Dly	HP @rpm	Torque @rpm (ft/lbs)	MPG Cty/Hwy	Years Avail
I-4	1.6	FI	113@6400	99@4800	26/32	87-87
I-4	1.6	FI	69@5000	94@2800	26/34	87-88
I-4	1.8	FI	125@5000	112@2800	23/29	88-88
I-4	1.8	FI	125@6400	115@4800	23/29	89-89
I-4	1.6	FI	90@6000	96@3200	26/34	89-90
I-4	1.6	FI	110@6000	108@4000	28/38	91-92
I-4	2.0	FI	140@6400	132@4800	23/30	91-92

KEY: I=in-line engine; V=V engine; F=flat engine; FI=fuel injection; bbl=barrel carburetor; T=turbo; D=diesel; HP=horsepower; MPG=estimated average miles per gallon.

EVALUATIONS, TESTS, AND RANKINGS

1992: ''[Nissan NX 2000 is] a sports coupe for adults . . . one of those rare automobiles that seem more expensive than they are . . . interior is rich, the dash tasteful.'' **Source:** ''The Bonsai GTs: Japan shrinks the American pony car and a new class is born,'' *Car and Driver*, November 1991, pp. 112-114, 116, 118-119, 122.

1992: ''almost elegant in its austerity . . . gearchange mechanism . . . works more like a good formula car's than an economy-minded people mover's.'' **Source:** ''Nissan NX2000: Balanced performance raises the NX out of econocoupe status,'' *Automobile Magazine*, January 1992, p. 54.

1991: ''precise and slick five-speed manual. . .ride and handling first-rate. . .excellent around town. . .firm, well controlled quality.'' **Source:** ''Nissan NX Coupe: Kiss the Pulsar bye-bye,'' *Motor Trend*, February 1991.

1991: ''quiet, stress-free ride. . .engine is not quite so silent. . .cockpit is fine.'' **Source:** ''Nissan NX Coupe,'' *Automobile Magazine*, December 1990.

1991: ''extremely nimble without being at all twitchy. . .an eye-opening little rat-racer. . .ergonomics are good. . .suspension is impressively supple.'' **Source:** ''Import Car of the Year: Around the world in eight days,'' *Motor Trend*, March 1991, pp. 34-50.

1991: ''NX 2000, new standard of goodness in a small

package.'' **Source:** "Getaway Coupes," *Popular Science,* July 1991, pp. 76-80, 82-83.

1991: "more interior volume, two more seats, and more power." **Source:** "Nissan's CRX Response," *Popular Mechanics,* May 1991, p. 115.

1988: "unique. . .creatively goes where no car has gone before. . .best in coupe/hatchback form. . .clean, simple, and cute. . .chassis is taut and its roadholding is impressive. . .trundle around town reliably and economically." **Source:** "Nissan Pulsar NX SE: Like the curate's egg, good in (its many different) parts," *Motor Trend,* September 1987, pp. 70-72, 74.

1987: "almost effortless acceleration for passing. . .feels more like a roadster than a sport coupe." **Source:** "Nissan Pulsar Pulsates with roof-raising fun," *Detroit Free Press,* July 20, 1987, p. 9C.

RECALLS

1987-88: (61,000 cars): Soldered joint where inlet pipe attaches to fuel tank may be cracked, resulting in fuel leak. **Corrective action:** Replace fuel tank. *(NHTSA Campaign No. 87V191000.)*

SAFETY AND REPAIRS

1989: "Car Clinic," *Popular Mechanics,* May 1990, p. 45. **Note:** Tip for position of wiring in early 1989 Pulsar and Sentra.

REPAIR MANUALS

1904 ● **Mitchell Glove Compartment Companion for Your Nissan**
Harcourt Brace Jovanovich, Inc.
6277 Sea Harbor Dr.
Orlando, FL 32821   Ph:(407)345-2000

Published 1988.

OTHER INFORMATION SOURCES

1905 ● **Z Club Bulletin**
Z Club of America
550 Lexington Ave.
Clifton, NJ 07011   Ph:(201)546-9200

Newsletter providing technical information on Datsun/Nissan automobiles. Contains new product reviews. Bimonthly. **Price:** Included in membership dues.

NISSAN PATHFINDER (1987-92)

A sports/utility truck that competes against the Ford Explorer, Jeep Cherokee, Toyota 4Runner, Chevy S-10, and Ford Bronco. The Nissan Pathfinder is currently produced in Kyoto, Japan.

1991 Nissan Pathfinder

MAJOR FEATURES

● Nissan Pathfinder XE 4x2 1992 standard equipment: five-speed manual or four-speed automatic transmission, anti-lock rear brakes, tilt steering column, power steering, rear window wiper/washer, front tow hooks, tinted glass, AM/FM cassette stereo system, and rear defogger.

● Nissan Pathfinder XE 4x4 adds as 1992 standard equipment: automatic locking front hubs and four-wheel drive.

● Nissan Pathfinder SE 4x4 adds as 1992 standard equipment: semi-automatic air conditioning, cruise control, power windows and locks, and upgraded interior.

PRICE HISTORY

The following new car prices reflect the approximate retail cost of the base model: **1987** - $12,524; **1988** - $15,399; **1989** - $15,399; **1990** - $15,720; **1991** - $16,635; **1992** - $17,265.

DIMENSIONS

Body Style	Years Avail	Wheel Base (in)	Lgth (in)	Ht (in)	Avg Wt (lbs)	Fuel Cap (gal)	Front Hdrm (in)	Front Legrm (in)
utl wgn	87-87	104.3	171.9	65.7	4,960	15.9	na	na
utl wgn	88-92	104.3	171.9	65.7	5,000	21.1	39.3	42.6

ENGINES

Type	Displacement (L)	Fuel Dly	HP @rpm	Torque @rpm (ft/lbs)	MPG Cty/Hwy	Years Avail
I-4	2.4	FI	106@na	na	16/20	87-89
V-6	3.0	FI	145@na	na	15/19	87-90
V-6	3.0	na	153@4800	180@4000	15/19	91-92

KEY: I=in-line engine; V=V engine; F=flat engine; FI=fuel injection; bbl=barrel carburetor; T=turbo; D=diesel; HP=horsepower; MPG=estimated average miles per gallon.

EVALUATIONS, TESTS, AND RANKINGS

1991: "blend of muscle and chic . . . Handling is superb . . . as far removed from a truck as an SUV in this class gets." **Source:** "Update: Sport-Utility Vehicles," *U.S. News and World Report,* May 13, 1991, pp. A4-A6, A8-A10, A12, A14-A15.

1990: "smooth and lively. . .excellent interior air circulation." **Source:** "'90 Nissan Pathfinder 4-door," *Popular Mechanics,* March 1990, p. 102.

1990: "one of the roomiest interiors. . .strong enough to pull a camping trailer to the mountains." **Source:** "Nissan Pathfinder 4-door: One more of something for everbody," *Motor Trend,* February 1990, pp. 110-11, 133.

1990: "a tall station wagon. . .quieter than low-budget cars and the ride is plusher than the truck tires would suggest."

Source: "Nissan Pathfinder SE: The freeway version of elevator shoes," *Car and Driver*, October 1989, pp. 147-9.

1990: "responsive steering, and smooth, quick braking power . . . aggressive styling and exceptional performance . . . ahead of the pack in ride and handling capabilities." **Source:** "Trailbreaker Pathfinder," *Outdoor Life*, March 1990, pp. 50, 52.

1990: "Ride and handling are the new Pathfinder's strong suits . . . engine a bit sluggish on the bottom end . . . dashboard and the working controls are all well placed." **Source:** "'90 Nissan Pathfinder 4-Door," *Popular Mechanics*, March 1990, p. 102.

1990: "part-time four-wheel-drive feature can be engaged on the fly at speeds up to 30 mph." **Source:** "4-Door Off-Roaders," *Sports Afield*, March 1990, pp. 120-122, 143-145.

1990: "absence of pavement won't slow them up a bit . . . engines . . . run as smoothly as a limousine, with ride quality to match." **Source:** "4-Doors for All Seasons," *New Choices for the Best Years*, December 1989, pp. 84, 86-87.

1989: "stylish, comfortable and strong . . . it's bog slow in acceleration . . . need[s] more horsepower." **Source:** "Dirt Rods: An expert torture test for the cream of the compact SUV crop," *Popular Mechanics*, March 1989, pp. 113-116, 120.

1989: "Perhaps the tightest, toughest, best put-together of the Japanese utilities." **Source:** "Sport Vehicles: Personal Pick," *Outdoor Life*, June 1989, pp. 20, 24-25.

1988: "big, macho and fun. . .tough. . .rugged. . .ability to get through nasty weather or to go where no BMW driver would dare to go." **Source:** "Nissan Pathfinder is macho but has a gentle touch, too," *The Detroit News*, August 26, 1987, pp. 1-2F.

RECALLS

1987-90: (750,000 cars and trucks; includes models made before 1987; includes other Nissan models): Incorrect tire inflation pressures printed on certification labels. **Corrective action:** Install corrected tire information label on doorpost certification label. (*NHTSA Campaign No. 90V072000.*)

1987: (3,996 vehicles): Male and female rear seat belt mismatched. **Corrective action:** Replace belt assemblies. (*NHTSA Campaign No. 87V137000.*)

REPAIR MANUALS

1906 ● **Mitchell Glove Compartment Companion for Your Nissan**
Harcourt Brace Jovanovich, Inc.
6277 Sea Harbor Dr.
Orlando, FL 32821   Ph:(407)345-2000

Published 1988.

1907 ● **Nissan Pick-up and Pathfinder 1989-91**
Chilton Co.
Chilton Way
Radnor, PA 19089   Ph:(215)964-4000

Total car care service. May 1991. **Price:** $19.95.

1908 ● **Nissan Pickups and Pathfinder, 1986-1988**
Clymer Publications
P.O. Box 1209
Overland Park, KS 66212   Ph:(913)541-6694

Published 1986. **Price:** $14.95.

OTHER INFORMATION SOURCES

1909 ● **Z Club Bulletin**
Z Club of America
550 Lexington Ave.
Clifton, NJ 07011   Ph:(201)546-9200

Newsletter providing technical information on Datsun/Nissan automobiles. Contains new product reviews. Bimonthly. **Price:** Included in membership dues.

NISSAN SENTRA (1987-1992)

A subcompact car that competes against the Honda Civic, Mazda Protege, and Toyota Corolla. Received a top ranking in customer satisfaction among cars under $20,000 in J.D. Powers & Associates Survey. The XE model was awarded the Best Coupe/Sedan less than $10,000 by *Road & Track* in 1990. XE was also ranked in the highest maintenance cost category for a subcompact wagon by *The Complete Car Cost Guide* in 1990. The SE-R model was named the 1991 Import Car of the Year by *Car and Driver*. Named the Import Car of the Year by *Motor Trend* in 1991. Rated a Best Bet of 1992 by *The Car Book*. The Nissan Sentra SE-R was selected to the *Car and Driver* Ten Best list in 1992. Currently built in Kyoto, Japan and Smyrna, Tennessee (Smyrna plant parts data: domestic parts - 35%, imported parts - 65%, *Federal Trade Zone Board*, 1989).

1991 Nissan Sentra GXE

MAJOR FEATURES

● Nissan Sentra E 1992 standard equipment: four-speed manual or three-speed automatic transmission, power-assisted front disc/rear drum brakes, rear defogger, active suspension, anti-roll bar, and various interior features.

● Nissan Sentra E 4-door adds as 1992 standard equipment: five-speed manual or three-speed automatic transmission, motorized front shoulder belts, and right visor mirror.

● Nissan Sentra XE adds to 1992 standard equipment: five-speed manual or four-speed automatic transmission, power steering, tilt steering, and power mirrors.

● Nissan Sentra GXE adds to 1992 standard equipment: power windows and locks, cruise control, AM/FM cassette stereo system, velour upholstery, and alloy wheels.

● Nissan Sentra SE adds to 1992 standard equipment: upgraded seats and upholstery and rear spoiler.

● Nissan Sentra SE-R adds to 1992 standard equipment: 2.0-liter engine, four-wheel disc brakes, limited slip sport suspension, fog lights, and alloy wheels.

PRICE HISTORY

The following new car prices reflect the approximate retail cost of the base model: **1987** - $6,199; **1988** - $6,699; **1989** - $6,999; **1990** - $7,399; **1991** - $9,225; **1992** - $8,495.

DIMENSIONS

Body Style	Years Avail	Wheel Base (in)	Lgth (in)	Ht (in)	Avg Wt (lbs)	Fuel Cap (gal)	Front Hdrm (in)	Front Legrm (in)
3d lbk	87-88	95.5	162.4	55.3	2,192	13.2	38.7	41.8
2d cpe	88-91	95.7	166.5	52.2	2,304	13.2	37.0	41.6
2d sdn	87-87	95.7	168.7	54.3	2,200	13.2	38.3	43.1
2d sdn	88-88	95.7	168.7	55.3	2,156	13.2	38.2	41.8
2d sdn	89-90	95.7	168.7	54.3	2,156	13.2	38.2	41.8
2d sdn	91-92	95.7	170.3	53.9	2,266	13.2	38.5	41.9
4d sdn	87-87	95.7	168.7	54.3	2,231	13.2	38.3	43.1
4d sdn	88-90	95.7	168.7	55.3	2,208	13.2	38.2	41.8
4d sdn	91-92	95.7	170.3	53.9	2,288	13.2	38.5	41.9
5d wgn	87-88	95.7	172.2	54.3	2,304	13.2	37.3	43.1
5d wgn	89-90	95.7	172.2	54.3	2,301	13.2	38.2	41.8

ENGINES

Type	Displacement (L)	Fuel Dly	HP @rpm	Torque @rpm (ft/lbs)	MPG Cty/Hwy	Years Avail
I-4	1.6	2-bbl	70@5000	92@2800	29/36	87-88
I-4	1.6	FI	69@5000	94@2800	22/27	88-88
I-4	1.6	FI	90@6000	96@3200	28/36	89-90
I-4	1.6	FI	110@6000	108@4000	29/39	91-92
I-4	2.0	FI	140@6400	132@4800	24/32	91-92

KEY: I=in-line engine; V=V engine; F=flat engine; FI=fuel injection; bbl=barrel carburetor; T=turbo; D=diesel; HP=horsepower; MPG=estimated average miles per gallon.

EVALUATIONS, TESTS, AND RANKINGS

1992: "delivered about as much fun for as little money as you could reasonably expect." **Source:** "Ten Best Cars," *Motor Trend,* January 1992, pp. 35-43.

1991: "silky steering . . . ride remains quiet, comfortable, even soft . . . protective understeer . . . handles potholes . . . seatbelts are clumsy." **Source:** "Nissan Sentra SE-R: The only thing it lacks is a prestigious hood ornament," *Car and Driver,* March 1991, pp. 53-7.

1991: "feels richer than its price. . .a fine family car. . .space is plentiful up front . . . adequate in the back seat. . .clean, simple, and attractive." **Source:** "Import Car of the Year: Around the world in eight days," *Motor Trend,* March 1991, pp. 33-50.

1991: "smooth-shifting . . . rigid body . . . spacious interior . . . only slight understeer." **Source:** "New-fashioned Nissans: A golden Sentra and a gilded 240SX," *Road & Track,* November 1990, pp. 145-6.

1991: "tasteful styling . . . better handling." **Source:** "Nissan Sentra," *Popular Mechanics,* December 1990, p. 28.

1991: " . . . for all the 2002 reasons and one more: you won't have to sell the farm." **Source:** "1991 Import Cars: Nissan Sentra SE-R: Poems to be written, ballads to be sung," *Car and Driver,* November 1990, p. 86.

1991: "reasonable power off the line combined with smooth, effortless passing at highway speeds . . . handling . . . a perfect compromise between road grip and passenger comfort." **Source:** "Fuel-Efficient Family Cars For 1991," *Home Mechanix,* March 1991, pp. 69-73.

1990: "[Sentra SE-R] solid appearance . . . fuel efficient for a

luxury model." **Source:** "Infiniti adds a low-end luxury model for 1991," *Detroit Free Press,* September 12, 1990, p. 1L.

RECALLS

1990-91: (165,000 vehicles equipped with two-point non-motorized passive front shoulder belts): Improper belt guide performance can cause fraying of shoulder safety belts near retractor, which could lead to inadequate protection of occupant. **Corrective action:** Modify safety belt guides to prevent fraying; and/or replace retractor assembly if fraying is present. (NHTSA Campaign No. 91V022000.)

SAFETY AND REPAIRS

1989: "Car Clinic," *Popular Mechanics,* May 1990, p. 45. **Note:** Tip for position of wiring in early 1989 Pulsar and Sentra.

REPAIR MANUALS

1910 ● **Chilton's Nissan Sentra, Datsun 1200 and B210, 1973-1987**
Chilton Co.
Chilton Way
Radnor, PA 19089   Ph:(215)964-4000

Published 1989. **Price:** $14.95.

1911 ● **Mitchell Glove Compartment Companion for Your Nissan**
Harcourt Brace Jovanovich, Inc.
6277 Sea Harbor Dr.
Orlando, FL 32821   Ph:(407)345-2000

Published 1988.

OTHER INFORMATION SOURCES

1912 ● **Z Club Bulletin**
Z Club of America
550 Lexington Ave.
Clifton, NJ 07011   Ph:(201)546-9200

Newsletter providing technical information on Datsun/Nissan automobiles. Contains new product reviews. Bimonthly. **Price:** Included in membership dues.

NISSAN STANZA (1987-1992)

A four-door sedan that competes against the Honda Accord, Subaru Legacy, Dodge Spirit, Plymouth Acclaim, Toyota Camry, Hyundai Sonata GLS, and Peugeot 405. The four-door wagon was dropped after 1988. Named one of the Best Sellers by *Popular Mechanics* in 1989. Nominated to the *Car and Driver* Ten Best Cars list in 1990. Currently produced in Japan.

1992 Nissan Stanza SE

MAJOR FEATURES

● Nissan Stanza XE 1992 standard equipment includes: five-speed manual transmission, four-wheel independent suspension, tilt steering wheel column, power steering, power front disc/rear drum brakes, front and rear stabilizer bars, wheel covers, tinted glass, rear window defroster, side window defoggers, and motorized shoulder seat belts.

● Nissan Stanza GXE adds as 1992 standard equipment: power windows and locks, air conditioning, power antenna, cruise control, AM/FM stereo system, and aluminum alloy wheels.

● Nissan Stanza SE adds as 1992 standard equipment: fog lights, rear spoiler, leather-wrapped steering wheel and shift knob, and sporty interior trim.

● Nissan Stanza Wagon had as 1988 standard equipment: sliding doors and part-time four-wheel drive.

PRICE HISTORY

The following new car prices reflect the approximate retail cost of the base model: **1987** - $10,749; **1988** - $11,499; **1989** - $12,199; **1990** - $11,650; **1991** - $12,380; **1992** - $12,750.

DIMENSIONS

Body Style	Years Avail	Wheel Base (in)	Lgth (in)	Ht (in)	Avg Wt (lbs)	Fuel Cap (gal)	Front Hdrm (in)	Front Legrm (in)
4d sdn	87-89	100.4	177.8	54.9	2,770	16.1	38.1	43.0
4d sdn	90-92	100.4	179.9	54.1	2,788	16.4	38.6	42.6
5d wgn	87-87	99.0	170.3	54.7	2,809	14.3	38.8	39.4
5d wgn	88-88	99.0	170.3	64.2	2,950	15.9	38.6	39.2

ENGINES

Type	Displace-ment (L)	Fuel Dly	HP @rpm	Torque @rpm (ft/lbs)	MPG Cty/Hwy	Years Avail
I-4	2.0	2-bbl	97@5200	114@3200	22/28	87-87
I-4	2.0	FI	94@5400	114@2800	22/28	87-89
I-4	2.0	FI	97@5200	114@3200	22/27	88-88
I-4	2.4	FI	138@5600	148@4400	22/29	90-92

KEY: I=in-line engine; V=V engine; F=flat engine; FI=fuel injection; bbl=barrel carburetor; T=turbo; D=diesel; HP=horsepower; MPG=estimated average miles per gallon.

EVALUATIONS, TESTS, AND RANKINGS

1992: "competent car with little soul . . . styling is clean, but displays limited imagination . . . boredom factor is likely to increase with each car payment." **Source:** "Stanza needs more inspiration," *Detroit News and Free Press*, October 24, 1991, p. 1D.

1990: "a quiet statement in uncluttered interior design . . . larger, quieter, and more rigid than the aging car it replaces." **Source:** "Compact Sedans Grow Up," *Popular Science*, April 1990, pp. 80-84.

1990: "plenty of glass area for good all-around visibility . . . ride is on the firm side and a tad noisy at times . . . fun to drive." **Source:** "Stanza GXE: Sedan with sports handling," *Design News*, June 11, 1990, p. 32.

1990: "accelerates briskly, handles securely, looks smart, feels solidly built, and takes fine care of its occupants . . . in close comparison with some of the compact (and not-so-compact) sedan alternatives, the Stanza goes a little flat." **Source:** "Nissan Stanza GXE: A conservative play in a hotly contested game," *Car and Driver*, April 1990, pp. 85-88.

1989: "except for cramped headroom, it's also quite cozy. . .logical controls and visible gauges." **Source:** "Best Sellers: A 13-car pitched battle for small sedan supremacy," *Popular Mechanics*, July 1989, pp. 60-3, 120-122.

1987: "adequate and bland lack of power. . .bit dull compared to the competition." **Source:** "Daily drivers: We pit Chevy's new Corsica against nine new-wave family sedans," *Popular Mechanics*, May 1987, pp. 71-4, 172.

RECALLS

1987-88: (750,000 cars and trucks; includes models made before 1987; includes other Nissan models): Incorrect tire inflation pressures printed on certification labels. **Corrective action:** Install corrected tire information label on doorpost certification label. *(NHTSA Campaign No. 90V072000.)*

REPAIR MANUALS

1913 ● **Mitchell Glove Compartment Companion for Your Nissan**
Harcourt Brace Jovanovich, Inc.
6277 Sea Harbor Dr.
Orlando, FL 32821   Ph:(407)345-2000
Published 1988.

OTHER INFORMATION SOURCES

1914 ● **Z Club Bulletin**
Z Club of America
550 Lexington Ave.
Clifton, NJ 07011   Ph:(201)546-9200

Newsletter providing technical information on Datsun/Nissan automobiles. Contains new product reviews. Bimonthly. **Price:** Included in membership dues.

NISSAN TRUCK (1987-92)

A pickup truck that competes against the Ford Ranger, Chevrolet S-10, Dodge Dakota, Jeep Comanche, and Toyota 4x4. Nissan Trucks come in a variety of configurations, transmission types, and engine sizes. The Nissan 4x4 (4WD) Trucks are offered in three different body configurations: Regular Cab, King Cab, and SE V6 King Cab. The Nissan 4x2 (2WD) Trucks add the Long Bed V-6 body configurations. Known as the Nissan Hardbody before 1990, the Nissan Truck is currently produced in Smyrna, Tennessee (plant parts data: domestic parts - 35%, imported parts - 65%, *Federal Trade Zone Board*, 1989).

1991 Nissan SE-V6 King Cab 4x4 Truck

MAJOR FEATURES

● Nissan Regular Cab and King Cab 4x4 Trucks have as 1992

standard equipment: 2.4 liter I-4 engine, five-speed manual transmission, power steering, front independent suspension, rear-wheel drive, power disc/drum brakes with ABS, towing hooks, chromed steel wheels, tinted glass, side window defoggers, and bench seat.

● Nissan Regular Cab and King Cab 4x2 Trucks 1992 standard equipment adds an optional four-speed automatic transmission, substitutes styled steel wheels, and deletes the ABS system.

● Nissan SE V-6 4x4 and 4x2 King Cab Trucks have as 1992 standard equipment: 3.0-liter V-6 engine, cruise control, numerous other exterior body stylings, reclining front bucket seats, and an upgraded interior.

● Nissan Long Bed V-6 4x2 Truck has the same chassis as the Nissan SE V-6 King Cab with fewer exterior and interior features and deletes cruise control in 1992.

Dimensions that follow represents those for the Regular Cab configuration.

PRICE HISTORY

The following new car prices reflect the approximate retail cost of the base model: **1987** - $6,699; **1988** - $7,399; **1989** - $7,549; **1990** - $8,149; **1991** - $8,545.

DIMENSIONS

Body Style	Years Avail	Wheel Base (in)	Lgth (in)	Ht (in)	Avg Wt (lbs)	Fuel Cap (gal)	Front Hdrm (in)	Front Legrm (in)
trk	87-88	104.3	174.2	62.0	4,200	15.9	na	na
trk	89-92	104.3	174.6	62.0	4,400	15.9	na	na

ENGINES

Type	Displace-ment (L)	Fuel Dly	HP @rpm	Torque @rpm (ft/lbs)	MPG Cty/Hwy	Years Avail
I-4	2.4	FI	134@na	na	23/27	90-92
V-6	3.0	FI	153@na	na	19/23	90-92
I-4	2.4	FI	106@na	na	21/26	87-89
V-6	3.0	FI	145@na	na	17/24	87-89

KEY: I=in-line engine; V=V engine; F=flat engine; FI=fuel injection; bbl=barrel carburetor; T=turbo; D=diesel; HP=horsepower; MPG=estimated average miles per gallon.

EVALUATIONS, TESTS, AND RANKINGS

1990: "low liftover on the 2WD model makes it easy to load and unload supplies and tools from the bed. . .In front, the split bench seat with armrest is supportive and comfortable for two people." **Source:** "Loadin' Up," *Organic Gardening*, April 1990, pp. 55-58.

1989: "distinctive. . .brawny. . .near the bottom of the pack in every performance test, coming across as slow and not much fun to drive." **Source:** "Compact Commandos: These muscular middleweights can haul a lot more than cargo," *Popular Mechanics*, February 1989, p. 122.

1989: "slower in acceleration tests than every truck except the Dodge Dakota. . .good braking and double-lane-change performance. . .softest ride of the group. . .at times the truck felt cheap and flimsy." **Source:** "Mudders," *Popular Mechanics*, July 1989, pp. 33-4, 38-40, 42, 44.

RECALLS

None to date.

REPAIR MANUALS

1915 ● **Datsun and Nissan Two and Four-Wheel Drive Pickups 1970-1987 Gas and Diesel**
Clymer Publications
P.O. Box 1209
Overland Park, KS 66212   Ph:(913)541-6694

With illustrations. Published 1987. **Price:** $26.95.

1916 ● **Mitchell Glove Compartment Companion for Your Nissan**
Harcourt Brace Jovanovich, Inc.
6277 Sea Harbor Dr.
Orlando, FL 32821   Ph:(407)345-2000

Published 1988.

1917 ● **Nissan Pick-up and Pathfinder 1989-91**
Chilton Co.
Chilton Way
Radnor, PA 19089   Ph:(215)964-4000

Total car care service. May 1991. **Price:** $19.95.

1918 ● **Nissan Pickups and Pathfinder, 1986-1988**
Clymer Publications
P.O. Box 1209
Overland Park, KS 66212   Ph:(913)541-6694

Published 1986. **Price:** $14.95.

OTHER INFORMATION SOURCES

1919 ● **Z Club Bulletin**
Z Club of America
550 Lexington Ave.
Clifton, NJ 07011   Ph:(201)546-9200

Newsletter providing technical information on Datsun/Nissan automobiles. Contains new product reviews. Bimonthly. **Price:** Included in membership dues.

NISSAN VAN (1987-90)

A compact van that competed against the Mitsubishi Wagon, Dodge Caravan, Plymouth Voyager, and Toyota Van. Produced in Japan through the 1990 model year.

MAJOR FEATURES

● XE had as 1990 standard equipment: five-speed manual or four-speed automatic transmission, power steering, power brakes, front and rear air conditioning, and various interior features.

● GXE added as 1990 standard equipment: four-speed automatic transmission, power windows and locks, privacy glass, dual power mirrors, and rear wiper/washer.

PRICE HISTORY

The following new car prices reflect the approximate retail cost of the base model: **1987** - $12,599; **1988** - $14,799.

DIMENSIONS

Body Style	Years Avail	Wheel Base (in)	Lgth (in)	Ht (in)	Avg Wt (lbs)	Fuel Cap (gal)	Front Hdrm (in)	Front Legrm (in)
5d van	87-90	92.5	178.0	72.4	4,800	17.7	na	na

ENGINES

Type	Displace-ment (L)	Fuel Dly	HP @rpm	Torque @rpm (ft/lbs)	MPG Cty/Hwy	Years Avail
I-4	2.4	FI	106@na	na	18/21	87-90

KEY: I=in-line engine; V=V engine; F=flat engine; FI=fuel injection; bbl=barrel carburetor; T=turbo; D=diesel; HP=horsepower; MPG=estimated average miles per gallon.

EVALUATIONS, TESTS, AND RANKINGS

1987: "slowly . . . accelerates . . . proved to be a comfortable place to spend time . . . not fun . . . not satisfying . . . but comfortable." **Source:** "Nissan Van GXE: It is the box it came in," *Car and Driver*, August 1987, pp. 123-5.

1987: "easy entry . . . delivered the smoothest ride . . . most truck-like in its mechanicals." **Source:** "Mini-vans: Maxi Versatility: De-cloning the people haulers from Toyota, Nissan, and Mitsubishi," *Motor Trend*, July 1987, pp. 87-91, 94-5.

RECALLS

1987-90: (33,000 trucks; includes models made before 1987): Power steering hoses may leak fluid that can spread to exhaust manifold and result in an engine compartment fire. **Corrective action:** Install new heat resistant power steering hoses. Also, install new fan coupling to increase air flow volume through engine compartment and replace any other damaged components. *(NHTSA Campaign No. 90V136000.)*

1987: (10,025 vehicles): Valve cover gasket may leak oil, possibly resulting in fire. **Corrective action:** Replace with redesigned valve cover gasket. *(NHTSA Campaign No. 87V109000.)*

REPAIR MANUALS

1920 ● **Mitchell Glove Compartment Companion for Your Nissan**
Harcourt Brace Jovanovich, Inc.
6277 Sea Harbor Dr.
Orlando, FL 32821   Ph:(407)345-2000

Published 1988.

OTHER INFORMATION SOURCES

1921 ● **Z Club Bulletin**
Z Club of America
550 Lexington Ave.
Clifton, NJ 07011   Ph:(201)546-9200

Newsletter providing technical information on Datsun/Nissan automobiles. Contains new product reviews. Bimonthly. **Price:** Included in membership dues.

OLDSMOBILE ACHIEVA (1992)

Introduced in 1992, the Oldsmobile Achieva replaces the Cutlass Calais. Corporate twins are the Buick Skylark and Pontiac Grand Am. Achieva is available in a 2-door coupe and 4-door sedan with either a 5-speed manual or 3-speed automatic transmission. Achieva is manufactured at the Lansing Car Assembly Plant in Lansing, Michigan.

1992 Oldsmobile Achieva SC

MAJOR FEATURES

● Achieva S has as 1992 standard equipment: 5-speed manual transmission, front independent suspension, power-assisted disc brakes with anti-lock braking system, power rack-and-pinion steering, reclining front bucket seats with driver's side lumbar support adjustments, full analog instrumentation, covered visor-vanity mirrors, rear heat ducts, and remote fuel filler and trunk release buttons.

● Achieva Sport Coupe adds as 1992 standard equipment: dual exhaust outlets, performance tires, 16-inch aluminum wheels, variable-effort power steering, fog lamps, grid-type radio antenna built into the rear window glass, and a decklid-mounted aero wing.

● Achieva SL adds as 1992 standard equipment: 3-speed automatic transmission, styled polycast road wheels, fold-down rear seat, and AM/FM cassette radio with 6-speaker dimensional sound.

● Achieva SCX is a special performance version of the Achieva, featuring a 5-speed manual heavy duty transmission with special gear ratios.

PRICE HISTORY

The following new car prices reflect the approximate retail cost of the base model: **1992 - $15,500.**

DIMENSIONS

Body Style	Years Avail	Wheel Base (in)	Lgth (in)	Ht (in)	Avg Wt (lbs)	Fuel Cap (gal)	Front Hdrm (in)	Front Legrm (in)
2d cpe	92-92	103.4	187.9	53.1	2690	15.2	37.8	43.1
4d sdn	92-92	103.4	187.9	53.1	2772	15.2	37.8	43.1

ENGINES

Type	Displace-ment (L)	Fuel Dly	HP @rpm	Torque @rpm (ft/lbs)	MPG Cty/Hwy	Years Avail
I-4	2.3	FI	120@5200	140@3200	24/33	92-92
I-4	2.3	FI	160@6000	155@4800	22/29	92-92
I-4	2.3	FI	180@6200	160@5200	22/29	92-92
V-6	3.3	FI	160@5200	185@2000	19/29	92-92

KEY: I=in-line engine; V=V engine; F=flat engine; FI=fuel injection; bbl=barrel carburetor; T=turbo; D=diesel; HP=horsepower; MPG=estimated average miles per gallon.

EVALUATIONS, TESTS, AND RANKINGS

1992: "a great deal better than the old Calais in the way it fits the driver . . . rear wheels tend to patter over the bumps . . .

structure of this car remains quite flexy, nowhere near as good as, say, a Honda Accord." **Source:** "Oldsmobile Achieva," *Car and Driver,* October 1991, pp. 49, 51.

1992: "outstanding style, attractive performance potential, and no pretension . . . ride quality and handling were fine . . . when pushed, the noise and vibration transmitted by the Quad 4 into the passenger cell is high and out of character." **Source:** "Oldsmobile Achieva SC," *Motor Trend,* October 1991, p. 78.

1992: "interior is simple and uncluttered, and the exterior is smart . . . Oldsmobile product with a distinct Japanese flavor . . . the most exciting Oldsmobile in a long time." **Source:** "Oldsmobile Achieva," *Automobile Magazine,* October 1991, pp. 98-99.

RECALLS

None to date.

OTHER INFORMATION SOURCES

1922 ● Journey With Olds
Oldsmobile Club of America
P.O. Box 16216
Lansing, MI 48901

Monthly.

1923 ● Oldsmobile Performance Chapter—Performance Roster
Oldsmobile Performance Chapter (OPC)
P.O. Box 4563
Chicago, IL 60680   Ph:(312)276-1006

Quarterly.

1924 ● W. Machines
Oldsmobile Performance Chapter (OPC)
P.O. Box 4563
Chicago, IL 60680   Ph:(312)276-1006

Monthly.

ASSOCIATIONS

1925 ● Oldsmobile Club of America
P.O. Box 16216
Lansing, MI 48901

Founded: 1970. **Membership:** 5,000. Owners and enthusiasts of Oldsmobile cars made from 1897 to the present. Promotes mutual assistance in keeping cars on the road and in locating parts and service. Encourages research into the old car hobby field. Bestows awards for competition in restoration and preservation. Maintains library of sales literature from the 1920s to the present. **Convention/Meeting:** Annual.

1926 ● Oldsmobile Performance Chapter
P.O. Box 4563
Chicago, IL 60680
Robert Gerometta, Editor   Ph:(312)276-1006

Founded: 1982. **Membership:** 1,200. A chapter of Oldsmobile Club of America. Seeks to promote and restore high performance Oldsmobiles. Maintains archives of performance data and articles from 1964 to 1985; operates 1,000 volume library including factory data on performance Oldsmobiles. **Convention/Meeting:** Annual car meet/show.

OLDSMOBILE BRAVADA (1991-1992)

Introduced as a 1991 model. Intended primarily for on-road operation, Bravada is essentially the luxury version of the Chevrolet S10 Blazer and GMC S15 Jimmy. Listed among five vehicles for Truck of the Year by *Motor Trend* in 1991.

1992 Oldsmobile Bravada

MAJOR FEATURES

● Oldsmobile Bravada has as 1992 standard equipment: 4-speed automatic transmission, front disc/rear drum brakes with anti-lock braking system, 4-wheel drive, power steering, air conditioning, power door locks and windows, AM/FM stereo cassette player, and rear window wiper/washer system.

PRICE HISTORY

The following new car prices reflect the approximate retail cost of the base model: **1991** - $23,795.

DIMENSIONS

Body Style	Years Avail	Wheel Base (in)	Lgth (in)	Ht (in)	Avg Wt (lbs)	Fuel Cap (gal)	Front Hdrm (in)	Front Legrm (in)
utl wgn	91-92	107.0	178.9	65.5	3,939	20	39.1	42.5

ENGINES

Type	Displacement (L)	Fuel Dly	HP @rpm	Torque @rpm (ft/lbs)	MPG Cty/Hwy	Years Avail
V-6	4.3	FI	160@4000	230@2800	17/22	91-92
V-6	4.3	FI	200@na	na	17/22	92-92

KEY: I=in-line engine; V=V engine; F=flat engine; FI=fuel injection; bbl=barrel carburetor; T=turbo; D=diesel; HP=horsepower; MPG=estimated average miles per gallon.

EVALUATIONS, TESTS, AND RANKINGS

1991: "offers handsome styling and a bevy of important safety features . . . that distinguish it among its peers . . . Steering is good." **Source:** "1991 Truck of the Year," *Motor Trend,* January 1991, pp. 79-84.

1991: "isn't intended for extremely rough going . . . But these drawbacks are more than overcome by . . . a combination of full-time four-wheel drive and four-wheel anti-lock brakes that operate on . . . ice-bound roads in amazing fashion." **Source:** "Bravo for Olds Bravada," *The Detroit News,* January 16, 1991, pp. 1F-2F.

1991: "offers impressive standard hardware . . . can handle trailers weighing up to 5500 pounds." **Source:** "Update: Sport-

Utility Vehicles,'' *Car and Driver*, May 13, 1991, pp. A4-A6, A8-A10, A12, A14-A15.

1991: ''look is definitely more luxury car than backwoods brush-buster ... seats are comfortable with ample back support ... heater and air-conditioner are very effective.'' **Source:** ''Bravada AWD,'' *Trailer Life*, July 1991, pp. 67-68, 128, 131-132, 137.

1991: ''One of the glaring omissions ... is the lack of an air bag ... big tires make it a trifle bouncy on the highway ... zero-to-60 accerlaration is a somewhat leisurely 12 seconds.'' **Source:** ''Oldsmobile Rolls Out a Sporty Truck,'' *The New York Times*, May 19, 1991.

RECALLS

1991: (102,885 light trucks and multi-purpose vehicles; includes the GMC Jimmy, Chevrolet S-10 Pickup, Chevrolet Blazer, and Oldsmobile Bravada): Vehicles have been shipped with the fuel tank sender seal out of position. In the event of a rollover accident, an out of position seal could allow fuel spillage in excess of the amount prescribed by FMVSS 301. Spilled fuel could ignite near an ignition source. **Corrective action:** Replace sender seals. *(NHTSA Campaign No. 91V108000.)*

REPAIR MANUALS

1927 ● **Get Your Oldsmobile Fixed Right**
Consumer Reports Books
51 E. 42nd St., Ste. 800
New York, NY 10017   Ph:(212)682-9280

Published 1989. **Editor(s):** Mort Schultz. **Price:** $8.95.

OTHER INFORMATION SOURCES

1928 ● **Chevrolet S-10 Blazer, GMC S-15, and Olds Bravada, 1982-1990**
Chilton Co.
Chilton Way
Radnor, PA 19089   Ph:(215)964-4000

Published 1991. **Price:** $19.95.

1929 ● **Illustrated Oldsmobile Buyer's Guide**
Motorbooks International
729 Prospect Ave
Osceola, WI 54020   Ph:(715)294-3345

Published 1987. **Editor(s):** R. Langworth. **Price:** $16.95.

1930 ● **Journey With Olds**
Oldsmobile Club of America
P.O. Box 16216
Lansing, MI 48901

Monthly.

ASSOCIATIONS

1931 ● **Oldsmobile Club of America**
P.O. Box 16216
Lansing, MI 48901

Founded: 1970. **Membership:** 5,000. Owners and enthusiasts of Oldsmobile cars made from 1897 to the present. Promotes mutual assistance in keeping cars on the road and in locating parts and service. Encourages research into the old car hobby field. Bestows awards for competition in restoration and preservation. Maintains library of sales literature from the 1920s to the present. **Convention/Meeting:** Annual.

OLDSMOBILE CUSTOM CRUISER (1987-92)

Introduced as part of B-car line, along with Buick Estate Wagon, Chevrolet Caprice, and Pontiac Safari. Chosen by *The Complete Car Cost Guide* as being one of the best overall values for a midsize/large wagon in 1990. Placed second in *Motor Trend's* 1991 Car of the Year competition.

1991 Oldsmobile Custom Cruiser

MAJOR FEATURES

● Oldsmobile Custom Cruiser has as 1992 standard equipment: 4-speed automatic transmission, power steering, front disc/rear drum brakes with anti-lock braking system, driver's side airbag, solar windshield, air conditioning, vista roof, and AM/FM stereo.

PRICE HISTORY

The following new car prices reflect the approximate retail cost of the base model: **1987** - $14,420; **1988** - $15,655; **1989** - $16,795; **1990** - $17,595; **1991** - $20,495.

DIMENSIONS

Body Style	Years Avail	Wheel Base (in)	Lgth (in)	Ht (in)	Avg Wt (lbs)	Fuel Cap (gal)	Front Hdrm (in)	Front Legrm (in)
5d wgn	87-90	116.0	220.3	58.5	4,136	22.0	39.6	42.2
5d wgn	91-91	115.9	217.5	60.1	4,435	22.0	39.7	42.2
5d wgn	92-92	115.9	217.5	60.3	4,434	na	39.6	42.2

ENGINES

Type	Displacement (L)	Fuel Dly	HP @rpm	Torque @rpm (ft/lbs)	MPG Cty/Hwy	Years Avail
V-8	5.0	4-bbl	140@3200	255@2000	17/24	87-90
V-8	5.0	FI	170@4200	255@2400	16/25	91-92
V-8	5.7	FI	180@4400	300@2400	16/25	92-92

KEY: I=in-line engine; V=V engine; F=flat engine; FI=fuel injection; bbl=barrel carburetor; T=turbo; D=diesel; HP=horsepower; MPG=estimated average miles per gallon.

EVALUATIONS, TESTS, AND RANKINGS

1991: ''the top point-getter in the objective scoring of instrumented testing ... ride quality and interior noise levels coddle the occupants.'' **Source:** ''Car of the Year,'' *Motor Trend*, February 1991, pp. 42-47, 50-52.

1991: ''Least convenient were ... stalk-mounted cruise controls ... power front seats ... are by far the widest and cushiest of this wagon group ... gets top honors for drivetrain smoothness.'' **Source:** ''Station to Station,'' *Home Mechanix*, June 1991, pp. 78-83.

RECALLS

1987: (11,936 vehicles with 200 4R transmissions; includes Chevrolet, Pontiac, Oldsmobile, Buick, Cadillac, and GMC models): Manual valve link in transmission may have been improperly formed. **Corrective action:** Replace manual valve detent lever link. *(NHTSA Campaign No. 87V168000.)*

REPAIR MANUALS

1932 ● **Buick-Olds-Pontiac Full-Size, 1975-87**
Chilton Co.
Chilton Way
Radnor, PA 19089   Ph:(215)964-4000

Price: $14.95.

1933 ● **Get Your Oldsmobile Fixed Right**
Consumer Reports Books
51 E. 42nd St., Ste. 800
New York, NY 10017   Ph:(212)682-9280

Published 1989. **Editor(s):** Mort Schultz. **Price:** $8.95.

OTHER INFORMATION SOURCES

1934 ● **Illustrated Oldsmobile Buyer's Guide**
Motorbooks International
729 Prospect Ave
Osceola, WI 54020   Ph:(715)294-3345

Published 1987. **Editor(s):** R. Langworth. **Price:** $16.95.

1935 ● **Journey With Olds**
Oldsmobile Club of America
P.O. Box 16216
Lansing, MI 48901

Monthly.

ASSOCIATIONS

1936 ● **Oldsmobile Club of America**
P.O. Box 16216
Lansing, MI 48901

Founded: 1970. **Membership:** 5,000. Owners and enthusiasts of Oldsmobile cars made from 1897 to the present. Promotes mutual assistance in keeping cars on the road and in locating parts and service. Encourages research into the old car hobby field. Bestows awards for competition in restoration and preservation. Maintains library of sales literature from the 1920s to the present. **Convention/Meeting:** Annual.

OLDSMOBILE CUTLASS CALAIS (1987-91)

Introduced as part of N-car line, along with Buick Skylark and Pontiac Grand Am. Prior to 1988, it was known as the Oldsmobile Calais. Produced at General Motors plant in Lansing, Michigan. Replaced in 1992 by the Achieva.

1991 Oldsmobile Cutlass Calais

MAJOR FEATURES

● Oldsmobile Cutlass Calais and Cutlass Calais S had as 1991 standard equipment: 5-speed manual transmission, power front disc/rear drum brakes, power rack-and-pinion steering, halogen headlamps, and AM/FM stereo.

● Oldsmobile Cutlass Calais S Quad 442 added as 1991 standard equipment: 15-inch aluminum wheels, upgraded suspension, and gas-charged rear shocks.

● Oldsmobile Cutlass Calais SL added as 1991 standard equipment: 3-speed automatic transmission, air conditioning, and AM/FM stereo cassette player.

● Oldsmobile Cutlass Calais International Series added as 1991 standard equipment: 5-speed manual transmission, anti-lock braking system, and 16-inch aluminum wheels.

● Oldsmobile Calais had as 1987 standard features: 3-speed automatic transmission, rack-and-pinion steering, and front disc/rear drum brakes.

● Oldsmobile Calais Supreme added as 1987 standard equipment: front-wheel drive, five-speed manual transmission, and upgraded interior.

PRICE HISTORY

The following new car prices reflect the approximate retail cost of the base model: **1988** - $10,320; **1989** - $9,995; **1990** - $9,995; **1991** - $10,295.

DIMENSIONS

Body Style	Years Avail	Wheel Base (in)	Lgth (in)	Ht (in)	Avg Wt (lbs)	Fuel Cap (gal)	Front Hdrm (in)	Front Legrm (in)
2d cpe	87-88	103.4	178.6	52.3	2,470	13.6	37.7	42.9
2d cpe	89-91	103.4	179.3	52.4	2,518	13.6	37.9	42.9
4d sdn	87-91	103.4	179.3	52.4	2,585	13.6	37.9	42.9

ENGINES

Type	Displacement (L)	Fuel Dly	HP @rpm	Torque @rpm (ft/lbs)	MPG Cty/Hwy	Years Avail
I-4	2.5	FI	98@4800	132@2800	22/33	87-87
I-4	2.5	FI	98@4800	135@3200	23/33	87-88
I-4	2.3	FI	150@5200	160@4000	24/35	88-89
I-4	2.5	FI	110@5200	135@3200	22/34	89-91
I-4	2.3	FI	180@6200	160@5200	22/33	89-91
I-4	2.3	FI	160@6200	155@5200	22/33	90-91
V-6	3.0	FI	125@4900	150@2400	19/27	87-88
V-6	3.3	FI	160@5200	185@2000	19/26	89-91

KEY: I=in-line engine; V=V engine; F=flat engine; FI=fuel injection; bbl=barrel carburetor; T=turbo; D=diesel; HP=horsepower; MPG=estimated average miles per gallon.

EVALUATIONS, TESTS, AND RANKINGS

1991: "still quick and is much more nimble and fuel efficient . . . engine ran smoothly . . . shifting action felt positive and fairly smooth with adequately short throws." **Source:** "Oldsmobile 442 returns lighter, leaner," *The Flint Journal*, August 7, 1991, pp. B1-B2.

1990: "when you consider how much it does do for how much it doesn't cost, the Calais makes a lot more sense." **Source:** "Bang for the Buck," *Motor Trend*, November 1989, pp. 42-46, 48, 52-55, 58-59, 62, 64, 66-68, 72, 76.

1990: "the appeal of this car is clearly in its performance . . . At speeds above 60 mph, the engine produces a faint whine . . . No complaints at all about the handling." **Source:** "The Rocket is Back," *Design News*, October 2, 1989, pp. 150-151.

1989: "mid-pack in every way, though it attacked the slalom with unexpected ferocity. . .inside of the Calais is very fancy." **Source:** "Best Sellers," *Popular Mechanics*, July 1989, pp. 60-63, 120-122.

1989: "More power, closer gears, firmer suspension, bigger tires, zoomier looks . . . the best American-designed engine on the market today . . . may not be perfect, but you won't find any shortcomings under the hood." **Source:** "Oldsmobile Cutlass Calais International Series Coupe," *Motor Trend*, March 1989, pp. 120-123, 125.

1988: "delivers good fuel economy . . . While its power characteristics are excellent . . . the Quad 4 has drawn some criticism for noise . . . fit and finish quality in our Calais seems exceptionally good." **Source:** "Long-Term Car Tests," *Popular Mechanics*, April 1988, pp. 154, 160.

1988: "engine . . . pulls well from bottom to top. If there's any criticism to be made at all, it's in the area of noise." **Source:** "Olds Calais Quad 4: A Calais that really cooks," *Road & Track*, January 1988, pp. 42-46, 48, 52-55, 58-59, 62, 64, 66-68, 72, 76.

1987: "reasonably innovative engine. . .heady blend of high revs and *haut*velour." **Source:** "Oldsmobile Calais Supreme," *Car and Driver*, May 1987, p. 131.

RECALLS

1990: (3,202 cars; includes Buick and Oldsmobile models): Improperly torqued connection of front fuel feed and return hoses may loosen causing fuel leakage. **Corrective action:** Properly torque the front fuel feed and return hoses at the body rail lines to prevent fuel leakage. *(NHTSA Campaign No. 90V119000.)*

1989: (5,459 cars equipped with electronic comfort control air conditioning): Electronic air conditioning control may not function when starting car that has been parked for a few hours with ignition off. Windshield may not defrost and car would not conform with FMVSS 103. **Corrective action:** Replace electronic comfort control assembly. *(NHTSA Campaign No. 89V122000.)*

1988-89: (61,765 cars with Quad-four engines; includes Buick, Pontiac, and Oldsmobile models): Cracking or separation of front fuel hose at coupling could allow fuel leakage and result in a fire. **Corrective action:** Replace front fuel feed hose assembly. *(NHTSA Campaign No. 90V042000.)*

1987-88: (1,755,897 vehicles equipped with cruise control and certain gasoline and diesel engines; includes several General Motors models; includes models made before 1987): Small nylon bushing in the cruise control servo bail may slip out of place, causing intermittent and unexpected increases in engine speed or dieseling (engine run on with ignition off). Servo rod assembly could catch on engine components and result in a stuck throttle with potential for a vehicle crash. **Corrective**

action: Install a new bushing in cruise control servo bail. *(NHTSA Campaign No. 89V102000.)*

1987: (39 cars; recall includes the Pontiac 6000 and Oldsmobile Cutlass): Poor bond adhesion between the windshield glass and mounting could allow the windshield to separate during a 30 mph frontal barrier test required by FMVSS 212. If windshield glass separation occurs during an accident, an unbelted occupant could be ejected from the vehicle and injured. **Corrective action:** Reinstall windshields to assure proper bond adhesion. *(NHTSA Campaign No. 87V034000.)*

1987: (22,300 passenger vehicles; includes Buick Skylark, Oldsmobile Calais, and Pontiac Grand Am): Fuel feed or fuel return hose at engine may rub against shift lever on five speed transaxle. In time a hole could be rubbed through hose and fuel could leak into engine compartment, possibly resulting in underhood fire. **Corrective action:** Replace fuel feed and return hose/pipe assemblies. *(NHTSA Campaign No. 88V032000.)*

REPAIR MANUALS

1937 ● **Get Your Oldsmobile Fixed Right**
Consumer Reports Books
51 E. 42nd St., Ste. 800
New York, NY 10017   Ph:(212)682-9280

Published 1989. **Editor(s):** Mort Schultz. **Price:** $8.95.

1938 ● **GM A-Cars Buick Century, Chevrolet Celebrity, Oldsmobile Cutlass Ciera, Pontiac 6000, 1982-87: Shop Manual**
Clymer Publications
P.O. Box 1209
Overland Park, KS 66212   Ph:(913)541-6694

Published 1987. **Price:** $14.95.

1939 ● **Haynes Oldsmobile Cutlass Owners Workshop Manual, No. 658: 1974-1989**
Haynes Publications, Inc.
861 Lawrence Dr.
Newbury Park, CA 91320   Ph:(818)889-5400

Published 1988. **Editor(s):** J. H. Haynes. **Price:** $15.95.

1940 ● **Pontiac Grand Prix-Oldsmobile Cutlass-Buick Regal, 1988 Repair and Tune-up Guide**
Chilton Co.
Chilton Way
Radnor, PA 19089   Ph:(215)964-4000

Published 1990. **Price:** $15.95.

OTHER INFORMATION SOURCES

1941 ● **Illustrated Oldsmobile Buyer's Guide**
Motorbooks International
729 Prospect Ave
Osceola, WI 54020   Ph:(715)294-3345

Published 1987. **Editor(s):** R. Langworth. **Price:** $16.95.

1942 ● **Journey With Olds**
Oldsmobile Club of America
P.O. Box 16216
Lansing, MI 48901

Monthly.

1943 ● Oldsmobile Performance Chapter—Performance Roster
Oldsmobile Performance Chapter (OPC)
P.O. Box 4563
Chicago, IL 60680   Ph:(312)276-1006

Quarterly.

1944 ● W. Machines
Oldsmobile Performance Chapter (OPC)
P.O. Box 4563
Chicago, IL 60680   Ph:(312)276-1006

Monthly.

ASSOCIATIONS

1945 ● Oldsmobile Club of America
P.O. Box 16216
Lansing, MI 48901

Founded: 1970. **Membership:** 5,000. Owners and enthusiasts of Oldsmobile cars made from 1897 to the present. Promotes mutual assistance in keeping cars on the road and in locating parts and service. Encourages research into the old car hobby field. Bestows awards for competition in restoration and preservation. Maintains library of sales literature from the 1920s to the present. **Convention/Meeting:** Annual.

1946 ● Oldsmobile Performance Chapter
P.O. Box 4563
Chicago, IL 60680
Robert Gerometta, Editor   Ph:(312)276-1006

Founded: 1982. **Membership:** 1,200. A chapter of Oldsmobile Club of America. Seeks to promote and restore high performance Oldsmobiles. Maintains archives of performance data and articles from 1964 to 1985; operates 1,000 volume library including factory data on performance Oldsmobiles. **Convention/Meeting:** Annual car meet/show.

OLDSMOBILE CUTLASS CIERA (1987-92)

Introduced as part of A-car line, along with Buick Century, Chevrolet Celebrity, and Pontiac 6000. Chosen by *The Complete Car Cost Guide* as having one of the lowest insurance costs for a midsize car in 1990. Produced at General Motors plants in Ramos Arispe, Mexico and Ste. Therese, Quebec, Canada.

1991 Oldsmobile Cutlass Ciera SL

MAJOR FEATURES

● Oldsmobile Cutlass Ciera has as 1992 standard equipment: 3-speed automatic transmission, power-assisted rack-and-pinion steering, power front disc/rear drum brakes, front independent suspension/rear rigid axle, AM/FM stereo, and power door locks.

● Oldsmobile Cutlass Ciera S and Cutlass Cruiser S Station Wagon add as 1992 standard equipment: upgraded interior.

● Oldsmobile Cutlass Ciera SL and Cutlass Cruiser SL Station Wagon add as 1992 standard equipment: air conditioning, AM/FM stereo cassette player, split-bench front seat, power recliners for the front seat backs, and visor mirrors.

PRICE HISTORY

The following new car prices reflect the approximate retail cost of the base model: **1987** - $10,940; **1988** - $10,995; **1989** - $11,695; **1990** - $11,995; **1991** - $12,495; **1992** - $12,755.

DIMENSIONS

Body Style	Years Avail	Wheel Base (in)	Lgth (in)	Ht (in)	Avg Wt (lbs)	Fuel Cap (gal)	Front Hdrm (in)	Front Legrm (in)
2d cpe	87-87	104.9	188.3	54.1	2,685	15.7	38.6	42.1
2d cpe	88-91	104.9	190.3	54.1	2,771	15.7	38.6	42.1
4d sdn	87-87	104.9	188.3	54.1	2,715	15.7	38.6	42.1
4d sdn	88-92	104.9	190.3	54.1	2,886	15.7	38.6	42.1
5d wgn	88-92	104.9	194.4	54.5	2,992	15.7	38.6	42.1

ENGINES

Type	Displacement (L)	Fuel Dly	HP @rpm	Torque @rpm (ft/lbs)	MPG Cty/Hwy	Years Avail
I-4	2.5	FI	92@4000	134@2800	22/32	87-87
I-4	2.5	FI	98@4800	135@3200	24/31	88-88
I-4	2.5	FI	110@5200	135@3200	22/31	89-92
V-6	2.8	FI	125@4800	155@3600	20/28	87-87
V-6	2.8	FI	125@4500	160@3600	20/29	87-89
V-6	3.8	FI	150@4400	200@2000	19/29	88-88
V-6	3.3	FI	160@5200	185@2000	19/30	89-92

KEY: I=in-line engine; V=V engine; F=flat engine; FI=fuel injection; bbl=barrel carburetor; T=turbo; D=diesel; HP=horsepower; MPG=estimated average miles per gallon.

EVALUATIONS, TESTS, AND RANKINGS

1988: "a deceptively fun car to drive . . . Because of its low-end torque. . .power is eminently useable . . . sheer sensibility." **Source:** "Oldsmobile Cutlass Ciera: A car that you, and your mother-in-law, could love," *Motor Trend*, April 1988, pp. 110, 112, 114.

RECALLS

1989: (5,459 cars equipped with electronic comfort control air conditioning): Electronic air conditioning control may not function when starting car that has been parked for a few hours with ignition off. Windshield may not defrost and car would not conform with FMVSS 103. **Corrective action:** Replace electronic comfort control assembly. *(NHTSA Campaign No. 89V122000.)*

1988: (27,369 passenger vehicles equipped with 2.8L V6 engine; includes several General Motors models): Fuel feed hose could leak at coupling on engine end of hose assembly. Fuel leakage into engine compartment could result in engine compartment fire that could spread to passenger compartment. **Corrective action:** Install new fuel feed hose assembly. *(NHTSA Campaign No. 88V164000.)*

1987-88: (1,755,897 vehicles equipped with cruise control and certain gasoline and diesel engines; includes several General Motors models; includes models made before 1987): Small nylon bushing in the cruise control servo bail may slip out of place, causing intermittent and unexpected increases in engine speed or dieseling (engine run on with ignition off). Servo rod assembly could catch on engine components and result in a stuck throttle with potential for a vehicle crash. **Corrective action:** Install a new bushing in cruise control servo bail. *(NHTSA Campaign No. 89V102000.)*

1987: (39 cars; recall includes the Pontiac 6000 and Oldsmobile Cutlass): Poor bond adhesion between the windshield glass and mounting could allow the windshield to separate during a 30 mph frontal barrier test required by FMVSS 212. If windshield glass separation occurs during an accident, an unbelted occupant could be ejected from the vehicle and injured. **Corrective action:** Reinstall windshields to assure proper bond adhesion. *(NHTSA Campaign No. 87V034000.)*

SAFETY AND REPAIRS

1992: ''GM Recalls '92 A-, W-Cars,'' *Automotive News*, December 2, 1991, p. 2. **Note:** Transmission problem could cause cars to remain in reverse when shifted into neutral.

REPAIR MANUALS

1947 ● **Chilton's Chevrolet Celebrity, Buick Century, Olds Cutlass Ciera, Pontiac 6000, 1982-1988**
Chilton Co.
Chilton Way
Radnor, PA 19089   Ph:(215)964-4000

Also available in Spanish edition. Published 1988. **Price:** $15.95.

1948 ● **Chilton's Cutlass 1970-1987**
Chilton Co.
Chilton Way
Radnor, PA 19089   Ph:(215)964-4000

Published 1987. **Price:** $15.95.

1949 ● **Get Your Oldsmobile Fixed Right**
Consumer Reports Books
51 E. 42nd St., Ste. 800
New York, NY 10017   Ph:(212)682-9280

Published 1989. **Editor(s):** Mort Schultz. **Price:** $8.95.

1950 ● **GM A-Cars Buick Century, Chevrolet Celebrity, Oldsmobile Cutlass Ciera, Pontiac 6000, 1982-87: Shop Manual**
Clymer Publications
P.O. Box 1209
Overland Park, KS 66212   Ph:(913)541-6694

Published 1987. **Price:** $14.95.

1951 ● **Haynes General Motor A-Cars Owner's Workshop Manual, No. 829**
Haynes Publishing, Inc.
861 Lawrence Dr.
Newbury Park, CA 91320   Ph:(818)889-5400

Published 1982 through 1989. **Price:** $15.95.

1952 ● **Haynes Oldsmobile Cutlass Owners Workshop Manual, No. 658: 1974-1989**
Haynes Publications, Inc.
861 Lawrence Dr.
Newbury Park, CA 91320   Ph:(818)889-5400

Published 1988. **Editor(s):** J. H. Haynes. **Price:** $15.95.

1953 ● **Pontiac Grand Prix-Oldsmobile Cutlass-Buick Regal, 1988 Repair and Tune-up Guide**
Chilton Co.
Chilton Way
Radnor, PA 19089   Ph:(215)964-4000

Published 1990. **Price:** $15.95.

OTHER INFORMATION SOURCES

1954 ● **Illustrated Oldsmobile Buyer's Guide**
Motorbooks International
729 Prospect Ave
Osceola, WI 54020   Ph:(715)294-3345

Published 1987. **Editor(s):** R. Langworth. **Price:** $16.95.

1955 ● **Journey With Olds**
Oldsmobile Club of America
P.O. Box 16216
Lansing, MI 48901

Monthly.

1956 ● **Oldsmobile   Performance   Chapter—Performance Roster**
Oldsmobile Performance Chapter (OPC)
P.O. Box 4563
Chicago, IL 60680   Ph:(312)276-1006

Quarterly.

1957 ● **W. Machines**
Oldsmobile Performance Chapter (OPC)
P.O. Box 4563
Chicago, IL 60680   Ph:(312)276-1006

Monthly.

ASSOCIATIONS

1958 ● **Oldsmobile Club of America**
P.O. Box 16216
Lansing, MI 48901

Founded: 1970. **Membership:** 5,000. Owners and enthusiasts of Oldsmobile cars made from 1897 to the present. Promotes mutual assistance in keeping cars on the road and in locating parts and service. Encourages research into the old car hobby field. Bestows awards for competition in restoration and preservation. Maintains library of sales literature from the 1920s to the present. **Convention/Meeting:** Annual.

1959 ● **Oldsmobile Performance Chapter**
P.O. Box 4563
Chicago, IL 60680
Robert Gerometta, Editor   Ph:(312)276-1006

Founded: 1982. **Membership:** 1,200. A chapter of Oldsmobile Club of America. Seeks to promote and restore high performance Oldsmobiles. Maintains archives of performance data and articles from 1964 to 1985; operates 1,000 volume library including factory data on performance Oldsmobiles. **Convention/Meeting:** Annual car meet/show.

OLDSMOBILE CUTLASS SUPREME (1987-92)

Introduced as part of W-car line, along with Buick Regal and Pontiac Grand Prix. Gained front-wheel drive in 1988; 4-door sedan rejoined the redesigned series in 1990; Cutlass Supreme

Classic discontinued in 1988. Produced at General Motors plant in Doraville, Georgia.

1991 Oldsmobile Cutlass Supreme International Series

MAJOR FEATURES

- Oldsmobile Cutlass Supreme S, formerly the Cutlass Supreme, has as 1992 standard equipment: 3.1 liter V6 engine, 3-speed automatic transmission, 4-wheel independent suspension, 4-wheel disc brakes, power rack-and-pinion steering, air conditioning, and electronic instrumentation.

- Oldsmobile Cutlass Supreme SL adds as 1992 standard equipment: 4-speed automatic transmission, cast aluminum wheels, fog lamps, upgraded stereo system, and upgraded interior.

- Oldsmobile Cutlass Supreme International Series adds as 1992 standard equipment: 5-speed manual transmission, upgraded suspension system, anti-lock brakes, fog lamps, cruise control, and tilt leather steering wheel with controls for radio and air conditioner.

- Oldsmobile Cutlass Supreme Convertible adds as 1992 standard equipment: SL level equipment plus front bucket seats and sport suspension.

- Oldsmobile Cutlass Supreme Classic had as 1988 standard equipment: other exterior body stylings.

PRICE HISTORY

The following new car prices reflect the approximate retail cost of the base model: **1987** - $11,539; **1988** - $12,846; **1989** - $14,370; **1990** - $14,495; **1991** - $14,995; **1992** - $15,695.

DIMENSIONS

Body Style	Years Avail	Wheel Base (in)	Lgth (in)	Ht (in)	Avg Wt (lbs)	Fuel Cap (gal)	Front Hdrm (in)	Front Legrm (in)
2d cpe	87-87	108.1	200.0	54.9	3,203	18.1	38.7	42.7
2d cpe	88-88	107.5	192.1	52.8	2,958	16.6	37.8	42.3
2d cpe	89-90	107.5	192.1	52.8	3,119	16.6	37.8	42.3
2d cpe	91-91	107.5	192.3	53.3	3,187	16.5	37.8	42.3
2d cpe	92-92	107.5	193.9	53.3	3,221	16.5	37.8	42.3
2d conv	90-91	107.5	192.3	54.3	3,602	16.5	37.8	42.3
2d conv	92-92	107.5	193.9	54.3	3,589	16.5	38.5	42.3
4d sdn	87-87	108.1	200.4	55.9	3,260	18.1	38.7	42.7
4d sdn	90-91	107.5	192.2	54.8	3,286	16.5	38.8	42.4
4d sdn	92-92	107.5	193.7	54.8	3,375	16.5	38.8	42.4

ENGINES

Type	Displacement (L)	Fuel Dly	HP @rpm	Torque @rpm (ft/lbs)	MPG Cty/Hwy	Years Avail
I-4	2.3	FI	180@6200	160@5200	22/29	90-90
I-4	2.3	FI	160@6200	155@5200	21/29	90-91
V-6	3.8	2-bbl	110@3800	190@1600	19/24	87-87
V-6	5.0	FI	170@4000	250@2600	17/23	87-87
V-6	5.0	FI	140@3200	255@2000	18/25	87-87
V-6	2.8	FI	125@4500	160@3600	19/28	88-88
V-6	2.8	FI	130@4500	170@3600	18/30	89-89
V-6	3.1	FI	140@4800	183@3600	na	89-89
V-6	3.1	FI	135@4400	180@3600	19/30	90-90
V-6	3.1	FI	140@4400	185@3200	19/29	91-92
V-6	3.4	FI	210@5200	215@4000	17/27	92-92
V-8	5.0	4-bbl	140@3200	255@2000	18/25	88-88

KEY: I=in-line engine; V=V engine; F=flat engine; FI=fuel injection; bbl=barrel carburetor; T=turbo; D=diesel; HP=horsepower; MPG=estimated average miles per gallon.

EVALUATIONS, TESTS, AND RANKINGS

1991: "ride is well controlled; the suspension never floats, but neither does it sting ... would have looked better without that giant basket handle that loops over the cabin." **Source:** "Olds Cutlass Supreme Convertible," *Car and Driver,* September 1991, p. 150.

1990: "Boulevard and highway ride quality is peachy keen, but hard cornering becomes an adventure in body roll." **Source:** "Oldsmobile Cutlass Supreme," *Motor Trend,* November 1989, pp. 118-120, 122.

1990: "top point-getter in the Ride and Drive category ... delivers its power output effortlessly, if a bit noisily." **Source:** "Sun, Sand, & Sedans," *Motor Trend,* June 1990, pp. 96-99, 102-104, 106.

1990: "immediately pleased by the Cutlass's overall stability in harsh conditions ... generous list of convenience items made long-distance cruises pleasant ... extremely poor radio reception." **Source:** "Life with Cutlass," *Car and Driver,* September 1990, pp. 165-166, 169.

1989: "smooth, aero-styled exterior ... all-around goodness that seems to defy being turned into a performance coupe if only because of the lack of power." **Source:** "Coupes," *Popular Science,* January 1989, pp. 42-44.

1988: "ride quality is acceptable for loafing around town, but the IS's sport suspension isn't as aggressive as one might hope." **Source:** "Oldsmobile Cutlass Supreme," *Car and Driver,* October 1987, p. 69.

1988: "shape is elegant and taut, its interior is tastefully tailored ... lines are fluid, lean and provocative." **Source:** "Oldsmobile Cutlass Supreme: Olds pins its hopes on a strong new contender," *Car and Driver,* March 1988, pp. 51-54.

RECALLS

1990: (412,792 vehicles; includes Chevrolet Lumina, Pontiac Grand Prix, Buick Regal, and Oldsmobile Cutlass Supreme): Front shoulder safety belt webbing may separate at front belt upper guide loops on either side of front seat. **Corrective action:** Install controlled rotation bracket on driver and passenger side front seat belt guide loops. *(NHTSA Campaign No. 91V005000.)*

1989-90: (476,422 vehicles; includes Buick, Chevrolet, Oldsmobile, and Pontiac models): Brake stoplamps may not illuminate or, in some cases, stoplamps will not stay illuminated all the time when brakes are applied due to a faulty stoplamp switch. **Corrective action:** Install an improved design stoplamp switch. *(NHTSA Campaign No. 90V185000.)*

1989: (5,459 cars equipped with electronic comfort control air conditioning): Electronic air conditioning control may not function when starting car that has been parked for a few hours with ignition off. Windshield may not defrost and car would not conform with FMVSS 103. **Corrective action:** Replace electronic comfort control assembly. *(NHTSA Campaign No. 89V122000.)*

1988-90: (673,000 passenger vehicles; includes the Pontiac Grand Prix, Buick Regal, Oldsmobile Cutlass Calais, and Chevrolet Lumina models): Front shoulder belt guide loop attachment fastener may pull through door mounted anchor plate. Seat belt may not properly restrain a passenger, resulting in increased risk of injury to occupant. **Corrective action:** Replace front shoulder belt guide loop attachment nuts and install new guide cover. *(NHTSA Campaign No. 90V054000.)*

1988: (3,857 passenger vehicles; includes Pontiac Grand Prix and Oldsmobile Cutlass): Parking brake cable may be disconnected from left rear brake caliper. Parking brake cannot be properly applied and vehicle will not meet grade holding requirements of FMVSS 105. **Corrective action:** Install retainer on left rear caliper if cable is not already retained with cotter pin and adjust parking brake system. *(NHTSA Campaign No. 88V175000.)*

1987-88: (1,755,897 vehicles equipped with cruise control and certain gasoline and diesel engines; includes several General Motors models; includes models made before 1987): Small nylon bushing in the cruise control servo bail may slip out of place, causing intermittent and unexpected increases in engine speed or dieseling (engine run on with ignition off). Servo rod assembly could catch on engine components and result in a stuck throttle with potential for a vehicle crash. **Corrective action:** Install a new bushing in cruise control servo bail. *(NHTSA Campaign No. 89V102000.)*

1987: (39 cars; recall includes the Pontiac 6000 and Oldsmobile Cutlass): Poor bond adhesion between the windshield glass and mounting could allow the windshield to separate during a 30 mph frontal barrier test required by FMVSS 212. If windshield glass separation occurs during an accident, an unbelted occupant could be ejected from the vehicle and injured. **Corrective action:** Reinstall windshields to assure proper bond adhesion. *(NHTSA Campaign No. 87V034000.)*

SAFETY AND REPAIRS

1992: "GM Recalls '92 A-, W-Cars," *Automotive News*, December 2, 1991, p. 2. **Note:** Transmission problem could cause cars to remain in reverse when shifted into neutral.

1991: "GM Recalls Cars for Belt Loops," *Automotive News*, February 10, 1992, p. 2. **Note:** May have cracked front-door shoulder belt guide loops.

1988: "Service Tips," *Popular Mechanics*, December 1989, p. 41. **Note:** Underhood lamp may be intermittent or constantly on.

1987: "Car Clinic," *Popular Mechanics*, August 1990, p. 26. **Note:** Tip for clashing starter motor gears in 1987-88 General Motors 4.3, 5.0, and 5.7 liter engines.

REPAIR MANUALS

1960 ● Chilton's Cutlass 1970-1987
Chilton Co.
Chilton Way
Radnor, PA 19089   Ph:(215)964-4000

Published 1987. **Price:** $15.95.

1961 ● General Motors 8-Cylinder
Peter Allen Video Productions
38-C Otis St.
West Babylon, NY 11704   Ph:(516)643-4372

A program demonstrating basic maintenance and tune-up procedures for the entitled engine. **Release date:** 1986. **Producer:** Peter Allen Productions. **Acquisition:** Purchase.

1962 ● Get Your Oldsmobile Fixed Right
Consumer Reports Books
51 E. 42nd St., Ste. 800
New York, NY 10017   Ph:(212)682-9280

Published 1989. **Editor(s):** Mort Schultz. **Price:** $8.95.

1963 ● Haynes Oldsmobile Cutlass Owners Workshop Manual, No. 658: 1974-1989
Haynes Publications, Inc.
861 Lawrence Dr.
Newbury Park, CA 91320   Ph:(818)889-5400

Published 1988. **Editor(s):** J. H. Haynes. **Price:** $15.95.

1964 ● Pontiac Grand Prix-Oldsmobile Cutlass-Buick Regal, 1988 Repair and Tune-up Guide
Chilton Co.
Chilton Way
Radnor, PA 19089   Ph:(215)964-4000

Published 1990. **Price:** $15.95.

OTHER INFORMATION SOURCES

1965 ● Illustrated Oldsmobile Buyer's Guide
Motorbooks International
729 Prospect Ave
Osceola, WI 54020   Ph:(715)294-3345

Published 1987. **Editor(s):** R. Langworth. **Price:** $16.95.

1966 ● Journey With Olds
Oldsmobile Club of America
P.O. Box 16216
Lansing, MI 48901

Monthly.

1967 ● Oldsmobile Performance Chapter—Performance Roster
Oldsmobile Performance Chapter (OPC)
P.O. Box 4563
Chicago, IL 60680   Ph:(312)276-1006

Quarterly.

1968 ● W. Machines
Oldsmobile Performance Chapter (OPC)
P.O. Box 4563
Chicago, IL 60680   Ph:(312)276-1006

Monthly.

ASSOCIATIONS

1969 ● Oldsmobile Club of America
P.O. Box 16216
Lansing, MI 48901

Founded: 1970. **Membership:** 5,000. Owners and enthusiasts of Oldsmobile cars made from 1897 to the present. Promotes mutual assistance in keeping cars on the road and in locating parts and service. Encourages research into the old car hobby field. Bestows awards for competition in restoration and preservation. Maintains library of sales literature from the 1920s to the present. **Convention/Meeting:** Annual.

1970 ● **Oldsmobile Performance Chapter**
P.O. Box 4563
Chicago, IL 60680
Robert Gerometta, Editor   Ph:(312)276-1006

Founded: 1982. **Membership:** 1,200. A chapter of Oldsmobile Club of America. Seeks to promote and restore high performance Oldsmobiles. Maintains archives of performance data and articles from 1964 to 1985; operates 1,000 volume library including factory data on performance Oldsmobiles. **Convention/Meeting:** Annual car meet/show.

OLDSMOBILE EIGHTY EIGHT ROYALE
(1987-92)

Introduced as part of H-car line, along with Buick LeSabre and Pontiac Bonneville. Oldsmobile Delta 88 was renamed the Eighty Eight Royale in 1989. Produced at General Motors plant in Flint, Michigan, and Wentzville, Missouri. Chosen by *The Complete Car Cost Guide* as having one of the lowest insurance costs for a large car.

1992 Oldsmobile Eighty Eight Royale LS

MAJOR FEATURES

● Oldsmobile Eighty Eight Royale has as 1992 standard equipment: 4-speed electronically controlled automatic transmission, 4-wheel independent suspension, power rack-and-pinion steering, power front disc/rear drum power brakes, tilt steering wheel, driver's-side airbag, and air conditioning.

● Oldsmobile Eighty Eight Royale LS adds as 1992 standard equipment: anti-lock brakes, cruise control, power operated outside rear-view mirrors, AM/FM stereo radio with cassette player, and a front-seat center armrest with storage.

● Oldsmobile Eighty Eight Royale Brougham had as 1991 standard equipment: 4-speed automatic transmission, power steering, air conditioning, tinted glass, AM/FM stereo cassette player, tilt steering wheel, and split bench front seat.

● Oldsmobile Delta 88 had as 1988 standard equipment: 4-speed automatic transmission, front disc/rear drum power brakes, four-wheel independent suspension, and rack-and-pinion power steering.

PRICE HISTORY

The following new car prices reflect the approximate retail cost of the base model: **1987** - $13,639; **1988** - $14,498; **1989** - $15,195; **1990** - $15,895; **1991** - $17,195; **1992** - $18,495.

DIMENSIONS

Body Style	Years Avail	Wheel Base (in)	Lgth (in)	Ht (in)	Avg Wt (lbs)	Fuel Cap (gal)	Front Hdrm (in)	Front Legrm (in)
2d cpe	87-88	110.8	196.1	54.7	3,176	18.0	38.1	42.4
2d cpe	89-91	110.8	196.1	54.6	3,248	18.0	38.3	39.1
4d sdn	87-88	110.8	196.1	55.5	3,216	18.0	38.9	42.4
4d sdn	89-91	110.8	196.1	54.6	3,292	18.0	38.9	42.4
4d sdn	92-92	110.8	200.4	55.7	3,404	18.0	39.1	42.0

ENGINES

Type	Displacement (L)	Fuel Dly	HP @rpm	Torque @rpm (ft/lbs)	MPG Cty/Hwy	Years Avail
V-6	3.8	FI	150@4400	200@2000	19/29	87-88
V-6	3.8	FI	165@5200	210@2000	19/28	88-89
V-6	3.8	FI	165@4800	210@2000	19/28	90-91
V-6	3.8	FI	170@4800	220@3200	18/28	92-92

KEY: I=in-line engine; V=V engine; F=flat engine; FI=fuel injection; bbl=barrel carburetor; T=turbo; D=diesel; HP=horsepower; MPG=estimated average miles per gallon.

EVALUATIONS, TESTS, AND RANKINGS

1992: "The car has a lighter, rounded and cohesive shape . . . High-speed passing is labored . . . In normal driving the Eighty Eight is composed, predictable, quiet." **Source:** "1992 Oldsmobile Eighty Eight," *Road & Track*, June 1991, p. 113.

1992: ""Solid" fairly describes its road behavior . . . You can barely feel it shift, and its gearing is a glove-fit to the engine's power . . . torque steer, the nastiest thing about front-wheel drive and with which the Eighty Eight is sadly afflicted." **Source:** "'92 Oldsmobile Eighty Eight Royale LS," *Motor Trend*, May 1991, pp. 104, 106.

1992: "This is a bumper-to-bumper freshening of one of Oldsmobile's popular six-passenger sedans . . . though all-new, it retains much of the previous model's character." **Source:** "New Olds Eighty Eight for Summer," *Motor Trend*, April 1991, p. 28.

1992: "new bodywork is contemporary and appealing . . . Power is good—not overwhelming . . . More than a little torque steer is noticeable at low speeds, but the demeanor of the car is one of resolute solidity." **Source:** "Oldsmobile Eighty Eight Royale LS," *Motor Trend*, November 1991, p. 90.

1992: "an all-new look and much new engineering. And it works . . . electronically controlled automatic executes creamy shifts . . . an uncommonly able-bodied four-door." **Source:** "1992 New Cars: Olds Eighty Eight Royale LS," *Car and Driver*, October 1991, pp. 83-85.

1992: "a well-equipped, full-size, front-wheel drive car . . . arguably the best looking Eighty Eight to roll down an expressway . . . has a stiffer body for '92, contributing to a more solid feel and better handling response." **Source:** "Eighty Eight goes for big style, small price," *The Flint Journal*, September 18, 1991, pp. E1-2.

1992: "interior isn't as smart and contemporary as the exterior . . . big, comfortable, roomy cars with excellent ride quality and a smooth powertrain . . . an excellent job of styling." **Source:** "Oldsmobile 88—A New Image Builder," *Popular Mechanics*, June 1991, p. 98.

1992: "trendier, more youthful shape . . . firm, controlled ride without much sacrifice in comfort . . . could use some work inside the cabin." **Source:** "Olds 88 Raises the Quality Stakes," *Detroit Free Press*, July 25, 1991, p. 1D.

1991: "will appeal to drivers of Oldsmobile midsized cars who want to trade up." **Source:** "Olds offers new family sedan," *The Detroit News*, January 9, 1991, p. 3H.

RECALLS

1991: (20,765 passenger cars; includes Oldsmobile Ninety Eight, Oldsmobile Eighty Eight, Buick Park Avenue, Pontiac Bonneville, and Buick LeSabre): When applied, the parking brake lever assembly may release one or more teeth, reducing the cable load to the rear brakes. Depending on the extent of the lever release and road level, the parking brake may not hold the vehicle, allowing it to roll. Vehicle does not comply with FMVSS 105. **Corrective action:** Replace parking brake lever assembly. *(NHTSA Campaign No. 91V167000.)*

1990: (116 Oldsmobile Eighty-Eight cars equipped with digital instrument cluster): Cars were built missing a wire between the digital cluster and dimmer control, thereby failing to provide at least two levels of lighting. **Corrective action:** Rewire connection between dimmer switch and digital cluster. *(NHTSA Campaign No. 91V034000.)*

1989: (1,655 passenger vehicles; includes several General Motors models): Fuel rollover valve assembly may not have been installed. In event of an accident in which vehicle becomes inverted missing valve could allow fuel spillage in excess of amount allowed by FMVSS 301 which could result in a fire. **Corrective action:** Replace fuel sender and pump assembly. *(NHTSA Campaign No. 88V143000.)*

1989: (6 passenger cars; includes the Oldsmobile 88 and Buick LeSabre): Welds in left rear rocker panel may break loose and cause excessive forward movement of the rear suspension. This could result in damage to the fuel tanks or lines possibly causing a fuel leak during or after a crash, which could result in fire. This is in violation of FMVSS 301. **Corrective action:** Install reinforcement kit. *(NHTSA Campaign No. 89V188000.)*

1989: (6 passenger cars; includes the Oldsmobile 88 and Buick LeSabre): Welds in the left rear rocker panel may break loose and cause excessive forward movement of the rear suspension. Increased deformation could cause the left rear safety belt anchorage to not achieve the load requirements of FMVSS 210. In the event of a vehicle crash, this would increase the likelihood of injury to the seat occupant. **Corrective action:** Install a reinforcement kit. *(NHTSA Campaign No. 89V188001.)*

1987: (35,057 passenger vehicles; includes several General Motors models): Excessive accelerator cable friction may restrict cables free movement between accelerator pedal and throttle body. This could prevent throttle from returning to closed (idle) position when accelerator pedal is released; thus, engine speed would not decrease, and loss of accelerator control could result in an accident. **Corrective action:** Replace accelerator cable. *(NHTSA Campaign No. 88V080000.)*

1987: (479,715 cars; includes Pontiac, Oldsmobile, and Buick models): In-line fusible link may melt down and ignite windshield washer fluid bottle bracket. **Corrective action:** Replace washer fluid bottle bracket. *(NHTSA Campaign No. 87V135000.)*

SAFETY AND REPAIRS

1992: "GM Recalls Cars for Belt, Brake Ills," *Automotive News*, December 9, 1991, p. 43. **Note:** Parking brake may partially release after being set.

REPAIR MANUALS

1971 ● **Buick-Olds-Pontiac Full-Size, 1975-87**
Chilton Co.
Chilton Way
Radnor, PA 19089　　　　　　　　Ph:(215)964-4000

Price: $14.95.

1972 ● **General Motors 8-Cylinder**
Peter Allen Video Productions
38-C Otis St.
West Babylon, NY 11704　　　　　Ph:(516)643-4372

A program demonstrating basic maintenance and tune-up procedures for the entitled engine. **Release date:** 1986. **Producer:** Peter Allen Productions. **Acquisition:** Purchase.

1973 ● **Get Your Oldsmobile Fixed Right**
Consumer Reports Books
51 E. 42nd St., Ste. 800
New York, NY 10017　　　　　　　Ph:(212)682-9280

Published 1989. **Editor(s):** Mort Schultz. **Price:** $8.95.

1974 ● **Haynes Buick, Olds, Pontiac, Full-Size Models: 1970-90**
Haynes Publications, Inc.
861 Lawrence Dr.
Newbury Park, CA 91320　　　　　Ph:(818)889-5400

Published 1989. **Price:** $15.95.

OTHER INFORMATION SOURCES

1975 ● **Illustrated Oldsmobile Buyer's Guide**
Motorbooks International
729 Prospect Ave
Osceola, WI 54020　　　　　　　　Ph:(715)294-3345

Published 1987. **Editor(s):** R. Langworth. **Price:** $16.95.

1976 ● **Journey With Olds**
Oldsmobile Club of America
P.O. Box 16216
Lansing, MI 48901

Monthly.

ASSOCIATIONS

1977 ● **Oldsmobile Club of America**
P.O. Box 16216
Lansing, MI 48901

Founded: 1970. **Membership:** 5,000. Owners and enthusiasts of Oldsmobile cars made from 1897 to the present. Promotes mutual assistance in keeping cars on the road and in locating parts and service. Encourages research into the old car hobby field. Bestows awards for competition in restoration and preservation. Maintains library of sales literature from the 1920s to the present. **Convention/Meeting:** Annual.

OLDSMOBILE FIRENZA (1987-88)

Introduced as part of J-car line, along with Buick Skyhawk, Chevrolet Cavalier, and Pontiac Sunbird. Produced at General Motors plant in Leeds, Missouri until discontinued in 1988.

MAJOR FEATURES

• Oldsmobile Firenza had as 1988 standard equipment: 4-speed manual transmission, 4-wheel independent suspension, and front disc/rear drum power brakes.

PRICE HISTORY

The following new car prices reflect the approximate retail cost of the base model: **1987** - $8,499; **1988** - $9,295.

DIMENSIONS

Body Style	Years Avail	Wheel Base (in)	Lgth (in)	Ht (in)	Avg Wt (lbs)	Fuel Cap (gal)	Front Hdrm (in)	Front Legrm (in)
2d cpe	87-88	101.2	174.3	51.7	2,327	13.6	37.7	42.1
4d sdn	87-88	101.2	176.2	53.7	2,381	13.6	38.6	42.2
wgn	87-88	101.2	176.2	55.2	2,438	13.6	38.1	42.2

ENGINES

Type	Displace-ment (L)	Fuel Dly	HP @rpm	Torque @rpm (ft/lbs)	MPG Cty/Hwy	Years Avail
I-4	2.0	FI	102@5200	130@2800	25/31	87-87
I-4	2.0	FI	90@5600	108@3200	27/38	87-88
I-4	2.0	FI	96@4800	118@3600	25/32	88-88
V-6	2.8	FI	125@4500	160@3600	19/27	87-87

KEY: I=in-line engine; V=V engine; F=flat engine; FI=fuel injection; bbl=barrel carburetor; T=turbo; D=diesel; HP=horsepower; MPG=estimated average miles per gallon.

EVALUATIONS, TESTS, AND RANKINGS

1988: "real and willing horsepower." **Source:** "Oldsmobile Firenza," *Car and Driver—Buyers Guide 1988*, 1988, p. 66.

RECALLS

1987: (131,476 cars with 2.0 L engines; includes Buick, Pontiac, and Oldsmobile models): Fuel feed and/or return hose assemblies could crack, causing underhood fire. **Corrective action:** Replace fuel feed/return hoses and assemblies. *(NHTSA Campaign No. 87V184000.)*

REPAIR MANUALS

1978 • **Chilton's Chevrolet Cavalier, Buick Skyhawk, Olds Firenza, Cadillac Cimarron, Pontiac 6000, 1982-88**
Chilton Co.
Chilton Way
Radnor, PA 19089   Ph:(215)964-4000

Published 1988. **Price:** $15.95.

1979 • **Get Your Oldsmobile Fixed Right**
Consumer Reports Books
51 E. 42nd St., Ste. 800
New York, NY 10017   Ph:(212)682-9280

Published 1989. **Editor(s):** Mort Schultz. **Price:** $8.95.

1980 • **GMC J Cars: Buick Skyhawk, Cadillac Cimarron, Chevrolet Cavalier, Oldsmobile Firenza, Pontiac J-2000, Sunbird Shop Manual, 1982-87**
Clymer Publications
P.O. Box 1209
Overland Park, KS 66212   Ph:(913)541-6694

Published 1987. **Price:** $14.95.

1981 • **Haynes General Motors J-Cars Owners Workshop Manual, No. 766: 1982-1989**
Haynes Publishing, Inc.
861 Lawrence Dr.
Newbury Park, CA 91320   Ph:(818)889-5400

Published 1989. **Price:** $15.95.

OTHER INFORMATION SOURCES

1982 • **Illustrated Oldsmobile Buyer's Guide**
Motorbooks International
729 Prospect Ave
Osceola, WI 54020   Ph:(715)294-3345

Published 1987. **Editor(s):** R. Langworth. **Price:** $16.95.

1983 • **Journey With Olds**
Oldsmobile Club of America
P.O. Box 16216
Lansing, MI 48901

Monthly.

1984 • **Oldsmobile Performance Chapter—Performance Roster**
Oldsmobile Performance Chapter (OPC)
P.O. Box 4563
Chicago, IL 60680   Ph:(312)276-1006

Quarterly.

1985 • **W. Machines**
Oldsmobile Performance Chapter (OPC)
P.O. Box 4563
Chicago, IL 60680   Ph:(312)276-1006

Monthly.

ASSOCIATIONS

1986 • **Oldsmobile Club of America**
P.O. Box 16216
Lansing, MI 48901

Founded: 1970. **Membership:** 5,000. Owners and enthusiasts of Oldsmobile cars made from 1897 to the present. Promotes mutual assistance in keeping cars on the road and in locating parts and service. Encourages research into the old car hobby field. Bestows awards for competition in restoration and preservation. Maintains library of sales literature from the 1920s to the present. **Convention/Meeting:** Annual.

1987 • **Oldsmobile Performance Chapter**
P.O. Box 4563
Chicago, IL 60680
Robert Gerometta, Editor   Ph:(312)276-1006

Founded: 1982. **Membership:** 1,200. A chapter of Oldsmobile Club of America. Seeks to promote and restore high performance Oldsmobiles. Maintains archives of performance data and articles from 1964 to 1985; operates 1,000 volume library including factory data on performance Oldsmobiles. **Convention/Meeting:** Annual car meet/show.

OLDSMOBILE NINETY EIGHT (1987-92)

Introduced as part of C-car line, along with Buick Electra, Buick Park Avenue, Cadillac Coupe DeVille, and Cadillac Fleetwood Coupe. Produced at General Motors plant in Lake Orion, Michigan. Two-door coupe ceased production after 1987 model year. Took sixth place in *Motor Trend's* 1991 Car of the Year competition.

1991 Oldsmobile Ninety-Eight Touring Sedan

MAJOR FEATURES

● Oldsmobile Ninety Eight Regency has as 1992 standard equipment: 4-speed automatic transmission, 4-wheel independent suspension, power-assisted rack-and-pinion steering, front disc/rear drum power brakes with anti-lock braking system, driver's side airbag, power windows and door locks, tilt steering, security system, automatic climate control system, and AM/FM stereo cassette player.

● Oldsmobile Ninety Eight Regency Elite adds as 1992 standard equipment: steering-wheel touch controls for climate control and entertainment systems, other exterior body stylings, and an upgraded interior.

● Oldsmobile Ninety Eight Touring Sedan adds as 1992 standard equipment: supercharged V6 engine, and upgraded suspension system, variable-assist rack-and-pinion power steering, multi-adjustable front bucket seats, leather upholstery, and full analog instrumentation.

PRICE HISTORY

The following new car prices reflect the approximate retail cost of the base model: **1987** - $17,371; **1988** - $17,995; **1989** - $19,295; **1990** - $19,995; **1991** - $23,695; **1992** - $24,595.

DIMENSIONS

Body Style	Years Avail	Wheel Base (in)	Lgth (in)	Ht (in)	Avg Wt (lbs)	Fuel Cap (gal)	Front Hdrm (in)	Front Legrm (in)
2d cpe	87-87	110.8	196.4	55.1	3,285	18.0	39.3	42.4
4d sdn	87-90	110.8	196.4	55.1	3,330	18.0	39.3	42.4
4d sdn	90-90	110.8	196.3	54.8	3,497	18.0	39.3	42.4
4d sdn	91-91	110.8	205.8	55.1	3,607	18.0	38.7	42.0
4d sdn	92-92	110.7	205.5	54.8	3,512	18.8	38.7	42.0

ENGINES

Type	Displacement (L)	Fuel Dly	HP @rpm	Torque @rpm (ft/lbs)	MPG Cty/Hwy	Years Avail
V-6	3.8	FI	150@4400	200@2000	19/29	87-87
V-6	3.8	FI	165@5200	215@2000	18/28	88-89
V-6	3.8	FI	165@4800	210@2000	19/28	90-91
V-6	3.8	FI	170@4800	220@3200	18/27	91-92
V-6	3.8	FI	205@4400	260@2600	18/25	92-92

KEY: I=in-line engine; V=V engine; F=flat engine; FI=fuel injection; bbl=barrel carburetor; T=turbo; D=diesel; HP=horsepower; MPG=estimated average miles per gallon.

EVALUATIONS, TESTS, AND RANKINGS

1991: "crisp, competent feeling . . . a good touring sedan at an affordable price; a large car with reasonably taut handling and quick steering." **Source:** "Car of the Year," *Motor Trend*, February 1991, pp. 41-47, 50-52.

1991: "handles well—far more crisply than most American luxury cruisers . . . impressive fuel economy." **Source:** "Olds Ninety Eight Touring Sedan," *Car and Driver*, October 1990, pp. 110, 112.

1991: "tight and well put together. Fit and finish, especially the paint job, are good. . .stable, predictable, and fairly responsive for its size." **Source:** "Sticker price puts Olds 98 in big leagues," *Flint Journal*, January 23, 1991, p. D2.

1990: "works agreeably, and it's in good taste. . .Unobtrusively doing the job. . .is great virtue of this automobile." **Source:** "Oldsmobile Touring Sedan," *Car and Driver*, September 1989, pp. 116, 118.

1989: "has plenty of grip for spirited touring . . . the ride motions are damped about right to give you a good sense of the road . . . it has the details that make a car seem special." **Source:** "Oldsmobile Touring Sedan," *Car and Driver*, September 1989, 115-118.

1988: "just about as posh as you can get, if you're shopping the Olds division product lineup. . .limited body roll, aggressive turn-in, diminished understeer and the absence of nasty surprises." **Source:** "American Posh," *Popular Mechanics*, August 1988, p. 57.

1987: "handles well for its size. . .responds to the helm quickly and precisely and never wallows or bucks." **Source:** "Oldsmobile Ninety Eight Touring Sedan: A small step on the long road from Lansing to Stuttgart," *Car and Driver*, March 1987, p. 127.

RECALLS

1991: (20,765 passenger cars; includes Oldsmobile Ninety Eight, Oldsmobile Eighty Eight, Buick Park Avenue, Pontiac Bonneville, and Buick LeSabre): When applied, the parking brake lever assembly may release one or more teeth, reducing the cable load to the rear brakes. Depending on the extent of the lever release and road level, the parking brake may not hold the vehicle, allowing it to roll. Vehicle does not comply with FMVSS 105. **Corrective action:** Replace parking brake lever assembly. *(NHTSA Campaign No. 91V167000.)*

1989: (26 passenger cars equipped with AJ3 supplemental inflatable restraint): Standard pad assembly for the supplemental inflatable restraint may have been incorrectly installed. In event of crash, lack of benefit of this special pad assembly could result in greater injury to driver than might otherwise occur. **Corrective action:** Replace parts as required and perform an electrical test. *(NHTSA Campaign No. 89V096000.)*

1988: (430 Oldsmobile Touring Sedan vehicles): Clip on shifter mechanism inside console may become dislodged preventing indication of correct gear selection under conditions of darkness. Clip could also bind part of shifter mechanism in way which could prevent gear detents from operating. This could cause undesired gear position, possibly leading to vehicle crash without prior warning. **Corrective action:** Clip will be replaced to preclude the condition from occuring. *(NHTSA Campaign No. 88V037000.)*

1987: (479,715 cars; includes Pontiac, Oldsmobile, and Buick models): In line fusible link may melt down and ignite windshield washer fluid bottle bracket. **Corrective action:** Replace washer fluid bottle bracket. *(NHTSA Campaign No. 87V135000.)*

1987: (6,004 passenger cars with anti-lock brakes. Recall includes the Cadillac DeVille, Oldsmobile 98, Buick Electra, Buick LeSabre, and Pontiac 6000): Anti-lock brake system (ABS) pressure/warning switch may exhibit brake fluid seepage which can lead to loss of brake system hydraulic pump motor. Additionally, hydraulic pump motor of ABS electrical relays may have been exposed to water contamination during vehicle assembly. Can cause loss of hydraulic pump motor and/or loss of ABS function. Loss of hydraulic pump would result in loss of rear brakes as well as power to assist to front brakes. **Corrective action:** ABS and hydraulic pump motor electrical relays and 30 amp fuses will be replaced. Hydraulic pump motor assembly and pressure/warning switch will be inspected and possibly replaced. (NHTSA Campaign No. 87V093000.)

1987: (35,057 passenger vehicles; includes several General Motors models): Excessive accelerator cable friction may restrict cables free movement between accelerator pedal and throttle body. This could prevent throttle from returning to closed (idle) position when accelerator pedal is released; thus, engine speed would not decrease, and loss of accelerator control could result in an accident. **Corrective action:** Replace accelerator cable. (NHTSA Campaign No. 88V080000.)

SAFETY AND REPAIRS

1991: "GM Recalls Cars for Belt, Brake Ills," *Automotive News*, December 9, 1991, p. 43. **Note:** Parking brake may partially release after being set.

REPAIR MANUALS

1988 ● **Buick-Olds-Pontiac Full-Size, 1975-87**
Chilton Co.
Chilton Way
Radnor, PA 19089　　　　　　Ph:(215)964-4000

Price: $14.95.

1989 ● **Get Your Oldsmobile Fixed Right**
Consumer Reports Books
51 E. 42nd St., Ste. 800
New York, NY 10017　　　　　　Ph:(212)682-9280

Published 1989. **Editor(s):** Mort Schultz. **Price:** $8.95.

1990 ● **Haynes Buick, Olds, Pontiac, Full-Size Models: 1970-90**
Haynes Publications, Inc.
861 Lawrence Dr.
Newbury Park, CA 91320　　　　Ph:(818)889-5400

Published 1989. **Price:** $15.95.

OTHER INFORMATION SOURCES

1991 ● **Illustrated Oldsmobile Buyer's Guide**
Motorbooks International
729 Prospect Ave
Osceola, WI 54020　　　　　　Ph:(715)294-3345

Published 1987. **Editor(s):** R. Langworth. **Price:** $16.95.

1992 ● **Journey With Olds**
Oldsmobile Club of America
P.O. Box 16216
Lansing, MI 48901

Monthly.

ASSOCIATIONS

1993 ● **Oldsmobile Club of America**
P.O. Box 16216
Lansing, MI 48901

Founded: 1970. **Membership:** 5,000. Owners and enthusiasts of Oldsmobile cars made from 1897 to the present. Promotes mutual assistance in keeping cars on the road and in locating parts and service. Encourages research into the old car hobby field. Bestows awards for competition in restoration and preservation. Maintains library of sales literature from the 1920s to the present. **Convention/Meeting:** Annual.

OLDSMOBILE SILHOUETTE VAN (1990-92)

Produced at General Motors plant in Tarrytown, New York. Placed third in *Motor Trend's* 1990 Truck of the Year competition. Listed as one of the Best Bets of 1992, and ranked among the best minivans in crash test performance by *The Car Book*.

1991 Oldsmobile Silhouette Van

MAJOR FEATURES

● Oldsmobile Silhouette has as 1992 standard equipment: 3-speed automatic transmission, power-assisted rack and pinion steering, front disc/rear drum power brakes with anti-lock braking system, air conditioning, and rear window wiper/washer system.

PRICE HISTORY

The following new car prices reflect the approximate retail cost of the base model: **1990** - $17,195; **1991** - $18,195; **1992** - $19,095.

DIMENSIONS

Body Style	Years Avail	Wheel Base (in)	Lgth (in)	Ht (in)	Avg Wt (lbs)	Fuel Cap (gal)	Front Hdrm (in)	Front Legrm (in)
3d van	90-92	109.8	194.2	65.7	3,648	20.0	35.7	40.7

ENGINES

Type	Displacement (L)	Fuel Dly	HP @rpm	Torque @rpm (ft/lbs)	MPG Cty/Hwy	Years Avail
V-6	3.1	FI	120@4200	175@2200	18/23	90-92
V-6	3.8	FI	165@na	na	16/24	92-92

KEY: I=in-line engine; V=V engine; F=flat engine; FI=fuel injection; bbl=barrel carburetor; T=turbo; D=diesel; HP=horsepower; MPG=estimated average miles per gallon.

EVALUATIONS, TESTS, AND RANKINGS

1991: "chassis and body construction are as radical as its exterior ... Styling also scored as the best-liked feature ... biggest pluses are ride comfort, interior spaciousness and the versatility of its seating arrangement." **Source:** "Oldsmobile Silhouette," *Popular Mechanics,* August 1991, pp. 37-39.

1991: "comfortable and distinctive looking, resilient plastic body panels ... bounce back from minor bumps ... engine is no better than tepid." **Source:** "Meet the New Minivans," *New Choices for the Best Years,* October 1990, pp. 86-87.

1991: "real beauty of this vehicle is in GM's daring use of innovative materials ... steep angle of the front end makes it very difficult to judge where the hood ends ... best of any minivan." **Source:** "Fairest Van in the Land," *Design News,* October 1, 1990, pp. 210-211.

1991: "luxury touches ... responds quickly, accurately and sure-footedly ... seats and interior offer a comfortable environment." **Source:** "Nose no problem for sweet-driving Silhouette," *The Flint Journal,* March 13, 1991, pp. B7-B8.

1990: "terrific styling ... dramatic, innovative and thoroughly visible ... Wind noise ... is higher than you'd expect." **Source:** "The Light Vantastics," *Popular Mechanics,* February 1990, pp. 64, 66-67.

1990: "light-footed expertise ... braking is stable and sure ... provides a degree of driving pleasure that's not always part of the bargain in mini-vans." **Source:** "Oldsmobile Silhouette: GM launches a family space shuttle," *Motor Trend,* June 1990, pp. 122-124, 126.

1990: "exhibits an impressive degree of road savvy even though its ride is smooth and pleasurable ... judged tops in handling ... offered somewhat less in hauling and load capability." **Source:** "Motor Trend's 1990 Truck of the Year: Invasion of the Space Cadets," *Motor Trend,* April 1990, pp. 115-124.

1990: "feels distinctly like an Oldsmobile car—soft ride over the bumps, smooth acceleration, an upscale experience." **Source:** "New Silhouette appeals with car-like qualities," *The Detroit News,* October 4, 1989, pp. 1F-2F.

1990: "a barely adequate three-speed transmission ... instrument panel seems cluttered ... the driver's seat offers superb support and comfort." **Source:** "You Don't Have to Pay the Maximum for a Minivan," *Business Week,* April 30, 1990, pp. 120-121.

RECALLS

1990: (343 multipurpose passenger vehicles; includes the Chevrolet Lumina APV, Pontiac Trans Sport, and Oldsmobile Silhouette): Rear modular seat frame hold-down hooks may not meet the required pull force at the rear set anchorage. **Corrective action:** Replace rear hold-down hooks and pivot rivets with heat treated hardware. *(NHTSA Campaign No. 89V164000.)*

1990: (400 passenger vans with grey interiors; includes Chevrolet Lumina APV, Oldsmobile Silhouette, and Pontiac Trans Sport models): Right hand seat/shoulder belt retractor may have been installed in the second row left hand seat position. Incorrect retractor may cause belts to lock up if van is parked on a steep grade. **Corrective action:** Replace shoulder belt assembly. *(NHTSA Campaign No. 91V046000.)*

REPAIR MANUALS

1994 ● Get Your Oldsmobile Fixed Right
Consumer Reports Books
51 E. 42nd St., Ste. 800
New York, NY 10017   Ph:(212)682-9280

Published 1989. **Editor(s):** Mort Schultz. **Price:** $8.95.

OTHER INFORMATION SOURCES

1995 ● Chevrolet   Lumina—Pontiac   Transport   Olds Silhouette, 1988-90
Chilton Co.
Chilton Way
Radnor, PA 19089   Ph:(215)964-4000

Published March 1991. **Price:** $15.95.

1996 ● Illustrated Oldsmobile Buyer's Guide
Motorbooks International
729 Prospect Ave
Osceola, WI 54020   Ph:(715)294-3345

Published 1987. **Editor(s):** R. Langworth. **Price:** $16.95.

1997 ● Journey With Olds
Oldsmobile Club of America
P.O. Box 16216
Lansing, MI 48901

Monthly.

ASSOCIATIONS

1998 ● Oldsmobile Club of America
P.O. Box 16216
Lansing, MI 48901

Founded: 1970. **Membership:** 5,000. Owners and enthusiasts of Oldsmobile cars made from 1897 to the present. Promotes mutual assistance in keeping cars on the road and in locating parts and service. Encourages research into the old car hobby field. Bestows awards for competition in restoration and preservation. Maintains library of sales literature from the 1920s to the present. **Convention/Meeting:** Annual.

OLDSMOBILE TORONADO (1987-92)

Introduced as part of E-car line, along with Buick Riviera and Cadillac Eldorado. Produced at General Motors plant in Hamtramck, Michigan. Named to *Car and Driver's* 1990 Ten Best Cars Nominees list. Listed as one of the Best Bets of 1992 by *The Car Book.*

1991 Oldsmobile Toronado

MAJOR FEATURES

● Oldsmobile Toronado has as 1992 standard equipment: 4-speed automatic transmission, 4-wheel independent suspension, power-assisted rack-and-pinion steering, 4-wheel disc brakes with anti-lock braking system, driver's side airbag, power windows, security system, automatic climate control system, and AM/FM stereo cassette player.

● Oldsmobile Toronado Trofeo adds as 1992 standard equipment: upgraded suspension system, aluminum wheels, tilt steering column, leather interior, and additional interior accessories.

PRICE HISTORY

The following new car prices reflect the approximate retail cost of the base model: **1987** - $19,938; **1988** - $20,598; **1989** - $21,995; **1990** - $21,995; **1991** - $23,795; **1992** - $24,695.

DIMENSIONS

Body Style	Years Avail	Wheel Base (in)	Lgth (in)	Ht (in)	Avg Wt (lbs)	Fuel Cap (gal)	Front Hdrm (in)	Front Legrm (in)
2d cpe	87-89	108.0	187.5	53.0	3,428	18.0	37.8	43.0
2d cpe	90-90	108.0	200.3	53.0	3,556	18.3	37.8	43.0
2d cpe	91-91	108.0	200.3	53.0	3,525	18.8	37.8	43.0
2d cpe	92-92	108.0	200.3	53.3	3,463	18.8	37.6	42.7

ENGINES

Type	Displacement (L)	Fuel Dly	HP @rpm	Torque @rpm (ft/lbs)	MPG Cty/Hwy	Years Avail
V-6	3.8	FI	140@4400	200@2000	19/24	87-87
V-6	3.8	FI	165@5200	210@2000	19/29	88-88
V-6	3.8	FI	165@4800	210@2000	18/27	88-90
V-6	3.8	FI	170@4800	220@3200	18/27	91-92

KEY: I=in-line engine; V=V engine; F=flat engine; FI=fuel injection; bbl=barrel carburetor; T=turbo; D=diesel; HP=horsepower; MPG=estimated average miles per gallon.

EVALUATIONS, TESTS, AND RANKINGS

1989: "absorbs the bumps and grinds of daily driving . . . In almost every event, the Trofeo encourages the driver to back away from aggressive driving." **Source:** "Oldsmobile Trofeo: A little light music," *Motor Trend,* November 1988, pp. 109-111, 113.

1989: "dashboard, which has no fewer than 52 buttons. . .just about every amenity imaginable. . .well-controlled ride after driving hundreds of miles under a wide variety of conditions." **Source:** "Olds stretches hopes for Trofeo," *The Detroit News,* December 20, 1989, pp. 10D-11D.

RECALLS

1992: (2,371 passenger cars; includes Buick Riviera, Oldsmobile Toronado, Cadillac Eldorado, and Cadillac Seville): The intermediate shaft to steering rack lower coupling pinch bolt may be missing. If this condition exists and shaft disengagement occurs, loss of steering control will result. **Corrective action:** Install pinch bolt. *(NHTSA Campaign No. 91V157000.)*

1990: (63,964 vehicles; includes Buick, Oldsmobile, and Cadillac models): Transaxle shift control cable may disengage from the floor shift control with loss of gear indicator reference and shift selector operation. Could result in unexpected vehicle movement and an accident. **Corrective action:** Install transaxle shift control cable retaining clip to prevent cable disengagement. *(NHTSA Campaign No. 90V164000.)*

1989: (634 passenger cars equipped with anti-lock brakes; includes the Cadillac Seville, Cadillac Eldorado, Buick Riviera, and Oldsmobile Toronado): One or both ABS hydraulic unit mounting bolts may not be properly seated and could loosen. Could lead to separation of the ABS hydraulic unit from the mounting bracket and result in loss of brake function and a crash without prior warning. **Corrective action:** Replace both ABS hydraulic unit mounting bolts. *(NHTSA Campaign No. 89V055000.)*

1989: (10,535 passenger cars equipped with 3,800 V-6 engines and anti-lock brakes; includes the Buick Riviera, Buick Reatta, and Oldsmobile Toronado): Left front brake pipe may contact the cruise control servo bracket. Brake line could wear through causing loss of brake fluid and partial loss of braking capability; could result in a vehicle crash. *(NHTSA Campaign No. 89V056000.)*

1987: (65,136 passenger vehicles; includes Oldsmobile Toronado and Buick Riviera; includes models made before 1987): Insufficient clearance between power steering pump pressure hose assembly and transmission governor/speed sensor connector could cause abrasion of hose. This could result in fluid leak, with potential for underhood fire. **Corrective action:** Replace power steering pump pressure hose. *(NHTSA Campaign No. 88V078000.)*

REPAIR MANUALS

1999 ● **Buick-Olds-Pontiac Full-Size, 1975-87**
Chilton Co.
Chilton Way
Radnor, PA 19089   Ph:(215)964-4000

Price: $14.95.

2000 ● **Get Your Oldsmobile Fixed Right**
Consumer Reports Books
51 E. 42nd St., Ste. 800
New York, NY 10017   Ph:(212)682-9280

Published 1989. **Editor(s):** Mort Schultz. **Price:** $8.95.

2001 ● **Haynes Buick, Olds, Pontiac, Full-Size Models: 1970-90**
Haynes Publications, Inc.
861 Lawrence Dr.
Newbury Park, CA 91320   Ph:(818)889-5400

Published 1989. **Price:** $15.95.

OTHER INFORMATION SOURCES

2002 ● **Illustrated Oldsmobile Buyer's Guide**
Motorbooks International
729 Prospect Ave
Osceola, WI 54020   Ph:(715)294-3345

Published 1987. **Editor(s):** R. Langworth. **Price:** $16.95.

2003 ● **Journey With Olds**
Oldsmobile Club of America
P.O. Box 16216
Lansing, MI 48901

Monthly.

2004 ● **Oldsmobile Performance Chapter—Performance Roster**
Oldsmobile Performance Chapter (OPC)
P.O. Box 4563
Chicago, IL 60680   Ph:(312)276-1006

Quarterly.

2005 ● W. Machines
Oldsmobile Performance Chapter (OPC)
P.O. Box 4563
Chicago, IL 60680   Ph:(312)276-1006
Monthly.

ASSOCIATIONS

2006 ● Oldsmobile Club of America
P.O. Box 16216
Lansing, MI 48901

Founded: 1970. **Membership:** 5,000. Owners and enthusiasts of Oldsmobile cars made from 1897 to the present. Promotes mutual assistance in keeping cars on the road and in locating parts and service. Encourages research into the old car hobby field. Bestows awards for competition in restoration and preservation. Maintains library of sales literature from the 1920s to the present. **Convention/Meeting:** Annual.

2007 ● Oldsmobile Performance Chapter
P.O. Box 4563
Chicago, IL 60680
Robert Gerometta, Editor   Ph:(312)276-1006

Founded: 1982. **Membership:** 1,200. A chapter of Oldsmobile Club of America. Seeks to promote and restore high performance Oldsmobiles. Maintains archives of performance data and articles from 1964 to 1985; operates 1,000 volume library including factory data on performance Oldsmobiles. **Convention/Meeting:** Annual car meet/show.

PEUGEOT 405 (1989-1991)

A midsize vehicle that competed against the Chrysler Imperial, Pontiac 6000 LE, Pontiac Grand Prix Turbo, and Mercury Sable GS. Awarded European Car of the Year by *Car and Driver* in 1989. The Mi 16 placed in the Highest Maintenance Cost category for a midsize vehicle by *Complete Car Cost Guide* in 1990. The S Sportswagon was placed in Highest Insurance Cost category for Midsize wagon by *Complete Car Cost Guide* in 1990. The DL Sportswagon was placed in Highest Maintenance Cost category for midsize wagon by *Complete Car Cost Guide* in 1990. Built in Sochaux, France, Peugeot Motors of America, Inc. discontinued offering all models to the U.S. market after 1991.

1991 Peugeot 405 S

MAJOR FEATURES

● Peugeot 405 DL 1991 standard equipment included: five-speed manual or four speed automatic transmission, rear defogger, rear wiper/washer, motorized front shoulder seat belts, air conditioning, power locks, and tilt steering.

● Peugeot 405 S added as 1991 standard equipment: anti-lock brakes, cruise control, power windows, moonroof, and alloy wheels.

● Peugeot 405 Mi 16 added as 1991 standard equipment: dual cam 16-valve 150-hp 1.9-liter engine, anti-lock brakes, rear spoiler, power moonroof, and various interior adjustments.

● Peugeot 405 DL Sportswagon added as 1991 standard equipment: five-door chassis, four-wheel disc brakes, fully independent suspension, central door-locking system.

● Peugeot 405 S Sportswagon added as 1991 standard equipment: five-door chassis, anti-theft system for the stereo with power antenna, and heated front seats.

PRICE HISTORY

The following new car prices reflect the approximate retail cost of the base model: **1989** - $14,500; **1990** - $15,390; **1991** - $15,490.

DIMENSIONS

Body Style	Years Avail	Wheel Base (in)	Lgth (in)	Ht (in)	Avg Wt (lbs)	Fuel Cap (gal)	Front Hdrm (in)	Front Legrm (in)
4d sdn	89-91	105.1	177.7	55.2	2,497	17.2	37.0	41.4
5d wgn	90-91	105.1	175.1	56.0	2,635	17.2	38.4	41.5

ENGINES

Type	Displacement (L)	Fuel Dly	HP @rpm	Torque @rpm (ft/lbs)	MPG Cty/Hwy	Years Avail
I-4	1.9	FI	110@5200	120@4250	21/28	89-91
I-4	1.9	FI	150@6400	128@5000	20/28	89-91

KEY: I=in-line engine; V=V engine; F=flat engine; FI=fuel injection; bbl=barrel carburetor; T=turbo; D=diesel; HP=horsepower; MPG=estimated average miles per gallon.

EVALUATIONS, TESTS, AND RANKINGS

1991: "aerodynamic . . . very fast . . . the hardest clutch this side of a Corvette . . . suspension is taut but very smooth." **Source:** "4-Cylinder Luxury in a Sporty Peugeot," *The New York Times*, February 24, 1991.

1991: "makes peak power at a high engine speed, 6,400 rpm . . . longer wheelbase yields more rearseat room." **Source:** "Entry-Level Luxury," *Popular Science*, April 1991, pp. 76-80, 96.

1990: "leisurely acceleration . . . the ride . . . soaks up holes, speed bumps and gutters." **Source:** "Peugeot 405 Sportswagon," *Road & Track*, June 1990, p. 75.

1990: "Large glass areas follow body lines and provide excellent visibility . . . unusually quiet and sturdy body . . . Good looks." **Source:** "Peugeot 405 wagon: Sports car flair, 'big car' ride," *Design News*, March 12, 1990, p.28.

1989: "clean, contemporary look . . . first-rate environment, with a solid sense of functionality . . . reassuringly stable . . . exceptional stopping power." **Source:** "Peugeot 405 Mi 16," *Motor Trend*, November 1988, p. 87-89.

1989: "consensus styling winner . . . Inside, excellence gives way to mere adequacy . . . won on the skidpad and ranked near top in the transient handling and braking." **Source:** "Best Sellers," *Popular Mechanics*, July 1989, pp. 60-63, 120-122.

1989: "rear spoiler in the Mi 16 model limits vision out of the back . . . long-legged drivers can't comfortably reach the nontelescoping steering wheel . . . biggest disappointment."

Source: "The Disappointing Peugeot 405," *Changing Times,* March 1989, pp. 122-123.

1989: "Mi 16 . . . follows the road like a sports car . . . Steering is light . . . engine . . . has tremendous power." **Source:** "Import Report," *Home Mechanix,* April 1989, pp. 84-86, 103-105.

RECALLS

1991: (689 passenger cars): Engine wiring harness may come in contact with the alternator housing. With normal engine movement over a period of time, the alternator housing could wear through the wire insulation of the harness. This could cause a short circuit which would affect engine operation by cutting off fuel delivery, possibly resulting in an electrical fire. **Corrective action:** Inspect and repair engine wiring harness. *(NHTSA Campaign No. 91V105000.)*

1989-90: (5,708 sedans and sports wagons): Fuel leakage in rear barrier crash exceeds specifications of FMVSS 301. **Corrective action:** Install protective buffers; relocate fuel pump and filter. *(NHTSA Campaign No. 89V161000.)*

1989-90: (2,888 cars and sports wagons): May be electrical interference between passive belt motor and electronic control unit, resulting in passive belt system failure. **Corrective action:** Repair passive belt system. *(NHTSA Campaign No. 89V158000.)*

1989: (4,664 vehicles): Child restraints information omitted from owner's manual. **Corrective action:** Send missing pages to owner. *(NHTSA Campaign No. 89V092000.)*

OTHER INFORMATION SOURCES

2008 ● **Lion of Belfort**
Peugeot Owners' Club (POC)
5113 Dickson Rd.
Indianapolis, IN 46226   Ph:(317)545-2825

Bimonthly.

2009 ● **Peugeot Owners' Club—Directory**
Peugeot Owners' Club (POC)
5113 Dickson Rd.
Indianapolis, IN 46226   Ph:(317)545-2825

Annual.

2010 ● **Peugeot Owner's Club Newsletter**
Peugeot Owner's Club
5113 Dickson Rd.
Indianapolis, IN 46226   Ph:(317)545-2825

Focuses on the Peugeot automobile. **Editor(s):** Franklin Grazeola. **Price:** $11.00/year.

ASSOCIATIONS

2011 ● **Peugeot Owners' Club**
6649 E. 65th St.
Indianapolis, IN 46220-4301
Marvin A. Needler Ph.D.,, Pres.   Ph:(317)845-5050

Founded: 1971. **Membership:** 600. Owners or enthusiasts of French-built Peugeot automobiles united for sharing of technical information and experiences.

PEUGEOT 505 (1987-1991)

A midsized vehicle that competed against the Mercury Sable Series, Chrysler Imperial, Mazda 626 Series, Mazda MX-6

Series, Ford LTD Crown Victorian Series, and Pontiac Grand Prix LE. 505 Series placed in the Highest Repair Costs category for a midsized car by *Complete Car Cost Guide* in 1990. Sedan production ceased after the 1989 model year, wagon model still in production. Produced in Sochaux, France, Peugeot Motors of America, Inc. discontinued offering all models to the U.S. market after 1991.

1991 Peugeot 505 SW8

MAJOR FEATURES

● Peugeot 505 DL 1991 standard equipment included: five-speed manual transmission, power steering, motorized front shoulder seat belts, air conditioning, power locks, rear defogger, rear wiper/washer, front and rear anti-sway bars, and roof rails.

● 505 Peugeot SW8 added as 1991 standard equipment: power windows, cruise control, anti-theft radio, and various interior and exterior adjustments.

● Peugeot 505 Turbo SW8 added as 1991 standard equipment: turbocharged engine, four-speed automatic transmission, keyless entry, alloy wheels, and various interior adjustments.

● Peugeot 505 S 2.2i 1990 standard equipment included: four-speed automatic transmission, anti-theft stereo, heated front seats, power sunroof, remote-control central door lock, and various interior features.

● Peugeot 505 S V6 added to 1990 S 2.2i standard equipment: V6 145hp engine, load sensitive rear braking system, alloy wheels, and various interior adjustments.

● Peugeot 505 SW8 2.2i added to 1990 S 2.2i standard equipment: front-wheel disc brakes, roof rails, green-tinted glass, and rear wiper/washer.

PRICE HISTORY

The following new car prices reflect the approximate retail cost of the base model: **1987** - $14,160; **1988** - $15,950; **1989** - $17,590; **1990** - $20,400; **1991** - $18,950.

DIMENSIONS

Body Style	Years Avail	Wheel Base (in)	Lgth (in)	Ht (in)	Avg Wt (lbs)	Fuel Cap (gal)	Front Hdrm (in)	Front Legrm (in)
4d sdn	87-87	108.0	186.7	56.7	2,870	18.0	33.9	41.0
4d sdn	88-88	108.0	186.7	57.0	2,870	18.0	37.5	40.0
4d sdn	89-89	108.0	181.4	57.0	2,998	18.0	37.5	40.0
5d wgn	87-87	114.2	198.9	60.9	3,175	18.0	34.8	32.4
5d wgn	88-88	114.2	198.9	60.1	3,130	18.0	38.1	40.0
5d wgn	89-91	114.2	194.5	60.9	3,230	18.0	38.1	40.0

ENGINES

Type	Displace-ment (L)	Fuel Dly	HP @rpm	Torque @rpm (ft/lbs)	MPG Cty/Hwy	Years Avail
I-4	2.2	FI	120@5000	131@3500	18/22	87-91
I-4T	2.2	FI	150@5000	180@2750	18/22	87-88
I-4T	2.2	FI	180@5200	205@2500	na	88-90
I-4T	2.2	FI	160@5000	205@2500	18/21	89-91
I-4TD	2.5	FI	95@4150	133@2000	24/27	87-87
V-6	2.8	FI	145@5000	173@3750	na	87-87
V-6	2.8	FI	145@5000	176@2800	na	88-89

KEY: I=in-line engine; V=V engine; F=flat engine; FI=fuel injection; bbl=barrel carburetor; T=turbo; D=diesel; HP=horsepower; MPG=estimated average miles per gallon.

EVALUATIONS, TESTS, AND RANKINGS

1988: "more road noise than preferred . . . good handling . . . Fit and finish inside and out were superb . . . seating was comfortable." **Source**: "Peugeot 505 Turbo S provides peppy intrigue," *Detroit News,* August 10, 1988, p. 2F.

1987: "carrying space . . . rivals an aircraft carrier . . . handling remains . . . excellent." **Source**: "Long-Term Test: Peugeot 505 Turbo Wagon," *Motor Trend,* May 1987, p. 126.

RECALLS

1989: (999 cars): Missing tire reserve load label, possibly resulting in overloading rear axle. **Corrective action**: Install correct placard. *(NHTSA Campaign No. 89V231000.)*

OTHER INFORMATION SOURCES

2012 ● **Lion of Belfort**
Peugeot Owners' Club (POC)
5113 Dickson Rd.
Indianapolis, IN 46226   Ph:(317)545-2825

Bimonthly.

2013 ● **Peugeot Owners' Club—Directory**
Peugeot Owners' Club (POC)
5113 Dickson Rd.
Indianapolis, IN 46226   Ph:(317)545-2825

Annual.

2014 ● **Peugeot Owner's Club Newsletter**
Peugeot Owner's Club
5113 Dickson Rd.
Indianapolis, IN 46226   Ph:(317)545-2825

Focuses on the Peugeot automobile. **Editor(s)**: Franklin Grazeola. **Price**: $11.00/year.

ASSOCIATIONS

2015 ● **Peugeot Owners' Club**
6649 E. 65th St.
Indianapolis, IN 46220-4301
Marvin A. Needler Ph.D.,, Pres.   Ph:(317)845-5050

Founded: 1971. **Membership**: 600. Owners or enthusiasts of French-built Peugeot automobiles united for sharing of technical information and experiences.

PLYMOUTH ACCLAIM (1989-92)

Introduced with its corporate twin the Dodge Spirit in 1989 as a replacement for the Plymouth Reliant and Dodge Aries,

respectively. Both A-cars are derivatives of the older K-car platform. Ranked among the lowest maintenance cost for a compact by *The Complete Car Cost Guide* in 1990. Listed as one of the Best Bets of 1992 by *The Car Book*. Produced at the Chrysler Motors plant in Newark, Delaware.

1991 Plymouth Acclaim

MAJOR FEATURES

● Acclaim has as 1992 standard equipment: 2.5 liter engine, five-speed manual transmission, Iso-strut front suspension, power rack-and-pinion steering, power front disc brakes, power rear drum brakes, Delta 14-inch steel wheels, tinted rear window, and restraint system including driver's air bag.

● Acclaim LE added as 1991 standard features: 3.0 liter engine, three-speed automatic transmission, Premium 14-inch steel wheels, all tinted windows, message center, electronic speed control, tilt steering column, and additional body stylings.

● Acclaim LX added as 1991 standard equipment: four-speed electronic automatic transmission, fascia integral fog lamps, luggage rack, 15-inch cast aluminum wheels, and a variety of accessories.

PRICE HISTORY

The following new car prices reflect the approximate retail cost of the base model: **1989** - $9,920; **1990** - $10,395; **1991** - $10,876; **1992** - $11,470.

DIMENSIONS

Body Style	Years Avail	Wheel Base (in)	Lgth (in)	Ht (in)	Avg Wt (lbs)	Fuel Cap (gal)	Front Hdrm (in)	Front Legrm (in)
4d sdn	89-92	103.5	181.2	53.5	2,784	16.0	38.4	41.9

ENGINES

Type	Displace-ment (L)	Fuel Dly	HP @rpm	Torque @rpm (ft/lbs)	MPG Cty/Hwy	Years Avail
I-4	2.5	FI	100@4800	135@2800	23/31	89-92
I-4T	2.5	FI	150@4800	180@2000	21/29	89-90
V-6	3.0	FI	141@5000	171@2800	20/28	89-92

KEY: I=in-line engine; V=V engine; F=flat engine; FI=fuel injection; bbl=barrel carburetor; T=turbo; D=diesel; HP=horsepower; MPG=estimated average miles per gallon.

EVALUATIONS, TESTS, AND RANKINGS

1989: "Well-equipped for the price, soundly constructed, quiet and thoughtfully designed." **Source**: "Chrysler wins Acclaim with new mid-size car," *The Detroit News,* April 26, 1989, pp. F1-F2.

1989: "offers a high order of ride quality, yet easily deals with harsh road surfaces." **Source:** "Plymouth Acclaim LX," *Motor Trend*, May 1989, pp. 197-198, 200, 210.

1989: "[Nominee Acclaim] offers a level of handling and performance that's a step above class-average." **Source:** "1989 Car of the Year: Detroit's back on track," *Motor Trend*, February 1989, pp. 48-56, 58.

1989: "not only is comfortable, peppy and quiet, but also manages to hold the road in the manner of European touring sedans." **Source:** "1989 offers an 8-pack of memorable cars," *The Detroit News*, July 2, 1989, p. H1.

RECALLS

1991: (398 passenger cars): The two air bag system front impact sensors may not be secured to their mounting brackets. Air bag will not deploy in a frontal collision if the front impact sensors are not attached. **Corrective action:** Repair to assure proper attachment of front impact sensors to brackets. *(NHTSA Campaign No. 90V194000.)*

1991: (18,000 passenger cars; includes several Chrysler, Dodge, and Plymouth models): Front disc brake caliper guide pin bolts may not have been adequately torqued and could loosen. This could cause reduced braking effectiveness and could result in an accident. **Corrective action:** Properly torque front brake caliper guide pin bolts to 250 lbs. *(NHTSA Campaign No. 90V162000.)*

1991: (130,000 passenger vehicles; includes Chrysler Imperial, Chrysler Fifth Avenue, Chrysler Salon, Chrysler LeBaron, Dodge Dynasty, Dodge Spirit, and Plymouth Acclaim): Front outboard safety belt may become difficult to latch or unlatch due to a webbing stiffener entering the buckle housing and dislodging the buckle latch guide. Latch may open during an accident or sudden stop. **Corrective action:** Replace buckle latch engagement. *(NHTSA Campaign No. 91V122000.)*

1989-90: (625,000 cars; includes several Plymouth, Dodge, and Chrysler vehicles): Engine valve cover gasket may dislocate and allow an engine oil leak at the gasket. Leakage of oil in the engine compartment could cause a fire. **Corrective action:** Replace gasket cover with revised cover, and RTV sealant will be applied in place of a gasket. *(NHTSA Campaign No. 89V237000.)*

OTHER INFORMATION SOURCES

2016 ● **How to Build Chrysler, Dodge, Plymouth**
Motorbooks International, Pubs. & Wholesalers, Inc.
729 Prospect Ave.
Osceola, WI 54020   Ph:(715)294-3345

Published 1990. **Editor(s):** Geoff Carter. **Price:** $17.95.

2017 ● **Torsion Bar**
Chrysler Product Owners Club
806 Winhall Way
Silver Spring, MD 20904

Promotes the collection, preservation, restoration, maintenance, exhibition, and enjoyment of Chrysler product cars, trucks, and other vehicles. Includes technical advice on the restoration of Chalmers, Chrysler, DeSoto, Dodge, Imperial, Maxwell, and Plymouth vehicles. Monthly. **Price:** Available to members only.

ASSOCIATIONS

2018 ● **Chrysler Product Owners Club**
5203 Edmondson Ave.
Baltimore, MD 21229
Brian K. Scott, Exec. Officer

Founded: 1978. **Membership:** 210. Collectors and restorers of

Chrysler-product automobiles. Promotes the collection, preservation, restoration, maintenance, exhibition, and enjoyment of all Chrysler product cars, trucks, and other vehicles, including Chrysler, DeSoto, Dodge, Imperial, and Plymouth. Offers technical advice; provides list of cars, parts, and services. Maintains library of service and parts manuals from the 1930s to 1989. **Convention/Meeting:** Annual.

2019 ● **WPC Club**
P.O. Box 3504
Kalamazoo, MI 49003-3504
Ralph Kendall, Pres.   Ph:(616)372-1067

Founded: 1969. **Membership:** 4,850. Individuals dedicated to the preservation, restoration, and enjoyment of Chrysler product cars. Conducts social activities; houses library. Awards annual trophies at national meets. **Convention/Meeting:** Annual; also sponsors International Winter Photo Meet.

PLYMOUTH CARAVELLE (1987-88)

Introduced as a replacement for the Chrysler E Class. This stretched K-car version was essentially similar to the Chrysler New Yorker and the Dodge 600. Produced through 1988 at the Chrysler Motors plant in Detroit, Michigan (Jefferson plant), and St. Louis, Missouri (No. 2).

MAJOR FEATURES

● Caravelle had as 1988 standard equipment: three-speed automatic transmission, front-drive, independent front strut suspension, vented front disc brakes, rear drum brakes, and power rack-and-pinion steering.

● Caravelle SE added as 1988 standard equipment: air conditioning, cruise control, and an assortment of interior accessories.

PRICE HISTORY

The following new car prices reflect the approximate retail cost of the base model: **1987** - $9,813; **1988** - $10,659.

DIMENSIONS

Body Style	Years Avail	Wheel Base (in)	Lgth (in)	Ht (in)	Avg Wt (lbs)	Fuel Cap (gal)	Front Hdrm (in)	Front Legrm (in)
4d sdn	87-88	103.3	185.2	53.1	2,589	14.0	38.6	42.2

ENGINES

Type	Displacement (L)	Fuel Dly	HP @rpm	Torque @rpm (ft/lbs)	MPG Cty/Hwy	Years Avail
I-4	2.2	FI	97@5200	122@3200	23/28	87-88
I-4	2.5	FI	96@4400	133@2800	23/28	87-88
I-4T	2.2	FI	146@5200	171@3600	19/24	87-87
I-4T	2.2	FI	146@5200	170@2400	20/25	88-88

KEY: I=in-line engine; V=V engine; F=flat engine; FI=fuel injection; bbl=barrel carburetor; T=turbo; D=diesel; HP=horsepower; MPG=estimated average miles per gallon.

EVALUATIONS, TESTS, AND RANKINGS

1988: "roomy, family-sized interior." **Source:** "Plymouth Caravelle," *Car and Driver—Buyers Guide 1988*, 1988, p. 74.

RECALLS

1987: (580,000 vehicles equipped with 2.2L turbocharged

engine; includes models made before 1987; includes Chrysler, Dodge, and Plymouth models): Fuel leakage may occur in low ambient temperature operation at connections of an engine compartment fuel supply hose to the pressure regulator and to the fuel rail. In the presence of an ignition source, fuel leakage could result in a fire. **Corrective action:** Relocate pressure regulator; replace fuel supply with formed hose with revised routing configuration to ensure sealing integrity. *(NHTSA Campaign No. 88V105000.)*

OTHER INFORMATION SOURCES

2020 ● How to Build Chrysler, Dodge, Plymouth
Motorbooks International, Pubs. & Wholesalers, Inc.
729 Prospect Ave.
Osceola, WI 54020   Ph:(715)294-3345

Published 1990. **Editor(s):** Geoff Carter. **Price:** $17.95.

2021 ● Torsion Bar
Chrysler Product Owners Club
806 Winhall Way
Silver Spring, MD 20904

Promotes the collection, preservation, restoration, maintenance, exhibition, and enjoyment of Chrysler product cars, trucks, and other vehicles. Includes technical advice on the restoration of Chalmers, Chrysler, DeSoto, Dodge, Imperial, Maxwell, and Plymouth vehicles. Monthly. **Price:** Available to members only.

ASSOCIATIONS

2022 ● Chrysler Product Owners Club
5203 Edmondson Ave.
Baltimore, MD 21229
Brian K. Scott, Exec. Officer

Founded: 1978. **Membership:** 210. Collectors and restorers of Chrysler-product automobiles. Promotes the collection, preservation, restoration, maintenance, exhibition, and enjoyment of all Chrysler product cars, trucks, and other vehicles, including Chrysler, DeSoto, Dodge, Imperial, and Plymouth. Offers technical advice; provides list of cars, parts, and services. Maintains library of service and parts manuals from the 1930s to 1989. **Convention/Meeting:** Annual.

2023 ● WPC Club
P.O. Box 3504
Kalamazoo, MI 49003-3504
Ralph Kendall, Pres.   Ph:(616)372-1067

Founded: 1969. **Membership:** 4,850. Individuals dedicated to the preservation, restoration, and enjoyment of Chrysler product cars. Conducts social activities; houses library. Awards annual trophies at national meets. **Convention/Meeting:** Annual; also sponsors International Winter Photo Meet.

PLYMOUTH COLT (1987-92)

An entry-level subcompact hatchback that competes against the Toyota Tercel, Nissan Sentra, Honda Civic, and Mazda 323. Corporate twin of the Dodge Colt and Eagle Summit. American cousin of the Mitsubishi Mirage. According to *The Complete Car Cost Guide*, the Plymouth Colt DL and Colt Vista were rated to have the lowest maintenance cost in the subcompact wagon and compact wagon classes, respectively, in 1990. At the same time, the Colt DL 4WD had the highest maintenance cost and the lowest resale value in 1990 in the subcompact wagon class. Currently produced at the Mitsubishi plants in Mizushima and Okazaki, Japan and sold under separate Dodge and Plymouth names.

1992 Plymouth Colt Vista

MAJOR FEATURES

● Colt has as 1992 standard equipment: 4-speed manual transmission, front independent strut suspension, rear three-link torsion axle suspension, manual rack-and-pinion steering, front power disc brakes, rear power drum brakes, Argent styled steel wheels, and restraint system.

● Colt GL adds as 1992 standard equipment: 5-speed manual transmission, outside dual manual remote mirrors, and Fabio wheelcovers.

● Colt Vista wagon has as 1992 standard equipment: 1.8 liter engine, 5-speed manual transmission, independent strut type front suspension, independent semi-trailing arm rear suspension, front-wheel drive, and removable rear seat.

● Colt Vista SE adds as 1992 standard features: tinted windows, rear seating area heat ducts, dual electric mirrors, and steel wheels with full wheel cover.

● Colt Vista AWD adds as 1992 standard equipment: all wheel drive, and front and rear mudguards.

● Colt GT had as 1990 standard equipment: 5-speed manual transmission, front independent strut suspension, anti-roll bar, rigid rear axle integral suspension, vented front disc brakes, and rear disc brakes.

● Colt DL and Colt DL Wagon had as 1990 standard equipment: front- or four-wheel drive, five-speed manual transmission, front independent suspension, rear rigid axle suspension, vented front disc brakes, and rear drum brakes.

● Colt E had as 1989 standard features: four-speed manual transmission, power brakes, and aero-style halogen headlamps.

● Colt Turbo had as 1989 standard features: front-wheel drive, 1.6 liter, turbocharged engine, and five-speed manual transmission.

● Colt Premier had as 1987 standard equipment: five-speed manual transmission and aero-style halogen headlamps.

PRICE HISTORY

The following new car prices reflect the approximate retail cost of the base model: **1987** - $5,949; **1988** - $5,998; **1989** - $6,678; **1990** - $6,851; **1991** - $7,067; **1992** - $7,302.

DIMENSIONS

Body Style	Years Avail	Wheel Base (in)	Lgth (in)	Ht (in)	Avg Wt (lbs)	Fuel Cap (gal)	Front Hdrm (in)	Front Legrm (in)
2d lbk	87-88	93.7	157.3	53.4	1,984	11.9	38.7	40.6
2d lbk	89-92	93.9	158.7	51.9	2,205	13.2	38.3	41.9
4d sdn	87-88	93.7	169.1	53.4	2,095	11.9	38.7	40.6
5d wgn	87-91	103.3	176.6	59.8	2,667	13.2	38.3	38.8
5d wgn	89-90	93.7	169.3	53.7	2,271	12.4	37.7	40.6
5d wgn	92-92	99.2	168.5	64.4	2,701	14.5	40.0	40.8

ENGINES

Type	Displacement (L)	Fuel Dly	HP @rpm	Torque @rpm (ft/lbs)	MPG Cty/Hwy	Years Avail
I-4	2.0	2-bbl	88@5000	108@3500	24/29	87-87
I-4	1.5	2-bbl	68@5500	85@3500	34/38	87-88
I-4	2.0	FI	99@5000	116@4000	23/29	87-90
I-4	2.0	FI	96@5000	113@3500	28/34	88-91
I-4	1.5	FI	81@5500	91@3000	28/34	89-90
I-4	1.5	FI	75@5500	87@2500	28/34	89-90
I-4	1.8	FI	87@5000	102@3000	na	89-90
I-4	1.6	FI	123@6500	101@5000	23/28	90-90
I-4	1.5	FI	92@6000	93@3000	29/35	91-92
I-4	1.8	FI	113@6000	116@4500	22/26	92-92
I-4	2.4	FI	116@5000	136@3500	21/27	92-92
I-4T	1.6	FI	105@5500	122@3000	25/31	87-88
I-4T	1.6	FI	135@6000	141@3000	23/29	89-89

KEY: I=in-line engine; V=V engine; F=flat engine; FI=fuel injection; bbl=barrel carburetor; T=turbo; D=diesel; HP=horsepower; MPG=estimated average miles per gallon.

EVALUATIONS, TESTS, AND RANKINGS

1992: "looks like a minivan, moves like a minivan and functions like a minivan . . . easy to drive with a slick five-speed gearbox, smooth clutch and peppy engine . . . body leans when it corners and its tall profile catches stiff crosswinds, but it's easy to keep things under control." **Source:** "Vista wagon is 'minivan' with soul," *The Flint Journal*, December 4, 1991, pp. E1-E2.

1991: "surprisingly spacious, especially in the rear . . . Its shifter is very smooth and its engine has ample pep and response for most needs . . . ride is also commendably smooth for a small car." **Source:** "Subcompact Colt has a spacious feel," *The Detroit News*, May 22, 1991, pp. 1F, 2F.

1990: "interior is airy and spacious." **Source:** "Plymouth Colt," *Motor Trend—1990 New Car Buyer's Guide*, 1990, p. 106.

1987: "handsome in styling." **Source:** "Dodge/Plymouth Colt Vista," *Road & Track—Buyer's Guide 1987*, 1986, p. 56.

RECALLS

None to date.

OTHER INFORMATION SOURCES

2024 ● How to Build Chrysler, Dodge, Plymouth
Motorbooks International, Pubs. & Wholesalers, Inc.
729 Prospect Ave.
Osceola, WI 54020   Ph:(715)294-3345

Published 1990. **Editor(s):** Geoff Carter. **Price:** $17.95.

2025 ● Torsion Bar
Chrysler Product Owners Club
806 Winhall Way
Silver Spring, MD 20904

Promotes the collection, preservation, restoration,

maintenance, exhibition, and enjoyment of Chrysler product cars, trucks, and other vehicles. Includes technical advice on the restoration of Chalmers, Chrysler, DeSoto, Dodge, Imperial, Maxwell, and Plymouth vehicles. Monthly. **Price:** Available to members only.

ASSOCIATIONS

2026 ● Chrysler Performance Parts Association
Box 1210
Azusa, CA 91702   Ph:(818)303-6220
Roland Osborne, Chm.   Fax:(818)303-2481

Founded: 1976. **Membership:** 5,000. Clearinghouse for information on from whom, where, and how to obtain vintage, muscle, and high-tech Chrysler performance parts. **Former Name(s):** (1979) National HEMI Owners; (1980) MOPAR Muscle Club. **Convention/Meeting:** Annual national meet.

2027 ● Chrysler Product Owners Club
5203 Edmondson Ave.
Baltimore, MD 21229
Brian K. Scott, Exec. Officer

Founded: 1978. **Membership:** 210. Collectors and restorers of Chrysler-product automobiles. Promotes the collection, preservation, restoration, maintenance, exhibition, and enjoyment of all Chrysler product cars, trucks, and other vehicles, including Chrysler, DeSoto, Dodge, Imperial, and Plymouth. Offers technical advice; provides list of cars, parts, and services. Maintains library of service and parts manuals from the 1930s to 1989. **Convention/Meeting:** Annual.

2028 ● Special Interest Auto Club
P.O. Box 681
Centreville, VA 22020
Stephen L. DiGiulian, Pres.   Ph:(703)631-0018

Founded: 1978. **Membership:** 2,000. Owners and enthusiasts of Chrysler high-performance automobiles manufactured from 1964 to the present including Dodge Challengers and Plymouth Barracudas. Purpose is to help restore and preserve Chrysler high-performance cars. Maintains merchandise department and parts program listing cars and parts wanted and for sale. Sponsors national and regional shows and meets; compiles statistics; maintains biographical archives and speakers' bureau. **Former Name(s):** (1981) T/A-AAR Special Interest Auto Club. **Convention/Meeting:** Annual (with exhibits) - always July, midwestern U.S.

2029 ● WPC Club
P.O. Box 3504
Kalamazoo, MI 49003-3504
Ralph Kendall, Pres.   Ph:(616)372-1067

Founded: 1969. **Membership:** 4,850. Individuals dedicated to the preservation, restoration, and enjoyment of Chrysler product cars. Conducts social activities; houses library. Awards annual trophies at national meets. **Convention/Meeting:** Annual; also sponsors International Winter Photo Meet.

PLYMOUTH GRAN FURY (1987-89)

Corporate twin of the Chrysler Fifth Avenue and the Dodge Diplomat. Variation on the rear-wheel design that started as the late Dodge Aspen/Plymouth Volare frame. It was popular mainly as police cars and taxis. Produced at the closed Chrysler Motors plant in Kenosha, Wisconsin until 1989.

MAJOR FEATURES

● Gran Fury had as standard equipment: three-speed Torqueflite automatic transmission, rear-wheel drive design, independent front suspension, vented front disc brakes, power steering, and restraint system with a passive driver's side air bag.

PRICE HISTORY

The following new car prices reflect the approximate retail cost of the base model: **1987** - $10,598; **1988** - $11,407; **1989** - $11,995.

DIMENSIONS

Body Style	Years Avail	Wheel Base (in)	Lgth (in)	Ht (in)	Avg Wt (lbs)	Fuel Cap (gal)	Front Hdrm (in)	Front Legrm (in)
4d sdn	87-89	112.6	204.6	55.1	3,559	18.0	39.3	42.5

ENGINES

Type	Displacement (L)	Fuel Dly	HP @rpm	Torque @rpm (ft/lbs)	MPG Cty/Hwy	Years Avail
V-8	5.2	2-bbl	140@3600	265@2000	17/23	87-88
V-8	5.2	4-bbl	175@4000	250@3200	16/22	87-89

KEY: I=in-line engine; V=V engine; F=flat engine; FI=fuel injection; bbl=barrel carburetor; T=turbo; D=diesel; HP=horsepower; MPG=estimated average miles per gallon.

EVALUATIONS, TESTS, AND RANKINGS

1988: "big cars. . .still substantial." **Source:** "Plymouth Gran Fury," *Car and Driver—Buyers Guide 1988*, 1987, p. 83.

RECALLS

1988-89: (12,000 passenger cars equipped with air bags; includes the Plymouth Gran Fury and Dodge Diplomat): Steering wheel may crack at its hub-weld attachment because of fatigue loading and eventually separate from the hub, resulting in loss of steering control. **Corrective action:** Replace steering wheels with revised wheel with arc welds added at the wheel stamping-to-hub attachment. *(NHTSA Campaign No. 91V051000.)*

1988: (12,000 passenger cars equipped with automatic speed control. Recall includes the Chrysler Fifth Avenue, Plymouth Fury, Dodge Diplomat): Engine compartment wiring harness fusible link wires may be trapped under the speed control servo bracket. Trapped wires may eventually cause a high resistance electrical short that can result in an underhood fire. **Corrective action:** Free any trapped wiring; then secure wiring with a tie strap to keep away from speed control bracket. *(NHTSA Campaign No. 87V164000.)*

REPAIR MANUALS

2030 ● **Chrysler, Dodge, Plymouth: 1972-1987 Rear Wheel Drive Tune-up Maintenance**
Clymer Publications
P.O. Box 1209
Overland Park, KS 66212   Ph:(913)541-6694

Published 1987. **Price:** $14.95.

OTHER INFORMATION SOURCES

2031 ● **How to Build Chrysler, Dodge, Plymouth**
Motorbooks International, Pubs. & Wholesalers, Inc.
729 Prospect Ave.
Osceola, WI 54020   Ph:(715)294-3345

Published 1990. **Editor(s):** Geoff Carter. **Price:** $17.95.

2032 ● **Torsion Bar**
Chrysler Product Owners Club
806 Winhall Way
Silver Spring, MD 20904

Promotes the collection, preservation, restoration, maintenance, exhibition, and enjoyment of Chrysler product cars, trucks, and other vehicles. Includes technical advice on the restoration of Chalmers, Chrysler, DeSoto, Dodge, Imperial, Maxwell, and Plymouth vehicles. Monthly. **Price:** Available to members only.

ASSOCIATIONS

2033 ● **Chrysler Product Owners Club**
5203 Edmondson Ave.
Baltimore, MD 21229
Brian K. Scott, Exec. Officer

Founded: 1978. **Membership:** 210. Collectors and restorers of Chrysler-product automobiles. Promotes the collection, preservation, restoration, maintenance, and enjoyment of all Chrysler product cars, trucks, and other vehicles, including Chrysler, DeSoto, Dodge, Imperial, and Plymouth. Offers technical advice; provides list of cars, parts, and services. Maintains library of service and parts manuals from the 1930s to 1989. **Convention/Meeting:** Annual.

2034 ● **WPC Club**
P.O. Box 3504
Kalamazoo, MI 49003-3504
Ralph Kendall, Pres.   Ph:(616)372-1067

Founded: 1969. **Membership:** 4,850. Individuals dedicated to the preservation, restoration, and enjoyment of Chrysler product cars. Conducts social activities; houses library. Awards annual trophies at national meets. **Convention/Meeting:** Annual; also sponsors International Winter Photo Meet.

PLYMOUTH HORIZON (1987-90)

Along with its corporate twin the Dodge Omni, the Plymouth Horizon was the first U.S.-made front-drive subcompact. Rated as having the lowest maintenance cost among compacts by *The Complete Car Cost Guide* in 1990. Produced until 1990 at the Chrysler Motors plants in Belvidere, Illinois, Kenosha, Wisconsin, and the Jefferson plant in Detroit, Michigan.

MAJOR FEATURES

● Horizon had as standard 1990 equipment: front-wheel drive, five-speed manual transmission, front independent strut suspension, power-assisted rack-and-pinion steering, and front disc brakes.

● Horizon America was offered in 1989 as part of a cost-cutting program to reduce manufacturing and retail costs by offering a single trim level with most options grouped into packages.

PRICE HISTORY

The following new car prices reflect the approximate retail cost

of the base model: **1987** - $5,799; **1988** - $5,995; **1989** - $6,595; **1990** - $6,995.

DIMENSIONS

Body Style	Years Avail	Wheel Base (in)	Lgth (in)	Ht (in)	Avg Wt (lbs)	Fuel Cap (gal)	Front Hdrm (in)	Front Legrm (in)
4d lbk	87-89	99.1	163.2	53.0	2,237	13.0	38.1	42.1
4d lbk	90-90	99.1	164.8	53.0	2,162	13.0	na	na

ENGINES

Type	Displace- ment (L)	Fuel Dly	HP @rpm	Torque @rpm (ft/lbs)	MPG Cty/Hwy	Years Avail
I-4	2.2	2-bbl	96@5600	119@3200	25/34	87-87
I-4	2.2	FI	93@4800	122@3200	26/35	88-90

KEY: I=in-line engine; V=V engine; F=flat engine; FI=fuel injection; bbl=barrel carburetor; T=turbo; D=diesel; HP=horsepower; MPG=estimated average miles per gallon.

EVALUATIONS, TESTS, AND RANKINGS

1989: "low cost, reasonable performance." **Source:** "Dodge Omni, Plymouth Horizon," *Road & Track—Buyer's Guide 1989*, 1988, p. 58.

1988: "Although the ride was better than average,. . .the handling suffered somewhat from rather sluggish and imprecise steering." **Source:** "Cheap Cars," *Changing Times*, May 1988, pp. 33-36, 37.

RECALLS

1989-90: (625,000 cars; includes several Plymouth, Dodge, and Chrysler vehicles): Engine valve cover gasket may dislocate and allow an engine oil leak at the gasket. Leakage of oil in the engine compartment could cause a fire. **Corrective action:** Replace gasket cover with revised cover, and RTV sealant will be applied in place of a gasket. *(NHTSA Campaign No. 89V237000.)*

1988: (120,000 cars; includes the Plymouth Horizon and Dodge Omni): Steering wheel horn pads do not contain the horn symbol display as required by FMVSS 101. Vehicles do not comply with FMVSS 101, controls and displays. **Corrective action:** Send notification postcard to owners to assist any future owners who might be unsure of horn location. *(NHTSA Campaign No. 89V091000.)*

1987: (95,000 passenger vehicles; includes Plymouth Horizon, Plymouth Turismo, Dodge Omni, and Dodge Charger): Pressure regulator installed in the fuel supply plumbing system leaks fuel into the engine compartment possibly resulting in fire. **Corrective action:** The fuel supply pressure regulator assembly will be replaced with a new assembly. *(NHTSA Campaign No. 91V132000.)*

REPAIR MANUALS

2035 ● **Dodge Omni, 024, Charger, Rampage, and Plymouth Horizon, TC3, Turismo and Scamp 1978-1987: Shop Manual**
Clymer Publications
P.O. Box 1209
Overland Park, KS 66212
Ph:(913)541-6694

Published 1987. **Price:** $14.95.

OTHER INFORMATION SOURCES

2036 ● **How to Build Chrysler, Dodge, Plymouth**
Motorbooks International, Pubs. & Wholesalers, Inc.
729 Prospect Ave.
Osceola, WI 54020
Ph:(715)294-3345

Published 1990. **Editor(s):** Geoff Carter. **Price:** $17.95.

2037 ● **Torsion Bar**
Chrysler Product Owners Club
806 Winhall Way
Silver Spring, MD 20904

Promotes the collection, preservation, restoration, maintenance, exhibition, and enjoyment of Chrysler product cars, trucks, and other vehicles. Includes technical advice on the restoration of Chalmers, Chrysler, DeSoto, Dodge, Imperial, Maxwell, and Plymouth vehicles. Monthly. **Price:** Available to members only.

ASSOCIATIONS

2038 ● **Chrysler Product Owners Club**
5203 Edmondson Ave.
Baltimore, MD 21229
Brian K. Scott, Exec. Officer

Founded: 1978. **Membership:** 210. Collectors and restorers of Chrysler-product automobiles. Promotes the collection, preservation, restoration, maintenance, exhibition, and enjoyment of all Chrysler product cars, trucks, and other vehicles, including Chrysler, DeSoto, Dodge, Imperial, and Plymouth. Offers technical advice; provides list of cars, parts, and services. Maintains library of service and parts manuals from the 1930s to 1989. **Convention/Meeting:** Annual.

2039 ● **WPC Club**
P.O. Box 3504
Kalamazoo, MI 49003-3504
Ralph Kendall, Pres.
Ph:(616)372-1067

Founded: 1969. **Membership:** 4,850. Individuals dedicated to the preservation, restoration, and enjoyment of Chrysler product cars. Conducts social activities; houses library. Awards annual trophies at national meets. **Convention/Meeting:** Annual; also sponsors International Winter Photo Meet.

PLYMOUTH LASER (1990-92)

Two-door sports coupe listed in the subcompact vehicle class. Voted one of *Car and Driver's* Ten Best Cars in 1990, 1991, and 1992.

Rated as having the highest maintenance cost among subcompacts by *The Complete Car Cost Guide*. First produced in 1990 in a joint venture with Mitsubishi at the Diamond-Star Motors plant in Normal, Illinois (plant parts data: domestic parts - 35%, imported parts - 65%; *Federal Trade Zone Board*, 1989). Shares basic components with the Mitsubishi Eclipse and the Eagle Talon.

1992 Plymouth Laser RS Turbo AWD

MAJOR FEATURES

• Laser has as 1992 standard equipment: 1.8 liter, I-4 SOHC engine, five-speed manual transmission, front MacPherson type strut suspension, rear sport suspension, manual rack-and-pinion steering, four-wheel power disc brakes, styled steel wheels, AM/FM stereo, restraint system with motorized front passive shoulder with active lap belt, and tilt steering column.

• Laser RS adds as 1992 standard equipment: 2.0 liter, 16-valve, I-4 DOHC engine, power variable assisted rack-and-pinion steering, AM/FM stereo cassette player, steel wheels with full wheel covers, and electric rear window defroster.

• Laser RS Turbo FWD adds as 1992 standard equipment: 2.0 liter, 16 valve, I-4 DOHC intercooled turbocharged engine, front-wheel drive, rear performance suspension, steel wheels with full turbine wheel covers, and additional interior accessories.

• Laser RS Turbo AWD adds as 1992 standard equipment: all-wheel-drive, rear enthusiast suspension, and 16-inch aluminum wheels.

PRICE HISTORY

The following new car prices reflect the approximate retail cost of the base model: **1990** - $10,855; **1991** - $10,864; **1992** - $11,184.

DIMENSIONS

Body Style	Years Avail	Wheel Base (in)	Lgth (in)	Ht (in)	Avg Wt (lbs)	Fuel Cap (gal)	Front Hdrm (in)	Front Legrm (in)
2d cpe	90-91	97.2	170.5	51.4	2,524	15.9	37.9	42.5
2d cpe	92-92	97.2	172.8	51.4	2,531	15.9	37.9	43.9

ENGINES

Type	Displace- ment (L)	Fuel Dly	HP @rpm	Torque @rpm (ft/lbs)	MPG Cty/Hwy	Years Avail
I-4	1.8	FI	92@5000	105@3500	23/32	90-92
I-4	2.0	FI	135@6000	125@5000	22/29	90-92
I-4T	2.0	FI	190@6000	203@3000	21/28	90-91
I-4T	2.0	FI	195@6000	203@3000	20/25	92-92

KEY: I=in-line engine; V=V engine; F=flat engine; FI=fuel injection; bbl=barrel carburetor; T=turbo; D=diesel; HP=horsepower; MPG=estimated average miles per gallon.

EVALUATIONS, TESTS, AND RANKINGS

1992: "[Diamond-Star Turbos] as fine a combination of value, good looks, and tummy-tightening performance as could be found anywhere at any price . . . [Laser RS Turbo AWD] can be enjoyed in everyday driving, looks good on social occasions, and provides a generous 195 horsepower." **Source:** "Ten Best Cars," *Car and Driver*, January 1992, pp. 35-43.

1992: "state of the art in small, affordable sports cars . . . all-wheel-drive system is a tad noisy at higher engine speeds . . . It's a pleasuremobile, nothing more." **Source:** "Laser Impresses the Less-Affluent Set," *Detroit Free Press*, September 26, 1991, p. 1E.

1991: "Turbo models deliver stunning acceleration. . .Rear seat room is abysmal, possibly the worst in the class." **Source:** "Diamond-Star Coupes: An All-Star Play," *Autoweek's AutoFile 1991 Edition*, 1990, pp. 34-38.

1991: "Another winner." **Source:** "Plymouth Laser," *Road & Track*, October 1990, p. 89.

1991: "this car works great. . .handsome, speedy." **Source:** "Life with Laser RS Turbo," *Car and Driver*, October 1990, pp. 147-150.

1991: "a handful under hard acceleration because of torque steer that's eliminated in the 4-wheel-drive version . . . testers had few criticisms about these well-made, high performance machines." **Source:** "Blind Taste Test," *Popular Mechanics*, November 1990, pp. 43-47, 124-125.

1990: "[RS Turbo is] holding its own in a forest of heavy artillery." **Source:** "Bang for the Buck," *Motor Trend*, November 1989, pp. 42-46, 48, 52-55, 58-59, 62, 64, 66-68, 72, 76.

1990: "highest top speed in the basic test group, and by an impressive margin." **Source:** "Coupes De Grace: The small, the quick and the slick in a high desert shootout," *Popular Mechanics*, May 1989, pp. 120-124, 212, 214.

1990: "handles extremely well. But on mountain roads its front-wheel drive makes it feel a bit twitchy . . . truly exhilarating to drive." **Source:** "Sizzling Performance— Without Sticker Shock," *Business Week*, February 6, 1989, p. 105.

1990: "Head-turning good looks . . . Very sporty performance . . . Good fuel economy . . . Turbocharged engine too powerful for car's front-drive chassis." **Source:** "Versatile Vehicles," *Home Mechanix*, July 1989, pp. 64-70.

1990: "built the Japanese way: darn near perfect . . . If you really step on the gas, you'll feel some torque steer or pulling to the side . . . Laser seems to be beamed directly at the bull's eye of the sports coupe market." **Source:** "2 for the Road," *Regardie's*, September 1989, pp. 169-170, 172-180, 182.

1990: "turbocharged-engine option that stretches the limits of power-handling capability for front-wheel drives . . . seemed to suffer from a mismatch between the free-revving engine and the automatic transmission in the lower gears." **Source:** "Power Coupes," *Popular Science*, April 1989, pp. 28-29, 32-34.

RECALLS

1990: (5,510 cars; includes Plymouth Laser and Mitsubishi Eclipse vehicles): Wiring harness for the headlamps may break due to the stress created by the headlamp pop-up devices. Causes loss of headlamp illumination which have a potential for an accident. **Corrective action:** Headlamp wiring harness routing will be modified and damaged wires repaired. *(NHTSA Campaign No. 89V128000.)*

1990: (210 cars; includes Eagle Talon, Mitsubishi Eclipse, and Plymouth Laser models. NHTSA Campaign Nos. 90V106001 and 90V106002 address same defect): Diluted primer may have been used on the windshield opening flanges prior to windshield glass installation which would not provide the retention required by FMVSS 212. Windshields would not prevent ejection of vehicle occupants during vehicle crash, which causes serious injuries and fatalities. **Corrective action:**

Replace windshields, associated parts, and primer. *(NHTSA Campaign No. 90V106000.)*

1990: (632 passenger cars equipped with Diamond-Star Motors sunroofs; includes Eagle Talon, Mitsubishi Eclipse, and Plymouth Laser models. NHTSA Campaign Nos. 90V056001 and 90V056002 address same defect): Operation of sunroof in non-standard manner may cause male hinge disengagement from the roof hinge receiver. Sunroof glass could detach from the roof and result in injury to occupants or persons in the vicinity. **Corrective action:** Replace male hinge with a modified version to increase roof hinge receiver retention ability. *(NHTSA Campaign No. 90V056000.)*

OTHER INFORMATION SOURCES

2040 ● How to Build Chrysler, Dodge, Plymouth
Motorbooks International, Pubs. & Wholesalers, Inc.
729 Prospect Ave.
Osceola, WI 54020   Ph:(715)294-3345

Published 1990. **Editor(s):** Geoff Carter. **Price:** $17.95.

2041 ● Torsion Bar
Chrysler Product Owners Club
806 Winhall Way
Silver Spring, MD 20904

Promotes the collection, preservation, restoration, maintenance, exhibition, and enjoyment of Chrysler product cars, trucks, and other vehicles. Includes technical advice on the restoration of Chalmers, Chrysler, DeSoto, Dodge, Imperial, Maxwell, and Plymouth vehicles. Monthly. **Price:** Available to members only.

ASSOCIATIONS

2042 ● Chrysler Performance Parts Association
Box 1210
Azusa, CA 91702   Ph:(818)303-6220
Roland Osborne, Chm.   Fax:(818)303-2481

Founded: 1976. **Membership:** 5,000. Clearinghouse for information on from whom, where, and how to obtain vintage, muscle, and high-tech Chrysler performance parts. **Former Name(s):** (1979) National HEMI Owners; (1980) MOPAR Muscle Club. **Convention/Meeting:** Annual national meet.

2043 ● Chrysler Product Owners Club
5203 Edmondson Ave.
Baltimore, MD 21229
Brian K. Scott, Exec. Officer

Founded: 1978. **Membership:** 210. Collectors and restorers of Chrysler-product automobiles. Promotes the collection, preservation, restoration, maintenance, exhibition, and enjoyment of all Chrysler product cars, trucks, and other vehicles, including Chrysler, DeSoto, Dodge, Imperial, and Plymouth. Offers technical advice; provides list of cars, parts, and services. Maintains library of service and parts manuals from the 1930s to 1989. **Convention/Meeting:** Annual.

2044 ● Special Interest Auto Club
P.O. Box 681
Centreville, VA 22020
Stephen L. DiGiulian, Pres.   Ph:(703)631-0018

Founded: 1978. **Membership:** 2,000. Owners and enthusiasts of Chrysler high-performance automobiles manufactured from 1964 to the present including Dodge Challengers and Plymouth Barracudas. Purpose is to help restore and preserve Chrysler high-performance cars. Maintains merchandise department and parts program listing cars and parts wanted and for sale. Sponsors national and regional shows and meets;

compiles statistics; maintains biographical archives and speakers' bureau. **Former Name(s):** (1981) T/A-AAR Special Interest Auto Club. **Convention/Meeting:** Annual (with exhibits) - always July, midwestern U.S.

2045 ● WPC Club
P.O. Box 3504
Kalamazoo, MI 49003-3504
Ralph Kendall, Pres.   Ph:(616)372-1067

Founded: 1969. **Membership:** 4,850. Individuals dedicated to the preservation, restoration, and enjoyment of Chrysler product cars. Conducts social activities; houses library. Awards annual trophies at national meets. **Convention/Meeting:** Annual; also sponsors International Winter Photo Meet.

PLYMOUTH RELIANT (1987-89)

Introduced as part of the K-car model line, along with its corporate twin the Dodge Aries. Produced until 1989 at, among other locations, the Chrysler Motors plants in Detroit, Michigan (Jefferson plant); St. Louis, Missouri; Newark, Delaware; and Toluca, Mexico.

MAJOR FEATURES

● Reliant had as 1989 standard features: five-speed manual transmission, power brakes, reclining front bucket seats, optical horn, and various interior accessories.

● Reliant America was offered through 1989 as part of a cost-cutting program to reduce manufacturing and retail costs by offering a single trim level with most options grouped into packages.

● Reliant LE added as 1989 standard equipment: three-speed automatic transmission, tinted glass, power steering, special sound insulation, wheel covers, and additional body stylings.

● Reliant LE wagon added as 1988 standard equipment: a special tonneau cover.

PRICE HISTORY

The following new car prices reflect the approximate retail cost of the base model: **1987** - $7,879; **1988** - $6,995; **1989** - $7,595.

DIMENSIONS

Body Style	Years Avail	Wheel Base (in)	Lgth (in)	Ht (in)	Avg Wt (lbs)	Fuel Cap (gal)	Front Hdrm (in)	Front Legrm (in)
2d sdn	87-89	100.3	178.6	52.5	2,375	14.0	38.2	42.2
4d sdn	87-89	100.3	178.6	52.9	2,402	14.0	38.6	42.2
5d wgn	87-88	100.4	178.5	53.2	2,480	14.0	38.5	42.2

ENGINES

Type	Displacement (L)	Fuel Dly	HP @rpm	Torque @rpm (ft/lbs)	MPG Cty/Hwy	Years Avail
I-4	2.2	2-bbl	97@5200	122@3200	25/32	87-87
I-4	2.5	FI	100@4800	136@2800	23/28	87-89
I-4	2.5	FI	96@4400	133@2800	23/27	88-88
I-4	2.2	FI	93@4800	122@3200	25/34	88-89

KEY: I=in-line engine; V=V engine; F=flat engine; FI=fuel injection; bbl=barrel carburetor; T=turbo; D=diesel; HP=horsepower; MPG=estimated average miles per gallon.

EVALUATIONS, TESTS, AND RANKINGS

1989: ''decent transportation.'' **Source:** ''Top 10 Cars of the 80's,'' *Motor Trend*, November 1989, pp. 100-103.

1988: ''still exemplifies the plain-wrapper approach to car styling. . .offers much more room than any other car in its price class.'' **Source:** ''Plymouth Reliant America,'' *Car and Driver*, August 1988, p. 109.

1988: ''proven engineering and low prices. . .a dated design. . .a basic transportation box.'' **Source:** ''Road Test Wagons: How Much Do You Have to Spend,'' *Home Mechanix*, September 1988, pp. 84-86, 88-89, 93.

RECALLS

None to date.

REPAIR MANUALS

2046 ● Haynes Dodge Aries and Plymouth Reliant Owners Workshop Manual, 1981-1988
Haynes Publications, Inc.
861 Lawrence Dr.
Newbury Park, CA 91320   Ph:(818)889-5400

Editor(s): J. H. Haynes and Larry Warren. **Price:** $15.95.

OTHER INFORMATION SOURCES

2047 ● How to Build Chrysler, Dodge, Plymouth
Motorbooks International, Pubs. & Wholesalers, Inc.
729 Prospect Ave.
Osceola, WI 54020   Ph:(715)294-3345

Published 1990. **Editor(s):** Geoff Carter. **Price:** $17.95.

2048 ● Torsion Bar
Chrysler Product Owners Club
806 Winhall Way
Silver Spring, MD 20904

Promotes the collection, preservation, restoration, maintenance, exhibition, and enjoyment of Chrysler product cars, trucks, and other vehicles. Includes technical advice on the restoration of Chalmers, Chrysler, DeSoto, Dodge, Imperial, Maxwell, and Plymouth vehicles. Monthly. **Price:** Available to members only.

ASSOCIATIONS

2049 ● Chrysler Product Owners Club
5203 Edmondson Ave.
Baltimore, MD 21229
Brian K. Scott, Exec. Officer

Founded: 1978. **Membership:** 210. Collectors and restorers of Chrysler-product automobiles. Promotes the collection, preservation, restoration, maintenance, exhibition, and enjoyment of all Chrysler product cars, trucks, and other vehicles, including Chrysler, DeSoto, Dodge, Imperial, and Plymouth. Offers technical advice; provides list of cars, parts, and services. Maintains library of service and parts manuals from the 1930s to 1989. **Convention/Meeting:** Annual.

2050 ● WPC Club
P.O. Box 3504
Kalamazoo, MI 49003-3504
Ralph Kendall, Pres.   Ph:(616)372-1067

Founded: 1969. **Membership:** 4,850. Individuals dedicated to the preservation, restoration, and enjoyment of Chrysler product cars. Conducts social activities; houses library. Awards annual trophies at national meets. **Convention/Meeting:** Annual; also sponsors International Winter Photo Meet.

PLYMOUTH SUNDANCE (1987-92)

Categorized in a compact vehicle class. Originally designed as a replacement for the Dodge Omni/Plymouth Horizon in 1987, along with its corporate twin the Dodge Shadow. Instead, it was elevated to the compact vehicle class. Named among intermediate vehicles as worst in the crash test rating index of *The Car Book*   in 1989. Listed as one of the Best Bets of 1992 by *The Car Book*. Produced at the Chrysler Motors plant at Sterling Heights, Michigan.

1992 Plymouth Sundance America

MAJOR FEATURES

● Sundance offers as 1992 standard equipment: 2.2 liter engine, five-speed manual transmission, front-wheel drive, Iso-strut front suspension, power rack-and-pinion steering, power front disc brakes, AM/FM radio, and restraint system with passive driver's side air bag.

● Sundance America is offered in 1992 as part of a cost-cutting program to reduce manufacturing and retail costs by offering a single trim level with most options grouped into package.

● Sundance RS had as 1991 standard features: 2.5 liter I-4 engine, intermittent windshield wiper/washer system, and enhanced body stylings and interior accessories.

PRICE HISTORY

The following new car prices reflect the approximate retail cost of the base model: **1987** - $7,599; **1988** - $7,995; **1989** - $8,395; **1990** - $8,845; **1991** - $7,699; **1992** - $7,984.

DIMENSIONS

Body Style	Years Avail	Wheel Base (in)	Lgth (in)	Ht (in)	Avg Wt (lbs)	Fuel Cap (gal)	Front Hdrm (in)	Front Legrm (in)
2d lbk	87-89	97.0	171.1	52.7	2,513	14.0	38.3	41.8
4d lbk	87-89	97.0	171.1	52.7	2,544	14.0	38.3	41.8
3d cpe	90-92	97.0	171.1	52.7	2,617	14.0	38.3	41.5
5d sdn	90-92	97.0	171.7	52.7	2,654	14.0	38.3	41.5

ENGINES

Type	Displace-ment (L)	Fuel Dly	HP @rpm	Torque @rpm (ft/lbs)	MPG Cty/Hwy	Years Avail
I-4	2.2	FI	97@5200	122@3200	25/33	87-87
I-4	2.2	FI	100@5200	133@3200	25/33	88-88
I-4	2.5	FI	96@4400	133@2800	23/31	88-88
I-4	2.2	FI	93@4800	122@3200	24/34	89-89
I-4	2.5	FI	100@4800	135@2800	23/31	89-92
I-4	2.2	FI	93@4800	122@3200	26/32	90-92
I-4T	2.2	FI	146@5200	171@3600	20/29	87-87
I-4T	2.2	FI	146@5200	170@2400	21/29	88-88
I-4T	2.5	FI	150@4800	180@2000	21/29	89-91

KEY: I=in-line engine; V=V engine; F=flat engine; FI=fuel injection; bbl=barrel carburetor; T=turbo; D=diesel; HP=horsepower; MPG=estimated average miles per gallon.

EVALUATIONS, TESTS, AND RANKINGS

1991: "singular advantage in this group is its size, with the longest wheelbase, overall length, width, and interior volume . . . driving dynamics of the Sundance America are mixed . . . engine is raucous, the shifter is vague and mushy, and the car is geared for marathons, not sprinting." **Source:** "No Frills," *Popular Science*, August 1991, pp. 60-63, 86-87.

1991: "the lowest-priced car with an airbag you can buy . . . The car has a feeling of soundness to it . . . The performance isn't captivating, but it's certainly adequate." **Source:** "Plymouth Sundance America," *Motor Trend*, September 1991, pp. 90, 92.

1990: "reasonable levels of refinement and performance." **Source:** "Eleven for Thirteen: Sportsters, $13,000 and under, that you can actually enjoy," *Car and Driver*, June 1990, pp. 46-50, 52, 61, 63-64, 66-69.

1989: "Pleasantly surprising are these cars' very crisp steering and handling. . .Brakes (disc front, drum rear) are very effective." **Source:** "Two Nifties by Chrysler: The Shadow-Sundance dilemma is resolved to the benefit of all," *The Detroit News*, October 22, 1986, pp. F1-F2.

1987: "cars are slightly bigger and more plush than most subcompacts." **Source:** "Shadow, Sundance roll at Chrysler," *The Detroit News*, September 11, 1986, pp. C1-C2.

1987: "[Fifth-place Sundance's] interior design is hardly cutting edge. . .Quality seems good, performance lively, but engine noise gets rather intrusive." **Source:** "1987 Car of the Year," *Motor Trend*, February 1987, pp. 27-41.

1987: "workmanship and overall quality of the Sundance/Shadow brought out some of the best marks. . .registered recently for a U.S. car." **Source:** "Ask the Man Who Owns One," *Popular Mechanics*, August 1987, pp. 59-62, 91-91.

RECALLS

1991: (18,000 passenger cars; includes several Chrysler, Dodge, and Plymouth models): Front disc brake caliper guide pin bolts may not have been adequately torqued and could loosen. This could cause reduced braking effectiveness and could result in an accident. **Corrective action:** Properly torque front brake caliper guide pin bolts to 250 lbs. *(NHTSA Campaign No. 90V162000.)*

1989-90: (625,000 cars; includes several Plymouth, Dodge, and Chrysler vehicles): Engine valve cover gasket may dislocate and allow an engine oil leak at the gasket. Leakage of oil in the engine compartment could cause a fire. **Corrective action:** Replace gasket cover with revised cover, and RTV sealant will be applied in place of a gasket. *(NHTSA Campaign No. 89V237000.)*

1988: (6,500 cars; includes Plymouth and Dodge models): Front passenger seat lap belt retractor, which incorporates a child seat belt locking feature, may malfunction. Seat belt lock would extract and child seat may move out of its restrained position. **Corrective action:** Redesign retractor. *(NHTSA Campaign No. 88V129000.)*

1987: (580,000 vehicles equipped with 2.2L turbocharged engine; includes models made before 1987; includes Chrysler, Dodge, and Plymouth models): Fuel leakage may occur in low ambient temperature operation at connections of an engine compartment fuel supply hose to the pressure regulator and to the fuel rail. In the presence of an ignition source, fuel leakage could result in a fire. **Corrective action:** Relocate pressure regulator; replace fuel supply with formed hose with revised routing configuration to ensure sealing integrity. *(NHTSA Campaign No. 88V105000.)*

OTHER INFORMATION SOURCES

2051 ● **How to Build Chrysler, Dodge, Plymouth**
Motorbooks International, Pubs. & Wholesalers, Inc.
729 Prospect Ave.
Osceola, WI 54020   Ph:(715)294-3345

Published 1990. **Editor(s):** Geoff Carter. **Price:** $17.95.

2052 ● **Torsion Bar**
Chrysler Product Owners Club
806 Winhall Way
Silver Spring, MD 20904

Promotes the collection, preservation, restoration, maintenance, exhibition, and enjoyment of Chrysler product cars, trucks, and other vehicles. Includes technical advice on the restoration of Chalmers, Chrysler, DeSoto, Dodge, Imperial, Maxwell, and Plymouth vehicles. Monthly. **Price:** Available to members only.

ASSOCIATIONS

2053 ● **Chrysler Product Owners Club**
5203 Edmondson Ave.
Baltimore, MD 21229
Brian K. Scott, Exec. Officer

Founded: 1978. **Membership:** 210. Collectors and restorers of Chrysler-product automobiles. Promotes the collection, preservation, restoration, maintenance, exhibition, and enjoyment of all Chrysler product cars, trucks, and other vehicles, including Chrysler, DeSoto, Dodge, Imperial, and Plymouth. Offers technical advice; provides list of cars, parts, and services. Maintains library of service and parts manuals from the 1930s to 1989. **Convention/Meeting:** Annual.

2054 ● **WPC Club**
P.O. Box 3504
Kalamazoo, MI 49003-3504
Ralph Kendall, Pres.   Ph:(616)372-1067

Founded: 1969. **Membership:** 4,850. Individuals dedicated to the preservation, restoration, and enjoyment of Chrysler product cars. Conducts social activities; houses library. Awards annual trophies at national meets. **Convention/Meeting:** Annual; also sponsors International Winter Photo Meet.

PLYMOUTH TURISMO (1987)

Corporate twin of the Dodge Charger. Produced until 1987 at, among other locations, the Chrysler Motors plant in Belvidere, Illinois. Dropped out after 1987 as production shifted to Dodge Omni/Plymouth Horizon models.

MAJOR FEATURES

• Turismo had as 1987 standard equipment: five-speed manual transmission, front independent suspension, front disc brakes, rack-and-pinion steering, rear-window heater, steel wheels, and a rallye instrument panel consisting of coolant temperature, oil pressure, voltage gauge, and tachometer.

PRICE HISTORY

The following new car prices reflect the approximate retail cost of the base model: **1987** - $7,199.

DIMENSIONS

Body Style	Years Avail	Wheel Base (in)	Lgth (in)	Ht (in)	Avg Wt (lbs)	Fuel Cap (gal)	Front Hdrm (in)	Front Legrm (in)
2d lbk	87-87	96.5	174.8	50.7	2,290	13.0	37.2	42.5

ENGINES

Type	Displacement (L)	Fuel Dly	HP @rpm	Torque @rpm (ft/lbs)	MPG Cty/Hwy	Years Avail
I-4	2.2	2-bbl	96@5200	119@3200	25/35	87-87

KEY: I=in-line engine; V=V engine; F=flat engine; FI=fuel injection; bbl=barrel carburetor; T=turbo; D=diesel; HP=horsepower; MPG=estimated average miles per gallon.

EVALUATIONS, TESTS, AND RANKINGS

1987: "low-price sporty transportation." **Source:** "Dodge Charger, Plymouth Turismo," *Road & Track—Buyer's Guide 1987*, 1986, p. 53.

RECALLS

1987: (95,000 passenger vehicles; includes Plymouth Horizon, Plymouth Turismo, Dodge Omni, and Dodge Charger): Pressure regulator installed in the fuel supply plumbing system leaks fuel into the engine compartment possibly resulting in fire. **Corrective action:** The fuel supply pressure regulator assembly will be replaced with a new assembly. *(NHTSA Campaign No. 91V132000.)*

REPAIR MANUALS

2055 ● **Dodge Omni, 024, Charger, Rampage, and Plymouth Horizon, TC3, Turismo and Scamp 1978-1987: Shop Manual**
Clymer Publications
P.O. Box 1209
Overland Park, KS 66212   Ph:(913)541-6694

Published 1987. **Price:** $14.95.

OTHER INFORMATION SOURCES

2056 ● **How to Build Chrysler, Dodge, Plymouth**
Motorbooks International, Pubs. & Wholesalers, Inc.
729 Prospect Ave.
Osceola, WI 54020   Ph:(715)294-3345

Published 1990. **Editor(s):** Geoff Carter. **Price:** $17.95.

2057 ● **Torsion Bar**
Chrysler Product Owners Club
806 Winhall Way
Silver Spring, MD 20904

Promotes the collection, preservation, restoration, maintenance, exhibition, and enjoyment of Chrysler product cars, trucks, and other vehicles. Includes technical advice on the restoration of Chalmers, Chrysler, DeSoto, Dodge, Imperial, Maxwell, and Plymouth vehicles. Monthly. **Price:** Available to members only.

ASSOCIATIONS

2058 ● **Chrysler Product Owners Club**
5203 Edmondson Ave.
Baltimore, MD 21229
Brian K. Scott, Exec. Officer

Founded: 1978. **Membership:** 210. Collectors and restorers of Chrysler-product automobiles. Promotes the collection, preservation, restoration, maintenance, exhibition, and enjoyment of all Chrysler product cars, trucks, and other vehicles, including Chrysler, DeSoto, Dodge, Imperial, and Plymouth. Offers technical advice; provides list of cars, parts, and services. Maintains library of service and parts manuals from the 1930s to 1989. **Convention/Meeting:** Annual.

2059 ● **WPC Club**
P.O. Box 3504
Kalamazoo, MI 49003-3504
Ralph Kendall, Pres.   Ph:(616)372-1067

Founded: 1969. **Membership:** 4,850. Individuals dedicated to the preservation, restoration, and enjoyment of Chrysler product cars. Conducts social activities; houses library. Awards annual trophies at national meets. **Convention/Meeting:** Annual; also sponsors International Winter Photo Meet.

PLYMOUTH VOYAGER (1987-92)

Along with its corporate twins, the Dodge Caravan and Chrysler Town & Country, the Voyager was the first compact van made by an American auto manufacturer. Nominated to *Car and Driver's* Ten Best Cars list in 1989. Listed as one of the Best Bets of 1992 by *The Car Book*. Built at the Chrysler Motors plants in St. Louis, Missouri (No. 2), and Windsor, Ontario, Canada.

1991 Plymouth Grand Voyager

MAJOR FEATURES

• Voyager has as 1992 standard equipment: 2.5-liter, 4-cylinder engine, five-speed manual transmission, front-wheel drive, front Iso-strut suspension, power-assisted rack-and-pinion steering, front power disc brakes, restraint system, Deluxe wheel covers, and additional accessories.

• Voyager SE adds as 1992 standard equipment: 3-speed automatic transmission, seven-passenger seating arrangement, power liftgate release, and sport wheel covers.

• Voyager LE adds as 1992 standard equipment: 3.0-liter, V-6 engine, 3-speed automatic transmission, front air conditioning, rear window electric defroster, deluxe body sound insulation, tilt steering wheel, and additional body stylings.

● Grand Voyager SE has as 1992 standard equipment: 3.3 liter V-6 engine, four-speed electronic automatic transmission, all-wheel drive, seven-passenger seating arrangement, and various interior accessories.

● Grand Voyager LE adds as 1992 standard features: same engine and transmission as Grand Voyager SE, all-wheel drive, front air conditioning, electric rear window defroster, deluxe body sound insulation, and an assortment of body stylings.

PRICE HISTORY

The following new car prices reflect the approximate retail cost of the base model: **1988** - $10,887; **1989** - $11,312; **1990** - $11,995; **1991** - $13,266; **1992** - $13,406.

DIMENSIONS

Body Style	Years Avail	Wheel Base (in)	Lgth (in)	Ht (in)	Avg Wt (lbs)	Fuel Cap (gal)	Front Hdrm (in)	Front Legrm (in)
4d van	87-88	112.0	175.9	64.4	4,060	15.0	na	na
4d van	89-90	112.0	175.9	64.6	4,070	20.0	na	na
4d van	91-91	112.3	175.9	66.0	na	20.0	37.3	38.2
4d van	92-92	112.3	178.1	66.0	na	20.0	39.1	37.3

ENGINES

Type	Displacement (L)	Fuel Dly	HP @rpm	Torque @rpm (ft/lbs)	MPG Cty/Hwy	Years Avail
I-4	2.2	2-bbl	95@na	na	22/29	87-87
I-4	2.6	2-bbl	104@na	na	19/22	87-87
I-4	2.5	FI	100@4800	135@2800	20/28	87-92
I-4T	2.5	FI	150@na	na	18/26	89-90
V-6	3.0	FI	142@5000	173@3600	18/24	87-92
V-6	3.3	FI	150@4800	185@3600	17/23	90-92

KEY: I=in-line engine; V=V engine; F=flat engine; FI=fuel injection; bbl=barrel carburetor; T=turbo; D=diesel; HP=horsepower; MPG=estimated average miles per gallon.

EVALUATIONS, TESTS, AND RANKINGS

1991: "Not a single competitive vehicle can handle the wide variety of tasks required of a minivan with the same equanimity." **Source:** "Dodge Caravan/Plymouth Voyager: An All-American five-time winner," *Automobile Magazine*, January 1991, p. 55.

1991: "[Car of the Year candidate Grand Voyager] on-road performance was wholly acceptable. . .solid steering feel and resolute stability. . .a pleasant driving companion regardless of the conditions." **Source:** "Car of the Year," *Motor Trend*, February 1991, pp. 41-52.

1991: "a more contemporary aerodynamic appearance . . . V-6 engine is smooth and powerful enough to keep pace with turnpike traffic . . . when it comes to all around drivability, they're still the best of the breed." **Source:** "Meet the new minivans," *New Choices for The Best Years*, October 1990, pp. 86-87.

1991: "seats exceptionally comfortable . . . A civilized, passenger-car chassis is perhaps the biggest advantage . . . K-car-based componentry provides the smoothest, most carlike ride of any minivan made today." **Source:** "Home Mechanix Versatile Vehicle Award," *Home Mechanix*, February 1991, pp. 72-77.

1987: "Voyager is still. . .the best passenger van around." **Source:** "The maxi challenge: stretched Voyager tackles Astro and Aerostar," *Popular Science*, October 1987, pp. 24-26, 78-79.

RECALLS

1990: (100 minivans; includes Dodge Caravan and Plymouth Voyager models): Incorrect screws may have been used in installing the load sensing brake proportioning valve to its bracket causing the clamping load to be less than intended. Could result in inconsistent front to rear brake balance with potential for rear brake skid under heavy braking conditions. **Corrective action:** Replace proportioning valve to bracket screws with proper length screws. *(NHTSA Campaign No. 90V145000.)*

1989-90: (625,000 cars; includes several Plymouth, Dodge, and Chrysler vehicles): Engine valve cover gasket may dislocate and allow an engine oil leak at the gasket. Leakage of oil in the engine compartment could cause a fire. **Corrective action:** Replace gasket cover with revised cover, and RTV sealant will be applied in place of a gasket. *(NHTSA Campaign No. 89V237000.)*

1989-90: (640,000 passenger vans; includes the Chrysler Town & Country, Dodge Caravan, and Plymouth Voyager): Inboard front seat belt assembly straps can suffer fatigue failure of the strap near its anchor position resulting in increased likelihood of injury to seat occupant. **Corrective action:** Replace fatigued straps or retrofit straps with a reinforcement plate and removal of an anti-rotation tab to prevent fatigue failure. *(NHTSA Campaign No. 91V053000.)*

1988: (4,000 cars; includes Plymouth and Dodge models): Fuel tanks may be constructed of improper material. Fuel could leak at the tank seam which, in presence of an ignition source, could result in a fire. **Corrective action:** Replace suspect fuel tanks. *(NHTSA Campaign No. 88V107000.)*

1988: (375 vans): Fuel tanks may have been damaged during tank manufacture, which may result in fuel leakage with the potential for a fire. **Corrective action:** Replace fuel tanks as necessary. *(NHTSA Campaign No. 88V010000.)*

SAFETY AND REPAIRS

1987: "Where Air And Water Don't Mix," *Popular Mechanics*, April 1989, p. 46. **Note:** Plymouth Voyager air conditioning compressor does not work.

1987: "Car Clinic," *Popular Mechanics*, June 1990, p. 49. **Note:** Tip for throttle plate sticking on 1987-88 Chrysler fwd cars and vans with 3.0-liter Mitsubishi engines.

REPAIR MANUALS

2060 ● **Chilton's Dodge Caravan-Plymouth Voyager, 1984-1988: Repair and Tune-Up Guide**
Chilton Co.
Chilton Way
Radnor, PA 19089   Ph:(215)964-4000

Published 1989. **Price:** $15.95.

2061 ● **Chilton's Dodge/Plymouth Vans 1967-1988**
Chilton Co.
Chilton Way
Radnor, PA 19089   Ph:(215)964-4000

Published 1989. **Price:** $15.95.

2062 ● **Dodge Caravan, Mini Ram Van, Plymouth Voyager, 1984-1987**
Clymer Publications
P.O. Box 1209
Overland Park, KS 66212   Ph:(913)541-6694

Published 1986. **Price:** $14.95.

2063 ● Haynes Dodge and Plymouth Vans Owners Workshop Manual, No. 349: 1971-1991
Haynes Publications, Inc.
861 Lawrence Dr.
Newbury Park, CA 91320   Ph:(818)889-5400

Published 1983. **Editor(s):** J. H. Haynes and P. Ward. **Price:** $15.95.

OTHER INFORMATION SOURCES

2064 ● How to Build Chrysler, Dodge, Plymouth
Motorbooks International, Pubs. & Wholesalers, Inc.
729 Prospect Ave.
Osceola, WI 54020   Ph:(715)294-3345

Published 1990. **Editor(s):** Geoff Carter. **Price:** $17.95.

2065 ● Torsion Bar
Chrysler Product Owners Club
806 Winhall Way
Silver Spring, MD 20904

Promotes the collection, preservation, restoration, maintenance, exhibition, and enjoyment of Chrysler product cars, trucks, and other vehicles. Includes technical advice on the restoration of Chalmers, Chrysler, DeSoto, Dodge, Imperial, Maxwell, and Plymouth vehicles. Monthly. **Price:** Available to members only.

ASSOCIATIONS

2066 ● Chrysler Product Owners Club
5203 Edmondson Ave.
Baltimore, MD 21229
Brian K. Scott, Exec. Officer

Founded: 1978. **Membership:** 210. Collectors and restorers of Chrysler-product automobiles. Promotes the collection, preservation, restoration, maintenance, exhibition, and enjoyment of all Chrysler product cars, trucks, and other vehicles, including Chrysler, DeSoto, Dodge, Imperial, and Plymouth. Offers technical advice; provides list of cars, parts, and services. Maintains library of service and parts manuals from the 1930s to 1989. **Convention/Meeting:** Annual.

2067 ● WPC Club
P.O. Box 3504
Kalamazoo, MI 49003-3504
Ralph Kendall, Pres.   Ph:(616)372-1067

Founded: 1969. **Membership:** 4,850. Individuals dedicated to the preservation, restoration, and enjoyment of Chrysler product cars. Conducts social activities; houses library. Awards annual trophies at national meets. **Convention/Meeting:** Annual; also sponsors International Winter Photo Meet.

PONTIAC 1000 (1987)

Produced at General Motors plant in Lakewood, Georgia until discontinued in 1987.

MAJOR FEATURES

● Pontiac 1000 had as 1987 standard equipment: 4-speed manual transmission, rack-and-pinion steering, front independent suspension/rear live axle, and front disc/rear drum brakes.

PRICE HISTORY

The following new car prices reflect the approximate retail cost of the base model: **1987 - $5,959.**

DIMENSIONS

Body Style	Years Avail	Wheel Base (in)	Lgth (in)	Ht (in)	Avg Wt (lbs)	Fuel Cap (gal)	Front Hdrm (in)	Front Legrm (in)
2d	87-87	94.3	161.9	52.8	2,114	12.2	37.8	41.7

ENGINES

Type	Displace- ment (L)	Fuel Dly	HP @rpm	Torque @rpm (ft/lbs)	MPG Cty/Hwy	Years Avail
I-4	1.6	2-bbl	65@5200	80@3200	27/35	87-87

KEY: I=in-line engine; V=V engine; F=flat engine; FI=fuel injection; bbl=barrel carburetor; T=turbo; D=diesel; HP=horsepower; MPG=estimated average miles per gallon.

RECALLS

None to date.

SAFETY AND REPAIRS

1987: ``In De Clutch,'' *Popular Mechanics*, January 1988, p. 34. **Note:** What could cause a 1987 Pontiac 1000 to stall when the clutch is disengaged while the car is in motion.

REPAIR MANUALS

2068 ● Chevrolet Chevette and Pontiac T 1000 Service Repair Handbook: All Models 1976-1987
Clymer Publications
P.O. Box 1209
Overland Park, KS 66212   Ph:(913)541-6694

Price: $14.95.

2069 ● Chilton's Chevette and Pontiac T1000 1976-1988
Chilton Co.
Chilton Way
Radnor, PA 19089   Ph:(215)964-4000

Published 1989. **Price:** $15.95.

2070 ● Get Your Pontiac Fixed Right
Consumer Reports Books
51 E. 42nd St., Ste. 800
New York, NY 10017   Ph:(212)682-9280

Published 1990. **Price:** $8.95.

2071 ● Haynes Chevrolet Chevette-Pontiac T1000 Owners Workshop Manuals, No. 449: 1976-1987
Haynes Publications, Inc.
861 Lawrence Dr.
Newbury Park, CA 91320   Ph:(818)889-5400

Editor(s): J.H. Haynes and R.G. Hawes. **Price:** $15.95.

OTHER INFORMATION SOURCES

2072 ● Badger Chatter
Pontiac-Oakland Club International, Badger State Chapter
5223 84th St.
Kenosha, WI 53142   Ph:(414)694-2500

Monthly.

2073 ● **Bison**
Pontiac-Oakland Club, Western New York Chapter
50 Cramer St.
North Tonawanda, NY 14120   Ph:(716)692-1564

Newsletter. Monthly.

2074 ● **Chiefly Pontiac**
Hoosier Pontiac-Oakland Club
1856 Gray Rd.
Mooresville, IN 46158   Ph:(317)831-1568

Newsletter. Bimonthly.

2075 ● **The Drumbeat**
Pontiac-Oakland Club, Nutmeg Chapter
Church Hill Rd.
Washington Depot, CT 06974   Ph:(203)868-7723

Periodic.

2076 ● **Finger Lakes News [New York]**
Pontiac-Oakland Club, Finger Lakes Chapter
14 Judd Ln.
Hilton, NY 14468   Ph:(716)392-3808

Periodic.

2077 ● **Hot Air**
Pontiac-Oakland Club International, Arizona Chapter
4348 E. Timrod
Tucson, AZ 85711   Ph:(602)795-0978

Newsletter. Monthly.

2078 ● **Illinois Newsletter**
Pontiac-Oakland Club International, Illinois Chapter
R.R. 1, Box 220
Beecher, IL 60401   Ph:(708)258-6017

Monthly.

2079 ● **Nebraskaland**
Pontiac-Oakland Club International, Nebraskaland Chapter
1603 Nebraska Ave.
York, NE 68467   Ph:(402)362-6413

Newsletter. Bimonthly.

2080 ● **On The Warpath**
Pontiac-Oakland Club International, National Capital Area
1509 Baltimore Rd.
Alexandria, VA 22308   Ph:(703)768-1569

Newsletter. Bimonthly.

2081 ● **Pontiac-Oakland Club International, Emerald Valley Chapter—Newsletter [Oregon]**
Pontiac-Oakland Club International, Emerald Valley Chapter
2411 Washington
Eugene, OR 97405   Ph:(503)485-0319

Monthly.

2082 ● **Pontiac-Oakland Club International, Garden State Chapter—Newsletter [New Jersey]**
Pontiac-Oakland Club International, Garden State Chapter
19 Earl St.
Denville, NJ 07834

Newsletter. Bimonthly.

2083 ● **Pontiac-Oakland Club International, Illinois Chapter—Annual Roster**
Pontiac-Oakland Club International, Illinois Chapter
R.R. 1, Box 220
Beecher, IL 60401   Ph:(708)258-6017

2084 ● **Pontiac-Oakland Club International, Kansas Chapter—Directory**
Pontiac-Oakland Club International, Kansas Chapter
Rt. 3, Box 421
Rose Hill, KS 67133   Ph:(316)776-2162

Periodic.

2085 ● **Pontiac-Oakland Club International, Kansas Chapter—Newsletter**
Pontiac-Oakland Club International, Kansas Chapter
Rt. 3, Box 421
Rose Hill, KS 67133   Ph:(316)776-2162

Periodic.

2086 ● **Pontiac-Oakland Club International, Kansas City Arrowhead Chapter—Directory [Kansas and Missouri]**
Pontiac-Oakland Club International, Kansas City
Arrowhead Chapter
104 Center Dr.
Silver Lake, KS 66539   Ph:(913)582-4207

Periodic

2087 ● **Pontiac-Oakland Club International—Membership Roster**
Pontiac-Oakland Club International
PO Box 4789
Culver City, CA 90230   Ph:(818)704-1580

Annual.

2088 ● **Pontiac-Oakland Club International, North Coast Ohio Chapter— Newsletter**
Pontiac-Oakland Club International, North Coast Ohio
Chapter
2500 Hetzel Dr.
Parma, OH 44134   Ph:(216)888-4867

Periodic.

2089 ● **Pontiac-Oakland Club International, Old Dominion Chapter—Newsletter [Virginia]**
Pontiac-Oakland Club International, Old Dominion Chapter
1400 Fortingale Circle
Sandstom, VA 23150   Ph:(804)737-3139

Bimonthly.

2090 ● **Pontiac-Oakland Club International, Yankee Chapter—Newsletter [Maine, Massachusetts, and Rhode Island]**
Pontiac-Oakland Club International, Yankee Chapter
44 Old Brook Rd.
Leonminster, MA 01453   Ph:(508)537-7066

Monthly.

2091 ● **The Scout**
Pontiac-Oakland Club International, Kansas City
Arrowhead Chapter
104 Center Dr.
Silver Lake, KS 66539   Ph:(913)582-4207

Newsletter. Monthly.

2092 ● Smoke Signals
Pontiac-Oakland Club International
PO Box 4789
Culver City, CA 90230   Ph:(818)704-1580

Aims to assist owners of Pontiac and Oakland automobiles with the restoration of their vehicles. Monthly. **Editor(s):** Larry Kummer, Editor and Publisher. **Price:** $22.00/yr.; $2.00/mo.

ASSOCIATIONS

2093 ● Pontiac-Oakland Club, Finger Lakes Chapter [New York]
14 Judd Ln.
Hilton, NY 14468
Deborah Arend, Sec.   Ph:(716)392-3808

Founded: 1972. Individuals interested in preserving and restoring Pontiac and Oakland automobiles manufactured between 1907 and the present.

2094 ● Pontiac-Oakland Club International
P.O. Box 4789
Culver City, CA 90230
Dick Hoyt, Exec.Sec.   Ph:(818)704-1580

Founded: 1972. **Membership:** 9,000. Persons interested in the history, restoration, and preservation of Pontiac and Oakland automobiles. Assists owners of Pontiac and Oakland automobiles with the restoration of their vehicles. Maintains staff of volunteer technical advisers. Conducts research pertaining to original specifications and production history. Maintains library. Sponsors competitions; bestows trophies; provides computerized services. **Former Name(s):** (1973) Pontiac Owners Club International. **Convention/Meeting:** Annual conference and auto show.

2095 ● Pontiac-Oakland Club, International, Arizona Chapter
4348 E. Timrod
Tucson, AZ 85711
Thom Sherwood, Pres.   Ph:(602)795-0978

Founded: 1982. **Membership:** 100. Automotive enthusiasts interested in the enjoyment, preservation, and restoration of Pontiac and Oakland automobiles.

2096 ● Pontiac-Oakland Club International, Emerald Valley Chapter [Oregon]
2411 Washington
Eugene, OR 97405
Ken W. Smith, Pres.   Ph:(503)485-0319

Founded: 1985. **Membership:** 52. Owners of Pontiac automobiles and other automobile enthusiasts. Promotes restoration and maintenance of Pontiacs. Assists in location of literature and parts. Conducts charitable and competitive car shows.

2097 ● Pontiac-Oakland Club International, Georgia Chapter
c/o Terry Hunt
139 Dials Dr.
Woodstock, GA 30188
Terry Hunt, Dir.   Ph:(404)929-2440

Persons interested in the history, restoration, and preservation of Pontiac and Oakland automobiles.

2098 ● Pontiac-Oakland Club International, Kansas Chapter
Rt. 3, Box 421
Rose Hill, KS 67133
Margaret Brinkley, Pres.   Ph:(316)776-2162

Individuals interested in collecting and preserving Oakland and Pontiac automobiles.

2099 ● Pontiac-Oakland Club International, Kansas City Arrowhead Chapter [Kansas and Missouri]
104 Center Dr.
Silver Lake, KS 66539

Founded: 1985. **Membership:** 40. Pontiac and Oakland automobiles owners in northeastern Kansas and western Missouri. Disseminates information; conducts charitable events; sponsors festival.

2100 ● Pontiac-Oakland Club International, National Capital Area [District of Columbia, Maryland, and Virginia]
c/o George Richardson
1509 Baltimore Rd.
Alexandria, VA 22308
George Richardson, Exec. Officer   Ph:(703)768-1569

Founded: 1979. **Membership:** 159. Pontiac automobile owners and enthusiasts in the District of Columbia, Maryland, and Virginia.

2101 ● Pontiac-Oakland Club International, Nebraskaland Chapter
1603 Nebraska Ave.
York, NE 68467
Jo Ann Kuester, Sec. Treas.   Ph:(402)362-6413

Founded: 1972. **Membership:** 30. To restore and enjoy Pontiac and Oakland automobiles.

2102 ● Pontiac-Oakland Club International, Southern California Chapter
c/o Daniel J. Santoro
419 Livingston Ave.
Placentia, CA 92670
Daniel J. Santoro, Exec. Officer   Ph:(714)524-8642

Owners of Oakland and Pontiac automobiles.

2103 ● Pontiac-Oakland Club International. Yankee Chapter [Maine, Massachusetts, and Rhode Island]
44 Old Brook Rd.
Lecminster, MA 01453
Steve Peluso, Editor   Ph:(508)537-7066

Founded: 1980. **Membership:** 150. Individuals in Maine, Massachusetts, and Rhode Island promoting restoration and preservation of Pontiac and Oakland automobiles.

2104 ● Pontiac-Oakland Club, Nutmeg Chapter [Connecticut]
Church Hill Rd.
Washington Depot, CT 06974
Starr F. Evans, Editor   Ph:(203)868-7723

Founded: 1976. **Membership:** 106. Owners of Pontiac-Oakland automobiles, built from 1909 to the present, organized to promote the model.

2105 ● Pontiac-Oakland Club, Western New York Chapter
50 Cramer St.
North Tonawanda, NY 14120
Brian Mertens, V. Pres.   Ph:(716)692-1564

Founded: 1976. **Membership:** 96. Owners and enthusiasts of

Pontiac/Oakland automobiles. To further the preservation of the automobiles.

PONTIAC 6000 (1987-91)

Introduced as part of A car line, along with Buick Century, Chevrolet Celebrity, and Oldsmobile Cutlass Calais. The 2-door coupe was discontinued after 1987 production year. The remaining vehicles in the lineup were produced at General Motors plant in Oklahoma City, Oklahoma until 1991.

MAJOR FEATURES

● Pontiac 6000 LE Sedan had as 1991 standard equipment: 3-speed automatic transmission, rack-and-pinion power steering, front independent suspension/rear rigid axle, front disc/rear drum power brakes, and AM/FM stereo.

● Pontiac 6000 LE Wagon added as 1991 standard equipment: 4-speed automatic transmission, upgraded suspension, and air conditioning.

● Pontiac 6000 S/E added as 1991 standard equipment: 15-inch aluminum wheels, power door locks and windows, and cruise control.

● Pontiac 6000 STE AWD had as 1990 standard equipment: 4-wheel drive.

PRICE HISTORY

The following new car prices reflect the approximate retail cost of the base model: **1987** - $10,499; **1988** - $11,199; **1989** - $11,969; **1990** - $12,149; **1991** - $12,999.

DIMENSIONS

Body Style	Years Avail	Wheel Base (in)	Lgth (in)	Ht (in)	Avg Wt (lbs)	Fuel Cap (gal)	Front Hdrm (in)	Front Legrm (in)
2d cpe	87-87	104.9	188.8	53.3	2,792	15.7	38.6	42.1
4d sdn	87-90	104.9	188.8	53.7	2,755	15.7	38.6	42.1
4d sdn	91-91	104.9	185.8	53.7	2,843	15.7	38.5	42.1
5d wgn	87-91	104.9	193.2	54.1	3,162	15.7	38.6	42.1

ENGINES

Type	Displacement (L)	Fuel Dly	HP @rpm	Torque @rpm (ft/lbs)	MPG Cty/Hwy	Years Avail
I-4	2.5	FI	112@4800	145@2100	24/31	87-87
I-4	2.5	FI	98@4800	135@3200	21/27	87-89
I-4	2.5	FI	110@5200	135@3200	22/31	90-91
V-6	2.8	FI	125@4500	160@3600	20/29	87-89
V-6	3.1	FI	140@4400	185@3200	19/30	89-91

KEY: I=in-line engine; V=V engine; F=flat engine; FI=fuel injection; bbl=barrel carburetor; T=turbo; D=diesel; HP=horsepower; MPG=estimated average miles per gallon.

EVALUATIONS, TESTS, AND RANKINGS

1989: "we like the 6000 AWD aesthetically, mechanically, and ergonomically. . .driving it was what we liked the most about the car." **Source**: "Pontiac 6000 STE AWD: The real beauty is under the skin," *Motor Trend*, July 1989, pp. 89-93, 128.

1988: "only steering flaw is a general numbness that provides very little input about the road's grip . . . 6000 provided impressively short stopping distances in the snow." **Source**: "Snow White and the Seven AWDs," *Road & Track*, May 1988, pp. 56-63, 67-70.

1988: "this is a great car made better the old-fashioned way, with shrewd engineering and careful development . . . braking performance was disappointing." **Source**: "Pontiac 6000 STE AWD," *Car and Driver*, March 1988, pp. 131-134.

RECALLS

1988: (27,369 passenger vehicles equipped with 2.8L V6 engine; includes several General Motors models): Fuel feed hose could leak at coupling on engine end of hose assembly. Fuel leakage into engine compartment could result in engine compartment fire that could spread to passenger compartment. **Corrective action**: Install new fuel feed hose assembly. *(NHTSA Campaign No. 88V164000.)*

1987: (39 cars; recall includes the Pontiac 6000 and Oldsmobile Cutlass): Poor bond adhesion between the windshield glass and mounting could allow the windshield to separate during a 30 mph frontal barrier test required by FMVSS 212. If windshield glass separation occurs during an accident, an unbelted occupant could be ejected from the vehicle and injured. **Corrective action**: Reinstall windshields to assure proper bond adhesion. *(NHTSA Campaign No. 87V034000.)*

1987: (6,004 passenger cars with anti-lock brakes. Recall includes the Cadillac DeVille, Oldsmobile 98, Buick Electra, Buick LeSabre, and Pontiac 6000): Anti-lock brake system (ABS) pressure/warning switch may exhibit brake fluid seepage which can lead to loss of brake system hydraulic pump motor. Additionally, hydraulic pump motor of ABS electrical relays may have been exposed to water contamination during vehicle assembly. Can cause loss of hydraulic pump motor and/or loss of ABS function. Loss of hydraulic pump would result in loss of rear brakes as well as power to assist to front brakes. **Corrective action**: ABS and hydraulic pump motor electrical relays and 30 amp fuses will be replaced. Hydraulic pump motor assembly and pressure/warning switch will be inspected and, if required, replaced. *(NHTSA Campaign No. 87V093000.)*

REPAIR MANUALS

2106 ● **Chilton's Chevrolet Cavalier, Buick Skyhawk, Olds Firenza, Cadillac Cimarron, Pontiac 6000, 1982-88**
Chilton Co.
Chilton Way
Radnor, PA 19089   Ph:(215)964-4000

Published 1988. **Price:** $15.95.

2107 ● **Chilton's Chevrolet Celebrity, Buick Century, Olds Cutlass Ciera, Pontiac 6000, 1982-1988**
Chilton Co.
Chilton Way
Radnor, PA 19089   Ph:(215)964-4000

Also available in Spanish edition. Published 1988. **Price:** $15.95.

2108 ● **Chilton's Cutlass 1970-1987**
Chilton Co.
Chilton Way
Radnor, PA 19089   Ph:(215)964-4000

Published 1987. **Price:** $15.95.

2109 ● **Get Your Pontiac Fixed Right**
Consumer Reports Books
51 E. 42nd St., Ste. 800
New York, NY 10017   Ph:(212)682-9280

Published 1990. **Price:** $8.95.

2110 ● GM A-Cars Buick Century, Chevrolet Celebrity, Oldsmobile Cutlass Ciera, Pontiac 6000, 1982-87: Shop Manual
Clymer Publications
P.O. Box 1209
Overland Park, KS 66212   Ph:(913)541-6694

Published 1987. **Price:** $14.95.

2111 ● Haynes General Motor A-Cars Owner's Workshop Manual, No. 829
Haynes Publishing, Inc.
861 Lawrence Dr.
Newbury Park, CA 91320   Ph:(818)889-5400

Published 1982 through 1989. **Price:** $15.95.

OTHER INFORMATION SOURCES

2112 ● Badger Chatter
Pontiac-Oakland Club International, Badger State Chapter
5223 84th St.
Kenosha, WI 53142   Ph:(414)694-2500

Monthly.

2113 ● Bison
Pontiac-Oakland Club, Western New York Chapter
50 Cramer St.
North Tonawanda, NY 14120   Ph:(716)692-1564

Newsletter. Monthly.

2114 ● Chiefly Pontiac
Hoosier Pontiac-Oakland Club
1856 Gray Rd.
Mooresville, IN 46158   Ph:(317)831-1568

Newsletter. Bimonthly.

2115 ● The Drumbeat
Pontiac-Oakland Club, Nutmeg Chapter
Church Hill Rd.
Washington Depot, CT 06974   Ph:(203)868-7723

Periodic.

2116 ● Finger Lakes News [New York]
Pontiac-Oakland Club, Finger Lakes Chapter
14 Judd Ln.
Hilton, NY 14468   Ph:(716)392-3808

Periodic.

2117 ● High Performance Pontiac
CSK Publishing Co., Inc.
299 Market St.   Ph:(201)712-9300
Saddle Brook, NJ 07662   Fax:(201)712-9899

Magazine for car enthusiasts, featuring collecting, restoring, modifying, and customizing of Pontiacs from 1950 to the present. Bimonthly. **Editor(s):** Sue Elliott. **Price:** $15.00/year; $3.25 per single issue.

2118 ● Hot Air
Pontiac-Oakland Club International, Arizona Chapter
4348 E. Timrod
Tucson, AZ 85711   Ph:(602)795-0978

Newsletter. Monthly.

2119 ● Illinois Newsletter
Pontiac-Oakland Club International, Illinois Chapter
R.R. 1, Box 220
Beecher, IL 60401   Ph:(708)258-6017

Monthly.

2120 ● Nebraskaland
Pontiac-Oakland Club International, Nebraskaland Chapter
1603 Nebraska Ave.
York, NE 68467   Ph:(402)362-6413

Newsletter. Bimonthly.

2121 ● On The Warpath
Pontiac-Oakland Club International, National Capital Area
1509 Baltimore Rd.
Alexandria, VA 22308   Ph:(703)768-1569

Newsletter. Bimonthly.

2122 ● Pontiac-Oakland Club International, Emerald Valley Chapter—Newsletter [Oregon]
Pontiac-Oakland Club International, Emerald Valley Chapter
2411 Washington
Eugene, OR 97405   Ph:(503)485-0319

Monthly.

2123 ● Pontiac-Oakland Club International, Garden State Chapter—Newsletter [New Jersey]
Pontiac-Oakland Club International, Garden State Chapter
19 Earl St.
Denville, NJ 07834

Newsletter. Bimonthly.

2124 ● Pontiac-Oakland Club International, Illinois Chapter—Annual Roster
Pontiac-Oakland Club International, Illinois Chapter
R.R. 1, Box 220
Beecher, IL 60401   Ph:(708)258-6017

2125 ● Pontiac-Oakland Club International, Kansas Chapter—Directory
Pontiac-Oakland Club International, Kansas Chapter
Rt. 3, Box 421
Rose Hill, KS 67133   Ph:(316)776-2162

Periodic.

2126 ● Pontiac-Oakland Club International, Kansas Chapter—Newsletter
Pontiac-Oakland Club International, Kansas Chapter
Rt. 3, Box 421
Rose Hill, KS 67133   Ph:(316)776-2162

Periodic.

2127 ● Pontiac-Oakland Club International, Kansas City Arrowhead Chapter—Directory [Kansas and Missouri]
Pontiac-Oakland Club International, Kansas City Arrowhead Chapter
104 Center Dr.
Silver Lake, KS 66539   Ph:(913)582-4207

Periodic

2128 ● Pontiac-Oakland Club International—Membership Roster
Pontiac-Oakland Club International
PO Box 4789
Culver City, CA 90230   Ph:(818)704-1580
Annual.

2129 ● Pontiac-Oakland Club International, North Coast Ohio Chapter— Newsletter
Pontiac-Oakland Club International, North Coast Ohio Chapter
2500 Hetzel Dr.
Parma, OH 44134   Ph:(216)888-4867
Periodic.

2130 ● Pontiac-Oakland Club International, Old Dominion Chapter—Newsletter [Virginia]
Pontiac-Oakland Club International, Old Dominion Chapter
1400 Fortingale Circle
Sandstom, VA 23150   Ph:(804)737-3139
Bimonthly.

2131 ● Pontiac-Oakland Club International, Yankee Chapter—Newsletter [Maine, Massachusetts, and Rhode Island]
Pontiac-Oakland Club International, Yankee Chapter
44 Old Brook Rd.
Leonminster, MA 01453   Ph:(508)537-7066
Monthly.

2132 ● The Scout
Pontiac-Oakland Club International, Kansas City Arrowhead Chapter
104 Center Dr.
Silver Lake, KS 66539   Ph:(913)582-4207
Newsletter. Monthly.

2133 ● Smoke Signals
Pontiac-Oakland Club International
PO Box 4789
Culver City, CA 90230   Ph:(818)704-1580
Aims to assist owners of Pontiac and Oakland automobiles with the restoration of their vehicles. Monthly. **Editor(s):** Larry Kummer, Editor and Publisher. **Price:** $22.00/yr.; $2.00/mo.

ASSOCIATIONS

2134 ● Pontiac-Oakland Club, Finger Lakes Chapter [New York]
14 Judd Ln.
Hilton, NY 14468
Deborah Arend, Sec.   Ph:(716)392-3808
Founded: 1972. Individuals interested in preserving and restoring Pontiac and Oakland automobiles manufactured between 1907 and the present.

2135 ● Pontiac-Oakland Club International
P.O. Box 4789
Culver City, CA 90230
Dick Hoyt, Exec.Sec.   Ph:(818)704-1580
Founded: 1972. **Membership:** 9,000. Persons interested in the history, restoration, and preservation of Pontiac and Oakland automobiles. Assists owners of Pontiac and Oakland automobiles with the restoration of their vehicles. Maintains staff of volunteer technical advisers. Conducts research pertaining to original specifications and production history.

Maintains library. Sponsors competitions; bestows trophies; provides computerized services. **Former Name(s):** (1973) Pontiac Owners Club International. **Convention/Meeting:** Annual conference and auto show.

2136 ● Pontiac-Oakland Club, International, Arizona Chapter
4348 E. Timrod
Tucson, AZ 85711
Thom Sherwood, Pres.   Ph:(602)795-0978
Founded: 1982. **Membership:** 100. Automotive enthusiasts interested in the enjoyment, preservation, and restoration of Pontiac and Oakland automobiles.

2137 ● Pontiac-Oakland Club International, Emerald Valley Chapter [Oregon]
2411 Washington
Eugene, OR 97405
Ken W. Smith, Pres.   Ph:(503)485-0319
Founded: 1985. **Membership:** 52. Owners of Pontiac automobiles and other automobile enthusiasts. Promotes restoration and maintenance of Pontiacs. Assists in location of literature and parts. Conducts charitable and competitive car shows.

2138 ● Pontiac-Oakland Club International, Georgia Chapter
c/o Terry Hunt
139 Dials Dr.
Woodstock, GA 30188
Terry Hunt, Dir.   Ph:(404)929-2440
Persons interested in the history, restoration, and preservation of Pontiac and Oakland automobiles.

2139 ● Pontiac-Oakland Club International, Kansas Chapter
Rt. 3, Box 421
Rose Hill, KS 67133
Margaret Brinkley, Pres.   Ph:(316)776-2162
Individuals interested in collecting and preserving Oakland and Pontiac automobiles.

2140 ● Pontiac-Oakland Club International, Kansas City Arrowhead Chapter [Kansas and Missouri]
104 Center Dr.
Silver Lake, KS 66539
Founded: 1985. **Membership:** 40. Pontiac and Oakland automobiles owners in northeastern Kansas and western Missouri. Disseminates information; conducts charitable events; sponsors festival.

2141 ● Pontiac-Oakland Club International, National Capital Area [District of Columbia, Maryland, and Virginia]
c/o George Richardson
1509 Baltimore Rd.
Alexandria, VA 22308
George Richardson, Exec. Officer   Ph:(703)768-1569
Founded: 1979. **Membership:** 159. Pontiac automobile owners and enthusiasts in the District of Columbia, Maryland, and Virginia.

2142 ● Pontiac-Oakland Club International, Nebraskaland Chapter

1603 Nebraska Ave.
York, NE 68467
Jo Ann Kuester, Sec. Treas.   Ph:(402)362-6413

Founded: 1972. **Membership:** 30. To restore and enjoy Pontiac and Oakland automobiles.

2143 ● Pontiac-Oakland Club International, Southern California Chapter

c/o Daniel J. Santoro
419 Livingston Ave.
Placentia, CA 92670
Daniel J. Santoro, Exec. Officer   Ph:(714)524-8642

Owners of Oakland and Pontiac automobiles.

2144 ● Pontiac-Oakland Club International, Yankee Chapter [Maine, Massachusetts, and Rhode Island]

44 Old Brook Rd.
Lecminster, MA 01453
Steve Peluso, Editor   Ph:(508)537-7066

Founded: 1980. **Membership:** 150. Individuals in Maine, Massachusetts, and Rhode Island promoting restoration and preservation of Pontiac and Oakland automobiles.

2145 ● Pontiac-Oakland Club, Nutmeg Chapter [Connecticut]

Church Hill Rd.
Washington Depot, CT 06974
Starr F. Evans, Editor   Ph:(203)868-7723

Founded: 1976. **Membership:** 106. Owners of Pontiac-Oakland automobiles, built from 1909 to the present, organized to promote the model.

2146 ● Pontiac-Oakland Club, Western New York Chapter

50 Cramer St.
North Tonawanda, NY 14120
Brian Mertens, V. Pres.   Ph:(716)692-1564

Founded: 1976. **Membership:** 96. Owners and enthusiasts of Pontiac/Oakland automobiles. To further the preservation of the automobiles.

PONTIAC BONNEVILLE (1987-92)

Four-door sedan is part of GM's H-car line, along with Buick LeSabre and Oldsmobile 88 Royale. The 1992 design is the first complete makeover and represents the 35th anniversary of the Bonneville nameplate. Produced at General Motors plant in Wentzville, Missouri. Named to *Car and Driver* 1987 Ten Best Cars list. Picked by *Motor Trend* as the best family sedan for 1990. Named to *Car and Driver* Ten Best Cars Nominees list for 1990. Received a very good mark for occupant injury history from *The Car Book* in 1992.

1992 Pontiac Bonneville SE

MAJOR FEATURES

● Pontiac Bonneville SE has as 1992 standard equipment: 4-speed automatic transmission, 4-wheel independent suspension, front disc/rear drum power brakes, rack-and-pinion power steering, theft-deterrent system, air conditioning, power windows and door locks, driver's side airbag, AM/FM stereo, and tilt-steering column.

● Pontiac Bonneville SSE adds as 1992 standard equipment: anti-lock brakes, 16-inch aluminum wheels, decklid spoiler, sport suspension, upgraded stereo system.

● Pontiac Bonneville SSEi adds as 1992 standard equipment: supercharged engine, traction control, passenger side air bag, leather seating, heated windshield, power sunroof, foglamps, and stereo system with compact disc player.

● Pontiac Bonneville LE had as 1991 standard equipment: 4-speed automatic transmission, 4-wheel independent suspension, front disc/rear drum power brakes, rack-and-pinion power steering, air conditioning, and AM/FM stereo.

PRICE HISTORY

The following new car prices reflect the approximate retail cost of the base model: **1987** - $13,399; **1988** - $14,099; **1989** - $14,829; **1990** - $15,774; **1991** - $16,834; **1992** - $18,599.

DIMENSIONS

Body Style	Years Avail	Wheel Base (in)	Lgth (in)	Ht (in)	Avg Wt (lbs)	Fuel Cap (gal)	Front Hdrm (in)	Front Legrm (in)
4d sdn	87-90	110.8	198.7	55.5	3,315	18.1	38.9	42.4
4d sdn	91-91	110.8	198.7	54.1	3,323	18.0	38.9	42.4
4d sdn	92-92	110.8	200.6	55.5	3,362	18.0	39.2	42.0

ENGINES

Type	Displacement (L)	Fuel Dly	HP @rpm	Torque @rpm (ft/lbs)	MPG Cty/Hwy	Years Avail
V-6	3.8	FI	150@4400	200@2000	19/29	87-88
V-6	3.8	FI	165@5200	210@2000	18/28	88-89
V-6	3.8	FI	165@4800	210@2000	18/28	90-91
V-6	3.8	FI	170@4800	220@3200	18/28	92-92
V-6	3.8	FI	205@4400	260@4800	16/25	92-92

KEY: I=in-line engine; V=V engine; F=flat engine; FI=fuel injection; bbl=barrel carburetor; T=turbo; D=diesel; HP=horsepower; MPG=estimated average miles per gallon.

EVALUATIONS, TESTS, AND RANKINGS

1992: "extremely fluid form . . . quality of the steering linkage also provides a sense of extraordinary straight-line stability . . . best thing about this car is the way it goes down the road." **Source:** "Pontiac Bonneville SSEi," *Automobile Magazine,* October 1991, p. 100.

1992: "there are serious improvements . . . new body has an aggressive look . . . "smooth" is Bonneville's operative word." **Source:** "Penguins and Pontiacs in Middle Age," *The New York Times,* September 15, 1991, Section 8, p. 14.

1992: "The supercharged V-6's strong suits are midrange performance—ideal for most suburban driving . . . predictable, competent handling . . . The interior is evolutionary in design." **Source:** "Pontiac Bonneville SSEi," *Road & Track,* November 1991, p. 56-60.

1992: "Inside, the SSEi bristles with thoughtful touches . . . spirited performance . . . highway ride quality is plush and pleasantly non-distracting." **Source:** "Pontiac Bonneville SSEi," *Motor Trend,* October 1991, pp. 70-71.

1992: "1992 is arguably the best of the run . . . had a solid feel and felt pressed to the road in high-speed cruising . . . ride comfort was good on regular roads." **Source:** "'92 Bonneville light years from predecessor," *The Flint Journal,* October 16, 1991, pp. B1-B2.

1992: "a more rigid but still very compliant ride over all surfaces . . . front seat support and driving position is excellent . . . gets high marks in all major areas: comfort, ride, handling and styling." **Source:** "'92 Bonneville a solid addition to sedan market," *The Detroit News,* July 31, 1991, pp. 1D, 2D.

1990: "pure family car offer[ing] technical sophistication, interior room, and handling and ride quality in a platform people can afford . . . Bonneville LE does it best." **Source:** "Top Ten New Car Buys—Domestic," *Motor Trend,* November 1989, pp. 80-83, 86-89.

1988: "impressive road car and comfortable large sedan . . . aerodynamically styled . . . wonderfully firm suspension . . . stable road handling and enjoyable ride." **Source:** "Bonneville SSE: An impressive road sedan," *The Detroit News,* April 27, 1988, pp. 1F-2F.

1988: "taut handling and well-bred road manners. . .SE has fallen off our Ten Best list this year. . .still consider it one of the most capable American touring sedans available." **Source:** "Life with Bonneville," *Car and Driver,* January 1988, pp. 121-123.

1987: "surprisingly good ergonomics and very comfortable seating position . . . there's too much understeer, the brakes are poor and there just isn't enough horsepower." **Source:** "This Sportin' Life," *Popular Mechanics,* January 1987, pp. 60-64, 114.

1987: "Pontiac Bonneville SE . . . Buick's venerable V-6 works hard but doesn't complain a bit. . .four-speed automatic transaxle makes all the right moves at the right time." **Source:** "Ten Best Cars: Fun work, but somebody's got to do it," *Car and Driver,* January 1987, pp. 36-41.

1987: "never driven a roomy, quiet comfortable sedan of anywhere near the Bonneville's size and weight that felt so good." **Source:** "Bonneville? Lemme tell ya," *The Detroit News,* June 3, 1987, pp. 1F-2F.

RECALLS

1992: (1,570 passenger cars with console shift automatic transmission): Transaxle shift control cable may disengage from shift control cable bracket, causing loss of gear indicator reference and shift selector operation. The disengaged cable could falsely indicate transmission gear position, creating the potential for an accident. **Corrective action:** Install a transaxle shift control cable retaining clip on the shift control cable bracket on top of transaxle. *(NHTSA Campaign No. 91V131000.)*

1992: (20,765 passenger cars; includes Oldsmobile Ninety Eight, Oldsmobile Eighty Eight, Buick Park Avenue, Pontiac Bonneville, and Buick LeSabre): When applied, the parking brake lever assembly may release one or more teeth, reducing the cable load to the rear brakes. Depending on the extent of the lever release and road level, the parking brake may not hold the vehicle, allowing it to roll. Vehicle does not comply with FMVSS 105. **Corrective action:** Replace parking brake lever assembly. *(NHTSA Campaign No. 91V167000.)*

1989: (1,655 passenger vehicles; includes several General Motors models): Fuel rollover valve assembly may not have been installed. In event of an accident in which vehicle becomes inverted missing valve could allow fuel spillage in excess of amount allowed by FMVSS 301 which could result in a fire. **Corrective action:** Replace fuel sender and pump assembly. *(NHTSA Campaign No. 88V143000.)*

1987: (5,162 cars): Intermittent headlamp circuit at low beam due to circuit breaker overheating. **Corrective action:** Revise foglamp circuit. *(NHTSA Campaign No. 87V103000.)*

1987: (479,715 cars; includes Pontiac, Oldsmobile, and Buick models): In line fusible link may melt down and ignite windshield washer fluid bottle bracket. **Corrective action:** Replace washer fluid bottle bracket. *(NHTSA Campaign No. 87V135000.)*

1987: (35,057 passenger vehicles; includes several General Motors models): Excessive accelerator cable friction may restrict cables free movement between accelerator pedal and throttle body. This could prevent throttle from returning to closed (idle) position when accelerator pedal is released; thus, engine speed would not decrease, and loss of accelerator control could result in an accident. **Corrective action:** Replace accelerator cable. *(NHTSA Campaign No. 88V080000.)*

SAFETY AND REPAIRS

1992: "GM Recalls Cars for Belt, Brake Ills," *Automotive News,* December 9, 1991, p. 43. **Note:** Parking brake may partially release after being set.

1987: "Car Clinic," *Popular Mechanics,* January 1990, p. 41. **Note:** Tip for valve clatter noise on 1987 3.8 liter Bonneville.

REPAIR MANUALS

2147 ● **Buick-Olds-Pontiac Full-Size, 1975-87**
Chilton Co.
Chilton Way
Radnor, PA 19089   Ph:(215)964-4000

Price: $14.95.

2148 ● **Get Your Pontiac Fixed Right**
Consumer Reports Books
51 E. 42nd St., Ste. 800
New York, NY 10017   Ph:(212)682-9280

Published 1990. **Price:** $8.95.

2149 ● **Haynes Buick, Olds, Pontiac, Full-Size Models: 1970-90**
Haynes Publications, Inc.
861 Lawrence Dr.
Newbury Park, CA 91320   Ph:(818)889-5400

Published 1989. **Price:** $15.95.

OTHER INFORMATION SOURCES

2150 ● **Badger Chatter**
Pontiac-Oakland Club International, Badger State Chapter
5223 84th St.
Kenosha, WI 53142   Ph:(414)694-2500

Monthly.

2151 ● Bison
Pontiac-Oakland Club, Western New York Chapter
50 Cramer St.
North Tonawanda, NY 14120   Ph:(716)692-1564

Newsletter. Monthly.

2152 ● Chiefly Pontiac
Hoosier Pontiac-Oakland Club
1856 Gray Rd.
Mooresville, IN 46158   Ph:(317)831-1568

Newsletter. Bimonthly.

2153 ● The Drumbeat
Pontiac-Oakland Club, Nutmeg Chapter
Church Hill Rd.
Washington Depot, CT 06974   Ph:(203)868-7723

Periodic.

2154 ● Finger Lakes News [New York]
Pontiac-Oakland Club, Finger Lakes Chapter
14 Judd Ln.
Hilton, NY 14468   Ph:(716)392-3808

Periodic.

2155 ● High Performance Pontiac
CSK Publishing Co., Inc.
299 Market St.   Ph:(201)712-9300
Saddle Brook, NJ 07662   Fax:(201)712-9899

Magazine for car enthusiasts, featuring collecting, restoring, modifying, and customizing of Pontiacs from 1950 to the present. Bimonthly. **Editor(s):** Sue Elliott. **Price:** $15.00/year; $3.25 per single issue.

2156 ● Hot Air
Pontiac-Oakland Club International, Arizona Chapter
4348 E. Timrod
Tucson, AZ 85711   Ph:(602)795-0978

Newsletter. Monthly.

2157 ● Illinois Newsletter
Pontiac-Oakland Club International, Illinois Chapter
R.R. 1, Box 220
Beecher, IL 60401   Ph:(708)258-6017

Monthly.

2158 ● Nebraskaland
Pontiac-Oakland Club International, Nebraskaland Chapter
1603 Nebraska Ave.
York, NE 68467   Ph:(402)362-6413

Newsletter. Bimonthly.

2159 ● On The Warpath
Pontiac-Oakland Club International, National Capital Area
1509 Baltimore Rd.
Alexandria, VA 22308   Ph:(703)768-1569

Newsletter. Bimonthly.

2160 ● Pontiac-Oakland Club International, Emerald Valley Chapter—Newsletter [Oregon]
Pontiac-Oakland Club International, Emerald Valley Chapter
2411 Washington
Eugene, OR 97405   Ph:(503)485-0319

Monthly.

2161 ● Pontiac-Oakland Club International, Garden State Chapter—Newsletter [New Jersey]
Pontiac-Oakland Club International, Garden State Chapter
19 Earl St.
Denville, NJ 07834

Newsletter. Bimonthly.

2162 ● Pontiac-Oakland Club International, Illinois Chapter—Annual Roster
Pontiac-Oakland Club International, Illinois Chapter
R.R. 1, Box 220
Beecher, IL 60401   Ph:(708)258-6017

2163 ● Pontiac-Oakland Club International, Kansas Chapter—Directory
Pontiac-Oakland Club International, Kansas Chapter
Rt. 3, Box 421
Rose Hill, KS 67133   Ph:(316)776-2162

Periodic.

2164 ● Pontiac-Oakland Club International, Kansas Chapter—Newsletter
Pontiac-Oakland Club International, Kansas Chapter
Rt. 3, Box 421
Rose Hill, KS 67133   Ph:(316)776-2162

Periodic.

2165 ● Pontiac-Oakland Club International, Kansas City Arrowhead Chapter—Directory [Kansas and Missouri]
Pontiac-Oakland Club International, Kansas City Arrowhead Chapter
104 Center Dr.
Silver Lake, KS 66539   Ph:(913)582-4207

Periodic

2166 ● Pontiac-Oakland Club International—Membership Roster
Pontiac-Oakland Club International
PO Box 4789
Culver City, CA 90230   Ph:(818)704-1580

Annual.

2167 ● Pontiac-Oakland Club International, North Coast Ohio Chapter— Newsletter
Pontiac-Oakland Club International, North Coast Ohio Chapter
2500 Hetzel Dr.
Parma, OH 44134   Ph:(216)888-4867

Periodic.

2168 ● Pontiac-Oakland Club International, Old Dominion Chapter—Newsletter [Virginia]
Pontiac-Oakland Club International, Old Dominion Chapter
1400 Fortingale Circle
Sandstom, VA 23150   Ph:(804)737-3139

Bimonthly.

2169 ● Pontiac-Oakland Club International, Yankee Chapter—Newsletter [Maine, Massachusetts, and Rhode Island]
Pontiac-Oakland Club International, Yankee Chapter
44 Old Brook Rd.
Leonminster, MA 01453   Ph:(508)537-7066

Monthly.

2170 ● **The Scout**
Pontiac-Oakland Club International, Kansas City
Arrowhead Chapter
104 Center Dr.
Silver Lake, KS 66539   Ph:(913)582-4207

Newsletter. Monthly.

2171 ● **Smoke Signals**
Pontiac-Oakland Club International
PO Box 4789
Culver City, CA 90230   Ph:(818)704-1580

Aims to assist owners of Pontiac and Oakland automobiles
with the restoration of their vehicles. Monthly. **Editor(s):** Larry
Kummer, Editor and Publisher. **Price:** $22.00/yr.; $2.00/mo.

ASSOCIATIONS

2172 ● **Pontiac-Oakland Club, Finger Lakes Chapter [New
    York]**
14 Judd Ln.
Hilton, NY 14468
Deborah Arend, Sec.   Ph:(716)392-3808

Founded: 1972. Individuals interested in preserving and
restoring Pontiac and Oakland automobiles manufactured
between 1907 and the present.

2173 ● **Pontiac-Oakland Club International**
P.O. Box 4789
Culver City, CA 90230
Dick Hoyt, Exec.Sec.   Ph:(818)704-1580

Founded: 1972. **Membership:** 9,000. Persons interested in the
history, restoration, and preservation of Pontiac and Oakland
automobiles. Assists owners of Pontiac and Oakland
automobiles with the restoration of their vehicles. Maintains
staff of volunteer technical advisers. Conducts research
pertaining to original specifications and production history.
Maintains library. Sponsors competitions; bestows trophies;
provides computerized services. **Former Name(s):** (1973)
Pontiac Owners Club International. **Convention/Meeting:**
Annual conference and auto show.

2174 ● **Pontiac-Oakland Club, International, Arizona
    Chapter**
4348 E. Timrod
Tucson, AZ 85711
Thom Sherwood, Pres.   Ph:(602)795-0978

Founded: 1982. **Membership:** 100. Automotive enthusiasts
interested in the enjoyment, preservation, and restoration of
Pontiac and Oakland automobiles.

2175 ● **Pontiac-Oakland Club International, Emerald Valley
    Chapter [Oregon]**
2411 Washington
Eugene, OR 97405
Ken W. Smith, Pres.   Ph:(503)485-0319

Founded: 1985. **Membership:** 52. Owners of Pontiac
automobiles and other automobile enthusiasts. Promotes
restoration and maintenance of Pontiacs. Assists in location of
literature and parts. Conducts charitable and competitive car
shows.

2176 ● **Pontiac-Oakland Club International, Georgia
    Chapter**
c/o Terry Hunt
139 Dials Dr.
Woodstock, GA 30188
Terry Hunt, Dir.   Ph:(404)929-2440

Persons interested in the history, restoration, and preservation
of Pontiac and Oakland automobiles.

2177 ● **Pontiac-Oakland Club International, Kansas Chapter**
Rt. 3, Box 421
Rose Hill, KS 67133
Margaret Brinkley, Pres.   Ph:(316)776-2162

Individuals interested in collecting and preserving Oakland and
Pontiac automobiles.

2178 ● **Pontiac-Oakland Club International, Kansas City
    Arrowhead Chapter [Kansas and Missouri]**
104 Center Dr.
Silver Lake, KS 66539

Founded: 1985. **Membership:** 40. Pontiac and Oakland
automobiles owners in northeastern Kansas and western
Missouri. Disseminates information; conducts charitable
events; sponsors festival.

2179 ● **Pontiac-Oakland Club International, National Capital
    Area [District of Columbia, Maryland, and Virginia]**
c/o George Richardson
1509 Baltimore Rd.
Alexandria, VA 22308
George Richardson, Exec. Officer   Ph:(703)768-1569

Founded: 1979. **Membership:** 159. Pontiac automobile owners
and enthusiasts in the District of Columbia, Maryland, and
Virginia.

2180 ● **Pontiac-Oakland Club International, Nebraskaland
    Chapter**
1603 Nebraska Ave.
York, NE 68467
Jo Ann Kuester, Sec. Treas.   Ph:(402)362-6413

Founded: 1972. **Membership:** 30. To restore and enjoy Pontiac
and Oakland automobiles.

2181 ● **Pontiac-Oakland Club International, Southern
    California Chapter**
c/o Daniel J. Santoro
419 Livingston Ave.
Placentia, CA 92670
Daniel J. Santoro, Exec. Officer   Ph:(714)524-8642

Owners of Oakland and Pontiac automobiles.

2182 ● **Pontiac-Oakland Club International, Yankee Chapter
    [Maine, Massachusetts, and Rhode Island]**
44 Old Brook Rd.
Lecminster, MA 01453
Steve Peluso, Editor   Ph:(508)537-7066

Founded: 1980. **Membership:** 150. Individuals in Maine,
Massachusetts, and Rhode Island promoting restoration and
preservation of Pontiac and Oakland automobiles.

2183 ● **Pontiac-Oakland Club, Nutmeg Chapter
    [Connecticut]**
Church Hill Rd.
Washington Depot, CT 06974
Starr F. Evans, Editor   Ph:(203)868-7723

Founded: 1976. **Membership:** 106. Owners of Pontiac-

Oakland automobiles, built from 1909 to the present, organized to promote the model.

2184 ● Pontiac-Oakland Club, Western New York Chapter
50 Cramer St.
North Tonawanda, NY 14120
Brian Mertens, V. Pres.   Ph:(716)692-1564

Founded: 1976. **Membership:** 96. Owners and enthusiasts of Pontiac/Oakland automobiles. To further the preservation of the automobiles.

PONTIAC FIERO (1987-88)

Plastic-body sports car produced at General Motors plant in Pontiac, Michigan. Because of sagging sales in final years, the Pontiac Fiero was discontinued in 1988.

MAJOR FEATURES

● Pontiac Fiero had as 1988 standard equipment: 5-speed manual transmission, 4-wheel disc brakes, and rack-and-pinion steering.

● Pontiac Fiero GT added as 1988 standard equipment: upgraded suspension.

● Pontiac Fiero Formula added as 1988 standard equipment: air conditioning, tilt steering, power windows, and AM/FM stereo.

PRICE HISTORY

The following new car prices reflect the approximate retail cost of the base model: **1987** - $8,299; **1988** - $8,999.

DIMENSIONS

Body Style	Years Avail	Wheel Base (in)	Lgth (in)	Ht (in)	Avg Wt (lbs)	Fuel Cap (gal)	Front Hdrm (in)	Front Legrm (in)
2d cpe	87-88	93.4	165.1	46.9	2,567	11.9	37.0	43.5

ENGINES

Type	Displacement (L)	Fuel Dly	HP @rpm	Torque @rpm (ft/lbs)	MPG Cty/Hwy	Years Avail
I-4	2.5	FI	98@4800	135@3200	24/35	87-88
V-6	2.8	FI	135@4500	165@3600	18/28	87-87
V-6	2.8	FI	135@4500	105@3600	17/27	88-88

KEY: I=in-line engine; V=V engine; F=flat engine; FI=fuel injection; bbl=barrel carburetor; T=turbo; D=diesel; HP=horsepower; MPG=estimated average miles per gallon.

EVALUATIONS, TESTS, AND RANKINGS

1988: "noticeable improvement over the 1987 Fiero, but still with a way to go." **Source:** "Fiero Formula vs MR2 Supercharged," *Road & Track,* October 1987, p. 55.

1988: "an agile, confident road-eater." **Source:** "The Gee Force," *Car and Driver,* April 1988, p. 45.

1987: "sporty image, economy, and a solid value for . . . those in the 2-seater car market." **Source:** "Pontiac Fiero GT: A champagne sports car on a light beer budget," *Motor Trend,* January 1987, p. 85.

RECALLS

1987-88: (244,000 cars; includes models made before 1987): Due to interaction of engine compartment environment and maintenance or service related factors, there is an unreasonable risk of connecting rod failure and engine compartment fires. Fire can spread to passenger compartment and injure occupants. **Corrective action:** Correct or install new engine components to prevent unreasonable fire risk. *(NHTSA Campaign No. 89V232000.)*

1987-88: (102,162 cars with 2.8L 6 cylinder engines; includes models made before 1987): Various fluid leaks and service related factors could cause engine fires. **Corrective action:** Correct or install new components to prevent unreasonable fire risk. *(NHTSA Campaign No. 90V104000.)*

REPAIR MANUALS

2185 ● Get Your Pontiac Fixed Right
Consumer Reports Books
51 E. 42nd St., Ste. 800
New York, NY 10017   Ph:(212)682-9280

Published 1990. **Price:** $8.95.

2186 ● Haynes Pontiac Fiero Owners Workshop Manual, No. 1232: 1984-1988
Haynes Publications, Inc.
861 Lawrence Dr.
Newbury Park, CA 91320   Ph:(818)889-5400

Published 1986. **Editor(s):** J. H. Haynes and Mike Stubblefield. **Price:** $15.95.

2187 ● Pontiac Fiero 1984-1988
Chilton Co.
Chilton Way
Radnor, PA 19089   Ph:(215)964-4000

Published 1989. **Price:** $15.95.

OTHER INFORMATION SOURCES

2188 ● Badger Chatter
Pontiac-Oakland Club International, Badger State Chapter
5223 84th St.
Kenosha, WI 53142   Ph:(414)694-2500

Monthly.

2189 ● Bison
Pontiac-Oakland Club, Western New York Chapter
50 Cramer St.
North Tonawanda, NY 14120   Ph:(716)692-1564

Newsletter. Monthly.

2190 ● Chiefly Pontiac
Hoosier Pontiac-Oakland Club
1856 Gray Rd.
Mooresville, IN 46158   Ph:(317)831-1568

Newsletter. Bimonthly.

2191 ● The Drumbeat
Pontiac-Oakland Club, Nutmeg Chapter
Church Hill Rd.
Washington Depot, CT 06974   Ph:(203)868-7723

Periodic.

2192 ● Fiero Owner
Fiero Owners Club of America
1541 Ritchey St.
Santa Ana, CA 92705-4730   Ph:(714)953-9400

Serves as a clearinghouse for information about Fiero automobiles produced by Pontiac since 1984. Covers technical aspects of the car, repair information, and news of rallies and local chapters. Quarterly. **Editor(s):** Philip Huff, Publisher.

2193 ● Fiero Owner
Fiero Owners Club of America
1541 S. Ritchey
Santa Ana, CA 92705   Ph:(714)953-9400

Magazine including updates and modification information. Quarterly.

2194 ● Fiero Secrets
Worldwide Fiero Club
835 E. 23rd Ave.
New Smyrna Beach, FL 32169

Newsletter. Quarterly.

2195 ● Finger Lakes News [New York]
Pontiac-Oakland Club, Finger Lakes Chapter
14 Judd Ln.
Hilton, NY 14468   Ph:(716)392-3808

Periodic.

2196 ● High Performance Pontiac
CSK Publishing Co., Inc.
299 Market St.
Saddle Brook, NJ 07662   Ph:(201)712-9300
                                Fax:(201)712-9899

Magazine for car enthusiasts, featuring collecting, restoring, modifying, and customizing of Pontiacs from 1950 to the present. Bimonthly. **Editor(s):** Sue Elliott. **Price:** $15.00/year; $3.25 per single issue.

2197 ● Hot Air
Pontiac-Oakland Club International, Arizona Chapter
4348 E. Timrod
Tucson, AZ 85711   Ph:(602)795-0978

Newsletter. Monthly.

2198 ● Illinois Newsletter
Pontiac-Oakland Club International, Illinois Chapter
R.R. 1, Box 220
Beecher, IL 60401   Ph:(708)258-6017

Monthly.

2199 ● Nebraskaland
Pontiac-Oakland Club International, Nebraskaland Chapter
1603 Nebraska Ave.
York, NE 68467   Ph:(402)362-6413

Newsletter. Bimonthly.

2200 ● On The Warpath
Pontiac-Oakland Club International, National Capital Area
1509 Baltimore Rd.
Alexandria, VA 22308   Ph:(703)768-1569

Newsletter. Bimonthly.

2201 ● Pontiac-Oakland Club International, Emerald Valley Chapter—Newsletter [Oregon]
Pontiac-Oakland Club International, Emerald Valley Chapter
2411 Washington
Eugene, OR 97405   Ph:(503)485-0319

Monthly.

2202 ● Pontiac-Oakland Club International, Garden State Chapter—Newsletter [New Jersey]
Pontiac-Oakland Club International, Garden State Chapter
19 Earl St.
Denville, NJ 07834

Newsletter. Bimonthly.

2203 ● Pontiac-Oakland Club International, Illinois Chapter—Annual Roster
Pontiac-Oakland Club International, Illinois Chapter
R.R. 1, Box 220
Beecher, IL 60401   Ph:(708)258-6017

2204 ● Pontiac-Oakland Club International, Kansas Chapter—Directory
Pontiac-Oakland Club International, Kansas Chapter
Rt. 3, Box 421
Rose Hill, KS 67133   Ph:(316)776-2162

Periodic.

2205 ● Pontiac-Oakland Club International, Kansas Chapter—Newsletter
Pontiac-Oakland Club International, Kansas Chapter
Rt. 3, Box 421
Rose Hill, KS 67133   Ph:(316)776-2162

Periodic.

2206 ● Pontiac-Oakland Club International, Kansas City Arrowhead Chapter—Directory [Kansas and Missouri]
Pontiac-Oakland Club International, Kansas City Arrowhead Chapter
104 Center Dr.
Silver Lake, KS 66539   Ph:(913)582-4207

Periodic

2207 ● Pontiac-Oakland Club International—Membership Roster
Pontiac-Oakland Club International
PO Box 4789
Culver City, CA 90230   Ph:(818)704-1580

Annual.

2208 ● Pontiac-Oakland Club International, North Coast Ohio Chapter— Newsletter
Pontiac-Oakland Club International, North Coast Ohio Chapter
2500 Hetzel Dr.
Parma, OH 44134   Ph:(216)888-4867

Periodic.

2209 ● Pontiac-Oakland Club International, Old Dominion Chapter—Newsletter [Virginia]
Pontiac-Oakland Club International, Old Dominion Chapter
1400 Fortingale Circle
Sandstom, VA 23150   Ph:(804)737-3139

Bimonthly.

2210 ● Pontiac-Oakland Club International, Yankee Chapter—Newsletter [Maine, Massachusetts, and Rhode Island]
Pontiac-Oakland Club International, Yankee Chapter
44 Old Brook Rd.
Leonminster, MA 01453   Ph:(508)537-7066

Monthly.

2211 ● The Scout
Pontiac-Oakland Club International, Kansas City
Arrowhead Chapter
104 Center Dr.
Silver Lake, KS 66539   Ph:(913)582-4207

Newsletter. Monthly.

2212 ● Smoke Signals
Pontiac-Oakland Club International
PO Box 4789
Culver City, CA 90230   Ph:(818)704-1580

Aims to assist owners of Pontiac and Oakland automobiles with the restoration of their vehicles. Monthly. **Editor(s):** Larry Kummer, Editor and Publisher. **Price:** $22.00/yr.; $2.00/mo.

ASSOCIATIONS

2213 ● Fiero Owners Club of America
1541 S. Ritchey
Santa Ana, CA 92705
Phil Huff, Dir.   Ph:(714)953-9400

Founded: 1983. **Membership:** 5,500. Pontiac Fiero automobile owners interested in learning more about the Fiero, produced by Pontiac between 1984 and 1988. Provides a network for the sharing of knowledge and information through publications, rallies, conventions, and local chapters. Bestows awards; maintains museum-archive. **Convention/Meeting:** Annual Fiero festival (with exhibits).

2214 ● Pontiac-Oakland Club, Finger Lakes Chapter [New York]
14 Judd Ln.
Hilton, NY 14468
Deborah Arend, Sec.   Ph:(716)392-3808

Founded: 1972. Individuals interested in preserving and restoring Pontiac and Oakland automobiles manufactured between 1907 and the present.

2215 ● Pontiac-Oakland Club International
P.O. Box 4789
Culver City, CA 90230
Dick Hoyt, Exec.Sec.   Ph:(818)704-1580

Founded: 1972. **Membership:** 9,000. Persons interested in the history, restoration, and preservation of Pontiac and Oakland automobiles. Assists owners of Pontiac and Oakland automobiles with the restoration of their vehicles. Maintains staff of volunteer technical advisers. Conducts research pertaining to original specifications and production history. Maintains library. Sponsors competitions; bestows trophies; provides computerized services. **Former Name(s):** (1973) Pontiac Owners Club International. **Convention/Meeting:** Annual conference and auto show.

2216 ● Pontiac-Oakland Club, International, Arizona Chapter
4348 E. Timrod
Tucson, AZ 85711
Thom Sherwood, Pres.   Ph:(602)795-0978

Founded: 1982. **Membership:** 100. Automotive enthusiasts

interested in the enjoyment, preservation, and restoration of Pontiac and Oakland automobiles.

2217 ● Pontiac-Oakland Club International, Emerald Valley Chapter [Oregon]
2411 Washington
Eugene, OR 97405
Ken W. Smith, Pres.   Ph:(503)485-0319

Founded: 1985. **Membership:** 52. Owners of Pontiac automobiles and other automobile enthusiasts. Promotes restoration and maintenance of Pontiacs. Assists in location of literature and parts. Conducts charitable and competitive car shows.

2218 ● Pontiac-Oakland Club International, Georgia Chapter
c/o Terry Hunt
139 Dials Dr.
Woodstock, GA 30188
Terry Hunt, Dir.   Ph:(404)929-2440

Persons interested in the history, restoration, and preservation of Pontiac and Oakland automobiles.

2219 ● Pontiac-Oakland Club International, Kansas Chapter
Rt. 3, Box 421
Rose Hill, KS 67133
Margaret Brinkley, Pres.   Ph:(316)776-2162

Individuals interested in collecting and preserving Oakland and Pontiac automobiles.

2220 ● Pontiac-Oakland Club International, Kansas City Arrowhead Chapter [Kansas and Missouri]
104 Center Dr.
Silver Lake, KS 66539

Founded: 1985. **Membership:** 40. Pontiac and Oakland automobiles owners in northeastern Kansas and western Missouri. Disseminates information; conducts charitable events; sponsors festival.

2221 ● Pontiac-Oakland Club International, National Capital Area [District of Columbia, Maryland, and Virginia]
c/o George Richardson
1509 Baltimore Rd.
Alexandria, VA 22308
George Richardson, Exec. Officer   Ph:(703)768-1569

Founded: 1979. **Membership:** 159. Pontiac automobile owners and enthusiasts in the District of Columbia, Maryland, and Virginia.

2222 ● Pontiac-Oakland Club International, Nebraskaland Chapter
1603 Nebraska Ave.
York, NE 68467
Jo Ann Kuester, Sec. Treas.   Ph:(402)362-6413

Founded: 1972. **Membership:** 30. To restore and enjoy Pontiac and Oakland automobiles.

2223 ● Pontiac-Oakland Club International, Southern California Chapter
c/o Daniel J. Santoro
419 Livingston Ave.
Placentia, CA 92670
Daniel J. Santoro, Exec. Officer   Ph:(714)524-8642

Owners of Oakland and Pontiac automobiles.

2224 ● Pontiac-Oakland Club International. Yankee Chapter [Maine, Massachusetts, and Rhode Island]
44 Old Brook Rd.
Lecminster, MA 01453
Steve Peluso, Editor   Ph:(508)537-7066

Founded: 1980. **Membership:** 150. Individuals in Maine, Massachusetts, and Rhode Island promoting restoration and preservation of Pontiac and Oakland automobiles.

2225 ● Pontiac-Oakland Club, Nutmeg Chapter [Connecticut]
Church Hill Rd.
Washington Depot, CT 06974
Starr F. Evans, Editor   Ph:(203)868-7723

Founded: 1976. **Membership:** 106. Owners of Pontiac-Oakland automobiles, built from 1909 to the present, organized to promote the model.

2226 ● Pontiac-Oakland Club, Western New York Chapter
50 Cramer St.
North Tonawanda, NY 14120
Brian Mertens, V. Pres.   Ph:(716)692-1564

Founded: 1976. **Membership:** 96. Owners and enthusiasts of Pontiac/Oakland automobiles. To further the preservation of the automobiles.

2227 ● Worldwide Fiero Club
835 E. 23rd Ave.
New Smyrna Beach, FL 32169
Matt Gruber, Pres.

Founded: 1984. **Membership:** 500. Owners and fans of the Fiero, a sports car manufactured by Pontiac from 1984 to 1988. Purposes are to: mediate the exchange of information; provide technical information on service and modifications; obtain quantity prices on parts and supplies. Researches and tests products. **Former Name(s):** (1985) National Fiero Owners' Association.

PONTIAC FIREBIRD (1987-92)

Introduced as part of the General Motors F-car line, along with its corporate twin the Chevrolet Camaro. A convertible version of the Firebird was introduced in mid-1991. Produced at the General Motors plant in Van Nuys, California, the Pontiac Firebird is also sold under Formula and Trans Am model versions.

1991 Pontiac Trans Am GTA

MAJOR FEATURES

● Pontiac Firebird 1992 standard equipment includes: 5-speed manual transmission, rack-and-pinion power steering, front disc/rear drum power brakes, driver's side airbag and security system.

● Pontiac Firebird Formula adds as 1992 standard equipment: sport suspension and air conditioning.

● Pontiac Trans Am adds as 1992 standard equipment: Rally Tuned Suspension, diamond spoke wheels, air conditioning, and the Aero Package with side treatment.

● Pontiac Trans Am GTA adds as 1992 standard equipment: 4-speed automatic transmission, sport suspension, diamond spoke wheels, air conditioning, Aero Package with side treatment, power door locks and windows, cruise control, power antenna, upgraded stereo system, and rear window defogger.

● Pontiac Formula Firehawk is a street-legal, SLP-modified Firebird. It has as 1992 standard equipment: 5.7 liter V-8 engine, 6-speed manual tansmission, independent front suspension, power-assisted steering, four-wheel disc brakes, cast aluminum wheels, and Firestone Firehawk tires.

PRICE HISTORY

The following new car prices reflect the approximate retail cost of the base model: **1987** - $10,359; **1988** - $10,999; **1989** - $11,999; **1990** - $11,985; **1991** - $12,690; **1992** - $12,505.

DIMENSIONS

Body Style	Years Avail	Wheel Base (in)	Lgth (in)	Ht (in)	Avg Wt (lbs)	Fuel Cap (gal)	Front Hdrm (in)	Front Legrm (in)
2d cpe	87-90	101.0	188.0	49.7	3,105	15.5	37.0	43.0
2d cpe	91-92	101.0	195.1	49.7	3,121	15.5	37.0	43.0
3d cpe	87-90	101.0	191.6	49.7	3,274	16.2	37.0	43.0
2d conv	91-92	101.0	195.1	49.7	3,280	15.5	37.0	43.0

ENGINES

Type	Displace- ment (L)	Fuel Dly	HP @rpm	Torque @rpm (ft/lbs)	MPG Cty/Hwy	Years Avail
V-6	2.8	FI	135@4900	160@3900	18/27	87-89
V-6	3.1	FI	140@4400	180@3600	18/27	90-91
V-6	3.1	FI	140@4400	185@3200	17/27	92-92
V-6T	3.8	FI	250@4400	340@2800	na	89-89
V-8	5.0	4-bbl	155@4200	245@2000	16/25	87-87
V-8	5.0	4-bbl	165@4400	250@2400	16/26	87-87
V-8	5.7	FI	210@4000	315@3200	16/25	87-87
V-8	5.0	FI	190@4000	290@2800	17/25	88-89
V-8	5.7	FI	225@4400	330@3200	17/25	88-89
V-8	5.0	FI	170@4000	255@2400	17/26	88-92
V-8	5.0	FI	215@4400	285@3200	na	89-89
V-8	5.7	FI	235@4400	340@3200	na	89-89
V-8	5.0	FI	230@4400	300@3200	na	89-91
V-8	5.0	FI	205@4200	285@3200	16/26	90-92
V-8	5.7	FI	240@4400	340@3200	17/25	90-92

KEY: I=in-line engine; V=V engine; F=flat engine; FI=fuel injection; bbl=barrel carburetor; T=turbo; D=diesel; HP=horsepower; MPG=estimated average miles per gallon.

EVALUATIONS, TESTS, AND RANKINGS

1992: "0-60 mph was acheived in a breathtaking 4.9 seconds ... sole performance disappointment was in braking ... The car is noisy, due to the stiff suspension and powerful V-8 ... virtually no body roll." **Source:** "Firebird Firepower [Pontiac Formula Firehawk]," *Motor Trend,* December 1991, p. 50-52.

1991: "A very powerful engine that provides impressive acceleration ... Reasonably low purchase price ... poor ergonomics." **Source:** "Pontiac Firebird 5.7: Shakes, Rattles, but Really Rolls," *Autoweek's Autofile 1991 Edition*, 1990, pp. 46-50.

1991: "plenty of torque at any rpm . . . and handling to back it all up." **Source:** "Here's one Firebird that can really fly," *Popular Mechanics*, September 1991, p. 96.

1991: "Wind buffeting is quite low at freeway speeds . . . radio . . . easily has the power to impress even mega-amp boombox fans at stoplights . . . blind spots created by the top's fabric . . . can easily hide a good-size car." **Source:** "Top-Down Showdown: We test the hottest cars under the sun," *Motor Trend*, June 1991, pp. 49-59, 62-63.

1991: "new drop-top edition . . . is noisy. It gulps gas . . . sport suspension will jar your dentures loose . . . But, boy, is it fun to drive." **Source:** "Soft-Top Firebird Has Youthful Spirit," *Detroit Free Press*, July 11, 1991, p. 11D.

1990: "What the Trans Am lacks in refinement, it more than makes up for with great howling blasts of acceleration." **Source:** "Bang for the Buck," *Motor Trend*, November 1989, pp. 42-46, 48, 52-55, 58-59, 62, 64, 66-68, 72, 76.

1989: "Trans Am Turbo . . . a balanced machine, with brakes and handling to match its awesome power." **Source:** "Motown Muscle," *Popular Mechanics*, January 1989, pp. 53-57, 116.

1989: "Firebird suspension and handling were real standouts. On the banking, at speed . . . was so precise it was hard to believe . . . steering was exactly linear." **Source:** "Top-Speed 10: Indulging our go-fast festish again," *Motor Trend*, September 1988, pp. 32-39, 42, 44.

1988: "transmission is the most precise-shifting . . . clear winner in both speed and handling . . . ride characteristics . . . on the harsh side." **Source:** "Playing the Ponycars," *Motor Trend*, January 1988, pp. 82-89.

1987: "handles like a go-cart but does not ride like one . . . ride is agreeably smooth." **Source:** "Joy: the Trans Am GTA: It's just the car to wander Indiana in search of an Outlaw race," *The Detroit News*, May 6, 1987, pp. 1F-2F.

1987: "preferred the Formula's ride to those of its competitors in most circumstances . . . could use more steering feel." **Source:** "The Best American GT: Camaro versus Mustang versus Firebird—and don't spare the brass knuckles," *Car and Driver*, June 1987, pp. 40-45, 47.

RECALLS

1991: (21 vehicles): Poor bond adhesion between windshield glass and mounting, which could allow the windshield to separate from vehicle during a collision. **Corrective action:** Remove all sealer from windshield and mounting; apply new bonding and sealant material, and reinstall windshield. *(NHTSA Campaign No. 91V031000.)*

1991: (40,696 coupes and convertibles; includes the Chevrolet Camaro and Pontiac Firebird): Metal latchplates may not engage the safety belt buckle assemblies. Movement of the seat occupant in this situation could cause latchplate release from the buckle subjecting the occupant to increased risk of injury in the event of a sudden stop or accident. **Corrective action:** Replace the retractor assembly for the safety belt (front and rear in coupes, and front only in convertibles). *(NHTSA Campaign No. 91V067000.)*

1990: (10,297 cars with 5.0L and 5.7L V8 engines; includes Chevrolet and Pontiac models): Fuel feed hoses may pull out of crimped coupling at engine allowing fuel leakage. **Corrective action:** Install a properly crimped fuel return hose. *(NHTSA Campaign No. 90V114000.)*

1988-89: (29,331 cars with 2.8L V6 engines; includes

Chevrolet and Pontiac models): Fuel feed hoses may pull out of crimped coupling at engine allowing fuel leakage. **Corrective action:** Install a redesigned fuel feed hose. *(NHTSA Campaign No. 90V115000.)*

1987-90: (1,500,000 cars; includes Chevrolet and Pontiac models; includes models made before 1987): Lack of ultraviolet stabilizer in plastic components of safety belt buckle assemblies could allow sunlight to weaken components. **Corrective action:** Replace or repair seat belt buckle. *(NHTSA Campaign No. 90V105000.)*

SAFETY AND REPAIRS

1987: "Car Clinic," *Popular Mechanics*, August 1990, p. 26. **Note:** Tip for clashing starter motor gears in 1987-88 General Motors 4.3, 5.0, and 5.7 liter engines.

REPAIR MANUALS

2228 ● Camaro 228 and Firebird Trans Am Shop Manual, 1982-1987
Clymer Publications
P.O. Box 1209
Overland Park, KS 66212   Ph:(913)541-6694

Published 1989. **Editor(s):** Kalton C. Lahue. **Price:** $14.95.

2229 ● Camaro and Firebird, 1982-1987: Super Shop Manual
Clymer Publications
P.O. Box 1209
Overland Park, KS 66212   Ph:(913)541-6694

Published 1988. **Editor(s):** Alan Ahlstrand. **Price:** $26.95.

2230 ● Chilton's Firebird, 1982-90: Repair and Tuneup Guide
Chilton Co.
Chilton Way
Radnor, PA 19089   Ph:(215)964-4000

Published 1990. **Price:** $15.95.

2231 ● General Motors 8-Cylinder
Peter Allen Video Productions
38-C Otis St.
West Babylon, NY 11704   Ph:(516)643-4372

A program demonstrating basic maintenance and tune-up procedures for the entitled engine. **Release date:** 1986. **Producer:** Peter Allen Productions. **Acquisition:** Purchase.

2232 ● Get Your Pontiac Fixed Right
Consumer Reports Books
51 E. 42nd St., Ste. 800
New York, NY 10017   Ph:(212)682-9280

Published 1990. **Price:** $8.95.

2233 ● Haynes Pontiac Firebird Owners Workshop Manual, No. 867: 1982-1989
Haynes Publications, Inc.
861 Lawrence Dr.
Newbury Park, CA 91320   Ph:(818)889-5400

Editor(s): J. H. Haynes and J. B. Raffa. **Price:** $15.95.

OTHER INFORMATION SOURCES

2234 ● Badger Chatter
Pontiac-Oakland Club International, Badger State Chapter
5223 84th St.
Kenosha, WI 53142   Ph:(414)694-2500

Monthly.

2235 ● Bison
Pontiac-Oakland Club, Western New York Chapter
50 Cramer St.
North Tonawanda, NY 14120   Ph:(716)692-1564

Newsletter. Monthly.

2236 ● Chiefly Pontiac
·Hoosier Pontiac-Oakland Club
1856 Gray Rd.
Mooresville, IN 46158   Ph:(317)831-1568

Newsletter. Bimonthly.

2237 ● The Drumbeat
Pontiac-Oakland Club, Nutmeg Chapter
Church Hill Rd.
Washington Depot, CT 06974   Ph:(203)868-7723

Periodic.

2238 ● The Eagle
National Firebird Club
P.O. Box 11238
Chicago, IL 60611

Newsletter. Includes calendar of events and membership list updates. Quarterly. **Price:** Included in membership dues.

2239 ● Finger Lakes News [New York]
Pontiac-Oakland Club, Finger Lakes Chapter
14 Judd Ln.
Hilton, NY 14468   Ph:(716)392-3808

Periodic.

2240 ● High Performance Pontiac
CSK Publishing Co., Inc.
299 Market St.   Ph:(201)712-9300
Saddle Brook, NJ 07662   Fax:(201)712-9899

Magazine for car enthusiasts, featuring collecting, restoring, modifying, and customizing of Pontiacs from 1950 to the present. Bimonthly. **Editor(s):** Sue Elliott. **Price:** $15.00/year; $3.25 per single issue.

2241 ● Hot Air
Pontiac-Oakland Club International, Arizona Chapter
4348 E. Timrod
Tucson, AZ 85711   Ph:(602)795-0978

Newsletter. Monthly.

2242 ● Illinois Newsletter
Pontiac-Oakland Club International, Illinois Chapter
R.R. 1, Box 220
Beecher, IL 60401   Ph:(708)258-6017

Monthly.

2243 ● Nebraskaland
Pontiac-Oakland Club International, Nebraskaland Chapter
1603 Nebraska Ave.
York, NE 68467   Ph:(402)362-6413

Newsletter. Bimonthly.

2244 ● On The Warpath
Pontiac-Oakland Club International, National Capital Area
1509 Baltimore Rd.
Alexandria, VA 22308   Ph:(703)768-1569

Newsletter. Bimonthly.

2245 ● Pontiac-Oakland Club International, Emerald Valley Chapter—Newsletter [Oregon]
Pontiac-Oakland Club International, Emerald Valley Chapter
2411 Washington
Eugene, OR 97405   Ph:(503)485-0319

Monthly.

2246 ● Pontiac-Oakland Club International, Garden State Chapter—Newsletter [New Jersey]
Pontiac-Oakland Club International, Garden State Chapter
19 Earl St.
Denville, NJ 07834

Newsletter. Bimonthly.

2247 ● Pontiac-Oakland Club International, Illinois Chapter—Annual Roster
Pontiac-Oakland Club International, Illinois Chapter
R.R. 1, Box 220
Beecher, IL 60401   Ph:(708)258-6017

2248 ● Pontiac-Oakland Club International, Kansas Chapter—Directory
Pontiac-Oakland Club International, Kansas Chapter
Rt. 3, Box 421
Rose Hill, KS 67133   Ph:(316)776-2162

Periodic.

2249 ● Pontiac-Oakland Club International, Kansas Chapter—Newsletter
Pontiac-Oakland Club International, Kansas Chapter
Rt. 3, Box 421
Rose Hill, KS 67133   Ph:(316)776-2162

Periodic.

2250 ● Pontiac-Oakland Club International, Kansas City Arrowhead Chapter—Directory [Kansas and Missouri]
Pontiac-Oakland Club International, Kansas City Arrowhead Chapter
104 Center Dr.
Silver Lake, KS 66539   Ph:(913)582-4207

Periodic

2251 ● Pontiac-Oakland Club International—Membership Roster
Pontiac-Oakland Club International
PO Box 4789
Culver City, CA 90230   Ph:(818)704-1580

Annual.

2252 ● Pontiac-Oakland Club International, North Coast Ohio Chapter— Newsletter
Pontiac-Oakland Club International, North Coast Ohio Chapter
2500 Hetzel Dr.
Parma, OH 44134   Ph:(216)888-4867

Periodic.

2253 ● Pontiac-Oakland Club International, Old Dominion Chapter—Newsletter [Virginia]
Pontiac-Oakland Club International, Old Dominion Chapter
1400 Fortingale Circle
Sandstom, VA 23150   Ph:(804)737-3139

Bimonthly.

2254 ● Pontiac-Oakland Club International, Yankee Chapter—Newsletter [Maine, Massachusetts, and Rhode Island]
Pontiac-Oakland Club International, Yankee Chapter
44 Old Brook Rd.
Leominster, MA 01453   Ph:(508)537-7066

Monthly.

2255 ● The Scout
Pontiac-Oakland Club International, Kansas City
Arrowhead Chapter
104 Center Dr.
Silver Lake, KS 66539   Ph:(913)582-4207

Newsletter. Monthly.

2256 ● Smoke Signals
Pontiac-Oakland Club International
PO Box 4789
Culver City, CA 90230   Ph:(818)704-1580

Aims to assist owners of Pontiac and Oakland automobiles with the restoration of their vehicles. Monthly. **Editor(s):** Larry Kummer, Editor and Publisher. **Price:** $22.00/yr.; $2.00/mo.

2257 ● Trans Ammer
Trans Am Club U.S.A. (TCUSA)
P.O. Box 99, Tufts Univ. Br.
Medford, MA 02153   Ph:(617)396-4424

Quarterly.

2258 ● TransAm Club U.S.A.—National Register
TransAm Club U.S.A.
PO Box 99
Tufts Univ. Branch
Medford, MA 02153   Ph:(617)396-4424

About 500 Pontiac TransAm, Formula, and Firebird automobile owners. Annual. **Editor(s):** Dick Hoyt.

ASSOCIATIONS

2259 ● National Firebird Club
P.O. Box 11238
Chicago, IL 60611
Thomas R. Scherer, Chm.

Founded: 1984. **Membership:** 1,500. Owners of Firebird automobiles, produced since 1967 by the Pontiac division of the General Motors Corporation. Promotes the magic of Firebird. Disseminates technical and historical information on the Firebird; acts as a Firebird registry. Conducts technical sessions; sponsors competitions; bestows awards. **Convention/Meeting:** Annual.

2260 ● Pontiac-Oakland Club, Finger Lakes Chapter [New York]
14 Judd Ln.
Hilton, NY 14468
Deborah Arend, Sec.   Ph:(716)392-3808

Founded: 1972. Individuals interested in preserving and restoring Pontiac and Oakland automobiles manufactured between 1907 and the present.

2261 ● Pontiac-Oakland Club International
P.O. Box 4789
Culver City, CA 90230
Dick Hoyt, Exec.Sec.   Ph:(818)704-1580

Founded: 1972. **Membership:** 9,000. Persons interested in the history, restoration, and preservation of Pontiac and Oakland

automobiles. Assists owners of Pontiac and Oakland automobiles with the restoration of their vehicles. Maintains staff of volunteer technical advisers. Conducts research pertaining to original specifications and production history. Maintains library. Sponsors competitions; bestows trophies; provides computerized services. **Former Name(s):** (1973) Pontiac Owners Club International. **Convention/Meeting:** Annual conference and auto show.

2262 ● Pontiac-Oakland Club, International, Arizona Chapter
4348 E. Timrod
Tucson, AZ 85711
Thom Sherwood, Pres.   Ph:(602)795-0978

Founded: 1982. **Membership:** 100. Automotive enthusiasts interested in the enjoyment, preservation, and restoration of Pontiac and Oakland automobiles.

2263 ● Pontiac-Oakland Club International, Emerald Valley Chapter [Oregon]
2411 Washington
Eugene, OR 97405
Ken W. Smith, Pres.   Ph:(503)485-0319

Founded: 1985. **Membership:** 52. Owners of Pontiac automobiles and other automobile enthusiasts. Promotes restoration and maintenance of Pontiacs. Assists in location of literature and parts. Conducts charitable and competitive car shows.

2264 ● Pontiac-Oakland Club International, Georgia Chapter
c/o Terry Hunt
139 Dials Dr.
Woodstock, GA 30188
Terry Hunt, Dir.   Ph:(404)929-2440

Persons interested in the history, restoration, and preservation of Pontiac and Oakland automobiles.

2265 ● Pontiac-Oakland Club International, Kansas Chapter
Rt. 3, Box 421
Rose Hill, KS 67133
Margaret Brinkley, Pres.   Ph:(316)776-2162

Individuals interested in collecting and preserving Oakland and Pontiac automobiles.

2266 ● Pontiac-Oakland Club International, Kansas City Arrowhead Chapter [Kansas and Missouri]
104 Center Dr.
Silver Lake, KS 66539

Founded: 1985. **Membership:** 40. Pontiac and Oakland automobiles owners in northeastern Kansas and western Missouri. Disseminates information; conducts charitable events; sponsors festival.

2267 ● Pontiac-Oakland Club International, National Capital Area [District of Columbia, Maryland, and Virginia]
c/o George Richardson
1509 Baltimore Rd.
Alexandria, VA 22308
George Richardson, Exec. Officer   Ph:(703)768-1569

Founded: 1979. **Membership:** 159. Pontiac automobile owners and enthusiasts in the District of Columbia, Maryland, and Virginia.

2268 ● Pontiac-Oakland Club International, Nebraskaland Chapter
1603 Nebraska Ave.
York, NE 68467
Jo Ann Kuester, Sec. Treas.   Ph:(402)362-6413

Founded: 1972. **Membership:** 30. To restore and enjoy Pontiac and Oakland automobiles.

2269 ● Pontiac-Oakland Club International, Southern California Chapter
c/o Daniel J. Santoro
419 Livingston Ave.
Placentia, CA 92670
Daniel J. Santoro, Exec. Officer   Ph:(714)524-8642

Owners of Oakland and Pontiac automobiles.

2270 ● Pontiac-Oakland Club International. Yankee Chapter [Maine, Massachusetts, and Rhode Island]
44 Old Brook Rd.
Lecminster, MA 01453
Steve Peluso, Editor   Ph:(508)537-7066

Founded: 1980. **Membership:** 150. Individuals in Maine, Massachusetts, and Rhode Island promoting restoration and preservation of Pontiac and Oakland automobiles.

2271 ● Pontiac-Oakland Club, Nutmeg Chapter [Connecticut]
Church Hill Rd.
Washington Depot, CT 06974
Starr F. Evans, Editor   Ph:(203)868-7723

Founded: 1976. **Membership:** 106. Owners of Pontiac-Oakland automobiles, built from 1909 to the present, organized to promote the model.

2272 ● Pontiac-Oakland Club, Western New York Chapter
50 Cramer St.
North Tonawanda, NY 14120
Brian Mertens, V. Pres.   Ph:(716)692-1564

Founded: 1976. **Membership:** 96. Owners and enthusiasts of Pontiac/Oakland automobiles. To further the preservation of the automobiles.

2273 ● Trans Am Club U.S.A.
P.O. Box 99, Tufts University Br.
Medford, MA 02153
M. F. Mills, Pres.   Ph:(617)396-4424

Founded: 1979. **Membership:** 500. Pontiac Trans Am, Formula, and Firebird automobile owners. Goal is to provide a personal and professional club for Pontiac high-performance car enthusiasts. Sponsors competitions and provides technical assistance. Offers discounts to members.

PONTIAC GRAND AM (1987-92)

Introduced as part of the General Motors N-car line, along with corporate twins Buick Skylark and Oldsmobile Cutlass Calais. In 1990, the 202,149 Grand Am registrations in the U.S. accounted for 30 percent of total Pontiac sales. Produced at the General Motors plant in Lansing, Michigan, the Pontiac Grand Am was dramatically redesigned for 1992.

1992 Pontiac Grand Am GT

MAJOR FEATURES

● Pontiac Grand Am SE coupe and sedan 1992 standard equipment includes: 5-speed manual transmission, rack-and-pinion power steering, front disc/rear drum power brakes with anti-lock braking system, wheel covers, fog lamps, and AM/FM stereo.

● Pontiac Grand Am GT coupe and sedan add as 1992 standard equipment: high output 16-valve 4-cyclinder engine, cast aluminum wheels, rally gauges with tachometer, tilt steering column, and cruise control.

● Pontiac Grand Am LE had as 1991 standard equipment: 5-speed manual transmission, rack-and-pinion power steering, front disc/rear drum power brakes, and AM/FM stereo.

PRICE HISTORY

The following new car prices reflect the approximate retail cost of the base model: **1987** - $9,299; **1988** - $9,869; **1989** - $10,469; **1990** - $10,544; **1991** - $10,174; **1992** - $11,899.

DIMENSIONS

Body Style	Years Avail	Wheel Base (in)	Lgth (in)	Ht (in)	Avg Wt (lbs)	Fuel Cap (gal)	Front Hdrm (in)	Front Legrm (in)
2d cpe	87-88	103.4	177.5	52.5	2,492	13.6	37.7	42.9
2d cpe	89-90	103.4	181.4	52.6	2,520	13.6	37.7	42.9
2d cpe	91-91	103.4	180.1	52.6	2,508	13.6	37.7	42.9
2d cpe	92-92	103.4	186.9	53.1	2,728	15.2	37.8	43.1
4d sdn	87-88	103.4	177.5	52.5	2,565	13.6	37.7	42.9
4d sdn	89-90	103.4	181.4	52.6	2,578	13.6	37.7	42.9
4d sdn	91-91	103.4	180.1	52.6	2,592	13.6	37.7	42.9
4d sdn	92-92	103.4	186.9	53.1	2,777	15.2	37.8	43.1

ENGINES

Type	Displacement (L)	Fuel Dly	HP @rpm	Torque @rpm (ft/lbs)	MPG Cty/Hwy	Years Avail
I-4	2.5	FI	98@4800	135@3200	23/33	87-89
I-4	2.3	FI	150@5200	160@4400	24/35	88-89
I-4	2.5	FI	110@5200	135@3200	22/33	89-91
I-4	2.3	FI	180@6200	160@5200	23/33	89-92
I-4	2.3	FI	160@6200	155@5200	23/33	90-92
I-4	2.3	FI	120@5200	140@3200	22/29	92-92
I-4T	2.0	FI	165@5600	175@4000	21/30	87-89
V-6	3.0	FI	125@4900	150@2400	19/27	87-87
V-6	3.3	FI	160@5200	185@2000	19/29	92-92

KEY: I=in-line engine; V=V engine; F=flat engine; FI=fuel injection; bbl=barrel carburetor; T=turbo; D=diesel; HP=horsepower; MPG=estimated average miles per gallon.

EVALUATIONS, TESTS, AND RANKINGS

1992: ''Above the beltline, we think the Grand Am is a success

... competent, but its drivetrain and chassis don't fulfill the promises the new body makes ... performance isn't the sedan's bag." **Source:** "Pontiac Grand Am SE," *Car and Driver*, January 1992, pp. 109-112.

1992: "The interior has been improved considerably ... better economy, performance, and smoothness ... covers pavement well and comfortably." **Source:** "Pontiac Grand Am GT," *Motor Trend*, October 1991, p. 62d.

1992: "On the road, the chassis feels more buttoned-down than in the old car ... front end is still floaty on quick roads ... interior is new, simple and clean." **Source:** "Pontiac Grand Am," *Car and Driver*, October 1991, p. 55.

1990: "competent and quick ... Cornering stability is good ... a drastic improvement over the last one we drove." **Source:** "Pontiac Grand Am SE," *Motor Trend*, January 1990, pp. 53-56.

1990: "does the most shaking and suffers the worst, making the Grand Am feel twitchy and unrefined ... tasteful interior layout." **Source:** "Three Translations of the Family Sedan," *Popular Science*, September 1990, pp. 79-83.

1987: "loves to go fast in a straight line. Anytime the wheels are off center and into high boost ... some effect is going to be felt in your hands ... you can have a lot of fun with this car." **Source:** "Pontiac Grand Am SE Turbo," *Motor Trend*, August 1987, pp. 91-92, 122.

RECALLS

1991: (35 vehicles): Steering column jackets may be 10mm short in overall length causing inadequate retention of column to the column support bracket. **Corrective action:** Replace steering column assembly. *(NHTSA Campaign No. 91V018000.)*

1988-89: (61,765 cars with Quad-4 engines; includes Buick, Pontiac, and Oldsmobile models): Cracking or separation of front fuel hose at coupling could allow fuel leakage and result in a fire. **Corrective action:** Replace front fuel feed hose assembly. *(NHTSA Campaign No. 90V042000.)*

1987: (131,476 cars with 2.0 L engines; includes Buick, Pontiac, and Oldsmobile models): Fuel feed and/or return hose assemblies could crack, causing underhood fire. **Corrective action:** Replace fuel feed/return hoses and assemblies. *(NHTSA Campaign No. 87V184000.)*

1987: (22,300 passenger vehicles; includes Buick Skylark, Oldsmobile Calais, and Pontiac Grand Am): Fuel feed or fuel return hose at engine may rub against shift lever on 5 speed transaxle. In time a hole could be rubbed through hose and fuel could leak into engine compartment, possibly resulting in underhood fire. **Corrective action:** Replace fuel feed and return hose/pipe assemblies. *(NHTSA Campaign No. 88V032000.)*

REPAIR MANUALS

2274 ● Get Your Pontiac Fixed Right
Consumer Reports Books
51 E. 42nd St., Ste. 800
New York, NY 10017   Ph:(212)682-9280

Published 1990. **Price:** $8.95.

OTHER INFORMATION SOURCES

2275 ● Badger Chatter
Pontiac-Oakland Club International, Badger State Chapter
5223 84th St.
Kenosha, WI 53142   Ph:(414)694-2500

Monthly.

2276 ● Bison
Pontiac-Oakland Club, Western New York Chapter
50 Cramer St.
North Tonawanda, NY 14120   Ph:(716)692-1564

Newsletter. Monthly.

2277 ● Chiefly Pontiac
Hoosier Pontiac-Oakland Club
1856 Gray Rd.
Mooresville, IN 46158   Ph:(317)831-1568

Newsletter. Bimonthly.

2278 ● The Drumbeat
Pontiac-Oakland Club, Nutmeg Chapter
Church Hill Rd.
Washington Depot, CT 06974   Ph:(203)868-7723

Periodic.

2279 ● Finger Lakes News [New York]
Pontiac-Oakland Club, Finger Lakes Chapter
14 Judd Ln.
Hilton, NY 14468   Ph:(716)392-3808

Periodic.

2280 ● High Performance Pontiac
CSK Publishing Co., Inc.
299 Market St.   Ph:(201)712-9300
Saddle Brook, NJ 07662   Fax:(201)712-9899

Magazine for car enthusiasts, featuring collecting, restoring, modifying, and customizing of Pontiacs from 1950 to the present. Bimonthly. **Editor(s):** Sue Elliott. **Price:** $15.00/year; $3.25 per single issue.

2281 ● Hot Air
Pontiac-Oakland Club International, Arizona Chapter
4348 E. Timrod
Tucson, AZ 85711   Ph:(602)795-0978

Newsletter. Monthly.

2282 ● Illinois Newsletter
Pontiac-Oakland Club International, Illinois Chapter
R.R. 1, Box 220
Beecher, IL 60401   Ph:(708)258-6017

Monthly.

2283 ● Nebraskaland
Pontiac-Oakland Club International, Nebraskaland Chapter
1603 Nebraska Ave.
York, NE 68467   Ph:(402)362-6413

Newsletter. Bimonthly.

2284 ● On The Warpath
Pontiac-Oakland Club International, National Capital Area
1509 Baltimore Rd.
Alexandria, VA 22308   Ph:(703)768-1569

Newsletter. Bimonthly.

2285 ● Pontiac-Oakland Club International, Emerald Valley Chapter—Newsletter [Oregon]
Pontiac-Oakland Club International, Emerald Valley Chapter
2411 Washington
Eugene, OR 97405   Ph:(503)485-0319

Monthly.

2286 ● Pontiac-Oakland Club International, Garden State Chapter—Newsletter [New Jersey]
Pontiac-Oakland Club International, Garden State Chapter
19 Earl St.
Denville, NJ 07834

Newsletter. Bimonthly.

2287 ● Pontiac-Oakland Club International, Illinois Chapter—Annual Roster
Pontiac-Oakland Club International, Illinois Chapter
R.R. 1, Box 220
Beecher, IL 60401   Ph:(708)258-6017

2288 ● Pontiac-Oakland Club International, Kansas Chapter—Directory
Pontiac-Oakland Club International, Kansas Chapter
Rt. 3, Box 421
Rose Hill, KS 67133   Ph:(316)776-2162

Periodic.

2289 ● Pontiac-Oakland Club International, Kansas Chapter—Newsletter
Pontiac-Oakland Club International, Kansas Chapter
Rt. 3, Box 421
Rose Hill, KS 67133   Ph:(316)776-2162

Periodic.

2290 ● Pontiac-Oakland Club International, Kansas City Arrowhead Chapter—Directory [Kansas and Missouri]
Pontiac-Oakland Club International, Kansas City
Arrowhead Chapter
104 Center Dr.
Silver Lake, KS 66539   Ph:(913)582-4207

Periodic

2291 ● Pontiac-Oakland Club International—Membership Roster
Pontiac-Oakland Club International
PO Box 4789
Culver City, CA 90230   Ph:(818)704-1580

Annual.

2292 ● Pontiac-Oakland Club International, North Coast Ohio Chapter— Newsletter
Pontiac-Oakland Club International, North Coast Ohio
Chapter
2500 Hetzel Dr.
Parma, OH 44134   Ph:(216)888-4867

Periodic.

2293 ● Pontiac-Oakland Club International, Old Dominion Chapter—Newsletter [Virginia]
Pontiac-Oakland Club International, Old Dominion Chapter
1400 Fortingale Circle
Sandstom, VA 23150   Ph:(804)737-3139

Bimonthly.

2294 ● Pontiac-Oakland Club International, Yankee Chapter—Newsletter [Maine, Massachusetts, and Rhode Island]
Pontiac-Oakland Club International, Yankee Chapter
44 Old Brook Rd.
Leonminster, MA 01453   Ph:(508)537-7066

Monthly.

2295 ● The Scout
Pontiac-Oakland Club International, Kansas City
Arrowhead Chapter
104 Center Dr.
Silver Lake, KS 66539   Ph:(913)582-4207

Newsletter. Monthly.

2296 ● Smoke Signals
Pontiac-Oakland Club International
PO Box 4789
Culver City, CA 90230   Ph:(818)704-1580

Aims to assist owners of Pontiac and Oakland automobiles with the restoration of their vehicles. Monthly. **Editor(s):** Larry Kummer, Editor and Publisher. **Price:** $22.00/yr.; $2.00/mo.

ASSOCIATIONS

2297 ● Pontiac-Oakland Club, Finger Lakes Chapter [New York]
14 Judd Ln.
Hilton, NY 14468
Deborah Arend, Sec.   Ph:(716)392-3808

Founded: 1972. Individuals interested in preserving and restoring Pontiac and Oakland automobiles manufactured between 1907 and the present.

2298 ● Pontiac-Oakland Club International
P.O. Box 4789
Culver City, CA 90230
Dick Hoyt, Exec.Sec.   Ph:(818)704-1580

Founded: 1972. **Membership:** 9,000. Persons interested in the history, restoration, and preservation of Pontiac and Oakland automobiles. Assists owners of Pontiac and Oakland automobiles with the restoration of their vehicles. Maintains staff of volunteer technical advisers. Conducts research pertaining to original specifications and production history. Maintains library. Sponsors competitions; bestows trophies; provides computerized services. **Former Name(s):** (1973) Pontiac Owners Club International. **Convention/Meeting:** Annual conference and auto show.

2299 ● Pontiac-Oakland Club, International, Arizona Chapter
4348 E. Timrod
Tucson, AZ 85711
Thom Sherwood, Pres.   Ph:(602)795-0978

Founded: 1982. **Membership:** 100. Automotive enthusiasts interested in the enjoyment, preservation, and restoration of Pontiac and Oakland automobiles.

2300 ● Pontiac-Oakland Club International, Emerald Valley Chapter [Oregon]
2411 Washington
Eugene, OR 97405
Ken W. Smith, Pres.   Ph:(503)485-0319

Founded: 1985. **Membership:** 52. Owners of Pontiac automobiles and other automobile enthusiasts. Promotes restoration and maintenance of Pontiacs. Assists in location of literature and parts. Conducts charitable and competitive car shows.

2301 ● Pontiac-Oakland Club International, Georgia Chapter

c/o Terry Hunt
139 Dials Dr.
Woodstock, GA 30188
Terry Hunt, Dir.   Ph:(404)929-2440

Persons interested in the history, restoration, and preservation of Pontiac and Oakland automobiles.

2302 ● Pontiac-Oakland Club International, Kansas Chapter

Rt. 3, Box 421
Rose Hill, KS 67133
Margaret Brinkley, Pres.   Ph:(316)776-2162

Individuals interested in collecting and preserving Oakland and Pontiac automobiles.

2303 ● Pontiac-Oakland Club International, Kansas City Arrowhead Chapter [Kansas and Missouri]

104 Center Dr.
Silver Lake, KS 66539

Founded: 1985. **Membership:** 40. Pontiac and Oakland automobiles owners in northeastern Kansas and western Missouri. Disseminates information; conducts charitable events; sponsors festival.

2304 ● Pontiac-Oakland Club International, National Capital Area [District of Columbia, Maryland, and Virginia]

c/o George Richardson
1509 Baltimore Rd.
Alexandria, VA 22308
George Richardson, Exec. Officer   Ph:(703)768-1569

Founded: 1979. **Membership:** 159. Pontiac automobile owners and enthusiasts in the District of Columbia, Maryland, and Virginia.

2305 ● Pontiac-Oakland Club International, Nebraskaland Chapter

1603 Nebraska Ave.
York, NE 68467
Jo Ann Kuester, Sec. Treas.   Ph:(402)362-6413

Founded: 1972. **Membership:** 30. To restore and enjoy Pontiac and Oakland automobiles.

2306 ● Pontiac-Oakland Club International, Southern California Chapter

c/o Daniel J. Santoro
419 Livingston Ave.
Placentia, CA 92670
Daniel J. Santoro, Exec. Officer   Ph:(714)524-8642

Owners of Oakland and Pontiac automobiles.

2307 ● Pontiac-Oakland Club International. Yankee Chapter [Maine, Massachusetts, and Rhode Island]

44 Old Brook Rd.
Lecminster, MA 01453
Steve Peluso, Editor   Ph:(508)537-7066

Founded: 1980. **Membership:** 150. Individuals in Maine, Massachusetts, and Rhode Island promoting restoration and preservation of Pontiac and Oakland automobiles.

2308 ● Pontiac-Oakland Club, Nutmeg Chapter [Connecticut]

Church Hill Rd.
Washington Depot, CT 06974
Starr F. Evans, Editor   Ph:(203)868-7723

Founded: 1976. **Membership:** 106. Owners of Pontiac-Oakland automobiles, built from 1909 to the present, organized to promote the model.

2309 ● Pontiac-Oakland Club, Western New York Chapter

50 Cramer St.
North Tonawanda, NY 14120
Brian Mertens, V. Pres.   Ph:(716)692-1564

Founded: 1976. **Membership:** 96. Owners and enthusiasts of Pontiac/Oakland automobiles. To further the preservation of the automobiles.

PONTIAC GRAND PRIX (1987-92)

Introduced as part of the General Motors W-car line, along with corporate twins Buick Regal and Oldsmobile Cutlass Supreme. Produced at General Motors plant in Fairfax, Kansas. Pontiac Grand Prix Turbo and STE Turbo named to *Car and Driver's* 1990 Ten Best Cars Nominees list. The Pontiac Grand Prix was listed as having the highest maintenance cost, fuel cost, and insurance cost among midsize vehicles in *The Complete Car Cost Guide* in 1990. In addition, the Pontiac Grand Prix LE was listed as having the lowest fuel cost and the Pontiac Grand Prix SE as having the lowest resale value among midsize vehicles in 1990 in the same publication.

1991 Pontiac Grand Prix GTP

MAJOR FEATURES

● Pontiac Grand Prix SE coupe 1992 standard equipment includes: 3.1L V6 engine, 3-speed automatic transmission, 4-wheel power disc brakes, rack-and-pinion power steering, air conditioning, power bucket front seats, and AM/FM stereo.

● Pontiac Grand Prix GT coupe adds as 1992 standard equipment: 4-speed automatic transmission, anti-lock brakes, rally tuned suspension, power door locks and windows, cruise control, 16-inch cast aluminum wheels, upgraded tires, and AM/FM stereo cassette player.

● Pontiac Grand Prix GTP coupe adds as 1992 standard equipment: 3.4l twin dual cam V6 engine, 5-speed manual transmission, rally tuned suspension, upgraded tires, and aero performance package.

● Pontiac Grand Prix LE coupe had as 1990 standard equipment: 2.3L I-4 engine.

● Pontiac Grand Prix LE sedan has as 1992 standard equipment includes: 3.1L V6 engine, 3-speed automatic transmission, four-wheel power disc brakes, rack-and-pinion power steering, integral fog lamps, front and rear fascias, other exterior body stylings, air-conditioning, and AM/FM stereo.

● Pontiac Grand Prix SE sedan adds as 1992 standard equipment: aero performance package, dual exhaust, cast aluminum wheels, and power reclining bucket front seats.

● Pontiac Grand Prix STE sedan adds as 1992 standard equipment: 4-speed automatic transmission, rally tuned suspension, anti-lock braking system, upgraded tires, electric information center, power windows and door locks, power driver's seat, cruise control, remote keyless entry system, and an upgraded stereo system.

● Pontiac Grand Prix Turbo and STE Turbo had as 1990 standard equipment: 3.1L V-6 turbo-charged engine. In addition, the STE turbo has other exterior body stylings.

PRICE HISTORY

The following new car prices reflect the approximate retail cost of the base model: **1987** - $11,069; **1988** - $12,539; **1989** - $13,975; **1990** - $14,564; **1991** - $14,294; **1992** - $14,890.

DIMENSIONS

Body Style	Years Avail	Wheel Base (in)	Lgth (in)	Ht (in)	Avg Wt (lbs)	Fuel Cap (gal)	Front Hdrm (in)	Front Legrm (in)
2d cpe	87-87	108.1	201.9	54.7	3,231	18.1	37.6	42.8
2d cpe	88-89	107.6	194.1	53.3	3,038	16.6	37.8	42.3
2d cpe	90-90	107.5	194.5	53.3	3,189	16.0	37.8	42.3
2d cpe	91-91	107.5	193.9	52.8	3,188	16.5	37.8	42.3
2d cpe	92-92	107.5	194.8	53.3	3,214	16.5	37.8	42.3
4d sdn	90-90	107.5	194.5	54.8	3,280	16.0	38.2	42.4
4d sdn	91-91	107.5	194.8	54.3	3,252	16.5	38.8	42.4
4d sdn	92-92	107.5	194.8	54.8	3,243	16.5	38.2	42.3

ENGINES

Type	Displacement (L)	Fuel Dly	HP @rpm	Torque @rpm (ft/lbs)	MPG Cty/Hwy	Years Avail
I-4	2.3	FI	160@6200	155@5200	21/29	90-91
V-6	3.8	2-bbl	110@3800	190@1600	19/24	87-87
V-6	4.3	FI	140@na	na	19/26	87-87
V-6	2.8	FI	130@4800	160@3600	19/28	88-88
V-6	2.8	FI	130@4500	170@3600	18/30	89-89
V-6	3.1	FI	140@4500	180@3600	18/23	89-89
V-6	3.1	FI	135@4400	180@3600	19/30	90-90
V-6	3.1	FI	140@4400	185@3200	19/29	91-92
V-6	3.4	FI	210@5200	215@4000	17/27	91-92
V-6T	3.1	FI	205@4800	220@3200	na	89-90
V-8	5.0	4-bbl	150@4000	245@2000	17/24	87-87

KEY: I=in-line engine; V=V engine; F=flat engine; FI=fuel injection; bbl=barrel carburetor; T=turbo; D=diesel; HP=horsepower; MPG=estimated average miles per gallon.

EVALUATIONS, TESTS, AND RANKINGS

1991: "engine power is well balanced . . . offers leading-edge styling, comfort . . . and performance." **Source:** "Pontiac Grand Prix GTP," *Motor Trend*, October 1990, pp. 88-91.

1991: "Headroom is tight for anyone of above-average height . . . seatbelts don't retract properly . . . A light constantly nags you to shift." **Source:** "Pontiac Grand Prix GTP," *Car and Driver*, October 1990, pp. 83, 86.

1991: "handled well up to its limits . . . plenty of steam available at low rpm . . . no performance match for its chief target, the Ford Taurus SHO." **Source:** "In Search of the Perfect 10," *Popular Science*, January 1991, pp. 76-80, 94.

1991: "surprisingly light and easily modulated clutch . . . Ride quality is very good . . . steering effort is on the high side." **Source:** "Pontiac has a powerful gem in Grand Prix," *The Detroit News*, July 3, 1991, pp. 1D-2D.

1991: "Y99 suspension package provided decent handling . . . keeps a solid grip on curves . . . has spirit." **Source:** "Sporty

Grand Prix STE grips curves; V-6 engine lends pep," *The Flint Journal*, April 17, 1991, p. D1-D2.

1990: "Acceleration is strong both off the line and in passing maneuvers, yet the motor is dead-silent at idle and tolerably quiet on the freeway . . . Numerous storage bins . . . add a dash of practicality." **Source:** "Turbo Grand Prix redefines Pontiac's performance image," *The Detroit News*, October 25, 1989, pp. 1F-2F.

1990: "a lot of this goodness is negated by the STE's insensible steering and the willing but still weak V-6 . . . engine quickly runs out of breath as the revs rise." **Source:** "Pontiac Grand Prix: A new sex symbol for sedanland," *Motor Trend*, October 1989, pp. 79-81.

1990: "engine begins to get rough during the end of the climb to its 6000-rpm redline . . . handling is something you can believe in . . . comes across as a performance sedan." **Source:** "Pontiac Grand Prix STE Turbo," *Car and Driver*, October 1989, pp. 40-44.

1989: "Turbo topped out at 128 mph . . . The car was stable and relatively quiet at these speeds." **Source:** "Grand McLaren Turbo Grand Prix," *Road & Track*, April 1989, pp. 110-113.

1989: "3.1-liter engine was the model of tractability and smoothness." **Source:** "Flat-out Fastest American cars II, the sequel," *Motor Trend*, June 1989, pp. 42-47, 50, 54.

1989: "corners with considerable understeer . . . fair amount of road feel through the high-effort rack-and-pinion power steering." **Source:** "Motown Muscle," *Popular Mechanics*, January 1989, pp. 53-57, 116.

RECALLS

1990: (1,121 SE turbo models): Exhaust system heat shield could puncture fuel tank in rear end collision. **Corrective action:** Remove rear exhaust system heat shield from the pipe assembly. *(NHTSA Campaign No. 90V036000.)*

1990: (412,792 vehicles; includes Chevrolet Lumina, Pontiac Grand Prix, Buick Regal, and Oldsmobile Cutlass Supreme): Front shoulder safety belt webbing may separate at front belt upper guide loops on either side of front seat. **Corrective action:** Install controlled rotation bracket on driver and passenger side front seat belt guide loops. *(NHTSA Campaign No. 91V005000.)*

1989-90: (476,422 vehicles; includes Buick, Chevrolet, Oldsmobile, and Pontiac models): Brake stoplamps may not illuminate or, in some cases, stoplamps will not stay illuminated all the time when brakes are applied due to a faulty stoplamp switch. **Corrective action:** Install an improved design stoplamp switch. *(NHTSA Campaign No. 90V185000.)*

1989: (247 cars with LG5 3.1 liter turbocharger engines): Misrouting of turbocharger oil feed pipe could allow pipe to contact the positive battery cable connecting stud on the starter motor. Could cause an electrical ground that could result in an engine compartment fire. **Corrective action:** Reroute oil feed pipe; also install a newly designed clamp and bracket to locate pipe away from the starter. *(NHTSA Campaign No. 89V108000.)*

1989: (3,784 passenger vehicles; includes Pontiac Grand Prix and Buick Regal): Fuel return lines could fracture and allow fuel to leak in area of fuel tank. In presence of ignition source, this condition could result in fire. **Corrective action:** Install new fuel return pipe assembly. *(NHTSA Campaign No. 88V188000.)*

1988-90: (673,000 passenger vehicles; includes the Pontiac Grand Prix, Buick Regal, Oldsmobile Cutlass Calais, and Chevrolet Lumina models): Front shoulder belt guide loop attachment fastener may pull through door mounted anchor plate. Seat belt may not properly restrain a passenger, resulting in increased risk of injury to occupant. **Corrective action:** Replace front shoulder belt guide loop attachment nuts and install new guide cover. *(NHTSA Campaign No. 90V054000.)*

1988: (7,775 cars): Wheel lug nuts were not properly torqued to specifications. Wheel lug nuts could loosen and/or come off wheel studs. This could eventually result in wheel separating from vehicle. Loss of vehicle control and vehicle crash could occur. **Corrective action:** Inspection of vehicle and assure proper torque replaces any missing lug nut or loose stud. *(NHTSA Campaign No. 88V03500.)*

1988: (1,559 cars): Front shoulder belt guide loop attached to upper rear corner of door may interfere with garnish molding. This interference could limit rotation of guide loop. If this condition exists and vehicle is involved in crash it could be possible for shoulder belt welding to be cut by guide. Loss of shoulder belt function during vehicle crash could increase risk of injuries to occupants. **Corrective action:** Newly designed guide loop nut and spacer will be installed to eliminate potential for interference conditions. *(NHTSA Campaign No. 88V049000.)*

1988: (17,745 passenger vehicles; includes Pontiac Grand Prix and Buick Regal): Interference between transmission shift cable and bellcrank clip in steering column can result in disengagement of transmission cable. This condition could allow transmission to be in gear other than displayed by shift indicator. Vehicle could move in unexpected direction and cause vehicle crash without prior warning. **Corrective action:** Newly designed bellcrank clip will be installed. *(NHTSA Campaign No. 88V045000.)*

1988: (12,457 passenger vehicles; includes Pontiac Grand Prix and Buick Regal): Secondary hood latch may not properly engage. If primary latch disengages, hood could unexpectantly open. If car was in motion, hood could contact windshield, reduce driver's forward vision area, and could result in accident. **Corrective action:** Replace secondary latch with new latch. *(NHTSA Campaign No. 88V065000.)*

1988: (3,857 passenger vehicles; includes Pontiac Grand Prix and Oldsmobile Cutlass): Parking brake cable may be disconnected from left rear brake caliper. Parking brake cannot be properly applied and vehicle will not meet grade holding requirements of FMVSS 105. **Corrective action:** Install retainer on left rear caliper if cable is not already retained with cotter pin and adjust parking brake system. *(NHTSA Campaign No. 88V175000.)*

SAFETY AND REPAIRS

1992: "GM Recalls '92 A-, W-Cars," *Automotive News*, December 2, 1991, P. 2. **Note:** Transmission problem may cause cars to remain in reverse when shifted into neutral.

1991: "GM Recalls Cars for Belt Loops," *Automotive News*, February 10, 1992, p. 2. **Note:** May have cracked front-door shoulder belt guide loops.

1987: "Car Clinic," *Popular Mechanics*, August 1990, p. 26. **Note:** Tip for clashing starter motor gears in 1987-88 General Motors 4.3, 5.0, and 5.7 liter engines.

REPAIR MANUALS

2310 ● Get Your Pontiac Fixed Right
Consumer Reports Books
51 E. 42nd St., Ste. 800
New York, NY 10017   Ph:(212)682-9280

Published 1990. **Price:** $8.95.

2311 ● Pontiac Grand Prix-Oldsmobile Cutlass-Buick Regal, 1988 Repair and Tune-up Guide
Chilton Co.
Chilton Way
Radnor, PA 19089   Ph:(215)964-4000

Published 1990. **Price:** $15.95.

OTHER INFORMATION SOURCES

2312 ● Badger Chatter
Pontiac-Oakland Club International, Badger State Chapter
5223 84th St.
Kenosha, WI 53142   Ph:(414)694-2500

Monthly.

2313 ● Bison
Pontiac-Oakland Club, Western New York Chapter
50 Cramer St.
North Tonawanda, NY 14120   Ph:(716)692-1564

Newsletter. Monthly.

2314 ● Chiefly Pontiac
Hoosier Pontiac-Oakland Club
1856 Gray Rd.
Mooresville, IN 46158   Ph:(317)831-1568

Newsletter. Bimonthly.

2315 ● The Drumbeat
Pontiac-Oakland Club, Nutmeg Chapter
Church Hill Rd.
Washington Depot, CT 06974   Ph:(203)868-7723

Periodic.

2316 ● Finger Lakes News [New York]
Pontiac-Oakland Club, Finger Lakes Chapter
14 Judd Ln.
Hilton, NY 14468   Ph:(716)392-3808

Periodic.

2317 ● High Performance Pontiac
CSK Publishing Co., Inc.
299 Market St.   Ph:(201)712-9300
Saddle Brook, NJ 07662   Fax:(201)712-9899

Magazine for car enthusiasts, featuring collecting, restoring, modifying, and customizing of Pontiacs from 1950 to the present. Bimonthly. **Editor(s):** Sue Elliott. **Price:** $15.00/year; $3.25 per single issue.

2318 ● Hot Air
Pontiac-Oakland Club International, Arizona Chapter
4348 E. Timrod
Tucson, AZ 85711   Ph:(602)795-0978

Newsletter. Monthly.

2319 ● Illinois Newsletter
Pontiac-Oakland Club International, Illinois Chapter
R.R. 1, Box 220
Beecher, IL 60401   Ph:(708)258-6017

Monthly.

2320 ● Nebraskaland
Pontiac-Oakland Club International, Nebraskaland Chapter
1603 Nebraska Ave.
York, NE 68467   Ph:(402)362-6413

Newsletter. Bimonthly.

2321 ● On The Warpath
Pontiac-Oakland Club International, National Capital Area
1509 Baltimore Rd.
Alexandria, VA 22308   Ph:(703)768-1569

Newsletter. Bimonthly.

**2322 ● Pontiac-Oakland Club International, Emerald Valley
Chapter—Newsletter [Oregon]**
Pontiac-Oakland Club International, Emerald Valley Chapter
2411 Washington
Eugene, OR 97405   Ph:(503)485-0319

Monthly.

**2323 ● Pontiac-Oakland Club International, Garden State
Chapter—Newsletter [New Jersey]**
Pontiac-Oakland Club International, Garden State Chapter
19 Earl St.
Denville, NJ 07834

Newsletter. Bimonthly.

**2324 ● Pontiac-Oakland Club International, Illinois
Chapter—Annual Roster**
Pontiac-Oakland Club International, Illinois Chapter
R.R. 1, Box 220
Beecher, IL 60401   Ph:(708)258-6017

**2325 ● Pontiac-Oakland Club International, Kansas
Chapter—Directory**
Pontiac-Oakland Club International, Kansas Chapter
Rt. 3, Box 421
Rose Hill, KS 67133   Ph:(316)776-2162

Periodic.

**2326 ● Pontiac-Oakland Club International, Kansas
Chapter—Newsletter**
Pontiac-Oakland Club International, Kansas Chapter
Rt. 3, Box 421
Rose Hill, KS 67133   Ph:(316)776-2162

Periodic.

**2327 ● Pontiac-Oakland Club International, Kansas City
Arrowhead Chapter—Directory [Kansas and Missouri]**
Pontiac-Oakland Club International, Kansas City
Arrowhead Chapter
104 Center Dr.
Silver Lake, KS 66539   Ph:(913)582-4207

Periodic

**2328 ● Pontiac-Oakland Club International—Membership
Roster**
Pontiac-Oakland Club International
PO Box 4789
Culver City, CA 90230   Ph:(818)704-1580

Annual.

**2329 ● Pontiac-Oakland Club International, North Coast
Ohio Chapter— Newsletter**
Pontiac-Oakland Club International, North Coast Ohio
Chapter
2500 Hetzel Dr.
Parma, OH 44134   Ph:(216)888-4867

Periodic.

**2330 ● Pontiac-Oakland Club International, Old Dominion
Chapter—Newsletter [Virginia]**
Pontiac-Oakland Club International, Old Dominion Chapter
1400 Fortingale Circle
Sandstom, VA 23150   Ph:(804)737-3139

Bimonthly.

**2331 ● Pontiac-Oakland Club International, Yankee
Chapter—Newsletter [Maine, Massachusetts, and Rhode
Island]**
Pontiac-Oakland Club International, Yankee Chapter
44 Old Brook Rd.
Leonminster, MA 01453   Ph:(508)537-7066

Monthly.

2332 ● The Scout
Pontiac-Oakland Club International, Kansas City
Arrowhead Chapter
104 Center Dr.
Silver Lake, KS 66539   Ph:(913)582-4207

Newsletter. Monthly.

2333 ● Smoke Signals
Pontiac-Oakland Club International
PO Box 4789
Culver City, CA 90230   Ph:(818)704-1580

Aims to assist owners of Pontiac and Oakland automobiles
with the restoration of their vehicles. Monthly. **Editor(s):** Larry
Kummer, Editor and Publisher. **Price:** $22.00/yr.; $2.00/mo.

ASSOCIATIONS

**2334 ● Pontiac-Oakland Club, Finger Lakes Chapter [New
York]**
14 Judd Ln.
Hilton, NY 14468
Deborah Arend, Sec.   Ph:(716)392-3808

Founded: 1972. Individuals interested in preserving and
restoring Pontiac and Oakland automobiles manufactured
between 1907 and the present.

2335 ● Pontiac-Oakland Club International
P.O. Box 4789
Culver City, CA 90230
Dick Hoyt, Exec.Sec.   Ph:(818)704-1580

Founded: 1972. **Membership:** 9,000. Persons interested in the
history, restoration, and preservation of Pontiac and Oakland
automobiles. Assists owners of Pontiac and Oakland
automobiles with the restoration of their vehicles. Maintains
staff of volunteer technical advisers. Conducts research
pertaining to original specifications and production history.
Maintains library. Sponsors competitions; bestows trophies;
provides computerized services. **Former Name(s):** (1973)
Pontiac Owners Club International. **Convention/Meeting:**
Annual conference and auto show.

2336 ● Pontiac-Oakland Club, International, Arizona Chapter
4348 E. Timrod
Tucson, AZ 85711
Thom Sherwood, Pres.   Ph:(602)795-0978

Founded: 1982. **Membership:** 100. Automotive enthusiasts interested in the enjoyment, preservation, and restoration of Pontiac and Oakland automobiles.

2337 ● Pontiac-Oakland Club International, Emerald Valley Chapter [Oregon]
2411 Washington
Eugene, OR 97405
Ken W. Smith, Pres.   Ph:(503)485-0319

Founded: 1985. **Membership:** 52. Owners of Pontiac automobiles and other automobile enthusiasts. Promotes restoration and maintenance of Pontiacs. Assists in location of literature and parts. Conducts charitable and competitive car shows.

2338 ● Pontiac-Oakland Club International, Georgia Chapter
c/o Terry Hunt
139 Dials Dr.
Woodstock, GA 30188
Terry Hunt, Dir.   Ph:(404)929-2440

Persons interested in the history, restoration, and preservation of Pontiac and Oakland automobiles.

2339 ● Pontiac-Oakland Club International, Kansas Chapter
Rt. 3, Box 421
Rose Hill, KS 67133
Margaret Brinkley, Pres.   Ph:(316)776-2162

Individuals interested in collecting and preserving Oakland and Pontiac automobiles.

2340 ● Pontiac-Oakland Club International, Kansas City Arrowhead Chapter [Kansas and Missouri]
104 Center Dr.
Silver Lake, KS 66539

Founded: 1985. **Membership:** 40. Pontiac and Oakland automobiles owners in northeastern Kansas and western Missouri. Disseminates information; conducts charitable events; sponsors festival.

2341 ● Pontiac-Oakland Club International, National Capital Area [District of Columbia, Maryland, and Virginia]
c/o George Richardson
1509 Baltimore Rd.
Alexandria, VA 22308
George Richardson, Exec. Officer   Ph:(703)768-1569

Founded: 1979. **Membership:** 159. Pontiac automobile owners and enthusiasts in the District of Columbia, Maryland, and Virginia.

2342 ● Pontiac-Oakland Club International, Nebraskaland Chapter
1603 Nebraska Ave.
York, NE 68467
Jo Ann Kuester, Sec. Treas.   Ph:(402)362-6413

Founded: 1972. **Membership:** 30. To restore and enjoy Pontiac and Oakland automobiles.

2343 ● Pontiac-Oakland Club International, Southern California Chapter
c/o Daniel J. Santoro
419 Livingston Ave.
Placentia, CA 92670
Daniel J. Santoro, Exec. Officer   Ph:(714)524-8642

Owners of Oakland and Pontiac automobiles.

2344 ● Pontiac-Oakland Club International. Yankee Chapter [Maine, Massachusetts, and Rhode Island]
44 Old Brook Rd.
Lecminster, MA 01453
Steve Peluso, Editor   Ph:(508)537-7066

Founded: 1980. **Membership:** 150. Individuals in Maine, Massachusetts, and Rhode Island promoting restoration and preservation of Pontiac and Oakland automobiles.

2345 ● Pontiac-Oakland Club, Nutmeg Chapter [Connecticut]
Church Hill Rd.
Washington Depot, CT 06974
Starr F. Evans, Editor   Ph:(203)868-7723

Founded: 1976. **Membership:** 106. Owners of Pontiac-Oakland automobiles, built from 1909 to the present, organized to promote the model.

2346 ● Pontiac-Oakland Club, Western New York Chapter
50 Cramer St.
North Tonawanda, NY 14120
Brian Mertens, V. Pres.   Ph:(716)692-1564

Founded: 1976. **Membership:** 96. Owners and enthusiasts of Pontiac/Oakland automobiles. To further the preservation of the automobiles.

PONTIAC LEMANS (1988-92)

Front-drive subcompact introduced in 1988, using the old LeMans nameplate. Produced in Pupyona, South Korea by Daewoo Motor Company (partially owned by General Motors). Similar to the Hyundai Excel, it is designed by GM's Opel division in West Germany.

MAJOR FEATURES

● Pontiac LeMans SE "Value Leader" Aerocoupe has as 1992 standard equipment: 1.6L engine, 4-speed manual transmission, power rack-and-pinion steering, McPherson struts suspension, front disc/rear drum brakes, and custom wheel covers.

● LeMans SE Aerocoupe, known in 1991 as the LE model, adds as 1992 standard equipment: 5-speed manual transmission fog lamps, rear deck lid spoiler, tinted glass, AM/FM stereo, and an upgraded interior.

● LeMans SE Sedan features similar standard equipment as the SE Aerocoupe and an upgraded interior.

● Pontiac LeMans SE had as 1990 standard equipment: 2.0-liter engine, sport suspension, and tilt steering column.

● Sport version Pontiac LeMans GSE, discontinued for 1991, had 1990 standard equipment: front air dam with fog lamps, sill extensions, rear spoiler, and alloy wheels.

PRICE HISTORY

The following new car prices reflect the approximate retail cost

of the base model: **1988** - $6,399; **1989** - $6,599; **1990** - $7,254; **1991** - $7,574; **1992** - $8,050.

DIMENSIONS

Body Style	Years Avail	Wheel Base (in)	Lgth (in)	Ht (in)	Avg Wt (lbs)	Fuel Cap (gal)	Front Hdrm (in)	Front Legrm (in)
cpe	88-92	99.2	163.7	53.5	2,164	13.2	38.8	42.0
4d sdn	88-92	99.2	172.4	53.7	2,241	13.2	38.8	42.0

ENGINES

Type	Displacement (L)	Fuel Dly	HP @rpm	Torque @rpm (ft/lbs)	MPG Cty/Hwy	Years Avail
I-4	1.6	FI	74@5600	90@2800	31/41	88-92
I-4	2.0	FI	96@4800	118@3600	25/31	89-90

KEY: I=in-line engine; V=V engine; F=flat engine; FI=fuel injection; bbl=barrel carburetor; T=turbo; D=diesel; HP=horsepower; MPG=estimated average miles per gallon.

EVALUATIONS, TESTS, AND RANKINGS

1990: "cheapness makes a stronger impression than the handling . . . chassis is benign, compliant, and well damped in hard cornering . . . engine is loud, rough, slow to rev, and generally happy only at low rpm." **Source:** "Eleven for Thirteen: Sportsters, $13,000 and under, that you can actually enjoy," *Car and Driver*, June 1990, pp. 46-50, 52, 61, 63, 64, 66-69.

1988: "It handles well, is easy to park, the doors are light . . . runs a pleasantly long way between stops at the gas pumps." **Source:** "Korean-built Opel bears proud old Pontiac name," *The Detroit News*, April 22, 1987, pp. 1F-2F.

1988: "provides a decent ride but is somewhat choppy and nervous . . . steering is especially annoying . . . the slightest nudge of the wheel produces a sharp deviation from straight ahead." **Source:** "Pontiac LeMans GSE," *Car and Driver*, May 1988, pp. 145, 147, 149.

1988: "surprisingly nice little car and very reasonably priced . . . It won our fuel economy test." **Source:** "Econo Commandos: The world's top pocket rockets in a fight to the finish," *Popular Mechanics*, July 1988, pp. 51-55, 119.

1988: "average performer." **Source:** "Asian Invasion," *Popular Mechanics*, July 1987, pp. 90-94, 148.

RECALLS

1988: (72,616 vehicles): Fuel filler neck may have been incompletely welded, allowing fuel to leak from neck assembly. In the event of collision impact, fuel spillage in excess of amount allowed by FMVSS 301 could result in fire. **Corrective action:** Replace fuel filler neck assembly. *(NHTSA Campaign No. 88V094000.)*

1988: (85,063 cars; includes models made before 1987): Seat belt buckles may not properly latch allowing latch plate to be removed from buckle without pressing release button. In event of sudden stop or collision, seat belt could release, increasing risk of injury to occupants. **Corrective action:** Replace seat belt buckles. *(NHTSA Campaign No. 88V163000.)*

REPAIR MANUALS

2347 ● **Get Your Pontiac Fixed Right**
Consumer Reports Books
51 E. 42nd St., Ste. 800
New York, NY 10017   Ph:(212)682-9280

Published 1990. **Price:** $8.95.

OTHER INFORMATION SOURCES

2348 ● **Badger Chatter**
Pontiac-Oakland Club International, Badger State Chapter
5223 84th St.
Kenosha, WI 53142   Ph:(414)694-2500

Monthly.

2349 ● **Bison**
Pontiac-Oakland Club, Western New York Chapter
50 Cramer St.
North Tonawanda, NY 14120   Ph:(716)692-1564

Newsletter. Monthly.

2350 ● **Chiefly Pontiac**
Hoosier Pontiac-Oakland Club
1856 Gray Rd.
Mooresville, IN 46158   Ph:(317)831-1568

Newsletter. Bimonthly.

2351 ● **The Drumbeat**
Pontiac-Oakland Club, Nutmeg Chapter
Church Hill Rd.
Washington Depot, CT 06974   Ph:(203)868-7723

Periodic.

2352 ● **Finger Lakes News [New York]**
Pontiac-Oakland Club, Finger Lakes Chapter
14 Judd Ln.
Hilton, NY 14468   Ph:(716)392-3808

Periodic.

2353 ● **Hot Air**
Pontiac-Oakland Club International, Arizona Chapter
4348 E. Timrod
Tucson, AZ 85711   Ph:(602)795-0978

Newsletter. Monthly.

2354 ● **Illinois Newsletter**
Pontiac-Oakland Club International, Illinois Chapter
R.R. 1, Box 220
Beecher, IL 60401   Ph:(708)258-6017

Monthly.

2355 ● **Nebraskaland**
Pontiac-Oakland Club International, Nebraskaland Chapter
1603 Nebraska Ave.
York, NE 68467   Ph:(402)362-6413

Newsletter. Bimonthly.

2356 ● **On The Warpath**
Pontiac-Oakland Club International, National Capital Area
1509 Baltimore Rd.
Alexandria, VA 22308   Ph:(703)768-1569

Newsletter. Bimonthly.

2357 ● **Pontiac-Oakland Club International, Emerald Valley Chapter—Newsletter [Oregon]**
Pontiac-Oakland Club International, Emerald Valley Chapter
2411 Washington
Eugene, OR 97405   Ph:(503)485-0319

Monthly.

2358 ● Pontiac-Oakland Club International, Garden State Chapter—Newsletter [New Jersey]
Pontiac-Oakland Club International, Garden State Chapter
19 Earl St.
Denville, NJ 07834

Newsletter. Bimonthly.

2359 ● Pontiac-Oakland Club International, Illinois Chapter—Annual Roster
Pontiac-Oakland Club International, Illinois Chapter
R.R. 1, Box 220
Beecher, IL 60401   Ph:(708)258-6017

2360 ● Pontiac-Oakland Club International, Kansas Chapter—Directory
Pontiac-Oakland Club International, Kansas Chapter
Rt. 3, Box 421
Rose Hill, KS 67133   Ph:(316)776-2162

Periodic.

2361 ● Pontiac-Oakland Club International, Kansas Chapter—Newsletter
Pontiac-Oakland Club International, Kansas Chapter
Rt. 3, Box 421
Rose Hill, KS 67133   Ph:(316)776-2162

Periodic.

2362 ● Pontiac-Oakland Club International, Kansas City Arrowhead Chapter—Directory [Kansas and Missouri]
Pontiac-Oakland Club International, Kansas City
Arrowhead Chapter
104 Center Dr.
Silver Lake, KS 66539   Ph:(913)582-4207

Periodic

2363 ● Pontiac-Oakland Club International—Membership Roster
Pontiac-Oakland Club International
PO Box 4789
Culver City, CA 90230   Ph:(818)704-1580

Annual.

2364 ● Pontiac-Oakland Club International, North Coast Ohio Chapter— Newsletter
Pontiac-Oakland Club International, North Coast Ohio Chapter
2500 Hetzel Dr.
Parma, OH 44134   Ph:(216)888-4867

Periodic.

2365 ● Pontiac-Oakland Club International, Old Dominion Chapter—Newsletter [Virginia]
Pontiac-Oakland Club International, Old Dominion Chapter
1400 Fortingale Circle
Sandstom, VA 23150   Ph:(804)737-3139

Bimonthly.

2366 ● Pontiac-Oakland Club International, Yankee Chapter—Newsletter [Maine, Massachusetts, and Rhode Island]
Pontiac-Oakland Club International, Yankee Chapter
44 Old Brook Rd.
Leonminster, MA 01453   Ph:(508)537-7066

Monthly.

2367 ● The Scout
Pontiac-Oakland Club International, Kansas City
Arrowhead Chapter
104 Center Dr.
Silver Lake, KS 66539   Ph:(913)582-4207

Newsletter. Monthly.

2368 ● Smoke Signals
Pontiac-Oakland Club International
PO Box 4789
Culver City, CA 90230   Ph:(818)704-1580

Aims to assist owners of Pontiac and Oakland automobiles with the restoration of their vehicles. Monthly. **Editor(s):** Larry Kummer, Editor and Publisher. **Price:** $22.00/yr.; $2.00/mo.

ASSOCIATIONS

2369 ● Pontiac-Oakland Club, Finger Lakes Chapter [New York]
14 Judd Ln.
Hilton, NY 14468
Deborah Arend, Sec.   Ph:(716)392-3808

Founded: 1972. Individuals interested in preserving and restoring Pontiac and Oakland automobiles manufactured between 1907 and the present.

2370 ● Pontiac-Oakland Club International
P.O. Box 4789
Culver City, CA 90230
Dick Hoyt, Exec.Sec.   Ph:(818)704-1580

Founded: 1972. **Membership:** 9,000. Persons interested in the history, restoration, and preservation of Pontiac and Oakland automobiles. Assists owners of Pontiac and Oakland automobiles with the restoration of their vehicles. Maintains staff of volunteer technical advisers. Conducts research pertaining to original specifications and production history. Maintains library. Sponsors competitions; bestows trophies; provides computerized services. **Former Name(s):** (1973) Pontiac Owners Club International. **Convention/Meeting:** Annual conference and auto show.

2371 ● Pontiac-Oakland Club, International, Arizona Chapter
4348 E. Timrod
Tucson, AZ 85711
Thom Sherwood, Pres.   Ph:(602)795-0978

Founded: 1982. **Membership:** 100. Automotive enthusiasts interested in the enjoyment, preservation, and restoration of Pontiac and Oakland automobiles.

2372 ● Pontiac-Oakland Club International, Emerald Valley Chapter [Oregon]
2411 Washington
Eugene, OR 97405
Ken W. Smith, Pres.   Ph:(503)485-0319

Founded: 1985. **Membership:** 52. Owners of Pontiac automobiles and other automobile enthusiasts. Promotes restoration and maintenance of Pontiacs. Assists in location of literature and parts. Conducts charitable and competitive car shows.

2373 ● Pontiac-Oakland Club International, Georgia Chapter
c/o Terry Hunt
139 Dials Dr.
Woodstock, GA 30188
Terry Hunt, Dir.   Ph:(404)929-2440

Persons interested in the history, restoration, and preservation of Pontiac and Oakland automobiles.

2374 ● Pontiac-Oakland Club International, Kansas Chapter
Rt. 3, Box 421
Rose Hill, KS 67133
Margaret Brinkley, Pres.   Ph:(316)776-2162

Individuals interested in collecting and preserving Oakland and Pontiac automobiles.

2375 ● Pontiac-Oakland Club International, Kansas City Arrowhead Chapter [Kansas and Missouri]
104 Center Dr.
Silver Lake, KS 66539

Founded: 1985. **Membership:** 40. Pontiac and Oakland automobiles owners in northeastern Kansas and western Missouri. Disseminates information; conducts charitable events; sponsors festival.

2376 ● Pontiac-Oakland Club International, National Capital Area [District of Columbia, Maryland, and Virginia]
c/o George Richardson
1509 Baltimore Rd.
Alexandria, VA 22308
George Richardson, Exec. Officer   Ph:(703)768-1569

Founded: 1979. **Membership:** 159. Pontiac automobile owners and enthusiasts in the District of Columbia, Maryland, and Virginia.

2377 ● Pontiac-Oakland Club International, Nebraskaland Chapter
1603 Nebraska Ave.
York, NE 68467
Jo Ann Kuester, Sec. Treas.   Ph:(402)362-6413

Founded: 1972. **Membership:** 30. To restore and enjoy Pontiac and Oakland automobiles.

2378 ● Pontiac-Oakland Club International, Southern California Chapter
c/o Daniel J. Santoro
419 Livingston Ave.
Placentia, CA 92670
Daniel J. Santoro, Exec. Officer   Ph:(714)524-8642

Owners of Oakland and Pontiac automobiles.

2379 ● Pontiac-Oakland Club International. Yankee Chapter [Maine, Massachusetts, and Rhode Island]
44 Old Brook Rd.
Lecminster, MA 01453
Steve Peluso, Editor   Ph:(508)537-7066

Founded: 1980. **Membership:** 150. Individuals in Maine, Massachusetts, and Rhode Island promoting restoration and preservation of Pontiac and Oakland automobiles.

2380 ● Pontiac-Oakland Club, Nutmeg Chapter [Connecticut]
Church Hill Rd.
Washington Depot, CT 06974
Starr F. Evans, Editor   Ph:(203)868-7723

Founded: 1976. **Membership:** 106. Owners of Pontiac-Oakland automobiles, built from 1909 to the present, organized to promote the model.

2381 ● Pontiac-Oakland Club, Western New York Chapter
50 Cramer St.
North Tonawanda, NY 14120
Brian Mertens, V. Pres.   Ph:(716)692-1564

Founded: 1976. **Membership:** 96. Owners and enthusiasts of Pontiac/Oakland automobiles. To further the preservation of the automobiles.

PONTIAC SAFARI WAGON (1987-89)

Wagon version of the now discontinued Parisienne, Safari was introduced in 1987. Produced at General Motors plant in Lakewood, Georgia until discontinued in 1989. Rated by *The Car Book* as having high repair costs.

MAJOR FEATURES

● Pontiac Safari had as 1989 standard equipment: 4-speed automatic transmission, front disc/rear drum power brakes, power steering, air conditioning, and AM/FM stereo.

PRICE HISTORY

The following new car prices reflect the approximate retail cost of the base model: **1987** - $13,959; **1988** - $14,519; **1989** - $15,659.

DIMENSIONS

Body Style	Years Avail	Wheel Base (in)	Lgth (in)	Ht (in)	Avg Wt (lbs)	Fuel Cap (gal)	Front Hdrm (in)	Front Legrm (in)
5d wgn	87-89	116.0	215.1	57.4	4,080	22.0	39.6	42.2

ENGINES

Type	Displacement (L)	Fuel Dly	HP @rpm	Torque @rpm (ft/lbs)	MPG Cty/Hwy	Years Avail
V-8	5.0	4-bbl	140@3200	255@2000	17/24	87-89

KEY: I=in-line engine; V=V engine; F=flat engine; FI=fuel injection; bbl=barrel carburetor; T=turbo; D=diesel; HP=horsepower; MPG=estimated average miles per gallon.

EVALUATIONS, TESTS, AND RANKINGS

1989: "in the 0-60 derby. . .checked in at a sleepy 13.74 sec." **Source:** "Wagon Train: The last rear-drive wagons in America," *Motor Trend*, September 1988, pp. 86-90, 92, 94-95.

RECALLS

None to date.

SAFETY AND REPAIRS

1987: "Car Clinic," *Popular Mechanics*, August 1990, p. 26. **Note:** Tip for clashing starter motor gears in 1987-88 General Motors 4.3, 5.0, and 5.7 liter engines.

REPAIR MANUALS

2382 ● Get Your Pontiac Fixed Right
Consumer Reports Books
51 E. 42nd St., Ste. 800
New York, NY 10017   Ph:(212)682-9280

Published 1990. **Price:** $8.95.

OTHER INFORMATION SOURCES

2383 ● Badger Chatter
Pontiac-Oakland Club International, Badger State Chapter
5223 84th St.
Kenosha, WI 53142   Ph:(414)694-2500

Monthly.

2384 ● Bison
Pontiac-Oakland Club, Western New York Chapter
50 Cramer St.
North Tonawanda, NY 14120   Ph:(716)692-1564

Newsletter. Monthly.

2385 ● Chiefly Pontiac
Hoosier Pontiac-Oakland Club
1856 Gray Rd.
Mooresville, IN 46158   Ph:(317)831-1568

Newsletter. Bimonthly.

2386 ● The Drumbeat
Pontiac-Oakland Club, Nutmeg Chapter
Church Hill Rd.
Washington Depot, CT 06974   Ph:(203)868-7723

Periodic.

2387 ● Finger Lakes News [New York]
Pontiac-Oakland Club, Finger Lakes Chapter
14 Judd Ln.
Hilton, NY 14468   Ph:(716)392-3808

Periodic.

2388 ● Hot Air
Pontiac-Oakland Club International, Arizona Chapter
4348 E. Timrod
Tucson, AZ 85711   Ph:(602)795-0978

Newsletter. Monthly.

2389 ● Illinois Newsletter
Pontiac-Oakland Club International, Illinois Chapter
R.R. 1, Box 220
Beecher, IL 60401   Ph:(708)258-6017

Monthly.

2390 ● Nebraskaland
Pontiac-Oakland Club International, Nebraskaland Chapter
1603 Nebraska Ave.
York, NE 68467   Ph:(402)362-6413

Newsletter. Bimonthly.

2391 ● On The Warpath
Pontiac-Oakland Club International, National Capital Area
1509 Baltimore Rd.
Alexandria, VA 22308   Ph:(703)768-1569

Newsletter. Bimonthly.

2392 ● Pontiac-Oakland Club International, Emerald Valley Chapter—Newsletter [Oregon]
Pontiac-Oakland Club International, Emerald Valley Chapter
2411 Washington
Eugene, OR 97405   Ph:(503)485-0319

Monthly.

2393 ● Pontiac-Oakland Club International, Garden State Chapter—Newsletter [New Jersey]
Pontiac-Oakland Club International, Garden State Chapter
19 Earl St.
Denville, NJ 07834

Newsletter. Bimonthly.

2394 ● Pontiac-Oakland Club International, Illinois Chapter—Annual Roster
Pontiac-Oakland Club International, Illinois Chapter
R.R. 1, Box 220
Beecher, IL 60401   Ph:(708)258-6017

2395 ● Pontiac-Oakland Club International, Kansas Chapter—Directory
Pontiac-Oakland Club International, Kansas Chapter
Rt. 3, Box 421
Rose Hill, KS 67133   Ph:(316)776-2162

Periodic.

2396 ● Pontiac-Oakland Club International, Kansas Chapter—Newsletter
Pontiac-Oakland Club International, Kansas Chapter
Rt. 3, Box 421
Rose Hill, KS 67133   Ph:(316)776-2162

Periodic.

2397 ● Pontiac-Oakland Club International, Kansas City Arrowhead Chapter—Directory [Kansas and Missouri]
Pontiac-Oakland Club International, Kansas City
Arrowhead Chapter
104 Center Dr.
Silver Lake, KS 66539   Ph:(913)582-4207

Periodic

2398 ● Pontiac-Oakland Club International—Membership Roster
Pontiac-Oakland Club International
PO Box 4789
Culver City, CA 90230   Ph:(818)704-1580

Annual.

2399 ● Pontiac-Oakland Club International, North Coast Ohio Chapter— Newsletter
Pontiac-Oakland Club International, North Coast Ohio
Chapter
2500 Hetzel Dr.
Parma, OH 44134   Ph:(216)888-4867

Periodic.

2400 ● Pontiac-Oakland Club International, Old Dominion Chapter—Newsletter [Virginia]
Pontiac-Oakland Club International, Old Dominion Chapter
1400 Fortingale Circle
Sandstom, VA 23150   Ph:(804)737-3139

Bimonthly.

2401 ● Pontiac-Oakland Club International, Yankee Chapter—Newsletter [Maine, Massachusetts, and Rhode Island]
Pontiac-Oakland Club International, Yankee Chapter
44 Old Brook Rd.
Leonminster, MA 01453   Ph:(508)537-7066

Monthly.

2402 ● The Scout
Pontiac-Oakland Club International, Kansas City
Arrowhead Chapter
104 Center Dr.
Silver Lake, KS 66539   Ph:(913)582-4207

Newsletter. Monthly.

2403 ● Smoke Signals
Pontiac-Oakland Club International
PO Box 4789
Culver City, CA 90230   Ph:(818)704-1580

Aims to assist owners of Pontiac and Oakland automobiles with the restoration of their vehicles. Monthly. **Editor(s):** Larry Kummer, Editor and Publisher. **Price:** $22.00/yr.; $2.00/mo.

ASSOCIATIONS

2404 ● Pontiac-Oakland Club, Finger Lakes Chapter [New York]
14 Judd Ln.
Hilton, NY 14468
Deborah Arend, Sec.   Ph:(716)392-3808

Founded: 1972. Individuals interested in preserving and restoring Pontiac and Oakland automobiles manufactured between 1907 and the present.

2405 ● Pontiac-Oakland Club International
P.O. Box 4789
Culver City, CA 90230
Dick Hoyt, Exec.Sec.   Ph:(818)704-1580

Founded: 1972. **Membership:** 9,000. Persons interested in the history, restoration, and preservation of Pontiac and Oakland automobiles. Assists owners of Pontiac and Oakland automobiles with the restoration of their vehicles. Maintains staff of volunteer technical advisers. Conducts research pertaining to original specifications and production history. Maintains library. Sponsors competitions; bestows trophies; provides computerized services. **Former Name(s):** (1973) Pontiac Owners Club International. **Convention/Meeting:** Annual conference and auto show.

2406 ● Pontiac-Oakland Club, International, Arizona Chapter
4348 E. Timrod
Tucson, AZ 85711
Thom Sherwood, Pres.   Ph:(602)795-0978

Founded: 1982. **Membership:** 100. Automotive enthusiasts interested in the enjoyment, preservation, and restoration of Pontiac and Oakland automobiles.

2407 ● Pontiac-Oakland Club International, Emerald Valley Chapter [Oregon]
2411 Washington
Eugene, OR 97405
Ken W. Smith, Pres.   Ph:(503)485-0319

Founded: 1985. **Membership:** 52. Owners of Pontiac automobiles and other automobile enthusiasts. Promotes restoration and maintenance of Pontiacs. Assists in location of literature and parts. Conducts charitable and competitive car shows.

2408 ● Pontiac-Oakland Club International, Georgia Chapter
c/o Terry Hunt
139 Dials Dr.
Woodstock, GA 30188
Terry Hunt, Dir.   Ph:(404)929-2440

Persons interested in the history, restoration, and preservation of Pontiac and Oakland automobiles.

2409 ● Pontiac-Oakland Club International, Kansas Chapter
Rt. 3, Box 421
Rose Hill, KS 67133
Margaret Brinkley, Pres.   Ph:(316)776-2162

Individuals interested in collecting and preserving Oakland and Pontiac automobiles.

2410 ● Pontiac-Oakland Club International, Kansas City Arrowhead Chapter [Kansas and Missouri]
104 Center Dr.
Silver Lake, KS 66539

Founded: 1985. **Membership:** 40. Pontiac and Oakland automobiles owners in northeastern Kansas and western Missouri. Disseminates information; conducts charitable events; sponsors festival.

2411 ● Pontiac-Oakland Club International, National Capital Area [District of Columbia, Maryland, and Virginia]
c/o George Richardson
1509 Baltimore Rd.
Alexandria, VA 22308
George Richardson, Exec. Officer   Ph:(703)768-1569

Founded: 1979. **Membership:** 159. Pontiac automobile owners and enthusiasts in the District of Columbia, Maryland, and Virginia.

2412 ● Pontiac-Oakland Club International, Nebraskaland Chapter
1603 Nebraska Ave.
York, NE 68467
Jo Ann Kuester, Sec. Treas.   Ph:(402)362-6413

Founded: 1972. **Membership:** 30. To restore and enjoy Pontiac and Oakland automobiles.

2413 ● Pontiac-Oakland Club International, Southern California Chapter
c/o Daniel J. Santoro
419 Livingston Ave.
Placentia, CA 92670
Daniel J. Santoro, Exec. Officer   Ph:(714)524-8642

Owners of Oakland and Pontiac automobiles.

2414 ● Pontiac-Oakland Club International, Yankee Chapter [Maine, Massachusetts, and Rhode Island]
44 Old Brook Rd.
Lecminster, MA 01453
Steve Peluso, Editor   Ph:(508)537-7066

Founded: 1980. **Membership:** 150. Individuals in Maine, Massachusetts, and Rhode Island promoting restoration and preservation of Pontiac and Oakland automobiles.

2415 ● Pontiac-Oakland Club, Nutmeg Chapter [Connecticut]
Church Hill Rd.
Washington Depot, CT 06974
Starr F. Evans, Editor   Ph:(203)868-7723

Founded: 1976. **Membership:** 106. Owners of Pontiac-Oakland automobiles, built from 1909 to the present, organized to promote the model.

2416 ● Pontiac-Oakland Club, Western New York Chapter
50 Cramer St.
North Tonawanda, NY 14120
Brian Mertens, V. Pres.   Ph:(716)692-1564

Founded: 1976. **Membership:** 96. Owners and enthusiasts of Pontiac/Oakland automobiles. To further the preservation of the automobiles.

PONTIAC SUNBIRD (1987-92)

Introduced as part of J-car line along with Buick Skyhawk and Chevrolet Cavalier. Formerly known as Pontiac J2000, the Pontiac Sunbird is produced at the General Motors plant in Lordstown, Ohio. A wagon version was available until 1989. Both the LE and SE models are available as coupe and sedan versions; a convertible version is also available on the SE model. Listed as one of the Best Bets of 1992 by *The Car Book*.

1991 Pontiac Sunbird GT

MAJOR FEATURES

● Pontiac Sunbird LE and SE have as 1992 standard equipment: 2.0L engine, 5-speed manual transmission, rack-and-pinion power steering, anti-lock brakes, MacPherson struts suspension, power door locks, and AM/FM stereo. In addition, the SE model offers other exterior body stylings and an upgraded interior.

● Pontiac Sunbird GT adds as 1992 standard equipment: 3.1L engine, performance suspension with front and rear stabilizer bars, 15-inch cast aluminum wheels, dual exhaust system, GT aero package, and tinted glass.

PRICE HISTORY

The following new car prices reflect the approximate retail cost of the base model: **1987** - $7,999; **1988** - $8,499; **1989** - $8,849; **1990** - $8,799; **1991** - $8,684; **1992** - $9,620.

DIMENSIONS

Body Style	Years Avail	Wheel Base (in)	Lgth (in)	Ht (in)	Avg Wt (lbs)	Fuel Cap (gal)	Front Hdrm (in)	Front Legrm (in)
2d cpe	87-87	101.2	173.7	51.9	2,353	13.6	37.7	42.2
2d cpe	88-88	101.2	178.2	50.4	2,394	13.6	37.7	42.2
2d cpe	89-91	101.2	181.3	52.0	2,570	13.6	37.8	42.9
2d cpe	92-92	101.3	180.7	52.0	2,484	15.2	37.8	42.2
2d conv	88-88	101.2	178.2	52.6	2,577	13.6	37.4	41.1
2d conv	89-91	101.2	181.3	52.1	2,775	13.6	39.1	42.9
2d conv	92-92	101.3	180.7	52.0	2,694	15.2	38.7	42.9
4d sdn	87-87	101.2	175.7	53.8	2,404	13.6	38.6	42.2
4d sdn	88-88	101.2	181.7	50.4	2,367	13.6	37.7	42.2
4d sdn	89-91	101.2	181.3	53.6	2,592	13.6	38.6	42.2
4d sdn	92-92	101.3	180.7	52.2	2,502	15.2	38.8	42.2
5d wgn	87-88	101.2	175.9	54.1	2,394	13.6	38.3	42.2

ENGINES

Type	Displacement (L)	Fuel Dly	HP @rpm	Torque @rpm (ft/lbs)	MPG Cty/Hwy	Years Avail
I-4	2.0	FI	96@4800	118@3600	26/36	87-91
I-4	2.0	FI	111@5200	125@3600	25/35	92-92
I-4T	2.0	FI	165@5600	175@4000	21/30	87-90
V-6	3.1	FI	140@4200	185@3600	19/28	91-92

KEY: I=in-line engine; V=V engine; F=flat engine; FI=fuel injection; bbl=barrel carburetor; T=turbo; D=diesel; HP=horsepower; MPG=estimated average miles per gallon.

EVALUATIONS, TESTS, AND RANKINGS

1990: "corners, stops, and accelerates with some fast company, for significantly less money." **Source:** "Pontiac Sunbird GT Sport Coupe: A pleasing arrangement of an old tune," *Motor Trend*, September 1989, pp. 55-58, 107.

1990: "with less mass up front and more horsepower, seems more twitchy . . . made better use of the available traction . . . ride quality . . . is super." **Source:** "Jammin' J-cars: Pontiac Turbo Sunbird GT meets Chevy 3.1L V6 Z/24," *Hot Rod*, May 1990, pp. 96-98, 100, 102.

1989: "Despite its drawbacks, driving. . .is fulfilling." **Source:** "Pontiac Sunbird GT Convertible," *Car and Driver*, August 1988, p. 115.

RECALLS

1992: (3,212 passenger cars; includes Chevrolet Cavalier, and Pontiac Sunbird): The secondary hood latch spring is improperly installed or missing. If this latch is not engaged, and the primary hood latch is also not engaged, the hood could open unexpectedly, possibly when the vehicle is in motion. **Corrective action:** Inspect hood latch assemblies and install a new secondary hood latch spring where necessary. *(NHTSA Campaign No. 91V166000.)*

1991: (41,718 passenger vehicles; includes Chevrolet Cavalier, and Pontiac Sunbird): Front door interlock striker may fail, causing door frame collapse and insufficient strength for the shoulder belt anchorage. Vehicle does not comply with FMVSS 210. **Corrective action:** Replace the passive restraint interlock striker studs on front doors. *(NHTSA Campaign No. 91V165000.)*

1989: (13,095 passenger vehicles with 2.0L or 2.8L engines; includes several General Motors models): Fuel tank leak could occur due to small creases on tank underside cracking during pressure cycling which occurs during normal operation. In presence of ignition source, this condition could result in fire. **Corrective action:** Replace fuel tank. *(NHTSA Campaign No. 88V189000.)*

1988: (14,840 coupe and convertible passenger vehicles; includes Chevrolet Cavalier and Pontiac Sunbird): Rear lamp wiring harness may contain open or intermittent circuits affecting back up lamp or license plate lamp operation. Lamps would flash or be inoperative; cars would not comply with FMVSS 108. **Corrective action:** Install new wiring harness. (NHTSA Campaign No. 88V095000.)

1988: (33 passenger vehicles; includes Chevrolet Cavalier and Pontiac Sunbird): There may be poor bond adhesion between windshield glass and mounting. Windshield could separate during a 30 mph frontal barrier test required by FMVSS 212. Such separation during an accident could result in unbelted occupant being ejected and injured. **Corrective action:** Reinstall windshield assuring proper adhesion. (NHTSA Campaign No. 88V121000.)

1987: (131,476 cars with 2.0L engines; includes Buick, Pontiac, and Oldsmobile models): Fuel feed and/or return hose assemblies could crack, causing underhood fire. **Corrective action:** Replace fuel feed/return hoses and assemblies. (NHTSA Campaign No. 87V184000.)

SAFETY AND REPAIRS

1991: ''GM Recalls Cars for Belt Loops,'' *Automotive News*, February 10, 1992, p. 2. **Note:** May have cracked front-door shoulder belt guide loops.

1991: ''GM Recalls Cars for Belt, Brake Ills,'' *Automotive News*, December 9, 1991, p. 43. **Note:** Substandard front door striker studs.

REPAIR MANUALS

2417 ● Get Your Pontiac Fixed Right
Consumer Reports Books
51 E. 42nd St., Ste. 800
New York, NY 10017   Ph:(212)682-9280

Published 1990. **Price:** $8.95.

2418 ● GMC J Cars: Buick Skyhawk, Cadillac Cimarron, Chevrolet Cavalier, Oldsmobile Firenza, Pontiac J-2000, Sunbird Shop Manual, 1982-87
Clymer Publications
P.O. Box 1209
Overland Park, KS 66212   Ph:(913)541-6694

Published 1987. **Price:** $14.95.

2419 ● Haynes General Motors J-Cars Owners Workshop Manual, No. 766: 1982-1989
Haynes Publishing, Inc.
861 Lawrence Dr.
Newbury Park, CA 91320   Ph:(818)889-5400

Published 1989. **Price:** $15.95.

2420 ● Haynes General Motors J-Cars Owners Workshop Manual, No. 766: 1982-1989
Haynes Publishing, Inc.
861 Lawrence Dr.
Newbury Park, CA 91320   Ph:(818)889-5400

Published 1989. **Price:** $15.95.

OTHER INFORMATION SOURCES

2421 ● Badger Chatter
Pontiac-Oakland Club International, Badger State Chapter
5223 84th St.
Kenosha, WI 53142   Ph:(414)694-2500

Monthly.

2422 ● Bison
Pontiac-Oakland Club, Western New York Chapter
50 Cramer St.
North Tonawanda, NY 14120   Ph:(716)692-1564

Newsletter. Monthly.

2423 ● Chiefly Pontiac
Hoosier Pontiac-Oakland Club
1856 Gray Rd.
Mooresville, IN 46158   Ph:(317)831-1568

Newsletter. Bimonthly.

2424 ● The Drumbeat
Pontiac-Oakland Club, Nutmeg Chapter
Church Hill Rd.
Washington Depot, CT 06974   Ph:(203)868-7723

Periodic.

2425 ● Finger Lakes News [New York]
Pontiac-Oakland Club, Finger Lakes Chapter
14 Judd Ln.
Hilton, NY 14468   Ph:(716)392-3808

Periodic.

2426 ● High Performance Pontiac
CSK Publishing Co., Inc.
299 Market St.   Ph:(201)712-9300
Saddle Brook, NJ 07662   Fax:(201)712-9899

Magazine for car enthusiasts, featuring collecting, restoring, modifying, and customizing of Pontiacs from 1950 to the present. Bimonthly. **Editor(s):** Sue Elliott. **Price:** $15.00/year; $3.25 per single issue.

2427 ● Hot Air
Pontiac-Oakland Club International, Arizona Chapter
4348 E. Timrod
Tucson, AZ 85711   Ph:(602)795-0978

Newsletter. Monthly.

2428 ● Illinois Newsletter
Pontiac-Oakland Club International, Illinois Chapter
R.R. 1, Box 220
Beecher, IL 60401   Ph:(708)258-6017

Monthly.

2429 ● Nebraskaland
Pontiac-Oakland Club International, Nebraskaland Chapter
1603 Nebraska Ave.
York, NE 68467   Ph:(402)362-6413

Newsletter. Bimonthly.

2430 ● On The Warpath
Pontiac-Oakland Club International, National Capital Area
1509 Baltimore Rd.
Alexandria, VA 22308   Ph:(703)768-1569

Newsletter. Bimonthly.

2431 ● Pontiac-Oakland Club International, Emerald Valley Chapter—Newsletter [Oregon]
Pontiac-Oakland Club International, Emerald Valley Chapter
2411 Washington
Eugene, OR 97405   Ph:(503)485-0319

Monthly.

2432 ● Pontiac-Oakland Club International, Garden State Chapter—Newsletter [New Jersey]
Pontiac-Oakland Club International, Garden State Chapter
19 Earl St.
Denville, NJ 07834

Newsletter. Bimonthly.

2433 ● Pontiac-Oakland Club International, Illinois Chapter—Annual Roster
Pontiac-Oakland Club International, Illinois Chapter
R.R. 1, Box 220
Beecher, IL 60401   Ph:(708)258-6017

2434 ● Pontiac-Oakland Club International, Kansas Chapter—Directory
Pontiac-Oakland Club International, Kansas Chapter
Rt. 3, Box 421
Rose Hill, KS 67133   Ph:(316)776-2162

Periodic.

2435 ● Pontiac-Oakland Club International, Kansas Chapter—Newsletter
Pontiac-Oakland Club International, Kansas Chapter
Rt. 3, Box 421
Rose Hill, KS 67133   Ph:(316)776-2162

Periodic.

2436 ● Pontiac-Oakland Club International, Kansas City Arrowhead Chapter—Directory [Kansas and Missouri]
Pontiac-Oakland Club International, Kansas City Arrowhead Chapter
104 Center Dr.
Silver Lake, KS 66539   Ph:(913)582-4207

Periodic

2437 ● Pontiac-Oakland Club International—Membership Roster
Pontiac-Oakland Club International
PO Box 4789
Culver City, CA 90230   Ph:(818)704-1580

Annual.

2438 ● Pontiac-Oakland Club International, North Coast Ohio Chapter— Newsletter
Pontiac-Oakland Club International, North Coast Ohio Chapter
2500 Hetzel Dr.
Parma, OH 44134   Ph:(216)888-4867

Periodic.

2439 ● Pontiac-Oakland Club International, Old Dominion Chapter—Newsletter [Virginia]
Pontiac-Oakland Club International, Old Dominion Chapter
1400 Fortingale Circle
Sandstom, VA 23150   Ph:(804)737-3139

Bimonthly.

2440 ● Pontiac-Oakland Club International, Yankee Chapter—Newsletter [Maine, Massachusetts, and Rhode Island]
Pontiac-Oakland Club International, Yankee Chapter
44 Old Brook Rd.
Leonminster, MA 01453   Ph:(508)537-7066

Monthly.

2441 ● The Scout
Pontiac-Oakland Club International, Kansas City Arrowhead Chapter
104 Center Dr.
Silver Lake, KS 66539   Ph:(913)582-4207

Newsletter. Monthly.

2442 ● Smoke Signals
Pontiac-Oakland Club International
PO Box 4789
Culver City, CA 90230   Ph:(818)704-1580

Aims to assist owners of Pontiac and Oakland automobiles with the restoration of their vehicles. Monthly. **Editor(s):** Larry Kummer, Editor and Publisher. **Price:** $22.00/yr.; $2.00/mo.

ASSOCIATIONS

2443 ● Pontiac-Oakland Club, Finger Lakes Chapter [New York]
14 Judd Ln.
Hilton, NY 14468
Deborah Arend, Sec.   Ph:(716)392-3808

Founded: 1972. Individuals interested in preserving and restoring Pontiac and Oakland automobiles manufactured between 1907 and the present.

2444 ● Pontiac-Oakland Club International
P.O. Box 4789
Culver City, CA 90230
Dick Hoyt, Exec.Sec.   Ph:(818)704-1580

Founded: 1972. **Membership:** 9,000. Persons interested in the history, restoration, and preservation of Pontiac and Oakland automobiles. Assists owners of Pontiac and Oakland automobiles with the restoration of their vehicles. Maintains staff of volunteer technical advisers. Conducts research pertaining to original specifications and production history. Maintains library. Sponsors competitions; bestows trophies; provides computerized services. **Former Name(s):** (1973) Pontiac Owners Club International. **Convention/Meeting:** Annual conference and auto show.

2445 ● Pontiac-Oakland Club, International, Arizona Chapter
4348 E. Timrod
Tucson, AZ 85711
Thom Sherwood, Pres.   Ph:(602)795-0978

Founded: 1982. **Membership:** 100. Automotive enthusiasts interested in the enjoyment, preservation, and restoration of Pontiac and Oakland automobiles.

2446 ● Pontiac-Oakland Club International, Emerald Valley Chapter [Oregon]
2411 Washington
Eugene, OR 97405
Ken W. Smith, Pres.   Ph:(503)485-0319

Founded: 1985. **Membership:** 52. Owners of Pontiac automobiles and other automobile enthusiasts. Promotes restoration and maintenance of Pontiacs. Assists in location of literature and parts. Conducts charitable and competitive car shows.

2447 ● Pontiac-Oakland Club International, Georgia Chapter
c/o Terry Hunt
139 Dials Dr.
Woodstock, GA 30188
Terry Hunt, Dir.   Ph:(404)929-2440

Persons interested in the history, restoration, and preservation of Pontiac and Oakland automobiles.

2448 ● Pontiac-Oakland Club International, Kansas Chapter
Rt. 3, Box 421
Rose Hill, KS 67133
Margaret Brinkley, Pres.   Ph:(316)776-2162

Individuals interested in collecting and preserving Oakland and Pontiac automobiles.

2449 ● Pontiac-Oakland Club International, Kansas City Arrowhead Chapter [Kansas and Missouri]
104 Center Dr.
Silver Lake, KS 66539

Founded: 1985. **Membership:** 40. Pontiac and Oakland automobiles owners in northeastern Kansas and western Missouri. Disseminates information; conducts charitable events; sponsors festival.

2450 ● Pontiac-Oakland Club International, National Capital Area [District of Columbia, Maryland, and Virginia]
c/o George Richardson
1509 Baltimore Rd.
Alexandria, VA 22308
George Richardson, Exec. Officer   Ph:(703)768-1569

Founded: 1979. **Membership:** 159. Pontiac automobile owners and enthusiasts in the District of Columbia, Maryland, and Virginia.

2451 ● Pontiac-Oakland Club International, Nebraskaland Chapter
1603 Nebraska Ave.
York, NE 68467
Jo Ann Kuester, Sec. Treas.   Ph:(402)362-6413

Founded: 1972. **Membership:** 30. To restore and enjoy Pontiac and Oakland automobiles.

2452 ● Pontiac-Oakland Club International, Southern California Chapter
c/o Daniel J. Santoro
419 Livingston Ave.
Placentia, CA 92670
Daniel J. Santoro, Exec. Officer   Ph:(714)524-8642

Owners of Oakland and Pontiac automobiles.

2453 ● Pontiac-Oakland Club International. Yankee Chapter [Maine, Massachusetts, and Rhode Island]
44 Old Brook Rd.
Lecminster, MA 01453
Steve Peluso, Editor   Ph:(508)537-7066

Founded: 1980. **Membership:** 150. Individuals in Maine, Massachusetts, and Rhode Island promoting restoration and preservation of Pontiac and Oakland automobiles.

2454 ● Pontiac-Oakland Club, Nutmeg Chapter [Connecticut]
Church Hill Rd.
Washington Depot, CT 06974
Starr F. Evans, Editor   Ph:(203)868-7723

Founded: 1976. **Membership:** 106. Owners of Pontiac-Oakland automobiles, built from 1909 to the present, organized to promote the model.

2455 ● Pontiac-Oakland Club, Western New York Chapter
50 Cramer St.
North Tonawanda, NY 14120
Brian Mertens, V. Pres.   Ph:(716)692-1564

Founded: 1976. **Membership:** 96. Owners and enthusiasts of Pontiac/Oakland automobiles. To further the preservation of the automobiles.

PONTIAC TRANS SPORT (1990-92)

Corporate twins include Chevrolet Lumina APV and Oldsmobile Silhouette. Produced at General Motors plant in Tarrytown, New York. Listed as one of the Best Bets of 1992, and ranked among the best minivans in crash test performance by *The Car Book*.

1991 Pontiac Trans Sport SE

MAJOR FEATURES

● Pontiac Trans Sport SE has as 1992 standard equipment: 3.1L V-6 engine, 3-speed automatic transmission, 5-passenger seating, front disc/rear drum power brakes with ABS, rack-and-pinion power steering, modular seating, and AM/FM stereo.

● Pontiac Trans Sport GT adds as 1992 standard equipment: 3.8L V-6 engine, 4-speed automatic transmission, electronic ride control, cast aluminum wheels, electronic control front air conditioning, 6-passenger seating, tilt steering, cruise control, tinted glass, and an upgraded stereo system.

PRICE HISTORY

The following new car prices reflect the approximate retail cost of the base model: **1990** - $14,995; **1991** - $15,619; **1992** - $16,225.

DIMENSIONS

Body Style	Years Avail	Wheel Base (in)	Lgth (in)	Ht (in)	Avg Wt (lbs)	Fuel Cap (gal)	Front Hdrm (in)	Front Legrm (in)
4d van	90-91	109.8	194.5	65.2	3,553	20.0	35.7	40.7
4d van	92-92	109.8	194.5	65.7	3,678	13.2	na	na

ENGINES

Type	Displace-ment (L)	Fuel Dly	HP @rpm	Torque @rpm (ft/lbs)	MPG Cty/Hwy	Years Avail
V-6	3.1	FI	120@4200	175@2200	18/23	90-92
V-6	3.8	FI	165@na	na	17/24	92-92

KEY: I=in-line engine; V=V engine; F=flat engine; FI=fuel injection; bbl=barrel carburetor; T=turbo; D=diesel; HP=horsepower; MPG=estimated average miles per gallon.

EVALUATIONS, TESTS, AND RANKINGS

1992: "Series 3800 V-6 engine . . . makes a noticeable and shining difference . . . balance of power, suspension, and tires give the vehicle a no-drama persona that lends itself to spirited driving . . . interior is well laid out and user-friendly." **Source:** "Pontiac Trans Sport," *Motor Trend*, October 1991, p. 96.

1991: "Although there are several minivans with more capacity, none can match the versatility." **Source:** "Long-Term Test Cars," *Popular Mechanics*, November 1990, pp. 56-59, 138.

1991: "comfortable and distinctive looking . . . resilient plastic body panels . . . bounce back from minor bumps . . . engine is no better than tepid." **Source:** "Meet the New Minivans," *New Choices for the Best Years*, October 1990, pp. 86-87.

1991: "handling on winding roads impressed us early . . . steering . . . wa s light and quick, but it felt loose on anything but smooth roads . . . Long-distance hauling is a breeze." **Source:** "Life with Trans Sport," *Car and Driver*, June 1991, pp. 107, 109, 113.

1990: "terrific styling . . . dramatic, innovative . . . Handling is competent." **Source:** "The Light Vantastics," *Popular Mechanics*, February 1990, pp. 64, 66-67.

1990: "easy to maneuver and extremely comfortable on long trips . . . impossible to see the front end . . . wide door post . . . impaired visibility." **Source:** "Best of the Minivans," *Changing Times*, July 1990, pp. 41-45.

1990: "woefully run-of-the-mill under its plastic skin . . . When the van is fully loaded, its performance is disappointing . . . top of the dashboard is a vast wasteland." **Source:** "Minivanguard," *Home Mechanix*, March 1990, pp. 56-60.

1990: "felt light and turned tightly . . . dark glass of the rear window made it difficult to see traffic in the rear-view mirror . . . decided lack of pick-up." **Source:** "Minivans, Maxi-space," *Travel Holiday*, March 1990, pp. 103-104.

RECALLS

1990: (343 multipurpose passenger vehicles; includes the Chevrolet Lumina APV, Pontiac Trans Sport, and Oldsmobile Silhouette): Rear modular seat frame hold-down hooks may not meet the required pull force at the rear set anchorage. **Corrective action:** Replace rear hold-down hooks and pivot rivets with heat treated hardware. *(NHTSA Campaign No. 89V164000.)*

1990: (400 passenger vans with grey interiors; includes Chevrolet Lumina APV, Oldsmobile Silhouette, and Pontiac Trans Sport models): Right hand seat/shoulder belt retractor may have been installed in the second row left hand seat position. Incorrect retractor may cause belts to lock up if van is parked on a steep grade. **Corrective action:** Replace shoulder belt assembly. *(NHTSA Campaign No. 91V046000.)*

REPAIR MANUALS

2456 ● Get Your Pontiac Fixed Right
Consumer Reports Books
51 E. 42nd St., Ste. 800
New York, NY 10017   Ph:(212)682-9280

Published 1990. **Price:** $8.95.

OTHER INFORMATION SOURCES

2457 ● Badger Chatter
Pontiac-Oakland Club International, Badger State Chapter
5223 84th St.
Kenosha, WI 53142   Ph:(414)694-2500

Monthly.

2458 ● Bison
Pontiac-Oakland Club, Western New York Chapter
50 Cramer St.
North Tonawanda, NY 14120   Ph:(716)692-1564

Newsletter. Monthly.

2459 ● Chevrolet Lumina—Pontiac Transport Olds Silhouette, 1988-90
Chilton Co.
Chilton Way
Radnor, PA 19089   Ph:(215)964-4000

Published March 1991. **Price:** $15.95.

2460 ● Chiefly Pontiac
Hoosier Pontiac-Oakland Club
1856 Gray Rd.
Mooresville, IN 46158   Ph:(317)831-1568

Newsletter. Bimonthly.

2461 ● The Drumbeat
Pontiac-Oakland Club, Nutmeg Chapter
Church Hill Rd.
Washington Depot, CT 06974   Ph:(203)868-7723

Periodic.

2462 ● Finger Lakes News [New York]
Pontiac-Oakland Club, Finger Lakes Chapter
14 Judd Ln.
Hilton, NY 14468   Ph:(716)392-3808

Periodic.

2463 ● Hot Air
Pontiac-Oakland Club International, Arizona Chapter
4348 E. Timrod
Tucson, AZ 85711   Ph:(602)795-0978

Newsletter. Monthly.

2464 ● Illinois Newsletter
Pontiac-Oakland Club International, Illinois Chapter
R.R. 1, Box 220
Beecher, IL 60401   Ph:(708)258-6017

Monthly.

2465 ● Nebraskaland
Pontiac-Oakland Club International, Nebraskaland Chapter
1603 Nebraska Ave.
York, NE 68467   Ph:(402)362-6413

Newsletter. Bimonthly.

2466 ● On The Warpath
Pontiac-Oakland Club International, National Capital Area
1509 Baltimore Rd.
Alexandria, VA 22308   Ph:(703)768-1569

Newsletter. Bimonthly.

2467 ● Pontiac-Oakland Club International, Emerald Valley Chapter—Newsletter [Oregon]
Pontiac-Oakland Club International, Emerald Valley Chapter
2411 Washington
Eugene, OR 97405   Ph:(503)485-0319

Monthly.

2468 ● Pontiac-Oakland Club International, Garden State Chapter—Newsletter [New Jersey]
Pontiac-Oakland Club International, Garden State Chapter
19 Earl St.
Denville, NJ 07834

Newsletter. Bimonthly.

2469 ● Pontiac-Oakland Club International, Illinois Chapter—Annual Roster
Pontiac-Oakland Club International, Illinois Chapter
R.R. 1, Box 220
Beecher, IL 60401   Ph:(708)258-6017

2470 ● Pontiac-Oakland Club International, Kansas Chapter—Directory
Pontiac-Oakland Club International, Kansas Chapter
Rt. 3, Box 421
Rose Hill, KS 67133   Ph:(316)776-2162

Periodic.

2471 ● Pontiac-Oakland Club International, Kansas Chapter—Newsletter
Pontiac-Oakland Club International, Kansas Chapter
Rt. 3, Box 421
Rose Hill, KS 67133   Ph:(316)776-2162

Periodic.

2472 ● Pontiac-Oakland Club International, Kansas City Arrowhead Chapter—Directory [Kansas and Missouri]
Pontiac-Oakland Club International, Kansas City
Arrowhead Chapter
104 Center Dr.
Silver Lake, KS 66539   Ph:(913)582-4207

Periodic.

2473 ● Pontiac-Oakland Club International—Membership Roster
Pontiac-Oakland Club International
PO Box 4789
Culver City, CA 90230   Ph:(818)704-1580

Annual.

2474 ● Pontiac-Oakland Club International, North Coast Ohio Chapter— Newsletter
Pontiac-Oakland Club International, North Coast Ohio
Chapter
2500 Hetzel Dr.
Parma, OH 44134   Ph:(216)888-4867

Periodic.

2475 ● Pontiac-Oakland Club International, Old Dominion Chapter—Newsletter [Virginia]
Pontiac-Oakland Club International, Old Dominion Chapter
1400 Fortingale Circle
Sandstom, VA 23150   Ph:(804)737-3139

Bimonthly.

2476 ● Pontiac-Oakland Club International, Yankee Chapter—Newsletter [Maine, Massachusetts, and Rhode Island]
Pontiac-Oakland Club International, Yankee Chapter
44 Old Brook Rd.
Leonminster, MA 01453   Ph:(508)537-7066

Monthly.

2477 ● The Scout
Pontiac-Oakland Club International, Kansas City
Arrowhead Chapter
104 Center Dr.
Silver Lake, KS 66539   Ph:(913)582-4207

Newsletter. Monthly.

2478 ● Smoke Signals
Pontiac-Oakland Club International
PO Box 4789
Culver City, CA 90230   Ph:(818)704-1580

Aims to assist owners of Pontiac and Oakland automobiles with the restoration of their vehicles. Monthly. **Editor(s):** Larry Kummer, Editor and Publisher. **Price:** $22.00/yr.; $2.00/mo.

ASSOCIATIONS

2479 ● Pontiac-Oakland Club, Finger Lakes Chapter [New York]
14 Judd Ln.
Hilton, NY 14468
Deborah Arend, Sec.   Ph:(716)392-3808

Founded: 1972. Individuals interested in preserving and restoring Pontiac and Oakland automobiles manufactured between 1907 and the present.

2480 ● Pontiac-Oakland Club International
P.O. Box 4789
Culver City, CA 90230
Dick Hoyt, Exec.Sec.   Ph:(818)704-1580

Founded: 1972. **Membership:** 9,000. Persons interested in the history, restoration, and preservation of Pontiac and Oakland automobiles. Assists owners of Pontiac and Oakland automobiles with the restoration of their vehicles. Maintains staff of volunteer technical advisers. Conducts research pertaining to original specifications and production history. Maintains library. Sponsors competitions; bestows trophies; provides computerized services. **Former Name(s):** (1973) Pontiac Owners Club International. **Convention/Meeting:** Annual conference and auto show.

2481 ● Pontiac-Oakland Club, International, Arizona Chapter
4348 E. Timrod
Tucson, AZ 85711
Thom Sherwood, Pres.   Ph:(602)795-0978

Founded: 1982. **Membership:** 100. Automotive enthusiasts interested in the enjoyment, preservation, and restoration of Pontiac and Oakland automobiles.

2482 ● Pontiac-Oakland Club International, Emerald Valley Chapter [Oregon]
2411 Washington
Eugene, OR 97405
Ken W. Smith, Pres.   Ph:(503)485-0319

Founded: 1985. **Membership:** 52. Owners of Pontiac automobiles and other automobile enthusiasts. Promotes restoration and maintenance of Pontiacs. Assists in location of literature and parts. Conducts charitable and competitive car shows.

2483 ● Pontiac-Oakland Club International, Georgia Chapter
c/o Terry Hunt
139 Dials Dr.
Woodstock, GA 30188
Terry Hunt, Dir.   Ph:(404)929-2440

Persons interested in the history, restoration, and preservation of Pontiac and Oakland automobiles.

2484 ● Pontiac-Oakland Club International, Kansas Chapter
Rt. 3, Box 421
Rose Hill, KS 67133
Margaret Brinkley, Pres.   Ph:(316)776-2162

Individuals interested in collecting and preserving Oakland and Pontiac automobiles.

2485 ● Pontiac-Oakland Club International, Kansas City Arrowhead Chapter [Kansas and Missouri]
104 Center Dr.
Silver Lake, KS 66539

Founded: 1985. **Membership:** 40. Pontiac and Oakland automobiles owners in northeastern Kansas and western Missouri. Disseminates information; conducts charitable events; sponsors festival.

2486 ● Pontiac-Oakland Club International, National Capital Area [District of Columbia, Maryland, and Virginia]
c/o George Richardson
1509 Baltimore Rd.
Alexandria, VA 22308
George Richardson, Exec. Officer   Ph:(703)768-1569

Founded: 1979. **Membership:** 159. Pontiac automobile owners and enthusiasts in the District of Columbia, Maryland, and Virginia.

2487 ● Pontiac-Oakland Club International, Nebraskaland Chapter
1603 Nebraska Ave.
York, NE 68467
Jo Ann Kuester, Sec. Treas.   Ph:(402)362-6413

Founded: 1972. **Membership:** 30. To restore and enjoy Pontiac and Oakland automobiles.

2488 ● Pontiac-Oakland Club International, Southern California Chapter
c/o Daniel J. Santoro
419 Livingston Ave.
Placentia, CA 92670
Daniel J. Santoro, Exec. Officer   Ph:(714)524-8642

Owners of Oakland and Pontiac automobiles.

2489 ● Pontiac-Oakland Club International, Yankee Chapter [Maine, Massachusetts, and Rhode Island]
44 Old Brook Rd.
Lecminster, MA 01453
Steve Peluso, Editor   Ph:(508)537-7066

Founded: 1980. **Membership:** 150. Individuals in Maine, Massachusetts, and Rhode Island promoting restoration and preservation of Pontiac and Oakland automobiles.

2490 ● Pontiac-Oakland Club, Nutmeg Chapter [Connecticut]
Church Hill Rd.
Washington Depot, CT 06974
Starr F. Evans, Editor   Ph:(203)868-7723

Founded: 1976. **Membership:** 106. Owners of Pontiac-Oakland automobiles, built from 1909 to the present, organized to promote the model.

2491 ● Pontiac-Oakland Club, Western New York Chapter
50 Cramer St.
North Tonawanda, NY 14120
Brian Mertens, V. Pres.   Ph:(716)692-1564

Founded: 1976. **Membership:** 96. Owners and enthusiasts of Pontiac/Oakland automobiles. To further the preservation of the automobiles.

PORSCHE 911 (1987-92)

Produced in Stuttgart, Germany. Made *Car and Driver* Ten Best Performers list for 1987 at 13.5 seconds for the quarter mile. Listed in *The Complete Car Cost Guide* in 1990 as having one of the highest maintenance, fuel, and insurance costs and one of the highest resale values among sports cars. Called one of the Ten Best Cars in the World, 1991 by *Road & Track*.

1991 Porsche 911 Turbo

MAJOR FEATURES

● Porsche 911 Carrera 2 1992 standard equipment includes: 5-speed manual transmission, rack-and-pinion power steering, 4-wheel disc brakes with anti-lock braking system, airbags for driver and passenger, air conditioning, power windows, cruise control, power sunroof, security system, and Blaupunkt AM/FM stereo cassette player.

• Porsche 911 Carrera 2 Cabriolet offers the same equipment, but in a two-door convertible body style.

• Porsche 911 Carrera 2 Targa adds as 1992 standard equipment: retracting rear spoiler.

• Porsche 911 Carrera 4, which was introduced in 1989 and weighs slightly more than the Porsche 911 Carrera 2, has as 1992 standard equipment: an upgraded engine, 5-speed manual transmission, all-wheel drive system, rack-and-pinion power steering, 4-wheel disc brakes with anti-lock braking system, airbags for driver and passenger, air conditioning, power windows, cruise control, power sunroof, security system, and Blaupunkt AM/FM stereo.

• Porsche 911 Carrera 4 Cabriolet offers the same equipment, but in a two-door convertible body style.

• Porsche 911 Carrera 4 Targa adds as 1992 standard equipment: retracting rear spoiler.

• Porsche 911 Turbo adds as 1992 standard equipment: rear-wheel drive and 3.3-liter turbo engine.

• Porsche 911 America Roadster adds to the Porsche 911 Carrera 2 in 1992: 3.6-liter Flat-6 engine and rear-wheel drive system.

The following price and dimension information is for the Porsche 911 Carrera 2.

PRICE HISTORY

The following new car prices reflect the approximate retail cost of the base model: **1987** - $41,440; **1988** - $45,895; **1989** - $51,205; **1990** - $58,500; **1991** - $61,915; **1992** - $63,155.

DIMENSIONS

Body Style	Years Avail	Wheel Base (in)	Lgth (in)	Ht (in)	Avg Wt (lbs)	Fuel Cap (gal)	Front Hdrm (in)	Front Legrm (in)
2d cpe	87-89	89.5	168.9	52.0	2,756	22.5	na	na
2d cpe	90-92	89.4	168.3	51.6	3,031	20.3	na	na
2d conv	90-92	89.4	168.3	51.6	3,031	20.3	na	na

ENGINES

Type	Displace-ment (L)	Fuel Dly	HP @rpm	Torque @rpm (ft/lbs)	MPG Cty/Hwy	Years Avail
Flat-6	3.2	FI	214@5900	195@4800	18/24	87-89
Flat-6	3.6	FI	247@6100	228@4800	16/23	89-92
Flat-6T	3.3	FI	282@4000	278@4000	16/22	87-87
Flat-6T	3.3	FI	282@5500	288@4000	14/21	88-91
Flat-6T	3.2	FI	315@5750	332@4500	na	92-92

KEY: I=in-line engine; V=V engine; F=flat engine; FI=fuel injection; bbl=barrel carburetor; T=turbo; D=diesel; HP=horsepower; MPG=estimated average miles per gallon.

EVALUATIONS, TESTS, AND RANKINGS

1991: "Stability at speed, steering response, and the enormously powerful brakes are ... impressive." **Source:** "Porsche 911 Turbo," *Automobile Magazine*, December 1990, pp. 54-57.

1991: "safer for the uninitiated, especially in cornering during throttle-drop ... turbo boasts some of the best brakes in the world." **Source:** "A Tale of Two Exotics," *Design News*, February 11, 1991, pp. 96-99.

1991: "has even more power, but is tractable and smooth, a pleasure even in commuter traffic ... freeway ride quality of the Porsche is its only serious flaw." **Source:** "Porsche 911 Turbo," *Motor Trend*, August 1991, pp. 54-57.

1991: "Carrera Cabriolet receives perfect marks for structural integrity. Weather tightness is also above reproach ... slightly weak air-conditioning system." **Source:** "Top-Down Showdown: We test the hottest cars under the sun," *Motor Trend*, June 1991, pp. 49-59, 62-63.

1990: "Porsche 911 Carrera 2 Tiptronic ... still turns heads and brings out the racer in people." **Source:** "Familiar Porsche packs surprise," *Detroit News*, September 5, 1990, pp. 1D-2D.

1990: "[Porsche 911 Carrera 4 has] bountiful torque, intuitive response to your every input ... Not much pizzaz for 80 grand." **Source:** "The Eroticars," *Car and Driver*, September 1990, pp. 42-45, 47-48, 50, 52-55, 57.

1989: "offers the warmth of familiarity and reliability ... It steadfastly refuses to be moody, hesitant, or faddish." **Source:** "Two Turbos, No Waiting! Lotus Esprit & Porsche 911," *Motor Trend*, December 1988, pp. 38-43, 46-47.

1989: "superb feedback through the steering; firm, linear brakes; good balance ... the faster you drive, the better it feels." **Source:** "Back to the Mother Lode," *Road & Track*, August 1989, pp. 38-49.

1989: "just about everything under the [Carrera 4's] skin is all ... a true driver's car ... sedate manners ... exquisite handling." **Source:** "Automotive Newsfront: Porsche 911— with 4WD," *Popular Science*, March 1989, pp. 20, 22.

1988: "reliable, fast, agile and fun ... The best all-round sports car." **Source:** "Five Exotic Convertibles," *Road & Track*, July 1988, pp. 52-59.

RECALLS

1990: (2,451 vehicles; includes Porsche 911 Carrera 2 and Porsche 911 Carrera 4 models): Luggage in luggage department and/or plastic trim surrounding safety latch may prevent latch on front hood from properly locking. **Corrective action:** Replace plastic trim piece and install a bracket behind the safety latch to prevent interference. *(NHTSA Campaign No. 91V012000.)*

1989: (975 Porsche 911 Turbo models): Due to routing of fuel line from the fuel tank to rear fuel pump, the fuel line may be damaged under certain driving conditions. on full travel of left rear suspension (jounce), the bracket for the brake pad wear indicator wire on left rear control arm could contact and damage fuel line, possibly resulting in a fuel leak and fire. **Corrective action:** Replace damaged fuel line: In addition, all fuel lines will be rerouted so that the brake pad wear indicator wire bracket cannot contact fu el line. *(NHTSA Campaign No. 91V103000.)*

REPAIR MANUALS

2492 ● **Haynes Porsche 911 Owners Workshop Manual, No. 264: 1965-1989**
Haynes Publications,Inc.
861 Lawrence Dr.
Newbury Park, CA 91320   Ph:(818)889-5400

Editor(s): J. H. Haynes and Peter G. Strasman. **Price:** $15.95.

2493 ● **Porsche 911, 944**
Peter Allen Video Productions
106 Charles Lindbergh Blvd.
Uniondale, NY 11553-3695   Ph:(516)222-1111

Two tapes on how to tune-up and maintain Porsche engines. **Release date:** 1986. **Producer:** Peter Allen Productions. **Acquisition:** Purchase.

2494 ● The Porsche 911 Video Manual
Peter Allen Video Productions
38-C Otis St.
West Babylon, NY 11704   Ph:(516)643-4372

Post-1970 Porsche 911 owners can learn helpful maintenance tips from this program. **Release date:** 1985. **Producer:** Videovision Productions. **Acquisition:** Purchase.

OTHER INFORMATION SOURCES

2495 ● European Car
Argus Publishers Corp.
12100 Wilshire Blvd., Ste. 250   Ph:(213)820-3601
Los Angeles, CA 90025   Fax:(213)207-9388

Magazine covering Volkswagen, Porsche, Mercedes-Benz, Audi, Ferrari, Jaguar, and BMW automobiles. Bimonthly. **Editor(s):** Greg N. Brown. **Price:** $11.00 per year; $2.75 per issue.

2496 ● Fantasy Cars
Increase Video
6860 Canby Ave., Ste. 117-118   Ph:(818)342-2880
Reseda, CA 91335   Fax:(818)342-4029

A Lamborghini, Ferrari, and Porsche are taken for a test drive. **Release date:** 1989. **Producer:** Increase Video. **Price:** $29.95.

2497 ● Four for the Road: Corvette, Ferrari, Mercedes-Benz, Porsche—The Greatest of the Survivors Series
Motorbooks International
729 Prospect Ave.
Osceola, WI 54020   Ph:(715)294-3345

Published 1989. **Editor(s):** Henry Rasmussen. **Price:** $19.95.

2498 ● Great Marques Porsche
Book Sales, Inc.
110 Enterprise Ave.
Secaucus, NJ 07094-1995   Ph:(201)864-6341

Published 1989. **Editor(s):** Chris Harvey. **Price:** $10.98.

2499 ● Illustrated Porsche Buyer's Guide
Motorbooks International
729 Prospect Ave.
Osceola, WI 54020   Ph:(715)294-3345

Published 1990. **Author(s):** Dean Batchelor. **Price:** $15.95.

2500 ● Porsche
Running Press Book Publishers
125 S. 22nd St.
Philadelphia, PA 19103   Ph:(215)567-5080

Published 1991. **Editor(s):** Malcolm Toogood. **Price:** $14.98.

2501 ● Porsche 911
Motorbooks Intl., Inc.
112 Madison Ave
New York, NY 10016   Ph:(212)532-6600

Published 1989. **Editor(s):** Clive Prew. **Price:** $15.95.

2502 ● A Porsche 911 & 930 Close-up
Driven by Design
225 Crossroads Blvd., No. 356   Ph:(408)625-1393
Carmel, CA 93923   Fax:(408)375-4699

A quality inspection video for the first time used Porsche buyer. Includes a step by step worksheet and method of

examining a Porsche before taking the big step of purchasing. **Release date:** 1990. **Price:** $39.95.

2503 ● Porsche 911 In All Its Forms
Haynes Publications, Inc.
861 Lawrence Dr.
Newbury Park, CA 91320   Ph:(818)889-5400

Published 1988. **Editor(s):** Chris Harvey. **Price:** $39.95.

2504 ● Porsche 911 Performance Handbook
Motorbooks International
729 Prospect Ave.
Osceola, WI 54020   Ph:(715)294-3345

Published 1987. **Editor(s):** Bruce Anderson. **Price:** $18.95.

2505 ● Porsche 911: The Complete Story
Motorbooks International, Inc.
6277 Sea Harbor Dr.
Orlando, FL 32821   Ph:(407)345-2000

Published 1990. **Editor(s):** David Vivian. **Price:** $32.95.

2506 ● Porsche Club of America—Annual Parade
Porsche Club of America (PCA)
P.O. Box 10402
Alexandria, VA 22310   Ph:(703)922-9300

2507 ● Porsche Market Letter
Porsche Market Letter
P.O. Box 60328
Oklahoma City, OK 73146-0328   Ph:(405)524-7880

Lists Porsche automobiles for sale; offers recommendations for models most likely to appreciate in worth and current market information. Monthly. **Editor(s):** John Hoke, Publisher. **Price:** $40.00 per year; $5.00 per issue.

2508 ● Porsche Owner
Marque Publications
P.O. Box 2791
Fullerton, CA 92633   Ph:(714)771-7126

Covers such topics as vehicles, European travel and lifestyles, and aftermarket accessories. Quarterly. **Editor(s):** R. Janis. **Price:** $12.00 per year; $3.95 per issue.

2509 ● Porsche Owners Club—Membership Roster
Porsche Owners Club (POC)
c/o Creative Motor Sports
425 W. Allen Ave., No. 115
San Dimas, CA 91773   Ph:(714)599-9288

Annual.

2510 ● Porsche Owners Club—Newsletter
Porsche Owners Club (POC)
c/o Creative Motor Sports
425 W. Allen Ave., No. 115
San Dimas, CA 91773   Ph:(714)599-9288

Bimonthly.

2511 ● Porsche Owner's Companion: A Manual of Preservation and Theft Protection
Post Publications
Box 459
Los Gatos, CA 95031   Ph:(408)395-7678

Published 1981. **Editor(s):** Dan W. Post. **Price:** $16.95.

2512 ● Porsche Panorama
Porsche Club of America, Inc.
912 Lullwater Rd.   Ph:(404)378-9823
Atlanta, GA 30307   Fax:(404)377-7041

Provides information on motor racing, Porsche road tests, new vehicle information, classic Porsche cars, and technical information. Monthly. **Editor(s):** Betty Jo Turner. **Price:** $36.00 per member.

2513 ● Porsche: Past and Present
Haynes Publications, Inc.
861 Lawrence Dr.
Newbury Park, CA 91320   Ph:(818)889-5400

Editor(s): Dennis Jenkinson. **Price:** $19.95.

2514 ● Porsche: Portrait of a Legend
Smithmark Publishers, Inc.
112 Madison Ave.
New York, NY 10016   Ph:(212)532-6600

Published 1989. **Editor(s):** Ingo Seiff. **Price:** $39.98.

2515 ● Porsche Uber Alles
Porsche Club of America, Western Michigan Region
1503 43rd St.
Wyoming, MI 49509

Ten times per year. **Price:** $5.00.

2516 ● The Story of Porsche
Simitar Entertainment
3850 Annapolis Ln.   Ph:(612)559-6660
Plymouth, MN 55447   Fax:(612)559-0210

Explores the evolution of the Porsche, from its initial concept to its most recent versions. **Release date:** 1990. **Producer:** Simitar Entertainment. **Price:** $9.95.

2517 ● Super Profile: Porsche 911 Carrera
Haynes Publications, Inc.
861 Lawrence Dr.
Newbury Park, CA 91320   Ph:(818)889-5400

Editor(s): Chris Harvey. **Price:** $11.95.

2518 ● Supercar Showdown
Simitar Entertainment
3850 Annapolis Ln.   Ph:(612)559-6660
Plymouth, MN 55447   Fax:(612)559-0210

A Porsche 911 Turbo, Ferrari Testarossa, and Lamborghini Countach are compared. **Release date:** 1988. **Producer:** Simitar Entertainment. **Price:** $9.95.

2519 ● VW and Porsche
Argus Publishers Corp.
12100 Wilshire Blvd., Ste. 250   Ph:(213)820-3601
Los Angeles, CA 90025   Fax:(213)207-9388

Offers articles of interest to enthusiasts of Volkswagen and Porsche models. Bimonthly. **Editor(s):** Greg Brown. **Price:** $11.00/yr.; $2.75/issue.

ASSOCIATIONS

2520 ● Porsche Club of America
P.O. Box 10402
Alexandria, VA 22310
Ruth R. Harte, Exec. Sec.   Ph:(703)922-9300

Founded: 1954. **Membership:** 30,000. Persons owning Porsche automobiles. **Convention/Meeting:** Annual, usually July or August.

2521 ● Porsche Owners Club
c/o Creative Motor Sports
425 W. Allen Ave., No. 115
San Dimas, CA 91773
Bill Follmer, Contact   Ph:(714)599-9288

Founded: 1955. **Membership:** 800. Porsche owners and related service groups, including dealers and parts, accessories, and repair facilities. Conducts time trials, slaloms, rallies, and parties. Sponsors driver training program and schools. Maintains biographical archives. Provides historical, restoration, competition, maintenance, and repair information. Bestows racing award annually; compiles statistics. **Convention/Meeting:** Bimonthly.

PORSCHE 924S (1987-88)

Produced in Stuttgart, Germany, until it was discontinued in 1988.

MAJOR FEATURES

● Porsche 924S had as 1988 standard equipment: 5-speed manual transmission, 4-wheel power disc brakes, power steering, air conditioning, and AM/FM stereo.

PRICE HISTORY

The following new car prices reflect the approximate retail cost of the base model: **1987** - $23,910; **1988** - $26,560.

DIMENSIONS

Body Style	Years Avail	Wheel Base (in)	Lgth (in)	Ht (in)	Avg Wt (lbs)	Fuel Cap (gal)	Front Hdrm (in)	Front Legrm (in)
3d cpe	87-88	94.5	168.9	50.2	2,734	17.4	na	na

ENGINES

Type	Displacement (L)	Fuel Dly	HP @rpm	Torque @rpm (ft/lbs)	MPG Cty/Hwy	Years Avail
I-4	2.5	FI	147@5800	140@3000	na	87-87
I-4	2.5	FI	158@5900	155@4500	20/28	88-88

KEY: I=in-line engine; V=V engine; F=flat engine; FI=fuel injection; bbl=barrel carburetor; T=turbo; D=diesel; HP=horsepower; MPG=estimated average miles per gallon.

EVALUATIONS, TESTS, AND RANKINGS

1987: "Rock-solid, harsh, heavy-duty, cramped, somewhat balky and occasionally hard to drive . . . a real sports car." **Source:** "'Entry-level,' but a Porsche," *The Detroit News*, April 22, 1987, pp. 1F-2F.

1987: "superior to its predecessor." **Source:** "'Cheap' Porsche 924S still bites wallet," *Detroit Free Press*, August 4, 1986, p. 1E.

RECALLS

1987-88: (53,427 cars; includes models made before 1987; includes other Porsche models): Fuel hose may harden and cause fuel leaks between hose and metal pipe fittings. **Corrective action:** Replace fuel line hose with hoses made of improved material. *(NHTSA Campaign No. 90V061000.)*

REPAIR MANUALS

2522 ● Porsche 924, 928, 944: The New Generation
Motorbooks International
729 Prospect Ave.
Osceola, WI 54020   Ph:(715)294-3345

Published 1987. **Editor(s):** Jerry Sloniger. **Price:** $29.95.

OTHER INFORMATION SOURCES

2523 ● European Car
Argus Publishers Corp.
12100 Wilshire Blvd., Ste. 250   Ph:(213)820-3601
Los Angeles, CA 90025   Fax:(213)207-9388

Magazine covering Volkswagen, Porsche, Mercedes-Benz,
Audi, Ferrari, Jaguar, and BMW automobiles. Bimonthly.
Editor(s): Greg N. Brown. **Price:** $11.00 per year; $2.75 per
issue.

2524 ● Fantasy Cars
Increase Video
6860 Canby Ave., Ste. 117-118   Ph:(818)342-2880
Reseda, CA 91335   Fax:(818)342-4029

A Lamborghini, Ferrari, and Porsche are taken for a test drive.
Release date: 1989. **Producer:** Increase Video. **Price:** $29.95.

**2525 ● Four for the Road: Corvette, Ferrari, Mercedes-Benz,
Porsche—The Greatest of the Survivors Series**
Motorbooks International
729 Prospect Ave.
Osceola, WI 54020   Ph:(715)294-3345

Published 1989. **Editor(s):** Henry Rasmussen. **Price:** $19.95.

2526 ● Great Marques Porsche
Book Sales, Inc.
110 Enterprise Ave.
Secaucus, NJ 07094-1995   Ph:(201)864-6341

Published 1989. **Editor(s):** Chris Harvey. **Price:** $10.98.

2527 ● Illustrated Porsche Buyer's Guide
Motorbooks International
729 Prospect Ave.
Osceola, WI 54020   Ph:(715)294-3345

Published 1990. **Author(s):** Dean Batchelor. **Price:** $15.95.

2528 ● Porsche
Running Press Book Publishers
125 S. 22nd St.
Philadelphia, PA 19103   Ph:(215)567-5080

Published 1991. **Editor(s):** Malcolm Toogood. **Price:** $14.98.

2529 ● Porsche Club of America—Annual Parade
Porsche Club of America (PCA)
P.O. Box 10402
Alexandria, VA 22310   Ph:(703)922-9300

2530 ● Porsche Market Letter
Porsche Market Letter
P.O. Box 60328
Oklahoma City, OK 73146-0328   Ph:(405)524-7880

Lists Porsche automobiles for sale; offers recommendations for
models most likely to appreciate in worth and current market
information. Monthly. **Editor(s):** John Hoke, Publisher. **Price:**
$40.00 per year; $5.00 per issue.

2531 ● Porsche Owner
Marque Publications
P.O. Box 2791
Fullerton, CA 92633   Ph:(714)771-7126

Covers such topics as vehicles, European travel and lifestyles,
and aftermarket accessories. Quarterly. **Editor(s):** R. Janis.
Price: $12.00 per year; $3.95 per issue.

2532 ● Porsche Owners Club—Membership Roster
Porsche Owners Club (POC)
c/o Creative Motor Sports
425 W. Allen Ave., No. 115
San Dimas, CA 91773   Ph:(714)599-9288

Annual.

2533 ● Porsche Owners Club—Newsletter
Porsche Owners Club (POC)
c/o Creative Motor Sports
425 W. Allen Ave., No. 115
San Dimas, CA 91773   Ph:(714)599-9288

Bimonthly.

**2534 ● Porsche Owner's Companion: A Manual of
Preservation and Theft Protection**
Post Publications
Box 459
Los Gatos, CA 95031   Ph:(408)395-7678

Published 1981. **Editor(s):** Dan W. Post. **Price:** $16.95.

2535 ● Porsche Panorama
Porsche Club of America, Inc.
912 Lullwater Rd.   Ph:(404)378-9823
Atlanta, GA 30307   Fax:(404)377-7041

Provides information on motor racing, Porsche road tests, new
vehicle information, classic Porsche cars, and technical
information. Monthly. **Editor(s):** Betty Jo Turner. **Price:** $36.00
per member.

2536 ● Porsche: Past and Present
Haynes Publications, Inc.
861 Lawrence Dr.
Newbury Park, CA 91320   Ph:(818)889-5400

Editor(s): Dennis Jenkinson. **Price:** $19.95.

2537 ● Porsche: Portrait of a Legend
Smithmark Publishers, Inc.
112 Madison Ave.
New York, NY 10016   Ph:(212)532-6600

Published 1989. **Editor(s):** Ingo Seiff. **Price:** $39.98.

2538 ● Porsche Uber Alles
Porsche Club of America, Western Michigan Region
1503 43rd St.
Wyoming, MI 49509

Ten times per year. **Price:** $5.00.

2539 ● The Story of Porsche
Simitar Entertainment
3850 Annapolis Ln.   Ph:(612)559-6660
Plymouth, MN 55447   Fax:(612)559-0210

Explores the evolution of the Porsche, from its initial concept
to its most recent versions. **Release date:** 1990. **Producer:**
Simitar Entertainment. **Price:** $9.95.

2540 ● VW and Porsche
Argus Publishers Corp.
12100 Wilshire Blvd., Ste. 250   Ph:(213)820-3601
Los Angeles, CA 90025   Fax:(213)207-9388

Offers articles of interest to enthusiasts of Volkswagen and Porsche models. Bimonthly. **Editor(s):** Greg Brown. **Price:** $11.00/yr.; $2.75/issue.

ASSOCIATIONS

2541 ● Porsche Club of America
P.O. Box 10402
Alexandria, VA 22310
Ruth R. Harte, Exec. Sec.   Ph:(703)922-9300

Founded: 1954. **Membership:** 30,000. Persons owning Porsche automobiles. **Convention/Meeting:** Annual, usually July or August.

2542 ● Porsche Owners Club
c/o Creative Motor Sports
425 W. Allen Ave., No. 115
San Dimas, CA 91773
Bill Follmer, Contact   Ph:(714)599-9288

Founded: 1955. **Membership:** 800. Porsche owners and related service groups, including dealers and parts, accessories, and repair facilities. Conducts time trials, slaloms, rallies, and parties. Sponsors driver training program and schools. Maintains biographical archives. Provides historical, restoration, competition, maintenance, and repair information. Bestows racing award annually; compiles statistics. **Convention/Meeting:** Bimonthly.

PORSCHE 928 (1987-92)

Produced in Stuttgart, Germany. Porsche 928 S4 made *Car and Driver's* 1987 Ten Best Performers list for braking from 70-0 mph in 164 ft. Listed in *The Complete Car Cost Guide* in 1990 as having one of the highest fuel and maintenance costs among sports cars.

1991 Porsche 928 GT

MAJOR FEATURES

● Porsche 928 S4 1992 standard equipment includes: 4-speed automatic transmission, 4-wheel power disc brakes with anti-lock braking system, rack-and-pinion power steering, driver and passenger airbags, automatic climate control system, power windows, cruise control, tilt steering, security system, leather seats, electric sunroof, and Blaupunkt AM/FM stereo cassette player.

● Porsche 928 GT adds as 1992 standard equipment: 5-speed manual transmission.

PRICE HISTORY

The following new car prices reflect the approximate retail cost of the base model: **1987** - $63,520; **1988** - $69,380; **1989** - $74,545; **1990** - $74,545; **1991** - $77,500; **1992** - $79,050.

DIMENSIONS

Body Style	Years Avail	Wheel Base (in)	Lgth (in)	Ht (in)	Avg Wt (lbs)	Fuel Cap (gal)	Front Hdrm (in)	Front Legrm (in)
2d lbk	87-92	98.4	178.1	50.5	3,505	22.7	na	na

ENGINES

Type	Displacement (L)	Fuel Dly	HP @rpm	Torque @rpm (ft/lbs)	MPG Cty/Hwy	Years Avail
V-8	5.0	FI	316@6000	317@3000	15/19	87-92
V-8	5.0	FI	326@6200	317@4100	13/19	90-92

KEY: I=in-line engine; V=V engine; F=flat engine; FI=fuel injection; bbl=barrel carburetor; T=turbo; D=diesel; HP=horsepower; MPG=estimated average miles per gallon.

EVALUATIONS, TESTS, AND RANKINGS

1991: "5.9 seconds to accelerate 0-60 mph . . . comforting stability . . . point and shoot agility . . . Braking is . . . amazing." **Source:** "Porsche S928 GT: The Gentleman's Express," *Motor Trend*, December 1990, pp. 98-102.

1990: "the top of the performance class . . . rocket from 0 to 60 mph in just 5.2 seconds . . . far more agile in curvy-road dicing and slicing than you'd expect such a hefty car to be." **Source:** "Porsche 928GT: Speed for the serious—and the solvent," *Car and Driver*, July 1990, pp. 133-134, 136, 139.

1989: "At 165 mph, the Porsche was stable as an aircraft carrier . . . entirely vibration-free . . . made 165 feel like 65." **Source:** "Top-Speed 10: Indulging our go-fast fetish again," *Motor Trend*, September 1988, pp. 32-39, 42, 44.

1987: "the fastest and best-handling two-plus-two on the road . . . cockpit is ergonomic perfection . . . comfort . . . is exemplary." **Source:** "Porsche 928S4: Vindicated at last," *Car and Driver*, May 1987, pp. 67, 69-70.

1987: "world-class handling dynamics and exemplary braking power and stability." **Source:** "Porsche 928S 4: Let's induldge our fantasies a little," *Motor Trend*, May 1987, pp. 61-62, 64, 160.

RECALLS

1990: (19 cars): Cracking of plastic fuel gauge mounting nut could allow fuel leakage and could result in a fire. **Corrective action:** Replace mounting nuts with nuts of an improved material. *(NHTSA Campaign No. 90V117000.)*

1987: (892 cars): Return fuel line hose may not be ozone resistant, resulting in cracked hose and fuel leak. **Corrective action:** Install ozone resistant hose. *(NHTSA Campaign No. 87V031000.)*

1987: (6,905 cars; includes models made before 1987): Inadequate heat shield above catalytic converter could overheat. May result in fire. **Corrective action:** Replace with improved heat shield. *(NHTSA Campaign No. 89V106000.)*

REPAIR MANUALS

2543 ● Porsche 924, 928, 944: The New Generation
Motorbooks International
729 Prospect Ave.
Osceola, WI 54020   Ph:(715)294-3345

Published 1987. **Editor(s):** Jerry Sloniger. **Price:** $29.95.

OTHER INFORMATION SOURCES

2544 ● European Car
Argus Publishers Corp.
12100 Wilshire Blvd., Ste. 250   Ph:(213)820-3601
Los Angeles, CA 90025   Fax:(213)207-9388

Magazine covering Volkswagen, Porsche, Mercedes-Benz, Audi, Ferrari, Jaguar, and BMW automobiles. Bimonthly. **Editor(s):** Greg N. Brown. **Price:** $11.00 per year; $2.75 per issue.

2545 ● Fantasy Cars
Increase Video
6860 Canby Ave., Ste. 117-118   Ph:(818)342-2880
Reseda, CA 91335   Fax:(818)342-4029

A Lamborghini, Ferrari, and Porsche are taken for a test drive. **Release date:** 1989. **Producer:** Increase Video. **Price:** $29.95.

2546 ● Four for the Road: Corvette, Ferrari, Mercedes-Benz, Porsche—The Greatest of the Survivors Series
Motorbooks International
729 Prospect Ave.
Osceola, WI 54020   Ph:(715)294-3345

Published 1989. **Editor(s):** Henry Rasmussen. **Price:** $19.95.

2547 ● Great Marques Porsche
Book Sales, Inc.
110 Enterprise Ave.
Secaucus, NJ 07094-1995   Ph:(201)864-6341

Published 1989. **Editor(s):** Chris Harvey. **Price:** $10.98.

2548 ● Illustrated Porsche Buyer's Guide
Motorbooks International
729 Prospect Ave.
Osceola, WI 54020   Ph:(715)294-3345

Published 1990. **Author(s):** Dean Batchelor. **Price:** $15.95.

2549 ● Porsche
Running Press Book Publishers
125 S. 22nd St.
Philadelphia, PA 19103   Ph:(215)567-5080

Published 1991. **Editor(s):** Malcolm Toogood. **Price:** $14.98.

2550 ● Porsche Club of America—Annual Parade
Porsche Club of America (PCA)
P.O. Box 10402
Alexandria, VA 22310   Ph:(703)922-9300

2551 ● Porsche Market Letter
Porsche Market Letter
P.O. Box 60328
Oklahoma City, OK 73146-0328   Ph:(405)524-7880

Lists Porsche automobiles for sale; offers recommendations for models most likely to appreciate in worth and current market information. Monthly. **Editor(s):** John Hoke, Publisher. **Price:** $40.00 per year; $5.00 per issue.

2552 ● Porsche Owner
Marque Publications
P.O. Box 2791
Fullerton, CA 92633   Ph:(714)771-7126

Covers such topics as vehicles, European travel and lifestyles, and aftermarket accessories. Quarterly. **Editor(s):** R. Janis. **Price:** $12.00 per year; $3.95 per issue.

2553 ● Porsche Owners Club—Membership Roster
Porsche Owners Club (POC)
c/o Creative Motor Sports
425 W. Allen Ave., No. 115
San Dimas, CA 91773   Ph:(714)599-9288

Annual.

2554 ● Porsche Owners Club—Newsletter
Porsche Owners Club (POC)
c/o Creative Motor Sports
425 W. Allen Ave., No. 115
San Dimas, CA 91773   Ph:(714)599-9288

Bimonthly.

2555 ● Porsche Owner's Companion: A Manual of Preservation and Theft Protection
Post Publications
Box 459
Los Gatos, CA 95031   Ph:(408)395-7678

Published 1981. **Editor(s):** Dan W. Post. **Price:** $16.95.

2556 ● Porsche Panorama
Porsche Club of America, Inc.
912 Lullwater Rd.   Ph:(404)378-9823
Atlanta, GA 30307   Fax:(404)377-7041

Provides information on motor racing, Porsche road tests, new vehicle information, classic Porsche cars, and technical information. Monthly. **Editor(s):** Betty Jo Turner. **Price:** $36.00 per member.

2557 ● Porsche: Past and Present
Haynes Publications, Inc.
861 Lawrence Dr.
Newbury Park, CA 91320   Ph:(818)889-5400

Editor(s): Dennis Jenkinson. **Price:** $19.95.

2558 ● Porsche: Portrait of a Legend
Smithmark Publishers, Inc.
112 Madison Ave.
New York, NY 10016   Ph:(212)532-6600

Published 1989. **Editor(s):** Ingo Seiff. **Price:** $39.98.

2559 ● Porsche Uber Alles
Porsche Club of America, Western Michigan Region
1503 43rd St.
Wyoming, MI 49509

Ten times per year. **Price:** $5.00.

2560 ● The Story of Porsche
Simitar Entertainment
3850 Annapolis Ln.   Ph:(612)559-6660
Plymouth, MN 55447   Fax:(612)559-0210

Explores the evolution of the Porsche, from its initial concept to its most recent versions. **Release date:** 1990. **Producer:** Simitar Entertainment. **Price:** $9.95.

2561 ● **VW and Porsche**
Argus Publishers Corp.
12100 Wilshire Blvd., Ste. 250   Ph:(213)820-3601
Los Angeles, CA 90025   Fax:(213)207-9388

Offers articles of interest to enthusiasts of Volkswagen and Porsche models. Bimonthly. **Editor(s):** Greg Brown. **Price:** $11.00/yr.; $2.75/issue.

ASSOCIATIONS

2562 ● **Porsche Club of America**
P.O. Box 10402
Alexandria, VA 22310
Ruth R. Harte, Exec. Sec.   Ph:(703)922-9300

Founded: 1954. **Membership:** 30,000. Persons owning Porsche automobiles. **Convention/Meeting:** Annual, usually July or August.

2563 ● **Porsche Owners Club**
c/o Creative Motor Sports
425 W. Allen Ave., No. 115
San Dimas, CA 91773
Bill Follmer, Contact   Ph:(714)599-9288

Founded: 1955. **Membership:** 800. Porsche owners and related service groups, including dealers and parts, accessories, and repair facilities. Conducts time trials, slaloms, rallies, and parties. Sponsors driver training program and schools. Maintains biographical archives. Provides historical, restoration, competition, maintenance, and repair information. Bestows racing award annually; compiles statistics. **Convention/Meeting:** Bimonthly.

PORSCHE 944 (1987-91)

Produced in Stuttgart, Germany, until it was replaced by the Porsche 968 in 1992. Listed in *The Complete Car Cost Guide* in 1990 as having one of the highest repair costs among sports cars over a five-year period.

1991 Porsche 944 S2 Cabriolet

MAJOR FEATURES

● Porsche 944 S2 1991 standard equipment included: 5-speed manual transmission, rack-and-pinion power steering, 4-wheel power disc brakes with anti-lock braking system, driver and passenger airbags, automatic climate control system, power windows, cruise control, security system, and Blaupunkt AM/FM stereo cassette player.

● Porsche 944 S2 Cabriolet offered the same standard equipment in 1991 but in a two-door convertible body style.

● Porsche 944 Turbo was discontinued in 1989.

● Porsche 944 S was discontinued in 1988.

PRICE HISTORY

The following new car prices reflect the approximate retail cost of the base model: **1987** - $27,840; **1988** - $30,995; **1989** - $33,245; **1990** - $41,900; **1991** - $43,350.

DIMENSIONS

Body Style	Years Avail	Wheel Base (in)	Lgth (in)	Ht (in)	Avg Wt (lbs)	Fuel Cap (gal)	Front Hdrm (in)	Front Legrm (in)
2d lbk	87-91	94.5	168.9	50.2	2,998	21.1	na	na

ENGINES

Type	Displace-ment (L)	Fuel Dly	HP @rpm	Torque @rpm (ft/lbs)	MPG Cty/Hwy	Years Avail
I-4	2.5	FI	147@5800	140@3000	21/27	87-87
I-4	2.5	FI	158@5900	155@4500	20/28	88-88
I-4	2.5	FI	188@6000	170@4300	19/26	88-88
I-4	2.7	FI	162@5800	166@4200	19/26	89-89
I-4	3.0	FI	208@5800	207@4100	17/26	89-91
I-4T	2.5	FI	217@5800	243@3500	19/27	87-88
I-4T	2.5	FI	247@6000	250@4000	19/27	88-89

KEY: I=in-line engine; V=V engine; F=flat engine; FI=fuel injection; bbl=barrel carburetor; T=turbo; D=diesel; HP=horsepower; MPG=estimated average miles per gallon.

EVALUATIONS, TESTS, AND RANKINGS

1991: "voted "most likely to be around 20 years from now." . . . exudes well-constructed quality." **Source:** "Carrying the Torch," *Road & Track*, November 1990, pp. 44-56.

1991: "cockpit is . . . simple and orderly and efficient . . . has perhaps the best steering in the world . . . supremely poised chassis." **Source:** "To What Shall I Compare Thee," *Car and Driver*, August 1991, p. 42.

1991: "not just a car but a motorized image . . . 5-speed manual was a disappointment." **Source:** "Porsche Convertible leaves envy in its wake," *Detroit Free Press*, June 3, 1991, F1.

1991: "ride is firm, bordering on harsh . . . top stayed snug through prolonged rain and didn't drum at high speeds . . . steering is quick and accurate." **Source:** "Porsche's true colors come out in driving," *The Flint Journal*, June 26, 1991, pp. E1-E2.

1990: "quiet, smooth power delivery . . . quality is widely evident . . . shifting action feels direct and accurate . . . easy to drive." **Source:** "Porsche 944 S2: Bigger, better, badder," *Motor Trend*, August 1989, pp. 60-66, 126.

1990: "a true driver's car, with excellent . . . balance, superb brakes and responsive, linear steering with good feedback from the road." **Source:** "Porsche 944 S2 Cabriolet," *Road & Track*, February 1990, pp. 84-85, 89.

1989: "all-aluminum 944-series engines dampen virtually all perceptible rotating vibration . . . extra torque . . . gives it more flexibility around town." **Source:** "Automotive Newsfront: Once and future Porsche," *Popular Science*, March 1989, pp. 20-22.

1989: "A precisely engineered suspension provides incredible cornering power and a very acceptable ride." **Source:** "2 for the Road," *Regardies*, September 1989, pp. 169-170, 172-180, 182.

1989: "A world-class driving machine that is sure to satisfy."

Source: "Two-Seat Heat," *Popular Science,* September 1989, pp. 38-40, 42, 44, 48.

1988: "by far the strongest-performing four-cylinder car in the world." **Source:** "Porsche 944 Turbo S," *Car and Driver,* June 1988, pp. 93-96.

RECALLS

1988: (1,936 vehicles): Possible defective alloy A-arms may crack and break, resulting in loss of control. **Corrective action:** Replace A-arms. *(NHTSA Campaign No. 89V133000.)*

1987-88: (53,427 cars; includes models made before 1987; includes other Porsche models): Fuel hose may harden and cause fuel leaks between hose and metal pipe fittings. **Corrective action:** Replace fuel line hose with hoses made of improved material. *(NHTSA Campaign No. 90V061000.)*

REPAIR MANUALS

2564 ● Haynes Porsche 944 Owners Workshop Manual, No. 1027: 1983-1989
Haynes Publications, Inc.
861 Lawrence Dr.
Newbury Park, CA 91320   Ph:(818)889-5400

Published 1987. **Editor(s):** J. H. Haynes. **Price:** $15.95.

2565 ● Porsche 911, 944
Peter Allen Video Productions
106 Charles Lindbergh Blvd.
Uniondale, NY 11553-3695   Ph:(516)222-1111

Two tapes on how to tune-up and maintain Porsche engines. **Release date:** 1986. **Producer:** Peter Allen Productions. **Acquisition:** Purchase.

2566 ● Porsche 924, 928, 944: The New Generation
Motorbooks International
729 Prospect Ave.
Osceola, WI 54020   Ph:(715)294-3345

Published 1987. **Editor(s):** Jerry Sloniger. **Price:** $29.95.

OTHER INFORMATION SOURCES

2567 ● European Car
Argus Publishers Corp.
12100 Wilshire Blvd., Ste. 250   Ph:(213)820-3601
Los Angeles, CA 90025   Fax:(213)207-9388

Magazine covering Volkswagen, Porsche, Mercedes-Benz, Audi, Ferrari, Jaguar, and BMW automobiles. Bimonthly. **Editor(s):** Greg N. Brown. **Price:** $11.00 per year; $2.75 per issue.

2568 ● Fantasy Cars
Increase Video
6860 Canby Ave., Ste. 117-118   Ph:(818)342-2880
Reseda, CA 91335   Fax:(818)342-4029

A Lamborghini, Ferrari, and Porsche are taken for a test drive. **Release date:** 1989. **Producer:** Increase Video. **Price:** $29.95.

2569 ● Four for the Road: Corvette, Ferrari, Mercedes-Benz, Porsche—The Greatest of the Survivors Series
Motorbooks International
729 Prospect Ave.
Osceola, WI 54020   Ph:(715)294-3345

Published 1989. **Editor(s):** Henry Rasmussen. **Price:** $19.95.

2570 ● Great Marques Porsche
Book Sales, Inc.
110 Enterprise Ave.
Secaucus, NJ 07094-1995   Ph:(201)864-6341

Published 1989. **Editor(s):** Chris Harvey. **Price:** $10.98.

2571 ● Illustrated Porsche Buyer's Guide
Motorbooks International
729 Prospect Ave.
Osceola, WI 54020   Ph:(715)294-3345

Published 1990. **Author(s):** Dean Batchelor. **Price:** $15.95.

2572 ● Porsche
Running Press Book Publishers
125 S. 22nd St.
Philadelphia, PA 19103   Ph:(215)567-5080

Published 1991. **Editor(s):** Malcolm Toogood. **Price:** $14.98.

2573 ● Porsche Club of America—Annual Parade
Porsche Club of America (PCA)
P.O. Box 10402
Alexandria, VA 22310   Ph:(703)922-9300

2574 ● Porsche Market Letter
Porsche Market Letter
P.O. Box 60328
Oklahoma City, OK 73146-0328   Ph:(405)524-7880

Lists Porsche automobiles for sale; offers recommendations for models most likely to appreciate in worth and current market information. Monthly. **Editor(s):** John Hoke, Publisher. **Price:** $40.00 per year; $5.00 per issue.

2575 ● Porsche Owner
Marque Publications
P.O. Box 2791
Fullerton, CA 92633   Ph:(714)771-7126

Covers such topics as vehicles, European travel and lifestyles, and aftermarket accessories. Quarterly. **Editor(s):** R. Janis. **Price:** $12.00 per year; $3.95 per issue.

2576 ● Porsche Owners Club—Membership Roster
Porsche Owners Club (POC)
c/o Creative Motor Sports
425 W. Allen Ave., No. 115
San Dimas, CA 91773   Ph:(714)599-9288

Annual.

2577 ● Porsche Owners Club—Newsletter
Porsche Owners Club (POC)
c/o Creative Motor Sports
425 W. Allen Ave., No. 115
San Dimas, CA 91773   Ph:(714)599-9288

Bimonthly.

2578 ● Porsche Owner's Companion: A Manual of Preservation and Theft Protection
Post Publications
Box 459
Los Gatos, CA 95031   Ph:(408)395-7678

Published 1981. **Editor(s):** Dan W. Post. **Price:** $16.95.

2579 ● Porsche Panorama
Porsche Club of America, Inc.
912 Lullwater Rd.   Ph:(404)378-9823
Atlanta, GA 30307   Fax:(404)377-7041

Provides information on motor racing, Porsche road tests, new vehicle information, classic Porsche cars, and technical information. Monthly. **Editor(s):** Betty Jo Turner. **Price:** $36.00 per member.

2580 ● Porsche: Past and Present
Haynes Publications, Inc.
861 Lawrence Dr.
Newbury Park, CA 91320   Ph:(818)889-5400

Editor(s): Dennis Jenkinson. **Price:** $19.95.

2581 ● Porsche: Portrait of a Legend
Smithmark Publishers, Inc.
112 Madison Ave.
New York, NY 10016   Ph:(212)532-6600

Published 1989. **Editor(s):** Ingo Seiff. **Price:** $39.98.

2582 ● Porsche Uber Alles
Porsche Club of America, Western Michigan Region
1503 43rd St.
Wyoming, MI 49509

Ten times per year. **Price:** $5.00.

2583 ● The Story of Porsche
Simitar Entertainment
3850 Annapolis Ln.   Ph:(612)559-6660
Plymouth, MN 55447   Fax:(612)559-0210

Explores the evolution of the Porsche, from its initial concept to its most recent versions. **Release date:** 1990. **Producer:** Simitar Entertainment. **Price:** $9.95.

2584 ● VW and Porsche
Argus Publishers Corp.
12100 Wilshire Blvd., Ste. 250   Ph:(213)820-3601
Los Angeles, CA 90025   Fax:(213)207-9388

Offers articles of interest to enthusiasts of Volkswagen and Porsche models. Bimonthly. **Editor(s):** Greg Brown. **Price:** $11.00/yr.; $2.75/issue.

ASSOCIATIONS

2585 ● Porsche Club of America
P.O. Box 10402
Alexandria, VA 22310
Ruth R. Harte, Exec. Sec.   Ph:(703)922-9300

Founded: 1954. **Membership:** 30,000. Persons owning Porsche automobiles. **Convention/Meeting:** Annual, usually July or August.

2586 ● Porsche Owners Club
c/o Creative Motor Sports
425 W. Allen Ave., No. 115
San Dimas, CA 91773
Bill Follmer, Contact   Ph:(714)599-9288

Founded: 1955. **Membership:** 800. Porsche owners and related service groups, including dealers and parts, accessories, and repair facilities. Conducts time trials, slaloms, rallies, and parties. Sponsors driver training program and schools. Maintains biographical archives. Provides historical, restoration, competition, maintenance, and repair information. Bestows racing award annually; compiles statistics. **Convention/Meeting:** Bimonthly.

PORSCHE 968 (1992)

The replacement for the 944 S2, the 968 is Porsche's entry-level sports car. A front-engine, rear-wheel drive passenger vehicle, the 968 is available in either 3-door coupe or 2-door convertible. About half of all 968s will be equipped with Porsche's Tiptronic transmission. This optional dual-function transmission system lets drivers utilize both the convenience of an automatic and the control of a manual. Selected to the *Automobile Magazine's* All-Stars list in 1992.

MAJOR FEATURES

● 968 Coupe has as 1992 standard equipment: 3.0-liter 16-valve 4-cylinder engine, 6-speed manual transmission, 4-wheel power-assisted vented disc brakes with ABS, power rack-and-pinion steering, driver- and passenger-side airbags, air conditioning, and cruise control.

● 968 Cabriolet adds as 1992 standard equipment: four-layer folding convertible top.

PRICE HISTORY

The following new car prices reflect the approximate retail cost of the base model: **1992** - $44,500.

DIMENSIONS

Body Style	Years Avail	Wheel Base (in)	Lgth (in)	Ht (in)	Avg Wt (lbs)	Fuel Cap (gal)	Front Hdrm (in)	Front Legrm (in)
2d cpe	92-92	94.5	170.1	50.2	3,086	19.6	38.0	44.5
2d conv	92-92	94.5	170.1	50.2	3,240	19.6	38.0	44.5

ENGINES

Type	Displace-ment (L)	Fuel Dly	HP @rpm	Torque @rpm (ft/lbs)	MPG Cty/Hwy	Years Avail
I-4	3.0	FI	236@6200	225@4100	17/25	92-92

KEY: I=in-line engine; V=V engine; F=flat engine; FI=fuel injection; bbl=barrel carburetor; T=turbo; D=diesel; HP=horsepower; MPG=estimated average miles per gallon.

EVALUATIONS, TESTS, AND RANKINGS

1992: "It is everything you might want a Porsche to be . . . quite handsome . . . shape blends elements of the 911 and 928 into a very pleasing whole." **Source:** "Porsche 968: A six-speed cabriolet, please. To go," *Automobile Magazine*, January 1992, p. 56.

1992: "less than perfect seats . . . precise steering offers plenty of feedback . . . anti-lift aerodynamics keep the car glued to the road." **Source:** "Porsche 968: You say you want an evolution," *Motor Trend*, November 1991, pp. 92-93.

1992: "Handling and braking are as good as ever . . . Ride is firm but not jarring with the standard suspension . . . Pleasant surprises are in store when you tip into the throttle." **Source:** "Porsche 968: If it looks like a Porsche and runs like a Porsche, then it must be . . . expensive," *Road & Track*, November 1991, p. 91.

1992: "the world's most powerful normally aspirated 3-liter engine . . . fuller front fenders and new-style 17-inch wheels give a more masculine stance." **Source:** "Porsche To Launch 968," *Motor Trend*, May 1991, p. 28.

1992: "ride is much friendlier than you'd expect . . . a suggestion of modular construction that's quite intriguing . . . the look is stylish." **Source:** "1992 Import Cars: Porsche 968; A

944 with 24 more,'' *Car and Driver*, November 1991, pp. 98-99.

1992: ''This road-eater gobbles ground like a fat guy in a pie-eating contest ... the front is roomy, the rear is tiny ... standard front seats, flattish at best, deliver little dynamic support.'' **Source:** ''Porsche 968: Days late and dollars high, but hot to trot,'' *Car and Driver*, March 1992, pp. 47-50.

RECALLS

None to date.

OTHER INFORMATION SOURCES

2587 ● Porsche Club of America—Annual Parade
Porsche Club of America (PCA)
P.O. Box 10402
Alexandria, VA 22310   Ph:(703)922-9300

2588 ● Porsche Market Letter
Porsche Market Letter
P.O. Box 60328
Oklahoma City, OK 73146-0328   Ph:(405)524-7880

Lists Porsche automobiles for sale; offers recommendations for models most likely to appreciate in worth and current market information. Monthly. **Editor(s):** John Hoke, Publisher. **Price:** $40.00 per year; $5.00 per issue.

2589 ● Porsche Owner
Marque Publications
P.O. Box 2791
Fullerton, CA 92633   Ph:(714)771-7126

Covers such topics as vehicles, European travel and lifestyles, and aftermarket accessories. Quarterly. **Editor(s):** R. Janis. **Price:** $12.00 per year; $3.95 per issue.

2590 ● Porsche Owners Club—Membership Roster
Porsche Owners Club (POC)
c/o Creative Motor Sports
425 W. Allen Ave., No. 115
San Dimas, CA 91773   Ph:(714)599-9288

Annual.

2591 ● Porsche Owners Club—Newsletter
Porsche Owners Club (POC)
c/o Creative Motor Sports
425 W. Allen Ave., No. 115
San Dimas, CA 91773   Ph:(714)599-9288

Bimonthly.

2592 ● Porsche Panorama
Porsche Club of America, Inc.
912 Lullwater Rd.   Ph:(404)378-9823
Atlanta, GA 30307   Fax:(404)377-7041

Provides information on motor racing, Porsche road tests, new vehicle information, classic Porsche cars, and technical information. Monthly. **Editor(s):** Betty Jo Turner. **Price:** $36.00 per member.

2593 ● Porsche: Past and Present
Haynes Publications, Inc.
861 Lawrence Dr.
Newbury Park, CA 91320   Ph:(818)889-5400

Editor(s): Dennis Jenkinson. **Price:** $19.95.

2594 ● Porsche Uber Alles
Porsche Club of America, Western Michigan Region
1503 43rd St.
Wyoming, MI 49509

Ten times per year. **Price:** $5.00.

2595 ● VW and Porsche
Argus Publishers Corp.
12100 Wilshire Blvd., Ste. 250   Ph:(213)820-3601
Los Angeles, CA 90025   Fax:(213)207-9388

Offers articles of interest to enthusiasts of Volkswagen and Porsche models. Bimonthly. **Editor(s):** Greg Brown. **Price:** $11.00/yr.; $2.75/issue.

ASSOCIATIONS

2596 ● Porsche Club of America
P.O. Box 10402
Alexandria, VA 22310
Ruth R. Harte, Exec. Sec.   Ph:(703)922-9300

Founded: 1954. **Membership:** 30,000. Persons owning Porsche automobiles. **Convention/Meeting:** Annual, usually July or August.

2597 ● Porsche Owners Club
c/o Creative Motor Sports
425 W. Allen Ave., No. 115
San Dimas, CA 91773
Bill Follmer, Contact   Ph:(714)599-9288

Founded: 1955. **Membership:** 800. Porsche owners and related service groups, including dealers and parts, accessories, and repair facilities. Conducts time trials, slaloms, rallies, and parties. Sponsors driver training program and schools. Maintains biographical archives. Provides historical, restoration, competition, maintenance, and repair information. Bestows racing award annually; compiles statistics. **Convention/Meeting:** Bimonthly.

RANGE ROVER (1987-92)

Manufactured in Solihull, England. Placed in the top ten in the Paris-Dakar Rally, the longest race in the world, in 1987. In 1989, this sport utility vehicle made the first north to south traverse of the Continental Divide off-pavement through Colorado, covering 1,123 miles. The event, called the Great Divide Expedition, was performed to promote the U.S. Forest Service's ''Tread Lightly'' program, which encourages safe, environmentally responsible off-pavement driving.

1990 Range Rover County

MAJOR FEATURES

● Range Rover has as 1992 standard equipment: 3.9 liter V-8 fuel-injected engine, four-speed automatic transmission, power steering, four-wheel disc brakes, four-wheel drive, sunroof, leather upholstery, power seats, and additional interior amenities.

● Range Rover County adds as 1992 standard equipment: anti-sway bar, anti-lock braking system, extensive burl walnut and leather trim, keyless entry/alarm system, heated seats, and CD sound system.

● Range Rover Hunter added as 1991 standard features: aluminum outer body panels, heated front and rear windows, and velour seats.

PRICE HISTORY

The following new car prices reflect the approximate retail cost of the base model: **1987** - $30,825; **1988** - $34,400; **1989** - $36,600; **1990** - $38,025; **1991** - $36,500; **1992** - $38,900.

DIMENSIONS

Body Style	Years Avail	Wheel Base (in)	Lgth (in)	Ht (in)	Avg Wt (lbs)	Fuel Cap (gal)	Front Hdrm (in)	Front Legrm (in)
utl wgn	87-92	100.0	175.0	70.8	6,019	21.6	38.4	41.0

ENGINES

Type	Displace-ment (L)	Fuel Dly	HP @rpm	Torque @rpm (ft/lbs)	MPG Cty/Hwy	Years Avail
V-8	3.5	FI	150@na	na	14/14	87-88
V-8	3.9	FI	178@4750	220@3000	13/16	89-91
V-8	3.9	FI	180@4750	227@3250	13/16	92-92

KEY: I=in-line engine; V=V engine; F=flat engine; FI=fuel injection; bbl=barrel carburetor; T=turbo; D=diesel; HP=horsepower; MPG=estimated average miles per gallon.

EVALUATIONS, TESTS, AND RANKINGS

1992: "finest feature is off-road comfort ... makes for unruffled travel over heavily ruffled terrain." **Source:** "Range Rover County SE," *Car and Driver*, October 1991, pp. 130, 134-135.

1991: "truly outstanding off-road capabilities ... an excellent customer service program ... once it overcomes inertia, the engines is smooth, quiet, and more than strong enough." **Source:** "Range Rover County SE," *Motor Trend*, July 1991, pp. 92-94.

1991: "built like a pre-war apartment building, sits news-radio-traffic chopper-high ... There is room for society inside a Range Rover." **Source:** "If Sherman McCoy had been driving a Range Rover ... He'd still be a Master of the Universe," *Forbes*, October 1, 1990, pp. 52-59.

1991: "sturdy, if somewhat ponderous, design ... world's most prestigious off-road vehicle ... There is nothing quite like it on the market." **Source:** "Range Rover aims for old money," *Detroit Free Press*, May 2, 1991, p. 12D.

1991: "can claim all the comforts of a European sedan ... excellent heating system ... rear bench seat offers a variety of passenger/storage combinations." **Source:** "Testing the Range Rover Hunter," *Sports Afield*, October 1991, p. 53.

1990: "comfortable ride and spacious interior." **Source:** "Range Rover," *Car and Driver—Buyers Guide 1990*, 1990, pp. 172-173.

1990: "suspension is as supple and adaptable as anything in the field today ... full-time 4-wheel-drive system is thoroughly user-friendly." **Source:** "4-Doors For all Seasons," *New Choices for the Best Years*, December 1989, pp. 84, 86-87.

1990: "outstanding off-road capabilities limit comfort on pavement ... When it comes to rough going ... Ranger Rover is first rate ... accelerates and brakes well by 4x4 standards ... price tends to limit our appreciation of this excellent vehicle." **Source:** "Suburban Chic," *Popular Mechanics*, August 1990, pp. 55-59, 109.

1990: "a vehicle in a class of its own ... reputation of tough off-road capability." **Source:** "4-Door Off-Roaders," *Sports Afield*, March 1990, pp. 120-122, 143-145.

1989: "amazed us with its creepy-crawly off-road prowess, tackling terrain that at first seemed impassable. . .be prepared to pay a steep admission price." **Source:** "Life with Range Rover," *Car and Driver*, June 1989, pp. 156, 158, 161-163.

1989: "smooth and powerful and, of course, the lap of luxury ... it's a beautiful machine." **Source:** "Sport Vehicles: Personal Pick," *Outdoor Life*, June 1989, pp. 20, 24-25.

1989: "thinks it's a luxury car ... soft ride ... one of the world's most capable vehicles when traveling far away from any paved path." **Source:** "Import Report: Off-Road Aplomb," *Home Mechanix*, April 1989, pp. 84-86, 103-105.

1989: "top of the line, as measured by cost, features, and prestige ... summons the kind of associations that melt the shrill noise of city business dead away." **Source:** "Driving," *Vogue*, August 1989, p. 248.

RECALLS

1990-91: (2,271 multi-purpose vehicles): The right rear metal brake line could come in contact with the top of the right rear shock absorber. This could lead to an eventual fluid leak in one of the two brake circuits. The leak of fluid from the rear metal brake line could cause reduced braking effectiveness and increase stopping distance. **Corrective action:** Reroute rear metal brake lines to avoid contact with the rear shock absorber, and replace brake lines that have contacted the shock absorbers. *(NHTSA Campaign No. 91V069000.)*

1987-88: (5,713 vehicles): Inflation pressure recommended for rear wheels will not support rear GAWR. Vehicles would not comply with FMVSS 120. **Corrective action:** Send notification letter with revised tire placard indicating appropriate tire inflation pressures. *(NHTSA Campaign No. 88V195000.)*

1987-88: (4,704 vehicles): Corrosion could occur between fuel filter and retaining bracket. Could result in perforation of filter casing and fuel leakage with potential for fire. **Corrective action:** Install modified fuel filter bracket. *(NHTSA Campaign No. 88V116000.)*

1987-88: (2,954 vehicles): Nylon pivot pin in seat belt retractor lock mechanism may be too large in diameter. Nylon material swells in presence of atmosphere humidity and can restrict movement of locking pawl which activates belt locking mechanism. **Corrective action:** Inspection of vehicles and replace suspect belt assembly. *(NHTSA Campaign No. 88V034000.)*

1987-88: (3,972 vehicles): Faculty installation of circlip holding brake pedal, resulting in position change of brake pedal. **Corrective action:** Repair circlip. *(NHTSA Campaign No. 89V012000.)*

1987: (114 vehicles): Master cylinder reservoir not equipped with a warning label. **Corrective action:** Affix warning label. *(NHTSA Campaign No. 87V146000.)*

REPAIR MANUALS

2598 ● The Land-Rover 1948-1988
Motorbooks International
729 Prospect Ave.
Osceola, WI 54020   Ph:(715)294-3345

Published 1988. **Editor(s):** James Taylor. **Price:** $24.95.

OTHER INFORMATION SOURCES

2599 ● Aluminum Workhorse
Land Rover Owners Association, U.S.A. (LROA, U.S.A.)
P.O. Box 6836
Oakland, CA 94603   Ph:(415)569-8879

Newsletter; includes technical information and calendar of regional events. Quarterly. **Price:** Included in membership dues; $15/year for nonmembers.

2600 ● Land Rover Owners
Land Rover Owners Association, U.S.A. (LROA, U.S.A.)
P.O. Box 6836
Oakland, CA 94603   Ph:(415)569-8879

Directory. Annual.

2601 ● Land Rover: The Unbeatable 4X4
Haynes Publications, Inc.
861 Lawrence Dr.
Newbury Park, CA 91320   Ph:(818)889-5400

Published 1989. **Editor(s):** K. Slavin and G. N. Mackie. **Price:** $34.95.

2602 ● Range Rover: Super Profile
Haynes Publications, Inc.
861 Lawrence Dr.
Newbury Park, CA 91320   Ph:(818)889-5400

Published 1987. **Editor(s):** Trevor Alder. **Price:** $11.95.

ASSOCIATIONS

2603 ● Land Rover Owners Association, U.S.A.
P.O. Box 6836
Oakland, CA 94603
Domingo Dias, Sec.   Ph:(415)569-8879

Founded: 1984. **Membership:** 500. Owners and enthusiasts of Land Rover and Range Rover vehicles. Seeks to bring Land Rover owners together for outdoor activities and information sharing. Provides parts and technical information. Exchanges newsletters with Land Rover organizations worldwide. Conducts technical sessions; coordinates social gatherings. **Former Name(s):** (1986) Land Rover Owners Association. **Convention/Meeting:** Annual outing.

RENAULT ALLIANCE (1987)

Produced in Kenosha, Wisconsin. Discontinued in 1987.

MAJOR FEATURES

● Renault Alliance had as 1987 standard equipment: 4-speed manual transmission, rack-and-pinion steering, 4-wheel independent suspension, and front disc/rear drum brakes.

● Renault Alliance L had as 1987 standard equipment: upgraded interior.

● Renault Alliance DL had as 1987 standard equipment: 5-speed manual transmission.

● Renault Alliance GS had as 1987 standard equipment: other exterior body stylings.

● Renault Alliance GTA Convertible added as 1987 standard equipment: upgraded suspension and other exterior body stylings.

PRICE HISTORY

The following new car prices reflect the approximate retail cost of the base model: **1987** - $6,399.

DIMENSIONS

Body Style	Years Avail	Wheel Base (in)	Lgth (in)	Ht (in)	Avg Wt (lbs)	Fuel Cap (gal)	Front Hdrm (in)	Front Legrm (in)
3d lbk	87-87	97.8	160.6	51.3	1,959	12.5	37.1	40.8
5d lbk	87-87	97.8	163.8	51.3	2,009	12.5	37.1	40.8
2d conv	87-87	97.8	163.8	51.3	2,206	12.5	38.5	40.8
2d sdn	87-87	97.8	163.8	51.3	2,097	12.5	37.1	40.8

ENGINES

Type	Displacement (L)	Fuel Dly	HP @rpm	Torque @rpm (ft/lbs)	MPG Cty/Hwy	Years Avail
I-4	1.4	FI	56@4200	75@2500	33/40	87-87
I-4	1.7	FI	78@5000	96@3000	29/37	87-87
I-4	2.0	FI	95@5250	144@2750	26/30	87-87

KEY: I=in-line engine; V=V engine; F=flat engine; FI=fuel injection; bbl=barrel carburetor; T=turbo; D=diesel; HP=horsepower; MPG=estimated average miles per gallon.

EVALUATIONS, TESTS, AND RANKINGS

1987: "level, controlled ride and sure, precise handling ... Instruments make sense." **Source:** "Franco-American GTA joins the 'pocket rockets," The Detroit News, November 12, 1986, pp. 1F-2F.

1987: "cute, fun and economical." **Source:** "Ragtop Fever," Popular Mechanics, June 1987, pp. 71-75, 123.

RECALLS

1987: (240,000 ; recall includes models manufactured prior to 1987): Cooling system pressures during overheated engine operation may exceed the strength capability of certain components due to inadequate venting capacity of the system pressure cap. Buildup of pressure may cause heater core to rupture and discharge hot coolant and steam in the proximity of the driver's legs. **Corrective action:** Replace all coolant system pressure caps with one having adequate venting capacity. (NHTSA Campaign No. 88V087000.)

OTHER INFORMATION SOURCES

2604 ● AM-XTRA
American Motorsport International
7963 Depew St.
Arvada, CO 80003   Ph:(303)428-8760

Newsletter. Bimonthly. **Price:** Available to members only.

2605 ● AMC Performance Car Club—Newsletter
AMC Performance Car Club
2000 25th Ave.
Marion, IA 52302   Ph:(319)377-7510

Bimonthly.

2606 ● American Motoring Magazine
American Motors Owners Association (AMO)
c/o Darryl A. Salisbury
517 New Hampshire
Portage, MI 49081   Ph:(616)342-9397

Bimonthly.

2607 ● American Motors Owners Association—Membership Roster
American Motors Owners Association (AMO)
517 New Hampshire   Ph:(616)342-9397
Portage, MI 49081   Fax:(616)387-4806

About 1,000 owners of American Motors Corporation vehicles; international coverage. Irregular; latest edition March 1990. **Editor(s):** Valerie Fleming. **Price:** Available to members only.

2608 ● Americana: The American Motors Magazine
American Motors Corp.
14250 Plymouth Rd.
Detroit, MI 48227

Bimonthly. **Editor(s):** Stephen Jacobs.

2609 ● Le Club News
Renault Club of America
2901 McGee Way
Olney, MD 20832   Ph:(301)942-9062

Serves as a clearinghouse to assist owners and enthusiasts of Renault automobiles with the location of automotive parts and technical information. Carries Club news, profiles of members and their cars, and a calendar of events. Bimonthly.

2610 ● Renault Owners Club of America—Membership Roster
Renault Owners Club of America (ROCOA)
1380-156 Ave. NE, Ste. 204
Bellevue, WA 98007   Ph:(206)882-0352

Periodic.

2611 ● Renault Owners Club of America—Newsletter
Renault Owners Club of America (ROCOA)
1380-156 Ave. NE, Ste. 204
Bellevue, WA 98007   Ph:(206)882-0352

Provides information on the Renault automobile. Bimonthly.

ASSOCIATIONS

2612 ● AMC Performance Car Club
2000 25th Ave.
Marion, IA 52302
Ralph W. Toms, Sec.-Treas.   Ph:(319)377-7510

Founded: 1983. **Membership:** 10. To preserve, promote, and enjoy automobiles built by the American Motors Corporation. Sponsors car shows. **Convention/Meeting:** Monthly (April-October).

2613 ● American Motors Owners Association
c/o Darryl A. Salisbury
517 New Hampshire
Portage, MI 49081
Darryl A. Salisbury, Pres.   Ph:(616)342-9397

Founded: 1974. **Membership:** 1,400. Owners and enthusiasts of AMC vehicles built from 1958 - 1988. To aid and encourage ownership, use, and enjoyment of AMC vehicles; to encourage preservation and restoration of these vehicles; and to increase communications and fellowship among owners. Maintains library; bestows awards. **Convention/Meeting:** Annual car show and swap meet - always July or August. 1992 Columbus, OH; 1993 Kenosha, WI.

2614 ● American Motorsport International
7963 Depew St.
Arvada, CO 80003
Larry G. Mitchell, Director   Ph:(303)428-8760

Founded: 1986. **Membership:** 751. Collectors and admirers of AMC cars and Jeeps. Functions as a clearinghouse of information on all AMC products. Provides technical assistance to members involved in restoring or preserving AMC automobiles. Maintains library and archive of sales and engineering literature and artifacts pertaining to AMC products. Sponsors concours for AMC cars and Jeeps. Makes available novelty items and memorabilia. Bestows awards. **Convention/Meeting:** Annual.

2615 ● Renault Club of America
2901 McGee Way
Olney, MD 20832
Paul Maraschiello, Pres.

Founded: 1978. **Membership:** 200. Owners and enthusiasts of Renault automobiles. Acts as clearinghouse and assists in locating parts. Maintains biographical archive and 200 volume library of books, newsletters, and photos of Renaults. Sponsors competitions; compiles statistics. **Convention/Meeting:** Annual - always April, Rockville, MD.

2616 ● Renault Owners Club of America
1380-156 Ave. NE, Ste. 204
Bellevue, WA 98007
George William Holt, Exec. Officer Ph:(206)882-0352

Founded: 1988. **Membership:** 200. Owners of Renault automobiles; individuals affiliated with service and sales companies in the automotive industry. Provides members with access to parts, services, sales, and literature on the Renault automobile from 1900 to the present. Maintains library and archives; offers placement services; compiles statistics.

RENAULT MEDALLION (1988)

Originally introduced in Europe as the Renault 21. Renault Medallion was imported by the American Motors Corporation in 1987 as a 1988 model. In August 1987, the Chrysler Motors Corporation purchased AMC, and sold the Medallion with the Jeep-Eagle badge (see separate entry). Finished ninth among thirteen vehicles in the *Motor Trend* Import Car of the Year ranking in 1987.

MAJOR FEATURES

● Renault Medallion DL had as 1988 standard equipment: 5-speed manual transmission, front-wheel drive system, independent front suspension, rack-and-pinion, power-assisted steering, power-assisted, vented front disc brakes, alloy wheels, tilt steering column, and rear defroster.

● Renault Medallion LX added as 1988 standard equipment: air-conditioning, cruise control, aluminum wheels, and upgraded exterior and interior styling.

● Renault Medallion Wagon added as 1988 standard equipment: tilt-steering wheel, tachometer, and a roofrack.

PRICE HISTORY

The following new car prices reflect the approximate retail cost of the base model: **1988 - $9,965.**

DIMENSIONS

Body Style	Years Avail	Wheel Base (in)	Lgth (in)	Ht (in)	Avg Wt (lbs)	Fuel Cap (gal)	Front Hdrm (in)	Front Legrm (in)
4d sdn	88-88	102.3	183.2	55.7	2,588	17.4	37.8	42.2
5d wgn	88-88	108.0	190.0	na	2,736	na	na	na

ENGINES

Type	Displace-ment (L)	Fuel Dly	HP @rpm	Torque @rpm (ft/lbs)	MPG Cty/Hwy	Years Avail
I-4	2.2	FI	103@5000	124@2500	26/33	88-88

KEY: I=in-line engine; V=V engine; F=flat engine; FI=fuel injection; bbl=barrel carburetor; T=turbo; D=diesel; HP=horsepower; MPG=estimated average miles per gallon.

EVALUATIONS, TESTS, AND RANKINGS

1988: "really a whole lot better nowadays . . . front seats are wide, the rear leg and head room is good. . .clings tenaciously to the asphalt with a surprisingly tolerable degree of body roll. . .the engine. . .is sadly lacking in outright power." **Source:** "Renault Medallion LX," *Motor Trend*, March 1987, pp. 61-62, 65, 68.

1988: "airy comfort for six-footers, front and rear. . .French cars are known for being comfortable above all, and the Medallion doesn't disappoint. . .steering is too undisciplined. . ." **Source:** "1988 Renault Medallion LX," *Car and Driver*, April 1987, pp. 64-65, 67-68, 71.

1988: "Good power. . .comfortable ride. . .spartan by comparison with most other wagons in the test group." **Source:** "Mid-Size Wagons [Renault Medallion Wagon]," *Changing Times*, June 1987, pp. 58-62.

1988: "lots of get-up in city driving and smooth highway performance. . .quiet. . .absent of the engine and road noise prevalent of Renault cars past." **Source:** "Say 'oui' to Medallion," *The Detroit News*, March 25, 1987, pp. 1F-2F.

1988: "excellent fuel economy. . .peak horsepower is only 103. . .could definitely use more oomph. . .lackluster interior styling." **Source:** "Motor Trend's 1987 Import Car of the Year," *Motor Trend*, April 1987, pp. 35-39, 41-42, 44, 46-47, 49, 51, 53.

RECALLS

1988: (30,000 passenger cars): Loss of retention of an integral over-travel spring on throttle cable could cause spring dislocation. Can cause increased idle position throttle opening and higher than normal idle speed. **Corrective action:** Replace throttle cables with cables designed to provide positive retention of the over-travel spring. *(NHTSA Campaign No. 90V138000.)*

1988: (30,000 vehicles; includes Renault Medallion and Eagle Medallion models): Fuse block wiring terminals may not adequately clamp the positive electrical connection of heater blower motor fuse blades. Increases electrical resistance that could overheat and ignite fuse block and terminal wiring. **Corrective action:** Modify fuse block terminal to ensure adequate retention clamp load on heater blower fuse blades. *(NHTSA Campaign No. 91V037000.)*

OTHER INFORMATION SOURCES

2617 ● AM-XTRA
American Motorsport International
7963 Depew St.
Arvada, CO 80003   Ph:(303)428-8760

Newsletter. Bimonthly. **Price:** Available to members only.

2618 ● AMC Performance Car Club—Newsletter
AMC Performance Car Club
2000 25th Ave.
Marion, IA 52302   Ph:(319)377-7510

Bimonthly.

2619 ● American Motoring Magazine
American Motors Owners Association (AMO)
c/o Darryl A. Salisbury
517 New Hampshire
Portage, MI 49081   Ph:(616)342-9397

Bimonthly.

2620 ● American Motors Owners Association—Membership Roster
American Motors Owners Association (AMO)
517 New Hampshire   Ph:(616)342-9397
Portage, MI 49081   Fax:(616)387-4806

About 1,000 owners of American Motors Corporation vehicles; international coverage. Irregular; latest edition March 1990. **Editor(s):** Valerie Fleming. **Price:** Available to members only.

2621 ● Americana: The American Motors Magazine
American Motors Corp.
14250 Plymouth Rd.
Detroit, MI 48227

Bimonthly. **Editor(s):** Stephen Jacobs.

2622 ● Le Club News
Renault Club of America
2901 McGee Way
Olney, MD 20832   Ph:(301)942-9062

Serves as a clearinghouse to assist owners and enthusiasts of Renault automobiles with the location of automotive parts and technical information. Carries Club news, profiles of members and their cars, and a calendar of events. Bimonthly.

2623 ● Renault Owners Club of America—Membership Roster
Renault Owners Club of America (ROCOA)
1380-156 Ave. NE, Ste. 204
Bellevue, WA 98007   Ph:(206)882-0352

Periodic.

2624 ● Renault Owners Club of America—Newsletter
Renault Owners Club of America (ROCOA)
1380-156 Ave. NE, Ste. 204
Bellevue, WA 98007   Ph:(206)882-0352

Provides information on the Renault automobile. Bimonthly.

ASSOCIATIONS

2625 ● AMC Performance Car Club
2000 25th Ave.
Marion, IA 52302
Ralph W. Toms, Sec.-Treas.   Ph:(319)377-7510

Founded: 1983. **Membership:** 10. To preserve, promote, and enjoy automobiles built by the American Motors Corporation. Sponsors car shows. **Convention/Meeting:** Monthly (April-October).

2626 ● American Motors Owners Association
c/o Darryl A. Salisbury
517 New Hampshire
Portage, MI 49081
Darryl A. Salisbury, Pres.   Ph:(616)342-9397

Founded: 1974. **Membership:** 1,400. Owners and enthusiasts of AMC vehicles built from 1958 - 1988. To aid and encourage ownership, use, and enjoyment of AMC vehicles; to encourage preservation and restoration of these vehicles; and to increase communications and fellowship among owners. Maintains library; bestows awards. **Convention/Meeting:** Annual car show and swap meet - always July or August. 1992 Columbus, OH; 1993 Kenosha, WI.

2627 ● American Motorsport International
7963 Depew St.
Arvada, CO 80003
Larry G. Mitchell, Director   Ph:(303)428-8760

Founded: 1986. **Membership:** 751. Collectors and admirers of AMC cars and Jeeps. Functions as a clearinghouse of information on all AMC products. Provides technical assistance to members involved in restoring or preserving AMC automobiles. Maintains library and archive of sales and engineering literature and artifacts pertaining to AMC products. Sponsors concours for AMC cars and Jeeps. Makes available novelty items and memorabilia. Bestows awards. **Convention/Meeting:** Annual.

2628 ● Renault Club of America
2901 McGee Way
Olney, MD 20832
Paul Maraschiello, Pres.

Founded: 1978. **Membership:** 200. Owners and enthusiasts of Renault automobiles. Acts as clearinghouse and assists in locating parts. Maintains biographical archive and 200 volume library of books, newsletters, and photos of Renaults. Sponsors competitions; compiles statistics. **Convention/Meeting:** Annual - always April, Rockville, MD.

2629 ● Renault Owners Club of America
1380-156 Ave. NE, Ste. 204
Bellevue, WA 98007
George William Holt, Exec. Officer   Ph:(206)882-0352

Founded: 1988. **Membership:** 200. Owners of Renault automobiles; individuals affiliated with service and sales companies in the automotive industry. Provides members with access to parts, services, sales, and literature on the Renault automobile from 1900 to the present. Maintains library and archives; offers placement services; compiles statistics.

ROLLS-ROYCE CORNICHE SERIES (1987-92)

Part of the Rolls-Royce line that is produced in London, England. Corniche II was manufactured until 1990, at which time Corniche III was introduced. Ranked fifth in *The Car Book* 1989 top ten list for fuel economy losers. Information on the 1992 model was not available at time of publication.

1991 Rolls-Royce Corniche III

MAJOR FEATURES

● Rolls-Royce Corniche III 1991 standard equipment included: 3-speed automatic transmission, 4-wheel disc brakes with anti-lock brake system, power-assisted rack-and-pinion steering, driver's side airbag, security system, leather interior, and AM/FM stereo/cassette/compact disc player with 10-speaker sound system.

● Rolls-Royce Corniche II 1989 equipment included: 3-speed automatic transmission, 4-wheel disc brakes with anti-lock brake system, power-assisted rack-and-pinion steering, leather interior, AM/FM stereo cassette, driver's side airbag, power windows, and power door locks.

PRICE HISTORY

The following new car prices reflect the approximate retail cost of the base model: **1987** - $173,800; **1988** - $183,500; **1989** - $205,500; **1990** - $215,800; **1991** - $226,700; **1992** - $228,300.

DIMENSIONS

Body Style	Years Avail	Wheel Base (in)	Lgth (in)	Ht (in)	Avg Wt (lbs)	Fuel Cap (gal)	Front Hdrm (in)	Front Legrm (in)
2d conv	87-88	120.5	207.5	59.8	5,200	26	36	39
2d conv	89-89	120.5	207.5	59.8	5,340	28.5	36	39
2d conv	90-91	120.5	207.5	59.8	5,360	28.5	37.7	41.2

ENGINES

Type	Displacement (L)	Fuel Dly	HP @rpm	Torque @rpm (ft/lbs)	MPG Cty/Hwy	Years Avail
V-8	6.8	FI	na	na	10/13	87-91

KEY: I=in-line engine; V=V engine; F=flat engine; FI=fuel injection; bbl=barrel carburetor; T=turbo; D=diesel; HP=horsepower; MPG=estimated average miles per gallon.

EVALUATIONS, TESTS, AND RANKINGS

1990: "ride is magnificent . . . paint quality on the car is stunning." **Source:** "Rolls-Royce Corniche II," *Road & Track*, February 1990, p. 61.

1990: "the essence of filthy-richness." **Source:** "Rolls-Royce Corniche III," *Car and Driver—Buyers Guide 1990*, 1989, p. 146.

RECALLS

None to date.

OTHER INFORMATION SOURCES

2630 ● The Flying Lady
Rolls-Royce Owners' Club (RROC)
191 Hempt Rd.
Mechanicsburg, PA 17055   Ph:(717)697-4671

Bimonthly.

2631 ● Illustrated Rolls-Royce and Bentley Buyer's Guide
Motorbooks International
729 Prospect Ave.
Osceola, WI 54020   Ph:(715)294-3345

Published 1987. **Editor(s):** Paul Woudenberg. **Price:** $15.95.

2632 ● Rolls-Royce/Bentley Marketletter
Mary Ann Liebert, Inc.
1651 3rd Ave.
New York, NY 10128   Ph:(212)289-2300

Provides extensive listings of Rolls-Royce and Bentley cars for sale or trade. Monthly. **Price:** $53.00.

2633 ● Rolls-Royce Owners' Club—Directory and Register
Rolls-Royce Owners' Club (RROC)
191 Hempt Rd.
Mechanicsburg, PA 17055   Ph:(717)697-4671

Annual.

ASSOCIATIONS

2634 ● Rolls-Royce Owners' Club
191 Hempt Rd.
Mechanicsburg, PA 17055
Timothy E. Younes, Exec.Dir.   Ph:(717)697-4671

Founded: 1951. **Membership:** 6,000. Persons interested in preserving and restoring automobiles produced by Rolls-Royce Ltd., Rolls-Royce Motors, Ltd., Rolls-Royce of America, and Bentley Motors (1931) Ltd. To exchange technical, historical, and general information. Reprints owners' manuals and technical materials.

ROLLS-ROYCE SILVER SPIRIT SERIES (1987-92)

Silver Spirit produced until 1990, at which time Silver Spirit II was introduced. Named to *Car and Driver's* Ten Best list in 1992. Information on the 1992 model was not available at time of publication.

1991 Rolls-Royce Silver Spirit II

MAJOR FEATURES

● Rolls-Royce Silver Spirit II had as 1991 standard equipment: 6.8L eight-cylinder engine, 3-speed automatic transmission, 4-wheel disc brakes with anti-lock brake system, power-assisted rack-and-pinion steering, driver's side airbag, security system, power windows, power door locks, climate control system, leather interior, AM/FM stereo cassette with 10-speaker sound system, and 235/70 VR15 tires.

● Rolls-Royce Silver Spirit had as 1989 standard equipment: 3-speed automatic transmission, 4-wheel disc brakes, power-assisted rack-and-pinion steering, and AM/FM stereo cassette.

PRICE HISTORY

The following new car prices reflect the approximate retail cost of the base model: **1987** - $109,700; **1988** - $117,500; **1989** - $129,800; **1990** - $140,200; **1991** - $151,700; **1992** - $157,800.

DIMENSIONS

Body Style	Years Avail	Wheel Base (in)	Lgth (in)	Ht (in)	Avg Wt (lbs)	Fuel Cap (gal)	Front Hdrm (in)	Front Legrm (in)
4d sdn	87-89	120.5	207.8	58.5	5,120	28.5	37.5	40
4d sdn	90-91	120.5	207.4	58.5	5,120	28.5	37.5	39

ENGINES

Type	Displacement (L)	Fuel Dly	HP @rpm	Torque @rpm (ft/lbs)	MPG Cty/Hwy	Years Avail
V-8	6.8	FI	na	na	10/13	87-91

KEY: I=in-line engine; V=V engine; F=flat engine; FI=fuel injection; bbl=barrel carburetor; T=turbo; D=diesel; HP=horsepower; MPG=estimated average miles per gallon.

EVALUATIONS, TESTS, AND RANKINGS

1992: "a leather seat of sofa proportions." **Source:** "Ten Best: Cars To Move You," *Car and Driver,* January 1992, pp. 63-65.

1990: "legendary creature comforts." **Source:** "Rolls-Royce Silver Spirit II/Silver Spur II," *Car and Driver—Buyers Guide 1990,* 1989, p. 133.

RECALLS

1990: (364 cars; includes other Rolls-Royce and Bentley models): Amperage overload could cause fuse failure, causing loss of rear stop lamps. **Corrective action:** Install an additional fused circuit to handle the main stop lamps. *(NHTSA Campaign No. 90V039000.)*

1989-90: (1,785 cars; includes other Rolls-Royce and Bentley models): Contact between right front brake caliper hydraulic line and engine oil cooler line may damage brake line. **Corrective action:** Add a protective shield to prevent contact and replace any damaged hydraulic pipe. *(NHTSA Campaign No. 90V073000.)*

OTHER INFORMATION SOURCES

2635 ● The Flying Lady
Rolls-Royce Owners' Club (RROC)
191 Hempt Rd.
Mechanicsburg, PA 17055   Ph:(717)697-4671

Bimonthly.

2636 ● **Illustrated Rolls-Royce and Bentley Buyer's Guide**
Motorbooks International
729 Prospect Ave.
Osceola, WI 54020   Ph:(715)294-3345

Published 1987. **Editor(s):** Paul Woudenberg. **Price:** $15.95.

2637 ● **Rolls-Royce/Bentley Marketletter**
Mary Ann Liebert, Inc.
1651 3rd Ave.
New York, NY 10128   Ph:(212)289-2300

Provides extensive listings of Rolls-Royce and Bentley cars for sale or trade. Monthly. **Price:** $53.00.

2638 ● **Rolls-Royce Owners' Club—Directory and Register**
Rolls-Royce Owners' Club (RROC)
191 Hempt Rd.
Mechanicsburg, PA 17055   Ph:(717)697-4671

Annual.

ASSOCIATIONS

2639 ● **Rolls-Royce Owners' Club**
191 Hempt Rd.
Mechanicsburg, PA 17055
Timothy E. Younes, Exec.Dir.   Ph:(717)697-4671

Founded: 1951. **Membership:** 6,000. Persons interested in preserving and restoring automobiles produced by Rolls-Royce Ltd., Rolls-Royce Motors, Ltd., Rolls-Royce of America, and Bentley Motors (1931) Ltd. To exchange technical, historical, and general information. Reprints owners' manuals and technical materials.

ROLLS-ROYCE SILVER SPUR SERIES (1987-92)

Silver Spur was produced until 1990, at which time the Silver Spur II was introduced. Information on the 1992 model was not available at time of publication.

1991 Rolls Royce Silver Spur II

MAJOR FEATURES

● Rolls-Royce Silver Spur II had as 1991 standard equipment: 6.8L, eight-cylinder engine, 3-speed automatic transmission, 4-wheel disc brakes with anti-lock brake system, security system, power-assisted rack-and-pinion steering, driver's side airbag, power windows, power door locks, climate control system, leather interior, AM/FM stereo/cassette/compact disc player with 10-speaker sound system, and 235/70 VR15 tires.

● Rolls-Royce Silver Spur had as 1989 standard equipment: 3-

speed automatic transmission, power-assisted rack-and-pinion steering, 4-wheel disc brakes, and AM/FM stereo cassette.

PRICE HISTORY

The following new car prices reflect the approximate retail cost of the base model: **1987** - $121,500; **1988** - $129,500; **1989** - $142,600; **1990** - $154,700; **1991** - $166,300.

DIMENSIONS

Body Style	Years Avail	Wheel Base (in)	Lgth (in)	Ht (in)	Avg Wt (lbs)	Fuel Cap (gal)	Front Hdrm (in)	Front Legrm (in)
4d sdn	87-89	124.5	211.8	58.5	5,180	28.5	37.5	40
4d sdn	90-91	124.5	211.4	58.5	5,180	28.5	37.5	39

ENGINES

Type	Displacement (L)	Fuel Dly	HP @rpm	Torque @rpm (ft/lbs)	MPG Cty/Hwy	Years Avail
V-8	6.8	FI	na	na	10/13	87-91

KEY: I=in-line engine; V=V engine; F=flat engine; FI=fuel injection; bbl=barrel carburetor; T=turbo; D=diesel; HP=horsepower; MPG=estimated average miles per gallon.

RECALLS

1990: (364 cars; includes other Rolls-Royce and Bentley models): Amperage overload could cause fuse failure, causing loss of rear stop lamps. **Corrective action:** Install an additional fused circuit to handle the main stop lamps. (NHTSA Campaign No. 90V039000.)

1989-90: (1,785 cars; includes other Rolls-Royce and Bentley models): Contact between right front brake caliper hydraulic line and engine oil cooler line may damage brake line. **Corrective action:** Add a protective shield to prevent contact and replace any damaged hydraulic pipe. (NHTSA Campaign No. 90V073000.)

OTHER INFORMATION SOURCES

2640 ● **The Flying Lady**
Rolls-Royce Owners' Club (RROC)
191 Hempt Rd.
Mechanicsburg, PA 17055   Ph:(717)697-4671

Bimonthly.

2641 ● **Illustrated Rolls-Royce and Bentley Buyer's Guide**
Motorbooks International
729 Prospect Ave.
Osceola, WI 54020   Ph:(715)294-3345

Published 1987. **Editor(s):** Paul Woudenberg. **Price:** $15.95.

2642 ● **Rolls-Royce/Bentley Marketletter**
Mary Ann Liebert, Inc.
1651 3rd Ave.
New York, NY 10128   Ph:(212)289-2300

Provides extensive listings of Rolls-Royce and Bentley cars for sale or trade. Monthly. **Price:** $53.00.

2643 ● **Rolls-Royce Owners' Club—Directory and Register**
Rolls-Royce Owners' Club (RROC)
191 Hempt Rd.
Mechanicsburg, PA 17055   Ph:(717)697-4671

Annual.

ASSOCIATIONS

2644 ● Rolls-Royce Owners' Club
191 Hempt Rd.
Mechanicsburg, PA 17055
Timothy E. Younes, Exec.Dir.   Ph:(717)697-4671

Founded: 1951. **Membership:** 6,000. Persons interested in preserving and restoring automobiles produced by Rolls-Royce Ltd., Rolls-Royce Motors, Ltd., Rolls-Royce of America, and Bentley Motors (1931) Ltd. To exchange technical, historical, and general information. Reprints owners' manuals and technical materials.

SAAB 900 (1987-92)

Listed in *The Complete Car Cost Guide* in 1990 for having one of the highest repair and insurance costs over a five-year period; Saab 900 SPG Turbo was also listed for having one of the lowest fuel costs. The Saab 900 is produced in Trollhattan, Sweden.

1992 Saab 900 Turbo Convertible

MAJOR FEATURES

● Saab 900 three-door hatchback has as 1992 standard equipment: 2.1-liter 16-valve engine, 5-speed manual transmission, 4-wheel disc brakes with anti-lock braking system, power steering, double wishbone front suspension, stabilizer bars, 16-spoke wheel covers, driver's side airbag, air conditioning, heated sideview mirrors, power windows and locks, and updated AM/FM cassette audio system; four-door sedan adds: fold-down rear seat, child door safety locks, and rear window child lock system.

● Saab 900 S three-door hatchback adds as 1992 standard equipment: cruise control, leather seats, power sunroof, 15-spoke alloy wheels, fog lamps, four-door sedans adds child door safety locks, and rear window child lock system.

● Saab 900 S Convertible adds as 1992 standard equipment: electric soft top with heated glass rear window, rear spoiler, dual front power seats, alarm system with keyless entry, and an upgraded interior.

● Saab 900 Turbo three-door hatchback adds as 1992 standard equipment: 2.0-liter turbocharged engine, 3-spoke alloy wheels, rear hatch spoiler, upgraded tires, upgraded modular audio system, driver's side power seat, and leather trim.

● Saab 900 Turbo Convertible adds for 1992: same equipment as Saab 900 Turbo plus an electric soft top with heated glass rear window.

● Saab 900 Turbo SPG had as 1991 standard equipment: upgraded turbo-charged engine and sport suspension.

PRICE HISTORY

The following new car prices reflect the approximate retail cost of the base model: **1987** - $14,395; **1988** - $15,432; **1989** - $16,995; **1990** - $16,995; **1991** - $18,295; **1992** - $19,395.

DIMENSIONS

Body Style	Years Avail	Wheel Base (in)	Lgth (in)	Ht (in)	Avg Wt (lbs)	Fuel Cap (gal)	Front Hdrm (in)	Front Legrm (in)
3d lbk	89-89	99.1	184.5	56.1	2,708	16.6	37.8	41.7
3d lbk	90-91	99.1	182.8	55.1	2,732	18	37.8	41.7
3d lbk	92-92	99.1	184.5	55.1	2,734	18	36.8	41.7
2d conv	89-89	99.1	184.3	55.1	2,967	16.6	37.8	41.7
2d conv	90-91	99.1	182.5	54.6	2,967	18	37.8	41.7
2d conv	92-92	99.1	184.3	55.1	2,947	18	36.8	41.7
4d sdn	87-89	99.1	184.3	56.1	2,763	16.6	37.8	41.7
4d sdn	90-91	99.1	182.5	55.1	2,787	18	37.8	41.7
4d sdn	92-92	99.1	184.3	56.1	2,776	18	36.8	41.7

ENGINES

Type	Displacement (L)	Fuel Dly	HP @rpm	Torque @rpm (ft/lbs)	MPG Cty/Hwy	Years Avail
I-4	2.0	FI	110@5250	119@3500	22/27	87-88
I-4	2.0	FI	125@5500	123@3000	21/27	87-88
I-4	2.0	FI	128@6000	128@3000	22/28	89-90
I-4	2.1	FI	140@6000	133@2900	20/27	91-92
I-4T	2.0	FI	165@5500	195@3000	21/27	87-88
I-4T	2.0	FI	160@5500	188@3000	21/28	87-92
I-4T	2.0	FI	175@5500	195@3000	20/28	90-91

KEY: I=in-line engine; V=V engine; F=flat engine; FI=fuel injection; bbl=barrel carburetor; T=turbo; D=diesel; HP=horsepower; MPG=estimated average miles per gallon.

EVALUATIONS, TESTS, AND RANKINGS

1991: "taut road manners and endearing personalities . . . Rear visibility is rather poor . . . standard heated seats for bun-warming on demand." **Source:** "Top-Down Showdown," *Motor Trend*, June 1991, pp. 49-59, 62-63.

1991: "engine revs smoothly, with a characteristic Saab whine . . . one of the most satisfying sun cars around." **Source:** "Saab 900S," *Car and Driver*, August 1991, p. 68.

1991: "ample performance and driving pleasure . . . engine . . . quiet at cruise and makes pleasing mechanical sounds . . . interior . . . too many hard plastic surfaces and rubber parts." **Source:** "Saab 900: More driving fun in the non-turbo version," *Road & Track*, May 1991, pp. 142-143.

1990: "craftsmanship and solidity . . . however . . . the car . . . feels outdated . . . Cargo capacity is awesome." **Source:** "Long-Magical Charm Is Wearing Out," *The New York Times*, June 10, p. 4.

1989: "engine was strong . . . an easy car to hustle around." **Source:** "Saab 900 Turbo: Part highbrow, part party animal," *Car and Driver*, February 1989, p. 59.

1987: "Left and right three-quarter visibility are severely limited . . . The brakes . . . perform impressively . . . sporty fun." **Source:** "Saab 900 Turbo Convertible," *Road & Track*, August 1987, pp. 80-82.

1987: "fun to drive . . . plush interior . . . incomparably comfortable seats . . . excellent climate control and stereo systems." **Source:** "Saab 900 Turbo: High-tech status," *The Detroit News*, August 19, 1987, pp. 1F-2F.

RECALLS

1989: (6,000 cars): Reverse current may flow cable between air recirculator and microswitch, resulting in heater fan resistor overheating and smoking. **Corrective action:** Disconnect cable and secure by tape around harness. *(NHTSA Campaign No. 89V104000.)*

1989: (1,586 passenger vehicles; includes Saab 9000s and Saab 900s): Fuel filter may not meet specification concerning leakage criteria due to low temperature during gluing process. Fuel filter may leak creating potential fire hazard. **Corrective action:** Replace fuel filter. *(NHTSA Campaign No. 88V185000.)*

1988: (3,000 cars): Bolts used in attachments of front suspension system control arms may be defective. If more than one of three bolts should fail, lower front control arm could come loose leading to loss of directional control of front wheel. **Corrective action:** Replace bolts with proper specification bolts. *(NHTSA Campaign No. 88V149000.)*

1987-88: (70,000 cars): Wiring harness may chafe against sharp edges under dashboard and against support under rear seat (1988 models only). This could cause short circuit; resulting heat buildup could cause smoke or fire in passenger compartment. **Corrective action:** Install rubber protective strips to sharp edges and completely encase wire harness in protective plastic tube. *(NHTSA Campaign No. 88V173000.)*

1987: (15,446 cars; includes models made before 1987): Fuel hose between pressure regulator and injector fuel rail may rupture under stress, resulting in fuel leak. **Corrective action:** Replace fuel hose. *(NHTSA Campaign No. 87V013000.)*

REPAIR MANUALS

2645 ● **Haynes Saab 900 Repair Manual, No. 980: 1979-1988**
Haynes Publications, Inc.
861 Lawrence Dr.
Newbury Park, CA 91320   Ph:(818)889-5400

1989. **Editor(s):** A. K. Legg. **Price:** $15.95.

2646 ● **Saab**
Peter Allen Video Productions
38-C Otis St.
West Babylon, NY 11704   Ph:(516)643-4372

How to tune-up and maintain the Saab engine. **Release date:** 1986. **Producer:** Peter Allen Productions. **Acquisition:** Purchase.

OTHER INFORMATION SOURCES

2647 ● **Nines**
Saab Club of North America
2416 London Rd., No. 900
Duluth, MN 55812   Ph:(218)724-1336

Newsletter. 11/year.

ASSOCIATIONS

2648 ● **Saab Club of North America**
2416 London Rd., No. 900
Duluth, MN 55812
Tim Winker, Editor   Ph:(218)724-1336

Founded: 1971. **Membership:** 3,900. Owners and enthusiasts of Swedish-manufactured Saab automobiles. Helps members exchange information on the care and maintenance of all Saab models. Holds technical sessions during convention. **Former Name(s):** Chicago Saab Club; Saab Clubs of America; Saab Clubs of North America. **Convention/Meeting:** Annual.

SAAB 9000 (1987-92)

A four-door sedan and five-door hatchback produced in Trollhattan, Sweden. Saab 9000 Turbo named to *Car and Driver's* Ten Best Cars list 1987-1989. Listed on *Car and Driver's* Ten Best Cars Nominees list 1990. *The Car Book* rated Saab 9000 a Best Bet and best in crash test performance in 1992.

1992 Saab 9000 S

MAJOR FEATURES

● Saab 9000 has as 1992 standard equipment: 2.3-liter 16-valve engine, 5-speed manual transmission, 4-wheel disc brakes with anti-lock braking system, rack-and-pinion power steering, driver's side airbag, power door locks and windows, air conditioning, power steel tilt/slide sunroof, velour upholstery, and 150-watt AM/FM stereo cassette player.

● Saab 9000 S adds as 1992 standard equipment: fog lights, electronic cruise control, power driver's seat, leather upholstery, and alloy wheels.

● Saab 9000 CD adds as 1992 standard equipment: 4-speed automatic transmission.

● Saab 9000 Turbo adds as 1992 standard equipment: turbocharged engine, traction control system, upgraded stereo system, and automatic climate control system.

● Saab 9000 Turbo CD adds 1992 standard equipment: same equipment as Saab 9000 Turbo plus rear passenger air conditioning.

● The limited production Saab 9000 CD Turbo Griffen Edition adds as 1992 standard equipment: Eucalyptus Green metallic paint, cross-spoke alloy wheels, leather seats, cellular telephone, and trunk-mounted six-disc CD changer.

PRICE HISTORY

The following new car prices reflect the approximate retail cost of the base model: **1987** - $17,935; **1988** - $24,037; **1989** - $24,445; **1990** - $25,495; **1991** - $22,895; **1992** - $24,845.

DIMENSIONS

Body Style	Years Avail	Wheel Base (in)	Lgth (in)	Ht (in)	Avg Wt (lbs)	Fuel Cap (gal)	Front Hdrm (in)	Front Legrm (in)
5d lbk	89-90	104.2	181.9	55.9	3,004	17.4	38.6	41.5
5d lbk	91-92	105.2	183.7	55.9	3,089	17.4	38.5	41.5
4d sdn	87-88	105.2	181.9	55.9	3,022	18	38.6	41.7
4d sdn	89-90	104.2	188.2	55.9	3,022	17.4	38.6	41.5
4d sdn	91-92	105.2	188.2	55.9	3,143	17.4	38.5	41.5

ENGINES

Type	Displace-ment (L)	Fuel Dly	HP @rpm	Torque @rpm (ft/lbs)	MPG Cty/Hwy	Years Avail
I-4	2.0	FI	125@5500	123@3000	21/27	87-88
I-4	2.0	FI	130@6000	128@3750	22/28	89-89
I-4	2.3	FI	150@5500	157@3800	20/26	90-92
I-4T	2.0	FI	160@5500	188@3000	22/28	87-89
I-4T	2.0	FI	165@5500	195@3000	20/26	90-90
I-4T	2.3	FI	200@5000	244@2000	19/26	91-92

KEY: I=in-line engine; V=V engine; F=flat engine; FI=fuel injection; bbl=barrel carburetor; T=turbo; D=diesel; HP=horsepower; MPG=estimated average miles per gallon.

EVALUATIONS, TESTS, AND RANKINGS

1992: "[9000 CS] styling is distinctly new." **Source:** "Saab Auto Unveils Its First Product As a GM Affiliate," *Wall Street Journal*, August 21, 1991, p. B5.

1992: "restyled nose and rear may well qualify as somewhat overly Saab ... extensive reinforcement of the central cabin ... traction control is also state-of-the-art." **Source:** "Saab 9000 CS," *Road & Track*, January 1992, pp. 82-83.

1992: "air-conditioning system ... ozone friendly ... aircraft-style instrumentation ... shape of the four-door sedan is a bit more mainstream." **Source:** "Saab 9000 CD Quick and Quirky," *Detroit Free Press*, October 3, 1991, p. 7D.

1991: "subtle stormer has the potential to deliver big-time thrills on demand." **Source:** "Saab 9000 Turbo," *Motor Trend*, February 1991, pp. 92-93.

1991: "small engine with big advantages ... quick, smooth acceleration ... torque steer is considerable." **Source:** "The Four That Roars," *Popular Science*, January 1991, p. 38.

1991: "9000 has shed its conservative image and how has a racy air about it ... more like a high-performance station wagon than a sedan ... interior is businesslike and functional." **Source:** "Saab 9000 makes the miles melt away," *Detroit News*, April 17, 1991, p. 1D.

1990: "alarm system apparently designed to do away with chivalry ... seats ... offer good thigh and back support ... interior scored high marks." **Source:** "Saab 9000 CD: Is there life after turbocharging," *Road & Track*, June 1990, pp. 78, 80-81.

1990: "doesn't look like your classic Saab ... doesn't have the soft, bumpless ride you'd expect from a luxury vehicle ... Inside is a gadgeteer's delight." **Source:** "Saab 9000 CD handles 'like a dream," *Design News*, June 25, 1990, p. 35.

1990: "feels agile and capable ... Back-seat occupants enjoy nearly as much room as those in front ... combination of a roomy, comfortable interior and responsive performance." **Source:** "Saab 9000CD: Maybe the "CD" should stand for "Civilized Disposition," *Car and Driver*, June 1990, pp. 141-145.

1990: "well-proven and highly competent suspension system ... most spacious interior of any European car sold in the U.S .... passenger compartment is well finished but with little ostentation." **Source:** "Saab 9000S: The Benefits of Motivational Therapy," *Motor Trend*, June 1990, pp. 64-67.

1989: "smooth and stylish." **Source:** "Ten Best Cars: And picking them wasn't easy," *Car and Driver*, January 1989, pp. 30-35.

1989: "astonishingly fast ... zips through the gears ... Steering feel is excellent ... a helluva nice car." **Source:** "Saab 9000 CD Turbo," *Motor Trend*, February 1989, pp. 101-103, 106.

1989: "big, spacious interior, comfortable seats, and well-controlled suspension ... brisk performer with more than adequate acceleration ... very pleasant car to drive." **Source:** "SAAB 9000S: Spacious, comfortable gas-saver," *Design News*, August 7, 1989, p. 32.

1987: "comfort ... is practically flawless." **Source:** "Ten Best Cars: Fun work, but somebody's got to do it," *Car and Driver*, January 1987, p. 41.

1987: "fit and finish were very good ... a thoroughly competent and predictable handler ... steering has a reassuringly positive feel." **Source:** "Saab 9000S: Even if you don't love it, you can't help but like it," *Motor Trend*, June 1987, pp. 91-92, 95.

RECALLS

1991: (250 vehicles): Improper assembly could cause ball of the gear selector arm not to be properly fixed to socket on end of gear selector cable; gear selector arm could separate from gear selector cable at ball socket joint. Gear position could not be selected or determined, resulting in sudden unexpected vehicle movement. **Corrective action:** Properly seat gear selector arm ball in selector cable socket and secure by lock ring inside socket. *(NHTSA Campaign No. 91V002000.)*

1989: (1,586 passenger vehicles; includes Saab 9000 and Saab 900 models): Fuel filter may not meet specification concerning leakage criteria due to low temperature during gluing process. Fuel filter may leak creating potential fire hazard. **Corrective action:** Replace fuel filter. *(NHTSA Campaign No. 88V185000.)*

1988: (14,000 cars with automatic transmissions): Chafing between throttle kickdown cable and steel brake fluid lines may occur, resulting in brake fluid leakage. **Corrective action:** Change cable routing and install new attachment bracket to prevent chafing. *(NHTSA Campaign No. 89V191000.)*

1988: (7,000 vehicles): Ball chain between cruise control vacuum regulator and accelerator pedal arm may catch on vacuum regulator attachment clip. If chain gets caught throttle could be prevented from returning to fully closed position when accelerator pedal is released. **Corrective action:** Plastic cap will be installed over vacuum regulator clip to cover openings. *(NHTSA Campaign No. 88V057000.)*

1987-90: (24,379 vehicles; includes models made before 1987): Abrasion on printed circuit card in combination neutral safety/backup lamp switch may cause an electrical fire in backup lamp circuit. **Corrective action:** Add an electrical circuit, including a relay, to the backup lamp circuit to reduce the current that can flow through the combination switch. *(NHTSA Campaign No. 90V001000.)*

REPAIR MANUALS

2649 ● Saab
Peter Allen Video Productions
38-C Otis St.
West Babylon, NY 11704   Ph:(516)643-4372

How to tune-up and maintain the Saab engine. **Release date:** 1986. **Producer:** Peter Allen Productions. **Acquisition:** Purchase.

OTHER INFORMATION SOURCES

2650 ● Nines
Saab Club of North America
2416 London Rd., No. 900
Duluth, MN 55812   Ph:(218)724-1336

Newsletter. 11/year.

ASSOCIATIONS

2651 ● Saab Club of North America
2416 London Rd., No. 900
Duluth, MN 55812
Tim Winker, Editor   Ph:(218)724-1336

Founded: 1971. **Membership:** 3,900. Owners and enthusiasts of Swedish-manufactured Saab automobiles. Helps members exchange information on the care and maintenance of all Saab models. Holds technical sessions during convention. **Former Name(s):** Chicago Saab Club; Saab Clubs of America; Saab Clubs of North America. **Convention/Meeting:** Annual.

SATURN (1991-92)

Introduced in late 1990 as a 1991 model. The Saturn division is an autonomous new sixth division at General Motors. Produced at plant in Spring Hill, Tennessee.

1991 Saturn SL1

MAJOR FEATURES

● Saturn SL 1992 standard equipment includes: 5-speed manual transmission, power front disc/rear drum power brakes, rack-and-pinion steering, independent MacPherson strut suspension, plastic vertical side panels, tilt steering, and AM/FM stereo.

● Saturn SL1 adds as 1992 standard equipment: power steering.

● Saturn SL2 and Saturn SC add as 1992 standard equipment: new instrument-cluster graphics, upgraded engine and tires.

PRICE HISTORY

The following new car prices reflect the approximate retail cost of the base model: **1991** - $7,995; **1992** - $8,195.

DIMENSIONS

Body Style	Years Avail	Wheel Base (in)	Lgth (in)	Ht (in)	Avg Wt (lbs)	Fuel Cap (gal)	Front Hdrm (in)	Front Legrm (in)
2d cpe	91-92	99.2	175.8	50.6	2,372	12.8	37.6	42.6
4d sdn	91-92	102.4	176.3	52.5	2,313	12.8	38.5	42.5

ENGINES

Type	Displace-ment (L)	Fuel Dly	HP @rpm	Torque @rpm (ft/lbs)	MPG Cty/Hwy	Years Avail
I-4	1.9	FI	85@5000	107@2400	28/38	91-92
I-4	1.9	FI	124@5600	119@2800	24/33	91-92

KEY: I=in-line engine; V=V engine; F=flat engine; FI=fuel injection; bbl=barrel carburetor; T=turbo; D=diesel; HP=horsepower; MPG=estimated average miles per gallon.

EVALUATIONS, TESTS, AND RANKINGS

1991: "sits at the head of the second echelon of small cars, solidly midpack but no better." **Source:** "Saturn: Finally, it's here. But is it good enough," *Car and Driver*, November 1990, pp. 132, 134-135, 138, 140.

1991: "gear ratios ... are tailored for economy, not excitement ... fit and finish are good ... surprisingly competent cars." **Source:** "Saturn Sports Coupe," *Road & Track*, November 1990, pp. 58-61, 63-64.

1991: "a small car that can satisfy the reasonable requirements of average American motorists." **Source:** "We have Liftoff! Saturn puts three cars into orbit," *Automobile Magazine*, November 1990, pp. 62, 64-67.

1991: "solid, well-built and nicely appointed ... a cut above ... garden-variety domestic small cars." **Source:** "Saturn shows it can hold its own against the Japanese imports," *Detroit Free Press*, September 27, 1990, p. 15A.

1991: "we ... like the overall handling." **Source:** "Halfway home: A competent compact car," *Detroit Free Press*, October 31, 1990, pp. 1A, 10A.

1991: "The Saturn coupe provides a pleasant visual interior environment ... handsome looks and respectable overall handling [are] its strongest suits ... engine transmission, suspension, and tires still create a symphony of dissonance." **Source:** "Getaway Coupes," *Popular Science*, July 1991, pp. 76-80, 82-83.

1991: "the Saturn is about as all new as it gets in terms of design, construction and marketing ... Performance isn't exactly breathtaking ... there's no mistaking Saturn for a Japanese car." **Source:** "A Peek at 1991," *New Choices*, September 1990, pp. 74-75.

1991: "The Saturn Sports Coupe is a down-to-earth vehicle with driving appeal ... A little quieting of the engine and damping of the suspension should provide refinement ... has the major pieces in place to appeal to consumers shopping sporty coupes." **Source:** "Saturn Sports Coupe stands up to imports," *Flint Journal*, March 20, 1991, pp. E1-E2.

1991: "seats are supportive ... handling is nimble and sporty ... manual shift is buttersmooth, though the lively four-cylinder engine is a bit noisier than the best from Japan." **Source:** "Test Drive: Taking Saturn out for a spin," *U.S. News & World Report*, October 22, 1990, p. 54.

1991: "quiet and roomy, given its small shell ... glossy paint is designed to be crack-proof as it bends with the plastic doors, fenders, and quarter-panels ... fuel economy is reasonable if not great." **Source:** "The New Saturn: Lustre Under the Skin," *New York Times*, April 14, 1991.

1991: "vertical side panels will be made of plastic, to eliminate annoying parking-lot dents and dings. The plastic molds can also be switched quickly making for faster styling changes in the future." **Source:** "Here Comes GM's Saturn," *Business Week*, April 9, 1990, pp. 56-62.

1991: "nice quick-wipe setting ... enables you to clear windshields splashes with one touch ... manages to deliver a smooth, comfortable ride . . . offers the most rear-passenger width and the most engine torque." **Source:** "Fuel-Efficient Family Cars for 1991," *Home Mechanix*, March 1991, pp. 69-73.

RECALLS

None to date.

STERLING 825 (1987-88)

Introduced as part of Austin Rover line; produced in partnership with Honda. Won 5th place in *Motor Trend's* 1987 Import Car of the Year. Sterling Motors discontinued offering all Sterling models to the U.S. market after 1991.

1988 Sterling 825SL

MAJOR FEATURES

● Sterling 825S had as 1988 standard equipment: air conditioning, power windows, power sunroof, 6-speaker AM/FM cassette stereo, power-assisted rack-and-pinion steering, and 4-wheel disc brakes.

● Sterling 825SL added as 1988 standard equipment: Anti-lock braking system and leather interior.

PRICE HISTORY

The following new car prices reflect the approximate retail cost of the base model: **1987** - $19,000; **1988** - $21,740.

DIMENSIONS

Body Style	Years Avail	Wheel Base (in)	Lgth (in)	Ht (in)	Avg Wt (lbs)	Fuel Cap (gal)	Front Hdrm (in)	Front Legrm (in)
4d sdn	87-88	108.6	188.8	54.8	3,164	18.0	37.8	41.2

ENGINES

Type	Displacement (L)	Fuel Dly	HP @rpm	Torque @rpm (ft/lbs)	MPG Cty/Hwy	Years Avail
V-6	2.5	FI	151@5800	154@4500	19/24	87-88

KEY: I=in-line engine; V=V engine; F=flat engine; FI=fuel injection; bbl=barrel carburetor; T=turbo; D=diesel; HP=horsepower; MPG=estimated average miles per gallon.

EVALUATIONS, TESTS, AND RANKINGS

1987: "very serious entry in the upscale sports/luxury sedan class . . . interior is luxurious . . . the best of the Japanese and

the British." **Source:** "Sterling: British get serious," *Detroit News*, July 22, 1987, pp. 1F-2F.

1987: "luxury and style at a price that won't curl your hair." **Source:** "1987 Import Car of the Year," *Motor Trend*, April 1987, p. 47.

1987: "The Sterling is . . . a car offering performance, comfort and handling . . . is noiser than other cars in this class." **Source:** "Austin Rover Sterling: Japanese technology with a British accent," *Home Mechanix*, March 1987, pp. 14-15.

1987: "[an Acura] Legend in English tweed." **Source:** "Sterling," *Road & Track—Buyers Guide 1987*, 1986, p. 144.

RECALLS

1987-88: (4,028 passenger cars with automatic shoulder belt systems): Automatic shoulder belt assembly may malfunction during abrupt braking or cornering. Also, the retractor driver unit may stall in any position, leaving the belt loose. In either case, the belt would not retract when the door is opened and would not allow the seat occupant to exit the vehicle. **Corrective action:** Replace the automatic safety belt assemblies. *(NHTSA Campaign No. 91V077000.)*

1987: (14,900 vehicles): Interrupted power supply to various electrical systems due to faulty ignition switch. **Corrective action:** Replace and lubricate ignition switch and electrical subharness. *(NHTSA Campaign No. 87V177000.)*

STERLING 827 (1988-91)

Introduced as part of Austin Rover line, successor to Sterling 825. Produced in partnership with Honda. Sterling Motor Cars discontinued offering all Sterling models to the U.S. market after 1991.

1991 Sterling 827SL

MAJOR FEATURES

● Sterling 827Si had as 1991 standard equipment: 5-speed manual transmission, 4-wheel disc brakes, anti-lock braking system, power moonroof, power locks, automatic climate control, power windows, cruise control, and 8-speaker AM/FM cassette stereo.

● Sterling 827SL 1991 standard equipment included: 4-speed automatic transmission and leather interior.

● Sterling 827SL Limited Edition added as 1991 standard equipment: metallic British Racing Green paint and upgraded leather seating.

● Sterling 827SLi, a high-performance hatchback version,

included the following 1991 standard equipment: 6Jx16 inch Roversport alloy wheels and rosewood veneer.

PRICE HISTORY

The following new car prices reflect the approximate retail cost of the base model: **1989** - $23,300; **1990** - $23,550; **1991** - $26,500.

DIMENSIONS

Body Style	Years Avail	Wheel Base (in)	Lgth (in)	Ht (in)	Avg Wt (lbs)	Fuel Cap (gal)	Front Hdrm (in)	Front Legrm (in)
4d lbk	88-91	108.6	188.8	54.8	3,153	17.0	37.8	41.2

ENGINES

Type	Displace-ment (L)	Fuel Dly	HP @rpm	Torque @rpm (ft/lbs)	MPG Cty/Hwy	Years Avail
V-6	2.7	FI	160@5900	162@4500	19/23	88-91

KEY: I=in-line engine; V=V engine; F=flat engine; FI=fuel injection; bbl=barrel carburetor; T=turbo; D=diesel; HP=horsepower; MPG=estimated average miles per gallon.

EVALUATIONS, TESTS, AND RANKINGS

1991: "A back-road burner the Sterling is not . . . interior has a cozy feel to it . . . Gauges are excellent." **Source:** "European Influence: Eight sporting sedans with price tags less than $30,000," *Road & Track*, August 1991, pp. 64-65, 78, 84.

1990: "suspension gives drivers a decent feel of the road while muffling many bumps . . . seats were wide and roomy." **Source:** "Venture Produces Sterling Car," *Detroit News*, August 15, 1990, pp. 1D-2D.

1990: "engine runs smoothly and quietly . . . stereo-system controls are also awkward . . . entire car turned off and on, engine and all, while cruising along the highway . . . for a split second . . . three times." **Source:** "Sterling 827Si: This silver lining has a cloud," *Car and Driver*, March 1990, pp. 108-110.

1989: "added roll stiffness and wider tires amounted to hefty payoffs in the handling department . . . a delightful, balanced car to drive . . . engine . . . made the 827SLi a joy to accelerate." **Source:** "Sterling 827SLi: All bets are on," *Road & Track*, June 1989, pp. 58-60, 62.

1989: "quite nimble and ready to thrust and jab with any traffic situation . . . solid, functional, and fun to drive." **Source:** "Sterling 827SLi," *Motor Trend*, May 1989, pp. 189-190, 193, 195.

RECALLS

None to date.

SUBARU BRAT (1987)

Subaru-Isuzu Automotive Inc. is the first U.S. joint venture between two Japanese auto manufacturing companies—Fuju Heavy Industries Ltd. (FHI) and Isuzu Motors Limited. Manufacturing operations for U.S.-marketed vehicles took place at FHI's home factory in Ota City, Japan, and at the U.S. joint venture facility located near Lafayette, Indiana. Discontinued in 1987.

MAJOR FEATURES

● Subaru Brat had as 1987 standard equipment: 4-speed manual transmission and 4-wheel drive.

PRICE HISTORY

The following new car prices reflect the approximate retail cost of the base model: **1987** - $8,338.

DIMENSIONS

Body Style	Years Avail	Wheel Base (in)	Lgth (in)	Ht (in)	Avg Wt (lbs)	Fuel Cap (gal)	Front Hdrm (in)	Front Legrm (in)
trk	87-87	96.3	174.2	56.9	2,205	14.5	38.2	39.3

ENGINES

Type	Displace-ment (L)	Fuel Dly	HP @rpm	Torque @rpm (ft/lbs)	MPG Cty/Hwy	Years Avail
Flat-4	1.8	2-bbl	73@4400	94@2400	24/29	87-87

KEY: I=in-line engine; V=V engine; F=flat engine; FI=fuel injection; bbl=barrel carburetor; T=turbo; D=diesel; HP=horsepower; MPG=estimated average miles per gallon.

RECALLS

None to date.

REPAIR MANUALS

2652 ● **Chilton's Subaru 1970-1988**
Chilton Co.
Chilton Way
Radnor, PA 19089   Ph:(215)964-4000

Published 1988. **Price:** $15.95.

SUBARU COUPE (1987-89)

Introduced as part of Subaru line. Discontinued in 1989.

MAJOR FEATURES

● Subaru DL Coupe 1989 standard equipment included: 5-speed manual transmission, rack-and-pinion steering, front disc/rear drum brakes, cloth upholstery, and trip odometer.

● Subaru GL Coupe added as 1989 standard equipment: power door locks, power windows, tilt steering, and AM/FM stereo.

● Subaru GL 4WD Turbo Coupe added as 1989 standard equipment: 4-wheel drive, 4-wheel disc brakes, power sunroof, air conditioning, cruise control, and upgraded stereo.

● Subaru RX Coupe added as 1989 standard equipment: upgraded suspension, analog instrument gauges, and performance tires.

PRICE HISTORY

The following new car prices reflect the approximate retail cost of the base model: **1987** - $9,108; **1988** - $9,201; **1989** - $9,731.

DIMENSIONS

Body Style	Years Avail	Wheel Base (in)	Lgth (in)	Ht (in)	Avg Wt (lbs)	Fuel Cap (gal)	Front Hdrm (in)	Front Legrm (in)
3d cpe	87-89	97.2	174.6	51.8	2,280	9.5	37.6	42.2

ENGINES

Type	Displace-ment (L)	Fuel Dly	HP @rpm	Torque @rpm (ft/lbs)	MPG Cty/Hwy	Years Avail
Flat-4	1.8	2-bbl	84@5200	101@3200	22/28	87-87
Flat-4	1.8	FI	90@5200	101@2800	23/29	88-89
Flat-4T	1.8	FI	115@5200	134@2800	22/25	87-89

KEY: I=in-line engine; V=V engine; F=flat engine; FI=fuel injection; bbl=barrel carburetor; T=turbo; D=diesel; HP=horsepower; MPG=estimated average miles per gallon.

EVALUATIONS, TESTS, AND RANKINGS

1987: ``snazzy styling, peppy performance and fuel efficiency ... excellent traction and road-holding ability.'' **Source:** ``Subaru RX leads new pack of hatchbacks,'' *Detroit Free Press,* July 27, 1987, p. 1E.

RECALLS

1987: (57,000 4-door sedans, 3-door coupes and station wagons, and 4-wheel drive carburetor-equipped vehicles; includes other Subaru models): Composition of certain non-genuine replacement preheat tubes may ignite. **Corrective action:** Install redesigned preheat tubes. *(NHTSA Campaign No. 89V103000.)*

REPAIR MANUALS

2653 ● **Chilton's Subaru 1970-1988**
Chilton Co.
Chilton Way
Radnor, PA 19089   Ph:(215)964-4000

Published 1988. **Price:** $15.95.

2654 ● **How to Keep Your Subaru Alive: A Manual of Step-by-Step Procedures for the Compleat Idiot**
John Muir Publications
P.O. Box 613
Santa Fe, NM 87504-0613   Ph:(505)982-4078

Published 1989. **Editor(s):** Larry Owens. **Price:** $19.95.

SUBARU HATCHBACK (1987-89)

Oldest model in the Subaru line. Discontinued in 1989.

MAJOR FEATURES

● Subaru GL Hatchback had as 1989 standard equipment: 5-speed manual transmission, power front disc/rear drum brakes, tilt steering, 4-wheel independent suspension, and trip odometer.

PRICE HISTORY

The following new car prices reflect the approximate retail cost of the base model: **1987** - $5,398; **1988** - $8,146; **1989** - $8,956.

DIMENSIONS

Body Style	Years Avail	Wheel Base (in)	Lgth (in)	Ht (in)	Avg Wt (lbs)	Fuel Cap (gal)	Front Hdrm (in)	Front Legrm (in)
3d lbk	87-87	93.7	156.9	53.7	2,050	13.2	38.2	39.3
3d lbk	88-89	93.7	157.9	53.7	2,120	13.2	38.2	39.3

ENGINES

Type	Displace-ment (L)	Fuel Dly	HP @rpm	Torque @rpm (ft/lbs)	MPG Cty/Hwy	Years Avail
Flat-4	1.6	2-bbl	69@4800	86@2800	28/32	87-87
Flat-4	1.8	2-bbl	73@4400	94@2400	26/31	87-89

KEY: I=in-line engine; V=V engine; F=flat engine; FI=fuel injection; bbl=barrel carburetor; T=turbo; D=diesel; HP=horsepower; MPG=estimated average miles per gallon.

EVALUATIONS, TESTS, AND RANKINGS

1988: ``four-wheel-drive rig.'' **Source:** ``Subaru Hatchback,'' *Car and Driver—Buyers Guide 1988,* 1988, p. 56.

RECALLS

None to date.

REPAIR MANUALS

2655 ● **Chilton's Subaru 1970-1988**
Chilton Co.
Chilton Way
Radnor, PA 19089   Ph:(215)964-4000

Published 1988. **Price:** $15.95.

2656 ● **How to Keep Your Subaru Alive: A Manual of Step-by-Step Procedures for the Compleat Idiot**
John Muir Publications
P.O. Box 613
Santa Fe, NM 87504-0613   Ph:(505)982-4078

Published 1989. **Editor(s):** Larry Owens. **Price:** $19.95.

SUBARU JUSTY (1987-92)

Produced in Japan. Chosen by *The Complete Car Cost Guide* as having one of the lowest insurance costs and best overall values for a subcompact (Subaru Justy Fun). Rated among the best in its class in Crash Test Performance and among the worst in Warranty Coverage by the 1992 *Car Book.* All models available with 4-wheel drive.

1991 Subaru Justy GL

MAJOR FEATURES

● Subaru Justy has as 1992 standard equipment: 5-speed manual transmission, rack-and-pinion steering, front disc/rear drum brakes, and remote hatch release.

● Subaru Justy GL adds as 1992 standard equipment: multi-point fuel injection, complete instrumentation including tachometer, AM/FM stereo, upgraded engine and suspension, rear defogger and wiper/washer, and folding rear seatback.

● Subaru Justy DL had as 1990 standard equipment: 5-speed manual transmission, locking fuel door, and reclining front bucket seats.

● Subaru Justy RS added as 1990 standard equipment: monochrome exterior, cloth and vinyl upholstery, and full wheel covers.

● Subaru Justy Fun added as 1990 standard equipment: other exterior body stylings.

PRICE HISTORY

The following new car prices reflect the approximate retail cost of the base model: **1987** - $5,495; **1988** - $5,666; **1989** - $5,866; **1990** - $5,866; **1991** - $6,295; **1992** - $6,645.

DIMENSIONS

Body Style	Years Avail	Wheel Base (in)	Lgth (in)	Ht (in)	Avg Wt (lbs)	Fuel Cap (gal)	Front Hdrm (in)	Front Legrm (in)
3d lbk	87-88	90.0	139.2	54.7	1,655	9.2	37.0	41.5
3d lbk	89-90	90.0	145.5	55.9	1,745	9.2	38.0	41.5
3d lbk	91-92	90.0	145.5	53.7	1,820	9.2	38.0	41.5
4d lbk	90-90	90.0	145.5	55.9	2,045	9.2	38.0	41.5
4d lbk	91-92	90.0	145.5	53.7	2,045	9.2	38.0	41.5

ENGINES

Type	Displacement (L)	Fuel Dly	HP @rpm	Torque @rpm (ft/lbs)	MPG Cty/Hwy	Years Avail
I-3	1.2	2-bbl	66@5200	70@3600	33/37	87-92
I-3	1.2	FI	73@5600	71@2800	33/37	90-92

KEY: I=in-line engine; V=V engine; F=flat engine; FI=fuel injection; bbl=barrel carburetor; T=turbo; D=diesel; HP=horsepower; MPG=estimated average miles per gallon.

EVALUATIONS, TESTS, AND RANKINGS

1989: "a kick to drive." **Source:** "Eight for Ten," *Car and Driver*, December 1988, pp. 54-58, 60, 63.

1989: "can climb hills steadily and without hesitation . . . sturdy but unexceptional . . . ride was overly rough . . . a good city car for the smaller driver." **Source:** "The Little Transmission That Could," *Changing Times*, May 1989, p. 100.

1989: "[Electronic Constantly Variable Transmission] provides the car's pint-size engine with an almost infinite number of forward speeds . . . transition is smooth." **Source:** "Import Report: Totally Shiftless," *Home Mechanix*, April 1989, pp. 84-86, 103-105.

1988: "handling in the snow is quite good . . . solid and rattle-free . . . lack of sound insulation." **Source:** "Snow White and the Seven AWDs," *Road & Track*, May 1988, pp. 56-63, 67-70.

1988: "willing, no-nonsense . . . unsophisticated operation . . . very efficient." **Source:** "3x3: Nine cylinders of basic transportation," *Road & Track*, July 1988, pp. 66-70, 74.

1987: "steering is precise and linear . . . a low-profile

workhorse." **Source:** "Subaru Justy GL," *Car and Driver*, April 1987, pp. 75-77, 79, 81.

RECALLS

1988-89: (15,000 cars with 5-speed manual transmission and 4-wheel drive): Insufficient lubrication of 4 wheel drive extension housing bearing due to transmission case dipstick design and fluid level checking method. May result in bearing seizure and rear wheel lock up. **Corrective action:** Install modified dipstick and insert information in manual on correct fluid level checking procedure. (NHTSA Campaign No. 89V028000.)

1988: (60,000 vehicles; includes the Subaru Justy, Subaru XT, Subaru XT-DL, and Subaru XT-GL): Omission of information specified by FMVSS 210 from owner manual. Fails to meet requirement of FMVSS 210 regarding child restraint systems. **Corrective action:** Adhesive backed inserts will be furnished with correct information. (NHTSA Campaign No. 88V052000.)

1988: (3,000 vehicles equipped with accessory Subaru air conditioning system): Insufficient clearance between relocated alternator wiring and solenoid hose alternator wiring stay bracket can cause wire chaffing and an electrical short. Could result in smoke and possibly an engine compartment fire. **Corrective action:** Modify by removing solenoid hose/alternator stay bracket. (NHTSA Campaign No. 88V029000.)

1987: (57,000 4-door sedans, 3-door coupes and station wagons, and 4-wheel drive carburetor equipped vehicles; includes other Subaru models): Composition of certain non-genuine replacement preheat tubes may ignite. **Corrective action:** Install redesigned preheat tubes. (NHTSA Campaign No. 89V103000.)

REPAIR MANUALS

2657 ● **Chilton's Subaru 1970-1988**
Chilton Co.
Chilton Way
Radnor, PA 19089　　　　　　　　Ph:(215)964-4000

Published 1988. **Price:** $15.95.

2658 ● **How to Keep Your Subaru Alive: A Manual of Step-by-Step Procedures for the Compleat Idiot**
John Muir Publications
P.O. Box 613
Santa Fe, NM 87504-0613　　　　　Ph:(505)982-4078

Published 1989. **Editor(s):** Larry Owens. **Price:** $19.95.

SUBARU LEGACY (1990-92)

Most Legacy vehicles are imported from Japan, but some sedans are built in Lafayette, Indiana, at a plant jointly operated by Subaru and Isuzu. Named to *Car and Driver's* List of Ten Best Cars Nominees. Competing models include: Honda Accord, Toyota Camry, and Mazda 626. The 1992 models feature new front and rear body styling. All models are available with all-wheel drive.

1992 Subaru Legacy L

MAJOR FEATURES

● Subaru Legacy L has as 1992 standard equipment: 5-speed manual transmission, 4-wheel independent suspension, 4-wheel power-assisted disc brakes, power steering, and tilt steering. Also available as a 5-door wagon.

● Subaru Legacy LS adds as 1992 standard equipment: 4-speed automatic transmission, anti-lock braking system, power door locks, power windows, cruise control, power moonroof, AM/FM stereo cassette player, and air conditioning. Also available as a 5-door wagon.

● Subaru Legacy LSi adds as 1992 standard equipment: compact disc player and leather upholstery and trim.

● Subaru Legacy Sport Sedan adds as 1992 standard equipment: 5-speed manual transmission, turbocharged engine, enhanced sport suspension, and upgraded tires.

PRICE HISTORY

The following new car prices reflect the approximate retail cost of the base model: **1990** - $11,499; **1991** - $12,924; **1992** - $11,999.

DIMENSIONS

Body Style	Years Avail	Wheel Base (in)	Lgth (in)	Ht (in)	Avg Wt (lbs)	Fuel Cap (gal)	Front Hdrm (in)	Front Legrm (in)
4d sdn	90-90	101.6	177.6	54.3	2,620	15.9	38.2	42.3
4d sdn	91-91	101.6	177.6	52.6	2,730	15.9	38.0	42.3
4d sdn	92-92	101.6	178.9	53.5	2,740	15.9	38.0	43.1
5d wgn	90-90	101.6	181.1	55.9	2,750	15.9	38.2	42.3
5d wgn	91-91	101.6	181.1	53.7	2,850	15.9	38.2	42.3
5d wgn	92-92	101.6	181.9	54.7	2,860	15.9	38.4	43.1

ENGINES

Type	Displacement (L)	Fuel Dly	HP @rpm	Torque @rpm (ft/lbs)	MPG Cty/Hwy	Years Avail
Flat-4	2.2	FI	130@5600	137@4400	23/30	90-92
Flat-4	2.2	FI	160@5600	181@2800	21/26	91-92

KEY: I=in-line engine; V=V engine; F=flat engine; FI=fuel injection; bbl=barrel carburetor; T=turbo; D=diesel; HP=horsepower; MPG=estimated average miles per gallon.

EVALUATIONS, TESTS, AND RANKINGS

1991: "Turn-in is quick and accurate . . . good chassis stiffness . . . Straight-line stability is good." **Source:** "Subaru Legacy Sport Sedan," *Road & Track*, January 1991, pp. 104-108.

1991: "a car of . . . sophistication." **Source:** "For '91, Subaru Sports a New Image," *The New York Times*, December 9, 1990.

1991: "leaning toward the luxury side of sport . . . more

compliant, less demanding." **Source:** "Mitsubishi Galant VR-4 VS. Subaru Legacy Sport Sedan," *Motor Trend,* February 1991, pp. 70-73.

1991: "Steering is accurate, responsive and adequately quick . . . a capable piece of machinery." **Source:** "Smooth or rough road, Subaru's Legacy all-wheel-drive turbo handles like a dream," *The Flint Journal*, December 26, 1990, pp. 1B-2B.

1991: "competent and confident mode of rapid transit . . . reserved exterior barely reveals its road-taming capabilities." **Source:** "Sport-Minded Subaru Legacy," *Popular Science,* January 1991, p. 34.

1991: "Exterior styling is clean, purposeful and pleasant . . . interior is functional, efficient and comfortable . . . responds decently to routine driving." **Source:** "Legacy may lack oomph but it's all right for family transportation," *The Flint Journal*, September 4, 1991, p. E1.

1990: "ranked near the top in most . . . performance tests." **Source:** "Best Sellers," *Popular Mechanics*, July 1989, pp. 60-63, 120-122.

1990: "comes on strong on the middle-class values of roominess and practicality." **Source:** "Subaru Legacy LS," *Motor Trend,* July 1989, pp. 97-101.

1990: "offers better than average engine access . . . components are easily accessible due to the engine's design." **Source:** "A Winning Legacy: Common sense and attention to detail make the Subaru Legacy HM's Easy-Maintenance Car of the Year," *Home Mechanix*, May 1990, pp. 58-61.

1990: "styling of the Legacy captures much of the glassy elegance that once was the exclusive domain of Honda . . . achieve[s] handling at the expense of a grumbling ride." **Source:** "Compact Sedans Grow Up," *Popular Science*, April 1990, pp. 80-84.

RECALLS

1990-91: (103,744 four-door sedans and station wagons): Torque of latch screws on front doors may loosen over time due to gap between latch base plate and inner door panel under screw head. Affected door may not be opened from inside, preventing exit from door. **Corrective action:** Replace front door latch screws with *lock-tight* screws. *(NHTSA Campaign No. 90V184000.)*

1990-91: (76,000 passenger cars with electronically controlled automatic transmissions; includes the Subaru Loyale, Subaru Legacy, and Subaru XT): Under certain load conditions the park gear may not disengage immediately when the transmission lever is moved from park to reverse, causing delayed and possibly abrupt vehicle movement. Could result in loss of vehicle control and an accident. **Corrective action:** Install a modified parking brake pawl to prevent delayed release into reverse gear. *(NHTSA Campaign No. 91V082000.)*

1990: (81,000 vehicles): Dislodged defroster pin may prevent shutter door from closing. **Corrective action:** Install a positioning stopper device to prevent dislocation of defroster lever pin to assure defroster operation. *(NHTSA Campaign No. 90V110000.)*

REPAIR MANUALS

2659 ● **How to Keep Your Subaru Alive: A Manual of Step-by-Step Procedures for the Compleat Idiot**
John Muir Publications
P.O. Box 613
Santa Fe, NM 87504-0613   Ph:(505)982-4078

Published 1989. **Editor(s):** Larry Owens. **Price:** $19.95.

SUBARU LOYALE (1990-92)

Replaced the Subaru Sedan. Subaru dropped the 3-door coupe and all turbocharged versions after 1990. Listed in *The Complete Car Cost Guide* as having one of the highest fuel costs for a subcompact wagon. Produced in Japan.

1991 Subaru Loyale Wagon

MAJOR FEATURES

● Subaru Loyale Sedan and Wagon have as 1992 standard equipment: 5-speed manual transmission, front disc/rear drum brakes, rack-and-pinion power steering, power door locks, power windows, AM/FM stereo cassette player, and air conditioning. All models available with 4-wheel drive.

PRICE HISTORY

The following new car prices reflect the approximate retail cost of the base model: **1990** - $9,299; **1991** - $9,499; **1992** - $9,799.

DIMENSIONS

Body Style	Years Avail	Wheel Base (in)	Lgth (in)	Ht (in)	Avg Wt (lbs)	Fuel Cap (gal)	Front Hdrm (in)	Front Legrm (in)
3d lbk	90-90	97.2	174.6	53.4	2,475	15.9	37.6	42.2
4d sdn	90-90	97.2	174.6	53.4	2,275	15.9	37.6	42.2
4d sdn	91-92	97.2	174.6	52.5	2,355	15.9	37.6	41.7
5d wgn	90-92	97.0	176.8	53.0	2,490	15.9	37.6	41.7

ENGINES

Type	Displacement (L)	Fuel Dly	HP @rpm	Torque @rpm (ft/lbs)	MPG Cty/Hwy	Years Avail
Flat-4	1.8	FI	90@5200	101@2800	25/32	90-92
Flat-4T	1.8	FI	115@5200	134@2800	22/24	90-90

KEY: I=in-line engine; V=V engine; F=flat engine; FI=fuel injection; bbl=barrel carburetor; T=turbo; D=diesel; HP=horsepower; MPG=estimated average miles per gallon.

EVALUATIONS, TESTS, AND RANKINGS

1990: "sporty." **Source:** "Subaru Loyale," *Car and Driver—Buyers Guide 1990*, 1989, p. 113.

RECALLS

1990-91: (19,763 cars including front and four-wheel drive vehicles equipped with the 3AT automatic transmission): Transmission shift linkage may be incorrectly adjusted and would not be engaged in a full park position when placed in park. A runaway situation would occur, possibly resulting in an

accident. **Corrective action:** Repair the transmission park mechanism. *(NHTSA Campaign No. 91V091000.)*

1990: (76,000 passenger cars with electronically controlled automatic transmissions; includes the Subaru Loyale, Subaru Legacy, and Subaru XT): Under certain load conditions, the park gear may not disengage immediately when the transmission lever is moved from park to reverse, causing delayed and possibly abrupt vehicle movement. Could result in loss of vehicle control and an accident. **Corrective action:** Install a modified parking brake pawl to prevent delayed release into reverse gear. *(NHTSA Campaign No. 91V082000.)*

REPAIR MANUALS

2660 ● **How to Keep Your Subaru Alive: A Manual of Step-by-Step Procedures for the Compleat Idiot**
John Muir Publications
P.O. Box 613
Santa Fe, NM 87504-0613   Ph:(505)982-4078

Published 1989. **Editor(s):** Larry Owens. **Price:** $19.95.

SUBARU SEDAN (1987-89)

Replaced in 1990 with the Subaru Loyale.

MAJOR FEATURES

● Subaru DL Sedan had as 1989 standard equipment: 5-speed manual transmission, rack-and-pinion power steering, 4-wheel independent suspension, front disc/rear drum power brakes, cloth upholstery, and trip odometer.

● Subaru GL Sedan added as 1989 standard equipment: power door locks, power windows, AM/FM stereo, and tilt steering.

● Subaru GL-10 Turbo Sedan added as 1989 standard equipment: 4-wheel disc brakes, power sunroof, air conditioning, cruise control, and upgraded stereo.

● Subaru RX 4WD Turbo Sedan added as 1989 standard equipment: 4-wheel drive, analog instrument gauges, and performance tires.

PRICE HISTORY

The following new car prices reflect the approximate retail cost of the base model: **1987** - $8,808; **1988** - $9,201; **1989** - $9,731.

DIMENSIONS

Body Style	Years Avail	Wheel Base (in)	Lgth (in)	Ht (in)	Avg Wt (lbs)	Fuel Cap (gal)	Front Hdrm (in)	Front Legrm (in)
4d sdn	87-89	97.2	174.6	52.5	2,195	15.9	37.6	41.7

ENGINES

Type	Displacement (L)	Fuel Dly	HP @rpm	Torque @rpm (ft/lbs)	MPG Cty/Hwy	Years Avail
Flat-4	1.8	FI	90@5200	101@2800	25/31	87-89
Flat-4T	1.8	2-bbl	84@5200	101@2800	22/25	87-87
Flat-4T	1.8	FI	115@5200	134@2800	22/25	88-89

KEY: I=in-line engine; V=V engine; F=flat engine; FI=fuel injection; bbl=barrel carburetor; T=turbo; D=diesel; HP=horsepower; MPG=estimated average miles per gallon.

EVALUATIONS, TESTS, AND RANKINGS

1988: ''host of convenience features.'' **Source:** ''Subaru Sedan/Wagon,'' *Car and Driver—Buyers Guide 1988*, 1988, p. 67.

RECALLS

1987: (57,000 4-door sedans, 3-door coupes and station wagons, and 4 wheel drive carburetor equipped vehicles; includes other Subaru models): Composition of certain non-genuine replacement preheat tubes may ignite. **Corrective action:** Install redesigned preheat tubes. *(NHTSA Campaign No. 89V103000.)*

REPAIR MANUALS

2661 ● **Chilton's Subaru 1970-1988**
Chilton Co.
Chilton Way
Radnor, PA 19089   Ph:(215)964-4000

Published 1988. **Price:** $15.95.

2662 ● **How to Keep Your Subaru Alive: A Manual of Step-by-Step Procedures for the Compleat Idiot**
John Muir Publications
P.O. Box 613
Santa Fe, NM 87504-0613   Ph:(505)982-4078

Published 1989. **Editor(s):** Larry Owens. **Price:** $19.95.

SUBARU SVX (1992)

A replacement for the XT6, the SVX marks Subaru's entry into the performance luxury coupe market. Assembled in Ota City, Japan.

1992 Subaru SVX

MAJOR FEATURES

● SVX has as 1992 standard equipment: 3.3-liter 6-cylinder engine, 4-speed automatic transmission, full-time all-wheel drive, 4-wheel disc brakes with ABS, power rack-and-pinion steering, driver-side air bag, automatic climate control, tilt steering column, power windows and locks, remote keyless entry system, AM/FM cassette audio system, and rear window defroster.

PRICE HISTORY

The following new car prices reflect the approximate retail cost of the base model: **1992** - $25,000.

DIMENSIONS

Body Style	Years Avail	Wheel Base (in)	Lgth (in)	Ht (in)	Avg Wt (lbs)	Fuel Cap (gal)	Front Hdrm (in)	Front Legrm (in)
2d lbk	92-92	102.8	182.1	51.2	3,525	18.5	38.0	43.5

ENGINES

Type	Displace-ment (L)	Fuel Dly	HP @rpm	Torque @rpm (ft/lbs)	MPG Cty/Hwy	Years Avail
Flat-6	3.3	FI	230@5,400	224@4,400	17/25	92-92

KEY: I=in-line engine; V=V engine; F=flat engine; FI=fuel injection; bbl=barrel carburetor; T=turbo; D=diesel; HP=horsepower; MPG=estimated average miles per gallon.

EVALUATIONS, TESTS, AND RANKINGS

1992: ''sleek, quick, comfortable, and it handles like a dream . . . a car with the hardware, versatility and even the looks to make it a star . . . looks like a solid value, as well as an impressive performer.'' **Source:** ''New Cars: SVX—A Sportier Subaru,'' *Popular Mechanics*, August 1991, p. 88.

1992: ''4-speed automatic . . . boasts takeoffs that are snappy . . . and shifts that are quick and direct . . . Small bumps can make the SVX feel a tad skittish. .interior is refreshingly devoid of gadgets.'' **Source:** ''Subaru SVX: Welcome to the big leagues,'' *Road & Track*, September 1991, pp. 85, 87-89, 90.

1992: ''interior is clean and simple . . . This is one smooth, competent car . . . even in gravel, snow, and deluges, can be driven fast and hard with little effort and great confidence.'' **Source:** ''Subaru SVX: A repli-jet strafes the luxocoupe market, and changes forever our understanding of the word 'Subaru,''' *Car and Driver*, September 1991, pp. 95-97, 99.

1992: ''body is spectacularly smooth . . . happy, solid, quiet and comfortable . . . Grocery bags will not stand up in the SVX trunk.'' **Source:** ''With Bells and Whistles, It's Subaru,'' *New York Times*, September 1, 1991, Section 8, p. 16.

1992: ''The most striking feature of SVX is a ''glass to glass'' canopy.'' **Source:** ''Car Capsules: Bruce Grant, McClatchy News Service, On The 1992 Subaru SVX,'' *Detroit Free Press*, October 24, 1991, p. 3D.

1992: ''driveline clunks occasionally . . . plastic wood in the cabin looks like the fake it is . . . driving experience is something to savor . . . car has character.'' **Source:** ''Subaru SVX: Sweet enough to have come from the fatherland,'' *Automobile Magazine*, January 1992, p. 59.

1992: ''A fast and smooth four-wheel-driver, it has a jet-fighter canopy-look to its styling, and it may just be politically correct.'' **Source:** ''Charting the Changes: Buy American. Or read this story.; Subaru,'' *Car and Driver*, November 1991, pp. 79-82, 86.

1992: ''Handling is superb . . . surprisingly limited forward ground clearance . . . unmistakable style and high degree of performance and class.'' **Source:** ''Subaru SVX: The Bold and the Beautiful,'' *Motor Trend*, September 1991, pp. 72-74.

RECALLS

None to date.

SUBARU WAGON (1987-89)

Subaru-Isuzu Automotive Inc. is the first U.S. joint venture between two Japanese auto manufacturing companies—Fuju Heavy Industries Ltd. (FHI) and Isuzu Motors Limited. Manufacturing operations for U.S.-marketed vehicles were located at FHI's home factory in Ota City, Japan, and at the U.S. joint venture facility near Lafayette, Indiana. Discontinued in 1989.

MAJOR FEATURES

● Subaru DL Wagon had as 1989 standard equipment: 5-speed manual transmission, rack-and-pinion steering, 4-wheel independent suspension, front disc/rear drum brakes, cloth upholstery, and trip odometer.

● Subaru GL Wagon added as 1989 standard equipment: power door locks, power windows, AM/FM stereo, and tilt steering.

● Subaru GL-10 Turbo Wagon added as 1989 standard equipment: 4-wheel disc brakes, 4-wheel drive, air conditioning, and cruise control.

PRICE HISTORY

The following new car prices reflect the approximate retail cost of the base model: **1987** - $9,208; **1988** - $9,651; **1989** - $10,181.

DIMENSIONS

Body Style	Years Avail	Wheel Base (in)	Lgth (in)	Ht (in)	Avg Wt (lbs)	Fuel Cap (gal)	Front Hdrm (in)	Front Legrm (in)
5d wgn	87-87	97.2	177.8	53.8	2,435	15.9	37.6	41.7
5d wgn	88-89	97.2	176.8	53.0	2,350	15.9	37.6	41.7

ENGINES

Type	Displacement (L)	Fuel Dly	HP @rpm	Torque @rpm (ft/lbs)	MPG Cty/Hwy	Years Avail
Flat-4	1.8	FI	90@5200	101@2800	25/31	87-89
Flat-4T	1.8	FI	115@5200	134@2800	20/26	88-89

KEY: I=in-line engine; V=V engine; F=flat engine; FI=fuel injection; bbl=barrel carburetor; T=turbo; D=diesel; HP=horsepower; MPG=estimated average miles per gallon.

RECALLS

1987: (57,000 4-door sedans, 3-door coupes and station wagons, and 4-wheel drive carburetor equipped vehicles; includes other Subaru models): Composition of certain non-genuine replacement preheat tubes may ignite. **Corrective action:** Install redesigned preheat tubes. *(NHTSA Campaign No. 89V103000.)*

REPAIR MANUALS

2663 ● *Chilton's Subaru 1970-1988*
Chilton Co.
Chilton Way
Radnor, PA 19089   Ph:(215)964-4000

Published 1988. **Price:** $15.95.

2664 ● **How to Keep Your Subaru Alive: A Manual of Step-by-Step Procedures for the Compleat Idiot**
John Muir Publications
P.O. Box 613
Santa Fe, NM 87504-0613   Ph:(505)982-4078

Published 1989. **Editor(s):** Larry Owens. **Price:** $19.95.

SUBARU XT (1987-89, 1991)

The 1.8L turbo was replaced with the I-6 2.7L engine, which is used in the Subaru XT6, in 1988. Due to an overabundance of 1989 models in dealer showrooms, Subaru suspended production of the XT in 1990. While production did resume in 1991, the XT was replaced by the Subaru SVX in 1992. Chosen by *The Complete Car Cost Guide* as having one of the highest fuel costs (Subaru XT6) for a subcompact in 1990.

1991 Subaru XT6

MAJOR FEATURES

● Subaru XT GL had as 1991 standard equipment: 5-speed manual transmission, 4-wheel independent suspension, rack-and-pinion power steering, front disc/rear drum power brakes, tilt steering, trip odometer, power door locks, power windows, and AM/FM stereo.

● Subaru XT6 added as 1991 standard equipment: 4-wheel disc brakes, air conditioning, cruise control, AM/FM stereo cassette player, and upgraded tires.

PRICE HISTORY

The following new car prices reflect the approximate retail cost of the base model: **1987** - $9,431; **1988** - $9,866; **1989** - $13,071; **1991** - $13,438.

DIMENSIONS

Body Style	Years Avail	Wheel Base (in)	Lgth (in)	Ht (in)	Avg Wt (lbs)	Fuel Cap (gal)	Front Hdrm (in)	Front Legrm (in)
2d cpe	87-87	97.1	175.2	49.4	2,280	15.9	37.4	43.3
2d cpe	88-88	97.0	177.6	49.4	2,375	15.9	37.4	43.3
2d cpe	89-91	97.0	177.6	49.4	2,455	15.9	37.4	43.3

ENGINES

Type	Displace- ment (L)	Fuel Dly	HP @rpm	Torque @rpm (ft/lbs)	MPG Cty/Hwy	Years Avail
I-4T	1.8	FI	115@5200	134@2800	23/28	87-87
I-6	2.7	FI	145@5200	156@4000	18/25	88-91
Flat-4	1.8	FI	94@5200	101@2800	24/28	87-89
Flat-4	1.8	FI	97@5200	103@3200	25/31	88-91

KEY: I=in-line engine; V=V engine; F=flat engine; FI=fuel injection; bbl=barrel carburetor; T=turbo; D=diesel; HP=horsepower; MPG=estimated average miles per gallon.

EVALUATIONS, TESTS, AND RANKINGS

1989: "reasonably well balanced and predictable." **Source:** "Coupes de Grace," *Popular Mechanics*, May 1989, pp. 120-124, 212, 214.

1989: "bizarre exterior . . . looks like a machine from another world . . . interior . . . becomes [a] reasonably efficient base of operations . . . XT6 has little appetite for hard driving." **Source:** "Two Times Four Equals Great: Eight of the best-performing bargains on the market," *Car and Driver*, July 1989, pp. 36-39, 41, 43, 45, 49, 51, 53, 56-57, 59.

1988: "a terrific sports coupe . . . rattle-free." **Source:** "Snow White and the Seven AWDs," *Road & Track*, May 1988, pp. 56-63, 67-70.

1988: "combination of . . . full-time four-wheel-drive . . . and the new 2.7-liter flat-six engine is superb." **Source:** "Subaru tones down gadgets and lets XT6's power shine," *Detroit Free Press*, December 28, 1987, p. 11C.

RECALLS

1989-91: (76,000 passenger cars with electronically controlled automatic transmissions; includes the Subaru Loyale, Subaru Legacy, and Subaru XT): Under certain load conditions, the park gear may not disengage immediately when the transmission lever is moved from park to reverse, causing delayed and possibly abrupt vehicle movement. Could result in loss of vehicle control and an accident. **Corrective action:** Install a modified parking brake pawl to prevent delayed release into reverse gear. *(NHTSA Campaign No. 91V082000.)*

1988: (60,000 vehicles; includes the Subaru Justy, Subaru XT, Subaru XT-DL, and Subaru XT-GL): Omission of information specified by FMVSS 210 from owner manual. Fails to meet requirement of FMVSS 210 regarding child restraint systems. **Corrective action:** Adhesive backed inserts will be furnished with correct information. *(NHTSA Campaign No. 88V052000.)*

REPAIR MANUALS

2665 ● **Chilton's Subaru 1970-1988**
Chilton Co.
Chilton Way
Radnor, PA 19089   Ph:(215)964-4000

Published 1988. **Price:** $15.95.

2666 ● **How to Keep Your Subaru Alive: A Manual of Step-by-Step Procedures for the Compleat Idiot**
John Muir Publications
P.O. Box 613
Santa Fe, NM 87504-0613   Ph:(505)982-4078

Published 1989. **Editor(s):** Larry Owens. **Price:** $19.95.

SUZUKI SAMURAI (1987-92)

Introduced to the U.S. market in the mid-1980s. Intended to appeal to young people who want an inexpensive 4-wheel drive vehicle. Produced in Japan.

1991 Suzuki Samurai

MAJOR FEATURES

● Suzuki Samurai JA 1992 standard equipment includes: 5-speed manual transmission and power-assisted front disc/rear drum brakes.

● Suzuki Samurai JL adds as 1992 standard equipment: 4-wheel drive, tinted glass, and 2-speed intermittent windshield wipers/washers.

● Suzuki Samurai JS had as 1991 standard equipment: fold-down rear seat

PRICE HISTORY

The following new car prices reflect the approximate retail cost of the base model: **1987** - $6,900; **1988** - $8,495; **1989** - $8,854; **1990** - $7,999; **1991** - $5,999; **1992** - $6,299.

DIMENSIONS

Body Style	Years Avail	Wheel Base (in)	Lgth (in)	Ht (in)	Avg Wt (lbs)	Fuel Cap (gal)	Front Hdrm (in)	Front Legrm (in)
utl wgn	87-92	79.9	135.0	64.2	2,935	10.6	na	na

ENGINES

Type	Displace- ment (L)	Fuel Dly	HP @rpm	Torque @rpm (ft/lbs)	MPG Cty/Hwy	Years Avail
I-4	1.3	2-bbl	64@na	na	28/29	87-89
I-4	1.3	FI	66@6000	76@3500	28/29	90-92

KEY: I=in-line engine; V=V engine; F=flat engine; FI=fuel injection; bbl=barrel carburetor; T=turbo; D=diesel; HP=horsepower; MPG=estimated average miles per gallon.

EVALUATIONS, TESTS, AND RANKINGS

1991: "sturdy machine for backcountry trails—but the highway ride is sacrificed . . . durable and economical vehicle . . . instrumentation and controls are easy to reach." **Source:** "Testing The New Mini 4x4s," *Sports Afield*, October 1990, pp. 110-112, 114-116.

1990: "Suzuki Samurai JL . . . Fourth Place . . . cute and cheap . . . just isn't enough." **Source:** "Dustbusters! Four small sport-utilities and four dusty editors tame the Mojave Road," *Car and Driver*, November 1989, pp. 136-140, 142, 146, 148, 152-153, 156, 158.

1990: "accelerated smoothly on the highway, but lacked the punch needed for confident lane changes . . . pulls with every passing semi . . . off road the car was fun." **Source:** "Suzuki Samurai: Weekend warrior," *Design News*, July 23, 1990, p. 28.

1989: "high center of gravity . . . tentative . . . didn't feel good . . . doesn't belong on a 55-mph highway." **Source:** "On the road with Suzuki's Samuri: A fun vehicle, but it should be limited to backroads," *Design News*, October 10, 1988, pp. 206-207.

1988: "Carpeting and insulation are minimal . . . ride and handling are both crude and rude." **Source:** "Suzuki's Little Warrior," *The Family Handyman*, December 1987, pp. 66-67.

1988: "continually pitches its occupants back and forth." **Source:** "Suzuki Samurai: Young, first-time buyers will soon outgrow it," *Home Mechanix*, March 1988, p. 94.

RECALLS

None to date.

SUZUKI SIDEKICK (1989-92)

Corporate twin is the Geo Tracker. Sidekick is available in two- or four-door models; the four-door model was introduced in 1992. Sidekick JL was discontinued in 1991. Produced in a Canadian plant jointly operated by General Motors and Suzuki. Nominated for 1989 and 1991 Truck of the Year by *Motor Trend*. Named to *Motor Trend's* Top Ten New Car Buys: Import for 1989.

1991 Suzuki Sidekick

MAJOR FEATURES

● Suzuki Sidekick JS has as 1992 standard equipment: 5-speed manual transmission, front independent suspension/rear live axle, rear-wheel anti-lock brakes, folding canvas top, and fold down rear seat.

● Suzuki Sidekick JX adds as 1992 standard equipment: 4-wheel drive, AM/FM stereo cassette player, tachometer, power steering, power mirrors, tinted glass, and rear defogger (hardtop).

● Suzuki Sidekick JLX adds as 1992 standard equipment: tilt wheel, power windows, power door locks, 2-place folding rear seat, and rear window wiper.

● Suzuki Sidekick JL had as 1991 standard equipment: 4-wheel drive.

PRICE HISTORY

The following new car prices reflect the approximate retail cost of the base model: **1989** - $8,995; **1990** - $9,999; **1991** - $10,299; **1992** - $10,699.

DIMENSIONS

Body Style	Years Avail	Wheel Base (in)	Lgth (in)	Ht (in)	Avg Wt (lbs)	Fuel Cap (gal)	Front Hdrm (in)	Front Legrm (in)
utl wgn	89-90	86.6	142.5	64.8	3,197	15.0	39.5	42.1
utl wgn	91-92	86.6	142.5	65.6	3,090	11.1	39.5	42.1

ENGINES

Type	Displacement (L)	Fuel Dly	HP @rpm	Torque @rpm (ft/lbs)	MPG Cty/Hwy	Years Avail
I-4	1.3	2-bbl	64@na	na	28/29	89-89
I-4	1.6	FI	80@5400	94@3000	25/27	89-92

KEY: I=in-line engine; V=V engine; F=flat engine; FI=fuel injection; bbl=barrel carburetor; T=turbo; D=diesel; HP=horsepower; MPG=estimated average miles per gallon.

EVALUATIONS, TESTS, AND RANKINGS

1992: "surprisingly high level of luxury and convenience features . . . On the freeway, it's quiet and stable . . . could seemingly climb up the side of the Empire State Building." **Source:** "Suzuki Sidekick: Catching the Next Wave," *Motor Trend*, December 1991, pp. 100, 102.

1991: "robust construction and low price." **Source:** "Suzuki Sidekick 4-Door," *Road & Track*, December 1990, p. 128.

1991: "a lot of fun to drive." **Source:** "1991 Truck of the Year," *Motor Trend*, January 1991, pp. 79-84.

1991: "small four-wheeler with the conveniences of a modern American passenger car . . . more than enough muscle for its weight." **Source:** "Testing The New Mini 4x4s," *Sports Afield*, October 1990, pp. 110-112, 114-116.

1991: "puppy-in-the-window looks . . . strong points are interior finish and appointments . . . power is not a strong point . . . choppy freeway ride." **Source:** "Beach Bandits," *Popular Mechanics*, July 1991, pp. 21-25.

1990: "a great package." **Source:** "Top 10 New Car Buys: Import," *Motor Trend*, November 1989, pp. 80-83, 86-89.

1990: "no mountain too steep . . . feels plenty strong . . . quite handy around a hunting camp." **Source:** "Best of the Rough Country 4x4s," *Sports Afield*, January 1990, pp. 36, 122.

1989: "handles rough roads with aplomb." **Source:** "Suzuki Sidekick: A Samurai for grown-ups," *Car and Driver*, November 1988, p. 95.

1989: "won't be accused of excessive rollover . . . bumpy ride and skimpy back seat limit its usefulness mostly to all-weather, around-town commuting." **Source:** "Import Report," *Home Mechanix*, April 1989, pp. 84-86, 103-105.

RECALLS

None to date.

SUZUKI SWIFT (1989-92)

Corporate twin is the Geo Metro. Suzuki Swift GTi nominated for 1989 Import Car of the Year by *Motor Trend*. Swift GTi and GLX models discontinued in 1989, GL discontinued in 1990. 1992 *Car Book* rates the Swift among the best in fuel economy based on most recent EPA mileage figures. For 1992, Suzuki Swift receives a slightly redesigned exterior, and a new interior on the GT model. Available in 3-door hatchback and 5-door sedan models.

1992 Suzuki Swift GT

MAJOR FEATURES

● Suzuki Swift GA has as 1992 standard equipment: 5-speed manual transmission, rack-and-pinion steering, power-assisted front disc/rear drum brakes, 4-wheel independent suspension, intermittent wipers, vanity mirrors, cloth interior, and rear window defogger.

● Suzuki Swift GS adds as 1992 standard equipment: power steering, tachometer, deluxe floor carpeting, and AM/FM stereo cassette player.

● Suzuki Swift GT adds as 1992 standard equipment: upgraded engine, 4-wheel disc brakes, rear window wiper/washer, and other exterior body stylings.

● Suzuki Swift GL had as 1990 standard equipment: other exterior body stylings.

● Suzuki Swift GLX added as 1989 standard equipment: upgraded interior and power locks.

● Suzuki Swift GTi had as 1989 standard equipment: 4-wheel disc brakes and alloy wheels.

PRICE HISTORY

The following new car prices reflect the approximate retail cost of the base model: **1989** - $7,495; **1990** - $6,399; **1991** - $6,699; **1992** - $6,899.

DIMENSIONS

Body Style	Years Avail	Wheel Base (in)	Lgth (in)	Ht (in)	Avg Wt (lbs)	Fuel Cap (gal)	Front Hdrm (in)	Front Legrm (in)
3d lbk	89-91	89.2	146.1	53.1	1,720	10.6	37.8	42.5
3d lbk	92-92	89.2	147.4	53.1	1,739	10.6	37.8	42.5
5d sdn	90-91	93.1	160.4	53.5	1,848	10.6	39.1	42.5
5d sdn	92-92	93.1	161.2	54.3	1,861	10.6	39.1	42.5

ENGINES

Type	Displacement (L)	Fuel Dly	HP @rpm	Torque @rpm (ft/lbs)	MPG Cty/Hwy	Years Avail
I-4	1.3	FI	70@6000	74@3300	39/43	89-92
I-4	1.3	FI	100@6500	83@5000	28/35	89-92

KEY: I=in-line engine; V=V engine; F=flat engine; FI=fuel injection; bbl=barrel carburetor; T=turbo; D=diesel; HP=horsepower; MPG=estimated average miles per gallon.

EVALUATIONS, TESTS, AND RANKINGS

1991: "truly quick . . . interior is depressingly plain and cheap." **Source:** "40 something: You can buy as much fuel economy as you want today. But what do you really pay," *Popular Mechanics*, February 1991, pp. 39-43.

1990: "nimble little scooter." **Source:** "Eleven for Thirteen," *Car and Driver*, June 1990, pp. 46-50, 52, 61, 63, 64, 66-69.

1990: "first-rate acceleration . . . 0-60 mph in 8.3 sec . . . firm, controlled suspension." **Source:** "Suzuki Swift GTi," *Motor Trend*, September 1989, pp. 65-68.

1989: "high fun-to-drive quotient." **Source:** "1989 Import Car of the Year," *Motor Trend*, March 1989, pp. 86-91, 94, 96, 98-100, 103-104.

1989: "well-equipped interior . . . feels fast . . . steering is unnecessarily heavy . . . cornering behavior, though predictable, is uninspiring." **Source:** "Suzuki Swift GTi: The nickel rocket we should have had Back Then," *Car and Driver*, February 1989, pp. 103-105, 107-108.

RECALLS

None to date.

TOYOTA 4-RUNNER (1987-92)

Built in Toyota City, Japan, the 4-Runner sport utility vehicle comes with a variety of options that can be added to the base model (SR5), including 2- or 4-door models, 2-wheel drive automatic transmission, 4-wheel drive automatic or manual transmissions, on-demand 4WD, and I-4 or V-6 engines.

1991 Toyota 4-Runner

MAJOR FEATURES

● The 1992 Toyota 4-Runner SR5 standard equipment includes: 2.4L SOHC, 4-cylinder engine, 4-speed automatic overdrive transmission, power-assisted, ventilated front-disc brakes, part-time 4-wheel drive, and an upgraded interior.

● Toyota 4-Runner SR5 V6 adds as standard equipment in

1992: 3.0 L V-6 engine, two-wheel or on-demand four-wheel drive, 5-speed manual overdrive transmission, anti-lock rear brakes, power steering, tilt steering column, and rear defogger.

PRICE HISTORY

The following new car prices reflect the approximate retail cost of the base model: **1987** - $12,998; **1988** - $13,618; **1989** - $13,988; **1990** - $16,218; **1991** - $15,998; **1992** - $18,218.

DIMENSIONS

Body Style	Years Avail	Wheel Base (in)	Lgth (in)	Ht (in)	Avg Wt (lbs)	Fuel Cap (gal)	Front Hdrm (in)	Front Legrm (in)
utl wgn	87-89	103.0	174.6	66.1	5,080	17.2	na	na
utl wgn	90-92	103.3	176.0	66.1	5,350	17.2	38.7	41.5

ENGINES

Type	Displacement (L)	Fuel Dly	HP @rpm	Torque @rpm (ft/lbs)	MPG Cty/Hwy	Years Avail
I-4	2.4	FI	116@4800	140@2800	19/22	87-92
I-4T	2.4	FI	na	na	17/19	87-87
V-6	3.0	FI	150@4800	180@3400	17/21	88-92

KEY: I=in-line engine; V=V engine; F=flat engine; FI=fuel injection; bbl=barrel carburetor; T=turbo; D=diesel; HP=horsepower; MPG=estimated average miles per gallon.

EVALUATIONS, TESTS, AND RANKINGS

1991: "Everything about the 4Runner smacks of quality ... highway ride is unfailingly glassy ... driving position takes some getting used to." **Source**: "Update: Sport-Utility Vehicles," *U.S. News and World Report*, May 13, 1991, pp. A4-A6, A8-A10, A12, A14-A15.

1991: "extra ground clearance comes in handy ... drivers and passengers must hoist themselves in and out of their seats ... stiff suspension ... hurts its ride and handling." **Source**: "Taking The High Road," *Home Mechanix*, December/January 1990, pp. 70-77.

1990: "new engineering features both inside and out ... definite aerodynamic look while retaining a rugged appearance ... Handling and ride comfort have been improved." **Source**: "4-Door Off-Roaders," *Sports Afield*, March 1990, pp. 120-122, 143-145.

1990: "the machinery lurking within thrives on rough stuff ... run as smoothly as a limousine, with ride quality to match." **Source**: "4-Doors For all Seasons," *New Choices for the Best Years*, December 1989, pp. 84, 86-87.

1990: "cabin is one of the quietest ... remarkably smooth ride on pavement ... you'll need the agility of a high-jumper to plant a foot inside." **Source**: "Keeping Pace: In the sport-utility world, those who stand pat fall behind," *Field and Stream*, December 1989, pp. 84-86.

1990: "dynamic, sleek look ... masculine appearance ... has not disappeared ... Practically no road noise." **Source**: "Trendy Toyota 4Runner," *Outdoor Life*, July 1989, pp. 32, 34-35.

1989: "capable where it counted on all kinds of roads ... Superb described the fit and finish inside and out ... decent legroom in back and generally pleasant surroundings." **Source**: "Toyota's new 4Runner adds more than 2 doors," *The Detroit News*, September 6, 1989, sec. F, pp. 1-2.

1989: "On the road ... well poised with a quiet and comfortable ride ... when the going gets tough, the suspension feels mushy." **Source**: "Automotive Newsfront: Split-personality 4x4," *Popular Science*, July 1991, p. 24.

1989: "durable and cheap to maintain ... handles more like a truck than a car ... 4Runner is not fast, and it drinks plenty of fuel." **Source**: "Long-Term Test: Life with 4Runner," *Car and Driver*, February 1991, pp. 96-99.

1989: "stiffest rear-end suspension in the business ... an off-roader that can take a licking and keep on ticking." **Source**: "Personal Pick," *Outdoor Life*, June 1989, pp. 20, 24-25.

1988: "Rather hard suspension ... excellent interior comforts." **Source**: "Toyota 4Runner: Dependable reputation spoiled by harsh ride," *Home Mechanix*, March 1988, p. 92.

RECALLS

1988: (4,842 Toyota Truck and Toyota 4-Runner models equipped with V6 engines): Improper routing of fuel hose could cause some fuel hoses to have inadequate clearance to EGR pipe. Heat from EGR could cause hose to crack and result in fuel leakage. **Corrective action:** Reroute fuel hose to ensure proper clearance and replace hose, if necessary. *(NHTSA Campaign No. 88V019000.)*

REPAIR MANUALS

2667 ● **Toyota Pick-ups and 4-Runner, 1984-88**
Clymer Publications
P.O. Box 1209
Overland Park, KS 66212   Ph:(913)541-6694

Published 1988. **Price**: $14.95.

2668 ● **Toyota Pickup, 4-Runner Service Manual: 1978-1988 Including Gasoline, Diesel, and Turbo Diesel, 4-cylinder and 6-cylinder Engines**
Robert Bentley Publishing, Inc.
1000 Massachusetts Ave.
Cambridge, MA 02138   Ph:(617)547-4170

Price: $29.95.

2669 ● **The Toyota Standard 4-Speed Transmission Explained**
Bergwall Productions, Inc.
106 Charles Lindbergh Blvd.
Uniondale, NY 11553-3695   Ph:(516)222-1111

On five tapes, the Toyota transmission is disassembled and assembled for trainee instruction. **Release date**: 1985. **Producer**: Bergwall Productions, Inc. **Acquisition**: Purchase.

TOYOTA CAMRY (1987-92)

Toyota's best-selling U.S. model, Camry is produced in Georgetown, Kentucky and Tsutsumi, Japan (plant parts data: domestic parts - 35%, imported parts - 65%; *Federal Trade Zone Board*, 1989). Chosen by *The Complete Car Cost Guide* in 1990 as having one of the best overall values for a compact under $15,000 and having one of the best overall values for a subcompact/compact wagon over $13,000 (Camry LE); also selected as having one of the lowest fuel, repair, and insurance costs (Camry DX); and highest resale value (Camry LE). Ranked the most trouble-free car built in America by J.D. Power & Associates' 1990 Initial Quality Study.

1992 Toyota Camry LE

MAJOR FEATURES

● Camry DLX 1992 standard equipment: 4-cylinder engine, front disc/rear drum brakes, 5-speed manual or 4-speed automatic transmission, 4-wheel independent suspension, power-assisted rack-and-pinion steering, tilt steering column, driver's side airbag, rear defogger, and tinted glass.

● Camry LE adds as 1992 standard equipment: power mirrors, illuminated entry with fadeout, air conditioning, cruise control, power windows and locks, and cassette player.

● Camry XLE adds as 1992 standard equipment: alloy wheels, tilt-and-slide moonroof, soft-touch heater controls, upgraded sound system, and anti-theft system.

● Camry SE adds as 1992 standard equipment: 3.0-liter V-6 engine, sport suspension, and other interior enhancements.

● Camry Wagon adds as 1992 standard equipment: rear wiper/washer. It is scheduled to debut in mid-1992.

● Camry All-Trac (available in DX and LE versions) added as 1991 standard equipment: permanent 4-wheel drive and 4-wheel disc brakes.

PRICE HISTORY

The following new car prices reflect the approximate retail cost of the base model: **1987** - $10,648; **1988** - $11,248; **1989** - $11,488; **1990** - $11,588; **1991** - $12,198; **1992** - $14,368.

DIMENSIONS

Body Style	Years Avail	Wheel Base (in)	Lgth (in)	Ht (in)	Avg Wt (lbs)	Fuel Cap (gal)	Front Hdrm (in)	Front Legrm (in)
4d sdn	87-91	102.4	182.1	54.1	2,734	15.9	37.9	42.9
4d sdn	92-92	103.1	187.8	55.1	2,943	18.5	38.4	43.5
5d wgn	87-91	102.4	183.1	54.5	2,855	15.9	38.2	42.9

ENGINES

Type	Displacement (L)	Fuel Dly	HP @rpm	Torque @rpm (ft/lbs)	MPG Cty/Hwy	Years Avail
I-4	2.0	FI	115@5200	124@4400	26/34	87-91
I-4	2.2	FI	130@5400	145@4400	22/29	92-92
V-6	2.5	FI	153@5600	155@4400	19/26	88-90
V-6	2.5	FI	156@5600	160@4400	19/25	91-91
V-6	3.0	FI	185@5200	195@4400	19/26	92-92

KEY: I=in-line engine; V=V engine; F=flat engine; FI=fuel injection; bbl=barrel carburetor; T=turbo; D=diesel; HP=horsepower; MPG=estimated average miles per gallon.

EVALUATIONS, TESTS, AND RANKINGS

1992: "au courant looks . . . superb interior appointments . . . excellent power and handling for a family sedan." **Source:** "Ten

Best Cars: And a glimpse into the future, too," *Car and Driver,* January 1992, pp. 35-43.

1992: "flashier and more luxurious . . . engineered specifically for American tastes." **Source:** "Toyota Hopes Bigger, Flashier Camry Will Help It Pass Honda in U.S. Market," *Wall Street Journal,* September 4, 1991, pp. B1, B6.

1992: "Exterior detailing shows an eye toward air-friendliness . . . interior ranks as sumptuously luxurious . . . handling is responsive and enjoyable." **Source:** "Toyota Camry: As new and improved as they get," *Motor Trend,* November 1991, pp. 102-103.

1992: "marvelously comfortable seats . . . moves its occupants through traffic and over all types of road with minimal fuss . . . SE . . . achieves a great balance between sport and comfort." **Source:** "New For '92," *Road & Track,* November 1991, pp. 92-94.

1992: "combines art and utility in the way it ought to be done . . . a look and feel of good breeding . . . feels far, far more expensive than it is." **Source:** "1992 Import Cars: Toyota Camry; Toyota's lead horse is a spirited runner," *Car and Driver,* November 1991, pp. 61-62.

1991: "engines are muted and distant . . . the car grips the road and handles well. Transitions . . . are world class." **Source:** "Toyota Camry," *Automobile Magazine,* December 1990, p.24.

1989: "a very competent, comfortable, high-quality automobile . . . interior is sedate, but seems like the interior from a more expensive luxury sedan." **Source:** "Best Sellers," *Popular Mechanics,* July 1989, pp.60-63, 120-122.

1989: "new All-Trac variant adds a degree of sure-footedness and stability . . . Ventilation is also outstanding." **Source:** "Toyota Camry All-Trac Deluxe," *Motor Trend,* August 1988, pp.69, 72-73, 76-77.

1989: "Camry power train set the standard of the group for ease of operation . . . felt solid, secure, and crisp." **Source:** "New Spirit in Family Cars," *Popular Science,* June 1989, pp. 48-50, 52, 54.

1988: "wagon holds quite a bit of cargo, despite the fact that it's still a compact family car . . . peppy performance." **Source:** "Toyota Camry," *Home Mechanix,* August 1987, pp.64-65.

1987: "sets a standard of engineering excellence by which all further automobiles in its class and market segment will be compared . . . all-around best sedan it's built to date . . . fit and finish that's second to none." **Source:** "Toyota Camry LE," *Motor Trend,* May 1987, pp.65, 68, 70.

RECALLS

1988: (11,486 vehicles): Due to design defect in thread profile of car jack, when wagon is raised, jack may be unable to sustain vehicle. Jack could lower itself with potential to cause personal injury. **Corrective action:** Replace jack. *(NHTSA Campaign No. 88V127000.)*

1987-89: (408,225 vehicles): Lap belt may lock at retracted and stowed position, resulting in inability to use. **Corrective action:** Replace with redesigned belt guide. *(NHTSA Campaign No. 89V175000.)*

REPAIR MANUALS

2670 ● Haynes Toyota Camry Owners Workshop Manual, No. 1023: 1983-1990
Haynes Publications, Inc.
861 Lawrence Dr.
Newbury Park, CA 91320   Ph:(818)889-5400

Editor(s): J. H. Haynes and Ken Freund. **Price:** $15.95.

2671 ● The Toyota Standard 4-Speed Transmission Explained
Bergwall Productions, Inc.
106 Charles Lindbergh Blvd.
Uniondale, NY 11553-3695   Ph:(516)222-1111

On five tapes, the Toyota transmission is disassembled and assembled for trainee instruction. **Release date:** 1985. **Producer:** Bergwall Productions, Inc. **Acquisition:** Purchase.

TOYOTA CELICA (1987-92)

Produced by Toyota Motor Corporation in Tahara, Japan. Chosen by *The Complete Car Cost Guide* as having one of the lowest fuel costs (Celica ST), highest insurance costs (Celica All-Trac), and highest resale values (Celica GT) for a compact in 1990.

1991 Toyota Celica GT

MAJOR FEATURES

● Celica ST 1992 standard equipment includes: 1.6 L 16-valve 4-cyclinder engine, 5-speed manual transmission, front disc/rear drum brakes, 4-wheel independent suspension, power steering, driver's side airbag, rear defogger, and tinted glass.

● Celica GT and GT convertible adds as 1992 standard equipment: 2.2L engine, 4-wheel disc brakes, tilt steering, full wheel covers, System 10 premium audio system, convertible has power top, and power rear quarter windows.

● Celica GT-S adds as 1992 standard equipment: 4-wheel disc brakes, 5-way adjustable sport seats, rear-window intermittent wiper, front air dam with fog lights, rear spoiler, cassette player, telescopic steering column with memory, and alloy wheels.

● Celica All-Trac Turbo adds as 1992 standard equipment: 2.0-liter turbocharged, intercooled engine, permanent 4-wheel drive, tilt steering column, and cruise control.

PRICE HISTORY

The following new car prices reflect the approximate retail cost of the base model: **1987** - $10,748; **1988** - $11,548; **1989** - $11,808; **1990** - $12,268; **1991** - $12,798; **1992** - $13,378.

DIMENSIONS

Body Style	Years Avail	Wheel Base (in)	Lgth (in)	Ht (in)	Avg Wt (lbs)	Fuel Cap (gal)	Front Hdrm (in)	Front Legrm (in)
3d lbk	87-89	99.4	171.9	49.8	2,555	15.9	37.8	44.4
3d lbk	90-92	99.4	173.6	50.6	2,646	15.9	37.7	42.9
4d lbk	88-89	99.4	171.9	49.8	3,197	15.9	37.8	44.4
2d cpe	87-87	99.4	173.6	49.8	2,455	15.9	37.8	44.4
2d cpe	88-89	99.4	171.9	49.8	2,600	15.9	37.8	44.4
2d cpe	90-92	99.4	176.0	50.6	2,447	15.9	37.7	42.9
2d conv	88-89	99.4	173.6	49.8	2,680	15.9	38.4	44.4
2d conv	90-92	99.4	176.0	50.6	2,844	15.9	37.7	42.9

ENGINES

Type	Displace-ment (L)	Fuel Dly	HP @rpm	Torque @rpm (ft/lbs)	MPG Cty/Hwy	Years Avail
I-4	2.0	FI	135@6000	125@4800	22/28	87-89
I-4	2.0	FI	115@5200	124@4400	26/32	87-89
I-4	2.2	FI	130@5400	140@4400	22/29	90-92
I-4	1.6	FI	103@6000	102@3200	25/32	90-92
I-4T	2.0	FI	190@6000	190@3200	19/26	88-89
I-4T	2.0	FI	200@6000	200@3200	19/24	90-92

KEY: I=in-line engine; V=V engine; F=flat engine; FI=fuel injection; bbl=barrel carburetor; T=turbo; D=diesel; HP=horsepower; MPG=estimated average miles per gallon.

EVALUATIONS, TESTS, AND RANKINGS

1992: "valiant companion . . . turbo comes up on boost quickly . . . all-weather crowd-pleaser." **Source:** "Toyota Celica All-Trac," *Motor Trend*, December 1991, p. 76.

1991: "clutch is remarkable . . . more comfortable than any suspension so firm has a right to be . . . Handling is sure-footed and benign." **Source:** "Toyota Celica: On the Horns of a Weighty Dilemma," *Autofile*, 1991, pp. 85-89.

1991: "power top is easy to raise and lower, and a clever plastic tonneau makes short work of the cover-up . . . isn't the cheapest convertible on the market, nor is it the most expensive." **Source:** "Toyota Celica Convertible," *Automobile Magazine*, 1991, p. 27.

1991: "Rear-seat shoulder room is heavily compromised by the top's storage well, but head room is generous. Carpeting is plush." **Source:** "Toyota Celica GT Convertible," *Road & Track*, December 1990, pp. 85-88.

1991: "performance better described as peppy than fast . . . soft top is sufficiently weather tight . . . aerodynamic shape rewards passengers with scant amounts of wind buffeting." **Source:** "Top-Down Showdown: We test the hottest cars under the sun," *Motor Trend*, June 1991, pp. 49-59, 62-63.

1991: "power-operated top is a snap to use . . . reasonably good fuel economy . . . delightful summertime vehicle. Quick, nimble and good-looking." **Source:** "Celica Convertible Great for Summer," *Detroit Free Press*, July 18, 1991, p. 1D.

1990: "stable under braking, but substantial fade set in after about three laps . . . free-revving engine is flexible and smooth." **Source:** "Bang for the Buck," *Motor Trend*, November 1989, pp. 42-46, 48, 52-55, 58-59, 62, 64, 66-68, 72, 76.

1990: "compact greenhouse, and softly rounded corners . . . heavy understeer characteristics . . . engine noise at times is quite annoying." **Source:** "Coupes Du Jour," *Popular Science*, February 1990, pp. 50-52, 56-57.

1989: "[Celica GT-S] more than its share of roll steer . . . Visibility is good, the car is well finished . . . brakes are excellent.'' **Source:** ''Coupes De Grace,'' *Popular Mechanics,* May 1989, pp. 120-124, 212, 214.

1989: ''car has a suppleness that makes it one of the best road cars in the group . . . has a nasty habit of getting its rear end loose when the throttle is lifted.'' **Source:** ''6 Quick Coupes,'' *Popular Science,* September 1988, pp. 32-34, 36, 40-41.

1989: ''vastly subdued tendency to get tail-happy compared with two-wheel-drive Celicas that we've driven in the past.'' **Source:** ''Wet Set,'' *Popular Science,* December 1988, pp. 36-37 40-42, 48.

1988: ''[Celica GT-S] delivers a great deal of performance and easily the best array of creature comforts in the bunch . . . one terrific value on your hands.'' **Source:** ''Catalina Express,'' *Motor Trend,* May 1988, pp. 54-58, 61, 64-66.

1988: ''All-Trac is powerful . . . has great brakes . . . handles well . . . 5-speed gearbox in the Celica was also not a crowd-pleaser . . . ride didn't draw much praise.'' **Source:** ''Snow White and the Seven AWDs,'' *Road & Track,* May 1988, pp. 56-63, 67-70.

1988: ''challenged the brake lane first. It was not impressive . . . front buckets are firm without being hard.'' **Source:** ''Performance Ragtops,'' *Popular Science,* August 1987, pp. 26-27, 32, 36, 38.

RECALLS

1990: (2,543 cars): Improperly machined airbag inflator case may not allow bag to deploy. **Corrective action:** Replace air bag inflator unit. *(NHTSA Campaign No. 90V078000.)*

SAFETY AND REPAIRS

1988: ''Car Clinic,'' *Popular Mechanics,* March 1990, p. 31. **Note:** Tip for improved cold driveability in 88-89 Celica All-Trac.

REPAIR MANUALS

2672 ● **Chilton's Toyota Celica-Supra, 1986-1990**
Chilton Co.
Chilton Way
Radnor, PA 19089   Ph:(215)964-4000

Published 1990. **Price:** $15.95.

2673 ● **Mitchell Glove Compartment Companion for Your Toyota Celica-Supra**
Harcourt Brace Jovanovich, Inc.
6277 Sea Harbor Dr.
Orlando, FL 32821   Ph:(407)345-2000

Published 1988.

2674 ● **The Toyota Standard 4-Speed Transmission Explained**
Bergwall Productions, Inc.
106 Charles Lindbergh Blvd.
Uniondale, NY 11553-3695   Ph:(516)222-1111

On five tapes, the Toyota transmission is disassembled and assembled for trainee instruction. **Release date:** 1985. **Producer:** Bergwall Productions, Inc. **Acquisition:** Purchase.

ASSOCIATIONS

2675 ● **Toyota Sport Car Club**
904 Silver Spur Rd., Ste. 482
Rolling Hills, CA 90274
Ralph Wenters, Pres.   Ph:(213)539-0595

Founded: 1983. **Membership:** 2,000. Owners of Toyota sports cars, especially the Celica and Supra models. Facilitates exchange of information among members; provides technical assistance. Makes available discount parts. **Former Name(s):** (1987) Toyota Celica Supra Club.

TOYOTA COROLLA (1987-92)

Japanese cousin of the Geo Prizm, the Toyota Corolla is built at New United Motor Manufacturing Inc. plants in Takaoka, Japan; Cambridge, Ontario, Canada; and in Fremont, California (Fremont plant parts data: domestic parts - 33%, imported parts - 67%; *Federal Trade Zone Board,* 1989). In 1989, the four-wheel drive sedan and wagon were the only versions equipped with the 100 hp fuel-injected engine; in 1990, all Corolla versions had this engine. Ranked the most trouble-free car in its class for the second year in a row, according to J.D. Power & Associates' 1990 Initial Quality Survey. Chosen as a Top Ten Best Sedan by *Road & Track* in 1987. Chosen by *The Complete Car Cost Guide* in 1990 as one of the best overall values for a subcompact under $10,000 (Corolla Standard and LE) and for a subcompact wagon under $13,000 (Corolla Deluxe); also selected for having the highest resale value (Corolla Deluxe) subcompact and subcompact wagon.

1991 Toyota Corolla

MAJOR FEATURES

● Corolla 1992 standard equipment: 5-speed manual transmission, 4-wheel independent suspension, power-assisted rack-and-pinion steering, power front disc/rear drum brakes, and door-mounted automatic front shoulder belts.

● Corolla DLX Sedan and Wagon add as 1992 standard equipment: rear defogger and split rear seat (wagon).

● Corolla LE adds as 1992 standard equipment: 4-speed automatic transmission, power steering, six-way driver's seat with lumbar support adjustment, tilt steering column, and full wheel covers.

● Corolla All-Trac DLX Wagon adds as 1992 standard equipment: front engine/All-Trac all wheel drive.

● Corolla GT-S had as 1991 standard equipment: 130 horsepower, 16-valve 1.6-liter four-cylinder engine.

● Corolla SR-5 added as 1991 standard equipment: 90-horsepower engine and front-wheel drive.

● Corolla Sport had as 1989 standard equipment: 5-speed manual or 4-speed automatic transmission and cloth reclining front bucket seats.

● Corolla FX, FX16, and FX16 GT-S had as 1988 standard equipment: four-wheel disc brakes and varying trim levels.

PRICE HISTORY

The following new car prices reflect the approximate retail cost of the base model: **1987** - $7,878; **1988** - $7,948; **1989** - $8,548; **1990** - $8,748; **1991** - $9,148; **1992** - $9,418.

DIMENSIONS

Body Style	Years Avail	Wheel Base (in)	Lgth (in)	Ht (in)	Avg Wt (lbs)	Fuel Cap (gal)	Front Hdrm (in)	Front Legrm (in)
3d lbk	87-87	94.5	168.7	52.6	2,346	13.2	37.6	43.5
5d lbk	87-87	95.7	166.3	52.8	2,163	13.2	37.8	42.4
2d cpe	87-87	94.5	168.7	52.6	2,224	13.2	37.6	43.5
2d cpe	88-91	95.7	172.2	49.6	2,242	13.2	37.9	42.9
3d cpe	87-88	95.7	160.0	52.8	2,141	13.2	38.3	42.4
4d sdn	87-87	95.7	166.3	53.0	2,145	13.2	38.3	42.4
4d sdn	88-92	95.7	170.3	52.4	2,253	13.2	38.4	40.9
5d wgn	88-92	95.7	171.5	54.5	2,299	13.2	39.6	40.9

ENGINES

Type	Displacement (L)	Fuel Dly	HP @rpm	Torque @rpm (ft/lbs)	MPG Cty/Hwy	Years Avail
I-4	1.6	2-bbl	74@5200	86@2800	30/35	87-87
I-4	1.6	FI	108@6600	96@4800	25/29	87-89
I-4	1.6	FI	115@6600	100@4800	na	87-89
I-4	1.6	2-bbl	90@6000	95@3600	30/35	88-89
I-4	1.6	FI	100@5600	101@4400	23/28	89-89
I-4	1.6	FI	130@6800	105@6000	25/31	90-91
I-4	1.6	FI	102@5800	101@4800	28/33	90-92

KEY: I=in-line engine; V=V engine; F=flat engine; FI=fuel injection; bbl=barrel carburetor; T=turbo; D=diesel; HP=horsepower; MPG=estimated average miles per gallon.

EVALUATIONS, TESTS, AND RANKINGS

1992: "a piranha determined to eat up the competition . . . flawless fit and finish . . . pleasant combination of suppleness and firm body control." **Source:** "Toyota Corolla: The twenty-valve four-banger," *Car and Driver,* October 1991, pp. 28-29.

1991: "left something to be desired in both head and leg room . . . soft, smooth ride . . . resolutely bland exterior styling." **Source:** "The World's Most Unfair Comparison Test," *Motor Trend,* April 1991, pp. 72-75, 78, 80, 82.

1991: "blind testers preferred the Corolla to the Prizm 8 to 3, with one ₉no preference." **Source:** "Blind Taste Test," *Popular Mechanics,* November 1990, pp. 43-47, 124-125.

1990: "a rather pleasant automobile . . . so-so seats, light controls, smooth power delivery and predictable handling traits combined with good ride quality." **Source:** "Letter from Japan," *Road & Track,* September 1987, pp. 100, 102, 104, 106, 108, 110.

1989: "[Corolla FX16] has exactly the right stuff . . . brakes are discs all around . . . seats are supportive and comfortable." **Source:** "Hitting for High Average," *Car and Driver,* August 1988, pp. 58-69.

1989: "easily clawed its way around and over ruts and small-to-medium dips . . . All-Trac's package is first-rate." **Source:** "Toyota Corolla All-Trac SR5 Wagon," *Car and Driver,* December 1988, p. 137.

1987: "offers the utility and roominess of a hatchback, providing the nimble handling usually associated with sportier models." **Source:** "An Aggressive Corolla from California," *Detroit Free Press,* September 1, 1986, p. 7C.

1987: "This puppy flies . . . roomy cockpit, quite impressive." **Source:** "Toyota FX16 GT-S," *Road & Track,* January 1987, pp. 46-48.

RECALLS

None to date.

REPAIR MANUALS

2676 ● **Chilton's Toyota Corolla, Carina, Tercel, Starlet, 1970-1987**
Chilton Co.
Chilton Way
Radnor, PA 19089   Ph:(215)964-4000

Published 1987. **Price:** $15.95.

2677 ● **Chilton's Toyota Corolla-Tercel-MR2, 1984-1990**
Chilton Co.
Chilton Way
Radnor, PA 19089   Ph:(215)964-4000

Published 1991. **Price:** $15.95.

2678 ● **Haynes Toyota Corolla Owners Workshop Manual, No. 1025: 1984-1988**
Haynes Publications, Inc.
861 Lawrence Dr.
Newbury Park, CA 91320   Ph:(818)889-5400

Editor(s): Peter G. Strasman. **Price:** $15.95.

2679 ● **Toyota Corolla**
Peter Allen Video Productions
38-C Otis St.
West Babylon, NY 11704   Ph:(516)643-4372

How to maintain and tune-up this one particular Toyota engine. **Release date:** 1986. **Producer:** Peter Allen Productions. **Acquisition:** Purchase.

2680 ● **The Toyota Standard 4-Speed Transmission Explained**
Bergwall Productions, Inc.
106 Charles Lindbergh Blvd.
Uniondale, NY 11553-3695   Ph:(516)222-1111

On five tapes, the Toyota transmission is disassembled and assembled for trainee instruction. **Release date:** 1985. **Producer:** Bergwall Productions, Inc. **Acquisition:** Purchase.

ASSOCIATIONS

2681 ● **Toyota Sport Car Club**
904 Silver Spur Rd., Ste. 482
Rolling Hills, CA 90274
Ralph Wenters, Pres.   Ph:(213)539-0595

Founded: 1983. **Membership:** 2,000. Owners of Toyota sports cars, especially the Celica and Supra models. Facilitates exchange of information among members; provides technical assistance. Makes available discount parts. **Former Name(s):** (1987) Toyota Celica Supra Club.

TOYOTA CRESSIDA (1987-92)

Modestly enlarged since its inception in 1987, however its basic shape and dimensions have not changed dramatically. Station wagon was available until 1988. Supply was limited in 1990, due to high demand for the automobile in Japan. Nominated to the *Car and Driver* Ten Best Cars List in 1990. Produced at the Toyota plant in Motomachi, Japan.

1991 Toyota Cressida

MAJOR FEATURES

● Cressida has as 1991 standard equipment: 3.0 liter fuel-injected I-6 engine, four-speed automatic overdrive transmission, speed-sensing rack-and-pinion power steering, 4-wheel power disc brakes, aluminum alloy wheels, cruise control, automatic climate control, AM/FM cassette stereo, tilt/telescopic steering column, and theft-deterrent system.

● Cressida Station Wagon had as 1987 standard features: 2.8 liter fuel injected I-6 engine, four-speed automatic overdrive transmission, rack-and-pinion steering, four-wheel disc brakes, and independent suspension.

PRICE HISTORY

The following new car prices reflect the approximate retail cost of the base model: **1987** - $19,850; **1988** - $20,998; **1989** - $21,498; **1990** - $21,498; **1991** - $22,698; **1992** - $23,488.

DIMENSIONS

Body Style	Years Avail	Wheel Base (in)	Lgth (in)	Ht (in)	Avg Wt (lbs)	Fuel Cap (gal)	Front Hdrm (in)	Front Legrm (in)
4d sdn	87-88	104.5	187.8	54.1	3,296	18.5	38.8	42.0
4d sdn	89-92	105.5	189.6	54.5	3,417	18.5	38.4	42.8
5d wgn	87-87	104.5	189.6	55.7	3,240	18.5	38.8	42.0

ENGINES

Type	Displacement (L)	Fuel Dly	HP @rpm	Torque @rpm (ft/lbs)	MPG Cty/Hwy	Years Avail
I-6	2.8	FI	156@5200	165@4500	19/24	87-88
I-6	3.0	FI	190@5600	185@4400	19/24	89-92

KEY: I=in-line engine; V=V engine; F=flat engine; FI=fuel injection; bbl=barrel carburetor; T=turbo; D=diesel; HP=horsepower; MPG=estimated average miles per gallon.

EVALUATIONS, TESTS, AND RANKINGS

1990: "hidden sporting flavor . . . exterior is best described as contemporary Japanese androgynous . . . impressive to drive." **Source:** "Toyota Cressida: Toyota's luxo . . . er, sport . . . er, top sedan," *Car and Driver,* April 1990, pp. 75-77, 80.

1989: "smooth and suave at all times." **Source:** "Japan Ups the Ante," *Popular Science,* December 1988, p. 52.

1989: "seats would look right at home in a La-Z-Boy showroom . . . dash [has] a bewildering array of buttons and dials . . . reworked power window switches make sense." **Source:** "Cressida vs. Maxima: If this is the preliminary, we can't wait for the main event," *Motor Trend,* June 1989, pp. 102-104, 106, 108-109.

1989: "ride that is excellent and a drivetrain that is impressively smooth and quiet . . . quick, well-balanced, high-speed performer . . . bulbous, conservatively styled body." **Source:** "Import Report: Crest of Luxury," *Home Mechanix,* April 1989, pp. 84-86, 103-105.

1987: "a flabby, unpredictable handler. The styling is boxy and unpretentious, but the interior is too glitzy." **Source:** "PM Comparison Test: This Sportin' Life," *Popular Mechanics,* January 1987, pp. 60-64, 114.

RECALLS

None to date.

REPAIR MANUALS

2682 ● **The Toyota Standard 4-Speed Transmission Explained**
Bergwall Productions, Inc.
106 Charles Lindbergh Blvd.
Uniondale, NY 11553-3695   Ph:(516)222-1111

On five tapes, the Toyota transmission is disassembled and assembled for trainee instruction. **Release date:** 1985. **Producer:** Bergwall Productions, Inc. **Acquisition:** Purchase.

TOYOTA LAND CRUISER WAGON (1987-92)

The Toyota Land Cruiser is Toyota's oldest U.S.-line model. Vehicle was completely redesigned in early 1990 as a 1991 model.

1991 Toyota Land Cruiser Wagon

MAJOR FEATURES

● The 1992 Land Cruiser includes the following standard equipment: 4.0L six-cylinder in-line engine, full-time four wheel drive, four-speed automatic transmission, power windows, door locks, and dual outside mirrors, AM/FM radio cassette, and child protector locks.

PRICE HISTORY

The following new car prices reflect the approximate retail cost

of the base model: **1987** - $16,498; **1988** - $20,398; **1989** - $20,898; **1990** - $21,998; **1991** - $23,488.

DIMENSIONS

Body Style	Years Avail	Wheel Base (in)	Lgth (in)	Ht (in)	Avg Wt (lbs)	Fuel Cap (gal)	Front Hdrm (in)	Front Legrm (in)
utl wgn	87-90	107.5	184.0	69.5	5,621	23.8	na	na
utl wgn	91-92	112.5	188.2	70.3	6,526	25.1	na	na

ENGINES

Type	Displace-ment (L)	Fuel Dly	HP @rpm	Torque @rpm (ft/lbs)	MPG Cty/Hwy	Years Avail
I-6	4.2	na	na	na	11/13	87-87
I-6	4.0	FI	155@na	na	12/14	88-92

KEY: I=in-line engine; V=V engine; F=flat engine; FI=fuel injection; bbl=barrel carburetor; T=turbo; D=diesel; HP=horsepower; MPG=estimated average miles per gallon.

EVALUATIONS, TESTS, AND RANKINGS

1991: "looks substantially different from its predecessor ... engine just hasn't got it ... Luxury touches abound." **Source:** "Cruising Upward: Upscale in style and biggest in its class, the new Toyota Land Cruiser goes off-road or on with luxury," *Outdoor Life,* October 1990, pp. 54, 58.

1991: "Despite its optional luxury equipment, the Land Cruiser ... is all truck ... has many features to recommend it ... true workhorse in stationwagon clothing." **Source:** "Strong And Sporty: These stylish vehicles are still trucks under the skin," *Organic Gardening,* November 1990, pp. 58-61.

1990: "less satisfactory in highway passing ... good rear legroom even with the front bucket seats all the way back ... fit and finish was good." **Source:** "Toyota's Land Cruiser provides rugged look, but smooth ride," *The Detroit News,* October 17, 1990, pp. 1D-2D.

1990: "The Land Cruiser FJ80 four-door is extremely well done ... ponderously slow ... Good braking distances ... Smooth and sure-footed." **Source:** "Toyota Land Cruiser," *Motor Trend,* October 1990, pp. 120-121.

1990: "Carlike comfort ... beautifully appointed cabin ... class-leading roominess." **Source:** "Toyota Land Cruiser: The old Crusher goes black-tie," *Car and Driver,* March 1990, p. 58.

RECALLS

1987-90: (38,500 multi-purpose vehicles; includes models made before 1987): Severe conditions of heavy loads and high ambient temperatures can create high pressure in the fuel tank. Can cause excessive load to the fuel tank separator weld attachment, which can result in cracks and fuel leakage. Fuel leakage can lead to fire when near an ignition source. **Corrective action:** Replace the fuel tank with an improved tank. *(NHTSA Campaign No. 91V110000.)*

1987-88: (30,256 vehicles; includes models made before 1987): Rear seat lap belt may not fully retract. **Corrective action:** Install belt guide. *(NHTSA Campaign No. 89V155000.)*

REPAIR MANUALS

2683 ● **The Toyota Standard 4-Speed Transmission Explained**
Bergwall Productions, Inc.
106 Charles Lindbergh Blvd.
Uniondale, NY 11553-3695   Ph:(516)222-1111

On five tapes, the Toyota transmission is disassembled and assembled for trainee instruction. **Release date:** 1985. **Producer:** Bergwall Productions, Inc. **Acquisition:** Purchase.

TOYOTA MR2 (1987-1992)

Redesigned for 1991 with new stylings, larger dimensions, and increased engine power. Supercharged MR2 was offered until 1990. Named as *Road & Track's* Ten Best Values as the Best Two-seat/High Performance Car, $12,500—$17,500 in 1987. Nominated to the 1991 *Motor Trend's* Import Car of the Year class. Manufactured in Sagamihara, Japan.

1991 Toyota MR2 Turbo

MAJOR FEATURES

● MR2 offers as 1992 standard features: 2.2 liter I-4 fuel-injected engine, five-speed manual overdrive transmission, four-wheel independent MacPherson strut suspension, driver side airbag, supplemental restraint system, four-wheel ventilated disc brakes, rack-and-pinion steering, rear defroster, and tilt steering column.

● MR2 Turbo adds as 1992 standard equipment: 2.0 liter I-4 fuel-injected turbocharged and air-cooled intercooler engine, 7-way adjustable sport seat, and rear spoiler.

● MR2 Supercharged had as 1990 standard equipment: 1.6 liter I-4 fuel-injected supercharged and intercooled engine and T-rooftop.

● MR2 1600G-Limited had as 1990 standard equipment: 1.6 liter I-4 fuel-injected supercharged and intercooled engine, T-rooftop, alloy wheels, and upgraded interior.

PRICE HISTORY

The following new car prices reflect the approximate retail cost of the base model: **1987** - $12,548; **1988** - $13,458; **1989** - $13,798; **1990** - $14,898; **1991** - $15,448; **1992** - $16,048.

DIMENSIONS

Body Style	Years Avail	Wheel Base (in)	Lgth (in)	Ht (in)	Avg Wt (lbs)	Fuel Cap (gal)	Front Hdrm (in)	Front Legrm (in)
2d cpe	87-90	91.3	155.5	48.6	2,350	10.8	37.4	43.0
2d cpe	91-92	94.5	164.2	48.8	2,559	14.3	37.5	43.3

ENGINES

Type	Displacement (L)	Fuel Dly	HP @rpm	Torque @rpm (ft/lbs)	MPG Cty/Hwy	Years Avail
I-4	1.6	FI	112@6600	97@4800	26/31	87-89
I-4	1.6	FI	145@6400	140@4000	24/30	89-89
I-4	2.2	FI	130@5400	140@4400	22/28	90-92
I-4T	2.0	FI	200@6000	200@3200	20/27	90-92

KEY: I=in-line engine; V=V engine; F=flat engine; FI=fuel injection; bbl=barrel carburetor; T=turbo; D=diesel; HP=horsepower; MPG=estimated average miles per gallon.

EVALUATIONS, TESTS, AND RANKINGS

1991: "body has been restyled in a frankly Ferrari-like vein . . . a refined, almost delicate feel to the controls . . . cleanly designed, user-friendly cockpit." **Source:** "Carrying The Torch: Toyota MR2," *Road & Track,* November 1990, pp. 44-53, 56.

1991: "interior . . . is generally without any sporting character . . . engine's sound is a bother, not a joy . . . This is a fast car." **Source:** "Toyota MR2 Turbo: Fauna and flora create a three-season test of our popular Mr. Two," *Automobile Magazine,* November 1991, pp. 120-122, 124-125.

1991: "a whole bunch of performance for your hard-earned dollars . . . nimble in the corners." **Source:** "Fast Five," *Motor Trend,* December 1990, pp. 38-45.

1990: "makes substantial power early in the rev range, but flattens out as redline approaches. . .can snap abruptly to oversteer if mishandled. . .front wheels lock early, requiring significant longer braking zones." **Source:** "Bang for the Buck!: In Search of the Top 10 Performance Coupes," *Motor Trend,* November 1989, pp. 42-46, 48, 52-55, 58-59, 62, 64, 66-68, 72, 76.

1990: "fun of acceleration is diminished only by the irritating whine of the turbo on boost. . .seats are comfortable, the analog gauges are plenty big and readable, and the controls come readily to hand." **Source:** "MR2 II: You'll be amazed at what Toyota has been doing behind your back," *Road & Track,* February 1990, pp. 38-45.

1990: "Probably the best all-around mid-engine car yet offered. . .Visibility suffers somewhat from the large rear pillars." **Source:** "Toyota MR2 Turbo: A Commitment to Terrific," *Motor Trend,* April 1990, pp. 58-60, 62.

1990: "offers luxury, comfort, handling and performance approaching that of bigger, more expensive GTs." **Source:** "Toyota MR2 Turbo: Second-generation sophistication, first-generation excitement," *Road & Track,* April 1990, pp. 81-84, 86.

1990: "bigger, faster, more capable and better looking . . . subtantially more power to offset the weight increases . . . an impressive piece of equipment." **Source:** "Toyota MR2: The new Mister-Two stretches the performance envelope," *Popular Mechanics,* April 1990, pp. 130, 132.

1988: "easier to get into and out of than many larger cars. . .With the supercharged engine. . .has matured into a more powerful but also heavier and less wieldy machine." **Source:** "Toyota MR2 Supercharged: Mister Two strives to be Superman Two," *Car and Driver,* December 1987, pp. 55-58.

1988: "overall excellence in craftsmanship, design and engineering. . .Supercharged engines tend to get lower fuel economy than turbocharged models." **Source:** "Supercharged MR2 packs power," *The Detroit News,* July 6, 1988, pp. F1-F2.

1987: "the essence of sporting fun: quick, agile, and always eager for a fling." **Source:** "Cars: Fun work, but somebody's got to do it," *Car and Driver,* January 1987, pp. 36-41.

1987: "any MR2 owner who has ever wished for more power should be pleased with the supercharger's contribution." **Source:** "Toyota MR2 1600G-Limited: Mister Two grows muscles," *Car and Driver,* January 1987, p. 27.

RECALLS

None to date.

SAFETY AND REPAIRS

1989: "Knock sensor and octane," *Road & Track,* September 1989, pp. 152, 154, 156. **Note:** MR2 has a knock sensor that retards timing.

REPAIR MANUALS

2684 ● **Chilton's Toyota Corolla-Tercel-MR2, 1984-1990**
Chilton Co.
Chilton Way
Radnor, PA 19089   Ph:(215)964-4000

Published 1991. **Price:** $15.95.

2685 ● **Haynes Toyota MR2 Owners Workshop Repair Manual, No. 1339: All Models, 1985-1987**
Haynes Publications, Inc.
861 Lawrence Dr.
Newbury Park, CA 91320   Ph:(818)889-5400

Published 1987. **Editor(s):** J. H. Haynes. **Price:** $15.95.

2686 ● **Toyota MR2, 1984-1988**
Motorbooks International, Inc.
729 Prospect Ave.
Osceola, WI 54020   Ph:(715)294-3345

Published 1988. **Editor(s):** R. M. Clarke. **Price:** $15.95.

2687 ● **The Toyota Standard 4-Speed Transmission Explained**
Bergwall Productions, Inc.
106 Charles Lindbergh Blvd.
Uniondale, NY 11553-3695   Ph:(516)222-1111

On five tapes, the Toyota transmission is disassembled and assembled for trainee instruction. **Release date:** 1985. **Producer:** Bergwall Productions, Inc. **Acquisition:** Purchase.

ASSOCIATIONS

2688 ● **Toyota Sport Car Club**
904 Silver Spur Rd., Ste. 482
Rolling Hills, CA 90274
Ralph Wenters, Pres.   Ph:(213)539-0595

Founded: 1983. **Membership:** 2,000. Owners of Toyota sports cars, especially the Celica and Supra models. Facilitates exchange of information among members; provides technical assistance. Makes available discount parts. **Former Name(s):** (1987) Toyota Celica Supra Club.

TOYOTA PASEO (1992)

Introduced in 1991 as a 1992 model, the Toyota Paseo is assembled in Takaoka, Japan. It replaces the Corolla SR5 and GT-S as Toyota's sporty, economical car. It is built on the same platform as the Toyota Tercel. Paseo competes against such coupes as the Geo Storm and Hyundai Scoupe.

1992 Toyota Paseo

MAJOR FEATURES

● Paseo has as 1992 standard equipment: 5-speed manual transmission, front independent MacPherson struts/rear trailing torsion beams, front and rear stabilizer bars, variable assist power rack-and-pinion steering, power-assisted ventilated disc/drum brakes, tinted glass, color-keyed front and rear bumpers, full wheel covers, high-back front seats, rear folding seat, and electronically tuned radio.

PRICE HISTORY

The following new car prices reflect the approximate retail cost of the base model: **1992** - $10,338.

DIMENSIONS

Body Style	Years Avail	Wheel Base (in)	Lgth (in)	Ht (in)	Avg Wt (lbs)	Fuel Cap (gal)	Front Hdrm (in)	Front Legrm (in)
2d cpe	92-92	93.7	163.2	50.2	2,075	11.9	37.7	41.1

ENGINES

Type	Displace-ment (L)	Fuel Dly	HP @rpm	Torque @rpm (ft/lbs)	MPG Cty/Hwy	Years Avail
I-4	1.5	FI	100@6400	91@3200	28/34	92-92

KEY: I=in-line engine; V=V engine; F=flat engine; FI=fuel injection; bbl=barrel carburetor; T=turbo; D=diesel; HP=horsepower; MPG=estimated average miles per gallon.

EVALUATIONS, TESTS, AND RANKINGS

1992: "packs a lot of value in its estimated $10,000 price . . . doesn't have the go-power of some of the other cars in this category, but it's not exactly sluggish either . . . seems likely to hold its own in the virtues that count over the long haul." **Source:** "New Cars," *Popular Mechanics*, June 1991, pp. 98-102.

1992: "smart exterior styling, responsive handling . . . surprisingly stable ride . . . rear seat was difficult to use." **Source:** "Sporty Paseo Styled for the Young at Heart," *The Detroit News*, June 1991, pp. 1F-2F.

1992: "feisty, affable, solid but light on its feet . . . a class above the chunky nickel-rocket sedanlets . . . the best power-to-weight ratio in the class." **Source:** "Toyota Paseo," *Car and Driver*, June 1991, pp. 79-80, 83.

1992: "front-three-quarter view looks dashing and sporty . . . well-appointed interior . . . On the highway, the Paseo's ride is on the firmer side." **Source:** "Toyota Paseo," *Road & Track*, October 1991, p. 46.

1992: "shift linkage is light and precise, and the driver's seat and steering wheel feel right . . . interior is lined with tweedy upholstery that would be at home in a Porsche . . . Hard

cornering over bumpy pavement does, however, unsettle the *front* tires' grip." **Source:** "Toyota Paseo," *Motor Trend*, June 1991, p. 104.

1992: "delivering such a car at such a price is a substantial achievement . . . engine offers a good combination of well-mannered driveability and torque . . . a nimble, predictable, fun-to-drive entry-level car." **Source:** "Toyota Paseo," *Road & Track*, December 1991, pp. 71-74.

1992: "underlying engineering, with a few exceptions . . . first-rate . . . there are other problems too big to overlook . . . If the Paseo were terrifically sporty, then we could overlook its lack of utility." **Source:** "Toyota Paseo," *Car and Driver*, November 1991, pp. 141-143.

1992: "aimed at young, first-time buyers who want something zippier than the Tercel." **Source:** "Toyota Breaks $10,000 Mark with Paseo," *The Detroit News*, May 3, 1991, Sec. E.

1992: "a head turner that drew lots of interest from passers-by . . . add a few options, and the price quickly jumps by $3,000." **Source:** "Paseo likeable, if not imperfect, way to go," *The Flint Journal*, August 28, 1991, p. D1.

1992: "a long way from loosely bound excitement . . . the sleek and brightly painted body wraps a core that is strictly econobox . . . oddly, in a car so basic, there are surprises." **Source:** "Selling Paseo's Sizzle Between the Lines," *The New York Times*, June 16, 1991.

RECALLS

None to date.

REPAIR MANUALS

2689 ● **The Toyota Standard 4-Speed Transmission Explained**
Bergwall Productions, Inc.
106 Charles Lindbergh Blvd.
Uniondale, NY 11553-3695   Ph:(516)222-1111

On five tapes, the Toyota transmission is disassembled and assembled for trainee instruction. **Release date:** 1985. **Producer:** Bergwall Productions, Inc. **Acquisition:** Purchase.

ASSOCIATIONS

2690 ● **Toyota Sport Car Club**
904 Silver Spur Rd., Ste. 482
Rolling Hills, CA 90274
Ralph Wenters, Pres.   Ph:(213)539-0595

Founded: 1983. **Membership:** 2,000. Owners of Toyota sports cars, especially the Celica and Supra models. Facilitates exchange of information among members; provides technical assistance. Makes available discount parts. **Former Name(s):** (1987) Toyota Celica Supra Club.

TOYOTA PREVIA (1991-92)

The Previa was introduced to the Toyota lineup in 1991, replacing the Toyota Van. The Previa was one of *Car and Driver's* Ten Best for 1991.

1991 Toyota Previa

MAJOR FEATURES

● 1992 Previa DLX standard equipment includes: 2.4L four-cyclinder engine, five-speed manual overdrive transmission, independent front suspension, power-assisted rack-and-pinion steering, ventilated front disc brakes, full wheel covers, tilt steering column, driver's side airbag, and tinted glass.

● 1992 Previa LE adds as 1992 standard equipment: four-speed automatic transmission, 4-wheel disc brakes, air conditioning, cruise control, rear window defogger, rear and upgraded tires. The Previa LE All-Trac offers full-time four-wheel drive in addition to the above standard equipment.

● The Previa Deluxe All-Trac offers full-time four-wheel drive in addition to the above standard equipment in both the DLX and LE models.

PRICE HISTORY

The following new car prices reflect the approximate retail cost of the base model: **1991** - $14,698; **1992** - $16,518.

DIMENSIONS

Body Style	Years Avail	Wheel Base (in)	Lgth (in)	Ht (in)	Avg Wt (lbs)	Fuel Cap (gal)	Front Hdrm (in)	Front Legrm (in)
van	91-92	112.8	187.0	68.7	5,215	19.8	39.4	40.1

ENGINES

Type	Displace-ment (L)	Fuel Dly	HP @rpm	Torque @rpm (ft/lbs)	MPG Cty/Hwy	Years Avail
I-4	2.4	FI	138@5000	154@4000	18/22	91-92

KEY: I=in-line engine; V=V engine; F=flat engine; FI=fuel injection; bbl=barrel carburetor; T=turbo; D=diesel; HP=horsepower; MPG=estimated average miles per gallon.

EVALUATIONS, TESTS, AND RANKINGS

1992: "1992 Previa will be equipped with air bags and be the first model to meet all U.S. passenger car safety standards." **Source:** "Toyota bringing air bags to minivans," *The Detroit News*, July 19, 1991, pp. 1E-2E.

1991: "Excellent carlike feel ... dash design is ... pleasingly modern." **Source:** "Ten Best Cars: Toyota Previa," *Car and Driver*, January 1991, pp 40-46.

1991: "Heating and audio controls [are] close at hand ... [Due to] a ceiling-mounted passenger fan, you have to bend over double to get from the front to rear seats." **Source:** "You Don't Have to Pay the Maximum for a Minivan," *Business Week*, April 30, 1990, pp. 120-121.

1991: "Classy cloth upholstery complements good seats ... steering ... feels truly coordinated ... side door slides with a

feathery ease." **Source:** "Life with Previa: Toyota's spacious minivan lives up to its romper-room reputation," *Car and Driver*, January 1992, pp. 119-121.

1991: "cohesively aerodynamic design approach ... ride is firm, though not harsh ... Inside, the layout is, in a word, different." **Source:** "Toyota Previa," *Trailer Life*, May 1990, p. 65.

1991: "as balanced and precise as anything in its class ... trifle noisy in hard acceleration ... Ride quality ranks near the top of the minivan class." **Source:** "Long-Term Test Cars: Toyota Previa LE," *Popular Mechanics*, June 1991, pp. 32-34.

1991: "one of the slickest profiles on the road ... excellent ride quality ... clever double-curved dashboard is like something out of The Jetsons." **Source:** "Meet The New Minivans: Cars for the long haul," *New Choices for the Best Years*, October 1990, pp. 86-87.

1991: "engine ... provided good (if not excellent) acceleration ... passengers can slide into and out of the seats easily ... dash arrangement is—ah, futuristic is probably a good word." **Source:** "Four For Fun," *Outdoor Life*, August 1990, pp. 52, 54.

1991: "more responsive than most vans ... mid-engine layout contributed to an annoying fore-and-aft pitching." **Source:** "The Wedge vs. The Box," *Popular Science*, August 1990, pp. 76-79, 81.

1991: "one-dimensional sound from the wimpy stereo ... enormous expanse of glass has a lot to do with its striking appearance ... remarkably composed and quiet at cruising speeds." **Source:** "Toyota Previa LE All-Trac," *Automobile Magazine*, January 1992, pp. 108-113.

RECALLS

None to date.

REPAIR MANUALS

2691 ● **The Toyota Standard 4-Speed Transmission Explained**
Bergwall Productions, Inc.
106 Charles Lindbergh Blvd.
Uniondale, NY 11553-3695   Ph:(516)222-1111

On five tapes, the Toyota transmission is disassembled and assembled for trainee instruction. **Release date:** 1985. **Producer:** Bergwall Productions, Inc. **Acquisition:** Purchase.

TOYOTA SUPRA (1987-92)

The 1992 Toyota Supra and Supra Turbo are produced in Tahara, Japan. The Supra Turbo was listed as one of *Car and Driver's* Ten Best Cars Nominees for 1990.

1991 Toyota Supra Turbo

MAJOR FEATURES

● The Supra 1992 standard equipment includes: 3.0L six-cylinder twin-cam engine, 5-speed manual transmission, power steering, four-wheel disc brakes, fog lights, theft deterrent system, rear defogger, cruise control, climate control, tilt and telescopic steering wheel, driver's side air bag, and outer-sliding sunroof.

● The Supra Turbo adds as 1992 standard equipment: turbocharged intercooled engine, four-wheel anti-lock brakes, and speed-sensitive power steering.

PRICE HISTORY

The following new car prices reflect the approximate retail cost of the base model: **1987** - $20,490; **1988** - $21,740; **1989** - $22,360; **1990** - $22,860; **1991** - $24,320; **1992** - $25,280.

DIMENSIONS

Body Style	Years Avail	Wheel Base (in)	Lgth (in)	Ht (in)	Avg Wt (lbs)	Fuel Cap (gal)	Front Hdrm (in)	Front Legrm (in)
3d lbk	87-92	102.2	181.9	51.2	3,463	18.5	37.5	43.6

ENGINES

Type	Displace-ment (L)	Fuel Dly	HP @rpm	Torque @rpm (ft/lbs)	MPG Cty/Hwy	Years Avail
I-6	3.0	FI	200@6000	185@4800	17/23	87-87
I-6	3.0	FI	200@6000	188@3600	18/23	88-92
I-6T	3.0	FI	230@5600	246@4000	18/23	87-88
I-6T	3.0	FI	232@5600	254@3200	17/23	89-92

KEY: I=in-line engine; V=V engine; F=flat engine; FI=fuel injection; bbl=barrel carburetor; T=turbo; D=diesel; HP=horsepower; MPG=estimated average miles per gallon.

EVALUATIONS, TESTS, AND RANKINGS

1991: "comfortable, functional interior treatment . . . adept at crisp lane changes . . . matches equal doses of performance with personal pampering." **Source:** "Toyota Supra Turbo: Muscle meets manners," *Motor Trend*, September 1991, pp. 82-83.

1990: "excellent power delivery and the first-rate stability under braking." **Source:** "Bang for the Buck," *Motor Trend*, November 1989, pp. 42-46, 48, 52-55, 58-59, 62, 64, 66-68, 72, 76.

1989: "best Japanese sports-coupe package around . . . steering effort is light (but not too light) . . . space in the trunk is ample." **Source:** "Toyota Supra Turbo," *Road & Track*, February 1989, pp. 68-70.

1987: "[With] the lift-off targa top . . . removed, the body could be felt flexing on rough roads." **Source:** "Driving Impression: Toyota Supra Turbo," *Road & Track*, February 1987, p. 85.

1987: "fully independent suspension . . . one of the car's strong points . . . handsome, inviting, and thoughtfully laid out . . . offers a mix of performance, luxury, and value." **Source:** "Toyota Supra Turbo," *Car and Driver*, April 1987, pp. 43-46.

RECALLS

None to date.

REPAIR MANUALS

2692 ● **Chilton's Toyota Celica-Supra, 1986-1990**
Chilton Co.
Chilton Way
Radnor, PA 19089   Ph:(215)964-4000

Published 1990. **Price:** $15.95.

2693 ● **Mitchell Glove Compartment Companion for Your Toyota Celica-Supra**
Harcourt Brace Jovanovich, Inc.
6277 Sea Harbor Dr.
Orlando, FL 32821   Ph:(407)345-2000

Published 1988.

2694 ● **The Toyota Standard 4-Speed Transmission Explained**
Bergwall Productions, Inc.
106 Charles Lindbergh Blvd.
Uniondale, NY 11553-3695   Ph:(516)222-1111

On five tapes, the Toyota transmission is disassembled and assembled for trainee instruction. **Release date:** 1985. **Producer:** Bergwall Productions, Inc. **Acquisition:** Purchase.

OTHER INFORMATION SOURCES

2695 ● **Supra-Sonicsl**
Toyota Sport Car Club
904 Silver Spur Rd., Ste. 482
Rolling Hills Estates, CA 90274

Magazine for Toyota owners. Quarterly. **Editor(s):** Ralph Wenters. **Price:** $25.00.

ASSOCIATIONS

2696 ● **Toyota Sport Car Club**
904 Silver Spur Rd., Ste. 482
Rolling Hills, CA 90274
Ralph Wenters, Pres.   Ph:(213)539-0595

Founded: 1983. **Membership:** 2,000. Owners of Toyota sports cars, especially the Celica and Supra models. Facilitates exchange of information among members; provides technical assistance. Makes available discount parts. **Former Name(s):** (1987) Toyota Celica Supra Club.

TOYOTA TERCEL (1987-92)

Toyota Tercel was completely restyled in 1991. The 4WD version last appeared in 1988 and the Tercel EZ in 1989. Produced in Takaoka, Japan.

1991 Toyota Tercel LE

MAJOR FEATURES

● Standard equipment for the 1992 Tercel includes: 1.5L SOHC 4-cylinder engine, 4-speed manual transmission, front independent suspension, and power-assisted front disc/rear drum brakes.

● The 1992 Tercel DLX adds: 5-speed manual transmission, other exterior body stylings child-protector rear door locks (4-door only), and upgraded tires.

● The Tercel LE adds for 1992 as standard equipment: upgraded upholstery, tinted glass, rear defogger, and other exterior body stylings.

PRICE HISTORY

The following new car prices reflect the approximate retail cost of the base model: **1987** - $5,848; **1988** - $5,998; **1989** - $6,328; **1990** - $6,488; **1991** - $6,588; **1992** - $6,998.

DIMENSIONS

Body Style	Years Avail	Wheel Base (in)	Lgth (in)	Ht (in)	Avg Wt (lbs)	Fuel Cap (gal)	Front Hdrm (in)	Front Legrm (in)
3d lbk	87-87	93.7	157.3	52.6	1,905	13.2	38.5	41.5
3d lbk	88-90	95.7	157.3	52.6	1,990	11.9	38.4	40.2
5d lbk	87-89	93.7	157.3	52.8	2,060	13.2	38.5	41.5
2d cpe	88-90	93.7	166.7	51.8	2,000	11.9	37.8	41.5
2d sdn	91-92	93.7	161.8	53.2	1,950	11.9	38.7	41.2
4d sdn	91-92	93.7	161.8	53.2	2,005	11.9	38.2	41.2
5d wgn	87-88	95.7	169.7	56.1	2,145	13.2	40.2	42.4

ENGINES

Type	Displacement (L)	Fuel Dly	HP @rpm	Torque @rpm (ft/lbs)	MPG Cty/Hwy	Years Avail
I-4	1.5	2-bbl	76@6000	85@3800	31/37	87-88
I-4	1.5	2-bbl	62@4800	76@2800	26/30	88-88
I-4	1.5	2-bbl	78@6000	87@4000	35/41	88-88
I-4	1.5	1-bbl	78@6000	87@4000	30/36	89-90
I-4	1.5	FI	82@5200	89@4400	29/36	91-92

KEY: I=in-line engine; V=V engine; F=flat engine; FI=fuel injection; bbl=barrel carburetor; T=turbo; D=diesel; HP=horsepower; MPG=estimated average miles per gallon.

EVALUATIONS, TESTS, AND RANKINGS

1991: "Rounder, smoother, sleeker shape ... heating and cooling systems perform nicely." **Source:** "Toyota Tercel," *Motor Trend*, February 1991, p. 24.

1991: "solid, affordable transportation with good fit and finish. . .handling is predictable and it copes smoothly with routine emergency manuevers." **Source:** "No-frills Toyota Tercel a good small economy car," *Flint Journal*, February 6, 1991, p. D1.

1991: "much rounder shape and higher bustle ... engine has lots of guts ... one well-screwed-together car." **Source:** "No Frills," *Popular Science*, August 1991, pp. 60-63, 86-87.

1987: "smooth and effortless shifter. . .simple, efficient transportation." **Source:** "Toyota Tercel: Not perfect, not bad (and a nice new boot out back), but almost perfectly invisible," *Car and Driver*, July 1987, pp. 99, 101-102, 104-105.

1987: "Ride quality is greatly improved from previous year models ... climate control is precise and comfortable." **Source:** "1987 Toyota Tercel: The more value for your dollar car," *Motor Trend*, March 1987, pp. 49, 53.

RECALLS

None to date.

REPAIR MANUALS

2697 ● **Chilton's Toyota Corolla, Carina, Tercel, Starlet, 1970-1987**
Chilton Co.
Chilton Way
Radnor, PA 19089   Ph:(215)964-4000

Published 1987. **Price:** $15.95.

2698 ● **Chilton's Toyota Corolla-Tercel-MR2, 1984-1990**
Chilton Co.
Chilton Way
Radnor, PA 19089   Ph:(215)964-4000

Published 1991. **Price:** $15.95.

2699 ● **The Toyota Standard 4-Speed Transmission Explained**
Bergwall Productions, Inc.
106 Charles Lindbergh Blvd.
Uniondale, NY 11553-3695   Ph:(516)222-1111

On five tapes, the Toyota transmission is disassembled and assembled for trainee instruction. **Release date:** 1985. **Producer:** Bergwall Productions, Inc. **Acquisition:** Purchase.

TOYOTA TRUCK (1987-92)

Toyota Trucks come in a variety of configurations, trim levels, transmission types, and engine sizes. All pickups are manufactured in Germany by Volkswagen AG. 1992 Toyota 4x2 (2WD) Trucks are offered in three trim levels: Standard, Deluxe, and SR5 V6. 1992 4x4 Trucks are offered in two trim levels: Deluxe and SR5 V6. In addition to multiple trim levels, the 1992 4x2 Trucks are available in five different configurations: Standard Bed, Long Bed, Xtracab, One Ton, and Cab Chassis. 1992 4x4 is only offered in the first three options.

1991 Toyota Truck

MAJOR FEATURES

● A 2.4L four-cylinder engine is standard in all 1992 Trucks, with the exception of the SR5 V6, One Ton, and Cab Chassis models, which have a 3.0L V6 engine as standard equipment. All models include electronic fuel injection, power-assisted, front disc brakes, three-point rear seatbelts, and upgraded interior as standard equipment. The 2WD Trucks use P195/75 R14 tires, while the four-wheel drives use P225/75 R15 tires.

● Toyota SR5 V6 4x4 adds as 1992 standard equipment: 3.0L

V6, rear-wheel anti-lock brakes and 4WDemand shift-on-the-move four-wheel drive.

Dimensions that follow represent those for the Standard Bed configuration.

PRICE HISTORY

The following new car prices reflect the approximate retail cost of the base model: **1987** - $6,598; **1988** - $7,698; **1989** - $7,998; **1990** - $7,998; **1991** - $8,448.

DIMENSIONS

Body Style	Years Avail	Wheel Base (in)	Lgth (in)	Ht (in)	Avg Wt (lbs)	Fuel Cap (gal)	Front Hdrm (in)	Front Legrm (in)
trk	87-92	103.0	174.6	60.8	4,400	13.7	38.3	41.5

ENGINES

Type	Displacement (L)	Fuel Dly	HP @rpm	Torque @rpm (ft/lbs)	MPG Cty/Hwy	Years Avail
I-4	2.4	FI	116@4800	140@2800	22/26	87-92
I-4	2.4	2-bbl	103@na	na	19/22	88-90
I-4T	2.4	FI	na	na	20/24	87-88
V-6	3.0	FI	150@na	na	18/23	88-92

KEY: I=in-line engine; V=V engine; F=flat engine; FI=fuel injection; bbl=barrel carburetor; T=turbo; D=diesel; HP=horsepower; MPG=estimated average miles per gallon.

EVALUATIONS, TESTS, AND RANKINGS

1991: "ride is typically rugged, and sometimes bone-jarring over broken pavement and uneven terrain . . . the most striking feature of the SR5 is its cockpit." **Source:** "Toyota SR5 Xtracab feels sporty," *Detroit Free Press,* 1991, p. E1.

RECALLS

1988: (4,842 Toyota Truck and Toyota 4-Runner models equipped with V6 engines): Improper routing of fuel hose could cause some fuel hoses to have inadequate clearance to EGR pipe. Heat from EGR could cause hose to crack and result in fuel leakage. **Corrective action:** Reroute fuel hose to ensure proper clearance and replace hose, if necessary. *(NHTSA Campaign No. 88V019000.)*

REPAIR MANUALS

2700 ● **Chilton's Toyota Trucks 1970-1987**
Chilton Co.
Chilton Way
Radnor, PA 19089   Ph:(215)964-4000

Published 1988. **Price:** $15.95.

2701 ● **Haynes Toyota Pick-up Owners Workshop Manual, No. 656: 1979-1990**
Haynes Publications, Inc.
861 Lawrence Dr.
Newbury Park, CA 91320   Ph:(818)889-5400

Editor(s): J. H. Haynes and John Raffa. **Price:** $15.95.

2702 ● **How to Keep Your Toyota Pick-Up Alive: A Manual of Step by Step Procedures for the Compleat Idiot**
John Muir Publications
P.O. Box 613
Santa Fe, NM 87504-0613   Ph:(505)982-4078

Published 1988. **Editor(s):** Larry Owens. **Price:** $19.95.

2703 ● **Toyota Pick-ups and 4-Runner, 1984-88**
Clymer Publications
P.O. Box 1209
Overland Park, KS 66212   Ph:(913)541-6694

Published 1988. **Price:** $14.95.

2704 ● **Toyota Pickup, 4-Runner Service Manual: 1978-1988 Including Gasoline, Diesel, and Turbo Diesel, 4-cylinder and 6-cylinder Engines**
Robert Bentley Publishing, Inc.
1000 Massachusetts Ave.
Cambridge, MA 02138   Ph:(617)547-4170

Price: $29.95.

2705 ● **The Toyota Standard 4-Speed Transmission Explained**
Bergwall Productions, Inc.
106 Charles Lindbergh Blvd.
Uniondale, NY 11553-3695   Ph:(516)222-1111

On five tapes, the Toyota transmission is disassembled and assembled for trainee instruction. **Release date:** 1985. **Producer:** Bergwall Productions, Inc. **Acquisition:** Purchase.

TOYOTA VAN (1987-1989)

Originally designed for the Japanese market, the Toyota Van was converted for passenger use to compete against the Chrysler minivans. The Van's last model year was 1989. A March 1990 model, sold as a 1991 family carrier, was called the Toyota Previa (see separate entry).

MAJOR FEATURES

● The 1989 Toyota Deluxe Van standard equipment included: 2.2L four-cylinder engine, 5-speed manual transmission, and P195/70 R14 tires.

PRICE HISTORY

The following new car prices reflect the approximate retail cost of the base model: **1987** - $11,988; **1988** - $13,198; **1989** - $13,608.

DIMENSIONS

Body Style	Years Avail	Wheel Base (in)	Lgth (in)	Ht (in)	Avg Wt (lbs)	Fuel Cap (gal)	Front Hdrm (in)	Front Legrm (in)
van	87-89	88	175.8	70.3	4,500	15.9	na	na

ENGINES

Type	Displacement (L)	Fuel Dly	HP @rpm	Torque @rpm (ft/lbs)	MPG Cty/Hwy	Years Avail
I-4	2.2	FI	101@na	na	22/24	87-89

KEY: I=in-line engine; V=V engine; F=flat engine; FI=fuel injection; bbl=barrel carburetor; T=turbo; D=diesel; HP=horsepower; MPG=estimated average miles per gallon.

EVALUATIONS, TESTS, AND RANKINGS

1989: "Great little family fun vehicle." **Source:** "Toyota Van and Wagon," *Road & Track—Buyer's Guide 1989,* 1988, p. 200.

1989: "Rides well . . . Steering is sharp . . . engine housing intrudes on the cockpit." **Source:** "Eeny, Meeny, Miney,

Mini,'' *Car and Driver*, May 1989, pp. 62-3, 65, 67, 71, 75-7, 81.

RECALLS

1987-88: (110,217 vans and cargo vans; includes models made before 1987): Steering bevel gear assembly may have water contamination, resulting in rust and erratic steering. **Corrective action:** Replace assembly and cover liquid gasket material with improved material. *(NHTSA Campaign No. 89V089000.)*

REPAIR MANUALS

2706 ● **The Toyota Standard 4-Speed Transmission Explained**
Bergwall Productions, Inc.
106 Charles Lindbergh Blvd.
Uniondale, NY 11553-3695   Ph:(516)222-1111

On five tapes, the Toyota transmission is disassembled and assembled for trainee instruction. **Release date:** 1985. **Producer:** Bergwall Productions, Inc. **Acquisition:** Purchase.

VOLKSWAGEN CABRIOLET (1987-92)

Built by Karmann Coachworks in Osnabrueck, Germany, the Volkswagen Cabriolet is based on the Rabbit design that was superceded by the Volkswagen Golf. Selected as a Best Buy among convertibles by *CAD* in 1990. The Insurance Institute for Highway Safety cited the Cabriolet best in its class of 2-door small cars in a 1991 report concerning fatality rates per 10,000 passenger cars. The study included 1984-88 model year vehicles.

1991 Volkswagen Cabriolet

MAJOR FEATURES

● Cabriolet has as 1992 standard equipment: 5-speed manual transmission, power steering, driver's side airbag, power front windows, sport suspension, power front disc/rear drum brakes, six-speaker theft-deterrent AM/FM stereo cassette, rear defogger, tinted glass and full wheel covers.

● Cabriolet Carat adds as 1992 standard equipment: leather sport seats, leather wrapped steering wheel and shift knob, cruise control, and alloy wheels.

● Cabriolet Etienne Aigner added as 1991 standard equipment: cloth and leather seat trim and forged alloy wheels.

● Cabriolet Bestseller had as 1990 standard equipment: upgraded tires.

● Cabriolet Boutique had as 1990 standard equipment: other exterior body stylings and an upgraded interior.

PRICE HISTORY

The following new car prices reflect the approximate retail cost of the base model: **1987** - $13,750; **1988** - $14,750; **1989** - $15,195; **1990** - $15,485; **1991** - $16,540; **1992** - $17,320.

DIMENSIONS

Body Style	Years Avail	Wheel Base (in)	Lgth (in)	Ht (in)	Avg Wt (lbs)	Fuel Cap (gal)	Front Hdrm (in)	Front Legrm (in)
2d conv	87-92	94.5	153.1	55.6	2,307	13.8	37.4	39.4

ENGINES

Type	Displace- ment (L)	Fuel Dly	HP @rpm	Torque @rpm (ft/lbs)	MPG Cty/Hwy	Years Avail
I-4	1.8	FI	90@5500	100@3000	25/32	87-89
I-4	1.8	FI	94@5400	100@3000	25/32	90-92

KEY: I=in-line engine; V=V engine; F=flat engine; FI=fuel injection; bbl=barrel carburetor; T=turbo; D=diesel; HP=horsepower; MPG=estimated average miles per gallon.

EVALUATIONS, TESTS, AND RANKINGS

1992: ''handling felt nimble, accurate, responsive, and teutonically taut . . . driving position . . . is hot in the vein of low-slung sports cars . . . steering wheel angle is fairly accommodating.'' **Source:** ''Not everyone will come to the Cabriolet,'' *The Flint Journal*, October 2, 1991, E1-E2.

1991: ''lovable but pricey.'' **Source:** ''Volkswagen Cabriolet,'' *Road & Track*, October 1990, p. 79.

1990: ''feels solid and tight . . . sprint is mediocore . . . trades some ease of open-air motoring for fine all-weather drivability.'' **Source:** ''Best Buys, 1990,'' *Car and Driver*, May 1990, pp. 37, 55, 57.

1989: ''The Karmann-built body looks good . . . Top down and windows up, the wind protection is impressive . . . ride quality is excellent, both firm and comfortable.'' **Source:** ''Volkswagen Cabriolet,'' *Car and Driver*, February 1989, p.67.

1989: ''When down . . . an easy one-person job . . . the top stack is a bit high . . . the 5-speed version goes from 0-60 mph in 10.8 seconds.'' **Source:** ''Volkswagen Cabriolet,'' *Road & Track*, March 1989, p. 68.

RECALLS

1990-91: (11,300 passenger cars): The center of the water separator panel located in the engine compartment between engine and firewall could bend if someone leans on it during engine maintenance. A bent panel could interfere with the free movement of the accelerator linkage, possibly causing unwanted acceleration. **Corrective action:** Install reinforcement bracket to secure separator panel. *(NHTSA Campaign No. 91V162000.)*

1987: (278,520 cars with dual fuel pump system; includes models made before 1987; includes other Volkswagen models): May stall due to fuel pump in fuel tank seizing up during high ambient temperatures. **Corrective action:** Install modified fuel pump and filter. *(NHTSA Campaign No. 87V053000.)*

SAFETY AND REPAIRS

1990: ''VW Recalls Sciroccos, Cabrios,'' *Automotive News*, December 16, 1991, p. 18. **Note:** 1987-90 models may have faulty fuel tanks.

REPAIR MANUALS

2707 ● Chilton's VW Front Wheel Drive, 1974-1990
Chilton Co.
Chilton Way
Radnor, PA 19089   Ph:(215)964-4000

Published 1990. **Price:** $15.95.

2708 ● Scirocco and Cabriolet Service Manual: 1985-1989, Including 16V
Robert Bentley Publishing, Inc.
1000 Massachusetts Ave.
Cambridge, MA 02138   Ph:(617)547-4170

Price: $39.95.

2709 ● Volkswagen   Electrical   Diagrams   and Troubleshooting Guide
Dianic Publications
P. O. Box 2527
Berkeley, CA 94702   Ph:(415)841-9622

Published 1987. **Editor(s):** Erik Bromberg. **Price:** $18.95.

2710 ● Volkswagen   Water-Cooled,   Front-Drive Performance Handbook
Motorbooks International, Inc.
729 Prospect Ave.
Osceola, WI 54020   Ph:(715)294-3345

Published 1987. **Editor(s):** Greg Haven. **Price:** $18.95.

OTHER INFORMATION SOURCES

2711 ● European Car
Argus Publishers Corp.
12100 Wilshire Blvd., Ste. 250   Ph:(213)820-3601
Los Angeles, CA 90025   Fax:(213)207-9388

Magazine covering Volkswagen, Porsche, Mercedes-Benz, Audi, Ferrari, Jaguar, and BMW automobiles. Bimonthly. **Editor(s):** Greg N. Brown. **Price:** $11.00 per year; $2.75 per issue.

2712 ● Small on Safety: The Design-In Danger of the Volkswagen
Center for Auto Safety
2001 S St. NW, Ste. 410
Washington, DC 20009   Ph:(202)328-7700

2713 ● VW and Porsche
Argus Publishers Corp.
12100 Wilshire Blvd., Ste. 250   Ph:(213)820-3601
Los Angeles, CA 90025   Fax:(213)207-9388

Offers articles of interest to enthusiasts of Volkswagen and Porsche models. Bimonthly. **Editor(s):** Greg Brown. **Price:** $11.00/yr.; $2.75/issue.

2714 ● VW Autoist
Volkswagen Club of America, Inc.
PO Box 154
N. Aurora, IL 60542   Ph:(314)821-9091

Carries news items from the national Club and from local chapters, technical advice on the Volkswagen, and "inside dope on new models" in a column from Europe. Bimonthly. **Editor(s):** Fred Ortlip. **Price:** Available to members only.

2715 ● VW Trends
McMullen Publishing, Inc.
2145 W. La Palma Ave.   Ph:(714)635-9040
Anaheim, CA 92801-1785   Fax:(714)533-9979

Magazine for Volkswagen enthusiasts. Monthly. **Editor(s):** Brian Noto.

2716 ● VW Trends
McMullen Publishing
2145 N. La Palma
Anaheim, CA 92801-1785   Ph:(714)635-9040

Features articles of interest to enthusiasts of Volkswagen models. Monthly. **Editor(s):** Robin Hartfiel. **Price:** $15.95/yr.; $2.25/mo.

ASSOCIATIONS

2717 ● Volkswagen Club of America
P.O. Box 154
North Aurora, IL 60542-0154
Shell Tomlin, Pres.   Ph:(708)896-2803

Founded: 1955. **Membership:** 4,000. Owners and enthusiasts of Volkswagen and Audi automobiles. Disseminates information on maintenance and restoration of Volkswagen vehicles. Local clubs hold rallies, parties, and other automotive and social events. **Convention/Meeting:** Annual, always summer.

2718 ● Volkswagen Convertible Owners of America
2650 Walnut St., Rm. H
Tustin, CA 92680
Rich Kimball, Pres.

Founded: 1983. **Membership:** 200. Individuals interested in Volkswagen convertibles. Shares information; aids in restoration efforts; promotes VW convertible events.

VOLKSWAGEN CORRADO (1990-92)

Introduced into Volkswagen's 1990 lineup, the Corrado model is made in Onsabrueck, Germany. According to *The Complete Car Cost Guide*, the Corrado was among the lowest in insurance costs and fuel costs for its vehicle category in 1990.

1991 Volkswagen Corrado

MAJOR FEATURES

● Standard equipment for the 1991 Corrado: 1.8L four-cylinder supercharged engine, five-speed manual transmission, four-wheel disc brakes, speed-activated retractable rear spoiler, air conditioning, cruise control, power windows and locks, AM-FM auto-reverse theft-protected cassette stereo, velour interior, tilt steering column, tinted glass, fog lamps, alarm system, rear wiper/washer, and alloy wheels.

PRICE HISTORY

The following new car prices reflect the approximate retail cost of the base model: **1990** - $17,900; **1991** - $19,100; **1992** - $19,860.

DIMENSIONS

Body Style	Years Avail	Wheel Base (in)	Lgth (in)	Ht (in)	Avg Wt (lbs)	Fuel Cap (gal)	Front Hdrm (in)	Front Legrm (in)
3d lbk	90-92	97.3	159.4	51.9	2,675	14.5	37.0	41.7

ENGINES

Type	Displace-ment (L)	Fuel Dly	HP @rpm	Torque @rpm (ft/lbs)	MPG Cty/Hwy	Years Avail
I-4	1.8	FI	158@5600	166@4000	20/28	90-92

KEY: I=in-line engine; V=V engine; F=flat engine; FI=fuel injection; bbl=barrel carburetor; T=turbo; D=diesel; HP=horsepower; MPG=estimated average miles per gallon.

EVALUATIONS, TESTS, AND RANKINGS

1991: "an impressive lack of torque steer . . . . [shifter] linkage is extremely notchy . . . Ride is firm, but not harsh . . . visibility isn't a strong point." **Source:** "VW Corrado: Settinc Course against the Wind," *Autoweek: AutoFile 1991,* 1990, pp. 72-77.

1991: "Radio greatl . . . Feel, sound (or lack of wind noise), handling and appearance are unique . . . Outside rearview mirrors are large and well-placed." **Source:** "Long-Term Update: Volkswagen Corrado," *Road & Track,* May 1991, p. 98.

1991: "Supercharger . . . provides added power at all rpms . . . does provide plenty of zip on the highway." **Source:** "Supercharger adds zip . . . not zoom . . . to VW's Corrado," *Design News,* October 1, 1990, p. 50.

1990: "fun to zip around in, and the power is surprising . . . . gearshift for the five speed manual transmission felt notchy but the transmission worked well with the four cylinder engine." **Source:** "Corrado Thinks Small, Fast and Fun," *The Detroit News,* April 18, 1990, pp. C1-C2.

1990: "one of the quietest Volkswagens we've ever driven . . . a financially attractive alternative to the all-too-common sports coupes of the Western world." **Source:** "Volkswagen Corrado G60: Shaped and driven by the wind," *Road & Track,* November 1989, pp. 66-70.

1990: "decidedly chopped appearance . . . often corners on three wheels . . . ragged unpredictable behavior at the limit of adhesion, particularly during aggressive maneuvers." **Source:** "Coupes du Jour," *Popular Science,* February 1990, pp. 50-52, 56-57.

1990: "cruises comfortably . . . stable ride on all road surfaces . . . wet and dry." **Source:** "Automotive Newsfront: Porche Challenger," *Popular Science,* March 1989, pp. 20,22.

RECALLS

1990-91: (8,500 passenger cars): The fuel filter housing, which serves as the base for the fuel pump could deform, resulting in the fuel pump becoming loose. Can cause reduced fuel flow to the engine, resulting in possible driveability problems and vehicle stalling. **Corrective action:** Replace fuel filter. *(NHTSA Campaign No. 91V068000.)*

REPAIR MANUALS

2719 ● **Volkswagen Corrado Official Factory Repair Manual: 1989-1990**
Robert Bentley Publishing, Inc.
1000 Massachusetts Ave.
Cambridge, MA 02138   Ph:(617)547-4170

Published 1989.

2720 ● **Volkswagen   Electrical   Diagrams   and Troubleshooting Guide**
Dianic Publications
P. O. Box 2527
Berkeley, CA 94702   Ph:(415)841-9622

Published 1987. **Editor(s):** Erik Bromberg. **Price:** $18.95.

2721 ● **Volkswagen   Water-Cooled,   Front-Drive Performance Handbook**
Motorbooks International, Inc.
729 Prospect Ave.
Osceola, WI 54020   Ph:(715)294-3345

Published 1987. **Editor(s):** Greg Haven. **Price:** $18.95.

OTHER INFORMATION SOURCES

2722 ● **European Car**
Argus Publishers Corp.
12100 Wilshire Blvd., Ste. 250   Ph:(213)820-3601
Los Angeles, CA 90025   Fax:(213)207-9388

Magazine covering Volkswagen, Porsche, Mercedes-Benz, Audi, Ferrari, Jaguar, and BMW automobiles. Bimonthly. **Editor(s):** Greg N. Brown. **Price:** $11.00 per year; $2.75 per issue.

2723 ● **Small on Safety: The Design-In Danger of the Volkswagen**
Center for Auto Safety
2001 S St. NW, Ste. 410
Washington, DC 20009   Ph:(202)328-7700

2724 ● **VW and Porsche**
Argus Publishers Corp.
12100 Wilshire Blvd., Ste. 250   Ph:(213)820-3601
Los Angeles, CA 90025   Fax:(213)207-9388

Offers articles of interest to enthusiasts of Volkswagen and Porsche models. Bimonthly. **Editor(s):** Greg Brown. **Price:** $11.00/yr.; $2.75/issue.

2725 ● **VW Autoist**
Volkswagen Club of America, Inc.
PO Box 154
N. Aurora, IL 60542   Ph:(314)821-9091

Carries news items from the national Club and from local chapters, technical advice on the Volkswagen, and "inside dope on new models" in a column from Europe. Bimonthly. **Editor(s):** Fred Ortlip. **Price:** Available to members only.

2726 ● **VW Trends**
McMullen Publishing, Inc.
2145 W. La Palma Ave.   Ph:(714)635-9040
Anaheim, CA 92801-1785   Fax:(714)533-9979

Magazine for Volkswagen enthusiasts. Monthly. **Editor(s):** Brian Noto.

ASSOCIATIONS

2727 ● Volkswagen Club of America
P.O. Box 154
North Aurora, IL 60542-0154
Shell Tomlin, Pres.   Ph:(708)896-2803

Founded: 1955. **Membership:** 4,000. Owners and enthusiasts of Volkswagen and Audi automobiles. Disseminates information on maintenance and restoration of Volkswagen vehicles. Local clubs hold rallies, parties, and other automotive and social events. **Convention/Meeting:** Annual, always summer.

VOLKSWAGEN FOX (1987-92)

Produced in San Paulo, Brazil since 1987, the Fox line is Volkswagen's entry-level car model. The Fox Wagon and Fox GL Sport were dropped after the 1990 model year.

1991 Volkswagen Fox

MAJOR FEATURES

● Fox standard equipment for 1991 includes: 1.8L engine, four-speed manual transmission, rear window defogger, and cloth reclining front bucket seats.

● Fox GL adds as 1992 standard equipment: five-speed manual transmission, child-safety rear door locks, tinted glass, upgraded carpet, velour upholstery, other exterior body stylings, and upgraded tires.

● Fox GL Wagon added to the Fox GL as 1990 standard equipment: folding rear seat.

● Fox GL Sport added as 1990 standard equipment: other exterior body stylings and an upgraded interior.

PRICE HISTORY

The following new car prices reflect the approximate retail cost of the base model: **1987** - $5,690; **1988** - $6,590; **1989** - $6,890; **1990** - $7,225; **1991** - $7,370; **1992** - $7,670.

DIMENSIONS

Body Style	Years Avail	Wheel Base (in)	Lgth (in)	Ht (in)	Avg Wt (lbs)	Fuel Cap (gal)	Front Hdrm (in)	Front Legrm (in)
2d cpe	87-92	92.8	163.4	53.7	2,172	12.4	36.6	41.1
4d sdn	89-92	92.8	163.4	53.7	2,238	12.4	36.6	41.1
3d wgn	90-90	92.8	163.4	54.5	2,249	12.4	36.6	41.1
3d wgn	89-89	92.8	163.4	53.7	2,214	12.4	36.6	41.1

ENGINES

Type	Displace-ment (L)	Fuel Dly	HP @rpm	Torque @rpm (ft/lbs)	MPG Cty/Hwy	Years Avail
I-4	1.8	FI	81@5500	93@3250	25/33	87-92

KEY: I=in-line engine; V=V engine; F=flat engine; FI=fuel injection; bbl=barrel carburetor; T=turbo; D=diesel; HP=horsepower; MPG=estimated average miles per gallon.

EVALUATIONS, TESTS, AND RANKINGS

1989: "5-speed makes the greatest contribution to the Fox's sporty feel ... gearshift linkage ... is more direct and less rubbery than anything else VW offers ... 11.7 seconds to reach 60 mph." **Source:** "Driving Impressions: Volkswagen Fox GL Sport," *Road & Track*, January 1989, p. 64.

1988: "[The Fox's] straight-lined sheetmetal could use a rounded edge or two .... Headroom is abundant, even for over-six-footers." **Source:** "Best Econosedan," *Car and Driver*, December 1988, pp. 54-58, 60, 63, 64-6, 68.

1988: "Fit and finish is solid and trim levels are extraordinarily high ... Steering is a tad heavy .... The engine's broad powerband makes it flexible enough. . .in the absence of a 5-speed's ratios." **Source:** "Volkswagen Fox GL Wagon," *Motor Trend*, February 1988, pp. 91-2, 94.

1987: "if the luster of ... Beetle rubs off ... could be Volkswagen's best year in the United States since 1980." **Source:** "Remember the Beetle! VW re-enters the low-priced market with a sly new Fox," *The Detroit News*, March 29, 1987, pp. D1-D4.

RECALLS

1991: (2,000 passenger cars): Metal fuel lines with an incorrect contour were installed in the engine compartment. Can cause the metal fuel line to rub against the intake manifold, which could cause a fuel line leak, and result in an engine compartment fire. **Corrective action:** Replace fuel line with correctly contoured fuel line. *(NHTSA Campaign No. 91V087000.)*

1987-89: (104,000 cars): Steering wheel/shaft designed to use surface friction may loose friction if grease or oil is present on coneshaped surface of steering shaft. Could result in loosening and separation of steering wheel. **Corrective action:** Remove steering wheel and clean friction surface and install spring retainer, replace steering wheel nut with self-locking nut. *(NHTSA Campaign No. 88V187000.)*

1987: (138 cars with alloy sport wheels): Rear tire sidewalls may chafe against wheel housing under heavy loading conditions. **Corrective action:** Install different type sport or standard wheels. *(NHTSA Campaign No. 87V162000.)*

REPAIR MANUALS

2728 ● Chilton's VW Front Wheel Drive, 1974-1990
Chilton Co.
Chilton Way
Radnor, PA 19089   Ph:(215)964-4000

Published 1990. **Price:** $15.95.

2729 ● Volkswagen Electrical Diagrams and Troubleshooting Guide
Dianic Publications
P. O. Box 2527
Berkeley, CA 94702   Ph:(415)841-9622

Published 1987. **Editor(s):** Erik Bromberg. **Price:** $18.95.

2730 ● Volkswagen Fox Service Manual: 1987-1989, Including Wagon and Sport
Robert Bentley Publishing, Inc.
1000 Massachusetts Ave.
Cambridge, MA 02138   Ph:(671)547-4170

Price: $39.95.

2731 ● Volkswagen Water-Cooled, Front-Drive Performance Handbook
Motorbooks International, Inc.
729 Prospect Ave.
Osceola, WI 54020   Ph:(715)294-3345

Published 1987. **Editor(s):** Greg Haven. **Price:** $18.95.

OTHER INFORMATION SOURCES

2732 ● European Car
Argus Publishers Corp.
12100 Wilshire Blvd., Ste. 250   Ph:(213)820-3601
Los Angeles, CA 90025   Fax:(213)207-9388

Magazine covering Volkswagen, Porsche, Mercedes-Benz, Audi, Ferrari, Jaguar, and BMW automobiles. Bimonthly. **Editor(s):** Greg N. Brown. **Price:** $11.00 per year; $2.75 per issue.

2733 ● Small on Safety: The Design-In Danger of the Volkswagen
Center for Auto Safety
2001 S St. NW, Ste. 410
Washington, DC 20009   Ph:(202)328-7700

2734 ● VW and Porsche
Argus Publishers Corp.
12100 Wilshire Blvd., Ste. 250   Ph:(213)820-3601
Los Angeles, CA 90025   Fax:(213)207-9388

Offers articles of interest to enthusiasts of Volkswagen and Porsche models. Bimonthly. **Editor(s):** Greg Brown. **Price:** $11.00/yr.; $2.75/issue.

2735 ● VW Autoist
Volkswagen Club of America, Inc.
PO Box 154
N. Aurora, IL 60542   Ph:(314)821-9091

Carries news items from the national Club and from local chapters, technical advice on the Volkswagen, and ``inside dope on new models'' in a column from Europe. Bimonthly. **Editor(s):** Fred Ortlip. **Price:** Available to members only.

2736 ● VW Trends
McMullen Publishing, Inc.
2145 W. La Palma Ave.   Ph:(714)635-9040
Anaheim, CA 92801-1785   Fax:(714)533-9979

Magazine for Volkswagen enthusiasts. Monthly. **Editor(s):** Brian Noto.

ASSOCIATIONS

2737 ● Volkswagen Club of America
P.O. Box 154
North Aurora, IL 60542-0154
Shell Tomlin, Pres.   Ph:(708)896-2803

Founded: 1955. **Membership:** 4,000. Owners and enthusiasts of Volkswagen and Audi automobiles. Disseminates information on maintenance and restoration of Volkswagen vehicles. Local clubs hold rallies, parties, and other automotive and social events. **Convention/Meeting:** Annual, always summer.

VOLKSWAGEN GOLF (1987-91)

The Volkswagen Golf, descendant of the Rabbit model, is produced in Volkswagen's Puebla, Mexico plant. According to the Highway Loss Data Institute, Volkswagen Golf had the most favorable score in the overall injury category in the small, four-door model class for 1988-90 models.

1991 Volkswagen Golf GL

MAJOR FEATURES

● Golf GL has as 1992 standard equipment: 1.8L engine, five-speed transmission, tinted glass, rear defogger, power-assisted brakes, tilt steering column, and radio prep (speakers, wiring, and antenna).

● Golf ECOdiesel adds as 1992 standard equipment: 1.6-liter turbo diesel engine.

PRICE HISTORY

The following new car prices reflect the approximate retail cost of the base model: **1987** - $8,390; **1988** - $7,990; **1989** - $8,465; **1990** - $8,695; **1991** - $9,270; **1992** - $9,640.

DIMENSIONS

Body Style	Years Avail	Wheel Base (in)	Lgth (in)	Ht (in)	Avg Wt (lbs)	Fuel Cap (gal)	Front Hdrm (in)	Front Legrm (in)
3d lbk	87-92	97.3	159.1	55.7	2,320	14.5	38.1	39.5
5d lbk	89-92	97.3	159.1	55.7	2,375	14.5	38.1	39.5

ENGINES

Type	Displacement (L)	Fuel Dly	HP @rpm	Torque @rpm (ft/lbs)	MPG Cty/Hwy	Years Avail
I-4	1.8	FI	85@5250	96@3000	na	87-87
I-4	1.8	FI	102@5250	110@3250	na	87-87
I-4	1.8	FI	105@5400	110@3400	na	88-88
I-4	1.8	FI	100@5400	107@3400	25/32	88-92
I-4D	1.6	FI	52@4800	71@2000	na	87-87

KEY: I=in-line engine; V=V engine; F=flat engine; FI=fuel injection; bbl=barrel carburetor; T=turbo; D=diesel; HP=horsepower; MPG=estimated average miles per gallon.

EVALUATIONS, TESTS, AND RANKINGS

1992: ``Golf is one impressive car: stylish, quiet, with great handling and a controlled yet supple ride.'' **Source:** ``New for '92: Volkswagen Golf and Golf VR6,'' *Road & Track*, December 1991, pp. 90, 92, 94.

1988: ``interior is a bit spartan ... All of the gauges are clear, and the controls are within easy reach .... terrific fun.''

Source: ''Eight for Ten,'' *Car and Driver*, December 1988, pp. 54-58, 60, 63, 64-66, 68.

RECALLS

1990: (11,000 vehicles): Omission of air ducts intended to guide flow of cooling air to left and right front brake calipers could allow brake fluid to exceed allowable operating temperature, resulting in reduced braking pressure. **Corrective action:** Install missing left and right front air ducts. *(NHTSA Campaign No. 90V142000.)*

1988: (1,900 cars with cruise control; includes other Volkswagen models): May not be marked with letters RES identifying resume function. **Corrective action:** Replace switch. *(NHTSA Campaign No. 87V175000.)*

1988: (784 cars with passive restraint seat belt systems; includes other Volkswagen models): Seat belt retractor pawl may not meet hardening specifications. **Corrective action:** Replace front passive restraint seat belt assembly. *(NHTSA Campaign No. 87V182000.)*

1987: (278,520 cars with dual fuel pump system; includes models made before 1987; includes other Volkswagen models): May stall due to fuel pump in fuel tank seizing up during high ambient temperatures. **Corrective action:** Install modified fuel pump and filter. *(NHTSA Campaign No. 87V053000.)*

1987: (10,000 cars with alloy wheels; includes other Volkswagen models): Front left wheel lug nuts possibly improperly torqued. Wheel may loosen over period of time. **Corrective action:** Re-torque left front wheel lug nuts. *(NHTSA Campaign No. 87V063000.)*

REPAIR MANUALS

2738 ● Chilton's VW Front Wheel Drive, 1974-1990
Chilton Co.
Chilton Way
Radnor, PA 19089   Ph:(215)964-4000

Published 1990. **Price:** $15.95.

2739 ● GTI, Golf and Jetta Service Manual: 1985-1989: Gasoline, Diesel, and Turbo Diesel, Including Golf, GT, Jetta GLI and 16V Models
Robert Bentley Publishing, Inc.
1000 Massachusetts Ave.
Cambridge, MA 02138   Ph:(617)547-4170

Price: $39.95.

2740 ● Improve and Modify Your VW Golf and Jetta (Including GTI)
Motorbooks International
729 Prospect Ave.
Osceola, WI 54020   Ph:(715)294-3345

Published 1988. **Editor(s):** Lindsay Porter and Dave Pollard. **Price:** $19.95.

2741 ● Volkswagen Electrical Diagrams and Troubleshooting Guide
Dianic Publications
P. O. Box 2527
Berkeley, CA 94702   Ph:(415)841-9622

Published 1987. **Editor(s):** Erik Bromberg. **Price:** $18.95.

2742 ● Volkswagen Water-Cooled, Front-Drive Performance Handbook
Motorbooks International, Inc.
729 Prospect Ave.
Osceola, WI 54020   Ph:(715)294-3345

Published 1987. **Editor(s):** Greg Haven. **Price:** $18.95.

OTHER INFORMATION SOURCES

2743 ● European Car
Argus Publishers Corp.
12100 Wilshire Blvd., Ste. 250   Ph:(213)820-3601
Los Angeles, CA 90025   Fax:(213)207-9388

Magazine covering Volkswagen, Porsche, Mercedes-Benz, Audi, Ferrari, Jaguar, and BMW automobiles. Bimonthly. **Editor(s):** Greg N. Brown. **Price:** $11.00 per year; $2.75 per issue.

2744 ● Small on Safety: The Design-In Danger of the Volkswagen
Center for Auto Safety
2001 S St. NW, Ste. 410
Washington, DC 20009   Ph:(202)328-7700

2745 ● VW and Porsche
Argus Publishers Corp.
12100 Wilshire Blvd., Ste. 250   Ph:(213)820-3601
Los Angeles, CA 90025   Fax:(213)207-9388

Offers articles of interest to enthusiasts of Volkswagen and Porsche models. Bimonthly. **Editor(s):** Greg Brown. **Price:** $11.00/yr.; $2.75/issue.

2746 ● VW Autoist
Volkswagen Club of America, Inc.
PO Box 154
N. Aurora, IL 60542   Ph:(314)821-9091

Carries news items from the national Club and from local chapters, technical advice on the Volkswagen, and ''inside dope on new models'' in a column from Europe. Bimonthly. **Editor(s):** Fred Ortlip. **Price:** Available to members only.

2747 ● VW Trends
McMullen Publishing, Inc.
2145 W. La Palma Ave.   Ph:(714)635-9040
Anaheim, CA 92801-1785   Fax:(714)533-9979

Magazine for Volkswagen enthusiasts. Monthly. **Editor(s):** Brian Noto.

ASSOCIATIONS

2748 ● Volkswagen Club of America
P.O. Box 154
North Aurora, IL 60542-0154
Shell Tomlin, Pres.   Ph:(708)896-2803

Founded: 1955. **Membership:** 4,000. Owners and enthusiasts of Volkswagen and Audi automobiles. Disseminates information on maintenance and restoration of Volkswagen vehicles. Local clubs hold rallies, parties, and other automotive and social events. **Convention/Meeting:** Annual, always summer.

2749 ● Volkswagen Convertible Owners of America
2650 Walnut St., Rm. H
Tustin, CA 92680
Rich Kimball, Pres.

Founded: 1983. **Membership:** 200. Individuals interested in

Volkswagen convertibles. Shares information; aids in restoration efforts; promotes VW convertible events.

VOLKSWAGEN GTI (1987-92)

Sportier variant of the Golf model, GTI is produced in Wolfsburg, Germany.

1991 Volkswagen GTI 16V

MAJOR FEATURES

● Volkswagen GTI has as 1992 standard equipment: 1.8L SOHC engine, 5-speed manual transmission, sport suspension, height-adjustable steering column, power-assisted steering, sport seats, radio prep (speakers, wiring, and antenna), rear window defogger, tinted glass, and upgraded tires.

● GTI 16V, in addition to the above, adds: 2.0-liter 16-valve DOHC engine, front and rear disc brakes, trip computer, split folding rear seats, and alloy wheels.

PRICE HISTORY

The following new car prices reflect the approximate retail cost of the base model: **1987** - $12,240; **1988** - $12,995; **1989** - $13,650; **1990** - $9,995; **1991** - $10,680; **1992** - $11,110.

DIMENSIONS

Body Style	Years Avail	Wheel Base (in)	Lgth (in)	Ht (in)	Avg Wt (lbs)	Fuel Cap (gal)	Front Hdrm (in)	Front Legrm (in)
3d lbk	87-92	97.3	159.1	55.7	2,346	14.5	38.1	39.5

ENGINES

Type	Displace-ment (L)	Fuel Dly	HP @rpm	Torque @rpm (ft/lbs)	MPG Cty/Hwy	Years Avail
I-4	1.8	FI	102@5250	110@3250	23/26	87-87
I-4	1.8	FI	123@5400	120@3400	19/25	88-88
I-4	1.8	FI	105@5400	110@3400	25/32	88-92
I-4	1.8	FI	123@5800	120@4250	22/29	89-89
I-4	2.0	FI	134@5800	133@4400	21/28	90-92

KEY: I=in-line engine; V=V engine; F=flat engine; FI=fuel injection; bbl=barrel carburetor; T=turbo; D=diesel; HP=horsepower; MPG=estimated average miles per gallon.

EVALUATIONS, TESTS, AND RANKINGS

1991: "lacks neither horsepower nor torque, but is somewhat lumpy at idle . . . engine will ping during hard acceleration . . . GTI trademark: a hike-up inside rear wheel dangling about a foot off the pavement." **Source**: "Battling Tops," *Road & Track*, February 1991, pp. 64-70.

1990: "its cockpit is so well set up for the business of driving . . . the GTI is extremely practical." **Source**: "Eleven for Thirteen: Volkswagen GTI," *Car and Driver*, June 1990, pp. 46-50, 52, 61, 63, 64, 66-69.

1988: "a driver's car, it's sturdy, it's a classic." **Source**: "Four Fun Fours: Volkswagen GTI 16V," *Road & Track*, September 1988, pp. 92-96, 99-101.

1988: "a hot performance car, yet with genuine room for four adults." **Source**: "Econo Commandos: Volkswagen GTI 16V," *Popular Mechanics*, July 1988, pp 51-55, 119.

1988: "continues to be one of the most cost-effective choices a budget-bound enthusiast can make." **Source**: "Volkswagen GTI: Farewell to a Favorite Flogger," *Motor Trend*, March 1988, p. 86.

1987: "At a highway cruise of 60 mph . . . the engine feels buzzy, as if it's spinning too hard . . . room for three skinny or two stout adults in the rear (bench) seat. The hatch is large . . . gearshift is light and sure." **Source**: "Volkswagen GTI 16V," *Road & Track*, June 1987, pp. 214-16, 18, 20.

1987: "the engine seems just a tad weak at very low revs . . . corners with aplomb . . . . The back seat is quite roomy. . .rear cargo area is both large and well concealed." **Source**: "Volkswagen GTI 16V," *Motor Trend*, April 1987, pp. 65-67.

RECALLS

1987: (10,000 cars with alloy wheels; includes other Volkswagen models): Front left wheel lug nuts possibly improperly torqued. Wheel may loosen over period of time. **Corrective action**: Re-torque left front wheel lug nuts. *(NHTSA Campaign No. 87V063000.)*

REPAIR MANUALS

2750 ● **Chilton's VW Front Wheel Drive, 1974-1990**
Chilton Co.
Chilton Way
Radnor, PA 19089   Ph:(215)964-4000

Published 1990. **Price**: $15.95.

2751 ● **GTI, Golf and Jetta Service Manual: 1985-1989: Gasoline, Diesel, and Turbo Diesel, Including Golf, GT, Jetta GLI and 16V Models**
Robert Bentley Publishing, Inc.
1000 Massachusetts Ave.
Cambridge, MA 02138   Ph:(617)547-4170

Price: $39.95.

2752 ● **Improve and Modify Your VW Golf and Jetta (Including GTI)**
Motorbooks International
729 Prospect Ave.
Osceola, WI 54020   Ph:(715)294-3345

Published 1988. **Editor(s)**: Lindsay Porter and Dave Pollard. **Price**: $19.95.

2753 ● **Volkswagen Electrical Diagrams and Troubleshooting Guide**
Dianic Publications
P. O. Box 2527
Berkeley, CA 94702   Ph:(415)841-9622

Published 1987. **Editor(s)**: Erik Bromberg. **Price**: $18.95.

**2754 ● Volkswagen   Water-Cooled,   Front-Drive
Performance Handbook**
Motorbooks International, Inc.
729 Prospect Ave.
Osceola, WI 54020   Ph:(715)294-3345

Published 1987. **Editor(s):** Greg Haven. **Price:** $18.95.

OTHER INFORMATION SOURCES

2755 ● European Car
Argus Publishers Corp.
12100 Wilshire Blvd., Ste. 250   Ph:(213)820-3601
Los Angeles, CA 90025   Fax:(213)207-9388

Magazine covering Volkswagen, Porsche, Mercedes-Benz,
Audi, Ferrari, Jaguar, and BMW automobiles. Bimonthly.
Editor(s): Greg N. Brown. **Price:** $11.00 per year; $2.75 per
issue.

**2756 ● Small on Safety: The Design-In Danger of the
Volkswagen**
Center for Auto Safety
2001 S St. NW, Ste. 410
Washington, DC 20009   Ph:(202)328-7700

2757 ● VW and Porsche
Argus Publishers Corp.
12100 Wilshire Blvd., Ste. 250   Ph:(213)820-3601
Los Angeles, CA 90025   Fax:(213)207-9388

Offers articles of interest to enthusiasts of Volkswagen and
Porsche models. Bimonthly. **Editor(s):** Greg Brown. **Price:**
$11.00/yr.; $2.75/issue.

2758 ● VW Autoist
Volkswagen Club of America, Inc.
PO Box 154
N. Aurora, IL 60542   Ph:(314)821-9091

Carries news items from the national Club and from local
chapters, technical advice on the Volkswagen, and ``inside
dope on new models'' in a column from Europe. Bimonthly.
Editor(s): Fred Ortlip. **Price:** Available to members only.

2759 ● VW Trends
McMullen Publishing, Inc.
2145 W. La Palma Ave.   Ph:(714)635-9040
Anaheim, CA 92801-1785   Fax:(714)533-9979

Magazine for Volkswagen enthusiasts. Monthly. **Editor(s):**
Brian Noto.

ASSOCIATIONS

2760 ● Volkswagen Club of America
P.O. Box 154
North Aurora, IL 60542-0154
Shell Tomlin, Pres.   Ph:(708)896-2803

Founded: 1955. **Membership:** 4,000. Owners and enthusiasts
of Volkswagen and Audi automobiles. Disseminates
information on maintenance and restoration of Volkswagen
vehicles. Local clubs hold rallies, parties, and other automotive
and social events. **Convention/Meeting:** Annual, always
summer.

VOLKSWAGEN JETTA (1987-92)

The Volkswagen Jetta is manufactured in Puebla, Mexico, and

is one of the few VW models assembled in North America. The
two-door model was dropped in 1992.

1991 Volkswagen Jetta GL

MAJOR FEATURES

● Volkswagen Jetta GL (both gasoline and diesel models)
1992 standard equipment: 1.8L four cylinder SOHC engine, 5-
speed manual transmission, front spoiler, power-assisted
brakes, power steering, height-adjustable steering column, and
velour upholstery.

● Volkswagen Jetta Carat adds as 1992 standard equipment:
cruise control, central locking, and power windows, locks, and
mirrors, and full wheel covers.

● Volkswagen Jetta GLI 16V adds as 1992 standard
equipment: 2.0L four cylinder 16-valve DOHC engine,
upgraded interior, AM/FM cassette stereo system, and alloy
wheels.

PRICE HISTORY

The following new car prices reflect the approximate retail cost
of the base model: **1987** - $9,590; **1988** - $9,195; **1989** -
$9,690; **1990** - $9,995; **1991** - $10,630; **1992** - $11,670.

DIMENSIONS

Body Style	Years Avail	Wheel Base (in)	Lgth (in)	Ht (in)	Avg Wt (lbs)	Fuel Cap (gal)	Front Hdrm (in)	Front Legrm (in)
2d sdn	87-90	97.3	171.7	55.7	2,275	14.5	38.1	39.5
2d sdn	91-91	97.3	172.6	55.7	2,275	14.5	38.1	39.5
4d sdn	87-90	97.3	171.7	55.7	2,367	14.5	38.1	39.5
4d sdn	91-92	97.3	172.6	55.7	2,330	14.5	38.1	39.5

ENGINES

Type	Displacement (L)	Fuel Dly	HP @rpm	Torque @rpm (ft/lbs)	MPG Cty/Hwy	Years Avail
I-4	1.8	FI	85@5250	96@3000	26/31	87-87
I-4	1.8	FI	102@5250	110@3250	26/31	87-87
I-4	1.8	FI	123@5800	120@4250	22/29	88-89
I-4	1.8	FI	100@5400	107@3400	25/32	88-92
I-4	2.0	FI	134@5800	133@4400	21/28	90-92
I-4D	1.6	FI	52@4800	81@2000	37/40	90-92

KEY: I=in-line engine; V=V engine; F=flat engine; FI=fuel injection;
bbl=barrel carburetor; T=turbo; D=diesel; HP=horsepower;
MPG=estimated average miles per gallon.

EVALUATIONS, TESTS, AND RANKINGS

1990: ``has even more horsepower . . . ride is nicely controlled
with a bit of stiffness but no harshness, and the steering
response . . . is excellent . . . brakes were up to the task.''

Source: "European Panache, Economy Car Price," *Motor Trend,* August 1990, pp. 90-92.

1989: "interior is very functional . . . shifter is suprisingly notchy . . . engine is a bit buzzy . . . fair amount of road noise."
Source: "Best Sellers: Volkswagen Jetta Carat," *Popular Mechanics,* July 1989, pp. 60-63, 120-122.

1989: "Recaro seats . . . are ideal for long-distance drives . . . will go from 0 to 60 mph in 9.3 seconds, and it has a top speed of 119 mph . . . anti-lock braking system worked flawlessly."
Source: "Volkswagen Jetta GLI 16V," *Motor Trend,* July 1989, pp. 127, 131.

1988: "Spirited performance; balanced, predictable handling . . . respectable braking; user-friendly interior with great ergonomics." **Source:** "Volkswagen Jetta GLI 16V," *Road & Track,* June 1988, pp. 70, 74, 76.

1988: "gear lever is . . . slow, notchy, and unreliable with respect to gear placement . . . . handling . . . is precise." **Source:** "Volkswagen Jetta GLI 16V," *Motor Trend,* January 1988, pp. 42-43.

RECALLS

1991: (465 vehicles): Front brake hoses of insufficient length were installed, which stretch and develop cracks. Could result in brake fluid leakage, with loss of fluid pressure and braking ability. **Corrective action:** Replace both brake hoses. *(NHTSA Campaign No. 90V173000.)*

1991: (550 passenger cars; California models equipped with cruise control): The lock nut of the cruise control rod for the operating servo may not have been properly torqued during manufacture. Inadequate torque of the lock nut could allow the rod adjustment to change. This could increase the engine idle speed, and possibly increase stopping distance with a potential for a vehicle accident. **Corrective action:** Check and ensure proper lock nut torque on the cruise control rod. *(NHTSA Campaign No. 91V064000.)*

1990: (225 cars): Power steering pump bracket breakage could allow pump to loosen and drive belt to slip, resulting in need for increased steering force with potential for an accident. **Corrective action:** Replace power steering pump bracket. *(NHTSA Campaign No. 90V007000.)*

1990: (11,000 vehicles): Omission of air ducts intended to guide flow of cooling air to left and right front brake calipers could allow brake fluid to exceed allowable operating temperature, resulting in reduced braking pressure. **Corrective action:** Install missing left and right front air ducts. *(NHTSA Campaign No. 90V142000.)*

1988: (1,900 cars with cruise control; includes other Volkswagen models): May not be marked with letters RES identifying resume functions. **Corrective action:** Replace switch. *(NHTSA Campaign No. 87V175000.)*

1988: (784 cars with passive restraint seat belt systems; includes other Volkswagen models): Seat belt retractor pawl may not meet hardening specifications. **Corrective action:** Replace front passive restraint seat belt assembly. *(NHTSA Campaign No. 87V182000.)*

1988: (1,700 passenger vehicles; includes the Volkswagen Jetta and Volkswagen Jetta GL): Brake roosters have been improperly assembled with two halves of booster unit insufficiently connected. Brake booster halves could separate under heavy brake application and braking power would suddenly diminish which could result in an accident. **Corrective action:** Replace brake boosters as necessary. *(NHTSA Campaign No. 88V144000.)*

1987-89: (8,000 cars): Incorrectly contoured metal brake line leading to right front wheel may be damaged by preheating tube chafing against it, resulting in leaking brake line. **Corrective action:** Curve or replace right front brake line. *(NHTSA Campaign No. 89V221000.)*

1987: (278,520 cars with dual fuel pump system; includes models made before 1987; includes other Volkswagen models): May stall due to fuel pump in fuel tank seizing up during high ambient temperatures. **Corrective action:** Install modified fuel pump and filter. *(NHTSA Campaign No. 87V053000.)*

REPAIR MANUALS

2761 ● **Chilton's VW Front Wheel Drive, 1974-1990**
Chilton Co.
Chilton Way
Radnor, PA 19089   Ph:(215)964-4000

Published 1990. **Price:** $15.95.

2762 ● **GTI, Golf and Jetta Service Manual: 1985-1989: Gasoline, Diesel, and Turbo Diesel, Including Golf, GT, Jetta GLI and 16V Models**
Robert Bentley Publishing, Inc.
1000 Massachusetts Ave.
Cambridge, MA 02138   Ph:(617)547-4170

Price: $39.95.

2763 ● **Improve and Modify Your VW Golf and Jetta (Including GTI)**
Motorbooks International
729 Prospect Ave.
Osceola, WI 54020   Ph:(715)294-3345

Published 1988. **Editor(s):** Lindsay Porter and Dave Pollard. **Price:** $19.95.

2764 ● **Volkswagen   Electrical   Diagrams   and Troubleshooting Guide**
Dianic Publications
P. O. Box 2527
Berkeley, CA 94702   Ph:(415)841-9622

Published 1987. **Editor(s):** Erik Bromberg. **Price:** $18.95.

2765 ● **Volkswagen   Water-Cooled,   Front-Drive Performance Handbook**
Motorbooks International, Inc.
729 Prospect Ave.
Osceola, WI 54020   Ph:(715)294-3345

Published 1987. **Editor(s):** Greg Haven. **Price:** $18.95.

OTHER INFORMATION SOURCES

2766 ● **European Car**
Argus Publishers Corp.
12100 Wilshire Blvd., Ste. 250   Ph:(213)820-3601
Los Angeles, CA 90025   Fax:(213)207-9388

Magazine covering Volkswagen, Porsche, Mercedes-Benz, Audi, Ferrari, Jaguar, and BMW automobiles. Bimonthly. **Editor(s):** Greg N. Brown. **Price:** $11.00 per year; $2.75 per issue.

2767 ● Small on Safety: The Design-in Danger of the Volkswagen
Center for Auto Safety
2001 S St. NW, Ste. 410
Washington, DC 20009   Ph:(202)328-7700

2768 ● VW and Porsche
Argus Publishers Corp.
12100 Wilshire Blvd., Ste. 250   Ph:(213)820-3601
Los Angeles, CA 90025   Fax:(213)207-9388

Offers articles of interest to enthusiasts of Volkswagen and Porsche models. Bimonthly. **Editor(s):** Greg Brown. **Price:** $11.00/yr.; $2.75/issue.

2769 ● VW Autoist
Volkswagen Club of America, Inc.
PO Box 154
N. Aurora, IL 60542   Ph:(314)821-9091

Carries news items from the national Club and from local chapters, technical advice on the Volkswagen, and "inside dope on new models" in a column from Europe. Bimonthly. **Editor(s):** Fred Ortlip. **Price:** Available to members only.

2770 ● VW Trends
McMullen Publishing, Inc.
2145 W. La Palma Ave.   Ph:(714)635-9040
Anaheim, CA 92801-1785   Fax:(714)533-9979

Magazine for Volkswagen enthusiasts. Monthly. **Editor(s):** Brian Noto.

ASSOCIATIONS

2771 ● Volkswagen Club of America
P.O. Box 154
North Aurora, IL 60542-0154
Shell Tomlin, Pres.   Ph:(708)896-2803

Founded: 1955. **Membership:** 4,000. Owners and enthusiasts of Volkswagen and Audi automobiles. Disseminates information on maintenance and restoration of Volkswagen vehicles. Local clubs hold rallies, parties, and other automotive and social events. **Convention/Meeting:** Annual, always summer.

VOLKSWAGEN PASSAT (1990-92)

Introduced early in 1990, the Volkswagen Passat is produced in Emden, Germany. According to *The Complete Car Cost Guide*, the Passat GL Wagon had the highest insurance cost for the compact wagon designation in 1990. Selected as nominee for 1990 *Motor Trend's* Import Car of the Year award.

1991 Volkswagen Passat GL Wagon

MAJOR FEATURES

● 1992 Passat GL standard equipment includes: 5-speed manual transmission, height-adjustable steering column, electric rear window defroster, air conditioning, motorized automatic shoulder belt system, power windows, and 195/60 VR14 tires.

● The Passat GL Wagon adds as 1992 standard equipment: rear wiper/washer and roof rails.

PRICE HISTORY

The following new car prices reflect the approximate retail cost of the base model: **1990** - $14,770; **1991** - $14,590; **1992** - $14,950.

DIMENSIONS

Body Style	Years Avail	Wheel Base (in)	Lgth (in)	Ht (in)	Avg Wt (lbs)	Fuel Cap (gal)	Front Hdrm (in)	Front Legrm (in)
4d sdn	90-92	103.3	180.0	56.2	2,985	18.5	38.2	42.5
5d wgn	90-92	103.3	179.9	56.2	3,029	18.5	38.7	42.5

ENGINES

Type	Displace- ment (L)	Fuel Dly	HP @rpm	Torque @rpm (ft/lbs)	MPG Cty/Hwy	Years Avail
I-4	2.0	FI	134@5800	133@4400	21/30	90-92

KEY: I=in-line engine; V=V engine; F=flat engine; FI=fuel injection; bbl=barrel carburetor; T=turbo; D=diesel; HP=horsepower; MPG=estimated average miles per gallon.

EVALUATIONS, TESTS, AND RANKINGS

1991: "excellent space utilization and comfort for both the front-and rear-seat occupants ... handling is crisp ... automatic transmission hinders its performance." **Source:** "New Car Test: Foreign Affairs," *Home Mechanix*, September 1990, pp. 74-76.

1991: "extremely roomy interior ... acceleration is good but fails to inspire ... handsome instrument panel, dashboard and steering wheel." **Source:** "European Influence: Eight sporting sedans with price tags less than $30,000," *Road & Track*, August 1991, pp. 64-65, 80, 84.

1990: "biggest selling points is an impressive interior volume ... interior look borders on austere ... the whole car hung in there and just hammered along." **Source:** "Volkswagen Passat GL," *Motor Trend*, April 1990, pp. 76-78, 82.

1990: "offers the comfort, roominess, cargo capacity, and chassis dynamics of more expensive and sportier sedans." **Source:** "Motor Trend's 1990 Import Car of the Year," *Motor Trend*, March 1990, pp. 44-45, 62-63.

1990: "predictably tart road manners ... impressively well utilized, allowing comfortable accommodations for five." **Source:** "Three Translations of the Family Sedan," *Popular Science*, September 1990, pp. 79-83.

RECALLS

None to date.

REPAIR MANUALS

**2772 ● Volkswagen   Electrical   Diagrams   and
   Troubleshooting Guide**
Dianic Publications
P. O. Box 2527
Berkeley, CA 94702   Ph:(415)841-9622

Published 1987. **Editor(s):** Erik Bromberg. **Price:** $18.95.

**2773 ● Volkswagen Passat Official Factory Repair Manual:
   1989-1991**
Robert Bentley Publishing, Inc.
1000 Massachusetts Ave.
Cambridge, MA 02138   Ph:(617)547-4170

Published 1989.

OTHER INFORMATION SOURCES

2774 ● European Car
Argus Publishers Corp.
12100 Wilshire Blvd., Ste. 250   Ph:(213)820-3601
Los Angeles, CA 90025   Fax:(213)207-9388

Magazine covering Volkswagen, Porsche, Mercedes-Benz,
Audi, Ferrari, Jaguar, and BMW automobiles. Bimonthly.
Editor(s): Greg N. Brown. **Price:** $11.00 per year; $2.75 per
issue.

**2775 ● Small on Safety: The Design-In Danger of the
   Volkswagen**
Center for Auto Safety
2001 S St. NW, Ste. 410
Washington, DC 20009   Ph:(202)328-7700

2776 ● VW and Porsche
Argus Publishers Corp.
12100 Wilshire Blvd., Ste. 250   Ph:(213)820-3601
Los Angeles, CA 90025   Fax:(213)207-9388

Offers articles of interest to enthusiasts of Volkswagen and
Porsche models. Bimonthly. **Editor(s):** Greg Brown. **Price:**
$11.00/yr.; $2.75/issue.

2777 ● VW Autoist
Volkswagen Club of America, Inc.
PO Box 154
N. Aurora, IL 60542   Ph:(314)821-9091

Carries news items from the national Club and from local
chapters, technical advice on the Volkswagen, and "inside
dope on new models" in a column from Europe. Bimonthly.
Editor(s): Fred Ortlip. **Price:** Available to members only.

2778 ● VW Trends
McMullen Publishing, Inc.
2145 W. La Palma Ave.   Ph:(714)635-9040
Anaheim, CA 92801-1785   Fax:(714)533-9979

Magazine for Volkswagen enthusiasts. Monthly. **Editor(s):**
Brian Noto.

ASSOCIATIONS

2779 ● Volkswagen Club of America
P.O. Box 154
North Aurora, IL 60542-0154
Shell Tomlin, Pres.   Ph:(708)896-2803

Founded: 1955. **Membership:** 4,000. Owners and enthusiasts
of Volkswagen and Audi automobiles. Disseminates
information on maintenance and restoration of Volkswagen
vehicles. Local clubs hold rallies, parties, and other automotive

and social events. **Convention/Meeting:** Annual, always
summer.

VOLKSWAGEN QUANTUM (1987-88)

Manufactured in Germany through the 1988 model year, the
Quantum was similar in looks to the Audi 4000.

MAJOR FEATURES

● Quantum GL and Quantum GL Wagon had as 1988
standard equipment: air conditioning, power-assisted brakes,
rack-and-pinion steering, tinted glass, dual mirrors, height-
adjustable driver's seat, and theft-protected AM/FM stereo
cassette.

● Quantum Syncro Wagon added as 1988 standard
equipment: five-speed manual transmission, extra-low first
gear, and various suspension adjustments.

PRICE HISTORY

The following new car prices reflect the approximate retail cost
of the base model: **1987** - $13,920; **1988** - $17,975.

DIMENSIONS

Body Style	Years Avail	Wheel Base (in)	Lgth (in)	Ht (in)	Avg Wt (lbs)	Fuel Cap (gal)	Front Hdrm (in)	Front Legrm (in)
4d sdn	87-88	100.4	179.5	54.8	2,646	15.8	38.2	42.3
5d wgn	87-88	100.4	180.7	58.0	2,745	15.8	38.1	42.3

ENGINES

Type	Displace- ment (L)	Fuel Dly	HP @rpm	Torque @rpm (ft/lbs)	MPG Cty/Hwy	Years Avail
I-5	2.2	FI	110@5500	122@2400	19/24	87-88
I-5	2.2	FI	115@5500	126@3000	17/21	87-88

KEY: I=in-line engine; V=V engine; F=flat engine; FI=fuel injection;
bbl=barrel   carburetor;   T=turbo;   D=diesel;   HP=horsepower;
MPG=estimated average miles per gallon.

EVALUATIONS, TESTS, AND RANKINGS

1988: "One of the Quantum [Syncro's] most impressive
features is its power assisted rack-and-pinion steering . . .
virtually no tail wagging . . . the Syncro's disc brakes . . .
[provide] powerful, fade-free stops." **Source:** "Snow White
and the Seven AWDs," *Road & Track*, May 1988, pp. 56-63,
67-70.

1987: "respectable power, better-than average stash space."
Source: "The Pick of the 4WD's," *Skiing*, October 1987, p.
250.

RECALLS

None to date.

REPAIR MANUALS

2780 ● Chilton's VW Front Wheel Drive, 1974-1990
Chilton Co.
Chilton Way
Radnor, PA 19089   Ph:(215)964-4000

Published 1990. **Price:** $15.95.

2781 ● Quantum Official Factory Repair Manual: 1982-1988, Gasoline and Turbo Diesel, including Wagon and Syncro

Robert Bentley Publishing, Inc.
1000 Massachusetts Ave.
Cambridge, MA 02138 Ph:(617)547-4170

Price: $89.95.

2782 ● Volkswagen Electrical Diagrams and Troubleshooting Guide

Dianic Publications
P. O. Box 2527
Berkeley, CA 94702 Ph:(415)841-9622

Published 1987. **Editor(s):** Erik Bromberg. **Price:** $18.95.

2783 ● Volkswagen Quantum

Peter Allen Video Productions
38-C Otis St.
West Babylon, NY 11704 Ph:(516)643-4372

The Quantum's engine is dissected for a demonstration of tune-up and basic maintenance. **Release date:** 1986. **Producer:** Peter Allen Productions. **Acquisition:** Purchase.

2784 ● Volkswagen Water-Cooled, Front-Drive Performance Handbook

Motorbooks International, Inc.
729 Prospect Ave.
Osceola, WI 54020 Ph:(715)294-3345

Published 1987. **Editor(s):** Greg Haven. **Price:** $18.95.

OTHER INFORMATION SOURCES

2785 ● European Car

Argus Publishers Corp.
12100 Wilshire Blvd., Ste. 250 Ph:(213)820-3601
Los Angeles, CA 90025 Fax:(213)207-9388

Magazine covering Volkswagen, Porsche, Mercedes-Benz, Audi, Ferrari, Jaguar, and BMW automobiles. Bimonthly. **Editor(s):** Greg N. Brown. **Price:** $11.00 per year; $2.75 per issue.

2786 ● Small on Safety: The Design-in Danger of the Volkswagen

Center for Auto Safety
2001 S St. NW, Ste. 410
Washington, DC 20009 Ph:(202)328-7700

2787 ● VW and Porsche

Argus Publishers Corp.
12100 Wilshire Blvd., Ste. 250 Ph:(213)820-3601
Los Angeles, CA 90025 Fax:(213)207-9388

Offers articles of interest to enthusiasts of Volkswagen and Porsche models. Bimonthly. **Editor(s):** Greg Brown. **Price:** $11.00/yr.; $2.75/issue.

2788 ● VW Autoist

Volkswagen Club of America, Inc.
PO Box 154
N. Aurora, IL 60542 Ph:(314)821-9091

Carries news items from the national Club and from local chapters, technical advice on the Volkswagen, and "inside dope on new models" in a column from Europe. Bimonthly. **Editor(s):** Fred Ortlip. **Price:** Available to members only.

2789 ● VW Trends

McMullen Publishing, Inc.
2145 W. La Palma Ave. Ph:(714)635-9040
Anaheim, CA 92801-1785 Fax:(714)533-9979

Magazine for Volkswagen enthusiasts. Monthly. **Editor(s):** Brian Noto.

ASSOCIATIONS

2790 ● Volkswagen Club of America

P.O. Box 154
North Aurora, IL 60542-0154
Shell Tomlin, Pres. Ph:(708)896-2803

Founded: 1955. **Membership:** 4,000. Owners and enthusiasts of Volkswagen and Audi automobiles. Disseminates information on maintenance and restoration of Volkswagen vehicles. Local clubs hold rallies, parties, and other automotive and social events. **Convention/Meeting:** Annual, always summer.

VOLKSWAGEN SCIROCCO (1987-88)

Made in Germany, the Scirocco was phased out of Volkswagen's model line in 1988, and replaced, in part, by the GTI.

MAJOR FEATURES

● The Scirocco had as 1988 standard equipment: 4-speed manual transmission, power steering, power-assisted brakes.

● The Scirocco 16V added as 1988 standard equipment: front air dam, fender flares, rocker-panel extensions, an upgraded sport suspension, four-wheel disc brakes, and upgraded tires.

PRICE HISTORY

The following new car prices reflect the approximate retail cost of the base model: **1987** - $11,110; **1988** - $14,440.

DIMENSIONS

Body Style	Years Avail	Wheel Base (in)	Lgth (in)	Ht (in)	Avg Wt (lbs)	Fuel Cap (gal)	Front Hdrm (in)	Front Legrm (in)
3d lbk	87-88	94.5	165.7	51.4	2,196	13.8	36.6	42.2

ENGINES

Type	Displacement (L)	Fuel Dly	HP @rpm	Torque @rpm (ft/lbs)	MPG Cty/Hwy	Years Avail
I-4	1.8	FI	90@5500	100@3000	24/29	87-87
I-4	1.8	FI	123@5800	120@4250	22/28	87-88

KEY: I=in-line engine; V=V engine; F=flat engine; FI=fuel injection; bbl=barrel carburetor; D=diesel; T=turbo; HP=horsepower; MPG=estimated average miles per gallon.

EVALUATIONS, TESTS, AND RANKINGS

1987: " ... heavyweight contender for the all-around-performance and satisfaction-per-dollar titles." **Source:** "Volkswagen Scirocco 16V," *Car and Driver—Buyers Guide 1988*, 1988, p. 39.

RECALLS

1987: (278,520 cars with dual fuel pump system; includes models made before 1987; includes other Volkswagen models):

May stall due to fuel pump in fuel tank seizing up during high ambient temperatures. **Corrective action:** Install modified fuel pump and filter. *(NHTSA Campaign No. 87V053000.)*

SAFETY AND REPAIRS

1988: "VW recalls Sciroccos, Cabrios," *Automotive News,* December 16, 1991, p. 18. **Note:** 1987-88 models may have faulty fuel tanks.

REPAIR MANUALS

2791 ● Chilton's VW Front Wheel Drive, 1974-1990
Chilton Co.
Chilton Way
Radnor, PA 19089   Ph:(215)964-4000

Published 1990. **Price:** $15.95.

2792 ● Volkswagen   Electrical   Diagrams   and Troubleshooting Guide
Dianic Publications
P. O. Box 2527
Berkeley, CA 94702   Ph:(415)841-9622

Published 1987. **Editor(s):** Erik Bromberg. **Price:** $18.95.

2793 ● Volkswagen   Water-Cooled,   Front-Drive Performance Handbook
Motorbooks International, Inc.
729 Prospect Ave.
Osceola, WI 54020   Ph:(715)294-3345

Published 1987. **Editor(s):** Greg Haven. **Price:** $18.95.

OTHER INFORMATION SOURCES

2794 ● European Car
Argus Publishers Corp.
12100 Wilshire Blvd., Ste. 250   Ph:(213)820-3601
Los Angeles, CA 90025   Fax:(213)207-9388

Magazine covering Volkswagen, Porsche, Mercedes-Benz, Audi, Ferrari, Jaguar, and BMW automobiles. Bimonthly. **Editor(s):** Greg N. Brown. **Price:** $11.00 per year; $2.75 per issue.

2795 ● Small on Safety: The Design-In Danger of the Volkswagen
Center for Auto Safety
2001 S St. NW, Ste. 410
Washington, DC 20009   Ph:(202)328-7700

2796 ● VW and Porsche
Argus Publishers Corp.
12100 Wilshire Blvd., Ste. 250   Ph:(213)820-3601
Los Angeles, CA 90025   Fax:(213)207-9388

Offers articles of interest to enthusiasts of Volkswagen and Porsche models. Bimonthly. **Editor(s):** Greg Brown. **Price:** $11.00/yr.; $2.75/issue.

2797 ● VW Autoist
Volkswagen Club of America, Inc.
PO Box 154
N. Aurora, IL 60542   Ph:(314)821-9091

Carries news items from the national Club and from local chapters, technical advice on the Volkswagen, and "inside dope on new models" in a column from Europe. Bimonthly. **Editor(s):** Fred Ortlip. **Price:** Available to members only.

2798 ● VW Trends
McMullen Publishing, Inc.
2145 W. La Palma Ave.   Ph:(714)635-9040
Anaheim, CA 92801-1785   Fax:(714)533-9979

Magazine for Volkswagen enthusiasts. Monthly. **Editor(s):** Brian Noto.

ASSOCIATIONS

2799 ● Volkswagen Club of America
P.O. Box 154
North Aurora, IL 60542-0154
Shell Tomlin, Pres.   Ph:(708)896-2803

Founded: 1955. **Membership:** 4,000. Owners and enthusiasts of Volkswagen and Audi automobiles. Disseminates information on maintenance and restoration of Volkswagen vehicles. Local clubs hold rallies, parties, and other automotive and social events. **Convention/Meeting:** Annual, always summer.

VOLKSWAGEN VANAGON (1987-91)

Introduced as a replacement to the Volkswagen Bus. Ranked seventh in a 1989 comparison test of eight mini-vans conducted by *Car and Driver*.   The Vanagon line was last produced in 1991 and consisted of seven models.

1991 Volkswagen Vanagon

MAJOR FEATURES

● Volkswagen Vanagon had as 1991 standard equipment: power steering, 185/70 R14 tires, electric rear window defogger, reclining front seats with headrests, two center, rear-facing removable seats with lap belts, rear bench seat that converts into a double bed with storage compartment, rear heater, four-speaker sound system, dual rear-view mirrors, and intermittent wipers.

● Vanagon Syncro included a viscous-coupling drive system, four-speed manual transmission with extra-low gear, electronically engaged rear differential lock, and a larger fuel tank than the standard Vanagon.

● Vanagon GL included all the standard equipment of the Vanagon, as well as: air conditioning, 205/70 R14 tires, power mirrors, rear window wiper/washer, full carpeting, digital clock, tachometer, adjustable armrests on front seats, center two-passenger folding bench seat, rear headrests, and wheel covers.

● Vanagon Carat included all of the standard equipment of the GL, as well as: cruise control, central locking system, power windows, privacy curtains, foldaway table, two center, rear-facing, removable seats with lap belts, and alloy wheels.

● Vanagon Multivan included all features of the Carat, plus: a pop-up top with double bed, rear clothes locker, window and rear hatch screens, skylight, and rooftop storage rack.

● Camper GL included all standard equipment of the GL, as well as: pop-up roof with skylight and double bed, kitched cabinet and sink, refrigerator with thermostat and 3-way power operation, double burner propane stove, external water hookup, 50-litre water tank with electric pump, 110v AC duplex power outlet, front swivel seats, and front and rearward stowaway tables.

● Camper GL Syncro included Syncro 4-wheel drive with locking differential, 6Jx14 alloy wheels, cruise control, and power windows.

PRICE HISTORY

The following new car prices reflect the approximate retail cost of the base model: **1987** - $11,560; **1988** - $16,245; **1989** - $17,035; **1990** - $14,080; **1991** - $14,930.

DIMENSIONS

Body Style	Years Avail	Wheel Base (in)	Lgth (in)	Ht (in)	Avg Wt (lbs)	Fuel Cap (gal)	Front Hdrm (in)	Front Legrm (in)
van	87-89	96.9	179.9	77.2	5,200	15.9	na	na
van	90-91	96.9	179.9	75.9	5,160	15.9	na	na

ENGINES

Type	Displace-ment (L)	Fuel Dly	HP @rpm	Torque @rpm (ft/lbs)	MPG Cty/Hwy	Years Avail
Flat-4	2.1	FI	90@4800	117@3200	18/19	87-91

KEY: I=in-line engine; V=V engine; F=flat engine; FI=fuel injection; bbl=barrel carburetor; T=turbo; D=diesel; HP=horsepower; MPG=estimated average miles per gallon.

EVALUATIONS, TESTS, AND RANKINGS

1991: "beautifully finished, inside and out . . . engine is anemic." **Source:** "Vans For All Seasons," *Popular Mechanics,* September 1990, pp. 24-27.

1990: "roomy, but its power was woefully inadequate . . . Beyond that, there was little to like." **Source:** "The Best of the Minivans," *Changing Times,* July 1990, pp. 41-45.

1989: "needs 16.9 seconds to reach 60 mph . . . poor highway performance resulted in large part from the wind noise that permeates the seven-passenger interior space." **Source:** "Eeny, Meeny, Miney, Mini," *Car and Driver,* May 1989, pp. 62-63, 65, 67, 71, 75-77, 81.

1987: "fit and finish were excellent . . . idling was erratic (especially at higher altitudes) and acceleration was lethargic . . . prime misgiving about the Vanagon is its cost." **Source:** "CAA Autopinions: 1987 Volkswagen Vanagon," *Canadian Consumer,* January 1987, pp. 30-31.

1987: "It has far more interior room than any of its competitors . . . . needs more horsepower." **Source:** "PM Comparison Test: Mass Transit," *Popular Mechanics,* November 1987, pp. 71-75.

RECALLS

1988: (600 vehicles): Improper jack furnished with vehicles. Jack may not reach far enough into jackets provided on both sides of the vehicle. If improper jack is used, it could slip and possibly injure person standing too close to vehicle. **Corrective action:** Replace jack with proper type for vehicle. *(NHTSA Campaign No. 88V056000.)*

1987-89: (300 vehicles; includes other Volkswagen models): Accelerator cable may become tangled with water pipe when using cruise control. **Corrective action:** Replace accelerator cable bracket. *(NHTSA Campaign No. 89V067000.)*

1987-88: (130 van and camper type vehicles; includes Volkswagen Vanagon and Volkswagen Camper; includes models made before 1987): Due to improper mounting process, semperit tires 20570R14 mounted on alloy wheel size 6J 14 could experience tiny cracks in bead area. Tires could lose air, creating potential for loss of vehicle control. **Corrective action:** Replace tires as necessary. *(NHTSA Campaign No. 88V076000.)*

1987: (15,500 vehicles; includes models made before 1987; includes other Volkswagen models): Usage of fuel with reid pressure up to 14 psi could lead to stalling under high engine load and high ambient temperatures due to fuel flow restriction. **Corrective action:** Install redesigned fuel tank and modified control units. *(NHTSA Campaign No. 87V052000.)*

1987: (2,397 vehicles): Seat brackets which anchor rearward passenger seats may not engage properly. **Corrective action:** Assure seat brackets are properly engaged. *(NHTSA Campaign No. 87V083000.)*

1987: (1,600 vans with automatic transmissions): Pin in shift locking pawl may not be properly welded, resulting in shifting gears without pressing safety button. **Corrective action:** Replace shift locking pin. *(NHTSA Campaign No. 87V085000.)*

1987: (12,000 vehicles; includes Volkswagen Truck Camper and Volkswagen Truck Vanagon; includes models made before 1987): In-line fuel filter located between fuel tank and fuel pump could seep fuel at seam of plastic casing. Should seepage occur, leaking fuel can cause risk of fire in presence of ignition source. **Corrective action:** In-line fuel filter will be replaced with straight fuel hose. *(NHTSA Campaign No. 88V038000.)*

REPAIR MANUALS

2800 ● **Chilton's VW Front Wheel Drive, 1974-1990**
Chilton Co.
Chilton Way
Radnor, PA 19089   Ph:(215)964-4000

Published 1990. **Price:** $15.95.

2801 ● **Vanagon Official Factory Repair Manual: 1980-1989, Including Air Cooled and Water-Cooled Gasoline Engines, Diesel Engine, Syncro, and Camper**
Robert Bentley Publishing, Inc.
1000 Massachusetts Ave.
Cambridge, MA 02138   Ph:(617)547-4170

Price: $74.95.

2802 ● **Volkswagen Electrical Diagrams and Troubleshooting Guide**
Dianic Publications
P. O. Box 2527
Berkeley, CA 94702   Ph:(415)841-9622

Published 1987. **Editor(s):** Erik Bromberg. **Price:** $18.95.

2803 ● **Volkswagen Water-Cooled, Front-Drive Performance Handbook**
Motorbooks International, Inc.
729 Prospect Ave.
Osceola, WI 54020   Ph:(715)294-3345

Published 1987. **Editor(s):** Greg Haven. **Price:** $18.95.

OTHER INFORMATION SOURCES

2804 ● European Car
Argus Publishers Corp.
12100 Wilshire Blvd., Ste. 250   Ph:(213)820-3601
Los Angeles, CA 90025   Fax:(213)207-9388

Magazine covering Volkswagen, Porsche, Mercedes-Benz, Audi, Ferrari, Jaguar, and BMW automobiles. Bimonthly. **Editor(s):** Greg N. Brown. **Price:** $11.00 per year; $2.75 per issue.

2805 ● Small on Safety: The Design-in Danger of the Volkswagen
Center for Auto Safety
2001 S St. NW, Ste. 410
Washington, DC 20009   Ph:(202)328-7700

2806 ● VW and Porsche
Argus Publishers Corp.
12100 Wilshire Blvd., Ste. 250   Ph:(213)820-3601
Los Angeles, CA 90025   Fax:(213)207-9388

Offers articles of interest to enthusiasts of Volkswagen and Porsche models. Bimonthly. **Editor(s):** Greg Brown. **Price:** $11.00/yr.; $2.75/issue.

2807 ● VW Autoist
Volkswagen Club of America, Inc.
PO Box 154
N. Aurora, IL 60542   Ph:(314)821-9091

Carries news items from the national Club and from local chapters, technical advice on the Volkswagen, and "inside dope on new models" in a column from Europe. Bimonthly. **Editor(s):** Fred Ortlip. **Price:** Available to members only.

2808 ● VW Trends
McMullen Publishing, Inc.
2145 W. La Palma Ave.   Ph:(714)635-9040
Anaheim, CA 92801-1785   Fax:(714)533-9979

Magazine for Volkswagen enthusiasts. Monthly. **Editor(s):** Brian Noto.

ASSOCIATIONS

2809 ● Volkswagen Club of America
P.O. Box 154
North Aurora, IL 60542-0154
Shell Tomlin, Pres.   Ph:(708)896-2803

Founded: 1955. **Membership:** 4,000. Owners and enthusiasts of Volkswagen and Audi automobiles. Disseminates information on maintenance and restoration of Volkswagen vehicles. Local clubs hold rallies, parties, and other automotive and social events. **Convention/Meeting:** Annual, always summer.

VOLVO 240 SERIES (1987-92)

The base model of Volvo's line, the 240 is manufactured in Torslanda, Sweden. The 240 GL, which was dropped in 1990, rejoins the 240 series lineup in 1992. The DL, dropped its suffix to become the base model. Rated a Best Bet by *The Car Book* in 1992.

1991 Volvo 240

MAJOR FEATURES

● Volvo 240 and 240 Wagon have as 1992 standard equipment: 2.3-liter four-cylinder engine, 5-speed manual transmission, power-assisted rack-and-pinion steering, anti-lock brakes, driver's air bag, air conditioning, power windows, anti-theft AM-FM radio cassette, and central locking.

● Volvo 240 GL adds as 1992 standard equipment: sunroof, power/heated outside mirrors, and heated front seats.

PRICE HISTORY

The following new car prices reflect the approximate retail cost of the base model: **1987** - $15,400; **1988** - $17,250; **1989** - $17,250; **1990** - $18,820; **1991** - $19,620; **1992** - $20,820.

DIMENSIONS

Body Style	Years Avail	Wheel Base (in)	Lgth (in)	Ht (in)	Avg Wt (lbs)	Fuel Cap (gal)	Front Hdrm (in)	Front Legrm (in)
4d sdn	87-92	104.3	189.9	56.3	2,919	15.8	37.9	40.1
5d wgn	87-92	104.3	190.7	57.5	3,051	15.8	37.9	40.1

ENGINES

Type	Displacement (L)	Fuel Dly	HP @rpm	Torque @rpm (ft/lbs)	MPG Cty/Hwy	Years Avail
I-4	2.3	FI	114@5400	136@2750	21/28	87-92

KEY: I=in-line engine; V=V engine; F=flat engine; FI=fuel injection; bbl=barrel carburetor; T=turbo; D=diesel; HP=horsepower; MPG=estimated average miles per gallon.

RECALLS

None to date.

REPAIR MANUALS

2810 ● Volvo 240 Series DL, GL, GLT and Turbo: 1975-1987—Service, Repair Handbook
Clymer Publications
P.O. Box 1209
Overland Park, KS 66212   Ph:(913)541-6694

Editor(s): Ray Hoy. **Price:** $14.95.

2811 ● Volvo 1970-1988: Repair and Tune-Up Guide
Chilton Co.
Chilton Way
Radnor, PA 19089   Ph:(215)964-4000

Published 1989. **Price:** $14.95.

2812 ● Volvo GL, DL
Peter Allen Video Productions
38-C Otis St.
West Babylon, NY 11704   Ph:(516)643-4372

How to tune-up and maintain the two Volvo engines. **Release date:** 1986. **Producer:** Peter Allen Productions. **Acquisition:** Purchase.

OTHER INFORMATION SOURCES

2813 ● Rolling
Volvo Club of America
P.O. Box 16
Afton, NY 13730   Ph:(607)639-2279

Promotes ownership of Volvo automobiles and communication among Volvo owners. Provides historical and technical items concerning Volvo automobiles produced from the 1930s to the present and outlines safe driving techniques. Bimonthly. **Editor(s):** Sharon Stasko. **Price:** Available to members only.

2814 ● Volvo
State Mutual Book and Periodical Service, Ltd.
521 Fifth Ave. 17th Fl.
New York, NY 10017   Ph:(212)682-5844

Published 1988. **Price:** $30.00.

2815 ● Volvo Club of America—Membership Directory
Volvo Club of America
P.O. Box 16
Afton, NY 13730   Ph:(607)639-2279

Approximately 1,700 member owners of Volvo automobiles. Annual, January. **Editor(s):** Duncan G. LaBay, President. **Price:** Available to members only.

2816 ● The Volvo Leader
Nils Sefeldt Volvo
11451 Katy Fwy.
Houston, TX 77079   Ph:(713)461-1600

Updates owners on new features, improvements, and services available for the Volvo automobile. Monthly. **Editor(s):** Bjorn O. Sefeldt. **Price:** Free.

ASSOCIATIONS

2817 ● Volvo Club of America
P.O. Box 16
Afton, NY 13730   Ph:(607)639-2279
Steve Seekins, Pres.   Fax:(607)639-2279

Founded: 1982. **Membership:** 1,500. Owners and enthusiasts of Volvo automobiles produced from the 1930s to the present. Promotes ownership of Volvos and communication among Volvo owners. Provides technical information and assistance. Encourages safe driving and the use of safety devices such as seat belts. Sponsors regional and national activities; conducts workshops, rallies, swap meets, and banquets. **Convention/Meeting:** Annual.

VOLVO 700 SERIES (1987-1992)

The 740 is manufactured in Ghent, Belgium, and Halifax, Nova Scotia, Canada. The 760 Series was replaced by the 940 Series, and the 780 Series name was changed to the Coupe in 1991, which was its last year of production. In addition, the 740 Turbo Sedan was discontinued in 1991.

1991 Volvo 740

MAJOR FEATURES

● The 740 Sedan and 740 Wagon standard equipment for 1992 includes: 2.3-liter four cylinder engine, 4-speed automatic transmission, anti-lock brakes, power-assisted rack-and-pinion steering, driver's airbag, air conditioning, power windows, anti-theft AM/FM stereo cassette, heated front seats, and central locking.

● The 740 Turbo Sedan and Wagon adds as 1992 standard equipment: turbo-charged engine, power sunroof, automatic climate control, and upgraded tires.

● The 740 Turbo Sedan added the same equipment in 1991 as the 740 Turbo Wagon.

● The 780 (Coupe) had as 1991 standard equipment: turbo-charged engine, driver's air bag, electronic climate control, cruise control, anti-lock brakes, power windows, anti-theft AM/FM cassette/radio CD, sunroof, power controlled and heated front seats, turbo boost gauge, automatic locking differential, central locking, leather upholstery, and 195/65 R15H MXV2 tires.

● The 760 GLE model for 1990 had: V-6 engine, automatic transmission, and 205/55 VR16 tires.

PRICE HISTORY

The following new car prices reflect the approximate retail cost of the base model: **1987** - $20,155; **1988** - $21,850; **1989** - $20,685; **1990** - $21,095; **1991** - $23,175; **1992** - $24,285.

DIMENSIONS

Body Style	Years Avail	Wheel Base (in)	Lgth (in)	Ht (in)	Avg Wt (lbs)	Fuel Cap (gal)	Front Hdrm (in)	Front Legrm (in)
2d cpe	88-91	109.1	188.8	55.5	3,415	21.0	37.2	41.0
4d sdn	87-90	109.1	188.4	55.5	3,067	15.8	38.6	41.0
4d sdn	91-92	109.1	189.3	55.5	2,954	15.8	38.6	41.0
5d wgn	87-90	109.1	188.4	56.5	3,082	15.8	38.6	41.0
5d wgn	91-92	109.1	189.3	56.5	3,082	15.8	38.6	41.0

ENGINES

Type	Displacement (L)	Fuel Dly	HP @rpm	Torque @rpm (ft/lbs)	MPG Cty/Hwy	Years Avail
I-4	2.3	FI	114@5400	136@2750	20/28	87-92
I-4	2.3	FI	153@5700	150@4450	18/23	89-91
I-4T	2.3	FI	160@5300	187@2900	20/25	87-89
I-4T	2.3	FI	175@5400	187@2900	19/23	89-89
I-4T	2.3	FI	188@5100	206@3900	19/22	90-91
I-4T	2.3	FI	162@4800	195@3450	19/22	90-92
V-6	2.8	FI	145@5100	173@3750	17/21	87-90

KEY: I=in-line engine; V=V engine; F=flat engine; FI=fuel injection; bbl=barrel carburetor; T=turbo; D=diesel; HP=horsepower; MPG=estimated average miles per gallon.

EVALUATIONS, TESTS, AND RANKINGS

1990: "clings to the square look . . . has lines that are uniquely Volvo." **Source:** "Volvo 740GL shows big-car form," *Design News,* May 21, 1990, p. 49.

1989: "handling is quite good . . . ride is surprisingly comfortable . . . power is always there when you need it." **Source:** "The People's Choice," *Regardie's,* July 1989, pp. 125-130.

1988: "well-controlled ride without undue harshness . . . climate control is easy to operate and within easy reach." **Source:** "Volvo 760/780: On the Road Again in the Luxury Touring Cars," *Motor Trend,* January 1988, pp. 67-68,70.

1987: "The interior is splendid . . . 780 is effortlessly competent and rock-solid." **Source:** "Volvo 780: Counterpoint," *Car and Driver,* May 1987, pp. 79-84.

1987: "Throttle response is good and the transmission ratios are well chosen . . . braking . . . was excellent." **Source:** "Volvo 780 Coupe: Swede Smell of Success," *Road & Track,* January 1987, p. 88.

RECALLS

1990: (253 of the Volvo 740 models): Fuel damper located behind fuel line and fuel rail may be improrerly assembled. Solder joints could allow fuel leakage, which could result in a fire. **Corrective action:** Replace fuel damper. *(NHTSA Campaign No. 90V165000.)*

1989-91: (19,286 vehicles equipped with 80 liter fuel tanks; includes Volvo 700 and Volvo 900 Series models): If conditions of high ambient temperature, overfilling of the fuel tank, and insufficient torque on the sending unit lock ring exist simultaneously, fuel seepage may occur. **Corrective action:** Retorque sending unit lock ring; replace lock ring gasket if fuel seepage is detected. *(NHTSA Campaign No. 91V010000.)*

1989: (475 Volvo 760 models): Tire information label is incorrect. **Corrective action:** Install proper labels. *(NHTSA Campaign No. 89V183000.)*

1988: (2,930 Volvo 760 models): Parts in headlight switch may become loose, causing short circuits. **Corrective action:** Replace headlight switch. *(NHTSA Campaign No. 87V195000.)*

1987-91: (485 station wagons; includes the Volvo 740, Volvo 760, and Volvo 940 models; includes models made before 1987): The instructional labels for the safety belt routing are inadequate and can result in an inadvertent release of the belt buckle. Could result in seat occupant being injured in a sudden stop or accident. **Corrective action:** Install labels to instruct the user in proper safety belt routing; also replace safety belt buckles. *(NHTSA Campaign No. 91V075000.)*

1987-88: (38,000 Volvo models; includes models made before 1987): Driveshaft and fuel tank may scrape, resulting in leak and possible fire. **Corrective action:** Replace fuel tank and/or install protective device between driveshaft and tank. *(NHTSA Campaign No. 89V204000.)*

1987-88: (1,883 Volvo 780 models with supplemental restraint system): Supplemental restraint electronic control unit may malfunction, resulting in airbag and safety belt pretensioner not working. **Corrective action:** Replace control unit. *(NHTSA Campaign No. 89V025000.)*

1987: (106,602 passenger sedans and wagons; includes the Volvo 740 and Volvo 760 models; includes models made before 1987): Engine wiring harness could chafe against air conditioning pipe, resulting in short circuit of electrical system. **Corrective action:** Relocate wiring harness and secure with bracket and clamp. *(NHTSA Campaign No. 87V064000.)*

REPAIR MANUALS

2818 ● **Volvo 1970-1988: Repair and Tune-Up Guide**
Chilton Co.
Chilton Way
Radnor, PA 19089　　　　　　Ph:(215)964-4000

Published 1989. **Price:** $14.95.

OTHER INFORMATION SOURCES

2819 ● **Rolling**
Volvo Club of America
P.O. Box 16
Afton, NY 13730　　　　　　Ph:(607)639-2279

Promotes ownership of Volvo automobiles and communication among Volvo owners. Provides historical and technical items concerning Volvo automobiles produced from the 1930s to the present and outlines safe driving techniques. Bimonthly. **Editor(s):** Sharon Stasko. **Price:** Available to members only.

2820 ● **Volvo**
State Mutual Book and Periodical Service, Ltd.
521 Fifth Ave. 17th Fl.
New York, NY 10017　　　　　　Ph:(212)682-5844

Published 1988. **Price:** $30.00.

2821 ● **Volvo Club of America—Membership Directory**
Volvo Club of America
P.O. Box 16
Afton, NY 13730　　　　　　Ph:(607)639-2279

Approximately 1,700 member owners of Volvo automobiles. Annual, January. **Editor(s):** Duncan G. LaBay, President. **Price:** Available to members only.

2822 ● **The Volvo Leader**
Nils Sefeldt Volvo
11451 Katy Fwy.
Houston, TX 77079　　　　　　Ph:(713)461-1600

Updates owners on new features, improvements, and services available for the Volvo automobile. Monthly. **Editor(s):** Bjorn O. Sefeldt. **Price:** Free.

ASSOCIATIONS

2823 ● **Volvo Club of America**
P.O. Box 16
Afton, NY 13730　　　　　　Ph:(607)639-2279
Steve Seekins, Pres.　　　　　　Fax:(607)639-2279

Founded: 1982. **Membership:** 1,500. Owners and enthusiasts of Volvo automobiles produced from the 1930s to the present. Promotes ownership of Volvos and communication among Volvo owners. Provides technical information and assistance. Encourages safe driving and the use of safety devices such as seat belts. Sponsors regional and national activities; conducts workshops, rallies, swap meets, and banquets. **Convention/Meeting:** Annual.

VOLVO 900 SERIES (1991-92)

Introduced in 1991 and similar to the 700 Series, the Volvo 900 Series adds only a few aerodynamic improvements. For 1992, 940 GLE Sedan and Wagon are replaced by the 940 GL; the 940 SE is replaced by the 960. Manufactured in Kalmar, Sweden; Uddevalla, Sweden; Ghent, Belgium; and Halifax, Nova Scotia, Canada.

1992 Volvo 940 GL

MAJOR FEATURES

● Volvo 940 GL has as 1992 standard equipment: 2.3-liter 4-cylinder engine, 4-speed automatic transmission, 4-wheel anti-lock disc brakes, Automatic Locking Differential, power steering, driver-side airbag, automatic climate control, and sunroof.

● Volvo 940 Turbo Sedan and Wagon add as 1992 standard equipment: turbo-charged engine, power mirrors, and alloy wheels.

● Volvo 960 Sedan and Wagon add as 1992 standard equipment: 2.9-liter 24-valve V-6 engine, leather upholstery, cruise control, upgraded tires, and alloy wheels.

● Volvo 940 GLE Sedan and Wagon had as 1991 standard equipment: 16-valve naturally aspirated engine, four-speed automatic transmission, driver's side airbag, air conditioning, anti-lock brakes, power windows, anti-theft AM/FM stereo cassette, sunroof, heated front seats, and central locking.

● Volvo 940 SE Sedan and Wagon added as 1991 standard equipment: turbo-charged engine, cruise control, turbo boost gauge, and automatic locking differential.

PRICE HISTORY

The following new car prices reflect the approximate retail cost of the base model: **1991** - $27,885; **1992** - $24,995.

DIMENSIONS

Body Style	Years Avail	Wheel Base (in)	Lgth (in)	Ht (in)	Avg Wt (lbs)	Fuel Cap (gal)	Front Hdrm (in)	Front Legrm (in)
4d sdn	91-92	109.1	191.7	55.5	3,009	15.8	38.6	41.0
5d wgn	92-92	109.1	189.3	56.5	3,177	15.8	38.6	41.0

ENGINES

Type	Displacement (L)	Fuel Dly	HP @rpm	Torque @rpm (ft/lbs)	MPG Cty/Hwy	Years Avail
I-4	2.3	FI	153@5700	150@4450	18/23	91-91
I-4	2.3	FI	114@5400	136@2750	20/28	92-92
I-4T	2.3	FI	162@4000	195@3450	19/22	91-92
I-6	3.0	FI	201@6000	197@4300	18/26	92-92

KEY: I=in-line engine; V=V engine; F=flat engine; FI=fuel injection; bbl=barrel carburetor; T=turbo; D=diesel; HP=horsepower; MPG=estimated average miles per gallon.

EVALUATIONS, TESTS, AND RANKINGS

1992: "shifts were smooth . . . paragon of luxury . . . excellent sound insulation." **Source:** "Volvo 960: The blessings of a six," *Road & Track*, November 1991, pp. 82, 84, 86.

1992: "car is a delight . . . a natural for any family that wants a luxury hauler . . . steady, stable and solid." **Source:** "Volvo Makes Its New 960 a Safe Bet," *New York Times*, December 15, 1991.

1991: "new lines deliver a fresh exterior . . . delivers a comfortable, soft ride." **Source:** "Volvo 940/960," *Automobile Magazine*, January 1991, pp. 100-104.

1991: "a luxury car that's been blessed with good handling . . . conservative but elegant interior . . . remind us of modern Danish furniture." **Source:** "Volvo 940 SE: Think of a 940 turbo, but with the works," *Road & Track*, July 1991, pp. 76, 80, 83.

1991: "look is fresh but the character is traditional . . . delivers clean handling and solid performance . . . windshield wipers . . . [offered] smeary, uneven coverage." **Source:** "Volvo 940 Turbo delivers crisp handling," *Design News*, August 5, 1991, p. 24.

1991: "cornered with minimal lean and responded instantly and predictably . . . European-style seats and road manners." **Source:** "Station To Station: HM tests four new-for-1991 family wagons," *Home Mechanix*, June 1991, pp. 78-83.

RECALLS

1991: (19,286 vehicles equipped with 80 liter fuel tanks; includes Volvo 700 and Volvo 900 Series models): If conditions of high ambient temperature, overfilling of the fuel tank, and insufficient torque on the sending unit lock ring exist simultaneously, fuel seepage may occur. **Corrective action:** Retorque sending unit lock ring; replace lock ring gasket if fuel seepage is detected. *(NHTSA Campaign No. 91V010000.)*

1991: (485 station wagons; includes the Volvo 740, Volvo 760, and Volvo 940 models): The instructional labels for the safety belt routing are inadequate and can result in inadvertent release of the belt buckle. Could result in seat occupant being injured in a sudden stop or accident. **Corrective action:** Install labels to instruct the user in proper safety belt routing; also replace safety belt buckles. *(NHTSA Campaign No. 91V075000.)*

OTHER INFORMATION SOURCES

2824 ● **Rolling**
Volvo Club of America
P.O. Box 16
Afton, NY 13730   Ph:(607)639-2279

Promotes ownership of Volvo automobiles and communication among Volvo owners. Provides historical and technical items concerning Volvo automobiles produced from the 1930s to the present and outlines safe driving techniques. Bimonthly. **Editor(s):** Sharon Stasko. **Price:** Available to members only.

2825 ● **Volvo**
State Mutual Book and Periodical Service, Ltd.
521 Fifth Ave. 17th Fl.
New York, NY 10017   Ph:(212)682-5844

Published 1988. **Price:** $30.00.

2826 ● **Volvo Club of America—Membership Directory**
Volvo Club of America
P.O. Box 16
Afton, NY 13730   Ph:(607)639-2279

Approximately 1,700 member owners of Volvo automobiles. Annual, January. **Editor(s):** Duncan G. LaBay, President. **Price:** Available to members only.

2827 ● The Volvo Leader
Nils Sefeldt Volvo
11451 Katy Fwy.
Houston, TX 77079   Ph:(713)461-1600

Updates owners on new features, improvements, and services available for the Volvo automobile. Monthly. **Editor(s):** Bjorn O. Sefeldt. **Price:** Free.

ASSOCIATIONS

2828 ● Volvo Club of America
P.O. Box 16
Afton, NY 13730   Ph:(607)639-2279
Steve Seekins, Pres.   Fax:(607)639-2279

Founded: 1982. **Membership:** 1,500. Owners and enthusiasts of Volvo automobiles produced from the 1930s to the present. Promotes ownership of Volvos and communication among Volvo owners. Provides technical information and assistance. Encourages safe driving and the use of safety devices such as seat belts. Sponsors regional and national activities; conducts workshops, rallies, swap meets, and banquets. **Convention/Meeting:** Annual.

YUGO (1987-92)

Built by Yugoslavian car manufacturer Zavodi Crvena Zastava. In 1990, GV model was discontinued, and the GVL, GVS, and GVX models were consolidated into the GV Plus.

MAJOR FEATURES

● Yugo GV Plus has as 1992 standard equipment: 5-speed manual transmission, power-assisted brakes, MacPherson front struts, rack-and-pinion steering, multi-port fuel injection, and 145 SR13 tires.

● Yugo Cabrio adds as 1992 standard equipment: power-operated top, tinted glass, glass rear window with electric defroster, and 155/70 SR13 tires.

PRICE HISTORY

The following new car prices reflect the approximate retail cost of the base model: **1987** - $3,990; **1988** - $4,349; **1989** - $4,349; **1990** - $4,435; **1991** - $4,825.

DIMENSIONS

Body Style	Years Avail	Wheel Base (in)	Lgth (in)	Ht (in)	Avg Wt (lbs)	Fuel Cap (gal)	Front Hdrm (in)	Front Legrm (in)
3d lbk	87-92	84.6	139.0	54.1	1,870	12.0	37.0	39.0
2d conv	90-92	84.6	139.0	55.2	1,947	12.0	37.0	39.0

ENGINES

Type	Displace- ment (L)	Fuel Dlv	HP @rpm	Torque @rpm (ft/lbs)	MPG Cty/Hwy	Years Avail
I-4	1.3	2-bbl	64@5800	68@4000	26/29	87-87
I-4	1.1	2-bbl	54@5000	52@4600	28/31	87-89
I-4	1.3	2-bbl	61@5000	68@4000	26/31	88-90
I-4	1.3	FI	67@5500	74@3750	27/34	90-92

KEY: I=in-line engine; V=V engine; F=flat engine; FI=fuel injection; bbl=barrel carburetor; T=turbo; D=diesel; HP=horsepower; MPG=estimated average miles per gallon.

EVALUATIONS, TESTS, AND RANKINGS

1988: "good price but not much in the way of ride and handling." **Source:** "Cheap Cars," *Changing Times,* May 1988, pp. 33-36, 37.

1988: "we can name fully a dozen small cars from the U.S., Japan, and Korea that deliver livelier performance ... and better assembly quality." **Source:** "Yugo GVX," *Car and Driver,* November 1988, pp. 159-160.

1987: "The styling is surprisingly neat and crisp ... awkward driving position ... choppy, harsh ride." **Source:** "Basic Transportation," *Home Mechanix,* August 1987, pp. 54-55, 58-59, 89.

RECALLS

1990-91: (3,676 passenger vehicles): The electronic control unit has a faulty rubber seal that allows water to infiltrate and short circuit the unit. The vehicle could stall and fail to restart without prior indication. **Corrective action:** Install a rubber seal between the unit and the firewall it is welded to. *(NHTSA Campaign No. 91V130000.)*

General Information Sources

This section describes associations and other sources of information on autos and auto-related topics. General associations comprise the first part of this section and appear in alphabetical order by name; publications and other materials containing general information on autos follow, and are categorized by specific subjects. Consult the User's Guide in the front of the book for a list of subject terms used in the General Information Sources section.

ASSOCIATIONS

2829 • AAA-Automobile Club of Maryland
126 S. Main St.
Bel Air, MD 21014   Ph:(301)838-5121

2830 • Afro-American Automobile Association
5125 Walnut St.
Philadelhia, PA 19139   Ph:(215)472-4250

2831 • Alfa Romeo Owners Club of Central California
705 Oakgrove Dr.
Santa Barbara, CA 93108
Leonard Tompkins, Pres.   Ph:(805)969-3435

2832 • Alliance Automobile Club
2322 S. Union Ave.
Alliance, OH 44601   Ph:(216)823-9820
Clem W. Atkins, Sec. & Mgr.   Fax:(216)823-5001

Founded: 1916. **Membership:** 14,200. Provides vehicle owners with services for travel by motor vehicles, rail, ship, and air. Promotes safety programs; works to improve highways; monitors legislation pertaining to motorists. Sponsors safety programs.

2833 • American Automobile Association
1000 AAA Dr.
Heathrow, FL 32746-5063   Ph:(407)444-7000
J. B. Creal, Pres.   Fax:(407)444-7380

Founded: 1902. **Membership:** 31,000,000. Federation of automobile clubs (1000 offices) providing domestic and foreign travel services, emergency road services, and insurance. Sponsors public services for traffic safety, better highways, more efficient and safer cars, energy conservation, and improvement of motoring and travel conditions. Maintains library of 13,000 volumes on travel, transportation safety, and business. **Convention/Meeting:** Annual.

2834 • Arkansas Automobile Club
PO Box 56128
Little Rock, AR 72215
Joe Pruitt, Mgr.   Ph:(501)223-9222

2835 • Association of International Automobile Manufacturers
1001 19th St. N., Ste. 1200
Arlington, VA 22209   Ph:(703)525-7788
George C. Nield, Pres.   Fax:(703)525-8817

Founded: 1964. **Membership:** 35. Companies that manufacture automobiles or automotive equipment and that import into, or export to, the U.S. Purposes are: to act as a clearinghouse for information, especially with regard to proposed state and federal regulations in the automobile industry as they bear upon imported automobiles; to report proposed regulations by state or federal governments pertaining to equipment standards, licensing, and other matters affecting members. **Former Name(s):** (1966) Imported Car Group; (1990) Automobile Importers of America. **Convention/Meeting:** Annual.

2836 • Auto Cap of Southern California
420 W. Culver Blvd., Ste. 300
Playa Del Ray, CA 90293
Scott Thomas Wilk, Admin.   Ph:(213)301-1554

Founded: 1979. **Membership:** 800. Franchised new car dealers. Provides arbitration in disputes involving members and their customers. **Additional Numbers:** Toll Free: 800-722-0579.

2837 • Automobile Club of Utah
560 East 500 South
Salt Lake City, UT 84102
Steve Zoumadakis, Pres. & CEO   Ph:(801)364-5615

Founded: 1919. **Membership:** 63,000. Represents members' interests; conducts lobbying activities. Holds seminars and workshops.

2838 • Automotive Consumer Action Program
National Automobile Dealers
  Association
8400 Westpark Dr.
McLean, VA 22102
Deborah M. Hopkins, Dir.   Ph:(703)821-7144

Founded: 1973. Acts as public service program providing dealers and their customers with consumer dispute resolution assistance. Panels of volunteers (usually 3 dealers and 3 consumer representatives) act as "mini-juries" in cases of customer dissatisfaction with dealers, when direct contact fails to resolve the problem. Sponsors professional development workshops. Compiles statistics.

2839 • Automotive Cooling Systems Institute
300 Sylvan Ave.
P.O. Box 1638
Englewood Cliffs, NJ 07632-0638   Ph:(201)569-8500
James J. Conner, Exec. V. Pres.   Fax:(201)569-0159

Founded: 1976. **Membership:** 20. A service activity of the Motor and Equipment Manufacturers Association. Manufacturers of automotive cooling system components and supplies. Educates the public on the proper care and maintenance of automotive cooling systems. **Convention/Meeting:** Semiannual.

2840 • Automotive Hall of Fame
P.O. Box 1727
Midland, MI 48641   Ph:(517)631-5760
Donald N. Richetti, Pres.   Fax:(517)631-0524

Founded: 1939. **Membership:** 2,700. Individuals who have been or are now engaged in the automotive industry or related industries. Dedicated in 1976, the Hall of Fame contains exhibits and histories of the people of the industry. Purpose is to perpetuate the memory of pioneers in the automotive industry among present and future generations. Cooperates with business schools and colleges that have automotive-related courses. Sponsors scholarship fund for automotive students. Awards Distinguished Service Citations, Young Leadership and Excellence Award annually to young automotive men or women between the ages of 25 and 35, and annual Automotive Industry Leader of the Year. Elects up to five automotive pioneers to Hall of Fame annually. Maintains library and collects books and other memorabilia on automotive pioneers. **Former Name(s):** (1957) Automobile Old Timers; (1971) Automotive Old Timers; (1982) Automotive Organization Team. **Convention/Meeting:** Annual.

2841 • Automotive Information Council
13505 Dulles Technology Dr.
Herndon, VA 22071-3415
Ronald H. Weiner, Pres.   Ph:(703)904-0700
                                           Fax:(703)904-0727

Founded: 1971. **Membership:** 600. Motor vehicle manufacturers, suppliers of original parts, replacement parts manufacturers, parts wholesalers and distributors, national automotive merchandisers, petroleum companies, auto repair facilities, automotive trade associations, and automotive advertising and consulting firms. Goals are to develop better relations between consumers and the automobile industry, encourage improved intra-industry relationships, promote consumer education programs that explain how the industry functions, and defend the industry against unwarranted attacks. Provides a central source of information about the motor vehicle industry for news media, government and consumer agencies, and the industry itself. Maintains reference library.

2842 • Automotive Safety Foundation
1776 Massachusetts Ave. NW, 5th Fl.
Washington, DC 20036
Jack C. Martin, Public Affairs Dir.   Ph:(202)857-1246
                                           Fax:(202)857-1220

Founded: 1937. **Membership:** 33. Supports the public education activities of individuals and organizations working to improve traffic safety at the national, state, and local levels.

2843 • Bluefield Automobile Club [West Virginia]
P.O. Box 1780
Bluefield, WV 24701
Laura Gooch Jr., Exec. Officer   Ph:(304)327-8187

2844 • British Car Union, Chicago Chapter [Illinois]
PO Box 486
Hinsdale, IL 60522-0486
Bill Kowalski, Exec. Officer

Founded: 1960. Owners and devotees of British automobiles organized to preserve and maintain the highest standard of the marques.

2845 • British Motorcars of New England
P.O. Box 666
North Dighton, MA 02764
Roger J. Jusseaume, Exec. Officer   Ph:(617)679-8252

Founded: 1984. **Membership:** 250. Automobile enthusiasts promoting interest in British automobiles. Provides network for information exchange regarding restoration. **Convention/Meeting:** Annual; also holds monthly meeting.

2846 • Car Care Council
One Grande Lake Dr.
Port Clinton, OH 43452
Donald B. Midgley, Pres.   Ph:(419)734-5343
                                           Fax:(419)732-3780

Founded: 1969. **Membership:** 145. Companies in the automotive aftermarket and related industries. Provides editorial and public service advertising material for use by newspapers, radio, television, and magazines that stress the importance of proper vehicle maintenance. **Convention/Meeting:** Annual - usually March.

2847 • Center for Auto Safety
2001 S St. NW, Ste. 410
Washington, DC 20009
Clarence M. Ditlow, Dir.   Ph:(202)328-7700

Founded: 1970. **Membership:** 12,000. Independent nonprofit organization founded by Ralph Nader and Consumers Union of United States. Monitors government agencies charged with regulation of the industry, supports safety standards, participates in the rule-making procedures of the National Highway Traffic Safety Administration, and the Federal Highway Administration, and occasionaly institutes legal action. **Convention/Meeting:** Annual - always spring, Washington, DC.

2848 • Central Pennsylvania Auto Club
2023 Market St.
Harrisburg, PA 17011
Thomas Miller, Pres. & CEO   Ph:(717)761-6811

Founded: 1909. **Membership:** 130,000. Provides domestic and foreign travel services, emergency road services, and insurance. Holds board meetings. **Convention/Meeting:** Periodic.

2849 • Citizens for Auto-Theft Responsibility
537 S. Sequoia Dr., Ste. 302
West Palm Beach, FL 33409-3670

Works to deter car thieves through changes in the law.

2850 • Diesel Automobile Association
PO Box 335
Ft. Lee, NJ 07024
Robert Gibbons, Pres.   Ph:(212)621-9898

Founded: 1977. Diesel auto amd light-vehicle owners; diesel manufacturing, service, and retail firms. Purpose is to advance automotive dieselization through: service and information; encouragement of research and technological development toward safety, efficiency, and enjoyment; public education legislation and input to government and regulatory agencies. Maintains speakers bureau; bestows Diesel Car of the Year Award. **Convention/Meeting:** Periodic symposium.

2851 • District of Columbia Automotive Consumer Action Program
15873 Crabbs Branch Way
Rockville, MD 20855
Gerard N. Murphy, Pres.   Ph:(301)670-1110

Founded: 1975. **Membership:** 200. New car dealers. Provides third party dispute mediation between car manufacturers, car dealers, and consumers.

2852 • Far East Auto Owners Association
108 E. Broadway
Port Jefferson, NY 11777
Louis V. Lehtonen, Pres.   Ph:(516)928-2818

Founded: 1981. Owners of Japanese-manufactured automobiles, including Datsuns, Hondas, Mazdas, Subarus, and Toyotas. To foster the care and maintenance of Japanese autos; to enhance enjoyment of the cars; and to protect their investment value. Provides members with discounts on purchases and services in all areas of the retailing aftermarket; also provides hotel/motel and insurance discounts. Plans to maintain an extensive research and educational program. Presently inactive.

2853 • Foreign Car Haters Club of America
4634 Desert Forest Trail
Cave Creek, AZ 85331
John Rosen, Pres.   Ph:(602)488-0330

Founded: 1983. **Membership:** 400. Individuals who own and drive American built cars. Tongue-in-cheek campaign whose goal is to ridicule, abuse, slander, and degrade foreign cars and owners of foreign cars. Seeks to ban the importation of all foreign cars to the United States or to impose taxes that would make them prohibitively expensive. Presents certificate of honor awards. **Convention/Meeting:** Annual foreign car bash.

2854 • Great American Station Wagon Owner's Association
2017 Manatee Ave., W.
Bradenton, FL 34205
Larry E. Kummer, Pres.   Ph:(813)747-9280

Founded: 1987. **Membership:** 300. Owners and enthusiasts of station wagons, sedan deliveries, and all enclosed rear body vehicles.

2855 • Inland Automobile Association [Washington State]
W. 1717 4th Ave.
Spokane, WA 99204
Dale Stedman, Pres.   Ph:(206)455-3400

Membership: 80,000. Auto club providing members with travel services including road maps, cruise and airline bookings, insurance, and emergency road assistance.

2856 • International Automotive Hall of Shame
515 Alpine Rd., Box 324
Fitchburg, MA 01420
Bernard A. Fossa, Founder & Chm.   Ph:(508)342-0731

Founded: 1986. **Membership:** 18. Seeks to discomfort persons who intentionally or unintentionally discredit or dishonor the American institution of the automobile. Bestows the IGGIE Award (Infamous, Grotesque, and Gratuitons Injury to Excellence) annually to the person or organization that commits the "most heinous act of desecration to our beloved automobile." **Convention/Meeting:** Periodic - 1993 February, Daytona Beach, FL; 1994 February, Chicago, Il; 1995 May, Indianapolis, IN.

2857 • Japan Automobile Manufacturers Association, Washington Office
1050 17th St. NW, Ste. 410
Washington, DC 20036
Akihiko Miyoshi, Gen.Dir.   Ph:(202)296-8537
     Fax:(202)872-1202

Founded: 1967. **Membership:** 13. Coalition of Japanese automobile manufacturers. Promotes the development of the automobile industry. Conducts research programs involving vehicle production, trade policy, overseas investment, and parts procurement; exchanges information with other sectors of the industry. Sponsors public service programs for consumers. JAMA headquarters: Otemachi Bldg., 1-6-1, Otemachi, Chiyoda-ku, Tokyo, Japan. **Convention/Meeting:** Periodic.

2858 • Massilion Auto Club [Ohio]
1972 Wales Rd., NE
Massillon, OH 44646
James Emmons, Gen. Mgr.   Ph:(216)833-1084

Founded: 1915. **Membership:** 17,000. Motor club members in western Stark County, OH. Provides travel and emergency road services and insurance.

2859 • North Carolina State Motor Club
PO Box 32697
Charlotte, NC 28206   Ph:(704)332-8507

Founded: 1929. Provides automobile insurance and road service.

2860 • North Dakota American Automobile Association
1801 38th St. SW
Fargo, ND 58103
John B. Wimbush, Bd.Chm.   Ph:(701)282-6222

Provides domestic and foreign travel services, emergency road services, and insurance.

2861 • Pennsylvania American Automobile Association Foundation
600 N. Third St.
PO Box 2865
Harrisburg, PA 17105
Elaine Sarrsell, Exec. Dir.   Ph:(717)238-7192

2862 • Registry of Italian Oddities
3305 Valley Vista Rd.
Walnut Creek, CA 94598
John de Boer, Contact   Ph:(415)458-1163

Founded: 1980. **Membership:** 400. Individuals, museums, and organizations owning or interested in preserving unusual Italian automobiles. Records histories of Italian cars. Conducts research; collects and distributes information. Maintains library.

2863 • Santa Fe Trail Auto Club [Kansas]
Baird Motors
Larned, KS 67550
Dennis Wilson, Contact

2864 • Schuylkill County Motor Club [Pennsylvania]
340 S. Centre
Pottsville, PA 17901
Mary Ann Garrity, Pres. & Gen. Mgr.   Ph:(717)622-4991

Founded: 1902. **Membership:** 24,000. Provides motoring services and information on automobile safety issues and touring. **Convention/Meeting:** Periodic.

2865 • Society of Automotive Historians
c/o Natl. Automotive History
   Collection
Detroit Public Library
5201 Woodward Ave.
Detroit, MI 48202

Founded: 1969. **Membership:** 480. Writers, researchers, librarians, students, educators, hobbyists, publishers, industry figures, museums, and other individuals. Purpose is the preservation and recording of the history of the automobile, the industry, its people, its attendant industries, and supporting structures. Conducts research. Activities include rescuing and placing historical material in publicly accessible libraries and archives. Presents annual Nicholas Joseph Cugnot Award for best book and Karl Benz Award for best article on automotive subjects; bestows James J. Bradley Memorial Award in recognition of outstanding work relating to the preservation of auto literature. **Convention/Meeting:** Annual social dinner - in conjunction with the fall Antique Automobile Club of America car show and flea market.

2866 • Society of Automotive Historians—Pioneer Chapter [New York State]
c/o John B. Montville
8 Mockingbird Ln.
Poughkeepsie, NY 12601
John B. Montville, Sec.   Ph:(914)462-6469

Founded: 1978. **Membership:** 20. Automotive hobbyists and historians in New York state and New England. To preserve important materials related to the automobile industry. Disseminates information. **Convention/Meeting:** Semiannual - spring and fall.

2867 • Society of Automotive Historians, Wisconsin Chapter
c/o Robert J. Gary
1316 4th Ave.
Stevens Point, WI 54481-1801
Robert J. Gary, Dir.-Treas.   Ph:(715)341-1085

Founded: 1979. Individuals and museums interested in the history of automobiles and the automobile industry. Offers seminars and plant tours.

2868 • South Carolina State Motor Club
Dutch Center
810 Dutch Sq. Blvd.
Columbia, SC 29210-7387
Mary Branch, Office Mgr.   Ph:(803)798-9205

Founded: 1936. Promotes the general welfare of its members.

2869 • Sports Car Collectors Society of America
1416 Pine Island View
Mt. Pleasant, SC 29464
Dan Badger, Pres.   Ph:(803)884-7490

Founded: 1970. **Membership:** 250. Sports car collectors, dealers, and clubs. **Convention/Meeting:** Annual car show - usually first Sunday in June, Washington, DC/Maryland area.

2870 • Tennessee Automotive Association
2521 White Ave.
Nashville, TN 37204
Roberts V. Weaver Jr., Pres.   Ph:(615)269-3433

2871 • Tri County Motor Club
1 S. Broad St.
Norwich, NY 13815   Ph:(607)334-9269

2872 • Tri County Motor Club
1 S. Broad St.
Norwich, NY 13815   Ph:(607)334-9269

2873 • U.S.A. Convertible Club
P.O. Box 40169
Cincinnati, OH 45240
Jim Grote, Editor

Founded: 1979. **Membership:** 1,575. Convertible owners and others interested in preserving existing convertible-top automobiles. Facilitates exchange of information among members; provides opportunity for the sale and exchange of cars. Maintains small collection of books on convertible cars and their values.

2874 • Warren County Motor Club [Pennsylvania]
201 Pennsylvania Ave., W.
Warren, PA 16365
James F. Miller, Mgr.   Ph:(814)723-6660

2875 • West Allis Auto Club [Wisconsin]
1721 S. 100 St.
West Allis, WI 53214
Tom Gorski, Pres.

2876 • West Pennsylvania Motor Club
192 Murtland Ave.
Washington, PA 15301   Ph:(412)222-3800

2877 • Youngstown Buicks of Yesteryear [Pennsylvania]
529 E. Judson Ave.
Youngstown, OH 44502
Steve Goricki, Exec. Officer   Ph:(216)757-4518

Founded: 1985. To develop, publish, and exchange technical, historical, and other information among individuals interested in Buick automobiles. **Convention/Meeting:** Annual car show.

AUTOMOTIVE INDUSTRY DIRECTORIES

Auto auctions

2878 • Motor Age Big I Who's Who
Fairchild Publications
201 King of Prussia Rd.
Radnor, PA 19089   Ph:(215)964-4225

Directory. Annual.

**2879 • National Auto Auction Association—
Membership Directory**
National Auto Auction Association
P.O. Box 129   Ph:(301)831-8072
Monrovia, MD 21770   Fax:(301)874-5701

Directory. 220 automobile auction firms. Annual, January.
Editor(s): Peter Lukasiak. **Price:** Free.

Automotive associations

2880 • All British Car Meets Program
Minor News Publishers
2311 30 Ave.
San Francisco, CA 94116   Ph:(415)566-6103

Directory. Covers clubs and businesses participating in the larger meets as well as history and club lists. Semiannual. **Editor(s):** Hendrik Idzerka, Production Manager. **Price:** $3.00 per issue.

**2881 • Automatic Transmission Rebuilders Association—
Membership Roster**
Automatic Transmission Rebuilders Association
2472 Eastman Ave., Ste. 23   Ph:(805)654-1700
Ventura, CA 93003   Fax:(805)654-0970

Directory. 2000 transmission rebuilders and suppliers. Every one to two years.

**2882 • Automotive Booster Clubs International—Roster
of Clubs and their Officers**
Automotive Booster Clubs Intl.
1545 Waukegan Rd.   Ph:(708)729-2227
Glenview, IL 60025-2187   Fax:(708)729-3670

Directory. Annual.

2883 • Automotive News—Market Data Book Issue
Crain Communications
1400 Woodbridge Ave.   Ph:(313)446-6000
Detroit, MI 48207   Fax:(313)446-0383

Directory. List of automobile, truck, parts, accessories, and dealership equipment manufacturers; "Who's Who in the Auto Industry" section gives brief biographical data and photographs of executives of major firms. Also includes production, sales, financial, price, automobile options and equipment, advertising expenditure, and other data; federal regulations; and domestic and import car specifications. Annual, May. **Editor(s):** Liz Pinto. **Price:** $35.00.

**2884 • Automotive Parts and Accessories Association—
Membership Directory**
Automotive Parts and Accessories Association
5100 Forbes Blvd.
Lanham, MD 20706   Ph:(301)459-9110

Directory. Lists APAA members by type of business, with information on the number of branches operated by each retailer and the market served; manufacturers' representatives' territories and the products and accounts they handle; jobber and warehouse distributor members, and each company's import/export status. Periodic. **Price:** Free, for members only.

2885 • Car Club Directory
Genesis Publishing Co.
5575 Baltimore Dr., Ste. 105-SF
Costa Mesa, CA 92042-1775

Directory. Over 1,000 U.S. and foreign car clubs. **Price:** $14.95.

**2886 • Collision—Automotive Association Directory
Issue**
Kruza Kaleidoscopix, Inc.
P.O. Box 389   Ph:(508)528-6211
Franklin, MA 02038   Fax:(508)528-3242

Directory. List of 500 automotive trade organizations. Every five years; latest edition December 1989. **Editor(s):** J. A. Kruza. **Price:** $10.00.

2887 • Hot Rod Annual
Petersen Publishing Co.
8490 Sunset Blvd.
Los Angeles, CA 90069   Ph:(213)657-5100

Directory. Lists of manufacturers, custom and speed shops, high-performance companies, engine builders, motorsport organizations. Annual, November. **Editor(s):** Bruce Caldwell. **Price:** $4.95, payment with order.

2888 • International Directory of Automotive Literature Collectors
Lloyd Motor Verlag
29 Froelich Ave.
Mountville, PA 17554   Ph:(717)285-4647

Directory. About 500 collectors of automotive promotional literature, including books, posters, and repair manuals; international coverage. Biennial, March of even years. **Editor(s):** John Lloyd. **Price:** $5.00.

2889 • International Motor Press Directory
Robert E. Lee
66689 Desert View Ave.
Desert Hot Springs, CA 92240-4047   Ph:(619)329-8596

Directory. About 1,900 automotive clubs that publish newsletters; international coverage. Annual. **Editor(s):** Robert E. Lee. **Price:** $10.00.

2890 • Jobber Retailer Aftermarket Manual
Bill Communications, Inc.
P.O. Box 3599   Ph:(216)867-4401
Akron, OH 44309   Fax:(216)867-0019

Directory. Program distribution groups of the automotive aftermarket industry; aftermarket associations; and aftermarket suppliers. Annual, May. **Editor(s):** Michael Mavrigian. **Price:** $62.00, plus $2.00 shipping.

2891 • Jobber Topics—Marketing/Directory Issue
Irving-Cloud Publishing Company
7300 N. Cicero Ave.   Ph:(708)588-7300
Chicago, IL 60646-1696   Fax:(708)674-7015

Directory. Manufacturers, remanufacturers, warehouse distributors, jobbers, manufacturers' agents, and trade associations in the automotive aftermarket field. Annual, July. **Editor(s):** Bob Weber, Editorial Director. **Price:** $60.00, postpaid.

2892 • Modern Tire Dealer—Facts/Directory Issue
Bill Communications, Inc.
PO Box 3599   Ph:(216)867-4401
Akron, OH 44309   Fax:(216)867-0019

Directory. Directories of tire and car service suppliers, tire shop jobbers, and national and state associations. Annual, January. **Editor(s):** Lloyd Stoyer. **Price:** $30.00.

2893 • Motor Age Big I Who's Who
Fairchild Publications
201 King of Prussia Rd.
Radnor, PA 19089   Ph:(215)964-4225

Directory. Annual.

2894 • MVMA Directory of Motor Vehicle Related Associations
Motor Vehicle Manufacturers Association
7430 Second Ave., Ste. 300
Detroit, MI 48202   Ph:(313)872-4311

Directory. 175 national associations which are active in business areas related to motor vehicles. Every 18-24 months; previous edition April 1986; latest edition April 1988. **Price:** Free.

2895 • National Automotive Radiator Service Association—Membership Directory
National Automotive Radiator Service Association
PO Box 97   Ph:(215)541-4500
East Greenville, PA 18041   Fax:(215)855-7257

Directory. Lists 1,800 operators of automotive radiator repair shops and cooling system service businesses. Annual.

2896 • NTDRA Dealer News—Who's Who Directory Issue
National Tire Dealers & Retreaders Association (NTDRA)
1250 I St., NW, Ste. 400   Ph:(202)789-2300
Washington, DC 20005   Fax:(202)682-3999

Directory. 5,000 tire dealers and retreaders, suppliers of related products and services, private brand groups, and local associations that are members of the National Tire Dealers and Retreaders Association; retread plants that have been rated "A" by the association. Annual, January. **Editor(s):** C. D. Hylton III, Director, Communications Services. **Price:** $50.00.

2897 • Old Cars Weekly—Car Club Special Issue
Krause Publications, Inc.
700 E. State St.   Ph:(715)445-2214
Iola, WI 54990   Fax:(715)445-4087

Directory. About 1,200 car collector and fancier clubs; coverage includes Canada and United Kingdom. Annual, April. **Editor(s):** Brad Bowling. **Price:** $1.50.

2898 • Special Interest Auto Club—Membership Directory
Special Interest Auto Club (SIAC)
P.O. Box 681
Centreville, VA 22020   Ph:(703)631-0018

Directory. Annual.

2899 • Sports Car Collectors Society of America— Directory
Sports Car Collectors Society of America
1416 Pine Island View
Mt. Pleasant, SC 29464   Ph:(803)884-7490

Directory. Periodic.

2900 • United Voice
United Four-Wheel Drive Associations
105 Highland Ave.
Battle Creek, MI 49015   Ph:(616)968-3994

Newsletter. Lists four-wheel drive associations; includes updates of activities of regional associations. Quarterly. **Price:** Included in membership dues.

2901 • Used Car Book
Fawcett Book Group
Random House, Inc.
201 E. 50th St.
New York, NY 10022   Ph:(212)872-8020

Directory. List of government agencies, trade organizations, and consumers' groups concerned with the buying and selling of used cars. Principal content of publication is discussion of methods for locating used cars and negotiating their prices. Irregular; latest edition 1985. **Price:** $6.95; Send orders to: Random House, Inc., 400 Hahn Road, Westminster, MD 21157.

Automotive body shops

2902 • Alabama Automotive Directory
Automotive Contact
Box 517
Terre Haute, IN 47808   Ph:(812)232-2441

Directory. Automotive aftermarket businesses, including body shops; brake, muffler, radiator, electrical and transmission repairs, as well as new car dealers, parts retailers, auto salvage companies, and automotive parts warehouses. Annual, January. **Editor(s):** T. L. Spelman, Publisher. **Price:** $30.95, plus $3.00 shipping.

2903 • Arizona/New Mexico Automotive Directory
Automotive Contact
P.O. Box 517
Terre Haute, IN 47808   Ph:(812)232-2441

Directory. Automotive aftermarket businesses, including body shops; brake, muffler, radiator, electrical and transmission repairs, as well as new car dealers, parts retailers, auto salvage companies, and automotive parts warehouses. Annual, January. **Editor(s):** T. L. Spelman, Publisher. **Price:** $30.95, plus $3.00 shipping.

2904 • Arkansas Automotive Directory
Automotive Contact
Box 517
Terre Haute, IN 47808   Ph:(812)232-2441

Directory. Automotive aftermarket businesses, including body shops; brake, muffler, radiator, electrical and transmission repairs, as well as new car dealers, parts retailers, auto salvage companies, and automotive parts warehouses. Annual, January. **Editor(s):** T. L. Spelman, Publisher. **Price:** $30.95, plus $3.00 shipping.

2905 • Automobile Body Shops Directory
American Business Directories, Inc.
American Business Information, Inc.
5711 S. 86th Circle   Ph:(402)593-4600
Omaha, NE 68127   Fax:(402)331-1505

Directory. Nearly 67,655 automotive body shops. Annual. **Price:** $2230.00, payment with order. Regional editions available: Eastern, $1,215.00; Western, $790.00. Significant discounts offered for standing orders.

2906 • Automobile Customizing Directory
American Business Directories, Inc.
American Business Information, Inc.
5711 S. 86th Circle   Ph:(402)593-4600
Omaha, NE 68127   Fax:(402)331-1505

Directory. About 7,210 automotive body shops. Annual. **Price:** $255.00, payment with order. Significant discounts offered for standing orders.

2907 • California Automotive Directory
Automotive Contact
P.O. Box 517
Terre Haute, IN 47808   Ph:(812)232-2441

Directory. Automotive aftermarket businesses, including body shops; brake, muffler, radiator, electrical and transmission repairs, as well as new car dealers, parts retailers, auto salvage companies, and automotive parts warehouses. Annual, January. **Editor(s):** T. L. Spelman, Publisher. **Price:** $30.95, plus $3.00 shipping.

2908 • Colorado/Utah/Nevada Automotive Directory
Automotive Contact
P.O. Box 517
Terre Haute, IN 47808   Ph:(812)232-2441

Directory. Automotive aftermarket businesses, including body shops; brake, muffler, radiator, electrical and transmission repairs, as well as new car dealers, parts retailers, auto salvage companies, and automotive parts warehouses. Annual, January. **Editor(s):** T. L. Spelman, Publisher. **Price:** $30.95, plus $3.00 shipping.

2909 • Connecticut/Rhode Island Automotive Directory
Automotive Contact
P.O. Box 517
Terre Haute, IN 47808   Ph:(812)232-2441

Directory. Automotive aftermarket businesses, including body shops; brake, muffler, radiator, electrical and transmission repairs, as well as new car dealers, parts retailers, auto salvage companies, and automotive parts warehouses. Annual, January. **Editor(s):** T. L. Spelman, Publisher. **Price:** $30.95, plus $3.00 shipping.

2910 • Delaware/District of Columbia/Maryland Automotive Directory
Automotive Contact
P.O. Box 517
Terre Haute, IN 47808   Ph:(812)232-2441

Directory. Automotive aftermarket businesses, including body shops; brake, muffler, radiator, electrical and transmission repairs, as well as new car dealers, parts retailers, auto salvage companies, and automotive parts warehouses. Annual, January. **Editor(s):** T. L. Spelman, Publisher. **Price:** $30.95, plus $3.00 shipping.

2911 • Florida Automotive Directory
Automotive Contact
P.O. Box 517
Terre Haute, IN 47808   Ph:(812)232-2441

Directory. Automotive aftermarket businesses, including body shops; brake, muffler, radiator, electrical and transmission repairs, as well as new car dealers, parts retailers, auto salvage companies, and automotive parts warehouses. Annual, January. **Editor(s):** T. L. Spelman, Publisher. **Price:** $30.95, plus $3.00 shipping.

2912 • Georgia Automotive Directory
Automotive Contact
Box 517
Terre Haute, IN 47808   Ph:(812)232-2441

Directory. Automotive aftermarket businesses, including body shops; brake, muffler, radiator, electrical and transmission repairs, as well as new car dealers, parts retailers, auto salvage companies, and automotive parts warehouses. Annual, January. **Editor(s):** T. L. Spelman, Publisher. **Price:** $30.95, plus $3.00 shipping.

2913 • Idaho/Montana/North Dakota/South Dakota/Wyoming Automotive Directory
Automotive Contact
P.O. Box 517
Terre Haute, IN 47808   Ph:(812)232-2441

Directory. Automotive aftermarket businesses, including body shops; brake, muffler, radiator, electrical and transmission repairs, as well as new car dealers, parts retailers, auto salvage companies, and automotive parts warehouses. Annual, January. **Editor(s):** T. L. Spelman, Publisher. **Price:** $30.95, plus $3.00 shipping.

2914 • Illinois Automotive Directory
Automotive Contact
Box 517
Terre Haute, IN 47808   Ph:(812)232-2441

Directory. Automotive aftermarket businesses, including body shops; brake, muffler, radiator, electrical and transmission repairs, as well as new car dealers, parts retailers, auto salvage companies, and automotive parts warehouses. Annual, January. **Editor(s):** T. L. Spelman, Publisher. **Price:** $30.95, plus $3.00 shipping.

2915 • Indiana Automotive Directory
Automotive Contact
Box 517
Terre Haute, IN 47808   Ph:(812)232-2441

Directory. Automotive aftermarket businesses, including body shops; brake, muffler, radiator, electrical and transmission repairs, as well as new car dealers, parts retailers, auto salvage companies, and automotive parts warehouses. Annual, January. **Editor(s):** T. L. Spelman, Publisher. **Price:** $30.95, plus $3.00 shipping.

2916 • Iowa Automotive Directory
Automotive Contact
Box 517
Terre Haute, IN 47808   Ph:(812)232-2441

Directory. Automotive aftermarket businesses, including body shops; brake, muffler, radiator, electrical and transmission repairs, as well as new car dealers, parts retailers, auto salvage companies, and automotive parts warehouses. Annual, January. **Editor(s):** T. L. Spelman, Publisher. **Price:** $30.95, plus $3.00 shipping.

2917 • Kansas/Nebraska Automotive Directory
Automotive Contact
P.O. Box 517
Terre Haute, IN 47808   Ph:(812)232-2441

Directory. Automotive aftermarket businesses, including body shops; brake, muffler, radiator, electrical and transmission repairs, as well as new car dealers, parts retailers, auto salvage companies, and automotive parts warehouses. Annual, January. **Editor(s):** T. L. Spelman, Publisher. **Price:** $30.95, plus $3.00 shipping.

2918 • Kentucky Automotive Directory
Automotive Contact
Box 517
Terre Haute, IN 47808   Ph:(812)232-2441

Directory. Automotive aftermarket businesses, including body shops; brake, muffler, radiator, electrical and transmission repairs, as well as new car dealers, parts retailers, auto salvage companies, and automotive parts warehouses. Annual, January. **Editor(s):** T. L. Spelman, Publisher. **Price:** $30.95, plus $3.00 shipping.

2919 • Louisiana Automotive Directory
Automotive Contact
Box 517
Terre Haute, IN 47808   Ph:(812)232-2441

Directory. Automotive aftermarket businesses, including body shops; brake, muffler, radiator, electrical and transmission repairs, as well as new car dealers, parts retailers, auto salvage companies, and automotive parts warehouses. Annual, January. **Editor(s):** T. L. Spelman, Publisher. **Price:** $30.95, plus $3.00 shipping.

2920 • Maine/New Hampshire/Vermont Automotive Directory
Automotive Contact
P.O. Box 517
Terre Haute, IN 47808   Ph:(812)232-2441

Directory. Automotive aftermarket businesses, including body shops; brake, muffler, radiator, electrical and transmission repairs, as well as new car dealers, parts retailers, auto salvage companies, and automotive parts warehouses. Annual, January. **Editor(s):** T. L. Spelman, Publisher. **Price:** $30.95, plus $3.00 shipping.

2921 • Massachusetts Automotive Directory
Automotive Contact
P.O. Box 517
Terre Haute, IN 47808   Ph:(812)232-2441

Directory. Automotive aftermarket businesses, including body shops; brake, muffler, radiator, electrical and transmission repairs, as well as new car dealers, parts retailers, auto salvage companies, and automotive parts warehouses. Annual, January. **Editor(s):** T. L. Spelman, Publisher. **Price:** $30.95, plus $3.00 shipping.

2922 • Michigan Automotive Directory
Automotive Contact
P.O. Box 517
Terre Haute, IN 47808   Ph:(812)232-2441

Directory. Automotive aftermarket businesses, including body shops; brake, muffler, radiator, electrical and transmission repairs, as well as new car dealers, parts retailers, auto salvage companies, and automotive parts warehouses. Annual, January. **Editor(s):** T. L. Spelman, Publisher. **Price:** $30.95, plus $3.00 shipping.

2923 • Minnesota Automotive Directory
Automotive Contact
P.O. Box 517
Terre Haute, IN 47808   Ph:(812)232-2441

Directory. Automotive aftermarket businesses, including body shops; brake, muffler, radiator, electrical and transmission repairs, as well as new car dealers, parts retailers, auto salvage companies, and automotive parts warehouses. Annual, January. **Editor(s):** T. L. Spelman, Publisher. **Price:** $30.95, plus $3.00 shipping.

2924 • Mississippi Automotive Directory
Automotive Contact
P.O. Box 517
Terre Haute, IN 47808   Ph:(812)232-2441

Directory. Automotive aftermarket businesses, including body shops; brake, muffler, radiator, electrical and transmission repairs, as well as new car dealers, parts retailers, auto salvage companies, and automotive parts warehouses. Annual, January. **Editor(s):** T. L. Spelman, Publisher. **Price:** $30.95, plus $3.00 shipping.

2925 • Missouri Automotive Directory
Automotive Contact
P.O. Box 517
Terre Haute, IN 47808   Ph:(812)232-2441

Directory. Automotive aftermarket businesses, including body shops; brake, muffler, radiator, electrical and transmission repairs, as well as new car dealers, parts retailers, auto salvage companies, and automotive parts warehouses. Annual, January. **Editor(s):** T. L. Spelman, Publisher. **Price:** $30.95, plus $3.00 shipping.

2926 • New Jersey Automotive Directory
Automotive Contact
P.O. Box 517
Terre Haute, IN 47808   Ph:(812)232-2441

Directory. Automotive aftermarket businesses, including body shops; brake, muffler, radiator, electrical and transmission repairs, as well as new car dealers, parts retailers, auto salvage companies, and automotive parts warehouses. Annual, January. **Editor(s):** T. L. Spelman, Publisher. **Price:** $30.95, plus $3.00 shipping.

2927 • New York Automotive Directory
Automotive Contact
P.O. Box 517
Terre Haute, IN 47808   Ph:(812)232-2441

Directory. Automotive aftermarket businesses, including body shops; brake, muffler, radiator, electrical and transmission repairs, as well as new car dealers, parts retailers, auto salvage companies, and automotive parts warehouses. Annual, January. **Editor(s):** T. L. Spelman, Publisher. **Price:** $30.95, plus $3.00 shipping.

2928 • North Carolina Automotive Directory
Automotive Contact
P.O. Box 517
Terre Haute, IN 47808   Ph:(812)232-2441

Directory. Automotive aftermarket businesses, including body shops; brake, muffler, radiator, electrical and transmission repairs, as well as new car dealers, parts retailers, auto salvage companies, and automotive parts warehouses. Annual, January. **Editor(s):** T. L. Spelman, Publisher. **Price:** $30.95, plus $3.00 shipping.

2929 • Ohio Automotive Directory
Automotive Contact
P.O. Box 517
Terre Haute, IN 47808   Ph:(812)232-2441

Directory. Automotive aftermarket businesses, including body shops; brake, muffler, radiator, electrical and transmission repairs, as well as new car dealers, parts retailers, auto salvage companies, and automotive parts warehouses. Annual, January. **Editor(s):** T. L. Spelman, Publisher. **Price:** $30.95, plus $3.00 shipping.

2930 • Oklahoma Automotive Directory
Automotive Contact
P.O. Box 517
Terre Haute, IN 47808   Ph:(812)232-2441

Directory. Automotive aftermarket businesses, including body shops; brake, muffler, radiator, electrical and transmission repairs, as well as new car dealers, parts retailers, auto salvage companies, and automotive parts warehouses. Annual, January. **Editor(s):** T. L. Spelman, Publisher. **Price:** $30.95, plus $3.00 shipping.

2931 • Oregon Automotive Directory
Automotive Contact
P.O. Box 517
Terre Haute, IN 47808   Ph:(812)232-2441

Directory. Automotive aftermarket businesses, including body shops; brake, muffler, radiator, electrical and transmission repairs, as well as new car dealers, parts retailers, auto salvage companies, and automotive parts warehouses. Annual, January. **Editor(s):** T. L. Spelman, Publisher. **Price:** $30.95, plus $3.00 shipping.

2932 • Pennsylvania Automotive Directory
Automotive Contact
P.O. Box 517
Terre Haute, IN 47808   Ph:(812)232-2441

Directory. Automotive aftermarket businesses, including body
shops; brake, muffler, radiator, electrical and transmission repairs,
as well as new car dealers, parts retailers, auto salvage companies,
and automotive parts warehouses. Annual, January. **Editor(s):** T. L.
Spelman, Publisher. **Price:** $30.95, plus $3.00 shipping.

2933 • South Carolina Automotive Directory
Automotive Contact
P.O. Box 517
Terre Haute, IN 47808   Ph:(812)232-2441

Directory. Automotive aftermarket businesses, including body
shops; brake, muffler, radiator, electrical and transmission repairs,
as well as new car dealers, parts retailers, auto salvage companies,
and automotive parts warehouses. Annual, January. **Editor(s):** T. L.
Spelman, Publisher. **Price:** $30.95, plus $3.00 shipping.

2934 • Tennessee Automotive Directory
Automotive Contact
P.O. Box 517
Terre Haute, IN 47808   Ph:(812)232-2441

Directory. Automotive aftermarket businesses, including body
shops; brake, muffler, radiator, electrical and transmission repairs,
as well as new car dealers, parts retailers, auto salvage companies,
and automotive parts warehouses. Annual, January. **Editor(s):** T. L.
Spelman, Publisher. **Price:** $30.95, plus $3.00 shipping.

2935 • Texas Automotive Directory
Automotive Contact
P.O. Box 517
Terre Haute, IN 47808   Ph:(812)232-2441

Directory. Automotive aftermarket businesses, including body
shops; brake, muffler, radiator, electrical and transmission repairs,
as well as new car dealers, parts retailers, auto salvage companies,
and automotive parts warehouses. Annual, January. **Editor(s):** T. L.
Spelman, Publisher. **Price:** $30.95, plus $3.00 shipping.

2936 • Virginia/West Virginia Automotive Directory
Automotive Contact
P.O. Box 517
Terre Haute, IN 47808   Ph:(812)232-2441

Directory. Automotive aftermarket businesses, including body
shops; brake, muffler, radiator, electrical and transmission repairs,
as well as new car dealers, parts retailers, auto salvage companies,
and automotive parts warehouses. Annual, January. **Editor(s):** T. L.
Spelman, Publisher. **Price:** $30.95, plus $3.00 shipping.

2937 • Washington Automotive Directory [State]
Automotive Contact
P.O. Box 517
Terre Haute, IN 47808   Ph:(812)232-2441

Directory. Automotive aftermarket businesses, including body
shops; brake, muffler, radiator, electrical and transmission repairs,
as well as new car dealers, parts retailers, auto salvage companies,
and automotive parts warehouses. Annual, January. **Editor(s):** T. L.
Spelman, Publisher. **Price:** $30.95, plus $3.00 shipping.

2938 • Wisconsin Automotive Directory
Automotive Contact
P.O. Box 517
Terre Haute, IN 47808   Ph:(812)232-2441

Directory. Automotive aftermarket businesses, including body
shops; brake, muffler, radiator, electrical and transmission repairs,
as well as new car dealers, parts retailers, auto salvage companies,
and automotive parts warehouses. Annual, January. **Editor(s):** T. L.
Spelman, Publisher. **Price:** $30.95, plus $3.00 shipping.

Automotive consultants

2939 • Automotive Consultants Directory
Society of Automotive Engineers (SAE)
400 Commonwealth Dr.   Ph:(412)776-4841
Warrendale, PA 15096-0001   Fax:(412)776-5760

Directory. About 390 consultants and consulting firms in
automotive engineering specialties, including safety,
manufacturing and quality control, engine design, emissions,
marketing, etc. Annual, December. **Price:** $22.00, postpaid,
payment with order.

2940 • Motor Age Big I Who's Who
Fairchild Publications
201 King of Prussia Rd.
Radnor, PA 19089   Ph:(215)964-4225

Directory. Annual.

Automotive dealers

2941 • Alabama Automotive Directory
Automotive Contact
Box 517
Terre Haute, IN 47808   Ph:(812)232-2441

Directory. Automotive aftermarket businesses, including body
shops; brake, muffler, radiator, electrical and transmission repairs,
as well as new car dealers, parts retailers, auto salvage companies,
and automotive parts warehouses. Annual, January. **Editor(s):** T. L.
Spelman, Publisher. **Price:** $30.95, plus $3.00 shipping.

2942 • Arizona/New Mexico Automotive Directory
Automotive Contact
P.O. Box 517
Terre Haute, IN 47808   Ph:(812)232-2441

Directory. Automotive aftermarket businesses, including body
shops; brake, muffler, radiator, electrical and transmission repairs,
as well as new car dealers, parts retailers, auto salvage companies,
and automotive parts warehouses. Annual, January. **Editor(s):** T. L.
Spelman, Publisher. **Price:** $30.95, plus $3.00 shipping.

2943 • Arkansas Automotive Directory
Automotive Contact
Box 517
Terre Haute, IN 47808   Ph:(812)232-2441

Directory. Automotive aftermarket businesses, including body
shops; brake, muffler, radiator, electrical and transmission repairs,
as well as new car dealers, parts retailers, auto salvage companies,
and automotive parts warehouses. Annual, January. **Editor(s):** T. L.
Spelman, Publisher. **Price:** $30.95, plus $3.00 shipping.

2944 • Automobile Dealers Directory [New Cars]
American Business Directories, Inc.
American Business Information, Inc.
5711 S. 86th Circle   Ph:(402)593-4600
Omaha, NE 68127   Fax:(402)331-1505

Directory. About 27,685 automotive dealers of new vehicles.
Annual. **Price:** $820.00, payment with order. Significant discounts
offered for standing orders. Franchise editions also available:
Buick, $150.00; Cadillac, $105.00; Chevrolet, $210.00;
Chrysler/Plymouth, $165.00; Datsun/Nissan, $105.00; Dodge,
$150.00; Ford, $210.00; Honda, $105.00; Isuzu, $105.00; Jeep,
$105.00; Lincoln/Mercury, $150.00; Mazda, $105.00; Oldsmobile,
$165.00; Pontiac, $165.00; Renault, $105.00; Subaru, $105.00;
Toyota, $105.00; Volkswagen, $105.00.

2945 • Automobile Dealers Directory [Used Cars]
American Business Directories, Inc.
American Business Information, Inc.
5711 S. 86th Circle   Ph:(402)593-4600
Omaha, NE 68127   Fax:(402)331-1505

Directory. About 76,070 automotive dealers of used vehicles.
Annual. **Price:** $2510.00, payment with order. Significant

discounts offered for standing orders. Regional editions available: Eastern, $1,295.00; Western, $850.00.

2946 • Automotive News—Market Data Book Issue
Crain Communications
1400 Woodbridge Ave.   Ph:(313)446-6000
Detroit, MI 48207   Fax:(313)446-0383

Directory. List of automobile, truck, parts, accessories, and dealership equipment manufacturers; "Who's Who in the Auto Industry" section gives brief biographical data and photographs of executives of major firms. Also includes production, sales, financial, price, automobile options and equipment, advertising expenditure, and other data; federal regulations; and domestic and import car specifications. Annual, May. **Editor(s):** Liz Pinto. **Price:** $35.00.

2947 • California Automotive Directory
Automotive Contact
P.O. Box 517
Terre Haute, IN 47808   Ph:(812)232-2441

Directory. Automotive aftermarket businesses, including body shops; brake, muffler, radiator, electrical and transmission repairs, as well as new car dealers, parts retailers, auto salvage companies, and automotive parts warehouses. Annual, January. **Editor(s):** T. L. Spelman, Publisher. **Price:** $30.95, plus $3.00 shipping.

2948 • Colorado/Utah/Nevada Automotive Directory
Automotive Contact
P.O. Box 517
Terre Haute, IN 47808   Ph:(812)232-2441

Directory. Automotive aftermarket businesses, including body shops; brake, muffler, radiator, electrical and transmission repairs, as well as new car dealers, parts retailers, auto salvage companies, and automotive parts warehouses. Annual, January. **Editor(s):** T. L. Spelman, Publisher. **Price:** $30.95, plus $3.00 shipping.

2949 • Connecticut/Rhode Island Automotive Directory
Automotive Contact
P.O. Box 517
Terre Haute, IN 47808   Ph:(812)232-2441

Directory. Automotive aftermarket businesses, including body shops; brake, muffler, radiator, electrical and transmission repairs, as well as new car dealers, parts retailers, auto salvage companies, and automotive parts warehouses. Annual, January. **Editor(s):** T. L. Spelman, Publisher. **Price:** $30.95, plus $3.00 shipping.

2950 • Delaware/District of Columbia/Maryland Automotive Directory
Automotive Contact
P.O. Box 517
Terre Haute, IN 47808   Ph:(812)232-2441

Directory. Automotive aftermarket businesses, including body shops; brake, muffler, radiator, electrical and transmission repairs, as well as new car dealers, parts retailers, auto salvage companies, and automotive parts warehouses. Annual, January. **Editor(s):** T. L. Spelman, Publisher. **Price:** $30.95, plus $3.00 shipping.

2951 • Directory of Foreign Automotive Companies in the United States
Mead Ventures, Inc.
P.O. Box 44952   Ph:(602)234-0044
Phoenix, AZ 85064   Fax:(602)234-0076

Directory. Over 600 foreign automotive manufacturers, distributors, and services in the United States. Irregular; latest edition June 1989. **Editor(s):** Dawn Erdos. **Price:** $295.00.

2952 • Florida Automotive Directory
Automotive Contact
P.O. Box 517
Terre Haute, IN 47808   Ph:(812)232-2441

Directory. Automotive aftermarket businesses, including body shops; brake, muffler, radiator, electrical and transmission repairs, as well as new car dealers, parts retailers, auto salvage companies,

and automotive parts warehouses. Annual, January. **Editor(s):** T. L. Spelman, Publisher. **Price:** $30.95, plus $3.00 shipping.

2953 • Georgia Automotive Directory
Automotive Contact
Box 517
Terre Haute, IN 47808   Ph:(812)232-2441

Directory. Automotive aftermarket businesses, including body shops; brake, muffler, radiator, electrical and transmission repairs, as well as new car dealers, parts retailers, auto salvage companies, and automotive parts warehouses. Annual, January. **Editor(s):** T. L. Spelman, Publisher. **Price:** $30.95, plus $3.00 shipping.

2954 • Idaho/Montana/North Dakota/South Dakota/Wyoming Automotive Directory
Automotive Contact
P.O. Box 517
Terre Haute, IN 47808   Ph:(812)232-2441

Directory. Automotive aftermarket businesses, including body shops; brake, muffler, radiator, electrical and transmission repairs, as well as new car dealers, parts retailers, auto salvage companies, and automotive parts warehouses. Annual, January. **Editor(s):** T. L. Spelman, Publisher. **Price:** $30.95, plus $3.00 shipping.

2955 • Illinois Automotive Directory
Automotive Contact
Box 517
Terre Haute, IN 47808   Ph:(812)232-2441

Directory. Automotive aftermarket businesses, including body shops; brake, muffler, radiator, electrical and transmission repairs, as well as new car dealers, parts retailers, auto salvage companies, and automotive parts warehouses. Annual, January. **Editor(s):** T. L. Spelman, Publisher. **Price:** $30.95, plus $3.00 shipping.

2956 • Indiana Automotive Directory
Automotive Contact
Box 517
Terre Haute, IN 47808   Ph:(812)232-2441

Directory. Automotive aftermarket businesses, including body shops; brake, muffler, radiator, electrical and transmission repairs, as well as new car dealers, parts retailers, auto salvage companies, and automotive parts warehouses. Annual, January. **Editor(s):** T. L. Spelman, Publisher. **Price:** $30.95, plus $3.00 shipping.

2957 • Iowa Automotive Directory
Automotive Contact
Box 517
Terre Haute, IN 47808   Ph:(812)232-2441

Directory. Automotive aftermarket businesses, including body shops; brake, muffler, radiator, electrical and transmission repairs, as well as new car dealers, parts retailers, auto salvage companies, and automotive parts warehouses. Annual, January. **Editor(s):** T. L. Spelman, Publisher. **Price:** $30.95, plus $3.00 shipping.

2958 • Kansas/Nebraska Automotive Directory
Automotive Contact
P.O. Box 517
Terre Haute, IN 47808   Ph:(812)232-2441

Directory. Automotive aftermarket businesses, including body shops; brake, muffler, radiator, electrical and transmission repairs, as well as new car dealers, parts retailers, auto salvage companies, and automotive parts warehouses. Annual, January. **Editor(s):** T. L. Spelman, Publisher. **Price:** $30.95, plus $3.00 shipping.

2959 • Kentucky Automotive Directory
Automotive Contact
Box 517
Terre Haute, IN 47808   Ph:(812)232-2441

Directory. Automotive aftermarket businesses, including body shops; brake, muffler, radiator, electrical and transmission repairs, as well as new car dealers, parts retailers, auto salvage companies, and automotive parts warehouses. Annual, January. **Editor(s):** T. L. Spelman, Publisher. **Price:** $30.95, plus $3.00 shipping.

2960 • Louisiana Automotive Directory
Automotive Contact
Box 517
Terre Haute, IN 47808   Ph:(812)232-2441

Directory. Automotive aftermarket businesses, including body shops; brake, muffler, radiator, electrical and transmission repairs, as well as new car dealers, parts retailers, auto salvage companies, and automotive parts warehouses. Annual, January. **Editor(s):** T. L. Spelman, Publisher. **Price:** $30.95, plus $3.00 shipping.

2961 • Maine/New Hampshire/Vermont Automotive Directory
Automotive Contact
P.O. Box 517
Terre Haute, IN 47808   Ph:(812)232-2441

Directory. Automotive aftermarket businesses, including body shops; brake, muffler, radiator, electrical and transmission repairs, as well as new car dealers, parts retailers, auto salvage companies, and automotive parts warehouses. Annual, January. **Editor(s):** T. L. Spelman, Publisher. **Price:** $30.95, plus $3.00 shipping.

2962 • Massachusetts Automotive Directory
Automotive Contact
P.O. Box 517
Terre Haute, IN 47808   Ph:(812)232-2441

Directory. Automotive aftermarket businesses, including body shops; brake, muffler, radiator, electrical and transmission repairs, as well as new car dealers, parts retailers, auto salvage companies, and automotive parts warehouses. Annual, January. **Editor(s):** T. L. Spelman, Publisher. **Price:** $30.95, plus $3.00 shipping.

2963 • Michigan Automotive Directory
Automotive Contact
P.O. Box 517
Terre Haute, IN 47808   Ph:(812)232-2441

Directory. Automotive aftermarket businesses, including body shops; brake, muffler, radiator, electrical and transmission repairs, as well as new car dealers, parts retailers, auto salvage companies, and automotive parts warehouses. Annual, January. **Editor(s):** T. L. Spelman, Publisher. **Price:** $30.95, plus $3.00 shipping.

2964 • Minnesota Automotive Directory
Automotive Contact
P.O. Box 517
Terre Haute, IN 47808   Ph:(812)232-2441

Directory. Automotive aftermarket businesses, including body shops; brake, muffler, radiator, electrical and transmission repairs, as well as new car dealers, parts retailers, auto salvage companies, and automotive parts warehouses. Annual, January. **Editor(s):** T. L. Spelman, Publisher. **Price:** $30.95, plus $3.00 shipping.

2965 • Mississippi Automotive Directory
Automotive Contact
P.O. Box 517
Terre Haute, IN 47808   Ph:(812)232-2441

Directory. Automotive aftermarket businesses, including body shops; brake, muffler, radiator, electrical and transmission repairs, as well as new car dealers, parts retailers, auto salvage companies, and automotive parts warehouses. Annual, January. **Editor(s):** T. L. Spelman, Publisher. **Price:** $30.95, plus $3.00 shipping.

2966 • Missouri Automotive Directory
Automotive Contact
P.O. Box 517
Terre Haute, IN 47808   Ph:(812)232-2441

Directory. Automotive aftermarket businesses, including body shops; brake, muffler, radiator, electrical and transmission repairs, as well as new car dealers, parts retailers, auto salvage companies, and automotive parts warehouses. Annual, January. **Editor(s):** T. L. Spelman, Publisher. **Price:** $30.95, plus $3.00 shipping.

2967 • Motor Age Big I Who's Who
Fairchild Publications
201 King of Prussia Rd.
Radnor, PA 19089   Ph:(215)964-4225

Directory. Annual.

2968 • National Tire Dealers and Retreaders Association—Who's Who Membership Directory
National Tire Dealers and Retreaders Assn.
1250 Eye St., NW, Ste. 400   Ph:(202)789-2300
Washington, DC 20005   Fax:(202)682-3999

Newsletter.

2969 • New Jersey Automotive Directory
Automotive Contact
P.O. Box 517
Terre Haute, IN 47808   Ph:(812)232-2441

Directory. Automotive aftermarket businesses, including body shops; brake, muffler, radiator, electrical and transmission repairs, as well as new car dealers, parts retailers, auto salvage companies, and automotive parts warehouses. Annual, January. **Editor(s):** T. L. Spelman, Publisher. **Price:** $30.95, plus $3.00 shipping.

2970 • New York Automotive Directory
Automotive Contact
P.O. Box 517
Terre Haute, IN 47808   Ph:(812)232-2441

Directory. Automotive aftermarket businesses, including body shops; brake, muffler, radiator, electrical and transmission repairs, as well as new car dealers, parts retailers, auto salvage companies, and automotive parts warehouses. Annual, January. **Editor(s):** T. L. Spelman, Publisher. **Price:** $30.95, plus $3.00 shipping.

2971 • North Carolina Automotive Directory
Automotive Contact
P.O. Box 517
Terre Haute, IN 47808   Ph:(812)232-2441

Directory. Automotive aftermarket businesses, including body shops; brake, muffler, radiator, electrical and transmission repairs, as well as new car dealers, parts retailers, auto salvage companies, and automotive parts warehouses. Annual, January. **Editor(s):** T. L. Spelman, Publisher. **Price:** $30.95, plus $3.00 shipping.

2972 • NTDRA Dealer News—Who's Who Directory Issue
National Tire Dealers & Retreaders Association (NTDRA)
1250 I St., NW, Ste. 400   Ph:(202)789-2300
Washington, DC 20005   Fax:(202)682-3999

Directory. 5,000 tire dealers and retreaders, suppliers of related products and services, private brand groups, and local associations that are members of the National Tire Dealers and Retreaders Association; retread plants that have been rated "A" by the association. Annual, January. **Editor(s):** C. D. Hylton III, Director, Communications Services. **Price:** $50.00.

2973 • Ohio Automobile Dealers Association—Directory
Ohio Automobile Dealers Association
1366 Dublin Rd.
Columbus, OH 43215   Ph:(614)487-9000

Directory. Lists of about 950 new car and truck dealers. Annual.

2974 • Ohio Automotive Directory
Automotive Contact
P.O. Box 517
Terre Haute, IN 47808   Ph:(812)232-2441

Directory. Automotive aftermarket businesses, including body shops; brake, muffler, radiator, electrical and transmission repairs, as well as new car dealers, parts retailers, auto salvage companies, and automotive parts warehouses. Annual, January. **Editor(s):** T. L. Spelman, Publisher. **Price:** $30.95, plus $3.00 shipping.

2975 • Oklahoma Automotive Directory
Automotive Contact
P.O. Box 517
Terre Haute, IN 47808   Ph:(812)232-2441

Directory. Automotive aftermarket businesses, including body shops; brake, muffler, radiator, electrical and transmission repairs, as well as new car dealers, parts retailers, auto salvage companies, and automotive parts warehouses. Annual, January. **Editor(s):** T. L. Spelman, Publisher. **Price:** $30.95, plus $3.00 shipping.

2976 • Oregon Automotive Directory
Automotive Contact
P.O. Box 517
Terre Haute, IN 47808   Ph:(812)232-2441

Directory. Automotive aftermarket businesses, including body shops; brake, muffler, radiator, electrical and transmission repairs, as well as new car dealers, parts retailers, auto salvage companies, and automotive parts warehouses. Annual, January. **Editor(s):** T. L. Spelman, Publisher. **Price:** $30.95, plus $3.00 shipping.

2977 • Pennsylvania Automotive Directory
Automotive Contact
P.O. Box 517
Terre Haute, IN 47808   Ph:(812)232-2441

Directory. Automotive aftermarket businesses, including body shops; brake, muffler, radiator, electrical and transmission repairs, as well as new car dealers, parts retailers, auto salvage companies, and automotive parts warehouses. Annual, January. **Editor(s):** T. L. Spelman, Publisher. **Price:** $30.95, plus $3.00 shipping.

2978 • Rhode Island Auto Dealers Association—Yearbook and Directory
Rhode Island Auto Dealers Association
335-D Centerville Rd.
Warwick, RI 02886   Ph:(401)732-6870

Directory. Lists 100 dealers of new automobiles.

2979 • South Carolina Automotive Directory
Automotive Contact
P.O. Box 517
Terre Haute, IN 47808   Ph:(812)232-2441

Directory. Automotive aftermarket businesses, including body shops; brake, muffler, radiator, electrical and transmission repairs, as well as new car dealers, parts retailers, auto salvage companies, and automotive parts warehouses. Annual, January. **Editor(s):** T. L. Spelman, Publisher. **Price:** $30.95, plus $3.00 shipping.

2980 • Tennessee Automotive Directory
Automotive Contact
P.O. Box 517
Terre Haute, IN 47808   Ph:(812)232-2441

Directory. Automotive aftermarket businesses, including body shops; brake, muffler, radiator, electrical and transmission repairs, as well as new car dealers, parts retailers, auto salvage companies, and automotive parts warehouses. Annual, January. **Editor(s):** T. L. Spelman, Publisher. **Price:** $30.95, plus $3.00 shipping.

2981 • Texas Automotive Directory
Automotive Contact
P.O. Box 517
Terre Haute, IN 47808   Ph:(812)232-2441

Directory. Automotive aftermarket businesses, including body shops; brake, muffler, radiator, electrical and transmission repairs, as well as new car dealers, parts retailers, auto salvage companies, and automotive parts warehouses. Annual, January. **Editor(s):** T. L. Spelman, Publisher. **Price:** $30.95, plus $3.00 shipping.

2982 • Truck Dealers Directory
American Business Directories, Inc.
American Business Information, Inc.
5711 S. 86th Circle   Ph:(402)593-4600
Omaha, NE 68127   Fax:(402)331-1505

Directory. 16,065 truck dealers. Annual. **Price:** $535.00, payment

with order. Significant discounts offered for standing orders. Franchise editions also available: GMC, $130.00.

2983 • Truck Dealers-Used Directory
American Business Directories, Inc.
American Business Information, Inc.
5711 S. 86th Circle   Ph:(402)593-4600
Omaha, NE 68127   Fax:(402)331-1505

Directory. Annual. **Price:** $215.00, payment with order. Significant discounts offered for standing orders.

2984 • Virginia/West Virginia Automotive Directory
Automotive Contact
P.O. Box 517
Terre Haute, IN 47808   Ph:(812)232-2441

Directory. Automotive aftermarket businesses, including body shops; brake, muffler, radiator, electrical and transmission repairs, as well as new car dealers, parts retailers, auto salvage companies, and automotive parts warehouses. Annual, January. **Editor(s):** T. L. Spelman, Publisher. **Price:** $30.95, plus $3.00 shipping.

2985 • Washington Automotive Directory [State]
Automotive Contact
P.O. Box 517
Terre Haute, IN 47808   Ph:(812)232-2441

Directory. Automotive aftermarket businesses, including body shops; brake, muffler, radiator, electrical and transmission repairs, as well as new car dealers, parts retailers, auto salvage companies, and automotive parts warehouses. Annual, January. **Editor(s):** T. L. Spelman, Publisher. **Price:** $30.95, plus $3.00 shipping.

2986 • Wisconsin Automotive Directory
Automotive Contact
P.O. Box 517
Terre Haute, IN 47808   Ph:(812)232-2441

Directory. Automotive aftermarket businesses, including body shops; brake, muffler, radiator, electrical and transmission repairs, as well as new car dealers, parts retailers, auto salvage companies, and automotive parts warehouses. Annual, January. **Editor(s):** T. L. Spelman, Publisher. **Price:** $30.95, plus $3.00 shipping.

Automotive Industry

2987 • Automotive News—Market Data Book Issue
Crain Communications
1400 Woodbridge Ave.   Ph:(313)446-6000
Detroit, MI 48207   Fax:(313)446-0383

Directory. List of automobile, truck, parts, accessories, and dealership equipment manufacturers; "Who's Who in the Auto Industry" section gives brief biographical data and photographs of executives of major firms. Also includes production, sales, financial, price, automobile options and equipment, advertising expenditure, and other data; federal regulations; and domestic and import car specifications. Annual, May. **Editor(s):** Liz Pinto. **Price:** $35.00.

Automotive parts retailers

2988 • ADP Parts Exchange
ADP Automotive Claims Services
2010 Crow Canyon Pl.
San Ramon, CA 94583   Ph:(415)866-1100

Database. Includes auto parts distributors, vehicle dismantlers, recyclers, and other sources of new and salvaged automobile parts and common repair items for vehicles manufactured since 1970. Formerly titled ADP Salvage Parts Locator; ADP Parts and Assemblies Locator. Daily updates.

2989 • Alabama Automotive Directory
Automotive Contact
Box 517
Terre Haute, IN 47808   Ph:(812)232-2441

Directory. Automotive aftermarket businesses, including body shops; brake, muffler, radiator, electrical and transmission repairs, as well as new car dealers, parts retailers, auto salvage companies, and automotive parts warehouses. Annual, January. **Editor(s):** T. L. Spelman, Publisher. **Price:** $30.95, plus $3.00 shipping.

2990 • Arizona/New Mexico Automotive Directory
Automotive Contact
P.O. Box 517
Terre Haute, IN 47808   Ph:(812)232-2441

Directory. Automotive aftermarket businesses, including body shops; brake, muffler, radiator, electrical and transmission repairs, as well as new car dealers, parts retailers, auto salvage companies, and automotive parts warehouses. Annual, January. **Editor(s):** T. L. Spelman, Publisher. **Price:** $30.95, plus $3.00 shipping.

2991 • Arkansas Automotive Directory
Automotive Contact
Box 517
Terre Haute, IN 47808   Ph:(812)232-2441

Directory. Automotive aftermarket businesses, including body shops; brake, muffler, radiator, electrical and transmission repairs, as well as new car dealers, parts retailers, auto salvage companies, and automotive parts warehouses. Annual, January. **Editor(s):** T. L. Spelman, Publisher. **Price:** $30.95, plus $3.00 shipping.

2992 • Automobile Air Conditioning Equipment Directory
American Business Directories, Inc.
American Business Information, Inc.
5711 S. 86th Circle   Ph:(402)593-4600
Omaha, NE 68127   Fax:(402)331-1505

Directory. About 13,630 suppliers and dealers of automobile air conditioning equipment. Annual. **Price:** $440.00, payment with order. Significant discounts offered for standing orders.

2993 • Automobile Components Aftermarket
Frost and Sullivan, Inc.
106 Fulton St.
New York, NY 10038   Ph:(212)233-1080

Directory. Two volume set. Published 1987. **Price:** $2,700.00.

2994 • Automobile Parts Retailers Directory
American Business Directories, Inc.
American Business Information, Inc.
5711 S. 86th Circle   Ph:(402)593-4600
Omaha, NE 68127   Fax:(402)331-1505

Directory. About 59,780 automotive parts retailers. Annual. **Price:** $1,975.00, payment with order. Significant discounts offered for standing orders. Regional editions available: Eastern, $945.00; Western, $765.00.

2995 • Automobile Radio/Stereo Systems Directory
American Business Directories, Inc.
American Business Information, Inc.
5711 S. 86th Circle   Ph:(402)593-4600
Omaha, NE 68127   Fax:(402)331-1505

Directory. About 7,300 retailers of automobile stereo systems. Annual. **Price:** $235.00, payment with order. Significant discounts offered for standing orders.

2996 • Automobile Seat Covers/Tops/Upholstery Directory
American Business Directories, Inc.
American Business Information, Inc.
5711 S. 86th Circle   Ph:(402)593-4600
Omaha, NE 68127   Fax:(402)331-1505

Directory. About 9,920 retail firms that offer automobile seat covers and other interior accessories. Annual. **Price:** $335.00, payment with order. Significant discounts offered for standing orders.

2997 • Automobile Smog Control Devices
American Business Directories, Inc.
American Business Information, Inc.
5711 S. 86th Circle   Ph:(401)593-4600
Omaha, NE 68127   Fax:(402)331-1505

Directory. 2,210 automotive manufacturers and retailers of smog control devices. Annual. **Price:** $75.00, payment with order. Significant discounts offered for standing orders.

2998 • Automotive Marketing—Retail Aftermarket Guide Issue
Chilton Co.
Chilton Way   Ph:(215)964-4000
Radnor, PA 19089   Fax:(215)964-4273

Directory. Lists of leading automotive retailers, wholesale distributors and suppliers, programmed distributors, franchises, discount stores, drug store chains, food store chains, hardware distributors, and marketing representatives dealing in aftermarket automotive products; list of paid advertisements from companies that publish product catalogs. Annual, April. **Editor(s):** Rosemarie Kitchin. **Price:** $55.00.

2999 • California Automotive Directory
Automotive Contact
P.O. Box 517
Terre Haute, IN 47808   Ph:(812)232-2441

Directory. Automotive aftermarket businesses, including body shops; brake, muffler, radiator, electrical and transmission repairs, as well as new car dealers, parts retailers, auto salvage companies, and automotive parts warehouses. Annual, January. **Editor(s):** T. L. Spelman, Publisher. **Price:** $30.95, plus $3.00 shipping.

3000 • Colorado/Utah/Nevada Automotive Directory
Automotive Contact
P.O. Box 517
Terre Haute, IN 47808   Ph:(812)232-2441

Directory. Automotive aftermarket businesses, including body shops; brake, muffler, radiator, electrical and transmission repairs, as well as new car dealers, parts retailers, auto salvage companies, and automotive parts warehouses. Annual, January. **Editor(s):** T. L. Spelman, Publisher. **Price:** $30.95, plus $3.00 shipping.

3001 • Connecticut/Rhode Island Automotive Directory
Automotive Contact
P.O. Box 517
Terre Haute, IN 47808   Ph:(812)232-2441

Directory. Automotive aftermarket businesses, including body shops; brake, muffler, radiator, electrical and transmission repairs, as well as new car dealers, parts retailers, auto salvage companies, and automotive parts warehouses. Annual, January. **Editor(s):** T. L. Spelman, Publisher. **Price:** $30.95, plus $3.00 shipping.

3002 • Delaware/District of Columbia/Maryland Automotive Directory
Automotive Contact
P.O. Box 517
Terre Haute, IN 47808   Ph:(812)232-2441

Directory. Automotive aftermarket businesses, including body shops; brake, muffler, radiator, electrical and transmission repairs, as well as new car dealers, parts retailers, auto salvage companies, and automotive parts warehouses. Annual, January. **Editor(s):** T. L. Spelman, Publisher. **Price:** $30.95, plus $3.00 shipping.

3003 • Directory of Automotive Aftermarket Suppliers
Chain Store Guide Information Services
3922 Coconut Palm Dr.
Tampa, FL 33519   Ph:(813)664-6700

Directory. Over 1,300 auto supply store chains operating 15,060 stores; over 960 warehouse distributors and branch offices; 15 buying/programming distribution groups. Biennial, December of even years. **Editor(s):** Michael Lambe. **Price:** $189.00. Also available in state editions.

3004 • Engine Dealers-Gasoline Directory
American Business Directories, Inc.
American Business Information, Inc.
5711 S. 86th Circle   Ph:(402)593-4600
Omaha, NE 68127   Fax:(402)331-1505

Directory. Nearly 13,640 automotive parts retailers and salvage dealers. Annual. **Price:** $440.00, payment with order. Significant discounts offered for standing orders.

3005 • Florida Automotive Directory
Automotive Contact
P.O. Box 517
Terre Haute, IN 47808   Ph:(812)232-2441

Directory. Automotive aftermarket businesses, including body shops; brake, muffler, radiator, electrical and transmission repairs, as well as new car dealers, parts retailers, auto salvage companies, and automotive parts warehouses. Annual, January. **Editor(s):** T. L. Spelman, Publisher. **Price:** $30.95, plus $3.00 shipping.

3006 • Georgia Automotive Directory
Automotive Contact
Box 517
Terre Haute, IN 47808   Ph:(812)232-2441

Directory. Automotive aftermarket businesses, including body shops; brake, muffler, radiator, electrical and transmission repairs, as well as new car dealers, parts retailers, auto salvage companies, and automotive parts warehouses. Annual, January. **Editor(s):** T. L. Spelman, Publisher. **Price:** $30.95, plus $3.00 shipping.

3007 • Hot Rod Annual
Petersen Publishing Co.
8490 Sunset Blvd.
Los Angeles, CA 90069   Ph:(213)657-5100

Directory. Lists of manufacturers, custom and speed shops, high-performance companies, engine builders, motorsport organizations. Annual, November. **Editor(s):** Bruce Caldwell. **Price:** $4.95, payment with order.

3008 • Idaho/Montana/North Dakota/South Dakota/Wyoming Automotive Directory
Automotive Contact
P.O. Box 517
Terre Haute, IN 47808   Ph:(812)232-2441

Directory. Automotive aftermarket businesses, including body shops; brake, muffler, radiator, electrical and transmission repairs, as well as new car dealers, parts retailers, auto salvage companies, and automotive parts warehouses. Annual, January. **Editor(s):** T. L. Spelman, Publisher. **Price:** $30.95, plus $3.00 shipping.

3009 • Illinois Automotive Directory
Automotive Contact
Box 517
Terre Haute, IN 47808   Ph:(812)232-2441

Directory. Automotive aftermarket businesses, including body shops; brake, muffler, radiator, electrical and transmission repairs, as well as new car dealers, parts retailers, auto salvage companies, and automotive parts warehouses. Annual, January. **Editor(s):** T. L. Spelman, Publisher. **Price:** $30.95, plus $3.00 shipping.

3010 • Indiana Automotive Directory
Automotive Contact
Box 517
Terre Haute, IN 47808   Ph:(812)232-2441

Directory. Automotive aftermarket businesses, including body shops; brake, muffler, radiator, electrical and transmission repairs, as well as new car dealers, parts retailers, auto salvage companies, and automotive parts warehouses. Annual, January. **Editor(s):** T. L. Spelman, Publisher. **Price:** $30.95, plus $3.00 shipping.

3011 • Iowa Automotive Directory
Automotive Contact
Box 517
Terre Haute, IN 47808   Ph:(812)232-2441

Directory. Automotive aftermarket businesses, including body shops; brake, muffler, radiator, electrical and transmission repairs, as well as new car dealers, parts retailers, auto salvage companies, and automotive parts warehouses. Annual, January. **Editor(s):** T. L. Spelman, Publisher. **Price:** $30.95, plus $3.00 shipping.

3012 • Jobber Retailer Aftermarket Manual
Bill Communications, Inc.
P.O. Box 3599   Ph:(216)867-4401
Akron, OH 44309   Fax:(216)867-0019

Directory. Program distribution groups of the automotive aftermarket industry; aftermarket associations; and aftermarket suppliers. Annual, May. **Editor(s):** Michael Mavrigian. **Price:** $62.00, plus $2.00 shipping.

3013 • Jobber Topics—Marketing/Directory Issue
Irving-Cloud Publishing Company
7300 N. Cicero Ave.   Ph:(708)588-7300
Chicago, IL 60646-1696   Fax:(708)674-7015

Directory. Manufacturers, remanufacturers, warehouse distributors, jobbers, manufacturers' agents, and trade associations in the automotive aftermarket field. Annual, July. **Editor(s):** Bob Weber, Editorial Director. **Price:** $60.00, postpaid.

3014 • Kansas/Nebraska Automotive Directory
Automotive Contact
P.O. Box 517
Terre Haute, IN 47808   Ph:(812)232-2441

Directory. Automotive aftermarket businesses, including body shops; brake, muffler, radiator, electrical and transmission repairs, as well as new car dealers, parts retailers, auto salvage companies, and automotive parts warehouses. Annual, January. **Editor(s):** T. L. Spelman, Publisher. **Price:** $30.95, plus $3.00 shipping.

3015 • Kentucky Automotive Directory
Automotive Contact
Box 517
Terre Haute, IN 47808   Ph:(812)232-2441

Directory. Automotive aftermarket businesses, including body shops; brake, muffler, radiator, electrical and transmission repairs, as well as new car dealers, parts retailers, auto salvage companies, and automotive parts warehouses. Annual, January. **Editor(s):** T. L. Spelman, Publisher. **Price:** $30.95, plus $3.00 shipping.

3016 • Louisiana Automotive Directory
Automotive Contact
Box 517
Terre Haute, IN 47808   Ph:(812)232-2441

Directory. Automotive aftermarket businesses, including body shops; brake, muffler, radiator, electrical and transmission repairs, as well as new car dealers, parts retailers, auto salvage companies, and automotive parts warehouses. Annual, January. **Editor(s):** T. L. Spelman, Publisher. **Price:** $30.95, plus $3.00 shipping.

3017 • Maine/New Hampshire/Vermont Automotive Directory
Automotive Contact
P.O. Box 517
Terre Haute, IN 47808   Ph:(812)232-2441

Directory. Automotive aftermarket businesses, including body shops; brake, muffler, radiator, electrical and transmission repairs, as well as new car dealers, parts retailers, auto salvage companies, and automotive parts warehouses. Annual, January. **Editor(s):** T. L. Spelman, Publisher. **Price:** $30.95, plus $3.00 shipping.

3018 • Massachusetts Automotive Directory
Automotive Contact
P.O. Box 517
Terre Haute, IN 47808   Ph:(812)232-2441

Directory. Automotive aftermarket businesses, including body shops; brake, muffler, radiator, electrical and transmission repairs, as well as new car dealers, parts retailers, auto salvage companies, and automotive parts warehouses. Annual, January. **Editor(s):** T. L. Spelman, Publisher. **Price:** $30.95, plus $3.00 shipping.

3019 • Michigan Automotive Directory
Automotive Contact
P.O. Box 517
Terre Haute, IN 47808   Ph:(812)232-2441

Directory. Automotive aftermarket businesses, including body shops; brake, muffler, radiator, electrical and transmission repairs, as well as new car dealers, parts retailers, auto salvage companies, and automotive parts warehouses. Annual, January. **Editor(s):** T. L. Spelman, Publisher. **Price:** $30.95, plus $3.00 shipping.

3020 • Minnesota Automotive Directory
Automotive Contact
P.O. Box 517
Terre Haute, IN 47808   Ph:(812)232-2441

Directory. Automotive aftermarket businesses, including body shops; brake, muffler, radiator, electrical and transmission repairs, as well as new car dealers, parts retailers, auto salvage companies, and automotive parts warehouses. Annual, January. **Editor(s):** T. L. Spelman, Publisher. **Price:** $30.95, plus $3.00 shipping.

3021 • Mississippi Automotive Directory
Automotive Contact
P.O. Box 517
Terre Haute, IN 47808   Ph:(812)232-2441

Directory. Automotive aftermarket businesses, including body shops; brake, muffler, radiator, electrical and transmission repairs, as well as new car dealers, parts retailers, auto salvage companies, and automotive parts warehouses. Annual, January. **Editor(s):** T. L. Spelman, Publisher. **Price:** $30.95, plus $3.00 shipping.

3022 • Missouri Automotive Directory
Automotive Contact
P.O. Box 517
Terre Haute, IN 47808   Ph:(812)232-2441

Directory. Automotive aftermarket businesses, including body shops; brake, muffler, radiator, electrical and transmission repairs, as well as new car dealers, parts retailers, auto salvage companies, and automotive parts warehouses. Annual, January. **Editor(s):** T. L. Spelman, Publisher. **Price:** $30.95, plus $3.00 shipping.

3023 • New Jersey Automotive Directory
Automotive Contact
P.O. Box 517
Terre Haute, IN 47808   Ph:(812)232-2441

Directory. Automotive aftermarket businesses, including body shops; brake, muffler, radiator, electrical and transmission repairs, as well as new car dealers, parts retailers, auto salvage companies, and automotive parts warehouses. Annual, January. **Editor(s):** T. L. Spelman, Publisher. **Price:** $30.95, plus $3.00 shipping.

3024 • New York Automotive Directory
Automotive Contact
P.O. Box 517
Terre Haute, IN 47808   Ph:(812)232-2441

Directory. Automotive aftermarket businesses, including body shops; brake, muffler, radiator, electrical and transmission repairs, as well as new car dealers, parts retailers, auto salvage companies, and automotive parts warehouses. Annual, January. **Editor(s):** T. L. Spelman, Publisher. **Price:** $30.95, plus $3.00 shipping.

3025 • North Carolina Automotive Directory
Automotive Contact
P.O. Box 517
Terre Haute, IN 47808   Ph:(812)232-2441

Directory. Automotive aftermarket businesses, including body shops; brake, muffler, radiator, electrical and transmission repairs, as well as new car dealers, parts retailers, auto salvage companies, and automotive parts warehouses. Annual, January. **Editor(s):** T. L. Spelman, Publisher. **Price:** $30.95, plus $3.00 shipping.

3026 • Ohio Automotive Directory
Automotive Contact
P.O. Box 517
Terre Haute, IN 47808   Ph:(812)232-2441

Directory. Automotive aftermarket businesses, including body shops; brake, muffler, radiator, electrical and transmission repairs, as well as new car dealers, parts retailers, auto salvage companies, and automotive parts warehouses. Annual, January. **Editor(s):** T. L. Spelman, Publisher. **Price:** $30.95, plus $3.00 shipping.

3027 • Oklahoma Automotive Directory
Automotive Contact
P.O. Box 517
Terre Haute, IN 47808   Ph:(812)232-2441

Directory. Automotive aftermarket businesses, including body shops; brake, muffler, radiator, electrical and transmission repairs, as well as new car dealers, parts retailers, auto salvage companies, and automotive parts warehouses. Annual, January. **Editor(s):** T. L. Spelman, Publisher. **Price:** $30.95, plus $3.00 shipping.

3028 • Oregon Automotive Directory
Automotive Contact
P.O. Box 517
Terre Haute, IN 47808   Ph:(812)232-2441

Directory. Automotive aftermarket businesses, including body shops; brake, muffler, radiator, electrical and transmission repairs, as well as new car dealers, parts retailers, auto salvage companies, and automotive parts warehouses. Annual, January. **Editor(s):** T. L. Spelman, Publisher. **Price:** $30.95, plus $3.00 shipping.

3029 • Pennsylvania Automotive Directory
Automotive Contact
P.O. Box 517
Terre Haute, IN 47808   Ph:(812)232-2441

Directory. Automotive aftermarket businesses, including body shops; brake, muffler, radiator, electrical and transmission repairs, as well as new car dealers, parts retailers, auto salvage companies, and automotive parts warehouses. Annual, January. **Editor(s):** T. L. Spelman, Publisher. **Price:** $30.95, plus $3.00 shipping.

3030 • Shock Absorbers-Retail Directory
American Business Directories, Inc.
American Business Information, Inc.
5711 S. 86th Circle   Ph:(402)593-4600
Omaha, NE 68127   Fax:(402)331-1505

Directory. About 4,840 automotive parts retailers that offer shock absorbers. Annual. **Price:** $180.00, payment with order. Significant discounts offered for standing orders.

3031 • South Carolina Automotive Directory
Automotive Contact
P.O. Box 517
Terre Haute, IN 47808   Ph:(812)232-2441

Directory. Automotive aftermarket businesses, including body shops; brake, muffler, radiator, electrical and transmission repairs, as well as new car dealers, parts retailers, auto salvage companies, and automotive parts warehouses. Annual, January. **Editor(s):** T. L. Spelman, Publisher. **Price:** $30.95, plus $3.00 shipping.

3032 • Specialty & Custom Dealer—Performance Warehouse Directory Issue
Babcox Automotive Publications
11 S. Forge St.   Ph:(216)535-6117
Akron, OH 44304   Fax:(216)535-0874

Directory. List of about 150-300 performance warehouses, suppliers of parts and accessories for hot rod and other high performance automobiles. Annual, June. **Editor(s):** Steve Cole. **Price:** $4.75, plus $1.00 shipping.

3033 • Starters—Engine Directory
American Business Directories, Inc.
American Business Information, Inc.
5711 S. 86th Circle   Ph:(402)593-4600
Omaha, NE 68127   Fax:(402)331-1505

Directory. Over 1,000 automotive manufacturers and retailers of engine starters. Annual. **Price:** $85.00, payment with order. Significant discounts offered for standing orders.

3034 • Tennessee Automotive Directory
Automotive Contact
P.O. Box 517
Terre Haute, IN 47808   Ph:(812)232-2441

Directory. Automotive aftermarket businesses, including body shops; brake, muffler, radiator, electrical and transmission repairs, as well as new car dealers, parts retailers, auto salvage companies, and automotive parts warehouses. Annual, January. **Editor(s):** T. L. Spelman, Publisher. **Price:** $30.95, plus $3.00 shipping.

3035 • Texas Automotive Directory
Automotive Contact
P.O. Box 517
Terre Haute, IN 47808   Ph:(812)232-2441

Directory. Automotive aftermarket businesses, including body shops; brake, muffler, radiator, electrical and transmission repairs, as well as new car dealers, parts retailers, auto salvage companies, and automotive parts warehouses. Annual, January. **Editor(s):** T. L. Spelman, Publisher. **Price:** $30.95, plus $3.00 shipping.

3036 • Tire Dealers-Retail Directory
American Business Directories, Inc.
American Business Information, Inc.
5711 S. 86th Circle   Ph:(402)593-4600
Omaha, NE 68127   Fax:(402)331-1505

Directory. 42,175 retail tire dealers. Annual. **Price:** $1,215.00, payment with order. Significant discounts offered for standing orders. Regional editions available: Eastern, $700.00; Western, $600.00. Franchise editions also available: Bridgestone, $130.00; Firestone, $165.00; Goodrich, $105.00; Goodyear, $230.00; Kelly Springfield, $105.00; Michelin, $210.00; Uniroyal, $150.00.

3037 • Tire Dealers-Used Directory
American Business Directories, Inc.
American Business Information, Inc.
5711 S. 86th Circle   Ph:(402)593-4600
Omaha, NE 68127   Fax:(402)331-1505

Directory. 2,875 tire dealers and automotive salvage dealers. Annual. **Price:** $110.00, payment with order. Significant discounts offered for standing orders.

3038 • Truck Canopies, Caps and Shells Directory
American Business Directories, Inc.
American Business Information, Inc.
5711 S. 86th Circle   Ph:(402)593-4600
Omaha, NE 68127   Fax:(402)331-1505

Directory. About 1,095 automotive manufacturers and retailers of truck canopies, caps, and shells. Annual. **Price:** $85.00, payment with order. Significant discounts offered for standing orders.

3039 • Truck Equipment & Parts Directory
American Business Directories, Inc.
American Business Information, Inc.
5711 S. 86th Circle   Ph:(402)593-4600
Omaha, NE 68127   Fax:(402)331-1505

Directory. Nearly 11,495 truck equipment and parts retailers. Annual. **Price:** $375.00, payment with order. Significant discounts offered for standing orders.

3040 • Virginia/West Virginia Automotive Directory
Automotive Contact
P.O. Box 517
Terre Haute, IN 47808   Ph:(812)232-2441

Directory. Automotive aftermarket businesses, including body shops; brake, muffler, radiator, electrical and transmission repairs, as well as new car dealers, parts retailers, auto salvage companies, and automotive parts warehouses. Annual, January. **Editor(s):** T. L. Spelman, Publisher. **Price:** $30.95, plus $3.00 shipping.

3041 • Washington Automotive Directory [State]
Automotive Contact
P.O. Box 517
Terre Haute, IN 47808   Ph:(812)232-2441

Directory. Automotive aftermarket businesses, including body shops; brake, muffler, radiator, electrical and transmission repairs, as well as new car dealers, parts retailers, auto salvage companies, and automotive parts warehouses. Annual, January. **Editor(s):** T. L. Spelman, Publisher. **Price:** $30.95, plus $3.00 shipping.

3042 • Wheels Directory
American Business Directories, Inc.
American Business Information, Inc.
5711 S. 86th Circle   Ph:(402)593-4600
Omaha, NE 68127   Fax:(402)331-1505

Directory. Nearly 2,695 automotive parts retailers. Annual. **Price:** $110.00, payment with order. Significant discounts offered for standing orders.

3043 • Wisconsin Automotive Directory
Automotive Contact
P.O. Box 517
Terre Haute, IN 47808   Ph:(812)232-2441

Directory. Automotive aftermarket businesses, including body shops; brake, muffler, radiator, electrical and transmission repairs, as well as new car dealers, parts retailers, auto salvage companies, and automotive parts warehouses. Annual, January. **Editor(s):** T. L. Spelman, Publisher. **Price:** $30.95, plus $3.00 shipping.

3044 • Wisconsin Automotive Parts Association— Directory
Wisconsin Automotive Parts Association
555 D'Onofrio Dr., Ste. 5
Madison, WI 53719   Ph:(608)833-6888

Directory. Lists about 190 automotive parts stores.

Automotive products manufacturers

3045 • Automobile International—Buyers' Guide Issue
Johnston International Publishing Corporation
386 Park Ave., S.   Ph:(212)689-0120
New York, NY 10016   Fax:(212)779-7475

Directory. List of over 1,000 manufacturers of automotive products; international coverage. Also includes worldwide vehicle census, including statistics on registrations of cars, trucks, and buses by country; and automotive show calendar, with listing of contacts and dates for automotive component, accessory and service equipment shows. Annual, November. **Editor(s):** Havis Dawson. **Price:** $50.00 per year; $80.00 per two years.

3046 • Automobile Smog Control Devices
American Business Directories, Inc.
American Business Information, Inc.
5711 S. 86th Circle   Ph:(401)593-4600
Omaha, NE 68127   Fax:(402)331-1505

Directory. 2,210 automotive manufacturers and retailers of smog control devices. Annual. **Price:** $75.00, payment with order. Significant discounts offered for standing orders.

3047 • Automotive Rebuilder—Purchasing Directory Issue
Babcox Automotive Publications
11 S. Forge St.   Ph:(216)535-6117
Akron, OH 44304   Fax:(216)535-0874

Directory. List of about 500 manufacturers of components, equipment, and supplies for rebuilding automotive parts. Annual, January. **Editor(s):** Dave Wooldridge. **Price:** $25.00.

3048 • Automotive Warehouse Distributors Association—Membership Directory
Automotive Warehouse Distributors Association
9140 Ward Pkwy.   Ph:(816)444-3500
Kansas City, MO 64114   Fax:(816)444-0330

Directory. Over 600 automotive parts distributors and 260 manufacturers of automotive parts. Annual, March. **Editor(s):** Charlotte Thomas. **Price:** $75.00, postpaid.

3049 • Brake and Front End—Buyers Guide to Brake Parts Issue
Babcox Automotive Publications
11 S. Forge St.
Akron, OH 44304   Ph:(216)535-6117

Directory. Manufacturers and suppliers of automotive brake parts and assemblies and friction products. Reported as annual; latest edition August 1988; suspended indefinitely. **Editor(s):** Jeffrey S. Davis. **Price:** $4.00.

3050 • Drive Shafts Wholesale and Manufacturers Directory
American Business Directories, Inc.
American Business Information, Inc.
5711 S. 86th Circle   Ph:(402)593-4600
Omaha, NE 68127   Fax:(402)331-1505

Directory. About 1,170 drive shaft wholesalers and manufacturers. Annual. **Price:** $85.00, payment with order. Significant discounts offered for standing orders.

3051 • Eastern Aftermarket Journal—Directory and Buyers Guide Issue
Stan Hubsher, Inc.
Box 373   Ph:(516)295-3680
Cedarhurst, NY 11516   Fax:(516)569-5296

Directory. List of about 1,500 manufacturers of automotive aftermarket parts, suppliers of services, manufacturers' representatives, and warehouse distributors on the eastern seaboard. Annual, January/February. **Editor(s):** Stan Hubsher. **Price:** $20.00, plus $2.00 shipping.

3052 • Eastern Aftermarket Journal—Foreign Parts Directory and Buyer's Guide Issue
Eastern Aftermarket Journal
PO Box 373   Ph:(516)295-3680
Cedarhurst, NY 11516   Fax:(516)569-5926

Directory. List of about 320 manufacturers, 240 warehouse distributors, and 100 representatives selling parts for foreign cars in the eastern United States. Annual, September/October. **Editor(s):** Stanley Hubsher, Publisher-Editor. **Price:** $15.00.

3053 • Hot Rod Annual
Petersen Publishing Co.
8490 Sunset Blvd.
Los Angeles, CA 90069   Ph:(213)657-5100

Directory. Lists of manufacturers, custom and speed shops, high-performance companies, engine builders, motorsport organizations. Annual, November. **Editor(s):** Bruce Caldwell. **Price:** $4.95, payment with order.

3054 • Installation News—Fact Book Issue
Bobit Publishing, Inc.
2512 Artesia Blvd.   Ph:(213)376-8788
Redondo Beach, CA 90278   Fax:(213)376-9043

Directory. Over 150 manufacturers and suppliers of automotive security, consumer electronics, and cellular products. Annual, October. **Editor(s):** Michele Guido and Michael Spivak. **Price:** $2.00.

3055 • International Mobile Air Conditioning Association—Membership/Industry Contact Directory
International Mobile Air Conditioning Association
2100 N. Hwy. 360, Ste. 1300   Ph:(214)988-6081
Grand Prairie, TX 75050   Fax:(214)641-8693

Directory. Member manufacturers and distributors in the mobile air conditioning industry. Biennial, February of odd years; irregular updates. **Editor(s):** Frank Allison, Executive Director. **Price:** $50.00, including updates.

3056 • Jobber Executive—Tool and Equipment Buyers Guide Issue
Hunter Publishing Limited Partnership
950 Lee St.   Ph:(708)296-0770
Des Plaines, IL 60016   Fax:(708)803-3328

Directory. List of manufacturers of automotive aftermarket tools and equipment. Annual, December. **Editor(s):** Jim Halloran.

3057 • Jobber Retailer Aftermarket Manual
Bill Communications, Inc.
P.O. Box 3599   Ph:(216)867-4401
Akron, OH 44309   Fax:(216)867-0019

Directory. Program distribution groups of the automotive aftermarket industry; aftermarket associations; and aftermarket suppliers. Annual, May. **Editor(s):** Michael Mavrigian. **Price:** $62.00, plus $2.00 shipping.

3058 • Jobber Topics—Marketing/Directory Issue
Irving-Cloud Publishing Company
7300 N. Cicero Ave.   Ph:(708)588-7300
Chicago, IL 60646-1696   Fax:(708)674-7015

Directory. Manufacturers, remanufacturers, warehouse distributors, jobbers, manufacturers' agents, and trade associations in the automotive aftermarket field. Annual, July. **Editor(s):** Bob Weber, Editorial Director. **Price:** $60.00, postpaid.

3059 • Performance Racing Engine Builder's Supplier Directory
Performance Builder
Box 1048
Norton, OH 44203   Ph:(216)825-8528

Directory. Nearly 2,800 manufacturers, chemical producers, warehouses and wholesalers, and distributors of products used in the building of engines for racing cars, boats, and high-performance and four-wheel-drive vehicles. Semiannual. **Editor(s):** Melanie Gross. **Price:** $25.00.

3060 • Starters—Engine Directory
American Business Directories, Inc.
American Business Information, Inc.
5711 S. 86th Circle   Ph:(402)593-4600
Omaha, NE 68127   Fax:(402)331-1505

Directory. Over 1,000 automotive manufacturers and retailers of engine starters. Annual. **Price:** $85.00, payment with order. Significant discounts offered for standing orders.

3061 • Tire Review—Tire Brands Issue
Babcox Publications
11 S. Forge St.
Akron, OH 44304
Ph:(216)535-6117
Fax:(216)535-0874

Directory. Listing of manufacturers of over 110 tire brands. Annual, November. **Editor(s):** Jim Davis. **Price:** $4.75.

3062 • Tire Review— Wheel Brand Profiles Issue
Babcox Publications
11 S. Forge St.
Akron, OH 44304
Ph:(216)535-6117
Fax:(216)535-0874

Directory. List of about 75 custom wheel manufacturers. Annual, February. **Editor(s):** Jim Davis. **Price:** $4.75.

3063 • Truck Canopies, Caps and Shells Directory
American Business Directories, Inc.
American Business Information, Inc.
5711 S. 86th Circle
Omaha, NE 68127
Ph:(402)593-4600
Fax:(402)331-1505

Directory. About 1,095 automotive manufacturers and retailers of truck canopies, caps, and shells. Annual. **Price:** $85.00, payment with order. Significant discounts offered for standing orders.

3064 • Undercar Digest—Buyer's Guide Issue
MD Publications, Inc.
Box 2210
Springfield, IL 65801
Ph:(417)866-3917
Fax:(417)866-2781

Directory. List of automotive aftermarket manufacturers and suppliers of mufflers, exhaust pipes, brakes, chassis, steering, suspension, driveline, shop equipment and tools, and other products. Annual, May. **Editor(s):** James R. Wilder. **Price:** $25.00.

3065 • Who Makes It and Where Directory
Tire Guides, Inc.
1101-6 S. Rogers Circle
Boca Raton, FL 33487
Ph:(407)997-9229
Fax:(407)997-9233

Directory. Over 600 tire, wheel, and tube manufacturers; international coverage. Also includes list of antique and odd size tire dealers; manufacturer toll-free phone numbers. Annual, January. **Editor(s):** Alfred Snyder. **Price:** $4.00, plus $1.00 shipping.

3066 • Who's Who Show Directory
Automotive Parts & Accessories Association
4600 East-West Hwy., Ste. 300
Bethesda, MD 20814
Ph:(301)654-6664
Fax:(301)654-3299

Directory. Manufacturers exhibiting at the association's annual show and member retailers, wholesalers, distributors, manufacturers' representatives, and export management companies. Annual, fall. **Editor(s):** Rebecca A. Wilcox, Director, Meeting & Program Planning. **Price:** Available free at annual show; $3.00 postage and handling after show.

Automotive road service

3067 • Automotive Road Service Directory
American Business Directories, Inc.
American Business Information, Inc.
5711 S. 86th Circle
Omaha, NE 68127
Ph:(402)593-4600
Fax:(402)331-1505

Directory. About 8,550 automotive road service firms. Annual. **Price:** $285.00, payment with order. Significant discounts offered for standing orders.

Automotive salvage dealers

3068 • ADP Parts Exchange
ADP Automotive Claims Services
2010 Crow Canyon Pl.
San Ramon, CA 94583
Ph:(415)866-1100

Database. Includes auto parts distributors, vehicle dismantlers, recyclers, and other sources of new and salvaged automobile parts

and common repair items for vehicles manufactured since 1970. Formerly titled ADP Salvage Parts Locator; ADP Parts and Assemblies Locator. Daily updates.

3069 • Alabama Automotive Directory
Automotive Contact
Box 517
Terre Haute, IN 47808
Ph:(812)232-2441

Directory. Automotive aftermarket businesses, including body shops; brake, muffler, radiator, electrical and transmission repairs, as well as new car dealers, parts retailers, auto salvage companies, and automotive parts warehouses. Annual, January. **Editor(s):** T. L. Spelman, Publisher. **Price:** $30.95, plus $3.00 shipping.

3070 • Arizona/New Mexico Automotive Directory
Automotive Contact
P.O. Box 517
Terre Haute, IN 47808
Ph:(812)232-2441

Directory. Automotive aftermarket businesses, including body shops; brake, muffler, radiator, electrical and transmission repairs, as well as new car dealers, parts retailers, auto salvage companies, and automotive parts warehouses. Annual, January. **Editor(s):** T. L. Spelman, Publisher. **Price:** $30.95, plus $3.00 shipping.

3071 • Arkansas Automotive Directory
Automotive Contact
Box 517
Terre Haute, IN 47808
Ph:(812)232-2441

Directory. Automotive aftermarket businesses, including body shops; brake, muffler, radiator, electrical and transmission repairs, as well as new car dealers, parts retailers, auto salvage companies, and automotive parts warehouses. Annual, January. **Editor(s):** T. L. Spelman, Publisher. **Price:** $30.95, plus $3.00 shipping.

3072 • Automobile Air Conditioning Equipment Directory
American Business Directories, Inc.
American Business Information, Inc.
5711 S. 86th Circle
Omaha, NE 68127
Ph:(402)593-4600
Fax:(402)331-1505

Directory. About 13,630 suppliers and dealers of automobile air conditioning equipment. Annual. **Price:** $440.00, payment with order. Significant discounts offered for standing orders.

3073 • Automobile Parts—Used/Salvage Directory
American Business Directories, Inc.
American Business Information, Inc.
5711 S. 86th Circle
Omaha, NE 68127
Ph:(402)593-4600
Fax:(402)331-1505

Directory. About 18,210 automotive salvage dealers. Annual. **Price:** $600.00, payment with order. Significant discounts offered for standing orders.

3074 • Automotive Dismantlers and Recyclers Association—Buyers Guide and Membership Roster
Automotive Dismantlers and Recyclers Association
1133 15th St., N.W.
Washington, DC 20005-2701
Ph:(202)293-2372

Buyers guide. Lists industry suppliers and ADRA members. Annual. **Editor(s):** Cindy Smith. **Price:** $150.00.

3075 • Automotive Dismantlers and Recyclers Association—Roster of Members
Automotive Dismantlers and Recyclers Association
10400 Eaton Pl., Ste. 203
Fairfax, VA 22030-2208
Ph:(703)385-1001

Directory. 5500 firms selling used auto, truck, motorcycle, bus, and farm and construction equipment parts, retail and wholesale. Annual.

3076 • Bumper Recycling Association of North America—Membership Directory
Bumper Recycling Association of North America
216 Country Club Rd.   Ph:(203)659-1762
South Glastonbury, CT 06073   Fax:(619)360-1290

Directory. List of firms which recondition and recycle vehicle bumpers. Annual, March. **Editor(s):** George E. Kermode, Executive Director. **Price:** Available to members only.

3077 • California Automotive Directory
Automotive Contact
P.O. Box 517
Terre Haute, IN 47808   Ph:(812)232-2441

Directory. Automotive aftermarket businesses, including body shops; brake, muffler, radiator, electrical and transmission repairs, as well as new car dealers, parts retailers, auto salvage companies, and automotive parts warehouses. Annual, January. **Editor(s):** T. L. Spelman, Publisher. **Price:** $30.95, plus $3.00 shipping.

3078 • Colorado/Utah/Nevada Automotive Directory
Automotive Contact
P.O. Box 517
Terre Haute, IN 47808   Ph:(812)232-2441

Directory. Automotive aftermarket businesses, including body shops; brake, muffler, radiator, electrical and transmission repairs, as well as new car dealers, parts retailers, auto salvage companies, and automotive parts warehouses. Annual, January. **Editor(s):** T. L. Spelman, Publisher. **Price:** $30.95, plus $3.00 shipping.

3079 • Connecticut/Rhode Island Automotive Directory
Automotive Contact
P.O. Box 517
Terre Haute, IN 47808   Ph:(812)232-2441

Directory. Automotive aftermarket businesses, including body shops; brake, muffler, radiator, electrical and transmission repairs, as well as new car dealers, parts retailers, auto salvage companies, and automotive parts warehouses. Annual, January. **Editor(s):** T. L. Spelman, Publisher. **Price:** $30.95, plus $3.00 shipping.

3080 • Delaware/District of Columbia/Maryland Automotive Directory
Automotive Contact
P.O. Box 517
Terre Haute, IN 47808   Ph:(812)232-2441

Directory. Automotive aftermarket businesses, including body shops; brake, muffler, radiator, electrical and transmission repairs, as well as new car dealers, parts retailers, auto salvage companies, and automotive parts warehouses. Annual, January. **Editor(s):** T. L. Spelman, Publisher. **Price:** $30.95, plus $3.00 shipping.

3081 • Florida Automotive Directory
Automotive Contact
P.O. Box 517
Terre Haute, IN 47808   Ph:(812)232-2441

Directory. Automotive aftermarket businesses, including body shops; brake, muffler, radiator, electrical and transmission repairs, as well as new car dealers, parts retailers, auto salvage companies, and automotive parts warehouses. Annual, January. **Editor(s):** T. L. Spelman, Publisher. **Price:** $30.95, plus $3.00 shipping.

3082 • Georgia Automotive Directory
Automotive Contact
Box 517
Terre Haute, IN 47808   Ph:(812)232-2441

Directory. Automotive aftermarket businesses, including body shops; brake, muffler, radiator, electrical and transmission repairs, as well as new car dealers, parts retailers, auto salvage companies, and automotive parts warehouses. Annual, January. **Editor(s):** T. L. Spelman, Publisher. **Price:** $30.95, plus $3.00 shipping.

3083 • Idaho/Montana/North Dakota/South Dakota/Wyoming Automotive Directory
Automotive Contact
P.O. Box 517
Terre Haute, IN 47808   Ph:(812)232-2441

Directory. Automotive aftermarket businesses, including body shops; brake, muffler, radiator, electrical and transmission repairs, as well as new car dealers, parts retailers, auto salvage companies, and automotive parts warehouses. Annual, January. **Editor(s):** T. L. Spelman, Publisher. **Price:** $30.95, plus $3.00 shipping.

3084 • Illinois Automotive Directory
Automotive Contact
Box 517
Terre Haute, IN 47808   Ph:(812)232-2441

Directory. Automotive aftermarket businesses, including body shops; brake, muffler, radiator, electrical and transmission repairs, as well as new car dealers, parts retailers, auto salvage companies, and automotive parts warehouses. Annual, January. **Editor(s):** T. L. Spelman, Publisher. **Price:** $30.95, plus $3.00 shipping.

3085 • Indiana Automotive Directory
Automotive Contact
Box 517
Terre Haute, IN 47808   Ph:(812)232-2441

Directory. Automotive aftermarket businesses, including body shops; brake, muffler, radiator, electrical and transmission repairs, as well as new car dealers, parts retailers, auto salvage companies, and automotive parts warehouses. Annual, January. **Editor(s):** T. L. Spelman, Publisher. **Price:** $30.95, plus $3.00 shipping.

3086 • Iowa Automotive Directory
Automotive Contact
Box 517
Terre Haute, IN 47808   Ph:(812)232-2441

Directory. Automotive aftermarket businesses, including body shops; brake, muffler, radiator, electrical and transmission repairs, as well as new car dealers, parts retailers, auto salvage companies, and automotive parts warehouses. Annual, January. **Editor(s):** T. L. Spelman, Publisher. **Price:** $30.95, plus $3.00 shipping.

3087 • Kansas/Nebraska Automotive Directory
Automotive Contact
P.O. Box 517
Terre Haute, IN 47808   Ph:(812)232-2441

Directory. Automotive aftermarket businesses, including body shops; brake, muffler, radiator, electrical and transmission repairs, as well as new car dealers, parts retailers, auto salvage companies, and automotive parts warehouses. Annual, January. **Editor(s):** T. L. Spelman, Publisher. **Price:** $30.95, plus $3.00 shipping.

3088 • Kentucky Automotive Directory
Automotive Contact
Box 517
Terre Haute, IN 47808   Ph:(812)232-2441

Directory. Automotive aftermarket businesses, including body shops; brake, muffler, radiator, electrical and transmission repairs, as well as new car dealers, parts retailers, auto salvage companies, and automotive parts warehouses. Annual, January. **Editor(s):** T. L. Spelman, Publisher. **Price:** $30.95, plus $3.00 shipping.

3089 • Louisiana Automotive Directory
Automotive Contact
Box 517
Terre Haute, IN 47808   Ph:(812)232-2441

Directory. Automotive aftermarket businesses, including body shops; brake, muffler, radiator, electrical and transmission repairs, as well as new car dealers, parts retailers, auto salvage companies, and automotive parts warehouses. Annual, January. **Editor(s):** T. L. Spelman, Publisher. **Price:** $30.95, plus $3.00 shipping.

3090 • Maine/New Hampshire/Vermont Automotive Directory
Automotive Contact
P.O. Box 517
Terre Haute, IN 47808   Ph:(812)232-2441

Directory. Automotive aftermarket businesses, including body shops; brake, muffler, radiator, electrical and transmission repairs, as well as new car dealers, parts retailers, auto salvage companies, and automotive parts warehouses. Annual, January. **Editor(s):** T. L. Spelman, Publisher. **Price:** $30.95, plus $3.00 shipping.

3091 • Massachusetts Automotive Directory
Automotive Contact
P.O. Box 517
Terre Haute, IN 47808   Ph:(812)232-2441

Directory. Automotive aftermarket businesses, including body shops; brake, muffler, radiator, electrical and transmission repairs, as well as new car dealers, parts retailers, auto salvage companies, and automotive parts warehouses. Annual, January. **Editor(s):** T. L. Spelman, Publisher. **Price:** $30.95, plus $3.00 shipping.

3092 • Michigan Automotive Directory
Automotive Contact
P.O. Box 517
Terre Haute, IN 47808   Ph:(812)232-2441

Directory. Automotive aftermarket businesses, including body shops; brake, muffler, radiator, electrical and transmission repairs, as well as new car dealers, parts retailers, auto salvage companies, and automotive parts warehouses. Annual, January. **Editor(s):** T. L. Spelman, Publisher. **Price:** $30.95, plus $3.00 shipping.

3093 • Minnesota Automotive Directory
Automotive Contact
P.O. Box 517
Terre Haute, IN 47808   Ph:(812)232-2441

Directory. Automotive aftermarket businesses, including body shops; brake, muffler, radiator, electrical and transmission repairs, as well as new car dealers, parts retailers, auto salvage companies, and automotive parts warehouses. Annual, January. **Editor(s):** T. L. Spelman, Publisher. **Price:** $30.95, plus $3.00 shipping.

3094 • Mississippi Automotive Directory
Automotive Contact
P.O. Box 517
Terre Haute, IN 47808   Ph:(812)232-2441

Directory. Automotive aftermarket businesses, including body shops; brake, muffler, radiator, electrical and transmission repairs, as well as new car dealers, parts retailers, auto salvage companies, and automotive parts warehouses. Annual, January. **Editor(s):** T. L. Spelman, Publisher. **Price:** $30.95, plus $3.00 shipping.

3095 • Missouri Automotive Directory
Automotive Contact
P.O. Box 517
Terre Haute, IN 47808   Ph:(812)232-2441

Directory. Automotive aftermarket businesses, including body shops; brake, muffler, radiator, electrical and transmission repairs, as well as new car dealers, parts retailers, auto salvage companies, and automotive parts warehouses. Annual, January. **Editor(s):** T. L. Spelman, Publisher. **Price:** $30.95, plus $3.00 shipping.

3096 • New Jersey Automotive Directory
Automotive Contact
P.O. Box 517
Terre Haute, IN 47808   Ph:(812)232-2441

Directory. Automotive aftermarket businesses, including body shops; brake, muffler, radiator, electrical and transmission repairs, as well as new car dealers, parts retailers, auto salvage companies, and automotive parts warehouses. Annual, January. **Editor(s):** T. L. Spelman, Publisher. **Price:** $30.95, plus $3.00 shipping.

3097 • New York Automotive Directory
Automotive Contact
P.O. Box 517
Terre Haute, IN 47808   Ph:(812)232-2441

Directory. Automotive aftermarket businesses, including body shops; brake, muffler, radiator, electrical and transmission repairs, as well as new car dealers, parts retailers, auto salvage companies, and automotive parts warehouses. Annual, January. **Editor(s):** T. L. Spelman, Publisher. **Price:** $30.95, plus $3.00 shipping.

3098 • North Carolina Automotive Directory
Automotive Contact
P.O. Box 517
Terre Haute, IN 47808   Ph:(812)232-2441

Directory. Automotive aftermarket businesses, including body shops; brake, muffler, radiator, electrical and transmission repairs, as well as new car dealers, parts retailers, auto salvage companies, and automotive parts warehouses. Annual, January. **Editor(s):** T. L. Spelman, Publisher. **Price:** $30.95, plus $3.00 shipping.

3099 • Ohio Automotive Directory
Automotive Contact
P.O. Box 517
Terre Haute, IN 47808   Ph:(812)232-2441

Directory. Automotive aftermarket businesses, including body shops; brake, muffler, radiator, electrical and transmission repairs, as well as new car dealers, parts retailers, auto salvage companies, and automotive parts warehouses. Annual, January. **Editor(s):** T. L. Spelman, Publisher. **Price:** $30.95, plus $3.00 shipping.

3100 • Oklahoma Automotive Directory
Automotive Contact
P.O. Box 517
Terre Haute, IN 47808   Ph:(812)232-2441

Directory. Automotive aftermarket businesses, including body shops; brake, muffler, radiator, electrical and transmission repairs, as well as new car dealers, parts retailers, auto salvage companies, and automotive parts warehouses. Annual, January. **Editor(s):** T. L. Spelman, Publisher. **Price:** $30.95, plus $3.00 shipping.

3101 • Oregon Automotive Directory
Automotive Contact
P.O. Box 517
Terre Haute, IN 47808   Ph:(812)232-2441

Directory. Automotive aftermarket businesses, including body shops; brake, muffler, radiator, electrical and transmission repairs, as well as new car dealers, parts retailers, auto salvage companies, and automotive parts warehouses. Annual, January. **Editor(s):** T. L. Spelman, Publisher. **Price:** $30.95, plus $3.00 shipping.

3102 • Pennsylvania Automotive Directory
Automotive Contact
P.O. Box 517
Terre Haute, IN 47808   Ph:(812)232-2441

Directory. Automotive aftermarket businesses, including body shops; brake, muffler, radiator, electrical and transmission repairs, as well as new car dealers, parts retailers, auto salvage companies, and automotive parts warehouses. Annual, January. **Editor(s):** T. L. Spelman, Publisher. **Price:** $30.95, plus $3.00 shipping.

3103 • South Carolina Automotive Directory
Automotive Contact
P.O. Box 517
Terre Haute, IN 47808   Ph:(812)232-2441

Directory. Automotive aftermarket businesses, including body shops; brake, muffler, radiator, electrical and transmission repairs, as well as new car dealers, parts retailers, auto salvage companies, and automotive parts warehouses. Annual, January. **Editor(s):** T. L. Spelman, Publisher. **Price:** $30.95, plus $3.00 shipping.

3104 • Tennessee Automotive Directory
Automotive Contact
P.O. Box 517
Terre Haute, IN 47808   Ph:(812)232-2441

Directory. Automotive aftermarket businesses, including body shops; brake, muffler, radiator, electrical and transmission repairs, as well as new car dealers, parts retailers, auto salvage companies, and automotive parts warehouses. Annual, January. **Editor(s):** T. L. Spelman, Publisher. **Price:** $30.95, plus $3.00 shipping.

3105 • Texas Automotive Directory
Automotive Contact
P.O. Box 517
Terre Haute, IN 47808   Ph:(812)232-2441

Directory. Automotive aftermarket businesses, including body shops; brake, muffler, radiator, electrical and transmission repairs, as well as new car dealers, parts retailers, auto salvage companies, and automotive parts warehouses. Annual, January. **Editor(s):** T. L. Spelman, Publisher. **Price:** $30.95, plus $3.00 shipping.

3106 • Tire Dealers-Used Directory
American Business Directories, Inc.
American Business Information, Inc.
5711 S. 86th Circle   Ph:(402)593-4600
Omaha, NE 68127   Fax:(402)331-1505

Directory. 2,875 tire dealers and automotive salvage dealers. Annual. **Price:** $110.00, payment with order. Significant discounts offered for standing orders.

3107 • Virginia/West Virginia Automotive Directory
Automotive Contact
P.O. Box 517
Terre Haute, IN 47808   Ph:(812)232-2441

Directory. Automotive aftermarket businesses, including body shops; brake, muffler, radiator, electrical and transmission repairs, as well as new car dealers, parts retailers, auto salvage companies, and automotive parts warehouses. Annual, January. **Editor(s):** T. L. Spelman, Publisher. **Price:** $30.95, plus $3.00 shipping.

3108 • Washington Automotive Directory [State]
Automotive Contact
P.O. Box 517
Terre Haute, IN 47808   Ph:(812)232-2441

Directory. Automotive aftermarket businesses, including body shops; brake, muffler, radiator, electrical and transmission repairs, as well as new car dealers, parts retailers, auto salvage companies, and automotive parts warehouses. Annual, January. **Editor(s):** T. L. Spelman, Publisher. **Price:** $30.95, plus $3.00 shipping.

3109 • Wisconsin Automotive Directory
Automotive Contact
P.O. Box 517
Terre Haute, IN 47808   Ph:(812)232-2441

Directory. Automotive aftermarket businesses, including body shops; brake, muffler, radiator, electrical and transmission repairs, as well as new car dealers, parts retailers, auto salvage companies, and automotive parts warehouses. Annual, January. **Editor(s):** T. L. Spelman, Publisher. **Price:** $30.95, plus $3.00 shipping.

Automotive service and maintenance firms

3110 • Alabama Automotive Directory
Automotive Contact
Box 517
Terre Haute, IN 47808   Ph:(812)232-2441

Directory. Automotive aftermarket businesses, including body shops; brake, muffler, radiator, electrical and transmission repairs, as well as new car dealers, parts retailers, auto salvage companies, and automotive parts warehouses. Annual, January. **Editor(s):** T. L. Spelman, Publisher. **Price:** $30.95, plus $3.00 shipping.

3111 • Arizona/New Mexico Automotive Directory
Automotive Contact
P.O. Box 517
Terre Haute, IN 47808   Ph:(812)232-2441

Directory. Automotive aftermarket businesses, including body shops; brake, muffler, radiator, electrical and transmission repairs, as well as new car dealers, parts retailers, auto salvage companies, and automotive parts warehouses. Annual, January. **Editor(s):** T. L. Spelman, Publisher. **Price:** $30.95, plus $3.00 shipping.

3112 • Arkansas Automotive Directory
Automotive Contact
Box 517
Terre Haute, IN 47808   Ph:(812)232-2441

Directory. Automotive aftermarket businesses, including body shops; brake, muffler, radiator, electrical and transmission repairs, as well as new car dealers, parts retailers, auto salvage companies, and automotive parts warehouses. Annual, January. **Editor(s):** T. L. Spelman, Publisher. **Price:** $30.95, plus $3.00 shipping.

3113 • Auto Smog Brake/Lamp Inspect Repair Directory
American Business Directories, Inc.
American Business Information, Inc.
5711 S. 86th Circle   Ph:(402)593-4600
Omaha, NE 68127   Fax:(402)331-1505

Directory. 3,220 automotive firms that offer emissions, brake, and electrical inspections and repair service. Annual. **Price:** $125.00, payment with order. Significant discounts offered for standing orders.

3114 • Auto Trim News—Directory of Product Sources Issue
National Association of Auto Trim Shops
3804 Gunn Hwy.   Ph:(813)960-1113
Tampa, FL 33624   Fax:(813)264-2158

Directory. Major suppliers, manufacturers, and installers of interior and exterior trim and accessory products used in customizing cars, trucks, vans, and boats. Annual, January. **Editor(s):** Nat Danas, Managing Editor. **Price:** $19.00.

3115 • Auto Undercoating & Rustproofing Directory
American Business Directories, Inc.
American Business Information, Inc.
5711 S. 86th Circle   Ph:(402)593-4600
Omaha, NE 68127   Fax:(402)331-1505

Directory. About 1,890 firms that offer automobile undercoating and rustproofing services. Annual. **Price:** $105.00, payment with order. Significant discounts offered for standing orders.

3116 • Automobile Brake Service Directory
American Business Directories, Inc.
American Business Information, Inc.
5711 S. 86th Circle   Ph:(402)593-4600
Omaha, NE 68127   Fax:(402)331-1505

Directory. About 34,950 automotive brake service firms. Annual. **Price:** $945.00, payment with order. Significant discounts offered for standing orders.

3117 • Automobile Detail & Clean-Up Service Directory
American Business Directories, Inc.
American Business Information, Inc.
5711 S. 86th Circle   Ph:(402)593-4600
Omaha, NE 68127   Fax:(402)331-1505

Directory. About 8,830 automotive detail and clean-up service firms. Annual. **Price:** $300.00, payment with order. Significant discounts offered for standing orders.

3118 • Automobile Diagnostic Service Directory
American Business Directories, Inc.
American Business Information, Inc.
5711 S. 86th Circle   Ph:(402)593-4600
Omaha, NE 68127   Fax:(402)331-1505

Directory. 2,875 automobile diagnostic service firms. Annual. **Price:** $110.00, payment with order. Significant discounts offered for standing orders.

3119 • Automobile Electric Service Directory
American Business Directories, Inc.
American Business Information, Inc.
5711 S. 86th Circle   Ph:(402)593-4600
Omaha, NE 68127   Fax:(402)331-1505

Directory. About 8,410 automotive electric service firms. Annual. **Price:** $285.00, payment with order. Significant discounts offered for standing orders.

3120 • Automobile Inspection Stations Directory
American Business Directories, Inc.
American Business Information, Inc.
5711 S. 86th Circle   Ph:(402)593-4600
Omaha, NE 68127   Fax:(402)331-1505

Directory. Approximately 8,950 automobile inspection stations. Annual. **Price:** $300.00, payment with order. Significant discounts offered for standing orders.

3121 • Automobile Lubrication Service Directory
American Business Directories, Inc.
American Business Information, Inc.
5711 S. 86th Circle   Ph:(402)593-4600
Omaha, NE 68127   Fax:(402)331-1505

Directory. About 2,400 automotive lubrication service firms. Annual. **Price:** $105.00, payment with order. Significant discounts offered for standing orders.

3122 • Automobile Muffler Repair Shops Directory
American Business Directories, Inc.
American Business Information, Inc.
5711 S. 86th Circle   Ph:(402)593-4600
Omaha, NE 68127   Fax:(402)331-1505

Directory. 17,680 automotive repair shops. Annual. **Price:** $565.00, payment with order. Significant discounts offered for standing orders. Franchise editions also available: Meineke, $105.00; Midas, $105.00; Walker, $130.00.

3123 • Automobile Radiator Repair Shops Directory
American Business Directories, Inc.
American Business Information, Inc.
5711 S. 86th Circle   Ph:(402)593-4600
Omaha, NE 68127   Fax:(402)331-1505

Directory. 11,840 radiator repair shops. Annual. **Price:** $375.00, payment with order. Significant discounts offered for standing orders.

3124 • Automobile Repair Shops Directory
American Business Directories, Inc.
American Business Information, Inc.
5711 S. 86th Circle   Ph:(402)593-4600
Omaha, NE 68127   Fax:(402)331-1505

Directory. Approximately 182,840 automobile repair shops. Annual. **Price:** $5530.00, payment with order. Significant discounts offered for standing orders. Regional editions available: Northeast (Connecticut, Maine, Massachusetts, New Hampshire, New Jersey, New York, Pennsylvania, Rhode Island, Vermont), $999.00; East North Central (Illinois, Indiana, Michigan, Ohio, Wisconsin), $835.00; West North Central (Iowa, Kansas, Minnesota, Missouri, Nebraska, North Dakota, South Dakota), $505.00; South Atlantic (District of Columbia, Delaware, Florida, Georgia, Maryland, North Carolina, South Carolina, Virginia, West Virginia), $865.00; South Central (Alabama, Arkansas,Kentucky, Louisiana, Mississippi, Oklahoma, Tennessee, Texas), $945.00; Mountain (Arizona, Colorado, Idaho, Montana, Nevada, New

Mexico, Utah, Wyoming), $345.00; Pacific (Alaska, California, Hawaii, Oregon, Washington), $835.00.

3125 • Automobile Service Stations Directory
American Business Directories, Inc.
American Business Information, Inc.
5711 S. 86th Circle   Ph:(402)593-4600
Omaha, NE 68127   Fax:(402)331-1505

Directory. About 102,615 automotive service stations. Annual. **Price:** $3,105.00, payment with order. Significant discounts offered for standing orders. Regional editions available: North East (Connecticut, Maine, Massachusetts, New Hampshire, New Jersey, Pennsylvania, Rhode Island, Vermont), $630.00; East North Central (Illinois, Indiana, Michigan, Ohio, Wisconsin), $630.00; West North Central (Iowa, Kansas, Minnesota, Missouri, Nebraska, North Dakota, South Dakota), $375.00; South Atlantic (District of Columbia, Delaware, Florida, Georgia, Maryland, North Carolina, South Carolina, Virginia, West Virginia), $600.00; South Central (Alabama, Arkansas,Kentucky, Louisiana, Mississippi, Oklahoma, Tennessee, Texas), $700.00; Mountain (Arizona, Colorado, Idaho, Montana, Nevada, New Mexico, Utah, Wyoming), $215.00; Pacific (Alaska, California, Hawaii, Oregon, Washington), $410.00. Franchise editions are also available, $105.00 to $270.00 per franchise.

3126 • Automobile Transmission Repair Shops Directory
American Business Directories, Inc.
American Business Information, Inc.
5711 S. 86th Circle   Ph:(402)593-4600
Omaha, NE 68127   Fax:(402)331-1505

Directory. About 18,895 automotive transmission repair shops. Annual. **Price:** $600.00, payment with order. Significant discounts offered for standing orders.

3127 • Automobile Transporters and Drive-Away Directory
American Business Directories, Inc.
American Business Information, Inc.
5711 S. 86th Circle   Ph:(402)593-4600
Omaha, NE 68127   Fax:(402)331-1505

Directory. About 1,035 firms that offer automobile transporting services. Annual. **Price:** $85.00, payment with order. Significant discounts offered for standing orders.

3128 • Automobile Upholstery Cleaning Directory
American Business Directories, Inc.
American Business Information, Inc.
5711 S. 86th Circle   Ph:(402)593-4600
Omaha, NE 68127   Fax:(402)331-1505

Directory. Nearly 1,480 firms that provide automobile upholstery cleaning services. Annual. **Price:** $85.00, payment with order. Significant discounts offered for standing orders.

3129 • Automotive Alternators and Generators Repair Directory
American Business Directories, Inc.
American Business Information, Inc.
5711 S. 86th Circle   Ph:(402)593-4600
Omaha, NE 68127   Fax:(402)331-1505

Directory. 1,330 firms that provide alternator and generator repair services. Annual. **Price:** $85.00, payment with order. Significant discounts offered for standing orders.

3130 • Automotive Engine Rebuilders Association— Membership Roster
Automotive Engine Rebuilders Assn.
330 Lexington Dr.   Ph:(708)541-6550
Buffalo Grove, IL 60089-6998   Fax:(708)541-5808

Directory. Annual.

3131 • Automotive Road Service Directory
American Business Directories, Inc.
American Business Information, Inc.
5711 S. 86th Circle   Ph:(402)593-4600
Omaha, NE 68127   Fax:(402)331-1505

Directory. About 8,550 automotive road service firms. Annual. **Price:** $285.00, payment with order. Significant discounts offered for standing orders.

3132 • California Automotive Directory
Automotive Contact
P.O. Box 517
Terre Haute, IN 47808   Ph:(812)232-2441

Directory. Automotive aftermarket businesses, including body shops; brake, muffler, radiator, electrical and transmission repairs, as well as new car dealers, parts retailers, auto salvage companies, and automotive parts warehouses. Annual, January. **Editor(s):** T. L. Spelman, Publisher. **Price:** $30.95, plus $3.00 shipping.

3133 • Carburetors-Service and Repair Directory
American Business Directories, Inc.
American Business Information, Inc.
5711 S. 86th Circle   Ph:(402)593-4600
Omaha, NE 68127   Fax:(402)331-1505

Directory. About 2,755 automotive service firms. Annual. **Price:** $110.00, payment with order. Significant discounts offered for standing orders.

3134 • Clutches Service and Repair Directory
American Business Directories, Inc.
American Business Information, Inc.
5711 S. 86th Circle   Ph:(402)593-4600
Omaha, NE 68127   Fax:(402)331-1505

Directory. About 1,510 automotive firms that offer clutch repair services. Annual. **Price:** $105.00, payment with order. Significant discounts offered for standing orders.

3135 • Colorado/Utah/Nevada Automotive Directory
Automotive Contact
P.O. Box 517
Terre Haute, IN 47808   Ph:(812)232-2441

Directory. Automotive aftermarket businesses, including body shops; brake, muffler, radiator, electrical and transmission repairs, as well as new car dealers, parts retailers, auto salvage companies, and automotive parts warehouses. Annual, January. **Editor(s):** T. L. Spelman, Publisher. **Price:** $30.95, plus $3.00 shipping.

3136 • Connecticut/Rhode Island Automotive Directory
Automotive Contact
P.O. Box 517
Terre Haute, IN 47808   Ph:(812)232-2441

Directory. Automotive aftermarket businesses, including body shops; brake, muffler, radiator, electrical and transmission repairs, as well as new car dealers, parts retailers, auto salvage companies, and automotive parts warehouses. Annual, January. **Editor(s):** T. L. Spelman, Publisher. **Price:** $30.95, plus $3.00 shipping.

3137 • Delaware/District of Columbia/Maryland Automotive Directory
Automotive Contact
P.O. Box 517
Terre Haute, IN 47808   Ph:(812)232-2441

Directory. Automotive aftermarket businesses, including body shops; brake, muffler, radiator, electrical and transmission repairs, as well as new car dealers, parts retailers, auto salvage companies, and automotive parts warehouses. Annual, January. **Editor(s):** T. L. Spelman, Publisher. **Price:** $30.95, plus $3.00 shipping.

3138 • Directory of Automotive Related Business Publishers
Motor & Equipment Manufacturing Assn.
300 Sylvan Ave.
Englewood Cliffs, NJ 07632   Ph:(201)569-8500

Directory. Lists publishers that serve all segments of the automotive industry. **Editor(s):** J.J. Conner, Publisher.

3139 • Directory of Foreign Automotive Companies in the United States
Mead Ventures, Inc.
P.O. Box 44952   Ph:(602)234-0044
Phoenix, AZ 85064   Fax:(602)234-0076

Directory. Over 600 foreign automotive manufacturers, distributors, and services in the United States. Irregular; latest edition June 1989. **Editor(s):** Dawn Erdos. **Price:** $295.00.

3140 • Directory of Korean Automotive Firms in the United States and Canada
Mead Ventures, Inc.
P.O. Box 44952   Ph:(602)234-0044
Phoenix, AZ 85064   Fax:(602)234-0076

Directory. About 50 Korean Automotive companies in the United States and Canada. Irregular, latest edition 1989. **Editor(s):** Christopher Mead and Dawn Erdos. **Price:** $25.00.

3141 • Engines-Rebuilding and Exchanging Directory
American Business Directories, Inc.
American Business Information, Inc.
5711 S. 86th Circle   Ph:(402)593-4600
Omaha, NE 68127   Fax:(402)331-1505

Directory. About 7,395 automotive firms specializing in rebuilt engines. Annual. **Price:** $255.00, payment with order. Significant discounts offered for standing orders.

3142 • Florida Automotive Directory
Automotive Contact
P.O. Box 517
Terre Haute, IN 47808   Ph:(812)232-2441

Directory. Automotive aftermarket businesses, including body shops; brake, muffler, radiator, electrical and transmission repairs, as well as new car dealers, parts retailers, auto salvage companies, and automotive parts warehouses. Annual, January. **Editor(s):** T. L. Spelman, Publisher. **Price:** $30.95, plus $3.00 shipping.

3143 • Gasoline and Automotive Service Dealers Association—Trade Directory and Buyers Guide
Gasoline and Automotive Service Dealers Association (GASDA)
6338 Ave. N
Brooklyn, NY 11234   Ph:(718)241-1111

Buyers guide. Directory comprised of randomly arranged advertisements of companies who offer services in the field. Indexed by subject and alphabetically by company name. Annual. **Price:** Free.

3144 • Gasoline and Automotive Service Dealers Association—Trade Directory and Buyers Guide
Gasoline and Automotive Service Dealers Association
6338 Ave. N.
Brooklyn, NY 11234   Ph:(718)241-1111

Directory. Annual. **Editor(s):** Stanley Schuer. **Price:** Free.

3145 • Georgia Automotive Directory
Automotive Contact
Box 517
Terre Haute, IN 47808   Ph:(812)232-2441

Directory. Automotive aftermarket businesses, including body shops; brake, muffler, radiator, electrical and transmission repairs, as well as new car dealers, parts retailers, auto salvage companies, and automotive parts warehouses. Annual, January. **Editor(s):** T. L. Spelman, Publisher. **Price:** $30.95, plus $3.00 shipping.

3146 • Glass-Auto, Plate, Window Directory
American Business Directories, Inc.
American Business Information, Inc.
5711 S. 86th Circle   Ph:(402)593-4600
Omaha, NE 68127   Fax:(402)331-1505

Directory. About 26,180 firms that provide automotive glass services. Annual. **Price:** $765.00, payment with order. Significant discounts offered for standing orders.

3147 • Idaho/Montana/North Dakota/South Dakota/Wyoming Automotive Directory
Automotive Contact
P.O. Box 517
Terre Haute, IN 47808   Ph:(812)232-2441

Directory. Automotive aftermarket businesses, including body shops; brake, muffler, radiator, electrical and transmission repairs, as well as new car dealers, parts retailers, auto salvage companies, and automotive parts warehouses. Annual, January. **Editor(s):** T. L. Spelman, Publisher. **Price:** $30.95, plus $3.00 shipping.

3148 • Illinois Automotive Directory
Automotive Contact
Box 517
Terre Haute, IN 47808   Ph:(812)232-2441

Directory. Automotive aftermarket businesses, including body shops; brake, muffler, radiator, electrical and transmission repairs, as well as new car dealers, parts retailers, auto salvage companies, and automotive parts warehouses. Annual, January. **Editor(s):** T. L. Spelman, Publisher. **Price:** $30.95, plus $3.00 shipping.

3149 • Indiana Automotive Directory
Automotive Contact
Box 517
Terre Haute, IN 47808   Ph:(812)232-2441

Directory. Automotive aftermarket businesses, including body shops; brake, muffler, radiator, electrical and transmission repairs, as well as new car dealers, parts retailers, auto salvage companies, and automotive parts warehouses. Annual, January. **Editor(s):** T. L. Spelman, Publisher. **Price:** $30.95, plus $3.00 shipping.

3150 • Iowa Automotive Directory
Automotive Contact
Box 517
Terre Haute, IN 47808   Ph:(812)232-2441

Directory. Automotive aftermarket businesses, including body shops; brake, muffler, radiator, electrical and transmission repairs, as well as new car dealers, parts retailers, auto salvage companies, and automotive parts warehouses. Annual, January. **Editor(s):** T. L. Spelman, Publisher. **Price:** $30.95, plus $3.00 shipping.

3151 • Kansas/Nebraska Automotive Directory
Automotive Contact
P.O. Box 517
Terre Haute, IN 47808   Ph:(812)232-2441

Directory. Automotive aftermarket businesses, including body shops; brake, muffler, radiator, electrical and transmission repairs, as well as new car dealers, parts retailers, auto salvage companies, and automotive parts warehouses. Annual, January. **Editor(s):** T. L. Spelman, Publisher. **Price:** $30.95, plus $3.00 shipping.

3152 • Kentucky Automotive Directory
Automotive Contact
Box 517
Terre Haute, IN 47808   Ph:(812)232-2441

Directory. Automotive aftermarket businesses, including body shops; brake, muffler, radiator, electrical and transmission repairs, as well as new car dealers, parts retailers, auto salvage companies, and automotive parts warehouses. Annual, January. **Editor(s):** T. L. Spelman, Publisher. **Price:** $30.95, plus $3.00 shipping.

3153 • Louisiana Automotive Directory
Automotive Contact
Box 517
Terre Haute, IN 47808   Ph:(812)232-2441

Directory. Automotive aftermarket businesses, including body shops; brake, muffler, radiator, electrical and transmission repairs, as well as new car dealers, parts retailers, auto salvage companies, and automotive parts warehouses. Annual, January. **Editor(s):** T. L. Spelman, Publisher. **Price:** $30.95, plus $3.00 shipping.

3154 • Maine/New Hampshire/Vermont Automotive Directory
Automotive Contact
P.O. Box 517
Terre Haute, IN 47808   Ph:(812)232-2441

Directory. Automotive aftermarket businesses, including body shops; brake, muffler, radiator, electrical and transmission repairs, as well as new car dealers, parts retailers, auto salvage companies, and automotive parts warehouses. Annual, January. **Editor(s):** T. L. Spelman, Publisher. **Price:** $30.95, plus $3.00 shipping.

3155 • Massachusetts Automotive Directory
Automotive Contact
P.O. Box 517
Terre Haute, IN 47808   Ph:(812)232-2441

Directory. Automotive aftermarket businesses, including body shops; brake, muffler, radiator, electrical and transmission repairs, as well as new car dealers, parts retailers, auto salvage companies, and automotive parts warehouses. Annual, January. **Editor(s):** T. L. Spelman, Publisher. **Price:** $30.95, plus $3.00 shipping.

3156 • Michigan Automotive Directory
Automotive Contact
P.O. Box 517
Terre Haute, IN 47808   Ph:(812)232-2441

Directory. Automotive aftermarket businesses, including body shops; brake, muffler, radiator, electrical and transmission repairs, as well as new car dealers, parts retailers, auto salvage companies, and automotive parts warehouses. Annual, January. **Editor(s):** T. L. Spelman, Publisher. **Price:** $30.95, plus $3.00 shipping.

3157 • Minnesota Automotive Directory
Automotive Contact
P.O. Box 517
Terre Haute, IN 47808   Ph:(812)232-2441

Directory. Automotive aftermarket businesses, including body shops; brake, muffler, radiator, electrical and transmission repairs, as well as new car dealers, parts retailers, auto salvage companies, and automotive parts warehouses. Annual, January. **Editor(s):** T. L. Spelman, Publisher. **Price:** $30.95, plus $3.00 shipping.

3158 • Mississippi Automotive Directory
Automotive Contact
P.O. Box 517
Terre Haute, IN 47808   Ph:(812)232-2441

Directory. Automotive aftermarket businesses, including body shops; brake, muffler, radiator, electrical and transmission repairs, as well as new car dealers, parts retailers, auto salvage companies, and automotive parts warehouses. Annual, January. **Editor(s):** T. L. Spelman, Publisher. **Price:** $30.95, plus $3.00 shipping.

3159 • Missouri Automotive Directory
Automotive Contact
P.O. Box 517
Terre Haute, IN 47808   Ph:(812)232-2441

Directory. Automotive aftermarket businesses, including body shops; brake, muffler, radiator, electrical and transmission repairs, as well as new car dealers, parts retailers, auto salvage companies, and automotive parts warehouses. Annual, January. **Editor(s):** T. L. Spelman, Publisher. **Price:** $30.95, plus $3.00 shipping.

3160 • Modern Tire Dealer—Facts/Directory Issue
Bill Communications, Inc.
PO Box 3599   Ph:(216)867-4401
Akron, OH 44309   Fax:(216)867-0019

Directory. Directories of tire and car service suppliers, tire shop jobbers, and national and state associations. Annual, January. **Editor(s):** Lloyd Stoyer. **Price:** $30.00.

3161 • National Tire Dealers and Retreaders Association—Who's Who Membership Directory
National Tire Dealers and Retreaders Assn.
1250 Eye St., NW, Ste. 400   Ph:(202)789-2300
Washington, DC 20005   Fax:(202)682-3999

Newsletter.

3162 • New Jersey Automotive Directory
Automotive Contact
P.O. Box 517
Terre Haute, IN 47808   Ph:(812)232-2441

Directory. Automotive aftermarket businesses, including body shops; brake, muffler, radiator, electrical and transmission repairs, as well as new car dealers, parts retailers, auto salvage companies, and automotive parts warehouses. Annual, January. **Editor(s):** T. L. Spelman, Publisher. **Price:** $30.95, plus $3.00 shipping.

3163 • New York Automotive Directory
Automotive Contact
P.O. Box 517
Terre Haute, IN 47808   Ph:(812)232-2441

Directory. Automotive aftermarket businesses, including body shops; brake, muffler, radiator, electrical and transmission repairs, as well as new car dealers, parts retailers, auto salvage companies, and automotive parts warehouses. Annual, January. **Editor(s):** T. L. Spelman, Publisher. **Price:** $30.95, plus $3.00 shipping.

3164 • North Carolina Automotive Directory
Automotive Contact
P.O. Box 517
Terre Haute, IN 47808   Ph:(812)232-2441

Directory. Automotive aftermarket businesses, including body shops; brake, muffler, radiator, electrical and transmission repairs, as well as new car dealers, parts retailers, auto salvage companies, and automotive parts warehouses. Annual, January. **Editor(s):** T. L. Spelman, Publisher. **Price:** $30.95, plus $3.00 shipping.

3165 • Ohio Automotive Directory
Automotive Contact
P.O. Box 517
Terre Haute, IN 47808   Ph:(812)232-2441

Directory. Automotive aftermarket businesses, including body shops; brake, muffler, radiator, electrical and transmission repairs, as well as new car dealers, parts retailers, auto salvage companies, and automotive parts warehouses. Annual, January. **Editor(s):** T. L. Spelman, Publisher. **Price:** $30.95, plus $3.00 shipping.

3166 • Oklahoma Automotive Directory
Automotive Contact
P.O. Box 517
Terre Haute, IN 47808   Ph:(812)232-2441

Directory. Automotive aftermarket businesses, including body shops; brake, muffler, radiator, electrical and transmission repairs, as well as new car dealers, parts retailers, auto salvage companies, and automotive parts warehouses. Annual, January. **Editor(s):** T. L. Spelman, Publisher. **Price:** $30.95, plus $3.00 shipping.

3167 • Oregon Automotive Directory
Automotive Contact
P.O. Box 517
Terre Haute, IN 47808   Ph:(812)232-2441

Directory. Automotive aftermarket businesses, including body shops; brake, muffler, radiator, electrical and transmission repairs, as well as new car dealers, parts retailers, auto salvage companies,

and automotive parts warehouses. Annual, January. **Editor(s):** T. L. Spelman, Publisher. **Price:** $30.95, plus $3.00 shipping.

3168 • Pennsylvania Automotive Directory
Automotive Contact
P.O. Box 517
Terre Haute, IN 47808   Ph:(812)232-2441

Directory. Automotive aftermarket businesses, including body shops; brake, muffler, radiator, electrical and transmission repairs, as well as new car dealers, parts retailers, auto salvage companies, and automotive parts warehouses. Annual, January. **Editor(s):** T. L. Spelman, Publisher. **Price:** $30.95, plus $3.00 shipping.

3169 • South Carolina Automotive Directory
Automotive Contact
P.O. Box 517
Terre Haute, IN 47808   Ph:(812)232-2441

Directory. Automotive aftermarket businesses, including body shops; brake, muffler, radiator, electrical and transmission repairs, as well as new car dealers, parts retailers, auto salvage companies, and automotive parts warehouses. Annual, January. **Editor(s):** T. L. Spelman, Publisher. **Price:** $30.95, plus $3.00 shipping.

3170 • Springs—Automotive Sales and Service Directory
American Business Directories, Inc.
American Business Information, Inc.
5711 S. 86th Circle   Ph:(402)593-4600
Omaha, NE 68127   Fax:(402)331-1505

Directory. 1,760 automotive firms that provide springs and service spring systems. Annual. **Price:** $105.00, payment with order. Significant discounts offered for standing orders.

3171 • Tennessee Automotive Directory
Automotive Contact
P.O. Box 517
Terre Haute, IN 47808   Ph:(812)232-2441

Directory. Automotive aftermarket businesses, including body shops; brake, muffler, radiator, electrical and transmission repairs, as well as new car dealers, parts retailers, auto salvage companies, and automotive parts warehouses. Annual, January. **Editor(s):** T. L. Spelman, Publisher. **Price:** $30.95, plus $3.00 shipping.

3172 • Texas Automotive Directory
Automotive Contact
P.O. Box 517
Terre Haute, IN 47808   Ph:(812)232-2441

Directory. Automotive aftermarket businesses, including body shops; brake, muffler, radiator, electrical and transmission repairs, as well as new car dealers, parts retailers, auto salvage companies, and automotive parts warehouses. Annual, January. **Editor(s):** T. L. Spelman, Publisher. **Price:** $30.95, plus $3.00 shipping.

3173 • Tire Retreading and Repair Directory
American Business Directories, Inc.
American Business Information, Inc.
5711 S. 86th Circle   Ph:(402)593-4600
Omaha, NE 68127   Fax:(402)331-1505

Directory. 5,295 automotive firms that offer tire retreading and repair services. Annual. **Price:** $200.00, payment with order. Significant discounts offered for standing orders.

3174 • Towing and Wrecker Service Directory
American Business Directories, Inc.
American Business Information, Inc.
5711 S. 86th Circle   Ph:(402)593-4600
Omaha, NE 68127   Fax:(402)331-1505

Directory. Nearly 39,080 firms that offer towing and wrecking services. Annual. **Price:** $1,080.00, payment with order. Significant discounts offered for standing orders. Regional editions available: Eastern, $790.00; Western, $440.00.

3175 • Truck-Frame and Axle Repair Association—Membership Directory
Truck-Frame and Axle Repair Assn.
915 E. 99th St.   Ph:(718)257-6133
Brooklyn, NY 11236   Fax:(718)272-9198

Directory. Lists automotive service firms that specialize in truck frame and axle repair. Annual. **Editor(s):** S. Licitra. **Price:** Free.

3176 • Truck Repairing and Service Directory
American Business Directories, Inc.
American Business Information, Inc.
5711 S. 86th Circle   Ph:(402)593-4600
Omaha, NE 68127   Fax:(402)331-1505

Directory. About 20,310 automotive firms that service and repair trucks. Annual. **Price:** $630.00, payment with order. Significant discounts offered for standing orders.

3177 • Truck Washing and Cleaning Directory
American Business Directories, Inc.
American Business Information, Inc.
5711 S. 86th Circle   Ph:(402)593-4600
Omaha, NE 68127   Fax:(402)331-1505

Directory. 2,055 firms that provide truck washing and cleaning services. Annual. **Price:** $105.00, payment with order. Significant discounts offered for standing orders.

3178 • Virginia/West Virginia Automotive Directory
Automotive Contact
P.O. Box 517
Terre Haute, IN 47808   Ph:(812)232-2441

Directory. Automotive aftermarket businesses, including body shops; brake, muffler, radiator, electrical and transmission repairs, as well as new car dealers, parts retailers, auto salvage companies, and automotive parts warehouses. Annual, January. **Editor(s):** T. L. Spelman, Publisher. **Price:** $30.95, plus $3.00 shipping.

3179 • Washington Automotive Directory [State]
Automotive Contact
P.O. Box 517
Terre Haute, IN 47808   Ph:(812)232-2441

Directory. Automotive aftermarket businesses, including body shops; brake, muffler, radiator, electrical and transmission repairs, as well as new car dealers, parts retailers, auto salvage companies, and automotive parts warehouses. Annual, January. **Editor(s):** T. L. Spelman, Publisher. **Price:** $30.95, plus $3.00 shipping.

3180 • Wheel Alignment/Frame Shops Directory
American Business Directories, Inc.
American Business Information, Inc.
5711 S. 86th Circle   Ph:(402)593-4600
Omaha, NE 68127   Fax:(402)331-1505

Directory. About 17,455 wheel alignment and frame shops. Annual. **Price:** $565.00, payment with order. Significant discounts offered for standing orders.

3181 • Wisconsin Automotive Directory
Automotive Contact
P.O. Box 517
Terre Haute, IN 47808   Ph:(812)232-2441

Directory. Automotive aftermarket businesses, including body shops; brake, muffler, radiator, electrical and transmission repairs, as well as new car dealers, parts retailers, auto salvage companies, and automotive parts warehouses. Annual, January. **Editor(s):** T. L. Spelman, Publisher. **Price:** $30.95, plus $3.00 shipping.

BUYERS GUIDES AND CLASSIFIEDS

3182 • Auto Trader
Auto Trader Magazine, Inc.
P.O. Box 17287   Ph:(502)447-8787
Louisville, KY 40217-0287 Fax:(502)447-8794

Magazine. Contains automotive photo classified ads. Weekly. **Editor(s):** Maurice Huber. **Price:** $120.00; 75¢ per single issue.

3183 • Autoguide
Edgell Communications
7500 Old Oak Blvd.
Cleveland, OH 44130   Ph:(216)243-8100

Buyers guide. Describes new automobile models. Annual, December. **Editor(s):** Daniel Ross. **Price:** $4.00.

3184 • Automobile Red Book
National Market Reports, Inc.
300 W. Adams St.
Chicago, IL 60606-5186   Ph:(312)726-2802

Book. Monthly.

3185 • Car and Driver—Buyers Guide
Hachette Publications, Inc.
2002 Hogback Rd.   Ph:(313)971-3600
Ann Arbor, MI 48105   Fax:(313)971-9188

Buyers guide. Contains information concerning all new automobile models as well as comparative tests and accessory buying guides. Annual. **Editor(s):** William Jeanes. **Price:** $4.95.

3186 • The Car Buyer's Handbook
Consumers Automotive Resource, Ltd.
9940 Main St., Suite 200
Fairfax, VA 22031   Ph:(202)783-7283

Buyers guide. **Author(s):** James A. Boerger. **Price:** $9.95.

3187 • Car Stereo Blue Book
Oryx Press
4041 N. Central
Phoenix, AZ 85102

Buyers guide.

3188 • Car Trader
Heartland Communications
1003 Central Ave.
Fort Dodge, IA 50501   Ph:(515)955-1600

Newspaper. Provides market information on antique, classic, and special interest automobiles. Weekly. **Editor(s):** Sheila Davis, Production Manager. **Price:** $59.00 per year; $2.00 per issue.

3189 • Cars and Parts Annual
Amos Press
911 Vandemark Rd.
Sidney, OH 45365   Ph:(513)498-0803

Magazine. Includes information on the hobby of car collecting. Annual. **Editor(s):** Robert Stevens. **Price:** $4.95.

3190 • CarTel
P.O. Box 2291
Topeka, KS 66603   Ph:(913)233-5662

Magazine. Advertises vehicles for sale and lists auto-related community events. Every other week. **Editor(s):** Reg Davis.

3191 • Complete Car Cost Guide
IntelliChoice, Inc.
1135 S. Saratoga-Sunnyvale Rd.
San Jose, CA 95129-3660 Ph:(408)554-8711

Buyers guide. Annual. **Price:** $39.00.

3192 • Complete Small Truck Cost Guide
IntelliChoice, Inc.
1135 S. Saratoga Sunnyvale Rd.
San Jose, CA 95129   Ph:(408)554-8711

Buyers guide. Published 1990. **Price:** $39.00.

3193 • Consumer Guide Automobile Book: The Complete New Car Buying Guide
NAL/Dutton
1633 Broadway
New York, NY 10019   Ph:(212)397-8000

Buyers guide. Annual. **Price:** $8.95.

3194 • Consumer Guide Used Car Book
NAL/Dutton
1633 Broadway
New York, NY 10019   Ph:(212)397-8000

Buyers guide. Annual. **Price:** $6.99.

3195 • Consumers Cars Guide
New American Library
1633 Broadway
New York, NY 10019   Ph:(212)397-8000

Buyers guide. Annual. **Price:** $4.95.

3196 • CPI: Cars of Particular Interest
CPI
PO Box 11409
Baltimore, MD 21239   Ph:(301)252-5759

Directory. Value guide to domestic and imported cars of interest. Quarterly. **Price:** $15.00.

3197 • Deals on Wheels: How to Buy, Care for and Sell a Car: Complete Buyer's Guide and Expose of the Automotive Jungle
Page Publishing Co.
P.O. Box 432
Brookfield, WI 53005

Buyers guide. Published 1984. **Author(s):** Gordon T. Page. **Price:** $9.95.

3198 • The duPont Registry
duPont Publishing, Inc.
2502 N. Rocky Point Dr., Ste. 1095   Ph:(813)281-5656
Tampa, FL 33607   Fax:(813)281-1215

Buyers guide. Full color catalog of classic, luxury, and exotic cars for sale from all over the U.S., Canada, and Europe. Monthly. **Editor(s):** Thomas L. duPont, Chmn. and Publisher. **Price:** $39.95.

3199 • Edmund's Car Price Buyer's Guide
St. Martin's Press, Inc.
175 5th Ave.
New York, NY 10010   Ph:(212)674-5151

Buyers guide. Annual. **Price:** $4.95.

3200 • Edmund's Economy Car Price Buying Guide
Edmund Publishers Corp.
515 Hempstead Tpke.
West Hempstead, NY 11552   Ph:(516)292-0044

Buyers guide. Lists the dealer cost and suggested retail prices for all economy cars and factory installed options. Annual. **Editor(s):** William Badnow. **Price:** $3.95.

3201 • Edmund's Foreign Car Prices
Edmund Publishers Corp.
515 Hempstead Tpke.
West Hempstead, NY 11552   Ph:(516)292-0044

Buyers guide. Lists dealer cost and suggested retail prices for imported cars and their factory installed options. Semiannual. **Editor(s):** William Badnow. **Price:** $3.95.

3202 • Edmund's New Car Prices
Edmund Publishers Corp.
515 Hempstead Tpke.
West Hempstead, NY 11552   Ph:(516)292-0044

Buyers guide. Lists dealer cost and suggested retail prices for domestic automobiles and their factory installed options. Annual. **Editor(s):** William Badnow. **Price:** $3.95.

3203 • Edmund's New Car Prices
St. Martin's Press, Inc.
175 5th Ave.
New York, NY 10010   Ph:(212)674-5151

Buyers guide. Annual. **Price:** $4.95.

3204 • Edmund's Used Car Prices
Edmund Publications Corp.
515 Hempstead Turnpike
W. Hempstead, NY 11552   Ph:(516)292-0044

Buyers guide. Lists original prices and current wholesale and retail prices of older model vehicles. Quarterly. **Editor(s):** William Badnow. **Price:** $13.40/yr.; $3.95/issue.

3205 • Edmund's Vans, Pickups/Off Road Buyer's Guide
Edmund Publishers Corp.
515 Hempstead Tpke.
West Hempstead, NY 11552   Ph:(516)292-0044

Buyers guide. Lists dealer cost and suggested retail prices for vans, pickups, and sport utility vehicles and factory options. Semiannual. **Editor(s):** William Badnow. **Price:** $3.95.

3206 • Four By Four Pickups and Vans [Year] Buying Guide
NAL/Dutton
1633 Broadway
New York, NY 10019   Ph:(212)397-8000

Buyers guide. Annual. **Price:** $6.99.

3207 • Guide to New Cars
Consumer Reports Books
51 E. 42nd St. Ste. 800
New York, NY 10017   Ph:(212)682-9280

Buyers guide. Published 1988. **Price:** $8.00.

3208 • Guide to Used Cars
NAL/Dutton
1633 Broadway
New York, NY 10019   Ph:(212)397-8000

Buyers guide. Annual. **Price:** $5.99.

3209 • Hemmings Motor News
Watering, Inc.
Box 256
Bennington, VT 05201   Ph:(802)442-3101

Buyers guide. Provides information on antique, classic, special interest, and vintage car marketplace. Monthly. **Editor(s):** David Brownell. **Price:** $23.95/year; $4.95 per single issue.

3210 • Kelley Blue Book Used Car Price Manual
Kelley Blue Book Co.
5 Oldfield
Irvine, CA 92718   Ph:(714)770-7704

Manual. Bimonthly.

3211 • Locator
John Holmes Publishing Co.
521 Main   Ph:800-457-0660
Whiting, IA 51063   Fax:(712)458-2687

Buyers guide. Provides information on used domestic, imported, and antique auto and truck parts. Monthly. **Editor(s):** John Holmes, Publisher. **Price:** $29.00 per year; $4.50 per issue.

3212 • Motor Trend—New Car Buyer's Guide
Petersen Publishing Co.
6725 Sunset Blvd.
Los Angeles, CA 90028   Ph:(213)854-2222

Buyers guide. Contains descriptions, prices, and photos on new automobiles. Annual. **Editor(s):** Ro McGonegal. **Price:** $3.95.

3213 • Motor Trend—Truck and Van Buyer's Guide
Petersen Publishing Co.
6725 Sunset Blvd.
Los Angeles, CA 90028   Ph:(213)854-2222

Buyers guide. Contains information on new trucks and vans. Annual. **Editor(s):** Ron Cogan. **Price:** $3.95.

3214 • National Auto Data Service
National Auto Data Service (NADS)
4211 S.E. International Way
Milwaukie, OR 97222   Ph:(503)652-3350

Database. Contains 1.8 million records of automobiles from more than 200 publications in the western United States. Each Computerized Vehicle Profile (CVP) record includes the year, make, model, body style, trim and optional equipment, and asking price of the vehicle, date and source of ad, and the telephone number of the seller. Also included are the wholesale auction data, public retail ads, dealer retail ads, local or regional market price trend graph, and the average vehicle pricing model. Each record is updated daily and maintained for 100 days.

3215 • New Car Buying Guide
Consumer Reports Books
51 E. 42nd St., Ste. 800
New York, NY 10017   Ph:(212)682-9280

Buyers guide. Annual. **Editor(s):** Guy Henle et al. **Price:** $8.95.

3216 • The Official Price Guide to Cars and Trucks
Ballantine Books, Inc.
201 E. 50th Street
New York, NY 10022   Ph:(212)751-2600

Buyers guide. Published 1987. **Price:** $5.95.

3217 • Official Used Car Guide Book
National Automobile Dealers Association (NADA)
8400 Westpark Dr.
McLean, VA 22102   Ph:(703)827-7407

Book. Monthly.

3218 • Old Cars Auction Results, 1989: Worldwide Model Years 1905-1988
Krause Publications, Inc.
700 E. State St.
Iola, WI 54990   Ph:(715)445-2214

Book. Published 1989. **Price:** $19.95.

3219 • Old Cars Price Guide
Krause Publications
700 E. State St.   Ph:(715)445-2214
Iola, WI 54990   Fax:(715)445-4087

Buyers guide. Lists current values to domestic cars since 1901 in five grading conditions. Bimonthly. **Editor(s):** Ken Buttolph. **Price:** $16.95 per year; $3.95 per issue.

3220 • Price Guide Presents
Krause Publications
700 E. State St.   Ph:(715)445-2214
Iola, WI 54990   Fax:(715)445-4087

Magazine. A series of specialized automotive price reference guides that cover domestic and imported cars and trucks. Quarterly. **Editor(s):** Kenny Boholph. **Price:** $14.95/yr.; $3.75/issue.

3221 • The Redbook: The Consumer's Automobile Purchasing Guide and Reference Manual
Vantage Press, Inc.
516 W. 34th St.
New York, NY 10001   Ph:(212)736-1767

Buyers guide. 1988. **Editor(s):** Michael L. Van Natten. **Price:** $12.95.

3222 • Standard Catalog of American Light Duty Trucks
Krause Publications, Inc.
700 E. State St.
Iola, WI 54990   Ph:(715)445-2214

Buyers guide. With illustrations. Published 1987. **Editor(s):** John Gunnel. **Price:** $24.95.

3223 • Standard Guide to Cars and Prices
Krause Publications, Inc.
700 E. State St.
Iola, WI 54990   Ph:(715)445-2214

Buyers guide. Published 1991. **Editor(s):** Jim Lenzke and Kenny Buttoph. **Price:** $14.95.

3224 • Truck & Equipment Trader
Landmark Classified Advertising Publications, Inc.
1450 Dixie Hwy.   Ph:(606)581-5500
Park Hills, KY 41011   Fax:(606)581-6837

Buyers guide. Magazine featuring photo ads of trucks and equipment for sale by individuals and dealers. Weekly (Thurs.). **Editor(s):** Mark Roehrig, Publisher and Advertising Mgr. **Price:** 75¢ per single issue.

3225 • Truck Guide
Macmillan Publishing Co.
866 Third Ave.
New York, NY 10022   Ph:(212)702-2000

Buyers guide. Three volume set: volume one, Engines; volume two, Transmissions; volume three, Steering and Brakes. Published 1984. **Editor(s):** Janese Brumbaugh. **Price:** $50.95 for the set.

3226 • Truck Trader
Cox Enterprises
1400 Lake Hearn Dr., N.E.
Atlanta, GA 30319   Ph:(404)843-5000

Buyers guide. Monthly. **Price:** $65.00.

3227 • The Underground Blue Book: A Guide to Buying And Selling New and Used Cars, Trucks, and R.V.s
Diamond S Publishing
P.O. Box 5998
Beaverton, OR 97006   Ph:(503)628-8588

Buyers guide. Published 1987. **Price:** $9.95.

3228 • The Used Car Book
Harper & Row Publishers, Inc.
10 E. 53rd St.
New York, NY 10022   Ph:(212)207-7000

Buyers guide. Annual. **Editor(s):** Jack Gillis. **Price:** $10.95.

3229 • Used Car Buying Guide
Consumer Reports Books
51 E. 42nd St., Ste. 800
New York, NY 10017   Ph:(212)682-9280

Buyers guide. Annual. **Editor(s):** Alex Markovich. **Price:** $8.95.

3230 • Vehicle Identification 1986-1987
Lee Books
PO Box 906
Novato, CA 94948   Ph:(415)897-3550

Book. Published 1986. **Editor(s):** Lee S. Cole. **Price:** $15.00.

3231 • Wheeler Dealer
Landmark Classified Advertising Publications, Inc.
1450 Dixie Hwy.   Ph:(606)581-5500
Park Hills, KY 41011   Fax:(606)581-6837

Buyers guide. Magazine featuring photo classified ads of automobiles for sale by individuals and dealers. Weekly. **Editor(s):** Mark Roehrig, Publisher and Advertising Mgr. **Price:** $1.00 per single issue.

3232 • Whole Car Catalog
Simon and Schuster, Inc.
1230 Ave. of the Americas
New York, NY 10020   Ph:(212)698-7000

Buyers guide. Published 1978. **Price:** $7.95.

3233 • Yo Money: A Very Fast Guide to Car Buying
Taos Bluewater Press
PO Box 529
Taos, NM 87571   Ph:(505)758-5671

Buyers guide. Published 1991. **Editor(s):** Paul D. Mallamo. **Price:** $10.00

OTHER INFORMATION SOURCES

Accessories

3234 • Chilton's Chassis Electronics and Power Accessories Service Manual, 1987-89: Motor-Age Professional Mechanic's Edition
Chilton Co.
Chilton Way
Radnor, PA 19089   Ph:(215)964-4000

Manual. Published 1988. **Price:** $77.00.

3235 • Orion Car Stereo Blue Book
Orion Research
1315 Main Ave.
Suite 230
Durango, CO 81301   Ph:(303)247-8855

Reference book. Published 1990. **Price:** $79.00.

3236 • Pinstriping Made Easy
Pinkston & Lusk Productions, Inc.
1422 Nelson Dr.
Derby, KS 67037   Ph:(316)788-3685

Audio-visual. An instructional program for pinstriping your car, complete with patterns of the basic strokes. **Release date:** 1987. **Producer:** Pinkston & Lusk Productions, Inc. **Acquisition:** Purchase.

3237 • Plastics in Automobile Instrument Panels, Trim, and Seating
Society of Automotive Engineers
400 Commonwealth Dr.
Warrendale, PA 15096   Ph:(412)776-4841

Book. **Price:** $54.00.

3238 • Plastics in Automobiles: Bumper Systems, Interior Trim, Instrument Panels and Exterior Panels
Society of Automotive Engineers, Inc.
400 Commonwealth Dr.
Warrendale, PA 15096   Ph:(412)776-4841

Book. Published 1989. **Price:** $72.00.

Automotive aftermarket parts

3239 • Aftermarket for Imported Cars and Light Trucks
Frost and Sullivan, Inc.
106 Fulton St.
New York, NY 10038   Ph:(212)233-1080

Audio-visual. Published 1984. **Price:** $1400.00.

3240 • Auto Owner's Supply Book
Northstar Books
P.O. Box 810
Lakeville, MN 55044-0810   Ph:(612)469-4928

Buyers guide. Published 1989. **Price:** $2.00.

3241 • Automotive Products Report
Irving-Cloud Publishing Co.
7300 N. Cicero Ave.   Ph:(708)674-7300
Lincolnwood, IL 60646-1696   Fax:(708)674-7015

Magazine. Bimonthly. **Editor(s):** Martin Schultz. **Price:** $30.00.

Automotive body shops

3242 • Truck Painting and Lettering Directory
American Business Directories, Inc.
American Business Information, Inc.
5711 S. 86th Circle   Ph:(402)593-4600
Omaha, NE 68127   Fax:(402)331-1505

Audio-visual. Approximately 5,975 firms that provide truck painting and lettering services. Annual. **Price:** $200.00, payment with order. Significant discounts offered for standing orders.

Automotive design

3243 • Automobile Aerodynamics: Wakes, Wind Effect, Vehicle Development
Society of Automotive Engineers, Inc.
400 Commonwealth Dr.
Warrendale, PA 15096   Ph:(412)776-4841

Book. Published 1984. **Price:** $44.00.

3244 • Automobile Design: Great Designers and Their Work
Robert Bentley, Inc., Pubs.
1000 Massachusetts Ave.
Cambridge, MA 02138   Ph:(617)547-4170

Book. **Editor(s):** Ronald Barker and Anthony Harding. **Price:** $16.50.

3245 • Automobile Design Liability
Lawyers Co-Operative Publishing, Co.
Aqueduct Bldg.
Rochester, NY 14694   Ph:(716)546-5530

Book. Published 1989. **Editor(s):** Richard M. Goodman. **Price:** $149.00; Supplement $54.00.

3246 • Automobile Frontal Impacts
Society of Automotive Engineers, Inc.
400 Commonwealth Dr.
Warrendale, PA 15096   Ph:(412)776-4841

Book. Published 1989. **Price:** $41.00.

3247 • Automotive Instrument Panels: Design, Materials, and Manufacturing
Society of Automotive Engineers, Inc.
400 Commonwealth Dr.
Warrendale, PA 15096   Ph:(412)776-4841

Book. Published 1987. **Price:** $44.00.

3248 • **Best of BAX: Collected Columns from Car and Driver**
TAB Books, Inc.
Blue Ridge Summit, PA 22301   Ph:(717)794-2191

Reference book. Published 1989. **Author(s):** Gordon Baxter. **Price:** 13.95.

3249 • **Computer Applications in Design and Manufacturing**
Society of Automotive Engineers, Inc.
400 Commonwealth Dr.
Warrendale, PA 15096   Ph:(412)776-4841

Manual. Published 1987. **Price:** $40.00.

3250 • **Computers in Design, Manufacture and Operation of Automobiles**
Computational Mechanics, Inc.
25 Bridge St.
Billerica, MA 01821   Ph:(508)667-5841

Manual. Published 1987. **Editor(s):** T.K. Murthy. **Price:** $72.00.

3251 • **Current and Future Directions of Supercomputer Applications in the Automobile Industry**
Society of Automotive Engineers, Inc.
400 Commonwealth Dr.
Warrendale, PA 15096   Ph:(412)776-4841

Book. Published 1985. **Price:** $27.00.

3252 • **Current Trends in Truck Suspension**
Society of Automotive Engineers, Inc.
400 Commonwealth Dr.
Warrendale, PA 15096   Ph:(412)776-4841

Report/bulletin. Six papers. Published 1980. **Price:** $33.00.

3253 • **Design Practices Passenger Car Automatic Transmission**
Society of Automotive Engineers, Inc.
400 Commonwealth Dr.
Warrendale, PA 15096   Ph:(412)776-4841

Book. Published 1988. **Price:** $79.00.

3254 • **Display Technology: Human Factors Concepts**
Society of Automotive Engineers, Inc.
400 Commonwealth Dr.
Warrendale, PA 15096   Ph:(412)776-4841

Manual. **Price:** $58.00.

3255 • **Displays, Electronics, and Sensors Technology**
Society of Automotive Engineers, Inc.
400 Commonwealth Dr.
Warrendale, PA 15096   Ph:(412)776-4841

Manual. Published 1984. **Price:** $64.00.

3256 • **Electronic Automotive Reliability**
Society of Automotive Engineers, Inc.
400 Commonwealth Dr.
Warrendale, PA 15096-0001   Ph:(412)776-4841

Manual. Published 1984. **Price:** $33.00.

3257 • **Electronic Displays and Information Systems**
Society of Automotive Engineers, Inc.
400 Commonwealth Dr.
Warrendale, PA 15096   Ph:(412)776-4841

Manual. Published 1981. **Price:** $46.00.

3258 • **Electronic Displays, Information Systems and On-Board Electronics**
Society of Automotive Engineers, Inc.
400 Commonwealth Dr.
Warrendale, PA 15096   Ph:(412)776-4841

Manual. Published 1982. **Price:** $58.00.

3259 • **Light Vehicle Fitting**
State Mutual Book & Periodical Service, Ltd.
521 Fifth Ave., 17th Fl.
New York, NY 10175   Ph:(212)682-5844

Manual. Published 1982. **Price:** $50.00.

3260 • **Lighting Systems for Motor Vehicles**
Society of Automotive Engineers, Inc.
400 Commonwealth Dr.
Warrendale, PA 15096   Ph:(412)776-4841

Manual. Published 1989. **Price:** $30.00.

3261 • **Manual for Incorporating Pneumatic Springs in Vehicle Suspension Designs**
Society of Automotive Engineers, Inc.
400 Commonwealth Dr.
Warrendale, PA 15096   Ph:(412)776-4841

Manual. Published 1989. **Price:** $33.00.

3262 • **Modern Automotive Structural Analysis**
Van Nostrand Reinhold Co., Inc.
115 Fifth Ave.
New York, NY 10003   Ph:(212)254-3232

Book. Published 1982. **Editor(s):** Mounir M. Kamal and Joseph A. Wolf. **Price:** $51.95.

3263 • **Multiplexing in Automobiles**
Society of Automotive Engineers, Inc.
400 Commonwealth Dr.
Warrendale, PA 15096   Ph:(412)776-4841

Manual. Published 1989. **Price:** $30.00.

3264 • **New Development and Requirements for Automotive Fabrics**
Industrial Fabrics Assn. Intl.
345 Cedar St.
St. Paul, MN 55101   Ph:(612)222-2508

Book. Published 1983. **Price:** $30.00.

3265 • **New Development in Automotive Fibers and Fabrics**
Industrial Fabrics Assn. Intl.
345 Cedar St.
St. Paul, MN 55101   Ph:(612)222-2508

Book. Published 1988. **Price:** $30.00.

3266 • **New Developments in Electronic Engine Management**
Society of Automotive Engineers, Inc.
400 Commonwealth Dr.
Warrendale, PA 15096   Ph:(412)776-4841

Book. Published 1984. **Price:** $56.00.

3267 • **New Developments in Polymer Composites for Automotive Applications**
Society of Automotive Engineers, Inc.
400 Commonwealth Dr.
Warrendale, PA 15096   Ph:(412)776-4841

Book. Published 1989. **Price:** $70.00.

3268 • **New Directions in Suspension Design: Making the Fast Car Faster**
Robert Bentley Inc., Pubs.
1000 Massachusetts Ave.
Cambridge, MA 02138   Ph:(617)547-4170

Book. Published 1981. **Editor(s):** Colin Campbell. **Price:** $21.95.

3269 • **New Engine and Advanced Component Design**
Society of Automotive Engineers, Inc.
400 Commonwealth Dr.
Warrendale, PA 15096   Ph:(412)776-4841

Book. **Price:** $54.00.

3270 • **New Polymer Technology for Auto Body Exteriors**
American Institute of Chemists, Inc.
7315 Wisconsin Ave.
Bethesda, MD 20814   Ph:(301)652-2447

Book. Published 1988. **Editor(s):** John Purcell. **Price:** $33.00.

3271 • **Past, Present & Future of Automotive Elastomer Applications**
Society of Automotive Engineers, Inc.
400 Commonwealth Dr.
Warrendale, PA 15096   Ph:(412)776-4841

Book. Published 1980. **Price:** $26.00.

3272 • **Plastics & Passenger Cars**
Society of Automotive Engineers, Inc.
400 Commonwealth Dr.
Warrendale, PA 15096   Ph:(412)776-4841

Book. Published 1984. **Price:** $56.00.

3273 • **Plastics in Automobile Bumper Systems and Exterior Panels**
Society of Automotive Engineers, Inc.
400 Commonwealth Dr.
Warrendale, PA 15096   Ph:(412)776-4841

Book. **Price:** $40.00.

3274 • **Plastics in Automobile Instrument Panels, Trim, and Seating**
Society of Automotive Engineers
400 Commonwealth Dr.
Warrendale, PA 15096   Ph:(412)776-4841

Book. **Price:** $54.00.

3275 • **Plastics in Automobiles: Bumper Systems, Interior Trim, Instrument Panels and Exterior Panels**
Society of Automotive Engineers, Inc.
400 Commonwealth Dr.
Warrendale, PA 15096   Ph:(412)776-4841

Book. Published 1989. **Price:** $72.00.

3276 • **Plastics in Automotive Applications**
Society of Automotive Engineers, Inc.
400 Commonwealth Dr.
Warrendale, PA 15096   Ph:(412)776-4841

Book. Published 1989. **Price:** $86.00.

3277 • **Polymers & Polymer Systems Used in Autos Market**
Frost & Sullivan, Inc.
106 Fulton St.
New York, NY 10038   Ph:(212)233-1080

Book. Published 1988.

3278 • **Powder Metal Parts**
Society of Automotive Engineers, Inc.
400 Commonwealth Dr.
Warrendale, PA 15096   Ph:(412)776-4841

Book. Published 1983. **Price:** $46.00.

3279 • **Power Behind the Wheel: Creativity and Evolution of the Automobile**
Abbeville Press, Inc.
488 Madison Ave.   Ph:(212)888-1969
New York, NY 10022   Fax:(212)644-5085

Book. Published 1991. **Editor(s):** Walter J. Boyne. **Price:** $19.98.

3280 • **Power Transmission Design**
Penton Publishing
1100 Superior Ave.   Ph:(216)696-7000
Cleveland, OH 44114-2543   Fax:(216)696-7648

Magazine. Aimed at people who design, apply, and maintain

motors, drives, bearings, controls, and power transmission accessories. Monthly. **Editor(s):** Phil Kingsley. **Price:** $40.00/year; $5.00 per single issue.

3281 • **Structural Design and Crashworthiness of Automobiles**
Computational Mechanics, Inc.
25 Bridge St.
Billerica, MA 01821   Ph:(508)667-5841

Manual. Published 1987. **Editor(s):** T.K. Murthy and C.A. Brebbia. **Price:** $72.00.

3282 • **Studies Relating Automobile Design & Vehicle Safety: An Annotated Bibliography**
Council of Planning Librarians
1313 E. 60th St.
Chicago, IL 60637   Ph:(312)942-2163

Reference book. Published 1982. **Editor(s):** Margaret E. Shepard. **Price:** $15.00.

3283 • **Transportation Energy Research**
National Technical Information Service (NTIS), U.S. Department of Commerce
5285 Port Royal Rd.
Springfield, VA 22161   Ph:(703)487-4630

Newsletter. Summarizes worldwide information on engineering and design of energy-efficient advanced automotive propulsion systems and other aspects of energy conservation measures involving transportation. Monthly. **Price:** $100.00/year, U.S., Canada, and Mexico; $200.00 elsewhere.

3284 • **Vehicle Lighting Trends**
Society of Automotive Engineers, Inc.
400 Commonwealth Dr.
Warrendale, PA 15096   Ph:(412)776-4841

Book. Published 1987. **Price:** $40.00

3285 • **Ward's Engine Update**
Ward's Communications, Inc.
28 W. Adams St.   Ph:(313)962-4433
Detroit, MI 48226   Fax:(313)962-4456

Report/bulletin. Reports on and monitors all engine and transmission technological developments relating to cars and trucks worldwide. Also discusses marketing and business strategies. Irregular. **Editor(s):** David C. Smith. **Price:** $550.00/year.

Automotive engineering

3286 • **Automobile Technology of the Future**
Society of Automotive Engineers, Inc.
400 Commonwealth Dr.
Warrendale, PA 15096-0001   Ph:(412)776-4841

Book. Published 1991. **Editor(s):** Ulrich Seiffert. **Price:** $69.00.

3287 • **Automotive Engineering**
Society of Automotive Engineers, Inc.
400 Commonwealth Dr.   Ph:(412)776-4841
Warrendale, PA 15096   Fax:(412)776-9765

Magazine. Provides technical and design information for automotive engineers. Monthly. **Editor(s):** Daniel J. Holt. **Price:** $72.00; $10.00 per single issue.

3288 • **Automotive Engineering and Litigation**
John Wiley & Sons, Inc.
136 Madison Ave.
New York, NY 10016   Ph:(212)686-7492

Book. Supplement edition in two volumes. Published 1984. **Editor(s):** George A. Peters and Barbara J. Peters. **Price:** $100.00.

3289 • Automotive Workbook
National Learning Corp.
212 Michael Dr.
Syosset, NY 11791   Ph:(516)921-8888

Manual. Published 1991. **Editor(s):** Jack Rudman. **Price:** $13.95.

3290 • Developments in Electronic Engine Management and Driveline Controls
Society of Automotive Engineers, Inc.
400 Commonwealth Dr.
Warrendale, PA 15096   Ph:(412)776-4841

Book. Published 1985. **Price:** $44.00.

3291 • Karl Benz
Franklin Watts, Inc.
387 Park Ave. S.
New York, NY 10016   Ph:(212)686-7070

Book. Published 1991. **Editor(s):** Brian Williams. **Price:** $12.40.

3292 • A Study of the Toyota Production System from an Industrial Engineering Viewpoint
Productivity Press, Inc.
P.O. Box 3007
Cambridge, MA 02140   Ph:(617)497-5146

Book. Published 1989. **Author(s):** Shigeo Shingo.

3293 • Transportation Energy Research
National Technical Information Service (NTIS), U.S.
    Department of Commerce
5285 Port Royal Rd.
Springfield, VA 22161   Ph:(703)487-4630

Newsletter. Summarizes worldwide information on engineering and design of energy-efficient advanced automotive propulsion systems and other aspects of energy conservation measures involving transportation. Monthly. **Price:** $100.00/year, U.S., Canada, and Mexico; $200.00 elsewhere.

3294 • Turbo and Hi-Tech Performance
MAG-TEC Productions, Inc.
9582 Hamilton   Ph:(714)962-7795
Huntington Beach, CA 92646   Fax:(714)965-2268

Magazine. Covers automotive performance and engineering. Bimonthly. **Editor(s):** Frank Balogh. **Price:** $14.97/year; $2.95 per issue.

3295 • Unsafe at Any Speed
Knightsbridge Publishing Co.
10513 W. Pico Blvd.
Los Angeles, CA 90064-2319   Ph:(213)275-4050

Book. Published 1991. **Editor(s):** Ralph Nader. **Price:** $4.95.

Automotive history

3296 • America on the Road
PBS Video
1320 Braddock Place
Alexandria, VA 22314-1698   Ph:(703)739-5380

Audio-visual. Bill Moyers shows how the auto became not only a means of transportation, but a new vision of ourselves. **Release date:** 1982. **Producer:** Corporation for Entertainment and Learning, Inc. **Acquisition:** Rent/Lease, Purchase, Off-Air Record.

3297 • An Auto Biography
Apt Books, Inc.
141 E. 44th St., Suite 511
New York, NY 10017   Ph:(212)697-0887

Book. Published 1987. **Author(s):** S. Sundaresan. **Price:** $22.50.

3298 • Auto Museums Directory: U.S.A., Supplement with Canadian Museums
Editorial Review
1009 Placer St.
Butte, MT 59701   Ph:(406)782-2546

Directory. Approximately 85 automobile museums in the U.S. and Canada. Irregular; previous edition 1983; latest edition 1989. **Editor(s):** William R. Taylor. **Price:** $8.50.

3299 • The Automobile Age
MIT Press
55 Hayward St.
Cambridge, MA 02142   Ph:(617)253-5646

Book. Published 1988. **Editor(s):** James J. Flink. **Price:** $30.00.

3300 • Automobile & Culture
Harry N. Abrams, Inc.
100 Fifth Ave.
New York, NY 10011   Ph:(212)206-7715

Book. Published 1984. **Editor(s):** Gerald Silk. **Price:** $45.00, hardbound; $29.95, paper.

3301 • Automobile Design: Great Designers and Their Work
Robert Bentley, Inc., Pubs.
1000 Massachusetts Ave.
Cambridge, MA 02138   Ph:(617)547-4170

Book. **Editor(s):** Ronald Barker and Anthony Harding. **Price:** $16.50.

3302 • Automobile Industry, 1885-1920
Facts on File, Inc.
460 Park Ave., S.
New York, NY 10016   Ph:(212)683-2244

Book. Published 1989. **Author(s):** George S. May. **Price:** $85.00.

3303 • The Automobile Industry, 1920-1980
Facts on File, Inc.
460 Park Ave., S.
New York, NY 10016   Ph:(212)683-2244

Book. Published 1989. **Editor(s):** George S. May. **Price:** $85.00.

3304 • The Automobile Industry since 1945
Books on Demand
University Microfilms International
300 N. Zeeb Rd.
Ann Arbor, MI 48106-1346   Ph:(313)761-4700

Book. **Author(s):** Lawrence J. White. **Price:** $90.50.

3305 • The Automobile—Its First 100 Years
New York State Education Dept.
Center for Learning Technologies
Media Distribution Network
Room C-7, Concourse Level
Cultural Education Center
Albany, NY 12230   Ph:(518)474-1265

Audio-visual. Rare footage documents the history of the automobile over the past century. **Release date:** 1981. **Producer:** Mercedes-Benz of North America. **Acquisition:** Purchase, Duplication.

3306 • Automotive Fine Arts Society—Quarterly
GP/Publishing
4140 S. Lapeer Rd.   Ph:(313)373-2500
Orion, MI 48359   Fax:(313)373-0565

Magazine. Dedicated to educating the public about the aesthetic value of automotive fine art and keeping collectors informed of field trends. Quarterly. **Editor(s):** Michael Sheridan, Publisher. **Price:** $16.00/year; $4.95 per single issue.

3307 • Automotive Hall of Fame—Membership Roster
Automotive Hall of Fame
P.O. Box 1727
Midland, MI 48641   Ph:(517)631-5760

Directory. Annual. **Price:** Free, for members only.

3308 • Automotive Hall of Fame—News
Automotive Hall of Fame
P.O. Box 1727
Midland, MI 48641   Ph:(517)631-5760

Newspaper. Includes articles about the auto industry and automobiles in general. Contains biographical information. Quarterly. **Price:** Free, for members only.

3309 • Automotive History Collection of the Detroit Public Library: A Simplified Guide to Its Holdings
G.K. Hall & Co., Inc.
70 Lincoln St.
Boston, MA 02111   Ph:(617)423-3990

Reference book. Two volume set. Published 1970. **Editor(s):** Detroit Public Library Staff. **Price:** $220.00.

3310 • Automotive History Review
Society of Automotive Historians (SAH)
c/o Natl. Automotive History
  Collection
Detroit Public Library
5201 Woodward Ave.
Detroit, MI 48202

Magazine. Semiannual.

3311 • Autos of Yesteryear
Visual Horizons
180 Metro Park   Ph:(716)424-5300
Rochester, NY 14623-2666   Fax:(716)424-5313

Audio-visual. The Model T and Duesenburg are just a few of the cars that can be seen in this video. **Release date:** 1988. **Producer:** Visual Horizons. **Acquisition:** Purchase.

3312 • Car Crazy: Wild Hour on Wheels
VidAmerica, Inc.
235 E. 55th St.
New York, NY 10022   Ph:(212)685-1300

Audio-visual. The 100th anniversary of the American automobile is celebrated with this rubber burnin' look at our fastest and most exotic cars. **Release date:** 1983. **Producer:** VidAmerica, Inc. **Price:** $19.98.

3313 • Car Wars: The Untold Story of the Great Automakers and the Giant 30-Year and Battle for Global Supremacy
McGraw-Hill Publishing Co.
11 W. 19th St.
New York, NY 10011   Ph:(212)337-6010

Book. Published 1985. **Author(s):** Robert Sobel. **Price:** $7.95.

3314 • Cars Detroit Never Built: Fifty Years of American Experimental Cars
Sterling Publishing Co., Inc.
387 Park Ave. S.
New York, NY 10016-8810   Ph:(212)532-7160

Book. Published 1991. **Editor(s):** Edward Janicki. **Price:** $30.00.

3315 • Changing Gears: The Development of the Automotive Transmission
Society of Automotive Engineers, Inc.
400 Commonwealth Dr.
Warrendale, PA 15096-0001   Ph:(412)776-4841

Book. Published 1991. **Editor(s):** Philip G. Gott. **Price:** $49.00.

3316 • Chevrolet: A History from 1911
Auto Quarterly, Inc.
15040 Kutztown Rd.
Kutztown, PA 19530   Ph:(215)683-3169

Book. Published 1987. **Editor(s):** Beverly R. Kimes and Robert C. Ackerson. **Price:** $34.95.

3317 • Chrysler: Once Upon a Time and Now
PBS Video
1320 Braddock Place
Alexandria, VA 22314-1698   Ph:(703)739-5380

Audio-visual. A comprehensive study of the Chrysler Corporation, from uncertain beginnings in the 1920's to becoming the tenth largest corporation in America. **Release date:** 1982. **Producer:** WTVS Detroit. **Acquisition:** Rent/Lease, Purchase, Off-Air Record.

3318 • Conspicuous Production: Automobiles & Elites in Detroit, 1899-1933
Temple University Press
1601 N. Broad St.
University Services Bldg., Rm. 306
Philadelphia, PA 19122   Ph:(215)787-8787

Book. Published 1988. **Author(s):** Donald F. Davis. **Price:** $37.95.

3319 • Dickinson and the Automobile: the Early Years 1903-1929
Dakota Western Auto Club
P.O. Box 725
Dickinson, ND 58601   Ph:(701)225-6757

Book.

3320 • Dinosaur Machine
Lionel Television Productions
66 1/2 Windward
Venice, CA 90291   Ph:(213)541-7342

Audio-visual. A celebratory film about America's love affair with automobiles and their meaning to succeeding generations of youth. **Release date:** 1982. **Producer:** David Lionel. **Acquisition:** Rent/Lease, Purchase.

3321 • Enzo Ferrari: The Man and the Machine
Doubleday & Co., Inc.
666 5th Ave.
New York, NY 10103   Ph:(212)984-7561

Book. Published 1991. **Editor(s):** Brock Yates. **Price:** $22.00.

3322 • Fifty Years of American Automobile, 1939-1989
Publications International, Ltd.
7373 N. Cicero Ave.
Lincolnwood, IL 60646   Ph:(312)676-3470

Book. Published 1989. **Price:** $49.95.

3323 • Ford: The Complete History
Publications International Ltd.
7373 N. Cicero Ave.
Lincolnwood, IL 60646   Ph:(312)676-3470

Book. Published 1989. **Price:** $49.95.

3324 • Ford: The Men and the Machine
Books on Tape, Inc.
P.O. Box 7900
Newport Beach, CA 92658

Audio-visual. Audiocassette read by Grover Gardner that describes the history of the Ford family and their automotive empire. **Release date:** 1989. **Author(s):** Robert Lacey.

3325 • The Golden Age of the Automobile
Increase Video
6914 Conby Ave., Suite 110   Ph:(818)342-2880
Reseda, CA 91335   Fax:(818)342-4029

Audio-visual. A documentary that remembers all those great

automobiles from days gone bye. **Release date:** 1983. **Producer:** Star Merchants. **Acquisition:** Purchase.

3326 • Henry Ford: The Mark of a Man
Two Star Films, Inc.
P.O. Box 495
St. James, NY 11780   Ph:(516)584-7283

Audio-visual. The life of Henry Ford, inventor of the automobile, is told in this program through classic newsreel footage. This is also the story of America growing up on wheels. **Release date:** 1954. **Producer:** Fox Movietone News. **Acquisition:** Purchase.

3327 • Henry Ford's America
Video Yesteryear
P.O. Box C
Sandy Hook, CT 06482   Ph:(203)426-2574

Audio-visual. A look at the history of the automobile, the dynastic Ford talent that created it, and the business empire that rules it. **Release date:** 1977. **Producer:** National Film Board of Canada. **Acquisition:** Purchase.

3328 • Henry: Life of Henry Ford II
Grove-Weidenfeld
920 Broadway
New York, NY 10010   Ph:(212)614-7850

Book. Published 1990. **Author(s):** Walter Hayes. **Price:** $19.95.

3329 • Honda: An American Success Story
Prentice Hall Press
1 Gulf and Western Plaza
New York, NY 10023   Ph:(212)373-8500

Book. Published 1989. **Author(s):** Robert Shook. **Price:** $12.95.

3330 • Karl Benz
Franklin Watts, Inc.
387 Park Ave. S.
New York, NY 10016   Ph:(212)686-7070

Book. Published 1991. **Editor(s):** Brian Williams. **Price:** $12.40.

3331 • Love and Revolution: The First Hundred & One Years of the Automobile Since 1888
HealthProInk and Thirty Three Publishing
582 Winddrift
Springlake, MI 49456   Ph:(616)847-2843

Book. Published 1988. **Author(s):** Richard Wright. **Price:** $9.95.

3332 • Merrily We Roll Again
The Center for Humanities, Inc.
Communications Park
Box 1000
Mount Kisco, NY 10549   Ph:(914)666-4100

Audio-visual. A comic look at automotive history, from horseless carriages to today's economy. **Release date:** 1971. **Producer:** Robert L Bendick. **Acquisition:** Purchase.

3333 • Model T Man from Michigan, America: Henry Ford and His Horseless Carriage
AIMS Media, Inc.
6901 Woodley Ave.
Van Nuys, CA 91406-4878   Ph:(818)785-4111

Audio-visual. Henry Ford, the man who altered the course of history, is profiled. **Release date:** 1988. **Producer:** Comco Productions. **Acquisition:** Purchase, Duplication License.

3334 • A Most Unique Machine: The Michigan Origins of the American Automobile Industry
Books on Demand
University Microfilms International
300 N. Zeeb Rd.
Ann Arbor, MI 48106-1346   Ph:(313)761-4700

Book. **Author(s):** George S. May. **Price:** $101.50.

3335 • New Deals: The Chrysler Revival and the American System
Penguin Books USA
1633 Broadway
New York, NY 10019   Ph:(212)397-8000

Book. Published 1986. **Author(s):** Robert B. Reich and John D. Donahue. **Price:** $7.95.

3336 • Porsche
Simitar Entertainment
3850 Annapolis Ln.   Ph:(612)559-6660
Plymouth, MN 55447   Fax:(612)559-0210

Audio-visual. The history of the sports car company is told, partially by using driver's eye footage of races. **Release date:** 1988. **Producer:** Simitar Entertainment. **Acquisition:** Purchase.

3337 • Power and Wheels: The Automobile in Modern Life
Britannica Films
310 S. Michigan Ave.   Ph:(312)347-7958
Chicago, IL 60604   Fax:(312)347-7966

Audio-visual. The history of the automobile and its influence on American culture is seen through the eyes of two visitors from outer space. **Release date:** 1972. **Producer:** Encyclopedia Britannica Educ. Corp. **Acquisition:** Rent/Lease, Purchase, Trade-in.

3338 • Power Behind the Wheel: Creativity and Evolution of the Automobile
Abbeville Press, Inc.
488 Madison Ave.   Ph:(212)888-1969
New York, NY 10022   Fax:(212)644-5085

Book. Published 1991. **Editor(s):** Walter J. Boyne. **Price:** $19.98.

3339 • Reckless Homicide: Ford's Pinto Trial
And Books
702 S. Michigan, Suite 836
South Bend, IN 46618   Ph:(219)232-3134

Book. Published 1980. **Editor(s):** Lee P. Strobel. **Price:** $8.95.

3340 • Reinventing the Wheels: Ford's Spectacular Comeback
HarperCollins Publishers, Inc.
10 E. 53rd St.
New York, NY 10022   Ph:(212)207-7000

Book. Published 1990. **Author(s):** Alton F. Doody and Ron Bingaman. **Price:** $8.95.

3341 • Road to Happiness
Films, Inc.
5547 N. Ravenwood Ave.
Chicago, IL 60640-1199   Ph:(312)878-2600

Audio-visual. Henry Ford's personal film collection leaves behind the story of a shy, nearly illiterate farm boy who became an American legend. The history of his era is also encompassed within his archives, the Ford Film Collection. **Release date:** 1980. **Producer:** Francis Gladstone, Patrick Griffin, WGBH Boston. **Acquisition:** Rent/Lease, Purchase.

3342 • Rude Awakening: General Motors in the 1980s
William Morrow & Co., Inc.
105 Madison Ave.
New York, NY 10016   Ph:(212)889-3050

Book. Published 1989. **Author(s):** Maryann Keller. **Price:** 19.95.

3343 • Society of Automotive Historians—Directory
Society of Automotive Historians (SAH)
c/o Natl. Automotive History
    Collection
Detroit Public Library
5201 Woodward Ave.
Detroit, MI 48202

Directory. Biennial.

3344 • Society of Automotive Historians—Journal
Society of Automotive Historians (SAH)
c/o Natl. Automotive History
  Collection
Detroit Public Library
5201 Woodward Ave.
Detroit, MI 48202

Magazine. Bimonthly.

3345 • Spark
Society of Automotive Historians, Wisconsin Chapter
c/o Robert J. Gary
1316 Fourth Ave.
Stevens Point, WI 54481   Ph:(715)341-1085

Newsletter. Periodic.

3346 • The Story of Ferrari
Simitar Entertainment
3850 Annapolis Ln.   Ph:(612)559-6660
Plymouth, MN 55447   Fax:(612)559-0210

Audio-visual. A visual history of Enzo Ferrari's world-renowned car company. **Release date:** 1988. **Producer:** Simitar Entertainment. **Price:** $9.95.

Automotive Industry

3347 • The American and Japanese Auto Industries in Transition: The Report of the Joint U.S.-Japan Automotive Study
Center for Japanese Studies
University of Michigan
108 Lane Hall
Ann Arbor, MI 48109-1290   Ph:(313)998-7265

Report/bulletin. Published 1984. **Editor(s):** Robert E. Cole and Taizo Yakushiji. **Price:** $60.00 hardbound; $17.95, paper.

3348 • The American Automobile Industry
G.K. Hall & Co., Inc.
70 Lincoln St.
Boston, MA 02111   Ph:(617)423-3990

Book. Published 1985. **Author(s):** John B. Rae. **Price:** $22.95, hardbound; $10.95, paper.

3349 • The American Automobile Industry: Rebirth or Requiem?
Center for Japanese Studies
University of Michigan
108 Lane Hall
Ann Arbor, MI 48109-1290   Ph:(313)998-7265

Book. Published 1984. **Editor(s):** Robert E. Cole. **Price:** $9.00.

3350 • American Made: Marysville and the Honda Plant
Ohio University Telecommunications Center
9 S. College St.
Athens, OH 45701

Audio-visual. This program examines why Honda chose the town of Marysville, Ohio, as its first site for an assembly plant in America and the effect it had on the town. **Release date:** 1984. **Producer:** Ohio University Telecommunications Center. **Acquisition:** Rent/Lease, Purchase.

3351 • American Technology and the British Vehicle Industry
Cambridge University Press
40 W. 20th St.
New York, NY 10011   Ph:(212)924-3900

Book. Published 1987. **Price:** $49.50.

3352 • Auto Inc.
Automotive Service Councils, Inc.
P.O. Box 929   Ph:(817)283-6205
Bedford, TX 76021-0929   Fax:(817)685-0225

Newsletter. Carries automotive technical material, news of the automotive industry, information on relevant legislation, and news of the Automotive Service Association. Monthly. **Editor(s):** Monica Buchholz. **Price:** Available to members only; $20.00/year for nonmembers.

3353 • Auto Industries of Europe, U.S., Japan to 1990
Abt Books, Inc.
146 Mt. Auburn St.
Cambridge, MA 02138   Ph:(617)661-1300

Book. Published 1982. **Author(s):** Richard Phillips and Arthur Way. **Price:** $40.00.

3354 • The Auto Industry Ahead: Who's Driving?
Center for Japanese Studies
University of Michigan
108 Lane Hall
Ann Arbor, MI 48109-1290   Ph:(313)998-7265

Book. Published 1989. **Editor(s):** Peter J. Arnesen. **Price:** $9.00.

3355 • Automobile Technology of the Future
Society of Automotive Engineers, Inc.
400 Commonwealth Dr.
Warrendale, PA 15096-0001   Ph:(412)776-4841

Book. Published 1991. **Editor(s):** Ulrich Seiffert. **Price:** $69.00.

3356 • Automotive Hall of Fame—Membership Roster
Automotive Hall of Fame
P.O. Box 1727
Midland, MI 48641   Ph:(517)631-5760

Directory. Annual. **Price:** Free, for members only.

3357 • Automotive Hall of Fame—News
Automotive Hall of Fame
P.O. Box 1727
Midland, MI 48641   Ph:(517)631-5760

Newspaper. Includes articles about the auto industry and automobiles in general. Contains biographical information. Quarterly. **Price:** Free, for members only.

3358 • Automotive Industries
Fairchild Publications
201 King of Prussia Rd.   Ph:(215)964-4255
Radnor, PA 19089   Fax:(215)964-4981

Magazine. Covers the entire automotive industry. Monthly. **Editor(s):** John McElroy, Editor-in-Chief. **Price:** $49.95 per year; $5.00 per issue.

3359 • Automotive Information Council—Newsletter
Automotive Information Council
13505 Dulles Technology Dr.
Herndon, VA 22071   Ph:(313)559-5922

Newsletter. Covers reports on legislation, marketing trends, and business activity affecting automotive industry. Monthly. **Editor(s):** Charles Charpie. **Price:** Free.

3360 • Automundo Magazine
Kogan E.A. Corp.
3305 W. 27th Ave., Ste. 403
Miami, FL 33135   Ph:(305)541-4198

Magazine. Spanish-language magazine that offers information on common automobile needs and developments; annual special section editions feature interviews with industry personalities. Monthly. **Editor(s):** Enrique A. Kogan. **Price:** $18.00 per year; $1.50 per issue.

3361 • Car Wars: The Untold Story of the Great Automakers and the Giant 30-Year and Battle for Global Supremacy
McGraw-Hill Publishing Co.
11 W. 19th St.
New York, NY 10011   Ph:(212)337-6010

Book. Published 1985. **Author(s):** Robert Sobel. **Price:** $7.95.

3362 • Cars Made in Upstate New York
Squire Hill Publishing Co.
PO Box 531
Andover, NY 14806   Ph:(607)478-8162

Book. Published 1988. **Author(s):** James F. Bellamy. **Price:** $24.95.

3363 • Chevrolet: A History from 1911
Auto Quarterly, Inc.
15040 Kutztown Rd.
Kutztown, PA 19530   Ph:(215)683-3169

Book. Published 1987. **Editor(s):** Beverly R. Kimes and Robert C. Ackerson. **Price:** $34.95.

3364 • Chrysler: Once Upon a Time and Now
PBS Video
1320 Braddock Place
Alexandria, VA 22314-1698   Ph:(703)739-5380

Audio-visual. A comprehensive study of the Chrysler Corporation, from uncertain beginnings in the 1920's to becoming the tenth largest corporation in America. **Release date:** 1982. **Producer:** WTVS Detroit. **Acquisition:** Rent/Lease, Purchase, Off-Air Record.

3365 • Honda: An American Success Story
Prentice Hall Press
1 Gulf and Western Plaza
New York, NY 10023   Ph:(212)373-8500

Book. Published 1989. **Author(s):** Robert Shook. **Price:** $12.95.

3366 • Honda Motor: The Men, the Management and the Machines
Kodansha International USA, Ltd.
114 Fifth Ave.
New York, NY 10011   Ph:(212)727-6460

Book. Published 1987. **Author(s):** Tetsuo Sakiya. **Price:** $5.95.

3367 • International
Wards Communications, Inc.
28 W. Adams   Ph:(313)962-4433
Detroit, MI 48226   Fax:(313)962-4456

Magazine. Journal of global automotive industry. Semimonthly. **Price:** $350.00/year.

3368 • International Automotive Hall of Shame— Newsletter
International Automotive Hall of Shame
515 Alpine Rd.
PO Box 324
Fitchburg, MA 01420   Ph:(508)342-0731

Newsletter. Periodic.

3369 • Is There Enough Business to Go Around? Overcapacity in the Auto Industry
Center for Japanese Studies
University of Michigan
108 Lane Hall
Ann Arbor, MI 48109-1290   Ph:(313)998-7265

Book. Published 1988. **Author(s):** Peter J. Arnesen. **Price:** $9.00.

3370 • Japan Transportation Scan
Kyodo News International, Inc.
50 Rockefeller Plaza, Ste. 382   Ph:(212)397-3723
New York, NY 10020   Fax:(212)307-1532

Newsletter. Reports on the Japanese automotive industry, including companies, manufacturing data, licensing, shipment statistics, and financial performance. Weekly.

3371 • The Japanese Auto Industry and the U.S. Market
Greenwood Press
88 Post Rd., W.
P.O. Box 5007
Westport, CT 06881   Ph:(203)226-3571

Book. Published 1981. **Author(s):** C.S. Chang. **Price:** $36.95.

3372 • The Japanese Competition: Phase Two
Center for Japanese Studies
University of Michigan
108 Lane Hall
Ann Arbor, MI 48109-1290   Ph:(313)998-7265

Book. Published 1987. **Author(s):** Peter J. Arnesen. **Price:** $17.00, hardbound; $9.00, paper.

3373 • Korea Automotive Review
Mead Ventures, Inc.
P.O. Box 44952
Phoenix, AZ 85064   Ph:(602)234-0044

Newsletter. Focuses on activity in the automotive industry in Korea. Provides information on producers and manufacturers, news of research and development, sales, distribution, and marketing strategies. Monthly.

3374 • Lindens Lines
Linden Assembly
General Motors Corp.
1016 W. Edgar Rd.
Linden, NJ 07036   Ph:(908)474-4877

Newsletter. Covers the automotive industry on the corporate level. Also available on diskette. Bimonthly. **Editor(s):** Paul Makuch.

3375 • Long Term Outlook for the World Automobile Industry
Organization for Economic Cooperation and Development
2001 L St., N.W., Suite 700
Washington, DC 20036   Ph:(202)785-6323

Book. Published 1984. **Price:** $15.00.

3376 • Motor City News [Detroit, Michigan]
Monday Morning Newspapers Group
1-218 General Motors Bldg.   Ph:(313)939-6800
Detroit, MI 48202   Fax:(313)939-5850

Newspaper. Contains automotive and business news. Serves Madison Heights and Troy, Michigan. Weekly. **Editor(s):** Peter Salinas.

3377 • The Motor Industry of Japan
Japan Automobile Manufacturers Association, Washington Office (JAMA)
1050 17th St. NW, Ste. 410
Washington, DC 20036   Ph:(202)296-8537

Report/bulletin. Annual.

3378 • The Motor Men: Pioneers of the British Car Industry
International Specialized Book Services
5602 N.E. Hassalo St.
Portland, OR 97213-3640   Ph:(503)287-3093

Book. Published 1989. **Author(s):** Peter King. **Price:** $36.95.

3379 • Motor Vehicle Facts and Figures
Motor Vehicle Manufacturers Association of the United States (MVMA)
7430 2nd Ave., Ste. 300
Detroit, MI 48202   Ph:(313)872-4311

Book. Statistics, charts, graphs, and editorial comment

documenting the year in the motor vehicle industry. Includes index. Annual. **Price:** $7.50.

3380 • Motor Vehicle Statistics
Japan Automobile Manufacturers Association
1050 17th St. NW, Ste. 410
Washington, DC 20036   Ph:(202)296-8537

Directory. Annual.

3381 • The Multinational Automobile Industry
St. Martin Press, Inc.
175 Fifth Ave.
New York, NY 10010   Ph:(212)674-5151

Book. Published 1981. **Author(s):** George Maxcy. **Price:** $35.00.

3382 • New Deals: The Chrysler Revival and the American System
Penguin Books USA
1633 Broadway
New York, NY 10019   Ph:(212)397-8000

Book. Published 1986. **Author(s):** Robert B. Reich and John D. Donahue. **Price:** $7.95.

3383 • News Focus
Automotive Information Council (AIC)
13505 Dulles Technology Dr.
Herndon, VA 22071-3415   Ph:(703)904-0700

Newsletter. Industry newsletter; reports on legislation, marketing trends, and business activities affecting the automotive industry. Monthly. **Price:** Free, for members only; also circulated to government agencies, members of Congress, state officials, and news media.

3384 • Porsche
Simitar Entertainment
3850 Annapolis Ln.   Ph:(612)559-6660
Plymouth, MN 55447   Fax:(612)559-0210

Audio-visual. The history of the sports car company is told, partially by using driver's eye footage of races. **Release date:** 1988. **Producer:** Simitar Entertainment. **Acquisition:** Purchase.

3385 • The Reckoning
Avon Books
105 Madison Ave.
New York, NY 10016   Ph:(212)481-5600

Book. Published 1987. **Author(s):** David Halberstam. **Price:** $5.95.

3386 • Reinventing the Wheels: Ford's Spectacular Comeback
HarperCollins Publishers, Inc.
10 E. 53rd St.
New York, NY 10022   Ph:(212)207-7000

Book. Published 1990. **Author(s):** Alton F. Doody and Ron Bingaman. **Price:** $8.95.

3387 • Rude Awakening: General Motors in the 1980s
William Morrow & Co., Inc.
105 Madison Ave.
New York, NY 10016   Ph:(212)889-3050

Book. Published 1989. **Author(s):** Maryann Keller. **Price:** 19.95.

3388 • SIS Automotive Industry Abstracts
Strategic Intelligence Systems, Inc. (SIS)
404 Park Ave. S., Ste. 1301
New York, NY 10016-8403   Ph:(212)725-4550

Newsletter. Summarizes and analyzes published articles from newspapers, industry-trade publications, magazines and other print media. Monitors new product activity, profiles of key competitors (domestic and international), developments in automotive technology and components, legislation/regulation, overall trends and issues, and market activity that affects the automotive industry. Weekly.

3389 • Tech Center News
Monday Morning Newspapers, Inc.
31201 Chicago Rd. S.
B-300   Ph:(313)939-6800
Warren, MI 48093   Fax:(313)939-5850

Newspaper. Contains automotive and business news for the business community, including General Motors Technical Center, Warren, Michigan. Weekly. **Editor(s):** Peter Salinas.

3390 • Transnational Corporations in the International Auto Industry
United Nations Publishing Service
Two United Nations Plaza, Rm. DC2-853
New York, NY 10017   Ph:(212)963-8302

Book. **Price:** $21.00.

3391 • Ward's Auto World
Ward's Communications, Inc.
28 W. Adams
Detroit, MI 48226   Ph:(313)962-4433

Magazine. Provides in-depth news coverage on the automotive industry. Monthly. **Editor(s):** Edward Miller. **Price:** $45.00 per year; $4.00 per issue.

3392 • Ward's Automotive International
Ward's Communications, Inc.
28 W. Adams St.   Ph:(313)962-4433
Detroit, MI 48226   Fax:(313)962-4532

Magazine. Provides a global view of news, technological developments, and trends in the automotive industry worldwide. Monthly. **Editor(s):** David E. Zoia. **Price:** $350.00/year.

3393 • Ward's Automotive Reports
Ward's Communications, Inc.
28 W. Adams St.   Ph:(313)962-4433
Detroit, MI 48226   Fax:(313)962-4532

Report/bulletin. Reports statistical information and news of interest to the automotive industry. Weekly. **Editor(s):** James W. Bush. **Price:** $795.00/year.

3394 • Wiretapper
General Motors Corp.
P.O. Box 260
Clinton, MS 39060   Ph:(601)924-8109

Newsletter. Covers news relating to local plants and divisions of General Motors Corporation. Monthly. **Editor(s):** Danny Greene.

3395 • World Automotive Market
Automobile Intl.
386 Park Ave., S.   Ph:(212)689-0120
New York, NY 10016   Fax:(212)779-7475

Reference book. Provides statistical data on the production, registration, and exportation of cars, trucks, and commercial buses. Annual. **Editor(s):** M. Havis Dawson. **Price:** $30.00.

3396 • World Guide to Automobile Manufacturers
Facts on File, Inc.
460 Park Ave., S.
New York, NY 10016   Ph:(212)683-2244

Directory. Published 1987. **Editor(s):** Brian Laban. **Price:** $50.00.

3397 • World Motor Vehicle Data Book
Motor Vehicle Manufacturers Association of the United States (MVMA)
7430 2nd Ave., Ste. 300
Detroit, MI 48202   Ph:(313)872-4311

Reference book. Provides motor vehicle production and assembly statistics on 157 countries as well as detailed import, export, sales, and registration data for 55 vehicle manufacturing nations. Annual. **Price:** $35.00.

Automotive law

3398 • Air Pollution, the Automobile, and Public Health
National Academy Press
2101 Constitution Ave. N.W.
Washington, DC 20418   Ph:(202)334-3318

Book. Published 1988. **Editor(s):** Richard Bates and Donald Kennedy. **Price:** $60.00.

3399 • Annual Supplement to Automobile Design Liability
Center for Auto Safety
2001 S St. NW, Ste. 410
Washington, DC 20009   Ph:(202)328-7700

Reference book. Supplements a reference book on automobile liability laws and consumer protection.

3400 • Auto Inc.
Automotive Service Councils, Inc.
P.O. Box 929   Ph:(817)283-6205
Bedford, TX 76021-0929   Fax:(817)685-0225

Newsletter. Carries automotive technical material, news of the automotive industry, information on relevant legislation, and news of the Automotive Service Association. Monthly. **Editor(s):** Monica Buchholz. **Price:** Available to members only; $20.00/year for nonmembers.

3401 • Automobiles
Knowles Law Book Publishing, Inc.
P.O. Box 911004
Forthworth, TX 76111   Ph:800-299-0202

Reference book. Published 1985. **Editor(s):** James L. Branton and Jim D. Lovett. **Price:** $135.00.

3402 • Automotive Engineering and Litigation
John Wiley & Sons, Inc.
136 Madison Ave.
New York, NY 10016   Ph:(212)686-7492

Book. Supplement edition in two volumes. Published 1984. **Editor(s):** George A. Peters and Barbara J. Peters. **Price:** $100.00.

3403 • Automotive Information Council—Newsletter
Automotive Information Council
13505 Dulles Technology Dr.
Herndon, VA 22071   Ph:(313)559-5922

Newsletter. Covers reports on legislation, marketing trends, and business activity affecting automotive industry. Monthly. **Editor(s):** Charles Charpie. **Price:** Free.

3404 • Automotive Litigation Reporter
Andrews Publications, Inc.
P.O. Box 1000   Ph:(215)399-6600
Westtown, PA 19395   Fax:(215)399-6610

Newsletter. Covers significant federal and state lawsuits, including pretrial, trial, and appeal proceedings, settlements, and class action suits. Offers complete texts of key decisions and pleadings. Semimonthly. **Price:** $700.00/year.

3405 • Car Audio Specialists Association—Government Action Bulletins
Car Audio Specialists Association (CASA)
2101 L St. NW, Ste. 800
Washington, DC 20037   Ph:(202)828-2270

Report/bulletin. Reports on federal, state, and local government actions affecting the mobile electronics industry. Monthly.

3406 • Digest of Motor Law
American Automobile Association (AAA)
1000 AAA Dr.
Heathrow, FL 32746-5063   Ph:(407)444-7000

Reference book. Annual.

3407 • Digest of Motor Laws
American Automobile Association
701 S. First Ave.
Suite 272
Arcadia, CA 91006   Ph:(818)446-6700

Reference book. Published 1990. **Price:** $3.50.

3408 • From the State Capitals: Motor Vehicle Regulation
Wakeman/Walworth, Inc.
300 N. Washington St., Suite 204
Alexandria, VA 22314   Ph:(703)549-8606

Newsletter. Examines state motor vehicle safety regulations, inspections, emission standards, drunken driving laws, motorist licensing, insurance, and education. Presented on a state-by-state basis and aimed toward lawyers, consultants, public officials, legislators, and company executives. **Editor(s):** Keyes Walworth. **Price:** $185.00/year; $102.00 per six months.

3409 • Handling Automobile Warranty and Repossesion Cases
Lawyers Co-Operative Publishing Co.
Aqueduct Bldg.
Rochester, NY 14694   Ph:(716)546-5530

Book. Published 1984. **Editor(s):** Roger D. Billings. **Price:** $79.50, hardbound; $31.00, paper.

3410 • How to Import-Convert-Legalize Your Investment Automobile
HIT Publications
1842 Irvine Ave.
Newport Beach, CA 92660   Ph:(714)722-7458

Book. Published 1984. **Editor(s):** Ingrid Mueller-Triol. **Price:** $30.00.

3411 • The Lemon Book: Auto Rights
Moyer Bell, Ltd.
Colonial Hill
R.F.D. One
Mount Kisco, NY 10549   Ph:(914)666-0084

Book. Published 1990. **Editor(s):** Ralph Nader and Clarence Ditlow. **Price:** $22.50.

3412 • Lemonaid
Oceana Publications, Inc.
75 Main St.   Ph:(914)693-1320
Dobbs Ferry, NY 10522   Fax:(914)693-0402

Report/bulletin. Published 1991. **Editor(s):** Andrew Faglio. **Price:** $20.00.

3413 • Michigan Motor Vehicle Laws: With Uniform Traffic Code
Gould Publications
199/300 State St.
Binghamton, NY 13901   Ph:(607)724-3000

Reference book. **Price:** $15.00

3414 • Michigan No-Fault Automobile Cases: Law and Practice
University of Michigan, Law School. Institute of Continuing Legal Education
1020 Greene St.
Ann Arbor, MI 48109-1444   Ph:(313)764-0533

Book. Published 1988. **Editor(s):** Robert E. Logeman. **Price:** $95.00; 1989 supplement, $35.00.

3415 • Motor Vehicle and Traffic Laws of New Jersey
Gould Publications
199-300 State St.
Binghamton, NY 13901-2782   Ph:(607)724-3000

Reference book. Lists New Jersey motor vehicle and traffic statutes. Annual. **Editor(s):** Kathleen Pichette. **Price:** $14.95.

3416 • Motor Vehicle Law of North Carolina
Institute of Government
University of North Carolina-Chapel
    Hill
C B Knapp Bldg. 3330
Chapel Hill, NC 27599-3330   Ph:(919)966-4119

Reference book. Published 1990. **Editor(s):** Ben F. Loeb, Jr.

3417 • Motor Vehicle Laws of Ohio
Gould Publications
199/300 State St.
Binghampton, NY 13901-2782   Ph:(607)724-3000

Reference book. **Price:** $14.95, loose-leaf bdg.; $5.00, slide rule.

3418 • The Motorist's Guide to the Law
State Mutual Books and Periodical Service, Ltd.
521 Fifth Ave.
17th Fl.
New York, NY 10017   Ph:(212)682-5844

Reference book. Published 1986. **Editor(s):** James Mathers. **Price:**
$40.00.

3419 • National Automobile Dealers Association—Title
    and Registration Book
National Appraisal Guides
3186 K Airway Ave.
Costa Mesa, CA 92626   Ph:(714)556-8511

Reference book. Summarizes the motor vehicle statutes and
regulations for each of the 50 states. Annual. **Editor(s):** Pat Phillips.
Price: $25.00.

3420 • New Hampshire Motor Vehicle and Boating
    Laws
Butterworth Publishers
80 Montvale Ave.
Stoneham, MA 02180   Ph:(617)438-8464

Reference book. Published 1990. **Price:** $24.00.

3421 • New York Vehicle and Traffic Law
Gould Publications
199/300 State St.
Binghampton, NY 13901-2782   Ph:(607)724-3000

Reference book. **Price:** $7.95, looseleaf; $7.95, pocket slide-rule.

3422 • News Focus
Automotive Information Council (AIC)
13505 Dulles Technology Dr.
Herndon, VA 22071-3415   Ph:(703)904-0700

Newsletter. Industry newsletter; reports on legislation, marketing
trends, and business activities affecting the automotive industry.
Monthly. **Price:** Free, for members only; also circulated to
government agencies, members of Congress, state officials, and
news media.

3423 • Peck's Title Book: Description of State Laws
    Regulating Motor Vehicle Titles, Registrations and
    Transfer of Same
Stephens-Peck, Inc.
366 S. 500 East, Ste. 104-105
Salt Lake City, UT 84102   Ph:(801)364-2312

Reference book. **Price:** $39.50.

3424 • Radar Reporter Newsletter
Radio Association Defending Airwave Rights, Inc.
4949 South 25A   Ph:(513)667-5472
Tipp City, OH 45371   Fax:(513)667-3178

Newsletter. Provides information on Association activities related
to police traffic radar and radar detectors. Also reports on other
transportation topics of interest to motorists. Monthly. **Editor(s):**
Janice Lee. **Price:** Available to members only.

3425 • Regulating the Automobile
Brookings Institution
1775 Massachusetts Ave., N.W.
Washington, DC 20036-2188   Ph:(202)797-6258

Book. Published 1986. **Editor(s):** Robert W. Crandall. **Price:** $29.95,
hardcover; $10.95, paper.

3426 • SIS Automotive Industry Abstracts
Strategic Intelligence Systems, Inc. (SIS)
404 Park Ave. S., Ste. 1301
New York, NY 10016-8403   Ph:(212)725-4550

Newsletter. Summarizes and analyzes published articles from
newspapers, industry-trade publications, magazines and other
print media. Monitors new product activity, profiles of key
competitors (domestic and international), developments in
automotive technology and components, legislation/regulation,
overall trends and issues, and market activity that affects the
automotive industry. Weekly.

3427 • Successful Automotive Litigation
Garland Publishing, Inc.
136 Madison Ave.
New York, NY 10016   Ph:(212)686-7492

Book. **Editor(s):** George A. Peters and Barbara J. Peters. **Price:**
$75.00

3428 • Vehicle Laws of Pennsylvania
Gould Publications
199/300 State St.
Binghampton, NY 13901-2782   Ph:(607)724-3000

Reference book. **Price:** $18.95, looseleaf; $7.95, flip code.

3429 • Washington Digest
Motor and Equipment Manufacturers Association
300 Sylvan Ave.
Englewood Cliffs, NJ 07632   Ph:(201)569-8500

Newsletter. Provides legislative updates and other news from the
nation's capitol concerning the automotive industry. Biweekly.
Editor(s): J.J. Conner, Publisher.

Automotive reconditioning

3430 • Auto Body Repairing and Repainting
Goodheart-Wilcox Co.
123 W. Taft Dr.
South Holland, IL 60473   Ph:(708)333-7200

Manual. Published 1982. **Editor(s):** Bill Toboldt. **Price:** $18.00.

3431 • Auto Restoration From Junker to Jewel
Motorbooks International
729 Prospect Ave.
Osceola, WI 54020   Ph:(715)294-3345

Book. Published 1980. **Editor(s):** Burt Mills. **Price:** $22.95.

3432 • Car Interior Restoration
Tab Books, Inc.
Blue Ridge Summit, PA 17294-0850   Ph:(717)794-2191

Manual. Published 1983. **Editor(s):** Terry Boyce. **Price:** $8.95.

3433 • Chilton's Guide to Auto Body Repair and
    Painting
Chilton Co.
Chilton Way
Radnor, PA 19089   Ph:(215)964-4000

Book. Published 1983. **Price:** $15.95.

3434 • The Complete Guide to Automotive Refinishing
Prentice-Hall
Rte. 9W
Englewood Cliffs, NJ 07632   Ph:(201)592-2000

Manual. Published 1988. **Editor(s):** Harry T. Chudy. **Price:** $46.00.

3435 • **The Glove Box Auto Reviver**
Chaparral Productions
636 Hermosa
Chaparral, NM 88021   Ph:(505)824-4213

Book. **Editor(s):** Wes Brewer and Ann Brewer. **Price:** $24.95.

3436 • **How to Chop Tops**
Motorbooks International
729 Prospect Ave.
Osceola, WI 54020   Ph:(715)294-3345

Manual. Published 1989. **Editor(s):** Leroi T. Smith. **Price:** $17.95.

3437 • **Moore's Recon Training Video**
Moore's Auto Reconditioning Employee Training
12 Laurel St.
Plains, PA 18705   Ph:(717)283-1377

Audio-visual. An instructional film on how to clean, buff, and totally recondition your car. **Release date:** 1987. **Producer:** Moore's Auto Reconditioning Employee Training. **Acquisition:** Purchase.

3438 • **Restoration**
International Society for Vehicle Preservation
PO Box 50046
Tucson, AZ 85703   Ph:(602)741-2121

Magazine. Covers the how-to of vehicle restoration. Quarterly. **Editor(s):** Walter Haessner, Editor/Publisher. **Price:** $15.00 includes membership; $3.00 per single issue.

3439 • **The Restoration Game**
Unicorn Video, Inc.
9811 Independence Ave.
Chatsworth, CA 91311   Ph:(818)407-1333

Audio-visual. A look at both professional car restoration, and amateur do-it-yourself techniques. **Release date:** 1986. **Producer:** Unicorn Video, Inc. **Price:** $14.95.

3440 • **Sheet Metal Handbook: How to Form, Shear, Roll and Shape Sheet Metal for Competition, Custom, and Restoration Use**
Price Stern Sloan, Inc.
400 Commonwealth Dr.
Warrendale, PA 15096   Ph:(412)776-4841

Manual. Published 1989. **Editor(s):** Ron Fournier and Susan Fournier. **Price:** $12.95.

3441 • **Tune Up America: Detailing**
Morris Video
2730 Monterey St., No. 105
Monterey Business Park
Torrance, CA 90503   Ph:(213)533-4800

Audio-visual. The steps needed to revitalize and maintain car interiors, exteriors, trim areas, and engine compartments are covered. **Release date:** 1986. **Producer:** Morris Video. **Price:** $19.95.

Automotive safety

3442 • **Airbags and Seat Belts**
Center for Auto Safety
2001 S St. NW, Ste. 410
Washington, DC 20009   Ph:(202)328-7700

Book.

3443 • **Ask Any Dummy: Seat Belts Make Sense**
AIMS Media, Inc.
6901 Woodley Ave.
Van Nuys, CA 91406-4878   Ph:(818)785-4111

Audio-visual. Film and videocassette starring the U.S. Department of Transportation crash dummies urging the use of seat belts and child restraint devices. **Release date:** 1989. **Producer:** John McDonald, Producer and Director.

3444 • **Auto Safety Series**
Phoenix/BFA Films
468 Park Ave., S.
New York, NY 10016   Ph:(212)684-5910

Audio-visual. This three-part series is an in-depth study of all facets of owning and operating an automobile. Subject matter includes car care, accident situation reactions, and driving tips that every driver should know. **Release date:** 1978. **Producer:** Greenhouse Films, William Boundey. **Acquisition:** Purchase.

3445 • **Automobile Safety**
Handel Film Corporation
8730 Sunset Blvd.
W. Hollywood, CA 90069   Ph:(213)657-8990

Audio-visual. Correct ways to work on cars while they are standing still are explained. **Release date:** 1981. **Producer:** Handel Film Corporation. **Acquisition:** Purchase.

3446 • **Center for Auto Safety—Impact**
Center for Auto Safety
2001 S St., N.W., Suite 410
Washington, DC 20009   Ph:(202)328-7700

Newsletter. Reports on product liability litigation; monitors the auto and highway safety work of the Center; and presents information on auto defects, recalls, and state and federal investigations, both regulatory and congressional. Analyzes National Highway Traffic Safety Administration investigations and the New Car Assessment Program. Recurring features include notices of publications available and news of research. Bimonthly. **Editor(s):** Debra Barclay. **Price:** $60.00/year.

3447 • **Children at Risk: Failure of the Federal Child Restraint Recall Program**
Center for Auto Safety
2001 S St. NW, Ste. 410
Washington, DC 20009   Ph:(202)328-7700

Book.

3448 • **Decade of Delay**
Wombat Productions, Inc.
250 W. 57th St., Ste. 916
New York, NY 10019   Ph:(212)315-2502

Audio-visual. Many devices and techniques have been developed to prevent serious injuries from automobile accidents. This program was featured on the PBS award-winning series "NOVA." **Release date:** 1980. **Producer:** CBC Productions. **Acquisition:** Release.

3449 • **Keystone AAA Motorist [Pennsylvania]**
AAA Mid-Atlantic, Inc.
2040 Market St.   Ph:(215)864-5455
Philadelphia, PA 19103-3302   Fax:(215)568-1153

Newspaper. Provides information on domestic and foreign travel and automotive safety. Bimonthly. **Editor(s):** Roy D. Hanhaw and J.C. Moyer. **Price:** $2.00.

3450 • **Lemon Times**
Center for Auto Safety
2001 S St., N.W.
Washington, DC 20009   Ph:(202)328-7700

Newsletter. Publicizes current findings on new car safety. Reports on recalls, class actions, arbitration, settlements, and defect investigations to alert consumers to potential problems. Includes reports of meetings, notices of publications available, coverage of the airbag issue, and tips for using small claims court. Quarterly. **Editor(s):** Debra Barclay. **Price:** $15.00/year.

3451 • **Safety Check Your Car**
Pyramid Film and Video
Box 1048   Ph:(213)828-7577
Santa Monica, CA 90406   Fax:(213)453-9083

Audio-visual. This program demonstrates effective auto maintenance for the average driver. Topics covered include: gas gauge precautions, tire maintenance, steering problems, muffler cracks, and brake problems. **Release date:** 1976. **Producer:** Pyramid; Lee Stanley. **Acquisition:** Rent/Lease, Purchase, Duplication License.

3452 • Seat Belts: Index of Modern Information
ABBE Publishing Assn.
4111 Gallows Rd.
Virginia Division
Annadale, VA 22003   Ph:(703)750-0255

Reference book. Published 1990. **Editor(s):** Lynn Chenn. **Price:** $37.50, hardbound; $29.50, paper.

3453 • Sportsmanlike Driving
American Automobile Association (AAA)
1000 AAA Dr.
Heathrow, FL 32746-5063   Ph:(407)444-7000

Magazine. Periodic (now in ninth edition).

3454 • Structural Design and Crashworthiness of Automobiles
Computational Mechanics, Inc.
25 Bridge St.
Billerica, MA 01821   Ph:(508)667-5841

Manual. Published 1987. **Editor(s):** T.K. Murthy and C.A. Brebbia. **Price:** $72.00.

3455 • Studies Relating Automobile Design & Vehicle Safety: An Annotated Bibliography
Council of Planning Librarians
1313 E. 60th St.
Chicago, IL 60637   Ph:(312)942-2163

Reference book. Published 1982. **Editor(s):** Margaret E. Shepard. **Price:** $15.00.

3456 • Take the Trouble
Film Library
3450 Wilshire Blvd., No. 700
Los Angeles, CA 90010-2215   Ph:(213)384-8114

Audio-visual. A description of why a driver should completely check his vehicle before attempting to drive it. **Producer:** National Safety Council. **Acquisition:** Release.

3457 • Unsafe at Any Speed
Knightsbridge Publishing Co.
10513 W. Pico Blvd.
Los Angeles, CA 90064-2319   Ph:(213)275-4050

Book. Published 1991. **Editor(s):** Ralph Nader. **Price:** $4.95.

3458 • Van & Light Truck Safety
Center for Auto Safety
2001 S St. NW, Ste. 410
Washington, DC 20009   Ph:(202)328-7700
Book.

3459 • Vehicle Occupant Restraint Systems and Components
Society of Automotive Engineers, Inc.
400 Commonwealth
Warrendale, PA 15096   Ph:(412)776-4841

Manual. Published 1991. **Price:** $44.00.

3460 • Your Quick and Easy Car Care and Safe Driving Handbook
Doubleday and Company, Inc.
666 Fifth Ave
New York, NY 10103   Ph:(212)984-7561

Manual. Published 1990. **Editor(s):** Laura F. McCarthy. **Price:** $9.95.

Body repair

3461 • Auto Body Repair
Bergwall Productions, Inc.
P.O. Box 238
Garden City, NY 11530   Ph:(201)592-2000

Manual. Published 1981. **Editor(s):** Robert Jenkins. **Price:** $5.00; $79.00, audio-visual package.

3462 • Auto Body Repair
Bennett Publishing Co.
866 Third Ave.
New York, NY 10022

Manual. Published 1984. **Price:** $26.00.

3463 • Auto Body Repair
Bergwall Productions, Inc.
106 Charles Lindbergh Blvd.
Uniondale, NY 11553-3695   Ph:(516)222-1111

Audio-visual. On four tapes for trainees, body repair instruction is demonstrated. **Release date:** 1985. **Producer:** Bergwall Productions, Inc. **Acquisition:** Purchase.

3464 • Auto Body Repair II
Bergwall Productions, Inc.
P.O. Box 238
Garden City, NY 11530   Ph:800-645-3565

Manual. Demonstrates body repair techniques. Published 1985. **Editor(s):** Charles Lauer. **Price:** $7.00; $229.00, audio-visual package.

3465 • Auto Body Repair—Procedure for Applying Plastic Filler
Allan Keith Productions
630 9th Ave.
New York, NY 10036   Ph:(212)246-0239

Audio-visual. Preparation of surfaces, mixing of plastic, and filling and sanding of the plastic filler are seen in this program for the auto body repair person. **Release date:** 1976. **Producer:** Allan Keith Productions. **Acquisition:** Purchase.

3466 • Auto Body Repairing and Repainting
Goodheart-Wilcox Co.
123 W. Taft Dr.
South Holland, IL 60473   Ph:(708)333-7200

Manual. Published 1982. **Editor(s):** Bill Toboldt. **Price:** $18.00.

3467 • Auto Body Rust Repair
Bergwall Productions, Inc.
106 Charles Lindbergh Blvd.
Uniondale, NY 11553-3695   Ph:(516)222-1111

Audio-visual. Rusted auto bodies are repaired to look like new, with discussions on such interesting topics as plastic filler and featheredging. **Release date:** 1988. **Producer:** Bergwall Productions, Inc. **Price:** $179.00.

3468 • Auto Body Series
RMI Media Productions, Inc.
2807 W. 47th St.
Shawnee Mission, KS 66205   Ph:(913)262-3974

Audio-visual. This series covers all aspects of automotive body repair with program lengths ranging from twelve minutes to forty-nine minutes. **Release date:** 1984. **Producer:** RMI Media Productions, Inc. **Acquisition:** Purchase.

3469 • Auto Body Tools Explained
Bergwall Productions, Inc.
106 Charles Lindbergh Blvd.
Uniondale, NY 11553-3695   Ph:(516)222-1111

Audio-visual. On two tapes, auto body tools are explicated for the mechanically minded viewer. **Release date:** 1982. **Producer:** Bergwall Productions, Inc. **Acquisition:** Purchase.

3470 • Autobody Refinishing Handbook
Prentice-Hall
Rte. 9W
Englewood Cliffs, NJ 07632   Ph:(201)592-2000

Manual. Published 1988. **Editor(s):** Andre G. Deroche. **Price:** $35.00.

3471 • Autobody Repair
Bennett Publishing Co.
866 Third Ave.
New York, NY 10022

Manual. Published 1984. **Editor(s):** Lester G. Duenk et al. **Price:** $18.60.

3472 • Autobody Repair and Refinishing
Prentice-Hall
Rte. 9W
Englewood Cliffs, NJ 07632   Ph:(201)592-2000

Manual. Published 1981. **Editor(s):** Robert P. Schmidt. **Price:** $47.00.

3473 • Automotive Body Repair and Refinishing
McGraw-Hill Publishing Co.
11 W. 19th St.
New York, NY 10011   Ph:(212)337-6010

Manual. Published 1985. **Price:** $34.95, text; $14.95, workbook.

3474 • Automotive Corrosion and Prevention Conference Proceedings
Society of Automotive Engineers
400 Commonwealth Dr.
Warrendale, PA 15096   Ph:(412)776-4841

Report/bulletin. Published 1989. **Price:** $71.00.

3475 • Automotive Glassfibre: A Practical Guide to Moulding and Repairing
Motorbooks International
729 Prospect Ave.
Osceola, WI 54020   Ph:(715)294-3345

Manual. Published 1987. **Editor(s):** Dennis Foy. **Price:** $19.95.

3476 • Chilton's Guide to Auto Body Repair and Painting
Chilton Co.
Chilton Way
Radnor, PA 19089   Ph:(215)964-4000

Book. Published 1983. **Price:** $15.95.

3477 • Chilton's Minor Auto Body Repair Manual
Chilton Co.
Chilton Way
Radnor, PA 19089   Ph:(215)964-4000

Manual. Published 1989. **Price:** $19.95.

3478 • Collision Repair Guide
McGraw-Hill Publishing Co.
11 W. 19th St.
New York, NY 10011   Ph:(212)337-6010

Manual. Published 1971. **Editor(s):** Robert C. MacPherson. **Price:** $32.95.

3479 • The Complete Guide to Automotive Refinishing
Prentice-Hall
Rte. 9W
Englewood Cliffs, NJ 07632   Ph:(201)592-2000

Manual. Published 1988. **Editor(s):** Harry T. Chudy. **Price:** $46.00.

3480 • Guide to Auto Body Sheet Metal Repair
Chilton Co.
Chilton Way
Radnor, PA 19089   Ph:(215)964-4000

Book. Published 1986. **Price:** $18.95.

3481 • Hammer and Dolly
Allan Keith Productions
630 Ninth Ave.
New York, NY 10036   Ph:(212)246-0239

Audio-visual. Techniques for using hammer and dolly for direct and indirect hammering in auto body repair work are presented. **Release date:** 1976. **Producer:** Allan Keith Productions. **Acquisition:** Purchase.

3482 • Haynes Body Repair and Painting Manual, No. 1479
Haynes Publications, Inc.
861 Lawrence Dr.
Newbury Park, CA 91320   Ph:(818)889-5400

Manual. Published 1989. **Price:** $15.95.

3483 • How to Paint Your Car
Motorbooks Intl.
729 Prospect Ave.
Osceola, WI 54020   Ph:(715)294-3345

Manual. Published 1991. **Price:** $14.95.

3484 • How to Restore Paintwork
Motorbooks International
729 Prospect Ave.
Osceda, WI 54020   Ph:(715)294-3345

Manual. Published 1984. **Editor(s):** Miles Wilkins. **Price:** $19.95.

3485 • How to Restore Wooden Body Framing
Motorbooks International
729 Prospect Ave.
Osceola, WI 54020   Ph:(715)294-3345

Manual. Published 1984. **Editor(s):** A. Alderwyck. **Price:** $19.95.

3486 • Pick and File
Allan Keith Productions
630 9th Ave.
New York, NY 10036   Ph:(212)246-0239

Audio-visual. How to use the pick and file is demonstrated, along with their importance in the finishing stages to eliminate unnecessary fill in auto body repair. **Release date:** 1976. **Producer:** Allan Keith Productions. **Acquisition:** Purchase.

3487 • The Principles of Auto Body Repairing and Repainting
Prentice-Hall
Rte. 9W
Englewood Cliffs, NJ 07632   Ph:(201)592-2000

Manual. Published 1986. **Editor(s):** Andre G. Deroche and N. N. Hildebrand. **Price:** $41.00.

3488 • Procedure for Applying Body Solder
Allan Keith Productions
630 Ninth Ave.
New York, NY 10036   Ph:(212)246-0239

Audio-visual. This program demonstrates the preparation, application, lubrication, filling in, and sanding of body solder for the auto repair person. **Release date:** 1976. **Producer:** Allan Keith Productions. **Acquisition:** Purchase.

3489 • Pull Rod Repair Method
Allan Keith Productions
630 Ninth Ave.
New York, NY 10036   Ph:(212)246-0239

Audio-visual. A step-by-step depiction of this method of repairing inaccessible areas of an auto body from the outside. **Release date:** 1976. **Producer:** Allan Keith Productions. **Acquisition:** Purchase.

3490 • Sheet Metal Handbook: How to Form, Shear, Roll and Shape Sheet Metal for Competition, Custom, and Restoration Use
Price Stern Sloan, Inc.
400 Commonwealth Dr.
Warrendale, PA 15096   Ph:(412)776-4841

Manual. Published 1989. **Editor(s):** Ron Fournier and Susan Fournier. **Price:** $12.95.

3491 • Slapper and File
Allan Keith Productions
630 Ninth Ave.
New York, NY 10036   Ph:(212)246-0239

Audio-visual. Practice habits for coordination between slapper and file are demonstrated, as well as techniques for using them. **Release date:** 1976. **Producer:** Allan Keith Productions. **Acquisition:** Purchase.

3492 • SMART Body Shop Talk: Dent Repair
Simitar Entertainment
3850 Annapolis Ln.   Ph:(612)559-6660
Plymouth, MN 55447   Fax:(612)559-0210

Audio-visual. A professional body mechanic shows how to repair dents with inexpensive, readily available tools. **Release date:** 1991. **Producer:** Simitar Entertainment. **Price:** $9.95.

3493 • SMART Body Shop Talk: Paint Tips
Simitar Entertainment
3850 Annapolis Ln.   Ph:(612)559-6660
Plymouth, MN 55447   Fax:(612)559-0210

Audio-visual. A guide to the wide variety of paint products available and how to properly use them. **Release date:** 1991. **Producer:** Simitar Entertainment. **Price:** $9.95.

3494 • SMART Body Shop Talk: Rust Repair
Simitar Entertainment
3850 Annapolis Ln.   Ph:(612)559-6660
Plymouth, MN 55447   Fax:(612)559-0210

Audio-visual. A guide to repairing rust damage using inexpensive and easy to find tools. **Release date:** 1991. **Producer:** Simitar Entertainment. **Price:** $9.95.

3495 • Total Auto Body Repair
MacMillan Publishing Co., Inc.
866 Third Ave.
New York, NY 10022   Ph:(212)702-2000

Manual. Published 1982. **Editor(s):** L.C. Rhone, and David H. Yates. **Price:** $28.99, text; $3.67, instructor's guide; $8.40, kit book.

3496 • Tune Up America: Body and Fender Repair
Morris Video
2730 Monterey St., No. 105
Monterey Business Park
Torrance, CA 90503   Ph:(213)533-4800

Audio-visual. A factory technician takes you through the steps necessary to repair simple dents and rust spots on steel body vehicles. **Release date:** 1986. **Producer:** Morris Video. **Price:** $19.95.

3497 • Vehicle Body Building
State Mutual Book & Periodical Service, Ltd.
521 Fifth Ave., 17th Fl.
New York, NY 10175   Ph:(212)682-5844

Manual. Two volume set. **Price:** $75.00.

Brakes

3498 • ABS Traction Control and Brake Components
Society of Automotive Engineers, Inc.
400 Commonwealth Dr.
Warrendale, PA 15096   Ph:(412)776-4841

Manual. **Price:** $47.00.

3499 • Anti Lock Braking Systems for Passenger Cars and Light Trucks: A Review
Society of Automotive Engineers, Inc.
400 Commonwealth Dr.
Warrendale, PA 15096   Ph:(412)776-4841

Manual. Published 1987. **Price:** $90.00.

3500 • Anti-Lock Up Brake Systems Explained, Vols. 1-5
Bergwall Productions, Inc.
106 Charles Lindbergh Blvd.
Uniondale, NY 11553-3695   Ph:(516)222-1111

Audio-visual. Videocassette series that explains the components, function, and servicing of brake systems. **Release date:** 1990.

3501 • Antilock Systems for Air-Braked Vehicles
Society of Automotive Engineers, Inc.
400 Commonwealth Dr.
Warrendale, PA 15096   Ph:(412)776-4841

Manual. Published 1989. **Price:** $20.00.

3502 • Auto Mechanics
RMI Media Productions, Inc.
2807 W. 47th St.
Shawnee Mission, KS 66205   Ph:(913)362-6910

Audio-visual. This series provides step-by-step instruction in auto mechanics, including set-up procedures, alignment techniques, and brake repair and installation. **Release date:** 1987. **Producer:** RMI Media Productions, Inc. **Acquisition:** Purchase.

3503 • Automobile Brakes and Braking Systems
Robert Bentley, Inc., Publishers
1000 Massachusetts Ave.
Cambridge, MA 02138   Ph:(617)547-4170

Manual. Part of the Motor Manuals Series, Volume Eight. **Price:** $10.95.

3504 • Automobiles Brakes and Braking Systems
Robert Bentley, Inc., Pubs.
1000 Massachusetts Ave.
Cambridge, MA 02138   Ph:(617)547-4170

Manual. **Editor(s):** T.P. Newcomb and R.T. Spurr. **Price:** $10.95.

3505 • Automotive Brake Systems
H. M. Gousha
10 E. 53rd St.
New York, NY 10022   Ph:(212)207-7000

Manual. Two volume set. Published 1987. **Price:** $40.50.

3506 • Automotive Brakes and Power Transmission Systems
Books On Demand
University Microfilms International
300 N. Zeeb Rd.
Ann Arbor, MI 48106-1346   Ph:(313)761-4700

Manual. **Editor(s):** Irving A. Frazee and Walter Billiet. **Price:** $69.30.

3507 • Automotive Brakes, Suspension and Steering
McGraw-Hill Publishing Co.
11 W. 19th. St.
New York, NY 10011   Ph:(212)337-6010

Manual. Published 1983. **Editor(s):** William H. Crouse and Donald L. Anglin. **Price:** $29.95.

3508 • Automotive Brakes: Text-Lab Manual
Glencoe Publishing Co.
15319 Chatsworth St.
Mission Hills, CA 91345   Ph:(818)898-1391

Manual. 1987. **Editor(s):** Sheldon L. Abbott. **Price:** $23.72; $4.28, teacher's manual.

3509 • Automotive Brakes: Theory and Service
Prentice-Hall
Rte. 9W
Englewood Cliffs, NJ 07632   Ph:(201)592-2000

Manual. Published 1988. **Editor(s):** Herbert E. Ellinger and Richard B. Hathaway. **Price:** $32.67.

3510 • Automotive Braking System
Prentice-Hall
Rte. 9W
Englewood Cliffs, NJ 07632   Ph:(201)592-2000

Manual. Published 1985. **Editor(s):** Carl T. Heller. **Price:** $32.80.

3511 • Automotive Braking Systems
Harcourt Brace Jovanovich, Inc.
1250 Sixth Ave.
San Diego, CA 92101   Ph:(619)231-6616

Manual. Published 1988. **Editor(s):** Thomas W. Birch. **Price:** $29.00.

3512 • Automotive Quick Test
L & K International Video Training
295 Evans Ave.
Toronto, ON M8Z 5P9   Ph:(416)252-6407

Audio-visual. Mechanics are taught how to quickly and efficiently check out a car. Titles include: Common Problems on Systems and Components; Electronic Ignition Systems; Emissions Controls; Brake Systems; FWD Axles Steering and Suspension; Air Conditioning; Carburetor and Fuel Injection Systems; Computerized Engine Controls. **Release date:** 1988. **Producer:** Leighton and Kidd. **Acquisition:** Purchase, Rent/Lease.

3513 • Automotive Steering, Suspension, and Braking Systems: Principles and Service
Prentice-Hall
Rte. 9W
Englewood Cliffs, NJ 07632   Ph:(201)592-2000

Manual. Published 1983. **Editor(s):** Frank J. Thiessen and David N. Dales. **Price:** $34.00.

3514 • Automotive Suspension, Steering and Brakes
Prentice-Hall
Rte. 9W
Englewood Cliffs, NJ 07632   Ph:(201)592-2000

Manual. Published 1980. **Editor(s):** Herbert E. Ellinger and Richard B. Hathaway. **Price:** $37.00.

3515 • Automotive Suspension, Steering and Brakes
Delmar Publishers, Inc.
Two Computer Dr., W.
Albany, NY 12212   Ph:(518)459-1150

Manual. Published 1987. **Editor(s):** Jay Webster. **Price:** $24.95; $6.00, instructor's guide.

3516 • Brake and Front End
Babcox Publications
11 S. Forge St.   Ph:(216)535-6117
Akron, OH 44304   Fax:(216)535-0874

Magazine. Covers automotive brake, front end, and chassis systems. Monthly. **Editor(s):** Mary Dellavelle. **Price:** $33.00/year; $56.00 two years. $4.75 per single issue. Free to qualified individuals.

3517 • Brake Block Identification Catalog
Friction Materials Standards Institute (FMSI)
588 Monroe Tpke.
Monroe, CT 06468   Ph:(203)452-1877

Reference book. Periodic.

3518 • Brakes
Harcourt Brace Jovanovich, Inc.
1250 Sixth Ave.
San Diego, CA 92101   Ph:(619)231-6616

Manual. Published 1987. **Editor(s):** James G. Hughes. **Price:** $28.00.

3519 • Brakes
Prentice-Hall
Rte. 9W
Englewood Cliffs, NJ 07632   Ph:(201)592-2000

Manual. Published 1983. **Editor(s):** John Remling. **Price:** $34.95.

3520 • Brakes, Steering, Front Suspension, Wheels and Tires
H. M. Gousha
2001 The Alameda
San Jose, CA 95126   Ph:(408)296-1060

Manual. Published 1981. **Editor(s):** Bob Leigh. **Price:** $9.95, workbook; $13.90, cassette.

3521 • Chilton's Guide to Brakes, Steering and Suspension 1980-1987: Domestic and Import Cars and Trucks
Chilton Co.
Chilton Way
Radnor, PA 19089   Ph:(215)964-4000

Manual. Published 1988. **Price:** $19.95.

3522 • The Hydraulic Brake System Explained
Bergwall Productions, Inc.
106 Charles Lindbergh Blvd.
Uniondale, NY 11553-3695   Ph:(516)222-1111

Audio-visual. On six tapes, a hydraulic brake system is dissected. **Release date:** 1984. **Producer:** Bergwall Productions, Inc. **Acquisition:** Purchase.

3523 • Mechanical Maintenance Training
Tel-A-Train
309 N. Market St.
P.O. Box 4752   Ph:(615)266-0113
Chattanooga, TN 37405   Fax:(615)267-2555

Audio-visual. After watching this series just about any viewer should be able to fix engines. **Release date:** 1989. **Producer:** Tel-A-Trail. **Acquisition:** Purchase, Rent/Lease.

3524 • Mitchell Automotive Braking Systems
Prentice-Hall
Rte. 9W
Englewood Cliffs, NJ 07632   Ph:(201)592-2000

Manual. Published 1989. **Price:** $28.00.

3525 • Safety Check Your Car
Pyramid Film and Video
Box 1048   Ph:(213)828-7577
Santa Monica, CA 90406   Fax:(213)453-9083

Audio-visual. This program demonstrates effective auto maintenance for the average driver. Topics covered include: gas gauge precautions, tire maintenance, steering problems, muffler cracks, and brake problems. **Release date:** 1976. **Producer:** Pyramid; Lee Stanley. **Acquisition:** Rent/Lease, Purchase, Duplication License.

3526 • Vehicle Dynamics Related to Braking and Steering
Society of Automotive Engineers, Inc.
400 Commonwealth Dr.
Warrendale, PA 15096   Ph:(412)776-4841

Manual. Published 1989. **Price:** $31.00.

Bumpers

3527 • Plastics in Automobile Bumper Systems and Exterior Panels
Society of Automotive Engineers, Inc.
400 Commonwealth Dr.
Warrendale, PA 15096   Ph:(412)776-4841

Book. **Price:** $40.00.

3528 • Plastics in Automobiles: Bumper Systems, Interior Trim, Instrument Panels and Exterior Panels
Society of Automotive Engineers, Inc.
400 Commonwealth Dr.
Warrendale, PA 15096   Ph:(412)776-4841

Book. Published 1989. **Price:** $72.00.

Buyers guides and classifieds

3529 • The Car Book
HarperCollins Publishers, Inc.
10 E. 53rd St.
New York, NY 10022   Ph:(212)207-7000

Buyers guide. Annual. **Editor(s):** Jack Gillis. **Price:** $10.95.

Crankshafts

3530 • Crankshaft Manual
Automotive Engine Rebuilders Association (AERA)
330 Lexington Dr.
Buffalo Grove, IL 60089-6998   Ph:(708)541-6550

Manual. Identifies automotive engine crankshafts by casting/forging number. Includes cross-references of casting/forging number to application, size of engine, years used, and bore and stroke of engine. Annual. **Price:** Free to members; $60.00 per copy to nonmembers.

3531 • Performance Tuning in Theory and Practice-Four Strokes
Haynes Publications, Inc.
861 Lawrence Dr.
Newbury Park, CA 91320   Ph:(818)889-5400

Manual. **Editor(s):** Graham A. Bell. **Price:** $19.95.

3532 • Performance Tuning in Theory and Practice-Two Strokes
Haynes Publications, Inc.
861 Lawrence Dr.
Newbury Park, CA 91320   Ph:(818)889-5400

Manual. **Price:** $19.95.

Diagnostics

3533 • Automotive Ignition Systems: Diagnosis and Repair
McGraw-Hill Publishing Co.
1221 Ave. of the Americas
New York, NY 10026   Ph:(212)512-2000

Manual. Published 1982. **Editor(s):** Frank Derato. **Price:** $29.95.

3534 • Chilton's Guide to Emission Diagnosis, Tune-Up and Vacuum Diagrams 1984-87
Chilton Co.
Chilton Way
Radnor, PA 19089   Ph:(215)964-4000

Manual. Volume one, domestic cars; volume two, import cars. Publications 1987. **Price:** Volume one, $19.95; volume two, $17.95.

3535 • Chilton's Tune-up Emission Diagnosis and Service Manual, 1988: Import Cars and Trucks
Chilton Co.
Chilton Way
Radnor, PA 19089   Ph:(215)964-4000

Manual. Published 1989. **Price:** $40.00.

3536 • Chilton's U.S. Emission Diagnostic and Service Manual, Vacuum Circuit, 1984-1987—Domestic Car: Motor-Age Professional Mechanic's Edition
Chilton Co.
Chilton Way
Radnor, PA 19089   Ph:(215)964-4000

Manual. Published 1987. **Price:** $52.00.

3537 • Emission Diagnosis Tune-up and Service Manual 1988 Import Cars and Trucks: Motor-Age Professional Mechanic's Edition
Chilton Co.
Chilton Way
Radnor, PA 19089   Ph:(215)964-4000

Manual. Published 1989. **Price:** $40.00.

3538 • Piper Tuning Manual
Haynes Publications, Inc.
861 Lawrence Dr.
Newbury Park, CA 91320   Ph:(818)889-5400

Manual. **Editor(s):** Bob Gayler. **Price:** $6.95.

Diesel engines

3539 • Automotive Diesel Engines
American Technical Publishers
1155 W. 175th St.
Homewood, IL 60430   Ph:(708)957-1100

Manual. Published 1982. **Editor(s):** J. Webster. **Price:** $15.96.

3540 • Car and Light Truck Diesel Engine Service Manual
H. M. Gousha
2001 The Alameda
San Jose, CA 95126   Ph:(408)296-1060

Manual. Published 1983. **Price:** $9.95.

3541 • Chilton's Guide to Diesel Cars and Trucks
Chilton Co.
Chilton Way
Radnor, PA 19089   Ph:(215)964-4000

Manual. Published 1983. **Editor(s):** James Joseph. **Price:** $15.95.

3542 • Diesel Car Digest
Diesel Car Journals
P.O. Box 160253
Sacramento, CA 95816

Magazine. Quarterly. **Price:** $6.00.

3543 • Diesel Engines for Automobiles, Small Trucks and Small Tractors
Prentice-Hall
Rte. 9W
Englewood Cliffs, NJ 07632   Ph:(201)592-2000

Manual. Published 1986. **Editor(s):** Tom Weathers, Jr. **Price:** $47.00.

3544 • Diesel Exhaust Emissions: Particulate Studies and Transient Cycle Testing
Society of Automotive Engineers, Inc.
400 Commonwealth Dr.
Warrendale, PA 15096   Ph:(412)776-4841

Book. Published 1984. **Price:** $56.00.

3545 • Diesel Magazine
McBain Publications, Inc.
47 Ontario St. S.
Kitchener, ON N2G 1X3   Ph:(519)744-4404

Magazine. Covers performance tests, new diesel cars and light trucks; describes new products and research in alternative fuels. Bimonthly. **Editor(s):** John A. McBain.

3546 • Diesel Mechanics
Bergwall Productions, Inc.
P.O. Box 238
Garden City, NY 11530   Ph:800-645-3565

Manual. Published 1981. **Editor(s):** Zdenko Geda. **Price:** $5.00, workbook; $369.00, audio visual package.

3547 • Diesel Mechanics II: Engine Assembly
Bergwall Productions, Inc.
P.O. Box 238
Garden City, NY 11530   Ph:800-645-3565

Manual. Published 1983. **Editor(s):** Zdenko Geda. **Price:** $7.00, workbook; $299.00, audio visual package.

3548 • Diesel Mechanics III
Bergwall Productions, Inc.
P.O. Box 238
Garden City, NY 11530   Ph:800-645-3565

Manual. Published 1983. **Editor(s):** Zdenko Gega. **Price:** $7.00, workbook; $299.00, audio visual package.

3549 • Diesel Particulates: An Update
Society of Automotive Engineers, Inc.
400 Commonwealth Dr.
Warrendale, PA 15096   Ph:(412)776-4841

Book. Published 1987. **Price:** $53.00.

3550 • Fuel Alternatives for S.I. and Diesel Engines
Society of Automotive Engineers, Inc.
400 Commonwealth Dr.
Warrendale, PA 15096   Ph:(412)776-4841

Book. Published 1983. **Price:** $40.00.

3551 • The Measurement and Control of Diesel Particulate Emissions
Society of Automotive Engineers, Inc.
400 Commonwealth Dr.
Warrendale, PA 15096   Ph:(412)776-4841

Book. Published 1982. **Price:** $72.00.

3552 • Modern Fuel for Modern Diesel Engines
Farmland Industries, Inc.
3315 N. Oak Trafficway
Kansas City, MO 64116

Audio-visual. After viewing this video anatomy of a diesel engine, one can better select its fuel. **Release date:** 1985. **Producer:** Farmland Industries, Inc. **Acquisition:** Purchase.

3553 • Multigrade Oils for Diesel Engines
Society of Automotive Engineers, Inc.
400 Commonwealth Dr.
Warrendale, PA 15096   Ph:(412)776-4841

Book. Published 1980. **Price:** $27.00.

3554 • New Diesel Engines, Combustion and Emissions Research in Japan
Society of Automotive Engineers, Inc.
400 Commonwealth Dr.
Warrendale, PA 15096   Ph:(412)776-4841

Book. Published 1980. **Price:** $51.00.

Drivetrains

3555 • Automatic, Manual Transmissions, Transaxles, and Drive Trains
H. M. Gousha
2001 The Alameda
San Jose, CA 95126   Ph:(408)296-1060

Manual. Published 1981. **Editor(s):** Roger L. Fennema and Kalton C. Lahue. **Price:** $9.95, workbook; $13.90, cassette.

3556 • Automotive Electronic Engine Management and Driveline Controls
Society of Automotive Engineers, Inc.
400 Commonwealth Dr.
Warrendale, PA 15096   Ph:(412)776-4841

Manual. Published 1987. **Price:** $36.00.

3557 • Automotive Manual Transmission and Power Trains
McGraw-Hill Publishing Co.
1221 Avenue of the Americas
New York, NY 10020   Ph:(212)512-2000

Manual. Published 1983. **Editor(s):** William Crouse and Donald Anglin. **Price:** $27.95.

3558 • Developments in Electronic Engine Management and Driveline Controls
Society of Automotive Engineers, Inc.
400 Commonwealth Dr.
Warrendale, PA 15096   Ph:(412)776-4841

Book. Published 1985. **Price:** $44.00.

Electrical systems

3559 • The Alternator Explained
Bergwall Productions, Inc.
106 Charles Lindbergh Blvd.
Uniondale, NY 11553-3695   Ph:(516)222-1111

Audio-visual. On five tapes, automobile alternators are shown for what they are. **Release date:** 1981. **Producer:** Bergwall Productions, Inc. **Acquisition:** Purchase.

3560 • Anatomy of a Battery
Farmland Industries, Inc.
3315 N. Oak Trafficway
Kansas City, MO 64116

Audio-visual. Describes the automobile battery, including maintenance and special care. **Release date:** 1985. **Producer:** Farmland Industries, Inc. **Acquisition:** Purchase.

3561 • Auto Dimensions
Cambridge Career Products
90 MacCorkle Ave. SW
South Charleston, WV 25311   Ph:(304)744-9323

Audio-visual. The viewer is reduced to miniature size so he can take a guided tour of a car's engine and electrical system. **Release date:** 1987. **Producer:** Cambridge Career Products. **Price:** $29.95.

3562 • Auto Electrical Handbook: How To Wire Your Car From Scratch
Price Stern Sloan, Inc.
360 N. La Cienega Blvd.
Los Angeles, CA 90048   Ph:(213)657-6100

Book. Published 1986. **Editor(s):** Jim Horner and Jim Barret. **Price:** $12.95.

3563 • Auto Electricity, Electronics, Computers
Goodheart-Wilcox Co.
123 W. Taft Dr.
South Holland, IL 60473   Ph:(708)533-7200

Manual. Published 1989. **Price:** $26.40.

3564 • Automobile Electrical and Electronic Equipment
Butterworth Publishers
80 Montvale Ave.
Stoneham, MA 02180   Ph:(617)438-8464
Manual. Published 1980. **Author(s):** A.P. Young and L. Griffiths.
Price: $26.95.

3565 • Automobile Electrical Manual: A Comprehensive Guide
Haynes Publications, Inc.
861 Lawrence Dr.
Newbury Park, CA 91320   Ph:(818)889-5400
Manual. **Editor(s):** Tony Tranter. **Price:** $15.95.

3566 • Automobile Electronics and Basic Electrical Systems
John Wiley & Sons, Inc.
605 Third Ave.
New York, NY 10158-0012   Ph:(212)850-6000
Manual. In two volumes. **Editor(s):** Ken Layne. **Price:** $22.95.

3567 • Automotive Electrical and Electronic Systems
Harper & Row Publishers, Inc.
10 E. 53rd St.
New York, NY 10022   Ph:(212)207-7000
Manual. Published 1987. **Price:** $40.50.

3568 • Automotive Electrical and Electronic Systems
McGraw-Hill Publishing Co.
11 W. 19th St.
New York, NY 10011   Ph:(212)337-6010
Manual. Published 1985. **Editor(s):** F.C. Derato. **Price:** $28.95.

3569 • Automotive Electrical and Electronic Systems
Prentice-Hall
Rte. 9W
Englewood Cliffs, NJ 07632   Ph:(201)592-2000
Manual. Published 1988. **Editor(s):** James D. Halderman. **Price:** $37.00.

3570 • Automotive Electrical and Electronic Systems Lab Manual
Prentice-Hall
Rte. 9W
Englewood Cliffs, NJ 07632   Ph:(201)592-2000
Manual. Published 1985. **Editor(s):** Ronald F. Gonzales. **Price:** $25.80.

3571 • Automotive Electrical Systems
Prentice-Hall
Rte. 9W
Englewood Cliffs, NJ 07632   Ph:(201)592-2000
Manual. Published 1985. **Editor(s):** Herbert E. Ellinger. **Price:** $35.00.

3572 • Automotive Electricity
Prentice-Hall
Rte. 9W
Englewood Cliffs, NJ 07632   Ph:(201)592-2000
Book. Published 1987. **Author(s):** John Remling. **Price:** $33.95.

3573 • Automotive Electronic and Computer Controlled Ignition Systems
Prentice—Hall
Rte. 9W
Englewood Cliffs, NJ 07632   Ph:(201)592-2000
Manual. Published 1988. **Editor(s):** Don Knowles. **Price:** $23.25.

3574 • Automotive Electronic-Electrical Systems: A Beginner's Troubleshooting and Repair Manual
Prentice-Hall
Rte. 9W
Englewood Cliffs, NJ 07632   Ph:(201)592-2000
Manual. Published 1985. **Editor(s):** Walter Billiet. **Price:** $18.95.

3575 • Automotive Electronics and Electrical Equipment
McGraw-Hill Publishing Co.
11 W. 19th St.
New York, NY 10020   Ph:(212)337-6010
Book. Published 1985. **Editor(s):** William Cruise and Donald L. Anglin. **Price:** $29.95.

3576 • Automotive Oscilloscope
L & K International Video Training
295 Evans Ave.
Toronto, ON M8Z 5P9
Audio-visual. This program presents a theory of operation of the automotive oscilloscope and its application through a detailed test procedure. **Release date:** 1984. **Producer:** Leighton and Kidd Ltd. **Acquisition:** Purchase.

3577 • Automotive Quick Test
L & K International Video Training
295 Evans Ave.
Toronto, ON M8Z 5P9   Ph:(416)252-6407
Audio-visual. Mechanics are taught how to quickly and efficiently check out a car. Titles include: Common Problems on Systems and Components; Electronic Ignition Systems; Emissions Controls; Brake Systems; FWD Axles Steering and Suspension; Air Conditioning; Carburetor and Fuel Injection Systems; Computerized Engine Controls. **Release date:** 1988. **Producer:** Leighton and Kidd. **Acquisition:** Purchase, Rent/Lease.

3578 • Autopower
Lindsay Publications, Inc.
P.O. Box 12
Bradley, IL 60915-0012   Ph:(815)933-3696
Book. **Author(s):** S.W. Duncan. **Price:** $4.95.

3579 • Basic Automotive Jobs Explained
Bergwall Productions, Inc.
106 Charles Lindbergh Blvd.
Uniondale, NY 11553-3695   Ph:(516)222-1111
Audio-visual. Simple automotive repairs are explained. Titles: Using Reference Material and Starter Replacement; Performing Road Service, Tie Road End and Idler Arm Replacement; Performing Underhood Services and Muffler Replacement; Changing Engine Oil, Automatic Transmission Fluid, Valve Cover Gasket, and Thermostat Replacement; and Alternator, Battery, Shocks and Spark Plug Replacement. **Release date:** 1985. **Producer:** Bergwall Productions, Inc. **Price:** $269.00.

3580 • Basic Electricity for Auto Mechanics
Bergwall Productions, Inc.
106 Charles Lindbergh Blvd.
Uniondale, NY 11553-3695   Ph:(516)222-1111
Audio-visual. Electrical basics are explained, with special emphasis on their importance to the auto mechanic. The series is also available on one tape for the same cost. **Release date:** 1989. **Producer:** Bergwall Productions, Inc. **Price:** $359.00.

3581 • Basic Electronic Test Equipment
Bergwall Productions, Inc.
106 Charles Lindbergh Blvd.
Uniondale, NY 11553-3695   Ph:(516)222-1111
Audio-visual. Devices for testing things on cars are demonstrated. Titles: Introduction to Multimeters; Resistance and Continuity Measurements; and Voltage and Current Measurements. **Producer:** Bergwall Productions, Inc. **Price:** $199.00.

3582 • The Battery and Its Electrical System
Farmland Industries, Inc.
3315 N. Oak Trafficway
Kansas City, MO 64116

Audio-visual. Information on battery activation, maintenance, and installation is included on this tape. **Release date:** 1985. **Producer:** Farmland Industries, Inc. **Acquisition:** Purchase.

3583 • Battery-Replacement Data Book
Battery Council Intl.
111 E. Wacker Dr., Ste. 600
Chicago, IL 60601   Ph:(312)644-6610

Reference book. Offers tables with sizing numbers for replacement batteries. Annual. **Price:** $5.25.

3584 • Battery Service Manual
Battery Council Intl.
111 E. Wacker Dr., Ste. 600
Chicago, IL 60601   Ph:(312)644-6610

Reference book. Technical service manual of automotive batteries. **Price:** $7.00.

3585 • Battery Technical Manual
Battery Council Intl.
111 E. Wacker Dr., Ste. 600
Chicago, IL 60601   Ph:(312)644-6610

Reference book. Technical information on automotive batteries. **Price:** $20.00.

3586 • Charging System Explained
Bergwall Productions, Inc.
P.O. Box 238
Garden City, NY 11530   Ph:800-645-3565

Manual. Published 1980. **Editor(s):** John Primi. **Price:** $7.00, workbook; $399.99, audio-visual package.

3587 • Chilton's Import Car Wiring Diagrams Manual, 1987-88: Motor-Age Professional Mechanic's Edition
Chilton Co.
Chilton Way
Radnor, PA 19089   Ph:(215)964-4000

Manual. Published 1988. **Price:** $69.00.

3588 • Chilton's Truck and Van Wiring Diagram Manual, 1989-1990: Motor Age Professional Mechanic's Edition
Chilton Co.
Chilton Way
Radnor, PA 19089   Ph:(215)964-4000

Manual. Published February 1991. **Price:** $69.00.

3589 • Chilton's Wiring Diagrams Manual, 1989: Domestic Cars
Chilton Co.
Chilton Way
Radnor, PA 19089   Ph:(215)964-4000

Manual. Published 1989. **Price:** $69.00.

3590 • Electric and Electronic Systems for Automobiles and Trucks
Prentice-Hall
Rte. 9W
Englewood Cliffs, NJ 07632   Ph:(201)592-2000

Manual. Published 1983. **Editor(s):** Robert N. Brady. **Price:** $50.00.

3591 • Electric Motors, Principles Controls, Service and Maintenance
Hobar Publications
1234 Tiller Ln.
Saint Paul, MN 55112   Ph:(612)633-3170

Manual. Published 1990. **Editor(s):** W. Forrest Bear. **Price:** $13.00, paper.

3592 • Electrical Systems
John Deere Service Publications
Dept. 333, John Deere Rd.
Moline, IL 61265   Ph:(309)765-2967

Manual. Discusses the basics of current, voltage, and resistance; shows various types of electrical circuits; explains generators and alternators; and tells how to maintain the circuits for safety and long service. Published 1984. **Price:** $16.73.

3593 • Electrical Systems, Heating, and Air Conditioning
H. M. Gousha
2001 The Alameda
San Jose, CA 95126   Ph:(408)296-1060

Manual. Published 1981. **Price:** $9.95, workbook; $13.90, cassette.

3594 • Electrics
International Film Bureau, Inc. (IFB)
332 S. Michigan Ave.
Chicago, IL 60604-4832   Ph:(312)427-4545

Audio-visual. Maintenance for electrical systems-ignition and lighting, including checking the battery water level and cable connections, and changing and cleaning plugs and points-is taught. **Release date:** 1981. **Producer:** International Film Bureau, Inc. **Acquisition:** Purchase.

3595 • Fundamentals of Electricity and Automotive Electrical Systems
Prentice-Hall
Rte. 9W
Englewood Cliffs, NJ 07632   Ph:(201)592-2000

Book. Published 1988. **Author(s):** Tom Weathers and Claud C. Hunter. **Price:** $36.00.

3596 • Haynes Automobile Electrical Manual: A Comprehensive Guide
Haynes Publications, Inc.
861 Lawrence Dr.
Newbury Park, CA 91320   Ph:(818)889-5400

Manual. Published 1988. **Editor(s):** Tony Tranter. **Price:** $15.95.

3597 • Haynes Automobile Electrical Manual No. 1654
Haynes Publications, Inc.
861 Lawrence Dr.
Newbury Park, CA 91320   Ph:(818)889-5400

Manual. Published 1988. **Price:** $15.95.

3598 • How to Do Electrical Systems
Motorbooks International
729 Prospect Ave.
Osceola, WI 54020   Ph:(715)294-3345

Manual. How-to series. Published 1989. **Editor(s):** Skip Readio. **Price:** $17.95.

3599 • Lighting Systems for Motor Vehicles
Society of Automotive Engineers, Inc.
400 Commonwealth Dr.
Warrendale, PA 15096   Ph:(412)776-4841

Manual. Published 1989. **Price:** $30.00.

3600 • Mitchell Automotive Electrical Systems
Prentice-Hall
Rte. 9W
Englewood Cliffs, NJ 07632   Ph:(201)592-2000

Manual. Published 1987. **Editor(s):** Mitchell International, Inc. Staff. **Price:** $41.00.

3601 • Motor Auto Engines and Electrical Systems
Delmar Publishers, Inc.
P. O. Box 15015
2 Computer Drive
Albany, NY 12212   Ph:(518)459-1150

Manual. **Price:** $28.00.

3602 • Petersen's Basic Ignition and Electrical Systems
Green Hill Publications
722 Columbus St.
Ottawa, IL 61350   Ph:(815)434-7905

Manual. Published 1985. **Price:** $9.95.

3603 • The Starting System Explained
Bergwall Productions, Inc.
106 Charles Lindbergh Blvd.
Uniondale, NY 11553-3695   Ph:(516)222-1111

Audio-visual. On four tapes, a car's starting system is made plain to the viewer. **Release date:** 1979. **Producer:** Bergwall Productions, Inc. **Acquisition:** Purchase.

3604 • Starting Systems Technology
Society of Automotive Engineers, Inc.
400 Commonwealth Dr.
Warrendale, PA 15096   Ph:(412)776-4841

Manual. Published 1984. **Price:** $51.00.

3605 • Troubleshooting Electrical Components
Bergwall Productions, Inc.
P.O. Box 238
Garden City, NY 11530   Ph:800-645-3565

Manual. Published 1983. **Editor(s):** Peter Novellino. **Price:** $5.00, workbook; $179.00, audio-visual package.

Electronic systems

3606 • Advanced Electronic Tune-Up
Bergwall Productions, Inc.
P.O. Box 238
Garden City, NY 11530   Ph:800-645-3565

Reference book. Published 1984. **Editor(s):** Peter Novellino. **Price:** $6.00, workbook; $199.00, audio visual package.

3607 • Auto Electricity, Electronics, Computers
Goodheart-Wilcox Co.
123 W. Taft Dr.
South Holland, IL 60473   Ph:(708)533-7200

Manual. Published 1989. **Price:** $26.40.

3608 • Automechanic's Guide to Electronic Instrumentation and Microprocessor
Prentice-Hall
Rte. 9W
Englewood Cliffs, NJ 07632   Ph:(201)592-2000

Manual. Published 1987. **Editor(s):** Lynn S. Mosher. **Price:** $40.00.

3609 • Automobile Electrical and Electronic Equipment
Butterworth Publishers
80 Montvale Ave.
Stoneham, MA 02180   Ph:(617)438-8464

Manual. Published 1980. **Author(s):** A.P. Young and L. Griffiths. **Price:** $26.95.

3610 • Automobile Electronics and Basic Electrical Systems
John Wiley & Sons, Inc.
605 Third Ave.
New York, NY 10158-0012   Ph:(212)850-6000

Manual. In two volumes. **Editor(s):** Ken Layne. **Price:** $22.95.

3611 • Automotive Chassis and Accessory Circuits
Prentice-Hall
Rte. 9W
Englewood Cliffs, NJ 07632   Ph:(201)592-2000

Manual. Published 1987. **Editor(s):** Mathias F. Brejcha and Clifford L. Samuels. **Price:** $42.00.

3612 • The Automotive Computer
Bergwall Productions, Inc.
106 Charles Lindbergh Blvd.
Uniondale, NY 11553-3695   Ph:(516)222-1111

Audio-visual. The evolution and uses of on-board automotive computers are examined. This series is also available as a single tape at the same cost. **Release date:** 1989. **Producer:** Bergwall Productions, Inc. **Price:** $299.00.

3613 • Automotive Computer Control Systems
Harcourt Brace Jovanovich, Inc.
6277 Sea Harbor Dr.
Orlando, FL 32821   Ph:(407)345-2000

Manual. Published 1989. **Editor(s):** William Husselbee. **Price:** $29.00.

3614 • Automotive Computers and Digital Instrumentation
Prentice-Hall
Rte. 9W
Englewood Cliffs, NJ 07632   Ph:(201)592-2000

Manual. Published 1988. **Editor(s):** Robert N. Brady. **Price:** $46.00.

3615 • Automotive Displays and Industrial Illumination
SPIE—International Society for Optical Engineering
PO Box 10
1022 19th St.
Bellingham, WA 98227   Ph:(206)676-3290

Book. Published 1988. **Editor(s):** B.J. Chang and T.M. Lemons. **Price:** $38.00.

3616 • Automotive Electrical and Electronic Systems
Harper & Row Publishers, Inc.
10 E. 53rd St.
New York, NY 10022   Ph:(212)207-7000

Manual. Published 1987. **Price:** $40.50.

3617 • Automotive Electrical and Electronic Systems
McGraw-Hill Publishing Co.
11 W. 19th St.
New York, NY 10011   Ph:(212)337-6010

Manual. Published 1985. **Editor(s):** F.C. Derato. **Price:** $28.95.

3618 • Automotive Electrical and Electronic Systems
Prentice-Hall
Rte. 9W
Englewood Cliffs, NJ 07632   Ph:(201)592-2000

Manual. Published 1988. **Editor(s):** James D. Halderman. **Price:** $37.00.

3619 • Automotive Electrical and Electronic Systems Lab Manual
Prentice-Hall
Rte. 9W
Englewood Cliffs, NJ 07632   Ph:(201)592-2000

Manual. Published 1985. **Editor(s):** Ronald F. Gonzales. **Price:** $25.80.

3620 • Automotive Electronic and Computer Controlled Ignition Systems
Prentice—Hall
Rte. 9W
Englewood Cliffs, NJ 07632   Ph:(201)592-2000

Manual. Published 1988. **Editor(s):** Don Knowles. **Price:** $23.25.

3621 • Automotive Electronic-Electrical Systems: A Beginner's Troubleshooting and Repair Manual
Prentice-Hall
Rte. 9W
Englewood Cliffs, NJ 07632   Ph:(201)592-2000

Manual. Published 1985. **Editor(s):** Walter Billiet. **Price:** $18.95.

3622 • Automotive Electronic Engine Management and Driveline Controls
Society of Automotive Engineers, Inc.
400 Commonwealth Dr.
Warrendale, PA 15096   Ph:(412)776-4841

Manual. Published 1987. **Price:** $36.00.

3623 • Automotive Electronics and Electrical Equipment
McGraw-Hill Publishing Co.
11 W. 19th St.
New York, NY 10020   Ph:(212)337-6010

Book. Published 1985. **Editor(s):** William Cruise and Donald L. Anglin. **Price:** $29.95.

3624 • Automotive Electronics and Engine Performance
Prentice-Hall
Rte. 9W
Englewood Cliffs, NJ 07632   Ph:(201)592-2000

Book. Published 1984. **Author(s):** Frank J. Thiessen and Davis Dales. **Price:** $40.00, hardcover; $39.00, paperback; solutions manual available.

3625 • Automotive Electronics Explained, Vols. 1-5
Bergwall Productions
106 Charles Lindbergh Blvd.
Uniondale, NY 11553-3695   Ph:(516)222-1111

Audio-visual. In this filmstrip, a 1988 Mercury Sable is used to demonstrate troubleshooting methods used by technicians to find, identify, and repair troublesome components in the automotive electronics system. **Release date:** 1988.

3626 • Automotive Electronics Reliability
Society of Automotive Engineers, Inc.
400 Commonwealth Dr.
Warrendale, PA 15096   Ph:(412)776-4841

Book. Published 1987. **Price:** $44.00.

3627 • Automotive Engine Electronics
Accuracy Publishing Co.
P.O. Box 514
Homestead, FL 33090   Ph:(305)245-2187

Manual. Guide to automotive computer control and fuel injection systems operation. Published 1990. **Editor(s):** Robert C. McElroy. **Price:** $13.95.

3628 • Automotive Microprocessors Explained
Bergwall Productions, Inc.
P.O. Box 238
Garden City, NY 11530   Ph:800-645-3565

Manual. Discusses the uses of microprocessors in automobile engines. Published 1984. **Editor(s):** Jim Hannemann. **Price:** $8.00, workbook; $269.00, audio-visual package.

3629 • Automotive Quick Test
L & K International Video Training
295 Evans Ave.
Toronto, ON M8Z 5P9   Ph:(416)252-6407

Audio-visual. Mechanics are taught how to quickly and efficiently check out a car. Titles include: Common Problems on Systems and Components; Electronic Ignition Systems; Emissions Controls; Brake Systems; FWD Axles Steering and Suspension; Air Conditioning; Carburetor and Fuel Injection Systems; Computerized Engine Controls. **Release date:** 1988. **Producer:** Leighton and Kidd. **Acquisition:** Purchase, Rent/Lease.

3630 • Chilton's Chassis Electronics and Power Accessories Service Manual, 1987-89: Motor-Age Professional Mechanic's Edition
Chilton Co.
Chilton Way
Radnor, PA 19089   Ph:(215)964-4000

Manual. Published 1988. **Price:** $77.00.

3631 • Chilton's Electronic Chassis Controls Manual, Import Cars and Trucks—1988-1990: Motor Age Professional Mechanic's Edition
Chilton Co.
Chilton Way
Radnor, PA 19089   Ph:(215)964-4000

Manual. Two volumes, A-M and N-Z. Published June 1991. **Price:** $72.00 per volume.

3632 • Chilton's Electronic Engine Controls Manual, 1988-90—Domestic Cars and Trucks: Motor-Age Professional Mechanic's Edition
Chilton Co.
Chilton Way
Radnor, PA 19089   Ph:(215)964-4000

Manual. Published 1989. **Price:** $72.00.

3633 • Chilton's Guide to Chassis Electronics, 1987-89
Chilton Co.
Chilton Way
Radnor, PA 19089   Ph:(215)964-4000

Manual. Published 1988. **Price:** $19.95.

3634 • Chilton's Guide to Fuel Injection and Electronic Engine Controls 1984-1988: Import Cars and Trucks
Chilton Co.
Chilton Way
Radnor, PA 19089   Ph:(215)964-4000

Manual. Published 1988. **Price:** $19.95.

3635 • Chilton's Guide to Fuel Injection and Electronic Engine Controls, 1988-90
Chilton Co.
Chilton Way
Radnor, PA 19089   Ph:(215)964-4000

Manual. In two volumes. Published 1989. **Price:** $19.95 per volume.

3636 • Computers in Design, Manufacture and Operation of Automobiles
Computational Mechanics, Inc.
25 Bridge St.
Billerica, MA 01821   Ph:(508)667-5841

Manual. Published 1987. **Editor(s):** T.K. Murthy. **Price:** $72.00.

3637 • Convergence 1988: Proceedings of the International Congress on Transportation Electronics
Society of Automotive Engineers, Inc.
400 Commonwealth Dr.
Warrendale, PA 15096   Ph:(412)776-4841

Report/bulletin. **Price:** $48.00.

3638 • Current and Future Directions of Supercomputer Applications in the Automobile Industry
Society of Automotive Engineers, Inc.
400 Commonwealth Dr.
Warrendale, PA 15096   Ph:(412)776-4841

Book. Published 1985. **Price:** $27.00.

3639 • Developments in Electronic Engine Management and Driveline Controls
Society of Automotive Engineers, Inc.
400 Commonwealth Dr.
Warrendale, PA 15096   Ph:(412)776-4841

Book. Published 1985. **Price:** $44.00.

3640 • Displays, Electronics, and Sensors Technology
Society of Automotive Engineers, Inc.
400 Commonwealth Dr.
Warrendale, PA 15096   Ph:(412)776-4841

Manual. Published 1984. **Price:** $64.00.

3641 • Domestic Electronic Fuel Injection and Computer Systems
Prentice-Hall
Rte. 9W
Englewood Cliffs, NJ 07632   Ph:(201)592-2000

Manual. Published 1988. **Editor(s):** Frederick Allen. **Price:** $38.00.

3642 • Electric and Electronic Systems for Automobiles and Trucks
Prentice-Hall
Rte. 9W
Englewood Cliffs, NJ 07632   Ph:(201)592-2000

Manual. Published 1983. **Editor(s):** Robert N. Brady. **Price:** $50.00.

3643 • Electronic Automotive Reliability
Society of Automotive Engineers, Inc.
400 Commonwealth Dr.
Warrendale, PA 15096-0001   Ph:(412)776-4841

Manual. Published 1984. **Price:** $33.00.

3644 • Electronic Displays and Information Systems
Society of Automotive Engineers, Inc.
400 Commonwealth Dr.
Warrendale, PA 15096   Ph:(412)776-4841

Manual. Published 1981. **Price:** $46.00.

3645 • Electronic Displays, Information Systems and On-Board Electronics
Society of Automotive Engineers, Inc.
400 Commonwealth Dr.
Warrendale, PA 15096   Ph:(412)776-4841

Manual. Published 1982. **Price:** $58.00.

3646 • Electronic Fuel Injection
Bergwall Productions, Inc.
106 Charles Lindbergh Blvd.
Uniondale, NY 11553-3695   Ph:(516)222-1111

Audio-visual. On two tapes, how fuel injection works is explained. **Release date:** 1986. **Producer:** Bergwall Productions, Inc. **Acquisition:** Purchase.

3647 • Electronic Ignition Explained
Bergwall Productions, Inc.
106 Charles Lindbergh Blvd.
Uniondale, NY 11553-3695   Ph:(516)222-1111

Audio-visual. On two tapes, the basic basics of electronic ignition are displayed. **Release date:** 1978. **Producer:** Bergwall Productions, Inc. **Acquisition:** Purchase.

3648 • Electronic Ignition Tune Up
Bergwall Publications, Inc.
P.O. Box 238
Garden City, NY 11530   Ph:800-645-3565

Manual. Published 1983. **Editor(s):** Peter Novellino. **Price:** Workbook costs $6.00; audio visual package costs $339.00.

3649 • Electronic Instrumentation Service Manual 1980-1987: Motor Age Professional Mechanic's Edition
Chilton Co.
Chilton Way
Radnor, PA 19089   Ph:(215)964-4000

Manual. Published 1988. **Price:** $59.00.

3650 • Mitchell's Electronic Fuel-Injection Troubleshooting Guide: Domestic Vehicles
Fisher Books
P.O. Box 445
Vienna, VA 22183   Ph:(703)448-0420

Manual. Published 1990. **Price:** $29.95.

3651 • Mitchell's Electronic Fuel-Injection Troubleshooting Guide: Import Vehicles
Fisher Books
P.O. Box 38040
Tuscon, AZ 85740-8040   Ph:(602)292-9080

Manual. Published 1990. **Price:** $29.95.

3652 • Mitchell's Electronic Ignition Troubleshooting Guide: Domestic Vehicles
Fisher Books
P.O. Box 445
Vienna, VA 22183   Ph:(703)448-0420

Manual. Published 1987. **Price:** $19.95.

3653 • Mitchell's Electronic Ignition Troubleshooting Guide: Import Vehicles
Fisher Books
P.O. Box 445
Vienna, VA 22183   Ph:(703)448-0420

Manual. Published 1988. **Price:** $14.95.

3654 • New Developments in Electronic Engine Management
Society of Automotive Engineers, Inc.
400 Commonwealth Dr.
Warrendale, PA 15096   Ph:(412)776-4841

Book. Published 1984. **Price:** $56.00.

3655 • New Technologies in Automotive Electronic Displays and Information Systems
Society of Automotive Engineers, Inc.
400 Commonwealth Dr.
Warrendale, PA 15096   Ph:(412)776-4841

Book. **Price:** $68.00.

3656 • Non-Entertainment Automotive Electronics Market
Frost and Sullivan, Inc.
106 Fulton St.
New York, NY 10038   Ph:(212)233-1080

Buyers guide. Published 1987. **Price:** $2,000.00.

3657 • Recent Developments in Automotive Electronic Displays and Information Systems
Society of Automotive Engineers, Inc.
400 Commonwealth Dr.
Warrendale, PA 15096   Ph:(412)776-4841

Book. Published 1987. **Price:** $59.00.

3658 • Recent Developments in Electronic Engine Control and Fuel Injection Management
Society of Automotive Engineers, Inc.
400 Commonwealth Dr.
Warrendale, PA 15096   Ph:(412)776-4841

Book. Published 1987. **Price:** $44.00.

3659 • Sensors and Actuators, 1989
Society of Automotive Engineers, Inc.
400 Commonwealth Dr.
Warrendale, PA 15096   Ph:(412)776-4841

Manual. Published 1989. **Price:** $64.00.

3660 • Sensors for Automotive Systems
Society of Automotive Engineers, Inc.
400 Commonwealth Dr.
Warrendale, PA 15096   Ph:(412)776-4841

Report/bulletin. Published 1980. **Price:** $53.00.

3661 • Truck Electronic Control Systems
Society of Automotive Engineers, Inc.
400 Commonwealth Dr.
Warrendale, PA 15096   Ph:(412)776-4841

Manual. Published 1985. **Price:** $24.00.

3662 • Understanding Automotive Electronics
Howard W. Sams and Co.
4300 W. 62nd Street
Indianapolis, IN 46288   Ph:800-428-7267

Manual. Published 1988. **Editor(s):** William B. Ribbens. **Price:** $19.95.

3663 • Vehicle Lighting Trends
Society of Automotive Engineers, Inc.
400 Commonwealth Dr.
Warrendale, PA 15096   Ph:(412)776-4841

Book. Published 1987. **Price:** $40.00

Emissions systems

3664 • Air Pollution, the Automobile, and Public Health
National Academy Press
2101 Constitution Ave. N.W.
Washington, DC 20418   Ph:(202)334-3318

Book. Published 1988. **Editor(s):** Richard Bates and Donald Kennedy. **Price:** $60.00.

3665 • Automobile Catalytic Converters
Springer-Verlag
175 Fifth Ave. 19th Floor
New York, NY 10010   Ph:(212)460-1500

Manual. Published 1984. **Editor(s):** K.C. Taylor. **Price:** $18.00.

3666 • Automotive Fuel Consumption in Actual Traffic Conditions
Organization for Economic Cooperation and Development
2001 L St.
NW Suite 700
Washington, DC 20036   Ph:(202)785-6323

Book. Published 1982. **Price:** $8.50.

3667 • Automotive Fuel, Cooling, Lubrication, and Exhaust Systems
Prentice-Hall
Rte. 9W
Englewood Cliffs, NJ 07632   Ph:(201)592-2000

Manual. Published 1985. **Editor(s):** William Husselbee. **Price:** $34.00.

3668 • Automotive Pollution Control
Bergwall Productions, Inc.
106 Charles Lindbergh Blvd.
Uniondale, NY 11553-3695   Ph:(516)222-1111

Audio-visual. On five tapes, car pollution systems are dissected and discussed. **Release date:** 1982. **Producer:** Bergwall Productions, Inc. **Acquisition:** Purchase.

3669 • Automotive Quick Test
L & K International Video Training
295 Evans Ave.
Toronto, ON M8Z 5P9   Ph:(416)252-6407

Audio-visual. Mechanics are taught how to quickly and efficiently check out a car. Titles include: Common Problems on Systems and Components; Electronic Ignition Systems; Emissions Controls; Brake Systems; FWD Axles Steering and Suspension; Air Conditioning; Carburetor and Fuel Injection Systems; Computerized Engine Controls. **Release date:** 1988. **Producer:** Leighton and Kidd. **Acquisition:** Purchase, Rent/Lease.

3670 • Chilton's Emission Control Manual 1992: Motor Age Professional Mechanic's Edition
Chilton Co.
Chilton Way
Radnor, PA 19089   Ph:(215)964-4000

Manual. Published 1991. **Price:** $80.00.

3671 • Chilton's Emission Controls Application Guide 1966-1992: Update
Chilton Co.
Chilton Way
Radnor, PA 19089   Ph:(215)964-4000

Manual. Published 1991. **Price:** $19.00.

3672 • Chilton's Guide to Emission Diagnosis, Tune-Up and Vacuum Diagrams 1984-87
Chilton Co.
Chilton Way
Radnor, PA 19089   Ph:(215)964-4000

Manual. Volume one, domestic cars; volume two, import cars. Publications 1987. **Price:** Volume one, $19.95; volume two, $17.95.

3673 • Chilton's IMP Emission Diagnostic and Service Manual, Vacuum Circuit, 1984-1987 Import Cars and Truck: Motor-Age Professional Mechanic's Edition
Chilton Co.
Chilton Way
Radnor, PA 19089   Ph:(215)964-4000

Manual. Published 1987. **Price:** $52.00.

3674 • Chilton's Tune-up Emission Diagnosis and Service Manual, 1988: Import Cars and Trucks
Chilton Co.
Chilton Way
Radnor, PA 19089   Ph:(215)964-4000

Manual. Published 1989. **Price:** $40.00.

3675 • Chilton's U.S. Emission Diagnostic and Service Manual, Vacuum Circuit, 1984-1987—Domestic Car: Motor-Age Professional Mechanic's Edition
Chilton Co.
Chilton Way
Radnor, PA 19089   Ph:(215)964-4000

Manual. Published 1987. **Price:** $52.00.

3676 • Diesel Exhaust Emissions: Particulate Studies and Transient Cycle Testing
Society of Automotive Engineers, Inc.
400 Commonwealth Dr.
Warrendale, PA 15096   Ph:(412)776-4841

Book. Published 1984. **Price:** $56.00.

3677 • Diesel Particulates: An Update
Society of Automotive Engineers, Inc.
400 Commonwealth Dr.
Warrendale, PA 15096   Ph:(412)776-4841

Book. Published 1987. **Price:** $53.00.

3678 • **Emission Diagnosis Tune-up and Service Manual 1988 Import Cars and Trucks: Motor-Age Professional Mechanic's Edition**
Chilton Co.
Chilton Way
Radnor, PA 19089   Ph:(215)964-4000

Manual. Published 1989. **Price:** $40.00.

3679 • **Emissions: Misfueling, Catalyst Deactivation and Alternative Catalyst**
Society of Automotive Engineers, Inc.
400 Commonwealth Dr.
Warrendale, PA 15096   Ph:(412)776-4841

Book. Published 1984. **Price:** $26.00.

3680 • **Exhaust News**
P.O. Box 120937
Arlington, TX 76012   Ph:(817)860-2375

Magazine. Monthly. **Editor(s):** Lee Cruse, Editor and Publisher. **Price:** $20.00/year; $3.00 per single issue.

3681 • **Fuel Systems and Emission Controls**
H. M. Gousha
10 E. 53rd St.
New York, NY 10022   Ph:(212)207-7000

Manual. Published 1988. **Price:** $40.50.

3682 • **Gaseous Fuels: Technology, Performance, and Emissions**
Society of Automotive Engineers, Inc.
400 Commonwealth Dr.
Warrendale, PA 15096   Ph:(412)776-4841

Book. Published 1989. **Price:** $50.00.

3683 • **Infrared Exhaust Analyzer**
Bergwall Productions, Inc.
106 Charles Lindbergh Blvd.
Uniondale, NY 11553-3695   Ph:(516)222-1111

Audio-visual. On six tapes, the method of analyzing exhaust with infrared is demonstrated. **Release date:** 1980. **Producer:** Bergwall Productions, Inc. **Acquisition:** Purchase.

3684 • **The Measurement and Control of Diesel Particulate Emissions**
Society of Automotive Engineers, Inc.
400 Commonwealth Dr.
Warrendale, PA 15096   Ph:(412)776-4841

Book. Published 1982. **Price:** $72.00.

3685 • **Motor Vehicle Pollution Control; A Global Perspective**
Society of Automotive Engineers, Inc.
400 Commonwealth Dr.
Warrendale, PA 15096   Ph:(412)776-4841

Book. Published 1987. **Price:** $44.00.

3686 • **New Diesel Engines, Combustion and Emissions Research in Japan**
Society of Automotive Engineers, Inc.
400 Commonwealth Dr.
Warrendale, PA 15096   Ph:(412)776-4841

Book. Published 1980. **Price:** $51.00.

3687 • **Present and Future Automotive Fuels: Performance and Exhaust Clarification**
John Wiley and Sons, Inc.
605 Third Ave.
New York, NY 10158   Ph:(212)850-6000

Book. Published 1988. **Editor(s):** Richard K. Pefley and Osamu Hirso. **Price:** $82.50.

3688 • **Recent Trends in Automotive Emissions Control**
Society of Automotive Engineers, Inc.
400 Commonwealth Dr.
Warrendale, PA 15096   Ph:(412)776-4841

Book. **Price:** $41.00.

3689 • **Safety Check Your Car**
Pyramid Film and Video
Box 1048   Ph:(213)828-7577
Santa Monica, CA 90406   Fax:(213)453-9083

Audio-visual. This program demonstrates effective auto maintenance for the average driver. Topics covered include: gas gauge precautions, tire maintenance, steering problems, muffler cracks, and brake problems. **Release date:** 1976. **Producer:** Pyramid; Lee Stanley. **Acquisition:** Rent/Lease, Purchase, Duplication License.

3690 • **Tune Up America: Replacing Exhaust Systems**
Morris Video
2730 Monterey St., No. 105
Monterey Business Park
Torrance, CA 90503   Ph:(213)533-4800

Audio-visual. Everything an individual needs to know to replace the muffler, or update the exhaust system in a car. **Release date:** 1986. **Producer:** Morris Video. **Price:** $19.95.

3691 • **Worldwide Emission Control: Automotive Catalysts**
Society of Automotive Engineers, Inc.
400 Commonwealth Dr.
Warrendale, PA 15096   Ph:(412)776-4841

Manual. Published 1985. **Price:** $36.00.

3692 • **Worldwide Emission Control: Automotive Catalysts**
Society of Automotive Engineers, Inc.
400 Commonwealth Dr.
Warrendale, PA 15096   Ph:(412)776-4841

Book. Published 1985. **Price:** $36.00.

Engines/transmissions

3693 • **Alternate Fuels for S.I. Engines**
Society of Automotive Engineers, Inc.
400 Commonwealth Dr.
Warrendale, PA 92101   Ph:(412)776-4841

Book. Published 1983. **Price:** $45.00.

3694 • **Auto Dimensions**
Cambridge Career Products
90 MacCorkle Ave. SW
South Charleston, WV 25311   Ph:(304)744-9323

Audio-visual. The viewer is reduced to miniature size so he can take a guided tour of a car's engine and electrical system. **Release date:** 1987. **Producer:** Cambridge Career Products. **Price:** $29.95.

3695 • **Automatic, Manual Transmissions, Transaxles, and Drive Trains**
H. M. Gousha
2001 The Alameda
San Jose, CA 95126   Ph:(408)296-1060

Manual. Published 1981. **Editor(s):** Roger L. Fennema and Kalton C. Lahue. **Price:** $9.95, workbook; $13.90, cassette.

3696 • **Automatic Transmission**
Prentice Hall
Chilton Way
Radnor, PA 19089   Ph:(215)964-4000

Manual. Published 1982. **Editor(s):** M. Brycha. **Price:** $41.00.

3697 • The Automatic Transmission
Bergwall Productions, Inc.
106 Charles Lindbergh Blvd.
Uniondale, NY 11553-3695   Ph:(516)222-1111

Audio-visual. The operation and maintenance of the automatic transmission of an automobile is the focus of this video series. **Release date:** 1985. **Producer:** Bergwall Productions, Inc. **Price:** $269.00.

3698 • Automatic Transmissions
McGraw Publishing Co.
1221 Ave. of the Americas
New York, NY 10020   Ph:(212)512-2000

Manual. Published 1983. **Editor(s):** William Crouse and Donald Anglin. **Price:** $28.95.

3699 • Automotive Brakes and Power Transmission Systems
Books On Demand
University Microfilms International
300 N. Zeeb Rd.
Ann Arbor, MI 48106-1346   Ph:(313)761-4700

Manual. **Editor(s):** Irving A. Frazee and Walter Billiet. **Price:** $69.30.

3700 • Automotive Chassis and Accessory Circuits
Prentice-Hall
Rte. 9W
Englewood Cliffs, NJ 07632   Ph:(201)592-2000

Manual. Published 1987. **Editor(s):** Mathias F. Brejcha and Clifford L. Samuels. **Price:** $42.00.

3701 • Automotive Cylinder Boring
Bergwall Productions, Inc.
106 Charles Lindbergh Blvd.
Uniondale, NY 11553-3695   Ph:(516)222-1111

Audio-visual. Automotive cylinder boring is performed before the video camera, including the use of the boring bar. **Release date:** 1987. **Producer:** Bergwall Productions, Inc. **Price:** $149.00.

3702 • Automotive Electronics and Engine Performance
Prentice-Hall
Rte. 9W
Englewood Cliffs, NJ 07632   Ph:(201)592-2000

Book. Published 1984. **Author(s):** Frank J. Thiessen and Davis Dales. **Price:** $40.00, hardcover; $39.00, paperback; solutions manual available.

3703 • Automotive Engine Electronics
Accuracy Publishing Co.
P.O. Box 514
Homestead, FL 33090   Ph:(305)245-2187

Manual. Guide to automotive computer control and fuel injection systems operation. Published 1990. **Editor(s):** Robert C. McElroy. **Price:** $13.95.

3704 • Automotive Engine Rebuilders Association— Technical Bulletin
Automotive Engine Rebuilders Association (AERA)
330 Lexington Dr.
Buffalo Grove, IL 60089-6998   Ph:(708)541-6550

Report/bulletin. Looseleaf bulletin describing technical changes in specification of light- and heavy-duty engines. Monthly. **Price:** Free, for members only.

3705 • Automotive Engine Repair and Overhaul
Prentice-Hall
Rte. 9W
Englewood Cliffs, NJ 07632   Ph:800-645-3565

Manual. Published 1980. **Editor(s):** Frederick Peacock and Thomas Gaston. **Price:** $40.00.

3706 • Automotive Engine Repair and Rebuilding
Prentice-Hall
Rte. 9W
Englewood Cliffs, NJ 07632   Ph:(201)592-2000

Manual. **Editor(s):** Frank J. Thiessen. **Price:** $35.00.

3707 • Automotive Engines: Maintenance and Repair
Books on Demand
University Microfilms International
300 N. Zeeb Rd.
Ann Arbor, MI 48106   Ph:(313)761-4700

Manual. **Editor(s):** Walter Billiet. **Price:** $131.50.

3708 • Automotive Manual Transmission and Power Trains
McGraw-Hill Publishing Co.
1221 Avenue of the Americas
New York, NY 10020   Ph:(212)512-2000

Manual. Published 1983. **Editor(s):** William Crouse and Donald Anglin. **Price:** $27.95.

3709 • Automotive Transmission
Glencoe Publishing Company
15319 Chatsworth St.
Mission Hills, CA 91345   Ph:(818)898-1391

Manual. Published 1988. **Editor(s):** Sheldon Abbott. **Price:** $21.60.

3710 • Bosch Fuel Injection and Engine Management
Robert Bentley, Inc., Publishers
1000 Massachusetts Ave.
Cambridge, MA 02138   Ph:(617)547-4170

Manual. **Editor(s):** Charles Probst. **Price:** $29.95.

3711 • Camshaft Identification Guide
Automotive Engine Rebuilders Association (AERA)
330 Lexington Dr.
Buffalo Grove, IL 60089-6998   Ph:(708)541-6550

Manual. Reference manual for identification and application of automotive engine camshafts by casting number. Annual. **Price:** Free to members; $14.00 for nonmembers.

3712 • Changing Gears: The Development of the Automotive Transmission
Society of Automotive Engineers, Inc.
400 Commonwealth Dr.
Warrendale, PA 15096-0001   Ph:(412)776-4841

Book. Published 1991. **Editor(s):** Philip G. Gott. **Price:** $49.00.

3713 • Chevrolet Small-Block V-8 Interchange Manual
Motorbooks International
729 Prospect Ave.
Osceola, WI 54020   Ph:(715)294-3345

Manual. Published 1989. **Editor(s):** David Lewis. **Price:** $17.95.

3714 • Chilton's Automatic Transmission Repair Manual, 1984-88: Motor-Age Professional Mechanics Edition
Chilton Co.
Chilton Way
Radnor, PA 19089   Ph:(215)964-4000

Manual. Published 1989. **Price:** $70.00.

3715 • Chilton's Automatic Transmission Repair Manual, 1984-1988: Import Cars and Trucks: Motor-Age Professional Mechanic's Edition
Chilton Co.
Chilton Way
Radnor, PA 19089   Ph:(215)964-4000

Manual. Published 1989. **Price:** $70.00.

3716 • Chilton's Automatic Transmission Service Manual 1984-88: Domestic Cars and Trucks: Motor-Age Professional Mechanic's Edition
Chilton Co.
Chilton Way
Radnor, PA 19089   Ph:(215)964-4000

Manual. Published 1989. **Price:** $70.00.

3717 • Chilton's Chassis Electronics and Power Accessories Service Manual, 1987-89: Motor-Age Professional Mechanic's Edition
Chilton Co.
Chilton Way
Radnor, PA 19089   Ph:(215)964-4000

Manual. Published 1988. **Price:** $77.00.

3718 • Chilton's Electronic Chassis Controls Manual, Import Cars and Trucks—1988-1990: Motor Age Professional Mechanic's Edition
Chilton Co.
Chilton Way
Radnor, PA 19089   Ph:(215)964-4000

Manual. Two volumes, A-M and N-Z. Published June 1991. **Price:** $72.00 per volume.

3719 • Chilton's Electronic Engine Controls Manual, 1988-90—Domestic Cars and Trucks: Motor-Age Professional Mechanic's Edition
Chilton Co.
Chilton Way
Radnor, PA 19089   Ph:(215)964-4000

Manual. Published 1989. **Price:** $72.00.

3720 • Chilton's Guide to Automatic Transmission Repair
Chilton Co.
Chilton Way
Radnor, PA 19089   Ph:(215)964-4000

Manual. Published 1985. **Price:** $19.95.

3721 • Chilton's Guide to Automatic Transmission Repair Manual, 1984-1989 Domestic Cars and Trucks
Chilton Co.
Chilton Way
Radnor, PA 19089   Ph:(215)964-4000

Manual. Published 1990. **Price:** $24.95.

3722 • Chilton's Guide to Chassis Electronics, 1987-89
Chilton Co.
Chilton Way
Radnor, PA 19089   Ph:(215)964-4000

Manual. Published 1988. **Price:** $19.95.

3723 • Chilton's Guide to Chassis Electronics 1989-91 (Asian Cars and Trucks)
Chilton Co.
Chilton Way
Radnor, PA 19089   Ph:(215)964-4000

Manual. Published 1991. **Price:** $19.95.

3724 • Chilton's Guide to Fuel Injection and Electronic Engine Controls 1984-1988: Import Cars and Trucks
Chilton Co.
Chilton Way
Radnor, PA 19089   Ph:(215)964-4000

Manual. Published 1988. **Price:** $19.95.

3725 • Connecting Rod Manual
Automotive Engine Rebuilders Association (AERA)
330 Lexington Dr.
Buffalo Grove, IL 60089-6998   Ph:(708)541-6550

Manual. Annual. **Price:** Free to members; $30.00 per copy to nonmembers.

3726 • Continuously Variable Transmissions for Passenger Cars
Society of Automotive Engineers, Inc.
400 Commonwealth Dr.
Warrenale, PA 15096   Ph:(412)776-4841

Manual. Published 1987. **Price:** $72.00.

3727 • Crankshaft Manual
Automotive Engine Rebuilders Association (AERA)
330 Lexington Dr.
Buffalo Grove, IL 60089-6998   Ph:(708)541-6550

Manual. Identifies automotive engine crankshafts by casting/forging number. Includes cross-references of casting/forging number to application, size of engine, years used, and bore and stroke of engine. Annual. **Price:** Free to members; $60.00 per copy to nonmembers.

3728 • Cylinder Head and Block Identification Guide
Automotive Engine Rebuilders Association (AERA)
330 Lexington Dr.
Buffalo Grove, IL 60089-6998   Ph:(708)541-6550

Manual. Identifies automotive engine cylinder heads and blocks by casting number. Includes cross-reference of casting numbers by application, size of engine, years used, and other special identifying features. Annual. **Price:** Free to members; $20.00 per copy for nonmembers.

3729 • Cylinder Head and Block Identification Guide
Automotive Engine Rebuilders Assn.
330 Lexington Dr.   Ph:(708)541-6550
Buffalo Grove, IL 60089-6998   Fax:(708)541-5808

Directory. Reference manual for identification of automotive engine cylinder heads and blocks. Annual. **Editor(s):** Joe Polich. **Price:** $25.00.

3730 • Deposit Formation in Gasoline Fuel Injected Engines
Society of Automotive Engineers
729 Prospect Ave.
Osceda, WI 54020   Ph:(715)294-3345

Book. Published 1987. **Price:** $27.00.

3731 • Design Practices Passenger Car Automatic Transmission
Society of Automotive Engineers, Inc.
400 Commonwealth Dr.
Warrendale, PA 15096   Ph:(412)776-4841

Book. Published 1988. **Price:** $79.00.

3732 • Developments in Electronic Engine Management and Driveline Controls
Society of Automotive Engineers, Inc.
400 Commonwealth Dr.
Warrendale, PA 15096   Ph:(412)776-4841

Book. Published 1985. **Price:** $44.00.

3733 • Drive Components
TPC Training Systems
310 S. Michigan Ave.
Chicago, IL 60604   Ph:(312)537-6610

Audio-visual. A program about how to recognize and fix various engine parts. **Release date:** 1988. **Producer:** TPC Training Systems. **Acquisition:** Purchase, Rent/Lease.

3734 • Electric Motors, Principles Controls, Service and Maintenance
Hobar Publications
1234 Tiller Ln.
Saint Paul, MN 55112   Ph:(612)633-3170
Manual. Published 1990. **Editor(s):** W. Forrest Bear. **Price:** $13.00, paper.

3735 • Engine Performance and Tune-Up
RMI Media Productions, Inc.
2807 W. 47th St.   Ph:(913)262-3974
Shawnee Mission, KS 66205   Fax:(913)362-6910
Audio-visual. This video covers the following topics: basic ignition theory, service procedures, trouble-shooting techniques, replacement of component parts, and electronics, including computer controls. **Release date:** 1988. **Producer:** RMI Media Productions, Inc. **Acquisition:** Purchase.

3736 • Engines, Fuels, and Lubricants: Perspectives on the Future
Society of Automotive Engineers, Inc.
400 Commonwealth Dr.
Warrendale, PA 15096   Ph:(412)776-4841
Book. A series of eight papers. Published 1980. **Price:** $32.00.

3737 • Engines, Lubricating and, Coding Systems
H. M. Gousha
2001 The Alameda
San Jose, CA 95126   Ph:(408)296-1060
Manual. Published 1981. **Editor(s):** Bob Leigh. **Price:** $9.95, paper; $13.90, cassette tape.

3738 • Foreign Car Engine Overhaul
Bergwall Productions, Inc.
P.O. Box 238
Garden City, NY 11530   Ph:800-645-3565
Manual. Published 1982. **Price:** $6.00, workbook; $139.00, audio visual package.

3739 • Front Wheel Drive Explained
Bergwall Productions, Inc.
106 Charles Lindbergh Blvd.
Uniondale, NY 11553-3695   Ph:(516)222-1111
Audio-visual. On three tapes, the basics of front wheel drive are discussed. **Release date:** 1983. **Producer:** Bergwall Productions, Inc. **Acquisition:** Purchase.

3740 • Front Wheel Drive: Transaxle Overhaul
Bergwall Productions, Inc.
106 Charles Lindbergh Blvd.
Uniondale, NY 11553-3695   Ph:(516)222-1111
Audio-visual. On five tapes, the ins and outs of overhauling a front wheel drive transaxle are demonstrated. **Release date:** 1984. **Producer:** Bergwall Productions, Inc. **Acquisition:** Purchase.

3741 • Fuel Alternatives for S.I. and Diesel Engines
Society of Automotive Engineers, Inc.
400 Commonwealth Dr.
Warrendale, PA 15096   Ph:(412)776-4841
Book. Published 1983. **Price:** $40.00.

3742 • Fuel Economy in Road Vehicles Powered by Spark Ignition Engines
Plenum Publishing Co.
233 Spring St.
New York, NY 10013   Ph:(212)620-8000
Manual. Published 1984. **Editor(s):** J.C. Hilliard. **Price:** $89.50.

3743 • Haynes Small Engine Repair Owners Workshop Manual
Haynes Publications, Inc.
861 Lawrence Dr.
Newbury Park, CA 91320   Ph:(818)889-5400
Manual. Published 1990. **Price:** $15.95.

3744 • High-Temperature, High-Shear (HTHS) Oil Viscosity: Measurement and Relationship to Engine Operation
American Society for Testing and Materials
1916 Race St.
Philadelphia, PA 19103   Ph:(215)299-5585
Book. Published 1989. **Editor(s):** James A. Spearot. **Price:** $25.00.

3745 • Horning Commemorative Volume: Award Winning Papers on Mutual Adaption of Fuels and IC Engines
Society of Automotive Engineers, Inc.
400 Commonwealth Dr.
Warrendale, PA 15096   Ph:(412)776-4841
Report/bulletin. **Price:** $60.00.

3746 • How to Do a Major Engine Tune Up
Bergwall Productions, Inc.
106 Charles Lindbergh Blvd.
Uniondale, NY 11553-3695   Ph:(516)222-1111
Audio-visual. On three tapes, a major engine tune-up is demonstrated. **Release date:** 1986. **Producer:** Bergwall Productions, Inc. **Acquisition:** Purchase.

3747 • How to Overhaul an Engine
Bergwall Productions, Inc.
106 Charles Lindbergh Blvd.
Uniondale, NY 11553-3695   Ph:(516)222-1111
Audio-visual. On six tapes, a complete overhaul made simple is shown. **Release date:** 1985. **Producer:** Bergwall Productions, Inc. **Acquisition:** Purchase.

3748 • How to Rebuild Small Block Chevys
Price Stern Sloan, Inc.
360 N. La Cienega Blvd.
Los Angeles, CA 90048   Ph:(213)657-6100
Manual. Published 1978. **Editor(s):** David Vizard. **Price:** $12.95.

3749 • How to Rebuild Your Big-Block Chevy
Price Stern Sloan, Inc.
360 N. La Cienega Blvd.
Los Angeles, CA 90048   Ph:(213)657-6100
Manual. Published 1983. **Editor(s):** Tom Wilson. **Price:** $12.95.

3750 • How to Use a Valve and Valve Seat Refacer
Bergwall Productions, Inc.
106 Charles Lindbergh Blvd.
Uniondale, NY 11553-3695   Ph:(516)222-1111
Audio-visual. On three tapes, valve and valve seat refacers are demonstrated. **Release date:** 1985. **Producer:** Bergwall Productions, Inc. **Acquisition:** Purchase.

3751 • The Internal Combustion Engine
Bergwall Productions, Inc.
106 Charles Lindbergh Blvd.
Uniondale, NY 11553-3695   Ph:(516)222-1111
Audio-visual. On five tapes, an internal combustion engine is studied in detail. **Release date:** 1984. **Producer:** Bergwall Productions, Inc. **Acquisition:** Purchase.

3752 • Lean Burn Engines
Cambridge University Press
40 W. 20th St.   Ph:(212)924-3900
New York, NY 10011   Fax:(212)691-3239
Book. Published 1991. **Editor(s):** Nick Collings and J. P. Pirault.

3753 • The Limited-Slip Differential: Pinion Operations and Service
Bergwall Productions, Inc.
106 Charles Lindbergh Blvd.
Uniondale, NY 11553-3695   Ph:(516)222-1111

Audio-visual. The entitled system is examined in great detail for mechanics. **Release date:** 1982. **Producer:** Bergwall Productions, Inc. **Acquisition:** Purchase.

3754 • Mechanical Maintenance Training
Tel-A-Train
309 N. Market St.
P.O. Box 4752   Ph:(615)266-0113
Chattanooga, TN 37405   Fax:(615)267-2555

Audio-visual. After watching this series just about any viewer should be able to fix engines. **Release date:** 1989. **Producer:** Tel-A-Trail. **Acquisition:** Purchase, Rent/Lease.

3755 • Mechanical Power Transmission
Bergwall Productions, Inc.
106 Charles Lindbergh Blvd.
Uniondale, NY 11553-3695   Ph:(516)222-1111

Audio-visual. On three tapes, the viewer learns how to work on and fix a mechanical power transmission. **Release date:** 1985. **Producer:** Bergwall Productions, Inc. **Acquisition:** Purchase.

3756 • Motor Auto Engines and Electrical Systems
Delmar Publishers, Inc.
P. O. Box 15015
2 Computer Drive
Albany, NY 12212   Ph:(518)459-1150

Manual. **Price:** $28.00.

3757 • New Developments in Electronic Engine Management
Society of Automotive Engineers, Inc.
400 Commonwealth Dr.
Warrendale, PA 15096   Ph:(412)776-4841

Book. Published 1984. **Price:** $56.00.

3758 • New Diesel Engines, Combustion and Emissions Research in Japan
Society of Automotive Engineers, Inc.
400 Commonwealth Dr.
Warrendale, PA 15096   Ph:(412)776-4841

Book. Published 1980. **Price:** $51.00.

3759 • New Engine and Advanced Component Design
Society of Automotive Engineers, Inc.
400 Commonwealth Dr.
Warrendale, PA 15096   Ph:(412)776-4841

Book. **Price:** $54.00.

3760 • Performance Tuning in Theory and Practice-Four Strokes
Haynes Publications, Inc.
861 Lawrence Dr.
Newbury Park, CA 91320   Ph:(818)889-5400

Manual. **Editor(s):** Graham A. Bell. **Price:** $19.95.

3761 • Performance Tuning in Theory and Practice-Two Strokes
Haynes Publications, Inc.
861 Lawrence Dr.
Newbury Park, CA 91320   Ph:(818)889-5400

Manual. **Price:** $19.95.

3762 • Power Transmission Design
Penton Publishing
1100 Superior Ave.   Ph:(216)696-7000
Cleveland, OH 44114-2543   Fax:(216)696-7648

Magazine. Aimed at people who design, apply, and maintain motors, drives, bearings, controls, and power transmission accessories. Monthly. **Editor(s):** Phil Kingsley. **Price:** $40.00/year; $5.00 per single issue.

3763 • Problems of Hydramatic Transmission
Bergwall Productions, Inc.
106 Charles Lindbergh Blvd.
Uniondale, NY 11553-3695   Ph:(516)222-1111

Audio-visual. On two tapes, hydramatic transmission problems are studied in detail. **Release date:** 1983. **Producer:** Bergwall Productions, Inc. **Acquisition:** Purchase.

3764 • Problems of Internal Combustion Engine
Bergwall Productions, Inc.
106 Charles Lindbergh Blvd.
Uniondale, NY 11553-3695   Ph:(516)222-1111

Audio-visual. On four tapes, an internal combustion engine's dilemmas are described and repaired. **Release date:** 1985. **Producer:** Bergwall Productions, Inc. **Acquisition:** Purchase.

3765 • Recent Developments in Electronic Engine Control and Fuel Injection Management
Society of Automotive Engineers, Inc.
400 Commonwealth Dr.
Warrendale, PA 15096   Ph:(412)776-4841

Book. Published 1987. **Price:** $44.00.

3766 • Small Engines
Bergwall Productions, Inc.
106 Charles Lindbergh Blvd.
Uniondale, NY 11553-3695   Ph:(516)222-1111

Audio-visual. Small engine construction and repair are explained for the benefit of auto mechanics. Also available as one tape at the same cost. **Release date:** 1989. **Producer:** Bergwall Productions, Inc. **Price:** $399.00.

3767 • Vehicle Maintenance
RMI Media Productions, Inc.
2807 W. 47th St.   Ph:(913)262-3974
Shawnee Mission, KS 66205   Fax:(913)362-6910

Audio-visual. Another series on the subject of fixing car engines is offered. **Release date:** 1989. **Producer:** RMI Media Productions, Inc. **Acquisition:** Purchase.

3768 • Ward's Engine Update
Ward's Communications, Inc.
28 W. Adams St.   Ph:(313)962-4433
Detroit, MI 48226   Fax:(313)962-4456

Report/bulletin. Reports on and monitors all engine and transmission technological developments relating to cars and trucks worldwide. Also discusses marketing and business strategies. Irregular. **Editor(s):** David C. Smith. **Price:** $550.00/year.

3769 • What's Under Your Hood?
AIMS Media, Inc.
6901 Woodley Ave.
Van Nuys, CA 91406-4878   Ph:(818)785-4111

Audio-visual. Shows how an automobile engine works. **Release date:** 1973. **Producer:** AIMS Media, Inc. **Acquisition:** Purchase, Duplication License.

3770 • Worldwide Trends in Engine Coolants, Cooling System Materials and Testing
Society of Automotive Engineers, Inc.
400 Commonwealth Dr.
Warrendale, PA 15096   Ph:(412)776-4841

Book. **Price:** $54.00.

Four-wheel drive

3771 • 4WD Action
McMullen Publishing
2145 N. La Palma
Anaheim, CA 92801-1785   Ph:(714)635-9040

Magazine. For off-road enthusiasts. Monthly. **Editor(s):** Bob Clark.
Price: $12.00 per year; $2.50 per issue.

3772 • All Wheel Drive High Performance Handbook
Motorbooks International
729 Prospect Ave.
Osceda, WI 54020   Ph:(715)294-3345

Manual. Published 1990. **Editor(s):** Jay Lamma. **Price:** $16.95.

3773 • Four Wheel and Off Road
Petersen Publishing Co.
6725 Sunset Blvd.
Los Angeles, CA 90028   Ph:(213)854-2222

Magazine. Provides information on two- and four-wheel drive
vehicles. Monthly. **Editor(s):** Steve Campbell. **Price:** $19.94 per
year; $2.95 per issue.

3774 • Four Wheeler Magazine
Penthouse Intl.
6728 Eton Ave.   Ph:(818)992-4777
Canoga Park, CA 91303   Fax:(818)992-4979

Magazine. Contains articles about four-wheel-drive vehicles.
Monthly. **Editor(s):** John Stewart. **Price:** $14.87.

3775 • Four Wheeler Specials
Penthouse Intl.
6728 Eton Ave.
P.O. Box 7116
Canoga Park, CA 91304   Ph:(212)496-6100

Magazine. Seven times per year. **Price:** $2.95.

3776 • Mid-Western 4-Wheeler
Midwest 4-Wheel Drive Association
1517 Sunset Ln.
New Holstein, WI 53061   Ph:(414)898-4598

Newsletter. Covers events and issues of interest to four-wheel
drive vehicle owners. Eight times/year. **Editor(s):** Linda Welch.
Price: $8.00/year.

3777 • National 4 Wheel Drive Association—Bulletin
National 4 Wheel Drive Association
3310 E. Shangrila Rd.
Phoenix, AZ 85028   Ph:(602)996-1124

Report/bulletin. Periodic.

3778 • National 4 Wheel Drive Association-News
National 4 Wheel Drive Association
3310 E. Shangrila
Phoenix, AZ 85028   Ph:(602)996-1124

Newsletter. Monthly.

3779 • National Four Wheel Drive Association News
National Four Wheel Drive Assn.
3310 E. Shangrila Rd.
Phoenix, AZ 85028   Ph:(602)996-1124

Newsletter.

3780 • Off-Road
Argus Publishers Corp.
12100 Wilshire Blvd., Ste. 250   Ph:(213)820-3601
Los Angeles, CA 90025   Fax:(213)207-9388

Magazine. Focuses on the sport of off-roading. Features four-
wheel drive vehicles, pick-ups, vans, and trail bikes. Includes trip
information, race reports, photos, technical tips, equipment and
accessories, and road tests. Monthly. **Editor(s):** Duanne Elliott.
Price: $15.00/year; $2.50 per single issue.

3781 • Off-Road Advertiser
Two Trees Publishing, Inc.
P.O. Box 1154
Arcata, CA 95521-1154   Ph:(213)860-7007

Magazine. Covers four-wheel drives, dune buggies, pickup trucks,
and sport utility vehicles. Contains articles on trail runs, jamborees,
and major off-road races. Monthly. **Editor(s):** Fred C. Horton. **Price:**
$15.00/year; $1.50 per single issue.

3782 • Off Road America
Intra-South Publications
4487 Ashton, Ste. A
Sarasota, FL 34233   Ph:(813)921-5687

Magazine. Covers four-wheel-drive and offroad racing activities
nationwide. Monthly. **Editor(s):** Patricia A. Sands, Editor. **Price:**
$18.00/year; $2.00 per single issue.

3783 • Petersen's 4 Wheel & Off Road
Petersen Publishing Co.
7750 Sunset Blvd.   Ph:(213)854-2360
Los Angeles, CA 90046   Fax:(213)854-2865

Magazine. Monthly. **Editor(s):** Steve Campbell. **Price:** $17.94/year;
$2.75 per single issue.

Fuel systems

3784 • Advanced Gas Turbine Systems for Automobiles
Society of Automotive Engineers, Inc.
400 Commonwealth
Warrendale, PA 15096   Ph:(412)776-4841

Book. Totaling seven papers. Published 1980. **Price:** $38.00.

3785 • Auto Fuel Systems
Goodheart—Wilcox Co.
123 W. Taft Dr.
South Holland, IL 60473   Ph:(301)333-7200

Book. Published 1987. **Editor(s):** James E. Duffy and Howard
Smith. **Price:** $26.00.

3786 • Automotive Engine Electronics
Accuracy Publishing Co.
P.O. Box 514
Homestead, FL 33090   Ph:(305)245-2187

Manual. Guide to automotive computer control and fuel injection
systems operation. Published 1990. **Editor(s):** Robert C. McElroy.
Price: $13.95.

3787 • Automotive Fuel and Ignition Systems
Books on Demand
University Microfilms International
300 N. Zeeb Rd.
Ann Arbor, MI 48106   Ph:(313)761-4700

Manual. Published 1987. **Editor(s):** William Landon and Irving A.
Frazee. **Price:** $128.00.

**3788 • Automotive Fuel, Cooling, Lubrication, and
Exhaust Systems**
Prentice-Hall
Rte. 9W
Englewood Cliffs, NJ 07632   Ph:(201)592-2000

Manual. Published 1985. **Editor(s):** William Husselbee. **Price:**
$34.00.

**3789 • Automotive Fuel, Lubricating and Cooling
Systems**
McGraw-Hill Publishing Co.
11 W. 19th St.
New York, NY 10011   Ph:(212)337-6010

Manual. Published 1981. **Editor(s):** William H. Crouse and Donald
L. Anglin. **Price:** $29.95.

3790 • **Automotive Quick Test**
L & K International Video Training
295 Evans Ave.
Toronto, ON M8Z 5P9   Ph:(416)252-6407

Audio-visual. Mechanics are taught how to quickly and efficiently check out a car. Titles include: Common Problems on Systems and Components; Electronic Ignition Systems; Emissions Controls; Brake Systems; FWD Axles Steering and Suspension; Air Conditioning; Carburetor and Fuel Injection Systems; Computerized Engine Controls. **Release date:** 1988. **Producer:** Leighton and Kidd. **Acquisition:** Purchase, Rent/Lease.

3791 • **Bosch Electronic Fuel Injection Systems**
Motorbooks International
729 Prospect Avenue
Osceda, WI 54020   Ph:(715)294-3345

Manual. Published 1986. **Price:** $14.95.

3792 • **Bosch Fuel Injection and Engine Management**
Robert Bentley, Inc., Publishers
1000 Massachusetts Ave.
Cambridge, MA 02138   Ph:(617)547-4170

Manual. **Editor(s):** Charles Probst. **Price:** $29.95.

3793 • **Chilton's Guide to Fuel Injection and Electronic Engine Controls 1984-1988: Import Cars and Trucks**
Chilton Co.
Chilton Way
Radnor, PA 19089   Ph:(215)964-4000

Manual. Published 1988. **Price:** $19.95.

3794 • **Chilton's Guide to Fuel Injection and Electronic Engine Controls, 1988-90**
Chilton Co.
Chilton Way
Radnor, PA 19089   Ph:(215)964-4000

Manual. In two volumes. Published 1989. **Price:** $19.95 per volume.

3795 • **Deposit Formation in Gasoline Fuel Injected Engines**
Society of Automotive Engineers
729 Prospect Ave.
Osceda, WI 54020   Ph:(715)294-3345

Book. Published 1987. **Price:** $27.00.

3796 • **Developments in Diesel Particulate Control Systems**
Society of Automotive Engineers
400 Commonwealth Dr.
Warrendale, PA 15096   Ph:(412)776-4841

Book. Published 1989. **Price:** $56.00.

3797 • **Domestic Electronic Fuel Injection and Computer Systems**
Prentice-Hall
Rte. 9W
Englewood Cliffs, NJ 07632   Ph:(201)592-2000

Manual. Published 1988. **Editor(s):** Frederick Allen. **Price:** $38.00.

3798 • **Electronic Fuel Injection**
Bergwall Productions, Inc.
106 Charles Lindbergh Blvd.
Uniondale, NY 11553-3695   Ph:(516)222-1111

Audio-visual. On two tapes, how fuel injection works is explained. **Release date:** 1986. **Producer:** Bergwall Productions, Inc. **Acquisition:** Purchase.

3799 • **Engines, Fuels, and Lubricants: Perspectives on the Future**
Society of Automotive Engineers, Inc.
400 Commonwealth Dr.
Warrendale, PA 15096   Ph:(412)776-4841

Book. A series of eight papers. Published 1980. **Price:** $32.00.

3800 • **Fuel and Induction System Deposits**
Society of Automotive Engineers, Inc.
400 Commonwealth Dr.
Warrendale, PA 15096   Ph:(412)776-4841

Book. Published 1989. **Price:** $34.00.

3801 • **Fuel Systems and Emission Controls**
H. M. Gousha
10 E. 53rd St.
New York, NY 10022   Ph:(212)207-7000

Manual. Published 1988. **Price:** $40.50.

3802 • **Gas Savers Guide**
NAL/Dutton
1633 Broadway
New York, NY 10019   Ph:(212)397-8000

Report/bulletin. Published 1991. **Price:** $2.95.

3803 • **How to Overhaul a Carburetor**
Bergwall Productions, Inc.
106 Charles Lindbergh Blvd.
Uniondale, NY 11553   Ph:(516)222-1111

Audio-visual. On three tapes, a carburetor overhaul is performed. **Release date:** 1985. **Producer:** Bergwall Productions, Inc. **Acquisition:** Purchase.

3804 • **How to Restore Fuel Systems and Carburetion**
Motorbooks International
729 Prospect Ave.
Osceda, WI 54020   Ph:(715)294-3345

Manual. Published 1988. **Editor(s):** I. Penberthy. **Price:** $19.95.

3805 • **Mitchell's Electronic Fuel-Injection Troubleshooting Guide: Domestic Vehicles**
Fisher Books
P.O. Box 445
Vienna, VA 22183   Ph:(703)448-0420

Manual. Published 1990. **Price:** $29.95.

3806 • **Mitchell's Electronic Fuel-Injection Troubleshooting Guide: Import Vehicles**
Fisher Books
P.O. Box 38040
Tuscon, AZ 85740-8040   Ph:(602)292-9080

Manual. Published 1990. **Price:** $29.95.

3807 • **Motor Vehicle Fuel Economy**
Scholium International
99 Seaview Blvd.
Port Washington, NY 11050   Ph:(516)484-3290

Book. Published 1989. **Editor(s):** Richard Stone. **Price:** $29.50.

3808 • **The Operation of the Fuel System**
Bergwall Productions, Inc.
106 Charles Lindbergh Blvd.
Uniondale, NY 11553-3695   Ph:(516)222-1111

Audio-visual. On six tapes, a car's fuel system is revealed in all of its functioning detail. **Release date:** 1974. **Producer:** Bergwall Productions, Inc. **Acquisition:** Purchase.

3809 • **Port Fuel Injection**
Bergwall Productions, Inc.
106 Charles Lindbergh Blvd.
Uniondale, NY 11553-3695   Ph:(516)222-1111

Audio-visual. Port fuel injection in automobiles is examined, both in theory and practice. This series is also available on a single tape for the same cost. **Release date:** 1988. **Producer:** Bergwall Productions, Inc. **Price:** $239.00.

3810 • Practical Gas Flow: Techniques for Low-Budget Performance Tuning
Motorbooks International
729 Prospect Ave.
Osceda, WI 54020   Ph:(715)294-3345

Manual. Published 1981. **Editor(s):** John Dalton. **Price:** $19.95.

3811 • Present and Future Automotive Fuels: Performance and Exhaust Clarification
John Wiley and Sons, Inc.
605 Third Ave.
New York, NY 10158   Ph:(212)850-6000

Book. Published 1988. **Editor(s):** Richard K. Pefley and Osamu Hirso. **Price:** $82.50.

3812 • The Problems of the Fuel System
Bergwall Productions, Inc.
106 Charles Lindbergh Blvd.
Uniondale, NY 11553-3695   Ph:(516)222-1111

Audio-visual. Many and varied fuel system problems are examined and fixed. Titles: Fuel Tank, Lines and Gauge; Fuel Pump, Filter and Vapor Lock; Carburetor Assembly-Part One; Carburetor Assembly-Part Two; Carburetor Assembly and Air Cleaner; and Manifolds and Combustion Problems. **Release date:** 1985. **Producer:** Bergwall Productions, Inc. **Price:** $269.00.

3813 • Recent Developments in Electronic Engine Control and Fuel Injection Management
Society of Automotive Engineers, Inc.
400 Commonwealth Dr.
Warrendale, PA 15096   Ph:(412)776-4841

Book. Published 1987. **Price:** $44.00.

3814 • Troubleshooting Port Fuel Injection
Bergwall Productions, Inc.
106 Charles Lindbergh Blvd.
Uniondale, NY 11553-3695   Ph:(516)222-1111

Audio-visual. The mechanics of finding breakdowns in a port fuel injection system are discussed. The series is also available as one tape, at the same cost. **Release date:** 1988. **Producer:** Bergwall Productions, Inc. **Price:** $399.00.

3815 • Tune-up Ignition and Fuel Induction Systems
H. M. Gousha
2001 The Alameda
San Jose, CA 95126   Ph:(408)296-1060

Manual. Published 1981. **Editor(s):** Bob Leigh. **Price:** $9.95, workbook; $13.90, cassette.

Fuels

3816 • Alternate Fuels for S.I. Engines
Society of Automotive Engineers, Inc.
400 Commonwealth Dr.
Warrendale, PA 92101   Ph:(412)776-4841

Book. Published 1983. **Price:** $45.00.

3817 • Automobile Fuel Economy
Autotronic Conversions
P.O. Box 17249
El Paso, TX 79917

Book. **Price:** $9.50.

3818 • Automotive Fuel, Lubrication, and Cooling Systems
Prentice-Hall
Rte. 9W
Englewood Cliffs, NJ 07632   Ph:(201)592-2000

Manual. Published 1985. **Editor(s):** Don Knowles. **Price:** $40.00, hardcover; $38.00, paper.

3819 • Developments in Diesel Particulate Control Systems
Society of Automotive Engineers
400 Commonwealth Dr.
Warrendale, PA 15096   Ph:(412)776-4841

Book. Published 1989. **Price:** $56.00.

3820 • Diesel Magazine
McBain Publications, Inc.
47 Ontario St. S.
Kitchener, ON N2G 1X3   Ph:(519)744-4404

Magazine. Covers performance tests, new diesel cars and light trucks; describes new products and research in alternative fuels. Bimonthly. **Editor(s):** John A. McBain.

3821 • Energy Demand Analysis and Alternative Fuels
Transportation Research Board
2101 Constitution Ave.
Washington, DC 20418   Ph:(202)334-3218

Book. Published 1986. **Price:** $7.60.

3822 • Fuel Alternatives for S.I. and Diesel Engines
Society of Automotive Engineers, Inc.
400 Commonwealth Dr.
Warrendale, PA 15096   Ph:(412)776-4841

Book. Published 1983. **Price:** $40.00.

3823 • Fuel Methanol
Society of Automotive Engineers, Inc.
400 Commonwealth Dr.
Warrendale, PA 15096   Ph:(412)776-4841

Book. **Price:** $68.00.

3824 • Gaseous Fuels: Technology, Performance, and Emissions
Society of Automotive Engineers, Inc.
400 Commonwealth Dr.
Warrendale, PA 15096   Ph:(412)776-4841

Book. Published 1989. **Price:** $50.00.

3825 • Horning Commemorative Volume: Award Winning Papers on Mutual Adaption of Fuels and IC Engines
Society of Automotive Engineers, Inc.
400 Commonwealth Dr.
Warrendale, PA 15096   Ph:(412)776-4841

Report/bulletin. **Price:** $60.00.

3826 • How to Convert Your Vehicle to Propane
Mother Earth News
105 Stoney Mountain Rd.
Hendersonville, NC 28791   Ph:(704)693-0211

Manual. Published 1981. **Editor(s):** Robert Hoffman. **Price:** $7.50.

3827 • Methanol: Promise and Problems
Society of Automotive Engineers
400 Commonwealth Dr.
Warrendale, PA 15096   Ph:(412)776-4841

Manual. published 1987. **Price:** $56.00.

3828 • Modern Fuel for Modern Diesel Engines
Farmland Industries, Inc.
3315 N. Oak Trafficway
Kansas City, MO 64116

Audio-visual. After viewing this video anatomy of a diesel engine, one can better select its fuel. **Release date:** 1985. **Producer:** Farmland Industries, Inc. **Acquisition:** Purchase.

3829 • Petroleum Products, Lubricants, and Fossil Fuels
American Society for Testing and Materials
1916 Race St.
Philadelphia, PA 19103   Ph:(215)299-5585

Book. Published 1986. **Price:** $34.00.

3830 • Present and Future Automotive Fuels: Performance and Exhaust Clarification
John Wiley and Sons, Inc.
605 Third Ave.
New York, NY 10158   Ph:(212)850-6000

Book. Published 1988. **Editor(s):** Richard K. Pefley and Osamu Hirso. **Price:** $82.50.

3831 • Transportation Fuel Alternative for North America into the 21st Century
Society of Automotive Engineers, Inc.
400 Commonwealth Dr.
Warrendale, PA 15096   Ph:(412)776-4841

Book. Published 1987. **Price:** $23.00.

General automotive

3832 • AAA Auto Club of Southern Pennsylvania— AAA Traveler
AAA Auto Club of Southern Pennsylvania
118 E. Market St.
PO Box 2387   Ph:(717)845-7676
York, PA 17405-2387   Fax:(717)845-5444

Magazine. Travel and motoring magazine for auto club membership. Quarterly. **Editor(s):** Kevin A. Forsythe.

3833 • AAA Cincinnati—AAA Today [Ohio]
AAA Cincinnati
15 W. Central Pkwy.   Ph:(513)762-3330
Cincinnati, OH 45202   Fax:(513)762-8741

Magazine. Auto club and travel magazine. Bimonthly. **Editor(s):** Mark Brackney.

3834 • AAA Today Magazine
AAA Automobile Club Publications
1380 Dublin Rd., Ste. 109
Columbus, OH 43215-1025   Ph:(614)481-8088

Magazine. Contains travel news and automotive information for members of American Automobile Association. Bimonthly. **Editor(s):** Johanna Guzik. **Price:** Available to members only.

3835 • AAA Washington Motor Club—Motorist [Washington state]
AAA Washington Motor Club
330 6th Ave. N.   Ph:(206)448-5353
Seattle, WA 98109   Fax:(206)448-8627

Newspaper. Coverage includes articles of interest to auto club members. Monthly. **Editor(s):** Janet E. Ray. **Price:** $3.00.

3836 • American Automobile Association—AAA World
American Automobile Association
8030 Excelsior Dr.   Ph:(608)257-0711
Madison, WI 53717   Fax:(608)257-1095

Magazine. Published for American Automobile Association membership. Bimonthly. **Editor(s):** Ernest Stetenfeld. **Price:** $4.00.

3837 • Auto and Truck News
BeAnCa Publishing
4346 SE Div.
Portland, OR 97206-1630   Ph:(503)238-1188

Magazine. Bimonthly. **Editor(s):** John Jangula. **Price:** $550.00.

3838 • Auto Club of Southern Pennsylvania—Motorist
Auto Club of Southern Pennsylvania
118 East Market St.
P.O. Box 2387
York, PA 17405

Newsletter. Monthly. **Editor(s):** Thomas W. Carr, Jr. **Price:** Free.

3839 • The Auto Index
7 Clinton Pl.
Suffern, NY 10901   Ph:(914)357-3695

Magazine. Provides a general purpose index to 14 automotive periodicals for consumers, do-it-yourself individuals, and researchers. Bimonthly. **Editor(s):** David F. Plump. **Price:** $5.00.

3840 • Auto Tiempo
Puerto Rico Almanacs, Inc.
P.O. Box 9582
Santurce, PR 00908   Ph:(809)725-3155

Magazine. Spanish-language automotive magazine covering automotive industry news, vehicle reviews, auto racing information, and maintenance tips. Monthly. **Editor(s):** Arturo Medina, Publisher. **Price:** $15.00 per year; $1.50 per issue.

3841 • Automobile Magazine
Murdoch Magazines
120 E. Liberty   Ph:(313)994-3500
Ann Arbor, MI 48104   Fax:(313)994-1153

Magazine. Monthly. **Editor(s):** David E. Davis, Jr. **Price:** $24.00.

3842 • Automobile Quarterly
Kutztown Publishing Co.
P. O. Box 346
Kutztown, PA 19530   Ph:(609)924-7555

Magazine. Offers in-depth stories, automobile histories, and photos. Quarterly. **Editor(s):** Lowell Paddock. **Price:** $49.95 per year; $16.95 per issue.

3843 • Automobiler
Automobile Club of Hartford
815 Farmington Ave.
West Hartford, CT 06119   Ph:(203)236-3261

Newsletter. Irregular. **Editor(s):** Michael Klein. **Price:** $2.00.

3844 • Automotive Contact
P.O. Box 517
Terre Haute, IN 47808   Ph:(812)232-2441

Magazine. Monthly. **Editor(s):** Tom Spelman, Publisher.

3845 • Automotive Encyclopedia
Goodheart-Wilcox Co.
123 W. Taft Dr.
South Holland, IL 60473   Ph:(708)333-7200

Reference book. Published 1989. **Editor(s):** William K. Toboldt. **Price:** $33.20, text; $3.00, instructor's guide; $7.60, workbook.

3846 • The Automotive Messenger
Hansen Publishing, Inc.
431 Chez Paree   Ph:(314)831-4000
Hazelwood, MO 63042   Fax:(314)831-3610

Magazine. Monthly. **Editor(s):** B. Hank Hansen, Publisher. **Price:** $10.00.

3847 • Automotive News
Crain Communications, Inc.
1400 Woodbridge Ave.   Ph:(313)446-6000
Detroit, MI 48207   Fax:(313)446-1680

Magazine. Reports on all facets of the automotive and truck industry, as well as related businesses. Weekly. **Editor(s):** Peter Brown. **Price:** $70.00; $2.00 per single issue.

3848 • Automotive Reference: A New Approach to the World of Auto & Related Information
Whitehorse
4154 Ticonderoga Way
Boise, ID 83706   Ph:(208)336-8650

Reference book. Published 1987. **Price:** $39.95, hardbound; $24.95, paper.

3849 • Automotive Seals: An Update
Society of Automotive Engineers, Inc.
400 Commonwealth Dr.
Warrendale, PA 15096   Ph:(412)776-4841

Book. Published 1989. **Price:** $45.00.

3850 • Automundo Magazine
Kogan E.A. Corp.
3305 W. 27th Ave., Ste. 403
Miami, FL 33135   Ph:(305)541-4198

Magazine. Spanish-language magazine that offers information on common automobile needs and developments; annual special section editions feature interviews with industry personalities. Monthly. **Editor(s):** Enrique A. Kogan. **Price:** $18.00 per year; $1.50 per issue.

3851 • Autoweek
Crain Communications, Inc.
1400 Woodbridge Ave.
Detroit, MI 48207   Ph:(313)446-6000

Magazine. Magazine for car enthusiasts includes news coverage and features on vehicles, personalities, and events. Provides coverage of Formula One, CART, and NASCAR racing. Weekly. **Editor(s):** Matt DeLorenzo. **Price:** $28.00; $1.95 single issue.

3852 • Bluefield Automobile Club—AAA Today [West Virginia]
Bluefield Automobile Club (AAA)
Box 1780
Bluefield, WV 24701-6780   Ph:(304)327-8187

Magazine. Motoring magazine. Quarterly. **Editor(s):** William D. Hostetter. **Price:** $1.50; $6.00 nonmembers.

3853 • Break It In Right! How to Make Your New Car Last
Avon Books
105 Madison Ave.
New York, NY 10016   Ph:(212)481-5600

Book. Published 1988. **Editor(s):** Robert Sikorsky. **Price:** $3.95.

3854 • Buy a New Car for Less
Academy Home Entertainment
1 Pine Haven Shore Rd.
PO Box 788   Ph:(802)985-2060
Shelburne, VT 05482   Fax:(802)985-3403

Audio-visual. Host Paul Rosa offers advice on how to get the most car for the least money. **Producer:** Info-Vid. **Price:** $14.95.

3855 • Buying A Used Car
RMI Media Productions, Inc.
2807 W. 47th St.   Ph:(913)262-3974
Shawnee Mission, KS 66205   Fax:(913)362-6910

Audio-visual. A program designed to prepare teenagers and others interested in purchasing a used car and familiarizes viewer with a car's main systems: engine, brakes, steering, power train, cooling, electrical, and auto body condition, and provides tips on routine maintenance, insurance budgeting, licensing, taxes, and operation.

Release date: 1988. **Producer:** RMI Media Productions, Inc. **Acquisition:** Purchase.

3856 • Car and Driver
Hachette Publications, Inc.
2002 Hogback Rd.   Ph:(313)971-3600
Ann Arbor, MI 48105   Fax:(313)971-9188

Magazine. Provides news on automobiles, accessories, road tests, and international coverage of races and other sports car events. Monthly. **Editor(s):** William Jeanes. **Price:** $19.94 /year; $2.95 per single issue.

3857 • Car and Driver—Road Test Annual
Hachette Publications, Inc.
2002 Hogback Rd.   Ph:(313)971-3600
Ann Arbor, MI 48105   Fax:(313)971-9188

Magazine. Offers detailed analysis and current evaluation of popular automobiles. Annual. **Editor(s):** William Jeanes. **Price:** $4.95.

3858 • Car & Parts Magazine
911 Vandemark Rd.   Ph:(513)498-0803
Sidney, OH 45365   Fax:(513)498-0808

Magazine. Includes articles on collector cars, restoration, and automotive history; show and auction reports; Ford Country column; classified marketplace. Monthly. **Editor(s):** Robert Jay Stevens. **Price:** $20.00/year; $2.50 per single issue.

3859 • Car Beautiful: A Complete Guide to a Shiny, Well-Protected Car
Loki Publishing Co.
849 Gary Ave.
Sunnyvale, CA 94086   Ph:(408)245-4040

Book. Published 1987. **Editor(s):** Henry A. Watts. **Price:** $7.95.

3860 • The Car Buyer's Art: How to Beat the Salesman at His Own Game
Book Express
P.O. Box 1249
Bellflower, CA 90706   Ph:(213)867-3723

Book. Published 1989. **Price:** $4.95.

3861 • The Car Buyers Guide
Book Express
P.O. Box 1249
Bellflower, CA 90706   Ph:(213)867-3723

Audio-visual. A consumer guide, instructing the viewer in how to buy a car wisely and cheaply without being manipulated by car salesmen, demonstrated through actual scenarios. **Release date:** 1988. **Producer:** Rodgers Prod. **Acquisition:** Purchase.

3862 • Car Care Guide
H. M. Gousha
2001 The Alameda
San Jose, CA 95126   Ph:(408)296-1060

Book. Published 1990. **Editor(s):** Roger L. Fennema. **Price:** $39.75.

3863 • Car Care Quarterly
Car Care Council
One Grande Lake Dr.   Ph:(419)734-5343
Port Clinton, OH 43452   Fax:(419)732-3780

Newspaper. Quarterly.

3864 • Car Life
Bond Publishing Co.
1499 Monrovia Ave.
Newport Beach, CA 92663

Magazine. Conducts road tests, evaluations, and reviews of domestic vehicles. Monthly. **Price:** $5.00 per year; 50¢ per issue.

3865 • Car Owners
Publishing and Business Consultants
951 S. Oxford, Ste. 109
Los Angeles, CA 90006   Ph:(213)732-3477

Magazine. Covers personal car maintenance with information on trends. Quarterly. **Editor(s):** Atia Napoleon. **Price:** $23.99.

3866 • The Car Owner's Diary
Dell Publishing Co., Inc.
666 Fifth Ave.
New York, NY 10103   Ph:(212)765-6500

Book. Published 1988. **Editor(s):** Peter Jones. **Price:** $3.95.

3867 • The Car Owner's Survival Guide
Fawcett Book Group
3801 23rd Ave.
Astoria, NY 11105   Ph:(718)204-0900

Book. Published 1986. **Editor(s):** Robert Appel. **Price:** $5.95.

3868 • Car Ownership and Use
Organization for Economic Cooperation and
    Development
2001 L. St., N.W., Ste. 700
Washington, DC 20036   Ph:(202)785-6323

Manual. Published 1982. **Price:** $7.50.

3869 • Car Savvy
Edmund Publishers Corp.
515 Hempstead Tpke.   Ph:(516)292-0044
W. Hempstead, NY 11552   Fax:(516)538-6767

Magazine. Provides general information about automobiles, along with specific recommendations on car buying, selling, insuring, driving, and maintenance. Annual. **Editor(s):** M.E. Groher. **Price:** $4.95.

3870 • The Car Show
Consumer Reports/Films
256 Washington St.
Mount Vernon, NY 10550   Ph:(914)664-6400

Audio-visual. Practical tips to help you reduce the expense of owning a car. **Release date:** 1981. **Producer:** Consumers Union. **Acquisition:** Purchase.

3871 • The CARR Buying System
Cambridge Career Products
One Players Club Dr.
Charleston, WV 25311   Ph:(304)344-8550

Audio-visual. A former car salesman explains to people how to avoid getting stuck with a high priced lemon. Comes with an audio tape and a book. **Release date:** 1988. **Producer:** Cambridge Video. **Acquisition:** Purchase.

3872 • Cars and Comments
Automotive Information Council
29200 Southfield Rd., Ste. 111
Southfield, MI 48076   Ph:(313)559-5922

Newsletter. Provides consumer-oriented automotive news and tips. Weekly. **Price:** Free.

**3873 • Cars: How to Buy a New or Used Car and
    Keep It Running**
Lorimar Home Video
17942 Cowan Ave.
Irvine, CA 92714   Ph:(714)474-0355

Audio-visual. An instructional tape designed to make clear the best ways to buy cars and maintain them for maximum performance. **Release date:** 1986. **Producer:** Consumer Reports TV; Major H. Prod.; George Paige Assoc. **Acquisition:** Purchase.

3874 • Cars Illustrated
CSK Publishing Co., Inc.
299 Market St.   Ph:(201)712-9300
Saddle Brook, NJ 07662   Fax:(201)712-9899

Magazine. Bimonthly. **Editor(s):** Stephen Schneider, Publisher. **Price:** $9.99.

3875 • Cartoons
Petersen Publishing Co.
7750 Sunset Blvd.
Los Angeles, CA 90046   Ph:(213)854-2222

Magazine. Depicts various automotive themes through comical satire. Bimonthly. **Editor(s):** Don Evans, Editorial Director. **Price:** $19.00/year; $1.95 per single issue.

3876 • Consumer Education: Buying an Automobile
AIMS Media, Inc.
6901 Woodley Ave.
Van Nuys, CA 91406-4878   Ph:(818)785-4111

Audio-visual. Do's and don't's in buying a car. **Release date:** 1973. **Producer:** AIMS Media, Inc. **Acquisition:** Purchase, Duplication License.

3877 • Consumer Reports—Cars
Cambridge Career Products
One Players Club Dr.
Charleston, WV 25311   Ph:(304)344-8550

Audio-visual. Viewers are told how they can get the most for their money when buying a car. Tips on maintaining cars are also included. **Release date:** 1986. **Producer:** Cambridge Career Products. **Price:** $34.95.

3878 • Consumer Survival Kit: Cars
Maryland Center for Public Broadcasting
11767 Bonita Ave.
Owings Mills, MD 21117   Ph:(301)356-5600

Audio-visual. Designed to inform the automobile investor about buying cars and basic repair jobs. Programs available individually. **Producer:** Maryland Center for Public Broadcasting. **Acquisition:** Rent/Lease, Purchase.

**3879 • Corrosion Prediction and Prevention in the
    Motor Vehicle**
Prentice-Hall
Rte. 9W
Englewood Cliffs, NJ 07632   Ph:(201)592-2000

Manual. Published 1988. **Editor(s):** Hugh McArthur. **Price:** $81.95.

**3880 • Don't Get Taken Every Time: The Insider's
    Guide to Buying or Leasing Your Next Car or Truck**
Viking Penguin, Inc.
40 W. 23rd St.
New York, NY 10010   Ph:(212)337-5200

Buyers guide. Published 1991. **Editor(s):** Remar Sutton. **Price:** $7.95.

3881 • Driving Newsletter
AAA New Jersey Automotive Club
One Hanover Rd.
Florham Park, NJ 07932-1899   Ph:(201)377-7200

Newsletter. Five times per year. **Price:** $2.75 per year; .50¢ per issue.

3882 • Fluid Conductors and Connectors
Society of Automotive Engineers, Inc.
400 Commonwealth Dr.
Warrendale, PA 15096   Ph:(412)776-4841

Book. **Price:** $36.00.

3883 • Getting a Better Buy in a Used Car
AIMS Media, Inc.
6901 Woodley Ave.
Van Nuys, CA 91406-4878   Ph:(818)785-4111

Audio-visual. A look at how to shop for a used car, including a checklist of important items, road testing, body and chassis test, and a mechanical check of a car. **Acquisition:** Purchase, Duplication License.

3884 • Glossary of Automotive Terms
Society of Automotive Engineers, Inc.
400 Commonwealth Dr.
Warrendale, PA 15096   Ph:(412)776-4841

Reference book. Published 1988. **Price:** $64.00.

3885 • The Glossary of Automotive Terms
Hall Automotive Services Co., Inc.
26072 Terra Bella
Laguna Hills, CA 92653   Ph:(714)643-3148

Report/bulletin. Published 1991. **Editor(s):** Richard H. Hall. **Price:** $49.95.

3886 • The Hartford Automobiler
AAA Automobile Club of Hartford
815 Farmington Ave.
West Hartford, CT 06119   Ph:(203)236-3261

Magazine. Bimonthly. **Editor(s):** Michael Klein. **Price:** $2.00.

3887 • Home & Away
P.O. Box 3535   Ph:(402)390-1000
Omaha, NE 68103   Fax:(402)390-0539

Magazine. Provides travel and recreation information to American Automobile Association members in the Midwest. Bimonthly. **Editor(s):** Barc Wade, Editor and Publisher. **Price:** Free to qualified subscribers; $3.00 for nonmembers. $1.00 per single issue.

3888 • Home & Away (Chicago Edition) [Illinois]
AAA Chicago Motor Club
999 E. Touhy Ave.   Ph:(708)390-9000
Des Plaines, IL 60018   Fax:(708)370-9112

Magazine. Official publication for members of AAA-Chicago Motor Club. Features include travel stories and articles on motoring. Bimonthly. **Editor(s):** B. Wade. **Price:** Free to qualified subscribers; $3.00 for nonmembers. $1.00 per single issue.

3889 • Home & Away (Hoosier Edition) [Indiana]
Midwest Magazine Network
P Box
Indianapolis, IN 46208   Ph:(317)923-1500

Magazine. Official publication for AAA Hoosier Motor Club members in Central Indiana. Bimonthly. **Editor(s):** Hugh Orr, Regional Editor (Indianapolis); James E. Parks. **Price:** $3.00 for nonmembers.

3890 • Home & Away (Minnesota Edition)
Minnesota State Automobile Assn.
7 Travelers Trail   Ph:(612)890-2500
Burnsville, MN 55337   Fax:(612)894-4079

Magazine. Official publication for Minnesota State Automobile Association members. Bimonthly. **Editor(s):** Ron Siegmund, Editor/Advertising Mgr. **Price:** $3.00.

3891 • Home & Away (Ohio Edition)
Ohio Auto Club
90 E. Wilson Bridge Rd.
Worthington, OH 43085   Ph:(614)431-7919

Magazine. Official publication for Ohio American Automobile Association members. Bimonthly. **Editor(s):** William J. Purpura. **Price:** Free to qualified subscribers; $6.00 for nonmembers.

3892 • Home Mechanix
Times Mirror Magazines, Inc.
2 Park Ave.   Ph:(212)779-5000
New York, NY 10016   Fax:(212)779-5468

Magazine. Intended for homeowners and automobile owners. Ten times per year. **Editor(s):** Michael Morris. **Price:** $11.94/year; $1.75 per single issue.

3893 • How the Automobile Works
Increase Video
6914 Conby Ave., Suite 110   Ph:(818)342-2880
Reseda, CA 91335   Fax:(818)342-4029

Audio-visual. A step by step breakdown on the interior workings of a car. **Release date:** 1984. **Producer:** Star Merchants. **Acquisition:** Purchase.

3894 • How to Avoid Getting Mugged by Mr. Badwrench
SFT Publishing
1014 Cassel Ave.
Bay Shore, NY 11706   Ph:(516)968-8565

Book. Published 1988. **Editor(s):** Sal Fariello and Vera Fariello. **Price:** $9.95.

3895 • How to Beat the Car Dealer at His Own Game: Buying a New or Used Car
B. M. Consumer Publications
P.O. Box 465
Kings Park, NY 11754   Ph:(516)979-9183

Book. Published 1982. **Editor(s):** L. J. Brum. **Price:** $5.95.

3896 • How to Buy a Car: The Essential Guide for Buying a New Car or Used Car
St. Martin's Press
175 Fifth Ave.
New York, NY 10010   Ph:(212)674-5151

Book. Published 1988. **Author(s):** James R. Ross. **Price:** $5.95.

3897 • How to Buy a Used Car—How to Sell a Used Car, Two Books in One
Putnam Berkley Group, Inc.
200 Madison Ave.
New York, NY 10016   Ph:(212)576-8900

Book. Published 1988. **Author(s):** Joel Makower. **Price:** $7.95.

3898 • How to Buy a Vehicle: Without Being Taken for a Ride
Quality Books
918 Sherwood Dr.
Lake Bluff, IL 60044-2204   Ph:(312)295-2010

Audio-visual. Videocassette hosted by Sheldon D. Joppru that offers helpful tips and suggestions. **Release date:** 1989.

3899 • How to Buy & Maintain a Used Car: For the Non-Mechanical Person
American Pacific Publishing Co.
16137 Sherman Way, Ste. 212
Van Nuys, CA 91406

Book. Published 1988. **Author(s):** Bradley W. Crouch. **Price:** $9.95.

3900 • How to Buy and Sell a Car by Long Distance
Motorbooks International
729 Prospect Ave.
Osceola, WI 54020   Ph:(715)294-3345

Book. Published 1987. **Author(s):** Hudson Adams. **Price:** $6.95.

3901 • How to Deal on an Automobile
Blue Mountain Publishing
P.O. Box 1575
Lyons, CO 80540   Ph:(303)823-6529

Book. Published 1990. **Author(s):** C.B. Robertson. **Price:** $7.95.

3902 • How to Outsmart the New-Car Salesman: A Legendary Salesman Reveals the Secrets to Negotiating a Great Deal
Macmillan Publishing Co., Inc.
866 Third Avenue
New York, NY 10022   Ph:(212)702-2000

Book. Published 1987. **Editor(s):** Gary Carr. **Price:** $8.95.

3903 • How to Squeeze More Miles From Your Car
Walter J. Klein Company Ltd.
6311 Carmel Rd.
P.O. Box 2087
Charlotte, NC 28211   Ph:(704)542-1403

Audio-visual. The many techniques that motorists can use to increase their car mileage are demonstrated in this program. **Release date:** 1976. **Producer:** Walter J. Klein Company Ltd. **Acquisition:** Purchase.

3904 • How to Test and Buy a Used Car
Used Car Publications
5502 Englishman Pl.
Rockville, MD 20852   Ph:(301)493-5686

Book. Published 1984. **Author(s):** J.K. Leon. **Price:** $4.95.

3905 • Introductory Auto Mechanics
EMC Publishing
300 York Ave.
Saint Paul, MN 55101   Ph:(612)771-1555

Manual. Published 1986. **Editor(s):** Dennis Karwatka. **Price:** $21.95, text; $5.95, workbook; $28.00, teacher's guide; $89.00, transparency masters.

3906 • Introductory Automechanics
John Wiley and Sons, Inc.
605 Third Ave.
New York, NY 10158-0012   Ph:(212)850-6000

Manual. Published 1988.

3907 • Keystone AAA Motorist [Pennsylvania]
AAA Mid-Atlantic, Inc.
2040 Market St.   Ph:(215)864-5455
Philadelphia, PA 19103-3302   Fax:(215)568-1153

Newspaper. Provides information on domestic and foreign travel and automotive safety. Bimonthly. **Editor(s):** Roy D. Hanhaw and J.C. Moyer. **Price:** $2.00.

3908 • Kicking Tires Is Not Enough
Consumer Reports/Films
256 Washington St.
Mount Vernon, NY 10550   Ph:(914)664-6400

Audio-visual. Backed by Consumer Reports' auto testing expertise, this program provides the basics of buying a good used car. **Release date:** 1975. **Producer:** Consumers Union. **Acquisition:** Purchase.

3909 • Lehigh Valley Motor Club—AAA Today [Pennsylvania]
Lehigh Valley Motor Club
1020 Hamilton St.
P.O. Box 1910   Ph:(215)434-5141
Allentown, PA 18105-1910   Fax:(215)434-7662

Magazine. Contains articles on consumer motoring and travel. Bimonthly. **Editor(s):** Floyd F. Fisher. **Price:** Free to members; $1.00 single issue.

3910 • Low-Cost Vehicles: Options for Moving People and Goods
Intermediate Technology Development Group of North America
777 United Nations Plaza
Suite 9A
New York, NY 10017   Ph:(212)972-9877

Book. Published 1985. **Editor(s):** Gordon Hathway. **Price:** $ 15.25.

3911 • The Mechanics Vest Pocket Reference Book
Prentice Hall
Rte. 9W
Englewood Cliffs, NJ 07632   Ph:(201)592-2000

Reference book. Published 1982. **Editor(s):** John H. Wolfe and E.R. Phelps. **Price:** $7.95.

3912 • Mechanisms of Car Choice: A Study of Learning by Using
Gower Publishing Co., Ltd.
Old Post Rd.
Brookfield, VT 05036   Ph:(802)276-3162

Book. Published 1989. **Author(s):** A.S. Lubulwa. **Price:** $49.95.

3913 • Miss Information's Automotive Calendar of Events
Bobbie'dine Rodda
1232 Highland Ave.
Glendale, CA 91202

Report/bulletin. Lists scheduled automotive events in Arizona, California, and Nevada. Monthly. **Editor(s):** Bobbie'dine Rodda, Publisher.

3914 • Motor Auto Repair Manual
Hearst Books
105 Madison Ave
New York, NY 10016   Ph:(212)889-3050

Manual. **Price:** $23.50.

3915 • Motor Club News
Motor Club of America Companies
484 Central Ave.
Newark, NJ 07107   Ph:(201)733-4030

Newspaper. Official publication of Motor Club of America. Bimonthly. **Editor(s):** Robert A. Green, Editor and Publisher. **Price:** $1.00 for members.

3916 • Motor Handbook
Hearst Corp.
645 Stewart Ave.
Garden City, NY 11530   Ph:(212)399-5655

Magazine. Provides over 400,000 manufacturer's specifications for domestic and imported cars and trucks. Annual. **Editor(s):** Wade Hoyt. **Price:** $5.00.

3917 • Motor Trend
Petersen Publishing Co.
7750 Sunset Blvd.
Los Angeles, CA 90046   Ph:(213)854-2222

Magazine. Consumer automotive publication that contains information on new vehicles, driving impressions, road tests, overseas reports, motor racing, historical perspectives, design and engineering trends, and repair tips. Monthly. **Editor(s):** Mike Anson. **Price:** $13.94/year; $2.75 per single issue.

3918 • Motor Trend—Road Tests
Petersen Publishing Co.
6725 Sunset Blvd.
Los Angeles, CA 90028   Ph:(213)854-2222

Magazine. Annual. **Editor(s):** David Fults. **Price:** $3.95.

3919 • Motor Vehicle
Butterworth Publishers
80 Montvale Ave.
Stoneham, MA 02180   Ph:(617)438-8464

Book. Published 1989. **Editor(s):** K. Newton and W. Steeds. **Price:** $65.00.

3920 • Motor Vehicle Identification Manual
Motor Vehicle Manufacturers Association of the United States (MVMA)
7430 2nd Ave., Ste. 300
Detroit, MI 48202   Ph:(313)872-4311

Reference book. Contains photographs of member company passenger cars, multipurpose passenger vehicles, and light trucks, as well as vehicle identification number information and their locations. Primarily for law enforcement and accident investigation agencies. Annual. **Price:** $5.00.

3921 • Motor Vehicle Size and Weight Regulations, Enforcement, and Permit Operations
Transportation Research Board
2101 Constitution Ave.
Washington, DC 20418   Ph:(212)334-3218

Reference book. Published 1980. **Price:** $6.00.

3922 • Motorland
AAA California State Automobile Assn.
150 Van Ness Ave.   Ph:(415)565-2620
San Francisco, CA 94102   Fax:(415)552-5825

Magazine. Magazine on automobile travel and recreation. Bimonthly. **Editor(s):** John G. Holmgren. **Price:** $3.00/year; 50¢ per single issue.

3923 • Motorweek
Maryland Center for Public Broadcasting
11767 Bonita Ave.
Owings Mills, MD 21117   Ph:(301)356-5600

Audio-visual. This is a video automotive magazine that features new car road tests, automotive maintenance, new tools, and money saving tips on buying a car. **Release date:** 1983. **Producer:** Maryland Center for Public Broadcasting. **Acquisition:** Rent/Lease, Purchase.

3924 • Mugged by Mr. Badwrench: An Insider's Guide to Getting Your Car Repaired
St. Martin's Press, Inc.
175 5th Ave.
New York, NY 10010   Ph:(212)674-5151

Book. Published 1991. **Editor(s):** Sal Fariello. **Price:** $9.95.

3925 • NAPA News
National Automotive Parts Assn.
2999 Circle
75 Parkway   Ph:(404)956-2200
Atlanta, GA 30339-3073   Fax:(404)956-2212

Newsletter. Offers articles on repair and maintenance tips and installation advice. **Editor(s):** Kathy Randall. **Price:** 10¢/copy.

3926 • Ohio Motorist
AAA Ohio Motorists Association
P.O. Box 6150   Ph:(216)361-6216
Cleveland, OH 44101   Fax:(216)361-6317

Magazine. Offers automotive and travel news. Monthly (except August and December). **Editor(s):** F. Jerome Turk, Editor and Publisher. **Price:** $1.50.

3927 • One Hundred One Things to Do with Your Car
TAB Books, Inc.
Blue Ridge Summit, PA 17294-0850   Ph:(717)794-2191

Book. Published 1986. **Price:** $15.95.

3928 • The One Hundred Seventy-Five Thousand-Mile Car
Grieco
P.O. Box 1262
San Juan Capistrano, CA 92693   Ph:(714)498-1536

Book. Published 1984. **Editor(s):** Mayre Myers and Joseph Grieco. **Price:** $7.95.

3929 • One Hundred Thousand Miles ... Two Hundred Thousand Miles ... or More: Practical Car Care
TAB Books, Inc.
Blue Ridge Summit, PA 17294-0850   Ph:(717)794-2191

Book. Published 1988. **Editor(s):** James Wesner and Joseph Ettwein. **Price:** $10.95.

3930 • Orange County Auto World [California]
Zigner Publications
27068 La Paz Rd., Ste. 621
Laguna Hills, CA 92654

Magazine. Provides news for car connoisseurs and enthusiasts. Monthly. **Editor(s):** Jeffrey L. Zigner, Editor and Publisher.

3931 • Pacific Automotive News
Northwest Motor Publishing Co.
811 1st Ave., Ste. 402   Ph:(206)624-3470
Seattle, WA 98104   Fax:(206)624-3360

Magazine. Bimonthly. **Editor(s):** J.B. Smith. **Price:** $4.00.

3932 • Popular Cars
McMullen Publishing, Inc.
2145 W. La Palma Ave.   Ph:(714)635-9040
Anaheim, CA 92801   Fax:(714)533-9979

Magazine. Offers information for late-model automobile enthusiasts. Monthly. **Editor(s):** Jim Kelso. **Price:** $17.98.

3933 • Quatrefoil
Kutztown Publishing Co.
P.O. Box 346
Kutztown, PA 19530   Ph:(714)720-5369

Magazine. Collection of selected readings aimed at the automobile enthusiast. Quarterly. **Editor(s):** Stephen Pearson. **Price:** 50¢ per copy.

3934 • Reading-Berks Auto Club Magazine
Roberts & Co.
920 Van Reed Rd.
Wyomissing, PA 19610   Ph:(215)375-4525

Magazine. Contains car, driver, and travel information. Bimonthly. **Editor(s):** Robert R. Gerhart, Jr., Editor and Publisher. **Price:** $2.00/year; 40¢ per single issue.

3935 • Rip-Off Tip-Offs: Winning the Auto Repair Game
TAB Books, Inc.
Blue Ridge Summit, PA 17294-0850   Ph:(717)794-2191

Book. Published 1990. **Editor(s):** Robert B. Sikorsky. **Price:** $16.95, hardbound; $9.95, paper.

3936 • Risks and Rewards of Purchasing a Grey Market Car
Center for Video Education
56 Lafayette Ave.
N. White Plains, NY 10603   Ph:(914)428-9620

Audio-visual. A comprehensive view of the ins and outs of grey market cars, and their viability for the individual consumer. **Release date:** 1985. **Producer:** Center for Video Education, Inc. **Acquisition:** Rent/Lease, Purchase.

3937 • Road & Track
Diamandis Communications, Inc.
1499 Monrovia Ave.   Ph:(714)720-5300
Newport Beach, CA 92663   Fax:(714)631-2374

Magazine. Contains an array of articles on domestic and import cars, trucks, vans, and sport utility vehicles, automobile road tests, vintage cars, maintenance advice, and special interest topics. Monthly. **Editor(s):** Thomas L. Bryant. **Price:** $19.94/year; $2.95 per single issue.

3938 • Road Reports
Contemporary Books, Inc.
180 N. Michigan Ave.
Chicago, IL 60601   Ph:(312)782-9181

Book. Published 1988. **Editor(s):** Daniel Heraud. **Price:** $12.95.

3939 • Rocky Mountain Motorist [Colorado]
Rocky Mountain Motorists, Inc.
4100 E. Arkansas Ave.   Ph:(303)753-8800
Denver, CO 80222   Fax:(303)758-8515

Magazine. Intended for members of the Colorado American Automobile Association. Contains articles on foreign and domestic travel as well as automotive issues. Monthly. **Editor(s):** Barbara Bauerle. **Price:** Available to members only.

3940 • SAE Cumulative Index
Society of Automotive Engineers, Inc.
400 Commonwealth Dr.   Ph:(412)776-4841
Warrendale, PA 15096-0001   Fax:(412)776-5760

Reference book. List all technical papers published by SAE from 1965 to the present; also available on microfiche, floppy disk, and an online service. **Price:** $145.00.

3941 • SAE Handbook 1990
Society of Automotive Engineers, Inc.
400 Commonwealth Dr.
Warrendale, PA 15096   Ph:(412)776-4841

Reference book. Vol. 1: Materials. Vol 2: Parts and Components. Vol 3: Engines, Emissions, Noise, Fuels, and Lubricants. Vol 4: On-Highway Vehicles and Off-Highway Equipment. Published 1990. **Price:** $175.00, set; $60.00, per volume.

3942 • SAE Technical Literature Abstracts
Society of Automotive Engineers, Inc.
400 Commonwealth Dr.   Ph:(412)776-4841
Warrendale, PA 15096-0001   Fax:(412)776-5760

Reference book. Listing of abstracts of SAE technical papers on developments in vehicular technology; also available on floppy disk and online service. Quarterly. **Price:** $92.00 per year; $14.00 per issue.

3943 • Save Big Money on a New Car: A Common Sense Buyers Guide
Maradia Press
228 Evening Star Dr.
Naugatuck, CT 06770   Ph:(203)723-0758

Buyers guide. Published 1990. **Author(s):** Peter Ciullo. **Price:** $6.95.

3944 • Seized, Surplus, Repos and Rentals: How to Get the Car of Your Dreams Without Ever Hasseling with a Salesman
Duane Shinn
5090 Dobrot St.
Central Point, OR 97502   Ph:(503)664-6037

Buyers guide. Published 1989. **Author(s):** Dunk Chen. **Price:** $10.00; $19.95, includes cassette.

3945 • SMART Buyer's Guide to Purchasing a New Car
Alexander Media Services
411 Video Information
3033 Comorant Rd.
Pebble Beach, CA 93953   Ph:(408)647-9253

Audio-visual. Protect yourself from dishonest car salesmen with this easy to understand video. Describes car dealership scams and gives advice for purchasing your new car at the lowest possible price. **Release date:** 1990. **Price:** $29.95.

3946 • So You Want to Buy a Secondhand Car?
State Mutual Book & Periodical Service, Ltd.
521 Fifth Ave., 17th Fl.
New York, NY 10017   Ph:(212)682-5844

Book. Published 1986. **Author(s):** Stephen McClymont. **Price:** $14.00.

3947 • Sparkplug: A Car Owner's Bible
Sutherland Publishing, Fl.
16956-6 McGregor Blvd.
Fort Myers, FL 33908   Ph:(813)466-1626

Manual. Published 1987. **Editor(s):** Dr. J. A. Anderson. **Price:** $14.95.

3948 • Tommy's First Car
Film Fair Communications
10900 Ventura Blvd.
P.O. Box 1728
Studio City, CA 91604   Ph:(818)985-0244

Audio-visual. Different clues to look for in the condition of a car when searching for a used or new one. **Release date:** 1972. **Producer:** California State Dept. of Education. **Acquisition:** Purchase, Duplication License.

3949 • Understanding Your Automobile
Handy Book Co.
2509 S. Padre Island Dr.
P.O. Box 721203
Corpus Christi, TX 78472-1203   Ph:(512)851-2240

Book. Published 1984. **Editor(s):** Robert G. Lozano. **Price:** $8.95, paper; $24.95 cassette.

3950 • Used Cars: Finding the Best Buy
Bonus Books
160 E. Illinois St.
Chicago, IL 60611   Ph:(312)467-0580

Book. Published 1988. **Author(s):** Jim Mateja. **Price:** $6.95.

3951 • The Valley Motorist
Valley Automobile Club
P.O. Box AAA
Wilkes-Barre, PA 18703   Ph:(717)824-2444

Magazine. Contains travel, auto, motoring articles. Bimonthly. **Editor(s):** Chas. J. Spitale, Managing Editor. **Price:** Included with membership.

3952 • Vehicle Painting
State Mutual Book and Periodical Service, Ltd.
521 Fifth Ave.
17th Floor
New York, NY 10017   Ph:(212)682-5844

Reference book. Two volume set. **Price:** $75.00.

3953 • Western Pennsylvania Motorist
West Penn AAA
202 Penn Circle W.   Ph:(412)362-3300
Pittsburgh, PA 15206   Fax:(412)362-8943

Newspaper. Provides motoring and travel information for auto club members. Monthly (except August and December). **Editor(s):** Ann Reed Rose. **Price:** $2.00.

3954 • What You Need to Know to Avoid Auto Repair Rip-Offs
H. Lee Stone Publications
P.O. Box 2857
Grapevine, TX 76051   Ph:(817)481-8089

Book. Published 1990. **Editor(s):** H. Lee Stone.

3955 • What Your Car Is Trying To Tell You
Bergwall Productions, Inc.
P.O. Box 238
Garden City, NY 11530   Ph:800-645-3565

Book. Published 1982. **Price:** $5.00, workbook; $179.00, audio visual package.

3956 • What's Wrong with My Car?: A Guide to Troubleshooting Common Mechanical and Performance Problems
Consumer Reports Books
51 E. 42nd St., Ste. 800
New York, NY 10017   Ph:(212)682-9280

Book. Published 1990. **Editor(s):** Mort Schultz. **Price:** $14.95.

3957 • Why Trade It In? How To Keep Your Car Running Almost Indefinitely
Liberty Publishing Co., Inc.
440 S. Federal Hwy., Ste. B3
Deerfield Beach, FL 33441   Ph:(305)360-9000

Book. Published 1991. **Editor(s):** George Fremon and Suzanne Fremon. **Price:** $9.95.

3958 • Women with Wheels—Newsletter
Patricia Stringer
1718 A Northfield Sq.
Northfield, IL 60093   Ph:(708)501-3519

Newsletter. Provides information on cars and their maintenance. Features articles on anti-lock brakes, safety, leasing, purchasing, and dealing with car salespeople. Quarterly. **Editor(s):** Susan Frissell, Ph.D. **Price:** $15.00/year for individuals; $20.00/year for institutions.

3959 • World of Wheels
World of Wheels Publishing, Inc.
2061 McCowan Rd., Rm. 207
Scarborough, ON M1S 3Y6   Ph:(416)297-9277

Magazine. Provides consumer-oriented information about automobiles. Bimonthly. **Editor(s):** Lynn Helpard, Managing Editor.

General repair/maintenance

3960 • Advanced Car Care: Belts, Hoses and Radiator
Video Tech
19346 Third Ave., N.W.
Seattle, WA 98177   Ph:(206)546-5401

Audio-visual. Advanced auto engine maintenance and repair techniques are described and performed. **Release date:** 1981. **Producer:** Cinema Associates. **Acquisition:** Purchase.

3961 • Advanced Car Care: Cooling System Service
RMI Media Productions, Inc.
2807 W. 47th St.
Shawnee Mission, KS 66205   Ph:(913)262-3974

Audio-visual. This program tells how to repair the car cooling system in a step by step manner. **Release date:** 1984. **Producer:** RMI Media Productions, Inc. **Acquisition:** Purchase.

3962 • Advanced Car Care: Plugs, Timing and Shocks
Video Tech
19346 Third Ave., N.W.
Seattle, WA 98177   Ph:(206)546-5401

Audio-visual. Advanced auto engine maintenance procedures are demonstrated. **Release date:** 1981. **Producer:** Cinema Associates. **Acquisition:** Purchase.

3963 • Advanced Car Care: Tune Up and Shocks
RMI Media Productions, Inc.
2807 W. 47th St.
Shawnee Mission, KS 66205   Ph:(913)262-3974

Audio-visual. This program tells how to tune up a car in a step by step manner. **Release date:** 1984. **Producer:** RMI Media Productions, Inc. **Acquisition:** Purchase.

3964 • Advanced Electronic Ignition Tune-Up
Bergwall Productions, Inc.
106 Charles Lindbergh Blvd.
Uniondale, NY 11553-3695   Ph:(516)222-1111

Audio-visual. On three tapes, ignition repair and tune-up are demonstrated. **Release date:** 1984. **Producer:** Bergwall Productions, Inc. **Acquisition:** Purchase.

3965 • Advanced Electronic Tune-Up
Bergwall Productions, Inc.
P.O. Box 238
Garden City, NY 11530   Ph:800-645-3565

Reference book. Published 1984. **Editor(s):** Peter Novellino. **Price:** $6.00, workbook; $199.00, audio visual package.

3966 • The Allen Smart Scope Explained
Bergwall Productions, Inc.
106 Charles Lindbergh Blvd.
Uniondale, NY 11553-3695   Ph:(516)222-1111

Audio-visual. The Allen Smart Scope, which tests automotive systems, is demonstrated. **Release date:** 1987. **Producer:** Bergwall Productions, Inc. **Price:** $119.00.

3967 • Anatomy of a Battery
Farmland Industries, Inc.
3315 N. Oak Trafficway
Kansas City, MO 64116

Audio-visual. Describes the automobile battery, including maintenance and special care. **Release date:** 1985. **Producer:** Farmland Industries, Inc. **Acquisition:** Purchase.

3968 • Auto-Know
Beacon Films
930 Pinter Ave.
Evanston, IL 60202   Ph:(312)328-6700

Audio-visual. Learn how to diagnose and fix basic auto problems. **Release date:** 1988. **Producer:** Beacon Films. **Acquisition:** Purchase.

3969 • Auto Maintenance for Everyone
Sales Focus, Inc.
P.O. Box 2477
Saratoga, CA 95070   Ph:(408)377-2277

Book. **Editor(s):** Kenneth Schock. **Price:** $26.95.

3970 • Auto Mechanics
RMI Media Productions, Inc.
2807 W. 47th St.
Shawnee Mission, KS 66205   Ph:(913)362-6910

Audio-visual. This series provides step-by-step instruction in auto mechanics, including set-up procedures, alignment techniques, and brake repair and installation. **Release date:** 1987. **Producer:** RMI Media Productions, Inc. **Acquisition:** Purchase.

3971 • Auto Mechanics for Everyone
Sales Focus, Inc.
P.O. Box 2477
Saratoga, CA 95070   Ph:(408)377-2277

Manual. **Editor(s):** Kenneth Schock. **Price:** $26.95.

3972 • Auto Repair
J. G. Ferguson Publishing Co.
200 W. Monroe, Suite 250
Chicago, IL 60606   Ph:(312)580-5480

Book. Published 1987. **Editor(s):** John Doyle.

3973 • Auto Repair for Dummies: The Maintenance Tape
Classic Telepublishing
PO Box 426
West Simsbury, CT 06092   Ph:(203)651-5257

Audio-visual. If you have absolutely no idea what goes on under the hood of your car, this video is for you. It will show and explain basic auto parts and teach you a routine to use in determining if your car needs maintenance or repair. **Release date:** 1990. **Price:** $19.95.

3974 • Auto Repair Manual
William Morrow and Co.
105 Madison Ave.
New York, NY 10016   Ph:(212)889-3050

Manual. 1988. **Price:** $23.00.

3975 • Auto Repair: The Costly Ride
Alfred Higgins Productions, Inc.
6350 Laurel Canyon Blvd.
N. Hollywood, CA 91606   Ph:(818)762-3300

Audio-visual. A guide designed to help the automobile owner obtain the best values in auto repair. **Release date:** 1977. **Producer:** Alfred Higgins Productions, Inc. **Acquisition:** Purchase.

3976 • Auto Repairs for Dummies
Ten Speed Press
11 W. 19th St.
New York, NY 10011   Ph:(212)337-6010

Book. Published 1989. **Editor(s):** Deanna Sclar. **Price:** $26.95.

3977 • Auto Service and Repair
Goodheart-Wilcox Co.
123 W. Taft Dr.
South Holland, IL 60473   Ph:(708)333-7200

Book. Published 1984. **Editor(s):** Martin W. Stockel and Martin T. Stockel. **Price:** $30.00.

3978 • Auto Video
Total Productions, Inc.
P.O. Box 906
Hixson, TN 37343   Ph:(615)842-7455

Audio-visual. A general survey of personal car care, from maintenance to the early warning signs of a breakdown. **Release date:** 1986. **Producer:** Larry Denauger. **Acquisition:** Purchase.

3979 • Automechanics
L & K International Video Training
295 Evans Ave.
Toronto, ON M8Z 5P9   Ph:(416)252-6407

Audio-visual. This program is designed for use by industry and concentrates on procedures used for testing and servicing the modern automobile. **Release date:** 1984. **Producer:** Leighton and Kidd Ltd. **Acquisition:** Purchase.

3980 • Automobile International
Johnston International Publishing Corp.
950 Lee St., No. 100
Des Plaines, IL 60016-6588

Magazine. Contains articles on auto service and repairs. Printed in English and Spanish; published quarterly in Arabic. Nine times per year. **Editor(s):** M. Havis Dawson. **Price:** $50.00.

3981 • Automotive Diagnosis and Tune-up
McGraw-Hill Publishing Co.
11 W. 19th St.
New York, NY 10011   Ph:(212)337-6010

Manual. Published 1983. **Editor(s):** Frank C. Derato and Lory V. Curtis. **Price:** $29.95.

3982 • Automotive Engines: Maintenance and Repair
Books on Demand
University Microfilms International
300 N. Zeeb Rd.
Ann Arbor, MI 48106   Ph:(313)761-4700

Manual. **Editor(s):** Walter Billiet. **Price:** $131.50.

3983 • Automotive Operation and Maintenance
Volunteers in Technical Assistance
P.O. Box 12438
Arlington, VA 22209-8438   Ph:(703)276-9411

Manual. Published 1991. **Editor(s):** E. Christopher Cone. **Price:** $14.95

3984 • Automotive Parts and Accessories Association—Tech Service Report
Automotive Parts and Accessories Association
5100 Forbes Blvd.
Lanham, MD 20706   Ph:(301)459-9110

Report/bulletin. Features bulletins on automobile service problems and repair procedures. Monthly. **Editor(s):** Timothy Tierney. **Price:** $50.00.

3985 • Automotive Principles: Repair and Service
Prentice-Hall
Rte. 9W
Englewood Cliffs, NJ 07632   Ph:(201)592-2000

Manual. In two volumes. Published 1988. **Editor(s):** Don Knowles. **Price:** $19.25.

3986 • Automotive Quick Test
L & K International Video Training
295 Evans Ave.
Toronto, ON M8Z 5P9   Ph:(416)252-6407

Audio-visual. Mechanics are taught how to quickly and efficiently check out a car. Titles include: Common Problems on Systems and Components; Electronic Ignition Systems; Emissions Controls; Brake Systems; FWD Axles Steering and Suspension; Air Conditioning; Carburetor and Fuel Injection Systems; Computerized Engine Controls. **Release date:** 1988. **Producer:** Leighton and Kidd. **Acquisition:** Purchase, Rent/Lease.

3987 • Automotive Tech Series
RMI Media Productions, Inc.
2807 W. 47th St.
Shawnee Mission, KS 66205   Ph:(913)262-3974

Audio-visual. This series demonstrates various aspects of auto mechanics using a step-by-step format. Developed by automotive instructors at the College of Du Page in Glen Ellyn, Illinois. **Release date:** 1987. **Producer:** RMI Media Productions, Inc. **Acquisition:** Purchase.

3988 • Automotive Tune-Up
McGraw-Hill Publishing Co.
1221 11 W. 19th St.
New York, NY 10011   Ph:(212)337-6010

Book. Published 1983. **Author(s):** Donald L. Anglin. **Price:** $28.95.

3989 • Automotive Tune-Up Guide
Associated Video Publishers
P.O. Box 381
Mill Valley, CA 94942   Ph:(415)381-3029

Audio-visual. All the basics of car care are shown on this one videotape. **Release date:** 1989. **Producer:** Associated Video Publishers. **Acquisition:** Purchase.

3990 • Automotive Tune-up Procedures
Prentice-Hall
Rte. 9W
Englewood Cliffs, NJ 07632   Ph:(201)592-2000

Manual. Published 1988. **Editor(s):** William Husselbee. **Price:** $42.00, hardbound; $39.00, pa per.

3991 • Automotive Workbook
National Learning Corp.
212 Michael Dr.
Syosset, NY 11791   Ph:(516)921-8888

Manual. Published 1991. **Editor(s):** Jack Rudman. **Price:** $13.95.

3992 • Basic Automobile Maintenance
Vision Productions Ltd.
P.O. Box 8778
Moscow, ID 83843   Ph:(208)883-0105

Audio-visual. Demonstrations are provided for the non-mechanic, including changing tires, battery care, checking sparkplugs, changing oil, replacing wiper blades, adjusting a fanbelt, and more.

Release date: 1981. **Producer:** Vision Productions Ltd. **Acquisition:** Purchase.

3993 • Basic Automotive Jobs Explained
Bergwall Productions, Inc.
106 Charles Lindbergh Blvd.
Uniondale, NY 11553-3695   Ph:(516)222-1111

Audio-visual. Simple automotive repairs are explained. Titles: Using Reference Material and Starter Replacement; Performing Road Service, Tie Road End and Idler Arm Replacement; Performing Underhood Services and Muffler Replacement; Changing Engine Oil, Automatic Transmission Fluid, Valve Cover Gasket, and Thermostat Replacement; and Alternator, Battery, Shocks and Spark Plug Replacement. **Release date:** 1985. **Producer:** Bergwall Productions, Inc. **Price:** $269.00.

3994 • Basic Car Care
Video Tech
19346 Third Ave., N.W.
Seattle, WA 98177   Ph:(206)546-5401

Audio-visual. Step-by-step instructions on basic car maintenance and repair procedures are given. Simple, easy-to-understand language is used. **Release date:** 1981. **Producer:** Cinema Associates. **Acquisition:** Purchase.

3995 • Basic Car Care
Time-Life Books
777 Duke St.
Alexandria, VA 22314   Ph:(703)838-7000

Manual. Published 1988. **Price:** $23.27.

3996 • Basic Car Care Illustrated
Hearst Books
105 Madison Ave.
New York, NY 10016   Ph:(212)889-3050

Manual. Published 1984. **Price:** $16.95.

3997 • Basics
Prentice-Hall
Rte. 9W
Englewood Cliffs, NJ 07632   Ph:(201)592-2000

Manual. Published 1989. **Editor(s):** John Remling. **Price:** $34.50.

3998 • Breakdown
Eastern Kentucky University
Division of Television and Radio
Richmond, KY 40475   Ph:(606)622-2474

Audio-visual. An instructional program outlining what one should do in the event of a car breakdown. **Release date:** 1982. **Producer:** Traffic Safety Institute at Eastern Kentucky University. **Acquisition:** Free Loan.

3999 • Car Care
Bullfrog Films, Inc.
Oley, PA 19547   Ph:(215)779-8226

Audio-visual. This program teaches the viewer how to service different parts of an automobile. **Producer:** Oklahoma Department of Economic and Community Affairs. **Acquisition:** Purchase, Duplication License.

4000 • Car Care News
Car Care News
4010 Airline Dr.
Houston, TX 77022

Newsletter. Monthly. **Editor(s):** Jay Hagins. **Price:** $24.00.

4001 • Car Maintenance Reminder and Record Book
Value Maintenance
600 S. Conklin
Sioux Falls, SD 57103   Ph:(605)335-1942

Book. Schedule of services and products to properly maintain your car, each 3,000 miles. Published 1990. **Editor(s):** George N. Berger. **Price:** $5.95.

4002 • Car Repair Book
HarperCollins Publishers, Inc.
10 E. 53rd St.
New York, NY 10022   Ph:(212)207-7000

Manual. Published 1990. **Editor(s):** Jack Gillis. **Price:** $10.95.

4003 • Car Service Manual
H. M. Gousha
2001 The Alameda
San Jose, CA 95126   Ph:(408)296-1060

Manual. Published 1984. **Editor(s):** Roger Fennema and Jennifer Phelps. **Price:** $9.15.

4004 • Car Talk
Dell Publishing Co., Inc.
666 5th Ave.
New York, NY 10103   Ph:(212)765-6500

Book. Published 1991. **Editor(s):** Tom Magliozzi. **Price:** $8.95.

4005 • Chevrolet Small-Block V-8 Interchange Manual
Motorbooks International
729 Prospect Ave.
Osceola, WI 54020   Ph:(715)294-3345

Manual. Published 1989. **Editor(s):** David Lewis. **Price:** $17.95.

4006 • Chilton's Auto Repair Manual, 1987-1991
Chilton Co.
Chilton Way
Radnor, PA 19089   Ph:(215)964-4000

Manual. Published 1990. **Price:** $25.75.

4007 • Chilton's Auto Repair Manual, 1988-92
Chilton Co.
Chilton Way
Radnor, PA 19089   Ph:(215)964-4000

Manual. Published 1991. **Price:** $26.95.

4008 • Chilton's Auto Service Manual 1988-1992: Motor Age Professional Mechanic's Edition
Chilton Co.
Chilton Way
Radnor, PA 19089   Ph:(215)964-4000

Manual. Published 1991. **Price:** $85.00.

4009 • Chilton's Easy Car Care Study Guide
Chilton Co.
Chilton Way
Radnor, PA 19089   Ph:(215)964-4000

Manual. Published 1984. **Price:** $6.60.

4010 • Chilton's Guide to Auto Tune-Up and Troubleshooting
Chilton Co.
Chilton Way
Radnor, PA 19089   Ph:(215)964-4000

Manual. Published 1983. **Price:** $15.95.

4011 • Chilton's Import Automotive Service Manual, 1982-1989
Chilton Co.
Chilton Way
Radnor, PA 19089   Ph:(215)964-4000

Manual. Published 1989. **Price:** $72.00.

4012 • Chilton's Import Car Repair Manual 1982-87: Motor Age Professional Mechanics Edition
Chilton Co.
Chilton Way
Radnor, PA 19089   Ph:(215)964-4000

Manual. Published 1991. **Price:** $55.00.

4013 • Chilton's Import Car Repair Manual 1987-91: Motor Age Professional Mechanics Edition
Chilton Co.
Chilton Way
Radnor, PA 19089   Ph:(215)964-4000

Manual. Published 1991. **Price:** $70.00.

4014 • Chilton's Import Car Repair Manual 1988-92
Chilton Co.
Chilton Way
Radnor, PA 19089   Ph:(215)964-4000

Manual. Published 1991. **Price:** $26.95.

4015 • Chilton's Import Car Service Manual, 1980-1987: Motor-Age Professional Mechanic's Edition
Chilton Co.
Chilton Way
Radnor, PA 19089   Ph:(215)964-4000

Manual. Published 1987. **Price:** $58.00.

4016 • Chilton's Labor Guide and Manual, 1988-1992: Motor Age Professional Mechanic's Edition
Chilton Co.
Chilton Way
Radnor, PA 19089   Ph:(215)964-4000

Manual. Published 1991. **Price:** $80.00.

4017 • Chilton's Labor Guide and Parts Manual 1986-90: Motor Age Professional Mechanic's Edition
Chilton Co.
Chilton Way
Radnor, PA 19089   Ph:(215)964-4000

Manual. Published 1991. **Price:** $69.00.

4018 • Chilton's Professional Truck and Van Repair Manual 1981-1988
Chilton Co.
Chilton Way
Radnor, PA 19089   Ph:(215)964-4000

Manual. Published 1988. **Price:** $65.00.

4019 • Chilton's Service Bay Handbook 1992: Motor Age Professional Mechanic's Edition
Chilton Co.
Chilton Way
Radnor, PA 19089   Ph:(215)964-4000

Manual. Published 1991. **Price:** $15.00.

4020 • Chilton's Truck and Van Repair Manual, 1982-1988
Chilton Co.
Chilton Way
Radnor, PA 19089   Ph:(215)964-4000

Manual. Published 1988. **Price:** $24.95.

4021 • Complete Automobile Mechanics Refresher Course
H. M. Gousha
2001 The Alameda
San Jose, CA 95126   Ph:(408)296-1060

Manual. Published 1981. **Editor(s):** Bob Leigh. **Price:** $79.95, workbook; $70.00, set of 5 cassettes.

4022 • Complete Automotive Service Library
H. M. Gousha
2001 The Alameda
San Jose, CA 95126   Ph:(408)296-1060

Manual. Published 1983. **Price:** $52.55.

4023 • The Complete Guide to Car Noises
Expim Co.
P.O. Box 23084
Washington, DC 20026   Ph:(703)768-5825

Manual. Published 1983. **Editor(s):** Jorge Lugo. **Price:** $2.95.

4024 • Consumer Car Care for the Wise, the Poor and the Helpless
ABBE Publishers Assn. of Washington, D.C.
4111 Gallows Rd.
Annandale, VA 22003-1862   Ph:(703)750-0255

Manual. Published 1991. **Editor(s):** John C. Bartone, II. **Price:** $34.50, hardbound; $29.50, paper.

4025 • Consumer Education: Maintaining an Automobile
AIMS Media, Inc.
6901 Woodley Ave.
Van Nuys, CA 91406-4878   Ph:(818)785-4111

Audio-visual. Choosing the right garage and mechanic in maintaining an automobile. **Release date:** 1973. **Producer:** AIMS Media, Inc. **Acquisition:** Purchase, Duplication License.

4026 • Consumer Reports—Cars
Cambridge Career Products
One Players Club Dr.
Charleston, WV 25311   Ph:(304)344-8550

Audio-visual. Viewers are told how they can get the most for their money when buying a car. Tips on maintaining cars are also included. **Release date:** 1986. **Producer:** Cambridge Career Products. **Price:** $34.95.

4027 • Consumer Survival Kit: Cars
Maryland Center for Public Broadcasting
11767 Bonita Ave.
Owings Mills, MD 21117   Ph:(301)356-5600

Audio-visual. Designed to inform the automobile investor about buying cars and basic repair jobs. Programs available individually. **Producer:** Maryland Center for Public Broadcasting. **Acquisition:** Rent/Lease, Purchase.

4028 • Consumers' Guide to Automotive Maintenance
Walter J. Klein Company Ltd.
6311 Carmel Rd.
P.O. Box 2087
Charlotte, NC 28211   Ph:(704)542-1403

Audio-visual. Viewers learn how to perform checks on their car to keep it running longer and free of cost. **Release date:** 1982. **Producer:** Walter J. Klein Company Ltd. **Acquisition:** Purchase.

4029 • Diesel Mechanics
Bergwall Productions, Inc.
P.O. Box 238
Garden City, NY 11530   Ph:800-645-3565

Manual. Published 1981. **Editor(s):** Zdenko Geda. **Price:** $5.00, workbook; $369.00, audio visual package.

4030 • Diesel Mechanics III
Bergwall Productions, Inc.
P.O. Box 238
Garden City, NY 11530   Ph:800-645-3565

Manual. Published 1983. **Editor(s):** Zdenko Gega. **Price:** $7.00, workbook; $299.00, audio visual package.

4031 • Do-It-Yourself Car Care
Tab Books, Inc.
Blue Ridge Summit, PA 17294-0850   Ph:(717)794-2191

Book. Published 1987. **Editor(s):** Larry W. Carley. **Price:** $12.95.

4032 • Drive It Forever: Your Key to Long Automobile Life
McGraw-Hill Publishing Co.
11 W. 19th St.
New York, NY 10011   Ph:(212)337-6010

Book. Published 1989. **Price:** $7.95.

4033 • Electric Motors, Principles Controls, Service and Maintenance
Hobar Publications
1234 Tiller Ln.
Saint Paul, MN 55112   Ph:(612)633-3170

Manual. Published 1990. **Editor(s):** W. Forrest Bear. **Price:** $13.00, paper.

4034 • Electrical Systems
John Deere Service Publications
Dept. 333, John Deere Rd.
Moline, IL 61265   Ph:(309)765-2967

Manual. Discusses the basics of current, voltage, and resistance; shows various types of electrical circuits; explains generators and alternators; and tells how to maintain the circuits for safety and long service. Published 1984. **Price:** $16.73.

4035 • Electrics
International Film Bureau, Inc. (IFB)
332 S. Michigan Ave.
Chicago, IL 60604-4832   Ph:(312)427-4545

Audio-visual. Maintenance for electrical systems-ignition and lighting, including checking the battery water level and cable connections, and changing and cleaning plugs and points-is taught. **Release date:** 1981. **Producer:** International Film Bureau, Inc. **Acquisition:** Purchase.

4036 • Electronic Ignition Tune Up
Bergwall Publications, Inc.
P.O. Box 238
Garden City, NY 11530   Ph:800-645-3565

Manual. Published 1983. **Editor(s):** Peter Novellino. **Price:** Workbook costs $6.00; audio visual package costs $339.00.

4037 • Emission Diagnosis Tune-up and Service Manual 1988 Import Cars and Trucks: Motor-Age Professional Mechanic's Edition
Chilton Co.
Chilton Way
Radnor, PA 19089   Ph:(215)964-4000

Manual. Published 1989. **Price:** $40.00.

4038 • Engine Performance and Tune-Up
RMI Media Productions, Inc.
2807 W. 47th St.   Ph:(913)262-3974
Shawnee Mission, KS 66205   Fax:(913)362-6910

Audio-visual. This video covers the following topics: basic ignition theory, service procedures, trouble-shooting techniques, replacement of component parts, and electronics, including computer controls. **Release date:** 1988. **Producer:** RMI Media Productions, Inc. **Acquisition:** Purchase.

4039 • Fix It/Get the Basics
Morris Video
2730 Monterey St., No. 105
Monterey Business Park
Torrance, CA 90503   Ph:(213)533-4800

Audio-visual. A must-see for all interested in simple automobile maintenance. Expert mechanic Ray Hill explains clearly and concisely the most fundamental procedures that once learned can save the layperson plenty of time and money. **Release date:** 1985. **Price:** $24.95.

4040 • Fix It/Running and Riding Smooth
Morris Video
2730 Monterey St., No. 105
Monterey Business Park
Torrance, CA 90503   Ph:(213)533-4800

Audio-visual. Ray Hill demonstrates some basics about the performance of a vehicle including spark plugs, timing, PVC systems, and much more. **Release date:** 1985. **Price:** $24.95.

4041 • Fix It Series: Keep Your Car Cool
Morris Video
2730 Monterey St., No. 105
Monterey Business Park
Torrance, CA 90503   Ph:(213)533-4800

Audio-visual. A guide through the basic car repair and maintenance steps. **Price:** $24.95.

4042 • Fixin' Facts News
Car Care News
4010 Airline Dr.
Houston, TX 77022   Ph:(713)691-6470

Newsletter. Quarterly. **Editor(s):** David Kaleh.

4043 • Fram/Autolite Car Care
Aqua-Field Publications, Inc.
656 Shrewsbury Ave.
Shrewsbury, NJ 07701   Ph:(908)842-8300

Magazine. **Editor(s):** Steve Ferber, Publisher and Editor.

4044 • How to Buy & Maintain a Used Car: For the Non-Mechanical Person
American Pacific Publishing Co.
16137 Sherman Way, Ste. 212
Van Nuys, CA 91406

Book. Published 1988. **Author(s):** Bradley W. Crouch. **Price:** $9.95.

4045 • How to Rebuild Small Block Chevys
Price Stern Sloan, Inc.
360 N. La Cienega Blvd.
Los Angeles, CA 90048   Ph:(213)657-6100

Manual. Published 1978. **Editor(s):** David Vizard. **Price:** $12.95.

4046 • How to Rebuild Your Big-Block Chevy
Price Stern Sloan, Inc.
360 N. La Cienega Blvd.
Los Angeles, CA 90048   Ph:(213)657-6100

Manual. Published 1983. **Editor(s):** Tom Wilson. **Price:** $12.95.

4047 • How to Save Thousands on Auto Repair Through Simple Maintenance
Northstar
4000 Robert E. Lee Dr.
Hopewell, VA 23860   Ph:800-458-0116

Book. Published 1990. **Editor(s):** Schuyler D. Wires.

4048 • Import Service
Gemini Communications
306 N. Cleveland Massillon Rd.   Ph:(216)666-9553
Akron, OH 44313-9302   Fax:(216)666-8912

Magazine. Provides information on service and repair of imported cars. Monthly. **Editor(s):** Karl Seyfert. **Price:** $36.00/year; $3.75 per single issue.

4049 • Keep It Running
NETCHE (Nebraska ETV Council for Higher Education)
P.O. Box 83111
Lincoln, NE 68501   Ph:(402)472-3611

Audio-visual. This 20-lesson course on consumer auto repair is designed to help the student gain a basic understanding of the automobile and the functions of its operating systems. **Release date:** 1982. **Producer:** University of Northern Virginia. **Acquisition:** Rent/Lease, Purchase, Subscription.

4050 • Keeping Your Car Alive: A Guide to Preventive Automotive Maintenance
National Center for Appropriate Technology
Box 3838
Butte, MT 59702   Ph:(406)494-4572

Manual. Published 1981. **Price:** $2.00.

4051 • Kirkwood Community College Auto Mechanics Series
RMI Media Productions, Inc.
2807 W. 47 St.   Ph:(913)262-3974
Shawnee Mission, KS 66205   Fax:(913)362-6910

Audio-visual. Instruction in auto mechanics is provided in this detailed series. **Release date:** 1987. **Producer:** RMI Media Productions, Inc. **Acquisition:** Purchase.

4052 • The Last Chance Garage
Harper and Row Publishers, Inc.
10 E. 53rd St.
New York, NY 10022   Ph:(212)207-7000

Manual. Demonstrates do-it-yourself car repairs from transmission to tune-ups; also available in audio-visual package. Published 1984. **Editor(s):** Brad Sears. **Price:** $14.95.

4053 • The Last Chance Garage
Crown Video
225 Park Ave. S.
New York, NY 10003   Ph:(201)382-7600

Audio-visual. In sequences culled from the television show of the same name, Brad Sears demonstrates twenty do-it-yourself car repairs, from transmission to tune-ups. **Release date:** 1986. **Producer:** PBS. **Acquisition:** Purchase.

4054 • Light Truck and Van Repair
Hearst Books
105 Madison Ave.
New York, NY 10016   Ph:(212)889-3050

Manual. Published 1987. **Price:** $27.50.

4055 • Love That Car
AIMS Media, Inc.
6901 Woodley Ave.
Van Nuys, CA 91406-4878   Ph:(818)785-4111

Audio-visual. A humorous approach to the importance of automobile maintenance, showing the consequences of failure to do so. **Release date:** 1967. **Producer:** AIMS Media, Inc. **Acquisition:** Purchase, Duplication License.

4056 • Lyn St. James' Car Owners Manual
Creative Images
4011 SW 47th Ave.
No. 1107
Fort Lauderdale, FL 33314   Ph:(305)565-8206

Manual. Published 1989. **Editor(s):** Lyn St. James. **Price:** $9.95.

4057 • Mitchell Automechanics
Prentice-Hall
Rte. 9W
Englewood Cliffs, NJ 07632   Ph:(201)592-2000

Manual. Published 1986. **Price:** $42.00, text; $16.80, workbook.

4058 • Motor Imported Car Repair
Hearst Books
105 Madison Ave.
New York, NY 10016   Ph:(212)889-3050

Manual. Published 1988. **Price:** $27.50.

4059 • Motor Imported Car Repair Manual: Up-to-Date Info for Imported Car Owners
William Morrow and Co.
105 Madison Ave.
New York, NY 10016   Ph:(212)889-3050

Manual. Published 1986. **Price:** $25.00.

4060 • Motortech
Motortech
555 W. 57th St., 17th Fl.
New York, NY 10019

Magazine. Contains articles on repair tips and advice. Quarterly. **Price:** $8.00.

4061 • National Automotive Parts Association—News
National Automotive Parts Association (NAPA)
2999 Circle 75 Pkwy.
Atlanta, GA 30339   Ph:(404)956-2200

Newspaper. Tabloid offered to the public through NAPA Auto Parts stores. Reports on subjects to help any professional mechanic or serious do-it-yourselfer with automotive repairs, including helpful hints. Three times per year. **Price:** Free.

4062 • New Automotive Mechanics Series
RMI Media Productions, Inc.
2807 W. 47th St.   Ph:(915)362-3974
Shawnee Mission, KS 66205   Fax:(915)362-6910

Audio-visual. These thirty three programs describe in step-by-step procedures how to repair an automobile, with program lengths varying from four to fifteen minutes each. **Release date:** 1984. **Producer:** RMI Media Productions, Inc. **Acquisition:** Purchase.

4063 • Performance Handling for the Nineties: How to Make Your Car Handle Better
Motorbooks Intl.
729 Prospect Ave.
Osceola, WI 54020   Ph:(715)294-3345

Manual. Published 1991. **Editor(s):** Don Alexander. **Price:** $17.95.

4064 • Petersen's Basic How to Tune Your Car
Green Hill Publications
722 Columbus St.
Ottawa, IL 61350   Ph:(815)434-7905

Manual. Published 1985. **Price:** $9.95.

4065 • A Run for Your Money
AIMS Media, Inc.
6901 Woodley Ave.
Van Nuys, CA 91406-4878   Ph:(818)785-4111

Audio-visual. Shows how the American driver can save in gasoline costs through regular car maintenance from tune-up to tires. **Release date:** 1976. **Producer:** AIMS Media, Inc. **Acquisition:** Purchase, Duplication License.

4066 • Safety Check Your Car
Pyramid Film and Video
Box 1048   Ph:(213)828-7577
Santa Monica, CA 90406   Fax:(213)453-9083

Audio-visual. This program demonstrates effective auto maintenance for the average driver. Topics covered include: gas gauge precautions, tire maintenance, steering problems, muffler cracks, and brake problems. **Release date:** 1976. **Producer:** Pyramid; Lee Stanley. **Acquisition:** Rent/Lease, Purchase, Duplication License.

4067 • Selecting and Maintaining Bearings
TPC Training Systems
310 S. Michigan Ave.
Chicago, IL 60604   Ph:(312)537-6610

Audio-visual. Installation, inspection, and repair of plain journal, ball, and roller bearings are covered in this series. **Release date:** 1988. **Producer:** TPC Training Systems. **Acquisition:** Purchase, Rent/Lease.

4068 • Troubleshooting with the Vat-40
Bergwall Productions, Inc.
106 Charles Lindbergh Blvd.
Uniondale, NY 11553-3695   Ph:(516)222-1111

Audio-visual. This five-tape program shows how to troubleshoot using this monitoring device. **Release date:** 1981. **Producer:** Bergwall Productions, Inc. **Acquisition:** Purchase.

4069 • Tune Up America: Tune Up and Maintenance
Morris Video
2730 Monterey St., No. 105
Monterey Business Park
Torrance, CA 90503   Ph:(213)533-4800

Audio-visual. Everything an individual needs to know to tune a car and keep it running smoothly. **Release date:** 1986. **Producer:** Morris Video. **Price:** $19.95.

4070 • Tune-up Service Manual
H. M. Gousha
2001 The Alameda
San Jose, CA 95126   Ph:(408)296-1060

Manual. Published 1986. **Editor(s):** Michael Calkins. **Price:** $9.19.

4071 • The Ultimate Owner's Manual: How to Buy, Finance and Take Care of Your Car
St. Martin's Press
175 5th Ave.
New York, NY 10010   Ph:(212)674-5151

Manual. Published 1991. **Price:** $8.95.

4072 • The Video Car Care Clinic
Morris Video
2730 Monterey St., Rm. 105
Monterey Business Park
Torrance, CA 90503

Audio-visual. This series offers lessons in various areas of automobiles and automotive repairs. **Release date:** 1985. **Producer:** Morris Video. **Acquisition:** Purchase.

4073 • Weekend Mechanic's Handbook: Complete Auto Repairs You Can Make
Prentice-Hall
Rte. 9W
Englewood Cliffs, NJ 07632   Ph:(201)592-2000

Book. Published 1988. **Editor(s):** Paul Weissler. **Price:** $16.95.

4074 • What Do You Know about Auto Mechanics
National Learning Corp.
212 Michael Dr.
Syosset, NY 11791   Ph:(516)921-8888

Book. Published 1991. **Editor(s):** Jack Rudman. **Price:** $15.00.

4075 • A Woman's Guide to Autos: Basics, Operation, Safety and Maintenance
Systems Co.
PO Box 876
Graham, WA 98338   Ph:(206)847-5775

Book. Published 1991. **Editor(s):** Betty Ostrander. **Price:** $39.95, hardbound; $25.00, paper.

4076 • Women with Wheels—Newsletter
Patricia Stringer
1718 A Northfield Sq.
Northfield, IL 60093   Ph:(708)501-3519

Newsletter. Provides information on cars and their maintenance. Features articles on anti-lock brakes, safety, leasing, purchasing, and dealing with car salespeople. Quarterly. **Editor(s):** Susan Frissell, Ph.D. **Price:** $15.00/year for individuals; $20.00/year for institutions.

4077 • Young Man's Guide to Autos: Basics, Operation, Safety and Maintenance
Systems Co.
PO Box 876
Graham, WA 98338   Ph:(206)847-5775

Book. Published 1991. **Editor(s):** Jeff S. Bouquet. **Price:** $39.95, hardbound; $25.00, paper.

4078 • Your Quick and Easy Car Care and Safe Driving Handbook
Doubleday and Company, Inc.
666 Fifth Ave
New York, NY 10103   Ph:(212)984-7561

Manual. Published 1990. **Editor(s):** Laura F. McCarthy. **Price:** $9.95.

Headlamps

4079 • Ground Vehicle Lighting Manual
Society of Automotive Engineers, Inc.
400 Commonwealth Dr.
Warrendale, PA 15096-0001   Ph:(412)776-4841

Manual. Published 1991.

4080 • Light Beam Alignment
Bergwall Productions, Inc.
P.O. Box 238
Garden City, NY 11530   Ph:800-645-3565

Manual. Published 1982. **Editor(s):** Peter Novellino. **Price:** $5.00, workbook; $119.00, audio visual package.

4081 • Lighting Systems for Motor Vehicles
Society of Automotive Engineers, Inc.
400 Commonwealth Dr.
Warrendale, PA 15096   Ph:(412)776-4841

Manual. Published 1989. **Price:** $30.00.

4082 • Vehicle Lighting Trends
Society of Automotive Engineers, Inc.
400 Commonwealth Dr.
Warrendale, PA 15096   Ph:(412)776-4841

Book. Published 1987. **Price:** $40.00

Heating/cooling systems

4083 • Advanced Car Care: Cooling System Service
RMI Media Productions, Inc.
2807 W. 47th St.
Shawnee Mission, KS 66205   Ph:(913)262-3974

Audio-visual. This program tells how to repair the car cooling system in a step by step manner. **Release date:** 1984. **Producer:** RMI Media Productions, Inc. **Acquisition:** Purchase.

4084 • Auto Air Conditioning
Doolco, Inc.
11252 Goodnight Ln., Suite 600
Dallas, TX 75229   Ph:(214)241-2326

Manual. Published 1982. **Editor(s):** James H. Doolin. **Price:** $15.00.

4085 • Auto Air Conditioning
Goodheart-Willcox Co.
123 W. Taft Dr.   Ph:(708)333-7200
South Holland, IL 60473   Fax:(708)331-9130

Manual. Published 1991. **Editor(s):** John Althouse. **Price:** $24.00.

4086 • Auto Heat Air Conditioning Manual
Motorbooks International
729 Prospect Ave.
Osceda, WI 54020   Ph:(715)294-3345

Manual. Published 1988. **Price:** $15.95.

4087 • The Automotive Air Conditioner
Bergwall Productions, Inc.
P.O. Box 238
Garden City, NY 11530   Ph:800-645-3565

Manual. Describes the parts and principles of automotive air conditioners. Published 1981. **Editor(s):** Peter Novellino. **Price:** $7.00; $179.00, audio-visual package.

4088 • Automotive Air Conditioning
McGraw-Hill Publishing Co.
11 W. 19th St.
New York, NY 10011   Ph:(212)337-6010

Manual. 1983. **Editor(s):** William H. Crouse and Donald L. Anglin. **Price:** $29.95.

4089 • Automotive Air Conditioning
Delmar Publishers, Inc.
Two Computer Dr., W.
Albany, NY 12212   Ph:(518)459-1150

Manual. Published 1988. **Editor(s):** Boyce Dwiggins. **Price:** $25.95.

4090 • Automotive Air Conditioning
Prentice-Hall
Rte. 9W
Englewood Cliffs, NJ 07632   Ph:(201)592-2000

Manual. Published 1981. **Editor(s):** Paul Weissler. **Price:** $37.00.

4091 • Automotive Air Conditioning Handbook
TAB Books, Inc.
Blue Ridge Summit, PA 17294-0850   Ph:(717)794-2191

Manual. Published 1988. **Editor(s):** John E. Traister. **Price:** $22.95, hardbound; $15.95, paper.

4092 • Automotive Cooling Journal
National Automotive Radiator Service Association (NARSA)
PO Box 1307
Lansdale, PA 19446   Ph:(215)362-5800

Magazine. Magazine containing news, views, profiles, and technology of the automotive heat repair and manufacturing industry. Includes advertisers index, book reviews, product news, obituaries, and employment listings. Monthly. **Price:** $25.00.

4093 • The Automotive Cooling System
Bergwall Productions, Inc.
106 Charles Lindbergh Blvd.
Uniondale, NY 11553-3695   Ph:(516)222-1111

Audio-visual. The construction and repair of automotive air conditioning systems is examined. **Release date:** 1988. **Producer:** Bergwall Productions, Inc. **Price:** $279.00.

4094 • Automotive Cooling Systems: Operation and Service
Prentice-Hall
Rte. 9W
Englewood Cliffs, NJ 07632   Ph:(201)592-2000

Manual. Published 1986. **Editor(s):** Thomas W. Birch. **Price:** $27.95.

4095 • Automotive Fuel, Cooling, Lubrication, and Exhaust Systems
Prentice-Hall
Rte. 9W
Englewood Cliffs, NJ 07632   Ph:(201)592-2000

Manual. Published 1985. **Editor(s):** William Husselbee. **Price:** $34.00.

4096 • Automotive Fuel, Lubricating and Cooling Systems
McGraw-Hill Publishing Co.
11 W. 19th St.
New York, NY 10011   Ph:(212)337-6010

Manual. Published 1981. **Editor(s):** William H. Crouse and Donald L. Anglin. **Price:** $29.95.

4097 • Automotive Fuel, Lubrication, and Cooling Systems
Prentice-Hall
Rte. 9W
Englewood Cliffs, NJ 07632   Ph:(201)592-2000

Manual. Published 1985. **Editor(s):** Don Knowles. **Price:** $40.00, hardcover; $38.00, paper.

4098 • Automotive Heating and Cooling
Society of Automotive Engineers, Inc.
400 Commonwealth Dr.
Warrendale, PA 15096   Ph:(412)776-4841

Book. Published 1986. **Price:** $44.00.

4099 • Automotive Quick Test
L & K International Video Training
295 Evans Ave.
Toronto, ON M8Z 5P9   Ph:(416)252-6407

Audio-visual. Mechanics are taught how to quickly and efficiently check out a car. Titles include: Common Problems on Systems and Components; Electronic Ignition Systems; Emissions Controls; Brake Systems; FWD Axles Steering and Suspension; Air Conditioning; Carburetor and Fuel Injection Systems; Computerized Engine Controls. **Release date:** 1988. **Producer:** Leighton and Kidd. **Acquisition:** Purchase, Rent/Lease.

4100 • Basic Air Conditioning
Bergwall Productions, Inc.
P.O. Box 238
Garden City, NY 11530   Ph:800-645-3565

Manual. Published 1980. **Editor(s):** Rocco Patella. **Price:** $6.00; $259.00, audio-visual package.

4101 • Chilton's Guide to Air Conditioning and Heating Manual, 1989-91: Professional Mechanics Edition
Chilton Co.
Chilton Way
Radnor, PA 19089   Ph:(215)964-4000

Manual. Published 1991. **Price:** $69.00.

4102 • Chilton's Guide to Air Conditioning and Heating Manual 1990-92: Motor Age Professional Mechanics Edition
Chilton Co.
Chilton Way
Radnor, PA 19089   Ph:(215)964-4000

Manual. Published April 1991. **Price:** $69.00.

4103 • Chilton's Guide to Air Conditioning Repair and Service, 1989-1991
Chilton Co.
Chilton Way
Radnor, PA 19089   Ph:(215)964-4000

Manual. Published June 1991. **Price:** $19.95.

4104 • Electrical Systems, Heating, and Air Conditioning
H. M. Gousha
2001 The Alameda
San Jose, CA 95126   Ph:(408)296-1060

Manual. Published 1981. **Price:** $9.95, workbook; $13.90, cassette.

4105 • Mitchell Automotive Heating and Air Conditioning Systems
Prentice-Hall
Rte. 9W
Englewood Cliffs, NJ 07632   Ph:(201)592-2000

Manual. Published 1987. **Price:** $41.00.

4106 • Principles and Service of Automotive Air Conditioning
Prentice-Hall
Rte. 9W
Englewood Cliffs, NJ 07632   Ph:(201)592-2000

Manual. Published 1984. **Editor(s):** Billy C. Langley. **Price:** $37.00, hardcover; $27.00, paper.

4107 • Quick Course in Car Cooling Systems
Automotive Cooling Systems Institute
300 Sylvan Ave.
P.O. Box 1638   Ph:(201)569-8500
Englewood Cliffs, NJ 07632-0638   Fax:(201)569-0159

Manual.

4108 • Quick Course in Car Cooling Systems
Automotive Cooling Systems Institute
300 Sylvan Ave.
PO Box 1638   Ph:(201)569-8500
Englewood Cliffs, NJ 07632-0638   Fax:(201)569-0159

Report/bulletin. Educates the public on the proper care and maintenance of automotive cooling systems.

4109 • Worldwide Trends in Engine Coolants, Cooling System Materials and Testing
Society of Automotive Engineers, Inc.
400 Commonwealth Dr.
Warrendale, PA 15096   Ph:(412)776-4841

Book. **Price:** $54.00.

Ignition systems

4110 • Advanced Electronic Ignition Tune-Up
Bergwall Productions, Inc.
106 Charles Lindbergh Blvd.
Uniondale, NY 11553-3695   Ph:(516)222-1111

Audio-visual. On three tapes, ignition repair and tune-up are demonstrated. **Release date:** 1984. **Producer:** Bergwall Productions, Inc. **Acquisition:** Purchase.

4111 • Automotive Electronic and Computer Controlled Ignition Systems
Prentice—Hall
Rte. 9W
Englewood Cliffs, NJ 07632   Ph:(201)592-2000

Manual. Published 1988. **Editor(s):** Don Knowles. **Price:** $23.25.

4112 • Automotive Fuel and Ignition Systems
Books on Demand
University Microfilms International
300 N. Zeeb Rd.
Ann Arbor, MI 48106   Ph:(313)761-4700

Manual. Published 1987. **Editor(s):** William Landon and Irving A. Frazee. **Price:** $128.00.

4113 • Automotive Ignition Systems: Diagnosis and Repair
McGraw-Hill Publishing Co.
1221 Ave. of the Americas
New York, NY 10026   Ph:(212)512-2000

Manual. Published 1982. **Editor(s):** Frank Derato. **Price:** $29.95.

4114 • Distributorless Ignition
Bergwall Productions, Inc.
106 Charles Lindbergh Blvd.
Uniondale, NY 11553-3695   Ph:(516)222-1111

Audio-visual. Various types of electronic ignition systems are examined from a mechanic's point of view. This series is also available as a single tape at the same cost. Titles: Point Type System; Electronic Ignition Systems and EST; Waste Spark Concept; Triggering Systems; and Troubleshooting. **Release date:** 1988. **Producer:** Bergwall Productions, Inc. **Price:** $369.00.

4115 • Electronic Ignition Explained
Bergwall Productions, Inc.
106 Charles Lindbergh Blvd.
Uniondale, NY 11553-3695   Ph:(516)222-1111

Audio-visual. On two tapes, the basic basics of electronic ignition are displayed. **Release date:** 1978. **Producer:** Bergwall Productions, Inc. **Acquisition:** Purchase.

4116 • Electronic Ignition Tune Up
Bergwall Publications, Inc.
P.O. Box 238
Garden City, NY 11530   Ph:800-645-3565

Manual. Published 1983. **Editor(s):** Peter Novellino. **Price:** Workbook costs $6.00; audio visual package costs $339.00.

4117 • Fuel Economy in Road Vehicles Powered by Spark Ignition Engines
Plenum Publishing Co.
233 Spring St.
New York, NY 10013   Ph:(212)620-8000

Manual. Published 1984. **Editor(s):** J.C. Hilliard. **Price:** $89.50.

4118 • The Ignition System Explained
Bergwall Productions, Inc.
106 Charles Lindbergh Blvd.
Uniondale, NY 11553-3695   Ph:(516)222-1111

Audio-visual. On six tapes, an explanation of ignition systems is given. **Release date:** 1985. **Producer:** Bergwall Productions, Inc. **Acquisition:** Purchase.

4119 • Mitchell's Electronic Ignition Troubleshooting Guide: Domestic Vehicles
Fisher Books
P.O. Box 445
Vienna, VA 22183   Ph:(703)448-0420

Manual. Published 1987. **Price:** $19.95.

4120 • Mitchell's Electronic Ignition Troubleshooting Guide: Import Vehicles
Fisher Books
P.O. Box 445
Vienna, VA 22183   Ph:(703)448-0420

Manual. Published 1988. **Price:** $14.95.

4121 • Petersen's Basic Ignition and Electrical Systems
Green Hill Publications
722 Columbus St.
Ottawa, IL 61350   Ph:(815)434-7905

Manual. Published 1985. **Price:** $9.95.

4122 • The Starting System Explained
Bergwall Productions, Inc.
106 Charles Lindbergh Blvd.
Uniondale, NY 11553-3695   Ph:(516)222-1111

Audio-visual. On four tapes, a car's starting system is made plain to the viewer. **Release date:** 1979. **Producer:** Bergwall Productions, Inc. **Acquisition:** Purchase.

4123 • Starting Systems Technology
Society of Automotive Engineers, Inc.
400 Commonwealth Dr.
Warrendale, PA 15096   Ph:(412)776-4841

Manual. Published 1984. **Price:** $51.00.

4124 • Tune-up Ignition and Fuel Induction Systems
H. M. Gousha
2001 The Alameda
San Jose, CA 95126   Ph:(408)296-1060

Manual. Published 1981. **Editor(s):** Bob Leigh. **Price:** $9.95, workbook; $13.90, cassette.

Import cars

4125 • Aftermarket for Imported Cars and Light Trucks
Frost and Sullivan, Inc.
106 Fulton St.
New York, NY 10038   Ph:(212)233-1080

Audio-visual. Published 1984. **Price:** $1400.00.

4126 • American Technology and the British Vehicle Industry
Cambridge University Press
40 W. 20th St.
New York, NY 10011   Ph:(212)924-3900

Book. Published 1987. **Price:** $49.50.

4127 • British Car
2D Publishing
7229 Remmet Ave.
PO Box 9099
Canoga Park, CA 91309   Ph:(818)710-1234
                               Fax:(818)710-1877

Magazine. Provides articles on British sports and luxury cars from classic to contemporary. Bimonthly. **Editor(s):** Dave Destler, Editor and Publisher. **Price:** $16.95/year; $2.95/year single issue.

4128 • Cabriolets
Motorbooks International
729 Prospect Ave.
Osceola, WI 54020   Ph:(715)294-3345

Book. Published 1986. **Editor(s):** Jean-Paul Thevenet and Peter Vann. **Price:** $9.95.

4129 • Chilton's Automatic Transmission Repair Manual, 1984-1988: Import Cars and Trucks: Motor-Age Professional Mechanic's Edition
Chilton Co.
Chilton Way
Radnor, PA 19089   Ph:(215)964-4000

Manual. Published 1989. **Price:** $70.00.

4130 • Chilton's Electronic Chassis Controls Manual, Import Cars and Trucks—1988-1990: Motor Age Professional Mechanic's Edition
Chilton Co.
Chilton Way
Radnor, PA 19089   Ph:(215)964-4000

Manual. Two volumes, A-M and N-Z. Published June 1991. **Price:** $72.00 per volume.

4131 • Chilton's Guide to Brakes, Steering and Suspension 1980-1987: Domestic and Import Cars and Trucks
Chilton Co.
Chilton Way
Radnor, PA 19089   Ph:(215)964-4000

Manual. Published 1988. **Price:** $19.95.

4132 • Chilton's Guide to Emission Diagnosis, Tune-Up and Vacuum Diagrams 1984-87
Chilton Co.
Chilton Way
Radnor, PA 19089   Ph:(215)964-4000

Manual. Volume one, domestic cars; volume two, import cars. Published 1987. **Price:** Volume one, $19.95; volume two, $17.95.

4133 • Chilton's Guide to Fuel Injection and Electronic Engine Controls 1984-1988: Import Cars and Trucks
Chilton Co.
Chilton Way
Radnor, PA 19089   Ph:(215)964-4000

Manual. Published 1988. **Price:** $19.95.

4134 • Chilton's IMP Emission Diagnostic and Service Manual, Vacuum Circuit, 1984-1987 Import Cars and Truck: Motor-Age Professional Mechanic's Edition
Chilton Co.
Chilton Way
Radnor, PA 19089   Ph:(215)964-4000

Manual. Published 1987. **Price:** $52.00.

4135 • Chilton's Import Automotive Service Manual, 1982-1989
Chilton Co.
Chilton Way
Radnor, PA 19089   Ph:(215)964-4000

Manual. Published 1989. **Price:** $72.00.

4136 • Chilton's Import Car Parts and Labor Guide, 1987-1991: Motor Age Professional Mechanics Edition
Chilton Co.
Chilton Way
Radnor, PA 19089   Ph:(215)964-4000

Manual. Published May 1991. **Price:** $70.00.

4137 • Chilton's Import Car Repair Manual 1982-87: Motor Age Professional Mechanics Edition
Chilton Co.
Chilton Way
Radnor, PA 19089   Ph:(215)964-4000

Manual. Published 1991. **Price:** $55.00.

4138 • Chilton's Import Car Repair Manual, 1987-91: Motor Age Professional Mechanic's Edition
Chilton Co.
Chilton Way
Radnor, PA 19089   Ph:(215)964-4000

Manual. Published 1991. **Price:** $24.95.

4139 • Chilton's Import Car Repair Manual 1987-91: Motor Age Professional Mechanics Edition
Chilton Co.
Chilton Way
Radnor, PA 19089   Ph:(215)964-4000

Manual. Published 1991. **Price:** $70.00.

4140 • Chilton's Import Car Repair Manual 1988-92
Chilton Co.
Chilton Way
Radnor, PA 19089   Ph:(215)964-4000

Manual. Published 1991. **Price:** $26.95.

4141 • Chilton's Import Car Service Manual, 1980-1987: Motor-Age Professional Mechanic's Edition
Chilton Co.
Chilton Way
Radnor, PA 19089   Ph:(215)964-4000

Manual. Published 1987. **Price:** $58.00.

4142 • **Chilton's Import Car Wiring Diagrams Manual,
1987-88: Motor-Age Professional Mechanic's Edition**
Chilton Co.
Chilton Way
Radnor, PA 19089   Ph:(215)964-4000

Manual. Published 1988. **Price:** $69.00.

4143 • **Emission Diagnosis Tune-up and Service Manual
1988 Import Cars and Trucks: Motor-Age
Professional Mechanic's Edition**
Chilton Co.
Chilton Way
Radnor, PA 19089   Ph:(215)964-4000

Manual. Published 1989. **Price:** $40.00.

4144 • **Far East Auto Owners Association—Newsletter**
Far East Auto Owners Association
108 E. Broadway
Port Jefferson, NY 11777   Ph:(516)928-2818

Newsletter. Quarterly.

4145 • **Fins, Chrome, and Steel**
Foreign Car Haters Club of America
P.O. Box 4500
Cave Creek, AZ 85331

Newsletter. Serves the Club's tongue-in-cheek campaign to
ridicule, abuse, slander, and degrade foreign cars and foreign car
owners. Seeks to ban the importation of all foreign cars in the U.S.
or to impose taxes that would make them prohibitively expensive.
Quarterly.

4146 • **Foreign Car Engine Overhaul**
Bergwall Productions, Inc.
P.O. Box 238
Garden City, NY 11530   Ph:800-645-3565

Manual. Published 1982. **Price:** $6.00, workbook; $139.00, audio
visual package.

4147 • **Foreign Interchange Manual**
Hollander Inc.
14800 28th Ave., Ste. 190
Plymouth, MN 55441   Ph:(612)553-0644

Manual. Published 1982. **Price:** $76.50.

4148 • **Honda Motor: The Men, the Management and
the Machines**
Kodansha International USA, Ltd.
114 Fifth Ave.
New York, NY 10011   Ph:(212)727-6460

Book. Published 1987. **Author(s):** Tetsuo Sakiya. **Price:** $5.95.

4149 • **Import Car Parts and Labor Guide 1982-89**
Chilton Co.
Chilton Way
Radnor, PA 19089   Ph:(215)964-4000

Book. Published 1989. **Price:** $70.00.

4150 • **Import Service**
Gemini Communications
306 N. Cleveland Massillon Rd.   Ph:(216)666-9553
Akron, OH 44313-9302   Fax:(216)666-8912

Magazine. Provides information on service and repair of imported
cars. Monthly. **Editor(s):** Karl Seyfert. **Price:** $36.00/year; $3.75 per
single issue.

4151 • **Import Update Newsletter**
Moog Automotive, Inc.
Dept. JT
P.O. Box 7224
St. Louis, MO 63177   Ph:(314)385-3400

Newsletter. Quarterly.

4152 • **Imported Car Reports**
United Communications Group
4550 Montgomery Ave., Ste. 700N
Bethesda, MD 20814   Ph:(313)851-1377

Newsletter. Weekly. **Editor(s):** Maynard Gordon, Editor and
Publisher. **Price:** $85.00.

4153 • **Mitchell's Electronic Fuel-Injection
Troubleshooting Guide: Import Vehicles**
Fisher Books
P.O. Box 38040
Tuscon, AZ 85740-8040   Ph:(602)292-9080

Manual. Published 1990. **Price:** $29.95.

4154 • **Mitchell's Electronic Ignition Troubleshooting
Guide: Import Vehicles**
Fisher Books
P.O. Box 445
Vienna, VA 22183   Ph:(703)448-0420

Manual. Published 1988. **Price:** $14.95.

4155 • **Motor Imported Car Repair**
Hearst Books
105 Madison Ave.
New York, NY 10016   Ph:(212)889-3050

Manual. Published 1988. **Price:** $27.50.

4156 • **Motor Imported Car Repair Manual: Up-to-Date
Info for Imported Car Owners**
William Morrow and Co.
105 Madison Ave.
New York, NY 10016   Ph:(212)889-3050

Manual. Published 1986. **Price:** $25.00.

4157 • **New Diesel Engines, Combustion and Emissions
Research in Japan**
Society of Automotive Engineers, Inc.
400 Commonwealth Dr.
Warrendale, PA 15096   Ph:(412)776-4841

Book. Published 1980. **Price:** $51.00.

4158 • **The Oil Spot**
British Motorcars of New England
P.O. Box 666
North Dighton, MA 02764   Ph:(617)679-8252

Newspaper. Periodic.

Instrument panels

4159 • **Automotive Instrument Panels: Design,
Materials, and Manufacturing**
Society of Automotive Engineers, Inc.
400 Commonwealth Dr.
Warrendale, PA 15096   Ph:(412)776-4841

Book. Published 1987. **Price:** $44.00.

4160 • **Electronic Displays and Information Systems**
Society of Automotive Engineers, Inc.
400 Commonwealth Dr.
Warrendale, PA 15096   Ph:(412)776-4841

Manual. Published 1981. **Price:** $46.00.

4161 • **Electronic Displays, Information Systems and
On-Board Electronics**
Society of Automotive Engineers, Inc.
400 Commonwealth Dr.
Warrendale, PA 15096   Ph:(412)776-4841

Manual. Published 1982. **Price:** $58.00.

4162 • Electronic Instrumentation Service Manual 1980-1987: Motor Age Professional Mechanic's Edition
Chilton Co.
Chilton Way
Radnor, PA 19089   Ph:(215)964-4000

Manual. Published 1988. **Price:** $59.00.

4163 • New Technologies in Automotive Electronic Displays and Information Systems
Society of Automotive Engineers, Inc.
400 Commonwealth Dr.
Warrendale, PA 15096   Ph:(412)776-4841

Book. **Price:** $68.00.

4164 • Plastics in Automobile Instrument Panels, Trim, and Seating
Society of Automotive Engineers
400 Commonwealth Dr.
Warrendale, PA 15096   Ph:(412)776-4841

Book. **Price:** $54.00.

4165 • Plastics in Automobiles: Bumper Systems, Interior Trim, Instrument Panels and Exterior Panels
Society of Automotive Engineers, Inc.
400 Commonwealth Dr.
Warrendale, PA 15096   Ph:(412)776-4841

Book. Published 1989. **Price:** $72.00.

4166 • Recent Developments in Automotive Electronic Displays and Information Systems
Society of Automotive Engineers, Inc.
400 Commonwealth Dr.
Warrendale, PA 15096   Ph:(412)776-4841

Book. Published 1987. **Price:** $59.00.

Lubricants

4167 • Automotive Fuel, Cooling, Lubrication, and Exhaust Systems
Prentice-Hall
Rte. 9W
Englewood Cliffs, NJ 07632   Ph:(201)592-2000

Manual. Published 1985. **Editor(s):** William Husselbee. **Price:** $34.00.

4168 • Automotive Fuel, Lubricating and Cooling Systems
McGraw-Hill Publishing Co.
11 W. 19th St.
New York, NY 10011   Ph:(212)337-6010

Manual. Published 1981. **Editor(s):** William H. Crouse and Donald L. Anglin. **Price:** $29.95.

4169 • Automotive Fuel, Lubrication, and Cooling Systems
Prentice-Hall
Rte. 9W
Englewood Cliffs, NJ 07632   Ph:(201)592-2000

Manual. Published 1985. **Editor(s):** Don Knowles. **Price:** $40.00, hardcover; $38.00, paper.

4170 • Basic Automotive Jobs Explained
Bergwall Productions, Inc.
106 Charles Lindbergh Blvd.
Uniondale, NY 11553-3695   Ph:(516)222-1111

Audio-visual. Simple automotive repairs are explained. Titles: Using Reference Material and Starter Replacement; Performing Road Service, Tie Road End and Idler Arm Replacement; Performing Underhood Services and Muffler Replacement; Changing Engine Oil, Automatic Transmission Fluid, Valve Cover Gasket, and Thermostat Replacement; and Alternator, Battery, Shocks and

Spark Plug Replacement. **Release date:** 1985. **Producer:** Bergwall Productions, Inc. **Price:** $269.00.

4171 • Engine Oil Effects on Vehicle Fuel Economy
Society of Automotive Engineers, Inc.
400 Commonwealth Dr.
Warrendale, PA 15096   Ph:(412)776-4841

Book. Published 1982. **Price:** $72.00.

4172 • Engines, Fuels, and Lubricants: Perspectives on the Future
Society of Automotive Engineers, Inc.
400 Commonwealth Dr.
Warrendale, PA 15096   Ph:(412)776-4841

Book. A series of eight papers. Published 1980. **Price:** $32.00.

4173 • Engines, Lubricating and, Cooling Systems
H. M. Gousha
2001 The Alameda
San Jose, CA 95126   Ph:(408)296-1060

Manual. Published 1981. **Editor(s):** Bob Leigh. **Price:** $9.95, paper; $13.90, cassette tape.

4174 • High-Temperature, High-Shear (HTHS) Oil Viscosity: Measurement and Relationship to Engine Operation
American Society for Testing and Materials
1916 Race St.
Philadelphia, PA 19103   Ph:(215)299-5585

Book. Published 1989. **Editor(s):** James A. Spearot. **Price:** $25.00.

4175 • How to Buy Motor Oil
Walter J. Klein Company Ltd.
6311 Carmel Rd.
P.O. Box 2087
Charlotte, NC 28211   Ph:(704)542-1403

Audio-visual. Viewers learn about types of motor oils and their uses and how to match oils to their cars' needs. **Release date:** 1978. **Producer:** Walter J. Klein Company Ltd. **Acquisition:** Purchase.

4176 • Hydraulics—Gear Oils—Grease
Farmland Industries, Inc.
3315 N. Oak Trafficway
Kansas City, MO 64116

Audio-visual. Here, the glories of proper mechanical lubrication are highlighted. **Release date:** 1985. **Producer:** Farmland Industries, Inc. **Acquisition:** Purchase.

4177 • Lube Recommendations and Capacities Booklet
H. M. Gousha
2001 The Alameda
San Jose, CA 95126   Ph:(408)296-1060

Book. Published 1986. **Price:** $5.55.

4178 • Master Lubrication Handbook
H. M. Gousha
2001 The Alameda
San Jose, CA 95126   Ph:(408)296-1060

Reference book. **Price:** $90.00.

4179 • Mechanical Maintenance Training
Tel-A-Train
309 N. Market St.
P.O. Box 4752   Ph:(615)266-0113
Chattanooga, TN 37405   Fax:(615)267-2555

Audio-visual. After watching this series just about any viewer should be able to fix engines. **Release date:** 1989. **Producer:** Tel-A-Train. **Acquisition:** Purchase, Rent/Lease.

4180 • Multicylinder Test Sequences for Evaluating Automotive Engine Oils
American Society for Testing and Materials
1916 Race St.
Philadelphia, PA 19103   Ph:(215)299-5585

Manual. In three parts: part one, Sequence IID-STP 315H; part two, Sequence IIID-STP 315H; part three, Sequence V-D-STP 315H. 1980. **Price:** $13.00, paperback; $16.00, looseleaf per volume.

4181 • Multigrade Oils for Diesel Engines
Society of Automotive Engineers, Inc.
400 Commonwealth Dr.
Warrendale, PA 15096   Ph:(412)776-4841

Book. Published 1980. **Price:** $27.00.

4182 • Passenger Car Motor Oils
Society of Automotive Engineers
400 Commonwealth Dr.
Warrendale, PA 15096   Ph:(412)776-4841

Book. Published 1989. **Price:** $46.00

4183 • Petroleum Products, Lubricants, and Fossil Fuels
American Society for Testing and Materials
1916 Race St.
Philadelphia, PA 19103   Ph:(215)299-5585

Book. Published 1986. **Price:** $34.00.

4184 • Selecting and Using Lubricants
TPC Training Systems
310 S. Michigan Ave.
Chicago, IL 60604   Ph:(312)537-6610

Audio-visual. The functions, characteristics, and ways of selecting lubricants are discussed. **Release date:** 1988. **Producer:** TPC Training Systems. **Acquisition:** Purchase, Rent/Lease.

4185 • Synthetic Automotive Engine Oils
Society of Automotive Engineers, Inc.
400 Commonwealth Dr.
Warrendale, PA 15096   Ph:(412)776-4841

Book. Published 1981. **Price:** $72.00.

4186 • Truck Lubrication Guide
H. M. Gousha
2001 The Alameda
San Jose, CA 95126   Ph:(408)296-1060

Book. Annual. **Editor(s):** Roger Fennema. **Price:** $35.80.

4187 • Tune Up America: Oil Change, Filters and Lube
Morris Video
2730 Monterey St., No. 105
Monterey Business Park
Torrance, CA 90503   Ph:(213)533-4800

Audio-visual. Learn how to save money by changing the oil and giving a car a lube job. **Release date:** 1986. **Producer:** Morris Video. **Price:** $19.95.

Parts

4188 • The Auto Parts Report
Cutter Information Corp.
1100 Massachusetts Ave.   Ph:(617)648-8700
Arlington, MA 02174   Fax:(617)648-8707

Newsletter. Provides news and information on auto parts. Semimonthly. **Editor(s):** Karen Fine Coburn. **Price:** $290.00/year.

4189 • Auto-Truck Interchange Manual: Body Parts
Hollander Inc.
14800 28th Ave., Suite 190
Plymouth, MN 55441   Ph:(612)553-0644

Manual. 1980. **Price:** $15.00.

4190 • Chilton's Import Car Parts and Labor Guide, 1987-1991: Motor Age Professional Mechanics Edition
Chilton Co.
Chilton Way
Radnor, PA 19089   Ph:(215)964-4000

Manual. Published May 1991. **Price:** $70.00.

4191 • Chilton's Labor Guide and Parts Manual 1986-90: Motor Age Professional Mechanic's Edition
Chilton Co.
Chilton Way
Radnor, PA 19089   Ph:(215)964-4000

Manual. Published 1991. **Price:** $69.00.

4192 • Crankshaft Manual
Automotive Engine Rebuilders Association (AERA)
330 Lexington Dr.
Buffalo Grove, IL 60089-6998   Ph:(708)541-6550

Manual. Identifies automotive engine crankshafts by casting/forging number. Includes cross-references of casting/forging number to application, size of engine, years used, and bore and stroke of engine. Annual. **Price:** Free to members; $60.00 per copy to nonmembers.

4193 • Cylinder Head and Block Identification Guide
Automotive Engine Rebuilders Association (AERA)
330 Lexington Dr.
Buffalo Grove, IL 60089-6998   Ph:(708)541-6550

Manual. Identifies automotive engine cylinder heads and blocks by casting number. Includes cross-reference of casting numbers by application, size of engine, years used, and other special identifying features. Annual. **Price:** Free to members; $20.00 per copy for nonmembers.

4194 • Filter Manufacturers Council—Technical Bulletin
Filter Manufacturers Council
300 Sylvan Ave.
P.O. Box 1638   Ph:(201)894-6809
Englewood Cliffs, NJ 07632   Fax:(201)569-0159

Report/bulletin. Contains information on the applications and uses of filters. Periodic. **Price:** Free.

4195 • Identification of Parts Failure
John Deere Service Publications
Dept. 333, John Deere Rd.
Moline, IL 61265   Ph:(309)765-2967

Manual. Text covers hundreds of parts failures, helps identify causes of damage, and gives examples of types of failures for different parts. Published 1987. **Price:** $11.14, paper; $117.45, slide set.

4196 • Import Car Parts and Labor Guide 1982-89
Chilton Co.
Chilton Way
Radnor, PA 19089   Ph:(215)964-4000

Book. Published 1989. **Price:** $70.00.

4197 • Powder Metal Parts
Society of Automotive Engineers, Inc.
400 Commonwealth Dr.
Warrendale, PA 15096   Ph:(412)776-4841

Book. Published 1983. **Price:** $46.00.

4198 • Selecting and Maintaining Bearings
TPC Training Systems
310 S. Michigan Ave.
Chicago, IL 60604   Ph:(312)537-6610

Audio-visual. Installation, inspection, and repair of plain journal, ball, and roller bearings are covered in this series. **Release date:** 1988. **Producer:** TPC Training Systems. **Acquisition:** Purchase, Rent/Lease.

Radiators

4199 • Advanced Car Care: Belts, Hoses and Radiator
Video Tech
19346 Third Ave., N.W.
Seattle, WA 98177   Ph:(206)546-5401

Audio-visual. Advanced auto engine maintenance and repair techniques are described and performed. **Release date:** 1981. **Producer:** Cinema Associates. **Acquisition:** Purchase.

Restraint systems

4200 • Airbags and Seat Belts
Center for Auto Safety
2001 S St. NW, Ste. 410
Washington, DC 20009   Ph:(202)328-7700

Book.

4201 • Children at Risk: Failure of the Federal Child Restraint Recall Program
Center for Auto Safety
2001 S St. NW, Ste. 410
Washington, DC 20009   Ph:(202)328-7700

Book.

4202 • Seat Belts: Index of Modern Information
ABBE Publishing Assn.
4111 Gallows Rd.
Virginia Division
Annadale, VA 22003   Ph:(703)750-0255

Reference book. Published 1990. **Editor(s):** Lynn Chenn. **Price:** $37.50, hardbound; $29.50, paper.

4203 • Vehicle Occupant Restraint Systems and Components
Society of Automotive Engineers, Inc.
400 Commonwealth
Warrendale, PA 15096   Ph:(412)776-4841

Manual. Published 1991. **Price:** $44.00.

Security systems

4204 • Automotive Security System—Design Handbook
TAB Books, Inc.
Blue Ridge Summit, PA 17294-0850   Ph:(717)794-2191

Manual. Published 1985. **Author(s):** Daniel J. Gifford. **Price:** $12.60.

4205 • Chilton's Guide to Auto Electronic Accessories: Sound, Security, and Safety
Chilton Co.
Chilton Way
Radnor, PA 19089   Ph:(215)964-4000

Manual. Published 1983. **Price:** $15.95.

4206 • Consumer Reports: Burglar Proofing Your Home and Car
Lorimar Home Video
17942 Cowan Ave.
Irvine, CA 92714   Ph:(714)474-0355

Audio-visual. A program sponsored by the consumer-advocative magazine designed to instruct the viewer in protecting his home and car from theft. **Release date:** 1987. **Producer:** Karl-Lorimar. **Acquisition:** Purchase.

4207 • How to Protect Yourself Against Automobile Theft
Car Audio Specialists Association (CASA)
2101 L St. NW, Ste. 800
Washington, DC 20037   Ph:(202)828-2270

Report/bulletin.

Shock absorbers

4208 • Advanced Car Care: Plugs, Timing and Shocks
Video Tech
19346 Third Ave., N.W.
Seattle, WA 98177   Ph:(206)546-5401

Audio-visual. Advanced auto engine maintenance procedures are demonstrated. **Release date:** 1981. **Producer:** Cinema Associates. **Acquisition:** Purchase.

4209 • Advanced Car Care: Tune Up and Shocks
RMI Media Productions, Inc.
2807 W. 47th St.
Shawnee Mission, KS 66205   Ph:(913)262-3974

Audio-visual. This program tells how to tune up a car in a step by step manner. **Release date:** 1984. **Producer:** RMI Media Productions, Inc. **Acquisition:** Purchase.

4210 • Basic Automotive Jobs Explained
Bergwall Productions, Inc.
106 Charles Lindbergh Blvd.
Uniondale, NY 11553-3695   Ph:(516)222-1111

Audio-visual. Simple automotive repairs are explained. Titles: Using Reference Material and Starter Replacement; Performing Road Service, Tie Road End and Idler Arm Replacement; Performing Underhood Services and Muffler Replacement; Changing Engine Oil, Automatic Transmission Fluid, Valve Cover Gasket, and Thermostat Replacement; and Alternator, Battery, Shocks and Spark Plug Replacement. **Release date:** 1985. **Producer:** Bergwall Productions, Inc. **Price:** $269.00.

4211 • Tune Up America: Replacing Shocks
Morris Video
2730 Monterey St., No. 105
Monterey Business Park
Torrance, CA 90503   Ph:(213)533-4800

Audio-visual. Everything an individual needs to know to replace the shocks on a car. **Release date:** 1986. **Producer:** Morris Video. **Price:** $19.95.

Sound systems

4212 • Audio Systems: Speakers, Receivers, Non-Audio Electronics
Society of Automotive Engineers, Inc.
400 Commonwealth Dr.
Warrendale, PA 15096   Ph:(412)776-4841

Manual. Published 1986. **Price:** $53.00.

4213 • Automobile Audio Systems
Society of Automotive Engineers, Inc.
400 Commonwealth Dr.
Warrendale, PA 15096   Ph:(412)776-4841

Book. Published 1989. **Price:** $74.00.

4214 • Automobile Audio Systems: Worldwide Developments
Society of Automotive Engineers, Inc.
400 Commonwealth Dr.
Warrendale, PA 15096   Ph:(412)776-4841

Book. Published 1985. **Price:** $71.00.

4215 • Car Audio Specialists Association—Government Action Bulletins
Car Audio Specialists Association (CASA)
2101 L St. NW, Ste. 800
Washington, DC 20037   Ph:(202)828-2270

Report/bulletin. Reports on federal, state, and local government actions affecting the mobile electronics industry. Monthly.

4216 • Car Audio Specialists Association—Special Bulletins
Car Audio Specialists Association (CASA)
2101 L St. NW, Ste. 800
Washington, DC 20037   Ph:(202)828-2270

Report/bulletin. Reports on original mobile electronics equipment; includes charts showing vehicle models of current year compared to those of the previous year. Periodic. **Price:** Free, for members only.

4217 • Car Stereo Review
Hachette Magazines, Inc.
1633 Broadway, 41st Fl.   Ph:(212)767-6020
New York, NY 10019   Fax:(212)767-5618

Magazine. Covers the buying, installation, maintenance, related accessories, and security of car sound systems, product reviews, and buyer's guides. **Price:** $16.98/year; $2.95 per single issue.

4218 • CARS
Viare Publishing
902 Broadway   Ph:(212)477-2200
New York, NY 10010   Fax:(212)529-3176

Magazine. Contains articles on mobile electronic systems and sound equipment. Monthly. **Editor(s):** Joseph Palenchar.

4219 • Chilton's Guide to Auto Electronic Accessories: Sound, Security, and Safety
Chilton Co.
Chilton Way
Radnor, PA 19089   Ph:(215)964-4000

Manual. Published 1983. **Price:** $15.95.

4220 • Guide to Radio Policy on Current Model Cars and Multi-Purpose Vehicles
Car Audio Specialists Association (CASA)
2101 L St. N.W., Ste. 800
Washington, DC 20037   Ph:(202)828-2270

Directory. Annual. **Price:** Free to members; $80.00 per issue for nonmembers.

4221 • How to Buy Car Stereo
Gray Publishers
703 E. Broadway Blvd.
Suite A1
Tucson, AZ 85719   Ph:(602)628-1965

Book. Published 1989. **Editor(s):** E. Duval Kopf.

4222 • Installation News
Bobit Publishing Co.
2512 Artesia Blvd.   Ph:(213)376-8788
Redondo Beach, CA 90278   Fax:(213)376-9043

Magazine. Technical journal of automotive electronics. Covers installation of autosound, security, cellular phones, and radar detectors. Monthly. **Editor(s):** Bill Florence. **Price:** Free.

4223 • Killer Car Stereo on a Budget
Audio Amateur Publications
P.O. Box 576
Peterborough, NH 03458   Ph:(603)924-9464

Manual. Published 1989. **Price:** $19.95.

4224 • Mobile Electronics Market Trends Guide
Car Audio Specialists Association (CASA)
2101 L St. NW, Ste. 800
Washington, DC 20037   Ph:(202)828-2270

Directory. Annual. **Price:** Free, for members only.

4225 • Orion Car Stereo Blue Book
Orion Research
1315 Main Ave.
Suite 230
Durango, CO 81301   Ph:(303)247-8855

Reference book. Published 1990. **Price:** $79.00.

4226 • RADAR
Radio Association Defending Airwave Rights
4949 S. 25A
Tipp City, OH 45371   Ph:(513)667-5472

Newsletter. Informs members of radar, radar detector, and transportation issues. Monthly. **Editor(s):** Janice Lee. **Price:** $20.00.

4227 • Radar Reporter Newsletter
Radio Association Defending Airwave Rights, Inc.
4949 South 25A   Ph:(513)667-5472
Tipp City, OH 45371   Fax:(513)667-3178

Newsletter. Provides information on Association activities related to police traffic radar and radar detectors. Also reports on other transportation topics of interest to motorists. Monthly. **Editor(s):** Janice Lee. **Price:** Available to members only.

Sport utility vehicles

4228 • California All Terrain Vehicle Association— Newsletter
California All Terrain Vehicle Assn.
401 Santa Barbara St.
Santa Barbara, CA 92101

Newsletter.

4229 • Four Wheel and Off Road
Petersen Publishing Co.
6725 Sunset Blvd.
Los Angeles, CA 90028   Ph:(213)854-2222

Magazine. Provides information on two- and four-wheel drive vehicles. Monthly. **Editor(s):** Steve Campbell. **Price:** $19.94 per year; $2.95 per issue.

4230 • Four Wheeler Magazine
Penthouse Intl.
6728 Eton Ave.   Ph:(818)992-4777
Canoga Park, CA 91303   Fax:(818)992-4979

Magazine. Contains articles about four-wheel-drive vehicles. Monthly. **Editor(s):** John Stewart. **Price:** $14.87.

4231 • Four Wheeler Specials
Penthouse Intl.
6728 Eton Ave.
P.O. Box 7116
Canoga Park, CA 91304   Ph:(212)496-6100

Magazine. Seven times per year. **Price:** $2.95.

4232 • The Great American Pickup Trucks: Stylesetter, Workhorse, Sport Truck
Motorbooks International
729 Prospect Ave.
Osceda, WI 54020   Ph:(715)294-3345

Book. Published 1988. **Editor(s):** Henry Rasmussen. **Price:** $24.95.

4233 • Guide to Radio Policy on Current Model Cars and Multi-Purpose Vehicles
Car Audio Specialists Association (CASA)
2101 L St. N.W., Ste. 800
Washington, DC 20037   Ph:(202)828-2270

Directory. Annual. **Price:** Free to members; $80.00 per issue for nonmembers.

4234 • Off-Road
Argus Publishers Corp.
12100 Wilshire Blvd., Ste. 250   Ph:(213)820-3601
Los Angeles, CA 90025   Fax:(213)207-9388

Magazine. Focuses on the sport of off-roading. Features four-wheel drive vehicles, pick-ups, vans, and trail bikes. Includes trip information, race reports, photos, technical tips, equipment and accessories, and road tests. Monthly. **Editor(s):** Duanne Elliott. **Price:** $15.00/year; $2.50 per single issue.

4235 • Off-Road Advertiser
Two Trees Publishing, Inc.
P.O. Box 1154
Arcata, CA 95521-1154   Ph:(213)860-7007

Magazine. Covers four-wheel drives, dune buggies, pickup trucks, and sport utility vehicles. Contains articles on trail runs, jamborees, and major off-road races. Monthly. **Editor(s):** Fred C. Horton. **Price:** $15.00/year; $1.50 per single issue.

4236 • Off Road America
Intra-South Publications
4487 Ashton, Ste. A
Sarasota, FL 34233   Ph:(813)921-5687

Magazine. Covers four-wheel-drive and offroad racing activities nationwide. Monthly. **Editor(s):** Patricia A. Sands, Editor. **Price:** $18.00/year; $2.00 per single issue.

4237 • Petersen's 4 Wheel & Off Road
Petersen Publishing Co.
7750 Sunset Blvd.   Ph:(213)854-2360
Los Angeles, CA 90046   Fax:(213)854-2865

Magazine. Monthly. **Editor(s):** Steve Campbell. **Price:** $17.94/year; $2.75 per single issue.

Sports and exotic cars

4238 • British Car
2D Publishing
7229 Remmet Ave.
PO Box 9099   Ph:(818)710-1234
Canoga Park, CA 91309   Fax:(818)710-1877

Magazine. Provides articles on British sports and luxury cars from classic to contemporary. Bimonthly. **Editor(s):** Dave Destler, Editor and Publisher. **Price:** $16.95/year; $2.95/year single issue.

4239 • Cabriolets
Motorbooks International
729 Prospect Ave.
Osceola, WI 54020   Ph:(715)294-3345

Book. Published 1986. **Editor(s):** Jean-Paul Thevenet and Peter Vann. **Price:** $9.95.

4240 • California Sports Car Club News
California Sports Car Club
12444 Victory Blvd., Ste. 405A
North Hollywood, CA 91606   Ph:(818)508-7811

Newspaper. Periodic.

4241 • Car Collector and Car Classics
Classic Publishing, Inc.
8601 Dunwoody Pl., Ste. 144
Atlanta, GA 30350   Ph:(404)998-4603

Magazine. Intended for collectors of antique, classic, milestone, and sports cars. Monthly. **Editor(s):** Donald R. Peterson. **Price:** $30.00/year; $3.75 per single issue.

4242 • Car Crazy: Wild Hour on Wheels
VidAmerica, Inc.
235 E. 55th St.
New York, NY 10022   Ph:(212)685-1300

Audio-visual. The 100th anniversary of the American automobile is celebrated with this rubber burnin' look at our fastest and most exotic cars. **Release date:** 1983. **Producer:** VidAmerica, Inc. **Price:** $19.98.

4243 • Elite Cars
Publications International Ltd.
7373 N. Cicero
Lincolnwood, IL 60646   Ph:(708)676-3470

Magazine. Magazine for luxury and sports car drivers. Bimonthly. **Editor(s):** Richard D. Hawthorne. **Price:** $4.95 per single issue.

4244 • The Encyclopedia of American Supercars
Bookman Publishing
1212 York Road, Suite C302
Lutherville, MD 21093   Ph:(301)321-6795

Reference book. Published 1981. **Editor(s):** Robert Ackerson. **Price:** $14.95.

4245 • Fast Facts
Auto Intl. Assn.
1575 S. Valley Vista Dr.
Diamond Bar, CA 91765-4173   Ph:(213)692-9402

Newsletter. Monthly. **Editor(s):** Tim Schneider.

4246 • Hot Rod Magazine
Petersen Publishing Co.
8490 Sunset Blvd.
Los Angeles, CA 90069   Ph:(213)854-2280

Magazine. Monthly. **Editor(s):** Jeff Smith. **Price:** $9.00.

4247 • Motor Trend—Sports Cars of the World
Petersen Publishing Co.
6725 Sunset Blvd.
Los Angeles, CA 90028   Ph:(213)854-2222

Magazine. Provides an in-depth analysis of current models as well as retrospectives on famous sports cars of the past. Annual. **Editor(s):** Ro McGonegal. **Price:** $2.95.

4248 • New Directions in Suspension Design: Making the Fast Car Faster
Robert Bentley Inc., Pubs.
1000 Massachusetts Ave.
Cambridge, MA 02138   Ph:(617)547-4170

Book. Published 1981. **Editor(s):** Colin Campbell. **Price:** $21.95.

4249 • Rag Top News
U.S.A. Convertible Club
P.O. Box 40169
Cincinnati, OH 45240

Newsletter. Semiannual.

4250 • Sports and Classics
Sports and Classics
512 Post Rd.   Ph:(203)655-8731
Darien, CT 06820   Fax:(203)656-1956

Magazine. Annual. **Editor(s):** John Peters. **Price:** $5.00.

4251 • Sports Car International
Sports Car International, Inc.
3901 Westerly Pl., Ste. 120   Ph:(714)851-3044
Newport Beach, CA 92660   Fax:(714)851-3924

Magazine. Features articles and graphics for car enthusiasts. Monthly. **Editor(s):** Mark Ewing. **Price:** $19.95/year; $2.50 per single issue.

4252 • SportsCar
Pfanner, Catheron & Brown Publications, Inc.
1385 E. Warner Ave., Bldg. 6, Ste. C   Ph:(714)259-8240
Tustin, CA 92680   Fax:(714)259-9377

Magazine. Official publication of the Sports Car Club of America. Monthly. **Editor(s):** John Zimmermann. **Price:** $35.40/year; $2.95 per single issue.

4253 • The Story of Ferrari
Simitar Entertainment
3850 Annapolis Ln.   Ph:(612)559-6660
Plymouth, MN 55447   Fax:(612)559-0210

Audio-visual. A visual history of Enzo Ferrari's world-renowned car company. **Release date:** 1988. **Producer:** Simitar Entertainment. **Price:** $9.95.

4254 • Superauto Illustrated
Publications Intl. Ltd.
7373 N. Cicero Ave.
Lincolnwood, IL 60646   Ph:(312)676-3470

Magazine. Contains articles on sports and exotic cars. Monthly. **Editor(s):** Richard Hawthorne. **Price:** $19.95 per year; $3.95 per issue.

4255 • Topwheels
TWC Publishing, Inc.
588 Broadway, Rm. 604   Ph:(212)972-7050
New York, NY 10012-5408   Fax:(212)370-4983

Magazine. Intended for enthusiasts of exotic and classic sports cars. Bimonthly. **Editor(s):** Richard S. Hollander. **Price:** $24.95/year; $4.95 per single issue.

4256 • Write Line
Sports Car Club of America, Salina Chapter
1513 Pershing
Salina, KS 67401   Ph:(913)827-5143

Newspaper. Periodic.

Station wagons

4257 • Tailgate News
Great American Station Wagon Owner's Association
2017 Manatee Ave., W.
Bradenton, FL 34205   Ph:(813)747-9280

Newsletter. Contains parts and sales listings. Monthly.

Steering systems

4258 • Automotive Brakes, Suspension and Steering
McGraw-Hill Publishing Co.
11 W. 19th. St.
New York, NY 10011   Ph:(212)337-6010

Manual. Published 1983. **Editor(s):** William H. Crouse and Donald L. Anglin. **Price:** $29.95.

4259 • Automotive Steering and Suspension Systems
Prentice—Hall
Rte. 9W
Englewood Cliffs, NJ 07632   Ph:(201)592-2000

Manual. Published 1988. **Editor(s):** William Husselbee. **Price:** $26.67.

4260 • Automotive Steering, Suspension, and Braking Systems: Principles and Service
Prentice-Hall
Rte. 9W
Englewood Cliffs, NJ 07632   Ph:(201)592-2000

Manual. Published 1983. **Editor(s):** Frank J. Thiessen and David N. Dales. **Price:** $34.00.

4261 • Automotive Suspension, Steering and Brakes
Prentice-Hall
Rte. 9W
Englewood Cliffs, NJ 07632   Ph:(201)592-2000

Manual. Published 1980. **Editor(s):** Herbert E. Ellinger and Richard B. Hathaway. **Price:** $37.00.

4262 • Automotive Suspension, Steering and Brakes
Delmar Publishers, Inc.
Two Computer Dr., W.
Albany, NY 12212   Ph:(518)459-1150

Manual. Published 1987. **Editor(s):** Jay Webster. **Price:** $24.95; $6.00, instructor's guide.

4263 • Brakes, Steering, Front Suspension, Wheels and Tires
H. M. Gousha
2001 The Alameda
San Jose, CA 95126   Ph:(408)296-1060

Manual. Published 1981. **Editor(s):** Bob Leigh. **Price:** $9.95, workbook; $13.90, cassette.

4264 • Chilton's Guide to Brakes, Steering and Suspension 1980-1987: Domestic and Import Cars and Trucks
Chilton Co.
Chilton Way
Radnor, PA 19089   Ph:(215)964-4000

Manual. Published 1988. **Price:** $19.95.

4265 • Safety Check Your Car
Pyramid Film and Video
Box 1048   Ph:(213)828-7577
Santa Monica, CA 90406   Fax:(213)453-9083

Audio-visual. This program demonstrates effective auto maintenance for the average driver. Topics covered include: gas gauge precautions, tire maintenance, steering problems, muffler cracks, and brake problems. **Release date:** 1976. **Producer:** Pyramid; Lee Stanley. **Acquisition:** Rent/Lease, Purchase, Duplication License.

4266 • Vehicle Dynamics Related to Braking and Steering
Society of Automotive Engineers, Inc.
400 Commonwealth Dr.
Warrendale, PA 15096   Ph:(412)776-4841

Manual. Published 1989. **Price:** $31.00.

Suspension systems

4267 • Advanced Truck Suspensions
Society of Automotive Engineers, Inc.
400 Commonwealth Dr.
Warrendale, PA 15096   Ph:(412)776-4841

Book. Published 1989. **Price:** $24.00.

4268 • All Wheel Drive High Performance Handbook
Motorbooks International
729 Prospect Ave.
Osceda, WI 54020   Ph:(715)294-3345

Manual. Published 1990. **Editor(s):** Jay Lamma. **Price:** $16.95.

4269 • Automotive Brakes, Suspension and Steering
McGraw-Hill Publishing Co.
11 W. 19th. St.
New York, NY 10011   Ph:(212)337-6010

Manual. Published 1983. **Editor(s):** William H. Crouse and Donald L. Anglin. **Price:** $29.95.

4270 • Automotive Steering and Suspension Systems
Prentice—Hall
Rte. 9W
Englewood Cliffs, NJ 07632   Ph:(201)592-2000

Manual. Published 1988. **Editor(s):** William Husselbee. **Price:** $26.67.

4271 • Automotive Steering, Suspension, and Braking Systems: Principles and Service
Prentice-Hall
Rte. 9W
Englewood Cliffs, NJ 07632   Ph:(201)592-2000

Manual. Published 1983. **Editor(s):** Frank J. Thiessen and David N. Dales. **Price:** $34.00.

4272 • Automotive Suspension, Steering and Brakes
Prentice-Hall
Rte. 9W
Englewood Cliffs, NJ 07632   Ph:(201)592-2000

Manual. Published 1980. **Editor(s):** Herbert E. Ellinger and Richard B. Hathaway. **Price:** $37.00.

4273 • Automotive Suspension, Steering and Brakes
Delmar Publishers, Inc.
Two Computer Dr., W.
Albany, NY 12212   Ph:(518)459-1150

Manual. Published 1987. **Editor(s):** Jay Webster. **Price:** $24.95; $6.00, instructor's guide.

4274 • Brakes, Steering, Front Suspension, Wheels and Tires
H. M. Gousha
2001 The Alameda
San Jose, CA 95126   Ph:(408)296-1060

Manual. Published 1981. **Editor(s):** Bob Leigh. **Price:** $9.95, workbook; $13.90, cassette.

4275 • Chilton's Guide to Brakes, Steering and Suspension 1980-1987: Domestic and Import Cars and Trucks
Chilton Co.
Chilton Way
Radnor, PA 19089   Ph:(215)964-4000

Manual. Published 1988. **Price:** $19.95.

4276 • Current Trends in Truck Suspension
Society of Automotive Engineers, Inc.
400 Commonwealth Dr.
Warrendale, PA 15096   Ph:(412)776-4841

Report/bulletin. Six papers. Published 1980. **Price:** $33.00.

4277 • The Front End
Bergwall Productions, Inc.
106 Charles Lindbergh Blvd.
Uniondale, NY 11553-3695   Ph:(516)222-1111

Audio-visual. On four tapes, an automobile front end is repaired. **Release date:** 1984. **Producer:** Bergwall Productions, Inc. **Acquisition:** Purchase.

4278 • Front Wheel Drive: Transaxle Overhaul
Bergwall Productions, Inc.
106 Charles Lindbergh Blvd.
Uniondale, NY 11553-3695   Ph:(516)222-1111

Audio-visual. On five tapes, the ins and outs of overhauling a front wheel drive transaxle are demonstrated. **Release date:** 1984. **Producer:** Bergwall Productions, Inc. **Acquisition:** Purchase.

4279 • Manual for Incorporating Pneumatic Springs in Vehicle Suspension Designs
Society of Automotive Engineers, Inc.
400 Commonwealth Dr.
Warrendale, PA 15096   Ph:(412)776-4841

Manual. Published 1989. **Price:** $33.00.

4280 • New Directions in Suspension Design: Making the Fast Car Faster
Robert Bentley Inc., Pubs.
1000 Massachusetts Ave.
Cambridge, MA 02138   Ph:(617)547-4170

Book. Published 1981. **Editor(s):** Colin Campbell. **Price:** $21.95.

4281 • Tires, Suspension and Handling
Cambridge Univ. Press
40 W. 20th St.
New York, NY 10011   Ph:(212)924-3900

Manual. Published 1991. **Editor(s):** J.C. Dixon.

4282 • Tune Up America: Replacing Struts
Morris Video
2730 Monterey St., No. 105
Monterey Business Park
Torrance, CA 90503   Ph:(213)533-4800

Audio-visual. Everything that is necessary to change struts on an automobile. **Release date:** 1986. **Producer:** Morris Video. **Price:** $19.95.

Tires

4283 • All Wheel Drive High Performance Handbook
Motorbooks International
729 Prospect Ave.
Osceda, WI 54020   Ph:(715)294-3345

Manual. Published 1990. **Editor(s):** Jay Lamma. **Price:** $16.95.

4284 • Brakes, Steering, Front Suspension, Wheels and Tires
H. M. Gousha
2001 The Alameda
San Jose, CA 95126   Ph:(408)296-1060

Manual. Published 1981. **Editor(s):** Bob Leigh. **Price:** $9.95, workbook; $13.90, cassette.

4285 • Safety Check Your Car
Pyramid Film and Video
Box 1048   Ph:(213)828-7577
Santa Monica, CA 90406   Fax:(213)453-9083

Audio-visual. This program demonstrates effective auto maintenance for the average driver. Topics covered include: gas gauge precautions, tire maintenance, steering problems, muffler cracks, and brake problems. **Release date:** 1976. **Producer:** Pyramid; Lee Stanley. **Acquisition:** Rent/Lease, Purchase, Duplication License.

4286 • Tire Retreading/Repair Journal
Tire Technical Services, Inc.
P.O. Box 17203   Ph:(502)361-9219
Louisville, KY 40217   Fax:(502)367-9570

Magazine. Contains technical information on tire retreading. Monthly. **Editor(s):** Edward J. Wagner. **Price:** $50.00.

4287 • Tire Wise
AIMS Media, Inc.
6901 Woodley Ave.
Van Nuys, CA 91406-4878   Ph:(818)785-4111

Audio-visual. What to know in buying a set of tires. **Release date:** 1976. **Producer:** AIMS Instructional Media Service. **Acquisition:** Purchase, Duplication License.

4288 • Tires, Suspension and Handling
Cambridge Univ. Press
40 W. 20th St.
New York, NY 10011   Ph:(212)924-3900

Manual. Published 1991. **Editor(s):** J.C. Dixon.

Trucks and vans

4289 • Advanced Truck Suspensions
Society of Automotive Engineers, Inc.
400 Commonwealth Dr.
Warrendale, PA 15096   Ph:(412)776-4841

Book. Published 1989. **Price:** $24.00.

4290 • Aftermarket for Imported Cars and Light Trucks
Frost and Sullivan, Inc.
106 Fulton St.
New York, NY 10038   Ph:(212)233-1080

Audio-visual. Published 1984. **Price:** $1400.00.

4291 • America's Light Trucks
Motor Vehicle Manufacturers Assn. of the United
  States
7430 Second Ave., Ste. 300
Detroit, MI 48202   Ph:(313)872-4311

Book. Published 1986. **Editor(s):** Sheridan Brinley.

4292 • Anti Lock Braking Systems for Passenger Cars and Light Trucks: A Review
Society of Automotive Engineers, Inc.
400 Commonwealth Dr.
Warrendale, PA 15096   Ph:(412)776-4841

Manual. Published 1987. **Price:** $90.00.

4293 • Auto and Truck News
BeAnCa Publishing
4346 SE Div.
Portland, OR 97206-1630   Ph:(503)238-1188

Magazine. Bimonthly. **Editor(s):** John Jangula. **Price:** $550.00.

4294 • Auto-Truck Interchange Manual: Body Parts
Hollander Inc.
14800 28th Ave., Suite 190
Plymouth, MN 55441   Ph:(612)553-0644

Manual. 1980. **Price:** $15.00.

4295 • Auto-Truck Interchange Manual: Wheel Covers
Hollander Inc.
14800 28th Ave., Ste. 190
Plymouth, MN 55441   Ph:(612)553-0644

Manual. Published 1982. **Price:** $15.95.

4296 • Auto-Truck Interchange Manual: Wheels
Hollander Inc.
14800 28th Ave., Ste. 190
Plymouth, MN 55447   Ph:(612)553-0644

Manual. Published 1981. **Price:** $5.95.

4297 • Car and Light Truck Diesel Engine Service Manual
H. M. Gousha
2001 The Alameda
San Jose, CA 95126   Ph:(408)296-1060

Manual. Published 1983. **Price:** $9.95.

4298 • Chilton's Automatic Transmission Repair Manual, 1984-1988: Import Cars and Trucks: Motor-Age Professional Mechanic's Edition
Chilton Co.
Chilton Way
Radnor, PA 19089   Ph:(215)964-4000

Manual. Published 1989. **Price:** $70.00.

4299 • Chilton's Automatic Transmission Service Manual 1984-88: Domestic Cars and Trucks: Motor-Age Professional Mechanic's Edition
Chilton Co.
Chilton Way
Radnor, PA 19089   Ph:(215)964-4000

Manual. Published 1989. **Price:** $70.00.

4300 • Chilton's Electronic Chassis Controls Manual, Import Cars and Trucks—1988-1990: Motor Age Professional Mechanic's Edition
Chilton Co.
Chilton Way
Radnor, PA 19089   Ph:(215)964-4000

Manual. Two volumes, A-M and N-Z. Published June 1991. **Price:** $72.00 per volume.

4301 • Chilton's Electronic Engine Controls Manual, 1988-90—Domestic Cars and Trucks: Motor-Age Professional Mechanic's Edition
Chilton Co.
Chilton Way
Radnor, PA 19089   Ph:(215)964-4000

Manual. Published 1989. **Price:** $72.00.

4302 • Chilton's Guide to Brakes, Steering and Suspension 1980-1987: Domestic and Import Cars and Trucks
Chilton Co.
Chilton Way
Radnor, PA 19089   Ph:(215)964-4000

Manual. Published 1988. **Price:** $19.95.

4303 • Chilton's Guide to Diesel Cars and Trucks
Chilton Co.
Chilton Way
Radnor, PA 19089   Ph:(215)964-4000

Manual. Published 1983. **Editor(s):** James Joseph. **Price:** $15.95.

4304 • Chilton's Guide to Fuel Injection and Electronic Engine Controls 1984-1988: Import Cars and Trucks
Chilton Co.
Chilton Way
Radnor, PA 19089   Ph:(215)964-4000

Manual. Published 1988. **Price:** $19.95.

4305 • Chilton's IMP Emission Diagnostic and Service Manual, Vacuum Circuit, 1984-1987 Import Cars and Truck: Motor-Age Professional Mechanic's Edition
Chilton Co.
Chilton Way
Radnor, PA 19089   Ph:(215)964-4000

Manual. Published 1987. **Price:** $52.00.

4306 • Chilton's Professional Truck and Van Repair Manual 1981-1988
Chilton Co.
Chilton Way
Radnor, PA 19089   Ph:(215)964-4000

Manual. Published 1988. **Price:** $65.00.

4307 • Chilton's Truck and Van Repair Manual, 1982-1988
Chilton Co.
Chilton Way
Radnor, PA 19089   Ph:(215)964-4000

Manual. Published 1988. **Price:** $24.95.

4308 • Chilton's Truck and Van Wiring Diagram Manual, 1989-1990: Motor Age Professional Mechanic's Edition
Chilton Co.
Chilton Way
Radnor, PA 19089   Ph:(215)964-4000

Manual. Published February 1991. **Price:** $69.00.

4309 • Chilton's Tune-up Emission Diagnosis and Service Manual, 1988: Import Cars and Trucks
Chilton Co.
Chilton Way
Radnor, PA 19089   Ph:(215)964-4000

Manual. Published 1989. **Price:** $40.00.

4310 • Current Trends in Truck Suspension
Society of Automotive Engineers, Inc.
400 Commonwealth Dr.
Warrendale, PA 15096   Ph:(412)776-4841

Report/bulletin. Six papers. Published 1980. **Price:** $33.00.

4311 • Diesel Engines for Automobiles, Small Trucks and Small Tractors
Prentice-Hall
Rte. 9W
Englewood Cliffs, NJ 07632   Ph:(201)592-2000

Manual. Published 1986. **Editor(s):** Tom Weathers, Jr. **Price:** $47.00.

4312 • Electric and Electronic Systems for Automobiles and Trucks
Prentice-Hall
Rte. 9W
Englewood Cliffs, NJ 07632   Ph:(201)592-2000

Manual. Published 1983. **Editor(s):** Robert N. Brady. **Price:** $50.00.

4313 • Emission Diagnosis Tune-up and Service Manual 1988 Import Cars and Trucks: Motor-Age Professional Mechanic's Edition
Chilton Co.
Chilton Way
Radnor, PA 19089   Ph:(215)964-4000

Manual. Published 1989. **Price:** $40.00.

4314 • Four Wheel and Off Road
Petersen Publishing Co.
6725 Sunset Blvd.
Los Angeles, CA 90028   Ph:(213)854-2222

Magazine. Provides information on two- and four-wheel drive vehicles. Monthly. **Editor(s):** Steve Campbell. **Price:** $19.94 per year; $2.95 per issue.

4315 • Four Wheeler Magazine
Penthouse Intl.
6728 Eton Ave.   Ph:(818)992-4777
Canoga Park, CA 91303   Fax:(818)992-4979

Magazine. Contains articles about four-wheel-drive vehicles. Monthly. **Editor(s):** John Stewart. **Price:** $14.87.

4316 • Four Wheeler Specials
Penthouse Intl.
6728 Eton Ave.
P.O. Box 7116
Canoga Park, CA 91304   Ph:(212)496-6100

Magazine. Seven times per year. **Price:** $2.95.

4317 • The Great American Pickup Trucks: Stylesetter, Workhorse, Sport Truck
Motorbooks International
729 Prospect Ave.
Osceda, WI 54020   Ph:(715)294-3345

Book. Published 1988. **Editor(s):** Henry Rasmussen. **Price:** $24.95.

4318 • Hot Truck
Peterson Publishing Co.
6725 Sunset Blvd.   Ph:(213)854-2222
Los Angeles, CA 90028   Fax:(213)854-2718

Magazine. Offers technical articles, event coverage, and new product information to enthusiasts of high performance and custom trucks. Bimonthly.

4319 • MiniTruckin'
McMullen Publishing, Inc.
2145 W. La Palma Ave.   Ph:(714)635-9040
Anaheim, CA 92801   Fax:(714)533-9979

Magazine. Intended for mini-truck enthusiasts. Quarterly. **Editor(s):** Steve Stillwell.

4320 • Off-Road
Argus Publishers Corp.
12100 Wilshire Blvd., Ste. 250   Ph:(213)820-3601
Los Angeles, CA 90025   Fax:(213)207-9388

Magazine. Focuses on the sport of off-roading. Features four-wheel drive vehicles, pick-ups, vans, and trail bikes. Includes trip information, race reports, photos, technical tips, equipment and accessories, and road tests. Monthly. **Editor(s):** Duanne Elliott. **Price:** $15.00/year; $2.50 per single issue.

4321 • Off-Road Advertiser
Two Trees Publishing, Inc.
P.O. Box 1154
Arcata, CA 95521-1154   Ph:(213)860-7007

Magazine. Covers four-wheel drives, dune buggies, pickup trucks, and sport utility vehicles. Contains articles on trail runs, jamborees, and major off-road races. Monthly. **Editor(s):** Fred C. Horton. **Price:** $15.00/year; $1.50 per single issue.

4322 • Off Road America
Intra-South Publications
4487 Ashton, Ste. A
Sarasota, FL 34233   Ph:(813)921-5687

Magazine. Covers four-wheel-drive and offroad racing activities nationwide. Monthly. **Editor(s):** Patricia A. Sands, Editor. **Price:** $18.00/year; $2.00 per single issue.

4323 • Petersen's 4 Wheel & Off Road
Petersen Publishing Co.
7750 Sunset Blvd.   Ph:(213)854-2360
Los Angeles, CA 90046   Fax:(213)854-2865

Magazine. Monthly. **Editor(s):** Steve Campbell. **Price:** $17.94/year; $2.75 per single issue.

4324 • Sport Truck
Peterson Publishing Co.
6725 Sunset Blvd.
Los Angeles, CA 90028   Ph:(213)854-2470

Magazine. Monthly. **Editor(s):** Drew Hardin. **Price:** $17.94/yr.; $2.95/mo.

4325 • Truck Electronic Control Systems
Society of Automotive Engineers, Inc.
400 Commonwealth Dr.
Warrendale, PA 15096   Ph:(412)776-4841

Manual. Published 1985. **Price:** $24.00.

4326 • Truck Lubrication Guide
H. M. Gousha
2001 The Alameda
San Jose, CA 95126   Ph:(408)296-1060

Book. Annual. **Editor(s):** Roger Fennema. **Price:** $35.80.

4327 • Truck 'N Van Power
M & O Communications, Inc.
P.O. Box 651
Murray Hill Stn.
New York, NY 10156

Magazine. Bimonthly. **Editor(s):** John Fasano. **Price:** $15.00 per year; $2.95 per issue.

4328 • Truckin' Magazine
McMullen Publishing, Inc.
2145 W. La Palma Ave.   Ph:(714)635-9040
Anaheim, CA 92801-1785   Fax:(714)533-9979

Magazine. Provides information about custom vans, mini trucks, and pickups. Monthly. **Editor(s):** Steve Stillwell. **Price:** $19.95/year; $34.95 per two years.

4329 • Vans and Trucks
Clark Kaho Media, Inc.
P.O. Box 2127
Yorba Linda, CA 92686   Ph:(714)970-8981

Magazine. Provides information on topics of interest to light truck enthusiasts. Bimonthly. **Editor(s):** Todd Kaho. **Price:** $12.95 per year; $2.50 per issue.

Turbocharging

4330 • Turbo and Hi-Tech Performance
MAG-TEC Productions, Inc.
9582 Hamilton   Ph:(714)962-7795
Huntington Beach, CA 92646   Fax:(714)965-2268

Magazine. Covers automotive performance and engineering. Bimonthly. **Editor(s):** Frank Balogh. **Price:** $14.97/year; $2.95 per issue.

4331 • The Turbocharger Explained
Bergwall Productions
106 Charles Lindbergh Blvd.
Uniondale, NY 11553-3695   Ph:(516)222-1111

Audio-visual. The functioning and repair of a turbocharger are explored. Titles: Operating Principles; Basic Parts I; Basic Parts II; Problem Diagnosis/Service Procedures-Part I; and Problem Diagnosis/Service Procedures-Part II. **Release date:** 1987. **Producer:** Bergwall Productions. **Price:** $289.00.

Undercar repair/maintenance

4332 • Basic Automotive Jobs Explained
Bergwall Productions, Inc.
106 Charles Lindbergh Blvd.
Uniondale, NY 11553-3695   Ph:(516)222-1111

Audio-visual. Simple automotive repairs are explained. Titles: Using Reference Material and Starter Replacement; Performing Road Service, Tie Road End and Idler Arm Replacement; Performing Underhood Services and Muffler Replacement; Changing Engine Oil, Automatic Transmission Fluid, Valve Cover Gasket, and Thermostat Replacement; and Alternator, Battery, Shocks and Spark Plug Replacement. **Release date:** 1985. **Producer:** Bergwall Productions, Inc. **Price:** $269.00.

4333 • Safety Check Your Car
Pyramid Film and Video
Box 1048   Ph:(213)828-7577
Santa Monica, CA 90406   Fax:(213)453-9083

Audio-visual. This program demonstrates effective auto maintenance for the average driver. Topics covered include: gas gauge precautions, tire maintenance, steering problems, muffler cracks, and brake problems. **Release date:** 1976. **Producer:** Pyramid; Lee Stanley. **Acquisition:** Rent/Lease, Purchase, Duplication License.

4334 • Total Auto Body Repair
MacMillan Publishing Co., Inc.
866 Third Ave.
New York, NY 10022   Ph:(212)702-2000

Manual. Published 1982. **Editor(s):** L.C. Rhone, and David H. Yates. **Price:** $28.99, text; $3.67, instructor's guide; $8.40, kit book.

Wheels

4335 • Auto-Truck Interchange Manual: Wheel Covers
Hollander Inc.
14800 28th Ave., Ste. 190
Plymouth, MN 55441   Ph:(612)553-0644

Manual. Published 1982. **Price:** $15.95.

4336 • Auto-Truck Interchange Manual: Wheels
Hollander Inc.
14800 28th Ave., Ste. 190
Plymouth, MN 55447   Ph:(612)553-0644

Manual. Published 1981. **Price:** $5.95.

4337 • Brakes, Steering, Front Suspension, Wheels and Tires
H. M. Gousha
2001 The Alameda
San Jose, CA 95126   Ph:(408)296-1060

Manual. Published 1981. **Editor(s):** Bob Leigh. **Price:** $9.95, workbook; $13.90, cassette.

4338 • Electronic Wheel Balancing
Bergwall Productions, Inc.
106 Charles Lindbergh Blvd.
Uniondale, NY 11553-3695   Ph:(516)222-1111

Audio-visual. This three-tape program studies an electronic wheel balancing procedure. **Release date:** 1984. **Producer:** Bergwall Productions, Inc. **Acquisition:** Purchase.

4339 • How to Balance Wheels
Bergwall Productions, Inc.
106 Charles Lindbergh Blvd.
Uniondale, NY 11553-3695   Ph:(516)222-1111

Audio-visual. This two-tape program shows how to recognize and fix unbalanced wheels. **Release date:** 1977. **Producer:** Bergwall Productions, Inc. **Acquisition:** Purchase.

4340 • Wheel and Rim Manual
National Wheel and Rim Association (NWRA)
5121 Bowden Rd., Ste. 303
Jacksonville, FL 32216   Ph:(904)737-2900

Manual.

Manufacturer Profiles

4340 • ACURA DIV., AMERICAN HONDA MOTOR CO.

1919 Torrance Blvd.
Torrance, CA 90501-2746

Ph:(310)783-2000

Acura Division, part of the American Honda Motor Company, is a subsidiary of Honda Motor Company Limited, Tokyo. The Division, formed in 1986, imports Legend and Integra cars and in 1990 was ranked first in customer satisfaction by J.D. Power and Associates for the fourth consecutive year. Preliminary sales figures show 143,700 Acura cars sold in the U.S. in 1991, up from 138,400 cars in 1990.

ADDITIONAL NUMBERS

Toll-free: 800-382-2238

CORPORATE CONTACTS

E. Taylor, Sales VP

4341 • ALFA ROMEO DISTRIBUTORS OF NORTH AMERICA

8259 Exchange Dr., Box 598026
Orlando, FL 32859-8026

Ph:(407)856-5000
Fax:(407)856-5075

Alfa Romeo Distributors of North America is a joint venture between Fiat Auto SpA (Alfa Romeo's parent in Turin) and Chrysler Corporation. The origins of Alfa Romeo can be traced back to 1910, when an Italian subsidiary of the French automaker Darracq was bought and renamed Anonima Lombarda Fabbrica Automobili—ALFA. The company was again purchased in 1916, this time by Italian industrialist and mining engineer Nicola Romeo. Throughout the years, Alfa Romeo gained popularity with its race cars and still produces race cars in addition to its sports car line. In 1991, Alfa Romeo Distributors of North America sold approximately 3,400 cars in the United States.

CORPORATE CONTACTS

Darrell L. Davis, Pres. & CEO
Joseph Hannan, Sales Dir.
Jamie F. Jameson, Mktg. Dir. & Sales Promo. Mgr.
Riccardo Brugnoli, Parts & Svc. Dir.
Craig Morningstar, Pub. Rel. Mgr.

CUSTOMER SERVICE CENTERS

Owner Relations Department
Alfa Romeo Distributors of North
  America
8259 Exchange Dr., PO Box 598026
Orlando, FL 32859-8026

Ph:(407)856-5000

4342 • AMERICAN HONDA MOTOR CO. INC.

1919 Torrance Blvd.
Torrance, CA 90501-2746

Ph:(213)783-2000
Fax:(301)783-3900

Subsidiary of Honda Motor Co. Ltd. of Tokyo. Parent company founded in 1948 and began car production in 1962. Began Canada production in 1986. Honda ranked as the most popular imported car in 1989, and the Honda Accord was the third best-selling car in the U.S. in 1991. Honda Motor Co. and Britain's Rover Group Ltd. have agreed to build three new cars together during the 1990s, beginning with the Synchro due out in late 1992. American Honda Motor Co. Inc. sold 659,700 cars in 1991, down from 716,500 in 1990.

CORPORATE CONTACTS

K. Amemiya, Pres.
M. Shinkai, Sr. VP
T. Elliott, Exec. VP
C. Hale, Exec. VP
T. Kobayashi, Exec. VP
J. Cardiges, Sales Sr. VP, Honda Division
E. Taylor, Sales Sr. VP, Acura Division
Y. Munekuni, Pres., Honda North America Inc.
K. Kadowaki, Pres., Honda Canada Inc.
National Hotline—(213)604-2584

CUSTOMER SERVICE ZONE OFFICES

Central Zone
101 South Stanfield Rd.
Troy, OH 45373

Ph:(513)332-6250

Mid-Atlantic Zone Office
902 Wind River Ln., Ste. 200
Gaithersburg, MD 20878

Ph:(301)990-2020

New England Zone Office
555 Old County Rd.
Windsor Locks, CT 06096

Ph:(203)623-3310

North Central Zone Office
601 Campus Dr., Suite A-9
Arlington Heights, IL 60004

Ph:(312)870-5600

Northeastern Zone Office
115 Gaither Dr.
P.O. Box 337
Moorestown, NJ 08057

Ph:(609)235-5533

Northwestern Zone Office
12439 N. E. Airport Way
P.O. Box 20186
Portland, OR 97220

Ph:(503)256-0943

South Central Zone Office   Ph:(214)929-5481
4529 Royal Lane
Irving, TX 75063

Southeastern Zone Office   Ph:(404)442-2045
1500 Morrison Parkway
Alpharetta, GA 30201

West Central Zone Office   Ph:(303)696-3935
1600 South Abilene St., Suite D
Aurora, CO 80012

Western Zone   Ph:(213)781-4565
700 Van Ness Ave.
P.O. Box 2260
Torrance, CA 90509

MANUFACTURING DIVISIONS

Honda of America Manufacturing Inc.   Ph:(513)642-5000
Honda Pkwy.
Marysville, OH 43040
H. Yoshino, Pres.

Honda of Canada Manufacturing Inc.   Ph:(705)435-5566
55 Tottenham Rd.
Box 5000
Alliston, ON, Canada L0M 1A0
H. Hayano, Pres.

4343 • AMERICAN ISUZU MOTORS INC.

13181 Crossroads Pkwy. N.   Ph:(213)699-0500
PO Box 2480
City of Industry, CA 91746

American Isuzu Motors Inc. is the U.S. marketing arm of Isuzu
Motors Ltd. of Tokyo. The parent company, founded in 1918,
signed a licensing agreement in the '50s to build British Hillman
cars. In the '70s, GM bought minority interest in Isuzu Motors Ltd.
(currently a 38% stake) and sells the Isuzu-built Geo Storm, a
version of the Impulse. In 1989 Subaru-Isuzu Automotive Inc. in
Lafayette, Indiana began building Subaru Legacy sedans and
wagons and Isuzu pickups and Amigos. American Isuzu Motors
sold 13,301 cars and 95,128 trucks in the U.S. in 1991, and
expects fiscal year losses for 1991 to be approximately $377
million.

ADDITIONAL NUMBERS

Toll-free: 800-255-6727

CORPORATE CONTACTS

Kozo Sakaino, Pres.
John E. Reilly, Chm.
E.F. Kern, VP and Gen. Mgr.
George Birk, Natl. Parts Opns. Mgr.
Charles Rayer, Nat. Svc. Opns. Mgr.

CUSTOMER SERVICE REGIONAL OFFICES

California Customer Relations   Ph:(714)770-2626
1 Autry St.
Irvine, CA 92718

Central Region   Ph:(312)952-8111
1830 Jarvis Ave.
Elk Grove Village, IL 60007

Mid-Atlantic Region   Ph:(301)761-2121
1 Isuzu Way
Glen Burnie, MD 21061

Northeast Region   Ph:(201)784-1414
156 Ludlow Ave.
Northvale, NJ 07647-0965

Northwest Region   Ph:(206)881-0203
8727 148th Ave., NE
Redmond, WA 98052

Southeast Region   Ph:(404)475-1995
205 Hembree Park Dr.
Roswell, GA 30076

Southwest Region   Ph:(214)647-2911
1150 Isuzu Pkwy.
Grand Prairie, TX 75050

4344 • ASTON MARTIN LAGONDA OF NORTH AMERICA INC.

1290 E. Main St.   Ph:(203)359-2259
Stamford, CT 06902   Fax:(203)323-2558

Aston Martin Lagonda of North America Inc. is a subsidiary of
Aston Martin Lagonda Ltd. of Newport Pagnell, England. The
background of the parent company comprises two separate
histories until the late 1940s: one for Aston Martin Company and
one for Lagonda Company. The first car produced by Robert
Bamford and Lionel Martin was completed in 1913 and was
originally designed to be a competitor to Bugatti. Subsequent cars
were named Aston Martin in honor of their success at the Aston
Clinton Hill Climb, a popular motoring competition in the days
after World War I. Throughout the years Aston Martin cars won
numerous competitions and broke several class and world records.

Like the Aston Martin Company, the Lagonda Company traces its
history back to England in the the early 1900s. Wilbur Gunn,
originally a motorcycle designer, developed the early Lagonda
Tricars, and in 1908 he won the London to Edinburgh reliability
trial. In 1909 Lagonda was the first British car to be designed with
an all steel body and chassis in one unit. Throughout the years the
Lagonda Company produced high performance cars that were
regularly successful in trials and other competitions.

In the late 1940s the Aston Martin and Lagonda Companies were
bought by the David Brown Corporation. The Company changed
hands two more times in the years that followed, and in 1987 it
was acquired by Ford Motor Company. Virage coupes are built by
hand in Newport Pagnell, Buckinghamshire, England at the rate of
five per week. U.S. car sales for 1990 topped out at 60 vehicles,
and the Company announced that it will not build any Lagondas in
1991.

CORPORATE CONTACTS

M.V. Gauntlett, Chm.
Michael R. Haysey, Mktg. Dir.
Simon T. Rodd, Tech. Dir.
Kathy L. Johnson, Sales Adm.

4345 • AUDI OF AMERICA INC.

3800 Hamlin Rd.   Ph:(313)340-5000
Auburn Hills, MI 48326

Importer of cars made by Audi AG of Ingolstadt, Germany, an auto
company founded by August Horch in 1909. Audi, a division of
the Volkswagen Group, entered the U.S. market in 1969. Audi of
America was formed in 1985 to replace Volkswagen of America's
Audi Division. Audi of America is expected to sell approximately
12,300 cars in the U.S. in 1991, down from approximately 21,100
cars sold in 1990. Audi announced that it will skip the 1992 model
year in Canada and resume marketing in March of 1993.

ADDITIONAL NUMBERS

Toll-free: 800-822-AUDI

CORPORATE CONTACTS

H. Hungerland, CEO
J. Kerr, CFO
Richard L. Mugg, VP
Ben Hilverda, Mktg. Dir.
Joseph Tate, Gen. Mgr. of Sales
Otto Sonnenschmidt, Svc. Mgr.
Joseph Bennett, Pub. Rel. Mgr.

CUSTOMER SERVICE ZONE OFFICES

Atlantic Zone   Ph:(301)459-7000
9300 Martin Luther King, Jr. Hwy.
Lanham, MD 20706

Audi Central Zone   Ph:(312)634-6000
420 Barclay Blvd.
Lincolnshire, IL 60069

Audi Eastern   Ph:(914)578-5000
Greenbush Rd.
Orangeburg, NY 10962

Audi Pacific Zone   Ph:(213)390-8011
11300 Playa St.
Culver City, CA 90230

Audi Southern Zone   Ph:(404)955-9261
1940 The Exchange
Atlanta, GA 30339

4346 • AVANTI AUTOMOTIVE CORP.

c/o Cafaro International   Ph:(216)448-4488
6874 Strinbu Dr.
Brookfield, OH 44403

CORPORATE CONTACTS

John J. Cafaro, Pres.
Gary Fielding, VP of Sales & Mktg.
Curt Cox, VP of Manufacturing
Keith Jones, Purchasing Dir.

4347 • BENTLEY MOTORS INC., ROLLS-ROYCE MOTOR CARS INC.

120 Chubb Ave.   Ph:(201)460-9600
Lyndhurst, NJ 07071   Fax:(201)460-9392

In 1919 W.O. Bentley, Harry Varley, and F.T. Burgess designed a 3-litre sports car at their London offices on Conduit Street, just opposite the showrooms of Rolls-Royce Limited. The first Bentleys, like the Rolls-Royces, were not complete cars but were built in the form of rolling chassis. Unable to pay back loans after the Depression of 1929, the assets of Bentley Motors were acquired by Rolls-Royce Limited in 1931. After World War II economics required that car models share a standard steel body type; the first standard steel-bodied Bentley of the postwar era was the Mark IV Bentley of 1946. Throughout the postwar period Bentley sales decreased dramatically to the point where they accounted for no more than 3% of the Company's total annual production. Sales showed signs of increasing, however, when the Bentley version of the Rolls-Royce Silver Spirit was named the Mulsanne in 1980. In 1986 a successful campaign in the United States promoted the Bentley Eight and later the Mulsanne S. In 1987 Bentley orders accounted for 48% of total sales in the United Kingdom.

ADDITIONAL NUMBERS

Toll-free: 800-777-6923

CORPORATE CONTACTS

Howard I. Mosher, Pres.

Robert Wharen, VP of Sales
Orson Munn, Mgr. of Adv. & Prom.
Donald J. Beck, CFO, Finance
Reg Abbiss, Sr. Exec. of Corp. Comm.

4348 • BMW OF NORTH AMERICA INC.

300 Chestnut Ridge Rd.   Ph:(201)307-4000
Woodcliff Lake, NJ 07675   Fax:(201)307-4045

BMW of North America, founded in 1975, is a subsidiary of BMW AG, Munich, Germany. BMWs are built at six sites in Germany and Austria by Bayerische Motoren Werke AG. BMW car sales in the U.S. were listed at 53,300 in 1991.

ADDITIONAL NUMBERS

Toll-free: 800-334-4BMW

CORPORATE CONTACTS

Karl Gerlinger, Pres. & CEO
Friedrich Hanau, Sr. VP of Corp. Aff.
Christian Penner, Sr. VP of Fin.
Carl Flescher, VP of Mktg.
James J. Ryan, VP of Reg. Opns. & Sales
Hans Duenzl, Svc. VP
Thomas O. McGurn, Gen. Mgr. of Corp. Comm.
Axel Mees, Parts VP

CUSTOMER SERVICE REGIONAL OFFICES

Central Region   Ph:(708)310-2700
498 E. Commerce Dr.
Schaumburg, IL 60173

Eastern Region   Ph:(201)573-2100
1 BMW Plaza
Montvale, NJ 07645

Southern Region   Ph:(404)552-3800
1280 Hightower Trail
Dunwoody, GA 30350

Western Region   Ph:(213)574-7300
12541 Beatrice St.
P.O. Box 66916
Los Angeles, CA 90066

4349 • BUICK MOTOR DIV., GENERAL MOTORS CORP.

Buick-Oldsmobile-Cadillac Group   Ph:(313)236-5000
902 E. Hamilton Ave.
Flint, MI 48550

Buick Motor Co. was organized in Flint, Michigan by David Dunbar Buick in 1903 and became part of General Motors Co. in 1908. In 1984 it became part of the Buick-Oldsmobile-Cadillac Group, giving the group complete responsibility for products, including engineering, manufacturing, assembly, and marketing. Buick sold 544,300 cars in 1991, up from 536,700 in 1990.

ADDITIONAL NUMBERS

Toll-free: 800-521-7300

CORPORATE CONTACTS

Edward H. Mertz, Gen. Mgr.
L.D. Robbins, Asst. Gen. Sales Mgr., Service
John C. Carlson, Mgr., Human Resources Adm.
Darwin E. Clark, General Mgr., Marketing
John E. DeCou, Director, Public Relations—(313)236-5844
Corby L. Casler, Mgr., Communications—(313)236-5892
Robert E. Coletta, Gen. Sales & Service Mgr.

Jack W. Qualman, Gen. Dir. of Adv.
Mark A. Rollinson, Mgr. of Product Publicity

OFF-SITE OPERATIONS

Flint Assembly Operation (Buick City)　　Ph:(313)236-5000
B-O-C Group
902 E. Hamilton Ave.
Flint, MI 48550

Lansing Assembly Plant (A Plant)　　Ph:(517)885-5000
B-O-C Group
401 N. Verlinden Ave.
Lansing, MI 48901

Oklahoma City Assembly Operation　　Ph:(405)733-6011
C-P-C Group
P.O. Box 26527
Oklahoma City, OK 73126

Wentzville Assembly Operation　　Ph:(314)327-5711
B-O-C Group
P.O. Box 444
Wentzville, MO 63385

CUSTOMER SERVICE ZONE OFFICES

Atlanta Zone Office
5730 Glenridge Dr.　　Toll-free: 800-521-7300
Atlanta, GA 30328

Boston Zone Office
35 Braintree Hill Park　　Toll-free: 800-521-7300
Ste. 202
Braintree, MA 02184-9152

Charlotte Zone Office
4201 Congress St.　　Toll-free: 800-521-7300
Ste. 465
Charlotte, NC 28209

Chicago Zone Office
475 Alexis R. Shuman Blvd.　　Toll-free: 800-521-7300
Naperville, IL 60563-0803

Cincinnati Zone Office
155 Tri-County Parkway　　Toll-free: 800-521-7300
Cincinnati, OH 45246

Dallas Zone Office
GM Building, Ste. 175　　Toll-free: 800-521-7300
130 E. Carpenter Freeway
Irving, TX 75062

Detroit Zone Office
New Center One Building　　Toll-free: 800-521-7300
3031 W. Grand Blvd., Ste. 505
Detroit, MI 48202

Kansas City Zone Office
General Motors Bldg.　　Toll-free: 800-521-7300
10800 Farley, Ste. 270
Overland Park, KS 66210

Los Angeles Zone Office
515 Marin St., Ste. 205　　Toll-free: 800-521-7300
Thousand Oaks, CA 91360

Memphis Zone Office
1770 Kirby Parkway, Ste. 222　　Toll-free: 800-521-7300
Memphis, TN 38138

New York Zone Office
2500 Westchester Ave.　　Toll-free: 800-521-7300
Purchase, NY 10577-0891

Orlando Zone Office
1900 Summit Tower Blvd., Ste. 450　　Toll-free: 800-521-7300
Orlando, FL 32810

Philadelphia Zone Office
851 Duportail Rd.　　Toll-free: 800-521-7300
Wayne, PA 19087

Pittsburgh Zone Office
One Penn Center West, Ste. 211　　Toll-free: 800-521-7300
Pittsburgh, PA 15230

San Francisco Zone Office
39465 Paseo Padre Parkway　　Toll-free: 800-521-7300
GM Bldg., Ste. 2900
Fremont, CA 94538

4350 • CADILLAC MOTOR CAR DIV., GENERAL MOTORS CORP.

Buick-Oldsmobile-Cadillac Group　　Ph:(313)554-5067
2860 Clark St.
Detroit, MI 48232

Organized in 1902 and became part of GM in 1908. Organized under the Buick-Oldsmobile-Cadillac Group (B-O-C) in 1984, giving the group complete responsibility for engineering, manufacturing, and marketing of products. Cadillac once again became responsible for its own engineering, manufacturing, and marketing of luxury cars on January 7, 1987. Employs more than 9,700 workers at its headquarters, six plant locations and zone sale offices. First U.S. automaker to introduce parts interchangeability, closed bodies, and the water-cooled V-8. The De Ville/Fleetwood is its best selling line. Cadillac won the Malcolm Baldrige National Quality Award in 1990. Cadillac Motor Car Division reported sales of 213,300 cars in the U.S. in 1991, down from 258,200 cars in 1990.

ADDITIONAL NUMBERS

Toll-free: 800-458-8006

CORPORATE CONTACTS

John O. Grettenberger, Gen. Mgr.
John M. Fleming, Gen. Dir., Mktg. & Product Planning
William J. O'Neill, Dir., Public Relations
Charles T. Harrington, Mgr., Public Relations, Western Region
Thomas H. Standen, Dir., Customer Satisfaction
Robert C. White, Dir., Human Resources
Peter R. Gerosa, Mgr. of Sales & Service
Peter R. Levin, Dir. of Adv.

OFF-SITE OPERATIONS

Arlington Assembly Operation　　Ph:(817)652-2200
Cadillac Motor Car Division
2525 E. Abram St.
Arlington, TX 76010

Detroit/Hamtramck Assembly　　Ph:(313)554-5067
 Operation
Cadillac Motor Car Division
2500 E. Grand Blvd.
Detroit, MI 48211-2002

Orion Assembly Operation　　Ph:(313)236-5912
Cadillac Motor Car Division
902 E. Hamilton Ave.
Flint, MI 48550

4351 • CHEVROLET/GEO MOTOR DIV., GENERAL MOTORS CORP.

Chevrolet-Pontiac-GM of Canada Group
30007 Van Dyke Ave.
Warren, MI 48090

Ph:(313)492-8841
Fax:(313)492-8853

Formed as the Chevrolet Motor Car Company in Detroit, on November 3, 1911 by Louis Chevrolet, Swiss engineer. Joined General Motors in 1918 and Chevrolet cars became the chief competition for low-priced Ford Motor Company vehicles. Introduced the first model with a plastic body to be produced in quantity in 1953. Organized under the Chevrolet-Pontiac-GM of Canada Group (C-P-C) in 1984, giving the group complete responsibility for products, including engineering, manufacturing, assembly, and marketing.

Introduced the Geo line of small vehicles in 1988 with Geo Metro, Geo Spectrum, and Geo Tracker. In cooperation with Suzuki, Isuzu, and Toyota, models are either imported from Japan or built in North America from a Japanese design, and are sold through Chevrolet dealers with Geo franchises. The Division sold 296,700 Geo cars and trucks in 1991, down from 325,100 cars and trucks in 1990. As a whole, the Division sold 2,229,600 Chevy and Geo vehicles in 1991, down from 2,607,100 vehicles in 1990.

ADDITIONAL NUMBERS

Toll-free: 800-222-1020

CORPORATE CONTACTS

Jimmie C. Perkins, Gen. Mgr.
Michael H. Erdman, Gen. Mgr., Marketing
Stephen D. McAvoy, Mktg. Mgr., Passenger Cars
F.F. Raine, Mktg. Mgr., Trucks
G.R. Hanley, Mktg. Mgr., Information & Research
Jeffrey P. Hurlbert, Dir., Area Mktg.
Michael W. Michalek, Dir., Personnel
Ralph J. Kramer, Dir., Public Relations—(313)492-8855
Suzanne M. Kane, Mgr., Public Relations, Western Region—(805)373-8440
A.J. Brock, Sales Mgr., Service & Customer Satisfaction

OFF-SITE OPERATIONS

Arlington Assembly Operation
C-P-C Group
2525 E. Abram St.
Arlington, TX 76010

Ph:(817)652-2200

Baltimore Assembly Operation
Truck & Bus Group
P.O. Box 148
2225 Broening Hwy.
Baltimore, MD 21203

Ph:(301)631-2000

Bowling Green Assembly Plant
C-P-C Group
600 Corvette Dr.
P.O. Box 90006
Bowling Green, KY 42102

Ph:(502)745-8000

Flint Assembly Operation
Truck & Bus Group
G-3100 Van Slyke
Flint, MI 48551

Ph:(313)236-5000

Fort Wayne Assembly Operation
Truck & Bus Group
12200 Lafayette Center Rd.
Roanoke, IN 46783

Ph:(219)673-2000

Janesville Assembly Operation
Truck & Bus Group
P.O. Box 629
1000 Industrial Ave.
Janesville, WI 53547

Ph:(608)756-7345

Lordstown Assembly Operation
B-O-C Group
P.O. Box 1406
Warren, OH 44482

Ph:(216)824-5000

Moraine Assembly Operation
Truck & Bus Group
2681 W. Stroop Rd.
Moraine, OH 45439

Ph:(513)455-5011

Pontiac East Assembly Operation
Truck & Bus Group
820 S. Opdyke
Pontiac, MI 48341-3123

Ph:(313)452-5059

Pontiac West Assembly Operation
Truck & Bus Group
600 S. Saginaw
Pontiac, MI 48058

Ph:(313)456-5000

Shreveport Assembly Operation
Truck & Bus Group
P.O. Box 30011
7600 GM Blvd.
Shreveport, LA 71130

Ph:(318)459-9000

Van Nuys Assembly Operation
C-P-C Group
8000 Van Nuys Blvd.
Van Nuys, CA 91409-2310

Ph:(818)997-5000

Wilmington Assembly Operation
B-O-C Group
P.O. Box 1512
Wilmington, DE 19899

Ph:(302)428-7000

CUSTOMER SERVICE CENTERS

Customer Assistance Department
P.O. Box 7047
Troy, MI 48009-7047

4352 • CHRYSLER CORP.

12000 Chrysler Dr.
Highland Park, MI 48288-1919

Ph:(313)956-5741

Chrysler Corp. was founded in 1925 by Walter P. Chrysler, a former GM executive. Manufacturing divisions include Chrysler/Plymouth, Dodge, and Jeep/Eagle. The company reported a $68 million loss in 1990, and a $795 million loss in 1991. Combined sales of cars and light trucks for the divisions worldwide were 1,866,100 in 1991, down 6% from 1,984,300 in 1990. In October 1991 Chrysler sold its 50% stake in Diamond-Star Motors, a joint venture with Mitsubishi, for $127 million. In November 1991 Chrysler dropped out of its 3-year joint venture with Fiat Auto S.p.A. Chrysler owns American Motors Corporation and Italian car maker Lamborghini, and continues its joint venture with Maserati. **See also:** Plymouth, Dodge, Jeep, Lamborghini.

CORPORATE CONTACTS

Lee Iacocca, CEO
Robert S. Miller Jr., V. Chm.
Robert A. Lutz, Pres., Chrysler Motors
T.G. Denomme, Exec. VP, Corp. Staff Group
S.J. Harris, Dir., Automotive Public Relations
G.E. White, VP, Personnel & Organization
A.P. St. John, VP, Human Resources
R.R. Boltz, VP, Product Strategy/Regulatory Affairs
T.C. Gale, VP, Product Design
Thomas Stallkamp, VP, Procurement/Supply
J.B. Damoose, VP, Brand Marketing—(313)956-5741
T.R. Cunningham, Exec. VP, Sales & Mktg.—(313)494-1014
E.Thomas Pappert, VP, Sales—(313)956-5741

G.J. Giocondi, VP, Quality/Productivity
CUSTOMER HOTLINE—(313)956-5970
Tom Kowaleski, Mgr. Prod. and Mktg. Pub. Rel.—(313)956-5342
Rita McKay, Mgr. Mktg. Pub. Rel.—(313)252-8794
Alan Miller, Mgr. Chrysler/Plymouth—(313)956-2566
Terri Houtman, Mgr. Dodge/Dodge Truck—(313)956-3667
Chris Pikulas, Mgr. Jeep/Eagle—(313)252-5781
Mike Aberlich, Mgr. Prod. Pub. Rel.—(313)956-2142
Tony Cervone, Mgr. Design and Motorsports—(313)956-3640
Jason Vines, Mgr. Eng. and Tech.—(313)956-5346

OFF-SITE OPERATIONS

Acustar Inc.   Ph:(313)528-6500
1850 Research Dr.   Fax:(313)528-6760
Troy, MI 48083
F. J. Farmer, Pres.

Chrysler Technologies   Ph:(703)979-6632
1725 Jefferson Davis Hwy., Ste. 500
Arlington, VA 22202

Fleet Operations   Ph:(313)244-3591
27777 Franklin Rd.
Southfield, MI 48034
H.L. Barton, Gen. Mgr.

Marketing Investment and Dealer   Ph:(313)952-1253
    Development
1450 W. Long Lake Rd., Ste. 270
Troy, MI 48098
J.J. Shady, Dir.

Service and Parts Operations, Chrysler   Ph:(313)497-1014
    Motors   Fax:(313)497-0718
P.O. Box 1718
Detroit, MI 48288
G.E. Blake, Gen. Mgr. of Svc. & Cust.
    Sat.

CUSTOMER SERVICE ZONE OFFICES

Atlanta Zone Office   Ph:(404)953-8880
900 Circle 75 Pkwy., Ste. 1600
Atlanta, GA 30339

Boston Zone Office   Ph:(508)261-2299
550 Forbes Blvd.
Mansfield, MA 02048-2038

Charlotte Zone Office   Ph:(704)357-7065
4944 Parkway Plaza Blvd., Ste. 470
Charlotte, NC 28217

Chicago Zone Office   Ph:(708)515-2450
650 Warrenville Rd., Ste. 502
Lisle, IL 60532

Cincinnati Zone Office   Ph:(513)530-1500
P.O. Box 41902
Cincinnati, OH 45241

Dallas Zone Office   Ph:(214)242-8462
P.O. Box 110162
Carrollton, TX 75011

Denver Zone Office   Ph:(303)373-8888
P.O. Box 39006
Denver, CO 80239

Detroit Zone Office   Ph:(313)879-3600
P.O. Box 3000
Troy, MI 48007-3000

Houston Zone Office   Ph:(713)820-7062
363 North Belt, Ste. 590
Houston, TX 77060-2405

Kansas City Zone Office   Ph:(913)469-3090
P.O. Box 25668
Overland Park, KS 66225-5668

Los Angeles Zone Office   Ph:(714)565-5200
P.O. Box 14112
Orange, CA 92613-1512

Memphis Zone Office   Ph:(901)797-3870
P.O. Box 18008
Memphis, TN 38181-0008

Milwaukee Zone Office   Ph:(414)797-3750
445 S. Moorland Rd., Ste. 470
Brookfield, WI 53008-0969

Minneapolis Zone Office   Ph:(612)553-2546
P.O. Box 1231
Minneapolis, MN 55440

New Orleans Zone Office   Ph:(504)838-8788
P.O. Box 157
Metairie, LA 70004

New York Zone Office   Ph:(914)359-0110
500 Rte. 303
Tappan, NY 10983-1592

Orlando Zone Office   Ph:(305)352-7402
8000 S. Orange Blossom Trail
Orlando, FL 32809

Philadelphia Zone Office   Ph:(215)251-2990
Valley Brooke Corporate Center
101 Lindenwood Dr., Ste. 320
Malvern, PA 19355

Phoenix Zone Office   Ph:(602)953-6899
11811 N. Tatum Blvd., Ste 4025
Phoenix, AZ 85028-1623

Pittsburgh Zone Office   Ph:(412)788-6622
Penn Center West 3, Ste. 420
Pittsburgh, PA 15276

Portland Zone Office   Ph:(503)526-5555
P.O. Box 744
Beaverton, OR 97075

St. Louis Zone Office   Ph:(314)895-0731
P.O. Box 278
Hazelwood, MO 63042

San Francisco Zone Office   Ph:(415)463-0656
P.O. Box 5009
Pleasanton, CA 94566-0509

Syracuse Zone Office   Ph:(315)445-6941
P.O. Box 603
Dewitt, NY 13214-0603

Washington, DC Zone Office   Ph:(301)464-4040
P.O. Box 1900
Bowie, MD 20716

FINANCE, INSURANCE, AND MORTGAGE UNITS

Chrysler Financial   Ph:(313)948-3890
27777 Franklin Rd.   Fax:(313)948-3437
Southfield, MI 48034

Chrysler Realty Corp.   Ph:(313)641-4504
5600 New King St., Ste 350
Troy, MI 48098

MANUFACTURING DIVISIONS

Belvidere Assembly Plant, Chrysler   Ph:(815)547-2200
  Motors
3000 W. Chrysler Dr.
Belvidere, IL 61008

Chrysler Motor Parts Dept.   Ph:(302)453-5619
500 S. College Ave.
Newark, DE 19713

Evart Products Plant 1, Chrysler   Ph:(616)734-5522
  Motors
601 W. 7th St.
Evart, MI 49631

Indianapolis Foundry, Chrysler Motors   Ph:(317)240-4800
1100 S. Tibbs Ave.
Indianapolis, IN 46241

Jefferson Assembly Plant, Chrysler   Ph:(313)823-8925
  Motors
P.O. Box 1658
Detroit, MI 48288

Kenosha Engine Plant, Chrysler Motors   Ph:(414)658-6011
56261 25th Ave.
Kenosha, WI 53140

Kokomo Transmission Plant, Chrysler   Ph:(317)454-1212
  Motors
P.O. Box 9007
Kokomo, IN 46901

New Process Gear Div., Chrysler   Ph:(315)432-4000
  Motors
6600 Chrysler Dr.
East Syracuse, NY 13057

St. Louis Assembly Plant 1, Chrysler   Ph:(314)343-3111
  Motors
1001 N. Hwy. Dr.
Fenton, MO 63026

St. Louis Assembly Plant 2, Chrysler   Ph:(314)349-4035
  Motors
1050 Dodge Dr.
Fenton, MO 63026

Sterling Stamping, Chrysler Motors
35777 Van Dyke Ave.
Sterling Hgts., MI 48077

Toledo Assembly Plant, Chrysler   Ph:(419)470-7182
  Motors
1000 Jeep Pkwy.
Toledo, OH 43657

Trenton Engine Plant, Chrysler Motors   Ph:(313)671-4129
P.O. Box 248
Trenton, MI 48183

Twinsburg Stamping Plant, Chrysler   Ph:(216)425-1777
  Motors
P.O. Box 152
Twinsburg, OH 44087

Warren Stamping Plant, Chrysler   Ph:(313)497-3690
  Motors
22800 Mound Rd.
Warren, MI 48091

Warren Truck Assembly Plant, Chrysler
  Motors
P.O. Box 2088
Detroit, MI 48288

4353 • CHRYSLER/PLYMOUTH DIV., CHRYSLER MOTORS CORP.

12000 Chrysler Dr.   Ph:(313)956-5741
Highland Park, MI 48288-1919

Chrysler/Plymouth Division of Chrysler Corp. was founded in 1928, when the Plymouth line of automobiles was created. The Division sold 365,600 Plymouth vehicles in 1991, down from 424,500 vehicles in 1990; and sold 131,600 Chrysler vehicles in 1991, down from 188,400 vehicles in 1990.

CORPORATE CONTACTS

Lee A. Iacocca, CEO, Chrysler Corp.
James P. Holden, Gen. Mgr., Chrysler/Plymouth Div.
Chris Hosford, Mgr., Chrysler/Plymouth Public Rel.—(313)956-5344

4354 • DAIHATSU AMERICA INC.

4422 Corporate Center Dr.   Ph:(714)761-7000
Los Alamitos, CA 90720   Fax:(714)952-3197

Subsidiary of Daihatsu Motor Company of Osaka, Japan. Parent company created in 1907 as Hatsudoki Seizo Company and renamed Daihatsu Motor Company in 1974. Built its 10 millionth vehicle in 1985 and sold its first vehicle in the U.S. in 1988. Toyota Motor Corp. has a 14% stake in Daihatsu. Daihatsu America Inc. sold approximately 9,000 cars and trucks in 1991, down from almost 15,000 in 1990.

ADDITIONAL NUMBERS

Toll-free: 800-777-7070

CORPORATE CONTACTS

S. "John" Fukunaka, Pres. and CEO
C.R. "Dick" Brown, Exec. VP and COO
Barry Jeshurin, Projects Mgr., Mktg.
Earl Campbell, Sales Dir. (West)
Richard Szamborski, Sales Dir. (East)
Edward Mooers, Svc. Dir.
Greg Dunlap, Parts Mgr.

CUSTOMER SERVICE REGIONAL OFFICES

Southeastern Region   Ph:(904)448-6800
8691 Western Way
Jacksonville, FL 32256

4355 • DODGE/DODGE TRUCK DIV., CHRYSLER MOTORS CORP.

12000 Chrysler Dr.   Ph:(313)956-5741
Highland Park, MI 48288-1919

Dodge Division of Chrysler Corp. was created in 1928 when Chrysler purchased Dodge Brothers, Inc., founded by John and Horace Dodge. Dodge minivan sales helped Chrysler retain the top spot in market share for minivans in 1989, with 54% of of all U.S. minivan sales. The sturdy reputation and continued popularity of Dodge trucks and minivans were major factors in Chrysler receiving the 1989 Forbes top ranking for most profitable automobile and truck companies in its Annual Report on American Industry. Dodge sold 773,400 cars and trucks in 1991, down from 827,600 cars and trucks in 1990. See Chrysler entry for additional contacts.

CORPORATE CONTACTS

Lee A. Iacocca, CEO, Chrysler
Martin R. Levine, Gen. Mgr., Dodge/Dodge Trucks
CUSTOMER HOTLINE—(313)956-5970
Mike Aberlich, Mgr./Prod. Pub. Rel., Dodge/Dodge Trucks

4356 • FERRARI NORTH AMERICA

250 Sylvan Ave.   Ph:(201)816-2600
Inglewood Cliffs, NJ 07632

Subsidiary of Ferrari SpA of Modena, Italy. Parent company formed by race car driver/entrepreneur Enzo Ferrari; first Ferrari (a race car) built in 1947. In 1990, added a 2-seater Ferrari 348TB with a 3.4 liter 32-valve V-8, 300hp engine to their line. Subsidiary sold 960 cars in 1991.

CORPORATE CONTACTS

Giuseppe Greco, Pres.
Kenneth McCay, Dir. of Svc. & Parts
Hugh Steward, Dir. of Mktg. & Sales

4357 • FORD MOTOR CO.

The American Road   Ph:(313)322-3000
Dearborn, MI 48121

Ford Motor Company was founded in 1903 in Detroit by the late Henry Ford and 11 associates. They started an industrial revolution with the introduction of the moving assembly line in the early 1900s and gained considerable success with the Model T in 1908. The company began producing trucks and tractors in 1917 and bought the Lincoln Motor company in 1922. In 1925 the company built the first of 196 Tri-Motor airplanes used by America's first commercial airlines. Ford contributed to the war effort in the '40s by building bombers, jeeps, tanks, and tank destroyers. The Ford Division was created in 1949 to give a central staff more control of administration and production. In 1990, Ford bought Jaguar plc, the holding company for Jaguar Cars Ltd., for $2.5 billion. Today Ford Motor Company is ranked as the second largest car and truck producer in the world and ranked second on the Fortune 500 list of the largest U.S. industrial corporations, based on sales. For the tenth straight year, the Ford F-series pickup was America's best-selling vehicle. Ford products accounted for five of the top 10 selling vehicles in 1991. Ford sold 2,867,200 cars and trucks in the U.S. in 1991, down from 3,317,100 in 1990. Ford reported a $2.3 billion loss for 1991. *Joint Ventures:* A Ford plant in Louisville, Kentucky builds sport-utilities badged as the Mazda Navajo and Ford Explorer. Ford currently sells a Kia Motor Corp. vehicle as the Ford Festiva, and owns 25 percent of Mazda. **See also:** Lincoln.

ADDITIONAL NUMBERS

Toll-free: 800-392-3673

CORPORATE CONTACTS

Harold A. Poling, Chm. & CEO
Philip E. Benton Jr., Pres. & COO
Stanley A. Seneker, Exec. VP & CFO
Lee R. Miskowski, Gen. Mgr., Ford Parts & Svc. Div.
Helen O. Petrauskas, VP, Environ. Safety & Eng.
David W. Scott, VP, Public Affairs
Edsel S. Ford II, Exec. Dir. of Mktg.
Robert L. Rewey, Sales Opns. VP
Edward E. Hagenlocker, Truck Opns. VP
Elliott S. Hall, VP of Washington Affairs
Ross Roberts, Ford Div. Gen. Mgr.
P.M. Novell, Ford Div. Gen. Mgr. of Sales
A.L. Kleinke, Ford Div. Mktg. Rep. Mgr.
W.C. Stangfield, Ford Div. Opns. Mgr.
J.B. Vanderzee, Ford Div. Adv. Mgr.
K.C. Magee, Ford Div. Mktg. Gen. Mgr.
B.S. Restuccia, Ford Div. Dir. of Mktg. Svcs.
L.A. Weis, Ford Div. Mgr. of Pub. Affairs

OFF-SITE OPERATIONS

Atlanta Assembly Plant   Ph:(404)763-6000
340 Henry Ford II Ave.
Hapeville, GA 30354
R.O. Anderson, Mgr.
J.C. McNeil, Controller

Automotive Components Group   Ph:(313)484-9009
PO Box 412
Ypsilanti, MI 48197
Frank E. Macher, Gen. Mgr.
John E. Jacobs, Controller
E.R. MacKethan, Mktg. Dir.

Dearborn Stamping Plant   Ph:(313)322-3000
(Body and Assembly Operations)
3001 Miller Rd.
Dearborn, MI 48121
James Agnew, Mgr.

Lorain Assembly Plant   Ph:(216)282-0200
(Body and Assembly Operations)
5401 Baumhart Rd.
Lorain, OH 44053
J.E. Akins, Mgr.
John Petropoulos, Controller
Ezra Carter, Dir. of Relations

Ohio Truck Plant (Body and Assembly   Ph:(216)933-1200
  Operations)
650 Miller Rd.
Avon Lake, OH 44012
J.E. Akins, Mgr.
John Petropoulos, Controller
Tom Harmon, Employee Relations Mgr.

Power Products Operations   Ph:(313)323-2123
PO Box 6011
3000 Schaefer Rd.
Dearborn, MI 48121
John J. Schlegel, Power Products Mgr.
Peter M. Dawson, Mgr. of Eng. &
  Plan.

Walton Hills Plant (Body and Assembly   Ph:(216)587-7961
  Operations)
7845 Northfield
Walton Hills, OH 44146
M.T. Sara, Mgr.
J.A. Berlinski, CFO

CUSTOMER SERVICE REGIONAL OFFICES

Atlanta District Office   Ph:(404)763-6440
PO Box 105003
Atlanta, GA 30348

Boston District Office   Ph:(508)481-2798
352 Turnpike Rd., Ste. 303
Southborough, MA 01772-1794

Buffalo District Office   Ph:(716)631-4430
PO Box 244
Buffalo, NY 14225

Charlotte District Office   Ph:(704)554-4501
PO Box 220307
Charlotte, NC 28222

Cincinnati District Office   Ph:(513)398-4884
PO Box 6308
Cincinnati, OH 45215-6308

Cleveland District Office   Ph:(216)526-6900
PO Box 41035
Brecksville, OH 44141

Dallas District Office   Ph:(214)323-6299
PO Box 110037
Carrollton, TX 75011

Denver District Office   Ph:(303)694-8600
PO Box 4028
Englewood, CO 80155

Houston District Office	Ph:(713)680-4260
PO Box 827	
Houston, TX 77001	
Indianapolis District Office	Ph:(317)353-8251
PO Box 19448	
Indianapolis, IN 46219	
Kansas City District Office	Ph:(913)888-0141
PO Box 501	
Shawnee Mission, KS 66201	
Los Angeles District Office	Ph:(714)520-8300
2200 W. Sequoia	
PO Box 4680-P	
Anaheim, CA 92803	
Louisville District Office	Ph:(502)456-3700
PO Box 32080	
Louisville, KY 40232	
Memphis District Office	Ph:(901)757-1076
PO Box 190	
Cordova, TN 38018	
Milwaukee District Office	Ph:(414)785-3100
PO Box 267	
Brookfield, WI 53005	
New Orleans District Office	Ph:(504)454-6764
PO Box 8630	
Metairie, LA 70011	
New York District Office	Ph:(201)288-9421
U.S. Hwy. 46	
Teterboro, NJ 07608	
Omaha District Office	Ph:(402)498-6050
PO Box 54440	
Omaha, NE 68154	
Philadelphia District Office	Ph:(609)662-8021
PO Box 5030	
Mt. Laurel, NJ 08054	
Phoenix District Office	Ph:(602)230-0784
PO Box 844	
Phoenix, AZ 85001	
St. Louis District Office	Ph:(314)569-4455
PO Box 24575	
St. Louis, MO 63141	
San Jose District Office	Ph:(408)262-9110
PO Box 4002	
Milpitas, CA 95035	
Seattle District Office	Ph:(206)244-5800
13555 South East 36th St., Ste. 200	
Bellevue, WA 98006	
Twin Cities District Office	Ph:(612)932-9799
PO Box 9303	
Minneapolis, MN 55440	
Washington District Office	Ph:(703)698-2052
8051 Gatehouse Rd.	
Falls Church, VA 22046	

MANUFACTURING DIVISIONS

Ford Division	Ph:(313)446-3800
Ford Motor Co.	
PO Box 43301	
300 Renaissance Center	
Detroit, MI 48243	
Thomas J. Wagner, VP & Gen. Mgr.	

4358 • GENERAL MOTORS CORP.

3044 W. Grand Blvd.	Ph:(313)556-5000
Detroit, MI 48202	

Formed in 1908 in Flint, Michigan. Has 240 operations in 33 states and 144 cities in the United States. Has plants in Canada and Mexico, and assembly, manufacturing, or distribution operations in 32 other countries. Delivered more than $12,300,000,000 worth of war material during World War II. Produced its 100,000,000th U.S.-made vehicle in 1967. Manufactured guidance and navigation systems which guided the Apollo II astronauts to man's first landing on the moon in 1969. In 1984, reorganized vehicle operations into Buick-Oldsmobile-Cadillac, Chevrolet-Pontiac-GM of Canada, and Truck & Bus Groups. Formed the Saturn Corp. in 1985. Currently has a 37.4 percent stake in Isuzu Motors Ltd.; Isuzu builds the Geo Storm for sale by GM in the United States, and markets Opels in Japan. GM has agreed to set up a joint venture with China's Jinbei Automotive Co. to produce compact pickup trucks in China. Maintains a 50-50 joint venture with Toyota and a Canadian joint venture with Suzuki. GM reported losses of $7.09 billion in the U.S. in 1991, on top of a $4.57 billion loss in the U.S. in 1990. Worldwide losses totaled $4.45 billion in 1991, compared with $2 billion in 1990. GM sold 4,319,700 cars and trucks in the U.S. in 1991, down from 4,934,300 in 1990. In early 1992 GM won two safety research awards presented by the Society of Automotive Engineers. **See also:** Buick, Cadillac, Chevrolet, GMC, Oldsmobile, Pontiac, Geo.

CORPORATE CONTACTS

Robert C. Stempel, Chm. & CEO
Lloyd E. Reuss, Pres., North American Automotive Operations
John F. Smith Jr., V. Chm. & Exec. VP, International Operations
William E. Hoglund, Exec. VP, Automotive Components & Power
    Products & Defense Operations Groups
F. Alan Smith, Exec. VP, Operating Staffs & Public Affairs and
    Marketing Groups
Robert C. O'Connell, Exec. VP & CFO, Finance Group & GMAC
Marina v.N. Whitman, VP & Group Exec., Public Affairs and
    Marketing Group
Shirley Young, VP, Consumer Market Development
Claude N. "Bud" Moore, VP, Customer Sales & Service Staff
Betsy Ancker-Johnson, VP, Environmental Activities Staff
James D. Johnston, VP, Industry-Government Relations Staff
Richard F. O'Brien, VP, Industrial Relations Staff
James B. Fitzpatrick, VP, Communications & Marketing Staff
Ronald H. Haas, VP of Quality & Reliability
Gerald A. Knechtel, VP, Personnel Admn. & Development Staff

OFF-SITE OPERATIONS

Automotive Components Group
901 Tower Dr.
Troy, MI 48098
W. Blair Thompson, VP and Group
    Exec.

Buick-Oldsmobile-Cadillac Group
30009 Van Dyke Ave.
Warren, MI 48090-9025
J.T. Battenberg III, VP and Group
    Exec.
James J. Williams, Group Director,
    Public Affairs

Chevrolet-Pontiac-GM of Canada
    Group
30001 Van Dyke Ave.
Warren, MI 48090-9020
E. Michael Mutchler, VP & Group
    Exec.
Edmond J. Dilworth Jr., Group
    Director, Public Affairs

Truck & Bus Group
31 Judson St.
Pontiac, MI 48342-2230
Clifford J. Vaughan, VP & Group
    Exec.
Donald C. Huss, Group Director, Public
    Affairs

FINANCE, INSURANCE, AND MORTGAGE UNITS

General Motors Acceptance Corp.
    (GMAC)
3044 W. Grand Blvd.
Detroit, MI 48202
John R. Edman, Chm.
Charles A. Krauss Jr., VP, Public
    Affairs and Advertising

GMAC Capital Corp.
4001 S. 700 East, Suite 380
Salt Lake City, UT 84107
Ralph J. Hall, Pres.

GMAC Mortgage Corp.
8360 Old York Rd.
Elkins Park, PA 19117-1590
Geoffrey C. Thomas, Pres.

Motors Insurance Corp.
3044 W. Grand Blvd.
Detroit, MI 48202
Joseph J. Pero, Pres.

MANUFACTURING DIVISIONS

New United Motor Mfg. Inc. (NUMMI)   Ph:(415)498-5500
45500 Fremont Blvd.
Fremont, CA 94538

4359 • GMC TRUCK DIVISION, GENERAL MOTORS CORP.

Truck & Bus Group   Ph:(313)456-5000
31 Judson St.
Pontiac, MI 48342-2230

Formed in 1946 as part of General Motors' Truck & Bus Group. GM entered the truck market in 1911, when it bought the Rapid Motor Vehicle Co. and Reliance Motor Car Co. GMC light trucks are identical to Chevrolet models, but are sold through the GMC marketing group and include no car-like minivans. The Division sold 286,400 trucks in the U.S. in 1991, down from 326,400 trucks in 1990. GMC plans to begin production of its new natural gas powered pickups in April of 1992 and has already received 2,000 advance orders.

CORPORATE CONTACTS

Lewis B. Campell, Gen. Mgr.
Thomas R. Klipstine, Dir., Public Relations—(313)456-2100
Richard M. Lee, Dir., Marketing
Ray E. Rota, Dir., Sales
John S. Kane, Dir., Service—(313)456-4547
Carl E. Rehm, Dir., Fleet Sales

OFF-SITE OPERATIONS

Baltimore Assembly Operation   Ph:(301)631-2000
Truck & Bus Group
P.O. Box 148
2225 Broening Hwy.
Baltimore, MD 21203

Detroit Assembly Operation   Ph:(313)974-3600
Truck & Bus Group
601 Piquette
Detroit, MI 48202

Fort Wayne Assembly Operation   Ph:(219)673-2000
Truck & Bus Group
12200 Lafayette Center Rd.
Roanoke, IN 46783

Moraine Assembly Operation   Ph:(513)455-5011
Truck & Bus Group
2681 W. Stroop Rd.
Moraine, OH 45439

Pontiac East Assembly Operation   Ph:(315)452-5059
Truck & Bus Group
820 S. Opdyke
Pontiac, MI 48341-3123

Pontiac West Assembly Operation   Ph:(313)456-5000
Truck & Bus Group
600 S. Saginaw
Pontiac, MI 48058

Shreveport Assembly Operation   Ph:(318)459-9000
Truck & Bus Group
P.O. Box 30011
7600 GM Blvd.
Shreveport, LA 71130

4360 • HYUNDAI MOTOR AMERICA

10550 Talbert Ave.   Ph:(714)965-3508
Fountain Valley, CA 92728   Fax:(714)965-3816

Subsidiary of Hyundai Motor Co. Ltd. of Seoul, Korea. Cars destined for the U.S. are built in Korea and in Quebec, Canada through Hyundai Auto Canada Inc. Expects to market a version of the Canadian-made Sonata in 1992 through Chrysler Corp.'s Jeep/Eagle Division. Hyundai sales in the U.S. were listed at 117,600 in 1991, down from 137,400 in 1990.

CORPORATE CONTACTS

D. O. Chung, Pres. and CEO
R. E. Hayden, Exec. VP
Bruce Campbell, Group VP and Svc. Dir.
Bob Parker, Sales Dir.
Tom Ryan, Mktg. VP
Bill Wolf, Pub. Rel. Dir.
Robert Rodgers, Reg. Mgr. (East)
James Hurban, Reg. Mgr. (Central)
Stephen Brown, Reg. Mgr. (West)
Jim Harrell, Reg. Mgr. (South)
Y.I. Lee, Pres., Hyundai Auto Canada Inc.
National Hotline—(416)477-0202

CUSTOMER SERVICE REGIONAL OFFICES

Central Region   Ph:(708)820-3100
700 N. Enterprise St.
Aurora, IL 60504

Eastern Region   Ph:(609)395-7347
1100 Cranbury South River Rd.
Jamesburg, NJ 08831

Southern Region   Ph:(404)739-9484
240 Thornton Rd.
Lithia Springs, GA 30057

Western Region   Ph:(714)965-3006
10550 Talbert Ave.
Fountain Valley, CA 92728-0850

4361 • INFINITI DIVISION, NISSAN MOTORS CORP. IN USA

18501 S. Figueroa St.   Ph:(213)532-3111
Carson, CA 90248-4500

Luxury car division of Nissan Motor Corp., founded in 1987. Sold 34,900 cars in the U.S. in 1991, up from 24,000 cars in 1990.

CORPORATE CONTACTS

William R. Bruce, VP and Gen. Mgr.
Richard Lueders, Natl. Parts and Svc. Mgr.
Pete McAvoy, Natl. Sales Opns. Mgr.
Robert Bibbs, Reg. Gen. Mgr. (West)
Patrick Doody, Reg. Gen. Mgr. (Central)
Ed Sherman, Reg. Gen. Mgr. (East)
Peter Bossis, Mktg. Dir.
Brad Bradshaw, Natl. Adv. Mgr.
Mary Lauwereins, Mgr. of Cust. Satisfaction
David Nakano, Mgr. of Cust. Satisfaction Planning,
    Public Relations—(213)719-5007
Thomas Eastwood, Gen. Sales Mgr.

4362 • JAGUAR CARS INC.

555 MacArthur Blvd.   Ph:(201)818-8500
Mahwah, NJ 07430-2327   Fax:(201)818-9781

Subsidiary of Jaguar Cars Ltd. of Coventry, England. Operates 140 dealers across the U.S., with most sales focused in Florida, California, and the three state area around New York. Jaguar plc, Jaguar's holding company, was purchased by Ford Motor Co. in 1990 for $2.5 billion. Jaguar sold approximately 9,400 cars in the U.S. in 1991, down from 18,700 in 1990.

CORPORATE CONTACTS

Michael B. Jackling, VP of Sales & Mktg.
Michael Dale, Pres.
D.E. Gambill, Customer Care
R.W. Burden, Mktg. VP
Michael Cook, Pub. Rel. Mgr.
R.R. Polakoski, Svc. VP
National Hotline—(201)592-5236
George J. Frame, VP of Finance & Adm.
John G. Crawford, VP of Public Affairs
Edward J. McCauley, Sr. VP

CUSTOMER SERVICE ZONE OFFICES

Eastern Zone   Ph:(201)818-8100
555 MacArthur Blvd.
Mahwah, NJ 07430-2327

Western Zone   Ph:(415)467-9402
422 Valley Dr.
Brisbane, CA 94005

4363 • JEEP/EAGLE DIV., CHRYSLER CORP.

12000 Chrysler Dr.   Ph:(313)956-5741
Highland Park, MI 48288-1919

Jeep/Eagle, a division of Chrysler Corp., celebrated its 50th year in 1991. Jeep history began in 1941 when Willys-Overland of Toledo, Ohio began contract production of the Jeep military vehicle for the U.S. Army. Eventually bought by American Motors Corp. (AMC), Jeep was acquired by Chrysler in 1987 as part of its own purchase of AMC. Jeep/Eagle sold 177,800 Jeep trucks in 1991, down from 196,900 in 1990; and sold 59,300 Eagle cars in 1991, down from 60,700 in 1990. *Joint ventures:* Eagle vehicle production done in partnership with Mitsubishi through the Diamond-Star Motor Corp. plant in Normal, Illinois. For additional contact information, see Chrysler Corp. entry.

CORPORATE CONTACTS

Lee A. Iacocca, CEO, Chrysler Corp.
Lawrence W. Baker, Gen. Mgr., Jeep/Eagle
    Public Relations—(313)252-8794

MANUFACTURING DIVISIONS

Diamond-Star Motor Corp.   Ph:(309)888-8000
100 N. Diamond-Star Pkwy.
Normal, IL 61761
Lino J. Piedra, Chm.
Yoichi Nakane, Pres.
Katsuhiko Kawasoe, Exec. VP/Human
    Resources

Jeep Corp.   Ph:(419)470-7182
1000 Jeep Pkwy.
Toledo, OH 43657

4364 • LAMBORGHINI U.S.A. INC.

7601 Centurion Parkway   Ph:(904)565-9100
Jacksonville, FL 32256

Founded in 1962 by Italian tractor magnate Ferruccio Lamborghini. Acquired by Chrysler Corp. in 1987; Chrysler also formed the subsidiary Lamborghini Engineering to develop a Formula One engine. The Lamborghini Diablo had a 1990 base price of $239,000. A total of 156 Lamborghini cars were sold in the U.S. in 1991. For additional contact information, see Chrysler Corp. entry.

CORPORATE CONTACTS

Lee A. Iacocca, CEO, Chrysler Corp.
A.D. Imber, Pres., Lamborghini U.S.A.
Jacque Kirk, CFO & Treas.
Bill Westlund, Natl. Mgr. of Svc./Warranty
Harvey Shepherd, Natl. Mgr. of Parts

4365 • LEXUS DIVISION, TOYOTA MOTOR SALES USA

19001 S. Western Ave.   Ph:(213)328-2075
Torrance, CA 90509

Division of Toyota Motor Sales USA Inc. established in 1987. Introduced two built-in Japan sedans in the fall of 1989. Sold 71,200 vehicles in the U.S. in 1991, up from 63,500 in 1990.

ADDITIONAL NUMBERS

Toll-free: 800-25—LEXUS

CORPORATE CONTACTS

J. Davis Illingworth, VP and Gen. Mgr.
K. Usuda, Sr. VP

4366 • LINCOLN-MERCURY DIVISION, FORD MOTOR CO.

P.O. Box 43322   Ph:(313)446-4450
300 Renaissance Center
Detroit, MI 48243

Lincoln Motor Company was bought by Ford Motor Company in 1922. The Lincoln-Mercury Division was formed October 22, 1945, in a company-wide restructuring orchestrated by Ford vice president Ernest R. Breech. Breech's goal was to modernize Ford Motor Company by creating divisions following a General Motors pattern of centralized administration. In 1987 Lincoln-Mercury was listed as the tenth largest auto dealer in the U.S. The company sold

178,700 Lincolns in 1991, down from 231,700 in 1990; and sold 375,900 Mercury cars in 1991, down from 390,800 in 1990.

ADDITIONAL NUMBERS

Toll-free: 800-521-4140

CORPORATE CONTACTS

Ross H. Roberts, VP & Gen. Mgr.
Steve C. Taylor, Adv. Mgr.
Ian G. McAllister, Gen. Mktg. Mgr.
B.S. Restuccia, Dir. of Mktg. Svcs.
George P. Tardiff, Mktg. Plans Mgr.
Ted C. Goellner, Mktg. Rep. Mgr.
Charles C. Snearly, Mgr. of Pub. Aff.
Mark W. Hutchins, Gen. Sales Mgr.
Myron Singer, Prog. Dist. Mgr.

CUSTOMER SERVICE REGIONAL OFFICES

Atlanta District Office · Ph:(404)763-6440
P.O. Box 105003
Atlanta, GA 30348

Boston District Office · Ph:(508)481-2798
352 Turnpike Rd., Ste. 303
Southborough, MA 01772-1794

Buffalo District Office · Ph:(716)631-4430
PO Box 244
Buffalo, NY 14225

Charlotte District Office · Ph:(704)554-4501
PO Box 220307
Charlotte, NC 28222

Cincinnati District Office · Ph:(513)398-4884
PO Box 6308
Cincinnati, OH 45215-6308

Cleveland District Office · Ph:(216)526-6900
PO Box 41035
Brecksville, OH 44141

Dallas District Office · Ph:(214)323-6299
PO Box 110037
Carrollton, TX 75011

Denver District Office · Ph:(303)694-8600
P.O.Box 4028
Englewood, CO 80155

Houston District Office · Ph:(713)680-4260
PO Box 827
Houston, TX 77001

Indianapolis District Office · Ph:(317)353-8251
P.O. Box 19448
Indianapolis, IN 46219

Kansas City District Office · Ph:(913)888-0141
P.O. Box 501
Shawnee Mission, KS 66201

Los Angeles District Office · Ph:(714)520-8300
2200 W. Sequoia
P.O. Box 4680-P
Anaheim, CA 92803

Louisville District Office · Ph:(502)456-3700
P.O. Box 32080
Louisville, KY 40232

Memphis District Office · Ph:(901)757-1076
PO Box 190
Cordova, TN 38018

Milwaukee District Office · Ph:(414)785-3100
PO Box 267
Brookfield, WI 53005

New Orleans District Office · Ph:(504)454-6764
P.O. Box 8630
Metairie, LA 70011

New York District Office · Ph:(201)288-9421
U.S. Hwy. 46
Teterboro, NJ 07608

Omaha District Office · Ph:(402)498-6050
P.O. Box 54440
Omaha, NE 68154

Philadelphia District Office · Ph:(609)662-8021
PO Box 5030
Mt. Laurel, NJ 08054

Phoenix District Office · Ph:(602)230-0784
P.O. Box 844
Phoenix, AZ 85001

St. Louis District Office · Ph:(314)569-4455
P.O. Box 24575
St. Louis, MO 63141

San Jose District Office · Ph:(408)262-9110
P.O. Box 4002
Milpitas, CA 95035

Seattle District Office · Ph:(206)244-5800
13555 South East 36th St., Ste. 200
Bellevue, WA 98006

Twin Cities District Office · Ph:(612)932-9799
P.O. Box 9303
Minneapolis, MN 55440

Washington District Office · Ph:(703)698-2052
8051 Gatehouse Rd.
Falls Church, VA 22046

4367 • LOTUS CARS USA INC.

1655 Lakes Pkwy. · Ph:(404)822-4566
Lawrenceville, GA 30243

Lotus Cars USA Inc. is an importer of Lotus autos, parts, and accessories. It is a subsidiary of the British company Group Lotus plc, which began as Lotus Cars Limited in 1955. Founded by Colin Chapman, Lotus Cars Limited gained reknown with its race cars and later applied the same engineering techniques to its luxury sports cars. The parent company was purchased by General Motors Corp. in 1986. Lotus sales in the U.S. for 1991 are estimated at 324 vehicles. Lotus will build about 2,000 cars in 1992, but will not market them in the U.S. The company plans to introduce 1993 models in 1992.

CORPORATE CONTACTS

Ronald L. Foster, Pres. & CEO
James R. Blackwell, VP of Fin. & Admin.
Mark O'Shaughnessy, Reg. Sales Mgr.
Arnold A. Johnson, Service VP
Uwe Lindner, Parts Mgr.
Jackson Pike, Reg. Sales Mgr.
Scott Sweeney, PR & Adv. Mgr.

4368 • MASERATI AUTOMOBILES INC.

1501 Caton Ave. · Ph:(301)646-6400
Baltimore, MD 21227 · Fax:(301)646-0406

Maserati Automobiles Inc. is the North American distributor of Maserati vehicles, owned in part by Fiat and Chrysler. The current Maserati line of high-performance, exotic sports vehicles includes the Spyder, Maserati 430, and the Shamal. In 1991, Maserati sold 2,100 cars worldwide, down 13.6 percent from 1990. Maserati Automobiles Inc. sold 240 cars in the U.S. in 1991.

CORPORATE CONTACTS

Mario Tozzi-Condivi, CEO
George A. Garbutt, Exec. VP

4369 • MAZDA MOTOR OF AMERICA INC.

7755 Irvine Center Dr.	Ph:(714)727-1990
Irvine, CA 92718	Fax:(714)727-6101

Mazda Motor of America Inc. is the importing arm of Mazda Motor Corp. in Hiroshima, Japan. The parent company was founded as Toyo Kogyo Co. in 1931 and was renamed Mazda in 1984. Ford Motor Co. acquired 25 percent interest in Mazda in 1979, and currently the two companies share production of Ford Probes at Mazda's plant in Flat Rock, Michigan. In 1987, Mazda cars were ranked as the fifth most popular imported cars in the United States. Mazda Motors of America Inc. sold 343,600 cars and trucks in the U.S. in 1991, down from 349,700 in 1990.

CORPORATE CONTACTS

Keiji Asano, Chm.
Yoshinori Taura, Pres.
Kensuke Kato, Exec. VP
Moto Katsube, Exec. VP
Clark Vitulli, Sen. VP & Gen. Mgr.
Kazuo Sonoguchi, Sen. VP & Dep. Gen. Mgr.
George McCabe, Group VP of Opns.
J. Badrtalei, VP of Fin.
Rick Balsiger, Dir. of Adv.
Duane Bowen, VP of Pub. Rel.
Duke Hale, VP of Sales Dev.
Janet Thompson, VP of Mktg.

OFF-SITE OPERATIONS

Gulf Regional Operations	Ph:(713)240-5800
10445 Corporate Dr.	
Sugar Land, TX 77478	
Peter F. Lassen, Reg. Opns. Mgr.	

Northeast Regional Operations	Ph:(201)865-1200
865 Centennial Ave.	Fax:(201)885-1324
Piscataway, NJ 08854	
William Goetz, Reg. Opns. Mgr.	
Steve Potter, Pub. Rel. Mgr.	

Northwest Regional Operations	Ph:(205)251-5920
8621 S. 180th St.	
Kent, WA 98032	
J. Nalley, Reg. Opns. Mgr.	

Pacific Regional Operations	Ph:(714)380-7705
9451 Toledo Way	
Irvine, CA 92714	
Jim Seidel, Reg. Opns. Mgr.	

Southeast Regional Operations	Ph:(904)731-0132
8318 Bay Center Rd.	Fax:(904)739-0753
Jacksonville, FL 32216	
F. Wallace, Reg. Opns. Mgr.	

CUSTOMER SERVICE REGIONAL OFFICES

Great Lakes Region	Ph:(616)949-9305
618 Kenmoor SE	
Grand Rapids, MI 49501-2008	

Gulf Region	Ph:(713)240-5800
10445 Corporate Dr.	
Sugar Land, TX 77478	

Northeast Region	Ph:(201)885-1200
865 Centennial Ave.	
Piscataway, NJ 08854	

Northwest Region	Ph:(206)251-5920
8621 S. 180th St.	
Kent, WA 98032	

Pacific Region	Ph:(714)380-7705
9451 Toledo Way	
Irvine, CA 92718	

Southeast Region	Ph:(904)731-4010
PO Box 16305	
Jacksonville, FL 32245-6345	

MANUFACTURING DIVISIONS

Mazda Motor Manufacturing (USA)	Ph:(313)782-7800
Corp.	
1 Mazda Dr.	
Flat Rock, MI 48134	
Osamu Nobuto, Pres.	
Masahiro Uchida, Exec. VP	
Takashi Itoh, VP of Manufacturing	

4370 • MERCEDES-BENZ OF NORTH AMERICA INC.

One Mercedes Dr.	Ph:(201)573-0600
Montvale, NJ 07645-0350	Fax:(201)573-6780

Mercedes-Benz of North America Inc. is a subsidiary of Mercedez-Benz in Stuttgart, Germany, which is in turn part of holding company Daimler-Benz AG. The company's origins can be traced back to German inventor Carl Benz, who built a three-wheel workable car in 1885, and to Gottlieb Daimler, who built a four-wheel car the following year. In 1988 Mercedes-Benz cars were ranked as the tenth most popular imported cars. Mercedes-Benz of North America Inc. sold 58,900 cars in the U.S. in 1991, down from 78,400 cars in 1990. 1992 S-Class models will be the first modern cars with CFC-free urethane foams, and activated charcoal filters to help prevent airborne pollutants from entering the passenger compartment.

CORPORATE CONTACTS

Werner Niefer, Chm.
Erich Krampe, Pres. & CEO
Wolfgang Hartung, Sen. VP of Fin.
Michael Jackson, Sen. VP of Sales & Mktg.
Karl-Heinz Schuering, Controller
Carol Gastaldi, Treasurer
Gerd Klauss, VP of Mktg.
Karl Heinz Faber Sr., VP of Prod. Compliance, Svc., & Parts
Paul Halata, VP of N. Amer. Aff.
Albert Weiss, Gen. Mgr. of Adv.
Kurt von Zumwalt, Gen. Mgr. of Pub. Rel.
A.B. Shuman, Mgr. of Pub. Rel.

CUSTOMER SERVICE REGIONAL OFFICES

North Central Region	Ph:(708)455-9131
3333 Charles St.	
Franklin Park, IL 60131	

Northeast Region	Ph:(301)859-9170
Baltimore Commons Business Park	
1300 Mercedes Drive (2nd Floor)	
P.O. Box 348	
Hanover, MD 21076	

Southern Region
8813 Western Way
P.O. Box 17604
Jacksonville, FL 32245

Ph:(904)443-2150

Western Region
6357 Sunset Boulevard
P.O. Box 93637
Hollywood, CA 90093-0637

Ph:(213)468-3040

4371 • MITSUBISHI MOTOR SALES OF AMERICA INC.

6400 Katella Ave.
Cypress, CA 90630-0064

Ph:(714)372-6000

Mitsubishi Motor Sales of America Inc. is a subsidiary of Mitsubishi Motors Corporation, Tokyo, Japan. The parent company, founded in 1917, was responsible for building Japan's first volume production car, the Mitsubishi Model A. Mitsubishi Motors Corporation of Japan has provided cars, trucks, and engines to Chrysler Corporation since 1971, and in 1981 Mitsubishi Motor Sales of America was formed to distribute a full range of subcompacts, compacts, sports coupes, light trucks, and sport/utility vehicles in the United States. Mitsubishi paid $450 million in late 1991 to take over Chrysler Corp's 50 percent share of Diamond Star Motors Inc., the two companies' joint-production venture in Normal, Illinois. In 1991, Mitsubishi Motor Sales of America Inc. sold 190,800 cars and trucks throughout the country, up from 190,700 cars and trucks in 1990.

ADDITIONAL NUMBERS

Toll-free: 800-222-0037

CORPORATE CONTACTS

Taiji Fukuda, Chm.
Kazue Naganuma, Pres. & CEO
Richard Recchia, Exec. VP of Gen. Opns. & COO
Tashiya Yamano, Exec. VP of Fin.
Hisashi Kunifusa, Sr. VP of Opns.
Robert LaBossiere, Parts VP
Thomas C. Benson, Svc. VP
Rick Lepley, Sr. VP of Sales
Garrett J. Nash, Mktg. Svcs. VP
Frances Oda, Adv. Dir.
Kim E. Custer, Pub. Rel. Mgr.
John E. Zorger, Controller

CUSTOMER SERVICE REGIONAL OFFICES

Eastern Regional Office
516 Heron Dr.
Bridgeport, NJ 08014

North Central Regional Office
555 Pierce, Ste. 195
Itasca, IL 60143

Southeastern Regional Office
6488 Currin Dr.
Orlando, FL 32811

Southwestern Regional Office
8100 Mesquite Bend Dr.
Irving, TX 75063

MANUFACTURING DIVISIONS

Diamond-Star Motors Corp.
100 N. Diamond-Star Parkway
Normal, IL 61761

Ph:(309)888-8000
Fax:(309)888-8150

4372 • NISSAN NORTH AMERICA INC.

990 W. 190th St.
Torrance, CA 90502

Ph:(310)768-3700
Fax:(310)327-2272

Nissan North America Inc. is an importer of Nissan cars, trucks, and parts. It is a subsidiary of Nissan Motor Company Limited, Japan, maker of cars, buses, trucks, industrial engines, boats, textile machinery, and high-lows. The first Nissan cars (then known as Datsun) were built in 1933. In 1966 the Japanese company merged with Prince Motors Limited. Currently, Nissan Motor Co. and Fuji Heavy Industries, parent company of Subaru of America, are working together to devise ways to share components and products. It is expected that the next-generation Nissan Micra/March, due in Japan in early 1992, and the Subaru Justy replacement, due in 1993, will share a number of common components. Nissan North America sold 549,000 cars and trucks in the U.S. in 1991, down from 597,600 in 1990. Nissan Motor Co. reported a 48.2 percent decline in net income in 1991. **See also:** Infiniti.

ADDITIONAL NUMBERS

Toll-free: 800-647-7261

CORPORATE CONTACTS

Yoshikazo Hanawa, Chm.
Thomas Mignanelli, Pres. & CEO
Sheleme Sendaba, VP of Fin.

FINANCE, INSURANCE, AND MORTGAGE UNITS

Nissan Motor Acceptance Corp.
990 W. 190th St., 7th Fl.
Torrance, CA 90502
Atsushi Muramatsu, Chm.
Masataka Matsamura, Pres.

Ph:(213)719-8000

MANUFACTURING DIVISIONS

Nissan Canada Inc.
5290 Orbitor Dr.
Mississauga, ON, Canada L4W 4Z5
Eisuke Toyama, Pres.
Y. Boyer, Sales VP

Ph:(416)629-9742
Fax:(416)629-9742

Nissan Motor Manufacturing Corp.
  U.S.A.
983 Nissan Dr.
Smyrna, TN 37167
Yoshikazu Hanawa, Chm.
Jerry L. Benefield, Pres.
Frederick F. Sommer, VP of
  Manufacturing

Ph:(615)459-1400
Fax:(615)459-1555

4373 • OLDSMOBILE DIVISION, GENERAL MOTORS CORP.

Buick-Oldsmobile-Cadillac Group
920 Townsend St.
Lansing, MI 48921

Ph:(517)377-5000

In 1897, the Olds Motor Vehicle Company was organized in Lansing, Michigan, and the first Oldsmobile was produced. The famous curved-dash Oldsmobile runabout, produced in 1901, was the first American car manufactured in quantity. The Company joined General Motors in 1908. In 1948 it introduced the first Cadillac with a high-compression V-8 and became known as GM's technology division, particularly in engine development. In 1984 it organized under the Buick-Oldsmobile-Cadillac Group (B-O-C), giving the group complete responsibility for their products, including engineering, manufacturing, assembly, and marketing. Oldsmobile Division sold 458,100 cars and trucks in 1991, down from 537,900 in 1990.

CORPORATE CONTACTS

J. Michael Losh, Gen. Mgr.
Michael A. Grimaldi, Gen. Mgr., Marketing
David E. Lahti, Gen. Mgr., Sales & Service

OFF-SITE OPERATIONS

Doraville Assembly Operation   Ph:(404)455-5255
C-P-C Group
3900 Motors Industrial Hwy.
Doraville, GA 30360-3163

Flint Assembly Operation (Buick City)   Ph:(313)236-5000
B-O-C Group
902 E. Hamilton Ave.
Flint, MI 48550

Lansing Assembly Operation   Ph:(517)885-5000
B-O-C Group
401 N. Verlinden Ave.
Lansing, MI 48901

Oklahoma City Assembly Operation   Ph:(405)733-6011
C-P-C Group
P.O. Box 26527
Oklahoma City, OK 73126

Wentzville Assembly Operation   Ph:(314)327-5711
B-O-C Group
P.O. Box 444
Wentzville, MO 63385

CUSTOMER SERVICE CENTERS

Customer Service Department   Ph:(517)377-5546
PO Box 30095
Lansing, MI 48909-7595

4374 • PEUGEOT MOTORS OF AMERICA INC.

One Peugeot Plaza   Ph:(201)935-8400
Lyndhurst, NJ 07071

Peugeot Motors of America Inc. is a subsidiary of Peugeot S.A. (PSA), Paris. PSA began as a textile mill in 1810. It was founded by two brothers, Jean-Frederic and Jean-Pierre Peugeot, who later invented the cold-roll steel process. In 1885 Armand Peugeot, a cycling enthusiast, persuaded the family to manufacture bicycles. The venture was an instant success. In 1889 the company built its first steam car as well as its first gasoline car. The company gained notice again in 1894 when it made and sold the world's first station wagon. Peugeot's later inventions included the first diesel-powered passenger car, produced in 1922, and the world's first production car with independent front-wheel suspension, introduced in the early 1930s. In 1978 Peugeot bought Chrysler Corporation's European operations.

Peugeot Motors of America Inc. was established in 1958 as the U.S. sales and marketing arm of Peugeut S.A. All Peugeot cars destined for the U.S. are built at Peugeot's main production center in Sochaux, France, and shipped via Antwerp, Belgium. Approximately 3,600 cars were sold in the U.S. in 1991, down from 4,300 in 1990. Due to declining sales, Peugeot Motors of America stopped importing cars in August of 1991. When dealers run out of new cars in mid-1992, the U.S. subsidiary will offer only parts and service.

ADDITIONAL NUMBERS

Toll-free: 800-345-5549

CORPORATE CONTACTS

Jean-Louis Saint Sevin, Pres.
Brad Helms, Natl. Sales Mgr.
Daniel Petit, Natl. Mktg. Mgr.
Kim Derderian, Natl. Pub. Rel. Mgr.

4375 • PONTIAC DIVISION, GENERAL MOTORS CORP.

Chevrolet-Pontiac-GM of Canada   Ph:(313)857-5000
  Group
One Pontiac Plaza
Pontiac, MI 48340

Named after Pottawatomis Indian Chief Pontiac. Dates back to 1893 when the Pontiac Buggy Company was formed in Pontiac, Michigan. Became the Oakland Motor Car Company, which joined General Motors in 1909. The first Pontiac was produced in 1926 under the Oakland name. Established from Oakland as the Pontiac Motor Division in 1932. Organized in 1984 under the Chevrolet-Pontiac-GM of Canada Group (C-P-C), giving the group complete responsibility for products, including engineering, manufacturing, assembly, and marketing. Sold 513,500 cars and trucks in the U.S. in 1991, down from 666,300 in 1990.

ADDITIONAL NUMBERS

Toll-free: 800-762-2737

CORPORATE CONTACTS

John G. Middlebrook, Gen. Mgr.
Elwood M. Schlesinger, Gen. Mgr., Sales & Service
Joe M. Hendrix, Gen. Mktg. Mgr., Market & Product Planning
Edward S. Lechtzin, Director, Public Relations—(313)857-1567
Carl Sheffer, Mgr., Public Relations, Western Region—(818)997-5444
Kirk H. Hobolth, Mgr., Personnel

OFF-SITE OPERATIONS

Lansing Assembly Operation (B Plant)   Ph:(517)885-5000
B-O-C Group
401 N. Verlinden Ave.
Lansing, MI 48901

Lordstown Assembly Operation   Ph:(216)824-5000
B-O-C Group
P.O. Box 1406
Warren, OH 44482

Oklahoma City Assembly Operation   Ph:(405)733-6011
C-P-C Group
P.O. Box 26527
Oklahoma City, OK 73126

4376 • PORSCHE CARS NORTH AMERICA INC.

100 W. Liberty St.   Ph:(702)348-3000
P.O. Box 30911   Fax:(702)348-3770
Reno, NV 89520-3911

Porsche Cars of North America Inc. is the U.S. marketing arm of the Porsche company in Germany. The parent company was founded in the early 1900s when German designer and inventor Ferdinand Porsche presented his electric car. His son Ferry Porsche also designed for the company, gaining acclaim with the Porsche 911. Porsche has worked with Volkswagen and Audi since the 1930s; in fact, the Porsche 914 was often considered a VW instead of a Porsche because of its Volkswagen components. In a 1988 survey, Porsche was voted as the fourth best-known and most highly regarded brand name in the world and the fifth most powerful global brand name in Europe. In 1991, Porsche Cars of North America Inc. sold 4,400 cars in the United States, down from 9,100 cars in 1990.

CORPORATE CONTACTS

Brian Bowler, Pres. & CEO
Hartmut Kristen, Mktg. VP
Frederick J. Schwab, Sr. Exec. VP of Fin. & Admin.
Larry Morris, VP of Parts & Svc.
Ed Triolo, Pub. Rel. Mgr.
Joel Ewanick, Adv. Mgr.

John Egan, Mgr. of Planning & Mkt. Dev.
Richard Ford, VP for Vehicle Sales & Opns.

4377 • RANGE ROVER OF NORTH AMERICA INC.

4390 Parliament Pl.   Ph:(301)731-9040
P.O. Box 1503   Fax:(301)731-9054
Lanham, MD 20706

Range Rover of North America Inc. was established in 1986 as a subsidiary of Land Rover UK Limited of Solihull, England. The parent group began as the Rover Car Company in 1906. The Land Rover truck was designed after World War II, and the Range Rover was introduced in 1970. In 1991 Range Rover of North America sold 3,300 trucks in the U.S., down from 4,600 in 1990.

CORPORATE CONTACTS

Charles Hughes, Pres.
Joel Greer, Sales VP
Richard P. Hubert, Natl. Parts Mgr.
David A. Schworm, Svc. Mgr.
William E. Baker, VP of Corp. Comm.
Russell T. Turnham, Mktg. VP
Roger J. Ball, VP of Opns.
Joel D. Scharfer, VP of Fin.

4378 • RENAULT USA INC.

4000 Town Center, Ste. 480   Ph:(313)358-8800
Southfield, MI 48075

In 1987, Renault was ranked the fourth top car manufacturer in Europe and the sixth leading vehicle producer worldwide.

CORPORATE CONTACTS

Herve Hauvespre, Chm.
Bernard Vernous, Pres.
R.J. Willman, VP of Fin. & Admin.
Robert Ferraris, VP of Prod. Dev. Group

4379 • ROLLS-ROYCE MOTOR CARS INC.

120 Chubb Ave.   Ph:(201)460-9600
P.O. Box 476   Fax:(201)460-9392
Lyndhurst, NJ 07071

Rolls-Royce Motor Cars Inc., Lyndhurst, New Jersey, imports Rolls-Royce and Bentley cars made by Rolls-Royce Motor Cars Ltd., Crewe, England. The British company, founded in 1906, acquired the Bentley company in 1931. In 1939 the company ceased production of cars and began producing engines for fighter planes. Rolls-Royce became a world leader in aviation as well as in luxury cars, but in 1971 financial difficulties overtook the company's aero engine production and the aviation interests were purchased by the British government. A new independent company, Rolls-Royce Motors, was created to continue car manufacturing, and in 1973 Rolls-Royce Motors became a publicly owned company. In 1980 Rolls-Royce merged with Vickers Ltd., now Vickers plc, a British engineering company. Rolls-Royce sold 1,200 cars in the U.S. in 1990. **See also:** Bentley.

ADDITIONAL NUMBERS

Toll-free: 800-777-6923

CORPORATE CONTACTS

Howard I. Mosher, Pres. & CEO
Robert Wharen, Sales VP
Orson Munn, Mgr. of Adv. & Promo.
Donald J. Beck, CFO & Treas.

Reg Abbiss, Sr. Exec./Corp. Comm.
Christopher O. Huffman, VP of Parts & Svc.

CUSTOMER SERVICE ZONE OFFICES

Zone 1   Ph:(201)469-9600
P.O. Box 476
Lyndhurst, NJ 07071

Zone 2   Ph:(312)529-5330
303 E. Army Trail Rd.
Suite 108
Bloomingdale, IL 60108

Zone 3   Ph:(214)241-1955
11225 Gemini Lane
Dallas, TX 75229

Zone 7   Ph:(407)750-8381
900 N. Federal Highway
Suite 360
Boca Raton, FL 33432

Zones 5 and 6   Ph:(805)499-4346
1909 Oak Terrace Lane
Thousand Oaks, CA 91320

4380 • SAAB CARS USA, INC.

P.O. Box 697   Ph:(203)795-5671
Orange, CT 06477-4451   Fax:(203)795-4451

Saab-Scania of America Inc., importer of Saab cars and Scania Class-8 trucks, is a subsidiary of Saab-Scania AB, Nykoping, Sweden. In 1989 Saab-Scania AB signed an agreement with General Motors Corporation to form an additional company, Saab Automobile AB in Sweden. Saab cars have been sold in the U.S. since 1957, and in 1991 Saab Cars USA sold 26,100 vehicles. Saab introduced its Saab 9000-CD Turbo Griffin Edition in 1992, but plans to produce only 400. Headquarters for Saab Cars USA will be moved from Connecticut to Atlanta, Georgia in 1992.

CORPORATE CONTACTS

Sten O. Helling, Pres. & COO
Robert J. Sinclair, Chm. & CEO
Daniel B. Chasins, Mktg. Dir.
Kenneth Adams, Treas. & VP of Fin.
William S. Kelly, VP of Sales & Mktg.
Roy Steinwolf, Mgr. of Mktg. & Opns.
Steven Rossi, Pub. Rel. Mgr.

4381 • SATURN CORP., GENERAL MOTORS CORP.

1420/1450 Stephenson Hwy.   Ph:(313)524-5000
PO Box 7025
Troy, MI 48083

Saturn Corporation was formed as a subsidiary of General Motors Corporation in 1985. Efforts began in 1983 when General Motors and the United Auto Workers (UAW) agreed to form a GM-UAW Study Center to explore new approaches to building small cars in the United States. The first Saturn demonstration vehicle was presented for evaluation in 1984. In 1986, a manufacturing and assembly complex was built in Spring Hill, Tennessee, and offices were opened in Troy, Michigan. Saturn sold 74,500 cars in 1991, up from 1,900 in 1990.

CORPORATE CONTACTS

Richard G. LeFauve, Pres.
Bruce G. MacDonald, VP of Comm.
Donald W. Hudler, VP of Mktg., Sales, & Svc.
Robert E. Boruff, VP of Manufacturing

4384 • SUZUKI

Thomas G. Manoff, VP of Finance
John J. Wetzel II, VP of Eng.

OFF-SITE OPERATIONS

Spring Hill Operations   Ph:(615)486-5050
Highway 31 South
P.O. Box 1502
Spring Hill, TN 37174
Laurie Kay, Corporate Communications
Dora Mack, Community Relations
Jennifer Schettler, Media Relations

4382 • STERLING MOTOR CARS, AUSTIN-ROVER CARS OF N.A.

8953 N.W. 23rd St.   Ph:(305)597-6400
Miami, FL 33172   Fax:(305)597-6475

Sterling Motor Cars is a subsidiary of Rover Group plc, England. Originally known as Austin Rover Cars of North America (ARCONA), the division's name was changed to Sterling Motor Cars in 1989 to more closely identify it with the Sterling sedans it sells. In late 1991 Rover Group and Honda Motor Corp. agreed to develop three cars during the 1990s, but no Rover or Sterling cars will be sold in the U.S. for five years or more due to declining sales. Sterling sold 2,700 cars in 1991, down from 4,000 cars in 1990.

CORPORATE CONTACTS

Graham Morris, Pres.
Stephen Arthur, Fin. Dir.
Michael Jackling, Mktg. & Sales VP
Rainer Fruechtnicht, Svc. Div. VP & Gen. Mgr.
Tim Tully, Parts Dir.
Anthony Cumming, Mktg. Comm. Dir.

4383 • SUBARU OF AMERICA INC.

Subaru Plaza   Ph:(609)488-8500
2235 Rte. 70 W.
Cherry Hill, NJ 08002

Subaru of America Inc. is a wholly-owned subsidiary of Fuji Heavy Industries Ltd. (FHI) of Tokyo, Japan. Manufacturing operations for U.S.-marketed vehicles are located at FHI's home factory in Ota City, Japan, and at the U.S. joint venture facility, Subaru-Isuzu Automotive Inc. near Lafayette, Indiana. FHI reportedly lost $15.8 million on the Lafayette plant in fiscal year 1991. Subaru of America sold 105,000 cars in 1991, down from 108,500 cars in 1990. Subaru was recently ranked eleventh overall by J.D. Power & Associates, compared to 38 domestic and foreign nameplates.

ADDITIONAL NUMBERS

Toll-free: 800-782-2783

CORPORATE CONTACTS

Takeshi Higurashi, Chm.
Thomas R. Gibson, Pres. & COO
Masaharu Masumitsu, Vice Chm. & CEO
Chris Wackman, VP of Mktg.
Herman Berg, Group VP of Info. & Admin. Svcs.
Sohei Matsukuma, Vice Chm.
George T. Muller, Sr. VP & CFO
Robert J. Whitehead, Group VP of Prod. Eng.
Walter D. Biggers, VP of Prod. Eng.
J. Paul Bubernak, Group VP of Parts & Svc.
Tom Braun, VP of Parts
D. Bearden, VP of Svc.
C.F. Worrell, Group Sales VP
W.K. Stanton, Sales VP
Fred Heiler, Dir. of Pub. Rel.

CUSTOMER SERVICE REGIONAL OFFICES

Penn Jersey Subaru, Inc.   Ph:(609)234-7600
1504 Glen Ave.
Moorestown, NJ 08057

Southeast Region Subaru   Ph:(404)732-3200
220 The Bluffs
Austell, GA 30001

Subaru Distributors Corporation   Ph:(914)359-2500
6 Ramland Rd.
Orangeburg, NY 10962

Subaru Mid-America Region   Ph:(708)953-1188
301 Mitchell Ct.
Addison, IL 60101

Subaru Northwest Region   Ph:800-878—6677
8040 E. 33rd Dr.
P.O. Box 11293
Portland, OR 97211

Subaru of New England, Inc.   Ph:(617)769-5100
95 Morse St.
Norwood, MA 02062

Subaru Southwest Region   Ph:(303)371-3820
15000 E. 39th Ave.
Aurora, CO 80011

Subaru Western Region   Ph:(714)951-6592
12 Whatney Dr.
Irvine, CA 92718-2895

4384 • SUZUKI OF AMERICA AUTOMOTIVE CORP.

3251 E. Imperial Hwy.   Ph:(714)996-7040
Brea, CA 92621-6722   Fax:(714)524-2512

Suzuki of America Automotive Corporation is a subsidiary of Suzuki Motor Company, Hamamatsu, Japan. The parent company was created in 1909 as Suzuki Loom Works. In 1952 the company produced its first motorcycles, followed by the production of its first automobiles in 1955. By 1985 Suzuki cars had reached the U.S. market, and by 1991 there were 305 Suzuki dealerships in 48 states. Suzuki maintains subsidiaries in Canada, Thailand, the Philippines, Indonesia, Australia, Colombia, New Zealand, France, and Germany; and joint ventures and assembly plants in Canada, Spain, India, Malaysia, Hungary, and several other countries. Suzuki of America sold 5,500 cars in 1991, down from 6,500 cars in 1990; however, combined car and truck sales for 1991 were 21,700, up from 20,500 in 1990.

ADDITIONAL NUMBERS

Toll-free: 800-934-0934

CORPORATE CONTACTS

Kenji Shimizu, Pres.
Yoshi Fujii, Exec. VP
Gary Anderson, Mktg. Dir.
John Dorsey, Sales Dir.
William A. Charles, Field Svc. Opns.
Thomas P. Meyers, Natl. Adv. & Pub. Rel. Mgr.
Tsuyoshi Naritomi, Dir. of Tech. Svc.

CUSTOMER SERVICE REGIONAL OFFICES

Atlanta Regional Office   Ph:(404)699-2400
3495 Bankhead Highway, N.W.
Atlanta, GA 30331

Los Angeles Regional Office	Ph:800-877—6900
3251 E. Imperial Highway	
Brea, CA 92621-6722	

New York Regional Office	Ph:(201)930-8668
50 Tice Boulevard	
Woodcliff Lake, NJ 07675	

4385 • TOYOTA MOTOR SALES USA INC.

19001 S. Western Ave.	Ph:(213)618-4000
Torrance, CA 90509	

Toyota Motor Sales USA Inc. is a subsidiary of Toyota Motor Corp., Toyota City, Japan. The company's history dates back to 1933 when an automotive division was created by Toyoda Automatic Loom Works in Toyoda City, Japan. An experimental car and truck were developed in 1935 and Toyota Motor was formed in 1937. In 1984 Toyota signed an agreement with General Motors to collaborate in the production of the Corolla and the Geo Prizm. Lexus Division was formed in 1987. In 1988 the company broke ground for two new plants, one in Cambridge, Ontario for the production of the Corolla and one in Georgetown, Kentucky for the production of the Camry. Soon after, Toyota entered a 50-50 joint venture with GM, called New United Motor Manufacturing Inc. (NUMMI). Toyota sold 939,300 cars and trucks in the U.S. in 1991, down from 994,500 in 1990. **See also:** Lexus.

ADDITIONAL NUMBERS

Toll-free: 800-331-4331

CORPORATE CONTACTS

Yukiyasu Togo, Pres.
Y. Gieszel, VP of Fin.
Robert McCurry, Exec. VP of Opns.
Robert Best, Group VP
Jim Lacy, VP of Human Resources
M. Maruhashi, Treas.
Hal Bracken, Group VP, Prts., Serv., Cust. Rel., & US Prods.
Albert Wagner, VP of Sales
George Borst, VP of Mktg.
Jim Olson, VP of Pub. Affrs.

CUSTOMER SERVICE REGIONAL OFFICES

Boston Regional Office	Ph:800-331—4331
440 Forbes Boulevard	
Mansfield, MA 02048	

Central Atlantic Toyota Distributors, Inc.	Ph:800-331—4331
6710 Baymeadow Dr.	
P.O. Box 608	
Glen Burnie, MD 21060	

Chicago Regional Office	Ph:800-331—4331
500 Kehoe Blvd.	
Carol Stream, IL 60188	

Cincinnati Regional Office	Ph:800-331—4331
4550 Creek Rd.	
Cincinnati, OH 45242	

Denver Regional Office	Ph:800-331—4331
9676 Maroon Circle	
Englewood, CO 80112	

Gulf States Private Distributor Office	Ph:800-331—4331
7701 Wilshire Place Dr.	
Houston, TX 77240-0306	

Kansas City Regional Office	Ph:800-331—4331
11111 N.W. Airworld Dr.	
Kansas City, MO 64153	

Los Angeles Regional Office	Ph:800-331—4331
2 Banting	
Irvine, CA 92718	

New York Regional Office	Ph:800-331—4331
16 Henderson Dr.	
West Caldwell, NJ 07006	

Portland Regional Office	Ph:800-331—4331
6111 N.E. 87th Ave.	
Portland, OR 97220	

San Francisco Regional Office	Ph:800-331—4331
2451 Bishop Dr.	
San Ramon, CA 94583	

Southeast Private Distributor Office	Ph:800-331—4331
8019 Bayberry Rd.	
Jacksonville, FL 32256	

FINANCE, INSURANCE, AND MORTGAGE UNITS

Toyota Motor Credit Corp.	Ph:(213)715-3700
1515 W. 190th St.	
Torrance, CA 90509	
R. Pitts, Gen. Mgr.	

MANUFACTURING DIVISIONS

New United Motor Mfg. Inc.	Ph:(415)498-5500
(NUMMI)	
45500 Fremont Blvd.	
Fremont, CA 94538	

Toyota Motor Manufacturing USA Inc.	Ph:(502)868-2000
1001 Cherry Blossom Way	
Georgetown, KY 40324	
Fujio Cho, Pres.	
Michael Dodge, Plant Mgr.	
Jim Wiseman, Pub. Affrs. Mgr.	

4386 • VOLKSWAGEN OF AMERICA INC.

3800 Hamlin Rd.	Ph:(313)340-5000
Auburn Hills, MI 48326	Fax:(313)340-5045

Volkswagen of America, Inc. (VWoA) is a wholly-owned subsidiary of Volkswagen AG, a German auto company. VWoA was founded in 1955, the first foreign manufacturer to establish automotive assembly operations in the United States. VWoA is the umbrella organization for two car divisions, Volkswagen United States and Audi of America. In 1991 the company sold 96,700 cars and trucks in the U.S., down from 136,400 in 1990. **See also:** Audi.

ADDITIONAL NUMBERS

Toll-free: 800-822-8987
Telex: 230628

CORPORATE CONTACTS

Carl H. Hahn, Chm.
William Young, Pres. & CEO
John Kerr, VP & Treas.
Ulrich Fahrun, VP, Prts. & Info. Org.
Peter Fischer, Central Mktg.
Philip A. Hutchinson, Gen. Counsel & Sec., Pub. Affrs.
Jennifer Hurshell, Dir. of Pub. Rel.

CUSTOMER SERVICE REGIONAL OFFICES

Volkswagen Mid-America Inc.	Ph:(314)429-8100
8825 Page Blvd.	
St. Louis, MO 63114	

World-Wide Volkswagen Corp.	Ph:(914)578-5000
39 N. Greenbush Rd.	
Orangeburg, NY 10962	

FINANCE, INSURANCE, AND MORTGAGE UNITS

Volkswagen Lease Finance Corp.   Ph:(313)362-7318
888 W. Big Beaver Rd.
Troy, MI 48084
J.R. Green, Pres.

MANUFACTURING DIVISIONS

Fort Worth Manufacturing Plant   Ph:(817)624-4949
4401 Blue Mound Rd.
Fort Worth, TX 76106
Robert P. Wood, Mgr.
John C. Belsly, Controller
U.J. Jonen, Dir. of Mktg.

4387 • VOLVO NORTH AMERICA CORP.

535 Madison Ave.   Ph:(212)754-3300
New York, NY 10022

Volvo North America Corporation is a subsidiary of Volvo AB, Gothenburg, Sweden. The company has imported cars to the United States for the past 35 years. In 1991 they sold 67,700 cars in the U.S., down from 89,900 in 1990.

CORPORATE CONTACTS

Pehr G. Gyllenhammar, Chm.
Albert R. Dowden, Pres. & CEO
Michael Duke, Sr. VP & CFO
Thomas Ericson, VP of Corp. Affairs
Robert Mercer, VP & Gen. Counsel
David Korpics, VP & Controller

4388 • YUGO AMERICA INC.

120 Pleasant Ave.   Ph:(201)825-4600
P.O. Box 730   Fax:(201)825-8979
Upper Saddle, NJ 07458-0730

Yugo America Inc. has been importing cars from Yugoslavia since 1985. Originally a subsidiary of Global Motors Inc., Upper Saddle, New Jersey, Yugo is now a fully owned subsidiary of the Yugoslavian manufacturer Zastava. Zastava, based in Kragujevac, is a 136-year-old diversified conglomerate producer of cars, trucks, defense systems, sporting arms, and machine tools. In 1991 Yugo sold 3,100 cars in the United States, down from 6,400 cars in 1990.

ADDITIONAL NUMBERS

Toll-free: 800-USA-YUGO

CORPORATE CONTACTS

John Spiech, Pres. & CEO
Jack Haywood, Serv. Mgr.
Mike Donato, Parts Dir.
Zoran Basaraba, Dir. of Pub. Rel. & Adv.
Ruth Gilleo, CFO

Rankings Appendix

The following is a list of select automotive rankings and statistics established by various sources during the years 1987-92. Model rankings and statistics are categorized by year; general automotive rankings and statistics follow model rankings.

1987 MODEL YEAR

1987 Ten Best Cars
Ranked by: Editorial staff evaluations.
(in alphabetical order)
1) Acura Integra
2) Audi 5000S/CS Turbo
3) Chevrolet Corvette
4) Ford Mustang GT
5) Ford Taurus
6) Honda Accord
7) Mazda RX-7 Turbo
8) Pontiac Bonneville SE
9) Saab 9000 Turbo
10) Toyota MR2
Source: *Car and Driver*, Jan 1987, pp. 36-41.

Top 10 Selling U.S. Make Cars for 1987
Ranked by: Sales by U.S. dealers.
1) Escort
2) Taurus
3) Cavalier
4) Celebrity
5) Ciera
6) Accord (U.S.)
7) Tempo
8) Corsica/Beretta
9) Grand Am
10) Caprice
Source: *Ward's Automotive Yearbook 1988*, Ward's Communications Inc., p. 154.

Ten Best Performers, 1987*

Acceleration, 0 to 60 mph	Buick GNX, 4.7 sec.
Quarter-mile	Buick GNX, 13.5 sec. @ 102 mph
	Porsche 911 Turbo Cabriolet 13.5 sec. @ 102 mph
Top-gear acceleration†	Buick GNX, 6.8 sec.
Top speed	Ferrari Testarossa, 173 mph
Braking, 70 to 0 mph	Porsche 928S4, 164 ft.
Roadholding	Chevrolet Corvette Z52, 0.87 g
Interior sound level @ 70 mph	BMW 735i, Cadillac Limousine, Jaguar XJ6, Mercedes-Benz 560SEL 66 dBA
Road horsepower @ 50 mph	Toyota Tercel, 9 hp
EPA city fuel economy	Ford Festiva LX, 39 mpg
C/D observed fuel economy	Ford Festiva LX, 35 mpg

* includes only U.S.-specification production cars tested by Car and Driver in 1987.
† sum of 30-to-50 mph and 50-to-70 mph acceleration times.
Source: *Car and Driver Buyers Guide*, 1988, p. 13.

Road & Track's 10 Best Cars (1987)
Ranked by: Price and editorial staff evaluations.

Best Sedan (under $7,500)	Honda Civic Hatchback
Best Sedan ($7,500-$12,500)	Toyota Corolla
Best Sedan ($12,500-$17,500)	Ford Taurus
Best Sedan ($17,500-$22,500)	Acura Legend
Best Sedan ($22,500-$27,500)	Merkur Scorpio
Best High-Performance Car (under $12,500)	Honda CRX Si
Best 2-seat/2+2 High Performance Car($12,500-$17,500)	Toyota MR2 Supercharged
Best 4-seat High Performance Car ($12,500-$17,500)	Ford Mustang GT 5.0
Best High-Performance Car ($17,500-$22-500)	Mazda RX-7 Turbo
Best High-Performance Car ($22,500-$27,500)	Acura Legend Coupe

Source: *Road & Track*, Dec 1987, pp. 46-53.

10 Best Cars in the World (1987)
Ranked by: Editorial staff evaluations.
Mercedes-Benz 300E
Ferrari Testarossa
Porsche 928S4
BMW 735i
Acura Legend Coupe
Toyota MR2 Supercharged
Chevrolet Corvette
Mercedes-Benz 560SEC
Porsche 911 Carrera
Honda CRX Si
Source: *Road & Track*, Dec 1987, pp. 54-57.

Top Ten Cars Most Likely to Be Stolen, 1987
Ranked by: Thefts per 1,000 cars manufactured in 1987.
1) Pontiac Firebird
2) Chevrolet Camaro
3) Chevrolet Monte Carlo
4) Toyota MR2
5) Buick Regal
6) Mitsubishi Starion
7) Ferrari Mondial
8) Mitsubishi Mirage
9) Pontiac Fiero
10) Oldsmobile Cutlass Supreme
Source: *Medical Economics*, Jan 16, 1989, p. 70.

1988 MODEL YEAR

Best Selling Cars in the United States (1988)
Ranked by: Number of auto sales in 1988.
1) Ford Escort, with 387,815
2) Chevrolet Corsica/Beretta, 380,301
3) Ford Taurus, 374,627
4) Honda Accord, 362,663

5) Chevrolet Cavalier, 306,267
6) Ford Tempo, 285,141
7) Hyundai, 264,282
8) Chevrolet Celebrity, 252,861
9) Nissan Sentra, 249,523
10) Oldsmobile Cutlass Ciera, 237,386
Source: *Automotive News,* Automotive News Market Data Book, May 31, 1989, p. 34.

Most Complained-About Cars (1988)

Ranked by: Complaints per 10,000 cars, 1987-88.
1) Oldsmobile Delta 88
2) Plymouth Horizon
3) Acura Legend
4) Pontiac Bonneville
5) Buick LaSabre
6) Oldsmobile 98
7) Mercury Sable
8) Nissan Maxima
9) Mazda 626
10) Ford Tempo
Source: *Chilton's Automotive Industries,* Jan 1990, p. 42.

Ten Best Performers, 1988 *

Acceleration, 0 to 60 mph	Lotus Esprit Turbo, 5.3 sec.
Quarter-mile	Porsche 911 Club Sport 13.9 sec. @ 99 mph
Top-gear acceleration†	Chevrolet Corvette Z52, 7.1 sec.
Top speed	BMW 750iL, 158 mph
Braking, 70 to 0 mph	Chevrolet Corvette Z52, Toyota MR2, 168 ft.
Roadholding	Chevrolet Corvette Z51, 0.89 g
Interior sound level @ 70 mph	Pontiac 6000 STE AWD, 65 dBA
Road horsepower @ 50 mph	Honda CRX Si, Toyota Corolla, 11 hp
EPA city fuel economy	Ford Festiva LX, 39 mpg
C/D observed fuel economy	Ford Festiva LX, Mitsubishi Mirage, 33 mpg

* includes only U.S.-specification production cars tested by Car and Driver in 1988.
† sum of 30-to-50 mph and 50-to-70 mph acceleration times.
Source: *Car and Driver,* Jan 1988, p. 35.

1988 Crash Results: Best 10 (Detroit News)

Ranked By: Repair costs for small cars after four 5 mph crashes.

Make and Model	Total Damage
1) Ford Escort EXP	$382
2) Ford Escort Pony	$407
3) Chevrolet Spectrum	$412
4) Toyota Corolla	$441
5) Toyota Celica ST	$570
6) Toyota Corolla FX	$713
7) Hyundai Excel GL	$767
8) Toyota Tercel EZ	$877
9) Mazda 323	$878
10) Subaru DL 3-door	$929

Source: *The Detroit News,* Feb 2, 1988, sec. A, p. 3, from Insurance Institute for Highway Safety.

1988 Crash Results: Worst 10 (Detroit News)

Ranked By: Repair costs for small cars after four 5 mph crashes.

Make and Model	Total Damage
1) Honda Civic CRX	$3,140
2) Yugo GV	$2,756
3) Pontiac LeMans	$2,121
4) VW Jetta	$1,966
5) Honda Civic	$1,960
6) Pontiac Fiero	$1,935
7) Subaru GL Hatchback	$1,800
8) Ford Festiva	$1,752
9) VW Fox	$1,705
10) Acura Integra LS	$1,657

Source: *The Detroit News,* Feb 2, 1988, sec. A, p. 3, from Insurance Institute for Highway Safety.

1988 Top-Speed 10

Ranked by: Editorial staff evaluations.
1) Ferrari Testarossa
2) Porsche 928S 4
3) Chevrolet Corvette
4) Nissan 300ZX Turbo
5) BMW M6
6) Chevrolet Camaro IROC-Z
7) Toyota Supra Turbo
8) Mercedes-Benz 560 SEC
9) Ford Mustang GT
10) Pontiac Firebird GTA
Source: *Motor Trend,* Sep 1988, pp. 32-39, 42, 44.

Cars with the Highest Occupant Death Rates

Ranked by: Death rates per 10,000 cars over 1986-88 period.
1) Chevrolet Corvette
2) Chevrolet Camaro
3) Dodge Charger/Shelby
4) Ford Mustang
5) Nissan 300ZX
6) Chevrolet Chevette 4-door
7) Chevrolet Sprint 2-door
8) Honda Civic CRX
9) Pontiac Firebird
10) Plymouth Turismo
11) Pontiac Fiero
Source: *U.S. News and World Report,* Jan 8, 1990, p. 66.

1989 MODEL YEAR

1989 Fuel Economy Winners

		MPG	Annual Fuel
	Make and Model	City/Hwy	Cost*
1)	Geo Metro (1.0L/3, M5)	53/58	$259
2)	Honda Civic CRX HF (1.5L/4, M5)	50/56	$274
3)	Geo Metro LSi (1.0L/3, M5)	46/50	$296
4)	Honda Civic CRX HF (1.5L/4, M5)†	45/52	$296
5)	Ford Festiva (1.3L/4, M5)	39/43	$348
6)	Daihatsu Charade (1.0L/3, M5)	38/42	$365
7)	Ford Festiva (1.3L/4, M4)	38/40	$365
8)	Geo Metro LSi (1.0L/3, A3)	38/40	$365
9)	Isuzu I-Mark (1.5L/4, M5)	37/41	$365
10)	Geo Spectrum (1.5L/4, M5)	37/41	$365

* based on driving 15,000 miles per year.
† manufactured with different fuel/emission system.
Source: *The Car Book,* 1989, p. 62.

1989 Fuel Economy Losers

		MPG	Annual Fuel
	Make and Model	City/Hwy	Cost*
1)	Aston Martin Lagonda (5.3L/8, L3)	8/11	$1583
2)	Aston Martin Sal./Vant./Vol. (5.3L/8, L3)	8/11	$1583
3)	Aston Martin Sal./Vant./Vol. (5.3L/8, M5)	8/11	$1583
4)	Rolls-Royce Bentley Turbo R (6.8L/8, A3)	10/13	$1500
5)	Rolls-Royce Corniche II (6.8L/8, A3)	10/12	$1425
6)	Rolls-Royce Bentley Convertible (6.8L/8, A3)	10/12	$1425
7)	Rolls-Royce Bentley 8/Mulsan (6.8L/8, A3)	10/12	$1295
8)	Rolls-Royce Silver Spirit/Spur (6.8L/8, A3)	10/15	$1295
9)	Ferrari Testarossa (4.9L/12, M5)	10/15	$1295
10)	BMW M6 (3.5L/6, M5)	10/19	$1269

* based on driving 15,000 miles per year.
Source: *The Car Book,* 1989, p. 62.

1989 10 Best Cars
Ranked by: Editorial staff evaluations.
(in alphabetical order)
Acura Legend Coupe
Chevrolet Corvette
Colt Turbo/Mitsubishi Mirage Turbo
Ford Probe GT
Ford Taurus/Taurus SHO
Honda Accord
Honda Civic
Lincoln Continental
Mitsubishi Eclipse Turbo/Plymouth Laser Turbo
Saab 9000 Turbo
Source: *Car and Driver*, Jan 1989, pp. 30-35.

Crash Tests: The Best (1989)
Ranked by: Editorial staff evaluation of U.S. Dept. of Transportation data.
(Best in Class)
　1) Ford Escort (subcompact)
　2) Toyota MR2 (compact)
　3) Volvo DL Wagon (intermediate)
　4) Dodge Caravan (minivan*)
* not all minivans tested
Source: *The Car Book*, 1989, p. 18.

Crash Tests: The Worst (1989)
Ranked by: Editorial staff evaluation of U.S. Dept. of Transportation data.
(Worst in class)
　1) Isuzu I-Mark/Geo Spectrum 4 dr. (subcompact)
　2) Chrysler LeBaron (compact)
　3) Peugeot 505 (intermediate)
　4) Chevy Astro (minivan*)
* not all minivans tested
Source: *The Car Book*, 1989, p. 18.

Least Safe Cars (1989)
Ranked by: Frequency of injuries as reported in medical insurance claims after accidents involving 1987-1989 models, regardless of the size of the claim.
　1) Chevrolet Spectrum
　2) Hyundai Excel
　3) Isuzu I-Mark (tied)
　3) Chevrolet Sprint (tied)
　5) Pontiac LeMans
　6) Subaru XT Coupe
　7) Nissan Sentra (tied)
　7) Ford Festiva (tied)
　9) Dodge Daytona
　10) Subaru Justy
Source: *Business Week*, Nov 26, 1990, p. 130.

Top Ten New Car Buys: Domestic (1989)
Ranked by: Editorial staff evaluations.
Econocar:	Ford Escort LX
GT/Sport Coupe:	Ford Mustang LX 5.0
2-Seat Sports Car:	Chevrolet Corvette
Luxury Sedan:	Cadillac Sedan de Ville
Personal Luxury Car:	Ford Thunderbird SC
Mini-Van:	Dodge Caravan/Plymouth Voyager
Econosport:	Dodge Shadow ES
Sport Sedan:	Ford Taurus SHO
Family Sedan:	Pontiac Bonneville LE
Sport/Utility:	Jeep Cherokee 4-liter
Source: *Motor Trend*, Nov 1989, pp. 80-83.

Top Ten New Car Buys: Import (1989)
Ranked by: Editorial staff evaluations.
Luxury Sedan:	Lexus LS400/Infiniti Q45
Sport Sedan:	Mitsubishi Galant GS
Personal Luxury Car:	Acura Legend Coupe L
Family Sedan:	Honda Accord
Mini-Van:	Mazda MPV
Sport/Utility:	Geo Tracker/Suzuki Sidekick
GT/Sport Coupe:	Mitsubishi Eclipse/ Plymouth Laser Turbos
Econocar:	Honda Civic Hatchback
Econosport:	Honda CRX Si
2-Seat Sports Car:	Mazda MX-5 Miata
Source: *Motor Trend*, Nov 1989, pp. 86-89.

Best Sellers (1989)
Ranked by: Number of sales.
　1) Toyota Camry Deluxe V6
　2) Honda Accord LXi
　3) Mitsubishi Galant GS
　4) Mazda 626 LX
　5) Volkswagen Jetta Carat
　6) Dodge Spirit ES
　7) Oldsmobile Cutlass Calais
　8) Chevrolet Corsica LTZ
　9) Hyundai Sonata GLS
　10) Peugeot 405 S
　11) Subaru Legacy L
　12) Ford Tempo GLS
　13) Nissan Stanza GXE
Source: *Popular Mechanics*, July 1989, pp. 60-63, 120-122.

Best-Selling Luxury Cars (1989)
Ranked by: 1989 unit sales, in thousands.
　1) Cadillac De Ville, 170 thousand unit sales
　2) Lincoln Town Car, 120
　3) Buick Electra, 78
　4) Acura Legend, 71
　5) Lincoln Continental, 56
Source: *Adweek's Marketing Week* (supplement), Superbrands: America's Top 2,000 Brands, 1990, p. 96.

1990 MODEL YEAR

World's Best Sedan (1990)
Ranked by: Editorial staff evaluations.
　1) BMW 750iL
　2) Mercedes-Benz 560 SEL
　3) Lexus LS400
　4) Bentley Turbo R
Source: *Car and Driver*, Nov 1990, pp.113-115, 118, 122-128.

Top Ten Cars (1990)
Ranked by: Number of sales.
　1) Honda Accord
　2) Ford Taurus
　3) Chevrolet Cavalier
　4) Toyota Camry
　5) Chevrolet Corsica/Beretta
　6) Ford Escort
　7) Ford Tempo
　8) Chevrolet Lumina
　9) Toyota Corolla
　10) Honda Civic
Source: *The Detroit News*, Oct 4, 1990, sec A, p. 16.

Top Ten Trucks (1990)
Ranked by: Number of sales.
　1) Ford F-Series
　2) Chevrolet C/K Series
　3) Ford Ranger
　4) Dodge Caravan/Mini Ram Van
　5) Chevrolet S-10
　6) Toyota Pickup
　7) Ford Aerostar
　8) Plymouth Voyager minivan

9) Chevrolet S-10 Blazer
10) Ford Econoline van
Source: *The Detroit News*, Oct 4, 1990, sec A, p. 16.

Top Cars in J.D. Power Survey (1990 cars)

Ranked by: Initial quality.
 1) Toyota Cressida
 2) Mercedes-Benz E-Series
 3) Toyota Camry
 4) Lexus LS400
 5) Mercedes-Benz S-Class
 6) Buick LeSabre
 7) Nissan Maxima
 8) Infiniti Q45
 9) Toyota Corolla
10) Mazda Miata
Source: *The New York Times*, Oct 13, 1990, p. 16, from J.D. Power and Associates.

Cars with the Best Resale Value (1990)

Ranked by: Retained value in 1994, in percent.
 1) Honda Prelude Coupe S, with 52%
 2) BMW 325i (convertible), 49%
 2) Porsche 911 Carrera, 49%
 4) Acura Integra, 47%
 4) Honda Accord DX, 47%
 4) Mercedes-Benz 300E sedan, 47%
 7) Lexus Infiniti Q45, 45%
 7) Lexus ES250, 45%
 9) Nissan Maxima, 43%
 9) Toyota Camry, 43%
Source: *Changing Times*, June 1990, p. 31.

Ten Best Performers, 1990*

Acceleration, 0 to 60 mph	Chevrolet Corvette ZR-1, 4.6 sec
Quarter-mile	Chevrolet Corvette ZR-1, 12.9 sec. @ 111 mph
Top-gear acceleration†	BMW 750iL, 7.4 sec.
Top speed	Chevrolet Corvette ZR-1, 176 mph
Braking, 70 to 0 mph	Acura NSX, 157 ft.
Roadholding	Chevrolet Corvette Z51 FX3, 0.91 g
Interior sound level @ 70 mph	Mercedes-Benz 560 SEL, 66 dBA
Road horsepower @ 50 mph	Ford Escort GT, 11 hp
EPA city fuel economy	Suzuki Swift GT, 29 mpg
C/D observed fuel economy	Honda CRX Si, Suzuki Swift GT, 32 mpg

* includes only U.S.-specification production cars tested by Car and Driver in 1990.
† sum of 30-to-50 mph and 50-to-70 mph acceleration times.
Source: *Car and Driver*, Jan 1991, p. 47.

Ten Worst Performers, 1990 *

Acceleration, 0 to 60 mph	Toyota 4Runner 4WD SR5 V6, 15.7 sec
Quarter-mile	Isuzu Trooper LS, 20.8 sec. @ 66 mph
Top-gear acceleration†	Dodge Colt GT 31.2 sec
Top speed	Jeep Wrangler Sahara, 81 mph
Braking, 70 to 0 mph	Isuzu Trooper LS, 235 ft.
Roadholding	Toyota 4Runner 4WD SR5 V6, 0.63 g
Interior sound level @ 70 mph	Geo Storm GSi, 87 dBA
Road horsepower @ 50 mph	Jeep Wrangler Sahara, 23 hp
EPA city fuel economy	Bentley Turbo R, 10 mpg
C/D observed fuel economy	Porsche 928GT, 13 mpg

* includes only U.S.-specification production cars tested by Car and Driver in 1990.
† sum of 30-to-50 mph and 50-to-70 mph acceleration times.
Source: *Car and Driver*, Jan 1991, p. 47.

1991 MODEL YEAR

Top 10 Sellers, Calendar Year 1991

Ranked by: Number of vehicles sold.
 1) Ford F-series pickup
 2) Chevrolet C/K pickup
 3) Honda Accord
 4) Ford Taurus
 5) Toyota Camry
 6) Chevrolet Cavalier
 7) Ford Explorer
 8) Ford Escort
 9) Ford Ranger
10) Chevrolet Corsica/Beretta
Source: *Automotive News*, Jan 13, 1992, p. 2.

Import Car of the Year (1991)

Ranked by: Editorial staff evaluations.
 1) Mitsubishi 3000 GT VR-4
 2) Acura Legend Sedan LS
 3) Nissan NX 2000
 4) Toyota MR2 Turbo
 5) Infiniti G20
 6) Mercury Capri XR2
 7) Alfa Romeo 164L
 8) Hyundai Scoupe
 9) Nissan Sentra
10) Isuzu Stylus XS
11) Isuzu Impulse RS
Source: *Motor Trend*, Mar 1991, p. 50.

Car of the Year (1991)

Ranked by: Editorial staff evaluations.
 1) Chevrolet Caprice Classic LTZ
 2) Oldsmobile Custom Cruiser
 3) Dodge Caravan ES
 4) Buick Park Avenue Ultra
 5) Ford Escort GT
 6) Oldsmobile Ninety Eight
 7) Mercury Tracer LTS
 8) Plymouth Grand Voyager LE
Source: *Motor Trend*, Feb 1991, p. 52.

Truck of the Year (1991)

Ranked by: Editorial staff evaluations.
 1) Mazda Navaho
 2) GMC Syclone
 3) Dodge Dakota V-8
 4) Oldsmobile Bravada
 5) Isuzu Rodeo LS
 6) Suzuki Sidekick JLX
Source: *Motor Trend*, Jan 1991, p. 86.

EPA Top 20 (1991)

Ranked by: Gas mileage.
 1) Geo Metro XFI
 2) Honda Civic CRX HF
 3) Geo Metro LSI *
 4) Geo Metro *
 5) Suzuki Swift
 6) Honda Civic CRX HF*
 7) Suzuki Swift GA*
 8) Volkswagen Jetta GL Diesel
 9) Daihatsu Charade SE
10) Ford Festiva
11) Geo Metro LSI (automatic)
12) Geo Metro (automatic)
13) Suzuki Swift (automatic)
14) Daihatsu Charade*
15) Honda Civic
16) Subaru Justy (2-barrel)

17) Subaru Justy (EFI)*
18) Toyota Tercel
19) Ford Escort FS
20) Subaru Justy (ECVT)*
* different versions of the same car model, due to certification of each differing engine/transmission and body configuration.
Source: *Popular Mechanics*, Feb 1991, p. 40.

EPA Bottom 10 (1991)
Ranked by: Gas mileage.
  1) Lamborghini Diablo
  2) Rolls-Royce Silver Spirit
  3) Rolls-Royce Corniche III
  4) Bentley Turbo
  5) Bentley Eight/Mulsanne
  6) Bentley Continental
  7) Ferrari Testarossa
  8) BMW M5
  9) Ferrari F40
  10) BMW 750iL/850i
Source: *Popular Mechanics*, Feb 1991, p. 40.

Ten Best Performers, 1991*
Acceleration, 0 to 60 mph	Ferrari F40, 4.2 sec
Quarter-mile	Ferrari F40, 12.1 sec @ 122 mph
Top-gear acceleration†	GMC Syclone, 7.6 sec
Top speed	Ferrari F40, 197 mph
Braking, 70 to 0 mph	Chevrolet Corvette ZR-1, 155 ft
Roadholding	Ferrari F40, 1.01 g
Interior sound level @ 70 mph	Mercedes-Benz 400SE, 66 dBA
Road horsepower @ 50 mph	Ford Escort LX, 10 hp
	Geo Metro LSi Convertible, 10 hp
EPA city fuel economy	Geo Metro LSi Convertible, 41 mpg
C/D observed fuel economy	Geo Metro LSi Convertible, 34 mpg

* includes only U.S. specification production cars tested by Car and Driver in 1991.
† sum of 30-to-50 mph and 50-to-70 mph acceleration times.
Source: *Car and Driver*, Jan 1992, p. 42.

1992 MODEL YEAR

All-Stars for 1992
Ranked by: Editorial staff evaluations.
(in alphabetical order)
Acura NSX
BMW 325i
Chevrolet Corvette LT1
Lexus ES300
Lexus SC400
Mazda MX-5 Miata
Nissan NX2000
Nissan 300ZX Turbo
Porsche 968
Subaru SVX
Source: *Automobile Magazine*, Jan 1992, pp. 46-59.

Top Ten New Car Buys: Domestic (1992)
Ranked by: Editorial staff evaluations.
Econocar:	Ford Escort LX
Econosport:	Dodge Shadow ES Turbo
Sport Sedan:	Dodge Spirit R/T
Luxury Sedan:	Cadillac Seville
Personal Luxury Car:	Mercury Cougar XR7
Family Sedan:	Buick LeSabre Custom (tie)
	Oldsmobile Eighty-Eight Royale (tie)
	Pontiac Bonneville SE (tie)

Two-Seat Sports Car:	Chevrolet Corvette
GT/Sport Coupe:	Ford Mustang LX 5.0
Minivan:	Dodge Caravan/Plymouth Voyager
Sport/Utility:	Ford Explorer
Source: *Motor Trend*, Nov 1991, pp. 40-43.

Top Ten New Car Buys: Import (1992)
Ranked by: Editorial staff evaluations.
Econocar:	Mazda 323
Econosport:	Toyota Paseo
Sport Sedan:	Mitsubishi Galant VR-4
Luxury Sedan:	Mitsubishi Diamante LS
Personal Luxury Car:	Lexus SC400
Family Sedan:	Toyota Camry
Two-Seat Sports Car:	Toyota MR2 Turbo
GT/Sport Coupe:	Eagle Talon/Plymouth Laser/ Mitsubishi Eclipse Turbos
Minivan:	Mazda MPV V-6
Sport/Utility:	Isuzu Rodeo
Source: *Motor Trend*, Nov 1991, pp. 46-51.

Ten Best Cars (1992)
Ranked by: Editorial staff evaluations.
(in alphabetical order)
BMW 325i
Cadillac Seville Touring Sedan
Diamond Star AWD Turbos (Plymouth Laser/Eagle Talon/Mitsubishi Eclipse)
Ford Taurus SHO
Honda Prelude Si
Lexus SC400
Mazda MX-5 Miata
Nissan Sentra SE-R
Nissan 300ZX Turbo
Toyota Camry V-6
Source: *Car and Driver*, Jan 1992, p. 35-42.

Cheapest Vehicles for 1992
Ranked by: Cost per vehicle as of October, 1991.
  1) Suzuki Samurai, $6,299
  2) Hyundai Excel, $6,595
  3) Daihatsu Charade, $6,633
  4) Subaru Justy, $6,645
  5) Suzuki Swift, $6,899
  6) Ford Festiva, $6,941
  7) Toyota Tercel, $6,998
  8) Mazda 323, $6,999
  9) Geo Metro, $7,284
  10) Dodge/Plymouth Colt, $7,302
Source: *Automobile Magazine*, Jan 1992, p.76.

Most Miles Per Tankful, 1992 Car Models
Ranked by: Number of miles.
  1) Honda Civic VX hatchback, 654.5 miles
  2) Cadillac Brougham, 625.0
  3) Geo Metro XFi, 614.8
  4) Chevrolet Caprice, 598.0
  5) Volkswagen Jetta, 580.0
  6) Buick Roadmaster, 575.0
  7) Mercedes-Benz 300D Turbo, 573.5
  8) Volvo 960, 566.8
  9) Volkswagen Passat, 555.0
  10) Volkswagen Passat wagon, 555.0
  11) Buick Roadmaster wagon, 550.0
  12) Chevrolet Caprice wagon, 550.0
  13) Oldsmobile Custom Cruiser wagon, 550.0
  14) Audi 100, 548.6
  15) Chevrolet Cavalier, 547.2
Source: *Automotive News* (Automotive News Insight supplement), Jan 27, 1992, p. 4i.

GENERAL AUTO RANKINGS

Top 10 Importers for 1987
Ranked by: Car registrations. Remarks: Figures for 1984-1986 also given
1) Toyota, with 612,621
2) Honda, 608,819
3) Nissan, 511,365
4) Hyundai, 259,325
5) Mazda, 213,091
6) Volkswagen, 177,728
7) Subaru, 172,152
8) Acura, 103,422
9) Volvo, 99,883
10) Mercedes-Benz, 92,378
Source: *Ward's Automotive Yearbook 1988*, Ward's Communications Inc., p. 170.

Largest Auto Companies in the U.S. (1988)
Ranked by: 1988 passenger car market share, in percent.
1) General Motors, 36.1%
2) Ford, 21.6%
3) Chrysler, 11.3%
4) Honda, 7.3%
5) Toyota, 6.5%
6) Nissan, 4.5%
7) Others, total 12.7%
Source: *Wall Street Journal*, Jan 6, 1989, p. B1.

Most Popular Imported Cars (1988)
Ranked by: 1988 new car registrations.
1) Honda, with 662,138
2) Toyota, 644,763
3) Nissan, 471,981
4) Hyundai, 263,248
5) Mazda, 253,272
6) Volkswagen, 166,344
7) Subaru, 159,894
8) Acura, 129,589
9) Volvo, 98,672
10) Mercedes-Benz, 84,557
Source: *Automotive News*, Apr 3, 1989, p. 22.

Leading Motor Vehicle Producers Worldwide (1988)
Ranked by: 1988 vehicle production.
1) General Motors, with 8,108,000
2) Ford, 6,517,186
3) Toyota, 3,854,186
4) Volkswagen, 2,848,000
5) Nissan, 2,713,234
6) Chrysler, 2,566,920
7) Fiat, 2,141,500
8) Peugeot-Citroen, 2,080,000
9) Renault, 1,850,667
10) Honda, 1,783,416
Source: *Automotive News*, May 1, 1989, p. 3.

Leading Sellers of Automobiles in the U.S. (1989)
Ranked by: Market share of total U.S. car sales from January 1 to March 20, 1989. Remarks: includes imported and domestic automobiles.
1) General Motors, 38.8%
2) Ford, 23.5%
3) Japanese companies, 23.1%
4) Chrysler, 10.5%
5) Other import companies, 7.1%
Source: *Wall Street Journal*, Mar 30, 1989, p. B1.

Leading Asian Auto Imports to the U.S. (1989)
Ranked by: 1989 total unit sales, in thousands
1) Toyota, 495 thousand units
2) Nissan, 405
3) Honda, 252
4) Mazda, 222
5) Hyundai, 183
Source: *Adweek's Marketing Week*, Superbrands: America's Top 2,000 Brands, 1990, p. 87.

Leading European Auto Imports to the U.S. (1989)
Ranked by: 1989 total unit sales, in thousands.
1) Volkswagen, 134 thousand units
2) Volvo, 103
3) Mercedes-Benz, 76
4) BMW, 65
5) Saab, 32
Source: *Adweek's Marketing Week*, Superbrands: America's Top 2,000 Brands, 1990, p. 87.

Top Ten States for New Car Registrations (1989)
Ranked by: Number of registrations in 1989.
1) California, with 1,136,430
2) Florida, 778,843
3) New York, 647,582
4) Illinois, 568,394
5) Texas, 566,688
6) Ohio, 473,801
7) Pennsylvania, 473,707
8) Michigan, 460,463
9) New Jersey, 416,503
10) Massachusetts, 282,233
Source: *Ward's Automotive Yearbook 1990*, p.228

Automobile Sales—1989 (Domestic)
Ranked by: Market share, in percent, based on domestic 1989 car sales of 9,848,496 units.
1) General Motors, 33.3%
2) Ford, 21.3%
3) Chrysler, 9.3%
4) Honda, 4%
5) Toyota, 2.2%
6) Nissan, 1.1%
7) Mazda, 0.4%
8) Mitsubishi, 0.3%
9) Volkswagen, 0.1%
Total Domestic, 71.9%
Source: *Investext*, Thomson Financial Networks, Apr 4, 1990, from Bear Stearns & Company.

Automobile Sales—1989 (Imports)
Ranked by: Market share, in percent, based on domestic 1989 car sales of 9,848,496 units.
1) Toyota, 5.1%
2) Nissan, 4.3%
3) Honda, 4%
4) Hyundai, 1.9%
5) Mazda, 1.9%
6) General Motors, 1.6%
7) Subaru, 1.4%
8) Volkswagen, 1.3%
9) Chrysler, 1%
10) Volvo, 1%
11) Mitsubishi, 0.9%
12) Ford, 0.8%
13) Mercedes, 0.8%
14) BMW, 0.7%
15) Saab, 0.3%
16) Audi, 0.2%
17) Daihatsu, 0.2%
18) Isuzu, 0.2%
19) Jaguar, 0.2%
20) Peugeot, 0.1%
21) Porsche, 0.1%
22) Sterling, 0.1%

23) Suzuki, 0.1%
24) Yugo, 0.1%
25) Alfa Romeo, 0.03%
26) Other, 0.01%
Total Imports, 28.1%
Source: *Investext*, Thomson Financial Networks, Apr 4, 1990, from Bear Stearns & Company.

Top Cars in J.D. Power Survey (1989 cars)
Ranked by: Customer satisfaction.
1) Acura
2) Mercedes-Benz
3) Toyota
4) Cadillac
5) Honda
6) Nissan
7) Subaru
7) Buick
9) Porsche
10) BMW
10) Mazda
10) Audi
Source: *The New York Times*, Oct 13, 1990, p. 16, from J.D. Power and Associates.

Favorite Car Colors (1989)
Ranked by: Percent of all vehicles.
1) Blue (22%)
2) Red (17%)
3) White (14%)
4) Gray (13%)
5) Black (11%)
6) other (21%)
Source: *Adweek's Marketing Week*, Dec 11, 1989, p. 10.

Most Popular Cars Among People Aged 50 and Over (1989)
Ranked by: Percent of owners aged 50+ buying the brand.
1) Chevrolet, with 19%
2) Ford, 16%
3) Buick, 12%
4) Oldsmobile, 10%
5) Pontiac, 7%
6) Mercury, 6%
7) Cadillac, 4%
7) Chrysler Corp., 4%
9) Toyota, 3%
10) others, total 19%
Source: *Advertising Age*, July 24, 1989, p. S-21.

Minivan Sales in the U.S. (1990)
Ranked by: Market share, in percent, of the 731,000 vehicles sold in the U.S. in 1989.
1) Chrysler, 54.0%
2) Ford, 23.0%
3) General Motors, 17.0%
4) Mazda, Mitsubishi, Toyota, 6.0%
Source: *The New York Times*, Jan 14, 1990, p. 10, from Ward's Automotive Reports.

Top Sellers of Cars in the U.S. (1990)
Ranked by: Number of vehicles sold.
1) General Motors, with 3,263,376
2) Ford, 1,945,241
3) Chrysler, 855,548
4) Honda, 849,549*
5) Nissan, 476,063*
6) Mitsubishi, 164,267
7) Toyota, 765,300
8) Mazda, 229,100
* includes Acura, Infiniti, and Lexus divisions
Source: *The Detroit Free Press*, Oct 4, 1990, Sec A, p. 16.

Top Sellers of Trucks in the U.S. (1990)
Ranked by: Number of vehicles sold.
1) General Motors, with 1,632,391
2) Ford, 1,383,170
3) Chrysler, 884,031
4) Nissan, 166,250
5) Mitsubishi, 28,588
6) Toyota, 277,200
7) Mazda, 213,000
Source: *The Detroit Free Press*, Oct 4, 1990, Sec A, p. 16.

Leading Japanese Automakers in the U.S. (1990)
Ranked by: 1990 U.S. market share.
1) Toyota, 7.64%
2) Honda, 6.12%
3) Nissan, 4.49%
4) Mazda, 2.52%
5) Mitsubishi, 1.38%
6) Subaru, 0.80%
7) Isuzu, 0.80%
8) Suzuki, 0.15%
9) Daihatsu, 0.11%
Source: *Business Week*, Jan 21, 1991, p. 37.

Most Popular Car Colors (1991)
Ranked by: DuPont survey of consumer preference for vehicle color.
1) White
2) Red
3) Black
4) Light blue
5) Silver
Source: *Automobile Magazine*, Jan 1992, p. 80.

Best Automotive Franchises (1991)
Ranked by: Dealer satisfaction.
1) Lexus
2) Saturn
3) Infiniti
4) Range Rover
5) Honda (tied)
5) Mercedes-Benz (tied)
7) Toyota
8) Audi
9) Acura (tied)
9) Saab (tied)
11) Mitsubishi
12) Mazda
Source: *Automotive News*, Jan 27, 1992, p. 2, from J.D. Power and Associates.

Most Popular Nameplates in Beverly Hills (1991)
Ranked by: Number of car registrations in the 90210 zip code area. Number listed: 43.
1) Mercedes-Benz
2) Lexus
3) BMW
4) Cadillac
5) Honda
6) Acura
7) Ford
8) Toyota
9) Infiniti
10) Nissan
11) Jaguar
12) Chevrolet
Source: *Automotive News*, Dec 16, 1991, p. 30, from R.L. Polk & Co.

Index to Information Sources

A

AAA Auto Club of Southern Pennsylvania—AAA Traveler **3832**

AAA-Automobile Club of Maryland **2829**

AAA Cincinnati—AAA Today Ohio **3833**

AAA Today Magazine **3834**

AAA Today Pennsylvania; Lehigh Valley Motor Club— **3909**

AAA Today West Virginia; Bluefield Automobile Club— **3852**

AAA Traveler; AAA Auto Club of Southern Pennsylvania— **3832**

AAA Washington Motor Club—Motorist Washington state **3835**

AAA World; American Automobile Association— **3836**

ABS Traction Control and Brake Components **3498**

Accessories Association—Membership Directory; Automotive Parts and **2884**

Accessory Circuits; Automotive Chassis and **3611, 3700**

Accord; Honda **1535**

Acura Div., American Honda Motor Co. **4340**

Acura Driving Club Magazine **1, 3, 5, 7**

Adirondack Shelby-Mustang Regional Club—Newsletter **1397**

ADP Parts Exchange **2988, 3068**

Advanced Car Care: Belts, Hoses and Radiator **3960, 4199**

Advanced Car Care: Cooling System Service **3961, 4083**

Advanced Car Care: Plugs, Timing and Shocks **3962, 4208**

Advanced Car Care: Tune Up and Shocks **3963, 4209**

Advanced Electronic Ignition Tune-Up **3964, 4110**

Advanced Electronic Tune-Up **3606, 3965**

Advanced Gas Turbine Systems for Automobiles **3784**

Advanced Truck Suspensions **4267, 4289**

Aerodynamics: Wakes, Wind Effect, Vehicle Development; Automobile **3243**

Aerostar, 1985-1990; Chilton's Ford **1289**

Aerostar Mini-Vans Owners Workshop Manual, No. 1476: 1986-1990; Haynes Ford **1294**

Afro-American Automobile Association **2830**

Aftermarket for Imported Cars and Light Trucks **3239, 4125, 4290**

Aftermarket Journal—Directory and Buyers Guide Issue; Eastern **3051**

Aftermarket Journal—Foreign Parts Directory and Buyer's Guide Issue; Eastern **3052**

Aftermarket Suppliers; Directory of Automotive **3003**

Air-Braked Vehicles; Antilock Systems for **3501**

Air Conditioner; The Automotive **4087**

Air Conditioning and Heating Manual, 1989-91: Professional Mechanics Edition; Chilton's Guide to **4101**

Air Conditioning and Heating Manual 1990-92: Motor Age Professional Mechanics Edition; Chilton's Guide to **4102**

Air Conditioning Association—Membership/Industry Contact Directory; International Mobile **3055**

Air Conditioning; Auto **4084, 4085**

Air Conditioning; Automotive **4088, 4089, 4090**

Air Conditioning; Basic **4100**

Air Conditioning; Electrical Systems, Heating, and **3593, 4104**

Air Conditioning Equipment Directory; Automobile **2992, 3072**

Air Conditioning Handbook; Automotive **4091**

Air Conditioning Manual; Auto Heat **4086**

Air Conditioning; Principles and Service of Automotive **4106**

Air Conditioning Repair and Service, 1989-1991; Chilton's Guide to **4103**

Air Conditioning Systems; Mitchell Automotive Heating and **4105**

Air Cooled and Water-Cooled Gasoline Engines, Diesel Engine, Syncro, and Camper; Vanagon Official Factory Repair Manual: 1980-1989, Including **2801**

Air Pollution, the Automobile, and Public Health **3398, 3664**

Airbags and Seat Belts **3442, 4200**

Alabama Alfa Romeo Owners Club **24, 49, 74**

Alabama Automotive Directory **2902, 2941, 2989, 3069, 3110**

Alfa Club of Colorado **25, 50, 75**

Alfa Club of Colorado—Newsletter **10, 35, 60**

Alfa Giornale **11, 36, 61**

Alfa—Newsletter; Tennessee **22, 47, 72**

Alfa Owner **12, 37, 62**

Alfa Romeo **9, 34, 59**

Alfa Romeo Club [Mississippi, Louisiana, and southwestern Tennessee]; Deep South **33, 58, 83**

Alfa Romeo Distributors of North America **4341**

Alfa Romeo Owners Club **26, 51, 76**

Alfa Romeo Owners Club; Alabama **24, 49, 74**

Alfa Romeo Owners Club, Atlanta Chapter [Georgia] **27, 52, 77**

Alfa Romeo Owners Club, Chicago Chapter—Membership Directory [Illinois] **13, 38, 63**

Alfa Romeo Owners Club—Membership Roster **14, 39, 64**

Alfa Romeo Owners Club, Northeastern Ohio Chapter **28, 53, 78**

Alfa Romeo Owners Club, Northern California Chapter **29, 54, 79**

Alfa Romeo Owners Club, Northern California Chapter— Journal **15, 40, 65**

Alfa Romeo Owners Club, Northern California Chapter— Newsletter **16, 41, 66**

Alfa Romeo Owners Club of Central California **2831**

Alfa Romeo Owners Club of Oklahoma **30, 55, 80**

Alfa Romeo Owners Club of Oklahoma—Newsletter **17, 42, 67**

Alfa Romeo Owners Club of Texas—Newsletter **18, 43, 68**

Alfa Romeo Owners Club, Orange County Chapter [California] **31, 56, 81**

Alfa Romeo Owners Club, Orange County Chapter— Newsletter [California] **19, 44, 69**

Alfa Romeo Owners Club, Washington D.C. Chapter **32, 57, 82**

Alfantics **20, 45, 70**

All British Car Meets Program **2880**

All Chevy 713, 719, 729, 741, 761, 771, 782, 790, 796,
   806, 840, 847, 856, 866, 878, 884, 894, 900, 913
All Wheel Drive High Performance Handbook 3772, 4268,
   4283
The Allen Smart Scope Explained 3966
Alliance Automobile Club 2832
Alternate Fuels for S.I. Engines 3693, 3816
The Alternator Explained 3559
Alternators and Generators Repair Directory;
   Automotive 3129
Aluminum Workhorse 2599
AM-XTRA 84, 2604, 2617
AMC Performance Car Club 89, 2612, 2625
AMC Performance Car Club—Newsletter 85, 2605, 2618
America on the Road 3296
The American and Japanese Auto Industries in Transition: The
   Report of the Joint U.S.-Japan Automotive Study 3347
American Automobile Association 2833
American Automobile Association—AAA World 3836
The American Automobile Industry 3348
The American Automobile Industry: Rebirth or Requiem? 3349
American Honda Motor Co. Inc. 4342
American Isuzu Motors Inc. 4343
American Made: Marysville and the Honda Plant 3350
American Motoring Magazine 86, 2606, 2619
American Motors Drivers and Racers Association; National 92
American Motors Magazine; Americana: The 88, 2608, 2621
American Motors Owners Association 90, 2613, 2626
American Motors Owners Association—Membership
   Roster 87, 2607, 2620
American Motorsport International 91, 2614, 2627
American Technology and the British Vehicle Industry 3351,
   4126
Americana: The American Motors Magazine 88, 2608, 2621
America's Light Trucks 4291
Anatomy of a Battery 3560, 3967
Annual Supplement to Automobile Design Liability 3399
Anti Lock Braking Systems for Passenger Cars and Light
   Trucks: A Review 3499, 4292
Anti-Lock Up Brake Systems Explained, Vols. 1-5 3500
Antilock Systems for Air-Braked Vehicles 3501
Appalachian Chapter [South central Pennsylvania]; Buick Club
   of America, 239, 275, 310, 343, 377, 417, 454, 488, 524,
   559, 592
Aries and Plymouth Reliant Owners Workshop Manual, 1981-
   1988; Haynes Dodge 1031, 2046
Arizona Chapter; Pontiac-Oakland Club, International, 2095,
   2136, 2174, 2216, 2262, 2299, 2336, 2371, 2406, 2445,
   2481
Arizona/New Mexico Automotive Directory 2903, 2942,
   2990, 3070, 3111
Arkansas Automobile Club 2834
Arkansas Automotive Directory 2904, 2943, 2991, 3071,
   3112
Arrowhead Chapter—Directory [Kansas and Missouri];
   Pontiac-Oakland Club International, Kansas City 2086,
   2127, 2165, 2206, 2250, 2290, 2327, 2362, 2397, 2436,
   2472
Arrowhead Chapter [Kansas and Missouri]; Pontiac-Oakland
   Club International, Kansas City 2099, 2140, 2178, 2220,
   2266, 2303, 2340, 2375, 2410, 2449, 2485
Asian Cars and Trucks); Chilton's Guide to Chassis Electronics
   1989-91 (3723
Ask Any Dummy: Seat Belts Make Sense 3443
Association of International Automobile Manufacturers 2835
Aston Martin and Lagonda 93
Aston Martin Lagonda of North America Inc. 4344
Aston Martin Owners Club—Membership List 94, 99, 100,
   101, 102, 103
Astro and GMC Safari; Chevrolet 709, 1518
Astro-GMC Safari, 1985-1990; Chevrolet 710, 1519
Atlanta Chapter [Georgia]; Alfa Romeo Owners Club, 27, 52,
   77
Auction Association—Membership Directory; National
   Auto 2879

Auction Results, 1989: Worldwide Model Years 1905-1988;
   Old Cars 3218
Audi 80, 90 Official Factory Repair Manual: 1988-91 104,
   108
Audi 100, 200 Official Factory Repair Manual: 1990, Including
   Quattro 112, 116
Audi 4000 Owners Workshop Manual, No. 165: 1980-1987;
   Haynes 121
Audi 4000S, 4000CS and Coupe GT Official Factory Repair
   Manual: 1984-1987, Including Quattro and Quattro
   Turbo 120, 131
Audi 5000 125
Audi 5000, 1984-1988; Haynes 127
Audi 5000S, 5000CS Official Factory Repair Manual: 1984-
   1988 Gasoline, Turbo and Turbo Diesel, Including Wagon
   and Quattro 126
Audi International Motor Car Club 107, 111, 115, 119, 124,
   130, 134, 135, 138
Audi of America Inc. 4345
Audi Quattro: The Development and Competition
   History 105, 109, 113, 117, 122, 128, 132, 136
Audio Specialists Association—Government Action Bulletins;
   Car 3405, 4215
Audio Specialists Association—Special Bulletins; Car 4216
Audio Systems: Speakers, Receivers, Non-Audio
   Electronics 4212
Audio Systems: Worldwide Developments; Automobile 4214
Auto Air Conditioning 4084, 4085
Auto and Truck News 3837, 4293
An Auto Biography 3297
Auto Body Repair 3461, 3462, 3463
Auto Body Repair II 3464
Auto Body Repair—Procedure for Applying Plastic Filler 3465
Auto Body Repairing and Repainting 3430, 3466
Auto Body Rust Repair 3467
Auto Body Series 3468
Auto Body Tools Explained 3469
Auto Cap of Southern California 2836
Auto Club of Southern Pennsylvania—Motorist 3838
Auto Dimensions 3561, 3694
Auto Electrical Handbook: How To Wire Your Car From
   Scratch 3562
Auto Electricity, Electronics, Computers 3563, 3607
Auto Fuel Systems 3785
Auto Heat Air Conditioning Manual 4086
Auto Inc. 3352, 3400
The Auto Index 3839
Auto Industries of Europe, U.S., Japan to 1990 3353
The Auto Industry Ahead: Who's Driving? 3354
Auto-Know 3968
Auto Maintenance for Everyone 3969
Auto Mechanics 3502, 3970
Auto Mechanics for Everyone 3971
Auto Museums Directory: U.S.A., Supplement with Canadian
   Museums 3298
Auto Owner's Supply Book 3240
The Auto Parts Report 4188
Auto Repair 3972
Auto Repair for Dummies: The Maintenance Tape 3973
Auto Repair Manual 3974
Auto Repair: The Costly Ride 3975
Auto Repairs for Dummies 3976
Auto Restoration From Junker to Jewel 3431
Auto Safety Series 3444
Auto Service and Repair 3977
Auto Smog Brake/Lamp Inspect Repair Directory 3113
Auto Tiempo 3840
Auto Trader 3182
Auto Trim News—Directory of Product Sources Issue 3114
Auto-Truck Interchange Manual: Body Parts 4189, 4294
Auto-Truck Interchange Manual: Wheel Covers 4295, 4335
Auto-Truck Interchange Manual: Wheels 4296, 4336
Auto Undercoating & Rustproofing Directory 3115
Auto Video 3978
Autobody Refinishing Handbook 3470
Autobody Repair 3471

Autobody Repair and Refinishing **3472**
Autocar on Bentley Since 1919 **143, 148, 153, 158**
Autoguide **3183**
Autolite Car Care; Fram/ **4043**
Automakers and the Giant 30-Year and Battle for Global
  Supremacy; Car Wars: The Untold Story of the
  Great **3313, 3361**
Automatic, Manual Transmissions, Transaxles, and Drive
  Trains **3555, 3695**
Automatic Transmission **3696**
The Automatic Transmission **3697**
Automatic Transmission; Design Practices Passenger
  Car **3253, 3731**
Automatic Transmission Rebuilders Association—Membership
  Roster **2881**
Automatic Transmission Repair; Chilton's Guide to **3720**
Automatic Transmission Repair Manual, 1984-88: Motor-Age
  Professional Mechanics Edition; Chilton's **3714**
Automatic Transmission Repair Manual, 1984-1988: Import
  Cars and Trucks: Motor-Age Professional Mechanic's Edition;
  Chilton's **3715, 4129, 4298**
Automatic Transmission Repair Manual, 1984-1989 Domestic
  Cars and Trucks; Chilton's Guide to **3721**
Automatic Transmission Service Manual 1984-88: Domestic
  Cars and Trucks: Motor-Age Professional Mechanic's Edition;
  Chilton's **3716, 4299**
Automatic Transmissions **3698**
Automechanics **3979**
Automechanic's Guide to Electronic Instrumentation and
  Microprocessor **3608**
Automobile Aerodynamics: Wakes, Wind Effect, Vehicle
  Development **3243**
The Automobile Age **3299**
Automobile Age; The **3299**
Automobile Air Conditioning Equipment Directory **2992,
  3072**
Automobile & Culture **3300**
Automobile Audio Systems **4213**
Automobile Audio Systems: Worldwide Developments **4214**
Automobile Body Shops Directory **2905**
Automobile Brake Service Directory **3116**
Automobile Brakes and Braking Systems **3503**
Automobile Catalytic Converters **3665**
Automobile Club of Utah **2837**
Automobile Components Aftermarket **2993**
Automobile Customizing Directory **2906**
Automobile Dealers Directory New Cars **2944**
Automobile Dealers Directory Used Cars **2945**
Automobile Design: Great Designers and Their Work **3244,
  3301**
Automobile Design Liability **3245**
Automobile Detail & Clean-Up Service Directory **3117**
Automobile Diagnostic Service Directory **3118**
Automobile Electric Service Directory **3119**
Automobile Electrical and Electronic Equipment **3564, 3609**
Automobile Electrical Manual: A Comprehensive Guide **3565**
Automobile Electronics and Basic Electrical Systems **3566,
  3610**
Automobile Frontal Impacts **3246**
Automobile Fuel Economy **3817**
Automobile Industry, 1885-1920 **3302**
The Automobile Industry, 1920-1980 **3303**
The Automobile Industry since 1945 **3304**
Automobile Inspection Stations Directory **3120**
Automobile International **3980**
Automobile International—Buyers' Guide Issue **3045**
The Automobile—Its First 100 Years **3305**
Automobile Lubrication Service Directory **3121**
Automobile Magazine **3841**
Automobile Muffler Repair Shops Directory **3122**
Automobile Parts Retailers Directory **2994**
Automobile Parts—Used/Salvage Directory **3073**
Automobile Quarterly **3842**
Automobile Radiator Repair Shops Directory **3123**
Automobile Radio/Stereo Systems Directory **2995**
Automobile Red Book **3184**

Automobile Repair Shops Directory **3124**
Automobile Safety **3445**
Automobile Seat Covers/Tops/Upholstery Directory **2996**
Automobile Service Stations Directory **3125**
Automobile Smog Control Devices **2997, 3046**
Automobile Technology of the Future **3286, 3355**
Automobile Transmission Repair Shops Directory **3126**
Automobile Transporters and Drive-Away Directory **3127**
Automobile Upholstery Cleaning Directory **3128**
Automobiler **3843**
Automobiles **3401**
Automobiles & Elites in Detroit, 1899-1933; Conspicuous
  Production: **3318**
Automobiles Brakes and Braking Systems **3504**
The Automotive Air Conditioner **4087**
Automotive Air Conditioning **4088, 4089, 4090**
Automotive Air Conditioning Handbook **4091**
Automotive Alternators and Generators Repair
  Directory **3129**
Automotive Body Repair and Refinishing **3473**
Automotive Booster Clubs International—Roster of Clubs and
  their Officers **2882**
Automotive Brake Systems **3505**
Automotive Brakes and Power Transmission Systems **3506,
  3699**
Automotive Brakes, Suspension and Steering **3507, 4258,
  4269**
Automotive Brakes: Text-Lab Manual **3508**
Automotive Brakes: Theory and Service **3509**
Automotive Braking System **3510**
Automotive Braking Systems **3511**
Automotive Chassis and Accessory Circuits **3611, 3700**
The Automotive Computer **3612**
Automotive Computer Control Systems **3613**
Automotive Computers and Digital Instrumentation **3614**
Automotive Consultants Directory **2939**
Automotive Consumer Action Program **2838**
Automotive Contact **3844**
Automotive Cooling Journal **4092**
The Automotive Cooling System **4093**
Automotive Cooling Systems Institute **2839**
Automotive Cooling Systems: Operation and Service **4094**
Automotive Corrosion and Prevention Conference
  Proceedings **3474**
Automotive Cylinder Boring **3701**
Automotive Diagnosis and Tune-up **3981**
Automotive Diesel Engines **3539**
Automotive Dismantlers and Recyclers Association—Buyers
  Guide and Membership Roster **3074**
Automotive Dismantlers and Recyclers Association—Roster of
  Members **3075**
Automotive Displays and Industrial Illumination **3615**
Automotive Electrical and Electronic Systems **3567, 3568,
  3569, 3616, 3617, 3618**
Automotive Electrical and Electronic Systems Lab
  Manual **3570, 3619**
Automotive Electrical Systems **3571**
Automotive Electricity **3572**
Automotive Electronic and Computer Controlled Ignition
  Systems **3573, 3620, 4111**
Automotive Electronic-Electrical Systems: A Beginner's
  Troubleshooting and Repair Manual **3574, 3621**
Automotive Electronic Engine Management and Driveline
  Controls **3556, 3622**
Automotive Electronics and Electrical Equipment **3575, 3623**
Automotive Electronics and Engine Performance **3624, 3702**
Automotive Electronics Explained, Vols. 1-5 **3625**
Automotive Electronics Reliability **3626**
Automotive Encyclopedia **3845**
Automotive Engine Electronics **3627, 3703, 3786**
Automotive Engine Rebuilders Association—Membership
  Roster **3130**
Automotive Engine Rebuilders Association—Technical
  Bulletin **3704**
Automotive Engine Repair and Overhaul **3705**
Automotive Engine Repair and Rebuilding **3706**

Automotive Engineering **3287**
Automotive Engineering and Litigation **3288, 3402**
Automotive Engines: Maintenance and Repair **3707, 3982**
Automotive Fine Arts Society—Quarterly **3306**
Automotive Fuel and Ignition Systems **3787, 4112**
Automotive Fuel Consumption in Actual Traffic
  Conditions **3666**
Automotive Fuel, Cooling, Lubrication, and Exhaust
  Systems **3667, 3788, 4095, 4167**
Automotive Fuel, Lubricating and Cooling Systems **3789,
  4096, 4168**
Automotive Fuel, Lubrication, and Cooling Systems **3818,
  4097, 4169**
Automotive Glassfibre: A Practical Guide to Moulding and
  Repairing **3475**
Automotive Hall of Fame **2840**
Automotive Hall of Fame—Membership Roster **3307, 3356**
Automotive Hall of Fame—News **3308, 3357**
Automotive Heating and Cooling **4098**
Automotive History Collection of the Detroit Public Library: A
  Simplified Guide to Its Holdings **3309**
Automotive History Review **3310**
Automotive Ignition Systems: Diagnosis and Repair **3533,
  4113**
Automotive Industries **3358**
Automotive Information Council **2841**
Automotive Information Council—Newsletter **3359, 3403**
Automotive Instrument Panels: Design, Materials, and
  Manufacturing **3247, 4159**
Automotive Litigation Reporter **3404**
Automotive Manual Transmission and Power Trains **3557,
  3708**
Automotive Marketing—Retail Aftermarket Guide Issue **2998**
The Automotive Messenger **3846**
Automotive Microprocessors Explained **3628**
Automotive News **3847**
Automotive News—Market Data Book Issue **2883, 2946,
  2987**
Automotive Operation and Maintenance **3983**
Automotive Oscilloscope **3576**
Automotive Parts and Accessories Association—Membership
  Directory **2884**
Automotive Parts and Accessories Association—Tech Service
  Report **3984**
Automotive Pollution Control **3668**
Automotive Principles: Repair and Service **3985**
Automotive Products Report **3241**
Automotive Quick Test **3512, 3577, 3629, 3669, 3790,
  3986, 4099**
Automotive Rebuilder—Purchasing Directory Issue **3047**
Automotive Reference: A New Approach to the World of
  Auto & Related Information **3848**
Automotive Road Service Directory **3067, 3131**
Automotive Safety Foundation **2842**
Automotive Seals: An Update **3849**
Automotive Security System—Design Handbook **4204**
Automotive Steering and Suspension Systems **4259, 4270**
Automotive Steering, Suspension, and Braking Systems:
  Principles and Service **3513, 4260, 4271**
Automotive Suspension, Steering and Brakes **3514, 3515,
  4261, 4262, 4272, 4273**
Automotive Tech Series **3987**
Automotive Terms; Glossary of **3884**
Automotive Transmission **3709**
Automotive Tune-Up **3988**
Automotive Tune-Up Guide **3989**
Automotive Tune-up Procedures **3990**
Automotive Warehouse Distributors Association—Membership
  Directory **3048**
Automotive Workbook **3289, 3991**
Automundo Magazine **3360, 3850**
Autopower **3578**
Autos of Yesteryear **3311**
Autoweek **3851**
Avanti **139**
Avanti Automotive Corp. **4346**

Avanti Owners Association International **142**
Avanti Owners Association International—Membership
  Roster **140**
Avanti Owners Association Newsletter **141**
Axle Repair Association—Membership Directory; Truck-Frame
  and **3175**

B

Badger Chatter **2072, 2112, 2150, 2188, 2234, 2275, 2312,
  2348, 2383, 2421, 2457**
Basic Air Conditioning **4100**
Basic Automobile Maintenance **3992**
Basic Automotive Jobs Explained **3579, 3993, 4170, 4210,
  4332**
Basic Car Care **3994, 3995**
Basic Car Care Illustrated **3996**
Basic Electricity for Auto Mechanics **3580**
Basic Electronic Test Equipment **3581**
Basics **3997**
Battery; Anatomy of a **3560, 3967**
The Battery and its Electrical System **3582**
Battery and its Electrical System; The **3582**
Battery-Replacement Data Book **3583**
Battery Service Manual **3584**
Battery Technical Manual **3585**
Bearings; Selecting and Maintaining **4067, 4198**
Bentley Buyer's Guide; Illustrated Rolls-Royce and **145, 150,
  155, 160, 2631, 2636, 2641**
Bentley Drivers Club—Members and Their Bentleys **144, 149,
  154, 159**
Bentley Marketletter; Rolls-Royce/ **146, 151, 156, 161, 2632,
  2637, 2642**
Bentley Motors Inc., Rolls-Royce Motor Cars Inc. **4347**
Bentley Since 1919; Autocar on **143, 148, 153, 158**
Bentleys; Bentley Drivers Club—Members and Their **144, 149,
  154, 159**
Benz; Karl **3291, 3330**
Beretta 1988; Chilton's Chevrolet Corsica and **717, 794**
Best of BAX: Collected Columns from Car and Driver **3248**
Big Bird **1499**
Big-Block Chevy; How to Rebuild Your **3749, 4046**
Bison **2073, 2113, 2151, 2189, 2235, 2276, 2313, 2349,
  2384, 2422, 2458**
Blazers, and Jimmy, 1982-1988 (Gas and Diesel); Chevy and
  GMC Two-Wheel Drive Mid-Size S- and T-Pickups, **726,
  872, 1510, 1523**
Block Identification Guide; Cylinder Head and **3728, 4193**
Blue Book: A Guide to Buying And Selling New and Used
  Cars, Trucks, and R.V.s; The Underground **3227**
Blue Book; Orion Car Stereo **3235, 4225**
Blue Book Used Car Price Manual; Kelley **3210**
Bluefield Automobile Club—AAA Today West Virginia **3852**
Bluefield Automobile Club West Virginia **2843**
Bluegrass Buick News **221, 257, 293, 325, 358, 396, 434,
  470, 506, 539, 574**
Bluegrass Chapter [Kentucky]; Buick Club of America, **240,
  276, 311, 344, 378, 418, 455, 489, 525, 560, 593**
BMW 6 Cylinder **165, 175, 185, 195, 205**
BMW Automobile Club of America **173, 183, 193, 203, 213**
BMW Automobile Club of America—Journal **166, 176, 186,
  196, 206**
BMW Car Club of America **174, 184, 194, 204, 214**
BMW; Friends of **169, 179, 189, 199, 209**
BMW; Great Marques **170, 180, 190, 200, 210**
BMW Magazine **167, 177, 187, 197, 207**
BMW of North America Inc. **4348**
Body and Fender Repair; Tune Up America: **3496**
Body Exteriors; New Polymer Technology for Auto **3270**
Body Framing; How to Restore Wooden **3485**
Body Parts; Auto-Truck Interchange Manual: **4189, 4294**
Body Repair and Painting; Chilton's Guide to Auto **3433,
  3476**
Body Repair and Painting Manual, No. 1479; Haynes **3482**

Body Repair and Refinishing; Automotive **3473**
Body Repair; Auto **3461, 3462**
Body Repair II; Auto **3464**
Body Repair Manual; Chilton's Minor Auto **3477**
Body Repair—Procedure for Applying Plastic Filler;
   Auto **3465**
Body Repair; Total Auto **3495, 4334**
Body Repairing and Repainting; Auto **3430, 3466**
Body Repairing and Repainting; The Principles of Auto **3487**
Body Sheet Metal Repair; Guide to Auto **3480**
Body Shop Talk: Dent Repair; SMART **3492**
Body Shop Talk: Paint Tips; SMART **3493**
Body Shop Talk: Rust Repair; SMART **3494**
Body Shops Directory; Automobile **2905**
Body Solder; Procedure for Applying **3488**
Bosch Electronic Fuel Injection Systems **3791**
Bosch Fuel Injection and Engine Management **3710, 3792**
Brake and Front End **3516**
Brake and Front End—Buyers Guide to Brake Parts
   Issue **3049**
Brake Block Identification Catalog **3517**
Brake Components; ABS Traction Control and **3498**
Brake/Lamp Inspect Repair Directory; Auto Smog **3113**
Brake Service Directory; Automobile **3116**
Brake System Explained; The Hydraulic **3522**
Brake Systems; Automotive **3505**
Brake Systems Explained, Vols. 1-5; Anti-Lock Up **3500**
Brakes **3518, 3519**
Brakes and Braking Systems; Automobile **3503**
Brakes and Braking Systems; Automobiles **3504**
Brakes and Power Transmission Systems; Automotive **3506,
3699**
Brakes; Automotive Suspension, Steering and **3514, 3515,
4261, 4262, 4272, 4273**
Brakes, Steering and Suspension 1980-1987: Domestic and
   Import Cars and Trucks; Chilton's Guide to **3521, 4131,
4264, 4275, 4302**
Brakes, Steering, Front Suspension, Wheels and Tires **3520,
4263, 4274, 4284, 4337**
Brakes, Suspension and Steering; Automotive **3507, 4258,
4269**
Brakes: Text-Lab Manual; Automotive **3508**
Brakes: Theory and Service; Automotive **3509**
Braking and Steering; Vehicle Dynamics Related to **3526,
4266**
Braking System; Automotive **3510**
Braking Systems; Automobile Brakes and **3503**
Braking Systems; Automobiles Brakes and **3504**
Braking Systems; Automotive **3511**
Braking Systems for Passenger Cars and Light Trucks: A
   Review; Anti Lock **3499, 4292**
Braking Systems; Mitchell Automotive **3524**
Braking Systems: Principles and Service; Automotive Steering,
   Suspension, and **3513, 4260, 4271**
Bravada, 1982-1990; Chevrolet S-10 Blazer, GMC S-15, and
   Olds **730, 1514, 1928**
Break It in Right! How to Make Your New Car Last **3853**
Breakdown **3998**
British Car **4127, 4238**
British Car Industry; The Motor Men: Pioneers of the **3378**
British Car Meets Program; All **2880**
British Car Union, Chicago Chapter Illinois **2844**
British Motorcars of New England **2845**
British Vehicle Industry; American Technology and the **3351,
4126**
Bronco 1987-1990; Ford Pickups and **1307, 1446**
Bronco and F-Series Pickups, 1969-1987; Ford Four-Wheel
   Drive **1305, 1319**
Bronco II 1983-1988: Includes Diesel and Four-Wheel Drive
   Shop Manual; Ford Ranger and **1321, 1447**
Bronco II 1983-1988: Repair and Tune-Up Guide; Ranger-
1324, 1451
Bronco II Owners Workshop Manual, No. 1026: 1983-1989;
   Haynes Ford Ranger and **1322, 1449**
Bronco Owners Workshop Manual, No. 880; Haynes Ford
   Pick-Ups and **1308, 1448**

The Buick: A Complete History **222, 258, 294, 326, 359,
397, 435, 471, 507, 540, 575**
Buick Century and Regal, 1975-87; Chilton's **215, 391**
Buick Century, Chevrolet Celebrity, Oldsmobile Cutlass Ciera,
   Pontiac 6000, 1982-87: Shop Manual; GM A-Cars **218,
780, 1938, 1950, 2110**
Buick Century, Olds Cutlass Ciera, Pontiac 6000, 1982-1988;
   Chilton's Chevrolet Celebrity, **216, 778, 1947, 2107**
Buick Club of America **238, 274, 309, 342, 376, 416, 453,
487, 523, 558, 591**
Buick Club of America, Appalachian Chapter [South central
   Pennsylvania] **239, 275, 310, 343, 377, 417, 454, 488,
524, 559, 592**
Buick Club of America, Bluegrass Chapter [Kentucky] **240,
276, 311, 344, 378, 418, 455, 489, 525, 560, 593**
Buick Club of America, Chicagoland Chapter [Illinois] **241,
277, 312, 345, 379, 419, 456, 490, 526, 561, 594**
Buick Club of America, Cream City Chapter [Wisconsin] **242,
278, 313, 346, 380, 420, 457, 491, 527, 562, 595**
Buick Club of America, Glass City Chapter [Ohio] **243, 279,
314, 347, 381, 421, 458, 492, 528, 563, 596**
Buick Club of America, Jersey Shore Chapter [New
   Jersey] **244, 280, 315, 348, 382, 422, 459, 493, 529,
564, 597**
Buick Club of America, Kansas Chapter **245, 281, 316, 349,
383, 423, 460, 494, 530, 565, 598**
Buick Club of America, Lone Star Chapter [Texas] **246, 282,
317, 350, 384, 424, 461, 495, 531, 566, 599**
Buick Club of America—Membership Roster **223, 259, 295,
327, 360, 398, 436, 472, 508, 541, 576**
Buick Club of America, National Pike Chapter
   [Pennsylvania] **247, 283, 318, 351, 385, 425, 462, 496,
532, 567, 600**
Buick Club of America, Nebraska Chapter **248, 284, 319,
352, 386, 426, 463, 497, 533, 568, 601**
Buick Club of America, Nebraska Chapter—Newsletter **224,
260, 296, 328, 361, 399, 437, 473, 509, 542, 577**
Buick Club of America, North Cascade Chapter—Newsletter
   [Washington state] **225, 261, 297, 329, 362, 400, 438,
474, 510, 543, 578**
Buick Club of America, North Texas Chapter **249, 285, 320,
353, 387, 427, 464, 498, 534, 569, 602**
Buick Club of America, Puget Sound Chapter [Washington
   state] **250, 286, 321, 354, 388, 428, 465, 499, 535, 570,
603**
Buick Club of America, San Gabriel Valley Chapter
   [California] **251, 287, 322, 355, 389, 429, 466, 500, 536,
571, 604**
Buick Club of America, San Gabriel Valley Chapter—
   Newsletter [California] **226, 262, 298, 330, 363, 401, 439,
475, 511, 544, 579**
Buick Club of America, Southwestern Ohio Chapter **252,
288, 323, 356, 390, 430, 467, 501, 537, 572, 605**
Buick Club of America, Southwestern Ohio Chapter—
   Newsletter **227, 263, 299, 331, 364, 402, 440, 476, 512,
545, 580**
Buick Fixed Right; Get Your **217, 255, 291, 324, 357, 393,
433, 469, 503, 538, 573**
Buick GS Club of America **431**
Buick GS Club of America—GS National Directory **403**
Buick GS Club of America, Indiana Chapter—Newsletter **404,
546**
Buick Mid-size Models Owners Workshop Manual No. 627:
   1974-1987; Haynes **219, 394**
Buick Motor Div., General Motors Corp. **4349**
Buick News; Bluegrass **221, 257, 293, 325, 358, 396, 434,
470, 506, 539, 574**
Buick-Olds-Pontiac Full-Size, 1975-87 **253, 289, 432, 1932,
1971, 1988, 1999, 2147**
Buick, Olds, Pontiac, Full-Size Models: 1970-90; Haynes **256,
292, 1974, 1990, 2001, 2149**
Buick Regal, 1988 Repair and Tune-up Guide; Pontiac Grand
   Prix-Oldsmobile Cutlass- **395, 1940, 1953, 1964, 2311**
Buick Skyhawk, Cadillac Cimarron, Chevrolet Cavalier,
   Oldsmobile Firenza, Pontiac J-2000, Sunbird Shop Manual,
   1982-87; GMC J Cars: **504, 640, 767, 1980, 2418**

Buick Skyhawk, Olds Firenza, Cadillac Cimarron, Pontiac 6000, 1982-88; Chilton's Chevrolet Cavalier, **502, 638, 765, 1978, 2106**

Buicks of Yesteryear Pennsylvania; Youngstown **2877**

Bumper Recycling Association of North America—Membership Directory **3076**

Bumper Systems and Exterior Panels; Plastics in Automobile **3273, 3527**

Bumper Systems, Interior Trim, Instrument Panels and Exterior Panels; Plastics in Automobiles: **3238, 3275, 3528, 4165**

Buy a New Car for Less **3854**

Buying A Used Car **3855**

C

Cabriolet Service Manual: 1985-1989, Including 16V; Scirocco and **2708**

Cabriolets **4128, 4239**

Cadillac 1967-89 Repair and Tune-up Guide **606, 623, 637, 653, 667, 681, 695**

Cadillac—American Luxury Car **608, 625, 641, 655, 669, 683, 697**

Cadillac Cimarron, Chevrolet Cavalier, Oldsmobile Firenza, Pontiac J-2000, Sunbird Shop Manual, 1982-87; GMC J Cars: Buick Skyhawk, **504, 640, 767, 1980, 2418**

Cadillac Cimarron, Pontiac 6000, 1982-88; Chilton's Chevrolet Cavalier, Buick Skyhawk, Olds Firenza, **502, 638, 765, 1978, 2106**

Cadillac Convertible Courier **609**

Cadillac Convertible Owners of America **620**

Cadillac Convertible Owners of America—Directory **610**

Cadillac Fixed Right; Get Your **607, 624, 639, 654, 668, 682, 696**

Cadillac; Great Marques **617, 632, 648, 662, 676, 690, 704**

Cadillac-LaSalle Club **621, 635, 651, 665, 679, 693, 707**

Cadillac-Lasalle Club—Directory **611, 626, 642, 656, 670, 684, 698**

Cadillac—LaSalle Club, Lake St. Clair Region—Membership Directory [Michigan] **612, 627, 643, 657, 671, 685, 699**

Cadillac-LaSalle Club, Lower Michigan Region **622, 636, 652, 666, 680, 694, 708**

Cadillac-LaSalle Club, Lower Michigan Region— Newsletter **613, 628, 644, 658, 672, 686, 700**

Cadillac Motor Car Div., General Motors Corp. **4350**

Cadillac Service Publication **614, 629, 645, 659, 673, 687, 701**

Cadillac: The Enduring Legend **615, 630, 646, 660, 674, 688, 702**

Cadillac the Heartbreak of America: Fifteen Years of Consumer Disillusionment **616, 631, 647, 661, 675, 689, 703**

California; Alfa Romeo Owners Club of Central **2831**

[California]; Alfa Romeo Owners Club, Orange County Chapter **31, 56, 81**

[California]; Alfa Romeo Owners Club, Orange County Chapter—Newsletter **19, 44, 69**

California All Terrain Vehicle Association—Newsletter **4228**

California; Auto Cap of Southern **2836**

California Automotive Directory **2907, 2947, 2999, 3077, 3132**

[California]; Buick Club of America, San Gabriel Valley Chapter **251, 287, 322, 355, 389, 429, 466, 500, 536, 571, 604**

[California]; Buick Club of America, San Gabriel Valley Chapter—Newsletter **226, 262, 298, 330, 363, 401, 439, 475, 511, 544, 579**

California Chapter; Alfa Romeo Owners Club, Northern **29, 54, 79**

California Chapter—Journal; Alfa Romeo Owners Club, Northern **15, 40, 65**

California Chapter—Newsletter; Alfa Romeo Owners Club, Northern **16, 41, 66**

California Chapter; Pontiac-Oakland Club International, Southern **2102, 2143, 2181, 2223, 2269, 2306, 2343, 2378, 2413, 2452, 2488**

California Sports Car Club News **4240**

Camaro 228 and Firebird Trans Am Shop Manual, 1982-1987 **734, 2228**

Camaro 1982-1988; Chilton's **736**

Camaro America **742**

Camaro and Firebird, 1982-1987: Super Shop Manual **735, 2229**

Camaro Buyer's Guide; Illustrated **748**

Camaro Club; International **755**

Camaro Club; United States **756**

Camaro Corral **743**

Camaro Owners of America **754**

Camaro Owners Workshop Manual, No. 866: 1982-1990; Haynes Chevrolet **740**

Camaro Parts Directory; A to Z **753**

Camaro; The Story of **751**

Camaro White Book 1967-1987 **744**

Camper; Vanagon Official Factory Repair Manual: 1980-1989, Including Air Cooled and Water-Cooled Gasoline Engines, Diesel Engine, Syncro, and **2801**

Camry Owners Workshop Manual, No. 1023: 1983-1990; Haynes Toyota **2670**

Camshaft Identification Guide **3711**

Canada; Directory of Korean Automotive Firms in the United States and **3140**

Canadian Museums; Auto Museums Directory: U.S.A., Supplement with **3298**

Capitals: Motor Vehicle Regulation; From the State **3408**

Capri 1979-1987: Includes Turbo Shop Manual; Ford Mustang and Mercury **1392**

Capri, 1979-1987: Super Shop Manual; Mustang and **1396**

Capri (In-Line) Owners Workshop Manual, No. 654: 1979-1990; Haynes Ford Mustang and Mercury **1393**

Capri-Merkur 1979-1988; Chilton's Mustang- **1389, 1885, 1889**

Capri]; The Sporting Fords [Mercury **1829**

Capri (V-6 and V-8) Owners Workshop Manual, No. 558: 1979-1989; Haynes Ford Mustang and Mercury **1394**

Car and Driver **3856**

Car and Driver; Best of BAX: Collected Columns from **3248**

Car and Driver—Buyers Guide **3185**

Car and Driver—Road Test Annual **3857**

Car and Light Truck Diesel Engine Service Manual **3540, 4297**

Car & Parts Magazine **3858**

Car Audio Specialists Association—Government Action Bulletins **3405, 4215**

Car Audio Specialists Association—Special Bulletins **4216**

Car Beautiful: A Complete Guide to a Shiny, Well-Protected Car **3859**

The Car Book **3529**

The Car Buyer's Art: How to Beat the Salesman at His Own Game **3860**

The Car Buyers Guide **3861**

The Car Buyer's Handbook **3186**

Car Care **3999**

Car Care Council **2846**

Car Care Guide **3862**

Car Care News **4000**

Car Care Quarterly **3863**

Car Club Directory **2885**

Car Collector and Car Classics **4241**

Car Crazy: Wild Hour on Wheels **3312, 4242**

Car Interior Restoration **3432**

Car Life **3864**

Car Maintenance Reminder and Record Book **4001**

Car Owners **3865**

The Car Owner's Diary **3866**

The Car Owner's Survival Guide **3867**

Car Ownership and Use **3868**

Car Repair Book **4002**

Car Savvy **3869**

Car Service Manual **4003**

The Car Show **3870**

Car Stereo Blue Book **3187**

Car Stereo Review **4217**

Car Talk **4004**

Car Trader **3188**

Car Wars: The Untold Story of the Great Automakers and the Giant 30-Year and Battle for Global Supremacy **3313, 3361**

Caravan, Mini Ram Van, Plymouth Voyager, 1984-1987; Dodge **1038, 2062**

Caravan-Plymouth Voyager, 1984-1988: Repair and Tune-Up Guide; Chilton's Dodge **1036, 2060**

Carburetion; How to Restore Fuel Systems and **3804**

Carburetor; How to Overhaul a **3803**

Carburetors-Service and Repair Directory **3133**

The CARR Buying System **3871**

CARS **4218**

Cars and Comments **3872**

Cars and Parts Annual **3189**

Cars Detroit Never Built: Fifty Years of American Experimental Cars **3314**

Cars Guide; Consumers **3195**

Cars: How to Buy a New or Used Car and Keep It Running **3873**

Cars Illustrated **3874**

Cars Made in Upstate New York **3362**

Cars of Lincoln-Mercury **1662, 1678, 1690, 1836, 1845, 1854, 1862, 1872, 1879**

CarTel **3190**

Cartoons **3875**

Catalyst Deactivation and Alternative Catalyst; Emissions: Misfueling, **3679**

Catalytic Converters; Automobile **3665**

Cavalier, Buick Skyhawk, Olds Firenza, Cadillac Cimarron, Pontiac 6000, 1982-88; Chilton's Chevrolet **502, 638, 765, 1978, 2106**

Cavalier, Oldsmobile Firenza, Pontiac J-2000, Sunbird Shop Manual, 1982-87; GMC J Cars: Buick Skyhawk, Cadillac Cimarron, Chevrolet **504, 640, 767, 1980, 2418**

Celebrity, Buick Century, Olds Cutlass Ciera, Pontiac 6000, 1982-1988; Chilton's Chevrolet **216, 778, 1947, 2107**

Celebrity, Oldsmobile Cutlass Ciera, Pontiac 6000, 1982-87: Shop Manual; GM A-Cars Buick Century, Chevrolet **218, 780, 1938, 1950, 2110**

Celica-Supra, 1986-1990; Chilton's Toyota **2672, 2692**

Celica-Supra; Mitchell Glove Compartment Companion for Your Toyota **2673, 2693**

Center for Auto Safety **2847**

Center for Auto Safety—Impact **3446**

Central Pennsylvania Auto Club **2848**

Century and Regal, 1975-87; Chilton's Buick **215, 391**

Century, Chevrolet Celebrity, Oldsmobile Cutlass Ciera, Pontiac 6000, 1982-87: Shop Manual; GM A-Cars Buick **218, 780, 1938, 1950, 2110**

Century, Olds Cutlass Ciera, Pontiac 6000, 1982-1988; Chilton's Chevrolet Celebrity, Buick **216, 778, 1947, 2107**

Changing Gears: The Development of the Automotive Transmission **3315, 3712**

Charger, Rampage, and Plymouth Horizon, TC3, Turismo and Scamp 1978-1987: Shop Manual; Dodge Omni, 024, **1044, 1097, 2035, 2055**

Charging System Explained **3586**

Chassis and Accessory Circuits; Automotive **3611, 3700**

Chassis Controls Manual, Import Cars and Trucks—1988-1990: Motor Age Professional Mechanic's Edition; Chilton's Electronic **3631, 3718, 4130, 4300**

Chassis Electronics, 1987-89; Chilton's Guide to **3633, 3722**

Chassis Electronics 1989-91 (Asian Cars and Trucks); Chilton's Guide to **3723**

Chassis Electronics and Power Accessories, 1988-1991 Ford/Chrysler/Jeep/Eagle; Chilton's Guide to **918, 935, 943, 952, 972, 991, 1002, 1019, 1158, 1161, 1164, 1167, 1292, 1303, 1317, 1332, 1344, 1359, 1365, 1376, 1388, 1432, 1443, 1461, 1478, 1493, 1596, 1605, 1613, 1621, 1630**

Chassis Electronics and Power Accessories Service Manual, 1987-89: Motor-Age Professional Mechanic's Edition; Chilton's **3234, 3630, 3717**

Cherokee, 1984-1989; Haynes Jeep **1597**

Cherokee 1984-1991; Jeep Wagoneer-Comanche- **1599, 1607, 1615, 1623**

Chevette and Pontiac T 1000 Service Repair Handbook: All Models 1976-1987; Chevrolet **785, 2068**

Chevette and Pontiac T1000 1976-1988; Chilton's **786, 2069**

Chevette-Pontiac T1000 Owners Workshop Manuals, No. 449: 1976-1987; Haynes Chevrolet **789, 2071**

Chevrolet 1968-1988; Chilton's **711, 716, 727, 737, 757, 764, 777, 787, 793, 802, 852, 864, 873, 882, 890, 898, 909**

Chevrolet: A History from 1911 **3316, 3363**

Chevrolet and GMC 4-Wheel Drive Tune-Up: 1967-1987 **725, 869, 906, 1509, 1517, 1529**

Chevrolet and GMC Pick-Ups Owners Workshop Manual, No. 420: 1967-1987; Haynes **876, 1512, 1527**

Chevrolet Astro and GMC Safari **709, 1518**

Chevrolet Astro-GMC Safari, 1985-1990 **710, 1519**

Chevrolet Camaro Owners Workshop Manual, No. 866: 1982-1990; Haynes **740**

Chevrolet Cavalier, Buick Skyhawk, Olds Firenza, Cadillac Cimarron, Pontiac 6000, 1982-88; Chilton's **502, 638, 765, 1978, 2106**

Chevrolet Cavalier, Oldsmobile Firenza, Pontiac J-2000, Sunbird Shop Manual, 1982-87; GMC J Cars: Buick Skyhawk, Cadillac Cimarron, **504, 640, 767, 1980, 2418**

Chevrolet Celebrity, Buick Century, Olds Cutlass Ciera, Pontiac 6000, 1982-1988; Chilton's **216, 778, 1947, 2107**

Chevrolet Celebrity, Oldsmobile Cutlass Ciera, Pontiac 6000, 1982-87: Shop Manual; GM A-Cars Buick Century, **218, 780, 1938, 1950, 2110**

Chevrolet Chevette and Pontiac T 1000 Service Repair Handbook: All Models 1976-1987 **785, 2068**

Chevrolet Chevette-Pontiac T1000 Owners Workshop Manuals, No. 449: 1976-1987; Haynes **789, 2071**

Chevrolet Corsica and Beretta 1988; Chilton's **717, 794**

Chevrolet Full-Size Sedans Owners Workshop Manual, No. 704: 1969-1990; Haynes **760, 768, 839**

Chevrolet/Geo Motor Div., General Motors Corp. **4351**

Chevrolet-GMC Fixed Right; Get Your **712, 718, 728, 739, 759, 766, 779, 788, 795, 804, 838, 846, 854, 865, 875, 883, 892, 899, 912, 1511, 1516, 1520, 1526**

Chevrolet/GMC Pick-ups and Suburban 1970-1987; Chilton's **874, 910, 1524, 1532**

Chevrolet GMC Trucks, 1988-90 **870, 1521**

Chevrolet High Performance **720, 745, 772, 797, 807, 841, 857, 885, 901**

Chevrolet Lumina—Pontiac Transport Olds Silhouette, 1988-90 **848, 1995, 2459**

Chevrolet Monte Carlo Owner's Manual, No. 626: 1970-1988; Haynes **855**

Chevrolet Nova 1985-1989 Repair and Tune-up Guide **863**

Chevrolet S-10 Blazer, GMC S-15, and Olds Bravada, 1982-1990 **730, 1514, 1928**

Chevrolet S-10, GMC S-15 Pickups 1982—90 **871, 1522**

Chevrolet Small-Block V-8 Interchange Manual **3713, 4005**

Chevrolet; Standard Catalog of **715, 723, 733, 750, 763, 775, 784, 792, 800, 829, 844, 851, 861, 868, 881, 888, 897, 904, 916**

Chevrolet V-8 Vans Owners Workshop Manual No. 345, 1968-1989; Haynes **893**

Chevy; All **713, 719, 729, 741, 761, 771, 782, 790, 796, 806, 840, 847, 856, 866, 878, 884, 894, 900, 913**

Chevy and GMC C-Series, Pickups, and Suburbans: 1967-1987: Includes Suburbans Shop Manual **907, 1530**

Chevy and GMC Two Wheel Drive C and R-Series Pickups, Suburbans, and Vans, 1970-1987 (Gas and Diesel) **908, 1531**

Chevy and GMC Two-Wheel Drive Mid-Size S- and T-Pickups, Blazers, and Jimmy, 1982-1988 (Gas and Diesel) **726, 872, 1510, 1523**

Chevy GMC Pickups, 1988-90; Haynes **877, 1513, 1528**

Chevy; How to Rebuild Your Big-Block **3749, 4046**

Chevy Outdoors **731, 849, 879, 895, 914**

Chevy Power **721, 746, 773, 798, 808, 842, 858, 886, 902**

Chevy; Super **724, 752, 776, 801, 831, 845, 862, 889, 905**

Chevys; How to Rebuild Small Block **3748, 4045**

Chicago Chapter Illinois; British Car Union, **2844**

Chicago Chapter—Membership Directory [Illinois]; Alfa Romeo Owners Club, **13, 38, 63**

(Chicago Edition) Illinois; Home & Away **3888**

Chicagoland Chapter [Illinois]; Buick Club of America, **241, 277, 312, 345, 379, 419, 456, 490, 526, 561, 594**

Chiefly Pontiac **2074, 2114, 2152, 2190, 2236, 2277, 2314, 2350, 2385, 2423, 2460**

Child Restraint Recall Program; Children at Risk: Failure of the Federal **3447, 4201**

Children at Risk: Failure of the Federal Child Restraint Recall Program **3447, 4201**

Chilton Ford-Mercury Front Wheel Drive 1981-1987 **1342, 1476, 1850, 1868**

Chilton's Auto Repair Manual, 1987-1991 **4006**

Chilton's Auto Repair Manual, 1988-92 **4007**

Chilton's Auto Service Manual 1988-1992: Motor Age Professional Mechanic's Edition **4008**

Chilton's Automatic Transmission Repair Manual, 1984-88: Motor-Age Professional Mechanics Edition **3714**

Chilton's Automatic Transmission Repair Manual, 1984-1988: Import Cars and Trucks: Motor-Age Professional Mechanic's Edition **3715, 4129, 4298**

Chilton's Automatic Transmission Service Manual 1984-88: Domestic Cars and Trucks: Motor-Age Professional Mechanic's Edition **3716, 4299**

Chilton's Buick Century and Regal, 1975-87 **215, 391**

Chilton's Camaro 1982-1988 **736**

Chilton's Chassis Electronics and Power Accessories Service Manual, 1987-89: Motor-Age Professional Mechanic's Edition **3234, 3630, 3717**

Chilton's Chevette and Pontiac T1000 1976-1988 **786, 2069**

Chilton's Chevrolet 1968-1988 **711, 716, 727, 737, 757, 764, 777, 787, 793, 802, 852, 864, 873, 882, 890, 898, 909**

Chilton's Chevrolet Cavalier, Buick Skyhawk, Olds Firenza, Cadillac Cimarron, Pontiac 6000, 1982-88 **502, 638, 765, 1978, 2106**

Chilton's Chevrolet Celebrity, Buick Century, Olds Cutlass Ciera, Pontiac 6000, 1982-1988 **216, 778, 1947, 2107**

Chilton's Chevrolet Corsica and Beretta 1988 **717, 794**

Chilton's Chevrolet/GMC Pick-ups and Suburban 1970-1987 **874, 910, 1524, 1532**

Chilton's Chrysler Front Wheel Drive 1981-1988 **951, 971**

Chilton's Colt/Challenger/Conquest/Vista, 1971-1988: Repair and Tune-Up Guide **917, 1053**

Chilton's Cutlass 1970-1987 **1948, 1960, 2108**

Chilton's Dodge Caravan-Plymouth Voyager, 1984-1988: Repair and Tune-Up Guide **1036, 2060**

Chilton's Dodge/Plymouth Trucks 1967-1988 **1061, 1110, 1124**

Chilton's Dodge/Plymouth Vans 1967-1988 **1037, 1118, 2061**

Chilton's Easy Car Care Study Guide **4009**

Chilton's Electronic Chassis Controls Manual, Import Cars and Trucks—1988-1990: Motor Age Professional Mechanic's Edition **3631, 3718, 4130, 4300**

Chilton's Electronic Engine Controls Manual, 1988-90—Domestic Cars and Trucks: Motor-Age Professional Mechanic's Edition **3632, 3719, 4301**

Chilton's Emission Control Manual 1992: Motor Age Professional Mechanic's Edition **3670**

Chilton's Emission Controls Application Guide 1966-1992: Update **3671**

Chilton's Firebird, 1982-90: Repair and Tuneup Guide **2230**

Chilton's Ford Aerostar, 1985-1990 **1289**

Chilton's Ford-Lincoln-Mercury Full-Size, 1968-1988 **1374, 1490, 1659, 1675, 1688, 1832, 1842**

Chilton's Ford Repair Manual 1980-1987 **1290, 1302, 1316, 1331, 1343, 1375, 1387, 1442, 1460, 1477, 1491**

Chilton's Ford Thunderbird, Mercury Cougar, Lincoln Continental-Mark VII, 1980-1987 **1492, 1660, 1676, 1833**

Chilton's Ford Vans, 1961-1988 **1291**

Chilton's Guide to Air Conditioning and Heating Manual, 1989-91: Professional Mechanics Edition **4101**

Chilton's Guide to Air Conditioning and Heating Manual 1990-92: Motor Age Professional Mechanics Edition **4102**

Chilton's Guide to Air Conditioning Repair and Service, 1989-1991 **4103**

Chilton's Guide to Auto Body Repair and Painting **3433, 3476**

Chilton's Guide to Auto Electronic Accessories: Sound, Security, and Safety **4205, 4219**

Chilton's Guide to Auto Tune-Up and Troubleshooting **4010**

Chilton's Guide to Automatic Transmission Repair **3720**

Chilton's Guide to Automatic Transmission Repair Manual, 1984-1989 Domestic Cars and Trucks **3721**

Chilton's Guide to Brakes, Steering and Suspension 1980-1987: Domestic and Import Cars and Trucks **3521, 4131, 4264, 4275, 4302**

Chilton's Guide to Chassis Electronics, 1987-89 **3633, 3722**

Chilton's Guide to Chassis Electronics 1989-91 (Asian Cars and Trucks) **3723**

Chilton's Guide to Chassis Electronics and Power Accessories, 1988-1991 Ford/Chrysler/Jeep/Eagle **918, 935, 943, 952, 972, 991, 1002, 1019, 1158, 1161, 1164, 1167, 1292, 1303, 1317, 1332, 1344, 1359, 1365, 1376, 1388, 1432, 1443, 1461, 1478, 1493, 1596, 1605, 1613, 1621, 1630**

Chilton's Guide to Diesel Cars and Trucks **3541, 4303**

Chilton's Guide to Emission Diagnosis, Tune-Up and Vacuum Diagrams 1984-87 **3534, 3672, 4132**

Chilton's Guide to Fuel Injection and Electronic Engine Controls 1984-1988: Import Cars and Trucks **3634, 3724, 3793, 4133, 4304**

Chilton's Guide to Fuel Injection and Electronic Engine Controls, 1988-90 **3635, 3794**

Chilton's Honda, 1973-1988 **1534, 1541, 1547, 1554**

Chilton's Hyundai 1985-1987 **1561**

Chilton's IMP Emission Diagnostic and Service Manual, Vacuum Circuit, 1984-1987 Import Cars and Truck: Motor-Age Professional Mechanic's Edition **3673, 4134, 4305**

Chilton's Import Automotive Service Manual, 1982-1989 **4011, 4135**

Chilton's Import Car Parts and Labor Guide, 1987-1991: Motor Age Professional Mechanics Edition **4136, 4190**

Chilton's Import Car Repair Manual 1982-87: Motor Age Professional Mechanics Edition **4012, 4137**

Chilton's Import Car Repair Manual 1987-91: Motor Age Professional Mechanics Edition **4013**

Chilton's Import Car Repair Manual, 1987-91: Motor Age Professional Mechanic's Edition **4138**

Chilton's Import Car Repair Manual 1987-91: Motor Age Professional Mechanics Edition **4139**

Chilton's Import Car Repair Manual 1988-92 **4014, 4140**

Chilton's Import Car Service Manual, 1980-1987: Motor-Age Professional Mechanic's Edition **4015, 4141**

Chilton's Import Car Wiring Diagrams Manual, 1987-88: Motor-Age Professional Mechanic's Edition **3587, 4142**

Chilton's Jeep CJ 1945-1987 **1631**

Chilton's Labor Guide and Manual, 1988-1992: Motor Age Professional Mechanic's Edition **4016**

Chilton's Labor Guide and Parts Manual 1986-90: Motor Age Professional Mechanic's Edition **4017, 4191**

Chilton's Minor Auto Body Repair Manual **3477**

Chilton's Mustang-Capri-Merkur 1979-1988 **1389, 1885, 1889**

Chilton's Nissan Sentra, Datsun 1200 and B210, 1973-1987 **1910**

Chilton's Professional Electronics Diagnostic Manual Ford Cars and Trucks 1984-1988: Motor-Age Professional Mechanic's Edition **1304, 1318, 1333, 1345, 1366, 1377, 1390, 1444, 1462, 1479, 1494**

Chilton's Professional Truck and Van Repair Manual 1981-1988 **4018, 4306**

Chilton's Service Bay Handbook 1992: Motor Age Professional Mechanic's Edition **4019**

Chilton's Subaru 1970-1988 **2652, 2653, 2655, 2657, 2661, 2663, 2665**

Chilton's Toyota Celica-Supra, 1986-1990 **2672, 2692**

Chilton's Toyota Corolla, Carina, Tercel, Starlet, 1970-1987 **2676, 2697**

Chilton's Toyota Corolla-Tercel-MR2, 1984-1990 **2677, 2684, 2698**

Chilton's Toyota Trucks 1970-1987 **2700**

Chilton's Truck and Van Repair Manual, 1982-1988 **4020, 4307**

Chilton's Truck and Van Wiring Diagram Manual, 1989-1990: Motor Age Professional Mechanic's Edition **3588, 4308**

Chilton's Tune-up Emission Diagnosis and Service Manual, 1988: Import Cars and Trucks **3535, 3674, 4309**

Chilton's U.S. Emission Diagnostic and Service Manual, Vacuum Circuit, 1984-1987—Domestic Car: Motor-Age Professional Mechanic's Edition **3536, 3675**

Chilton's VW Front Wheel Drive, 1974-1990 **2707, 2728, 2738, 2750, 2761, 2780, 2791, 2800**

Chilton's Wiring Diagrams Manual, 1989: Domestic Cars **3589**

Chrysler 1924-1990; Standard Catalog of **929, 939, 946, 964, 984, 997, 1012, 1022**

Chrysler Corp. **4352**

Chrysler, Dodge, Plymouth: 1972-1987 Rear Wheel Drive Tune-up Maintenance **919, 936, 992, 1076, 2030**

Chrysler, Dodge, Plymouth; How to Build **924, 938, 944, 958, 978, 995, 1020, 1027, 1032, 1040, 1045, 1055, 1063, 1068, 1077, 1081, 1085, 1093, 1098, 1106, 1114, 1120, 1125, 1129, 1137, 1152, 2016, 2020, 2024, 2031, 2036, 2040, 2047, 2051, 2056, 2064**

Chrysler Front Wheel Drive 1981-1988; Chilton's **951, 971**

Chrysler/Jeep/Eagle; Chilton's Guide to Chassis Electronics and Power Accessories, 1988-1991 Ford/ **918, 935, 943, 952, 972, 991, 1002, 1019, 1158, 1161, 1164, 1167, 1292, 1303, 1317, 1332, 1344, 1359, 1365, 1376, 1388, 1432, 1443, 1461, 1478, 1493, 1596, 1605, 1613, 1621, 1630**

Chrysler Mid-Size Cars Owners Workshop Manual, 1982-1989; Haynes **953, 973, 993**

Chrysler; Motor Auto Repair 1983-1989 **920, 937, 954, 974, 994, 1003**

Chrysler: Once Upon a Time and Now **3317, 3364**

Chrysler Performance Parts Association **931, 966, 986, 1014, 1048, 1057, 1071, 1088, 1101, 1132, 1139, 1147, 1154, 1168, 2026, 2042**

Chrysler Performance Parts Association Newsletter **921, 955, 975, 1004, 1144**

Chrysler/Plymouth Div., Chrysler Motors Corp. **4353**

Chrysler Power Magazine **922, 956, 976, 1005, 1145**

Chrysler Product Owners Club **932, 941, 948, 967, 987, 999, 1015, 1024, 1029, 1034, 1042, 1058, 1065, 1072, 1079, 1083, 1089, 1095, 1102, 1108, 1116, 1122, 1127, 1133, 1140, 1148, 1155, 1159, 1162, 1165, 1169, 1602, 1610, 1618, 1627, 1636, 2018, 2022, 2027, 2033, 2038, 2043, 2049, 2053, 2058, 2066**

Chrysler Revival and the American System; New Deals: The **3335, 3382**

Ciera, Pontiac 6000, 1982-1988; Chilton's Chevrolet Celebrity, Buick Century, Olds Cutlass **216, 778, 1947, 2107**

Cimarron, Chevrolet Cavalier, Oldsmobile Firenza, Pontiac J-2000, Sunbird Shop Manual, 1982-87; GMC J Cars: Buick Skyhawk, Cadillac **504, 640, 767, 1980, 2418**

Cimarron, Pontiac 6000, 1982-88; Chilton's Chevrolet Cavalier, Buick Skyhawk, Olds Firenza, Cadillac **502, 638, 765, 1978, 2106**

Cincinnati—AAA Today Ohio; AAA **3833**

Citizens for Auto-Theft Responsibility **2849**

The Class of Monte Carlo **859**

Classic Jaguar Association **1578, 1593**

Classic Jaguar Association—News and Technical Bulletin **1567, 1583**

Cleaning Directory; Truck Washing and **3177**

Clutches Service and Repair Directory **3134**

Collectors Society of America; Sports Car **2869**

Collision—Automotive Association Directory Issue **2886**

Collision Repair Guide **3478**

Colorado; Alfa Club of **25, 50, 75**

Colorado—Newsletter; Alfa Club of **10, 35, 60**

Colorado/Utah/Nevada Automotive Directory **2908, 2948, 3000, 3078, 3135**

Colt/Challenger/Conquest/Vista, 1971-1988: Repair and Tune-Up Guide; Chilton's **917, 1053**

Colt-Plymouth Champ FWD Owners Workshop Manual, No. 610: 1978-1987; Haynes Dodge **1054**

Comanche-Cherokee 1984-1991; Jeep Wagoneer- **1599, 1607, 1615, 1623**

Combustion and Emissions Research in Japan; New Diesel Engines, **3554, 3686, 3758, 4157**

Complete Automobile Mechanics Refresher Course **4021**

Complete Automotive Service Library **4022**

The Complete Book of Ferrari **1172, 1195, 1218, 1241, 1264**

The Complete Book of Mustang **1398**

Complete Buyer's Guide and Expose of the Automotive Jungle; Deals on Wheels: How to Buy, Care for and Sell a Car: **3197**

Complete Car Cost Guide **3191**

The Complete Guide to Automotive Refinishing **3434, 3479**

The Complete Guide to Car Noises **4023**

The Complete Lamborghini **1639, 1647, 1653**

Complete Small Truck Cost Guide **3192**

Components Aftermarket; Automobile **2993**

Computer Applications in Design and Manufacturing **3249**

Computer Control Systems; Automotive **3613**

Computer Controlled Ignition Systems; Automotive Electronic and **3573, 3620, 4111**

Computer Systems; Domestic Electronic Fuel Injection and **3641, 3797**

Computers; Auto Electricity, Electronics, **3563, 3607**

Computers in Design, Manufacture and Operation of Automobiles **3250, 3636**

[Connecticut]; Pontiac-Oakland Club, Nutmeg Chapter **2104, 2145, 2183, 2225, 2271, 2308, 2345, 2380, 2415, 2454, 2490**

Connecticut/Rhode Island Automotive Directory **2909, 2949, 3001, 3079, 3136**

Connecting Rod Manual **3725**

Conquest/Vista, 1971-1988: Repair and Tune-Up Guide; Chilton's Colt/Challenger/ **917, 1053**

Conspicuous Production: Automobiles & Elites in Detroit, 1899-1933 **3318**

Consultants Directory; Automotive **2939**

Consumer Action Program; Automotive **2838**

Consumer Action Program; District of Columbia Automotive **2851**

Consumer Car Care for the Wise, the Poor and the Helpless **4024**

Consumer Education: Buying an Automobile **3876**

Consumer Education: Maintaining an Automobile **4025**

Consumer Guide Automobile Book: The Complete New Car Buying Guide **3193**

Consumer Guide Used Car Book **3194**

Consumer Reports: Burglar Proofing Your Home and Car **4206**

Consumer Reports—Cars **3877, 4026**

Consumer Survival Kit: Cars **3878, 4027**

Consumers Cars Guide **3195**

Consumers' Guide to Automotive Maintenance **4028**

Continental Bulletin **1663**

Continental Comments **1664, 1665**

Continental-Mark VII, 1980-1987; Chilton's Ford Thunderbird, Mercury Cougar, Lincoln **1492, 1660, 1676, 1833**

Continental Owners Club—Authenticity Manual; Lincoln and **1668, 1681, 1693**

Continental Owners Club—Directory; Lincoln and **1669, 1682, 1694**

Continental Owners Club; Lincoln and **1674, 1687, 1699**

Continental Owners Club, Southern Region—Bulletin; Lincoln and **1670, 1683, 1695**

Continental Owners Club, Southern Region—Comments; Lincoln and **1671, 1684, 1696**

Continuously Variable Transmissions for Passenger Cars **3726**

Control Systems; Automotive Computer **3613**

Convergence 1988: Proceedings of the International Congress on Transportation Electronics **3637**

Convertible Club; U.S.A. **2873**

Convertible Courier; Cadillac **609**

Convertible Owners of America; Cadillac **620**
Convertible Owners of America—Directory; Cadillac **610**
Convertible Owners of America; Volkswagen **2718, 2749**
Coolants, Cooling System Materials and Testing; Worldwide
  Trends in Engine **3770, 4109**
Cooling; Automotive Heating and **4098**
Cooling Journal; Automotive **4092**
Cooling, Lubrication, and Exhaust Systems; Automotive
  Fuel, **3667, 3788, 4095, 4167**
Cooling System; The Automotive **4093**
Cooling System Materials and Testing; Worldwide Trends in
  Engine Coolants, **3770, 4109**
Cooling System Service; Advanced Car Care: **3961, 4083**
Cooling Systems; Automotive Fuel, Lubricating and **3789,
  4096, 4168**
Cooling Systems; Automotive Fuel, Lubrication, and **3818,
  4097, 4169**
Cooling Systems Institute; Automotive **2839**
Cooling Systems; Operation and Service; Automotive **4094**
Cooling Systems; Quick Course in Car **4107, 4108**
Corolla, Carina, Tercel, Starlet, 1970-1987; Chilton's
  Toyota **2676, 2697**
Corolla Owners Workshop Manual, No. 1025: 1984-1988;
  Haynes Toyota **2678**
Corolla-Tercel-MR2, 1984-1990; Chilton's Toyota **2677, 2684,
  2698**
Corolla; Toyota **2679**
Corrado Official Factory Repair Manual: 1989-1990;
  Volkswagen **2719**
Corrosion Prediction and Prevention in the Motor
  Vehicle **3879**
Corsica and Beretta 1988; Chilton's Chevrolet **717, 794**
Corvette **809**
Corvette: A Complete Story **810**
Corvette: America's Sports Car Legend **811**
Corvette: America's Supercar **812**
Corvette Association—Newsletter; Mississippi Valley **826**
The Corvette Black Book: 1953-92 **813**
Corvette Buyer's Guide; Illustrated **824**
Corvette Club—Newsletter; Valley Vettes **832**
Corvette Clubs—Handbook; National Council of **827**
Corvette Clubs; National Council of **837**
Corvette Detailing; Secrets of **828**
Corvette Driver-Owner Guide for 1953-1988 Models:
  Maximizing Your Corvette's Potential **814**
Corvette, Ferrari, Mercedes-Benz, Porsche—The Greatest of
  the Survivors Series; Four for the Road: **822, 1187, 1210,
  1233, 1256, 1280, 1777, 1784, 1792, 1800, 1808, 1816,
  2497, 2525, 2546, 2569**
Corvette Fever—Directory of Corvette-Related Businesses
  Issue **815**
Corvette Fever Magazine **816**
Corvette Illustrated **817**
Corvette Owners Association; National **836**
Corvette Owners Workshop Manual, No. 1336: All Models
  1984-1989; Haynes **805**
Corvette: Portrait of a Legend **818**
Corvette Quarterly **819**
Corvette; The Story of **830**
Corvette: The Legend Lives On **820**
Cougar, Lincoln Continental-Mark VII, 1980-1987; Chilton's
  Ford Thunderbird, Mercury **1492, 1660, 1676, 1833**
Cougar, No. 1338: 1983-1988; Haynes Ford Thunderbird and
  Mercury **1497**
Countach: Super Profile; Lamborghini **1644**
CPI: Cars of Particular Interest **3196**
Crankshaft Manual **3530, 3727, 4192**
Cream City Chapter [Wisconsin]; Buick Club of America, **242,
  278, 313, 346, 380, 420, 457, 491, 527, 562, 595**
Cream City Chronicle [Wisconsin] **228, 264, 300, 332, 365,
  405, 441, 477, 513, 547, 581**
Current and Future Directions of Supercomputer Applications
  in the Automobile Industry **3251, 3638**
Current Trends in Truck Suspension **3252, 4276, 4310**
Customizing Directory; Automobile **2906**
Cutlass 1970-1987; Chilton's **1948, 1960, 2108**

Cutlass-Buick Regal, 1988 Repair and Tune-up Guide; Pontiac
  Grand Prix-Oldsmobile **395, 1940, 1953, 1964, 2311**
Cutlass Ciera, Pontiac 6000, 1982-87: Shop Manual; GM A-
  Cars Buick Century, Chevrolet Celebrity, Oldsmobile **218,
  780, 1938, 1950, 2110**
Cutlass Ciera, Pontiac 6000, 1982-1988; Chilton's Chevrolet
  Celebrity, Buick Century, Olds **216, 778, 1947, 2107**
Cutlass Owners Workshop Manual, No. 658: 1974-1989;
  Haynes Oldsmobile **1939, 1952, 1963**
Cylinder Head and Block Identification Guide **3728, 3729,
  4193**

D

Daihatsu America Inc. **4354**
Datsun and Nissan Two and Four-Wheel Drive Pickups 1970-
  1987 Gas and Diesel **1915**
Daytona and Chrysler Laser Owners Workshop Manual, No.
  1140: 1984-1989; Haynes Dodge **1067**
Dealer at His Own Game: Buying a New or Used Car; How
  to Beat the Car **3895**
Dealers Association—Yearbook and Directory; Rhode Island
  Auto **2978**
Dealers Directory New Cars; Automobile **2944**
Dealers Directory Used Cars; Automobile **2945**
Deals on Wheels: How to Buy, Care for and Sell a Car:
  Complete Buyer's Guide and Expose of the Automotive
  Jungle **3197**
Decade of Delay **3448**
Deep South Alfa Romeo Club [Mississippi, Louisiana, and
  southwestern Tennessee] **33, 58, 83**
Delaware/District of Columbia/Maryland Automotive
  Directory **2910, 2950, 3002, 3080, 3137**
Deposit Formation in Gasoline Fuel Injected Engines **3730,
  3795**
Design and Crashworthiness of Automobiles; Structural **3281,
  3454**
Design and Manufacturing; Computer Applications in **3249**
Design & Vehicle Safety: An Annotated Bibliography; Studies
  Relating Automobile **3282, 3455**
Design: Great Designers and Their Work; Automobile **3244,
  3301**
Design, Manufacture and Operation of Automobiles;
  Computers in **3250, 3636**
Design Practices Passenger Car Automatic Transmission **3253,
  3731**
Detailing; Tune Up America: **3441**
Detroit, 1899-1933; Conspicuous Production: Automobiles &
  Elites in **3318**
Detroit Public Library: A Simplified Guide to Its Holdings;
  Automotive History Collection of the **3309**
Developments in Diesel Particulate Control Systems **3796,
  3819**
Developments in Electronic Engine Management and Driveline
  Controls **3290, 3558, 3639, 3732**
Diagnostic Service Directory; Automobile **3118**
Dickinson and the Automobile: the Early Years 1903-
  1929 **3319**
Diesel and Four-Wheel Drive Shop Manual; Ford Ranger and
  Bronco II 1983-1988: Includes **1321, 1447**
Diesel, and Turbo Diesel, 4-cylinder and 6-cylinder Engines;
  Toyota Pickup, 4-Runner Service Manual: 1978-1988
  Including Gasoline, **2668, 2704**
Diesel, and Turbo Diesel, Including Golf, GT, Jetta GLI and
  16V Models; GTI, Golf and Jetta Service Manual: 1985-
  1989: Gasoline, **2739, 2751, 2762**
Diesel Automobile Association **2850**
Diesel Car Digest **3542**
Diesel Cars and Trucks; Chilton's Guide to **3541, 4303**
Diesel]; Chevy and GMC Two Wheel Drive C and R-Series
  Pickups, Suburbans, and Vans, 1970-1987 (Gas and **908,
  1531**

Diesel); Chevy and GMC Two-Wheel Drive Mid-Size S- and T-Pickups, Blazers, and Jimmy, 1982-1988 (Gas and **726, 872, 1510, 1523**

Diesel; Datsun and Nissan Two and Four-Wheel Drive Pickups 1970-1987 Gas and **1915**

Diesel Engine Service Manual; Car and Light Truck **3540, 4297**

Diesel Engine, Syncro, and Camper; Vanagon Official Factory Repair Manual: 1980-1989, Including Air Cooled and Water-Cooled Gasoline Engines, **2801**

Diesel Engines; Automotive **3539**

Diesel Engines, Combustion and Emissions Research in Japan; New **3554, 3686, 3758, 4157**

Diesel Engines for Automobiles, Small Trucks and Small Tractors **3543, 4311**

Diesel Engines; Fuel Alternatives for S.I. and **3550, 3741, 3822**

Diesel Engines; Modern Fuel for Modern **3552, 3828**

Diesel Engines; Multigrade Oils for **3553, 4181**

Diesel Exhaust Emissions: Particulate Studies and Transient Cycle Testing **3544, 3676**

Diesel, Including Wagon and Quattro; Audi 5000S, 5000CS Official Factory Repair Manual: 1984-1988 Gasoline, Turbo and Turbo **126**

Diesel Magazine **3545, 3820**

Diesel Mechanics **3546, 4029**

Diesel Mechanics II: Engine Assembly **3547**

Diesel Mechanics III **3548, 4030**

Diesel; Mercedes **1775, 1790**

Diesel Particulate Control Systems; Developments in **3796, 3819**

Diesel Particulate Emissions; The Measurement and Control of **3551, 3684**

Diesel Particulates: An Update **3549, 3677**

Digest of Motor Law **3406**

Digest of Motor Laws **3407**

Digital Instrumentation; Automotive Computers and **3614**

Dinosaur Machine **3320**

Directory of Automotive Aftermarket Suppliers **3003**

Directory of Automotive Related Business Publishers **3138**

Directory of Foreign Automotive Companies in the United States **2951, 3139**

Directory of Korean Automotive Firms in the United States and Canada **3140**

Dismantlers and Recyclers Association—Roster of Members; Automotive **3075**

Display Technology: Human Factors Concepts **3254**

Displays and Industrial Illumination; Automotive **3615**

Displays, Electronics, and Sensors Technology **3255, 3640**

Distributorless Ignition **4114**

District of Columbia Automotive Consumer Action Program **2851**

[District of Columbia, Maryland, and Virginia]; Pontiac-Oakland Club International, National Capital Area **2100, 2141, 2179, 2221, 2267, 2304, 2341, 2376, 2411, 2450, 2486**

District of Columbia/Maryland Automotive Directory; Delaware/ **2910, 2950, 3002, 3080, 3137**

Do-It-Yourself Car Care **4031**

Dodge and Plymouth Vans Owners Workshop Manual, No. 349: 1971-1991; Haynes **1039, 1111, 1119, 2063**

Dodge Aries and Plymouth Reliant Owners Workshop Manual, 1981-1988; Haynes **1031, 2046**

Dodge Automobile Club; Shelby **1050, 1073, 1090, 1103, 1134**

Dodge Caravan, Mini Ram Van, Plymouth Voyager, 1984-1987 **1038, 2062**

Dodge Caravan-Plymouth Voyager, 1984-1988: Repair and Tune-Up Guide; Chilton's **1036, 2060**

Dodge Colt-Plymouth Champ FWD Owners Workshop Manual, No. 610: 1978-1987; Haynes **1054**

Dodge Daytona and Chrysler Laser Owners Workshop Manual, No. 1140: 1984-1989; Haynes **1067**

Dodge/Dodge Truck Div., Chrysler Motors Corp. **4355**

Dodge Omni, 024, Charger, Rampage, and Plymouth Horizon, TC3, Turismo and Scamp 1978-1987: Shop Manual **1044, 1097, 2035, 2055**

Dodge Pick-ups Owner's Workshop Manuals, No. 912: 1974-1990; Haynes **1062, 1113**

Dodge, Plymouth: 1972-1987 Rear Wheel Drive Tune-up Maintenance; Chrysler, **919, 936, 992, 1076, 2030**

Dodge, Plymouth; How to Build Chrysler, **924, 938, 944, 958, 978, 995, 1020, 1027, 1032, 1040, 1045, 1055, 1063, 1068, 1077, 1081, 1085, 1093, 1098, 1106, 1114, 1120, 1125, 1129, 1137, 1152, 2016, 2020, 2024, 2031, 2036, 2040, 2047, 2051, 2056, 2064**

Dodge/Plymouth Trucks 1967-1988; Chilton's **1061, 1110, 1124**

Dodge/Plymouth Vans 1967-1988; Chilton's **1037, 1118, 2061**

Domestic Cars and Trucks; Chilton's Guide to Automatic Transmission Repair Manual, 1984-1989 **3721**

Domestic Electronic Fuel Injection and Computer Systems **3641, 3797**

Don't Get Taken Every Time: The Insider's Guide to Buying or Leasing Your Next Car or Truck **3880**

Drive Components **3733**

Drive It Forever: Your Key to Long Automobile Life **4032**

Drive Shafts Wholesale and Manufacturers Directory **3050**

Drive Trains; Automatic, Manual Transmissions, Transaxles, and **3555, 3695**

Driveline Controls; Automotive Electronic Engine Management and **3556, 3622**

Driveline Controls; Developments in Electronic Engine Management and **3290, 3558, 3639, 3732**

Driving Newsletter **3881**

The Drumbeat **2075, 2115, 2153, 2191, 2237, 2278, 2315, 2351, 2386, 2424, 2461**

The duPont Registry **3198**

Dyna's Chatter **229, 230, 265, 266, 301, 333, 334, 366, 367, 406, 407, 442, 443, 478, 479, 514, 515, 548, 549, 582, 583**

E

The Eagle **2238**

Eagle; Chilton's Guide to Chassis Electronics and Power Accessories, 1988-1991 Ford/Chrysler/Jeep/ **918, 935, 943, 952, 972, 991, 1002, 1019, 1158, 1161, 1164, 1167, 1292, 1303, 1317, 1332, 1344, 1359, 1365, 1376, 1388, 1432, 1443, 1461, 1478, 1493, 1596, 1605, 1613, 1621, 1630**

Eastern Aftermarket Journal—Directory and Buyers Guide Issue **3051**

Eastern Aftermarket Journal—Foreign Parts Directory and Buyer's Guide Issue **3052**

Economy Car Price Buying Guide; Edmund's **3200**

Edmund's Car Price Buyer's Guide **3199**

Edmund's Economy Car Price Buying Guide **3200**

Edmund's Foreign Car Prices **3201**

Edmund's New Car Prices **3202, 3203**

Edmund's Used Car Prices **3204**

Edmund's Vans, Pickups/Off Road Buyer's Guide **3205**

Ejag News Magazine **1568, 1584**

Elan, Cortina, and Europa; Lotus: The **1704**

Elan; Super Profile: Lotus **1707**

Elan: The Complete Story; Lotus **1701**

Elastomer Applications; Past, Present & Future of Automotive **3271**

Electric and Electronic Systems for Automobiles and Trucks **3590, 3642, 4312**

Electric Motors, Principles Controls, Service and Maintenance **3591, 3734, 4033**

Electric Service Directory; Automobile **3119**

Electrical and Electronic Equipment; Automobile **3564, 3609**

Electrical and Electronic Systems; Automotive **3567, 3568, 3569, 3616, 3617, 3618**

Electrical and Electronic Systems Lab Manual; Automotive **3570, 3619**

Electrical Components; Troubleshooting **3605**

Electrical Diagrams and Troubleshooting Guide; Volkswagen **2709, 2720, 2729, 2741, 2753, 2764, 2772, 2782, 2792, 2802**

Electrical Equipment; Automotive Electronics and **3575, 3623**

Electrical Handbook: How To Wire Your Car From Scratch; Auto **3562**

Electrical Manual: A Comprehensive Guide; Automobile **3565**

Electrical Manual: A Comprehensive Guide; Haynes Automobile **3596**

Electrical Manual No. 1654; Haynes Automobile **3597**

Electrical System; The Battery and its **3582**

Electrical Systems **3592, 4034**

Electrical Systems: A Beginner's Troubleshooting and Repair Manual; Automotive Electronic- **3574, 3621**

Electrical Systems; Automobile Electronics and Basic **3566, 3610**

Electrical Systems; Automotive **3571**

Electrical Systems; Fundamentals of Electricity and Automotive **3595**

Electrical Systems, Heating, and Air Conditioning **3593, 4104**

Electrical Systems; How to Do **3598**

Electrical Systems; Mitchell Automotive **3600**

Electrical Systems; Motor Auto Engines and **3601, 3756**

Electrical Systems; Petersen's Basic Ignition and **3602, 4121**

Electricity and Automotive Electrical Systems; Fundamentals of **3595**

Electricity; Automotive **3572**

Electricity, Electronics, Computers; Auto **3563, 3607**

Electricity for Auto Mechanics; Basic **3580**

Electrics **3594, 4035**

Electronic Accessories: Sound, Security, and Safety; Chilton's Guide to Auto **4205, 4219**

Electronic and Computer Controlled Ignition Systems; Automotive **3573, 3620, 4111**

Electronic Automotive Reliability **3256, 3643**

Electronic Chassis Controls Manual, Import Cars and Trucks—1988-1990: Motor Age Professional Mechanic's Edition; Chilton's **3631, 3718, 4130, 4300**

Electronic Control Systems; Truck **3661, 4325**

Electronic Displays and Information Systems **3257, 3644, 4160**

Electronic Displays and Information Systems; New Technologies in Automotive **3655, 4163**

Electronic Displays and Information Systems; Recent Developments in Automotive **3657, 4166**

Electronic Displays, Information Systems and On-Board Electronics **3258, 3645, 4161**

Electronic-Electrical Systems: A Beginner's Troubleshooting and Repair Manual; Automotive **3574, 3621**

Electronic Engine Control and Fuel Injection Management; Recent Developments in **3658, 3765, 3813**

Electronic Engine Controls 1984-1988: Import Cars and Trucks; Chilton's Guide to Fuel Injection and **3634, 3724, 3793, 4133, 4304**

Electronic Engine Controls, 1988-90; Chilton's Guide to Fuel Injection and **3635, 3794**

Electronic Engine Controls Manual, 1988-90—Domestic Cars and Trucks: Motor-Age Professional Mechanic's Edition; Chilton's **3632, 3719, 4301**

Electronic Engine Management and Driveline Controls; Automotive **3556, 3622**

Electronic Engine Management and Driveline Controls; Developments in **3290, 3558, 3639, 3732**

Electronic Engine Management; New Developments in **3266, 3654, 3757**

Electronic Equipment; Automobile Electrical and **3564, 3609**

Electronic Fuel Injection **3646, 3798**

Electronic Fuel Injection and Computer Systems; Domestic **3641, 3797**

Electronic Fuel Injection Systems; Bosch **3791**

Electronic Fuel-Injection Troubleshooting Guide: Domestic Vehicles; Mitchell's **3650, 3805**

Electronic Fuel-Injection Troubleshooting Guide: Import Vehicles; Mitchell's **3651, 3806, 4153**

Electronic Ignition Explained **3647, 4115**

Electronic Ignition Troubleshooting Guide: Domestic Vehicles; Mitchell's **3652, 4119**

Electronic Ignition Troubleshooting Guide: Import Vehicles; Mitchell's **3653, 4120, 4154**

Electronic Ignition Tune Up **3648, 4036, 4116**

Electronic Ignition Tune-Up; Advanced **3964, 4110**

Electronic Instrumentation and Microprocessor; Automechanic's Guide to **3608**

Electronic Instrumentation Service Manual 1980-1987: Motor Age Professional Mechanic's Edition **3649, 4162**

Electronic Systems; Automotive Electrical and **3567, 3568, 3569, 3616, 3617, 3618**

Electronic Systems for Automobiles and Trucks; Electric and **3590, 3642, 4312**

Electronic Systems Lab Manual; Automotive Electrical and **3570, 3619**

Electronic Test Equipment; Basic **3581**

Electronic Tune-Up; Advanced **3606, 3965**

Electronic Wheel Balancing **4338**

Electronics, 1987-89; Chilton's Guide to Chassis **3633, 3722**

Electronics and Basic Electrical Systems; Automobile **3566, 3610**

Electronics and Electrical Equipment; Automotive **3575, 3623**

Electronics and Engine Performance; Automotive **3624, 3702**

Electronics and Power Accessories, 1988-1991 Ford/Chrysler/Jeep/Eagle; Chilton's Guide to Chassis **918, 935, 943, 952, 972, 991, 1002, 1019, 1158, 1161, 1164, 1167, 1292, 1303, 1317, 1332, 1344, 1359, 1365, 1376, 1388, 1432, 1443, 1461, 1478, 1493, 1596, 1605, 1613, 1621, 1630**

Electronics and Power Accessories Service Manual, 1987-89: Motor-Age Professional Mechanic's Edition; Chilton's Chassis **3234, 3630, 3717**

Electronics, and Sensors Technology; Displays, **3255, 3640**

Electronics; Automotive Engine **3627, 3703, 3786**

Electronics, Computers; Auto Electricity, **3563, 3607**

Electronics; Convergence 1988: Proceedings of the International Congress on Transportation **3637**

Electronics Diagnostic Manual Ford Cars and Trucks 1984-1988: Motor-Age Professional Mechanic's Edition; Chilton's Professional **1304, 1318, 1333, 1345, 1366, 1377, 1390, 1444, 1462, 1479, 1494**

Electronics Explained, Vols. 1-5; Automotive **3625**

Electronics Market; Non-Entertainment Automotive **3656**

Electronics Market Trends Guide; Mobile **4224**

Electronics Reliability; Automotive **3626**

Electronics; Understanding Automotive **3662**

Elite Cars **4243**

Emerald Valley Chapter—Newsletter [Oregon]; Pontiac-Oakland Club International, **2081, 2122, 2160, 2201, 2245, 2285, 2322, 2357, 2392, 2431, 2467**

Emerald Valley Chapter [Oregon]; Pontiac-Oakland Club International, **2096, 2137, 2175, 2217, 2263, 2300, 2337, 2372, 2407, 2446, 2482**

Emission Control: Automotive Catalysts; Worldwide **3691, 3692**

Emission Control Manual 1992: Motor Age Professional Mechanic's Edition; Chilton's **3670**

Emission Controls Application Guide 1966-1992: Update; Chilton's **3671**

Emission Controls; Fuel Systems and **3681, 3801**

Emission Diagnosis and Service Manual, 1988: Import Cars and Trucks; Chilton's Tune-up **3535, 3674, 4309**

Emission Diagnosis Tune-up and Service Manual 1988 Import Cars and Trucks: Motor-Age Professional Mechanic's Edition **3537, 3678, 4037, 4143, 4313**

Emission Diagnosis, Tune-Up and Vacuum Diagrams 1984-87; Chilton's Guide to **3534, 3672, 4132**

Emission Diagnostic and Service Manual, Vacuum Circuit, 1984-1987—Domestic Car: Motor-Age Professional Mechanic's Edition; Chilton's U.S. **3536, 3675**

Emission Diagnostic and Service Manual, Vacuum Circuit, 1984-1987 Import Cars and Truck: Motor-Age Professional Mechanic's Edition; Chilton's IMP **3673, 4134, 4305**

Emissions Control; Recent Trends in Automotive **3688**

Emissions; Gaseous Fuels: Technology, Performance, and **3682, 3824**

Emissions; The Measurement and Control of Diesel Particulate **3551, 3684**

Emissions: Misfueling, Catalyst Deactivation and Alternative Catalyst **3679**

Emissions: Particulate Studies and Transient Cycle Testing; Diesel Exhaust **3544, 3676**

Emissions Research in Japan; New Diesel Engines, Combustion and **3554, 3686, 3758, 4157**

The Encyclopedia of American Supercars **4244**

Energy Demand Analysis and Alternative Fuels **3821**

Engine and Advanced Component Design; New **3269, 3759**

Engine Assembly; Diesel Mechanics II: **3547**

Engine Builder's Supplier Directory; Performance Racing **3059**

Engine Control and Fuel Injection Management; Recent Developments in Electronic **3658, 3765, 3813**

Engine Controls 1984-1988: Import Cars and Trucks; Chilton's Guide to Fuel Injection and Electronic **3634, 3724, 3793, 4133, 4304**

Engine Controls, 1988-90; Chilton's Guide to Fuel Injection and Electronic **3635, 3794**

Engine Controls Manual, 1988-90—Domestic Cars and Trucks: Motor-Age Professional Mechanic's Edition; Chilton's Electronic **3632, 3719, 4301**

Engine Coolants, Cooling System Materials and Testing; Worldwide Trends in **3770, 4109**

Engine Dealers-Gasoline Directory **3004**

Engine Electronics; Automotive **3627, 3703, 3786**

Engine; How to Overhaul an **3747**

Engine; The Internal Combustion **3751**

Engine Management and Driveline Controls; Automotive Electronic **3556, 3622**

Engine Management and Driveline Controls; Developments in Electronic **3290, 3558, 3639, 3732**

Engine Management; Bosch Fuel Injection and **3710, 3792**

Engine Management; New Developments in Electronic **3266, 3654, 3757**

Engine Oil Effects on Vehicle Fuel Economy **4171**

Engine Oils; Multicylinder Test Sequences for Evaluating Automotive **4180**

Engine Operation; High-Temperature, High-Shear (HTHS) Oil Viscosity: Measurement and Relationship to **3744, 4174**

Engine Overhaul; Foreign Car **3738, 4146**

Engine Performance and Tune-Up **3735, 4038**

Engine Performance; Automotive Electronics and **3624, 3702**

Engine; Problems of Internal Combustion **3764**

Engine Rebuilders Association—Technical Bulletin; Automotive **3704**

Engine Repair and Overhaul; Automotive **3705**

Engine Repair and Rebuilding; Automotive **3706**

Engine Repair Owners Workshop Manual; Haynes Small **3743**

Engine Tune Up; How to Do a Major **3746**

Engineering and Litigation; Automotive **3288, 3402**

Engineering; Automotive **3287**

Engineering Viewpoint; A Study of the Toyota Production System from an Industrial **3292**

Engines and Electrical Systems; Motor Auto **3601, 3756**

Engines, Combustion and Emissions Research in Japan; New Diesel **3554, 3686, 3758, 4157**

Engines; Deposit Formation in Gasoline Fuel Injected **3730, 3795**

Engines for Automobiles, Small Trucks and Small Tractors; Diesel **3543, 4311**

Engines; Fuel Alternatives for S.I. and Diesel **3550, 3741, 3822**

Engines; Fuel Economy in Road Vehicles Powered by Spark Ignition **3742, 4117**

Engines, Fuels, and Lubricants: Perspectives on the Future **3736, 3799, 4172**

Engines; Lean Burn **3752**

Engines, Lubricating and, Cooling Systems **3737, 4173**

Engines: Maintenance and Repair; Automotive **3707, 3982**

Engines; Modern Fuel for Modern Diesel **3552, 3828**

Engines-Rebuilding and Exchanging Directory **3141**

Engines; Small **3766**

Enzo Ferrari: The Man and the Machine **3321**

Escort and Mercury Lynx Owners Manual Workshop Manual, No. 789: 1981-1988; Haynes Ford **1348, 1853**

Escort-EXP and Mercury Lynx-LN7, 1981-1989: Shop Manual; Ford **1346, 1851**

Europe, U.S., Japan to 1990; Auto Industries of **3353**

European Car **106, 110, 114, 118, 123, 129, 133, 137, 168, 178, 188, 198, 208, 1173, 1196, 1219, 1242, 1265, 1569, 1585, 1776, 1783, 1791, 1799, 1807, 1815, 1822, 2495, 2523, 2544, 2567, 2711, 2722, 2732, 2743, 2755, 2766, 2774, 2785, 2794, 2804**

Excel: 1986-1989; Haynes Hyundai **1562**

Exhaust Analyzer; Infrared **3683**

Exhaust Clarification; Present and Future Automotive Fuels: Performance and **3687, 3811, 3830**

Exhaust News **3680**

Exhaust Systems; Automotive Fuel, Cooling, Lubrication, and **3667, 3788, 4095, 4167**

Exhaust Systems; Tune Up America: Replacing **3690**

Exotic Cars of the World: Fabulous Ferraris **1174, 1197, 1220, 1243, 1266**

Exterior Panels; Plastics in Automobile Bumper Systems and **3273, 3527**

Exterior Panels; Plastics in Automobiles: Bumper Systems, Interior Trim, Instrument Panels and **3238, 3275, 3528, 4165**

F

Fabrics; New Development and Requirements for Automotive **3264**

Fabrics; New Development in Automotive Fibers and **3265**

Fabulous Mustangs and Exotic Fords **1399**

Fantasy Cars **1175, 1198, 1221, 1244, 1267, 1640, 1648, 1654, 2496, 2524, 2545, 2568**

Far East Auto Owners Association **2852**

Far East Auto Owners Association—Newsletter **4144**

Fast Facts **4245**

Fender Repair; Tune Up America: Body and **3496**

Ferrari Club Magazine **1176, 1199, 1222, 1245, 1268**

Ferrari Club of America **1191, 1214, 1237, 1260, 1285**

Ferrari Club of America—Bulletin **1177, 1200, 1223, 1246, 1269**

Ferrari Club of America—Membership Roster **1178, 1201, 1224, 1247, 1270**

Ferrari Club of America, Northwest Region **1192, 1215, 1238, 1261, 1286**

Ferrari; The Complete Book of **1172, 1195, 1218, 1241, 1264**

Ferrari Data Bank **1193, 1216, 1239, 1262, 1287**

Ferrari: Forty Years on the Road **1179, 1202, 1225, 1248, 1271**

Ferrari; Great Marques **1188, 1211, 1234, 1257, 1281**

Ferrari: Guide to Performance **1180, 1203, 1226, 1249, 1272**

Ferrari Index **1181, 1204, 1227, 1250, 1273**

Ferrari; Inside **1189, 1212, 1235, 1258, 1282**

Ferrari Journal **1182, 1205, 1228, 1251, 1274**

Ferrari, Mercedes-Benz, Porsche—The Greatest of the Survivors Series; Four for the Road: Corvette, **822, 1187, 1210, 1233, 1256, 1280, 1777, 1784, 1792, 1800, 1808, 1816, 2497, 2525, 2546, 2569**

Ferrari North America **4356**

Ferrari Owners Club **1194, 1217, 1240, 1263, 1288**

Ferrari Owners Club—Directory and Yearbook **1183, 1206, 1229, 1252, 1275**

Ferrari Owners Club—Newsletter **1184, 1207, 1230, 1253, 1276**

Ferrari Register **1185, 1208, 1231, 1254, 1277**

Ferrari; The Story of **3346, 4253**

Ferrari Testarossa **1278**

Ferrari: The Man and the Machine; Enzo **3321**

Ferrari: The Road Cars **1186, 1209, 1232, 1255, 1279**

Ferraris; Exotic Cars of the World: Fabulous **1174, 1197, 1220, 1243, 1266**

Fibers and Fabrics; New Development in Automotive 3265
Fiero 1984-1988; Pontiac 2187
Fiero Club; Worldwide 2227
Fiero Owner 2192, 2193
Fiero Owners Club of America 2213
Fiero Owners Workshop Manual, No. 1232: 1984-1988;
    Haynes Pontiac 2186
Fiero Secrets 2194
Fifty Years of American Automobile, 1939-1989 3322
File; Slapper and 3491
Filter Manufacturers Council—Technical Bulletin 4194
Filters and Lube; Tune Up America: Oil Change, 4187
Finger Lakes Chapter [New York]; Pontiac-Oakland
    Club, 2093, 2134, 2172, 2214, 2260, 2297, 2334, 2369,
    2404, 2443, 2479
Finger Lakes News [New York] 2076, 2116, 2154, 2195,
    2239, 2279, 2316, 2352, 2387, 2425, 2462
Fins, Chrome, and Steel 4145
Fireball Flash 231, 267, 302, 335, 368, 408, 444, 480, 516,
    550, 584
Fireball News 232, 268, 303, 336, 369, 409, 445, 481, 517,
    551, 585
Firebird, 1982-90: Repair and Tuneup Guide; Chilton's 2230
Firebird, 1982-1987: Super Shop Manual; Camaro and 735,
    2229
Firebird Club; National 2259
Firebird Owners Workshop Manual, No. 867: 1982-1989;
    Haynes Pontiac 2233
Firebird Trans Am Shop Manual, 1982-1987; Camaro 228
    and 734, 2228
Firenza, Cadillac Cimarron, Pontiac 6000, 1982-88; Chilton's
    Chevrolet Cavalier, Buick Skyhawk, Olds 502, 638, 765,
    1978, 2106
Firenza, Pontiac J-2000, Sunbird Shop Manual, 1982-87; GMC
    J Cars: Buick Skyhawk, Cadillac Cimarron, Chevrolet
    Cavalier, Oldsmobile 504, 640, 767, 1980, 2418
Fix It/Get the Basics 4039
Fix It/Running and Riding Smooth 4040
Fix It Series: Keep Your Car Cool 4041
Fixin' Facts News 4042
Florida Automotive Directory 2911, 2952, 3005, 3081, 3142
Fluid Conductors and Connectors 3882
The Flying Lady 2630, 2635, 2640
FOMOCO Owners Club 1301, 1315, 1330, 1341, 1357,
    1364, 1373, 1386, 1428, 1440, 1459, 1474, 1489, 1507,
    1673, 1686, 1698, 1830, 1840, 1848, 1858, 1866, 1876,
    1883, 1888, 1892
FOMOCO Owners Club—Newsletter 1296, 1310, 1325,
    1336, 1350, 1360, 1368, 1381, 1400, 1434, 1452, 1466,
    1484, 1500, 1666, 1679, 1691, 1827, 1837, 1855, 1863,
    1873, 1880, 1886, 1890
For Vetts Only 821
Ford 1896-1990; Standard Catalog of 1299, 1313, 1328,
    1339, 1354, 1363, 1371, 1384, 1424, 1438, 1456, 1470,
    1487, 1504
Ford Aerostar, 1985-1990; Chilton's 1289
Ford Aerostar Mini-Vans Owners Workshop Manual, No.
    1476: 1986-1990; Haynes 1294
Ford and His Horseless Carriage; Model T Man from Michigan,
    America: Henry 3333
Ford and Mercury Full-Size Owners Workshop Manual, No.
    754: 1975-1987; Haynes 1379, 1496, 1835, 1844
Ford Cars and Trucks 1984-1988: Motor-Age Professional
    Mechanic's Edition; Chilton's Professional Electronics
    Diagnostic Manual 1304, 1318, 1333, 1345, 1366, 1377,
    1390, 1444, 1462, 1479, 1494
Ford/Chrysler/Jeep/Eagle; Chilton's Guide to Chassis
    Electronics and Power Accessories, 1988-1991 918, 935,
    943, 952, 972, 991, 1002, 1019, 1158, 1161, 1164, 1167,
    1292, 1303, 1317, 1332, 1344, 1359, 1365, 1376, 1388,
    1432, 1443, 1461, 1478, 1493, 1596, 1605, 1613, 1621,
    1630
Ford Club of America, Inc.; Performance 1358, 1431, 1441,
    1475, 1508
Ford Enthusiast Magazine 1351, 1401, 1435, 1453, 1467,
    1501

Ford Escort and Mercury Lynx Owners Manual Workshop
    Manual, No. 789: 1981-1988; Haynes 1348, 1853
Ford Escort-EXP and Mercury Lynx-LN7, 1981-1989: Shop
    Manual 1346, 1851
Ford Four-Wheel Drive Bronco and F-Series Pickups, 1969-
    1987 1305, 1319
Ford II; Henry: Life of Henry 3328
Ford: Including Lincoln-Mercury: Essential Service Information
    for Owners and Mechanics; Your 1300, 1314, 1329, 1340,
    1356, 1372, 1385, 1427, 1458, 1473, 1488, 1506, 1672,
    1685, 1697, 1839, 1847, 1857, 1865, 1875, 1882
Ford Legends 1402
Ford, Lincoln, Mercury Car Repair and Tune-Up Guide: 1972-
    1987 1293, 1306, 1320, 1334, 1347, 1378, 1391, 1463,
    1480, 1495, 1661, 1677, 1689, 1834, 1843, 1852, 1860,
    1869, 1878
Ford-Lincoln-Mercury Club of Florida—Newsletter 1297,
    1311, 1326, 1337, 1352, 1361, 1369, 1382, 1403, 1436,
    1454, 1468, 1485, 1502, 1667, 1680, 1692, 1828, 1838,
    1846, 1856, 1864, 1874, 1881, 1887, 1891
Ford-Lincoln-Mercury Full-Size, 1968-1988; Chilton's 1374,
    1490, 1659, 1675, 1688, 1832, 1842
Ford-Mercury Front Wheel Drive 1981-1987; Chilton 1342,
    1476, 1850, 1868
Ford; Motor Auto Repair 1983-1989 1295, 1309, 1323,
    1335, 1349, 1367, 1380, 1395, 1433, 1450, 1465, 1483,
    1498
Ford Motor Co. 4357
Ford Mustang and Mercury Capri 1979-1987: Includes Turbo
    Shop Manual 1392
Ford Mustang and Mercury Capri (In-Line) Owners Workshop
    Manual, No. 654: 1979-1990; Haynes 1393
Ford Mustang and Mercury Capri (V-6 and V-8) Owners
    Workshop Manual, No. 558: 1979-1989; Haynes 1394
Ford/Mustang Buyer's Guide 1404
Ford-O-Gram 1298, 1312, 1327, 1338, 1353, 1362, 1370,
    1383, 1405, 1437, 1455, 1469, 1486, 1503
Ford Pick-Ups and Bronco Owners Workshop Manual, No.
    880; Haynes 1308, 1448
Ford Pickups: 1969-1987 Shop Manual 1445
Ford Pickups and Bronco 1987-1990 1307, 1446
Ford Ranger and Bronco II 1983-1988: Includes Diesel and
    Four-Wheel Drive Shop Manual 1321, 1447
Ford Ranger and Bronco II Owners Workshop Manual, No.
    1026: 1983-1989; Haynes 1322, 1449
Ford Repair Manual 1980-1987; Chilton's 1290, 1302, 1316,
    1331, 1343, 1375, 1387, 1442, 1460, 1477, 1491
Ford; Super 1355, 1426, 1439, 1457, 1471, 1505
Ford Taurus and Mercury Sable Owners Workshop Manual,
    No. 1421: 1986-1991; Haynes 1464, 1861
Ford; Taurus: The Making of the Car That Saved 1472
Ford Tempo and Mercury Topaz, 1984-1987 1481, 1870
Ford Tempo-Mercury Topaz Owners Workshop Manual, No.
    1418: 1984-1989; Haynes 1482, 1871
Ford: The Complete History 3323
Ford: The Mark of a Man; Henry 3326
Ford: The Men and the Machine 3324
Ford Thunderbird and Mercury Cougar, No. 1338: 1983-1988;
    Haynes 1497
Ford Thunderbird, Mercury Cougar, Lincoln Continental-Mark
    VII, 1980-1987; Chilton's 1492, 1660, 1676, 1833
Ford Vans, 1961-1988; Chilton's 1291
Ford's America; Henry 3327
Fords; Fabulous Mustangs and Exotic 1399
Fords [Mercury Capri]; The Sporting 1829
Ford's Spectacular Comeback; Reinventing the Wheels: 3340,
    3386
Foreign Automotive Companies in the United States; Directory
    of 2951, 3139
Foreign Car Engine Overhaul 3738, 4146
Foreign Car Haters Club of America 2853
Foreign Car Prices; Edmund's 3201
Foreign Interchange Manual 4147
Ft. Worth [Texas]; Mercedes-Benz Club of 1782, 1789, 1797,
    1805, 1813, 1821, 1826
Fossil Fuels; Petroleum Products, Lubricants, and 3829, 4183

Four By Four Pickups and Vans Year Buying Guide 3206
Four for the Road: Corvette, Ferrari, Mercedes-Benz,
    Porsche—The Greatest of the Survivors Series 822, 1187,
    1210, 1233, 1256, 1280, 1777, 1784, 1792, 1800, 1808,
    1816, 2497, 2525, 2546, 2569
4-Runner, 1984-88; Toyota Pick-ups and 2667, 2703
4-Runner Service Manual: 1978-1988 Including Gasoline,
    Diesel, and Turbo Diesel, 4-cylinder and 6-cylinder Engines;
    Toyota Pickup, 2668, 2704
Four Wheel and Off Road 3773, 4229, 4314
4 Wheel & Off Road; Petersen's 3783, 4237, 4323
4WD Action 3771
4 Wheel Drive Association—Bulletin; National 3777
4 Wheel Drive Association-News; National 3778
Four Wheel Drive Association News; National 3779
4-Wheel Drive Tune-Up: 1967-1987; Chevrolet and
    GMC 725, 869, 906, 1509, 1517, 1529
Four Wheeler Magazine 3774, 4230, 4315
Four Wheeler Specials 3775, 4231, 4316
Fox Service Manual: 1987-1989, Including Wagon and Sport;
    Volkswagen 2730
Fram/Autolite Car Care 4043
Frame Shops Directory; Wheel Alignment/ 3180
Friends Magazine 714, 722, 732, 747, 762, 774, 783, 791,
    799, 823, 843, 850, 860, 867, 880, 887, 896, 903, 915
Friends of BMW 169, 179, 189, 199, 209
From the State Capitals: Motor Vehicle Regulation 3408
The Front End 4277
Front End; Brake and 3516
Front End—Buyers Guide to Brake Parts Issue; Brake
    and 3049
Front Suspension, Wheels and Tires; Brakes, Steering, 3520,
    4263, 4274, 4284, 4337
Front Wheel Drive, 1974-1990; Chilton's VW 2707, 2728,
    2738, 2750, 2761, 2780, 2791, 2800
Front Wheel Drive 1981-1987; Chilton Ford-Mercury 1342,
    1476, 1850, 1868
Front Wheel Drive 1981-1988; Chilton's Chrysler 951, 971
Front Wheel Drive Explained 3739
Front Wheel Drive: Transaxle Overhaul 3740, 4278
Fuel Alternative for North America into the 21st Century;
    Transportation 3831
Fuel Alternatives for S.I. and Diesel Engines 3550, 3741,
    3822
Fuel and Ignition Systems; Automotive 3787, 4112
Fuel and Induction System Deposits 3800
Fuel, Cooling, Lubrication, and Exhaust Systems;
    Automotive 3667, 3788, 4095, 4167
Fuel Economy; Automobile 3817
Fuel Economy; Engine Oil Effects on Vehicle 4171
Fuel Economy in Road Vehicles Powered by Spark Ignition
    Engines 3742, 4117
Fuel Economy; Motor Vehicle 3807
Fuel for Modern Diesel Engines; Modern 3552, 3828
Fuel Induction Systems; Tune-up Ignition and 3815, 4124
Fuel Injected Engines; Deposit Formation in Gasoline 3730,
    3795
Fuel Injection and Computer Systems; Domestic
    Electronic 3641, 3797
Fuel Injection and Electronic Engine Controls 1984-1988:
    Import Cars and Trucks; Chilton's Guide to 3634, 3724,
    3793, 4133, 4304
Fuel Injection and Electronic Engine Controls, 1988-90;
    Chilton's Guide to 3635, 3794
Fuel Injection and Engine Management; Bosch 3710, 3792
Fuel Injection; Electronic 3646, 3798
Fuel Injection Management; Recent Developments in Electronic
    Engine Control and 3658, 3765, 3813
Fuel Injection Systems; Bosch Electronic 3791
Fuel-Injection Troubleshooting Guide: Domestic Vehicles;
    Mitchell's Electronic 3650, 3805
Fuel-Injection Troubleshooting Guide: Import Vehicles;
    Mitchell's Electronic 3651, 3806, 4153
Fuel Injection; Troubleshooting Port 3814

Fuel, Lubricating and Cooling Systems; Automotive 3789,
    4096, 4168
Fuel, Lubrication, and Cooling Systems; Automotive 3818,
    4097, 4169
Fuel Methanol 3823
Fuel System; The Operation of the 3808
Fuel System; The Problems of the 3812
Fuel Systems and Carburetion; How to Restore 3804
Fuel Systems and Emission Controls 3681, 3801
Fuel Systems; Auto 3785
Fuels and IC Engines; Horning Commemorative Volume:
    Award Winning Papers on Mutual Adaption of 3745, 3825
Fuels, and Lubricants: Perspectives on the Future;
    Engines, 3736, 3799, 4172
Fuels; Energy Demand Analysis and Alternative 3821
Fuels for S.I. Engines; Alternate 3693, 3816
Fuels: Performance and Exhaust Clarification; Present and
    Future Automotive 3687, 3811, 3830
Fuels: Technology, Performance, and Emissions;
    Gaseous 3682, 3824
Fundamentals of Electricity and Automotive Electrical
    Systems 3595

G

Garden State Chapter—Newsletter [New Jersey]; Pontiac-
    Oakland Club International, 2082, 2123, 2161, 2202, 2246,
    2286, 2323, 2358, 2393, 2432, 2468
Gas Flow: Techniques for Low-Budget Performance Tuning;
    Practical 3810
Gas Savers Guide 3802
Gaseous Fuels: Technology, Performance, and Emissions 3682,
    3824
Gasoline and Automotive Service Dealers Association—Trade
    Directory and Buyers Guide 3143, 3144
Gasoline Directory; Engine Dealers- 3004
Gear Oils—Grease; Hydraulics— 4176
General Motors 8-Cylinder 254, 290, 392, 468, 738, 758,
    803, 853, 891, 911, 1515, 1525, 1533, 1961, 1972, 2231
General Motors Corp. 4358
General Motors in the 1980s; Rude Awakening: 3342, 3387
Generators Repair Directory; Automotive Alternators
    and 3129
[Georgia]; Alfa Romeo Owners Club, Atlanta Chapter 27, 52,
    77

Georgia Automotive Directory **2912, 2953, 3006, 3082, 3145**

Georgia Chapter; Pontiac-Oakland Club International, **2097, 2138, 2176, 2218, 2264, 2301, 2338, 2373, 2408, 2447, 2483**

Get Your Buick Fixed Right **217, 255, 291, 324, 357, 393, 433, 469, 503, 538, 573**

Get Your Cadillac Fixed Right **607, 624, 639, 654, 668, 682, 696**

Get Your Chevrolet-GMC Fixed Right **712, 718, 728, 739, 759, 766, 779, 788, 795, 804, 838, 846, 854, 865, 875, 883, 892, 899, 912, 1511, 1516, 1520, 1526**

Get Your Oldsmobile Fixed Right **1927, 1933, 1937, 1949, 1962, 1973, 1979, 1989, 1994, 2000**

Get Your Pontiac Fixed Right **2070, 2109, 2148, 2185, 2232, 2274, 2310, 2347, 2382, 2417, 2456**

Getting a Better Buy in a Used Car **3883**

Glass-Auto, Plate, Window Directory **3146**

Glass City Chapter [Ohio]; Buick Club of America, **243, 279, 314, 347, 381, 421, 458, 492, 528, 563, 596**

Glossary of Automotive Terms **3884**

The Glossary of Automotive Terms **3885**

The Glove Box Auto Reviver **3435**

GM A-Cars Buick Century, Chevrolet Celebrity, Oldsmobile Cutlass Ciera, Pontiac 6000, 1982-87: Shop Manual **218, 780, 1938, 1950, 2110**

GMC 4-Wheel Drive Tune-Up: 1967-1987; Chevrolet and **725, 869, 906, 1509, 1517, 1529**

GMC C-Series, Pickups, and Suburbans: 1967-1987: Includes Suburbans Shop Manual; Chevy and **907, 1530**

GMC Fixed Right; Get Your Chevrolet- **712, 718, 728, 739, 759, 766, 779, 788, 795, 804, 838, 846, 854, 865, 875, 883, 892, 899, 912, 1511, 1516, 1520, 1526**

GMC J Cars: Buick Skyhawk, Cadillac Cimarron, Chevrolet Cavalier, Oldsmobile Firenza, Pontiac J-2000, Sunbird Shop Manual, 1982-87 **504, 640, 767, 1980, 2418**

GMC Pick-ups and Suburban 1970-1987; Chilton's Chevrolet/ **874, 910, 1524, 1532**

GMC Pick-Ups Owners Workshop Manual, No. 420: 1967-1987; Haynes Chevrolet and **876, 1512, 1527**

GMC Pickups, 1988-90; Haynes Chevy **877, 1513, 1528**

GMC S-15, and Olds Bravada, 1982-1990; Chevrolet S-10 Blazer, **730, 1514, 1928**

GMC S-15 Pickups 1982—90; Chevrolet S-10, **871, 1522**

GMC Safari, 1985-1990; Chevrolet Astro- **710, 1519**

GMC Safari; Chevrolet Astro and **709, 1518**

GMC Truck Division, General Motors Corp. **4359**

GMC Trucks, 1988-90; Chevrolet **870, 1521**

GMC Two Wheel Drive C and R-Series Pickups, Suburbans, and Vans, 1970-1987 (Gas and Diesel); Chevy and **908, 1531**

GMC Two-Wheel Drive Mid-Size S- and T-Pickups, Blazers, and Jimmy, 1982-1988 (Gas and Diesel); Chevy and **726, 872, 1510, 1523**

The Golden Age of the Automobile **3325**

Golf and Jetta (Including GTI); Improve and Modify Your VW **2740, 2752, 2763**

Golf and Jetta Service Manual: 1985-1989: Gasoline, Diesel, and Turbo Diesel, Including Golf, GT, Jetta GLI and 16V Models; GTI, **2739, 2751, 2762**

Grand Prix-Oldsmobile Cutlass-Buick Regal, 1988 Repair and Tune-up Guide; Pontiac **395, 1940, 1953, 1964, 2311**

Grease; Hydraulics—Gear Oils— **4176**

The Great American Pickup Trucks: Stylesetter, Workhorse, Sport Truck **4232, 4317**

Great American Station Wagon Owner's Association **2854**

Great Marques BMW **170, 180, 190, 200, 210**

Great Marques Cadillac **617, 632, 648, 662, 676, 690, 704**

Great Marques Ferrari **1188, 1211, 1234, 1257, 1281**

Great Marques Jaguar **1570, 1586**

Great Marques Mercedes-Benz **1778, 1785, 1793, 1801, 1809, 1817**

Great Marques Porsche **2498, 2526, 2547, 2570**

Grey Market Car; Risks and Rewards of Purchasing a **3936**

Ground Vehicle Lighting Manual **4079**

GS Club of America—GS National Directory; Buick **403**

GS Directory **370, 410, 446, 552**

GTI, Golf and Jetta Service Manual: 1985-1989: Gasoline, Diesel, and Turbo Diesel, Including Golf, GT, Jetta GLI and 16V Models **2739, 2751, 2762**

Guide to Auto Body Sheet Metal Repair **3480**

Guide to Mazda Miata MX-5 **1767**

Guide to New Cars **3207**

Guide to Radio Policy on Current Model Cars and Multi-Purpose Vehicles **4220, 4233**

Guide to Used Cars **3208**

H

Hall of Fame; Automotive **2840**

Hall of Shame; International Automotive **2856**

Hall of Shame—Newsletter; International Automotive **3368**

Hammer and Dolly **3481**

Handbook; Volvo 240 Series DL, GL, GLT and Turbo: 1975-1987—Service, Repair **2810**

Handling Automobile Warranty and Repossesion Cases **3409**

The Hartford Automobiler **3886**

Haynes Audi 4000 Owners Workshop Manual, No. 165: 1980-1987 **121**

Haynes Audi 5000, 1984-1988 **127**

Haynes Automobile Electrical Manual: A Comprehensive Guide **3596**

Haynes Automobile Electrical Manual No. 1654 **3597**

Haynes Body Repair and Painting Manual, No. 1479 **3482**

Haynes Buick Mid-size Models Owners Workshop Manual No. 627: 1974-1987 **219, 394**

Haynes Buick, Olds, Pontiac, Full-Size Models: 1970-90 **256, 292, 1974, 1990, 2001, 2149**

Haynes Chevrolet and GMC Pick-Ups Owners Workshop Manual, No. 420: 1967-1987 **876, 1512, 1527**

Haynes Chevrolet Camaro Owners Workshop Manual, No. 866: 1982-1990 **740**

Haynes Chevrolet Chevette-Pontiac T1000 Owners Workshop Manuals, No. 449: 1976-1987 **789, 2071**

Haynes Chevrolet Full-Size Sedans Owners Workshop Manual, No. 704: 1969-1990 **760, 768, 839**

Haynes Chevrolet Monte Carlo Owner's Manual, No. 626: 1970-1988 **855**

Haynes Chevrolet V-8 Vans Owners Workshop Manual No. 345, 1968-1989 **893**

Haynes Chevy GMC Pickups, 1988-90 **877, 1513, 1528**

Haynes Chrysler Mid-Size Cars Owners Workshop Manual, 1982-1989 **953, 973, 993**

Haynes Corvette Owners Workshop Manual, No. 1336: All Models 1984-1989 **805**

Haynes Dodge and Plymouth Vans Owners Workshop Manual, No. 349: 1971-1991 **1039, 1111, 1119, 2063**

Haynes Dodge Aries and Plymouth Reliant Owners Workshop Manual, 1981-1988 **1031, 2046**

Haynes Dodge Colt-Plymouth Champ FWD Owners Workshop Manual, No. 610: 1978-1987 **1054**

Haynes Dodge D-50 and Plymouth Arrow and Mitsubishi Pick-ups Owner's Workshop Manual, No. 556: 1979-1988 **1112**

Haynes Dodge Daytona and Chrysler Laser Owners Workshop Manual, No. 1140: 1984-1989 **1067**

Haynes Dodge Pick-ups Owner's Workshop Manuals, No. 912: 1974-1990 **1062, 1113**

Haynes Ford Aerostar Mini-Vans Owners Workshop Manual, No. 1476: 1986-1990 **1294**

Haynes Ford and Mercury Full-Size Owners Workshop Manual, No. 754: 1975-1987 **1379, 1496, 1835, 1844**

Haynes Ford Escort and Mercury Lynx Owners Manual Workshop Manual, No. 789: 1981-1988 **1348, 1853**

Haynes Ford Mustang and Mercury Capri (In-Line) Owners Workshop Manual, No. 654: 1979-1990 **1393**

Haynes Ford Mustang and Mercury Capri (V-6 and V-8) Owners Workshop Manual, No. 558: 1979-1989 **1394**

Haynes Ford Pick-Ups and Bronco Owners Workshop Manual, No. 880 **1308, 1448**

Haynes Ford Ranger and Bronco II Owners Workshop Manual, No. 1026: 1983-1989 **1322, 1449**

Haynes Ford Taurus and Mercury Sable Owners Workshop Manual, No. 1421: 1986-1990 **1464, 1861**

Haynes Ford Tempo-Mercury Topaz Owners Workshop Manual, No. 1418: 1984-1989 **1482, 1871**

Haynes Ford Thunderbird and Mercury Cougar, No. 1338: 1983-1988 **1497**

Haynes General Motor A-Cars Owner's Workshop Manual, No. 829 **220, 781, 1951, 2111**

Haynes General Motors J-Cars Owners Workshop Manual, No. 766: 1982-1989 **505, 769, 770, 1981, 2419, 2420**

Haynes Honda Prelude CVCC Owners Workshop Manuals, No 601: 1979-1989 **1555**

Haynes Hyundai Excel: 1986-1989 **1562**

Haynes Jeep Cherokee, 1984-1989 **1597**

Haynes Mazda B-Series Pick-ups Owners Workshop Manual, No. 267: 1972-1990 **1761**

Haynes Mazda RX-7 Owners Workshop Manual, No. 1419: 1986-1989 **1769**

Haynes Oldsmobile Cutlass Owners Workshop Manual, No. 658: 1974-1989 **1939, 1952, 1963**

Haynes Pontiac Fiero Owners Workshop Manual, No. 1232: 1984-1988 **2186**

Haynes Pontiac Firebird Owners Workshop Manual, No. 867: 1982-1989 **2233**

Haynes Porsche 911 Owners Workshop Manual, No. 264: 1965-1989 **2492**

Haynes Porsche 944 Owners Workshop Manual, No. 1027: 1983-1989 **2564**

Haynes Saab 900 Repair Manual, No. 980: 1979-1988 **2645**

Haynes Small Engine Repair Owners Workshop Manual **3743**

Haynes Toyota Camry Owners Workshop Manual, No. 1023: 1983-1990 **2670**

Haynes Toyota Corolla Owners Workshop Manual, No. 1025: 1984-1988 **2678**

Haynes Toyota MR2 Owners Workshop Repair Manual, No. 1339: All Models, 1985-1987 **2685**

Haynes Toyota Pick-up Owners Workshop Manual, No. 656: 1979-1990 **2701**

Heart of America Jaguar Club [Kansas] **1579, 1594**

Heart of America Jaguar Club—Newsletter **1571, 1587**

Heat Air Conditioning Manual; Auto **4086**

Heating, and Air Conditioning; Electrical Systems, **3593, 4104**

Heating and Air Conditioning Systems; Mitchell Automotive **4105**

Heating and Cooling; Automotive **4098**

Heating Manual, 1989-91: Professional Mechanics Edition; Chilton's Guide to Air Conditioning and **4101**

Heating Manual 1990-92: Motor Age Professional Mechanics Edition; Chilton's Guide to Air Conditioning and **4102**

Hemmings Motor News **3209**

Henry Ford: The Mark of a Man **3326**

Henry Ford's America **3327**

Henry: Life of Henry Ford II **3328**

Hi-Tech Performance; Turbo and **3294, 4330**

High Performance Mopar **923, 957, 977, 1006**

High Performance Pontiac **2117, 2155, 2196, 2240, 2280, 2317, 2426**

High-Temperature, High-Shear (HTHS) Oil Viscosity: Measurement and Relationship to Engine Operation **3744, 4174**

Historians—Directory; Society of Automotive **3343**

Historians—Pioneer Chapter New York State; Society of Automotive **2866**

Historians; Society of Automotive **2865**

Historians, Wisconsin Chapter; Society of Automotive **2867**

History Collection of the Detroit Public Library: A Simplified Guide to Its Holdings; Automotive **3309**

History Review; Automotive **3310**

Home & Away **3887**

Home & Away (Chicago Edition) Illinois **3888**

Home & Away (Hoosier Edition) Indiana **3889**

Home & Away (Minnesota Edition) **3890**

Home & Away (Ohio Edition) **3891**

Home Mechanix **3892**

Honda, 1973-1988; Chilton's **1534, 1541, 1547, 1554**

Honda Accord **1535**

Honda: An American Success Story **3329, 3365**

Honda Car Club **1539, 1545, 1552, 1559**

Honda Car Club Newsletter **1537, 1543, 1550, 1557**

Honda CRX Shop Manual, 1983-1987 **1548**

Honda; Mitchell Glove Compartment Companion for Your **1536, 1542, 1549, 1556**

Honda Motor: The Men, the Management and the Machines **3366, 4148**

Honda Plant; American Made: Marysville and the **3350**

Honda Prelude CVCC Owners Workshop Manuals, No 601: 1979-1989; Haynes **1555**

Hondacar **1538, 1544, 1551, 1558**

Hondacar International **2, 4, 6, 8, 1540, 1546, 1553, 1560**

(Hoosier Edition) Indiana; Home & Away **3889**

Hoosier Mustang Club News [Indiana] **1406**

Horizon, TC3, Turismo and Scamp 1978-1987: Shop Manual; Dodge Omni, 024, Charger, Rampage, and Plymouth **1044, 1097, 2035, 2055**

Horning Commemorative Volume: Award Winning Papers on Mutual Adaption of Fuels and IC Engines **3745, 3825**

Hot Air **2077, 2118, 2156, 2197, 2241, 2281, 2318, 2353, 2388, 2427, 2463**

Hot Rod Annual **2887, 3007, 3053**

Hot Rod Magazine **4246**

Hot Truck **4318**

How the Automobile Works **3893**

How to Avoid Getting Mugged by Mr. Badwrench **3894**

How to Balance Wheels **4339**

How to Beat the Car Dealer at His Own Game: Buying a New or Used Car **3895**

How to Build Chrysler, Dodge, Plymouth **924, 938, 944, 958, 978, 995, 1020, 1027, 1032, 1040, 1045, 1055, 1063, 1068, 1077, 1081, 1085, 1093, 1098, 1106, 1114, 1120, 1125, 1129, 1137, 1152, 2016, 2020, 2024, 2031, 2036, 2040, 2047, 2051, 2056, 2064**

How to Buy a Car: The Essential Guide for Buying a New Car or Used Car **3896**

How to Buy a Used Car—How to Sell a Used Car, Two Books in One **3897**

How to Buy a Vehicle: Without Being Taken for a Ride **3898**

How to Buy & Maintain a Used Car: For the Non-Mechanical Person **3899, 4044**

How to Buy and Sell a Car by Long Distance **3900**

How to Buy Car Stereo **4221**

How to Buy Motor Oil **4175**

How to Chop Tops **3436**

How to Convert Your Vehicle to Propane **3826**

How to Deal on an Automobile **3901**

How to Do a Major Engine Tune Up **3746**

How to Do Electrical Systems **3598**

How to Import-Convert-Legalize Your Investment Automobile **3410**

How to Keep Your Subaru Alive: A Manual of Step-by-Step Procedures for the Compleat Idiot **2654, 2656, 2658, 2659, 2660, 2662, 2664, 2666**

How to Keep Your Toyota Pick-Up Alive: A Manual of Step by Step Procedures for the Compleat Idiot **2702**

How to Outsmart the New-Car Salesman: A Legendary Salesman Reveals the Secrets to Negotiating a Great Deal **3902**

How to Overhaul a Carburetor **3803**

How to Overhaul an Engine **3747**

How to Paint Your Car **3483**

How to Protect Yourself Against Automobile Theft **4207**

How to Rebuild Small Block Chevys **3748, 4045**

How to Rebuild Your Big-Block Chevy **3749, 4046**

How to Restore Fuel Systems and Carburetion **3804**

How to Restore Paintwork **3484**

How to Restore Wooden Body Framing **3485**

How to Save Thousands on Auto Repair Through Simple Maintenance **4047**

How to Squeeze More Miles From Your Car **3903**

How to Test and Buy a Used Car **3904**

How to Use a Valve and Valve Seat Refacer **3750**
Hydramatic Transmission; Problems of **3763**
The Hydraulic Brake System Explained **3522**
Hydraulics—Gear Oils—Grease **4176**
Hyundai 1985-1987; Chilton's **1561**
Hyundai Excel: 1986-1989; Haynes **1562**
Hyundai Motor America **4360**

I

IC Engines; Horning Commemorative Volume: Award Winning
   Papers on Mutual Adaption of Fuels and **3745, 3825**
Idaho/Montana/North Dakota/South Dakota/Wyoming
   Automotive Directory **2913, 2954, 3008, 3083, 3147**
Identification of Parts Failure **4195**
Ignition and Electrical Systems; Petersen's Basic **3602, 4121**
Ignition and Fuel Induction Systems; Tune-up **3815, 4124**
Ignition; Distributorless **4114**
Ignition Explained; Electronic **3647, 4115**
The Ignition System Explained **4118**
Ignition Systems; Automotive Electronic and Computer
   Controlled **3573, 3620, 4111**
Ignition Systems; Automotive Fuel and **3787, 4112**
Ignition Systems: Diagnosis and Repair; Automotive **3533,
   4113**
Ignition Troubleshooting Guide: Domestic Vehicles; Mitchell's
   Electronic **3652, 4119**
Ignition Troubleshooting Guide: Import Vehicles; Mitchell's
   Electronic **3653, 4120, 4154**
Ignition Tune-Up; Advanced Electronic **3964, 4110**
Ignition Tune Up; Electronic **3648, 4036, 4116**
[Illinois]; Alfa Romeo Owners Club, Chicago Chapter—
   Membership Directory **13, 38, 63**
Illinois Automotive Directory **2914, 2955, 3009, 3084, 3148**
[Illinois]; Buick Club of America, Chicagoland Chapter **241,
   277, 312, 345, 379, 419, 456, 490, 526, 561, 594**
Illinois Chapter—Annual Roster; Pontiac-Oakland Club
   International, **2083, 2124, 2162, 2203, 2247, 2287, 2324,
   2359, 2394, 2433, 2469**
Illinois Newsletter **2078, 2119, 2157, 2198, 2242, 2282,
   2319, 2354, 2389, 2428, 2464**
Illustrated Camaro Buyer's Guide **748**
Illustrated Corvette Buyer's Guide **824**
Illustrated Jaguar Buyer's Guide **1572, 1588**
Illustrated Jeep Buyer's Guide **1600, 1608, 1616, 1624, 1633**
Illustrated Lamborghini Buyer's Guide **1641, 1649, 1655**
Illustrated Maserati Buyer's Guide **1722, 1728, 1734, 1740,
   1750**
Illustrated Mustang Buyer's Guide **1407**
Illustrated Oldsmobile Buyer's Guide **1929, 1934, 1941, 1954,
   1965, 1975, 1982, 1991, 1996, 2002**
Illustrated Porsche Buyer's Guide **2499, 2527, 2548, 2571**
Illustrated Rolls-Royce and Bentley Buyer's Guide **145, 150,
   155, 160, 2631, 2636, 2641**
Import Car Parts and Labor Guide 1982-89 **4149, 4196**
Import Car Parts and Labor Guide, 1987-1991: Motor Age
   Professional Mechanics Edition; Chilton's **4136, 4190**
Import Car Repair Manual 1982-87: Motor Age Professional
   Mechanics Edition; Chilton's **4012, 4137**
Import Car Repair Manual 1987-91: Motor Age Professional
   Mechanics Edition; Chilton's **4013**
Import Car Repair Manual, 1987-91: Motor Age Professional
   Mechanic's Edition; Chilton's **4138**
Import Car Repair Manual 1987-91: Motor Age Professional
   Mechanics Edition; Chilton's **4139**
Import Car Repair Manual 1988-92; Chilton's **4014, 4140**
Import Car Service Manual, 1980-1987: Motor-Age
   Professional Mechanic's Edition; Chilton's **4015, 4141**
Import Car Wiring Diagrams Manual, 1987-88: Motor-Age
   Professional Mechanic's Edition; Chilton's **3587, 4142**
Import Cars and Truck: Motor-Age Professional Mechanic's
   Edition; Chilton's IMP Emission Diagnostic and Service
   Manual, Vacuum Circuit, 1984-1987 **3673, 4134, 4305**

Import Cars and Trucks—1988-1990: Motor Age Professional
   Mechanic's Edition; Chilton's Electronic Chassis Controls
   Manual, **3631, 3718, 4130, 4300**
Import Cars and Trucks; Chilton's Guide to Brakes, Steering
   and Suspension 1980-1987: Domestic and **3521, 4131,
   4264, 4275, 4302**
Import Cars and Trucks; Chilton's Guide to Fuel Injection and
   Electronic Engine Controls 1984-1988: **3634, 3724, 3793,
   4133, 4304**
Import Cars and Trucks; Chilton's Tune-up Emission Diagnosis
   and Service Manual, 1988: **3535, 3674, 4309**
Import Cars and Trucks: Motor-Age Professional Mechanic's
   Edition; Emission Diagnosis Tune-up and Service Manual
   1988 **3537, 3678, 4037, 4143, 4313**
Import Service **4048, 4150**
Import Update Newsletter **4151**
Import Vehicles; Mitchell's Electronic Fuel-Injection
   Troubleshooting Guide: **3651, 3806, 4153**
Import Vehicles; Mitchell's Electronic Ignition Troubleshooting
   Guide: **3653, 4120, 4154**
Imported Car Reports **4152**
Imported Cars and Light Trucks; Aftermarket for **3239, 4125,
   4290**
Improve and Modify Your VW Golf and Jetta (Including
   GTI) **2740, 2752, 2763**
In the Fast Lane **749**
Indiana Automotive Directory **2915, 2956, 3010, 3085, 3149**
Indiana Chapter—Newsletter; Buick GS Club of
   America, **404, 546**
[Indiana]; Hoosier Mustang Club News **1406**
[Indiana, Michigan]; Michiana Mustangs—Newsletter **1408**
Induction System Deposits; Fuel and **3800**
Industrial Illumination; Automotive Displays and **3615**
Infiniti Division, Nissan Motors Corp. in USA **4361**
Information Council; Automotive **2841**
Information Systems and On-Board Electronics; Electronic
   Displays, **3258, 3645, 4161**
Information Systems; Electronic Displays and **3257, 3644,
   4160**
Infrared Exhaust Analyzer **3683**
Inland Automobile Association Washington State **2855**
Inside Ferrari **1189, 1212, 1235, 1258, 1282**
Inspection Stations Directory; Automobile **3120**
Installation News **4222**
Installation News—Fact Book Issue **3054**
Instrument Panels and Exterior Panels; Plastics in Automobiles:
   Bumper Systems, Interior Trim, **3238, 3275, 3528, 4165**
Instrument Panels: Design, Materials, and Manufacturing;
   Automotive **3247, 4159**
Instrument Panels, Trim, and Seating; Plastics in
   Automobile **3237, 3274, 4164**
Instrumentation Service Manual 1980-1987: Motor Age
   Professional Mechnanic's Edition; Electronic **3649, 4162**
Interior Restoration; Car **3432**
Interior Trim, Instrument Panels and Exterior Panels; Plastics in
   Automobiles: Bumper Systems, **3238, 3275, 3528, 4165**
The Internal Combustion Engine **3751**
Internal Combustion Engine; Problems of **3764**
International **3367**
International Automobile Manufacturers; Association of **2835**
International Automotive Hall of Shame **2856**
International Automotive Hall of Shame—Newsletter **3368**
International Camaro Club **755**
International Directory of Automotive Literature
   Collectors **2888**
International Mobile Air Conditioning Association—
   Membership/Industry Contact Directory **3055**
International Motor Press Directory **2889**
Introductory Auto Mechanics **3905**
Introductory Automechanics **3906**
Iowa Automotive Directory **2916, 2957, 3011, 3086, 3150**
Is There Enough Business to Go Around? Overcapacity in the
   Auto Industry **3369**
Italian Oddities; Registry of **2862**

J

Jaguar 6 Cylinder **1563, 1581**
Jaguar Association; Classic **1578, 1593**
Jaguar Association—News and Technical Bulletin;
   Classic **1567, 1583**
Jaguar Buyer's Guide; Illustrated **1572, 1588**
Jaguar Cars Inc. **4362**
Jaguar Club [Kansas]; Heart of America **1579, 1594**
Jaguar Club—Newsletter; Heart of America **1571, 1587**
Jaguar Clubs of North America **1580, 1595**
Jaguar; Great Marques **1570, 1586**
Jaguar Journal **1573, 1589**
Jaguar: Roaring to Victory **1574, 1590**
The Jaguar Scrapbook **1575, 1591**
Jaguar Sports Cars **1576, 1592**
Jaguar XJ-6 and XJ-12 Series 3 **1564**
The Jaguar XJ-6 Series 1, 2.8, and 4.2 Litre Workshop
   Manual **1565**
Jaguar XJ-6 Series 2 **1566**
The Jaguar XJ-6 Series 3 Driver's Handbook **1577**
Jaguar XJ-S Workshop Manual **1582**
Japan Automobile Manufacturers Association, Washington
   Office **2857**
Japan; The Motor Industry of **3377**
Japan; New Diesel Engines, Combustion and Emissions
   Research in **3554, 3686, 3758, 4157**
Japan to 1990; Auto Industries of Europe, U.S., **3353**
Japan Transportation Scan **3370**
Japanese Auto Industries in Transition: The Report of the
   Joint U.S.-Japan Automotive Study; The American
   and **3347**
The Japanese Auto Industry and the U.S. Market **3371**
The Japanese Competition: Phase Two **3372**
Jeep 6-Cylinder **1598, 1606, 1614, 1622, 1632**
Jeep Buyer's Guide; Illustrated **1600, 1608, 1616, 1624,
   1633**
Jeep Cherokee, 1984-1989; Haynes **1597**
Jeep CJ 1945-1987; Chilton's **1631**
Jeep Club [Washington state]; Yakima Ridgerunners **1604,
   1612, 1620, 1629, 1638**
Jeep/Eagle; Chilton's Guide to Chassis Electronics and Power
   Accessories, 1988-1991 Ford/Chrysler/ **918, 935, 943,
   952, 972, 991, 1002, 1019, 1158, 1161, 1164, 1167, 1292,
   1303, 1317, 1332, 1344, 1359, 1365, 1376, 1388, 1432,
   1443, 1461, 1478, 1493, 1596, 1605, 1613, 1621, 1630**
Jeep/Eagle Div., Chrysler Corp. **4363**
Jeep: Mechanical Mule to People's Plaything **1601, 1609,
   1617, 1625, 1634**
Jeep: The Fifty Year History **1626, 1635**
Jeep Wagoneer-Comanche-Cherokee 1984-1991 **1599, 1607,
   1615, 1623**
Jersey Shore Chapter News [New Jersey] **233, 269, 304,
   337, 371, 411, 447, 482, 518, 553, 586**
Jetta (Including GTI); Improve and Modify Your VW Golf
   and **2740, 2752, 2763**
Jetta Service Manual: 1985-1989: Gasoline, Diesel, and Turbo
   Diesel, Including Golf, GT, Jetta GLI and 16V Models; GTI,
   Golf and **2739, 2751, 2762**
Jimmy, 1982-1988 (Gas and Diesel); Chevy and GMC Two-
   Wheel Drive Mid-Size S- and T-Pickups, Blazers, and **726,
   872, 1510, 1523**
Jobber Executive—Tool and Equipment Buyers Guide
   Issue **3056**
Jobber Retailer Aftermarket Manual **2890, 3012, 3057**
Jobber Topics—Marketing/Directory Issue **2891, 3013, 3058**
Journey With Olds **1922, 1930, 1935, 1942, 1955, 1966,
   1976, 1983, 1992, 1997, 2003**

K

[Kansas and Missouri]; Pontiac-Oakland Club International,
   Kansas City Arrowhead Chapter **2099, 2140, 2178, 2220,
   2266, 2303, 2340, 2375, 2410, 2449, 2485**

[Kansas and Missouri]; Pontiac-Oakland Club International,
   Kansas City Arrowhead Chapter—Directory **2086, 2127,
   2165, 2206, 2250, 2290, 2327, 2362, 2397, 2436, 2472**
Kansas Chapter; Buick Club of America, **245, 281, 316, 349,
   383, 423, 460, 494, 530, 565, 598**
Kansas Chapter—Directory; Pontiac-Oakland Club
   International, **2084, 2125, 2163, 2204, 2248, 2288, 2325,
   2360, 2395, 2434, 2470**
Kansas Chapter—Newsletter; Pontiac-Oakland Club
   International, **2085, 2126, 2164, 2205, 2249, 2289, 2326,
   2361, 2396, 2435, 2471**
Kansas Chapter; Pontiac-Oakland Club International, **2098,
   2139, 2177, 2219, 2265, 2302, 2339, 2374, 2409, 2448,
   2484**
Kansas City Arrowhead Chapter—Directory [Kansas and
   Missouri]; Pontiac-Oakland Club International, **2086, 2127,
   2165, 2206, 2250, 2290, 2327, 2362, 2397, 2436, 2472**
Kansas City Arrowhead Chapter [Kansas and Missouri];
   Pontiac-Oakland Club International, **2099, 2140, 2178,
   2220, 2266, 2303, 2340, 2375, 2410, 2449, 2485**
[Kansas]; Heart of America Jaguar Club **1579, 1594**
Kansas/Nebraska Automotive Directory **2917, 2958, 3014,
   3087, 3151**
Karl Benz **3291, 3330**
Keep It Running **4049**
Keepin' Track of Vettes **825**
Keeping Your Car Alive: A Guide to Preventive Automotive
   Maintenance **4050**
Kelley Blue Book Used Car Price Manual **3210**
Kentucky Automotive Directory **2918, 2959, 3015, 3088,
   3152**
[Kentucky]; Buick Club of America, Bluegrass Chapter **240,
   276, 311, 344, 378, 418, 455, 489, 525, 560, 593**
Keystone AAA Motorist Pennsylvania **3449, 3907**
Kicking Tires Is Not Enough **3908**
Killer Car Stereo on a Budget **4223**
Kirkwood Community College Auto Mechanics Series **4051**
Korea Automotive Review **3373**
Korean Automotive Firms in the United States and Canada;
   Directory of **3140**

L

Lagonda; Aston Martin and **93**
Lagonda Club, U.S. Section **98**
Lagonda Club, U.S. Section—Bulletin **95**
Lagonda Club, U.S. Section—Magazine **96**
Lagonda Club, U.S. Section—Newsletter **97**
Lake St. Clair Region—Membership Directory [Michigan];
   Cadillac—LaSalle Club, **612, 627, 643, 657, 671, 685, 699**
Lamborghini **1642, 1650, 1656**
Lamborghini Buyer's Guide; Illustrated **1641, 1649, 1655**
Lamborghini Club America **1646, 1652, 1658**
Lamborghini Club Magazine **1643, 1651, 1657**
Lamborghini; The Complete **1639, 1647, 1653**
Lamborghini Countach: Super Profile **1644**
Lamborghini U.S.A. Inc. **4364**
The Land-Rover 1948-1988 **2598**
Land Rover Owners **2600**
Land Rover Owners Association, U.S.A. **2603**
Land Rover: The Unbeatable 4X4 **2601**
The Last Chance Garage **4052, 4053**
Law; Digest of Motor **3406**
Law; New York Vehicle and Traffic **3421**
Laws; New Hampshire Motor Vehicle and Boating **3420**
Laws of New Jersey; Motor Vehicle and Traffic **3415**
Laws of Pennsylvania; Vehicle **3428**
Laws Regulating Motor Vehicle Titles, Registrations and
   Transfer of Same; Peck's Title Book: Description of
   State **3423**
Laws: With Uniform Traffic Code; Michigan Motor
   Vehicle **3413**
Le Club News **2609, 2622**
Lean Burn Engines **3752**

Lehigh Valley Motor Club—AAA Today Pennsylvania **3909**
The Lemon Book: Auto Rights **3411**
Lemon Times **3450**
Lemonaid **3412**
Lexus Division, Toyota Motor Sales USA **4365**
Light Beam Alignment **4080**
Light Duty Trucks; Standard Catalog of American **3222**
Light Truck and Van Repair **4054**
Light Trucks; Aftermarket for Imported Cars and **3239, 4125, 4290**
Light Vehicle Fitting **3259**
Lighting Manual; Ground Vehicle **4079**
Lighting Systems for Motor Vehicles **3260, 3599, 4081**
Lighting Trends; Vehicle **3284, 3663, 4082**
The Limited **234, 270, 305, 338, 372, 412, 448, 483, 519, 554, 587**
The Limited-Slip Differential: Pinion Operations and Service **3753**
Lincoln and Continental Owners Club **1674, 1687, 1699**
Lincoln and Continental Owners Club—Authenticity Manual **1668, 1681, 1693**
Lincoln and Continental Owners Club—Directory **1669, 1682, 1694**
Lincoln and Continental Owners Club, Southern Region—Bulletin **1670, 1683, 1695**
Lincoln and Continental Owners Club, Southern Region—Comments **1671, 1684, 1696**
Lincoln Continental-Mark VII, 1980-1987; Chilton's Ford Thunderbird, Mercury Cougar, **1492, 1660, 1676, 1833**
Lincoln, Mercury Car Repair and Tune-Up Guide: 1972-1987; Ford, **1293, 1306, 1320, 1334, 1347, 1378, 1391, 1463, 1480, 1495, 1661, 1677, 1689, 1834, 1843, 1852, 1860, 1869, 1878**
Lincoln-Mercury; Cars of **1662, 1678, 1690, 1836, 1845, 1854, 1862, 1872, 1879**
Lincoln-Mercury Club of Florida—Newsletter; Ford- **1297, 1311, 1326, 1337, 1352, 1361, 1369, 1382, 1403, 1436, 1454, 1468, 1485, 1502, 1667, 1680, 1692, 1828, 1838, 1846, 1856, 1864, 1874, 1881, 1887, 1891**
Lincoln-Mercury Division, Ford Motor Co. **4366**
Lincoln-Mercury Full-Size, 1968-1988; Chilton's Ford- **1374, 1490, 1659, 1675, 1688, 1832, 1842**
Lindens Lines **3374**
Lion of Belfort **2008, 2012**
Literature Collectors; International Directory of Automotive **2888**
Litigation; Automotive Engineering and **3288, 3402**
Litigation Reporter; Automotive **3404**
Litigation; Successful Automotive **3427**
Locator **3211**
Lone Star Chapter [Texas]; Buick Club of America, **246, 282, 317, 350, 384, 424, 461, 495, 531, 566, 599**
Long Term Outlook for the World Automobile Industry **3375**
Lotus **1708, 1715**
Lotus Cars USA Inc. **4367**
Lotus Elan; Super Profile: **1707**
Lotus Elan: The Complete Story **1701**
Lotus—Membership Roster **1702, 1711**
Lotus Remarque **1703, 1712**
Lotus: The Elan, Cortina, and Europa **1704**
Lotus Twin-Cam Engine **1700, 1710**
Lotus West **1709, 1716**
Lotus West—Directory **1705, 1713**
Louisiana, and southwestern Tennessee]; Deep South Alfa Romeo Club [Mississippi, **33, 58, 83**
Louisiana Automotive Directory **2919, 2960, 3016, 3089, 3153**
Love and Revolution: The First Hundred & One Years of the Automobile Since 1888 **3331**
Love That Car **4055**
Low-Cost Vehicles: Options for Moving People and Goods **3910**
Lube Recommendations and Capacities Booklet **4177**
Lube; Tune Up America: Oil Change, Filters and **4187**
Lubricants, and Fossil Fuels; Petroleum Products, **3829, 4183**

Lubricants: Perspectives on the Future; Engines, Fuels, and **3736, 3799, 4172**
Lubricants; Selecting and Using **4184**
Lubricating and, Cooling Systems; Engines, **3737, 4173**
Lubricating and Cooling Systems; Automotive Fuel, **3789, 4096, 4168**
Lubrication, and Cooling Systems; Automotive Fuel, **3818, 4097, 4169**
Lubrication, and Exhaust Systems; Automotive Fuel, Cooling, **3667, 3788, 4095, 4167**
Lubrication Guide; Truck **4186, 4326**
Lubrication Handbook; Master **4178**
Lubrication Service Directory; Automobile **3121**
Lumina—Pontiac Transport Olds Silhouette, 1988-90; Chevrolet **848, 1995, 2459**
Lyn St. James' Car Owners Manual **4056**
Lynx-LN7, 1981-1989: Shop Manual; Ford Escort-EXP and Mercury **1346, 1851**
Lynx Owners Manual Workshop Manual, No. 789: 1981-1988; Haynes Ford Escort and Mercury **1348, 1853**

M

[Maine, Massachusetts, and Rhode Island]; Pontiac-Oakland Club International Yankee Chapter **2103, 2144, 2182, 2224, 2270, 2307, 2344, 2379, 2414, 2453, 2489**
[Maine, Massachusetts, and Rhode Island]; Pontiac-Oakland Club International, Yankee Chapter—Newsletter **2090, 2131, 2169, 2210, 2254, 2294, 2331, 2366, 2401, 2440, 2476**
Maine/New Hampshire/Vermont Automotive Directory **2920, 2961, 3017, 3090, 3154**
Maintenance; Consumers' Guide to Automotive **4028**
Manual for Incorporating Pneumatic Springs in Vehicle Suspension Designs **3261, 4279**
Manual Transmission and Power Trains; Automotive **3557, 3708**
Manual Transmissions, Transaxles, and Drive Trains; Automatic, **3555, 3695**
Mark VII, 1980-1987; Chilton's Ford Thunderbird, Mercury Cougar, Lincoln Continental- **1492, 1660, 1676, 1833**
Maryland; AAA-Automobile Club of **2829**
Maryland, and Virginia]; Pontiac-Oakland Club International, National Capital Area [District of Columbia, **2100, 2141, 2179, 2221, 2267, 2304, 2341, 2376, 2411, 2450, 2486**
Maryland Automotive Directory; Delaware/District of Columbia/ **2910, 2950, 3002, 3080, 3137**
Maserati Automobiles Inc. **4368**
Maserati Buyer's Guide; Illustrated **1722, 1728, 1734, 1740, 1750**
Maserati Information Exchange **1720, 1726, 1732, 1738, 1744, 1754**
Maserati Market Letter **1717, 1723, 1729, 1735, 1741, 1746, 1751**
Maserati Owners Club of North America **1721, 1727, 1733, 1739, 1745, 1749, 1755**
Maserati Owners Club of North America Quarterly **1718, 1724, 1730, 1736, 1742, 1747, 1752**
Massachusetts, and Rhode Island]; Pontiac-Oakland Club International, Yankee Chapter [Maine, **2103, 2144, 2182, 2224, 2270, 2307, 2344, 2379, 2414, 2453, 2489**
Massachusetts, and Rhode Island]; Pontiac-Oakland Club International, Yankee Chapter—Newsletter [Maine, **2090, 2131, 2169, 2210, 2254, 2294, 2331, 2366, 2401, 2440, 2476**
Massachusetts Automotive Directory **2921, 2962, 3018, 3091, 3155**
Massillon Auto Club Ohio **2858**
Master Lubrication Handbook **4178**
Maxima 1985-1989; Nissan **1902**
Mazda 626, 1983-1988 **1757**
Mazda 1971-1989 Repair and Tune-Up Guide **1756, 1758, 1760, 1762, 1766, 1768, 1770**

Mazda B-Series Pick-ups Owners Workshop Manual, No. 267: 1972-1990; Haynes **1761**

Mazda GLC, 626, RX 7 **1759, 1771**

Mazda Miata MX-5; Guide to **1767**

Mazda Motor of America Inc. **4369**

Mazda Pick-Ups 1971-1989: Repair and Tune-Up Guide **1763**

Mazda Pickups, 1972-1988 **1764**

Mazda Pickups Two and Four Wheel Drive, 1979-1989 **1765**

Mazda RX-7 Owners Workshop Manual, No. 1419: 1986-1989; Haynes **1769**

The Measurement and Control of Diesel Particulate Emissions **3551, 3684**

Mechanical Maintenance Training **3523, 3754, 4179**

Mechanical Power Transmission **3755**

The Mechanics Vest Pocket Reference Book **3911**

Mechanisms of Car Choice: A Study of Learning by Using **3912**

Mercedes 8-Cylinder **1798, 1806, 1814**

Mercedes-Benz Club of America **1781, 1788, 1796, 1804, 1812, 1820, 1825**

Mercedes-Benz Club of Ft. Worth [Texas] **1782, 1789, 1797, 1805, 1813, 1821, 1826**

Mercedes-Benz; Great Marques **1778, 1785, 1793, 1801, 1809, 1817**

Mercedes-Benz of North America Inc. **4370**

Mercedes-Benz, Porsche—The Greatest of the Survivors Series; Four for the Road: Corvette, Ferrari, **822, 1187, 1210, 1233, 1256, 1280, 1777, 1784, 1792, 1800, 1808, 1816, 2497, 2525, 2546, 2569**

Mercedes-Benz Star **1779, 1786, 1794, 1802, 1810, 1818, 1823**

Mercedes Diesel **1775, 1790**

Mercedes Magazine **1780, 1787, 1795, 1803, 1811, 1819, 1824**

Mercury Capri 1979-1987: Includes Turbo Shop Manual; Ford Mustang and **1392**

Mercury Capri (In-Line) Owners Workshop Manual, No. 654: 1979-1990; Haynes Ford Mustang and **1393**

[Mercury Capri]; The Sporting Fords **1829**

Mercury Capri (V-6 and V-8) Owners Workshop Manual, No. 558: 1979-1989; Haynes Ford Mustang and **1394**

Mercury Car Repair and Tune-Up Guide: 1972-1987; Ford, Lincoln, **1293, 1306, 1320, 1334, 1347, 1378, 1391, 1463, 1480, 1495, 1661, 1677, 1689, 1834, 1843, 1852, 1860, 1869, 1878**

Mercury; Cars of Lincoln- **1662, 1678, 1690, 1836, 1845, 1854, 1862, 1872, 1879**

Mercury Club **1831, 1841, 1849, 1859, 1867, 1877, 1884**

Mercury Club of Florida—Newsletter; Ford-Lincoln- **1297, 1311, 1326, 1337, 1352, 1361, 1369, 1382, 1403, 1436, 1454, 1468, 1485, 1502, 1667, 1680, 1692, 1828, 1838, 1846, 1856, 1864, 1874, 1881, 1887, 1891**

Mercury Cougar, Lincoln Continental-Mark VII, 1980-1987; Chilton's Ford Thunderbird, **1492, 1660, 1676, 1833**

Mercury Cougar, No. 1338: 1983-1988; Haynes Ford Thunderbird and **1497**

Mercury Front Wheel Drive 1981-1987; Chilton Ford- **1342, 1476, 1850, 1868**

Mercury Full-Size, 1968-1988; Chilton's Ford-Lincoln- **1374, 1490, 1659, 1675, 1688, 1832, 1842**

Mercury Full-Size Owners Workshop Manual, No. 754: 1975-1987; Haynes Ford and **1379, 1496, 1835, 1844**

Mercury Lynx-LN7, 1981-1989: Shop Manual; Ford Escort-EXP and **1346, 1851**

Mercury Lynx Owners Manual Workshop Manual, No. 789: 1981-1988; Haynes Ford Escort and **1348, 1853**

Mercury Sable Owners Workshop Manual, No. 1421: 1986-1990; Haynes Ford Taurus and **1464, 1861**

Mercury Topaz, 1984-1987; Ford Tempo and **1481, 1870**

Mercury Topaz Owners Workshop Manual, No. 1418: 1984-1989; Haynes Ford Tempo- **1482, 1871**

Merkur 1979-1988; Chilton's Mustang-Capri- **1389, 1885, 1889**

Merrily We Roll Again **3332**

Methanol: Promise and Problems **3827**

Miata MX-5; Guide to Mazda **1767**

Michiana Mustangs—Newsletter [Indiana, Michigan] **1408**

Michigan, America: Henry Ford and His Horseless Carriage; Model T Man from **3333**

Michigan Automotive Directory **2922, 2963, 3019, 3092, 3156**

[Michigan]; Cadillac—LaSalle Club, Lake St. Clair Region—Membership Directory **612, 627, 643, 657, 671, 685, 699**

Michigan]; Michiana Mustangs—Newsletter [Indiana, **1408**

Michigan Motor Vehicle Laws: With Uniform Traffic Code **3413**

Michigan—Newsletter; Mustang Owners Club of Southeastern **1417**

Michigan No-Fault Automobile Cases: Law and Practice **3414**

Michigan Origins of the American Automobile Industry; A Most Unique Machine: The **3334**

Michigan Region; Cadillac-LaSalle Club, Lower **622, 636, 652, 666, 680, 694, 708**

Michigan Region—Newsletter; Cadillac-LaSalle Club, Lower **613, 628, 644, 658, 672, 686, 700**

Microprocessors Explained; Automotive **3628**

Mid-Western 4-Wheeler **3776**

Mighty Mopars **925, 959, 979, 1007**

Mini Ram Van, Plymouth Voyager, 1984-1987; Dodge Caravan, **1038, 2062**

Mini-Vans Owners Workshop Manual, No. 1476: 1986-1990; Haynes Ford Aerostar **1294**

MiniTruckin' **4319**

Minnesota Automotive Directory **2923, 2964, 3020, 3093, 3157**

(Minnesota Edition); Home & Away **3890**

Miss Information's Automotive Calendar of Events **3913**

Mississippi Automotive Directory **2924, 2965, 3021, 3094, 3158**

[Mississippi, Louisiana, and southwestern Tennessee]; Deep South Alfa Romeo Club **33, 58, 83**

Mississippi Valley Corvette Association—Newsletter **826**

Missouri Automotive Directory **2925, 2966, 3022, 3095, 3159**

Missouri]; Pontiac-Oakland Club International, Kansas City Arrowhead Chapter—Directory [Kansas and **2086, 2127, 2165, 2206, 2250, 2290, 2327, 2362, 2397, 2436, 2472**

Missouri]; Pontiac-Oakland Club International, Kansas City Arrowhead Chapter [Kansas and **2099, 2140, 2178, 2220, 2266, 2303, 2340, 2375, 2410, 2449, 2485**

Mitchell Automechanics **4057**

Mitchell Automotive Braking Systems **3524**

Mitchell Automotive Electrical Systems **3600**

Mitchell Automotive Heating and Air Conditioning Systems **4105**

Mitchell Glove Compartment Companion for Your Honda **1536, 1542, 1549, 1556**

Mitchell Glove Compartment Companion for Your Nissan **1893, 1895, 1897, 1899, 1901, 1904, 1906, 1911, 1913, 1916, 1920**

Mitchell Glove Compartment Companion for Your Toyota Celica-Supra **2673, 2693**

Mitchell's Electronic Fuel-Injection Troubleshooting Guide: Domestic Vehicles **3650, 3805**

Mitchell's Electronic Fuel-Injection Troubleshooting Guide: Import Vehicles **3651, 3806, 4153**

Mitchell's Electronic Ignition Troubleshooting Guide: Domestic Vehicles **3652, 4119**

Mitchell's Electronic Ignition Troubleshooting Guide: Import Vehicles **3653, 4120, 4154**

Mitsubishi Motor Sales of America Inc. **4371**

Mitsubishi Pick-ups Owner's Workshop Manual, No. 556: 1979-1988; Haynes Dodge D-50 and Plymouth Arrow and **1112**

Mobile Air Conditioning Association—Membership/Industry Contact Directory; International **3055**

Mobile Electronics Market Trends Guide **4224**

Model T Man from Michigan, America: Henry Ford and His Horseless Carriage **3333**

Modern Automotive Structural Analysis **3262**

Modern Fuel for Modern Diesel Engines **3552, 3828**

Modern Tire Dealer—Facts/Directory Issue **2892, 3160**

Montana/North Dakota/South Dakota/Wyoming Automotive Directory; Idaho/ **2913, 2954, 3008, 3083, 3147**

Monte Carlo; The Class of **859**

Monte Carlo Owner's Manual, No. 626: 1970-1988; Haynes Chevrolet **855**

Moore's Recon Training Video **3437**

MOPAR **926, 960, 980, 1008**

Mopar; High Performance **923, 957, 977, 1006**

Mopar Muscle **927, 961, 981, 1009**

Mopars; Mighty **925, 959, 979, 1007**

MoPerformance **928, 962, 982, 1010**

A Most Unique Machine: The Michigan Origins of the American Automobile Industry **3334**

Motor Age Big I Who's Who **2878, 2893, 2940, 2967**

Motor Age Professional Mechanics Edition; Chilton's Import Car Parts and Labor Guide, 1987-1991: **4136, 4190**

Motor-Age Professional Mechanic's Edition; Chilton's IMP Emission Diagnostic and Service Manual, Vacuum Circuit, 1984-1987 Import Cars and Truck: **3673, 4134, 4305**

Motor Age Professional Mechanic's Edition; Chilton's Auto Service Manual 1988-1992: **4008**

Motor-Age Professional Mechanics Edition; Chilton's Automatic Transmission Repair Manual, 1984-88: **3714**

Motor-Age Professional Mechanic's Edition; Chilton's Automatic Transmission Repair Manual, 1984-1988: Import Cars and Trucks: **3715, 4129, 4298**

Motor-Age Professional Mechanic's Edition; Chilton's Automatic Transmission Service Manual 1984-88: Domestic Cars and Trucks: **3716, 4299**

Motor-Age Professional Mechanic's Edition; Chilton's Chassis Electronics and Power Accessories Service Manual, 1987-89: **3234, 3630, 3717**

Motor Age Professional Mechanic's Edition; Chilton's Electronic Chassis Controls Manual, Import Cars and Trucks—1988-1990: **3631, 3718, 4130, 4300**

Motor-Age Professional Mechanic's Edition; Chilton's Electronic Engine Controls Manual, 1988-90—Domestic Cars and Trucks: **3632, 3719, 4301**

Motor Age Professional Mechanic's Edition; Chilton's Emission Control Manual 1992: **3670**

Motor Age Professional Mechanics Edition; Chilton's Guide to Air Conditioning and Heating Manual 1990-92: **4102**

Motor Age Professional Mechanics Edition; Chilton's Import Car Repair Manual 1982-87: **4012, 4137**

Motor Age Professional Mechanics Edition; Chilton's Import Car Repair Manual 1987-91: **4013**

Motor Age Professional Mechanics Edition; Chilton's Import Car Repair Manual, 1987-91: **4138**

Motor Age Professional Mechanics Edition; Chilton's Import Car Repair Manual 1987-91: **4139**

Motor-Age Professional Mechanic's Edition; Chilton's Import Car Service Manual, 1980-1987: **4015, 4141**

Motor-Age Professional Mechanic's Edition; Chilton's Import Car Wiring Diagrams Manual, 1987-88: **3587, 4142**

Motor Age Professional Mechanic's Edition; Chilton's Labor Guide and Manual, 1988-1992: **4016**

Motor-Age Professional Mechanic's Edition; Chilton's Labor Guide and Parts Manual 1986-90: **4017, 4191**

Motor-Age Professional Mechanic's Edition; Chilton's Professional Electronics Diagnostic Manual Ford Cars and Trucks 1984-1988: **1304, 1318, 1333, 1345, 1366, 1377, 1390, 1444, 1462, 1479, 1494**

Motor-Age Professional Mechanic's Edition; Chilton's Service Bay Handbook 1992: **4019**

Motor-Age Professional Mechanic's Edition; Chilton's Truck and Van Wiring Diagram Manual, 1989-1990: **3588, 4308**

Motor-Age Professional Mechanic's Edition; Chilton's U.S. Emission Diagnostic and Service Manual, Vacuum Circuit, 1984-1987—Domestic Car: **3536, 3675**

Motor-Age Professional Mechanic's Edition; Emission Diagnosis Tune-up and Service Manual 1988 Import Cars and Trucks: **3537, 3678, 4037, 4143, 4313**

Motor Age Professional Mechnanic's Edition; Electronic Instrumentation Service Manual 1980-1987: **3649, 4162**

Motor Auto Engines and Electrical Systems **3601, 3756**

Motor Auto Repair 1983-1989 Chrysler **920, 937, 954, 974, 994, 1003**

Motor Auto Repair 1983-1989 Ford **1295, 1309, 1323, 1335, 1349, 1367, 1380, 1395, 1433, 1450, 1465, 1483, 1498**

Motor Auto Repair Manual **3914**

Motor City News Detroit, Michigan **3376**

Motor Club News **3915**

Motor Handbook **3916**

Motor Imported Car Repair **4058, 4155**

Motor Imported Car Repair Manual: Up-to-Date Info for Imported Car Owners **4059, 4156**

The Motor Industry of Japan **3377**

The Motor Men: Pioneers of the British Car Industry **3378**

Motor Trend **3917**

Motor Trend—New Car Buyer's Guide **3212**

Motor Trend—Road Tests **3918**

Motor Trend—Sports Cars of the World **4247**

Motor Trend—Truck and Van Buyer's Guide **3213**

Motor Vehicle **3919**

Motor Vehicle and Traffic Laws of New Jersey **3415**

Motor Vehicle Facts and Figures **3379**

Motor Vehicle Fuel Economy **3807**

Motor Vehicle Identification Manual **3920**

Motor Vehicle Law of North Carolina **3416**

Motor Vehicle Laws of Ohio **3417**

Motor Vehicle Pollution Control; A Global Perspective **3685**

Motor Vehicle Size and Weight Regulations, Enforcement, and Permit Operations **3921**

Motor Vehicle Statistics **3380**

Motorist; Auto Club of Southern Pennsylvania— **3838**

Motorist Washington state; AAA Washington Motor Club— **3835**

The Motorist's Guide to the Law **3418**

Motorland **3922**

Motors, Principles Controls, Service and Maintenance; Electric **3591, 3734, 4033**

Motortech **4060**

Motorweek **3923**

Muffler Repair Shops Directory; Automobile **3122**

Mugged by Mr. Badwrench: An Insider's Guide to Getting Your Car Repaired **3924**

Multi-Purpose Vehicles; Guide to Radio Policy on Current Model Cars and **4220, 4233**

Multicylinder Test Sequences for Evaluating Automotive Engine Oils **4180**

Multigrade Oils for Diesel Engines **3553, 4181**

The Multinational Automobile Industry **3381**

Multiplexing in Automobiles **3263**

Museums Directory: U.S.A., Supplement with Canadian Museums; Auto **3298**

Mustang **1409, 1410**

Mustang, 1965-1989 GT-MACH One Guide **1411**

Mustang: A Living Legend **1412**

Mustang and Capri, 1979-1987: Super Shop Manual **1396**

Mustang and Mercury Capri 1979-1987: Includes Turbo Shop Manual; Ford **1392**

Mustang and Mercury Capri (In-Line) Owners Workshop Manual, No. 654: 1979-1990; Haynes Ford **1393**

Mustang and Mercury Capri (V-6 and V-8) Owners Workshop Manual, No. 558: 1979-1989; Haynes Ford **1394**

Mustang Annual **1413**

Mustang Buyer's Guide; Ford/ **1404**

Mustang Buyer's Guide; Illustrated **1407**

Mustang-Capri-Merkur 1979-1988; Chilton's **1389, 1885, 1889**

Mustang Club News [Indiana]; Hoosier **1406**

Mustang Club of America **1429**

Mustang Club of America, Northeastern Ohio Regional Group—Newsletter **1414**

Mustang; The Complete Book of **1398**

Mustang Illustrated **1415**

Mustang Monthly **1416**

Mustang Owners Club International **1430**

Mustang Owners Club of Southeastern Michigan— Newsletter **1417**

Mustang Red Book, 1965-1990 **1418**

Mustang Regional Club—Newsletter; Adirondack Shelby- **1397**

Mustang; The Story of **1425**

Mustang: The 25th Silver Anniversary **1419**

Mustang: The Enduring Legend **1420**

Mustang Times **1421**

Mustang Times Magazine [South Carolina] **1422**

Mustangs and Exotic Fords; Fabulous **1399**

Mustangs—Newsletter [Indiana, Michigan]; Michiana **1408**

MVMA Directory of Motor Vehicle Related Associations **2894**

N

NAPA News **3925**

National 4 Wheel Drive Association—Bulletin **3777**

National 4 Wheel Drive Association-News **3778**

National American Motors Drivers and Racers Association **92**

National Auto Auction Association—Membership Directory **2879**

National Auto Data Service **3214**

National Automobile Dealers Association—Title and Registration Book **3419**

National Automotive Parts Association—News **4061**

National Automotive Radiator Service Association— Membership Directory **2895**

National Corvette Owners Association **836**

National Council of Corvette Clubs **837**

National Council of Corvette Clubs—Handbook **827**

National Firebird Club **2259**

National Four Wheel Drive Association News **3779**

National Tire Dealers and Retreaders Association—Who's Who Membership Directory **2968, 3161**

Nebraska Automotive Directory; Kansas/ **2917, 2958, 3014, 3087, 3151**

Nebraska Chapter; Buick Club of America, **248, 284, 319, 352, 386, 426, 463, 497, 533, 568, 601**

Nebraska Chapter—Newsletter; Buick Club of America, **224, 260, 296, 328, 361, 399, 437, 473, 509, 542, 577**

Nebraskaland **2079, 2120, 2158, 2199, 2243, 2283, 2320, 2355, 2390, 2429, 2465**

Nebraskaland Chapter; Pontiac-Oakland Club International, **2101, 2142, 2180, 2222, 2268, 2305, 2342, 2377, 2412, 2451, 2487**

Nevada Automotive Directory; Colorado/Utah/ **2908, 2948, 3000, 3078, 3135**

New Automotive Mechanics Series **4062**

New Car: A Common Sense Buyers Guide; Save Big Money on a **3943**

New Car Buyer's Guide; Motor Trend— **3212**

New Car Buying Guide **3215**

New Car for Less; Buy a **3854**

New Car or Used Car; How to Buy a Car: The Essential Guide for Buying a **3896**

New Car Prices; Edmund's **3203**

New-Car Salesman: A Legendary Salesman Reveals the Secrets to Negotiating a Great Deal; How to Outsmart the **3902**

New Car; SMART Buyer's Guide to Purchasing a **3945**

New Deals: The Chrysler Revival and the American System **3335, 3382**

New Development and Requirements for Automotive Fabrics **3264**

New Development in Automotive Fibers and Fabrics **3265**

New Developments in Electronic Engine Management **3266, 3654, 3757**

New Developments in Polymer Composites for Automotive Applications **3267**

New Diesel Engines, Combustion and Emissions Research in Japan **3554, 3686, 3758, 4157**

New Directions in Suspension Design: Making the Fast Car Faster **3268, 4248, 4280**

New Engine and Advanced Component Design **3269, 3759**

New England; British Motorcars of **2845**

New Hampshire Motor Vehicle and Boating Laws **3420**

New Hampshire/Vermont Automotive Directory; Maine/ **2920, 2961, 3017, 3090, 3154**

New Jersey Automotive Directory **2926, 2969, 3023, 3096, 3162**

[New Jersey]; Buick Club of America, Jersey Shore Chapter **244, 280, 315, 348, 382, 422, 459, 493, 529, 564, 597**

[New Jersey]; Jersey Shore Chapter News **233, 269, 304, 337, 371, 411, 447, 482, 518, 553, 586**

New Jersey; Motor Vehicle and Traffic Laws of **3415**

[New Jersey]; Pontiac-Oakland Club International, Garden State Chapter—Newsletter **2082, 2123, 2161, 2202, 2246, 2286, 2323, 2358, 2393, 2432, 2468**

New Mexico Automotive Directory; Arizona/ **2903, 2942, 2990, 3070, 3111**

New or Used Car; How to Beat the Car Dealer at His Own Game: Buying a **3895**

New Polymer Technology for Auto Body Exteriors **3270**

New Technologies in Automotive Electronic Displays and Information Systems **3655, 4163**

New York Automotive Directory **2927, 2970, 3024, 3097, 3163**

New York; Cars Made in Upstate **3362**

New York Chapter; Pontiac-Oakland Club, Western **2105, 2146, 2184, 2226, 2272, 2309, 2346, 2381, 2416, 2455, 2491**

[New York]; Finger Lakes News **2076, 2116, 2154, 2195, 2239, 2279, 2316, 2352, 2387, 2425, 2462**

[New York]; Pontiac-Oakland Club, Finger Lakes Chapter **2093, 2134, 2172, 2214, 2260, 2297, 2334, 2369, 2404, 2443, 2479**

New York Vehicle and Traffic Law **3421**

News Focus **3383, 3422**

911 & 930 Close-up; A Porsche **2502**

Nines **2647, 2650**

Nissan Maxima 1985-1989 **1902**

Nissan; Mitchell Glove Compartment Companion for Your **1893, 1895, 1897, 1899, 1901, 1904, 1906, 1911, 1913, 1916, 1920**

Nissan North America Inc. **4372**

Nissan Pick-up and Pathfinder 1989-91 **1907, 1917**

Nissan Pickups and Pathfinder, 1986-1988 **1908, 1918**

Nissan Sentra, Datsun 1200 and B210, 1973-1987; Chilton's **1910**

Nissan Two and Four-Wheel Drive Pickups 1970-1987 Gas and Diesel; Datsun and **1915**

Non-Audio Electronics; Audio Systems: Speakers, Receivers, **4212**

Non-Entertainment Automotive Electronics Market **3656**

North Carolina Automotive Directory **2928, 2971, 3025, 3098, 3164**

North Carolina; Motor Vehicle Law of **3416**

North Carolina State Motor Club **2859**

North Dakota American Automobile Association **2860**

North Dakota/South Dakota/Wyoming Automotive Directory; Idaho/Montana/ **2913, 2954, 3008, 3083, 3147**

Nova 1985-1989 Repair and Tune-up Guide; Chevrolet **863**

NTDRA Dealer News—Who's Who Directory Issue **2896, 2972**

Nutmeg Chapter [Connecticut]; Pontiac-Oakland Club, **2104, 2145, 2183, 2225, 2271, 2308, 2345, 2380, 2415, 2454, 2490**

O

Off-Road 3780, 4234, 4320
Off-Road Advertiser 3781, 4235, 4321
Off Road America 3782, 4236, 4322
Off Road Buyer's Guide; Edmund's Vans, Pickups/ 3205
Off Road; Four Wheel and 3773, 4229, 4314
The Official Price Guide to Cars and Trucks 3216
Official Used Car Guide Book 3217
Ohio Automobile Dealers Association—Directory 2973
Ohio Automotive Directory 2929, 2974, 3026, 3099, 3165
[Ohio]; Buick Club of America, Glass City Chapter 243, 279, 314, 347, 381, 421, 458, 492, 528, 563, 596
Ohio Chapter; Alfa Romeo Owners Club, Northeastern 28, 53, 78
Ohio Chapter; Buick Club of America, Southwestern 252, 288, 323, 356, 390, 430, 467, 501, 537, 572, 605
Ohio Chapter—Newsletter; Buick Club of America, Southwestern 227, 263, 299, 331, 364, 402, 440, 476, 512, 545, 580
Ohio Chapter— Newsletter; Pontiac-Oakland Club International, North Coast 2088, 2129, 2167, 2208, 2252, 2292, 2329, 2364, 2399, 2438, 2474
(Ohio Edition); Home & Away 3891
Ohio; Motor Vehicle Laws of 3417
Ohio Motorist 3926
Ohio Regional Group—Newsletter; Mustang Club of America, Northeastern 1414
Oil Change, Filters and Lube; Tune Up America: 4187
Oil Effects on Vehicle Fuel Economy; Engine 4171
Oil; How to Buy Motor 4175
The Oil Spot 4158
Oil Viscosity: Measurement and Relationship to Engine Operation; High-Temperature, High-Shear (HTHS) 3744, 4174
Oils for Diesel Engines; Multigrade 3553, 4181
Oils; Multicylinder Test Sequences for Evaluating Automotive Engine 4180
Oils; Passenger Car Motor 4182
Oils; Synthetic Automotive Engine 4185
Oklahoma; Alfa Romeo Owners Club of 30, 55, 80
Oklahoma Automotive Directory 2930, 2975, 3027, 3100, 3166
Oklahoma—Newsletter; Alfa Romeo Owners Club of 17, 42, 67
Old Cars Auction Results, 1989: Worldwide Model Years 1905-1988 3218
Old Cars Price Guide 3219
Old Cars Weekly—Car Club Special Issue 2897
Old Dominion Chapter—Newsletter [Virginia]; Pontiac-Oakland Club International, 2089, 2130, 2168, 2209, 2253, 2293, 2330, 2365, 2400, 2439, 2475
Olds Bravada, 1982-1990; Chevrolet S-10 Blazer, GMC S-15, and 730, 1514, 1928
Olds Cutlass Ciera, Pontiac 6000, 1982-1988; Chilton's Chevrolet Celebrity, Buick Century, 216, 778, 1947, 2107
Olds Firenza, Cadillac Cimarron, Pontiac 6000, 1982-88; Chilton's Chevrolet Cavalier, Buick Skyhawk, 502, 638, 765, 1978, 2106
Olds; Journey With 1922, 1930, 1935, 1942, 1955, 1966, 1976, 1983, 1992, 1997, 2003
Olds-Pontiac Full-Size, 1975-87; Buick- 253, 289, 432, 1932, 1971, 1988, 1999, 2147
Olds, Pontiac, Full-Size Models: 1970-90; Haynes Buick, 256, 292, 1974, 1990, 2001, 2149
Olds Silhouette, 1988-90; Chevrolet Lumina—Pontiac Transport 848, 1995, 2459
Oldsmobile Buyer's Guide; Illustrated 1929, 1934, 1941, 1954, 1965, 1975, 1982, 1991, 1996, 2002
Oldsmobile Club of America 1925, 1931, 1936, 1945, 1958, 1969, 1977, 1986, 1993, 1998, 2006
Oldsmobile Cutlass-Buick Regal, 1988 Repair and Tune-up Guide; Pontiac Grand Prix- 395, 1940, 1953, 1964, 2311
Oldsmobile Cutlass Ciera, Pontiac 6000, 1982-87: Shop Manual; GM A-Cars Buick Century, Chevrolet Celebrity, 218, 780, 1938, 1950, 2110
Oldsmobile Cutlass Owners Workshop Manual, No. 658: 1974-1989; Haynes 1939, 1952, 1963
Oldsmobile Division, General Motors Corp. 4373
Oldsmobile Firenza, Pontiac J-2000, Sunbird Shop Manual, 1982-87; GMC J Cars: Buick Skyhawk, Cadillac Cimarron, Chevrolet Cavalier, 504, 640, 767, 1980, 2418
Oldsmobile Fixed Right; Get Your 1927, 1933, 1937, 1949, 1962, 1973, 1979, 1989, 1994, 2000
Oldsmobile Performance Chapter 1926, 1946, 1959, 1970, 1987, 2007
Oldsmobile Performance Chapter—Performance Roster 1923, 1943, 1956, 1967, 1984, 2004
Omni, 024, Charger, Rampage, and Plymouth Horizon, TC3, Turismo and Scamp 1978-1987: Shop Manual; Dodge 1044, 1097, 2035, 2055
On-Board Electronics; Electronic Displays, Information Systems and 3258, 3645, 4161
On The Warpath 2080, 2121, 2159, 2200, 2244, 2284, 2321, 2356, 2391, 2430, 2466
One Hundred One Things to Do with Your Car 3927
The One Hundred Seventy-Five Thousand-Mile Car 3928
One Hundred Thousand Miles.Two Hundred Thousand Miles.or More: Practical Car Care 3929
The Operation of the Fuel System 3808
Orange County Auto World California 3930
Orange County Chapter [California]; Alfa Romeo Owners Club, 31, 56, 81
Orange County Chapter—Newsletter [California]; Alfa Romeo Owners Club, 19, 44, 69
Oregon Automotive Directory 2931, 2976, 3028, 3101, 3167
[Oregon]; Pontiac-Oakland Club International, Emerald Valley Chapter 2096, 2137, 2175, 2217, 2263, 2300, 2337, 2372, 2407, 2446, 2482
[Oregon]; Pontiac-Oakland Club International, Emerald Valley Chapter—Newsletter 2081, 2122, 2160, 2201, 2245, 2285, 2322, 2357, 2392, 2431, 2467
Orion Car Stereo Blue Book 3235, 4225

P

Pacific Automotive News 3931
Paint Tips; SMART Body Shop Talk: 3493
Paint Your Car; How to 3483
Painting and Lettering Directory; Truck 3242
Painting; Chilton's Guide to Auto Body Repair and 3433, 3476
Painting Manual, No. 1479; Haynes Body Repair and 3482
Paintwork; How to Restore 3484
Parts and Accessories Association—Membership Directory; Automotive 2884
Parts and Labor Guide 1982-89; Import Car 4149, 4196
Parts Association—News; National Automotive 4061
Parts Exchange; ADP 2988, 3068
Parts Failure; Identification of 4195
Parts Report; The Auto 4188
Parts Retailers Directory; Automobile 2994
Parts—Used/Salvage Directory; Automobile 3073
Passenger Car Motor Oils 4182
Past, Present & Future of Automotive Elastomer Applications 3271
Pathfinder, 1986-1988; Nissan Pickups and 1908, 1918
Pathfinder 1989-91; Nissan Pick-up and 1907, 1917
Peck's Title Book: Description of State Laws Regulating Motor Vehicle Titles, Registrations and Transfer of Same 3423
Pennsylvania—AAA Traveler; AAA Auto Club of Southern 3832
Pennsylvania American Automobile Association Foundation 2861
Pennsylvania Auto Club; Central 2848
Pennsylvania Automotive Directory 2932, 2977, 3029, 3102, 3168

Pennsylvania]; Buick Club of America, Appalachian Chapter [South central **239, 275, 310, 343, 377, 417, 454, 488, 524, 559, 592**

[Pennsylvania]; Buick Club of America, National Pike Chapter **247, 283, 318, 351, 385, 425, 462, 496, 532, 567, 600**

Pennsylvania Motor Club; West **2876**

Pennsylvania—Motorist; Auto Club of Southern **3838**

Pennsylvania Motorist; Western **3953**

Pennsylvania; Vehicle Laws of **3428**

Performance Ford Club of America, Inc. **1358, 1431, 1441, 1475, 1508**

Performance Handling for the Nineties: How to Make Your Car Handle Better **4063**

Performance Racing Engine Builder's Supplier Directory **3059**

Performance Tuning in Theory and Practice-Four Strokes **3531, 3760**

Performance Tuning in Theory and Practice-Two Strokes **3532, 3761**

Petersen's 4 Wheel & Off Road **3783, 4237, 4323**

Petersen's Basic How to Tune Your Car **4064**

Petersen's Basic Ignition and Electrical Systems **3602, 4121**

Petroleum Products, Lubricants, and Fossil Fuels **3829, 4183**

Peugeot Motors of America Inc. **4374**

Peugeot Owners' Club **2011, 2015**

Peugeot Owners' Club—Directory **2009, 2013**

Peugeot Owner's Club Newsletter **2010, 2014**

Pick and File **3486**

Pick-up and Pathfinder 1989-91; Nissan **1907, 1917**

Pick-up Owners Workshop Manual, No. 656: 1979-1990; Haynes Toyota **2701**

Pick-Ups 1971-1989: Repair and Tune-Up Guide; Mazda **1763**

Pick-ups and 4-Runner, 1984-88; Toyota **2667, 2703**

Pick-Ups and Bronco Owners Workshop Manual, No. 880; Haynes Ford **1308, 1448**

Pick-ups and Suburban 1970-1987; Chilton's Chevrolet/GMC **874, 910, 1524, 1532**

Pick-ups Owners Workshop Manual, No. 267: 1972-1990; Haynes Mazda B-Series **1761**

Pick-Ups Owners Workshop Manual, No. 420: 1967-1987; Haynes Chevrolet and GMC **876, 1512, 1527**

Pick-ups Owner's Workshop Manual, No. 556: 1979-1988; Haynes Dodge D-50 and Plymouth Arrow and Mitsubishi **1112**

Pick-ups Owner's Workshop Manuals, No. 912: 1974-1990; Haynes Dodge **1062, 1113**

Pickup, 4-Runner Service Manual: 1978-1988 Including Gasoline, Diesel, and Turbo Diesel, 4-cylinder and 6-cylinder Engines; Toyota **2668, 2704**

Pickup Trucks: Stylesetter, Workhorse, Sport Truck; The Great American **4232, 4317**

Pickups, 1969-1987; Ford Four-Wheel Drive Bronco and F-Series **1305, 1319**

Pickups: 1969-1987 Shop Manual; Ford **1445**

Pickups 1970-1987 Gas and Diesel; Datsun and Nissan Two and Four-Wheel Drive **1915**

Pickups, 1972-1988; Mazda **1764**

Pickups 1982—90; Chevrolet S-10, GMC S-15 **871, 1522**

Pickups, 1988-90; Haynes Chevy GMC **877, 1513, 1528**

Pickups and Bronco 1987-1990; Ford **1307, 1446**

Pickups and Pathfinder, 1986-1988; Nissan **1908, 1918**

Pickups, and Suburbans: 1967-1987: Includes Suburbans Shop Manual; Chevy and GMC C-Series **907, 1530**

Pickups and Vans Year Buying Guide; Four By Four **3206**

Pickups/Off Road Buyer's Guide; Edmund's Vans, **3205**

Pickups, Suburbans, and Vans, 1970-1987 (Gas and Diesel); Chevy and GMC Two Wheel Drive C and R-Series **908, 1531**

Pickups Two and Four Wheel Drive, 1979-1989; Mazda **1765**

Pike Press **235, 271, 306, 339, 373, 413, 449, 484, 520, 555, 588**

Pinstriping Made Easy **3236**

Pioneer Chapter New York State; Society of Automotive Historians— **2866**

Piper Tuning Manual **3538**

Plastics & Passenger Cars **3272**

Plastics in Automobile Bumper Systems and Exterior Panels **3273, 3527**

Plastics in Automobile Instrument Panels, Trim, and Seating **3237, 3274, 4164**

Plastics in Automobiles: Bumper Systems, Interior Trim, Instrument Panels and Exterior Panels **3238, 3275, 3528, 4165**

Plastics in Automotive Applications **3276**

Plymouth: 1972-1987 Rear Wheel Drive Tune-up Maintenance; Chrysler, Dodge, **919, 936, 992, 1076, 2030**

Plymouth Horizon, TC3, Turismo and Scamp 1978-1987: Shop Manual; Dodge Omni, 024, Charger, Rampage, and **1044, 1097, 2035, 2055**

Plymouth; How to Build Chrysler, Dodge, **924, 938, 944, 958, 978, 995, 1020, 1027, 1032, 1040, 1045, 1055, 1063, 1068, 1077, 1081, 1085, 1093, 1098, 1106, 1114, 1120, 1125, 1129, 1137, 1152, 2016, 2020, 2024, 2031, 2036, 2040, 2047, 2051, 2056, 2064**

Plymouth Reliant Owners Workshop Manual, 1981-1988; Haynes Dodge Aries and **1031, 2046**

Plymouth Trucks 1967-1988; Chilton's Dodge/ **1061, 1110, 1124**

Plymouth Vans 1967-1988; Chilton's Dodge/ **1037, 1118, 2061**

Plymouth Vans Owners Workshop Manual, No. 349: 1971-1991; Haynes Dodge and **1039, 1111, 1119, 2063**

Plymouth Voyager, 1984-1987; Dodge Caravan, Mini Ram Van, **1038, 2062**

Plymouth Voyager, 1984-1988: Repair and Tune-Up Guide; Chilton's Dodge Caravan- **1036, 2060**

Pneumatic Springs in Vehicle Suspension Designs; Manual for Incorporating **3261, 4279**

Pollution Control; A Global Perspective; Motor Vehicle **3685**

Polymer Composites for Automotive Applications; New Developments in **3267**

Polymer Technology for Auto Body Exteriors; New **3270**

Polymers & Polymer Systems Used in Autos Market **3277**

Pontiac 6000, 1982-87: Shop Manual; GM A-Cars Buick Century, Chevrolet Celebrity, Oldsmobile Cutlass Ciera, **218, 780, 1938, 1950, 2110**

Pontiac 6000, 1982-88; Chilton's Chevrolet Cavalier, Buick Skyhawk, Olds Firenza, Cadillac Cimarron, **502, 638, 765, 1978, 2106**

Pontiac 6000, 1982-1988; Chilton's Chevrolet Celebrity, Buick Century, Olds Cutlass Ciera, **216, 778, 1947, 2107**

Pontiac; Chiefly **2074, 2114, 2152, 2190, 2236, 2277, 2314, 2350, 2385, 2423, 2460**

Pontiac Division, General Motors Corp. **4375**

Pontiac Fiero 1984-1988 **2187**

Pontiac Fiero Owners Workshop Manual, No. 1232: 1984-1988; Haynes **2186**

Pontiac Firebird Owners Workshop Manual, No. 867: 1982-1989; Haynes **2233**

Pontiac Fixed Right; Get Your **2070, 2109, 2148, 2185, 2232, 2274, 2310, 2347, 2382, 2417, 2456**

Pontiac Full-Size, 1975-87; Buick-Olds- **253, 289, 432, 1932, 1971, 1988, 1999, 2147**

Pontiac, Full-Size Models: 1970-90; Haynes Buick, Olds, **256, 292, 1974, 1990, 2001, 2149**

Pontiac Grand Prix-Oldsmobile Cutlass-Buick Regal, 1988 Repair and Tune-up Guide **395, 1940, 1953, 1964, 2311**

Pontiac; High Performance **2117, 2155, 2196, 2240, 2280, 2317, 2426**

Pontiac J-2000, Sunbird Shop Manual, 1982-87; GMC J Cars: Buick Skyhawk, Cadillac Cimarron, Chevrolet Cavalier, Oldsmobile Firenza, **504, 640, 767, 1980, 2418**

Pontiac-Oakland Club, Finger Lakes Chapter [New York] **2093, 2134, 2172, 2214, 2260, 2297, 2334, 2369, 2404, 2443, 2479**

Pontiac-Oakland Club International **2094, 2135, 2173, 2215, 2261, 2298, 2335, 2370, 2405, 2444, 2480**

Pontiac-Oakland Club, International, Arizona Chapter **2095, 2136, 2174, 2216, 2262, 2299, 2336, 2371, 2406, 2445, 2481**

Pontiac-Oakland Club International, Emerald Valley Chapter— Newsletter [Oregon] 2081, 2122, 2160, 2201, 2245, 2285, 2322, 2357, 2392, 2431, 2467

Pontiac-Oakland Club International, Emerald Valley Chapter [Oregon] 2096, 2137, 2175, 2217, 2263, 2300, 2337, 2372, 2407, 2446, 2482

Pontiac-Oakland Club International, Garden State Chapter— Newsletter [New Jersey] 2082, 2123, 2161, 2202, 2246, 2286, 2323, 2358, 2393, 2432, 2468

Pontiac-Oakland Club International, Georgia Chapter 2097, 2138, 2176, 2218, 2264, 2301, 2338, 2373, 2408, 2447, 2483

Pontiac-Oakland Club International, Illinois Chapter—Annual Roster 2083, 2124, 2162, 2203, 2247, 2287, 2324, 2359, 2394, 2433, 2469

Pontiac-Oakland Club International, Kansas Chapter 2098, 2139, 2177, 2219, 2265, 2302, 2339, 2374, 2409, 2448, 2484

Pontiac-Oakland Club International, Kansas Chapter— Directory 2084, 2125, 2163, 2204, 2248, 2288, 2325, 2360, 2395, 2434, 2470

Pontiac-Oakland Club International, Kansas Chapter— Newsletter 2085, 2126, 2164, 2205, 2249, 2289, 2326, 2361, 2396, 2435, 2471

Pontiac-Oakland Club International, Kansas City Arrowhead Chapter—Directory [Kansas and Missouri] 2086, 2127, 2165, 2206, 2250, 2290, 2327, 2362, 2397, 2436, 2472

Pontiac-Oakland Club International, Kansas City Arrowhead Chapter [Kansas and Missouri] 2099, 2140, 2178, 2220, 2266, 2303, 2340, 2375, 2410, 2449, 2485

Pontiac-Oakland Club International—Membership Roster 2087, 2128, 2166, 2207, 2251, 2291, 2328, 2363, 2398, 2437, 2473

Pontiac-Oakland Club International, National Capital Area [District of Columbia, Maryland, and Virginia] 2100, 2141, 2179, 2221, 2267, 2304, 2341, 2376, 2411, 2450, 2486

Pontiac-Oakland Club International, Nebraskaland Chapter 2101, 2142, 2180, 2222, 2268, 2305, 2342, 2377, 2412, 2451, 2487

Pontiac-Oakland Club International, North Coast Ohio Chapter— Newsletter 2088, 2129, 2167, 2208, 2252, 2292, 2329, 2364, 2399, 2438, 2474

Pontiac-Oakland Club International, Old Dominion Chapter— Newsletter [Virginia] 2089, 2130, 2168, 2209, 2253, 2293, 2330, 2365, 2400, 2439, 2475

Pontiac-Oakland Club International, Southern California Chapter 2102, 2143, 2181, 2223, 2269, 2306, 2343, 2378, 2413, 2452, 2488

Pontiac-Oakland Club International, Yankee Chapter [Maine, Massachusetts, and Rhode Island] 2103, 2144, 2182, 2224, 2270, 2307, 2344, 2379, 2414, 2453, 2489

Pontiac-Oakland Club International, Yankee Chapter— Newsletter [Maine, Massachusetts, and Rhode Island] 2090, 2131, 2169, 2210, 2254, 2294, 2331, 2366, 2401, 2440, 2476

Pontiac-Oakland Club, Nutmeg Chapter [Connecticut] 2104, 2145, 2183, 2225, 2271, 2308, 2345, 2380, 2415, 2454, 2490

Pontiac-Oakland Club, Western New York Chapter 2105, 2146, 2184, 2226, 2272, 2309, 2346, 2381, 2416, 2455, 2491

Pontiac T 1000 Service Repair Handbook: All Models 1976- 1987; Chevrolet Chevette and 785, 2068

Pontiac T1000 1976-1988; Chilton's Chevette and 786, 2069

Pontiac T1000 Owners Workshop Manuals, No. 449: 1976- 1987; Haynes Chevrolet Chevette- 789, 2071

Pontiac Transport Olds Silhouette, 1988-90; Chevrolet Lumina— 848, 1995, 2459

The Pony Express 1423

Popular Cars 3932

Porsche 2500, 2528, 2549, 2572, 3336, 3384

Porsche 911 2501

Porsche 911, 944 2493, 2565

A Porsche 911 & 930 Close-up 2502

Porsche 911 Carrera; Super Profile: 2517

Porsche 911 In All Its Forms 2503

Porsche 911 Owners Workshop Manual, No. 264: 1965-1989; Haynes 2492

Porsche 911 Performance Handbook 2504

Porsche 911: The Complete Story 2505

The Porsche 911 Video Manual 2494

Porsche 924, 928, 944: The New Generation 2522, 2543, 2566

Porsche 944 Owners Workshop Manual, No. 1027: 1983- 1989; Haynes 2564

Porsche Buyer's Guide; Illustrated 2499, 2527, 2548, 2571

Porsche Cars North America Inc. 4376

Porsche Club of America 2520, 2541, 2562, 2585, 2596

Porsche Club of America—Annual Parade 2506, 2529, 2550, 2573, 2587

Porsche; Great Marques 2498, 2526, 2547, 2570

Porsche Market Letter 2507, 2530, 2551, 2574, 2588

Porsche Owner 2508, 2531, 2552, 2575, 2589

Porsche Owners Club 2521, 2542, 2563, 2586, 2597

Porsche Owners Club—Membership Roster 2509, 2532, 2553, 2576, 2590

Porsche Owners Club—Newsletter 2510, 2533, 2554, 2577, 2591

Porsche Owner's Companion: A Manual of Preservation and Theft Protection 2511, 2534, 2555, 2578

Porsche Panorama 2512, 2535, 2556, 2579, 2592

Porsche: Past and Present 2513, 2536, 2557, 2580, 2593

Porsche: Portrait of a Legend 2514, 2537, 2558, 2581

Porsche; The Story of 2516, 2539, 2560, 2583

Porsche—The Greatest of the Survivors Series; Four for the Road: Corvette, Ferrari, Mercedes-Benz, 822, 1187, 1210, 1233, 1256, 1280, 1777, 1784, 1792, 1800, 1808, 1816, 2497, 2525, 2546, 2569

Porsche Uber Alles 2515, 2538, 2559, 2582, 2594

Porsche; VW and 2519, 2540, 2561, 2584, 2595, 2713, 2724, 2734, 2745, 2757, 2768, 2776, 2787, 2796, 2806

Port Fuel Injection 3809

Port Fuel Injection; Troubleshooting 3814

Powder Metal Parts 3278, 4197

Power and Wheels: The Automobile in Modern Life 3337

Power Behind the Wheel: Creativity and Evolution of the Automobile 3279, 3338

Power Trains; Automotive Manual Transmission and 3557, 3708

Power Transmission Design 3280, 3762

Practical Gas Flow: Techniques for Low-Budget Performance Tuning 3810

Prancing Horse 1190, 1213, 1236, 1259, 1283

Prelude CVCC Owners Workshop Manuals, No 601: 1979- 1989; Haynes Honda 1555

Present and Future Automotive Fuels: Performance and Exhaust Clarification 3687, 3811, 3830

Price Guide Presents 3220

Principles and Service of Automotive Air Conditioning 4106

The Principles of Auto Body Repairing and Repainting 3487

Problems of Hydramatic Transmission 3763

Problems of Internal Combustion Engine 3764

The Problems of the Fuel System 3812

Procedure for Applying Body Solder 3488

Propane; How to Convert Your Vehicle to 3826

Puget Sound Chapter [Washington state]; Buick Club of America, 250, 286, 321, 354, 388, 428, 465, 499, 535, 570, 603

Pull Rod Repair Method 3489

Q

Quantum Official Factory Repair Manual: 1982-1988, Gasoline and Turbo Diesel, including Wagon and Syncro 2781

Quantum; Volkswagen 2783

Quatrefoil 3933

Quick Course in Car Cooling Systems 4107, 4108

R

Racing Engine Builder's Supplier Directory; Performance **3059**
RADAR **4226**
Radar Reporter Newsletter **3424, 4227**
Radiator; Advanced Car Care: Belts, Hoses and **3960, 4199**
Radiator Repair Shops Directory; Automobile **3123**
Radiator Service Association—Membership Directory; National
    Automotive **2895**
Radio Policy on Current Model Cars and Multi-Purpose
    Vehicles; Guide to **4220, 4233**
Radio/Stereo Systems Directory; Automobile **2995**
Rag Top News **4249**
Range Rover of North America Inc. **4377**
Range Rover: Super Profile **2602**
Ranger and Bronco II 1983-1988: Includes Diesel and Four-
    Wheel Drive Shop Manual; Ford **1321, 1447**
Ranger and Bronco II Owners Workshop Manual, No. 1026:
    1983-1989; Haynes Ford **1322, 1449**
Ranger-Bronco II 1983-1988: Repair and Tune-Up
    Guide **1324, 1451**
Reading-Berks Auto Club Magazine **3934**
Rear Wheel Drive Tune-up Maintenance; Chrysler, Dodge,
    Plymouth: 1972-1987 **919, 936, 992, 1076, 2030**
Rebuilder—Purchasing Directory Issue; Automotive **3047**
Recall Program; Children at Risk: Failure of the Federal Child
    Restraint **3447, 4201**
Receivers, Non-Audio Electronics; Audio Systems:
    Speakers, **4212**
Recent Developments in Automotive Electronic Displays and
    Information Systems **3657, 4166**
Recent Developments in Electronic Engine Control and Fuel
    Injection Management **3658, 3765, 3813**
Recent Trends in Automotive Emissions Control **3688**
Reckless Homicide: Ford's Pinto Trial **3339**
The Reckoning **3385**
Recon Training Video; Moore's **3437**
Recyclers Association—Roster of Members; Automotive
    Dismantlers and **3075**
The Redbook: The Consumer's Automobile Purchasing Guide
    and Reference Manual **3221**
Refinishing; Autobody Repair and **3472**
Refinishing; Automotive Body Repair and **3473**
Refinishing; The Complete Guide to Automotive **3434, 3479**
Refinishing Handbook; Autobody **3470**
The Reflector **236, 272, 307, 340, 374, 414, 450, 485, 521,
    556, 589**
Regal, 1975-87; Chilton's Buick Century and **215, 391**
Regal, 1988 Repair and Tune-up Guide; Pontiac Grand Prix-
    Oldsmobile Cutlass-Buick **395, 1940, 1953, 1964, 2311**
Registrations and Transfer of Same; Peck's Title Book:
    Description of State Laws Regulating Motor Vehicle
    Titles, **3423**
Registry of Italian Oddities **2862**
Regulating the Automobile **3425**
Regulation; From the State Capitals: Motor Vehicle **3408**
Reinventing the Wheels: Ford's Spectacular Comeback **3340,
    3386**
Reliant Owners Workshop Manual, 1981-1988; Haynes Dodge
    Aries and Plymouth **1031, 2046**
Renault Club of America **2615, 2628**
Renault Owners Club of America **2616, 2629**
Renault Owners Club of America—Membership Roster **2610,
    2623**
Renault Owners Club of America—Newsletter **2611, 2624**
Renault USA Inc. **4378**
Rentals: How to Get the Car of Your Dreams Without Ever
    Hasseling with a Salesman; Seized, Surplus, Repos
    and **3944**
Repainting; Auto Body Repairing and **3430, 3466**
Repainting; The Principles of Auto Body Repairing and **3487**
Repair Game; Rip-Off Tip-Offs: Winning the Auto **3935**
Repair Handbook; Volvo 240 Series DL, GL, GLT and Turbo:
    1975-1987—Service, **2810**

Repair Manual: 1980-1989, Including Air Cooled and Water-
    Cooled Gasoline Engines, Diesel Engine, Syncro, and
    Camper; Vanagon Official Factory **2801**
Repair Shops Directory; Automobile **3124**
Repair; SMART Body Shop Talk: Dent **3492**
Report of the Joint U.S.-Japan Automotive Study; The
    American and Japanese Auto Industries in Transition:
    The **3347**
Repos and Rentals: How to Get the Car of Your Dreams
    Without Ever Hasseling with a Salesman; Seized,
    Surplus, **3944**
Repossesion Cases; Handling Automobile Warranty and **3409**
Restoration **3438**
Restoration; Car Interior **3432**
Restoration From Junker to Jewel; Auto **3431**
The Restoration Game **3439**
Restraint Systems and Components; Vehicle Occupant **3459,
    4203**
Rhode Island Auto Dealers Association—Yearbook and
    Directory **2978**
Rhode Island Automotive Directory; Connecticut/ **2909,
    2949, 3001, 3079, 3136**
Rhode Island]; Pontiac-Oakland Club International, Yankee
    Chapter [Maine, Massachusetts, and **2103, 2144, 2182,
    2224, 2270, 2307, 2344, 2379, 2414, 2453, 2489**
Rhode Island]; Pontiac-Oakland Club International, Yankee
    Chapter—Newsletter [Maine, Massachusetts, and **2090,
    2131, 2169, 2210, 2254, 2294, 2331, 2366, 2401, 2440,
    2476**
Rim Manual; Wheel and **4340**
Rip-Off Tip-Offs: Winning the Auto Repair Game **3935**
Risks and Rewards of Purchasing a Grey Market Car **3936**
Riviera Owners Association—Review **451**
Road & Track **3937**
Road Reports **3938**
Road to Happiness **3341**
Rocky Mountain Motorist Colorado **3939**
Rolling **2813, 2819, 2824**
Rolls-Royce and Bentley Buyer's Guide; Illustrated **145, 150,
    155, 160, 2631, 2636, 2641**
Rolls-Royce/Bentley Marketletter **146, 151, 156, 161, 2632,
    2637, 2642**
Rolls-Royce Motor Cars Inc. **4379**
Rolls-Royce Owners' Club **147, 152, 157, 162, 2634, 2639,
    2644**
Rolls-Royce Owners' Club—Directory and Register **2633,
    2638, 2643**
Rotary Review **1772**
Rotary Rocket **1773**
Roundel Magazine **171, 181, 191, 201, 211**
Rude Awakening: General Motors in the 1980s **3342, 3387**
A Run for Your Money **4065**
Running Board **237, 273, 308, 341, 375, 415, 452, 486,
    522, 557, 590**
Rust Repair; SMART Body Shop Talk: **3494**
Rustproofing Directory; Auto Undercoating & **3115**
RX-7 Report **1774**

S

S-10 Blazer, GMC S-15, and Olds Bravada, 1982-1990;
    Chevrolet **730, 1514, 1928**
S-10, GMC S-15 Pickups 1982—90; Chevrolet **871, 1522**
S-15, and Olds Bravada, 1982-1990; Chevrolet S-10 Blazer,
    GMC **730, 1514, 1928**
S-15 Pickups 1982—90; Chevrolet S-10, GMC **871, 1522**
Saab **2646, 2649**
Saab 900 Repair Manual, No. 980: 1979-1988; Haynes **2645**
Saab Cars USA, Inc. **4380**
Saab Club of North America **2648, 2651**
Sable Owners Workshop Manual, No. 1421: 1986-1990;
    Haynes Ford Taurus and Mercury **1464, 1861**
SAE Cumulative Index **3940**
SAE Handbook 1990 **3941**

SAE Technical Literature Abstracts **3942**
Safari, 1985-1990; Chevrolet Astro-GMC **710, 1519**
Safari; Chevrolet Astro and GMC **709, 1518**
Safety: An Annotated Bibliography; Studies Relating
    Automobile Design & Vehicle **3282, 3455**
Safety; Center for Auto **2847**
Safety Check Your Car **3451, 3525, 3689, 4066, 4265, 4285,
    4333**
Safety; Chilton's Guide to Auto Electronic Accessories: Sound,
    Security, and **4205, 4219**
Safety Foundation; Automotive **2842**
Safety: The Design-In Danger of the Volkswagen; Small
    on **2712, 2723, 2733, 2744, 2756, 2767, 2775, 2786,
    2795, 2805**
Salesman at His Own Game; The Car Buyer's Art: How to
    Beat the **3860**
San Gabriel Valley Chapter [California]; Buick Club of
    America, **251, 287, 322, 355, 389, 429, 466, 500, 536,
    571, 604**
San Gabriel Valley Chapter—Newsletter [California]; Buick
    Club of America, **226, 262, 298, 330, 363, 401, 439, 475,
    511, 544, 579**
Santa Fe Trail Auto Club Kansas **2863**
Saturn Corp., General Motors Corp. **4381**
Save Big Money on a New Car: A Common Sense Buyers
    Guide **3943**
Schuylkill County Motor Club Pennsylvania **2864**
Scirocco and Cabriolet Service Manual: 1985-1989, Including
    16V **2708**
The Scout **2091, 2132, 2170, 2211, 2255, 2295, 2332,
    2367, 2402, 2441, 2477**
Seat Belts: Index of Modern Information **3452, 4202**
Seat Belts Make Sense; Ask Any Dummy: **3443**
Seat Covers/Tops/Upholstery Directory; Automobile **2996**
Seating; Plastics in Automobile Instrument Panels, Trim,
    and **3237, 3274, 4164**
Secondhand Car?; So You Want to Buy a **3946**
Secrets of Corvette Detailing **828**
Security, and Safety; Chilton's Guide to Auto Electronic
    Accessories: Sound, **4205, 4219**
Seized, Surplus, Repos and Rentals: How to Get the Car of
    Your Dreams Without Ever Hasseling with a
    Salesman **3944**
Selecting and Maintaining Bearings **4067, 4198**
Selecting and Using Lubricants **4184**
Self Starter **618, 633, 649, 663, 677, 691, 705**
Sensors and Actuators, 1989. **3659**
Sensors for Automotive Systems **3660**
Sensors Technology; Displays, Electronics, and **3255, 3640**
Sentra, Datsun 1200 and B210, 1973-1987; Chilton's
    Nissan **1910**
Service, Repair Handbook; Volvo 240 Series DL, GL, GLT and
    Turbo: 1975-1987— **2810**
Service Stations Directory; Automobile **3125**
Sheet Metal Handbook: How to Form, Shear, Roll and Shape
    Sheet Metal for Competition, Custom, and Restoration
    Use **3440, 3490**
Shelby Dodge Automobile Club **1050, 1073, 1090, 1103,
    1134**
Shelby Times **1046, 1069, 1086, 1099, 1130**
Shock Absorbers-Retail Directory **3030**
Shocks; Advanced Car Care: Plugs, Timing and **3962, 4208**
Shocks; Advanced Car Care: Tune Up and **3963, 4209**
Shocks; Tune Up America: Replacing **4211**
S.I. and Diesel Engines; Fuel Alternatives for **3550, 3741,
    3822**
S.I. Engines; Alternate Fuels for **3693, 3816**
Silhouette, 1988-90; Chevrolet Lumina—Pontiac Transport
    Olds **848, 1995, 2459**
SIS Automotive Industry Abstracts **3388, 3426**
Skyhawk, Cadillac Cimarron, Chevrolet Cavalier, Oldsmobile
    Firenza, Pontiac J-2000, Sunbird Shop Manual, 1982-87;
    GMC J Cars: Buick **504, 640, 767, 1980, 2418**
Skyhawk, Olds Firenza, Cadillac Cimarron, Pontiac 6000,
    1982-88; Chilton's Chevrolet Cavalier, Buick **502, 638,
    765, 1978, 2106**

Slant 6 Club of America **949, 968, 988, 1000, 1016, 1025,
    1151**
Slant 6 News **945, 963, 983, 996, 1011, 1021, 1146**
Slapper and File **3491**
Small Block Chevys; How to Rebuild **3748, 4045**
Small-Block V-8 Interchange Manual; Chevrolet **3713, 4005**
Small Engines **3766**
Small on Safety: The Design-In Danger of the
    Volkswagen **2712, 2723, 2733, 2744, 2756, 2767, 2775,
    2786, 2795, 2805**
SMART Body Shop Talk: Dent Repair **3492**
SMART Body Shop Talk: Paint Tips **3493**
SMART Body Shop Talk: Rust Repair **3494**
SMART Buyer's Guide to Purchasing a New Car **3945**
Smog Control Devices; Automobile **2997, 3046**
Smoke Signals **2092, 2133, 2171, 2212, 2256, 2296, 2333,
    2368, 2403, 2442, 2478**
So You Want to Buy a Secondhand Car? **3946**
Society of Automotive Historians **2865**
Society of Automotive Historians—Directory **3343**
Society of Automotive Historians—Journal **3344**
Society of Automotive Historians—Pioneer Chapter New York
    State **2866**
Society of Automotive Historians, Wisconsin Chapter **2867**
Sotto Veloce **21, 46, 71**
South Carolina Automotive Directory **2933, 2979, 3031,
    3103, 3169**
[South Carolina]; Mustang Times Magazine **1422**
South Carolina State Motor Club **2868**
South Dakota/Wyoming Automotive Directory;
    Idaho/Montana/North Dakota/ **2913, 2954, 3008, 3083,
    3147**
Southern California; Auto Cap of **2836**
Southern California Chapter; Pontiac-Oakland Club
    International, **2102, 2143, 2181, 2223, 2269, 2306, 2343,
    2378, 2413, 2452, 2488**
Spark **3345**
Sparkplug: A Car Owner's Bible **3947**
Speakers, Receivers, Non-Audio Electronics; Audio
    Systems: **4212**
Special Interest Auto Club **933, 969, 989, 1017, 1051, 1059,
    1074, 1091, 1104, 1135, 1141, 1149, 1156, 1170, 2028,
    2044**
Special Interest Auto Club—Membership Directory **2898**
Specialty & Custom Dealer—Performance Warehouse Directory
    Issue **3032**
Sport Truck **4324**
The Sporting Fords [Mercury Capri] **1829**
Sports and Classics **4250**
Sports Car Collectors Society of America **2869**
Sports Car Collectors Society of America—Directory **2899**
Sports Car International **4251**
Sports Cars; Jaguar **1576, 1592**
Sports Cars of the World; Motor Trend— **4247**
SportsCar **4252**
Sportsmanlike Driving **3453**
Springs—Automotive Sales and Service Directory **3170**
The Standard **619, 634, 650, 664, 678, 692, 706**
Standard 4-Speed Transmission Explained; The Toyota **2669,
    2671, 2674, 2680, 2682, 2683, 2687, 2689, 2691, 2694,
    2699, 2705, 2706**
Standard Catalog of American Light Duty Trucks **3222**
Standard Catalog of Chevrolet **715, 723, 733, 750, 763,
    775, 784, 792, 800, 829, 844, 851, 861, 868, 881, 888,
    897, 904, 916**
Standard Catalog of Chrysler 1924-1990 **929, 939, 946, 964,
    984, 997, 1012, 1022**
Standard Catalog of Ford 1896-1990 **1299, 1313, 1328,
    1339, 1354, 1363, 1371, 1384, 1424, 1438, 1456, 1470,
    1487, 1504**
Standard Guide to Cars and Prices **3223**
Starters—Engine Directory **3033, 3060**
The Starting System Explained **3603, 4122**
Starting Systems Technology **3604, 4123**
Station Wagon Owner's Association; Great American **2854**

Steering and Brakes; Automotive Suspension, **3514, 3515, 4261, 4262, 4272, 4273**

Steering and Suspension 1980-1987: Domestic and Import Cars and Trucks; Chilton's Guide to Brakes, **3521, 4131, 4264, 4275, 4302**

Steering and Suspension Systems; Automotive **4259, 4270**

Steering; Automotive Brakes, Suspension and **3507, 4258, 4269**

Steering, Front Suspension, Wheels and Tires; Brakes, **3520, 4263, 4274, 4284, 4337**

Steering, Suspension, and Braking Systems: Principles and Service; Automotive **3513, 4260, 4271**

Steering; Vehicle Dynamics Related to Braking and **3526, 4266**

Stereo Blue Book; Car **3187**

Stereo Blue Book; Orion Car **3235, 4225**

Stereo; How to Buy Car **4221**

Stereo on a Budget; Killer Car **4223**

Stereo Review; Car **4217**

Stereo Systems Directory; Automobile Radio/ **2995**

Sterling Motor Cars, Austin-Rover Cars of N.A. **4382**

The Story of Camaro **751**

The Story of Corvette **830**

The Story of Ferrari **3346, 4253**

The Story of Mustang **1425**

The Story of Porsche **2516, 2539, 2560, 2583**

Stress Cracks **1706, 1714**

Structural Design and Crashworthiness of Automobiles **3281, 3454**

Struts; Tune Up America: Replacing **4282**

Studies Relating Automobile Design & Vehicle Safety: An Annotated Bibliography **3282, 3455**

A Study of the Toyota Production System from an Industrial Engineering Viewpoint **3292**

Subaru 1970-1988; Chilton's **2652, 2653, 2655, 2657, 2661, 2663, 2665**

Subaru Alive: A Manual of Step-by-Step Procedures for the Compleat Idiot; How to Keep Your **2654, 2656, 2658, 2659, 2660, 2662, 2664, 2666**

Subaru of America Inc. **4383**

Suburban 1970-1987; Chilton's Chevrolet/GMC Pick-ups and **874, 910, 1524, 1532**

Suburbans: 1967-1987: Includes Suburbans Shop Manual; Chevy and GMC C-Series, Pickups, and **907, 1530**

Suburbans, and Vans, 1970-1987 (Gas and Diesel); Chevy and GMC Two Wheel Drive C and R-Series Pickups, **908, 1531**

Suburbans Shop Manual; Chevy and GMC C-Series, Pickups, and Suburbans: 1967-1987: Includes **907, 1530**

Successful Automotive Litigation **3427**

Sunbird Shop Manual, 1982-87; GMC J Cars: Buick Skyhawk, Cadillac Cimarron, Chevrolet Cavalier, Oldsmobile Firenza, Pontiac J-2000, **504, 640, 767, 1980, 2418**

Super Chevy **724, 752, 776, 801, 831, 845, 862, 889, 905**

Super Ford **1355, 1426, 1439, 1457, 1471, 1505**

Super Profile: Lotus Elan **1707**

Super Profile: Porsche 911 Carrera **2517**

Superauto Illustrated **4254**

Supercar Showdown **1284, 1645, 2518**

Supercars; The Encyclopedia of American **4244**

Supercomputer Applications in the Automobile Industry; Current and Future Directions of **3251, 3638**

Supra, 1986-1990; Chilton's Toyota Celica- **2672, 2692**

Supra; Mitchell Glove Compartment Companion for Your Toyota Celica- **2673, 2693**

Supra-Sonicsl **2695**

Suspension 1980-1987: Domestic and Import Cars and Trucks; Chilton's Guide to Brakes, Steering and **3521, 4131, 4264, 4275, 4302**

Suspension, and Braking Systems: Principles and Service; Automotive Steering, **3513, 4260, 4271**

Suspension and Handling; Tires, **4281, 4288**

Suspension and Steering; Automotive Brakes, **3507, 4258, 4269**

Suspension; Current Trends in Truck **3252, 4276, 4310**

Suspension Design: Making the Fast Car Faster; New Directions in **3268, 4248, 4280**

Suspension Designs; Manual for Incorporating Pneumatic Springs in Vehicle **3261, 4279**

Suspension, Steering and Brakes; Automotive **3514, 3515, 4261, 4262, 4272, 4273**

Suspension Systems; Automotive Steering and **4259, 4270**

Suspensions; Advanced Truck **4267, 4289**

Suzuki of America Automotive Corp. **4384**

Syncro, and Camper; Vanagon Official Factory Repair Manual: 1980-1989, Including Air Cooled and Water-Cooled Gasoline Engines, Diesel Engine, **2801**

Synthetic Automotive Engine Oils **4185**

T

Tailgate News **4257**

Take the Trouble **3456**

Taurus and Mercury Sable Owners Workshop Manual, No. 1421: 1986-1990; Haynes Ford **1464, 1861**

Taurus: The Making of the Car That Saved Ford **1472**

Tech Center News **3389**

Technical Literature Abstracts; SAE **3942**

Technology; Starting Systems **3604, 4123**

Tempo and Mercury Topaz, 1984-1987; Ford **1481, 1870**

Tempo-Mercury Topaz Owners Workshop Manual, No. 1418: 1984-1989; Haynes Ford **1482, 1871**

Tennessee Alfa—Newsletter **22, 47, 72**

Tennessee Automotive Association **2870**

Tennessee Automotive Directory **2934, 2980, 3034, 3104, 3171**

Tennessee]; Deep South Alfa Romeo Club [Mississippi, Louisiana, and southwestern **33, 58, 83**

Tercel-MR2, 1984-1990; Chilton's Toyota Corolla- **2677, 2684, 2698**

Tercel, Starlet, 1970-1987; Chilton's Toyota Corolla, Carina, **2676, 2697**

Testarossa; Ferrari **1278**

Texas Automotive Directory **2935, 2981, 3035, 3105, 3172**

[Texas]; Buick Club of America, Lone Star Chapter **246, 282, 317, 350, 384, 424, 461, 495, 531, 566, 599**

Texas Chapter; Buick Club of America, North **249, 285, 320, 353, 387, 427, 464, 498, 534, 569, 602**

[Texas]; Mercedes-Benz Club of Ft. Worth **1782, 1789, 1797, 1805, 1813, 1821, 1826**

Texas—Newsletter; Alfa Romeo Owners Club of **18, 43, 68**

Thunderbird and Mercury Cougar, No. 1338: 1983-1988; Haynes Ford **1497**

Thunderbird, Mercury Cougar, Lincoln Continental-Mark VII, 1980-1987; Chilton's Ford **1492, 1660, 1676, 1833**

Tire Dealer—Facts/Directory Issue; Modern **2892, 3160**

Tire Dealers and Retreaders Association—Who's Who Membership Directory; National **2968, 3161**

Tire Dealers-Retail Directory **3036**

Tire Dealers-Used Directory **3037, 3106**

Tire Retreading and Repair Directory **3173**

Tire Retreading/Repair Journal **4286**

Tire Review—Tire Brands Issue **3061**

Tire Review— Wheel Brand Profiles Issue **3062**

Tire Wise **4287**

Tires; Brakes, Steering, Front Suspension, Wheels and **3520, 4263, 4274, 4284, 4337**

Tires, Suspension and Handling **4281, 4288**

Titles, Registrations and Transfer of Same; Peck's Title Book: Description of State Laws Regulating Motor Vehicle **3423**

A to Z Camaro Parts Directory **753**

Tommy's First Car **3948**

Topaz, 1984-1987; Ford Tempo and Mercury **1481, 1870**

Topaz Owners Workshop Manual, No. 1418: 1984-1989; Haynes Ford Tempo-Mercury **1482, 1871**

Tops/Upholstery Directory; Automobile Seat Covers/ **2996**

Topwheels **4255**

Torsion Bar 930, 940, 947, 965, 985, 998, 1013, 1023, 1028, 1033, 1041, 1047, 1056, 1064, 1070, 1078, 1082, 1087, 1094, 1100, 1107, 1115, 1121, 1126, 1131, 1138, 1143, 1153, 2017, 2021, 2025, 2032, 2037, 2041, 2048, 2052, 2057, 2065

Total Auto Body Repair 3495, 4334

Towing and Wrecker Service Directory 3174

Toyota Camry Owners Workshop Manual, No. 1023: 1983-1990; Haynes 2670

Toyota Celica-Supra, 1986-1990; Chilton's 2672, 2692

Toyota Celica-Supra; Mitchell Glove Compartment Companion for Your 2673, 2693

Toyota Corolla 2679

Toyota Corolla, Carina, Tercel, Starlet, 1970-1987; Chilton's 2676, 2697

Toyota Corolla Owners Workshop Manual, No. 1025: 1984-1988; Haynes 2678

Toyota Corolla-Tercel-MR2, 1984-1990; Chilton's 2677, 2684, 2698

Toyota Motor Sales USA Inc. 4385

Toyota MR2, 1984-1988 2686

Toyota MR2 Owners Workshop Repair Manual, No. 1339: All Models, 1985-1987; Haynes 2685

Toyota Pick-Up Alive: A Manual of Step by Step Procedures for the Compleat Idiot; How to Keep Your 2702

Toyota Pick-up Owners Workshop Manual, No. 656: 1979-1990; Haynes 2701

Toyota Pick-ups and 4-Runner, 1984-88 2667, 2703

Toyota Pickup, 4-Runner Service Manual: 1978-1988 Including Gasoline, Diesel, and Turbo Diesel, 4-cylinder and 6-cylinder Engines 2668, 2704

Toyota Production System from an Industrial Engineering Viewpoint; A Study of the 3292

Toyota Sport Car Club 2675, 2681, 2688, 2690, 2696

The Toyota Standard 4-Speed Transmission Explained 2669, 2671, 2674, 2680, 2682, 2683, 2687, 2689, 2691, 2694, 2699, 2705, 2706

Toyota Trucks 1970-1987; Chilton's 2700

Trans Am Club U.S.A. 2273

Trans Am Shop Manual, 1982-1987; Camaro 228 and Firebird 734, 2228

Trans Ammer 2257

TransAm Club U.S.A.—National Register 2258

Transaxle Overhaul; Front Wheel Drive: 3740, 4278

Transaxles, and Drive Trains; Automatic, Manual Transmissions, 3555, 3695

Transmission and Power Trains; Automotive Manual 3557, 3708

Transmission; Automatic 3696

Transmission; Automotive 3709

Transmission; Changing Gears: The Development of the Automotive 3315, 3712

Transmission Design; Power 3280, 3762

Transmission; Design Practices Passenger Car Automatic 3253, 3731

Transmission Explained; The Toyota Standard 4-Speed 2669, 2671, 2674, 2680, 2682, 2683, 2687, 2689, 2691, 2694, 2699, 2705, 2706

Transmission; Mechanical Power 3755

Transmission; Problems of Hydramatic 3763

Transmission Rebuilders Association—Membership Roster; Automatic 2881

Transmission Repair; Chilton's Guide to Automatic 3720

Transmission Repair Manual, 1984-88: Motor-Age Professional Mechanics Edition; Chilton's Automatic 3714

Transmission Repair Manual, 1984-1988: Import Cars and Trucks: Motor-Age Professional Mechanic's Edition; Chilton's Automatic 3715, 4129, 4298

Transmission Repair Manual, 1984-1989 Domestic Cars and Trucks; Chilton's Guide to Automatic 3721

Transmission Repair Shops Directory; Automobile 3126

Transmission Service Manual 1984-88: Domestic Cars and Trucks: Motor-Age Professional Mechanic's Edition; Chilton's Automatic 3716, 4299

Transmission Systems; Automotive Brakes and Power 3506, 3699

Transmissions for Passenger Cars; Continuously Variable 3726

Transmissions, Transaxles, and Drive Trains; Automatic, Manual 3555, 3695

Transnational Corporations in the International Auto Industry 3390

Transport Olds Silhouette, 1988-90; Chevrolet Lumina—Pontiac 848, 1995, 2459

Transportation Electronics; Convergence 1988: Proceedings of the International Congress on 3637

Transportation Energy Research 3283, 3293

Transportation Fuel Alternative for North America into the 21st Century 3831

Transporters and Drive-Away Directory; Automobile 3127

Tri County Motor Club 2871, 2872

Trim, and Seating; Plastics in Automobile Instrument Panels, 3237, 3274, 4164

Troubleshooting Electrical Components 3605

Troubleshooting Port Fuel Injection 3814

Troubleshooting with the Vat-40 4068

Truck & Equipment Trader 3224

Truck and Van Buyer's Guide; Motor Trend— 3213

Truck and Van Repair; Light 4054

Truck and Van Repair Manual 1981-1988; Chilton's Professional 4018, 4306

Truck and Van Repair Manual, 1982-1988; Chilton's 4020, 4307

Truck and Van Wiring Diagram Manual, 1989-1990: Motor Age Professional Mechanic's Edition; Chilton's 3588, 4308

Truck Canopies, Caps and Shells Directory 3038, 3063

Truck Cost Guide; Complete Small 3192

Truck Dealers Directory 2982

Truck Dealers-Used Directory 2983

Truck Diesel Engine Service Manual; Car and Light 3540, 4297

Truck Electronic Control Systems 3661, 4325

Truck Equipment & Parts Directory 3039

Truck-Frame and Axle Repair Association—Membership Directory 3175

Truck Guide 3225

Truck; Hot 4318

Truck Interchange Manual: Body Parts; Auto- 4189, 4294

Truck Interchange Manual: Wheel Covers; Auto- 4295, 4335

Truck Interchange Manual: Wheels; Auto- 4296, 4336

Truck Lubrication Guide 4186, 4326

Truck: Motor-Age Professional Mechanic's Edition; Chilton's IMP Emission Diagnostic and Service Manual, Vacuum Circuit, 1984-1987 Import Cars and 3673, 4134, 4305

Truck 'N Van Power 4327

Truck News; Auto and 3837, 4293

Truck Painting and Lettering Directory 3242

Truck Repairing and Service Directory 3176

Truck Suspension; Current Trends in 3252, 4276, 4310

Truck Suspensions; Advanced 4267, 4289

Truck Trader 3226

Truck Washing and Cleaning Directory 3177

Truckin' Magazine 4328

Trucks 1967-1988; Chilton's Dodge/Plymouth 1061, 1110, 1124

Trucks 1970-1987; Chilton's Toyota 2700

Trucks 1984-1988: Motor-Age Professional Mechanic's Edition; Chilton's Professional Electronics Diagnostic Manual Ford Cars and 1304, 1318, 1333, 1345, 1366, 1377, 1390, 1444, 1462, 1479, 1494

Trucks, 1988-90; Chevrolet GMC 870, 1521

Trucks—1988-1990: Motor Age Professional Mechanic's Edition; Chilton's Electronic Chassis Controls Manual, Import Cars and 3631, 3718, 4130, 4300

Trucks: A Review; Anti Lock Braking Systems for Passenger Cars and Light 3499, 4292

Trucks; America's Light 4291

Trucks, and R.V.s; The Underground Blue Book: A Guide to Buying And Selling New and Used Cars, 3227

Trucks and Small Tractors; Diesel Engines for Automobiles, Small 3543, 4311

Trucks; Chilton's Guide to Automatic Transmission Repair Manual, 1984-1989 Domestic Cars and 3721

Trucks; Chilton's Guide to Brakes, Steering and Suspension
1980-1987: Domestic and Import Cars and **3521, 4131,
4264, 4275, 4302**
Trucks; Chilton's Guide to Diesel Cars and **3541, 4303**
Trucks; Chilton's Guide to Fuel Injection and Electronic Engine
Controls 1984-1988: Import Cars and **3634, 3724, 3793,
4133, 4304**
Trucks; Chilton's Tune-up Emission Diagnosis and Service
Manual, 1988: Import Cars and **3535, 3674, 4309**
Trucks; Electric and Electronic Systems for Automobiles
and **3590, 3642, 4312**
Trucks: Motor-Age Professional Mechanic's Edition; Chilton's
Automatic Transmission Repair Manual, 1984-1988: Import
Cars and **3715, 4129, 4298**
Trucks: Motor-Age Professional Mechanic's Edition; Chilton's
Automatic Transmission Service Manual 1984-88: Domestic
Cars and **3716, 4299**
Trucks: Motor-Age Professional Mechanic's Edition; Chilton's
Electronic Engine Controls Manual, 1988-90—Domestic Cars
and **3632, 3719, 4301**
Trucks: Motor-Age Professional Mechanic's Edition; Emission
Diagnosis Tune-up and Service Manual 1988 Import Cars
and **3537, 3678, 4037, 4143, 4313**
Trucks; The Official Price Guide to Cars and **3216**
Trucks; Standard Catalog of American Light Duty **3222**
Trucks; Vans and **4329**
Tune Up America: Body and Fender Repair **3496**
Tune Up America: Detailing **3441**
Tune Up America: Oil Change, Filters and Lube **4187**
Tune Up America: Replacing Exhaust Systems **3690**
Tune Up America: Replacing Shocks **4211**
Tune Up America: Replacing Struts **4282**
Tune Up America: Tune Up and Maintenance **4069**
Tune Up; How to Do a Major Engine **3746**
Tune-up Ignition and Fuel Induction Systems **3815, 4124**
Tune-up Service Manual **4070**
Turbine Systems for Automobiles; Advanced Gas **3784**
Turbo and Hi-Tech Performance **3294, 4330**
Turbo and Turbo Diesel, Including Wagon and Quattro; Audi
5000S, 5000CS Official Factory Repair Manual: 1984-1988
Gasoline, **126**
Turbo Diesel, 4-cylinder and 6-cylinder Engines; Toyota Pickup,
4-Runner Service Manual: 1978-1988 Including Gasoline,
Diesel, and **2668, 2704**
Turbo Diesel, Including Golf, GT, Jetta GLI and 16V Models;
GTI, Golf and Jetta Service Manual: 1985-1989: Gasoline,
Diesel, and **2739, 2751, 2762**
Turbo Diesel, including Wagon and Syncro; Quantum Official
Factory Repair Manual: 1982-1988, Gasoline and **2781**
The Turbocharger Explained **4331**

U

The Ultimate Owner's Manual: How to Buy, Finance and Take
Care of Your Car **4071**
Undercar Digest—Buyer's Guide Issue **3064**
Undercoating & Rustproofing Directory; Auto **3115**
The Underground Blue Book: A Guide to Buying And Selling
New and Used Cars, Trucks, and R.V.s **3227**
Understanding Automotive Electronics **3662**
Understanding Your Automobile **3949**
United States Camaro Club **756**
United Voice **2900**
Unsafe at Any Speed **3295, 3457**
Upholstery Cleaning Directory; Automobile **3128**
Upholstery Directory; Automobile Seat Covers/Tops/ **2996**
U.S.A. Convertible Club **2873**
Used Car Book **2901**
The Used Car Book **3228**
Used Car Book; Consumer Guide **3194**
Used Car Buying Guide **3229**
Used Car: For the Non-Mechanical Person; How to Buy &
Maintain a **3899, 4044**
Used Car; Getting a Better Buy in a **3883**

Used Car Guide Book; Official **3217**
Used Car; How to Beat the Car Dealer at His Own Game:
Buying a New or **3895**
Used Car; How to Buy a Car: The Essential Guide for Buying
a New Car or **3896**
Used Car—How to Sell a Used Car, Two Books in One; How
to Buy a **3897**
Used Car; How to Test and Buy a **3904**
Used Car Prices; Edmund's **3204**
Used Cars: Finding the Best Buy **3950**
Used Cars; Guide to **3208**
Used/Salvage Directory; Automobile Parts— **3073**
Utah; Automobile Club of **2837**
Utah/Nevada Automotive Directory; Colorado/ **2908, 2948,
3000, 3078, 3135**

V

V-8 Interchange Manual; Chevrolet Small-Block **3713, 4005**
Vacuum Circuit, 1984-1987—Domestic Car: Motor-Age
Professional Mechanic's Edition; Chilton's U.S. Emission
Diagnostic and Service Manual, **3536, 3675**
Vacuum Circuit, 1984-1987 Import Cars and Truck: Motor-Age
Professional Mechanic's Edition; Chilton's IMP Emission
Diagnostic and Service Manual, **3673, 4134, 4305**
Vacuum Diagrams 1984-87; Chilton's Guide to Emission
Diagnosis, Tune-Up and **3534, 3672, 4132**
The Valley Motorist **3951**
Valley Vettes Corvette Club—Newsletter **832**
Valve Seat Refacer; How to Use a Valve and **3750**
Van & Light Truck Safety **3458**
Van Buyer's Guide; Motor Trend—Truck and **3213**
Van Power; Truck 'N **4327**
Van Repair; Light Truck and **4054**
Van Repair Manual 1981-1988; Chilton's Professional Truck
and **4018, 4306**
Van Repair Manual, 1982-1988; Chilton's Truck and **4020,
4307**
Van Wiring Diagram Manual, 1989-1990: Motor Age
Professional Mechanic's Edition; Chilton's Truck and **3588,
4308**
Vanagon Official Factory Repair Manual: 1980-1989, Including
Air Cooled and Water-Cooled Gasoline Engines, Diesel
Engine, Syncro, and Camper **2801**
Vans, 1961-1988; Chilton's Ford **1291**
Vans 1967-1988; Chilton's Dodge/Plymouth **1037, 1118,
2061**
Vans, 1970-1987 (Gas and Diesel); Chevy and GMC Two
Wheel Drive C and R-Series Pickups, Suburbans, and **908,
1531**
Vans and Trucks **4329**
Vans Owners Workshop Manual No. 345, 1968-1989; Haynes
Chevrolet V-8 **893**
Vans Owners Workshop Manual, No. 349: 1971-1991;
Haynes Dodge and Plymouth **1039, 1111, 1119, 2063**
Vans, Pickups/Off Road Buyer's Guide; Edmund's **3205**
Vans Year Buying Guide; Four By Four Pickups and **3206**
Vehicle Body Building **3497**
Vehicle Dynamics Related to Braking and Steering **3526,
4266**
Vehicle Identification 1986-1987 **3230**
Vehicle Laws of Pennsylvania **3428**
Vehicle Lighting Trends **3284, 3663, 4082**
Vehicle Maintenance **3767**
Vehicle Occupant Restraint Systems and Components **3459,
4203**
Vehicle Painting **3952**
Vermont Automotive Directory; Maine/New
Hampshire/ **2920, 2961, 3017, 3090, 3154**
Vette **833**
Vette Vues **834**
Vetten USA **835**
Vettes Corvette Club—Newsletter; Valley **832**
Vettes; Keepin' Track of **825**

Vetts Only; For **821**

Viale Ciro Menotti **1719, 1725, 1731, 1737, 1743, 1748, 1753**

The Video Car Care Clinic **4072**

Virginia]; Pontiac-Oakland Club International, National Capital Area [District of Columbia, Maryland, and **2100, 2141, 2179, 2221, 2267, 2304, 2341, 2376, 2411, 2450, 2486**

[Virginia]; Pontiac-Oakland Club International, Old Dominion Chapter—Newsletter **2089, 2130, 2168, 2209, 2253, 2293, 2330, 2365, 2400, 2439, 2475**

Virginia/West Virginia Automotive Directory **2936, 2984, 3040, 3107, 3178**

Vista, 1971-1988: Repair and Tune-Up Guide; Chilton's Colt/Challenger/Conquest/ **917, 1053**

Volkswagen Club of America **2717, 2727, 2737, 2748, 2760, 2771, 2779, 2790, 2799, 2809**

Volkswagen Convertible Owners of America **2718, 2749**

Volkswagen Corrado Official Factory Repair Manual: 1989-1990 **2719**

Volkswagen Electrical Diagrams and Troubleshooting Guide **2709, 2720, 2729, 2741, 2753, 2764, 2772, 2782, 2792, 2802**

Volkswagen Fox Service Manual: 1987-1989, Including Wagon and Sport **2730**

Volkswagen of America Inc. **4386**

Volkswagen Passat Official Factory Repair Manual: 1989-1991 **2773**

Volkswagen Quantum **2783**

Volkswagen; Small on Safety: The Design-In Danger of the **2712, 2723, 2733, 2744, 2756, 2767, 2775, 2786, 2795, 2805**

Volkswagen Water-Cooled, Front-Drive Performance Handbook **2710, 2721, 2731, 2742, 2754, 2765, 2784, 2793, 2803**

Volvo **2814, 2820, 2825**

Volvo 240 Series DL, GL, GLT and Turbo: 1975-1987— Service, Repair Handbook **2810**

Volvo 1970-1988: Repair and Tune-Up Guide **2811, 2818**

Volvo Club of America **2817, 2823, 2828**

Volvo Club of America—Membership Directory **2815, 2821, 2826**

Volvo GL, DL **2812**

The Volvo Leader **2816, 2822, 2827**

Volvo North America Corp. **4387**

Voto Veloce **23, 48, 73**

Voyager, 1984-1987; Dodge Caravan, Mini Ram Van, Plymouth **1038, 2062**

Voyager, 1984-1988: Repair and Tune-Up Guide; Chilton's Dodge Caravan-Plymouth **1036, 2060**

VW and Porsche **2519, 2540, 2561, 2584, 2595, 2713, 2724, 2734, 2745, 2757, 2768, 2776, 2787, 2796, 2806**

VW Autoist **2714, 2725, 2735, 2746, 2758, 2769, 2777, 2788, 2797, 2807**

VW Front Wheel Drive, 1974-1990; Chilton's **2707, 2728, 2738, 2750, 2761, 2780, 2791, 2800**

VW Golf and Jetta (Including GTI); Improve and Modify Your **2740, 2752, 2763**

VW Trends **2715, 2716, 2726, 2736, 2747, 2759, 2770, 2778, 2789, 2798, 2808**

W

W. Machines **1924, 1944, 1957, 1968, 1985, 2005**

Wagoneer-Comanche-Cherokee 1984-1991; Jeep **1599, 1607, 1615, 1623**

Ward's Auto World **3391**

Ward's Automotive International **3392**

Ward's Automotive Reports **3393**

Ward's Engine Update **3285, 3768**

Warranty and Repossesion Cases; Handling Automobile **3409**

Warren County Motor Club Pennsylvania **2874**

Washing and Cleaning Directory; Truck **3177**

Washington Automotive Directory State **2937, 2985, 3041, 3108, 3179**

Washington D.C. Chapter; Alfa Romeo Owners Club, **32, 57, 82**

Washington Digest **3429**

Washington Motor Club—Motorist Washington state; AAA **3835**

Washington Office; Japan Automobile Manufacturers Association, **2857**

[Washington state]; Buick Club of America, Puget Sound Chapter **250, 286, 321, 354, 388, 428, 465, 499, 535, 570, 603**

[Washington state]; Yakima Ridgerunners Jeep Club **1604, 1612, 1620, 1629, 1638**

Water-Cooled Gasoline Engines, Diesel Engine, Syncro, and Camper; Vanagon Official Factory Repair Manual: 1980-1989, Including Air Cooled and **2801**

Weekend Mechanic's Handbook: Complete Auto Repairs You Can Make **4073**

West Allis Auto Club Wisconsin **2875**

West Pennsylvania Motor Club **2876**

West Virginia Automotive Directory; Virginia/ **2936, 2984, 3040, 3107, 3178**

Western Pennsylvania Motorist **3953**

What Do You Know about Auto Mechanics **4074**

What You Need to Know to Avoid Auto Repair Rip-Offs **3954**

What Your Car Is Trying To Tell You **3955**

What's Under Your Hood? **3769**

What's Wrong with My Car?: A Guide to Troubleshooting Common Mechanical and Performance Problems **3956**

Wheel Alignment/Frame Shops Directory **3180**

Wheel and Rim Manual **4340**

Wheel Balancing; Electronic **4338**

Wheel Brand Profiles Issue; Tire Review— **3062**

Wheel Covers; Auto-Truck Interchange Manual: **4295, 4335**

Wheeler Dealer **3231**

Wheels and Tires; Brakes, Steering, Front Suspension, **3520, 4263, 4274, 4284, 4337**

Wheels; Auto-Truck Interchange Manual: **4296, 4336**

Wheels Directory **3042**

Wheels; How to Balance **4339**

Whispering Bomb **172, 182, 192, 202, 212**

Who Makes It and Where Directory **3065**

Whole Car Catalog **3232**

Who's Who; Motor Age Big I **2878, 2893, 2940, 2967**

Who's Who Show Directory **3066**

Why Trade It In? How To Keep Your Car Running Almost Indefinitely **3957**

Wiretapper **3394**

Wiring Diagram Manual, 1989-1990: Motor Age Professional Mechanic's Edition; Chilton's Truck and Van **3588, 4308**

Wiring Diagrams Manual, 1987-88: Motor-Age Professional Mechanic's Edition; Chilton's Import Car **3587, 4142**

Wiring Diagrams Manual, 1989: Domestic Cars; Chilton's **3589**

Wisconsin Automotive Directory **2938, 2986, 3043, 3109, 3181**

Wisconsin Automotive Parts Association—Directory **3044**

[Wisconsin]; Buick Club of America, Cream City Chapter **242, 278, 313, 346, 380, 420, 457, 491, 527, 562, 595**

Wisconsin Chapter; Society of Automotive Historians, **2867**

[Wisconsin]; Cream City Chronicle **228, 264, 300, 332, 365, 405, 441, 477, 513, 547, 581**

A Woman's Guide to Autos: Basics, Operation, Safety and Maintenance **4075**

Women with Wheels—Newsletter **3958, 4076**

Wooden Body Framing; How to Restore **3485**

World Automotive Market **3395**

World Guide to Automobile Manufacturers **3396**

World Motor Vehicle Data Book **3397**

World of Wheels **3959**

Worldwide Emission Control: Automotive Catalysts **3691, 3692**

Worldwide Fiero Club **2227**

Worldwide Trends in Engine Coolants, Cooling System Materials and Testing **3770, 4109**

WPC Club 934, 942, 950, 970, 990, 1001, 1018, 1026,
1030, 1035, 1043, 1052, 1060, 1066, 1075, 1080, 1084,
1092, 1096, 1105, 1109, 1117, 1123, 1128, 1136, 1142,
1150, 1157, 1160, 1163, 1166, 1171, 1603, 1611, 1619,
1628, 1637, 2019, 2023, 2029, 2034, 2039, 2045, 2050,
2054, 2059, 2067
Wrecker Service Directory; Towing and 3174
Write Line 4256
Wyoming Automotive Directory; Idaho/Montana/North
Dakota/South Dakota/ 2913, 2954, 3008, 3083, 3147

X

X1/9 Car Club 164
X1/9 Newsletter 163

Y

Yakima Ridgerunners Jeep Club [Washington state] 1604,
1612, 1620, 1629, 1638
Yankee Chapter [Maine, Massachusetts, and Rhode Island];
Pontiac-Oakland Club International 2103, 2144, 2182,
2224, 2270, 2307, 2344, 2379, 2414, 2453, 2489
Yankee Chapter—Newsletter [Maine, Massachusetts, and
Rhode Island]; Pontiac-Oakland Club International, 2090,
2131, 2169, 2210, 2254, 2294, 2331, 2366, 2401, 2440,
2476
Yo Money: A Very Fast Guide to Car Buying 3233
Young Man's Guide to Autos: Basics, Operation, Safety and
Maintenance 4077
Youngstown Buicks of Yesteryear Pennsylvania 2877
Your Ford: Including Lincoln-Mercury: Essential Service
Information for Owners and Mechanics 1300, 1314, 1329,
1340, 1356, 1372, 1385, 1427, 1458, 1473, 1488, 1506,
1672, 1685, 1697, 1839, 1847, 1857, 1865, 1875, 1882
Your Quick and Easy Car Care and Safe Driving
Handbook 3460, 4078
Yugo America Inc. 4388

Z

Z Club Bulletin 1894, 1896, 1898, 1900, 1903, 1905, 1909,
1912, 1914, 1919, 1921